JOURNALISM

IN THE

UNITED STATES,

FROM 1690 TO 1872.

JOURNALISM

IN THE

UNITED STATES,

FROM 1690 TO 1872.

By FREDERIC HUDSON.

J. & J. HARPER EDITIONS
HARPER & ROW, PUBLISHERS
NEW YORK AND EVANSTON

THE PRESS,

The Argus of the World, the Ear-Gallery of the Globe, the Reporter of the Universe.

JOURNALISM IN THE UNITED STATES, by Frederic Hudson. Introduction copyright © 1969 by Harper & Row, Publishers, Incorporated.

Printed in the United States of America. All rights reserved. No part of this book may be used or reproduced in any manner whatsoever without written permission except in the case of brief quotations embodied in critical articles and reviews. For information address Harper & Row, Publishers, Incorporated, 49 East 33rd Street, New York, N.Y. 10016.

FIRST J. & J. HARPER EDITION 1969
Printed on long-life, acid-free paper, with reinforced bindings

LIBRARY OF CONGRESS CATALOG CARD NUMBER: 7-4474

THESE SKETCHES

ARE

RESPECTFULLY INSCRIBED

TO THE

JOURNALISTS

OF THE

UNITED STATES OF AMERICA.

NOTE.

THE reader will find various styles of typography and various modes of spelling proper names and words on the pages of this work. Our purpose has been to follow the fashion of printing which prevailed at the time the newspapers, from which extracts have been taken, were printed, and also to adhere to the orthography of those journals as indulged in during the whole of the eighteenth century. This will be particularly observable in the advertisements of the almanacs which appeared towards the close of that century, in which, as well as in other instances, we have endeavored to give an idea of the manner of display prevalent at the time.

CONTENTS.

Introduction to the J. & J. Harper Edition .... xva
INTRODUCTION...Page xv
OUR OWN OPENING.. xxi

THE FIRST NEWSPAPERS IN THE WORLD.

The Proof-Sheet.—News Circulars and Letters.—The Newspaper.—The first in the World.—The first in America.—The Prospectus.—The Official Organ.—The Journal.—Advertisements.—The Penny Press.—News-boys.—Now and Then.. xxviii

NEWSPAPERS IN AMERICA.

FIRST ERA.
1690—1704.
THE BEGINNING IN MASSACHUSETTS.

CHAPTER I.
THE INITIAL NEWSPAPER.

Harris's Publick Occurrences in Boston.—Its Editor and Publisher.—Its Contents.—Its one Day's Existence.—The reprinted London Gazette in New York, by William Bradford 43

SECOND ERA.
1704—1748.
THE COLONIAL PRESS.

CHAPTER II.
THE EARLY PRESS OF BOSTON AND PHILADELPHIA.

The Boston News-Letter.—Dependence of Printers on the Authorities.—John Campbell.—His News Circulars.—The early Postmasters the first Editors.—Circulation of the News-Letter.—The first Reporting.—Home Intelligence.—Appeals to Subscribers.—Boston Gazette and Philadelphia Mercury.—William Brooker.—James and Benjamin Franklin.—Andrew Bradford.—Conflicts with the governing Classes.—The first Newspaper War.—Busy Body.—The Original Jenkins.—Fashions.—Troubles with the Clergy.—Increase and Cotton Mather.—Imprisonment of James Franklin, etc........................ 51

CHAPTER III.
THE FIRST NEWSPAPER IN NEW YORK.

The Gazette.—Its Commencement by William Bradford.—The Bible.—Premiums for Subscribers.—New England Weekly Journal.—Samuel Kneeland.—The Mails.—Difficulties in circulating Newspapers.—Style of Writers, etc.. 72

CHAPTER IV.
REAPPEARANCE OF THE FRANKLINS.

The Way Benjamin Franklin started a Paper in Philadelphia.—Samuel Keimer.—The Pennsylvania Gazette.—The Fleets in Boston.—Mother Goose Melodies.—The Fashions.—More Trouble with the Authorities.—Boston Evening Post.—Zenger's New York Journal.—Arrest of Zenger.—The first Libel Suit in America.—Andrew Hamilton's great Speech.—The popular Verdict.—The Joy of the People.—The Dawn of Liberty.—The New York Gazette.—William Bradford.—The Post-Boy.—James Parker.—Personal Description of an early New York Editor.—James Franklin in Newport.—The Rhode Island Gazette.—Newport then and now, etc.................................Page 77

CHAPTER V.
THE PRESS AT THE SOUTH.

Commencement in South Carolina.—The Gazette.—The first Newspaper in Virginia.—The Gazette.—Boston Weekly Post-Boy.—Ellis Huske.—The Bradfords of Pennsylvania.—The Stamp Act.—Indignation in Printing-offices.—John Hughes, the Stamp Commissioner.—Carriers' Addresses.—The first Paper in Maryland.—The Gazette again.—Toujours Perdrix.—Very old Printing-press.—The Beginning of the German Newspapers, etc.................. 96

THIRD ERA.
1748—1783.
THE REVOLUTIONARY PRESS.
CHAPTER VI.
THE PRE-REVOLUTIONARY NEWSPAPERS.

Our Patriotic Editors and Publishers.—The Sons of Liberty.—Who Wrote for the Newspapers.—Opening of the Revolutionary Ball.—The Boston Independent Advertiser.—Samuel Adams.—New York Mercury.—Hugh Gaine's Gazette.—Philip Freneau, the Poet.—The Adamses, Warrens, and Quincys.—Boston Gazette.—Shed's Grocery-store.—Boston Massacre.—Throwing the Tea overboard.—Imprisonment of Daniel Fowle.—Newport (R. I.) Mercury.—James Franklin, Jr.—Ann Franklin.—The Franklin Printing-presses.—Imprisonment of Alexander M'Dougall, etc................................ 102

CHAPTER VII.
SPREAD OF THE REVOLUTIONARY SPIRIT.

The Connecticut Courant.—Scarcity of Rags for Paper-mills.—Appeals for old Cotton and Linen.—Curiosities of the old Rag Shops.—History repeating itself.—The American Rag-bag.—The Maryland Gazette.—Charles Carroll, of Carrollton.—The Virginia Resolutions.—Mottoes and Devices.—Opinions of Sir William Berkeley and Henry A. Wise.—New York Journal.—Alexander M'Dougall.—Royal Gazetteer.—James Rivington.—Attack on Rivington's Office.—Alexander Hamilton.—Boston Chronicle.—John Mein.—Salem Gazette.—Harvard College.—Nathaniel Willis, etc........................... 113

CHAPTER VIII.
THE REVOLUTIONARY CRISIS.

The Massachusetts Spy.—Isaiah Thomas.—The British Organ.—Massachusettensis.—Join or Die.—Paul Revere's Midnight Ride.—The Concord Fight.—Worcester Spy.—Rivington's Royal Gazette.—Curious Interview with Colonel Ethan Allen.—Major André and the Cow Chase.—Freneau's Satires, etc, 127

CHAPTER IX.
CLOSE OF THE REVOLUTIONARY PERIOD.

Increase of Newspapers.—The Independent Chronicle.—Death of General Warren.—William Gordon, the Historian.—Publication of Histories and Geographies.—New York Packet.—Samuel Loudon.—Death of James Otis.—Newspapers in New Jersey.—The first New York Directory.—The Greenbacks of the last Century.—Number of Papers printed at the close of the Revolutionary Struggle, etc..Page 136

FOURTH ERA.
1783—1832.
THE POLITICAL PARTY PRESS.
CHAPTER X.
ORGANIZATION OF THE GREAT POLITICAL PARTIES.

After the Revolution.—The Beginning of the Federal and Republican Parties.—Metternich's Opinion.—Stamp Acts.—Names of Cliques.—Contributors to the Press.—Newspapers in Existence.—Independent Gazette.—American Citizen.—James Cheetham.—State of Society.—Aaron Burr's Suit against the Citizen.—Theatre in New York.—"Vivat Respublica."—Box 8s., Pit 6s., Gallery 4s.—Massachusetts Centinel.—Major Benjamin Russell.—Shay's Rebellion.—Federal Constitution.—Real and imaginary Processions.—The War of Editors.—King Louis Philippe.—The Black Cockade.—Death of the Federal Party.—Gerrymandering.—New Hampshire Gazette.—Connecticut Courant..... 141

CHAPTER XI.
THE NEWSPAPERS ON THE PENDING QUESTIONS.

The Restoration of the Tories to Citizenship.—Society of Cincinnati.—The Alien and Sedition Laws. —Virginia Resolutions.—Prosecutions of Newspapers.—Law of Libel in Massachusetts.—The Common Law of England "the Birthright of every American."—Benjamin Austin and Thomas O. Selfridge.—Assassination of Charles Austin.—The Massachusetts Stamp Act.—Tax on Advertisements.—Benjamin Edes and Isaiah Thomas.—Worcester Spy.—American Titles.—The Rise and Fall of Newspapers.—The first Express.—Salem Register and Salem Gazette.—Chief Justice Story on Newspaper Personalities... 158

CHAPTER XII.
THE FIRST DAILY NEWSPAPERS.

The American Daily Advertiser of Philadelphia.—Zachariah Poulson.—The New York Daily Advertiser.—Washington in New York.—Freneau.—The Portland Daily Courier.—Junius and the Federalist.—When and where published.—Interesting Incidents.—New York Gazette.—John Lang.—Shipping News.—Old Lang's Sign.—United States Gazette and North American of Philadelphia.—John Fenno.—Joseph R. Chandler.—Newspaper Enterprise.—Ten Journals in one.—Impartial Intelligencer..................................... 175

CHAPTER XIII.
NOTABLE JOURNALS.

National Gazette of Philadelphia.—The celebrated Philip Freneau.—Organ of Thomas Jefferson. — Violent Attacks on Washington. — His Complaints in Cabinet Council.—New York Time-piece.—Matthew L. Davis.—Newspapers in New Jersey. — Massachusetts Mercury. — "Immutably Impartial." — Harry Blake, the Ship-news Compiler.—Incidents in his Life.—Topliff's News-room in Boston. — Noah Webster. — New York Commercial Advertiser. — Colonel William L. Stone. — Anecdote of James G. Percival. — Thurlow Weed and Hugh Hastings. 185

CHAPTER XIV.
THE·PRESS AT THE WEST.

The Centinel of the Northwestern Territory.—First Journalist of the Northwest.—Posmasters as Publishers.—Western Spy and Sol. Smith.—Newspapers in Cincinnati.—The Gazette.—Charles Hammond.—The first daily Paper.—Introduction of Steam Presses.—Symmes's Hole.—Horse Expresses.—Cash Receipts of Newspapers.—Cincinnati Commercial.—Murat Halsted.—The Thomases in Journalism. — Cincinnati Chronicle and Times. — Ohio Statesman.—Newspapers in Indiana and Missouri. — St. Louis Republican. — Sale of the Democrat.—Journalism in Chicago.—War with the Blondes. — The Press in Wisconsin.—Thurlow Weed and William L. Stone.—Newspapers in Kansas.—The Frontier Index, etc.. Page 195

CHAPTER XV.
TWO REMARKABLE NEWSPAPERS.

The Philadelphia Aurora.—Benjamin Franklin Bache and William Duane.—Savage Attack on Washington.—Curious Incident in India.—Expulsion of Duane.—The Alien and Sedition Laws.—Trials and Convictions of Editors.—Serious Riots in Philadelphia. — Alexander Hamilton's Libel Suit against the New York Argus.—New York Evening Post.—William Coleman.—Extraordinary Duel.—Interesting Coincident.—Theodore Dwight.—Fitz Greene Halleck and John Rodman Drake. — William Cullen Bryant and William Leggett. — The Food of an Editor.—The Bee and Columbian.—Newspaper Circulation.—Gales and Seaton.—James Montgomery, the Poet.—The Lay Preacher, etc..... 210

CHAPTER XVI.
THE OFFICIAL ORGANS IN WASHINGTON.

The Organs of the World.—The first Newspaper in the National Capital.—National Intelligencer.—Gales and Seaton.—Organs of the Government.—Congressional Printing. — National Journal. — Advent of Jackson. — The United States Telegraph and Duff Green.—The Quarrel of Jackson and Calhoun.—Thomas H. Benton.—The Globe.—Francis P. Blair and Amos Kendall.—John C. Rives.—The Spectator and Constitution. — Intrigues and Incidents.—The Union.—Thomas Ritchie.—Congressional Globe.—Interesting Reminiscences.—The Nullification Proclamation.—The Madisonian.—The Republic.—Newspapers of To-day, etc... 230

CHAPTER XVII.
THE DEMOCRATIC TRIUMVIRATE.

The Charleston (S. C.) Courier, James Gordon Bennett's Newspaper Cradle.—Morning Chronicle of New York.—Washington Irving and Charles Dickens.—Jonathan Oldstyle and Boz.—Singular Duel.—Harry Croswell, of the Hudson Balance.—Suit against him for an Attack on Jefferson.—Opinions of Alexander Hamilton.—The Triumvirate.—Richmond Enquirer.—Thomas Ritchie.—Andrew Jackson on Ritchie.—Tragical Duel between John H. Pleasants and Thomas Ritchie, Jr.—New Hampshire Patriot and Isaac Hill.—"Origin" of the War on the United States Bank.—The Albany Register and Solomon Southwick.—Nathaniel H. Carter.—Mobbing the Baltimore Republican.—The Albany Argus and Edwin Croswell.—Public Printing.—The Regency.—Judge Kent on Newspapers.—James Gordon Bennett and the Courier and Enquirer.. 262

CHAPTER XVIII.
THE NATIONAL ADVOCATE AND ENQUIRER.

Troubles of Politicians.—New Party Organs.—The Advocate.—Henry Wheaton. —Henry Eckford.—The Enquirer.—Major Noah.—Washington Correspondence and James Gordon Bennett.—Horace Walpole's Letters.—Niblo's Coffeehouse.—The Duel between William Graham and Dr. Barton.—Ingathering of the Jews at Grand Island.—The City of Ararat.—Noah's grand Procession and Oration.—Evening Star.—Newspaper Editors in General..........Page 282

CHAPTER XIX.
THE RELIGIOUS PRESS.

Origin of religious Journalism.—The first in the Field.—Chillicothe Recorder and John Andrews.—Boston Recorder and Nathaniel Willis.—Autobiography of Willis.—The Claims of Sidney E. Morse.—New York Observer.—Watchman and Reflector.—Zion's Herald.—Christian Register.—Christian Herald.—Christian Advocate.—Tilt between the Evangelist and Independent.—Christian Union.—Henry Ward Beecher and Wendell Phillips as Journalists.—Organs of Churches.—Character of the Religious Press.—Its Ups and Downs.—Archbishop Hughes and the Catholic Press.—Jewish Organs.—The Daily Witness.—New York Herald as a religious Paper.—Newspapers for Children, etc.. 289

CHAPTER XX.
SOME OF THE REPRESENTATIVE NEWSPAPERS.

Inkling of an Independent Press.—Judge Bouvier and the American Telegraph. —Niles's Register.—Hartford Times.—John M. Niles and Gideon Welles.—Funny Fight for a Post-office.—Thomas H. Benton and Duff Green in Missouri.—St. Louis Enquirer.—William Cobbett.—The Porcupine.—Cobbett as a Host.—New York American and Charles King.—The Providence Journal,—Wonderful Change of Base on the Tariff Question.—New York Albion.—Organs of other Nations in the United States.—The Poets as Journalists.—Stop my Paper!—Fashionable Journalism.—The Louisville Journal.—George D. Prentice and John Greenleaf Whittier.—The Courier-Journal.—Henry Watterson.—The Wits of the Press.—The Initial Sheet west of Albany.—John I. Mumford.—Fanny Wright.—Opinion of Richard Cobden, etc........... 306

CHAPTER XXI.
SPECIAL OR CLASS JOURNALISM.

Organs of the Farmers.—Number of Agricultural Newspapers.—What they have accomplished.—Commercial and Financial Press.—Origin of the Boston Commercial Bulletin.—Its Character and Value.—The Sunday Newspapers.—What are they?—The Sporting Press.—What it has done for the Turf and the Field.—The Telegraph Organs.—Our Society Journals............. 329

CHAPTER XXII.
THE BLANKET SHEETS OF NEW YORK.

The Morning Courier and New York Enquirer.—James Watson Webb.—Newspaper Enterprise.—Size of the Sheets.—The Quadruple Constellation.—The Graves and Cilley Duel.—Colonel Webb and Duff Green.—The Woods Riot. —The Marshall Duel.—Sentence of Colonel Webb.—The Bankrupt Act.—William L. Marcy and James Gordon Bennett.—The Mackenzie Pamphlet.—The Editor of the Courier as a Diplomat.—Webb and Napoleon.—The Journal of Commerce.—Its Origin.—David Hale and Gerard Hallock.—News Schooners and Pony Expresses.—Abolition Riots in New York.—Lewis Tappan's

Escape. — Origin of the Associated Press.—The Rebellion.—Advertisements. —The Bogus Proclamation.—Suspension of New York Papers.—The Present Manager and Editor of the Journal of Commerce.................Page 344

CHAPTER XXIII.
SOME OF THE BOSTON NEWSPAPERS.

The Boston Daily Advertiser.—Horatio Biglow and Nathan Hale.—The first Daily Newspaper in New England.—Origin of Editorial Articles.—North American Review.—The Evening Traveller.—Its Introduction to News-boys.—The Boston Courier.—Joseph Tinker Buckingham. — New England Galaxy.—The Transcript.—The Liberator.—William Lloyd Garrison.—Old Files of Newspapers.—The Boston Pilot.—Charles G. Greene.—" All Sorts" of Wit.—The Atlas.—Richard Haughton and John H. Eastburn.—Samuel Bowles, of Springfield.—The Mercantile Journal.—The stunning News Placards.—The Herald. —The last Newspaper Enterprise.—The Globe....................... 378

CHAPTER XXIV.
ANTI-MASONRY AND NULLIFICATION.

Thurlow Weed and the Albany Evening Journal.—The Anti-Masonic Party.— Seward, Weed & Co.—Who wrote the Junius Letters?—The Roorback Hoax. —The Nashville Union.—Duels and Offices.—The Charleston (S. C.) Mercury. —The chief Organ of the Nullifiers and Secessionists.—More Duels.—Nice Points of Honor.—The Code.—The "Independence" of the Press.—The Tariff Question... 397

FITFH ERA.
1832—1835.
JOURNALISM IN A TRANSITION STATE.

CHAPTER XXV.
THE BEGINNING OF THE NEWSPAPER REVOLUTION.

Size of Newspapers in 1832.—Waste of Space. — Smaller Papers. — The New York Globe.—James Gordon Bennett.—Signs of a Change.—The Pennsylvanian.—The Mackenzie Pamphlet.—The Hoyt, Van Buren, and Bennett Correspondence.—Inside View of the Party Press.—Blair's Opinion of Bennett.—Opposition of Politicians.—Incoming of the Independent Press.—Seward, Weed, and Greeley... 408

CHAPTER XXVI.
THE PENNY PRESS.

Where did it originate?—The Cent of Philadelphia.—The Morning Post of New York.—Its Failure.—Dr. Horatio D. Shepard and Horace Greeley.—The New York Sun. — Its Success. — Speech of its Originator. —Contents of the first Number.—The Moon Hoax.— Richard Adams Locke.—The Man without a Country.—Enterprise of the Sun.—Opinion of a "Blanket Sheet" on the Cheap Press.—The Citizen and Miles O'Reilly............................. 416

SIXTH ERA.
1835—1872.
THE INDEPENDENT PRESS.
CHAPTER XXVII.
THE NEW YORK HERALD.

James Gordon Bennett, Senior.—Newspaper Autobiography.—His Prospectus.—What he promised to do.—How he started the Herald.—It came with Steamboats and Railroads. — Origin of the Money Articles. — News Agencies and News Companies.—Burned out.—Another Prospectus.—Ocean Steam Navigation. — The Extradition Treaty.—The Cash System.— Sam. Houston and Texas.—Amos Kendall and Nicholas Biddle. — Personal Assaults.—Illustrations and War Maps.—The Religious Anniversary Meetings.—Opposition of the Clergy.—Harbor News Arrangements.—Visit to Europe—European Correspondence.—The Harrison Hard-Cider Campaign. . . . . Page 428

CHAPTER XXVIII.
MORE OF THE NEW YORK HERALD.

The great Moral War.—Tremendous Struggle between the old and new Class of Journals.—The Forces in the Field.—Anecdotes.—The curious Result.—John Howard Payne. — Attempted Assassination. — An Infernal Machine. — New Mode of Advertising.—Interesting Incidents.—The Mexican War.—Overland Expresses.—Discovery of Gold in California.—Silver Plate to Mr. Bennett. — Libel Suits.—The Policy of the Herald.—Obituary Notices.—Curious Incident with Sir Henry Bulwer.—Style of Editorials.—The Telegraphic Era. —The Great Rebellion.—The Herald War Correspondents.—News from the South. — Letter from Secretary Stanton. — The French Mission. — What did Pierce, Buchanan, and Lincoln do?—Death of the Founder of the Herald.—Cheap Press in New York.—James Gordon Bennett, Jr.—Wonderful Enterprise in Europe and Africa.—The Anglo-Abyssinian Expedition.—The News Steam Yachts.—The Herald Exploring Expeditions in Africa.—What next?.... 456

CHAPTER XXIX.
NEWSPAPERS IN NEW ORLEANS AND MOBILE.

The Initial Papers of the Crescent City.—Journalism in French and English.—New Orleans Bee.—The Picayune.—George Wilkins Kendall.—War Correspondence from Mexico.—Decline of Journalism in New Orleans.—Its Cause.—Newspaper Architecture.—The first Paper in Mobile.—Newspapers in that City.—The first Penny Paper.—The Register and John Forsyth. 491

CHAPTER XXX.
FEMALE JOURNALISTS.

The Ladies' Magazine.—The Lowell Offering.—Early Female Periodical Writers. —Sarah Josepha Hale.—The Woman's Rights Movement.—The Revolution. —The Sorosis. — Woman's Journal. — Woodhull & Claflin's Weekly. — The True Woman.—Free Love.—Female Suffrage.—The Troubles of the Reformers. 497

CHAPTER XXXI.
THE CHEAP PRESS IN PHILADELPHIA AND BALTIMORE.

The Public Ledger of Philadelphia.—The Sun of Baltimore.—Swain, Abell, and Simmons.—Their wonderful Success.—The way George W. Childs purchased the Ledger. — His manifest Destiny. — His Management of the Paper. — The

splendid Ledger Building.—Anecdotes of Swain and Childs.—Political Hoax.
—" The Pen is mightier than the Sword."—The Ledger Almanac... Page 505

CHAPTER XXXII.
THE EXPRESS NEWSPAPER AND THE EXPRESS LINES.

The New York Express.—Willis Hall and James Brooks.—The European Correspondent.—The Man with the big Hat.—Erastus Brooks.—The Express Lines.—Harnden, Adams, Dinsmore, and Sanford.—Importance of the Expresses to Newspaper Publishers 517

CHAPTER XXXIII.
THE NEW YORK TRIBUNE.

Horace Greeley.—What he has done in Journalism.—The Daily Tribune.—The Weekly Tribune.—Inducements to Subscribers.—Associated Ownership.—Circulation and Advertisements.—The Isms of the Tribune.—Contests with the Herald.—The Great Halifax Express.—The Atlantic Ocean Express.—The Firm of Seward, Weed, and Greeley.—Its Dissolution.—Greeley before a Parliamentary Committee.—His Slap at the Herald.—The Kansas Question.—"Just once."—What it costs to publish the Tribune.—Managing Editors.—Interviewing and its Advantages.—The Inititial Editors.—Greeley's Penmanship.—Thirty Years in the Tribune.—Tour through the South.—Aspirations for the Presidency.—Nomination for the White House.—Withdrawal from the Tribune.—Newspaper Almanacs.. 522

CHAPTER XXXIV.
ALL SORTS OF POLITICAL PAPERS.

The first Newspaper in Tennessee.—The Knoxville Whig.—Parson Brownlow and Andrew Johnson.—The Albany Register.—The Plebeian, New Era, Morning News, Globe, and Aurora.—Slamm, Bang & Co.—The Republic.—Chevalier Wikoff and Duff Green.—The Albany Atlas.—The War of the Roses.—The Springfield Republican.—Samuel Bowles.—Arrest in New York.—Controversy with David Dudley Field.—The first Journal in the Oil Regions. 574

CHAPTER XXXV.
CHEAP LITERATURE.

Novels made into News and sold by News-boys.—The Brother Jonathan and New World.—The Boston Notion.—Competition for the last Novel by the last Steamer.—Dickens's American Notes and the Queen's Speech.—Effect of the Copyright Law in Canada.. 587

CHAPTER XXXVI.
NEWSPAPERS ON THE PACIFIC.

The Flumgudgeon Gazette, of Oregon.—Stevenson's Expedition.—Type and Presses go with the Troops.—The Discovery of Gold.—Specimens sent to the New York Herald.—Tremendous Gold Excitement.—How Newspapers in California originated.—Eastern Journals in the Mines.—How early News from California was obtained.—The Present.—The Future................... 590

CHAPTER XXXVII.
THE TELEGRAPHIC ERA.

Various Modes of transmitting Intelligence for Newspapers.—Carrier Pigeons and Balloons.—Introduction of the Telegraph.—Its Struggles.—Opinion of a Wall-Street Millionaire.—Nomination of Silas Wright.—Influence of the Telegraph on the Press.—Curious Prediction of Lamartine.—The Battles in Mexico.—Marvelous Progress.—The Battles in Europe.—Affairs of the World daily Electrotyped for the Journalist. — Balloons as News and Mail Carriers from Paris.—The Lightning Express Lines...................... Page 595

CHAPTER XXXVIII.
THE NEW YORK ASSOCIATED PRESS.

Its Origin.—Its Necessity.—Its Object.—Its Operations.—War with the Telegraph Companies.—Attempt at Monopoly.—Lease of the Newfoundland Line.—Intercepting Steamers off Halifax and Cape Race.—Will the Association be a permanent Institution?... 608

CHAPTER XXXIX.
THE NEW YORK TIMES.

How it originated.—Negotiations on the Ice.—The Tilsit Raft of the Times.—Henry J. Raymond its Editor.—His Ability as a Reporter.—His early Career in Politics.—Why he was called "Little Villain" by Horace Greeley.—Trouble with James Watson Webb.—Threatened Duel with Thomas Francis Meagher.—Sharp Controversy with Archbishop Hughes.—The Elbows of the Mincio.—The Draft Riots.—Fortifying Newspaper Offices.—Manners in Journalism.—Sudden Death of Mr. Raymond.—Henry Ward Beecher's Eulogy.—The new Management of the Times.—George Jones.—The Gold Speculations of 1869.—John Bigelow.—The War on the Tammany Ring.—Its great and important Result... 618

CHAPTER XL.
THE NEW YORK LEDGER.

Its Origin.—Its first Name.—Curious Names of Papers.—Why Bonner bought the Ledger.—How he brought it into Notice.—Mrs. Sigourney the first Contributor.—Who writes for the Ledger?—Bonner's Advertisements.—How he managed the Herald.—His System.—Anxiety of his Pastor.—Novels by Telegraph.—Interesting Incident.—Correspondence with General Grant and Henry Ward Beecher.—His Horses.—His Country Seat and the Fever and Ague.—The Circulation of the Ledger.. 646

CHAPTER XLI.
THE PRESS CLUBS AND ASSOCIATIONS.

Origin of the Press Club of New York.—Kossuth's Reception and Speech.—The Dickens Banquet.—Speeches of Greeley, Dickens, Raymond, Curtis, and Hawley. — The Press Social Associations in the Country. — What they do. — No Connection with the News Associations............................... 656

CHAPTER XLII.
THE NEW YORK WORLD.

How it was Started.—Its religious Character.—Two hundred thousand Dollars lost in the Enterprise.—Its Change of Base.—Its Union with the Courier and Enquirer.—The Bogus Proclamation.—Suspension of the World by the Government. — Its Reappearance and Manifesto. — Repudiation of Seymour and Blair.—The Literary Character of the Paper.—Its Enterprise.—Manton Marble, its Editor... 667

CHAPTER XLIII.
THE NEW YORK SUN.

Its modern Character.—Its Sale to Charles A. Dana and Associates.—It is no longer a Penny Paper. — Who is Editor Dana? — His Connection with the Tribune.—Assistant Secretary of War.—Editor of the Chicago Republican.—Editor of the New York Sun.—Trouble with John Russell Young.—Circula-

tion of the Sun. — Its Platform. — Marriages, Divorces, Births, and Deaths.—
Summoned before Congress................................... Page 677

CHAPTER XLIV.
THE COMIC PAPERS.

Their Failure in the United States and Success in Europe.—The Cause.—Wit and Humor here and elsewhere.—Mark Twain on Artemus Ward.—Interview with Petroleum V. Nasby.—What one Humorist says of another.—Abundance of Wit in America.. 688

CHAPTER XLV.
THE PRESS IN CONGRESS.

Journalists in the Senate and House of Representatives.—Newspaper Representatives in the national Capital.—The two Congresses.—Editors as M. C.'s, Correspondents, and Reporters... 697

CHAPTER XLVI.
THE ILLUSTRATED NEWSPAPERS.

News pictorially reported and described.—Wood-engraving in the United States.—Harper's Family Bible.—The first Illustrated Newspapers.—Frank Leslie's Illustrated News, Harper's Weekly, and Harper's Bazar. — Sinclair's Photo-Zinco.—The new Art.—Exchange of Engravings.—Our National Gallery. 705

CHAPTER XLVII.
THE TRANSIENT PRESS.

Newspapers in the Army and Navy.—Newspapers in Colleges.—The Schools of Journalism.—Newspapers with the Troops in the Field.—Amateur Journalism. —The Avant Coureurs of America................................... 710

CHAPTER XLVIII.
THE WAR CORRESPONDENTS.

What have they accomplished?—Their Labors and Dangers.—Their Capture and Imprisonment.—Journalists in Action.—What is thought of them.—They are the Historians of the great Conflicts of the World.—The Rebellion.—The Abyssinian Expedition.—The Franco-German War.—The Search for Livingstone.. 715

CHAPTER XLIX.
THE REPORTERS OF THE PRESS.

Their early Struggles in reporting Speeches and Debates.—The Revolution.—Value of Reports.—Number of Reporters............................ 720

CHAPTER L.
THE COPYRIGHT IN NEWS.

What Protection has a Newspaper with its News?—Colonel Thomas H. Benton's Lecture. — Weekly Papers entered at the Office of the Librarian.—The Proposed International Copyright Treaty of 1853. — Important Lawsuits. — The real Copyright in News.—What is it?—The new Copyright Treaty...... 723

CHAPTER LI.
ADVERTISEMENTS.

The first Advertisement.—Annual Value of a Column of Advertisements.—The professional Advertisement Writer.—Various Modes of Advertisements.—Placards on the Face of Nature.—Curious Advertisements.—The Spread of Religion by Advertisements. — The Philosophy of the Business.—The Advertising Agencies.—Their Expansion... 728

CHAPTER LII.
THE MOTTOES OF THE PRESS.

Are they the Editors' Platforms of Principles?—Specimen Mottoes.—The Pope's Motto for Journalists..Page 738

CHAPTER LIII.
THE LAW OF LIBEL.

Trials and Responsibilities of the Press.—What is the Law of Libel?—Interesting and instructive Cases.—The editorial Right to criticise.—The Suits of J. Fenimore Cooper, Charles Reade, and George Augustus Sala.—The Russian Law.—Eating his own Words.—The Emperor of Germany and the Press.—The Organic Law of the United States.............................. 741

CHAPTER LIV.
THE CASH VALUE OF NEWSPAPERS.

Values in the United States.—Sale of the Bulletin in Philadelphia at Public Auction.—Offers for the New York Herald and Times.—Millionaires in Newspapers and Dry Goods... 758

CHAPTER LV.
THE DUELS OF EDITORS.

Assaults and Assassinations.—The Code of Honor among Journalists.—Several extraordinary Duels.—State of Feeling at the South since the Rebellion.. 761

CHAPTER LVI.
THE END.

Statistics of the Press in the United States.—Our Progress.—Newspapers a Half Century old.—Number of Periodicals in the World.—The Future........ 769

ADDENDA.

Horace Greeley's Return to the Tribune after the Presidential Election of November, 1872.—His Death.—The new Editor of the New Orleans Picayune.—Change in the Form of the St. Louis Republican...................... 777

INTRODUCTION
TO THE J. & J. HARPER EDITION

Frederic Hudson, managing editor of the New York *Herald* in the mid-nineteenth century, had the bad luck to call his book *Journalism in the United States*. Even with the qualifying appendage—"from 1690 to 1872"—it had a grand theme, and though it was the standard text for many years after its publication in 1873 it became a monumental target for criticism by later historians.

It is a book with defects.

Hudson was euphoric to the point of giddiness, an emotion maintained today only by the more oleaginous lobbyists for the trade. His dedication is: "THE PRESS, The Argus of the World, the Ear-Gallery of the Globe, the Reporter of the Universe."

Hudson's introduction, also in the Victorian style, is a series of grandiloquent and fulsome quotations on the press, among them Thomas Jefferson's famous dictum of 1787—"I would rather live in a country with newspapers and without a government, than in a country with a government but without newspapers"—but not including Jefferson's not-so-famous dictum of 20 years later: "Nothing can now be believed which is seen in a newspaper."

Hudson's history is not always accurate, and he was an imperfect prophet. He predicted that pneumatic tubes would deliver the New York papers to San Francisco "on the day of publication." He said that the Associated Press would soon disintegrate. "It will go out of existence as soon as the network of electric wires and cables are capable of transmitting easily and without delay the news correspondence of the Press. . . ." But with the passage of time these defects have become unimportant, some of them understandable from the perspective of his own career and the rest forgivable because of other qualities in the book. The imprecision in some dates and circumstances have since been remedied in books that lack Hudson's detail and sense of excitement.

He was a working editor and a good one and compiled this encyclopedic work when, graduate students not having been invented, men still did their own research. Meticulous historical study of journalism was still 50 years away, the work, for example, of the two Lees—James Melvin Lee, who disputed Hudson on some of his facts, and Alfred McClung Lee, who said the differences were unimportant—and Frank Luther Mott, who said that Hudson was "diffuse and unreliable, but extensive and valuable for suggestions."

If Hudson had given his work a title more in the style of the century before his own, such as *Some Observations and Contemplations Upon Being an Actor in the Evolution of a New Medium of Human Communication,* it would have expressed the value of reading his book a hundred years after he wrote it. Looked at in this way, Hudson's work has insights for those of us participating in the start of another, and probably more radical, change in the way men exchange information.

We would do well to understand why the author felt so satisfied with the prospects of journalism in his time. For one thing, he wrote during a special period, after the mud-slinging of a previous period and before the yellow journalism in the circulation wars of Hearst and Pulitzer.

Hudson was 54 years old when he published *Journalism in the United States,* but he had been a newspaperman since the age of 17, when he was hired by the flamboyant James Gordon Bennett. Bennett was a favorite target for accusations of irresponsibility, and was looked down on for turning his *Herald* into a "ribald vehicle" of "moral leprosy."

Bennett was no saintly character breathing the beatitudes on his daily pages. When Hudson went to work for him in 1836, there were no professional reporters in journalism. Editors listened to gossip and clipped items from other papers that had done the same thing. The news collection system of the American newspaper at the time consisted of an editor with a free mail franchise, a pair of scissors, a glue pot and, in the case of Bennett, a talent for inventing stories when the truth disappointed him.

Hudson became Bennett's managing editor. The *Herald* hired full-time reporters. At first the reporters spent a lot of time covering the juiciest cases in court, but Bennett and Hudson gradually turned them to other things, including the printing of stenographic accounts of major Sunday sermons (a practice that brought howls of rage from the clergy, who later came to like the idea so well that they got indignant if Hudson's men didn't cover their church services). The Mexican War in 1846 was covered by correspondents, and then telegraph brought systematic coverage of major events.

The *Herald* under Hudson became the leading newspaper in New York. Hence at his prime, when he conceived his book, Hudson had reason to think grandly of the improvement of the press and to believe that the future would be a succession of triumphs.

It was a time of strong editors who saw themselves as arbiters of ideas. Journalism was still a professional activity, and editors were analysts of social development. The time had not yet come when journalism would be a corporate activity and editors administrative executives.

Hudson could remember when out-of-town papers carried by stagecoach were the standard communications link for the news, and the most dramatic means of speeding communication were the carrier pigeon and the free-floating balloon. Once the information drifted in, it was reproduced on expensive paper through cumbersome presses. Yet by the time Hudson wrote the book, a generation later, professional correspondents were sending dispatches by telegraph and cable, and printing speeds were going up exponentially while the price of paper was going down.

It was a span of time long enough for one to see enormous change, with all the pleasure and excitement of radical improvement, but not long enough to see clearly some of the less pleasant implications that would later become obvious.

Hudson, living at the start of the Industrial Revolution, expressed the euphoria of his time over the wonders of the steam locomotive, the telegraph, and high-speed printing. It was a time of innocent faith in the inexorable improvement of civilization by the march of technology and commerce, with little suspicion that the new machines might merely spread error more efficiently or that corporate decision making might ever be divorced from social good. When Hudson's book was published, Lincoln Steffens was only seven years old, and William Randolph Hearst only ten.

Hudson reminds us of our own time, when the introduction of the computer wed to electronic communication in the home is imminent, with at least as much promise for human growth and social benefit as had the earlier Industrial Revolution, but also, with as much opportunity for stultification and perversion.

Beyond this, Hudson provides fascinating detail of journalistic changes, detail often lost in the modern, more tightly constructed histories. He was plainly not a rushed man when he wrote and he assumed that the reader too was not rushed. The result is a work that is often wordy but often full of rich, detailed accounts. For example, he prints the verbatim testimony of Horace Greeley before a British parliamentary inquiry into the press in 1851. (Greeley: "... when a town grows to have as many as 15,000 inhabitants, or thereabouts, it has a daily paper ... At 20,000 they have two, and so on.")

To those in awe of contemporary experiments with microfiche, the miniaturization of printed or other graphic matter on film, the following report by Hudson will be of interest.

> On one occasion, during the siege of the French capital in 1870, a carrier pigeon carried into that city a newspaper 4 3/4 inches square, with 226 dispatches microscopically photographed upon it, embracing the news of the day, from all parts of the world. This paper had to be read by the aid of a powerful microscope and the magic lantern.

Hudson saw advertising as an unblemished joy, including its tricks. "How many are deceived by the first few lines of a business notice in a New York paper!" he wrote, adding, "No one gets angry over these modern cheats." Account executives and copywriters for modern advertising agencies will enjoy Hudson's report on the new growth of ads in newspapers: "There was one Duncan Mousseux lately died in the French capital who devoted himself exclusively to this peculiar kind of business."

Some of Hudson's speculations have meaning today:

> Now what will be the effect of the universal extension of the telegraph on the Press? Will it make newspapers greater intellectual powers than they were previous to 1844?... Will not the common property in news compel journalists to employ better, brighter, broader brains? With the events of the world hourly placed before the conductor of a leading newspaper, will he not have to be a man of greater and more comprehensive grasp of intellect than has yet been seen?

Today, of course, the "events of the world" are "hourly placed," not only before the editor but before the consumer himself as well. And Hudson's observations still apply.

Today, on the threshold of radical changes in printed and broadcast news, we are less innocent about men and machines. We know a little bit more about the relation between communications and behavior. But we are still inclined to believe that new machines are ordained by some natural law to create unalloyed human benefit and that uninfluenced by social concerns and untended by public involvement, they still automatically enrich the human spirit. With mass communications about to change in ways as radical and as exciting as those that had taken place in Frederic Hudson's time, his euphoria is a warning and his perceptions are a guide.

BEN H. BAGDIKIAN

February, 1969

INTRODUCTION.

No book is without a preface. It opens the subject with the reader as the state of the weather begins a conversation among strangers. When a new journal is contemplated it has its prospectus. When a new theatre is opened the manager speaks a piece called a prologue. New goods are anticipated by an advertisement. Sermons are preached from texts. Oaks start from acorns. This volume, therefore, requires an introduction. What shall it be? What the compiler may say would not, incipiently, amount to much. What the ablest intellects of the world have thought will have more weight. What these writers have expressed must consequently be our grand proem. Our readers will be sufficiently satisfied, we think, with the preface which our distinguished colaborers have prepared, at divers times, since Job, and which we insert, as the pearl and diamond settings in our Dutch gold, and the rich frames of our imperfect sketches. These are the

MEMORABILIA.

Who is most thought of in London, Sir Marmaduke—the Lord Chancellor, or the editor of the *Jupiter?*

The Lord Chancellor, a great deal, said Sir Marmaduke, quite dismayed by the audacity of the question.

* * * * * * *

Nobody cares for the Lord Chancellor!

* * * * * * *

I do not say so. He may be a great lawyer, and very useful; but his lordship, and his wig, and his woolsack are tinsel in comparison with the real power possessed by the editor of a leading newspaper. If the Lord Chancellor were to go to bed for a month, would he be much missed?

I don't know, sir; I'm not in the secrets of the Cabinet. I should think he would.

About as much as my grandmother; but if the editor of the *Jupiter* were to be taken ill, it would work quite a commotion.

Anthony Trollope, "*He knew he was right.*"

Eh bien! quelle place occupe dans ces libertés nécessaires la liberté de la presse?

Elle n'est pas la plus attrayante, mais elle est la plus nécessaire. C'est la liberté de penser.

Quand une nation veut faire ses affaires, il faut qu'elle y pense, qu'elle y puisse penser librement, former des volontés et les faire prévaloir. Donc, la liberté de la presse est théoriquement et pratiquement la plus nécessaire de toutes.

* * * * * * *

Eh bien, Messieurs, le véritable juge du juge, c'est l'opinion publique ; comment alors interdire la publicité ?
Adolphe Thiers, Censor of the Press in France in 1872.

I would rather live in a country with newspapers and without a government, than in a country with a government but without newspapers.
Thomas Jefferson.

Give me the liberty to know, to alter, and to argue freely, according to conscience, above all liberties.
John Milton, the Cromwellian Editor.

A journalist! That means a grumbler, a censurer, a giver of advice, a regent of sovereigns, a tutor of nations! Four hostile newspapers are more to be dreaded than a hundred thousand bayonets!
Napoleon the First.

Il est de la nature du journalisme de susciter plus de griefs et de créer plus de ressentimens que l'éloquence délibérative ; mais quand on a cité le glorieux pseudonyme de Junius, les noms de Swift et de Bolingbroke en Angleterre, et chez nous les noms de Chateaubriand et de Benjamin Constant, sans ajouter d'autres noms présens à toutes les mémoires, il est bien difficile de contester que ce soit un genre de littérature qui a, comme tous les genres, ses règles, ses modèles et ses chefs d'œuvre même, bien qu'en général la durée leur fasse défaut. C'est qu'un journal, comme le mot l'indique, est surtout la chose du jour, et vise à produire un effet immédiat plutôt qu'à laisser un long souvenir. Néanmoins, Messieurs, je demande avec quelque confiance à quiconque s'est jamais mêlé d'écrire si ce sont de médiocres qualités littéraires que la clarté, la concision et la force, et ce sont là les vraies conditions de l'art du journalisme. Si vous ajoutez à ces qualités littéraires la belle condition que Caton imposait à l'orateur en l'appelant *vir bonus dicendi peritus*, et si vous supposez que le journaliste est intègre, de bonne foi, indépendant à l'égard du pouvoir, ferme contre les passions injustes, et dédaigneux d'une popularité trop facile, n'aurez vous point porté assez haut cet art indispensable aux sociétés modernes pour lui donner pleinement droit de cité dans les régions élevées de la littérature ? Mais, dira-t-on, ces conditions sont rarement atteintes.
Prevost-Paradol, the Journalist and Publicist.

We do not belong to our patrons ;
Our paper is wholly our own ;
Whoever may like it, may take it ;
Who don't, may just let it alone.
Anonymous Bohemian.

The Press all lands shall sing ;
The Press, the Press we bring,
All lands to bless ;
O pallid Want, O Labor stark,
Behold, we bring the second Ark—
The Press, the Press, the Press !
Ebenezer Elliot, the Corn-law Rhymer.

—— that mine adversary had written a book.
Newspaper Critic after Job.

'Tis pleasant, sure, to see one's name in print ;
A book's a book, altho' there's nothing in't.
Byron after the Newspaper Critics.

What is it but a map of busy life,
Its fluctuations, and its vast concerns.
Cowper on Newspapers.

I'll put a girdle around about the earth in forty minutes.
Puck, the first Telegraph Operator.

Great is journalism! Is not every able editor a ruler of the world, being a persuader of it?
Thomas Carlyle.

I wish no other herald,
No other speaker of my living actions,
To keep mine honor from corruption,
But such an honest chronicler.
Henry VIII., reported by Shakspeare.

La presse n'a d'autre puissance que celle qui resulte de l'expression de l'opinion publique.
Jules Favre.

In this one sheet how much for thought profound,
How much for feeling deep doth meet the eye!
Here man's decease, here empire's fate is found,
And yet with careless glance we pass them by!
Perchance upon one page enough we find
On which through a long life we well might muse:
But oft with husks we fill the hungry mind,
When men the gifts of speech and thought abuse.
Not in the many words, or books we read,
Is knowledge gained of Nature, or of man;
Oft in a single word lies wrapped the seed
Of changes vast, would we its meaning scan;
But lacking still the wisdom to be wise,
The Truth we seek is hidden from our eyes.
The Christian Register.

In Neuilly the doorways were crowded with people, chiefly women and children, timidly venturing into daylight after nearly three weeks' close imprisonment in their houses and even cellars. * * * * One man begged for a newspaper, declaring he had heard nothing from the outside world for many days.
Paris Letter, April 25, 1871, in London Times.

How doth the little busy bee
Improve each shining hour,
And gather honey all the day
From every opening flower.
Isaac Watts's Eulogy on Newspaper Reporters.

At last the floundering carrier bore
The village paper to our door.
Lo! broadening outward as we read,
To warmer zones the horizon spread;
In panoramic length unrolled,
We saw the marvels that it told.
. . . Its monthly gauge of snow and rain,
Its record, mingling in a breath
The wedding-knell and dirge of death;
Jest, anecdote, and love-lorn tale,
The latest culprit sent to jail;
Its hue and cry of stolen and lost,
Its vendue sales and goods at cost,
And traffic calling loud for gain.
We felt the stir of hall and street,
The pulse of life that round us beat;
The chill embargo of the snow
Was melted in the genial glow;

> Wide swung again our ice-locked door,
> And all the world was ours once more!
>
> *John Greenleaf Whittier, the "Snow-bound" Carrier.*

In the United States every worthy citizen reads a newspaper, and owns the paper which he reads. A newspaper is a window through which men look out on all that is going on in the world. Without a newspaper a man is shut up in a small room, and knows little or nothing of what is happening outside of himself. In our day newspapers keep pace with history and record it. * * * A good newspaper will keep a sensible man in sympathy with the world's current history. It is an ever-unfolding encyclopædia; an unbound book forever issuing and never finished.

Henry Ward Beecher.

> Mightiest of the mighty means
> On which the arm of Progress leans—
> Man's noblest mission to advance,
> His woes assuage, his weal enhance,
> His rights enforce, his wrongs redress—
> Mightiest of the mighty is the Press!
>
> *Bowring on the Fourth Estate.*

A newspaper can drop the same thought into a thousand minds at the same moment. A newspaper is an adviser who does not require to be sought, but comes to you briefly every day of common weal, without distracting your private affairs. Newspapers, therefore, become more necessary in proportion as men become more equal individuals, and more to be feared. To suppose that they only serve to protect freedom would be to diminish their importance: they maintain civilization.

Alexis de Tocqueville.

It is a momentous, yes, a fearful truth, that the millions have no literature, no school, and almost no pulpit but the press. Not one man in ten reads books. * * * * * * * * But every one of us, except the very few helpless poor, poisons himself every day with a newspaper. It is parent, school, college, pulpit, theatre, example, counselor, all in one. Every drop of our blood is colored by it. Let me make the newspapers, and I care not who makes the religion or the laws.

Wendell Phillips on Journalism.

> Leaf by leaf the roses fall,
>   Dime by dime the purse runs dry;
> One by one beyond recall,
>   Mushroom papers droop and die.
>
> *Obituary Notice of Newspapers.*

I believe that we could produce a visible change in the public mind if, against the encroachments of our German confederates, we touch the chord of an independent Prussian policy in the Press.

Count Bismarck, May 12, 1859.

Were the starry heavens deficient of one constellation, the vacuum could not be better supplied than by the introduction of a printing-press.

Astronomical View of Journalism.

> Hear, land o' cakes and brither Scots,
> Frae Maidenkirk to Johnny Groats',
> If there's a hole in a' your coats,
>   I rede ye tent it;
> A chiel's amang ye takin' notes,
>   An' faith he'll prent it!
>
> *Robert Burns.*

Give me but the liberty of the press, and I will give to the minister a venal House of Peers—I will give him a corrupt and servile House of Commons—I will give him the full sway of the patronage of office—I will give him the whole host of ministerial influence—I will give him all the power that place can confer upon him to purchase up submission and overawe resistance—and yet, armed with the liberty of the press, I will go forth to meet him undismayed—I will attack the mighty fabric he has reared with that mightier engine—I will shake down from its height corruption, and bury it amidst the ruins of the abuses it was meant to shelter.

Sheridan.

There she is; she never sleeps. She has her ambassadors in every quarter of the world—her couriers upon every road. Her officers march along with armies, and her envoys walk into statesmen's cabinets. They are ubiquitous. Yonder journal has an agent at this moment giving bribes at Madrid, and another inspecting the price of potatoes at Covent Garden.

W. M. Thackeray.

More solid things do not show the complexion of the Times so well as ballads and libels.

Selden.

Its liberties and the liberties of the people must stand or fall together.

David Hume.

After all, the Press is king.
It is the Press that creates public opinion.
It is the grand fact of the hour that popular sentiment has been educated by the Press up to the point of spurning party trammels and voting on principle.
Who, then, shall keep our custodians? If journalism is so powerful, who shall save us from such journalism as made the Commune possible in Paris?

The Bishop of Western New York.

These two centuries have been dealt with too much as fashionable travelers accomplish a Swiss tour. They go straight to Mont Blanc, then to the Oberland, then to the Righi, and care nothing for the country except as it may be seen from those glorious heights. The details of history, in truth, can only be gathered from a study of the immense and varied surface which the literature of newspapers presents.

Sainte Beuve, the Essayist and Critic.

Ever enlightening, always confirming grand truths, ever baptizing infant peoples, and always new.

Archbishop Hughes, of New York.

OUR OWN OPENING.

JOURNALISM! what is it? Newspapers! what are they? *Qu'est-ce la presse? C'est la voix de la nation.*
It is said that fifty thousand volumes and pamphlets have been written about America, and yet there is no history of the American Press.
Writers have accomplished more than this for England. F. Knight Hunt has given us "The Fourth Estate;" Alexander Andrews, "The History of British Journalism;" and James Grant published last year "The Newspaper Press: its Origin, Progress, and present Position." Speeches and pamphlets innumerable on the Stamp Act, the freedom of the press, and the law of libel have appeared, but they form no connected history, although they have had great influence in bringing the newspapers of England far above the fourth estate in that kingdom. "What does the *Times* say?" is a question that indicates the power of the newspaper in that country. Junius, in the *Public Advertiser*, aided largely in accomplishing this great result.

Writers have been even more industrious and effective in France. Eugene Hatin has attractively filled no less than eight large volumes with interesting details of the origin and growth of newspapers in that fertile country, where every eminent man in politics, poetry, philosophy, or science is a journalist. M. Hatin has also published a "Manual of the Liberty of the Press in France," which embraces a history of the struggles of the newspaper publishers to obtain their freedom, from the time of Francis I. to the overthrow of Napoleon III., including the famous debate of 1868 in the French Legislature on a new press law. This work contains a frightful accumulation of oppressive and restrictive measures to crush the liberty of the press in that country during the last three hundred years. Other works on the press have been published in France. Germain prepared the "*Martyrologe de la Presse*, 1789–1864;" Fernand Girardin issued, in 1868, "*La Presse périodique de* 1789 à 1867;" and Léon Vingtain wrote "*De la liberté de la Presse*, 1848–1868." Several *brochures* have also appeared: "*La Presse et la Législation de* 1852," by Edouard Hervé, and "*La liberté de la Presse et la Suffrage universal*," by Dupont White. Writers in France are so intimately associated with journalism, that the subject is always a fascinating one to them. So influential are the newspapers there, that the republican government of M. Thiers, himself originally an editor, felt compelled to suppress half a dozen radical journals in Paris by one decree in 1871, even before the Germans had evacuated Versailles.

What have we, in the United States, to compare with these works on journalism? Isaiah Thomas published the first volume on this subject in 1810. "Thomas's History of Printing" was its title. Joseph Tinker Buckingham furnished us the second in 1852. It was known as "Buckingham's Reminiscences," and related mostly to the Press of New England. These books are now out of print, and can rarely be found in a library or at a book-stall. They were exceedingly entertaining and valuable in facts, but neither full enough to satisfy the present generation. Other attempts have been made to furnish some idea of the American Press: one in the "Memoirs of Bennett and His Times," and another in the "Life of Horace Greeley." There are others, such as the lives of David Hale and Gerard Hallock, of the *Journal of Commerce*. Since these have appeared, "Henry J. Raymond and the New York Press for Thirty Years," and the "Life of Mark W. Pomeroy," have been sold throughout the country. "The *Richmond Examiner* during the War," embracing the leading articles of its editor, John T. Daniels, has been published. "The *Public Ledger* Building," filled with facts about that well-known penny paper, was issued in 1868. In Griswold's "American Literature" there are many items of interest relating to journals and editors. The "Life and Correspondence of William Seaton, of the *National Intelligencer*," and the "Newspaper Press of Philadelphia from 1719 to 1872," illustrated with portraits, have appeared, the latter, from time to time, in the *Proof-Sheet*. So far as these works go, they are acquisitions to the newspaper history and literature of the country; but they are local and incomplete. More is wanted to fill up the gaps in the chronology of events.

It is now modestly proposed to compile a history of the Newspaper Press of the United States a little more comprehensive and connected in its scope. It will begin with Benjamin Harris's *Publick Occurrences*, which appeared in Boston in 1690, and end with the *Daily Globe*, the last new paper, which was issued in the same city early in 1872. This will embrace a period of nearly two hundred years. Not to reach the number of volumes of M. Hatin's work on the French Press, this history will be less discursive, less in details, and with fewer and shorter extracts from the newspapers described.

There will be omissions, and how can they be avoided? In all great battles there are thousands of men on the field of operations, formed into companies, regiments, brigades, divisions, and *corps*, with private soldiers, captains, colonels, brigadier generals, major generals, and marshals. In describing these conflicts the newspaper correspondent and the historian mention the chief officers, the *corps*, the divisions, the brigades, sometimes a regiment, but rarely a company or a private soldier. Space, on the pages of history, has never permitted a detailed description of Waterloo or Gettysburg. Waterloo, where all Europe were engaged, was described in one third of a column of the London *Morning Chronicle* in 1815! Not quite a column was devoted to a list of the killed and wounded! Sedan, where three hundred thousand men were engaged, an empire overthrown, and one hundred and twenty thousand prisoners taken, occupied only five columns of the New York *Tribune* and New York *Herald* in a comprehensive and graphic account of the fight. One of these great battles, in full detail, would weary even Gradgrinds. So it is with the Press. Where there are five or six thousand newspapers in actual existence in the United States, and five or six thousand journals, each with its history, on the melancholy lists of newspaper mortality, the public and the Press will see the impossibility of describing the fields of journalism any more fully than others have described the fields of battle. "*Nommer tout le monde, c'était ne distinguer personne. Oublier quelqu'un, quelle injustice!*"

There are the Napoleons, the Bennetts, the Wellingtons, the Blairs, the Grants, the Greeleys, the Von Moltkes, the Raymonds, in the armies and in the press. They are prominent characters, and must appear on the pages of history as illustrative facts. There they stand. But neither the name of the farmer's boy who led Rosecrans to the rear of the rebel works on Rich Mountain, nor that of the writer of the letter which led to the capture of Fort M'Allister by Hazen are known to fame. Rosecrans's and Hazen's names are in gold and glory; nowhere are to be found that of the rustic guide or the rebel letter-writer. Achievements of leading soldiers, leading statesmen, and leading journalists are described because they illustrate the fact that comprehends the whole event of the time, but there is no space for the name of that humble guide who lost an empire to Napoleon by leading Blücher by the shortest road to the field of Waterloo. Bismarck's name, in our day, is on every tongue, but how many can tell that of the inventor of the famous needle-gun, which accomplished so much at Sadowa, Gravelotte, and Sedan? Bismarck is a nation; Dreyse was simply a gunsmith.

Thus with newspapers. We must describe the leading journals. Some of these, indeed, as important in their way as the inventor of the needle-gun, or as Blücher's guide at Waterloo, may be omitted in our story. Thousands of newspapers and journalists must continue to live "unhonored and unsung," except in their own offices, at their own town meetings, and at their own election districts, where the good they have done, and the good they may yet do, can be felt and appreciated, and be amply remunerated in subscriptions and advertisements.

AUTHORITIES.

It is the custom, in preparing works of this kind, to give, in notes at the foot of pages, the sources of the information used in illustration and description. This custom has its disadvantages as well as advantages. One of its greatest disadvantages is in the size of the volume to make room for these notes, which have often to be repeated. Another is the distraction of the reader's attention, and the breaking of the continuity of the narrative, as is frequently done on the telegraph lines when interesting news is coming over the wires, much to the vexation and annoyance of every one. The chief advantage is to enable the doubter to verify the statements made, and obtain more information on the subject, if such be desirable. It is our purpose not to cumber our pages with these footnotes. Newspapers, books, letters, memory, pamphlets, individuals, had to be consulted, and the facts thus obtained make up this compilation.

Several years ago, if there be any truth in tradition, Lord Timothy Dexter, of Newburyport—he who made a fortune in sending warming-pans to the West Indies—wrote a book, on the pages of which not a comma, semicolon, colon, or period appeared. Instead, he devoted four or five pages at the end of his work to these points of punctuation, with the request to the reader to throw them into the preceding pages as best suited his tastes and inclinations. It is our intention to copy, in part, the plan of this distinguished nobleman, by giving a list of the authorities for the facts and poetry, dates and data of these historical sketches, all on one page, not exactly for the reader to throw in where he pleases, but to show him that the statements come from good sources, and can be relied on as fully and as faithfully as any historical facts can be, outside of Sir Walter Raleigh's prison-yard, in this world of partisanship, exaggeration, and doubt. Here is our list :

Dunton's Life and Errors.
Isaiah Thomas.
Washington Irving.
Several Thousand Newspapers.
James Gordon Bennett.

Benjamin Franklin.
Joseph T. Buckingham.
Henry J. Raymond.
Mackenzie's Correspondence of Jesse Hoyt.

Authorities.

Edward Everett.
Tait's Edinburg Magazine.
Private Letters.
F. Knight Hunt.
Henry W. Bellows.
Newspaper Directories.
Bennett's Memoirs.
The Reporters.
Boston Athenæum.
Valentine's Manual.
Eugene H. Munday.
Edward E. Hale.
American Literary Gazette.
Horace Greeley.
William T. Coggeshall.
Anson Herrick.
Memory.
Joseph B. Felt.
Philadelphia Proof-Sheet.
John W. Francis.
Rufus W. Griswold.
Cuvillier Fleury.
North American Review.
Historical Magazine.
Watson's Men and Times.
Nathaniel Willis.
Niles's Register.
Parton's Life of Horace Greeley.
American Statesmen.
U. S. Agricultural Report.
James Kent.
George Borrow.
Lippincott's Magazine.
Charles Lanman.
Henry A. Wise.
Maverick's Life of Raymond.
Eugene Hatin.
William M. Swain.
Duff Green.
Fitz Greene Halleck.
The Printer.
John C. Hamilton.
Massachusetts Historical Society.
Henry R. Boss.
New York Annual Register.
Athenæum Français.
Robert Bonner.
Historical Society of Pennsylvania.
American Almanac.
English State Trials.
John C. Rives.
Horatio Gates Jones.
Colonial Records.
William C. Bryant.
Newspaper Press Directory.
Edwin Williams.
Jabez D. Hammond.
Henry W. Longfellow.
Harper's New Monthly.
Benton's Thirty Years.
New England Genealogical Antiquarian Record.
W. F. G. Shanks.
Administration of John Adams.
William C. Rives.
Gideon J. Tucker.
Adolphe Thiers.
Charles G. Shanks.
John Tyler.
Alexander Jones.
E. S. Thomas's Reminiscences.
William Gowan.
Democratic Review.
Archbishop Hughes.
Francis P. Blair.
John Mullaly.

This work is incomplete, even in the face of this array of names. It is, indeed, only an outline of a History of Journalism, to aid, so far as it may, a future Hume, or a Thiers, or a Macaulay, or a Prescott. When the indefatigable Dr. Coggswell collected the books which now form the magnificent Astor Library in New York, his effort and purpose was to have every department of literature, art, history, science, religion, as perfect and as complete as human wisdom, unlimited means, and unflagging industry could make them. When he came to Ethnology, a knowledge of which was not so widespread then in this country as it is now, he succeeded in purchasing fifty-nine works, by fifty-nine different authors, on this interesting science. On carefully consulting the foot-notes of these volumes, he discovered, much to his joy, that he had obtained all but two of all the works on this subject that had been written to that time. Now, with the list of authorities which we here give, it strikes us that we have been nearly as fortunate on the Press as Dr. Coggswell was on the human race, although we may not make the same good use of them as he has done with his. He placed his on his shelves. We have put ours in a book.

If editors, finding errors and omissions in this work, will send their corrections and additions to the compiler, at the office of the publisher, he will either make use of the new data in another edition, or reserve them for the Thiers or the Macaulay of the Press, when he appears and is prepared for work. In a republic where the newspaper is so imperial an element, a complete history of its rise and progress should not be omitted in the catalogue of the literature of the nation. In this view, journalists will bear in mind that anecdotes and incidents of newspaper offices, newspaper men, and newspaper enterprise are, in a work of this sort, like the etchings and illustrations of Darley, and Doré, and Leach, and Nast, and M'Lenan to other historical and social sketches. They should be rescued from oblivion and private note-books. They are the lights and shades, the wit and philosophy of the editorial sanctums, the printing-offices, and press-rooms of the land.

THE EPOCHS OF JOURNALISM.

Often what is of the most importance to us in our daily life receives the least notice. Thousands living in a metropolis never visit its wonders. Hundreds never go beyond their native town. No one looks at the telegraph wires strung along our streets and railroads with any thought of the mighty power of the thin thread of galvanized iron which now runs from pole to pole on our thoroughfares, and soon, indeed, to stretch from pole to pole on our planet. Telegrams are transmitted every second from the most distant points of the world without our special wonder.

Newspapers are daily read by millions at their breakfast tables, in the railway cars, at the counting-room, and thrown aside as soon as read, without apparent thought of the medium through which the affairs of the world, the events of the day, the gossip of the hour are conveyed to their minds, forming their opinions, leading them to fame and fortune, saving them from disaster, and governing their actions. But as the polyp of the sea industriously and unceasingly works in building up the coral reefs and beds into islands and peninsulas, so does the journalist slowly and surely work on the minds of the world, producing heroes and statesmen, navigators and merchants, mechanics and philosophers. Those who use the telegraph condemn the unsightly poles that stand like sentinels along our sidewalks. Those most influenced by the Press heap upon it the most abuse in public. Yet the newspaper is the most appreciated of all human productions. Small matters sometimes indicate great facts. No public dinner is given in honor of a military hero, or of an inventor, or of a statesman, or of a novelist, that "the Press" is not a regular toast. This is seen on every programme at every banquet. It is a stereotyped acknowledgment of the power and influence of the newspaper. On such occasions, too, is not the accomplished stenographer the most important listener to the efforts of the orators in their estimation? Is he not the ear of the Great Public?

Such an institution as the newspaper is, in this view, an important one. Its origin, and its intellectual and material development and progress, can not be otherwise than interesting. It has its epochs with those of peoples and nations. Acting as the historical photographer of national acts, it forms a necessary part of national government, of national machinery, indeed, of national existence. These journalistic periods, or epochs, are thus indicated in the history of North America:

First.—The first American newspapers—1690-1704.
Second.—The Colonial Press—1704-1755.
Third.—The Revolutionary Press—1755-1783.
Fourth.—The Political Party Press, the Religious Press, the Agricultural Press, the Sporting Press, the Commercial Press—1783-1833.
Fifth.—The Transition Press, the Cheap Press—1833-1835.
Sixth.—The Independent Press, the Telegraph Press—1835-1872.

Six periods of marvelous intellectual development and enterprise in the United States. All kinds of newspapers, with all sorts of characteristics, are embraced in these epochs. We find every interest with its organ—each its circle, like the oak; its strata, like the earth; its policy, like the political party; its cycle, like the sun. We look through the lens of the camera obscura for a perfect image of man. Do we get it? We look through the newspaper, as the camera obscura of the world, for a perfect idea of all time, past and present. Are we as successful? But who does not look upon an old newspaper as upon an old picture? We appreciate a Michael Angelo or a Rubens, and hang it up in our Art Gallery or Academy of Design. We read with peculiar interest a *Boston News-Letter* of 1704, or a *New York Gazette* of 1725, and file away the treasure in the Astor Library or the Athenæum.

THE FIRST NEWSPAPERS.

THE PROOF-SHEET.—THE NEWS CIRCULAR.—THE NEWSPAPER.—THE PROSPECTUS.—THE OFFICIAL ORGAN.—THE JOURNAL.—THE ADVERTISEMENT.—THE PENNY PRESS.—THE NEWS-BOY.

There is an excellent painting by Hillemacher hanging up in the house of some one, representing the *atélier* of John Gutenburg, in Mayence, where he is showing the first proof-sheet to John Faust. It is a very suggestive picture. It represents Gutenburg, in the year 1441, in his small work-cap, handing the impression to the man of dollars of that ancient town, so famous for its Rhenish wine, to induce him to join in the business of printing by investing some of his capital therein. It is a scene of a simple business transaction. Faust appears inspecting the proof-sheet with curious wonder, very much as Cornelius Vanderbilt would look at the first steam-engine, or Cave Johnson or Amos Kendall at the first telegraph instrument, without, perhaps, a thought beyond the moment or the pocket—without an idea of the revolution it was destined to create. The apprentice, with his shirt-sleeves rolled up, and one hand resting on a small, rude press, stops work to see the effect the sheet produces on Faust, whose name, from that day, is to be linked with that of Koster, Gutenburg, and Schœffer in all the printing-offices, school-houses, book-stores, libraries, and press-rooms of the world throughout all time. If the picture of Harvey demonstrating the circulation of blood to Charles the First; if that of Luther and the first Reformers presenting the famous protest to the Diet at Spires; if that of signing the compact in the cabin of the Mayflower are great historical scenes, this unpretending painting, in its bits of light and shade, must far surpass them in interest, as representing the introduction of an art which was to preserve all arts, and which was to elevate the human race, and spread intelligence, education, the Bible, the almanac, and the newspaper throughout the world.

It is not a little singular that this "art preservative of all arts" should have failed in transmitting to succeeding generations a more accurate and reliable account of its own origin than we have in our records. Much that we do know comes to us, after all, through tradition, and is exceedingly misty and opaque, and many of the legal documents affecting Gutenburg's claims, sad to say, were destroyed in 1870 at Strasburg by the Prussians. It is only till lately that we have become even satisfied of the origin of newspapers—where the first one was printed, and when it was issued. These interesting facts have been almost as much in doubt as the birthplace of Homer, or the name of the first Northman that landed on the shores of North America, or of the inventor of lucifer matches, or the authorship of Junius, or of the name of the inventor of bronze. It is not our intention to go back to the times anterior to the introduction of printing in Europe in 1438–40. Journalists undoubtedly first made their appearance in Rome. The *Acta Diurna*, in manuscript, of course, gave accounts of fires, executions, and remarkable hail-storms. There were bankruptcies then, as now, which were noticed; and the Roman *Tribune* had its House, and its Winter, and its Wilkins to criticise public plays, and its Jenkins to describe the *fêtes* of that happy period. But this is enough of the *Diurna*. We start with printing-ink and metal types in Europe, and not with the writing-fluid of Rome or the wooden types of the Celestials. Out of all these enterprises, however, and out of the desire of mankind to hear the gossip and news of the day, sprung the modern newspaper, with its annually increasing perfection.

News was distributed, before the era of newspapers, by news-letters and news circulars, written in Venice, Nuremberg, Augsburg, Amsterdam, Cologne, Frankfort, Leipsic, Paris, London, and Boston, as it had previously been done in Rome by paid letter-writers in those news centres, and sent to their principals in other places; not unlike the correspondence from London, or Canton, or Washington at the present time, by the bankers, merchants, and editors of Boston, or New York, or Chicago, or Cincinnati. There is evidence of their being circulated in Venice in 1536, a century after Koster introduced his rude style of type and ink. There are thirty volumes of these news-letters preserved in the Magliabecchi Library in Florence. Some, we believe, are filed away in the British Museum. The news circulars of Augsburg were started towards the close of the sixteenth century. There appeared the *Ordinari Zeittunger* and the *Extraordinari Zeittunger*. There is a collection of these journals from 1568 to 1604 in the Vienna Library. They were issued by the mercantile house of the Messrs. Függer, who had agents scattered every where—merchants and traders well posted on the current events of the day. Nine of John Campbell's news-letters, written in Boston in 1703, the year before he resorted to the printing-press, have lately been added to the collection of the Massachusetts Historical Society. These news-letters were, of course, the pioneers of the newspapers of the world.

Encyclopædists have given the credit to Queen Elizabeth and Lord Burleigh, whose shake of the head was such authority, for the first printed newspaper. It had been claimed that the British Museum had a copy of the earliest paper in its collection. It was called the *English Mercurie*, and printed July 23, 1588; but it has been shown that this copy, like specimens of rare old coins, was

spurious, and gotten up for sale. Watts, the bibliographer of the
Museum, who saw, on examination, that the type and paper were of
modern origin, and did not belong to the sixteenth century, exposed
the forgery. It was an ingenious fabrication, pretending to give the
news of the Spanish Armada, which was destroyed in the English
Channel by Drake and Howard a day or two previous to the date
of the sheet. There were seven numbers of this spurious *Mercurie*
produced—four in manuscript, and three in print.

It has also been claimed that the first newspaper was printed in
Venice. The *Gazzetta*, thus named because it sold for a small piece
of money called gazzetta, it is asserted, was printed there in 1570,
and it is pretended that copies of this paper of that date are in one
or two collections in London. There were printed books in Venice
a century earlier than this, and we have an account of a sale, a few
years ago, at auction, of a copy of Valdarfer's Boccaccio, a small folio, printed in Venice in 1471, which brought $10,000. There were
printed books in London as early as this date. William Caxton set
up a press in Westminster in the same year, and published "Recuyel
of the Historyes of Troye" in 1471. If a book was printed in 1471,
it would not be strange to see a newspaper emanate from the same
place in 1570, and yet no paper appeared in London for over half a
century after this last period. But, if we may believe *Galignani's
Messenger*, always a reliable chronicler, neither Venice nor London
have any claims to this great honor of issuing the first newspaper.
According to a statement in the *Messenger*, a paper called the *Gazette* was printed as early as 1457, five years after Peter Schœffer cast
the first metal type in matrices, in Nuremberg, Bavaria, a place celebrated for many mechanical inventions, and where the Reformation
made great progress at a later period. Nuremberg, with the first
paper in the fifteenth century, also claims, in our researches, the hon-
or of the first paper in the sixteenth century. There is an ancient-
ly printed sheet in the Libri collection which antedates all others
except the sheet of 1457 and the *Chronicle* of Cologne. It is called
the *Neue Zeitung aus Hispanien und Italien,* and bears the date of
February, 1534. The British Museum, it is said, has a duplicate of
this sheet. The catalogue of this collection, when it was offered for
sale, contained this description of this specimen of one of the incu-
nabula of the press:

> An exceedingly rare journal, which appears to have been printed at Nurem-
> berg. It contains the first announcement of the discovery of Peru, and has re-
> mained unknown to all the bibliographists that we have been able to consult. In
> this printed sheet it is said that the Governor of Panumyra (Panama), in the In-
> dies, wrote to his majesty, Charles V., that a vessel had arrived from Peru, with a
> letter from the regent, Francisco Piscara (Pizarro), announcing that he had taken
> possession of the country; that, with about two hundred Spaniards, infantry and

cavalry, he had repaired to the possessions of a great seignor, named Cassiko (who refused peace), and attacked him; that the Spaniards were the victors, and that he had seized upon five thousand castillons (gold pieces), and of twenty thousand silver marks; and, lastly, that he had obtained two millions in gold from the said Cassiko.

Thus even the second newspaper of which we have any record was printed in that imperial city where Albert Durer and many other distinguished men first saw the light of heaven. It is not unlikely that the *Gazette* continued to be published at intervals during the period between 1457 and 1534. Nuremberg was manifestly the spot where a newspaper would first appear and be appreciated.

"In the valley of the Pegnitz, where, across broad meadow lands,
Rise the blue Franconian mountain, Nuremberg, the ancient, stands;
Quaint old town of toil and traffic, quaint old town of art and song,
Memories haunt thy pointed gables, like the works that round them throng.

Memories of the Middle Ages, where the emperors, rough and bold,
Had their dwelling in thy castle, time defying centuries old;
And thy brave and thrifty burghers boasted, in their uncouth rhyme,
That their great imperial city *stretched its hand through every clime.*"

There was a printing-press in Copenhagen as early as 1493, but we have no knowledge of a newspaper in that city at that time. It is well ascertained that Ulric Zell printed the *Chronicle* in Cologne in 1499. There was a sheet called the *Mercurius Gallo Belgicus* issued in Cologne in 1598, and afterward in Frankfort in 1605, and immortalized in Fletcher's Fair Maid of the Inn. So to Germany belongs the honor not only of the first printers and the first printing, but of the first printed newspaper. *Die Frankfurter Oberpostamts Zeitung* was published in Germany in 1615, and is claimed to have been the first daily paper in the world. This journal is still published. Frankfort is to erect a monument in honor of its editor, Egenolf Eurmel, as the father of Newspapers. In the United States Benjamin Franklin is celebrated in monuments, and paintings, and engravings, as if he was the father of Printing and Newspapers in this country, wholly ignoring the superior claims of the Greens, the Harrises, the Campbells, the Bradfords, and the elder Franklin. The last monument to Benjamin Franklin was unveiled in Printing House Square, in New York, in 1872, the ceremony closing with a banquet at which nearly all the leading journalists and printers of that city were present. Monuments to the Press are going up every where. There is a fine one to Gutenburg in Mayence, and one to Koster in the Town-house in Haarlem. There is one to be erected, opposite Franklin's, in New York, to Horace Greeley. There has been erected in Brussels a column in honor of the constitutional liberties enjoyed in Belgium. At the four corners of the base of this column are placed four allegorical figures of colossal size. Two of these were confided to M. Geefs, the Professor of Sculpture of the

Royal Academy at Antwerp. One represents the "Liberty of the Press," and the other "The Liberty of Instruction." That to the Press is thus described:

> This statue of the Liberty of the Press is an imposing composition, measuring three metres fifty-nine centimetres in height. The great organ of the intelligence of the age is typified in the form of a female of muscular mould, and with severe and energetic features, wearing a composed and firm expression—all admirably suggestive of force and grandeur, of power and high resolve. And this grandiose character is maintained in every part of the work. The grandeur and severity of the contour, the imposing and daring character of the pose, irresistibly fill the mind of the spectator with the feelings of awe and veneration which the representation of the emblems of public liberty ought to inspire. Even in the draperies there is nothing small or frivolous; every fold is broad, bold, massive, indicating at once free will and the power to execute it. The left arm of this colossal figure rests upon a printing-press, while the hand holds a wreath of flowers, signifying that every thing flourishes under the auspices of Liberty. The right hand rests upon the knee, grasping the fragments of a broken chain, the other portions of which are trampled under foot by the goddess. Her head is crowned with laurels, beneath which is the fillet usually attributed to divine personages, in the middle of which is the star of immortality. Altogether this is a very stately, complete, and intelligent production.

But there are three monuments to the Press in Germany that have exceeded any of these in age and appropriateness. On the 1st of January, 1860, two of the oldest newspapers in that country celebrated—one, the *Leipsic Gazette*, its two hundredth anniversary, and the other, the *Rostock Gazette*, its one hundred and fiftieth birthday! The *Leipsic Gazette*, on that interesting event, presented to its subscribers *fac-similes* of its publication on the 1st of January, 1660 and 1760, respectively. The *Vassische Zeitung*, of Berlin, reached its one hundredth and fiftieth year in 1872. There are not many more than twenty or thirty newspapers in the world that have lived over a hundred years. We annex the names of several as they occur to us:

THE CENTURY NEWSPAPERS OF THE WORLD.

Established.
1. Frankfort Gazette, ——, 1615.
2. Leipsic Gazette, January, 1660.
3. London Gazette, November, 1665.
4. Stamford (Eng.) Mercury, ——, 1695.
5. Edinburg Courant, February, 1705.
6. Rostock Gazette, January, 1710.
7. Newcastle (Eng.) Courant, ——, 1711.
8. Leeds (Eng.) Mercury, ——, 1718.

Established.
9. Berlin Gazette, March, 1722.
10. Leicester (Eng.) Journal, ——, 1752.
11. Dublin Freeman's Journal, ——, 1755.
12. New Hampshire Gazette, Oct., 1756.
13. Newport (R. I.) Mercury, June, 1758.
14. Connecticut Gazette, November, 1763.
15. Connecticut Journal, October, 1767.
16. Salem (Mass.) Gazette, Aug. 5, 1768.
17. Worcester (Mass.) Spy, July, 1770.

These are monuments, not in bronze, or marble, or brass, or granite, but in living words that endure forever.

The fifth newspaper in the world appeared in England in 1622, toward the close of the reign of James the First, and shortly after Sir Walter Raleigh's unsuccessful voyage to America. It was published by Nicholas Bourne and Thomas Archer. The earliest sheet known of this paper is dated May 23, 1622. It was entitled *The Weekley Newes*. Although the name of Nathaniel Butters does not appear till September 28, he is called the father of the English Press because of his earlier efforts in this profession. Nicholas Bourne, Thomas Archer, Nathaniel Newbury, William Sheffard, Bartholomew Downes, and Edward Alide were associates of Butters. They met with indifferent success. Ben Jonson, in "The Staple of News," ridiculed these half-fledged newspaper men. So did Fletcher and Shirley. The playwrights were then the censors of the public, and newspapers were considered enterprising to obtain the earliest copies of play-bills. Other wits made fun of the *Newes*. But since that period the journalists have changed places with the playwrights, and have become not only the critics and the arbiters on the stage, but in the cars, at the breakfast table, in the drawing-room, in presidential conventions, in cabinet councils, indeed every where. In spite of the wits, the *Newes* lived longer than many papers of more modern date.

One of the curiosities in newspapers, if not in literature, is the close resemblance of the names of the publishers of the first regularly printed papers in England and America. The imprint of the *Weekley Newes* in 1622 was as follows:

London: printed by I. D., for Nicholas Bourne and Thomas Archer.

The imprint of the *News-Letter* was in 1704:

Boston: Printed by B. Green. Sold by Nicholas Boone at his Shop near the Old Meeting House.

Ninety-two years elapsed between the publication of these two papers, one by Nicholas Bourne and the other by Nicholas Boone. Names, as well as history, it thus appears, repeat themselves over the globe.

In the capacity of a news-carrier, his original profession, as a hired letter-writer in the pay of a few country gentlemen to gather the news in London and send a weekly written sheet of his intelligence and gossip to his employers, Butters prepared the way for the first English newspaper. He had printed news pamphlets now and then as far back as 1611, and on the 9th of October, 1621, he published, on a half sheet, one or two numbers of *The Courant, or Weekley Newes from Forain Partes*. It seems that he was one of the originators of the present mode of selling papers in the streets. "Mercury women" and "hawkers," the news-venders of his day, were introduced by him. We now have news-boys, although many of the news-venders of the present time in New York and other cities are women and girls. Women keep the *kiosques* in Paris where all the papers are daily sold, and these women, some of whom have been news-venders for thirty years, are perfectly *au courant* in the political upheavals of France in that time. So important has this class become in England, that in 1839 the male portion formed a Newsvenders' Benevolent and Provident Association in London, and celebrated its tenth anniversary in 1849 by a public dinner in that city, at which Charles Dickens presided.

Butters having given an impulse to this new intellectual movement, newspapers increased in number. In the civil wars, periodicals, organs of the two parties, and edited by men of ability, were largely circulated. There was one named the *Impartial Intelligencer*, which we mention because it contained the first advertisement ever published. This original business notice appeared in March, 1648, and offered a reward for the recovery of two stolen horses. Among other papers, we can not omit the *Public Intelligencer*, established by Sir Roger l'Estrange on the 31st of August, 1663, and made famous at the time by the ability of its editor, and the immense power given him as the Licenser of the Press, a power which he greatly abused. It enjoyed the reputation, in some of the encyclopædias, of being the first real newspaper in England, and afterward, with change of name, became the official *Gazette* of England. Sir Roger was strongly opposed to Butters's mode of selling newspapers in the streets. In his prospectus in 1663 he said:

> The way as to the sale that has been found most beneficial to the master of the book has been to cry and expose it about the streets by mercuries and hawkers; but whether they may be so advisable in some other respects may be a question, for under countenance of that employment is carried on the private trade of treasonous and seditious libels; nor, effectually, has any thing been dispersed against either Church or State without the aid and privity of this sort of people; wherefore, without ample assurance and security against this inconvenience, I shall adventure to steer another course.

Notwithstanding this early onslaught, the system of mercuries was popular, and continued in vogue, as the Sweeneys of 1765, who sold the *Courant* in the streets of New York, and the Mark Maguires, the "King of the Newsboys," a century later, who sold the *Sun, Herald*, and *Times*, are ample and wealthy proofs. Our data do not develop the fact of the elevation of the "mercuries" of the time of Butters and L'Estrange to high offices of honor and trust, but we have records of numerous instances of the "newsboys" who have sold the *Transcript, Herald*, and *Sun* in the streets of New York, becoming sheriffs, Common Council-men, members of the state Legislature, police magistrates, eminent lawyers, distinguished actors, millionaires, and members of the national Congress. Some, it is true, went to the States Prisons, but these were the accidents of the profession. In a sketch of Charles O'Conor, in the *New York Herald*, in October, 1869, appeared the following incidents of his life:

Released from debt and jail, the elder O'Conor soon after established a weekly newspaper called the *War*, which name, however, after the publication of a few numbers, was changed to the *Military Monitor*. This was at the outbreak of the war of 1812. O'Conor was a vigorously epigrammatic writer, though at times showing a wonderful capacity at ornate description. In the columns of his paper he availed himself of the broad opportunity afforded him of giving vent to his burning indignation against the English government, which time and his years of residence here had not abated. Charles, who was then eight years old, was his father's office boy, a position that not only enforced keeping charge of the office in his father's absence, but also delivering the papers to subscribers. At this time New York had ninety thousand inhabitants, the population of Brooklyn was about two thousand, and Jersey City was a small country village; and between it and New York, as also between here and Brooklyn, the communication was by rowboats. Newspapers were not then what they are now. The subscription list of the *Military Monitor* was not very large, but it was sufficiently large to keep young Charles busily employed every Saturday in delivering the papers to subscribers.

"Sometimes the publication was delayed beyond the usual time, and to get through my circuit of delivery would take all night," he recently remarked to a gentleman, in speaking of this epoch of his early days; "but I boldly went up door-steps, chucking papers under the doors; plunged into areas and down through alleyways, fearless of the police and every body, for my bundle of papers was a perfect safeguard, as good to me as the ægis and crested helmet to Hector."

"So you commenced your career as a newsboy?" queried the gentleman.

"A newsboy of the old school," rejoined Mr. O'Conor, with a merry twinkle of the eye; "for between newsboys of the old and modern school there is as marked a difference as between old and modern school gentlemen."

After the *Public Intelligencer*, the *Oxford Gazette*, now so venerable, was published in November, 1665. It was and is the organ of the court. This was the first official organ in the form of a newspaper, although L'Estrange pretended to be such. On the return of the court to London, after its flight from the plague, the name was changed to *London Gazette*, and has ever since remained as such. It is a mere reprint of laws and proclamations. There is no editorial labor, yet its editor, as late as 1869, received a salary of $4000 per year. When a vacancy occurred in that year there were numerous applications for the situation. It was then proposed to abolish the office and the paper, after an existence of over two hundred years; but the proposition did not find favor, and finally Thomas Walker, for many years on the editorial staff of the *London News*, received the sinecure appointment from William Gladstone, the premier.

The first daily newspaper printed in English appeared in the reign of Queen Anne. It was the *Daily Courant*, a morning paper, and issued in March, 1702. It was not till 1777 that the first daily paper appeared in Paris. It was the *Journal de Paris ou Poste au Soir*. Colletet published a paper a century earlier, named the *Journal de la Ville de Paris*, in which daily occurrences were recorded, hence the name of journal, but the sheet, we think, was not issued oftener than once a week. The first daily newspaper in the United States was the *American Daily Advertiser*, published in Philadelphia in 1784.

The earliest Scottish newspaper appeared in 1652, under the auspices of Cromwell, when Milton was his private secretary and wrote political articles. One authority states that the initial paper was the *Mercurius Politicus*, and issued in Leith in October, 1653. There was an *Edinburg Gazette* in 1699. In February, 1705, the *Edinburg Courant* was published, by authority, semi-weekly. The copy of February 19 of that year, now before us, is a half sheet of the size of letter paper. Its contents are advices from the camp before Gibraltar, and accounts of the war in Austria, and of a battle at Rivoli, in Piedmont. This paper was printed by James Watson, in Craig's Close, and sold at the Exchange Coffee-house. Its news shows the existence of other newspapers in Holland than the *Harlemm Courant*, which made its appearance in 1656, as it quotes from the *Amsterdam Gazette* of February 17, 1705, and the *Amsterdam Courant* of the same month and year. We know that a newspaper was published in Russia in 1703. It was printed under the authority of Peter the Great, who not only took an active part in its direction, but it is asserted that he corrected many of the proof-sheets! It was named the *St. Petersburg Gazette*. The initial paper in Spain appeared in 1704, and was called the *Gaceta de Madrid*.

The conciseness and quaintness of the prospectus of the Scottish publisher, in view of the modern announcements of the kind, induces us to give it entire:

> The Author hereof having upon the 13, instant, got an Act of Her Majesty's most Honorable Privy Council, to Print and Publish the Foreign and Home News thrice-Weekly, viz., Monday, Wednesday, and Friday; the same will be continued from this day forward.
>
> NOTA. Advertisements may be put in this *Courant*, and for that end, attendance will be given from ten o'Clock in the Forenoon till twelve, and from two in the Afternoon till four, at the Exchange Coffee House in Edinburg.

There were three advertisements in the sheet of the 19th of February, and, if any evidence were needed to show the early existence of "patent medicines," advertisements of which now fill our papers at a yearly cost of over a million dollars, we would refer those with coughs and colds to one of the three paid notices left at the Coffee-house, Edinburg, on the 18th of February, 1705, for insertion in the *Courant* of the next day. Among the first advertisements in the first newspapers were those of patent medicines. Life Pills, Soothing Sirups, and Bronchial Troches, it would seem, existed then as now. Here is the one in the *Courant*:

> That the Famous Loozengees for Curing the Cold, stopping and pains in the Breast, the Kinkpost; Are to be sold by George Anderson at the foot of the Fish Mercal, and at George Mowbray's Shop, opposit to the Main Gaard. Price 8 sh. the box.

The *Courant* was a famous sheet, as it once had Daniel de Foe, author of Robinson Crusoe, for its editor. It came under his management in 1710, and he created a sensation as a political journalist. He had an active share in the *Mercurius Politicus*, in *Dorner's News-Letter*, and in *Mail's Journal*. In 1714 he wrote a letter for *Hurst's Flying Post* which caused him temporary imprisonment. In 1720 he contributed to *Applebee's Weekly Journal*, and continued to do so till 1726, and also for the *Director*. He established the *Whitehall Evening Post* in 1720, and was connected with that paper for two years. De Foe manifestly had journalism on the brain, for at one time he had six or seven papers on his hands for which he was an active contributor. It is a wonder that he did not "set up a press," and establish Robinson Crusoe as an editor on his wonderful island.

The *Orange Postman* was the first penny paper. It was started in England in 1706, and sold for half a penny. It is, therefore, probably the first ONE-CENT paper ever published. It was unquestionably the father of the Penny Press.

The first newspaper printed in Ireland was *Pue's Occurrences*, published in Dublin in 1700. It was said that it became a daily paper, and lived for half a century. Some authorities claim that there was a *Dublin News-Letter* in 1685.

After Germany and England, is it not time that France, then in the most flourishing period of her literature, should appear on the historic roll? Strange as it may seem, in view of the progress of that great nation in art, science, literature, and industry, France, in journalism, occupies the same rank now in merit as she did chronologically two hundred years ago, both periods showing an abundance of journalistic ability and an utter absence of journalistic enterprise.

On the 30th of May, 1631, Théophraste Renaudot published the *Gazette de France* in Paris, the first regular newspaper printed in France. The *Mercure François* appeared in 1613, but it was never called a newspaper. The official bulletins of the first grand expedition of the French in Italy, under the command of Charles the Eighth, in 1494 and 1495, were printed, and formed a sort of *Moniteur* in that period of French renown. These were military bulletins, and do not deprive Renaudot of any of his glory. The *Gazette* lived nearly two centuries and a half. Indeed, there has always been a *Gazette de France*, from Louis XIII. to Napoleon III., the oldest periodical in name in the world. Pére Renaudot of French journalism, like Father Butters of English newspapers, killed off, almost with one *coup de presse*, the written news-slips and club manuscripts, those slow, irregular, meagre chroniclers of their day. Newspapers then came into power. Since then, Louis XVI., Napoleon

I., Charles X., Louis Philippe, Napoleon III., have all been overthrown by this power. So their adherents have persistently asserted. Yet the newspaper in France is apparently controlled by the government. Richelieu, Mazarin, and Louis XIII. wrote for the *Gazette*, as Edward Everett, Henry Ward Beecher, and Sylvanus Cobb for the *Ledger*, and Guizot, Thiers, and Napoleon for the *Moniteur* and *La Patrie*.

But to return to Renaudot and his *Gazette*. Twelve months after the establishment of the paper, its originator issued, in 1632, a prospectus, which we annex. The quaint and simple manner of expressing his views on the duties of a journalist gives it a peculiar charm and attraction:

The novelty of this design, its utility, its difficulty, and its purpose, my reader, deserve a preface.

The publication of *Gazettes* is indeed new; but in France only can this novelty find favor which it can always easily retain. Above all will these gazettes be sustained for their utility to the public and to individuals: to the public, because they will prevent the circulation of false reports, which often serve to kindle intestine and seditious movements; indeed, if we may believe Cæsar in his Commentaries, our ancestors often undertook wars precipitately, to repent of them at leisure, on the mere rumors of the day; to individuals, because each one willingly adjusts his affairs on the model of the times. Thus no merchant would go to a besieged or ruined city to trade or traffic, nor would a soldier seek employment in a country where there are no wars. It is not necessary to speak of the advantages of these gazettes to those who heretofore have been obliged to write to their friends to satisfy their curiosity, and to laboriously describe news which is often invented at pleasure, and founded on simple rumor. Besides the gratification which the variety of news which these gazettes will give, and which will serve as an agreeable diversion in company, they will prevent slanders and other vices which idlers produce, and this ought to render them acceptable. They are, on this point at least, free from blame, and are no more injurious or hurtful to the mass of the people than my other innocent inventions, each one standing on its own merits.

The difficulty I encounter in the composition of my gazettes and my news is not paraded in advance to make the public esteem my labor more highly than it ought to be. Those who know me can say to others that if I do not find as honorable employment elsewhere as in these sheets, they must excuse my style if it does not always reach the dignity of the subject, and if the subject be not to their mind, and both style and subject of sufficient merit to meet their approbation. All can not be satisfied. Captains wish for battles, and sieges raised or cities captured; lawyers are anxious for judgments; devout persons seek the names of renowned preachers and confessors. Those who hear nothing of the mysteries of court wish to see them mentioned in great letters. If one carries a parcel to court, or leads a company of soldiers from one village to another without losing a man, or performs the duties of a small office, he frets himself if the king does not see his name in the *Gazette*. Others wish to have the title of monseigneur or monsieur prefixed to each person of whom I speak, without thinking that these titles are too common, and, being omitted in all cases, can give jealousy to none. There are some who take to a flowery language, while others wish to have my descriptions a fleshless skeleton, in order that the relation be naked and simple. It is my effort to please all.

Is it fair, then, oh my reader, to complain of all my doings, and find no excuse for my pen if it fails to please the world, no matter what I say or do, like the peasant and his son, who placed themselves first alone and then together, sometimes on foot and sometimes on the back of their ass? And if the fear of displeasing the age in which they live has prevented many good authors from touching the history of their time, what ought to be the difficulty of writing that of the week, indeed of the day even, in which it is published? Add to this the shortness of time that your impatience gives me, and I am much deceived if the rudest of censors will not find some excuse for a work which has to be accomplished in four hours, the only time given me by the arrival of the couriers every week in gathering, arranging, and printing these lines.

But no, I deceive myself in estimating that I hold the bridle of your censure by my remonstrances. It can not be done; and if I could do it, my reader, I ought not to do it, for this liberty of reproving not being one of the smallest pleasures of this class of readers, and a pleasure and a gratification, as we may call it, is really one of the causes which led to the invention of this novelty. Enjoy, then, at your ease, this French liberty, and let each one speak as boldly as he pleases of removing this or changing that, which he would have done much better than I have or can do. I submit.

In one thing, however, I will cede to no one, and that is in seeking the truth; of which, nevertheless, I make no guarantee, it being difficult in the midst of five hundred news-letters, written in haste from one clime to another, to always escape a correction from Father Time; and yet there are some curious persons who will always hold to the truth of the news thus published.

This is a remarkable prospectus. It is rather a postscript to the original idea of the newspaper. No one can say that Renaudot was not a first-class journalist for the age in which he lived. The *Gazette* was evidently more of a newspaper than the *Weekley Newes*. It described events, expressed opinions, and had special correspondents. It was sold for five sous a copy. Women sold it in the streets. It was issued daily after May 1, 1792.

The official gazette of Sweden next made its appearance. The *Postosch Inrikes Tidning* was its name. It was founded in 1644, in the reign of Christine, daughter of Gustavus Adolphus the Great. We believe it is still published. Then there was the *Harlemm Courant*, which was established on the 8th of January, 1656.

These were the earliest newspapers in Europe; and now America steps into the ranks of journalism.

Tenth on the list in the seventeenth century, in their colonial condition, chronologically considered, the United States, in their independent condition, are first, in every attribute of a newspaper, in the nineteenth century. The *avant courier* of the thousands of journals that have appeared on this side of the Atlantic was printed in Boston on the 25th of September, 1690, by Richard Pierce, for Benjamin Harris. It was called *Publick Occurrences*, and was immediately suppressed by the government. The first permanent newspaper was the *Boston News-Letter*. The latter did not make its appearance till the 20th of April, 1704. In all records it incorrectly stands as the initial American newspaper. It was, indeed, the first sheet regularly and persistently issued, but it was not the pioneer. It was not like its predecessor in the character of its contents. It gave no local news. Its whole aim seemed to be to keep its readers *au courant* with the affairs of Europe only. In this way it escaped local censure and persecution. Another paper, called the *Gazette*, was issued in Boston in 1719. The *American Mercury* appeared in

Philadelphia in the same year. Then James Franklin started the *Boston Courant* in 1721, but, after some persecution from the authorities, it passed nominally under the management of Benjamin Franklin. It ceased to exist in 1727. It was too independent.

The first newspaper in New York made its *entrée* in 1725. It was the *New York Gazette*, and was the pioneer of the wonderfully enterprising newspapers of the great metropolis of the present time. Another *Gazette*, then the favorite name for newspapers, came out in Annapolis, Maryland, in 1727. Another in Charleston, South Carolina, in 1731, and yet another, the *Rhode Island Gazette*, in Newport, in 1733. There was very little originality in names in this early period of newspapers, for we find that the first one printed in Virginia was the *Gazette*, and published in Williamsburg in 1736. Twenty years later, in 1756, the *New Hampshire Gazette*, yet in existence, was published in Portsmouth, N. H.

Thus, with the discovery of printing, the initial printed newspapers of the world appeared in the following order:

THE FIRST NEWSPAPERS.

Name.	Town.	Year.
0. Printing introduced,	Mayence,	1438
1. Gazette	Nuremberg,	1457
2. Chronicle,	Cologne,	1499
3. Gazette,	Venice,	1570
4. Die Frankfurter Oberpostamts Zeitung,	Frankfort,	1615
5. Weekley Newes,	London,	1622
6. Gazette de France,	Paris,	1631
7. Postosch Inrikes Tidning,	Sweden,	1644
8. Mercurius Politicus,	Leith, Scotland,	1653
9. Courant,	Harlemm, Holland,	1656
10. Publick Occurrences,	Boston,	1690
11. Pue's Occurrences,	Dublin, Ireland,	1700
12. Gazette,	St. Petersburg, Russia,	1703
13. News-Letter,	Boston,	1704
14. Gaceta de Madrid,	Madrid, Spain,	1704
15. Mercury,	Philadelphia, Pa.,	1719
16. Gazette,	New York,	1725
17. Gazette,	Annapolis, Md.,	1727
18. Gazette,	Charleston, S. C.,	1731
19. Gazette,	Williamsburg, Va.,	1736
20. Gazette,	Calcutta,	1781

Other papers were of course published in Europe and in the United States prior to the Revolution of 1776, but the object we have in view, in this introductory chapter, is to give the first sheets as they appeared in the world. These twenty *Gazettes*, and *News-Letters*, and *Occurrences* were the pioneers. Although they were the merest chroniclers of brief items of news, bits of history, without philosophy, to be used and rearranged in after ages, they were the originators of the palladiums of the people, now so numerous and necessary wherever the rights of man are recognized, and corrupt corporations, and political leaders and "rings" are to be exposed. Very little space was devoted, in these early days, to editorial articles, or communications, or expression of opinions. News, with an advertisement here and there, filled the short columns in the small half sheets of the sixteenth and seventeenth centuries. It was in the next epoch, between 1755 and 1783, that intellect began to manifest itself, and political and religious liberty receive its great impulse from the public press, particularly in the United States, resulting in the Revolution of 1776. If, as in the case of Benjamin Harris in 1690, or James Franklin in 1721, those journals indulged in the modern luxury of publicly uttering their political sentiments, or even in a free publication of news affecting the authorities, they were doomed to persecution and punishment, as in England under Charles the First and Second in the sixteenth, and in France under Napoleon the Third and Thiers in the nineteenth century.

These initial sheets were an illustration of the papers, and the people, and the times of those early periods, as the leading journals of to-day are the illustration of the papers, and people, and the times of our epoch. Our modern organs of public opinion—the *Augsburg Gazette*, the *London Times*, the Paris *Journal des Débats*, and the *New York Herald* of 1872, with their *daily circulation of a quarter of a million sheets, or a million and a half of readers*, are the natural and progressive result and historical contrast of the *Nuremberg Gazette* of 1457, the London *Weekley Newes* of 1622, the *Gazette de France* of 1631, and the *Boston News-Letter* of 1704, with their *weekly circulation of less than two thousand copies, or ten thousand readers.* Slow chroniclers and imperfect impressions of 1457 and 1622 compared with the rapidity of steam, the flash of electricity, and the perfect photographic impressions of 1872!

JOURNALISM IN AMERICA.

THE FIRST EPOCH.

1690—1704.

CHAPTER I.
THE INITIAL NEWSPAPER.

HARRIS'S PUBLICK OCCURRENCES IN BOSTON.—ONE DAY'S EXISTENCE ONLY.
—ITS CONTENTS.—THE REPRINTED LONDON GAZETTE IN NEW YORK.

THERE is always a beginning in every nation and with every individual. The primer is every where. All created things have an origin. Where there is a necessity in a community, some one supplies the want. The activity of the human intellect is constantly meeting the requirements of the human family. When ideas, and signs, and words came, something was necessary to put words into shape to communicate ideas with greater rapidity. Type were invented for this purpose. Ink and rude presses came with type, as gutta-percha with the telegraph. Written news-slips were too slowly prepared even for the slow age of Gutenburg and Schœffer. Newspapers, therefore, became a necessity, and were invented in their turn. Then came steam and electricity as auxiliary powers to intellect. What next? The pneumatic tunnel—the universal newspaper carrier!

With the progress of civilization and the increase of population in America, the same elements, the same manners, the same customs, the same wants, the same desires that existed in Europe were required here. We imported them and paid taxes on them. Newspapers had become a necessity in England, France, and Germany; they were equally so in America. We therefore imported the idea, and the type, and the ink, and the press, and the paper. So a newspaper was established on this side of the Atlantic. It made its first appearance in Boston, and that city has the honor and the glory of bringing into existence this useful and popular institution.

Seventy years after the landing of the Pilgrims on Plymouth

Rock, and two hundred and fifty years after the invention of printing, a newspaper was issued in that colony. It lived one day, and one copy only is known to have been preserved. That specimen sheet—that great curiosity in newspaper literature, is in the Colonial State Paper Office in London. It is not mentioned in any history that we have seen, nor in Disraeli's Curiosities of Literature, that the capital of Massachusetts derived its *sobriquets* of Athens of America, or the Hub of the Universe, from the important fact that the first American newspaper was printed there. It is not altogether unlikely that such is the fact. All we need say is that Boston enjoys these titles to fame, and she gave birth to the first newspaper. The people of that labyrinthine city feel that these titles belong to them. They are so much accustomed to the sound of the names that they hear them without visible emotion and with the utmost placidity.

The historian of Salem, the Rev. J. B. Felt, in his researches for facts connected with that ancient commercial town, discovered the copy of the "original newspaper" in the State Paper Office. Till then it was believed that the *News-Letter*, issued fourteen years later, was the first gazette printed on this side of the Atlantic. The pioneer of American journalism was published by Benjamin Harris at the London Coffee-house, and was printed for him by Richard Pierce on Thursday, the 25th of September, 1690, nearly two centuries after Columbus discovered this continent. This newspaper was printed on three pages of a folded sheet, leaving one page blank, with two columns to a page, and each page about eleven inches by seven in size. It was intended by its enterprising projector as a monthly, which, in his "journalistic" dreams, might do to start with in that progressive town. We give the editor's prospectus, which is a model in its way. It exhibits a comprehensiveness, common in the early days of newspapers, that must be charming and refreshing to many journalists of the more modern era:

NUMB. I.   PUBLICK
             OCCURRENCES
        Both FORREIGN and DOMESTICK.
          Boston, Thursday, *Sept.* 25th, 1690.

It is designed that the Countrey shall be furnished once a moneth (or if any Glut *of* Occurrences *happen* oftener) *with an Account of such considerable things as have arrived unto our Notice.*

In order here unto, the Publisher will take what pains he can to obtain a Faithful Relation *of all such things ; and will particularly make himself beholden to such Persons in* Boston *whom he knows to have been for their own use the diligent Observers of such matters.*

That which is herein proposed, is, First, *That* Memorable Occurrents *of* Divine Providence *may not be neglected or forgotten, as they too often are.* Secondly, *That people everywhere may better understand the Circumstances of Publique Affairs, both*

Contents of the First Newspaper. 45

abroad and at home; which may not only direct their Thoughts *at all times, but at some times also to assist their* Business *and* Negotiations.

Thirdly, *That some thing may be done towards the* Curing, *or at least the* Charming *of that* Spirit of Lying, *which prevails among us, wherefore nothing shall be entered, but what we have reason to believe is true, repairing to the best fountains for our Information. And when there appears any* material mistake *in any thing that is collected, it shall be* corrected *in the next.*

Moreover, *the Publisher of these* Occurrences is willing to engage, *that whereas, there are many* False Reports, *maliciously made, and spread among us, if any well minded person will be at the pains to trace any such* false Report, *so far as to find out and Convict the* First Raiser *of it, he will in this Paper* (*unless just Advice be given to the contrary*) *expose the Name of such person, as* A malicious Raiser of a False Report. *It is supposed that none will dislike this Proposal, but such as intend to be guilty of so villanous a Crime.*

This chronicle seems to have had no name, but it is not unlikely that the intention of the proprietor was to have it called *Publick Occurrences.* That appears prominent in his public announcement. Ten years afterward a paper with a similar name, *Pue's Occurrences,* was published in Dublin. The Genius for names, who has flourished so extensively in these latter days, had not been born at that early period. What Editor Harris's idea of public occurrences were may be judged by reading the contents of his first and only number. We annex them entire :

[The figures inclosed in brackets denote the ends of the columns.]

THE Christianized *Indians* in some parts of *Plimouth,* have newly appointed a day of Thanksgiving to God for his mercy in supplying their extream and pinching Necessities under their late want of Corn, and for His giving them now a prospect of a very *Comfortable Harvest.* Their Example may be worth Mentioning.

'Tis observed by the Husbandmen, that altho' the With-draw of so great a strength [1] from them, as what is in the Forces lately gone for *Canada,* made them think it almost impossible for them to get well through the Affairs of their Husbandry at this time of the year, yet the season has been so unusually favorable that they scarce find any want of the many hundred of hands, that are gone from them; which is looked upon as a merciful Providence.

While the barbarous *Indians* were lurking about *Chelmsford,* there were missing about the beginning of this Month a couple of Children belonging to a man of that Town, one of them aged about eleven, the other aged about nine years, both of them supposed to be fallen into the hands of the *Indians.*

A very *Tragical Accident* happened at *Watertown* the beginning of this Month, an *Old man,* that was of somewhat a Silent and Morose Temper, but one that had long Enjoyed the reputation of a *Sober* and a *Pious Man,* having newly buried his Wife, The Devil took advantage of the Melancholy which he thereupon fell into, his wives discretion and industry had long been the support of his Family, and he seemed hurried with an impertinent fear that he should now come to want before he dyed, though he had very careful friends to look after him who kept a strict eye upon him, lest he should do himself any harm. But one evening escaping from them into the Cow-house, they there quickly followed him, found *hanging by a Rope,* which they had used to tye their *Calves* withal, he was dead with his feet near touching the Ground.

Epidemical *Fevers* and *Agues* grow very common, in some parts of the Country, whereof, tho' many dye not, yet they are sorely unfitted for their imployments; but in some parts a more *malignant Fever* seems to prevail in such sort that it usually goes thro' a Family where it comes, and proves mortal unto many.

The *Small pox* which has been raging in *Boston,* after a manner very Extraordinary, is now very much abated. It is thought that far more have been sick of it than were visited with it, when it raged so much twelve years ago, nevertheless it has not been so Mortal. The number of them that have [2] dyed in *Boston* by this last Visitation is about *three hundred and twenty*, which is not perhaps half so many as fell by the former. The time of its being most *General*, was in the Months *June, July* and *August*, then 'twas that sometimes in some one Congregation on a Lords-day there would be Bills desiring prayers for above an *hundred sick*. It seized upon all sorts of people that came in the way of it. 'Tis not easy to relate the Trouble and Sorrow that poor *Boston* has felt by this *Epidemical Contagion*. But we hope it will be pretty nigh Extinguished, by that time twelve-month when it first began to Spread. It now unhappily spreads in several other places, among which our Garrisons in the *East* are to be reckoned some of the Sufferers.

Altho' *Boston* did a few weeks ago, meet with a Disaster by *Fire*, which consumed about *twenty Houses* near the *Mill-Creek*, yet about midnight, between the sixteenth and seventeenth of this Instant, *another Fire* broke forth near the *South-Meeting-House*, which consumed about five or six houses, and had almost carried the Meeting-house itself, one of the fairest Edifices in the Country, if God had not remarkably assisted the Endeavours of the People to put out the Fire. There were two more considerable Circumstances in the Calamities of this Fire, one was that a young man belonging to the House where the Fire began, unhappily perished in the Flames; it seems that tho' he might sooner awake than some others who did escape, yet he some way lost those Wits that should have taught him to help himself. Another was that the best furnished PRINTING PRESS, of those few that we know of in *America* was lost; a loss not presently to be repaired.

There lately arrived at *Piscataqua*, one *Papoon* from *Penobscot*, in a small Shallop, wherein he had used to attend upon the pleasure of *Casteen*, but took his opportunity to run away, and reports: That a Vessel of small Bulk bound from *Bristol* to *Virginia*, having been so long at Sea, till they were prest with want, put in at *Penobscot* instead of *Piscataqua*, where the *Indians* and *French* seized her, and Butchered the Master, and several of the men; but that himself who belonged unto the Ships Crew, being a *Jersey*-man, was more favorably used and found at length an advantage to make his Escape.

The chief discourse of this month has been about the affairs of the Western Expedition against *Canada*. The *Albanians, New Yorkers* and the *five Nations* of *Indians*, in the *West*, had long been pressing of the *Massachusetts* to make an Expedition by Sea into *Canada*, and still made us believe, that they stayed for us, and that while we assaulted [3] *Quebeck*, they would pass the *Lake*, and by Land make a Descent upon Mount *Real*. Accordingly this Colony with some assistance from our kind Neighbours of *Plimouth;* fitted an Army of near *five and twenty hundred men*, and a Navy of two and thirty Sail: which went from hence the beginning of the last *August* under the Command of the Honourable Sir *William Phips*.

In the mean time the *English* Colonies and Provinces in the West raised Forces, the Numbers whereof have been reported five or six hundred. The Honourable General *Winthrop* was in the Head of these, and advanced within a few miles of the *Lake;* He there had some good number of *Maquas* to joyn his Forces, but contrary to his Expectation, it was found that the Canoo's to have been ready for the transportation of the Army over the *Lake*, were not prepared, and the other Nations of Indians, that should have come to this *Campaign*, sent their Excuses, pretending that the Small-pox was among them, and some other Trifles. The General Meeting with such vexing disappointment called a Councel of War, wherein 'twas agreed, That it was impossible for them to prosecute their Intended Expedition. However he despatched away the Maqua's to the *French Territories*, who returned with some Success, having slain several of the *French*, and brought home several Prisoners, whom they used in a manner too barbarous for any *English* to approve. The General coming back to *Albany*, there happened a misunderstanding between him and the Lieutenant Governor of *New York* which occasioned much discourse, but produced not those effects which were feared of it. Where lay the bottom of these miscarriages is variously conjectured, if any people further West than *Albany*, have been tampering with the Indians, to desert the business of *Canada*, we hope time will discover it. And if Almighty God will have *Canada* to be subdued without the assistance of those miserable Salvages, in whom we have too much confided, we shall be glad, that there will be no sacrifice offered up to the Devil, upon this occasion; God alone will have all the glory.

'Tis possible we have not so exactly related the Circumstances of this business, but the Account, is as near exactness, as any that could be had, in the midst of many various reports about it.

Another late matter of discourse, has been an unaccountable destruction befalling a body of *Indians*, that were our Enemies. This body of *French Indians* had a Fort somewhere far up the River, and a party of Maqua's returning from the *East Country*, where they have at a great rate pursued and terrified those *Indians* which have been invading of our *North East* Plantations, and Killed their General *Hope Hood* among the rest; resolved [4] to visit this Fort; but they found the Fort ruined, the Canoo's cut to pieces, and the people all either Butchered or Captived. This gave them no little surprise and they gave the *English* this account of it. That a body of *Maqua's* lately returning from the spoil of *Canada* brought several *French Prisoners* with them; That calling at this Fort in their way, the *Indians* there seeing themselves unable to resist them did pass divers Complements with them and partake of their Booties. That a *French* Captive after this, escaping from the *Maqua's* informed the *French* that these *Indians* had revolted unto the *Maqua's*, and hereupon the *French* or their *Indians* made a sudden Sally forth upon them, and utterly destroyed them, tho' they were in reality of their own party still.

Two *English Captives* escaped from the hands of *Indians* and *French* at *Pscadamoquady*, came into Portsmouth on the sixteenth Instant & say, That when Capt. Mason was at *Port Real*, he cut the faces, and ript the bellies of two *Indians*, and threw a third over board in the sight of the *French*, who informing the other *Indians* of it, they have in revenge barbarously Butcher'd forty Captives of ours that were in their hands.

These two captives escaped in a Shallop, which our enemies intended to have set out with all the Circumstances of a Fishing Shallop but to have indeed filled with *Indians* that should have Clap't on board any *English* Vessel that came in their way; They say that about three or four weeks ago, some *Indians* were coming this way to War, but crossing a path which they supposed to be of the *Maqua's*, they followed it untill they discovered a place where some Canoo's were making, whereupon twenty *Kennebeck Indian*-Warriors went to look further after the business, who never yet returned, Which gives hope that they may come short home but upon this the *Squaws* are sent to *Penobscot*, and the men stand on their Defence.

Portsmouth, Sept. 20*th.* Two days since arrived here a small Vessel from *Barbadoes*, in which is a letter to Captain H. K. of 19th *August* that speaks thus,

Christophers is wholly taken from the *French* as also a small island called *Stacia:* we are very strong in Shipping, and our Ships of War are now gone for *Tobago*, a very good place to shelter from any Storms, after the suspicious months are over, they will Attack the rest of the *French* places. We have. News here that K. *William* is safe arrived in *Ireland*, and is marched with *one hundred* and *forty thousand Foot and Horse. Himself leads the Body*, Duke *Scomburgh* the right Wing, and the Earl of *Oxford* the left Wing, Duke *Hamilton* of *Scotland* leads the forlorn Hope with *ten thousand men* under him. Great victory they dayly have, and much people daily come in to him, with submission; He has [5] 200 Shipping with him of one sort or other, above one hundred Sail dayly run between *Ireland* and *England*, with meat for Man and Beast; His Majesty being unwilling to trust false *Ireland* for it. *France* is in much trouble (and fear not only with us but also with his Son, who has revolted against him lately, and has great reason) if reports be true. He has got all the *Hugonots*, and all the dissatisfied Papists, with the great force of the D. of Loraign, and are now against him, resolving to depose him of his Life and Kingdom.

It's Reported the City of *Cork* in *Ireland* has proclaimed K. *William*, and turned their *French* Landlords out of Doors: of this there wants further confirmation.

From *Plimouth* Sept. 22, We have an Account that on *Friday* the 12th Instant, in the night, our Forces Landing privately, forthwith surrounded *Pegypscot* Fort; but finding no *Indians* there, they March'd to *Amonoscoggin*. There on the Lordsday, they kill'd and took 15 or 16 of the Enemy, and recovered five *English* Captives, mostly belonging to Oyster River; who advised, that the men had been gone about ten days down to a River, to meet with the *French*, and the *French Indians:* where they expected to make up a Body of 300 men, and design first against Wells or *Piscataqua*.

On *Tuesday*, the Army came to our Vessels at *Macquoit*, but one of the Vessels touching a Ground stopt a Tide; by which means young *Bracket*, who was a considerable distance up the River, above *Amonoscoggin* Fort, being advised by an Indian that ran away from *Amonoscoggin*, that an *English* Army was there attempted his Escape, and came down to the Sloop just as they came on their Sail.

On Thursday, they landed at *Saco;* a Scout of 60 men of ours discover a party of the enemy, and had the Advantage of killing three of them, and of taking *nine Canoo's*, and an English captive named, *Thomas Baker*, who informed, that the Enemy had left a considerable Plunder at *Pegypscot*-Plains, which he supposed the Enemy was gone to secure.

Whereupon, the Army immediately embark'd, and arriving there that night, the next morning found the Bever Plunder accordingly.

While our Vessels where [were] at Anchor in *Cascoe Bay*, our Auxiliary Indians lodging on shore, and being too careless in their Watch, the Enemy made an Attaque upon them. The English forthwith repair'd to their Relief; but were sorely galled by an Embuscade of Indians. The Enemy soon quitted the field, escaping with their *Canoo's* whereof ours took several. In the Surprise, we lost 9 men, and had about 20 wounded; the blow chiefly fell on our dear *Friends*, the *Plimouth Forces*, 15 being killed and wounded of Captain *Southworth's* Company.

The imprint of the paper was as follows:

Boston, Printed by *R. Pierce* for *Benjamin Harris*, at the *London-Coffee-House.* 1690.

This specimen number attracted especial official notice. Editor Harris had touched upon local and military matters. It was frowned upon at once by the authorities, and killed outright within twenty-four hours. In alluding to this fact, Buckingham, in his Reminiscences, says:

Immediately on its publication it was noticed by the legislative authorities. Four days after, they spoke of it as a pamphlet; stated that it came out contrary to law, and contained "reflections of a very high nature." They strictly forbade "any thing in print, without license first obtained from those appointed by the government to grant the same."

This nipped Harris's enterprise in the bud, and no other effort was made to establish a paper in America till 1704. The authorities, it would seem, were peculiarly sensitive to any infringement of their power. They feared the influence even of a sheet simply giving the news of the day. There was nothing very offensive in any of the intelligence published by Harris. There was no effort at sensation. The news, some of which was really important, and which would be given with startling head-lines and learned editorial comments nowadays, is very quaintly and quietly told. There was evidently no excitement in the printing-office at the London Coffee-house, Boston; and it is clear that the system of paying so much a line was not in vogue with the proprietor of *Publick Occurrences*. If any of the expressions of 1690 reflected in any way upon the conduct of the office-holders then, it is a fortunate circumstance that none of them live and hold office now, to read and act upon some of the matter of many of the journals of the present day. What would become of such men as Emile de Girardin, of *La Liberté;* or James Gordon Bennett, *père et fils,* of the *Herald;* or James Walter, of the *Times;* or Henri Rochefort, of *La Lanterne* and *Mot d'Ordre;* or Horace Greeley, of the *Tribune?*

But, simple and guileless as Harris's paper appeared to be in a political point of view, there was something more about the, man and his antecedents, we think, than about his publication *per se,* that alarmed the provincial authorities, and led them to suppress the initial number so summarily. They feared the future issues of the paper. An English bookseller, named Dunton, in a curious work called "Life and Errors," published in London in 1705, in speaking of Harris, states:

> He was a brisk asserter of English liberties, and once printed a book with that very title. He sold a Protestant Petition in King Charles's reign, for which he was fined five pounds; and he was once set in the pillory, but his wife (like a kind Rib) stood by him to defend her husband against the mob. After this (having a deal of mercury in his natural temper) he traveled to New England, where he followed book selling, and then coffee selling, and then printing, but continued Ben Harris still, and is now both bookseller and printer in Grace Church street, as we find by his *London Post;* so that his conversation is general (but never impertinent) and his wit pliable to all inventions. But yet his vanity, if he has any, gives no alloy to his wit, and is no more than might justly spring from conscious virtue; and I do him but justice in this part of his character, for in once travelling with him from Bury Fair, I found him to be the most ingenious and innocent companion, that I had ever met with.

Manifestly the authorities of Massachusetts felt that such a man should not be permitted to create a new power and a new influence in that province, and in their midst. They therefore crushed the new enterprise in its cradle. But Harris was a good printer, and a man of energy and ability as a publisher; he must dabble in some public work. Two years after the suppression of his paper he was appointed " Printer to His Excellency the Governor and Council." This may have been balm to him for a time, as such appointments have since been to the journalists of Washington, New York, and Albany. Here is Harris's commission as State Printer:

> By his Excellency.—I order Benjamin Harris to print the Acts and Laws made by the Great and General Court, or Assembly of Their Majesties Province of Massachusetts-Bay in New England, that we the People may be informed thereof.
> WILLIAM PHIPPS.
> Boston, December 16, 1692.

Harris, however, was too restless to remain in Boston merely as a printer of laws. He returned to London in 1694 or thereabouts, and was not only a printer and bookseller in that metropolis as late as 1705, but publisher of the *Post*, showing his progressive spirit, for he had found a name for a newspaper which has lived to this day.

This effort of Harris in Boston forms an epoch in itself in the history of newspapers in America. It was the beginning. In 1692, when Benjamin Fletcher, who had faith in types and printing-ink, became Governor of New York, feeling a little jealous of the progress of Massachusetts and Pennsylvania in the typographical art, induced William Bradford, of Philadelphia, to migrate to that state and set up a printing-office in New York City, and in 1696 he had the *London Gazette*, which contained an account of an engagement with the French previous to the general peace of Ryswick, reprinted and circulated in that city. There was, we believe, only one issue. Of course the reprint had no local news. Its contents embraced merely the events in Europe. It was not intended for an American newspaper. It was issued to give a piece of important news to the people toward the close of a great war which the governor could not keep to himself. But the fact indicated the necessity of newspapers.

Nearly fourteen years elapsed after Harris's *Occurrences*, and eight years after Bradford's republication, before another attempt was made to give the news of the day to the American people in printed sheets! Meanwhile the newspapers of England arrived from time to time, feeding the public mind with news from home, and creating a desire for such an institution in the colonies. It was impossible for every one to get copies of the few London publications sent across the Atlantic, and the contents of those received had to be retailed in coffee-houses and on the streets. Written news circulars were also used to disseminate the latest intelligence. No doubt there was as much interest, all things considered, in Boston and New York on the arrival of an English mail, to get hold of a London paper, as there was in California, in the early days of the gold fever, to hear from the Atlantic slope, when a single copy of the *New York Herald*, received in San Francisco overland by the way of Mazatlan, sold for five dollars, and when the fortunate possessor of a copy of that paper had to mount a stump and read its contents to the assembled miners of 1848–9, and afterward pass it through the "diggings" till it was worn threadbare, with scarcely a printed word remaining visible on the sheet.

Thus was the necessity for a newspaper created in Massachusetts Bay and in America, as in all other parts of the world, and this brings us down to 1704.

THE SECOND EPOCH.

1704—1748.

CHAPTER II.
THE COLONIAL PRESS.

THE BOSTON NEWS-LETTER.—THE DEPENDENCE OF THE PRINTER ON THE GOVERNING CLASSES.—THE EARLY POSTMASTERS THE FIRST EDITORS.—THE FIRST REPORTING.—THE BOSTON GAZETTE AND PHILADELPHIA MERCURY.—THE FRANKLINS.—CONFLICTS WITH THE AUTHORITIES.—THE FIRST NEWSPAPER WAR.—THE ORIGINAL JENKINS IN AMERICA.

THIS period of nearly half a century embraces the Colonial Press —a period of the incipient newspapers of the country. Now and then there was an exhibition of independent opinion, a premonition of what was coming, but the repressive acts of the public authorities did not permit this to proceed far, or become in any way chronic. The few newspapers published in this epoch were, therefore, as a general thing, mere chroniclers of bald facts that did not affect the government. Society, too, was puritanical, and the press, under these circumstances, could not be free and unfettered. We will mention an incident which happened on the eve of this period which will illustrate this point.

Increase Mather, in March, 1700, published a treatise called "The Order of the Gospel Professed and Practiced by the Churches of Christ in New England Justified." Shortly after, a pamphlet appeared under the title of "Gospel Order Revived, being an Answer to a Book lately set forth by the Rev. Mr. Increase Mather, President of Harvard College, etc., by sundry Ministers of the Gospel in New England." It was remarkable for its calm and candid spirit. Yet it could not be printed in Boston. It was issued in New York with this advertisement:

> The Reader is desired to take Notice, that the Press in Boston is so much under the aw of the Reverend Author whom we answer, and his Friends, that we could not obtain of the Printer there to Print the following Sheets, which is the only true Reason why we have sent the Copy so far for its Impression, and where it is Printed with some Difficulty.

The printer in Boston was Bartholomew Green. It was necessary for him to vindicate himself, and this he did in a hand-bill which appeared in December, 1700, with some remarks prefaced by

Cotton Mather. This led to a paper war in pamphlets and handbills, which materially aided in breaking the sanctity and inviolability of the opinions of the controlling classes, and leading, in the course of time, to the establishment of newspapers in the colonies.

There were other circumstances tending to the same result. The colonists, in the absence of reliable intelligence printed at home, depended upon the English papers, sparingly received, official publications of proclamations and oppressive laws, and the gossip of the street and coffee-houses, and mostly on the latter source of information, for intelligence. The postmasters were the newsmen of the day. They were the ones that "told you so." They supplied their friends and patrons with the news, as the news-letter writers of Rome and Venice did in their time, and as Butters and Renaudot did in England and France prior to the establishment of newspapers in those countries. They used the Pen instead of the Press.

John Campbell, in virtue of his office as Postmaster of Boston, was the news-vender of Massachusetts Bay, and, indeed, of all New England on the opening of the eighteenth century. It soon became evident to him, from experience, that the time had come for the establishment of a newspaper as a better mode of circulating "publick intelligence" than written news circulars, so laborious to prepare and tedious to multiply, and the necessity was too apparent to be overlooked by a man of ordinary spirit and energy. After fourteen years of deprivation, the tastes and opinions of the public had sufficiently ripened for the authorities to tolerate and authorize the enterprise, under great restrictions however, such as prevailed in England a century before, and the newspaper was accordingly started, which became from that time a permanent institution in the country.

Approaching this important event, we find, in the "Proceedings of the Massachusetts Historical Society of 1866–67," nine of Campbell's news-letters or circulars, which had been written to Governor Fitz John Winthrop, of Connecticut, beginning in April and ending in October, 1703, the last one only six months prior to the issue of his newspaper. One of these letters, the first of the nine, we give entire, as a specimen, to enable our readers to see what sort of news was circulated, and how it was spread among the people in colonial times on this continent:

JOHN CAMPBELL TO GOV. WINTHROP.

Boston . Aprill 12th 1703.

Last week arrived a Vessell from ffyall and tells that about nine weeks from this time Two Vessells arrived from Scotland and one from Corke, in Ireland, that gave an Acco.[t] that the Union between England and Scotland was concluded upon and said master from ffyall sayes he see it in publick prints.

Capt Smith In the Gospert ffrigett from Jamaica arrived here also Last Week, and by him are we Informed of the union being Concluded upon, he came from Jamaica about midle or tenth of March.

Wee do apprehend that the union is only agreed upon by the Commissioners, which if true will be a great step Towards both parliam^{ts} Concluding it being the Commissioners are some of the greatest men of both nations.

They Talk from Jamaica of the Spaniards sueing for a peace. That about 20 Grandees were come to Portugal, to get the King of Portugale to Interceed with her mag^e of England to appoint Plenipotentiary to mediat. Capt Lawrence is arrived at Rhode Island & a Bermudas Sloop, both Privateers, who In Comp^e with Capt Blue an other privateer, took a Spanish Ship of 8 guns, Loaden with Canary and Brandy, and other goods, bound for the Havanne, who had on board 12 families consisting of above 130 Soules. The Prisoners they put on shore in N. Spain, all to about 7. The Three Consorts put 17 men an a Quarter Master on board. Capt Blue attended her with his sloop or vessell. The Prize is not yet arrived. The Prize said to Come from Spain and touched at the Canary's.

Capt Southack with our Western fleett arrived yesterday.

Capt Delbridge will sayle for London In 20 days, Ten guns, & Capt Dows, lyke guns, in a moneth.

BOSTON. April 12. 1703.

Hono^{ble} Sir :

I'm favoured with you^r ho^{ns} of the 9 Instant. Came in too day about ii a cloucke & do despatch him again at ffiue because should have no excuise to hinder his Coming In on Satterday, so have no tyme, either for selfe or man, to go to Mad^m Richards, but the Letter I sent theire Two days after its receipt.

On other Syde is what occurrs, with the Inclosed print, and with humble service am Sr   Yo^r ho^{rs} humble Servt

J^{no} CAMPBEL.

Go^r Winthrop.

[Superscribed]

To the Hono^{ble} John Winthrop, Esqr Govr of Connecticut, New London.

ffranck.

[Indorsed by Gov Winthrop]

Publick Occurrences & the adres to her Maj^e. Aprill 12th 1703.

The other eight letters, so interesting as the precursors of journalism in America, embraced the news of the day, mostly foreign, accounts of the stirring events of that eventful period, briefly related, and in a style similar to the above letter. These circulars were sent to each governor of the New England provinces, and must have been prepared with considerable labor. The writer made use of them, as journalists now make use of their columns, as a means to influence the authorities of that period to accomplish some reform or good to the public, or perhaps for themselves. In his letter of Sept. 20, for instance, he asked some aid for the post-office in Boston. He made the same sort of appeal to Governor Winthrop for this public institution that he afterward, in his paper, so often made to the people for the support of the *News-Letter*. On the 20th of September, 1703, he wrote :

I must represent to your ho^r and Assembly The state of the post office, as I have done to this Gov^{nt} and New Hampshire ; In order to have some encouragement for the support of it, as they have done ; else of necessity it must drop.

Those veteran journalists who became postmaster generals of this country in after years, one before and two since the Revolution— Benjamin Franklin, Amos Kendall, and John M. Niles—could scarce-

ly have had more trouble, even with the chronic financial distress
of that department in their day, than this primitive postmaster and
journalist had in his small local institution, with his fears lest the
office should "drop."

But thus prepared, with experience as a news correspondent, and
the machinery of the post-office in his hands for the distribution of
his paper, John Campbell, on Monday, the 24th of April, 1704, issued the initial number of the *Boston News-Letter.* It was an event
in Boston. Its appearance was a feature of that period. There
was a visible sensation. The first sheet of the first number was
taken damp from the press by Chief Justice Sewall to show to President Willard, of Harvard University, as a wonderful curiosity in the
colony. When this occurred the population of Boston was only
eight thousand.

The *News-Letter* was printed sometimes on a single sheet, foolscap size, and oftener on a half sheet, with two columns on each side.
No subscription price was mentioned. It was "printed by authority," and the following was the prospectus, advertisement as Campbell called it, as it appeared in the first number:

Advertisement.

THis News-Letter is to be continued Weekly; and all Perſons who have any
Houſes, Lands, Tenements, Farms, Ships, Veſſels, Goods, Wares or Merchan-
dizes, &c. to be Sold, or Let ; or Servants Run-away, or Goods Stole or Loſt ; may
have the ſame inſerted at a Reaſonable Rate, from *Twelve Pence* to *Five Shillings,*
and not to exceed : Who may agree with *John Campbel* Poſt-maſter of *Boſton.*

All Perſons in Town and Country may have ſaid News-Letter every Week,
Yearly, upon reaſonable terms, agreeing with *John Campbel,* Poſt-maſter for the
ſame.

There were no useless words in this announcement. There were
no great promises of what the publisher intended to do, as we now
often see. It is practical and to the purpose. No advertisement
was to be inserted costing over five shillings for its insertion ! John
Campbell, who then spelt his name with one l, thus burst upon the
world as the father of the American Press. We suppose that Harris must have been its grandfather. All that is known of Campbell
is that he was a Scotchman, a son of Duncan Campbell, the organ-
izer of the postal system of America, a bookseller, and the postmaster of Boston. The printer was Bartholomew Green, our handbill
hero of 1700, eldest son of Thomas Green, printer to Cambridge
University, where the Greens had been located, as such, since 1649,
and where Samuel Green printed the first Bible in America, not in
English, but in the Indian language, a copy of which recently sold
in New York for $300. Bartholomew Green was a member in "good
standing" of the Old South Church.

The *News-Letter*, in spite of its vicissitudes and troubles, lived seventy-two years. There is a complete file of it, the only one in existence, in the collection of the New York Historical Society. There are only two other copies of the first number known to be extant: one with the Massachusetts Historical Society, and the other with the American Antiquarian Society. It was under Campbell's management eighteen years. The first number contained news taken from the *London Flying Post* from December 2 to 4, 1703, and from the *London Gazette* from December 16 to 20. These extracts were "concerning the present Danger of the Kingdom and of the Protestant Religion," in consequence of the movements, and intrigues, and "talking big" of the friends of "the pretended King James VIII." This intelligence, with a short speech of Queen Anne to Parliament on the same subject, occupied three fourths of the printed part of the paper. The domestic news filled the remainder of the space. We insert this home intelligence in full, to place it in contrast with the contents of Harris's *Publick Occurrences*, published in 1690, and of the leading journals of 1872:

Boston, April 18. Arrived Capt. *Sill* from *Jamacia* about 4 Weeks Paſſage, ſays, they continue there very Sickly.

Mr. *Nathanael Oliver*, a principal Merchant of this place dyed *April* 15 & was decently inter'd April. 18. Ætatis 53.

The Honourable Col. *Nathanael Byfield* Eſq. is Commiſſioned Judge of the Admiralty for the Provinces of *Maſſachuſetts-Bay, New Hampſhire*, and *Rhod-Iſland*. And *Thomas Newton* Eſq. Judge-Deputy for the Colony of *Maſſachuſetts-Bay*.

The 20. the R'd. Mr. *Pemberton* Preach'd an Excellent Sermon on 1 *Thes.* 4. 11. *And do your own buſineſs*: Exhorting all Ranks & Degrees of Perſons to do their own work, in order to a REFORMATION: which His Excellency has ordered to be Printed.

The 21. His Excellency Diſſolved the Gen. Aſſembly.

Rhode-Iſland 22. The Rd. Mr. *Lockyer* dyed on Thurs. laſt.

Capt. *Toungrello* has taken Five Prizes off of *Curraſo*, one of which is come in to *Rhode-Iſland* moſtly Loaden with *Cocco, Tobacco, Liquors* &c. She is a *Curraſo* Trader, as all the reſt were. One of the Five was one *Larew* a *French-man*, a Sloop of 8 Guns & 8 Patteraro's 76 Men, Fought him Board and Board three Glaſſes; Captain *Larew* was kill'd, and 20 of his Men kill'd & wounded: Capt. *Toungrello* wounded thro' the Body, and five of his men, but none kill'd, he had but 40 Fighting Men, when he took Larew.

The 18 Currant, came in a Sloop to this Port from *Virginia*, the Maſter informed Governour *Cranſton* Eſq. he was Chaſed by a Topſail Shallop off of *Block Iſland*, which he judged to be a *French* Privateer, and that there was two other Veſſels in her Company, which he judged to be her Prizes. Whereupon his Honour being concerning for the Publick Weal and Safty of Her Majeſties good Subjects, immediately cauſed the Drum to beat for Voluntiers, under the Command of Capt. *Wanton*, and in 3 or 4 hours time, Fitted and Man'd a Brigantine, with 70 briſk young men well Arm'd, who Sail'd the following Night; returned laſt Evening, and gave his Honour an Account, that they found the aforeſaid Shallop, with one other, and a Ketch at T*arpolian* Cove, who were all Fiſhing Veſſels belonging to *Marblehead* or *Salem*, who were Fiſhing off of *Block-Iſland*, one of them was a *French* built Shallop with a Topſail, which gave the great ſuſpician that they were Enemies.

New-York, April 17. By a Barque from *Jamaica* (laſt from *Burmuda*, 7 Weeks Paſſage,) ſays, there was an Imbargo in that Iſland ſeveral Months, occaſioned by News they had of a deſign the *French & Spaniards* had, to make a deſcent upon them: She came out with the Homeward bound *London* Fleet, who are gone home without Convoy.

Capt. *Daviſon* in the Eagle Gally, Sailes for *London*, in a Month, if the *Virginia* Fleet ſtays ſo long, he intends to keep them Company Home, if not, to run for it, being Built for that Service.

Philadelphia, April, 14. An Account that the *Dreadnaught* Man of War was Arrived in *Marryland.*

N. London April, 20. The Adventure, A Veſſel 60 Tuns, will Sail from thence to London, in three Weeks or a Months time.

There was not an advertisement in the paper. None of the interesting local news now so copiously given in the numerous advertisements of the present day—bits of information of merchants, mechanics, milliners, millionaires, servants, *modistes*, ship-owners, railroads, steam-ships, boot-makers, tailors, theatres, churches, hotels, bankers, fortune-tellers, patent medicines, horses, races, auction sales, lectures, balls, real-estate sales, houses to let, and personals, so full of hope, and joy, and sorrow, which now fill column after column of the newspapers. One omission is quite noticeable in this, and, indeed, in all of the primitive papers, that would be greatly missed in modern journals. Marriages were not announced at all, and deaths rarely mentioned. Only two deaths, one of a leading merchant in Boston, and the other of a clergyman in Rhode Island, are announced in the first *News-Letter.* These important social events were afterward, and till quite recently, considered so interesting and necessary that publishers inserted them gratuitously. Now, however, these items of home news, so absorbingly attractive to so large a class of newspaper readers, are treated as advertisements, and their insertion is paid for as such at the highest rates, and there is never less than one column of these items published daily in the *New York Herald* alone.

In one of the October news circulars of 1703, Campbell speaks of the London "Gazet" of the previous July. This "Gazet," as we have already mentioned, was the official organ of the British government, smaller than the *News-Letter* generally, but printed on a half sheet. In style and arrangement the two papers were not unlike. One publisher would copy the style and manner of the "make-up" of another, in the absence partly of any taste of his own, but mostly, probably, in consequence of the expense and want of variety in type. Some of the *News-Letters,* indeed many of them, in contents, were a mere transcript of the *London Gazette,* giving no local news beyond the arrival and departure of a few vessels, and two or three advertisements. As an instance of the enterprise of that day, the editor announced, with as much regret as simplicity, that he was "thirteen months behind in giving the news from Europe." It was the only paper in existence, and had no rival for upward of fifteen years, yet it did not appear to have thrived abundantly in a pecuniary point of view, not sufficiently to enable its proprietor to publish such a paper as he planned in his dreams. Appeals for support were repeatedly made to the public. There were more readers than paying subscribers. The publisher found it difficult, in his small sheet, to give all the news: it was impossible, he said, "with half a sheet a week, to carry on all the Publick News of Europe."

The first effort at reporting in this country was made for the *News-Letter* shortly after it was established. Six pirates were executed on Charles River on Friday, June 30, 1704. In describing the scene, the "exhortations to the malefactors," and the prayer made by one of the ministers, after the pirates were on the scaffold, "as near as it could be taken in writing in the great crowd," filled nearly one half of the paper.

After urging the public to support him in all sorts of ways, Campbell made a strong appeal, on the 10th of August, 1719, giving an interesting statement of his affairs, to induce his readers to aid him sufficiently to publish a paper that would keep them fully posted in the affairs of the world. Here is the appeal, and a singular one it is:

The Undertaker of this News-Letter, the 12th January last being the Second Week of this Currant Years Intelligence gave then Intimation that after 14 (now upwards of 15) years experience, it was impossible with half a Sheet a Week to carry on all the Publick Occurrences of Europe, with those of this, our Neighbouring Provinces, and the West Indies. To make up which Deficiency, and the News Newer and more acceptable, he has since Printed every other Week a Sheet, whereby that which seem'd Old in the former half Sheets, becomes New now by the Sheet, which is easy to be seen by any One who will be at the pains to trace back former years, and even this time 12 Months, we were then 13 Months behind with the Foreign News beyond Great Britain, and now less than Five Months, so that by the Sheet we have retrieved about 8 months since January last, and any One that has the News-Letter since that time, to January next (life permitted) will be accommodated with all the News of Europe, &c. contained in the Publick Prints of London that are needful for to be known in these Parts. And in regard the Undertaker had not suitable encouragement, even to Print half a Sheet Weekly, seeing that *he cannot vend* 300 *at an Impression, tho' some ignorantly concludes he Sells upwards of a Thousand;* far less is he able to Print a Sheet every other Week, without an Addition of 4, 6, or 8 Shillings a Year, as every one thinks fit to give payable Quarterly, which will only help to pay for Press and Paper, giving his Labour for nothing. And considering the great Charge he is at for several Setts of Publick Prints, by sundry Vessels from London, with the Price of Press, Paper, Labour, carrying out the News Papers, and his own Trouble, in collecting and composing, &c. It is afforded by the Year, or by the Piece or Paper, including the difference of money far cheaper than in England, where they Sell several Hundreds nay Thousands of Copies to a very small number vended here. Such therefore as have not already paid for the half Year past the last Monday of June, are hereby desired to send or pay in the same to John Campbell at his House in Cornhill, Boston.
August 10, 1719.

So much is this, in spirit, like Nathaniel Butters, in his *Weekley Newes*, three quarters of a century earlier, that we must give Nathaniel's last appeal to the people of London for support. Butters had been terribly annoyed with the unaccommodating spirit and ignorance of the Licenser of the Press:

The Printer to the Reader:

Courteous Reader: We had thought to have given over printing our foreign avisoes, for that the licenser (out of a partiall affection) would not oftentimes let pass apparant truth, and in other things (oftentimes) so crosse, and alter, which made us almost weary of printing, but he being vanished, (and that office fallen upon another, more understanding in these Forraine Affaires, and as you will find more candid.) We are againe (by the favour of his Majestie and the State) resolved to go on printing, if we shall finde the World to give a better acceptation of them, (than of late,) by their Weekly buying them. It is well known these Novels are well esteemed in all parts of the World, (but heere), by the more judicious, which we can impute to no other but the discontinuance of them, and the uncertaine days of publishing them, which, if the poste fail us not, we shall keepe a constant day every weeke therein, whereby every man may constantly expect them, and so we take leave.

January the 9th 1640.

And Nathaniel did "take leave," for we see no more of him in the journalistic world; but Campbell continued three years longer on the *News-Letter*, long enough to inaugurate the "war of editors," which has continued intermittently from that day to this, sometimes ending in a farce, and sometimes in a funeral.

Notwithstanding the apparent want of success, financially, of the *News-Letter*, journalism, technically, if not in fact, had become, by its establishment, an organized business in America. The troubles of Campbell, who in 1711 added another l to his name, did not deter others then, any more than the numerous failures since have deterred thousands from rushing to the printing-office for fame and fortune in these latter days. Supreme for sixteen years, without a rival of any sort on this continent, his feelings can be imagined, especially in newspaper offices and post-offices, when other papers and other office-seekers made their appearance in opposition to him and his paper, and to take from him some of the public honor, public favor, and public pay.

In 1719 Campbell was removed from the post-office, and William Brooker was appointed Postmaster of Boston. On the 21st of December of that year the new Postmaster, in accordance with the custom inaugurated by his predecessor, began the publication of a paper, the *Boston Gazette*, the second newspaper in America, the father of the innumerable *Gazettes* issued from that day to this throughout the land. It was the name of the first paper printed in France. It was the name of the first paper in Venice and in Nuremberg. Some hold that the name come sfrom the Italian word gazza or gazzara, which means a magpie, a chatterer, a gossip, and not from the small piece of money called gazzetta.

The *Boston Gazette* was printed on a half sheet of foolscap. In consequence of the dismissal of Mr. Campbell from the post-office, and the establishment of the *Gazette* by his rival in office, some ill feeling, ending in a "paper war," grew up between the two concerns. "I pity the readers of the new paper," said John Campbell, in bitterness and chagrin; "its sheets smell stronger of beer than of midnight oil. It is not reading fit for people!" Campbell's indignation on his removal from office was so great that he even refused to send his paper through the mails to his subscribers, and it is said to have been partly in consequence of this that the new Postmaster was induced to start the *Gazette*. This fact, indeed, was mentioned in the first number of that paper. Then Campbell rejoined. On the 11th of January, 1720, the *Gazette* thus replied:

The good manners and caution that has been observed in writing this paper, 'twas hoped would have prevented any occasion for controversies of this kind; but finding a very particular advertisement published by Mr. Campbell in his Boston News-Letter of the 4th current, lays me under an absolute necessity of giving the following answer thereunto.

Mr. Campbell begins in saying, *The* Nameless Author—Intimating as if the not mentioning the author's name was a fault: But if he will look over the papers wrote in England, (such as the London Gazette, Postman, and other papers of reputation) he will find their authors so. As this part of his advertisement is not very material, I shall say no more thereon; but proceed to matters of more moment. Mr. Campbell seems somewhat displeased that the author says he was *removed* from being Postmaster. I do hereby declare I was the person that wrote the said Preamble, as he calls it; and think I could not have given his being *turned out* a softer epithet. And to convince him (and all mankind) that it was so, I shall give the following demonstrations of it.

Many months before John Hamilton, Esq. Deputy-Postmaster-General of North-America displaced the said Campbell, he received letters from the secretary of the Right Honorable the Postmaster-General of Great Britain, &c. that there had been several complaints made against him, and therefore the removal of him from being Postmaster was thought necessary. Mr. Hamilton for some time delayed it, 'till on the 13th of September, 1718, he appointed me to succeed him, with the same salary and other just allowances, according to the establishment of the office; and if Mr. Campbell had any other, they were both unjust and unwarrantable, and he ought not to mention them. As soon as I was put in possession of the office, Mr. Hamilton wrote a letter to the Right Honorable the Postmaster-General, acquainting him that he had removed Mr. Campbell and appointed me in his room.

Mr. Campbell goes on: saying, *I was superseded by Mr. Musgrave from England.* To make him appear also mistaken in this point: Mr. Hamilton not displacing him as soon as was expected, the Right Honorable the Postmaster-General appointed Mr. Phillip Musgrave, by their deputation dated June 27, 1718, to be their Deputy-Postmaster of Boston; and in a letter brought by him from the Right Honorable the Postmaster-General to John Hamilton, Esq. mention is made, that for the many complaints that were made against Mr. Campbell, they had thought it fit to remove him, and appoint Mr. Musgrave in his stead, who was nominated Postmaster of Boston almost three months before I succeeded Mr. Campbell, which has obliged me to make it appear that he was either *removed, turned out, displaced,* or *superseded.*

The last thing I am to speak to, is, Mr. Campbell says, *it is amiss to represent that people remote have been prevented from having the News-Paper.* I do pray he will again read over my introduction, and then he will find there is no word there advanced that will admit of such an *interpretation.*

There is nothing herein contained but what is *unquestionably true;* therefore I shall take leave of him, wishing him all *desirable success in his agreeable News-Letter,* assuring him I have neither capacity nor inclination to answer any more of his like Advertisements.

The *Gazette* became the Postmaster's organ. It was owned and conducted by no less than five between the years 1719 and 1739, and for the heirs of the last Postmaster till 1741, when it was merged with the *New England Weekly Journal.* The *Gazette,* when owned by Brooker, was printed by James Franklin. When it passed into the hands of Philip Musgrave, the printing was taken away from Franklin and given to Samuel Kneeland, who afterwards owned the establishment.

On the appearance of the *Gazette* the proprietor of the *News-Letter* once more addressed his patrons, stating comprehensively enough that he had published his "Publick Letter of Intellegence" for nearly sixteen years with "Universal Approbation" and "for the Interest and advantage of the Post Office, Gentlemen, Merchants, and others, both in town and country; and preventing a great many false Reports."

The day after the issue of the first number of the *Gazette* the third newspaper in the colonies was established in Philadelphia. Its title was the *American Weekly Mercury,* and its birthday was the 22d of December, 1719. This paper was "Printed and sold by Andrew Bradford, at the Bible, in the Second Street, and John Copson, in the High Street, 1719-20." Bradford was the Postmaster of Philadelphia. He was a son of William Bradford, who opened the first printing-office in the colonies outside of New England. The *Mercury,* like the *News-Letter,* had soon to compete with a Franklin. It had also its troubles with the authorities. On the 2d of January, 1721, the following paragraph appeared in the *Mercury:*

> Our General Assembly are now sitting, and we have great expectations from them, at this juncture, that they will find some effectual remedy to revive the dying credit of this Province, and restore us to our former happy circumstances.

Apparently this was a harmless paragraph. Moderation was the tone of these few lines; but on the 21st of February the editor and publisher was summoned before the Provincial Council. Stating that the paragraph was written and inserted by a journeyman without his knowledge, and regretting its publication, he was discharged with a reprimand, and a warning never to publish any thing more relative to the affairs of any of the colonies. Afterward he had to pass through a severer ordeal. Benjamin Franklin had written a series of essays, over the signature of Busy Body, for the *Mercury,* and in one of them, near an annual election, the following remarks were made:

> To the friends of liberty, firmness of mind and public spirit are absolutely requisite; and this quality, so essential and necessary to a noble mind, proceeds from a just way of thinking that we are not born for ourselves alone, nor our own private advantages alone, but likewise and principally for the good of others and service of civil society. This raised the genius of the Romans, improved their virtue, and made them protectors of mankind. This principle, according to the motto of these papers, animated the Romans—Cato and his followers—and it was impossible to be thought great or good without being a patriot; and none

could pretend to courage, gallantry, and greatness of mind, without being first of all possessed with a public spirit and love of their country.

This simple matter produced such an effect on the Governor and Council that they ordered Bradford to be arrested, committed to prison, and bound over to the court. But Bradford showed some pluck on this occasion, and the matter ended there. It is probable that Franklin infused some of the boldness manifested in the *Mercury* at this time.

There was one feature in the *Mercury* that characterizes few of the enterprising papers of the modern school. On the 17th of October, 1734, the particulars of the battle of Phillipsburg were given with diagrams, such as those published in the *Tribune*, and *Times*, and *Herald* of Bull Run and Gettysburg.

Andrew Bradford died on the 24th of November, 1742. The *Mercury* was suspended a week after his death, and its column-rules, on its reappearance, were inverted for six weeks. His widow conducted the paper after her husband's decease.

But the era of journalism, with a character a little above that of merely publishing the news of the week with an occasional sensation, now commenced. On the 7th of August, 1721, the Franklins dawned upon the world and became famous. On that day James Franklin, having lost the printing of the *Gazette*, issued a paper which he called the *New England Courant*. It was the fourth newspaper on this continent. The appearance of the *Courant* was the saddest blow John Campbell received. It brought out a few sparks of originality and vitality, and then the father of the American Press abdicated, and subsided into a Justice of the Peace. But Campbell had a few last words before he surrendered the *News-Letter* to Bartholomew Green.

On the issue of the *Courant*, it was evident Franklin intended to make it a readable paper. Speaking of the *News-Letter* in his first number, he asserted that it was "a dull vehicle of intelligence." This was considered so severe by Campbell that it completely aroused the old editor, and a broadside, in answer, in Latin and English, appeared in the *News-Letter* on the 14th of August, 1721:

On Monday last the 7th Currant, came forth a Third Newspaper in this Town, Entitled, The New England Courant, by *Homo non unius Negotii;* Or Jack of all Trades, and it would seem, Good at none; giving some very, very frothy fulsome Account of himself, but lest the continuance of that style should offend his readers; wherein with submission (I speak for the Publisher of this Intelligence, whose endeavours has always been to give no offence, not meddling with things out of his Province.) The said Jack promises in pretence of Friendship to the other News Publishers to amend like soure Ale in Summer, Reflecting too, too much that my performances are now and then, very, very dull, Misrepresenting my candid endeavors (according to the Talent of my Capacity and Education; not soaring above my Sphere) in giving a true and genuine account of all Matters of Fact, both Foreign and Domestick, as comes any way well Attested, for these

Seventeen Years and an half past. It is often observed, a bright Morning is succeeded by a dark Rainy Day, and so much Mercury in the beginning may end in *Album Græcum*. And seeing our New Gentleman seems to be a Scholar of Academical Learning, (which I pretend not to, the more my unhappiness; and too late to say, *O mihi præteritos referat si Jupiter Annos*) and better qualified to perform a work of this Nature, for want whereof out of a Design for publick good made me at first at the Sollicitation of several Gentlemen, Merchants, and Others, come into it, according to the Proverb, thinking that half a Loaf was better than no Bread; often wishing and desiring in Print that such a one would undertake it, and then no one should sooner come into it and pay more Yearly to carry it on than the Publisher, and none appearing then, nor since, (others being judges) to excell him in their performances, made him to continue. And our New Publisher being a Scholler and Master, he should (me thinks) have given us (whom he terms low, flat and dull) Admonition and told one and the other wherein our Dulness lay, (that we might be better Proficients for the future, Whither in reading, hearing, or pains taking, to write, gather, collect and insert the Public Occurrences) before publick Censure, and a good example to copy and write after, and not tell us and the World at his first setting out, that he'll be like us in doing as we have done. *Turpe est Doctori cum culpa nedarguit ipsum*. And now all my Latin being spent excepting what I design always to remember *Nemo sine crimine vivit*, I promise for my part so soon as he or any Scholler will Undertake my hitherto Task, and Endeavours, giving proof that he will not be very, very Dull, I shall not only desist for his Advantage, but also so far as capable Assist such a good Scribe.

Very few of the *Courant* are in existence: none of those containing Franklin's articles on the *News-Letter*. But it is believed that Franklin had the best of the controversy. We can obtain the spirit of his reply to Campbell's first article from the rejoinder which appeared in the *News-Letter* on the 28th of August:

☞ J. C. to Jack Dullman *sendeth* Greeting.
Sir, What you call a Satyrical Advertisement was a just Vindication of my News-Letter, from some unfair Reflections, in your Introduction to your first Courant; Your reply in hobling Verse, had they more Reason and less Railing might possibly have inclined me to think you was some Man of great Learning, or as you please to Word it, a *Meikle Man;* but Railery is the talent of a mean Spirit, and not to be returned by me. In honour to the Muses I dare not acknowledge your Poem to be from Parnassus; but as a little before the Composure you had been Rakeing in the Dunghill, its more probable the corrupt Steams got into your Brains, and your Dullcold Skul precipitate them into Ribaldry. I observe you are not always the same, your History of Inoculation intends the Publick Good, but your Letter to Mr. Compton and Rhyme to me smell more of the Ale Tub than the Lamp. I do not envy your skill in Anatomy, and your accurate discovery of the Gall Bladder, nor your Geography of the Dunghill (*natale solum*.) You say your Ale grows better, but have a care you do not Bottle it too New, Lest the Bottles fly and wet your Toyes. You say you are the Wiseman, and his Advice is, Prov. xxvi. Ver. 4. *Answer not a fool according to his folly, lest thou be like unto him.* And not very disagreeable to what I learned when a School Boy.

Contra verbosos, noli contendere verbis.
Against a man of wind spend not thy Breath.

Therefore I conclude with *Verbum Sapienti,*

Tutius est, igitur fictis contendere verbis,
Quam pugnare manu.   Vale.

Since like the Indian Natives, you Delight,
to Murder in the Dark, eshun and fly the light,
Farewel.

The "war of the papers" did not have its origin on this continent. Although it has been more violent here than in any other country, leading to duels and street-fights. It began in England as far back as 1642. Previously, the wits of the theatres and coffee-houses made butts of the newspapers. The war was the first sign of intellectual vitality in the Press. It was a conflict of brains. Those editors who accuse others of being villains, liars, forgers, blasphemers in our day, are not originals. Such epithets were applied to the *Mercurius Aulicus* and *Mercurius Aquaticus* by the *Mercurius Britannicus* in 1642, when the editor of the latter said, "I have discovered the lies, forgeries, insolencies, impieties, prophanities, blasphemies of the two sheets." Our modern pen-warriors use no stronger expressions. They are a little more sententiously thrown at each other. They use one epithet at a time. That is all the difference. There is more force and point in the modern mode. When a political friend of Governor Marcy told him of his mistake in the expression of "To the victors belong the spoil," in the heated campaign of Jackson's time, he replied that all politicians held the same opinion. "Yes, yes," said his friend, "but they are not so silly as to put it in half a dozen words that every body can remember." When Horace Greeley applied to William Cullen Bryant or John Bigelow the epithet "You lie, villain, you know you lie," he merely condensed the expression of the *Mercurius Britannicus* of 1642.

Such a warfare was not an evil. It was needed two centuries ago. It vitalized the press. Abuse, like every thing else, can be overdone. It will correct itself. All difference of opinion is healthy. All elements need disturbance. If a newspaper goes too far in its criticisms, it suffers. Other newspapers do not. All trades and professions differ in views and in opinion of each other. There is no more *esprit du corps* among clergymen, lawyers, physicians, or merchants, than among editors. Journalists parade their jealousies and differences on the public clothes-line, where every body can see them. They wash their "dirty linen" before the people, and in the most exposed places. Other professions simply use their own premises for this purpose.

After a few weeks the contest between the *Courant* and Campbell ended, and the *News-Letter* passed into the hands of Bartholomew Green, in accordance with the subjoined announcement, which was published on the 31st of December, 1721:

⁎⁎* These are to give Notice, That Mr. *Campbell*, Designing not to Publish any more News-Letters, after this Monday the 31st Currant, *Bartholomew Green* the Printer thereof for these 18 Years past, having had Experience of his Practice therein; intends (Life permitted) to carry on the same, (using his Method on the Arrival of Vessels from *Great Britain*, &c., *to give a Summary of the most Remarkable Occurrences of Europe, and afterwards the Thread of the News,*) provided he can have due Encouragement by competent Numbers taking it by the Year, so as to enable him to defray the necessary Charges. And all those who have a Mind (either in Town or Country) to Promote and Encourage the Con-

tinuation of the abovesaid Intelligence, are hereby desired to Agree with the said *Green*, either by Word or Writing; who may have it on reasonable Terms, left at any House in Town, Sealed or Unsealed.

The last, on earth, of John Campbell is thus modestly announced in the *News-Letter* of March 7, 1728 :

On Monday last, the 4th inst, died here, at the age of seventy five years, John Campbell, Esquire, formerly director of the post in this town, many years editor of the *Boston News-Letter*, and one of her Majesty's justice of the peace for the County of Suffolk.

There was no other obituary notice. None of the column-rules of the paper were turned. None of the "sticks" of the compositors were reversed. It was not deemed even necessary to say that he was the proprietor or founder of the first regular newspaper on this continent. He was simply editor "for many years." So passed away the glory of John Campbell.

When Green assumed the management of the *News-Letter*, he designed giving it a semi-religious character. On the 21st of January, 1723, he issued the following as

An Advertisement from the Publisher.

It being my Desire to make this as profitable and entertaining to the good people of this country as I can, I propose to give not only the most material articles of intelligence, both foreign and domestic, which concern the political state of the world; but also because this is a country, that has yet, through the mercy of God, many people in it, that have the State of religion in the world very much at heart, and would be glad, if they knew how to order their prayers and praises to the Great God thereupon, I shall endeavour, now and then, *to insert an article upon the state of religion*. I shall, therefore, from time to time, wait upon such as I may know to cultivate a correspondence with the most eminent persons in several nations, who may please to communicate to me, and thereby to the public, such things as all good men cannot but receive with satisfaction.

In 1733 Bartholomew Green died, and the paper passed into the hands of his son-in-law, John Draper, who continued to maintain the semi-religious character of its columns.

One of the *News-Letters* of 1757, now before us, that of October 20th, then issued by John Draper, published on a half sheet, with naval news, and the following advertisement printed on the margin :

Any gentlewoman and others that want Stays made or mended after the best and neatest Manner in their Houses, may have them done Cheap for the sake of ready Money by John Banks ; or he will take Stays to mend or make at his House opposite Deacon Barrett's Shop near the Mill Bridge.

It was then the custom for men to make stays. There were the inimitable Banks and Slaughters then as there is the inimitable Worth that governs the fashionable world now. Moses Slaughter advertised in the *New York Gazette*, October 3, 1737, to the same effect. His advertisement will be interesting to the *modistes* of the present day. Slaughter, as he lodged with the publisher of the *Gazette*, ought to have furnished him with a regular article on the fashions, after the style of those we now see in *Le Follet*. But here is his notice on Stays:

Moses Slaughter, Stay Maker, from *London*, has brought with him a Parcel of extraordinary good and Fashionable Stays of his own making, of several Sizes and Prices. The Work of them he will warrant to be good, and for Shape, Inferiour to none that are made.

He lodges at present at the House of *William Bradford* next door but one to the Treasurer's near the *Fly Market*, where he is ready to suit those that want, with extraordinary good Stays. Or he is ready to wait upon any Ladys or Gentlewomen that please to send for him to their Houses. If any desire to be informed of the Work he has done, let them enquire of Mrs. *Elliston* in the Broadstreet, or of Mrs. *Nichols* in the *Broadway*, who have had his work.

John Draper died in 1762, and was succeeded by his son, Richard Draper, who changed the title of the paper to that of the *Boston Weekly News-Letter and New England Chronicle*. The name was again changed to the *Massachusetts Gazette and Boston News-Letter*. In 1768 it was united with the *Boston Post-Boy*. The union was a mongrel affair, and did not last long. Although the united papers were called the *Massachusetts Gazette*, each paper continued a separate publication—the *Post-Boy*, as such, appearing on Mondays, and the *News-Letter* on Thursdays—one half being called by its own name, and the other half by the name of the united concerns. One half was the official organ of the government, and published the laws; the contents of the other half were in accordance with the interests, opinions, and fancy of each publisher. These Siamese Twins in journalism were separated in 1769, and Draper fell back on his old title, and continued to publish the *News-Letter* till the 6th of June, 1774, when he died, and was succeeded by his widow, Margaret Draper, and John Boyle, whom he had taken into partnership a month previously. John Howe afterward assumed Boyle's share, and with the widow Draper carried on the paper till March, 1776, when, with the evacuation of Boston by the British troops, the *News-Letter*, after a life of seventy-two years, ceased to exist.

The *News-Letter* was loyal to the home government, and was the only paper published in Boston during the siege of that city by Washington. While the British troops occupied that town, the original Jenkins made his appearance, and wrote for the *News-Letter*. On the 22d of February, 1776, it contained the following notice:

MASQUERADE.

On Monday, the 11th of March will be given at Concert-Hall, a SUBSCRIPTION MASKED BALL. By the sixth of March a Number of Different Masks will be prepared, and sold by almost all the Milliners and Mantua Makers in Town.

In speaking of this "grand affair," the *News-Letter* said that "ten Capital Cooks are already engaged in preparing supper for the Masquerade, which is to be the most brilliant Thing ever seen in America." This affair was on the 11th of March. On the 17th the entire British army, including the "ten Capital Cooks," evacuated Boston, and Washington, with the American troops, marched in and took possession of the city.

After the tilt with the *News-Letter*, the *Courant* opened its pen and ink batteries upon the authorities, clerical and lay, and soon got into trouble. Whatever may be the judgment of mankind on Franklin's course, he certainly initiated a new era in journalism. While he suffered in purse and person, the press gained in freedom and independence. The *News-Letter* and *Gazette* in Boston, and the *Mercury* in Philadelphia, the other papers then published, being in the hands of office-holders, were circumspect in the utterance of their views, and confined themselves to a mere rehash of foreign news and a few unimportant local items. But Franklin was made of different stuff. His paper was the first rebel organ in America. With the leaven of 1776 in his soul, he was bold and outspoken, and commented on the abuses of the times as he saw them. Satire was the effective weapon of Franklin and his writers. In less than a year of the existence of the *Courant*, its proprietor was arrested and in prison for the boldness of his language. More outspoken than ever after his release, he was forbidden to print any thing without authority from his majesty's secretary of the province. About this time Benjamin Franklin made his appearance. In speaking of the *Courant* and of his brother James, the autobiography of Benjamin Franklin says:

> My brother had, in 1720 or 1721, begun to print a newspaper. It was the second that appeared in America, and was called the *New England Courant*. The only one before it was the *Boston News-Letter*. I remember his being dissuaded by some of his friends from the undertaking, as not likely to succeed, one newspaper being in their judgment enough for America. At this time, 1771, there are not less than five-and-twenty. He went on, however, with the undertaking. I was employed to carry the papers to the customers, after having worked in composing the types and printing off the sheets.
>
> He (James Franklin) had some ingenious men among his friends, who amused themselves by writing little pieces for his paper, which gained it credit, and made it more in demand, and these gentlemen often visited us. Hearing their conversation, and their accounts of the approbation their papers were received with, I was excited to try my hand among them. But, being still a boy, and suspecting that my brother would object to printing any thing of mine in his paper, if he knew it to be mine, I contrived to disguise my hand, and, writing an anonymous paper, I put it at night under the door of the printing-house. It was found in the morning, and communicated to his writing friends when they called in as usual. They read it, commented on it in my hearing, and I had the exquisite pleasure of finding it met with their approbation, and that, in their different guesses at the author, none were named but men of some character among us for learning and ingenuity. I suppose that I was rather lucky in my judges, and that they were not really so very good as I then believed them to be. Encouraged, however, by this attempt, I wrote and sent in the same way to the press several other pieces, that were equally approved; and I kept my secret till all my fund of sense for such performances was exhausted, and then discovered it, when I began to be considered a little more by my brother's acquaintance.
>
> However, that did not quite please him, as he thought it tended to make me

too vain. This might be one occasion of the difference we began to have about this time. * * * * * *

One of the pieces in our newspaper on some political point, which I have now forgotten, gave offense to the Assembly. He was taken up, censured, and imprisoned for a month by the Speaker's warrant, I suppose because he would not discover the author. I too was taken up and examined before the Council; but, though I did not give them any satisfaction, they contented themselves with admonishing me, and dismissed me, considering me perhaps as an apprentice, who was bound to keep his master's secrets. During my brother's confinement, which I resented a good deal notwithstanding our private differences, I had the management of the paper; and I made bold to give our rulers some rubs in it, which my brother took very kindly, while others began to consider me in an unfavorable light, as a youth that had a turn for libelling and satire.

My brother's discharge was accompanied with an order, and a very odd one, that "*James Franklin* no longer print the newspaper called *The New England Courant.*" On consultation held in our printing-office amongst his friends, what he should do in this conjuncture, it was proposed to elude the order by changing the name of the paper. But my brother, seeing inconvenience in this, came to a conclusion, as a better way, to let the paper in future be printed in the name of *Benjamin Franklin;* and in order to avoid the censure of the Assembly, that might fall on him, as still printing it by his apprentice, he contrived and consented that my old indenture should be returned to me with a discharge on the back of it, to show in case of necessity; and, in order to secure to him the benefit of my service, I should sign new indentures for the remainder of my time, which were to be kept private. A very flimsy scheme it was; however, it was immediately executed, and the paper was printed accordingly, under my name, for several months.

The *Courant* was not the second paper even in Boston. It was the fourth in America.

Inoculation for the smallpox was the great point in dispute between the *Courant* on one side, and the authorities and clergy, with the *News-Letter* and *Gazette,* on the other. It had been introduced into England by Lady Mary Wortley Montague in 1718, and had just reached the colonies when James Franklin issued his paper. While the practice was preached against by many of the bishops and clergy in England, it was strongly advocated by Increase and Cotton Mather, and other clergymen in America.

It was manifest that there was a staff on the *Courant* of free thinkers, free writers, and free talkers. They were called the Hell-Fire Club by the Mathers, who seemed to have the care and control of the souls and consciences of the people of Boston at that time. These writers, including the youthful Benjamin Franklin, had many fights, on paper, with the clergy and their adherents. Increase Mather, with the experience of eighty-four years on his shoulders, recognized the "inspiration of the devil" in the third number of the *Courant,* and thus denounced it to the world through the columns of the *Gazette:*

Advice to the Publick from Dr. Increase Mather.

Whereas a wicked Libel called the *New England Courant,* has represented me as one among the Supporters of it; I do hereby declare, that altho' I had paid for two or three of them, I then, (before the last Courant was published) sent him word I was *extreamly offended* with it! In special, because in one of his *Vile Courants* he insinuates, that if *the Ministers of God approve of a thing, it is a Sign it is of the Devil;* which is a horrid thing to be related! And altho' in one of the *Courants* it is declared, that the London Mercury Sept. 16, 1721, affirms that Great Numbers of Persons in the City and Suburbs are under the Inoculation of the Small Pox; In his next Courant he asserts, that it was some *Busy Inoculator, that imposed on the Publick in saying so;* Whereas I myself saw and read those words in the London Mercury: And he doth frequently abuse the Ministers of Religion, and many other worthy Persons in a manner, which is intolerable. For these and such like Reasons I signified to the Printer, that I would have no more of their *Wicked Courants.* I that have known what New-England was from the Beginning, cannot but be troubled to see the Degeneracy of this Place. I can well remember when the Civil Government would have taken an effectual Course to suppress such a *Cursed Libel!* which if it be not done I am afraid that some *Awful Judgment* will come upon this Land, and the *Wrath of God will arise, and there will be no Remedy.*

I cannot but pity poor *Franklin,* who tho' but a *Young Man* it may be *Speedily* he must appear before the Judgment Seat of God, and what answer will he give for printing things so vile and abominable? And I cannot but Advise the Supporters of this Courant to consider the Consequences of being *Partakers in other Mens Sins,* and no more Countenance such a Wicked *Paper.*

The war of words went on for some time, until Franklin became still more involved with the authorities. The reply of the *Courant* to the charge that it was carried on by a Hell-Fire Club will give the public some idea of the style of the original articles published by the *Courant.* On the 22d of January, 1722, it said:

* * * * * * * *

These, with many other endeavors, proceeding from an arbitrary and selfish temper, have been attended with their hearty curses on the Courant and its publisher; but all to no purpose; for, as a Connecticut trader once said of his onions, *The more they are cursed, the more they grow.* Notwithstanding which, a young scribbling collegian, [Mather Byles] who has just learning enough to make a fool of himself, has taken it in his head *to put a stop to this wickedness,* (as he calls it) by a letter in the last week's Gazette. Poor Boy! When your letter comes to be *seen in other countries,* (under the umbrage of authority) *what indeed will they think of* New-England! They will certainly conclude, *There is bloody fishing* for nonsense at Cambridge, and *sad work at the* College. The young wretch, when he calls those who wrote the several pieces in the Courant the Hell-Fire Club of Boston, and finds a godfather for them, (which, by the way, is a Hellish mockery of the ordinance of baptism, as administered by the Church of England,) and tells us, *That all the supporters of the paper will be looked upon as destroyers of the religion of the country, and enemies to the faithful ministers of it,* little thinks what a cruel reflection he throws on his reverend grandfather, who was then and for some time before, a subscriber for the paper.

* * * * * * * *

It is a pleasure to me, that I never inserted any thing in the Courant, which charged any man, or society of men, with being guilty of the crimes, which were peculiar to the Hell-Fire Club in London, and which the devils themselves are not capable of perpetrating. And whether Mr. M———e [Mr. Musgrave, Postmaster and Publisher of the *Gazette*] or his young champion know it or no 'tis looked upon as a gross reflection on the government) that they should be told of a Hell-Fire Club in Boston (in a paper *published by authority*) and not use their endeavors to discover who they are, in order to punish them.

On the 14th of January, 1722, the *Courant* was especially emphatic in regard to religion and the clergy, and respecting the sudden departure of Governor Shute for England. In regard to the latter, it asked,

Whether (pursuant to the Charter) the ministers of this province ought now to pray for Samuel Shute Esq as our immediate Governor, and, at the same time, pray for the Lieutenant-Governor as commander-in-chief? Or, Whether their praying for his *success* in his voyage, if he designs to hurt the province (as some suppose) be not in effect to pray for destruction?

On that day the General Court took the matter in hand, and appointed a committee to consider what should be done with Franklin. Here is their report:

> The Committee appointed to consider of the paper called, The New-England Courant, published Monday the fourteenth current, are *humbly of opinion* that the tendency of the said paper is to mock religion, and bring it into contempt, that the Holy Scriptures are therein profanely abused, that the revered and faithful ministers of the gospel are injuriously reflected on, His Majesty's Government affronted, and the peace and good order of His Majesty's subjects of this Province disturbed, by the said Courant ; and for precaution of the like offence for the future, the Committee *humbly propose*, That James Franklin, the printer and publisher thereof, be strictly forbidden by this Court to print or publish the New-England Courant, or any other pamphlet or paper of the like nature, except it be first supervised by the Secretary of this Province ; and the Justices of His Majesty's Sessions of the Peace for the County of Suffolk, at their next adjournment, be directed to take sufficient bonds of the said Franklin, for Twelve Months time.

The next number of the *Courant*, by innuendo, was more severe than ever on the officials, and Franklin had refused to submit the manuscript to the Secretary of the Province previous to publication. This created more difficulty and another short imprisonment. It was then decided that "James Franklin no longer print the newspaper." On the 11th of February, 1722, Benjamin Franklin, "in his teens," became a journalist. On that day the *Courant* appeared with the following salutatory:

> The late publisher of this paper, finding so many inconveniences would arise by his carrying the manuscripts and public news to be supervised by the Secretary, as to render his carrying it on unprofitable, has entirely dropt the undertaking. The present publisher having received the following piece, desires the readers to accept of it as a preface to what they may hereafter meet with in this paper.
>
> > Non ego mordaci distrinxi Carmine quemquam,
> > Nulla venenato Litera mista joco est.
>
> Long has the Press groaned in bringing forth an hateful brood of party pamphlets, malicious scribblers, and billingsgate ribaldry. The rancor and bitterness it has unhappily infused into men's minds, and to what a degree it has soured and leavened the tempers of persons formerly esteemed some of the most sweet and affable, is too well known here to need any further proof or representation of the matter.
>
> No generous and impartial person, then, can blame the present undertaking, which is designed purely for the diversion and merriment of the reader. Pieces of pleasancy and mirth have a secret charm in them to allay the heats and tumors of our spirits and to make a man forget his restless resentments. They have a strange power in them to hush disorders of the soul, and reduce us to a serene and placid state of mind.
>
> The main design of this weekly paper will be to entertain the town with the most comical and diverting incidents of human life, which, in so large a place as Boston, will not fail of a universal exemplification : Nor shall we be wanting to fill up these papers with a grateful interspersion of more serious morals, which may be drawn from the most ludicrous and odd parts of life.
>
> As for the author, that is the next question. But though we profess ourselves ready to oblige the ingenious and courteous reader with most sorts of intelligence, yet here we beg a reserve. Nor will it be of any advantage either to them or to the writers, that their names should be published ; and therefore in this matter we desire the favor of you to suffer us to hold our tongues : which though at this

time of day it may sound like a very uncommon request, yet it proceeds from the very hearts of your humble servants.

By this time the reader perceives that more than one are engaged in the present undertaking. Yet there is one person, an inhabitant of this town of Boston, whom we honor as a doctor in the chair, or a perpetual dictator.

The society had designed to present the public with his effigies, but that the Limner, to whom he was presented for a draught of his countenance, descried (and this he is ready to offer upon oath) nineteen features in his face, more than he ever beheld in any human visage before; which so raised the price of his picture, that our master himself forbid the extravagance of coming up to it. And then, besides, the Limner objected a schism in his face, which split it from his forehead in a straight line down to his chin, in such sort, that Mr. Painter protests it is a double face, and he'll have four pounds for the portraiture. However, though his double face has spoilt us of a pretty picture, yet we all rejoiced to see Old James in our company. There is no man in Boston better qualified than Old Janus for a *Couranteer*, or, if you please, an *Observator*, being a man of such remarkable *optics* as to look two ways at once.

As for his morals, he is a cheerly Christian, as the country phrase expresses it. A man of good temper, courteous deportment, sound judgement, a mortal hater of nonsense, foppery, formality, and endless ceremony. As for his Club, they aim at no greater happiness or honor, than the public be made to know, that it is the utmost of their ambition to attend upon and do all imaginable good offices to good Old Janus the Couranteer, who is and always will be the reader's humble servant.

P. S. Gentle Reader, we design never to let a paper pass without a Latin motto if we can possibly pick one up, which carries a charm in it to the vulgar, and the learned admire the pleasure of construing. We should have obliged the world with a Greek scrap or two, but the printer has no types, and therefore we entreat the candid reader not to impute the defect to our ignorance, for our doctor can say all the Greek letters by heart.

There was no change in the tone or the policy of the paper as marked out by James Franklin. Other troubles came upon the *Courant* and its proprietor, but they ultimately became the seed of a Free Press.

In June, 1722, a pirate appeared off Block Island. In a letter from Newport, speaking of the energetic action there in sending out vessels to catch the marauder, the *Courant* charged the Massachusetts authorities with tardiness. On the 12th, the Council took the matter up and ordered James Franklin before them. He "owned that he had published said paper." The Council then "resolved that the said paragraph is a high affront to this government," and that Franklin be imprisoned in the jail in Boston. After a week's confinement the state of his health constrained him to seek some mitigation, and the records of the General Court contain the following entry:

In Council, 20th June, 1722, a petition of James Franklyn, printer, humbly shewing, that he is truly sensible and heartily sorry for the offence he has given to this court in the late Courant, relating to the fitting out of a ship by the government, and truly acknowledges his inadvertency and folly therein in affronting the government, as also his indiscretion and indecency when before the court, for all which he intreats the court's forgiveness, and praying a discharge from the stone prison where he is confined by order of the court, and that he may have the liberty of the yard, he being much indisposed and suffering in his health by the said confinement; a certificate of Dr. Zabdiel Boylston being offered with the said petition.

In the House of Representatives, read, and
Voted, that James Franklyn, now a prisoner in the stone gaol, may have the liberty of the prison house and yard, upon his giving security for his faithful abiding there.
In Council, read and concurred; consented to.
SAMUEL SHUTE.

The warfare with the clergy was also taken notice of in Council, and efforts made to crush the paper and editor in the interest of religion, but it appears by the following that this failed :

In Council July 5th, 1722.

Whereas in the Paper called the *New-England Courant* printed Weekly by James Franklin, many passages have been published boldly reflecting on His Majesty's Government and on the Administration of it in this Province, the Ministry, Churches and College ; and it very often contains Paragraphs that tend to fill the Readers' minds with vanity to the Dishonor of God, and disservice of Good Men.

Resolved, that no such Weekly Paper be hereafter Printed or Published without the same be first perused and allowed by the Secretary, as has been usual. And that the said Franklin give Security before the Justices of the Superior Court in the Sum of 100*l*. to be of the good Behaviour to the End of the next Fall Sessions of this Court. Sent down for Concurrence.

Read and Non-concurred.

These Orders in Council sufficiently indicate the relative attitude of the press and the government a little over a century ago. There was not a very large opportunity for expansion. These movements and prosecutions were of considerable importance to journalism, especially in connection with the *New England Courant*, and, a few years later, with the *New York Weekly Journal*, which was of the same stamp and character as the *Courant*. Neither of the Franklins sacrificed their independence on the altar of power. They could not go very far publicly, but they accomplished a good deal for the time. Benjamin Franklin was only sixteen years of age at this period of his career, and even then he seemed to combine, *in petto*, all the elements of a modern newspaper establishment—brains, steam, courage, and electricity.

CHAPTER III.
THE FIRST PAPER IN NEW YORK.

THE NEW YORK GAZETTE.—ITS COMMENCEMENT BY WILLIAM BRADFORD.—PREMIUMS FOR SUBSCRIBERS.—ANOTHER NEWSPAPER IN BOSTON.—THE NEW ENGLAND WEEKLY JOURNAL.—THE DIFFICULTIES IN CIRCULATING NEWSPAPERS.—THE WANT OF MAIL FACILITIES.

ALTHOUGH Governor Fletcher, in having a copy of the *London Gazette* reprinted in New York in 1696, must have infused a little journalistic spirit in that city, the first newspaper there did not make its appearance till 1725.

William Bradford, a printer in Philadelphia, in consequence of litigations with the authorities there, growing out of his polemical publications, or a difference or two perhaps with the Society of Friends, was induced by Governor Fletcher to leave that city in 1690, and open a printing-office in New York. He there became the official printer, and after publishing Almanacs, the laws, the English Prayer-book, and official proclamations, and erecting the first paper-mill, he issued in October, 1725, the *New York Gazette*, which was, like the other papers then in existence, published weekly. The contents of the first number embraced the news from October 16 to October 23. Bradford believed that a man was never too old to work, for he was seventy years of age when he started the *Gazette*. The paper, for some time, was under the influence and control of William Cosby, the governor of that province.

William Bradford was the fourth printer in America, having been preceded by Stephen Daye, our Caxton, at Cambridge, Massachusetts, in 1638, Samuel Green in the same town in 1640, and by John Foster in Boston in 1675. Bradford established a printing-press in Philadelphia in 1687, and published a sheet Almanac in that year, and made preparations to print the first Bible in the English language in America somewhere about 1688. The inducements held forth in his proposals for printing the Holy Scriptures, one would imagine, have been the basis for most of the modern appeals to the public for the support of newspapers, magazines, and books. Our Pennsylvania Caxton thus announced:

Propoſals for the Printing of a large BIBLE, by *William Bradford.*

T Heſe are to give Notice, that it is propoſed for a large houſe-Bible to be Printed by way of Subſcriptions [a method usual in *England* for the printing of large Volumns, becaufe Printing is very chargeable] therefore to all that are willing to forward fo good (and great) a Work, as the Printing of the holy Bible, are offered thefe Propofals, *viz.*

1. That it fhall be printed in a fair Character, on good Paper, and well bound.
2. That it fhall contain the Old and New Teftament, with the Apocraphy, and all to have ufeful Marginal Notes.
3. That it fhall be allowed (to them that fubfcribe) for Twenty Shillings *per Bible* : [A Price which one of the fame volumn in *England* would coft.]
4. That the pay fhall be half Silver Money, and half Country Produce at Money price. One half down now, and the other half on the delivery of the Bibles.
5. That thofe who do fubfcribe for fix, fhall have the Seventh gratis, and have them delivered one month before any above that number fhall be fold to others.
6. To thofe which do not fubfcribe, the faid Bibles will not be allowed under 26 *s.* a piece.
7. Thofe who are minded to have the Common-Prayer, fhall have the whole bound up for 22 *s.* and thofe that do not fubfcribe 28 *s.* and 6 d. *per* Book.
8. That as encouragement is given by Peoples fubfcribing and paying down one half, the faid Work will be put forward with what Expedition may be.
9. That the Subfcribers may enter their Subfcriptions and time of Payment, at *Pheneas Pemberton*'s and *Robert Halls* in the County of *Bucks.* At *Malen Stacy*'s Mill at the Falls. At *Thomas Budds* House in *Burlington.* At *John Hafting's* in the County of *Chefter.* At *Edward Blake's* in *New - Caftle.* At *Thomas VVoodrooffs* in *Salem.* And at *William Bradford's* in *Philadelphia*, Printer & Undertaker of the faid Work. At which places the Subfcribers fhall have a Receipt for fo much of their Subfcriptions as paid, and an obligation for the delivery of the number of Bibles (fo Printed and Bound as aforefaid) as the refpective Subfcribers fhall depofit one half for.

Alfo this may further give notice, that *Samuell Richardfon* and *Samuell Carpenter* of *Philadelphia*, are appointed to take care and be affiftant in the laying out of the Subfcription Money, and to fee that it be imploy'd to the ufe intended, and confequently that the whole Work be expedited. Which is promifed by
William Bradford.

Philadelphia, the 14th of
the 1ft Month, 1688.

There has been some improvement, in the shape of premiums, on this prospectus of 1688, but William Bradford is entitled to the credit of introducing this system of newspaper and book subscriptions. Some of our modern periodicals, religious as well as secular, run far ahead of Bradford in inducements to subscribe for their publications, but there were no sewing-machines, melodeons, or life-insurance companies in the amiable Bradford's time. The *New York Express* of December 12, 1868, for instance, contained the following immensely comprehensive advertisement :

THE CHURCH UNION.

THIS PAPER HAS BEEN RECENTLY ENLARGED TO MAMmoth proportions. IT IS THE LARGEST RELIGIOUS PAPER IN THE WORLD. Is the leading organ of the Union Movement, and opposes ritualism, close communion, exclusiveness and church caste. It is the only paper that publishes HENRY WARD BEECHER'S Sermons, which it does every week, just as delivered,— without qualification or correction by him. It advocates universal suffrage ; a union of Christians at the polls ; and the rights of labor. It has the best Agricultural Department of any paper in the world ; publishes stories for the family, and for the destruction of social evils. Its editorial management is impersonal ; its writers and editors are from every branch of the Church and from every grade of society. It has been aptly termed the freest organ of thought in the world.

Such a paper, offering premiums of Sewing Machines, Dictionaries, Appleton's

Cyclopedia, Pianos, Organs for Churches, etc., makes one of the best papers for canvassers in the world.

Every Congregation may obtain a Communion Service, an Organ, a Melodeon, a Bible, or a Life Insurance Policy for its Pastor, or almost any other needful thing, by a club of subscribers.

This system of drumming for patrons has become so wide-spread that scarcely a paper is started that does not offer some premium more attractive than the preceding one. Some one published a parody on all these advertisements which covers the whole ground. It is given as a

MODEL FOR "PREMIUMS TO SUBSCRIBERS."

Subscribers for one copy of the —— will be presented with a box of Patent Petroleum Paste Blacking. This is a superior article. It blacks boots or stoves, and may be used as a hair dye.

Subscribers for two copies will receive a box of sardines.

Subscribers for five copies will be presented with a pair of iron-clad spectacles, with glass eyes, warranted to suit one age as well as another.

Subscribers for ten copies will be entitled to a patent adjustable bootjack, which can also be used as a corkscrew, a coffee-mill, or inkstand.

Subscribers for twenty-five copies will receive a marble bureau with a mahogany top.

Subscribers for fifty copies will receive a seven-octave sewing-machine with the Agraff attachment.

Subscribers for seventy-five copies will receive a basswood parlor suit of furniture.

Subscribers for one hundred copies will receive a burial plot, with an order for tombstones delivered when required.

Subscribers for five hundred copies will receive a nomination for Congress.

Subscribers for a thousand copies will be presented with a farm in New Jersey, fenced and mortgaged.

The French are as peculiar and as characteristic in their premiums. The *Gaulois* offered two bottles of Champagne for every new subscriber for six months. Four bottles of the Widow Cliquot for sending the *Gaulois* for one year! Sparkling inducement! The *Figaro*, not to be outdone, offered a small pocket revolver at half price for every new subscriber. Thus every reader of that paper would have a six-shooter at half cock for reading its brilliant articles for twelve months.

But this is anticipating. William Bradford emigrated from England to Pennsylvania before Philadelphia was laid out. For half a century he was printer to the colonial government. Notwithstanding his controversy with the *Weekly Journal*, Bradford was a champion of the freedom of the press. Members of his family, for four generations, distinguished themselves in various ways. The senior Bradford died in New York in 1752, at the age of 92, and was buried in Trinity Church-yard under the following epitaph:

Here lies the Body of Mr. William Bradford—Printer who departed this Life May 23 1752 aged 92 Years He was born in Leicester Shire in Old England in 1660 and came over to America in 1680 before Philadelphia was laid out. He was Printer to the Government for upward of 50 years and being quite worn out with Old age and labor he left this mortal state in the lively hopes of a blessed Immortality.

> Reader reflect how soon you'll quit this stage
> You'll find but few atain to such an Age
> Life's full of Pain Lo here's a Place of Rest
> Prepare to meet your GOD then you are blest

The New York Historical Society and Trinity Church, with the municipal authorities of the metropolis, united, in May, 1863, on the two hundredth anniversary of the birth of William Bradford, to do honor to his name and services as the first printer and first editor of New York; and a commemorative address was delivered on that occasion by John William Wallace, the President of the Historical Society of Pennsylvania. The latter society, at its annual meeting in February, 1869, paid similar honors—not on his natal day, however—to Andrew Bradford, as the founder of the Newspaper Press of the Middle States of America, Horatio Gates Jones delivering an excellent and appropriate address. We are not aware that the Massachusetts Historical Society has taken any notice of either Benjamin Harris or John Campbell, the first editors of New England.

Newspapers began to increase in the colonies. In 1727, on the 20th of March, the fourth paper appeared in Boston, named the *New England Weekly Journal*, "Containing the most Remarkable Occurrences Foreign and Domestick." It was published by Samuel Kneeland, who succeeded James Franklin as printer of the *Gazette*. The famous Whitefield, and the equally celebrated Edwards, exercised great influence over this establishment. Kneeland, in his prospectus, promised a number of new features in journalism; proposed the organization of a corps of correspondents of "the most knowing and ingenious gentlemen in several noted towns" to send news; made arrangements for the regular weekly publication of "the Number of Persons Buried and Baptized in the town of Boston;" the prospectus closing thus:

☞ This may serve as a Notification, that a Select number of Gentlemen, who have had the happiness of a liberal Education, and some of them considerably improv'd by their Travels into distant Countries; are now concerting some regular Schemes for the Entertainment of the ingenious Reader, and the Encouragement of Wit and Politeness; and may in a very short time, open upon the Public in a variety of pleasing and profitable Speculations.

On the 8th of April, 1728, the publisher held out the following inducements for subscribers:

☞ *There are Meaſures concerting for rendring this Paper yet more univerſally eſteemed, and uſeful, in which 'tis hop'd the Publick will be gratifi'd, and by which thoſe Gentlemen who deſire to be improv'd in Hiſtory, Philoſophy, Poetry, &c. will be greatly advantaged. We will take the liberty at this time to inſert the following paſſage of Hiſtory.*

Then followed a very curious and quaint account of the invention of the stocking-loom.

Quite a number of essays were published by Kneeland, after the style of the *Tattler, Spectator,* and *Freeholder.* Indeed, the style of the newspaper writers of those days imitated that of Addison, Steele, Swift, and Bolingbroke. Mather Byles, Judge Danforth, Governor Burnet, and the Rev. Thomas Prince, of the Old South Church, were contributors to the *Journal.* It was, in 1741, united with the *Gazette,* and published till 1752, when it was discontinued.

It seems to have been one of the objects of John Campbell, if we rely upon his appeals to the public, in publishing the *News-Letter,* "to prevent the spreading of false reports." Other publishers, no doubt, were governed by the same laudable motive. But this was evidently slow work. Circulating the paper outside of the city limits was then any thing but a speedy or certain process. Mails were mostly monthly and half monthly in going from point to point. Bulk was a matter of importance in the time of post-horses, and stage-coaches, and imperfect roads. Those who live along the banks of the Hudson, or on the line of any railroad running out of Boston, or New York, or Chicago, within one hundred miles of these news centres, and receiving at their own doors their morning city journals as regularly and as early as subscribers living in the upper wards of these cities receive their papers, scarcely realize the advantages they enjoy over their ancestors. Some idea of this may be obtained from the following official notice:

By Order of the Post Master General of North-America.

These are to give Notice, that on Monday Night the Sixth of this Instant December, *The Western Post between* Boston *and* New-York *sets out once a Fortnight the Three Winter Months of* December, January *and* February, *and to go Alternately from* Boston *to* Saybrook *and* Hartford, *to Exchange the Mayle of Letters with the* New-York *Ryder, the first Turn for* Say-Brook, *to meet the* New-York *Ryder on Saturday Night the* 11th *Currant.* And the *Second Turn he sets out at* Boston, *on Monday Night the* 20th *Currant to meet the* New-York *Ryder at* Hartford *on Saturday Night the* 25th *Currant, to Exchange Mayles.*

And all Persons that sends Letters from Boston *to* Connecticut, *from and after the* 13th *Instant, are hereby Notified, first to pay the Portage on the same.*

What a contrast with the numerous railroad trains, with their splendid family cars, and three or four steam-boats, floating palaces in fact, running daily, morning and evening, between New York and Boston, in addition to the fifteen or twenty telegraph wires which now connect these two important cities! All the wonders of Aladdin pale before these realities. There could be no extended circulation of newspapers with such facilities of transportation as Campbell and the Bradfords had. But as the colonies grew in population and wealth, there was an improvement in the mails and in the roads, and an increased desire for more news, and other journals came into existence.

CHAPTER IV.

THE REAPPEARANCE OF THE FRANKLINS.

The Way Benjamin Franklin started a Paper in Philadelphia.—The Fleets in Boston.—The Fashions.—Zenger's New York Journal.—The first Libel Suit.—Andrew Hamilton's great Speech.—The popular Verdict.—The Dawn of Liberty.—The New York Gazette again.—The Post-Boy.—James Franklin in Newport.—The Rhode Island Gazette.—Newport then and now.

BENJAMIN FRANKLIN now reappeared as a journalist. In 1728 another paper was established in Philadelphia—the second in that city. It was entitled the *Universal Instructor in all the Arts and Sciences and Pennsylvania Gazette*, a title sufficiently long to satisfy any newspaper subscriber. It was published by Samuel Keimer. There is a story connected with this paper which had better be told in the words of one of the parties most interested. Speaking of his job printing-office, which he had just started, Benjamin Franklin, in his autobiography, gives these facts:

George Webb, who had found a female friend that lent him wherewithal to purchase his time of Keimer, now came to offer himself as a journeyman to us. We could not then employ him; but I foolishly let him know as a secret, that I soon intended to begin a newspaper, and might then have work for him. My hopes of success, as I told him, were founded on this; that the then only newspaper, printed by Bradford, was a paltry thing, wretchedly managed, no way entertaining, and yet was profitable to him; I therefore freely thought a good paper would scarcely fail of good encouragement. I requested Webb not to mention it; but he told it to Keimer, who immediately, to be beforehand with me, published proposals for one himself, on which Webb was to be employed. I was vexed at this; and, to counteract them, not being able to commence our paper, I wrote several amusing pieces for Bradford's paper, under the title of Busy Body, which Breintnal continued some months. By this means the attention of the public was fixed on that paper, and Keimer's proposals which we burlesqued and ridiculed, were disregarded. He began his paper, however; and, before carrying it on three quarters of a year, with at most only ninety subscribers, he offered it to me for a trifle; and I, having been ready some time to go on with it, took it in hand directly; and it proved in a few days extremely profitable to me. * * * * * * Our first papers made quite a different appearance from any before in the province; a better type, and better printed; but some remarks of my writing, on the dispute then going on between Governor Burnet, and the Massachusetts Assembly, struck the principal people, occasioned the paper and the manager of it to be much talked of, and in a few weeks brought them all to be our subscribers.

Their example was followed by many, and our number went on growing continually. This was one of the first good effects of my having learned a little to scribble; another was, that the leading men, seeing a newspaper now in the hands of those who could handle a pen, thought it convenient to oblige and encourage me. Bradford still printed the votes, and laws, and other public business. He had printed an address of the House to the Governor, in a coarse, blundering manner; we reprinted it elegantly and correctly, and sent one to every member. They were sensible of the difference, it strengthened the hands of our friends in the House, and they voted us their printers for the year ensuing.

Among my friends in the House, I must not forget Mr. Hamilton, before mentioned, who was then returned from England, and had a seat in it. He interested himself for me strongly in that instance, as he did in many others afterwards, continuing his patronage till his death.

This was Franklin's first really independent attempt at the management of a newspaper on his own responsibility; and it is evident, from his opinion of the *Mercury*, "a paltry thing," as he called it, that he felt equal to the enterprise. One of his first acts was to condense the title of his paper to that of the *Pennsylvania Gazette*, which he did on the 28th of September, 1729, and under that name it continued under his management till 1765. In spite of what he says in his autobiography, it has been asserted that Franklin wrote but little for the *Gazette*. He dabbled in politics and electricity, and set up printing-offices in other places, so that his time was pretty well occupied. Many of the articles published in the *Gazette* and attributed to Franklin were, in the opinion of Sparks, manifestly written by others. On one occasion, in 1734, Bradford, of the *Mercury*, rebuked the publication in the *Gazette* of some vulgar communications. Franklin stated that he inserted them because "by being too nice in the choice of little pieces sent him by correspondents, he had almost discouraged them from writing to him any more."

The Franklins appreciated, above all others, what a newspaper should be. "My friends," said Benjamin Franklin to a number of gentlemen who had constituted themselves his censors, "any one who can subsist upon sawdust pudding and water, as I can, needs no man's patronage." This was his code.

In 1748, David Hall, a Scotchman, became Franklin's partner. Hall carried on the establishment till his death in 1772. After Hall the concern passed into the hands of Andrew Brown, an Irishman, and was called the *Philadelphia Gazette*. The establishment was destroyed by fire when Mr. Brown owned it, and nearly his whole family perished in the flames. It was afterward continued by a son of Mr. Brown, who came out from Ireland for that purpose, in connection with Samuel Relf. This was in 1802. It ceased to exist for a time in 1804, but was re-established with the same title, and was, for some time, the oldest paper in the United States. Mr. Relf then purchased his partner's interest and conducted the paper alone. He was considered an able writer in his early journalistic days. The paper, under his management, was called *Relf's Gazette*. In 1824 or '25 Mr. Relf died. Stevenson Smith then became the publisher and editor, and the *Gazette* was the advocate of the political principles of the Jackson democracy. After this period the establishment was sold to Willis Gaylord Clark and James Russell. Mr. Clark had married a niece of Samuel Relf, and the Relf family were again, though indirectly, interested in the paper. It had now become the champion of Whig principles. It was an evening paper. Willis Gaylord Clark, the editor, was twin brother of Lewis Gaylord Clark, the wit, and for many years the genial editor of the *Knickerbocker Magazine* of New York. Willis was proprietor of the *Gazette* to the time of his death in 1841. On the 3d of November, 1845, it was merged with the *North American*. It had been, for some time, a branch, a sort of an evening edition to that journal. Thus closed the career of Franklin's *Gazette*, after an existence of one hundred and seventeen years.

The old paper-mill in which the paper used by Franklin was made was still in existence a few years ago. It was erected on Chester Creek, Delaware County, in 1713. The paper was made then by hand, as it was as late as 1853. There had been no change in one hundred and forty years in that little old mill, notwithstanding the great improvements and changes in paper-making since that period.

Newspapers enjoyed one or two privileges in the days of Franklin that would be seriously damaging to the revenue of the Post-office Department if tolerated now. In the *Gazette* of the 28th of January, 1735, Franklin said:

By the indulgence of the Honorable Colonel Spotswood, Post-Master-General, the printer hereof is allowed to send the *Gazettes* by the post, *postage free*, to all parts of the postroad, from Virginia to New England.

The five or six thousand newspapers of 1872, with their millions of circulation, with a privilege like the above, would utterly ruin the Post-office Department of to-day. Only a small part of the newspapers go through the mails now. They are sent as freight and by newsboys over the numerous railroads, and delivered at the different news centres by express lines and news agents here, there, and every where.

Maryland next fell into line with the old name on its title-page. The *Maryland Gazette* was the first paper published in that state. William Parks, one of the migratory printers of that century, issued the first number in Annapolis in 1727, and the paper was regularly published till 1736, when Parks went to Virginia to establish a newspaper there.

Another paper appeared in Boston on the 27th of September, 1731. It was styled the *Weekly Rehearsal*, and started by Jeremy Gridley, "a young man of fine literary accomplishments," who became Attorney General of the Province, Member of the General Court, Colonel of Militia, President of the Marine Society, and

Grand Master of Freemasons. He died in 1767. The *Rehearsal* was printed by "J. Draper, for the Author," as editors were frequently called in those primitive days. It was filled with Addisonian essays, and exhibited large pretensions to literary taste and culture. In one article on the prevailing fashions in dress in 1732, it spoke of the crinolines of that period, which seemed to swell beyond the proportions of those of a hundred and thirty-five years later. The writer said:

> I shall not busy myself with the ladies' shoes and stockings at all; but I can't so easily pass over the *Hoop*, when 'tis in my way, and therefore I must beg pardon of my fair readers, if I begin my attack here. 'Tis now some years since this remarkable fashion made a figure in the world, and from its first beginning divided the public opinion as to its convenience and beauty. For my part, I was always willing to indulge it, under some restrictions: that is to say, if 'tis not a rival to the dome of St. Paul's, to incumber the way, or a tub for the residence of a new Diogenes: if it does not eclipse too much beauty above, or discover too much below. In short, I am for living in peace, and I am afraid a fine lady, with too much liberty in this particular, would render my own imagination an enemy to my repose.

The *Rehearsal*, after two years of literary effort, became a record of passing events, and was owned and managed by Thomas Fleet. On the 21st of August, 1735, the name was changed to that of the *Boston Evening Post*. Fleet was the original publisher of the famous nursery rhymes of Mother Goose. The *Post* was conducted with energy, and became popular. If, as in the case of Franklin and Bradford, the government was at all censured, by implication even, the editor was prosecuted. On the 8th of March, 1741, the following proceedings took place in the Athens of America:

> At a Council, held at the Council Chamber in Boston, upon Tuesday the 9th day of March, 1741.
> Whereas there is published in the weekly paper called the Boston Evening Post of yesterday's date, a paragraph in the following words:
> "Last Saturday Capt. Gibbs arrived here from Madeira, who informs us, that before he left that Island, Capt. Dandridge, in one of His Majesty's ships of forty guns, came in there from England, and gave an account, that the Parliament had called for all the Papers relating to the War, and 'twas expected the Right Hon. Sir Robert Walpole would be taken into custody in a very few days. Capt. Dandridge was going upon the Virginia station to relieve the valiant and vigilant Knight there, almost worn out in the service of his country, and for which he has a chance to be rewarded with a *Flag*."
> Which paragraph contains a scandalous and libelous Reflection upon his Majesty's Administration, and may tend very much to inflame the minds of his Majesty's subjects here and disaffect them to his Government;
> Therefore, *Ordered*, That the Attorney-General do, as soon as may be, file an Information against Thomas Fleet, the Publisher of the said Paper, in his Majesty's Superior Court of Judicature, Court of Assize and General Gaol Delivery, in order to his being prosecuted for his said offence, as Law and Justice requires.
> W. SHIRLEY.
> Copy Examin'd, per *J. Willard*, Sec.

This affair resulted in nothing because of the truth of the paragraph, but the animus dictating the proceedings was the same.

Fleet had his troubles with the clergy. He published John Wesley's sermon on Free Grace. For this he was denounced from the pulpit by the Rev. John Morehead, who not only thundered against the unfortunate Fleet, but against the printing-press also. It appears that the editor of the *Post* was fully equal to any of these assaults upon him or upon the liberty of the Press. In his replies Fleet was good-natured, and therefore the more severe and the more effective.

On the death of Thomas Fleet the *Evening Post* was carried on by his sons Thomas and John, and they continued to publish it till 1775. It was stopped then in consequence of the discontent growing out of the attempted neutrality of the paper in the great agitation leading to the Revolution. Then, as now, the press were accused of being corrupted and improperly influenced by money. On the 10th of March, 1775, the *Post* said:

> Whereas it hath been hinted in several letters lately received from England, that one or more printers of the public newspapers in the principal towns in America are hired, or rather bribed, (from a fund said to be established for that use) for the vile purpose of publishing pieces in their respective papers tending to favor despotism and the present arbitrary and tyrannical proceedings of the ministry relative to America; The publishers of the Boston *Evening Post* (whose papers have always been conducted with the utmost freedom and impartiality) do, for themselves, thus publicly declare, that no application has ever been made to them to prostitute their paper to such a base and mean purpose; and should they hereafter be applied to for that design, they shall despise the offer and those who make it, with the greatest contempt; not but that their paper shall, as usual, be open for the insertion of all pieces that shall tend to amuse or instruct, or to the promoting of useful knowledge and the general good of mankind, as they themselves (who are the sole directors and proprietors thereof) shall think prudent, profitable, or entertaining to their numerous readers.

The battles of Concord and Lexington were fought on the 19th of April, 1775. Without giving any of the particulars of that fight, the paper appeared on the 24th of April for the last time. These scenes of action were only two or three hours' drive from the printing-office of the *Post!* The British troops had returned to their barracks in Boston on the 20th of that month.

John Peter Zenger, with the *New York Weekly Journal*, next appeared before the public. The first number of that paper was issued on the 5th of November, 1733. It was established in opposition to Bradford's *Gazette* for a political purpose, and published by Zenger, who was a good printer, the importer of the first piano-forte in America, something of a scholar, and a famous editor in his day. He came from Germany when he was thirteen years of age, and was an apprentice of Bradford's. For three years the *Journal* was in a state of bitter war with the administration of Governor William Cosby, and his successor, Lieutenant Governor George Clarke. Zenger, as a politician, was in the interest of Rip Van Dam, a wealthy merchant of New York, and in virtue of his office as President of the Council, acting Governor of the Province till the arrival of Cosby. In settling Van Dam's accounts, one half of his salary as governor had to be paid to his successor. This led to the formation of an opposition colonial party. The *Gazette*, under the management of William Bradford, was the government organ.

After repeated animadversions on the authorities in the *Journal*, its editor was arrested on the charge of libel on Sunday, November 17, 1734. He was imprisoned by the government, and kept in confinement nearly nine months before he could obtain a trial. The arrest produced great excitement, and the affair obtained wide-spread notoriety. It was the first action for newspaper libel on this continent. It created the most intense interest in the public mind, and the result was, in the opinion of Gouverneur Morris, "the dawn of that liberty which afterwards revolutionized America." In this view, as well as in the interest of journalism, we devote some space to this important event.

On the 6th of November the governor issued two proclamations on the subject. Here is one of them:

By his Excellency William Cosby, *Capt. General and Governour in Chief of the Provinces* of New York, New Jersey, *and Territories thereon depending* in America, *Vice Admiral of the same, and Colonel in his Majesty's Army,* &c.

A PROCLAMATION.

WHEREAS by the Contrivance of some evil Disposed and Disafected Persons, divers Journals or Printed News-Papers (entitled *The New-York Weekly Journal, containing the freshest Advices, foreign and Domestick*) have been caused to be Printed and Published by *John Peter Zenger*, in many of which Journals or Printed News-Papers (but more particularly those numbered 7, 47, 48, 49) are contained divers Scandalous, Virulent, False and Seditious Reflections, not only upon the whole Legislature, in general, and upon the most considerable Persons in the most distinguish'd Stations in the Province, but also upon his Majesty's lawful and rightful Government, and just Prerogative. Which said Reflections seem contrived by the Wicked Authors of them, not only to create Jealousies, Discontents and Animosities in the Minds of his Majesty's Liege People of this Province to the Subversion of the Peace and Tranquility thereof but to alienate their Affection from the best of Kings, and raise *Factions, Tumults* and *Sedition* among them. Wherefore I have thought fit, by and with the Advice of his Majesty's Council, to issue this Proclamation, hereby Promising a Reward of *Fifty Pounds* to such Person or Persons who shall discover the Author or Authors of the said Scandalous, Virulent and Seditious Reflections contained in the said Journals or Printed News-Papers, to be paid to the said Person or Persons discovering the same as soon as such Author shall be convicted of having been the Author or Authors thereof.

Given under my Hand and Seal at Fort George, in New York, the sixth day of November, in the 8th year of his Majesty's Reign, Annoq Domini, 1734.

W. COSBY.

The other proclamation offered a reward of £20 for the discovery of "the Author of two late scandalous Songs or Ballads, Printed and dispersed in this City, &c., highly defaming the Administration of his Majesty's Government in this Province." The arrest of Zenger was the result of these official documents. The specific libel complained of was, in substance, that "the people of this city (New

The First Libel Suit.

York) and province think, as matters now stand, that their liberties and properties are precarious, and that slavery is like to be entailed on them and their posterity, if some past things be not amended."

On the 20th of November Zenger was brought, by a writ of habeas corpus, before the Chief Justice at his chamber, where the writ was returnable. The argument of that matter was ordered to be at the City Hall on the 23d. After a long debate on that day, the Chief Justice directed that Zenger should be admitted to bail, and bound by recognizance, with two securities, in the sum of $2000. He was remanded to prison in default thereof. It does not appear that Zenger at all wilted under this persecution, for on the 25th of November the *Journal* contained the following card to his readers:

To all my Subscribers and Benefactors who take my weekly Journall: Gentlemen, Ladies and Others:

As you last week were Disappointed of my Journall, I think it incumbent upon me, to publish my Apoligy which is this. On the Lords Day, the Seventeenth of this Instant, I was Arrested, taken and Imprisoned in the common Gaol of this City, by Virtue of a Warrant from the *Governour*, and the Honourable *Francis Harrison*, Esq; and others in Council of which (God willing) you'l have a Coppy, whereupon I was put under such Restraint that I had not the Liberty of Pen, Ink, or Paper, or to see, or speak with People, till upon my Complaint to the Honourable the Chief Justice, at my appearing before him upon my *Habeas Corpus* on the *Wednesday* following. Who discountenanced that Proceeding, and therefore I have had since that Time, the Liberty of Speaking through the Hole of the Door, to my Wife and Servants by which I doubt not you'l think me sufficiently Excused for not sending my last week's *Journall*, and I hope for the future by the Liberty of Speaking to my Servants thro' the Hole of the Door of the Prison, to entertain you with my weekly *Journall* as formerly

And am your obliged,
Humble Servant
J. PETER ZENGER.

The *Journal* continued to be published, and Zenger to write for it, in spite of his imprisonment. Indeed, the event made that paper the most popular of the two then printed in New York. Bradford, as publisher of the official organ, the *Gazette,* was compelled to print articles and communications reflecting on his rival in business; but Zenger manfully met his opponents, giving blow for blow, and a little more. Some idea of his style may be had in the annexed communication, which appeared in the *Journal* after he had been one month in jail:

From my Prison, December 20th, 1734.

Oh cruelty unknown before
To any barbarous savage shore,
Much more when Men so much profess
Humanity and Godliness

It is no new Thing for even a Man of Vertue to fall under Distress; but to mock him when distress'd or under Misfortunes, is what has been accounted a Vice among the more civilized Heathens; however it is my case at present, and my Adversaries are not content with my Imprisonment, but I am made their laughing Stock.

There is a great Noise made in that ridiculous Letter in Mr. *Bradford's* last *Gazette* about setting *the Province in Flames, raising of Sedition and Tumults, &c.*

I know of none, either past or intended; if my Adversaries know of any, they'l do well to discover them and prevent ill Consequences. I have printed some Complaints to the Public, those complain'd of had a Remedy to answer without coming to me; and had they come to me, they would have found the same Fidelity some of them experienc'd before; They may tax me with Weaknesses accident to human Nature; but it is out of their Power (and I hope ever will be) truly to prove me guilty of any premeditated Wickedness.

That Author begins the Confession he would have me make with a very puny Witticism on my Address to my Readers; by saying *It sounds like the Language of the Prize-fighter or Poppet Show Man.* I can assure him that many *Gentlemen and Ladies* read my *Journals;* there is also some *others* and among them some S——s, witness that Author. I might tell him that the Whole of his Performance sounds too much like the Language of a bankrupt Vinter or ——— &c.

That I was brought over at the charitable Expence of the Crown is the only Truth that groaping Fumbler found when he studied that clumsy Performance. I acknowledge it; Thanks to QUEEN ANNE whose Name I Mention with Reverence, her Bounty to me and my distress'd County Folks is to be gratefully remembered. If that Author has contributed any Thing towards it, I begg to be informed. I assure him that my Acknowledgement shall not be wanting, notwithstanding his ill Treatment: If he has not, I begg leave to tell him, that it is mean for him to twit me with Benefits that I am no ways beholden to him for.

That my Friends are pretendedly so, will (I hope) prove as false as my Enemies are malicious; whatever some of my Adversaries may be, I beleive my Friends to be Men of Honour and Probity. And if they even should forsake me, I would say of them as *Cicero* said in Answer to the Notion the *Epicureans* had of a God, *fi tales sint Amici, ut nulla gratia, nulla hominum, charitate teneantur valeant.* I'll trust to the Laws of the Realm and my country, and still retain my Integrity: FOR HONESTY IS THE BEST POLICY.

My Sword was never intended to protect me against a sworn Officer in the Discharge of his Duty: But since this Scribbler must needs make himself merry with it, I think it may not be amiss to tell my Readers a serious but true Story. About 8 Weeks agoe the Honourable *Francis Harrison*, came to my House, and swore by the God that made him he would lay his Cane over me the first Time he met me in the Street, with some scurrilous Expressions more fit to be uttered by a Dray Man than a Gentleman. Against such Assaults my Sword not only could but would have protected me, and shall while I have it, against any Man that has Impudence enough to attempt any thing of that Nature—*Veni vi repellore licet.*

What private Orders the Sheriff had concerning me are best known to himself. This I know that from the time of my being apprehended till the Return of the Precept by virtue of which I was taken, I was deny'd the Use of Pen, Ink, and Paper; Alterations were purposely Made on my Account, to put me in a Place by myself, where I was strictly confin'd above 50 Hours, that my Wife might not speak to me but in presence of the Sub-sheriff; to say this was done without Orders is Lybelling the Sheriff, and I hope he will resent it.

To conclude, I begg of this indifferent Gentleman (indifferent indeed but how impartial!) That if he needs will continue Author, to write Ballads for Children if he has the Knack of Versifying; if he has not, then let him write some Thing in Imitation of *Tom Thum, Jack,* the Giant Killer, or any Thing, the more nonsensical it is the better it will suit his Genius; let him bring his Lucubrations to me, and on the Word of an honest Man, I'll earn his Money as faithfully as any Printer in *America:* But let him leave Lampooning of me, a Task equally mean as wicked, for I think no honest Man can be guilty of deriding his Fellow mortal when he sees him struggling in the Waves of Adversities, Laughing is catching, what has hapned to me may befall him & perhaps with double weight. I am,

J. PETER ZENGER.

The *Gazettes* containing the libels and the ballads were ordered to be burnt by the common hangman. The mayor and magistrates of the city were directed to be present at this holocaust to the freedom of the Press. The corporation refused to attend. The Provincial Assembly also declined to join in this crusade against the Press. It was in consequence of this rebellion that the government party made up their minds to crush the editor under the weight of legal proceedings, and, to accomplish this more effectually, Zenger's counsel, on some quibble, and in the most arbitrary manner, was "thrown over the bar" by the judge, who had been named by Cosby alone, without the sanction of his council, on the plea of Zenger's counsel that he could not have an impartial trial before a court thus constituted. But the friends of the editor met this contingency. They quietly engaged Andrew Hamilton, the celebrated jurist of Philadelphia, the warm personal friend of Franklin, and the sturdy upholder of the rights of the Press and the people, to defend Zenger. The court met on the 4th of August, 1735. The chamber was crowded. The unexpected appearance of Hamilton by the side of Zenger increased the excitement in the case. The publication of the article was admitted. Mr. Hamilton offered to prove the truth of the statements embraced in the alleged libel, but this proposition was overruled by the court, which was unmistakably on the government side of the question. It was optional with judges in England to admit or refuse evidence in such cases, and they were sustained in this action by the government. Indeed, they were encouraged to do so. On the trial of Franklin in 1731, in London, for the publication of a libel in the *Craftman*, Lord Raymond refused, as the chief justice in the case of Zenger did, to admit any evidence to prove the matter to be true, and stated that he was only following precedents in cases of a similar character. But Pemberton permitted evidence to be given as to the truth of an alleged libel in protesting that Sir Edmondbury Godfrey had murdered himself; and Holt repeatedly offered to let Fuller, on a similar charge, prove the truth of what he said. Interest regulated these rulings. It was not for the interest of Governor Cosby that the truth of the alleged libels of Zenger should be proved. There being no evidence, therefore, in the case, Mr. Hamilton proceeded to sum up, and addressed the jury as follows:

Then, gentlemen of the jury, it is to you we must now appeal for witnesses to the truth of the facts we have offered, and are denied the liberty to prove; and let it not seem strange that I apply myself to you in this manner; I am warranted so to do, both by law and reason. The law supposes you to be summoned out of the neighborhood where the fact is alleged to be committed; and the reason of your being taken out of the neighborhood is because you are supposed to have the best knowledge of the fact that is to be tried; and were you to find a verdict against my client, you must take upon you to say that the papers referred to in the information, and which we acknowledge we printed and published, are false, scandalous and seditious; but of this I can have no apprehension. You are citizens of New York; you are really what the law supposes you to be, honest and lawful men; and the facts which we offer to prove were not committed in a corner. They are notoriously known to be true; and, therefore, in your justice lies our safety. And as we are denied the liberty of giving evidence to prove the truth of what we have published, I will beg leave to lay it down as a standing rule in such cases, that the suppressing of evidence ought always to be taken for the strongest evidence, and I hope it will have weight with you. But since we are not admitted to examine our witnesses, I will endeavor to shorten the dispute with Mr. Attorney, and to that end I desire he would favor us with some standard definition of a libel, by which it may be certainly known whether a writing be a libel, yea or not.

Attorney-General.—The books, I think, have given a very full definition of a libel. They say it is in a strict sense taken for a malicious defamation, expressed either in writing or printing, and tending either to blacken the memory of one who is dead or the reputation of one who is alive, and to expose him to public hatred, contempt or ridicule. But it is said that, in a larger sense, the notion of a libel may be applied to any defamation whatsoever, expressed either by signs or pictures; as by fixing up a gallows against a man's door, or by painting him in a shameful and ignominious manner; and since the chief cause for which the law so severely punishes all offences of this nature is the direct tendency of them to a breach of the public peace, by provoking the parties injured, their friends and families to acts of revenge, which it would be impossible to restrain by the severest laws, were there no redress from public justice for injuries of this kind, which of all others are most seriously felt; and since the plain meaning of such scandal, as is expressed by signs or pictures, is as obvious to common sense and as easily understood by every common capacity, and altogether as provoking as that which is expressed by writing or printing, why should it not be equally criminal? From the same ground it also appears to follow that such scandal as is expressed in a scoffing and ironical manner makes a writing as properly a libel as that which is expressed in direct terms; as where a writing in a taunting mannner, reckoning up several acts of public charity done by one, says: "You shall not play the Jew nor the hypocrite," and so goes on in a strain of ridicule to insinuate that what he did was owing to his vain glory; or where a writing, pretending to recommend to one the character of several great men for his imitation, instead of taking notice of what they are generally esteemed famous for, pitched on such qualities only which their enemies charge them with the want of, as by proposing such a one to be imitated for his courage who is known to be a great statesman, but no soldier; and another to be imitated for his learning who is known to be a great general but no scholar &c, which kind of writing is as well understood to mean only to upbraid the parties with the want of these qualities, as if it had directly and expressly said so.

Hamilton.—Ay, Mr. Attorney, but what certain standard rule have the books laid down by which we can certainly know whether the words or the signs are malicious? Whether they are defamatory? Whether they tend to a breach of the peace, and are a sufficient ground to provoke a man, his family or friends to acts of revenge, especially those of the ironical sort of words? And what rule have you to know when I write ironically? I think it would be hard when I say such a man is a very worthy, honest gentleman, and of fine understanding, that therefore I meant he was a knave or a fool.

After a brief discussion on the question whether the jury or the judges were to find the libelous character of the publication, the court intimated that "the jury could find that Zenger printed and published those papers, and leave it to the court to judge whether they were libelous," Mr. Hamilton continued:

I.know, may it please your Honor, the jury may do so; but I likewise know they may do otherwise. I know they have the right, beyond all dispute, to determine both the law and the fact, and where they do not doubt the law they ought to do so. This manner of leaving it to the judgement of the Court whether the words are libellous or not, in effect renders juries useless, to say no worse, in many cases; but this I shall have occasion to speak to by-and-by; and I will, with the Court's leave, proceed to examine the inconveniences that must inevitably arise from the doctrines Mr. Attorney has laid down; and I observe in support of this prosecution, he has frequently repeated the words taken from the case *de libellis famosis*, in the fifth of Coke. This is indeed the leading case to which almost all the cases upon the subject of libels refer; and I must insist upon saying that, according as this case seems to be understood by the Court and Mr. Attorney, it is not law at this day. For though I own it to be base and unworthy to scandalize any man, yet I think it is even villainous to scandalize a person of public character, and I will go so far into Mr. Attorney's doctrine as to agree, that if the faults, mistakes, nay, even the vices of such a person be private and personal, and do not affect the peace of the public, or the liberty or property of our neighbor, it is unmanly and unmannerly to expose them either by word or writing. But when a ruler of a people brings his personal feelings, but much more his vices into his administration, and the people find themselves affected by them either in their liberties or properties, that will alter the case mightily; and all the high things that are said in favor of rulers and of dignities, and upon the side of power, will not be able to stop people's mouths when they feel themselves oppressed—I mean in a free government. It is true, in times past it was a crime to speak truth, and in that terrible court of star chamber many worthy and brave men suffered for so doing; and yet, even in that court, and in those bad times, a great and good man durst say what I hope will not be taken amiss of me to say in this place, that the practice of informations for libels is a sword in the hands of a wicked King, and an arrant coward to cut down and destroy the innocent; the one cannot because of his high station, and the other dares not, because of his want of courage, revenge himself in another manner.

Attorney-General.—Pray, Mr. Hamilton, have a care what you say, do not go too far, either! I do not like those liberties.

Hamilton.—Sure, Mr. Attorney, you will not make any applications; all men agree that we are governed by the best of Kings, and I cannot see the meaning of Mr. Attorney's caution; my well known principles, and the sense I have of the blessings we enjoy under his present Majesty, make it impossible for me to err, and I hope, even to be suspected, in that point of duty to my King. May it please your honor, I was saying, that notwithstanding all the duty and reverence claimed by Mr. Attorney to men in authority, they are not exempt from observing the rules of common justice, either in their private or public capacities; the laws of our mother country know no exemption. It is true, men in power are harder to be come at for wrongs they do either to a private person or to the public, especially a governor in the plantations, where they insist upon an exemption from answering complaints of any kind in their own government. We are indeed told, and it is true, they are obliged to answer a suit in the King's Courts at Westminster for a wrong done to any person here; but do we not know how impracticable this is to most men among us, to leave their families, who depend upon their labor and care for their livelihood, and carry evidence to Britain, and at a great, nay a far greater expense than almost any of us are able to bear, only to prosecute a governor for an injury done here. But when the oppression is general, there is no remedy even in that way; no, our Constitution has, (blessed be God) given us an opportunity, if not to have such wrongs redressed, yet by our prudence and resolution to prevent in a great measure the committing of such wrongs, by making a governor sensible that it is his interest to be just to those under his care; for such is the sense that men in general (I mean freemen) have of common justice, that when they come to know that a chief magistrate abuses the power with which he is trusted for the good of the people, and is attempting to turn that very power against the innocent, whether of high or low degree, I say, mankind in general seldom fail to interpose, and as far as they can, prevent the destruction of their fellow subjects. And has it not often been seen (and I hope it will always be seen) that when the representatives of a free people, are by just representations or remonstrances made sensible of the sufferings of their fellow subjects, by the abuse of power in the hands of a governor, they have declared (and loudly too) that they were not obliged by any law to support a governor who goes about to destroy a province or a colony, or their privileges, which by his Majesty he was appointed, and by the law he is bound to protect and encourage. But I pray it may be considered, of what use is this mighty privilege if every man that suffers must be silent, and if a man must be taken up as a libeler for telling his sufferings to his neighbor? I know I may be answered, have you not a legislature? Have you not a house of representatives to whom you may complain? And to this I answer, we have. But what then: is an assembly to be troubled with every injury done by a governor? Or are they to hear of nothing but what those in the administration will please to tell them? Or what sort of a trial must a man have? And how is he to be remedied: especially if the case were as I have known it to happen in America in my time; that a governor who has places, (I will not say pensions, for I believe they seldom give that to another which they can take to themselves) to bestow, and can or will keep the same assembly, after he has modeled them so as to get a majority of the house in his interest, for near twice seven years together? I pray what redress is to be expected for an honest man, who makes his complaint against a governor, to an assembly who may properly enough be said to be made by the same governor against whom the complaint is made? The thing answers itself. No, it is natural, it is a privilege. I will go further, it is a right which all freemen claim, and are entitled to, to complain when they are hurt; they have a right publicly to remonstrate against abuses of power in the strongest terms; to put their neighbors upon their guard against the craft or open violence of men in authority, and to assert with courage the sense they have of the blessings of liberty, the value they put upon it, and their resolution at all hazards to preserve it as one of the greatest blessings Heaven can bestow. And when a house of assembly, composed of honest freemen, sees the general bent of the people's inclinations, that is it which must and will—I am sure it ought to—weigh with a legislature in spite of all the craft caressing and cajoling, made use of by a governor to divert them from hearkening to the voice of their country.

Mr. Hamilton then examined the law of libel at some length, and continued:

From all which, I insist, it is plain that the jury are by law at liberty (without any affront to the judgement of the Court) to find both the law and the fact in our case, as they did in the case I am speaking to, which I will beg leave just to mention, and it is this:—Messrs. Penn and Mead, being Quakers, and having met in a peaceable manner, and after being shut out of their meeting-house, preached in Grace Church street, in London, to the people of their own persuasion, and for this they were indicted; and it was said, "that they, with other persons, to the number of three hundred, unlawfully and tumultuously assembled, to the disturbance of the peace, &c." To which they pleaded not guilty. And the petit jury being sworn to try the issue between the king and the prisoners, that is, whether they were guilty according to the form of the indictment; here there was no dispute but that they were assembled together to the number mentioned in the indictment; but, whether that meeting together was riotously, tumultuously and to the disturbance of the peace was the question. And the Court told the jury it was, and ordered the jury to find it so; "for," said the Court, "the meeting was the matter of fact, and that is confessed, and we tell you it is unlawful, for it is against the statute; and the meeting being unlawful, it follows, of course, that it was tumultuous and to the disturbance of the peace." But the jury did not think fit to take the Court's word for it; for they could find neither riot, tumult or anything tending to breach of the peace committed at that meeting, and they acquitted Messrs. Penn and Mead. In doing of which they took upon them to judge both the law and the fact, at which the Court (being themselves true courtiers) were so much offended that they fined the jury forty marks a piece, and committed them till paid. But Mr. Bushel, who valued the right of a juryman, and the liberty of his country more than his own, refused to pay the fine, and was resolved (though at a great expense and trouble too,) to bring, and did bring his *habeas corpus*, to be relieved from his fine and imprisonment, and he was released accordingly; and this being the judgement in his case it is established for law, "that the judges how great soever they be, have no right to fine, imprison and punish a jury for not finding a verdict according to the discretion of the Court." And this, I hope, is sufficient to prove that jurymen are to see with their own eyes, to hear with their own ears, and to make use of their own consciences and understandings, in judging of the lives, liberties, or estates of their fellow subjects; and so I have done with this point.

This is the second information for libelling of a governor that I have ever known in America, and the first, though it may look like a romance, yet, as it is true, I will beg leave to mention it :—Governor Nicholson, who happened to be offended with one of his clergy, met him one day upon the road, and, as was usual with him, under the protection of his commission, used the parson with the worst of language, threatened to cut off his ears, slit his nose, and at last to shoot him through the head. The parson being a reverend man, continued all this time uncovered in the heat of the sun, until he found an opportunity to fly for it, and coming to a neighbor's house, felt himself very ill of a fever, and immediately writes for a doctor, and, that his physician might be the better judge of his distemper, he acquainted him with the usage he had received, concluding that the governor was certainly mad, for that no man in his senses would have acted in that manner. The doctor unhappily shows the parson's letter; the governor came to hear it, and so an information was preferred against the poor man for saying he believed the governor was mad; and it was laid in the information to be false, scandalous and wicked, and wrote with intent to move sedition among the people, and bring his Excellency in contempt. But by an order from the late Queen Anne, there was put a stop to that prosecution, with sundry others set on foot by the same governor, against gentlemen of the greatest worth and honor in that government.

And, may I not be allowed, after all this, to say that by a little countenance, almost any thing which a man writes may, with the help of that useful term of art, called an inuendo, be construed to be a libel, according to Mr. Attorney's definition of it; that whether the words are spoken of a person of a public character, or of a private man, whether dead or living, good or bad, true or false, all make a libel, for according to Mr. Attorney, after a man hears a writing read, or reads or repeats it, or laughs at it, they are all punishable. It is true, Mr. Attorney is so good as to allow, after the party knows it to be a libel; but he is not so kind as to take the man's word for it.

If a libel is understood in the large and unlimited sense urged by Mr. Attorney, there is scarce a writing I know that may not be called a libel, or scarce any person safe from being called to an account as a libeller; for Moses, meek as he was, libelled Cain, and who is it that has not libelled the devil; for according to Mr. Attorney, it is no justification to say one has a bad name. Echard was libelled by our good King William. Burnet has libelled, among many others, King Charles and King James, and Rapin has libelled them all. How must a man speak or write, or what must he hear, read or sing, or when must he laugh, so as to be secure from being taken up as a libeller? I sincerely believe, that were some persons to go through the streets of New York now-a-days, and read a part of the Bible, if it was not known to be such, Mr. Attorney, with the help of his inuenedos, would easily turn it into a libel. As for instance, the sixteenth verse of the ninth chapter of Isaiah: "The leaders of the people caused them to err and they that are led by them are destroyed." But, should Mr. Attorney go about to make this a libel he would read it thus: "The leaders of the people (inuendo, the Governor and Council of New York) cause them (inuendo, the people of this province) to err, and they (the people of this province meaning) are destroyed (inuendo, are deceived into the loss of their liberty), which is the worst kind of destruction. Or, if some person should publicly repeat, in a manner not pleasing to his betters, the tenth and eleventh verses of the fifty-fifth chapter of the same book, there Mr. Attorney would have a large field to display his skill, in the artful application of his inuendos. The words are, "His watchmen are all blind, they are ignorant; yea, they are greedy dogs, that can never have enough." But, to make them a libel no more is wanting but the aid of his skill in the right adapting his inuendos. As for instance, "His watchmen (inuendo, the Governor, Council and Assembly,) are blind, they are ignorant, (inuendo, will not see the dangerous designs of his Excellency,) yea, they, (the Governor and Council meaning,) are greedy dogs which can never have enough, (inuendo, enough of riches and power.)

Such an instance as this seems only fit to be laughed at; but I may appeal to Mr. Attorney himself, whether these are not at least equally proper to be applied to his Excellency and his ministers, as some of the inferences and inuendos in his information against my client. Then, if Mr. Attorney is at liberty to come into court and file an information in the king's name, without leave, who is secure, whom he is pleased to prosecute as a libeller? And, as the crown law is contended for in bad times, there is no remedy for the greatest oppression of this sort, even though the party prosecuted is acquitted with honor. And give me leave to say, as great men as any in Britain have boldly asserted that the mode of prosecution by information, when a grand jury will not find a bill of indictment, is a national grievance, and greatly inconsistent with that freedom which the subjects of England enjoy in most other cases. But, if we are so unhappy as not to be able to ward off this stroke of power directly, yet let us take care not to be cheated out of our liberties by forms and appearances; let us always be sure that the charge in the information is made out clearly, even beyond a doubt; for though matters in the information may be called form, upon trial, yet they may be and often have been found to be matters of substance upon giving judgment.

Gentlemen the danger is great in proportion to the mischief that may happen through our too great credulity. A proper confidence in a court is commendable; but as the verdict (whatever it is) will be yours, you ought to refer no part of your duty to the discretion of other persons. If you should be of opinion that there is no falsehood in Mr. Zenger's papers, you will, nay, (pardon me for the expression,) you ought to say so; because you do not know whether others, (I mean the Court,) may be of that opinion. It is your right to do so, and there is much depending upon your resolution, as well as upon your integrity.

* * * * * * * *

I am truly unequal to such an undertaking, on many accounts. And you see I labor under the weight of many years, and am borne down by many infirmaties of body; yet old and weak as I am I should think it my duty, if required, to go to the utmost part of the land, where my service could be of any use in assisting to quench the flame of prosecutions upon informations set on foot by the government, to deprive a people of the right of remonstrating, (and complaining too,) of the arbitrary attempts of men in power. Men who injure and oppress the people under their administration provoke them to cry out and complain, and then make that very complaint the foundation for new oppressions and prosecutions. I wish I could say there were no instances of this kind. But to conclude, the question before the Court and you, gentlemen of the jury, is not of small or private concern; it is not the cause of a poor printer, nor of New York alone, which you are trying. No! it may, in its consequences, affect every freeman that lives under a British government, on the main of America. It is the best cause; it is the cause of liberty; and I make no doubt but your upright conduct, this day, will not only intitle you to the love and esteem of your fellow citizens, but every man who prefers freedom to a life of slavery, will bless and honor you as men who have baffled the attempts of tyranny; and by an impartial and uncorrupt verdict, have laid a noble foundation for securing to ourselves, our posterity, and our neighbors, that to which nature and the laws of our country have given us a right—the liberty—both of exposing and opposing arbitrary power in those parts of the world at least, by speaking and writing truth.

Mr. Hamilton was heard with intense interest. His address was in tone, sentiment, and eloquence equal to that of the celebrated Erskine in 1792, in the great libel suit of Thomas Paine for the publication of the Rights of Man in London. On the conclusion of Mr. Hamilton's remarks, the Attorney General briefly replied. The Chief Justice charged the jury, and again said that as the defendant had confessed the publication of the words, the only question for them was whether or not the words were libelous, and as this was a question of law, the jury could safely leave it to the Court. After a short absence, the jury returned with a verdict of Not Guilty.

The reception of the verdict by the crowd was immense. Shouts filled the court. When the Chief Justice admonished the audience, and threatened the leader with imprisonment, a son of Admiral Norris declared himself the leader, and called for more cheers; and they were repeated with a strong and significant will. Mr. Hamilton was conducted by the crowd to a splendid entertainment. When he left the city for his home in Philadelphia, a grand salute was fired on starting in the barge across the North River. He was presented with the freedom of the city by the Common Council for "the remarkable service done by him to the city and colony by his learned and generous defence of the rights of mankind, and the liberty of the Press." On the splendid gold box in which the certificate of the freedom of the city was inclosed were these words, encircling the arms of the city:

Demensæ Sleges—Timefacta Libertas—Hæc tandem emergunt.

In a flying garter:

Non nummis, virtute paratur.

On the front:

Ita cuique eveniat ut de republica meruit.

Thus concluded this remarkable case, important in every aspect to the Press, and the key-note to the revolutionary spirit that was then springing up throughout the colonies.

The *Journal* was a small-sized sheet, and printed on much-worn Pica type. Sometimes one, and sometimes two or three advertisements would appear in this famous paper. Among the few thus published was the following, which would indicate that Orange County butter has, in later times, perhaps by the introduction of Tricopherous, lost some of its virtues:

₊†₊ To be sold, by Peter Lynch, near Mr. Rutgers' Brewhouse, very good Orange Butter. It is excellent for Gentlewomen to comb up their hair with. It also cures children's sore heads.

Zenger continued to publish the *Journal* till his death in 1746. His widow then managed the paper for a time. It afterward passed into the hands of his son, John Zenger, who conducted it till 1752. On the 28th of February, 1751, the following curious announcement appeared:

The country subscribers are earnestly entreated to send in their arrears; if they do not pay promptly, I shall leave off sending the paper, and try to recover my money otherwise. Some of these easy subscribers are in arrear for more than seven years. After serving them so long, I fancy it is time, and high time, that they should repay me my advances; for the truth is—and they may believe me—I have worn my clothes threadbare.

N.B. Gentlemen, if you have no money to spare, still think of your printer. When you have read this Advertisement, and thought on it, you cannot do less than say, "Come, wife!" (I address myself principally to married folk, but let bachelors take it to heart also), "Come, wife, let us send the poor printer some flour, or a few hams, butter, cheese, poultry, etc."

In the mean while, I am your obedient servant,   JOHN ZENGER.

In spite of this appeal for bread and butter, in spite of the fame of his father's trial in 1735, in spite of the freedom of the city in a gold box, in spite of all these things, the *Journal* languished, and finally died of starvation in 1752. *Ainsi va le monde.*

Meanwhile the *Gazette* remained the official organ of the government of New York. Occasionally Bradford felt constrained to vindicate himself and his paper to the people. In March, 1736, several months after Zenger's acquittal, the *Gazette* published the following manifesto:

New York, March 28, 1736.

The PRINTER *To his Readers:*

Gentlemen it is but too well Known to you all that for above 2 years past, there has been a Difference between the late Governour *Cosby* and some other Persons in this Province, which has been exposed in print with some warmth, but as to the merit of the Cause I meddle not with it, nor will I enter into Controversie about it, having declared myself to be of neither party, from the beginning, yet as I am and have been above forty years last past a Servant to the Government (and consequently to the several Governours during that Time) so I have according to my duty, some times printed in my *Gazette* some observations which the late Governour's Friends, thought proper to make upon what the other Party printed against him, and for so doing Mr. *Zenger*, or some of the Party, have been angry with me, as I may suppose, (for I know not of any thing else that I have done by which they could be offended with me, they having formerly been my very good Friends) they have from time to time, Reflected upon me and against my *Gazette*, insinuating that what I published was not true. That I *published nothing but what the Governour does allow of,* &c., whereas the contrary is most true, for neither his late Excellency Governour *Cosby* nor any other Person ever directed me, or ever saw what News I put into my Paper before it was published to the World; only what Answers on Observations were sent to me against what the other Party *printed* against the Governour &c. (as before mentioned) and sometimes (when I was not present) some Friend of mine would send me an account of what passed and how the Royal Healths were drank on Publick Days, and sometimes would say, *That most of the principal Merchants and Gentlemen at the Fort,* &c. This *Zenger's* Journal oftentimes would contradict and say, *the greatest number were not at the Fort,* whereas perhaps neither party had made an exact calculation how many were at the Fort, or how many absent; however, this and such like trivial matters *Zenger's Journal* would magnifie to be a Lie, in order to discredit *Will. Bradford's* News Paper, that People should not believe what he publishes, and consequently not buy his *Gazette.* The like Treatment he has met with, at times, for two years, without contradiction, which has induced some to believe what *Zenger's Journal* insinuates, is True, particularly his two last Journals *Numb.* 123, 124, where they charge *W. Bradford with his constant respect to Falsehood and dislike of Truth. His Integrity has been so long established, and the Falsity of his Assertions so often proved that I* (says the Journal) *as a Lover of Truth, a Friend to my Country, and one who is in Charity with all Men,* take the liberty [lax liberty] *of passing a few genuine Remarks upon what he* (Bradford) *has said.* Why what has he said? Why in his *Gazette,* Number 540, he has pleased on Tuesday last to inform his Readers, that his Excellency (our then Governour) was in a fair way of Recovery; whereas *on Wednesday last* (says the Journal) *he resigned his last breath ;* Ergo *Bradford* has a constant respect to falsehood and a dislike of *Truth ;* the consequence of which is, that what he publishes is not to be believed. But as I have not concerned myself with the present Differences, nor given just occasion for these Reflections and false Charges, so I do assure my *Unprejudiced Readers,* that as I have had a regard to Truth, so for the future I shall be cautious what I do publish. But as all men are liable to Mistakes, so more especially the Publisher of a News Paper; for let him be never so careful, he will sometimes have wrong Intelligence; and therefore we very often find the *English* Papers that they give notice that they had wrong information in such an affair mentioned in such a Paper, and this is allowed of. and the Publisher not charged with *Falsehood,* or a *Publisher of Untruths.* And I hereby acquaint my Friends and Readers, that if at any time I am made sensible that thro' wrong Information I have published anything not true, I shall readily make known the true matter of facts. But as to what I published concerning the *Governour's being in a fair way of Recovery after his Imposthume was lanced* is True, accordingly to the then Opinion of his Physicians and Friends about him, as I then had it from some of them, in writing, and still have it by me. But if my account of the Governour's Indisposition has been wrong, was any body hurt by it? I suppose my Friends nor enemies will not say it. So also what I related concerning his Excellency's Funeral I find, upon enquiry, to be true, altho' Mr. *Zenger's* Journal insinuates the contrary. They cite my words *The Gentlemen of the Council &c., Voluntarily assisted in paying their last Duty to His Remains;* and then ask *W. Bradford, were none of the Gentlemen of the Council invited to that Funeral?* To which W. B. answers. That he is informed that some of the Council were invited to be Pawl-bearers, and yet he will not allow that he gave a false account, when he says, *They Voluntarily Assisted,* &c., because he is very well informed, that the several Degrees of Persons there mentioned, did come to said Funeral of their *own Voluntarily good Will.* To conclude, altho' I apprehend myself to be wronged by their or his false Charges, I am obliged to him for his good Advice, (and which I hope I shall follow) where he says, *I advise Mr. Bradford not rake any more in the Ashes of the Dead.* The giver of which Advice will do well to apply it.

Kind Reader, I thought myself obliged to say something to take off the edge of some of the unworthy Reflections cast upon me in *Zenger's* late Journals, and that without the least cause given them; nor can I think of any design they could have in their so abusing me, but with intent (what in them lyes) to deprive me of Bread; for who will buy my Papers if they can be induced to believe that I have a *constant respect* to (or am Constant Publisher of) *Falsehood, and Dislike to Truth;* but as I profess to be a *Lover of Truth,* I hope to practise the same. I make this short Apology in my own defence, and not to begin a Controversie or Paper War with *Zenger's Journal,* or its Coadjutors (to use their own word) for as there is nothing that can be done or said, but something may be said against it, so if they make any Reflections or Observations upon what I here say, I do not intend to answer it or take any Notice of it, but do my endeavour to serve my Superiours in my Place and Station, as I have done for above Forty years last past, and also collect and publish such News and Occurrences as shall happen to come to my knowledge, in the best manner I can, be obedient to the King and to all that are put in Authority under him, and to my power, am
A Friend and Well-Wisher To all Men,
WILL. BRADFORD.

These two newspapers are thus made prominent because in history they occupy an important niche, and because the policy adopted by Zenger, like that of Franklin, and Fleet, and Thomas, and Edes, was "the dawn" not only "of that liberty which afterward revolutionized America," but of the independence of the Press, which we now see so splendidly illustrated and exemplified in so many of the leading newspapers of the present day.

The *Gazette* was carried on by Bradford till 1742. In January, 1743, the name was changed to *New York Gazette or Weekly Post-Boy*, and published by James Parker. The *Post-Boy* was a new paper, and only connected with the *Gazette* for the use of its name, and by the purchase of the material of that office. In proof of this, the name of the paper was changed in January, 1747, to that of the *New York Gazette, Revived in the Weekly Post-Boy.* As this occurred several years prior to the death of Bradford, it was undoubtedly done by arrangement with him. There were only two printing-offices in New York at that time, according to Professor Kalm, who described the city in a letter written in 1748. "There are two printers in the town," said Kalm, "and every week some gazettes, in English, are published, which contain news from all parts of the world."

Parker, like Zenger, who was "a forward boy," had been apprentices to Bradford. Indeed, nearly all the printers of newspapers in New York, New Jersey, and Pennsylvania had been taught in his offices either in New York or Philadelphia. It appears that Parker had run away from Bradford, as Franklin had from his brother's office. On the disappearance of Parker, the following advertisement was inserted in the *Gazette* of May 23, 1733, ten years before the *Post-Boy* was started, giving a full description of one of our earliest journalists. Our modern newspaper proprietors are not often publicly described in this way:

> Ran away on the 17th of this Instant *May*, from the Printer hereof, an Apprentice Lad, named *James Parker*, by Trade a Printer, aged about 19 years; he is of a fresh Complection, with short yellowish Hair, having on a yellowish Bengall Coat, Jacket and Breeches, lined with the same, and has taken with him a brown colour'd coarse Coat, with flat Mettal Buttons, Two Frocks, Two Shirts, One Pair of strip'd Ticken Jacket and Breeches. Whoever takes up and secures the said Apprentice, so that his said Master may have him again, shall have *Twenty Shillings* as a Reward, and all reasonable Charges Paid by
> WILLIAM BRADFORD.

The *Post-Boy* had the support of what was called the opposition party. It became involved in a difficulty with the Episcopal Church, which it severely attacked. It died shortly after. Its proprietor was a partner of Franklin's, who had spread himself over the colonies with his type and presses. One printing-office was started in South Carolina, others in different provinces, and that of James Parker in New York. These partnerships lasted for six years, and all accounts were settled quarterly. Franklin would send a printing-press and a certain quantity of type, and take one third of the profits and debts for his share. Quite a number of the early papers were established in this way.

On the 27th of September, 1732, the *Rhode Island Gazette* was issued in Newport, the first in that state. It was printed on a half sheet of cap paper, by James Franklin. After his failure in Boston, in consequence of the persecutions of the authorities, he thought, as Roger Williams did, that he would leave the original Puritans, and try the atmosphere and people of Rhode Island for more freedom of mind and conscience; but he was soon discouraged, partly from ill health, for only twelve numbers are known to have been published. The *Gazette* did not survive three months, and Franklin died in 1735. The *Gazette* contained no advertisements. There were no

Helmbolds, Knoxes, Brandreths, opera-houses or theatres, steamship lines, or Schiedam schnapps in those days. There was very little local news. In that period of hebdominalism the arrivals and departures of vessels were given briefly—so briefly, indeed, that the sea-captains of the last century were not enrolled on the pages of history as they have since been. There were no gentlemanly captains then, nor polite pursers. Newport was not a fashionable watering-place, *per se*, in 1732, as it is in this fast and elegant age. It promised then to be the Commercial Emporium of the Western World. It could boast of its foreign commerce, and bid fair to be more than a rival to New York, in consequence of possessing one of the finest harbors on the North Atlantic coast. There was no idea then of simply being wealthy in magnificent summer residences, and having its splendid bay merely the summer rendezvous of the New York Yacht squadron.

One number of the *Gazette*, in 1732, contained the following marine report of Newport for one week:

Entered Inward.—*Vincent* from Virginia, *Dyer & Sears* from Eustatia, *Gullin* from Hispaniola, and *Walters* from Boston.
Outward Bound.—*Briggs* for Barbados.
Cleared Out.—*Bell* for Barbados, *Linsey* for Leward Islands, and *Fame* for Antigua.

One number of the *Newport Mercury* of 1871 contained, in amount of tonnage as well as in number of vessels, more arrivals in one day, of pleasure yachts alone, than is embraced in the above list of arrivals and departures for a week. If any Rip van Winkle, who saw the Vincent, and Gullin, and Walters enter that port in 1732, stood at the railroad dépôt in the summer of 1871, and saw the Sappho, and Cambria, and Dauntless, and Fleetwing come bouncing up that expansive and beautiful bay, he must have been bewildered with the sight, or believed it all a dream.

CHAPTER V.

APPEARANCE OF THE PRESS AT THE SOUTH.

THE FIRST NEWSPAPER IN SOUTH CAROLINA.—THE FIRST IN VIRGINIA.—THE BRADFORD FAMILY IN PENNSYLVANIA.—THE STAMP ACT.—ITS ORIGINATOR IN BOSTON.—OPPOSITION OF JOURNALS.—THE FIRST PAPER IN MARYLAND.—VERY OLD PRESS.—THE FIRST CARRIERS' ADDRESS.—THE GERMAN PRESS.

OUR sketches of the Press of the colonial period must necessarily be written with a running pen.

The South must have her chronicles. On the 8th of January, 1731, the *South Carolina Gazette* was published in Charleston by Thomas Whitemarsh. It was printed on a half sheet for about a year, and died with its proprietor. In February, 1734, it reappeared in name, and was published for several years by Lewis Timothy.

The first paper in Virginia made its *début* in Williamsburg in 1736 —a rare old town, the society of which has been graphically described by Wirt in his Life of Patrick Henry. This newspaper was the *Virginia Gazette*, and printed by William Parks, sometimes on half a sheet of foolscap, and sometimes on a whole sheet. It was continued till Parks's death in 1750, and during that time was under the influence of the governor. After the death of Parks the *Gazette* was revived under new auspices, and issued in February, 1751, as the *Virginia Gazette, with the freshest advices, Foreign and Domestic*. The new paper was printed on a crown sheet, and had a cut of the arms of Virginia incorporated with the title. It bore this imprint :

Williamsburg : Printed by Wm. Hunter, at the Post Office, by whom persons may be supplied with this paper. Advertisements of a moderate length for Three shillings for the first week, and Two shillings each week after.

With Hunter's death in 1761 the *Gazette* was enlarged, and published by Joseph Royle. On his demise it was conducted by Purdie and Dixon till the Revolution. It was managed by Purdie alone during the war.

The *Boston Weekly Post-Boy*, in imitation of Parker's paper, was published by Ellis Huske. Its first number appeared in 1734. Huske was Postmaster of Boston. It was believed that he recommended the obnoxious Stamp Act of 1765 to the British government. He must have been astonished with the excitement and indignation that his measure created in the colonies. The *Post-Boy* lived nearly a quarter of a century, but did not reach the period of the odious act he had suggested to the home government to inflict on the colonial Press.

Nearly ten years elapsed before another paper appeared in the colonies. Then William Bradford, grandson of the one who printed the *Gazette* in New York, issued the *Pennsylvania Journal and Weekly Advertiser* in 1742. Bradford was father of William Bradford who was Attorney General of the United States in 1794-5. This Bradford family, like the Franklins, had newspaper on the brain, as much so as De Foe had in the earlier part of the century in Scotland. They were ready to print one or edit one wherever and whenever such an institution was wanted. The *Journal* was established at an important era in American journalism—shortly before the passage of the famous Stamp Act. It was devoted to the interests of the colonies, and was a strong advocate of freedom from England. On the 31st of October, the day before the Stamp Act was to take effect, the pages of the *Journal* were inclosed in black lines, with a picture of a skull and cross-bones over the title, and with these words printed beneath : "EXPIRING : In Hopes of a Resurrection to Life again." On the border of the first page were printed, " Adieu, adieu, to the Liberty of the Press." On the last column of the third page were the words "FAREWELL LIBERTY." On the fourth page was an engraving of a coffin, under which was this epitaph :

The last Remains of
THE PENNSYLVANIA JOURNAL,
Which departed this Life, the 31st of October, 1765,
Of a STAMP in her Vitals,
Aged 23 years.

With these typographical demonstrations the publisher issued the following patriotic card :

I am sorry to be obliged to acquaint my readers, that, as the Stamp act is feared to be obligatory upon us after the *First of November* evening, (the *fatal* To-morrow,) the Publisher, unable to bear the Burthen, has thought it expedient to STOP awhile, in order to deliberate, whether any methods can be found to elude the chains forged for us, and escape the insupportable Slavery ; which, it is hoped, from the just representations now made against this Act, may be effected. Meanwhile I must earnestly request every individual of my Subscribers, that they would immediately discharge their respective arrears, that I may be able, not only to support myself during the Interval, but be the better prepared to proceed again with the paper, whenever an opening for that purpose appears, which I hope will be soon. WILLIAM BRADFORD.

PHILADELPHIA, Oct. 31, 1765.

No resurrection was necessary, for Bradford continued the publication of the *Journal;* but in the next issue, in place of its regular title, "No *Stamp-Paper* to be had" appeared, and the paper came out as usual after this. Thomas Bradford, a son of the publisher, was taken into partnership in 1766, and the firm then became William & Thomas Bradford.

In the conflict with the authorities in regard to the unpopular Stamp Act, a member of the Pennsylvania Assembly, named John Hughes, sent a communication to the *Journal*, defending Franklin on the charge that he was an instigator of this infamous act. Hughes also wrote several letters to the commissioner of the Stamp Office in London. He was afterward appointed Commissioner of Stamps for Pennsylvania. These letters appeared in September, 1766, and were pronounced forgeries by Hughes. He commenced actions against the *Journal*, on a charge of libel, for their publication. As Selden said that "more solid things do not show the complexion of the Times so well as Ballads and Libels," we insert the remarks of the *Journal* on this attempt of Hughes to disown his own letters in his prosecution of Bradford:

* * * * * * * * *

His suing the Printers of the Pennsylvania Journal, for printing an exact copy of his own letters, is no more than the ill-judged effect of that insatiable passion which he has, to trample upon the most sacred Rights and Privileges of British subjects in America. The letters themselves, which are but the history of his own conduct for a considerable time past, plainly discover how heartily and passionately he wished for the favourable opportunity which would put it into the power of this excellent patriot, to execute the detestable STAMP ACT, which no American can mention without abhorrence, and to reduce the free born Sons of Britain to a state of the most wretched slavery. What else can be the meaning of his barefaced Falsehood, in representing North-America as in a state of absolute rebellion against the best of Kings, and in using all his feeble endeavours to excite his Majesty and his Ministers to send over an armed force to quell us, as he modestly terms it? But such is his insensibility to all the dictates of Honour or publick Virtue, that to compleat his character, he would now attempt to demolish the Liberty of the Press, that invaluable privilege of a free people; because through that channel his hidden arts are brought to Light.

'Tis but a piece of justice to the public, to let them know his last effort to prop his sinking character, which has long laboured under violent suspicions. He procured a writ for the printers of his letters, on Saturday last, which was executed by the Sheriff on Monday morning following; as twelve hundred pounds damages were marked upon the writ, the printers sent him a notice about 12 o'clock, to appear before a Magistrate to shew cause of action; but he refused to appear. At 4 o'clock, the same afternoon, they sent him another notice, to appear for the same purpose at 10 o'clock the next day, and informed him, that unless he appeared, they would move for a discharge from the arrest. But such was the consciousness of his guilt, that he refused again to appear, and as he could not be compelled by law to shew cause of action, the arrest was accordingly discharged. We are only the printers of a free and impartial paper, and we challenge Mr. Hughes and the world, to convict us of partiality in this respect, or of even an inclination to restrain the freedom of the press in any instance. We can appeal to North-America not only for our impartiality as printers, but also for the great advantages derived to us very lately from the unrestrained liberty, which every Briton claims of communicating his sentiments to the public thro' the channel of the press. What would have become of the liberties of the British Colonies in North-America, if Mr. Hughes's calls on Great Britain had been heard, to restrain the printers here from publishing what he is pleased to stile *inflammatory pieces*, and if every prostitute scribbler, and enemy to his country had been suffered, without control from the pens of true patriots, to rack their distempered brains, to find out arguments to gull a free-born people into a tame submission to perpetual slavery, and to impose their flimsy cobwebs upon us, instead of solid and substantial reasoning? To the freedom of the press in America we may in a great measure attribute the continuance of those inherent and constitutional privileges, which we yet enjoy and which every Briton, who is not inslaved to private or party interests, prefers to his life. We cannot therefore doubt, but that the happiness, which now reigns through all the British plantations, will inspire every friend of his country with an honest and generous indignation against the wretch that would attempt to enslave his countrymen by restraints on the press.

We would now inform the publick, that the letters of Mr. Galloway and Mr. Hughes, which we printed in our last week's paper, were transmitted to Philadelphia, by Capt. Sparks, from a gentleman in London of character and integrity, who is a friend of North-America, and never was accounted capable of imposing upon the publick. They were publickly seen and read in the Coffee-Houses in London by great numbers, were laid before the Parliament, and are copied verbatim in their Books. They came as genuine into our hands, as such we laid them before the publick, and such, we have it in our power to prove them. But were there no other evidences of his writing the letters we printed, there may be sufficient Proofs of the Fact taken from the very letters themselves, to show them the genuine Productions of his accurate pen.—Let not Mr. Hughes therefore think that his weak and faint denial of the Genuineness of the Letters will pass with the impartial world, as sufficient to overthrow such a Variety and Strength of Evidence, as the Publick is already possessed of against him. Let him reconcile the assurances he has given to the Commissioners of the Stamp Office, *that he would faithfully execute the stamp-office when it would be in his power*, with his full resignation of it which he made to the public, before he can expect to be believed in any matter by his fellow citizens.   WILLIAM & THOMAS BRADFORD.

"Carriers' Addresses," which are now going out of use as scarcely dignified and proper enough for the Press of 1872 to indorse or encourage, originated with Bradford in 1776, nearly a century ago, as an indirect means of making the public pay more than the regular subscription price of his paper. The first address was headed,

THE NEW-YEAR VERSES
OF
THE PRINTER'S LADS, WHO CARRY
THE
PENNSYLVANIA JOURNAL,
TO THE CUSTOMERS,
PHILADELPHIA, JANUARY 1, 1776.

What oceans of ink have been pressed into the service of Thalia since she stepped forward in aid of the "Printer's Lads" of the *Philadelphia Journal!* Not much money was paid, it is true, in those times of limited means, but in 1860 or 1865, the carriers of the New York papers, in English, German, French, Irish, Welsh, Political, Literary, Theatrical, Scientific, and Religious, with their enormous issue, no doubt received, on a single New Year's Day, no less than $5000 in *pour-boires* at the doors of newspaper subscribers in that city alone. The Newspaper Carriers' Address is probably the last of its class. Thirty or forty years ago, the Lamplighters, the

Watchmen, and others employed by the authorities of Boston, annually issued addresses in rhyme, but without reason, and received considerable sums of money. The *New York Herald* was the first to put a stop to those of the Carriers in New York. The *Journal of Commerce* followed. The *Philadelphia Ledger*, instead of an address in rhyme, got out, in 1870, a very useful and valuable Almanac, which Mr. Childs, its proprietor, sent to each subscriber free. He printed ninety thousand of the Almanac in 1872.

But Bradford deserved well of his country. His family was one of patriots. He served the nation well and boldly in his newspaper, and he served it well and nobly on the field of battle. He was a major of militia at Trenton. He came out of the affair at Princeton a colonel. He was at Fort Mifflin. He fought for his principles, and aided in gaining splendid victories for the Press and the country.

Another family of printers made their mark in the ranks of journalism during this interesting epoch. One of the Greens, famous in New England as far back in the annals of time as 1649, revived the *Maryland Gazette*, the original of which closed its career under Parks in 1736. It was revived in 1745 under the proprietorship of Jonas Green, who had, for many years previously, a printing-office in Annapolis. The *Gazette*, thus re-established, continued, with the exception of a brief suspension in 1765, in consequence of the odious Stamp Act, under the same name, and was published weekly by Mr. Green and his descendants until the year 1839, nearly a century, when, while in the hands of Jonas Green, the great-grandson of the original proprietor, it was discontinued, and the *St. Mary's Gazette* took its place. Any one can see a copy of this Century Newspaper in the Maryland State Library. Its original shape was quarto.

The *Gazette* was printed on the same press throughout its long career. On October 30, 1848, the *St. Mary's Gazette* said:

> But few of our readers are aware, we expect, that the press upon which our little sheet is printed, is the oldest now in use in the United States, and probably in the world. Yet such is the fact. The press now used by us has been in almost constant service for more than a hundred years. Upon it was printed the *Maryland Gazette*, the earliest paper published in the province of Maryland, and one among the very first in America. Upon it, also, was printed the first volume of the laws of Maryland that ever appeared. It is constructed somewhat on the Ramage principle, and requires three pulls, though two were originally sufficient to produce a good impression. It is truly a venerable object.

The next in order of time, and the last in this epoch, was the *New York Evening Post*. Henry de Forrest issued the initial number in 1746. This paper lived about a year only.

Two newspapers, printed in German, appeared in Pennsylvania during this period. One was published by Sower, in Germantown, in 1739, and the other by Ambruster, in Philadelphia, in 1743. The

German newspaper literature of the country has since increased to one hundred and forty-two superior journals printed in that language, some of which have daily circulations, like the *Staats Zeitung* of New York, of thirty, forty, and fifty thousand copies. They are now a political and literary power in the United States.

This closes the colonial period of newspapers. They were imperfect and incomplete in a journalistic, as the colonies were in a national point of view. Only here and there, as in the case of Franklin and Fleet in Boston, of the Bradfords in Philadelphia, and Zenger in New York, did they exhibit any fire or vitality, and in these few instances the sparks were nearly smothered in persecutions and imprisonment. But, happily, these sparks were only smouldering. They brightened up in the next epoch, and kindled the revolutionary fire of 1776, which made this a great nation of popular sovereignty and popular rights.

THE THIRD EPOCH.

1748—1783.

CHAPTER VI.
THE REVOLUTIONARY PRESS.

THE SONS OF LIBERTY.—OUR PATRIOTIC EDITORS AND PUBLISHERS.—WHO WROTE FOR THE NEWSPAPERS.—OPENING OF THE REVOLUTIONARY BALL.—THE PROGRESS OF JOURNALISM.—THE INDEPENDENT ADVERTISER.—NEW YORK MERCURY. — HUGH GAINE'S GAZETTE. — THE BOSTON GAZETTE OF EDES AND GILL. — THE NEW HAMPSHIRE GAZETTE. — NEWPORT (R. I.) MERCURY. — THE FRANKLIN PRESSES. — IMPRISONMENT OF ALEXANDER M'DOUGALL.

REVOLUTION! A.D. 1748 opened the campaign for 1776. The Revolutionary Press dawned upon the colonies. This was an important era in journalism and liberalism every where. Newspapers had been in existence for less than half a century. They were few in number. They were published in Boston, New York, Philadelphia, Annapolis, Williamsburg, Virginia, and Charleston, South Carolina. Nowhere else on this continent had a newspaper appeared. These news centres had now become the revolutionary centres of America. The arbitrary acts of the agents of the home government, the Stamp Act, the persecutions of the Franklins and the Zengers, began to react upon the people. The vigorous growth of a spirit of independence among the colonists began to develop itself in clubs and in newspaper offices. Sons of Liberty were active in Boston, New York, and elsewhere. Men of brains became constant and fearless contributors to the Press, and the result—the gun at Concord, "which was heard around the world"—was to startle the crowned heads of Europe.

Samuel Adams, of whom Napoleon borrowed the epithet he applied to England as a "nation of shopkeepers," established the *Independent Advertiser* in 1748. He was assisted by a club of ardent young rebels. It was full of free thought and free speech. The first number was printed on the 4th of January by Rogers and Fowle. Among its contributors was Jonathan Mayhew, the founder of Unitarianism in America. We have seen it somewhere stated that the *Advertiser* reproduced Mayhew's sermons as the *Boston*

Traveller now publishes those of Henry Ward Beecher. This pioneer of the revolutionary Press was managed with great skill and good sense for several years. Notwithstanding the spirit with which the paper was conducted, it did not come in direct and dangerous collision with the government till 1752. In 1750 Rogers and Fowle dissolved partnership, when David Fowle became the printer for these early rebels.

One of Mayhew's sermons, on the occasion of an election, strongly advocated the republican form of government. It was published. Shortly after the Legislative Assembly passed a bill imposing certain custom duties. This bill was severely denounced in a pamphlet from the office of the *Advertiser*, in which it was called the "Monitor of Monitors," and the Legislature somewhat tartly handled. This onslaught, immediately after the publication of such a sermon, was too much for the authorities to overlook. Fowle, the printer, was arrested, and, for refusing to divulge the name of the writer of the newspaper article, was sent to jail, where he was confined for several days, and harshly treated while there. This decided action on the part of government checked the originators of the *Advertiser* for a time, but a fresh impulse was soon given to the vigorous young writers of that eventful period.

Sandwiched between the *Advertiser* and the next newspaper enterprise in New England was the *New York Mercury*, the publication of which was commenced by Hugh Gaine on the 3d of August, 1752. With a short intermission it was continued in existence for thirty-one years, having been published till after the Revolution. After John Holt revived the *Journal* in 1767, Gaine added the name of *Gazette* to his paper, and it was called *Gaine's New York Gazette and Mercury* from that time.

Philip Freneau, the poet of the Revolution, had very little affection for Gaine. When he was editing the *Freeman's Journal* in Philadelphia, he overflowed with verses on the public characters of that era, and, among others, Hugh Gaine, a vicar of Bray in newspapers, "who lied at the sign of the Bible and Crown," came in for his share. Freneau published "Gaine's Life" in rhyme. Here is an extract:

> Now, if I was ever so given to lie,
> My dear native country I would n't deny;
> (I know you love Teagues) and I shall not conceal,
> That I came from the kingdom where Phelim O'Neil
> And other brave worthies ate butter and cheese,
> And walked in the clover-fields up to their knees:
> Full early in youth, without basket or burden,
> With staff in my hand, I pass'd over Jordan,
> (I remember my comrade was Doctor Magraw,
> And many strange things on the water we saw,

>   Sharks, dolphins and sea dogs, bonettas and whales,
>   And birds at the tropic, with quills in their tails,)
>   And came to your city and government seat,
>   And found it was true, you had something to eat !
>   When thus I wrote home : " The country is good,
>   They have plenty of victuals and plenty of wood ;
>   The people are kind, and whate'er they may think,
>   I shall make it appear I can swim where they'll sink ;
>   And yet they're so brisk, and so full of good cheer,
>   By my soul ! I suspect they have always New Year,
>   And, therefore, conceive it is good to be here."
>   So said, and so acted : I put up a press,
>   And printed away with amazing success ;
>   Neglected my person and looked like a fright,
>   Was bothered all day, and was busy all night,
>   Saw money come in, as the papers went out,
>   While Parker and Weyman were driving about,
>   And cursing and swearing and chewing their cuds,
>   And wishing Hugh Gaine and his press in the suds—
>   Thus life ran away, so smooth and serene—
>   Ah ! these were the happiest days I had seen !
>   But the saying of JACOB I've found to be true,
>   " The days of thy servant are evil and few !"
>   The days that to me were joyous and glad,
>   Are nothing to those which are dreary and sad !
>   The feuds of the stamp act foreboded foul weather,
>   And woe and vexation, all coming together.
>   Those days were the days of riots and mobs,
>   Tar, feathers, and tories, and troublesome jobs—
>   Priests preaching up war for the good of our souls,
>   And libels, and lying, and liberty-poles,
>   From which when some whimsical colors you waved
>   We had nothing to do, but look up and be saved !
>   But this was the reason that I must lament ;
>   I first was a whig, with an honest intent—
>   Yes, I *was* a whig, and a whig from my heart—
>   But still was unwilling with Britain to part.
>   I thought to oppose her was foolish and vain,
>   I thought she would turn and embrace us again,
>   And make us as happy as happy could be,
>   By renewing the era of mild sixty-three ;
>   And yet, like a cruel, undutiful son,
>   Who evil returns for the good to be done,
>   Unmerited odium on Britain to throw,
>   I printed some treason for PHILIP FRENEAU !

Hugh Gaine was an Irishman and an industrious journalist. He not only collected his own news and set up his own types, but he did his own press-work, folded his own papers, and delivered them to his subscribers. No man could now accomplish so much.

After the *Advertiser* ceased to exist, the *Boston Gazette, or Weekly Advertiser*, made its appearance. The first number was published January 3, 1753, and lived till March, 1755, and was then stopped in consequence of the provincial Stamp Act. It was printed by Samuel Kneeland after the dissolution of the firm of Kneeland and Green, mentioned in our preceding chapter.

Symptoms of the approaching political storm now began to show themselves more distinctly on the horizon. Thought and speech in coffee-houses and club-rooms became more free. Otis, the Adamses, Mayhews, Warrens, and Quincys were bolder and stronger. But talk and pamphlets were not sufficient for the public mind. Something better was needed. On the 7th of April, 1755, therefore, the real organ of the Revolutionary Party, which brought about the great conflict of 1766, made its appearance. On that day the *Boston Gazette and Country Gentleman* was established by Edes and Gill. The *Connecticut Gazette* was started in New Haven on the 1st of January of that year, by James Parker, of New York, and John Holt, who migrated from Virginia, but the great organ of the Revolutionary Party at that time was the *Boston Gazette*. It was printed on two pages folio, on a crown half sheet. On its first appearance its title-page was decorated with two cuts—one representing an Indian with bow and arrow ready for instant use, evidently scouting; the other represented Britannia liberating a bird confined by a cord to the arms of France. All the writers for the *Independent Advertiser*, with Samuel Adams at the head, became the brains of the *Gazette.* There was Jonathan Mayhew, James Otis, John Adams, Joseph Warren, Thomas Cushing, Samuel Dexter, Oxenbridge Thatcher, and Samuel Cooper. They were the Sons of Liberty of Massachusetts. There they stood, the real Bunker Hill Monument of history. Indicative of the progress of events, the *Gazette* appeared in 1760 with a new device. This struck out Britannia, and, instead, represented Minerva holding a spear surmounted with the cap of Liberty in her left hand, seated at a pedestal on which was a cage. With her right hand she opens the cage and liberates the bird, which is depicted as flying towards a tree—the Tree of Liberty. This was ten years before the Boston Massacre, and fifteen years before the fight at Concord.

The office of the *Gazette* was the resort of the leading spirits of that day. Another rendezvous during the intense excitement of the time, when the Stamp Act aroused the popular indignation to the highest point, was a small building in Milk Street, near the Old South Church, occupied by Samuel Shed as a grocery. Shed and his family lived in the rear part of the building. His parlor was the Inner Temple of Freedom. No one passed the old wooden building in after years without making a sign of respectful and grateful recognition. Mammon has since destroyed the place. There these patriots met and consulted. One day a communication appeared in the *Gazette* which did not emanate from any of those in the habit of meeting with this little band of brothers. It was bold and fearless in tone. Shed's parlor was in commotion. After an effort the author was discovered. It was Benjamin Austin, Jr. He was immediately enrolled as one of their number, and he became one of the most active and effective minds of the Revolutionary Press and cause.

Benjamin Edes and John Gill, the publishers of the *Gazette*, were bold, fearless men, inflexible in their patriotism, the right men, indeed, in the right place. With such managers and such writers, this paper became the powerful organ of the Whigs. The Stamp Act, the Boston Massacre, the Tea Tax, the closing of the port of Boston, the letters of Governor Hutchinson, the measures of the provincial government, the conduct of the British soldiers, were the grievances which furnished the material for these brilliant writers to arouse the indignation of the colonists, and make rebels, patriots, and freemen of them all. The most faithful description of the massacre in King Street, Boston, on the 5th of March, 1770, was given in the *Gazette*. The first anniversary of this massacre and outrage was observed in Boston in 1771, with great solemnity. It is thus described in the *Gazette*, which gives the reader a fair idea of the local reporting at that time:

Tuesday last was the Anniversary of the never-to-be-forgotten Fifth of March, 1770, when Messieurs *Gray, Maverick, Caldwell, Carr*, and *Attucks* were inhumanly murdered by a Party of Soldiers of the XXIXth Regiment in King-Street:—The Bells of the several Congregational Meeting-Houses were tolled from XII o'clock at Noon till I:—In the Evening there was a very striking Exhibition at the Dwelling-House of Mr. PAUL REVERE, fronting the Old North Square.—At one of the Chamber-Windows was the appearance of the Ghost of the unfortunate young Seider, with one of his Fingers in the Wound, endeavoring to stop the Blood issuing therefrom: Near him his Friends weeping: And at a small distance a monumental Obelisk, with his Bust in Front:—On the Front of the Pedestal, were the Names of those killed on the Fifth of March: Underneath the following Lines,

*Seider's pale Ghost fresh bleeding stands,
And Vengeance for his Death demands.*

In the next Window were represented the Soldiers drawn up, firing at the People assembled before them—the Dead on the Ground—and the Wounded falling, with the Blood running in Streams from their Wounds: Over which was wrote FOUL PLAY. In the third Window was the Figure of a Woman, representing AMERICA, sitting on the Stump of a Tree, with a Staff in her Hand, and the Cap of Liberty on the Top thereof,—one Foot on the Head of a Grenadier lying prostrate grasping a Serpent—Her Finger pointing to the Tragedy.

The whole was so well executed, that the Spectators, which amounted to many Thousands, were struck with solemn Silence, and their Countenances covered with a melancholy Gloom. At nine o'clock the Bells tolled a doleful Peal, until Ten; when the Exhibition was withdrawn, and the People retired to their respective Habitations.

Another specimen of newspaper description of the pre-Revolutionary time is the following simple and unpretending account, from the *Gazette* of December 20, 1773, of the famous exploit of destroying the tea in Boston Harbor:

On Tuesday last the body of the people of this and all the adjacent towns, and others from the distance of twenty miles, assembled at the Old South meeting-house, to inquire the reason of the delay in sending the ship Dartmouth, with the

East-India Tea, back to London; and having found that the owner had not taken the necessary steps for that purpose, they enjoined him at his peril to demand of the collector of the customs a clearance of the ship, and appointed a committee of ten to see it performed: after which they adjourned to the Thursday following, ten o'clock. They then met, and being informed by Mr. Rotch, that a clearance was refused him, they enjoined him immediately to enter a protest and apply to the Governor for a passport by the castle, and adjourned again till three o'clock for the same day. At which time they again met, and after waiting till near sunset, Mr. Rotch came in and informed them that he had accordingly entered his protest and waited on the Governor for a pass, but his excellency told him he could not consistent with his duty grant it until his vessel was qualified. The people finding all their efforts to preserve the property of the East-India Company and return it safely to London, frustrated by the tea consignees, the collector of the customs, and the Governor of the Province, DISSOLVED their meeting.—But, BEHOLD what followed! A number of brave and resolute men, determined to do all in their power to save their country from the ruin which their enemies had plotted, in less than four hours, emptied every chest of tea overboard the three ships commanded by Captains Hull, Bruce, and Coffin, amounting to 342 chests, into the Sea!! without the least damage done to the ships or any other property. The masters and owners are well pleased that their ships are thus cleared; and the people are almost universally congratulating each other on this happy event.

John Adams, in January, 1775, commenced the publication, in the *Gazette*, of a series of papers over the signature of "Novauglus." These communications were brought out in reply to another series, written by Jonathan Sewall, an eminent jurist, who wrote over the signature of "Massachusettensis." One authority, in speaking of these two prominent men, said:

He and John Adams were bosom friends. He attempted to dissuade Mr. Adams from attending the first continental congress; and it was in reply to his arguments, and as they walked on the Great Hill at Portland, that Adams used the memorable words: "The die is now cast; I have now passed the Rubicon; swim or sink, live or die, survive or perish with my country is my unalterable determination." They parted and met no more, until Sewall came to America in 1788. The one, the high-souled, the lion-hearted Adams, had a country, and a free country; the eloquent and gifted Sewall lived and died a colonist.

The *Gazette* was removed to Watertown in 1775, as the British troops had possession of Boston. The Provincial Congress was sitting there, and the *Gazette* was filled with the proceedings of that body. On the evacuation of Boston the establishment returned to that city, and the paper continued to be published by Edes and his two sons. But the vigor of the paper began to fall off. Warren, killed on Bunker Hill; Quincy, dead of disease; Otis, disabled from writing by a ruffianly assault; John Adams, busy in Congress; and Samuel Adams, active also in other departments, and then more interested in the *Chronicle*, where were the vigorous intellects to keep up the spirit and tone of the paper? Edes's patriotism was unflagging. Occasionally the columns of the *Gazette* would flare up, like the aurora borealis, with a brilliant article; but the persistent energy of its early days, which did so much for the country, were dying out in the midst of the more active scenes in Congress and on the field. It continued to give the news of the day, faithful accounts of the stirring and important events of that great epoch in the history of the world. But the close of the life of the *Gazette* belongs to the next period of journalism, and we will leave it till then.

These old papers are the resource of historians, and their preservation is of prime importance. We are glad to learn, therefore, that a large volume of these Revolutionary newspapers has lately been presented to the public library of Taunton, Mass. This volume embraces the *Boston Gazette and Country Journal*, and the *United States Chronicle*, printed in Providence, R. I., from July 4, 1768, to June 21, 1792.

The *North Carolina Gazette*, which was issued in Newbern in December, 1755, was the next newspaper published in the colonies, and the first in the Old North State. It was printed about six years, and then discontinued for a time. On the 27th of May, 1768, it was revived, and continued in existence till after the commencement of the war.

The imprisonment of Daniel Fowle, in Boston, as the publisher of the *Independent Advertiser*, having disgusted him with the authorities of that province, he migrated, with printing material, to Portsmouth, N. H., where he established the *New Hampshire Gazette*, in 1756. The first number was issued on the 7th of October. Of this number there is probably not a copy now in existence. Its own autobiography is interesting. The *Gazette* is now the oldest paper in the Union which has been continued without interruption of issue or change of name. It has often had a second title, but never gave up the first. Number one was called "The New Hampshire Gazette and Historical Chronicle, containing the Freshest Advices, Foreign & Domestic." Among the material carried to Portsmouth by Mr. Fowle was a set of wood or metal cuts belonging to Æsop's Fables. One of these, the Crow and the Fox, adorned the head of his paper. After this had performed its duty, the cut of Jupiter and the Peacock took its place. Then the Royal Arms occupied the post of honor till the Revolution overthrew all signs of royalty. Mr. Fowle confined himself mostly to his paper. He printed the laws of the province and a few pamphlets. His short stay in the Boston jail made him a very discreet man. He was appointed a justice of the peace shortly after his arrival in Portsmouth. His manners were agreeable, his sentiments liberal, his disposition pacific. He was attached to the cause of his country. For thirty years he published the *Gazette*. In 1785 it passed into the hands of Melcher and Osborn. Mr. Fowle died in 1787. He lived long enough to see the principles of Samuel Adams and the Caucus Club, enunciated in the *Independent Advertiser* in 1752, sustained by the colonists, and incorporated in a free and independent nation.

On the 22d of August, 1757, the *Boston Weekly Advertiser* appeared from the office of Green & Russell. It was contemplated by its proprietors not only to make a newspaper, but a literary paper as well. Very little success attended their effort in literature. After the second year its name was changed to *Green & Russell's Post-Boy and Advertiser*. Subsequently it was again altered, and it appeared as the *Massachusetts Gazette and Post-Boy and Advertiser*. In 1768 it was united with the *News-Letter*, but was disunited in 1769. In 1773 it was published by Mills and Hicks, and continued by them till 1775, when the war commenced. It soon after ceased to exist. It had several good writers on its staff of contributors, and an excellent advertising patronage for that period. It is recorded that Hicks was one of the young men who had the difficulty with the British soldiers which led to the Boston massacre of 1770, and that his father was one of the first who fell in the fight of the 19th of April, 1775; yet the *Advertiser* and young Hicks adhered to the Tory interest, and sustained the home government.

South Carolina could now boast of its third newspaper. It was published in Charleston, by Robert Wells, in 1758, and was called the *South Carolina and American General Gazette*.

Another of those long-lived papers, so few in number, appeared in the same year. On the 12th of June, 1758, James Franklin, son of James Franklin who printed the *Courant* in Boston in 1721, and the *Gazette* in Newport in 1732, more successful than his father, established a newspaper, which, with the *New Hampshire Gazette*, should have *Esto perpetua* for their motto. In that year he issued the *Newport* (R. I.) *Mercury*.

It was a seven by nine sheet, with a wood-cut representing Mercury flying over a ship and fort. With this device was the title of the paper, *Newport Mercury, or Weekly Advertiser*. The printing-office of the elder James Franklin had been carried on by Mrs. Ann Franklin during the illness of her husband, after the suspension of the *Gazette*, and it is probable that the *Mercury* was originally published on the old type of that office. On the 16th of June, 1866, in giving a sketch of its history, the *Mercury* thus described its initial number:

It was about the size of a letter sheet containing eight columns three and-a-half inches wide and twelve inches in length. For a frontispiece it showed a ship leaving the harbor, a fortification in the rear with the British flag flying and a figure of mercury passing through the air, holding in his hand a package, signifying a news-carrier. Six columns were devoted to news and CHARLES HANDY, JOSEPH GARDNER, SARAH OSBORNE, GEORGE HAZARD, JOB ALMY, WILLIAM STEVENS, BENJAMIN WILBUR, MARY TATE, CHRISTOPHER ELLERY, GIDEON and JOHN WANTON occupied the other columns with advertisements; JAMES FRANKLIN reserving two-thirds of a column to proclaim the contents of "Poor Richard's Almanac, for 1759."

The younger Franklin, when he entered upon his new enterprise, had evidently acquired some experience in his profession. As was customary with the earlier journalists, he often asked indulgence of his patrons. In one instance he stated that he had received a new font of types from England, and that he hoped, in the next four months, to bring up the arrears of foreign news. This font of types was presented to him by his uncle, Benjamin Franklin, who thus made his brother James "ample amends for the service" he had "deprived him of by leaving him so early." In these ancient sheets there are always paragraphs of interest. One finds in the *Mercury*, for instance, a detailed account of Arnold's treason, and then the news of Andre's execution. Here a piece of scandal from the court of Louis XV. Then an item of a ball given by Washington, and the particulars of one of Nelson's victories. In a number issued in 1759 appeared a suggestion which was adopted three quarters of a century later in our famous Florida War. It was this:

> The great Columbus, we are informed, in his expeditions against the Indians, made use of dogs with great success. The same experiment might be practised at this time against the wild Canadians and Indians, who, on account of the impenetrableness of the woods, have too successfully hitherto surprised our regular forces, &c.

James Franklin the second suddenly left Newport and never returned. Mrs. Ann Franklin, his mother, immediately placed her imprint on the paper, and issued it regularly as before. She was a woman of energy, industry, and experience. She carried on the business till the marriage of her daughter to Samuel Hall. He then took charge of the establishment. Subsequently he sold out to Solomon Southwick, who continued to publish the *Mercury* till December, 1776, when it was discontinued for a time for fear that the British, on landing, would destroy his office and material. Southwick was a patriot. He early took up the cause of his country with much vigor and effect. Three years before the affair at the North Bridge, in Concord, he published a communication in which the following bold paragraph appeared:

> To the Printer of the Newport Mercury.
>
> We are much mistaken if there be not something *now* brewing, in some parts of Europe, which will infallibly free this country from the worst of temporal curses, under which it at present groans, the curse of being tyrannized over by a parcel of dependant tools of arbitrary power, sent hither to enrich themselves and their MASTERS, on the *spoils* of the honest and industrious of these colonies; whom Satan envies as he did Adam and Eve in paradise; and therefore has let loose *his* Legions to work their final overthrow.

The press on which the elder James Franklin and his brother, Benjamin Franklin, so often worked in Boston, remained in the *Mercury* office over one hundred years. In 1859 it was sold to John B. Murray, Esq., he agreeing to place it in the Patent-office at

Washington, or some equally public and safe place, the desire being to insure its preservation for future generations as the first press on which Benjamin Franklin worked. Mr. Murray decided, in 1864, to present it to the Massachusetts Charitable Mechanics' Association on the one hundred and fifty-eighth anniversary of the birthday of Franklin. The press will be recognized as the original of the front panel of the Franklin statue in front of the City Hall, in School Street, Boston. Another press, on which Franklin worked in London in 1725–6, was obtained by Mr. Murray in 1841, and placed in the Patent-office at Washington.

On the title-page of the *Mercury* it is now published that the paper was "Established by Franklin, A.D. 1758."

The New London *Summary* was added to the list of newspapers on the 8th of August, 1758. Timothy Green was its publisher till 1763, when both paper and printer died.

Our records state that another *New York Gazette* was started on the 16th of February, 1759. William Weyman was its printer. This paper was a revival of the old G*azette* of Bradford and the *Gazette and Post-Boy* of Parker. The latter, after a short banishment to Connecticut, returned and became a partner of Weyman's, and the new *Gazette* was conducted by the new firm, and, as such, was immortalized by Freneau in verse. In 1763–4 Parker retired from journalism, but continued his printing-office and became secretary of the Post-office.

In the excitement growing out of the efforts of Sir Henry Moore to enforce the Mutiny Act in 1768–9, and the favorable action of the Assembly on the subject, an inflammatory handbill, charging the Assembly with a betrayal of its trust, was issued in the interests of the Sons of Liberty. In the search for the author, its publication was traced to the printing-office of Parker, and he was arrested and confined in the fort. Threats to deprive him of his office and promises of indemnity induced him to disclose the name of Alexander M'Dougall as the author. M'Dougall afterwards became famous in the annals of the patriotic press as the editor of the *Journal*. He was, of course, arrested. He was taken before the chief justice, and, refusing to give bail, was confined in the new jail, now the Hall of Records, opposite the old Tammany Hall, where the *Sun* Building now stands. The Assembly voted the handbill libelous, and the proceedings were printed on the forty-fifth page of the journal of that body. "Forty-five" became, therefore, the countersign of the Sons of Liberty. M'Dougall was overrun with visitors. They were so numerous, as in the case of Leigh Hunt, of the *London Examiner*, in 1812, that he was compelled to publish the following card:

Many of my Friends who have honored me with their Visits since my oppressive Confinement in this Place, have advised me, as I intend to devote a considerable Part of my Time to do Justice to the Public, in the Cause for which I am imprisoned, to appoint an Hour from which will be most convenient for me to see my Friends; I do therefore, hereby notify them, that I shall be glad of the Honor of their Company, from Three o'Clock in the Afternoon till Six.

I am, Gentlemen,
With great Esteem and Gratitude
Your very humble Servant,

New Goal
Feb. 10, 1770.

Alex. M'Dougall.

The *Journal* of February 15, 1770, in giving an idea of the character of these visits, says:

Yesterday, the forty-fifth day of the year, forty-five gentlemen, real enemies to internal taxation, by, or in obedience to external authority, and cordial friends to Captain McDougal, and the glorious cause of American liberty, went in decent procession to the New Gaol; and dined with him on forty-five pounds of beef stakes, cut from a bullock of forty-five months old, and with a number of other friends, who joined them in the afternoon, drank a variety of toasts, expressive not only of the most undissembled loyalty, but of the warmest attachment to Liberty, its renowned advocates in Great Britain and America, and the freedom of the press. Before the evening the company, who conducted themselves with great decency, seperated in the most cordial manner, but not without the firmest resolution to continue united in the glorious cause.

The only newspaper printed in Delaware, during this epoch, was the *Wilmington Courant*, which was published for about six months in 1761, by James Adams, who introduced printing in that state.

The third paper in Rhode Island was published in Providence in 1762, and was named the *Providence Gazette and Country Journal*. It was in the *Gazette* of 1822 that the well-known song of "Old Grimes," written by Albert C. Greene, was first published. Greene was one of the writers, if not the editor, of the modern *Gazette*. In 1833-4 he edited the *Literary Journal and Weekly Register*. He afterward became a judge, and died in 1868.

Away down South the next journalistic enterprise appeared. James Johnston, a native of Scotland, began the publication of the *Georgia Gazette* in Savannah on the 17th of April, 1763. It was published by Johnston for twenty-seven years, and was the only newspaper in that state before the Revolution.

On the death of the *Summary* the New London *Gazette* made its appearance. It was issued on the 1st of November, 1763. Its name was changed in 1773 to that of the *Connecticut Gazette*, and is the oldest paper in that state.

CHAPTER VII.

SPREAD OF THE REVOLUTIONARY SPIRIT.

NEW PAPERS ESTABLISHED.—SCARCITY OF RAGS.—APPEALS TO THE PEOPLE.
—HOW PAPER-MILLS WERE SUPPLIED.—CHARLES CARROLL, OF CARROLLTON.—EARLY OPINION OF NEWS IN VIRGINIA.—THOMAS JEFFERSON AND THE PRESS.

ANOTHER century newspaper is now announced.

On the 29th of October, 1764, a specimen number of the *Connecticut Courant* was published by Thomas Green "at the Heart and Crown, near the North Meeting House," in Hartford. The first regular issue of the paper, which has continued without interruption or change of name to the present time, was on the 19th of November, 1764.

Its prospectus read as follows :

OF all the Arts which have been introduc'd amongſt Mankind, for the civilizing Human-Nature, and rendering Life agreeable and happy, none appear of greater Advantage than that of Printing : for hereby the greateſt Genius's of all Ages, and Nations, live and ſpeak for the Benefit of future Generations.—

Was it not for the Preſs, we ſhould be left almoſt intirely ignorant of all thoſe noble Sentiments which the Antients were endow'd with.

By this Art, Men are brought acquainted with each other, though never ſo remote, as to Age or Situation ; it lays open to View, the Manners, Genius and Policy of all Nations and Countries and faithfully tranſmits them to Poſterity.—But not to inſiſt upon the Uſefulneſs of this Art in general, which muſt be obvious to every One, whoſe Thoughts are the leaſt extefive.

The Benefit of a Weekly Paper, muſt in particular have its Advantages, as it is the Channel which conveys the History of the preſent Times to every Part of the World.

The Articles of News from the different Papers (which we ſhall receive every Saturday, from the neighbouring Provinces) that ſhall appear to us, to be moſt authentic and intereſting ſhall always be carefully inferted ; and great Care will be taken to collect from Time to Time all domeſtic Occurrences, that are worthy the Notice of the Publick ; for which, we ſhall always be obliged to any of our Correſpondents, within whoſe Knowledge they may happen.

The CONNECTICUT COURANT, (a Specimen of which, the Publick are now preſented with) will, on due Encouragement be continued every Monday, beginning on Monday, the 19th of November, next : Which Encouragement we hope to deſerve, by a coſtant Endeavour to render this Paper uſeful, and entertaining, not only as a Channel for News, but aſſiſting to all Thoſe who may have Occaſion to make uſe of it as an Advertiſer.

On the 25th of April, 1768, Ebenezer Watson became a partner in the concern, and its sole publisher in December, 1770. On the 2d of March, 1779, Hudson and Goodwin were the publishers, Mr. Watson having died. Barzillai Hudson married the widow Watson, and assumed her interest. Various changes have occurred, since the first issue of the paper, in the condition of the country and the Press. In running over the early files of a century newspaper, one can trace the growth of that sentiment which led to such great results on this continent. The *Courant*, in alluding to its past history, said :

> When the COURANT was started, the utmost deference was paid in *words* to the English government, and "His Gracious Majesty's most loyal and dutiful subjects" were full of expressions which now grate harshly on an American ear of fealty to the British throne. As the time wore along, the "Loyal Sons of Liberty" whose doings are faithfully reported by their organ the COURANT, toned up the public mind to the great issue which all sagacious men knew to be not far in the future, and when the war of Independence broke out, the COURANT was bold as the boldest in sustaining the American doctrine. * * * * The early publishers of the COURANT were patriotic and courageous in opposing the tyranny of the ministers of George 3d, the stamp act, the tea tax, &c.—Historians like Bancroft, Trumbull, Stuart, Hollister and other writers and politicians have freely quoted and cited from the files of the COURANT. At the time when the acceptance or rejection of the Constitution of the United States was pending, the debate is fully reported, and as such men as Oliver Ellsworth, Jeremiah Wadsworth and Roger Sherman took part in it, no abler debate can be found.

The proprietors of the *Courant*, during the War of Independence, erected a paper-mill in Hartford, and made the paper on which they printed, and numerous appeals and entreaties are to be seen in the files of the paper to the people to save every scrap of rags or other material that could be converted into paper, and take it to the *Courant* paper-mill. The want of rags was the great *desideratum* of the early publishers of newspapers. After starting a paper-mill, it was difficult to supply it with the raw material. Rags were gathered on a very limited scale. Increase of population is an increase of rags. Fashion aids the paper-maker. But to gather the cast-off tatters was a task. Peddlers' wagons now go through towns and villages, and buy up all they can find. They purchase old books, old papers, old manuscripts, for money or tin-ware. Bell-carts go about the cities and collect all they can, but the quantity is too small to supply the great demand. Our paper-makers, therefore, resort to Italy and other foreign countries. Immense quantities are imported. Bell-carts were used in the last century for the collection of rags only. Old books and old newspapers were a rarity then. One bell-cart, and no more, it appears by the following advertisement in the *News-Letter* of March 6, 1769, and only one paper-mill, in New England in that year:

ADVERTISEMENT.

> The Bell Cart will go through Boston before the end of next month, to collect Rags for the Paper-Mill at Milton, when all people that will encourage the Paper Manufactory, may dispose of them. They are taken in at Mr. Caleb Davis's Shop, at the Fortification ; Mr. Andrew Gillespie's, near Dr. Clark's ; Mr. Andras Randalis, near Phillips's Wharf ; and Mr. John Boies's in Long Lane ; Mr. Frothingham's in Charlestown ; Mr. Williams's in Marblehead ; Mr. Edson's in Salem ; Mr. John Harris's in Newbury ; Mr. Daniel Fowle's in Portsmouth ; and at the Paper-Mill in Milton.

> *Rags are as beauties, which concealed lie,*
> *But when in Paper, how it charms the eye:*
> *Pray save your rags, new beauties to discover,*
> *For Paper truly, every one's a lover:*
> *By the Pen and Press such knowledge is displayed,*
> *As wouldn't exist, if Paper was not made,*
> *Wisdom of things, mysterious, divine,*
> *Illustriously doth on Paper shine.*

Ten years later, when the war was in full force, the issue of newspapers was very irregular in consequence of the scarcity of paper. Every effort was made to secure stock for the mills, and the publisher of the *Massachusetts Spy* of the 16th of November, 1780, appealed to the women of the nation in these words:

CASH GIVEN FOR LINEN AND COTTON AND LINEN RAGS, AT THE PRINTING OFFICE.

It is earnestly requested that the fair Daughters of Liberty in this extensive country would not neglect to serve their country, by saving for the Paper-Mill, all Linen and Cotton and Linen Rags, be they ever so small, as they are equally good for the purpose of making paper, as those that are larger. A bag hung up in one corner of a room, would be the means of saving many which would be otherwise lost. If the Ladies should not make a fortune by this piece of economy they will at least have the satisfaction of knowing they are doing an essential service to the community, which with TEN SHILLINGS per pound, the price now given for clean white rags, they must be sensible will be a sufficient reward.

ISAIAH THOMAS.

The Supreme Executive Council of Pennsylvania subscribed for Loudon's *New York Packet*, and Secretary Mallack wrote to have it sent regularly, "in order to have the files compleat." Publisher Loudon replied as follows:

FISHKILL 25th Feby. 1779.

Sir,—Agreeable to your desire the paper shall be sent to you. I have published but few papers for the past three months, owing to scarcity of Paper, but now have a parcel on the way hither and in two weeks shall begin to forward them to you. I am s[r]

Your h'ble serv't
SAM LOUDON.

Imagine such a letter from the *New York Herald* or the *Philadelphia Ledger* in February, 1872! But these were only a few of the early struggles of the Newspaper Press of this country. The journalists of the South experienced the same sort of troubles in 1861–65, during the rebellion, and many of the Paris papers were compelled to suspend their issue during the siege in 1870–71. More than half the papers in the Southern States were stopped entirely. Others were printed on light brown paper of no better quality than those of the last century were printed on. Many of the Southern journals were printed on common house-paper, with the news on one side and handsome figured patterns on the reverse. Several of the war correspondents of the *New York Herald* and other papers wrote their descriptions of Union victories on the backs of rebel state bonds and Confederate scrip representing hundreds of thousands of dollars in an account of a single battle. They took notes on the backs of exploded bank-notes. With cotton every where, they had not mills enough to turn it into paper.

"Water, water, every where,
And not a drop to drink."

All sorts of material are now used. Old blank-books and ledgers, footing up fortunes for their owners in days gone by, old newspapers, old speeches, old sermons, old letters, Congressional documents without end, are made into pulp for the enlightenment of the present age. Old history is ground into new history. There is one concern in New York City alone that has had more curious revelations in old letters on love, politics, religion, and trade, in the tons of old papers and manuscript that they have purchased, than would fill as many novels and histories as are now on the shelves of our libraries with their wit and wisdom, plots and philosophy, schemes and sentiment, humor and humbug. The advertisement of this concern appears daily in the *Evening Telegram* of New York, headed with a capital O, a picture of a human eye, and a capital C, and it has paid five hundred dollars for a single page of the *New York Herald* for one insertion of an advertisement calling for old books and old papers. Here is the advertisement that appears in the *Telegram:*

The Highest Cash Prices
PAID FOR
OLD NEWSPAPERS OF EVERY DESCRIPTION, OLD PAMPHLETS of every kind,
OLD BLANK BOOKS AND LEDGERS that are written full, and all kinds of WASTE PAPER from bankers, insurance companies, brokers, patent medicine depots, printing offices, book binders, public and private libraries, hotels, steamboats, railroad companies, express offices, &c.
J. C. STOCKWELL,
25 Ann street, N. Y.

Some of the "stuff" thus obtained is valuable. Some of the old volumes of newspapers are of considerable importance in a historical point of view. Some old files have been rescued from oblivion in this way. There was a curious philosopher living a few years ago in Brooklyn named Eben Merriam. He was the veritable clerk of the weather. He kept the New York journals meteorologically posted daily and semi-daily. E. M. came with every rain and every change of wind with his atmospheric "perturbations." So enthusiastic was he in the pursuit of his hobby, that he would often leave a warm bed and ascend to the roof of his house almost *in puris naturalibus*, to see how many degrees below zero the mercury had fallen. This singular man saved every scrap of newspaper that contained an idea of any value. When he died his attic was filled with this salt. All was sold to this Ann Street gatherer in bulk by the pound.

Nearly five hundred dollars were paid for the lot. Imagine the quantity! When the rebellion of 1861 burst upon us, thousands of attics were filled with such rubbish. The almost fabulous prices of manufactured paper, owing to the scarcity of the raw material, emptied these attics into the paper-mills. Not, however, at ten shillings a pound, as in 1780.

But, as we have said, Italy is our rag-bag. It is a perfect wonder to see the constant supply poured out of that lovely country into the storehouses of the Crockers, Butlers, and Rices of the United States. If the lazzaroni are always in rags, how can they supply America with the article? Has this problem ever been solved? Other nations have rags, but the exportation has been prohibited in France and Belgium in order that their paper-mills may not run short, even under the oppressive and suppressive press-laws of imperial France. We now import thirty millions of pounds annually, half of which comes from Italy. One would suppose that a year's exportation would completely strip the lazzaroni to the very dirt on their skin, and yet, if you visit that beautiful country of art and song, you will not miss a rag. Nothing has yet been found to take the place of rags except paper itself. Straw, bark, and several fibrous plants have been introduced as substitutes, but nothing approaches cotton and linen rags for this purpose. In the early days of press persecutions the obnoxious publications were burnt in some public square by the common hangman. Zenger's *Gazette*, and others, were thus treated by the authorities. This was a wanton waste of raw material. Napoleon III., with an eye to economy, managed better with the proscribed newspapers of his reign. These unfortunate sheets, when seized, were placed in an immense storeroom. When filled, the papers were taken out, and carried, under guard, to the suburbs of Paris, and thrown into caldrons of boiling water, where they were reduced to a pulp. The mass was then sold to the paper and card-board makers. Half a million copies of the *Independance Belge*, the *Gazette de Francfort*, the *Gazette de Moscow*, the *Kladderadatch*, the comic paper of Berlin, and the *Lanterne*, were thus served just before the war with Germany. Thus all the Bourbonism, Orleanism, and *sans culottism* were boiled out of them.

About the time the *Courant* was started in Hartford, Andrew Stewart, who had opened a printing-office in Wilmington, N. C., issued a newspaper in that place. He named it the *Cape Fear Gazette and Wilmington Advertiser*. It was first issued in 1763, and lived till 1767.

The second newspaper of New Hampshire made its *début* in Portsmouth, which was the important commercial centre of that state, a thrifty little place with a history attached to it. The new aspirant for journalistic honors was entitled the *Portsmouth Mercury and Weekly Advertiser.* It was born in 1765, and died in 1768. It was published by Ezekiel Russell, of the firm of Russell and Furber, who was afterward, it was asserted, in the employment of the home government to write against the wide-awake Whigs of New England.

The *Maryland Gazette,* started in the last epoch, now loomed up under the inspiration of Charles Carroll, of Carrollton. In March, 1765, the famous Stamp Act was passed in Parliament, by which all instruments in writing were to be executed on stamped paper, to be purchased of the agents of the English government, and all offenses against the act were to be tried in any royal marine or admiralty court in any part of the colonies, no matter how distant from the place of offense, thus interfering with the right of trial by jury. The colonies were aroused, as our pages have already indicated. On the 29th of May of that year, when Washington occupied a seat in the House of Burgesses of Virginia, Patrick Henry rose and introduced his celebrated resolutions declaring that the General Assembly of that state had the exclusive right and power to lay taxes and impositions upon the inhabitants thereof, and whoever maintained the contrary was an enemy to the colony. On the speaker's objecting to them as inflammatory, Henry vindicated them in a clear exposition of colonial rights, and how they had been assailed, closing with that brilliant flight which startled the House and was heard throughout the colonies: "Cæsar had his Brutus; Charles his Cromwell; and George the Third—(Treason! Treason! from the neighborhood of the chair) may profit by their examples. Sir, if this be treason (bowing to the speaker), make the most of it!"

After some slight modifications to meet the objections of the speaker, the resolutions were adopted. Fauquier, the governor, alarmed and indignant, dissolved the Assembly, but it was too late. The resolutions appeared in full in the next number of the *Maryland Gazette,* accompanied with an article strongly approving them. Charles Carroll was then one of the writers for the *Gazette,* and a member of the Assembly of Maryland. Educated at St. Omer and Bourges, he returned home at this critical period in our history, and with no very strong attachment for England, he indorsed these resolutions with his signature, and had them published. Thence they run through the colonies. They were printed in Benjamin Franklin's *Pennsylvania Gazette;* then in the *Newport Mercury,* which number was instantly suppressed as a traitorous publication; then the *South Carolina Gazette,* the *American General Gazette,* and the *Gazette and Country Journal,* all printed in Charleston, published them. When they appeared in Massachusetts, the Sons of Liberty took them up and indorsed them; and the comments of John Adams, which were published in the *Boston Gazette*, were afterward printed in pamphlet form in London. Efforts were made, without success, to have it suppressed by act of Parliament, on the plea that the language was traitorous and seditious. The Stamp Act was repealed, but the revolutionary ball was opened. All this was accomplished by the few newspapers then in existence, and in the hands of bold and patriotic men.

The *Gazette and Country Journal* was established in Charleston, S. C., by Charles Crouch, in 1765, in special opposition to the Stamp Act. It was his widow, Mary Crouch, who, twenty years later, moved to Salem, and started one of the *Gazettes* there with the type used by her husband in Charleston.

There was published in New Jersey, in 1765, on Saturday, the 21st of September, a paper under the title of *The Constitutional Courant*. It was printed in Burlington "by Andrew Marvel, at the sign of the Bribe refused, on Constitution Hill, North America." The real printer, however, was William Goddard, who afterward published the *Pennsylvania Chronicle and Universal Advertiser*. It contained three articles only—the address of "Andrew Marvel" and two editorials. With its title it had for a device a cut representing a snake divided into eight parts, each part denoting a section or colony—the head and neck representing New England, and the body New York, New Jersey, Pennsylvania, Maryland, Virginia, North Carolina, and South Carolina, with the motto "Join or Die." Isaiah Thomas adopted, in 1774, for a time, a similar device for the *Massachusetts Spy*. It was an allegorical appeal to the colonists to be united in the coming struggle with the home government. The *Constitutional Courant* was sold in the streets of New York, and produced a sensation. It was noticed by the government. There was a "council of war" on the paper. One of the "news-boys" of that day, Samuel Sweeney—there are many of that name nowadays—on being asked by one of the council "where that incendiary paper was printed," answered, "At Peter Hassenclever's Iron Works, please your honor." Only one number was issued, but that number made its mark.

Virginia was very backward in the encouragement of newspapers. Indeed, from the earliest period she discouraged free-schools and printing alike. Settled first of the American colonies, she was from half a century to a century behind Massachusetts in material progress. It was ninety years after the introduction of printing in Massachusetts that the art was carried into Virginia. Sir William Berkeley, the governor of that province for nearly forty years, said in 1661, "I thank God we have no free-schools nor printing, and I hope we shall not have these hundred years; for learning has brought disobedience, and heresy, and sects into the world, and printing has devulged them and libels against the government." Another distinguished governor of that state, the Hon. Henry A. Wise, as late as 1842, uttered a similar sentiment in thanking God there were neither schools nor newspapers in the Accomac District, the enlightened voters of which had sent him to Congress. In alluding to this statement, and some later boasts of the same gentleman on the floor of the House of Representatives touching the intelligence of the people in this same district, a correspondent of the *Baltimore Patriot* said :

> Hast ever been, gentle reader of newspapers, in Accomac County of Virginia ? If you had been there one day in the year 1840, you would have seen how good it is to have no newspaper to announce coming events. Mr. Wise was expected to speak in a tavern porch in Drummond Town, and whigs and locos were notified of it by a man riding through the town on horseback who lifted up his voice and thus proclaimed : "*O yese, O yese*, this *here* is *fur* to give *notis* that the honorable Henry A. Wise, is *fur* to be delivered of a speech this afternoon at 4 o'clock, right in misty Waddy's pe-az, and I want you all for to cum."

But, in spite of these drawbacks, several very excellent newspapers, for one or two of which the Wise family have written some brilliant articles, have existed in Virginia. One, it will be recollected, was established in the first epoch, and now we have to chronicle another, called by the familiar name of *Virginia Gazette*, the first number of which was issued in 1766. In May of that year the new *Gazette* appeared with this imprint :

> Williamsburg : Printed by William Rind, at the New Printing Office, on the Main Street, All persons may be supplied with this *Gazette* at 12s. 6d. per year.

Its title was "*The Virginia Gazette*, published by Authority ; Open to all Parties, but influenced by none." The arms of the colony formed the device with the title. Nearly all the papers of that early period had representative cuts with their titles. Some had two, and they changed the designs and devices with the changes in the sentiments of the editors and the people. Thomas Jefferson was the prime instigator in the establishment of the second *Gazette*. In consequence of the other *Gazette* being entirely under the influence of the governor, the author of the Declaration of Independence saw the necessity of another newspaper. Jefferson said : " Till the beginning of our Revolutionary disputes we had but one press, and that, having the whole business of the government, and no competitor for public favor, nothing disagreeable to the governor could find its way into it. We procured Rind to come from Maryland to publish a free paper." After the first year, "published by Authority" was not printed with the title, its tone not being loyal enough for the home government. William Rind published the paper till his death in 1773. His widow, Clementina Rind, carried it on for some time. Then John Pinckney conducted the establishment. In April, 1775, it was published by John Clarkson and Augustine Davis.

It is stated that the first printed statement of the adoption of the Declaration of Independence of the Fourth of July by Congress was made in the *Virginia Gazette* of the 19th of July, 1776, and then only a synopsis was given. The document in full was first published in the *Gazette* on the 26th of July. The fact of the passage of the Declaration was known by private letters as early as the 10th or 12th of the month.

There were published in Virginia at the beginning of the Revolution two newspapers only, while in Massachusetts there were seven, and four in New York.

On the 29th of May, 1767, John Holt commenced the *New York Journal, or General Advertiser.* It was brought into existence under the inspiration of George Clinton and Philip Schuyler, two leaders of the Revolutionary Party. It was, indeed, a revival of Zenger's paper of the same name, and its columns soon amplified the doctrines of Andrew Hamilton, and became a bold and enthusiastic organ of the Whigs. Its editor was a Scotchman named Alexander M'Dougall, previously mentioned in these pages. Holt had published Parker's *Gazette*, first in company with Parker, and afterward on his own account, from 1760 to 1766. He was a native of Virginia, received a good education, and was bred to the mercantile life. He followed commercial pursuits for several years, and was elected mayor of the ancient city of Williamsburg, Virginia. Not successful as a merchant, Holt left Virginia and went to New Haven, where our records unite him with James Parker in the *Connecticut Gazette* in 1755. On his arrival in New York he managed the *New York Gazette and Post-Boy* and kept a book-store till 1766. The *Gazette* was a strong opponent of the Stamp Act. Its columns gave excellent accounts of the exciting proceedings of the people in New York in 1765-66 in opposition to that obnoxious measure. The *Journal* was numbered continuously from the *Gazette*, and was, in fact, a continuation of that paper under other auspices. It soon had a very extensive circulation.

The *Journal* was a zealous advocate for the cause of America during the Revolution. It maintained its ground until the British army took possession of the city of New York in 1776, when the publisher removed to Kingston, which was called Esopus, and revived the paper there in July, 1777. When Esopus was burned by the British in October, 1777, Holt removed to Poughkeepsie, where he published the *Journal* until the termination of the war.

Holt was printer to the state during the Revolution, and his widow, at his decease, was appointed to that office. He was brother-in-law to Robert Hunter, printer at Williamsburg, Virginia, who was deputy postmaster general with Benjamin Franklin. The *Massachusetts Spy* of the 17th of July, 1770, disposed of Holt's partner in announcing the death of "James Parker, Esquire : Printer, Comptroller and Secretary of the Post Office, for the Northern District of the British Colonies."

The government in New York, as in Boston, sought to use the Press to counteract the influence of the Press. Without much difficulty they obtained control of the *Royal Gazetteer*, which was established by James Rivington originally in 1762. It was managed with more skill and tact than the *Chronicle*, also a royal organ, was in Boston by John Mein. The principal contributors of the *Gazetteer* were Attorney General Seabury ; Isaac Wilkins, a man of talent and influence ; the Rev. Samuel Chandler ; Myles Cooper, President of Kings, now Columbia College ; the Rev. John Vardill, the great satirist, and one or two others. The contributors to the opposition paper, the *Journal*, were the most distinguished men of the Whig party ; and among those who entered the ranks of the rebels and journalism at that time was Alexander Hamilton, then only sixteen years of age. Alone he was a match for the writers on the other side. It was in the beginning of this Revolutionary excitement, with King Sears as the chief of the Sons of Liberty, that the people decided to proceed to the college, seize Myles Cooper, and cool his ardor for the home government by ducking him in the Collect, where the Tombs now stand. It was then that Hamilton performed the chivalric deed of rushing to the college, reaching there before the populace, and making a speech to them on their arrival, enabling Cooper to escape on board a British man-of-war in the harbor, and thus saving his old preceptor from popular indignation and bodily harm. But the safety of Cooper was the destruction of the office of the *Gazetteer* and the house of its proprietor. The people had become so much exasperated and excited that somebody had to suffer to appease their wrath.

The *Connecticut Journal and New Haven Post-Boy* made its *début* in October, 1767. It was printed by Thomas and Samuel Green till 1799. *New Haven Post-Boy* was dropped from its title in 1775. It was published by Thomas Green & Son till 1809. It was a strong Whig paper, and helped along the Revolution. The paper is still in existence.

On the 21st of December, 1767, the *Boston Chronicle*, mentioned in connection with the *Royal Gazetteer*, came out, under the auspices of the English authorities, by Mein and Fleming. On its appearance it created quite a sensation by its literary character and fine typographical arrangement. It was printed on a whole sheet, in quarto, and sold at six shillings and eight pence per year. John Mein, one of the publishers, was very severe on the Whigs of Boston, and, having been charged with insulting the people, he was compelled to leave the country. Mein was assisted in the editorial department by Joseph Green, a pre-Revolutionary wit of Boston, and Samuel Waterhouse, who filled a superior post in the Custom-house. They ridiculed the piety and Puritanism of their opponents, the Whigs, and endeavored in this way to shatter the influence of the leading spirits of the Revolutionary Party with the masses. But in vain. Mein fled, leaving his business with Fleming, his partner, who soon followed the former to England.

It was the custom at that time for the people to amuse themselves on the 5th of November in processions and displays in the streets, and in carrying effigies depicting the pope and the devil. In 1769 there was an additional effigy representing Mein. On his right side was a label with the following acrostic:

>   I—nsulting wretch, we'll him expose—
>   O—'er the whole world his deeds disclose;
>   H—ell now gapes wide to take him in;
>   N—ow he is ripe—O lump of Sin!
>
>   M—ean is the man—Mein is his name;
>   E—nough he's spread his hellish fame;
>   I—nfernal furies hurl his soul,
>   N—ine million times, from pole to pole!

On the left side were labels denouncing the Tories in general. On the lantern illuminating the group was a perfect Danterian epitaph on Mein. No wonder, after these poetic and patriotic demonstrations, that the *Chronicle*, in 1770, with the loss of public support and public sympathy, made the following announcement:

₊ The Printers of the Boston Chronicle return thanks to the gentlemen, who have so long favored them with their subscriptions, and now inform them that, as the Chronicle, in the present state of affairs, cannot be carried on, either for their entertainment or the emolument of the Printers, it will be discontinued for some time.

Mein landed in Boston in 1764 from Glasgow in company with Robert Sandeman, a theological and controversial writer of notoriety, and the founder of a religious sect known as the Sandemanians, sufficiently numerous in Boston at one time. Mein was a bookseller, of good education, and full of enterprise. Sometimes he would fill an entire page of his paper with advertisements of his books for sale. On his return home the English government indemnified him for his losses, and employed him on one of the newspapers of London.

The *Pennsylvania Chronicle and Universal Advertiser* was next issued. It was published in Philadelphia in 1767 by William Goddard, who, it will be recollected, created a sensation in New York in 1765 by throwing a political bomb into the streets of that city in the form of the *Constitutional Courant*. The title of *Universal Advertiser* seemed a misnomer, for the business notices of the paper were few, and very local in their character and scope.

One of the oldest papers now printed appeared in Salem, Massachusetts, and was called the *Essex Gazette*. On the 5th of August, 1868, the *Salem Gazette* gave an interesting account of its life of a hundred years. Without much enterprise—without, indeed, much need of any—it has maintained itself respectably during this long period of time, in which a great republic has been born and grown to greatness, El Dorado of Walter Raleigh discovered and developed, and the map of Europe changed a dozen times by such mapmakers as the Catharines, the Napoleons, the Victor Emanuels, and the Bismarcks. What a panorama of wonderful events the columns of such a paper unfolds to public view!

The *Salem Gazette* claims to be a centenarian, but its early history is somewhat mixed and muddled. Our researches develop these facts:

1st. Samuel Hall established a paper called the *Essex Gazette*, August 5, 1768.

2d. The *Salem Gazette and Newbury and Marblehead Advertiser* was commenced in June, 1774, by Russell. Ceased to exist.

3d. The *American Gazette, or Constitutional Journal*, in 1776.

4th. Mary Crouch started the *Salem Gazette and General Advertiser* January 1, 1781. Merged with Hall's *Gazette*.

The *Essex Gazette* was published by Hall in Salem till May, 1775, when, on the recommendation of the leading members of the Whig, or Revolutionary Party, the material of the paper was taken to Cambridge, where it was issued under the name of the *New England Chronicle, or the Weekly Gazette*, and was an influential supporter of the independence of the nation. In 1776 the office was again moved, and the types and press carried to Boston. Its last number printed in Cambridge contained the following interesting document in both Latin and English:

The Corporation of HARVARD COLLEGE in Cambridge, in New England, to all the Faithful in Christ, to whom these Presents shall come,
GREETING.

Whereas Academical Degrees were originally instituted for this Purpose, That men eminent for Knowledge, Wisdom, and Virtue, who have highly merited of the Republic of Letters and of the Common Wealth, should be rewarded with the Honors of these Laurels; there is the greatest Propriety in conferring such Honor on that very illustrious Gentleman, GEORGE WASHINGTON, Esq.; the accomplished General of the confederated Colonies in America, whose Knowledge and patriotic Ardor are manifest to all: Who, for his distinguished Virtue, both Civil and Military, in the first Place, being elected by the Suffrages of the Virginians, one of their Delegates, exerted himself with Fidelity and singular Wisdom in the celebrated *Congress of America*, for the Defence of Liberty, when in the utmost Danger of being for ever lost, and for the Salvation of his Country; and then, at the earnest Request of that Grand Council of Patriots, without Hesitation, left all the Pleasures of his delightful Seat in Virginia, and the Affairs of his own Estate, that through all the Fatigues and Dangers of a Camp, without accepting any Reward, he might deliver New-England from the unjust and cruel Arms of Britain, and defend the other Colonies; and who, by the most signal Smiles of Divine Providence on his Military Operations, drove the Fleet and Troops of the Enemy with disgraceful Precipitation from the Town of Boston, which, for Eleven Months had been shut up, fortified and defended by a Garrison of above Seven Thousand Regulars; So that the Inhabitants, who suffered a great variety of Hardships and Cruelties while under the Power of the Oppressors, now rejoice in their Deliverance, and the neighboring Towns are freed from the Tumult of Arms, and our University has the agreeable Prospect of being restored to its antient Seat.

Know ye therefore, that We, the President and Fellows of Harvard College in Cambridge, (with the Consent of the Honored and Reverend Overseers of our Academy) have constituted and created the aforesaid Gentleman, GEORGE WASHINGTON, who merits the highest Honor, DOCTOR OF LAWS, the Law of Nature and Nations, and the Civil Law; and have given and granted unto him at the same Time all Rights, Privileges, and Honors to the said Degree pertaining.

In Testimony whereof, We have affixed the Seal of our University to these Letters, and subscribed with our Hand writing this Third Day of April in the Year of our Lord One Thousand Seven Hundred and Seventy-six.

SAMUEL LANGDON, S. T. D. Præses.
NATHANAEL APPLETON, S. T. D.
JOHANNES WINTHROP, Math. et Phil. P. Hol. LL.D.
ANDREAS ELIOT, S. T. D. } Socii.
SAMUEL COOPER, S. T. D.
JOHANNES WADSWORTH, Log. et Eth. Pre. Thesaurarius.

On the appearance of the paper in Boston the second title was omitted. Shortly after the *Chronicle* was sold to Powers and Willis. Willis was the father of Nathaniel Willis, who has the reputation of having established the first religious newspaper in the United States, and grandfather of Nathaniel Parker Willis, the poet and editor, the associate of George P. Morris in the *New York Mirror* and *Home Journal*. Hall, subsequent to the sale of the *Chronicle*, still retaining the name of *Gazette*, returned to Salem, where he found, in 1781, a paper of that name which had just been brought out by Mrs. Crouch. She had issued thirty-five numbers. On the arrival of Mr. Hall in October of that year the two *Gazettes* were united, and the publication of the consolidated paper, under the title of the *Salem Gazette*, was continued by Hall till November 22, 1785, when he returned to Boston in consequence of the obnoxious tax on newspaper advertisements, and the general decline in trade, which deprived him of nearly three fourths of that necessary branch of newspaper business. But the *Gazette* still lives, as our pages will show.

There is an old English press in the attic of the *Gazette* office that is covered with the dust and cobwebs of tradition. It was a part of Mr. Hall's material, and the story is that the *Essex Gazette* was printed upon it over a hundred years ago. There is a legend in the office that Benjamin Franklin had worked on that press; but Franklin left Massachusetts fifty years before the establishment of the

Gazette. Still, the story may be true, for Samuel Hall had worked in the office of James Franklin in Newport, and had married his daughter, a niece of Benjamin Franklin. On that event he became the publisher of the *Mercury*, in which was the old material used in Boston when Benjamin Franklin was an apprentice with his brother. But, in the face of this, the original press on which Franklin worked is now in possession of the Mechanics' Society of Boston. Yet, if we believe all the newspapers, there are now no less than seventeen old presses in different parts of the country on which Franklin originally worked when he was a printer!

The pre-Revolutionary newspapers were so few in number that it is our desire to mention each one. A paper called the *New York Chronicle* was issued in 1768 by Alexander and James Robertson. It did not long survive, and very little is known of its affairs.

On the 13th of October, 1769, the third paper in North Carolina was published. It was printed by Adam Boyd, at Wilmington, and named the *Cape Fear Mercury*.

CHAPTER VIII.
THE REVOLUTIONARY CRISIS.

THE MASSACHUSETTS SPY.—ISAIAH THOMAS.—RIVINGTON'S ROYAL GAZETTE.—MAJOR ANDRÉ AND THE COW CHASE.—ETHAN ALLEN'S INTERVIEW WITH RIVINGTON.—FRENEAU'S SATIRES.

IMPORTANT events were now culminating in America. All the leading minds had become editors, pamphleteers, and agitators. All others readers and believers. The Press was the power and the fulcrum.

Quite a remarkable newspaper came into existence at this time, which, with the *Gazette*, and others then in circulation, gave great aid and comfort to the prevailing sentiment of the people. In July, 1770, Isaiah Thomas, in connection with Zechariah Fowle, issued the *Massachusetts Spy*, named after several of the earlier papers in England, which bore the title of *Spye*. We annex their prospectus:

TO THE PUBLIC.

IT has always been cuſtomary for Printers and Publiſhers of new periodical Publications, to introduce them to the World with an Account of the Nature and End of their Defign. We, therefore, beg Leave to obſerve, That this ſmall Paper, under the name of THE MASSACHUSETTS SPY, is calculated on an entire NEW PLAN. If it meets with a favorable Reception, it will be regularly publiſhed THREE Times every Week, viz. *Tueſdays*, *Thurſdays* and *Saturdays*, (on two of which Days no News-Paper is published in this Town) by which Means, thoſe who favour this Undertaking with their Subſcription, will always have the moſt material of the News, which may from Time to Time arrive from Europe and from the other Parts of this Continent, on the Day of its Arrival, or the next Day following, (Sundays excepted) which will be ſooner through this Channel than any other. Great Care will be taken in collecting and inſerting the freſheſt and choiceſt Intelligence from Europe, and the material Tranſactions of this Town and Province : Twice every Week will be given a Liſt of the Arrival and Departure of Ships and other Veſſels, alſo a List of Marriages and Deaths, &c. and occaſionally will be inſerted ſelect Pieces in Proſe and Verſe, curious Inventions and new Diſcoveries in Nature and Science. Those who chooſe to advertiſe herein, may depend on having their ADVERTISEMENTS inſerted in a neat and conſpicuous Manner, at the moſt reaſonable Rates. When there happens to be a larger Quantity of News and a greater Number of Advertiſements than can well be contained in one Number, at its usual Bigneſs, it will be enlarged to double its Size at ſuch Times, in order that our Readers may not be diſappointed of Intelligence.

This is a brief Sketch of the Plan on which we propoſe to publiſh this Paper, and we readily flatter ourſelves the Public will honour it with that Regard the Execution of it may deſerve ; and doubt not, it will be executed with ſuch Judgment and Accuracy as to merit a favourable Reception.

Three months' experience led to a dissolution of the partnership, and Thomas carried on the paper alone, increasing its size to four pages, and publishing twice a week. With three months more of trial it was changed to a weekly paper. On the 7th of March, 1771, it adopted for its motto, "Open to all parties, but influenced by none." Although the editor apparently made an effort to be neutral and impartial in the political character of his columns, and published communications from each side, it was evident to his readers that Thomas was a Whig, and with the people heartily and cordially. This soon became patent to his Tory patrons, and they withdrew their support. The *Spy* then came out fully and boldly for the Revolutionary Party. Mean attempts were made to crush the paper by threats of libel suits and personal violence, and the government officers refused to allow Thomas the privileges of the Custom-house to obtain the arrivals and departures of vessels. There were no newsboats or steam yachts in those days. In noticing this folly on the part of the authorities, the *Spy* contained the following card:

TO THE PUBLIC.

A Tyrant may be justly compared to a Polypus, of which the smallest portion broken off becomes almost immediately as big, as voracious, and as deformed a *thing*, as the original ; entangling, plaguing, and engulphing every thing within its reach and power. How applicable this may be to our *petty lords*, the custom-house officers, every one is left to judge, after being informed that THEY, *to discourage this paper*, as they phrase it, have denied THIS Press the SHIP LIST, notwithstanding, according to the title, pieces from *all* sides have been inserted in it. The Printer conceives himself in no wise to blame if the Court side are now at a loss for writers, it being his province only to publish.

The office of the *Spy* was styled "the sedition foundery" by the Royalists, and Joseph Greenleaf was dismissed from the office of justice of the peace for writing for the paper. On the 8th of October, 1772, nearly three years before the fight at Concord, he closed an article in this bold manner:

Should the liberty of the press be once destroyed, farewell the remainder of our invaluable rights and privileges ! We may next expect padlocks on our lips, fetters on our legs, and only our hands left at liberty to slave for our *worse than Egyptian taskmasters*, or—or—FIGHT OUR WAY TO CONSTITUTIONAL FREEDOM.

The government made great efforts to counteract the influence of the *Boston Gazette*, and such writers as the Adamses and the Quincys, and the *Spy*, with its staff of contributors equally bold and resolute. After the failure of the *Chronicle*, another paper, called the *Censor*, with Ezekiel Russell to manage it, was started, but it scarcely survived the year. The authorities then fell back entirely on the old *News-Letter*, which was called the *Massachusetts Gazette* and *Weekly News-Letter*. All the Tory writers concentrated their power on this paper. Andrew Oliver, William Brattle, Daniel Leonard, and Jonathan Sewall opened their batteries on the Whigs. Sewall and Leonard, in a series of articles over the signature of "Massachusettensis," were considered the smartest and most important of their contributors. These articles, as we have already stated, were answered by John Adams in the *Boston Gazette.* Some of the contributions in the *Spy* were very powerful. "Centinel," "Leonidas," and "Mucius Scævola" were terribly severe on the Tories. The *Spy*, as early as 1771, urged a recourse to arms. "Mucius Scævola" denounced Governor Hutchinson as "an usurper, and should be punished as such," and showed Lieutenant Governor Oliver to be a "recorded perjured traitor." Attorney General Sewall was directed to prosecute the printer for libel, but the grand jury refused to find a bill. So the thunders of the *Spy* continued to roll and mutter over the heads of the doomed authorities.

It was in 1774 that Thomas introduced the device, borrowed from the *Constitutional Courant* of 1765, which represented a snake divided into nine parts, one part denoting New England, and each of the remaining parts denoting the other colonies — the Immortal Thirteen in all. Over this, in large letters, extending the entire width of the page, was the motto, "JOIN OR DIE." This device had created a sensation in the streets of New York nine years previously. It increased the excitement in 1774.

More British troops having landed in Boston, the place became too warm for Thomas. Threats of personal violence were uttered against him by some of the red-coated soldiers. He was on the list of twelve, with Samuel Adams and John Hancock, who were to be summarily executed when taken. To avoid this difficulty and unpleasantness, and to do more good with more safety, he sent his type and press across the Charles River one night preceding the eventful day of the affair at Lexington and Concord, and had them conveyed to Worcester. The last number of the *Spy* printed in Boston was on the 6th of April, 1775.

It was Isaiah Thomas, the bold journalist, who was, on the 18th of April, 1775, concerned with that modest and determined patriot, Paul Revere, in conveying information, by his "midnight ride," to the inhabitants of the interior towns, of the crossing of Charles River by the unfortunate British troops, under Major Pitcairn, on their secret expedition to destroy the military stores which had been gathered by the rebel authorities, and stored at Concord. Thomas's own types and press had only a short time previously passed over the same historic stream. It was the opening incident of the Revolutionary drama, and is thus celebrated by Longfellow:

> Listen, my children, and you shall hear
> Of the midnight ride of Paul Revere,
> On the eighteenth of April, in Seventy-five;
> Hardly a man is now alive
> Who remembers that day and year.

> He said to his friend, "If the British march
> By land or sea from the town to-night,
> Hang a lantern aloft in the belfry arch
> Of the North Church tower as a signal light,—
> One, if by land, and two, if by sea;
> And I on the opposite shore will be,
> Ready to ride and spread the alarm
> Through every Middlesex village and farm,
> For the country-folk to be up and to arm."

It was by Paul Revere's famous rides that the Sons of Liberty of New York and New England were kept advised of the important steps taken by those in Massachusetts. One of the New York papers of 1765 announced his arrival there with the action in Boston in regard to the Stamp Act. He was two days and a few hours in riding from one city to the other—

> "To spread the alarm
> Through every New England village and farm."

On the 3d of May, 1775, the *Spy* made its appearance in Worcester. Its motto, in large type, over the title of the paper, was,

AMERICANS! LIBERTY OR DEATH! JOIN OR DIE!

In this number, with a fancy head, and a small device representing the cap of liberty, the following notice was printed:

To the PUBLIC.

THE good People of this County, at a Meeting some Time since, voted to encourage the Establishment of a Printing-Office in this Place: In Consequence thereof, Application was made to me, then in Boston, to issue Proposals for publishing a weekly NEWS-PAPER in this Town, to be entitled, The WORCESTER GAZETTE, or AMERICAN ORACLE of LIBERTY: This I accordingly did; since that Time, Things have worn a different Face in our distressed Capital, and it was thought highly necessary that I should remove my Printing Materials from Boston to this Place, and instead of publishing the intended WORCESTER GAZETTE, &c. continue the Publication of the well-known MASSACHUSETTS SPY, or THOMAS'S BOSTON JOURNAL: I accordingly removed my Printing Utensils to this Place, and escaped myself from Boston on the memorable 19th of April, 1775, which will be remembered in future as the Anniversary of the BATTLE of LEXINGTON! I intend publishing this Paper regularly every Wednesday, and have made an Alteration in the Title, in order to take in Part of that intended for the Gazette.

I beg the Assistance of all the Friends to our righteous Cause to circulate this Paper.—They may rely that the utmost of my poor Endeavours shall be used to maintain those Rights and Priviledges for which we and *our Fathers have bled*! and that all possible Care will be taken to procure the most interesting and authentic Intelligence.

I am the Public's most obedient Servant,   ISAIAH THOMAS.
Worcester, May 2d, 1775.

When Boston was evacuated by the English troops in the following year, it was proposed to remove the *Spy* to that city; but on the 21st of June the establishment was taken by William Stearns and Daniel Bigelow "under a lease from the proprietor." With a fresh motto, "Undaunted by Tyrants, we will die or be free," and some very wholesome views on journalism, these new publishers managed the paper about a year. They said:

The liberty and free exercise of the Press, is the greatest temporal safeguard of the State. It assists the civil magistrate in wielding the sword of justice—holds up to public view the vicious, in their truly odious colors—and "is a praise and encouragement to them that do well." It detects political impostors, and is a terrific scourge to tyrants. None can notoriously transgress the line of duty, who may not be hereby subjected to public contempt and ignominy. It is one grand mean of promoting public virtue. It conveys knowledge to mankind, by acquainting them with the state of the community to which they belong, whereby they are better able to regulate their police—to supply its defects, or lop off its excrescences. It serves to increase *the majesty of the people*, by giving them understanding in the times, and conveying to them "the knowledge of what Israel ought to do." In fine, it is capable of being made the source of general literature.

Then Anthony Haswell carried on the establishment for a year. Then Thomas returned to Worcester and resumed the management of the *Spy*, with another new motto: "Unanimity at Home, and Bravery and Perseverance in the Field, will secure the Independence of America." These mottoes seemed to be the very concentration of the thought and feelings of the people—a series of strong patriotic editorial articles, illustrative of the time, compressed into a few words—into pointed revolutionary epigrams, that became the watchwords throughout the colonies.

What better appeal than the following could an editor make to the public? Its refreshing quaintness ought to have increased his subscription-list largely:

TO THE LOVERS OF LITERATURE IN THE COUNTY OF WORCESTER.

PRINTING OFFICE, Worcester, Nov. 1, 1780.

For twelve months past the number of customers for this paper has been so small as to be no ways adequate to the support of such a work, by which means the printer has absolutely sunk money by its publication. Books, Newspapers, and schools, are become too much neglected, and of consequence the rising generation will be great sufferers thereby, if these necessary things, which tend to learning, are not more encouraged.

Many people are so mistaken that they image that there will be but little intelligence of consequence contained in News-Papers in winter and therefore cease to become customers for them in that season of the year, not thinking that it is, on many accounts, a public benefit for News-Papers to circulate. It is an understood fact, that the expence to a Printer in publishing a News-Paper weekly, is very great, and more so in the winter than in the summer ; and it is also true, that such a publication cannot be laid bye and taken up again, at leisure. The Printer of this paper, therefore, begs leave to request all those who are desirous of having the Press and the publication of a News-paper continued in this town, to be so kind as to procure as large a number of customers for the Massachusetts Spy, as they conveniently can (by the last Thursday in this month) in the several towns where they reside, who will take said News-Paper for six months to come ; and if the number shall then appear only barely sufficient to defray the necessary expences of publishing said News-Paper, through the winter, it shall be continued; otherwise, said publication must cease in this town, and the press of course be removed out of this county to another where it has been solicited.

Should proper encouragement appear for continuing the publication of the Massachusetts Spy in this place, the Printer engages on his part to do all in his power to make it worthy of perusal and support.

ISAIAH THOMAS.

The title of the paper was changed in 1781 to *Thomas's Massa-*

chusetts Spy, or the Worcester Gazette, with yet a new device and another motto: "The noble Efforts of a Virtuous, Free, and United People, shall extirpate Tyranny, and establish Liberty and Peace." One of the new devices represented a chain of thirteen links, with a star in each link, the Union of the thirteen states: the chain is placed in a circular form, leaving an opening for the *fleur de lis* of France, to which the ends of the chain were attached. Above the arms of France were two hands clasped, and over them a sword with its hilt resting on the hands.

The *Spy* continued its powerful support of the Union, and the patriotic measures of the people and of the Revolutionary Party, till it saw the independence of the country acknowledged and its journalistic efforts fully secured and rewarded. As this paper is still in existence, and known as the *Worcester Spy*, we shall have occasion to speak of it again.

The Robertsons, who published the *Chronicle* in New York in 1768, established the *Post-Boy* in Albany in 1772. It was in circulation in 1775, at the beginning of the War of the Revolution.

In speaking of the *New York Journal* and its controversy with the *Royal Gazetteer*, it was stated that the publication of the latter was commenced in 1762. It became notorious in the colonies, and especially in New York, during the Revolutionary conflict. It was first called *Rivington's New York Gazetteer, or the Connecticut, New Jersey, Hudson River, and Quebec Weekly Advertiser.* It was established in April, 1762, by James Rivington. He had been a successful printer and bookseller with his brother John in London, where he made about $50,000. After losing most of this in his love for horses and horse-racing, he came to America in 1760, when he settled first in Philadelphia, and afterward in New York. The *Gazette* was a zealous Royalist organ, and had its office twice mobbed for its zeal, once by the Sons of Liberty, as we have already described, and once by a party of Connecticut militia. After this Rivington returned to London and obtained the appointment of king's printer for America, when he came back with new type, new presses, and renewed energy, and re-established his paper under the name of *Rivington's Royal Gazette.*

In the early part of the Revolution Rivington conducted his paper with as much impartiality and fairness as most of the editors did in that period, and it may be added that no newspaper in the colonies was better printed, or more copiously furnished with foreign intelligence. In October, 1773, Rivington informed his readers that each impression of his weekly *Gazette* amounted to 3600 copies. In that year a census of the city was taken, and showed that it contained a population of 21,876 inhabitants. In Boston, with a population of 8000, Campbell succeeded in selling but 300 copies of his *News-Letter* when it was the only newspaper printed in America.

While New York was occupied by the British troops four papers were published there. In order to have a newspaper issued daily, the proprietors made an arrangement by which one was published every day, except Sunday and Tuesday of each week, in the following manner:

Rivington's *Royal Gazette*, Wednesdays and Saturdays.
Hugh Gaine's *Gazette, or Mercury*, Mondays.
Robertson, Mills, and Hicks's *Royal American Gazette*, Thursdays.
Lewis's *New York Mercury and General Advertiser*, Fridays.

And, according to another authority, one of these papers was published on Tuesday. These papers were all published under the sanction of the British commander-in-chief, but none of the printers assumed the title of "printer to the king" except Rivington, who had a government appointment.

Major André was a frequent contributor to the columns of Rivington's paper. In his leisure moments he would employ his time in lampooning the American generals. He was the author of the famous satire "The Cow Chase," which appeared in the *Gazette*. It was in three cantos, and contained a few specimens of genuine humor. It was soon after the completion of the third canto that André left New York on his fatal visit to Arnold at West Point. It was published in the *Gazette* on the very day of his capture.

> "And now I've clos'd my epic strain,
> I tremble as I show it,
> Lest this same warrior-drover, Wayne,
> Should ever catch the poet."

Before the three thousand subscribers of the *Gazette* had read this canto the poet was indeed caught, and in the hands of these very "warrior-drovers" and "dung-born tribes" that he had been so facetiously lampooning.

The *American Literary Gazette* relates the following incident in Rivington's journalistic career:

The wit of Rivington's *Gazette* appears to have been very offensive to some of the Americans, and they were very liberal of their promises as to what they would do when they got him into their power; but he had a large amount of tact, and we suspect was very much of the gentleman also. He used to tell a capital story of his interview with Ethan Allen, one of the republican heroes who paid him a visit for the purpose of administering a "licking." He says, "I was sitting alone, after a good dinner, with a bottle of Madeira before me, when I heard an unusual noise in the street and a huzza from the boys. I was in the second story, and stepping to the window saw a tall figure in tarnished regimentals, with a large cocked hat and an enormous long sword, followed by a crowd of boys, who occasionally cheered him with huzzas of which he seemed insensible. He came up to my door and stopped. I could see no more, my heart told me it was Ethan Allen. I shut my window and retired behind my table and my bottle. I was certain the hour of reckoning had come. There was no retreat. Mr. Staples, my clerk, came in paler than ever, and clasping his hands, said, 'Master, he has come!'

'I know it.' 'He entered the store and asked if James Rivington lived there. I answered yes, sir. Is he at home? I will go and see, sir, I said, and now master what is to be done? There he is in the store and the boys peeping at him from the street.' I had made up my mind. I looked at the Madeira—possibly took a glass. Show him up, said I, and if such Madeira cannot mollify him he must be harder than adamant. There was a fearful moment of suspense. I heard him on the stairs, his long sword clanking at every step. In he stalked. 'Is your name James Rivington?' It is, sir, and no man could be more happy to see Colonel Ethan Allen. 'Sir, I have come ——' Not another word, my dear Colonel, until you have taken a seat and a glass of old Madeira. 'But, sir, I don't think it proper ——' Not another word, Colonel; taste this wine, I have had it in glass for ten years : old wine you know, unless it is originally sound, never improves by age. He took the glass, swallowed the wine, smacked his lips and shook his head approvingly. 'Sir, I come——' Not another word until you have taken another glass, and then, my dear Colonel, we will talk of old affairs, and I have some queer events to detail. In short, we finished two bottles of Madeira, and parted as good friends as if we had never had cause to be otherwise."

When the war was about to close Rivington threw away the appendages of royalty. The arms of Great Britain no longer appeared on his office. It was no more the *Royal Gazette*, but a plain Republican newspaper, entitled *Rivington's New York Gazette and Universal Advertiser*. But the people put very little trust in its editor; the public patronage fell off, and the paper ended in 1783. There were few men better qualified in energy and enterprise than Rivington to publish a newspaper. His sagacity during the war in keeping clear of difficulties, after King Sears and his men had destroyed his types before the Revolution, was remarkable. The following appeared in the *Gazette* of July 10, 1782, when there was a prospect of peace, as an instance of the tact of its editor :

To the Public.

The publisher of this paper, sensible that his zeal for the success of his Majesty's arms, his sanguine wishes for the good of his country, and his friendship for individuals, have at times led him to credit and circulate paragraphs, without investigating the facts so closely as his duty to the public demanded, trusting to their feelings, and depending on their generosity, he begs them to look over past errors, and depend on future correctness. From henceforth he will neither expect nor solicit their favours longer than his endeavours shall stamp the same degree of authenticity and credit on the Royal Gazette of New-York, as all Europe allow to the Royal Gazette of London.

Freneau, who was then editing a paper in Philadelphia, frequently satirized Rivington and his *Royal Gazette*. On one occasion, when the title to the *Gazette* was scarcely legible, Freneau wrote :

> Says Satan to Jemmy, "I hold you a bet,
> That you mean to abandon our *Royal Gazette;*
> Or, between you and me, you would manage things better,
> Than the title to print in so sneaking a letter.
> Now, being connected so long in the art,
> It would not be prudent at present to part;
> And the people, perhaps, would be frightened, and fret
> If the devil alone carried on the *Gazette*."
> Says Jemmy to Satan (by way of a wipe,)
> "Who gives me the matter, should furnish the type ;
> And why you find fault I can scarcely divine,
> For the types, like the printer, are certainly thine."

After the *Gazette* had somewhat improved in its typographical appearance, Freneau proceeded :

> From the regions of night with his head in a sack
> Ascended a person accoutred in black.
> * * * * * *
> "My mandates are fully complied with at last,
> New arms are engraved, and new letters are cast ;
> I therefore determine and fully accord,
> This servant of mine shall receive his reward."
> Then turning about, to the printer he said,
> "Who late was my *servant*, shall now be my *aid ;*
> Kneel down ! for your merits I dub you a knight ;
> From a passive subaltern I bid you to rise—
> The inventor, as well as the printer, of lies."

Although Rivington discontinued the *Gazette* soon after the peace of 1783, he uninterruptedly traded largely in books and stationery for several years subsequent to that period. He finally failed in that business, and retired. He died in July, 1802, at the age of seventy-eight. One of the old thoroughfares of New York City is still named Rivington Street.

In August, 1773, the *Maryland Journal and Baltimore Advertiser* appeared. It was published by William Goddard, the old printer of the ephemeral and sensational *Constitutional Courant* at "Peter Hassenclever's Iron Works," and the *Pennsylvania Chronicle* in 1767. Goddard was one of the itinerant journalists of his day.

The *Norwich* (Connecticut) *Packet* was published for the first time in October, 1773.

Isaiah Thomas, like Franklin, and Goddard, and Parks, and Rind, did not confine his enterprise to one paper. He established others wherever he thought he could accomplish any thing. On the 4th of December, 1773, he issued the *Essex Journal and Merrimack Packet, or the Massachusetts and New Hampshire General Advertiser.* It was published in Newburyport. Thomas had for partner in this enterprise Henry Walton Tinges. In a few months Thomas sold his share to Ezra Lunt, and in two years and a half the whole concern passed into the hands of John Mycall, who published the paper for a number of years—twenty or more.

CHAPTER IX.

THE CLOSE OF THE REVOLUTIONARY PERIOD.

INCREASE OF NEWSPAPERS. — NAMES. — LINES ON THE DEATH OF WARREN. — WILLIAM GORDON, THE HISTORIAN OF THE REVOLUTION. — DEATH OF JAMES OTIS. — PUBLICATION OF HISTORIES AND GEOGRAPHIES. — NEWSPAPERS IN NEW JERSEY AND VERMONT. — THE GREENBACKS OF THE LAST CENTURY.

ANNO DOMINI 1775 not only inaugurated the Revolution, giving birth to a new nation, but it imparted new life to journalism. Newspapers had become an important institution in the colonies. It was the *vox populi* of that eventful period.

No great wealth had been acquired by either printers or editors, but many became easy in their circumstances. Not much capital was required to carry on an establishment then. Journalists run no expensive expresses; they employed no European correspondents; they did not enjoy the luxury of a staff of paid writers. The Atlantic cable, with tolls at five, three, or two dollars a word, was not then laid; they had not even dreamed, as Shakspeare had, of Puck's "putting a girdle around about the earth in forty minutes." It is positive that the expense of a common news-boat would have ruined John Campbell and the *News-Letter* outright, and sent him to an insane asylum, if there had been one in Boston at that time. But the spirit of the colonies was revolutionary. Wonderful achievements of the Press were in the womb of time. They were beginning to develop themselves in the increase of newspaper readers, and the consequent increase of newspapers and newspaper enterprise. The progress was slow, but sure. No less than eight newspapers were established during the first year of the Revolution. Four of these appeared in Philadelphia, where the Continental Congress sat, and where Thomas Paine and Philip Freneau lived. John Dunlop published the *Pennsylvania Packet, or General Advertiser;* James Humphreys, Jr., the *Pennsylvania Ledger, or the Virginia, Maryland, Pennsylvania, and New Jersey Weekly Advertiser;* B. Towne the *Pennsylvania Evening Post;* and Story and Humphreys the *Pennsylvania Mercury and Universal Advertiser,* the latter endeavoring evidently to outstrip the *Ledger,* which modestly asked, in its title, for advertisements from four provinces only. Another German paper in Philadelphia was established at this time.

The *Constitutional Gazette* was issued in New York in 1775, its first number appearing in August. John Anderson was its publisher.

The other paper originating in this year was *A New Hampshire Gazette*, called so because there was a newspaper then in existence entitled *The New Hampshire Gazette*. The latter was sometimes called *Freeman's Journal, or New Hampshire Gazette*, and sometimes *Fowle's Gazette*. It appears to have been the custom in those days to repeat the names of papers, regardless of principle, proprietorship, meaning, property, or originality. The only two papers published in Virginia before the Revolution bore the same name, the *Virginia Gazette*, and were issued at the same time and in the same town. Occasionally a weekly paper would be styled the *Journal*. Time, and experience, and necessity, and genius, perhaps, have made an improvement—a change, at all events, in the title-pages of the Press, for our newspapers now display many curious and some very ludicrous names.

The *New England Chronicle*, which had been published in Cambridge, and afterward sold to Powers & Willis by Samuel Hall, appeared in the summer of 1776 under the title of *The Independent Chronicle*. In November of that year *Universal Advertiser* was added to its name. The *Chronicle* was a strong Whig paper. With all the papers of the last century, it had a pictorial device at the head of the paper, with the motto, " Appeal to Heaven. Independence." John Hancock, William Gordon, and Samuel Adams wrote for its columns. It was influential in the cause of the Revolution, and powerful in its support of the principles of that great struggle. After the *Boston Gazette* and *Massachusetts Spy*, no paper in New England accomplished more for the cause of the country and its independence than the *Chronicle*. In one of its numbers it published a few verses on the death of Warren on Bunker Hill, one of which we give, embracing the sentiment " of his soul marching on" of the famous John Brown song. It embodied the spirit of the times:

> Columbia, forbear ! not a sigh to alloy,
>   For thy Warren, so justly beloved ;
> Thy griefs shall be changed into triumphs of joy,
>   Thy Warren's not dead, but removed.
>
> The sons of the earth, the proud giants of old,
>   Have broke from their darksome abode ;
> And this is the news—for in heaven it is told—
>   They are marching to war with the gods.
> A council was held in the chambers of Jove,
>   And this was the final decree,
> That Warren should soar to the armies above—
>   And the charge was entrusted to me.

On the second year of the publication of the paper, early in 1777, the proprietors said:

The Printers and publishers of the Independent Chronicle and Universal Advertiser, (to keep pace with others of their profession of more ancient standing) beg leave, through this channel, to congratulate their customers on the arrival of the New Year,—being the first that has rolled over since their publication.

At the same time that they welcome in the New Year, they cannot pass over, in silent forgetfulness, the cruel, inhuman treatment, that America has experienced, during a series of months, without mentioning the desolating conflagration of Charleston, Falmouth, Norfolk, &c. from those, whom she *once* embraced as her bosom friends; and whose interest would, to this day, have been considered as inseperably connected with her own, had not a sincere love to America, in general, and to the great and good law of self-preservation, dictated a *total* seperation: Which the Grand Council of these Confederated States, in their Wisdom, have seen fit *for ever* to dissolve.

That America may prove victorious, and all, who have spirit, resolution, fortitude, and virtue, sufficient to assist her much injured (though glorious) cause, obtain what the whole collective wisdom of these States say they have an "inalienable right" to, viz. "PEACE, LIBERTY, and SAFETY" is the ardent wish of the Public's much obliged, and most devoted, humble servants,

THE PRINTERS.

One of the contributors to the *Chronicle*, the Rev. William Gordon, was the author of the first "History of the American Revolution." He was chaplain of the Provincial Congress of Massachusetts, and took a great interest in the Constitution of that state, a draft of which was then before the Convention.

The *Chronicle* was published by Powars and Willis till near the close of the war, and by Willis alone till the end of 1783.

Samuel Loudon, in January, 1776, issued the *New York Packet and American Advertiser*. It was a revival in name of the *Pacquet* of 1763. Loudon was born in Ireland, and settled in New York several years before the Revolution, establishing himself there as a ship-chandler. He bought a printing-office and material of Frederick Shober, a German, in 1775. With this material he opened a bookstore in Water Street, near Old Slip, and started the *Packet*. He was a decided Whig. Just before the British took possession of New York he removed with his press and types to Fishkill, where he published his paper till the peace of 1783, when he returned to the city. The *Packet*, having been established in January, 1776, was the last paper started in New York before the Declaration of Independence.

There was a paper published in Boston in 1776 under the title of *The Continental Journal and Weekly Advertiser*. Its first number was issued on the 30th of May of that year by John Gill, the former partner of Edes, of the *Boston Gazette*. Gill was a sound Whig, and aided the Revolutionary cause so far as he could. When James Otis was killed by lightning in Andover in 1783, a fate which, it seems, he singularly desired, Thomas Dawes wrote a poem on his death which was published in the *Journal*. Otis, a master-spirit of the Revolution, was one of the glorious band which gave the *Gazette* so much influence in shaping the policy of the colonies in their struggle with England. Here is an extract from Dawes's apotheosis:

> When flushed with conquest and elate with pride,
> Britannia's monarch Heaven's high will defied,
> And, bent on blood, by lust of rule inclined
> With odious chains to vex the freeborn mind,—
> On these young shores set up unjust command,
> And spread the slaves of office round the land;
> Then OTIS rose, and, great in patriot fame,
> To listening crowds resistance dared proclaim.
> From soul to soul the bright idea ran,
> The fire of freedom flew from man to man;
> His pen, like Sydney's, made the doctrine known,
> His tongue, like Tully's, shook a tyrant's throne:
> Then men grew bold, and, in the public eye,
> The right divine of monarchs dared to try;
> Light shone on all, despotic darkness fled,
> And, for a *sentiment*, a nation bled,
> * * * * * * * *
> Hark! the deep thunders echo round the skies!
> On wings of flame the eternal errand flies;
> One chosen *charitable* bolt is sped,
> And OTIS mingles with the glorious dead.

It was considered enterprising to publish histories and geographies in full in the columns of the papers. The *Journal*, for instance, like the *Spy*, published the whole of Robertson's History of America. It took two years to accomplish this typographical feat.

The first regular newspaper issued in New Jersey was published there on the 3d of December, 1777, the *New Jersey Gazette*. In 1758, James Parker, the New York printer, established a literary periodical, called the *New American Magazine*, which was edited by Samuel Nevil, a judge of the Supreme Court of that state, and who had been editor of the *London Evening Post*. But the first newspaper was published in 1777 by an enterprising Quaker named Isaac Collins, a printer, for a number of years, in that remarkable and respectable province. It was regularly issued till crowded out of existence by other more pretentious papers in November, 1786. Collins, like Franklin in Pennsylvania, printed the paper money of that state, the greenbacks of the last century, with this important exception: the greenbacks of this century are redeemed; those of the Revolution are in public and private museums and collections of curiosities, and unredeemed.

There was a paper, entitled the *New Jersey Journal*, established at Chatham, N. J., in 1778, by David Franks. It was continued till the close of the Revolution. Franks afterward removed to New York, and issued a weekly paper there. He also published, in connection with Shepard Kollock, the first Directory of that city. He then returned to New Jersey and his first love, and revived the *Journal* at Elizabethtown, and remained its editor till 1818.

On the 15th of June, 1778, the first number of the *Independent Ledger and American Advertiser* appeared in Boston—Draper and Folsom publishers. It was revolutionary in sentiment. Its prospectus was modest. Like other papers, it had a motto: "All hands with one inflamed and enlightened Heart." In 1779 the people began to reflect on what kind of government and what code of laws they should have after they had acquired their independence. Indicative of the prevailing sentiment, the *Ledger* published a peculiar communication on the subject. These communications were the editorials of the newspapers. Original articles, such as fill a page of the *Tribune* or *Sun* to-day, on the prevailing topics, were unknown then. Communications from the most distinguished writers were the opinions and sentiments of the paper publishing them.

In 1783 the *Ledger* was published by John W. Folsom alone.

Edward E. Powars, who had been connected with Nathaniel Willis in the publication of the *Independent Chronicle*, started the *American Herald* in Boston in 1781, which he continued till 1788, when he removed to Worcester, Mass., and published the paper there for a couple of years with the additional name of *Worcester Recorder*.

Mississippi began to enjoy the luxury of a newspaper in 1779. There was one published there in that year.

Vermont now entered the field of journalism, and closes our epoch of the Revolutionary Press by the publication of the *Vermont Gazette, or Green Mountain Post-Boy*, in 1781. It was printed at Westminster by Judah Paddock Spooner and Timothy Green. The establishment was removed to Windsor in 1783.

The forty-nine newspapers which were established in the colonies from 1748 to 1783 were all weekly or semi-weekly publications—not a daily, not a journal, was issued to this time in America. One paper had been started as a tri-weekly, but failed on that plan, and was then issued semi-weekly, and finally weekly. While New York was occupied by the English troops, the several papers there arranged their days of publication, as has since been done in Liverpool, England, so that one paper was issued each day, thus giving the public a daily newspaper. Of all the newspapers published on this continent to the end of this period, sixty-seven in number, from 1690 to 1783, only forty-three were in existence in 1783, when the independence of the United States was acknowledged by George the Third, and the young republic commenced its career of greatness and glory.

THE FOURTH EPOCH.

1783—1832.

THE POLITICAL PARTY PRESS.
CHAPTER X.
ORGANIZATION OF THE GREAT POLITICAL PARTIES.

AFTER THE REVOLUTION.—THE BEGINNING OF THE FEDERAL AND REPUBLICAN PARTIES.—METTERNICH'S OPINION.—THE PARTY PRESS.—ITS TROUBLES.—ITS LIBELS.—ITS DUELS AND ASSAULTS.—THE NATIONAL CONSTITUTION.—THE MASSACHUSETTS CENTINEL.—MAJOR BENJAMIN RUSSELL.—LOUIS PHILIPPE AND TALLEYRAND IN BOSTON.—THE BLACK AND TRI-COLORED COCKADES.—THE METHUSELAHS OF JOURNALISM.

THE printer and the Press have ceased to be martyrs in England and America. The time when journalists were dragged through the streets to Tyburn, or had their ears cut off as with Prynne, or put in the pillory as with Defoe, or had their papers burned by the common hangman as with Zenger, has passed with the Anglo-Saxon race. Occasionally, it is true, by the blunders and passions of those in power, as in the enactment of the Alien and Sedition laws in 1798, in the suspension of the *New York World* and *Journal of Commerce* in 1864, and in the arrest of Samuel Bowles, of the *Springfield Republican*, in New York in 1868, there is a glimmering of the despotism of the seventeenth and eighteenth centuries. But this is all. Such mistakes as these are not likely to be repeated on this side of the Atlantic.

After numerous persecutions of the Press in England, more freedom began to dawn on journalism there; and in the great struggle for the abolition of the stamp duty, which originated in an effort to muzzle the Press in 1712, the journalists of Great Britain made rapid progress in acquiring their rights. This struggle began in 1828, and ended, for a time, in 1836, in a reduction of the tax from fourpence to one penny, and its final abolition in 1871. But in obtaining this result there were nearly a thousand prosecutions, imprisonments, and fines for selling unstamped publications. So decisive a victory was only finally achieved after a fierce contest, and through the early exertions of Hetherington, the cheap journalist, aided by such men as Hume, Grote, Bulwer, Birkbeck, Cobden, and others, at a later day.

There was now greater latitude in the United States. Some of the best intellects of the country continued their contributions to the newspapers in the organization of society, of parties, of politics, of literature, and of religion. It was necessary to place the nation on a solid foundation. Newspapers were necessary to accomplish this desirable result. Scarcely had the echo of the last hostile gun of the Revolution died away when the country became divided into two great political camps, with newspapers as their needle-guns, and pamphlets as their chassepôts. Journalism, however, had not yet become a profession. It was a power with the people, but it was managed by ambitious political chiefs, as armies are manœuvred by their generals. It was, during these fifty years, a Party Press. It had more enterprise, more reading matter, more advertisements, more originality, but its views and opinions on public affairs were the inspiration of politicians and statesmen. Editors were free of prisons; they were in no danger of having their ears cut off; they could fight duels; they had their legal rights; they felt their power in all elections, and in all great questions that agitated the public mind, but they were bound to party. Independence of opinion and expression, outside of party, was political and financial ruin. But the world was moving, and its soul was marching on.

When the independence of the United States was acknowledged in 1783, the people, solid and compact during the war, began to disintegrate, and, from a grand Revolutionary Party, with one sublime object in view, formed themselves into two political parties. Each was a safety-valve to the country; each was honest and patriotic in its purposes, but each entertained different views on the policy and form of government deemed best for the republic. With the close of the Revolution, fought out on military principles, the organization of the nation and its political progress and improvement were to be arranged and settled by lesser contests and revolutions, which would take place every four years, and peacefully accomplish their objects and purposes at the ballot-box. This was the course of things during this epoch.

The remarkable events in our national history, nowhere else so splendidly achieved as on this continent, were results obtained by the political leaders and political parties through the Press. Thus the pen became "mightier than the sword." But the people had not acquired, any more than the newspaper, their full freedom of thought and action, for they had become, in the heats and passions of political campaigns, strong partisans. Through the light of time, however, and with the spread of that great national school-book, the

Newspaper, the masses have become educated to think and act more independently.

In the organization of parties after the Revolution, one was called the Federalist, under the lead of Alexander Hamilton, and the other the Republican, under the guidance of Thomas Jefferson. The term Democrat was then applied to the Republicans as one of reproach. In retaliation, the term Aristocrat was given to the Federalists. The names of the parties were changed in 1824. The Republicans, in the campaign resulting in the election of John Quincy Adams, accepted the name of Democrat, and the party has ever since been known as such, with a few local distinctions, such as Hard Shells, Soft Shells, Barn-burners, Hard-fisted, Locofocos, Tammanyites, Huge Paws, etc. The Federalists also changed their name to National Republicans, and since then the opposition party to the democracy has gone through several revolutions and changes. It has been known since 1789 as Federalist, National Republican, and Whig, and since the Fremont campaign of 1856 it has assumed the original name of the Democratic Party, and fought its political battles as Republicans. Splits, in certain localities, have taken independent names, such as Conservatives and Silver Grays in New York—Nathaniel P. Talmadge at the head of one, and Millard Fillmore the representative man of the other. Attempts have been made to rally the masses under the names of popular candidates, without, however, much success. Adams men and Jackson men were known, but the titles remained only for an election. There were Hard-Cider and Log-Cabin Whigs in the Harrison campaign, but "principles, not men," seemed to be the governing idea of the people.

One day Dr. Nehemiah Niles, our chargé d'affaires to Sardinia, was in Vienna, and had an interview with the venerable Metternich. "If I lived in the United States," said Metternich, "I would be a Locofoco." "Why so?" asked Dr. Niles. "Why?" continued the prime minister; "because that is the party of your people; their interests are democratic, and the people govern the nation. I am in favor of absolutism here. One is as necessary to America as the other is to Austria." Wise old diplomat! Swept away in the revolution of 1848, he died before Sadowa semi-liberalized the absolutism of the Hapsburg empire.

On the conclusion of peace North America was under the government of the Articles of Confederation which had been adopted by the colonies, and which went into operation on the 2d of March, 1781. It was demonstrated, after the war was over, that this form of government was too weak and too defective to build a great and powerful nation upon, leading to serious confusion in the intercourse and commerce of the several states. This experience resulted in the calling of a Convention, which met in Philadelphia on the 25th of May, 1787, and gave the world, on the 17th of September of that year, the present Constitution of the United States. In the political contest growing out of the immature condition of the nation from 1783 to the final adoption of the Constitution, the first two parties, the Federalists and Anti-Federalists, came into existence. It was during this period of public excitement and popular agitation that the newspapers were arrayed on either side, and it was in this important and vital political conflict that the Party Press had its origin in the United States.

Of those papers that passed through the fire of the Revolution and entered the new political arena, the *New York Journal*, the *New York Packet*, the *Massachusetts Spy*, the *Boston Gazette*, the *Newport Mercury*, the *Connecticut Courant*, the *Maryland Gazette*, the *Boston Independent Chronicle*, the *Salem Gazette*, the *New Hampshire Gazette*, the *Pennsylvania Gazette*, the *Pennsylvania Journal*, were the most prominent. Other journals were soon established, and many of the most distinguished men who have since held high positions started in political life and distinction with these papers.

The several New York journals which were removed from that city during its occupancy by the British troops were returned to their old quarters on the conclusion of peace. Among others was the *New York Journal*, published by John Holt. It was now named the *Independent Gazette, or the New York Journal revived*. In the following January it was printed on new and handsome Bourgeois type, and issued twice a week. Holt died before the end of the year, and the paper passed into the hands of Elizabeth Holt, his widow. Holt was a man of ardent feelings, a High-Churchman, a good writer, and a firm Whig. Soon after his death his widow printed a memorial of him on cards for distribution among her friends. It was as follows:

A due tribute to the memory of JOHN HOLT, printer to this State; a native of Virginia; who patiently obeyed Death's awful summons, on the 30th of January 1784, in the 64th year of his age. To say that his family lament him, is needless; that his friends bewail him, useless; that all regret him, unnecessary; for, that he merited every esteem, is certain. The tongue of slander cannot say less, though justice might say more. In token of sincere affection, his disconsolate widow hath caused this memorial to be erected.

Mrs. Holt continued the *Journal* till 1785, but it was published only once a week. Eleazar Oswald, a kinsman of Mrs. Holt, who had been a colonel in the American army, conducted the paper for her from 1785 to 1786, after which Oswald printed it in his own name, Mrs. Holt receiving a proportion of the profits. In January, 1787, Mrs. Holt and Oswald sold the *Journal* and their printing establishment to Thomas Greeenleaf. Oswald died in September, 1795.

Soon after Greenleaf took possession of the *Journal* he made the establishment the foundation of two papers. The paper intended for city circulation was called *The New York Journal and Daily Patriotic Register;* the other, with the same title, was published weekly, on Thursday, for the country. The titles of these papers were afterward altered; the daily was called *The Argus, or Greenleaf's New Daily Advertiser;* and *Greenleaf's New York Journal and Patriotic Register* was published twice a week. When the two great political parties were forming, the measures of Washington's administration were attacked with virulence in Greenleaf's paper. It was, in fact, the first Democratic organ in the country.

Thomas Greenleaf was born in Abington, Massachusetts, and learned to set type of Isaiah Thomas. He was the son of Joseph Greenleaf, who was a printer in Boston in 1774. The *Journal and Argus* were published by Greenleaf in New York till 1798, when he died of yellow fever, at the age of forty-two. He was a good printer, enterprising, and of an amiable character. He was elected one of the sachems of the Tammany Society in 1789. He had been an editor on the *Independent Chronicle*, of Boston, prior to 1787. That paper, on the 24th of September, 1798, in noticing his death, said:

> He was a steady, uniform, zealous supporter of the Rights of Humanity; a warm friend to civil and religious liberty, unawed by persecution or prosecution, both of which it has, not unfrequently, been his lot to experience. He loved his country; and if, at any time, as Editor of this paper, he dipped his pen in gall, and exercised it with unusual severity, it was occasioned by that strong abhorrence he felt against political apostacy, and the fervor of his wishes to preserve the Constitution from encroachment.

Mrs. Greenleaf, his widow, published both the daily and semi-weekly papers for some time, but finally disposed of the establishment to James Cheetham, an Englishman, who altered the titles of both papers; the daily to the *American Citizen*, and the semi-weekly to the *American Watchman*.

These papers flourished from 1801 to 1810. They were edited with marked ability by Cheetham, who acted with that portion of the Democratic party of which George Clinton, De Witt Clinton, and Judge Spencer were leaders, in opposition to Aaron Burr. Violent quarrels took place between the Van Nesses, Swartwouts, Matthew L. Davis, and other friends of Colonel Burr on one side, and Cheetham, Richard Riker, afterward Recorder of New York, De Witt Clinton, and Judge Spencer on the other. Several duels took place. On one occasion, Matthew L. Davis sallied forth in Wall Street with pistol in hand, expecting to be constrained to shoot Cheetham at sight. The latter, however, kept out of the way of Davis, and the affair ended without bloodshed. In 1805 Colonel Burr instituted a suit against Cheetham for libel, growing out of the

Presidential election in the House of Representatives in 1801, which created considerable excitement. There were some able writers for Cheetham's paper, and he always stood high with his section of the Democratic party as a ready writer and skillful tactician. He wrote a life of Thomas Paine, which was distasteful to Paine's followers. In opposing the embargo the *Citizen* declined, and ceased to be the organ of the Republican or Democratic Party the year previous to Cheetham's death.

Cheetham was not a professional printer, but he was an able editor, and acquired great distinction as a writer. Occasionally the vigor and pungency of his style caused his productions to be compared with the letters of Junius, which were long considered a model for political writers here as well as in England. But Junius was not alone his model. Dr. Francis, who was with him when he died, thus described his death-bed scene:

> He had removed with his family to a country residence, some three miles from the city, in the summer of 1809.—Within a few days after he exposed himself to malaria, by walking uncovered by his hat, through the fields, under a burning September sun. He was struck with a complication of ills: fever, congestion of the brain, and great cerebral distress. The malignancy of his case soon foretold to his physician the impossibility of his recovery. Being at that time a student of medicine, I was requested to watch him; on the second day of his malady, his fever raging higher, he betrayed a disturbed intellect. On the night of the third day, raving mania set in. Incoherently he called his family around him: addressed his sons as to their peculiar avocations for life: giving advice to one ever to be temperate in all things: upon another urging the importance of knowledge. After midnight he became much worse, and ungovernable. With herculean strength he now raised himself from his pillow: with eyes of meteoric fierceness, he grasped his bed covering, and in a most vehement but rapid articulation, exclaimed to his sons, "Boys, study Bolingbroke for style, and Locke for sentiment." He spoke no more. In a moment life had departed.

The personal appearance of Cheetham was remarkable: tall and athletic. None of his political difficulties ever made him a principal in an actual duel, but in 1804 he challenged William Coleman, of the *Evening Post*. Mutual friends interfered, preventing a meeting, which, however, resulted in a duel, in which Cheetham was a second. This remarkable affair of honor we shall fully describe in our sketch of the *Post*. Mrs. Cheetham died about the same time that her husband departed this life. We believe that his orphan daughter, a very beautiful girl, was sent to Norwich, Connecticut, for education, after the death of her parents.

The *New York Packet*, published by Samuel Loudon, returned to New York with the others. Shortly after its publication was changed from a weekly to a daily, and was continued for several years. It was called, as late as 1793, the *Diary, or Loudon's Register*. In the number of February 12 of that year it contained the following dramatic advertisement:

THEATRE.

By the OLD AMERICAN COMPANY
THIS EVENING, the 12th of February,
A COMEDY,
CALLED, THE
ROAD TO RUIN.
To which will be added,
A COMIC OPERA,
called, the
ROMP;
Or, A Cure for the SPLEEN.

PLACES in the BOXES may be had of Mr. *Faulkner*, at the Box Office from *Ten* to *Twelve* A. M. and on the Days of Performance from *t hre* to *five*, P. M. where alfo Tickets may be had, and at Mr. Gaine's book-ftore at the Bible in Hanover-Square.

☞ The Doors will be opened at a quarter of an hour after Five, and the Curtain drawn up precifely at a quarter of an hour after Six o'clock.
BOX 8s. PIT 6s. GALLERY 4s.
VIVAT RESPUBLICA.

On the 12th of February, 1869, there were four columns of advertisements of theatres and other places of public amusement in the *New York Herald*, and there were twenty-three theatres open nightly in that city. One religiously inclined would say that the Road to Ruin was an open thoroughfare in 1869 in that metropolis.

The *Packet* was the political opponent of the *Journal*, and strongly advocated the Federal side, and the adoption of the Constitution. Loudon was an elder in the Scotch Seceders' Church in New York. He lived to an advanced age. Several years previous to his death he had retired from business.

The most influential and enterprising paper in Massachusetts after the Revolution was the *Massachusetts Centinel and the Republican Journal*, started as a semi-weekly by Warden and Russell in 1784, and managed for forty-two years by Major Benjamin Russell, who was the master-spirit of the establishment. Its first number was issued on the 24th of March. It was, after the war, what the *Spy* and *Gazette* were before the war—the popular guide in Massachusetts. Major Russell learned the art of printing in the office of Isaiah Thomas, and served six months in the Continental Army as a substitute for Thomas. He was one of the guard at the execution of André. The *Centinel* was immediately recognized as a good newspaper, and its proprietors endeavored to keep up with the progress of the times. It was established at an important period in the world's history: when Europe was being remapped and reorganized by revolutions and Napoleon's victories, and this country moulded into a great republic.

Major Russell, with the true instinct of a journalist, made politics and the interests of the merchant and mechanic the standard matter of his paper. But he did not lose sight of literature. Nearly all of Goldsmith's poems, the narrative of Cook's voyages, Cunningham's Pastorals, and portions of Cowper, Gray, and other British poets, were published by him. Original poetry also found a place in his columns. The *Centinel* was in favor of protection to all domestic manufactures. The British factors and agents made great efforts to establish themselves in the United States. Having lost the country, they endeavored to save the trade. Several public meetings were held in Boston to deliberate on the subject. One, of merchants and mechanics, was held in Faneuil Hall in 1785, when it was voted, as many opposed to the extravagance of our day and the course of England during the late rebellion, would have voted in 1863-4,

> That we do pledge our honor, that we will not directly or indirectly, purchase any goods of, or have any commercial connections whatever, with, such British merchants, agents, or factors, as are now residing among us, or may hereafter arrive; and that we will not let, or sell, any warehouse, shop, house, or any other place, for the sale of such goods, nor will we employ any persons, who will assist said merchants, factors, or agents, by trucks, carts, barrows, or labor, (except in the reshipment of their merchandize) but will *discountenance* all such persons, who shall in any way advise, or in the least degree help or support such merchants, factors, or agents, in the prosecution of their business; *as we conceive all such British importations are calculated to drain us of our currency, and have a direct tendency to impoverish this country.*

These meetings and these appeals had very little more effect then than they would now have. Fashion was more potent.

The *Centinel* also opposed the return of the refugees. Other papers favored their restoration to political and property rights, because other states, more liberal than Massachusetts, would allow their return, and reap the advantages of their property and industry. Some of the newspaper paragraphs on this subject, which we have lately seen in regard to the Southern rebels, remind one of those published eighty-five years ago. The *Centinel*, in August, 1784, said:

> However the principles of common benevolence, and the desire of curing the calamities of our fellow citizens, might operate in favor of an act of amnesty and naturalization to the ill-fated body of men, the refugees; yet the antipathies nurtured during the war have taken so deep a root, as will, we are apprehensive, be very difficult to remove.

In our sketch of the *Gazette*, the course of the venerable Edes in regard to the threats against the editor of the *Centinel* is noticed. In the latter paper of January 19th, 1785, the assault, then anticipated, was made on Major Russell, which is thus *naïvely* paragraphed:

A few days since we were requested to publish a small performance on the institution of the Sans Souci. After carefully perusing it, and perceiving it to be only intended to display the dangerous tendency of that society, not the vehicle of personal abuse, (as has been too common) we determined to publish it and advertised our intentions of so doing. This roused the passions of those who conceived themselves deserving the lash of satire, and urged them to endeavor to suppress it in embryo. A variety of injuries was threatened us, if we persisted in our determination of publishing it. In the afternoon of Saturday we were waited upon by Mr. Samuel Jarvis, who desired to speak with one of us in another apartment; being attended thither, he demanded to know whether or not we intended publishing 'A Farce,' and being answered in the affirmative, exclaimed, "By God, I'll kill you if you do," and endeavored to put his threat into execution, *but found his efforts inadequate to the task.*

In the political contests of those days the newspapers were frequently more violent in coarse invective and ribaldry than even in our modern political campaigns. With an exception here and there, an improvement in this respect, as well as in many others, affecting the character and dignity of the Press of America, has certainly taken place. When the local Stamp Act of 1785 was passed, the *Centinel* was quite tame on the subject. Major Russell thought the tax on newspapers injudicious, but was really in favor of the tax on advertisements!

Shay's rebellion was denounced, but the great feature of the *Centinel* was its course in favor of the acceptance of the Federal Constitution by the people. From the adoption of this instrument in National Convention till its adoption in State Conventions, the *Centinel* kept up a constant fire in its favor. One is reminded, in reading its paragraphs and illustrations, of the energy and persistency of the *New York Herald* in carrying through an important measure in after years. Meetings of mechanics, a series of them indeed, were held in Boston by the influence of Major Russell, to represent their sentiments to the State Convention, then in session, and the petition from this class which was submitted on that occasion turned the scale, said John Hancock, in favor of the Constitution. The *Centinel* announced with great enthusiasm, as the news came in, the fact of the ratification of the Constitution by the several states. According to Russell, little Delaware was the first, and he based large hopes on the result in this small state. He said:

The State of Delaware being the first to adopt, ratify, and confirm the American Constitution, argues well. It is a good maxim, which inculcates the practice of '*entering at the little end of the horn ;*'—as, at every step we take, our circle is increased, and our basis progressively growing broader and broader.

Delaware was the eighth state; New Jersey was the first.

The Massachusetts Convention met in an old church, on the spot where William Ellery Channing afterward preached, in Federal Street. Its proceedings were reported by Russell. He thus describes his own labors and a scene in the Convention:

I had never studied stenography, nor was there any person then in Boston that understood reporting. The presiding officer of the Convention sat in the Deacon's seat, under the pulpit. I took the pulpit for my reporting desk, and a very good one it was. I succeeded well enough in this my first effort to give a tolerably fair report in my next paper; but the puritanical notions had not entirely faded away, and I was voted out of the pulpit. A stand was fitted up for me in another place, and I proceeded with my reports, generally to the acceptance of the Convention. The doubts that still existed as to whether enough of the states would come into the compact as to make the constitution binding, made the proceedings of the Convention intensely interesting. When the news arrived of the acceptance of it by the State of Virginia, there was a most extraordinary outbreak of rejoicing. It seemed as if the meeting-house would burst with the acclamation.

On the adoption of the Constitution there were celebrations every where. When it was evident that a sufficient number of states had voted in its favor, New York had a grand pageant. This was on the 23d of July, 1788. There was, of course, a procession. All the trades turned out in costume. Among the others, numerously represented, were the printers, bookbinders, stationers, and all those connected with the Press. They marched in this order, with the other trades and professions:

THE PRESS SECTION.
MARSHALS.
Hugh Gaine of the *Gazette*.
Samuel Loudon of the *Register*,
on horseback.

The standard was alternately supported by Messrs. Bryce, Carroll, Harrison and Purdy.

A handsome stage, drawn by four horses.

Upon the stage, the federal printing-press complete; cases, and other typographical implements, with pressmen and compositors at work. During the procession, many hundred copies of a song and an ode, adapted to the occasion, were struck off, and distributed, by Messrs. A. M'Lean and J. Russel, among the multitude. A small flag on the top of the press, on which was inscribed the word "Publius," in gold letters. Mr. John Loudon, representing a herald, mounted on the back of the press, dressed in a flowing robe, and a cap, on which were written the words, "The Liberty of the Press;" with a brazen trumpet in the right hand, proclaiming, "The epocha of Liberty and Justice," pending from the mouth of the trumpet. In the left hand, a parchment scroll, representing the new constitution.

The master Printers, Booksellers and Bookbinders, with their journeymen and apprentices, four abreast, following the stage.

Description of the Standard.
Fame, blowing her trumpet, and supporting the medallion of his excellency Doctor Franklin; Liberty attending, holding her cap over his head; the electric fluid darting from below; on the upper corner, the union flag, and Stationers' arms; and below, the Bible and federal constitution, representing the religious and civil constitution of our country.

Mottos,

1st. "*Ars artium omnium conservatrix.*"

2d. "May the liberty of the Press be inviolably preserved, as the palladium of the constitution, and the centinel of freedom."

Surrounding the medallion of his excellency Doctor Franklin, the following words:

"Where liberty dwells, there is my country."

With the adoption of the Constitution the Federal Party considered itself fully organized, and prepared to sit *en permanence* over the destinies of the nation. On the inauguration of Washington and Adams, the Boston *Centinel* formally announced the death of the Anti-Federalists after the following manner :

> Notwithstanding the medical exertions of a *celebrated Physician*—the prescriptions of three *gubernatorial* Esculapians—and the endeavors of the whole fraternity of *State Quacks* and *Mountebanks* to prolong its existence—in convulsions the most violent—in contortions and wreathings the most painful, on *Wednesday* last, finished its wicked career,
>
> The Genius of Antifederalism.
>
> It was born in August, 1787—was aged 17 months. Though thus cut off in its childhood, it still lived to do much mischief; and to have grown so detestable, that even its friends—its foster-parents, shewed the utmost resentment whenever called by its name : It has, however expired, a striking instance of the truth of the adage,—"*The wicked shall not live half their days.*"
>
> On WEDNESDAY, MARCH 4th, the funeral obsequies will be consummated—when a GRAND PROCESSION will be formed.
>
> ---
>
> ORDER OF THE PROCESSION.
> The DEMON of REBELLION,
> drawn in a flaming Car, by <i>Ignorance, Knavery,</i> and <i>Idleness.</i>
> DANIEL SH-YS, and JOHN FR-NKLIN,
> armed with <i>levelers</i> in their right, and halters in their left hands.
> DAY, SHATTUCK, &c. &c. their followers, two and two, each with
> <i>caps</i> and <i>bells.</i>
> Several "<i>great men</i>" their abettors, in <i>disguise.</i>
> CHIEF PHYSICIAN—
>
> | Supporters, | | Supporters, |
> |---|---|---|
> | Injustice, | The | Knavery, |
> | Abuse, | BODY. | Defamation, |
> | Prevarication, | | Falsehood. |
>
> His SATANIC MAJESTY—Chief Mourner.
> His standard—motto—"<i>The prop of my
> Empire is fallen.</i>"
> A KNOW-YE Rhode-Islander—and a <i>pine-barren</i> Carolinian, in sackcloth, with brazen helmets—crest "<i>A Highwayman robbing by law,</i>" motto—"'Tis power which <i>sanctifies</i> a crime."
> A cart drawn by <i>Fraud</i>—with Paper-Money, Tender-Laws, &c. the sides painted, "<i>Be it enacted,</i>" &c.
> The GODDESS of DISCORD—in weepers.
> —In her right hand a torch expiring—in her left a bloody sword broken.
> BENEDICT ARNOLD, SILAS DEANE, &c. with swords embossed, "<i>In '75 we were right.</i>"
> A standard, motto, "<i>Birds of a feather flock together.</i>"
> Hon. PATRICK H-NRY, of Virginia,
> Bearing a scroll, with the words, "<i>In the creation of</i> TWO <i>Confederacies are all my hopes of greatness.</i>"
> His Excel. G. CL-NT-N, Esq.
> In both hands a Purse, tied up. The words thereon, "<i>If New-York loses the Impost, I lose thee.</i>"
> The GENIUS of IMBECILITY,
>
> In a car—painted on both sides with hieroglyphicks. "*A ship rotting in the harbor.—An English Crow picking the Eagle's eyes out—the Eagle asleep ; his talons cut—an American fort, with English colors—a rusty sword—a broken ploughshare—starving mechanics—broken merchants, &c.*"

<blockquote>
200 Wrongheads, two and two
"*While we're in, let's keep in.*"
A WOLF, covered with the golden fleece of a LAMB, marked 4000l. per ann.
The Geniuses of the Philad. Gazetteer—New-York Journal—Boston Gazette, &c. in their original *blackness;*
"*The days of our years are evil and few.*"
A cart, with antifederal Pamphlets, Essays, Protests, &c. in reams, marked "*waste-paper.*"
GALEN and the Junto—two and two.
The GODDESS of POVERTY—in tatters—
"*Follow me, my sons,*" she cries,
"*We do,*" each scribbler replies.
A dray with stumps of pens, broken inkstands, &c.
Antifederal Scribblers, in dishabille, two and two, chaunting the following lines:—*Who will close the Procession.*
</blockquote>

There was a singular prediction of the recent rebellion in the Virginia scroll borne by Patrick Henry in this imaginary procession.

On the 16th of June, 1790, the name of the paper was changed to *Columbian Centinel*. Very few of the journals of the last century continued long under one title. Some of the newspapers had as many *aliases* as an English nobleman. Major Russell and Isaiah Thomas were ever inventing some new title or some new device for their figure-heads. In the progress of the republic, and in the progress of journalism, the broader views of Russell suggested the more comprehensive name of *Columbian Centinel*, and so it was thereafter called. It became more national in its character. It was strongly in favor of Washington, Adams, and Hamilton. It was full of Federalism and patriotism. On one occasion Russell printed all the public laws gratuitously. When called upon for his bill, he sent it to the State Department receipted. "This must not be," said Washington on learning the fact. "When Mr. Russell offered to publish the laws without pay, we were poor. It was a generous offer. We are now able to pay our debts. This is a debt of honor, and must be discharged." Shortly after, a check for seven thousand dollars was sent to Major Russell.

The "war of editors," which began in England in 1645, and in America in 1719, continued at this period of our history. Wherever and whenever two newspapers come in competition in politics, circulation, or advertisements, there is a fight. Such was the case with the *Centinel* and *Chronicle* in 1790–3, and such is the case with the *Times*, and *Tribune*, and *World*, and *Sun* now. There was a disgraceful scene in Faneuil Hall and on 'Change in 1793 between Major Russell and Benjamin Austin, Jr., of the *Chronicle*. Austin publicly, in Faneuil Hall, called his opponent "such a fellow as Ben Russell." Shortly after, Russell met Austin on 'Change, and spat in his face. There was an action for damages, and the jury awarded Austin twenty shillings.

The Citizen-king of France in 1830, Louis Philippe, was an exile in Boston, teaching school there, in 1793–4. Talleyrand was also in that city at that time. They often visited the office of the *Centinel*, especially on the arrival of news from Europe. In return for the privilege of looking over the *Moniteur*, Louis Philippe presented an Atlas to Russell, then a rare book in the colonies, and it was by the aid of the maps thus obtained that he was enabled to make his compilations of the movements of the armies on the Continent of Europe so clear and comprehensive that the reader could easily trace the operations of Napoleon and his opponents in all the great battles of the Empire. In this way the *Centinel* acquired a high reputation throughout the country.

In the Presidential contest of 1796, the *Centinel*, true to its party, although Federalism began to show evident signs of weakness, advocated the claim of John Adams. The aggressions of the French on our commerce were the irritating and exciting topics. Adams was elected. But the Democratic Party began its real existence in that contest, and secured the office of Vice-president for Jefferson. It was at the instigation of Russell that the Federalists of Massachusetts wore the black cockade. In the *Centinel* of July 4, 1798, it was strongly recommended :

> It has been repeatedly recommended, that our citizens wear in their hats on the day of Independence, the American Cockade, (which is a *Rose*, composed of black ribbon, with a white button, or fastening) and that the Ladies should add to the attraction of their dress (the Ladies' cockade should be a *white rose*,) this symbol of their attachment to the government, which cherishes and protects them—either on their breasts or in their bonnets. The measure is innocent ; but the effect will be highly important. It will add cement to the *Union*, which so generally and so happily exists. Every cockade will be another edition of the *Declaration of Independence*, and the demonstration of it, by this national emblem now, will be as highly laudable as the display of the immortal instrument of 1776 was then : Those who signed the Address to the President are pledged to display this evidence of it to the world—and they may be assured, that the influence of their example in this measure will be productive of as great good, as the influence of their names was on the paper. All those, who have not had opportunity to sign the address, and who feel themselves Independent Americans, cannot hesitate to show by some outward mark, that they love their country better than any other in the world ; this mark ought to be the black cockade. The Ladies, we understand, are universally in favor of the measure ; and if they lead, who will not follow ?

This suggestion arose from the order of Adet, which had previously appeared in the Philadelphia *Aurora*, for all Frenchmen in the United States to wear the tri-colored cockade. In the heat of political excitement many Americans wore the same emblem. After the appearance of the above, the *Centinel* said :

> The Jacobins have the impudence to say, that the people of Boston were really divided, and they give as a proof, that not more than half of them wear the American Cockade. This being the case, let every Bostonian, attached to the constitution and government of the United States, immediately mount the COCKADE,

and swear that he will not relinquish it, until the infamous projects of the external and internal enemies of our country shall be destroyed.

Again Russell came to the rescue of the black cockade:

> The Cockade is generally worn by every class of citizens in almost every town in the United States. It is considered as a token of patriotism and union. It will enliven our commencement at Cambridge this day. It will receive the smiles and approbation of the Fair Daughters of Columbia; and will convince the Gallic spies, now in our country, that we are not a divided people.

It appears that William Cobbett, although in the interests of the Federalists, had hit Russell several times in the columns of the *Porcupine*, then published in Philadelphia. In reply, the *Centinel* said:

> * * * * * COBBETT was never encouraged and supported by the Federalists as a solid, judicious writer in their cause; but was kept merely to hunt Jacobinic *foxes*, *skunks*, and *serpents*. The Federalists found the Jacobins had the *Aurora*, *Argus*, and *Chronicle*, through which they ejected their mud, filth, and venom, and attacked and blackened the best characters the world ever boasted; and they perceived that these vermin were not to be operated on by reason or decency. It was therefore thought *necessary* that the opposite party should keep, and *feed* a *suitable beast* to hunt down these *skunks* and *foxes*; and "*the fretful Porcupine*" was selected for this business. This imported, or transported beast has been kept as gentlemen keep a fierce *bull Dog*, to guard his house and property against thieves, Jacobins and Frenchmen, and as such he has been a good and faithful dog, and has been *fed* and caressed accordingly. * * * * *

In the next great political contest, which resulted in the overthrow of the Federal party and the election of Thomas Jefferson, the *Centinel*, and many of the Federalists of Massachusetts, declared in favor of Aaron Burr. On the 4th of March, 1801, Major Russell published an epitaph for the tombstone of his party under the head of

Monumental Inscription.

"*That life is long which answers Life's great end.*"

YESTERDAY EXPIRED,
Deeply regretted by MILLIONS of grateful Americans,
And by *all* GOOD MEN,
The FEDERAL ADMINISTRATION
Of the
GOVERNMENT of the *United States*;
Animated by
A WASHINGTON, an ADAMS;—a HAMILTON, KNOX,
PICKERING, WOLCOTT, M'HENRY, MARSHALL,
STODDERT and DEXTER.
Æt. 12 years.

Its death was occasioned by the
Secret Arts and Open Violence,
Of Foreign and Domestic Demagogues:
Notwithstanding its whole Life
Was devoted to the Performance of every Duty
to promote
The UNION, CREDIT, PEACE, PROSPERITY,
HONOR, and
FELICITY OF ITS COUNTRY.

The remainder of the inscription is very long, and gives an elaborate epitome of the political history of the United States for the previous twelve years, showing how much good the Federalists accomplished for the country. It ends by saying

> The "Sun of Federalism is set for ever."
> "*Oh shame, where is thy blush?*"

The *Centinel* opposed all the measures of Jefferson and Madison, and strongly denounced the war with England. With Russell originated, during Madison's administration, that famous political term "Gerrymandering." The incident is thus related by Buckingham:

<blockquote>
In 1811, when Mr. Gerry was governor of the commonwealth, the Legislature made a new division of the districts for the election of representatives to Congress. Both branches had then a democratic majority. For the purpose of securing a democratic representative, an absurd and singular arrangement of towns in the county of Essex was made to compose a district. Russell took a map of the county, and designated by a particular coloring the towns thus selected. He then hung the map on the wall of his editorial closet. One day, Gilbert Stuart, the celebrated painter, looked at the map, and said the towns, which Russell had thus distinguished, formed a picture resembling some monstrous animal. He took a pencil, and, with a few touches, added what might be supposed to represent claws. "There," said Stuart, "that will do for a salamander." Russell, who was busy with his pen, looked up at the hideous figure, and exclaimed, "Salamander! call it Gerrymander." The word became a proverb, and, for many years, was in popular use among the Federalists as a term of reproach to the democratic Legislature, which had distinguished itself by this act of political turpitude. An engraving of the "Gerrymander" was made, and hawked about the State, which had some effect in annoying the democratic party.
</blockquote>

De Witt Clinton was the Federal candidate, in opposition to Madison, for the presidency in 1812. The *Centinel* gave him a very weak support. On the election of Monroe in 1816–17, the "era of good feelings," a phrase which also originated with Russell, commenced, and the Federalists were no longer known as a party. The *Centinel* began then to lose its hold upon the public. It had changed its name by adding "American Federalist" to the principal title. It advocated the election of John Quincy Adams in 1824, and his re-election in 1828. With the incoming of the Democratic Party again under the lead of Andrew Jackson, the influence of the *Centinel* became still less potential. In November, 1828, Russell sold the establishment to Adams and Hudson, and, with a farewell banquet given him at the Exchange Coffee-house by the editors and printers of Boston, he retired to private life.

In 1830 the *New England Palladium*, and in 1836 the *Boston Gazette*, were merged with the *Centinel*. In 1840 the *Centinel* disappeared in the embrace of the *Boston Daily Advertiser*.

That Methuselah of newspapers, the *New Hampshire Gazette*, started in the last, lives through this, and runs through all our epochs. After the death of Daniel Fowle the establishment passed into the hands of two of his apprentices, John Melcher and George Jerry Osborne, in 1785. Shortly after Osborne retired, and Melcher carried it on till February 9, 1802, when he sold the establishment to Nathaniel S. and Washington Pierce. The Pierces began to print the *Gazette* February 9, 1802, when they changed its politics from Federal to Republican, or Democratic, as it would now be called. They, in connection with Benjamin Hill and Samuel Gardner, published it till May 21, 1805, when they sold it to William Weeks. Up to this time little or no editorial writing had appeared in the paper, except a little political matter at certain seasons. The scissors did most of the work. The news and selected matter were all that was expected. Mr. Weeks wrote more than his predecessors, and remained editor more than four years of a stormy period, and until December 14, 1813, when he was succeeded by Beck and Foster. This firm continued the publication till it was dissolved by the death of David C. Foster, which occurred in 1823. From that time to 1834 Gideon Beck was the publisher. He then admitted Albert Greenleaf as a partner, and published it with him till July 14, 1835, when Mr. Beck finally left the business.

In conducting their paper and managing their business, Beck and Foster were industrious and successful. Both of them were members of the Legislature of the state, and the decease of Mr. Foster was felt to be a public loss. On the 14th of July, 1835, the imprint bore the names of Thomas B. Laighton and Abner Greenleaf, Jr.; from 1836 to 1841 the name of A. Greenleaf, Jr. On the 15th of June, 1841, it was changed to Virgin and Moses, who published it to 1843, when Virgin left, and S. W. Moses appears as publisher. In 1844 Abner Greenleaf is named as editor; then A. Greenleaf and Son, editors. The year closed without any imprint whatever, and the paper was published without any during the year 1845–6. Abner Greenleaf died in September, 1869, aged eighty-three. In 1847 the *N. H. Gazette and Republican Union* was published by William P. Hill, who began in March, and remained till August 13, 1850, when he was succeeded by Gideon Rundlett. The present publisher, Edward N. Fuller, commenced in March, 1852. Several of these numerous editors were men of talent and energy; but the sudden and frequent changes of conductors and printers have operated against the profit of the proprietors.

The *Connecticut Courant*, which became the property of Hudson and Goodwin in 1779, was printed by them till November 21, 1815, when George Goodwin and Sons appeared as printers. That interval of excitement and anxiety between the peace with Great Britain of 1783 and the practical operation of the new Constitution in 1789 is vividly outlined in the files of the *Courant*, and the beneficent influence of Washington's administrations clearly traced through its columns. It was a supporter of Washington and Adams. The paper remained in the hands of the Goodwin family until September 12, 1836. When the last Goodwin retired in that year he was eighty years of age, and had been in the establishment, as apprentice, journeyman, and owner, for seventy years! In 1836 the concern passed into the hands of John L. Boswell, and was published by him until January 1, 1850, when William Faxon was associated, and the paper appeared in the name of Boswell and Faxon until the 1st of January, 1855, when it passed into the hands of Thomas M. Day. It appeared in the sole name of Mr. Day until the 1st of January, 1857, when A. N. Clark was taken in, and the paper appeared in the names of Day and Clark. In 1865 the firm was again changed, and the paper published by A. N. Clark and Company.

CHAPTER XI.
THE NEWSPAPERS ON THE PENDING QUESTIONS.

THE RESTORATION OF THE TORIES TO CITIZENSHIP.—SOCIETY OF CINCINNATI.—THE ALIEN AND SEDITION LAWS.—PROSECUTIONS OF NEWSPAPERS.—LAW OF LIBEL IN MASSACHUSETTS.—THE COMMON LAW OF ENGLAND "THE BIRTHRIGHT OF EVERY AMERICAN.—ASSASSINATION OF CHARLES AUSTIN.—THE MASSACHUSETTS STAMP ACT.—TAX ON ADVERTISEMENTS.—AMERICAN TITLES.—THE RISE AND FALL OF NEWSPAPERS.—THE FIRST EXPRESS.—JUDGE STORY ON NEWSPAPER PERSONALITIES.

ON the conclusion of the Revolution the *Independent Chronicle* of Boston became the property of Adams and Nourse. This journal was the strong opponent of two measures which came up for the action and indorsement of the people. In the *Chronicle* of May 22d, 1783, the following article appeared, which, in view of recent events, is interesting. It was inspired by the efforts in the Massachusetts Legislature to restore the Tories, who had left the country, to their original rights. It is an illustration of the spirit of the times in New England after the war:

As Hannibal swore never to be at peace with the Romans, so let every Whig swear—by the abhorrence of Slavery—by liberty and religion—by the shades of those departed friends who have fallen in battle—by the ghosts of those of our brethren who have been destroyed on board of prison-ships and in loathsome dungeons—by the names of a Hayne and other virtuous citizens whose lives have been wantonly destroyed—by every thing that a freeman holds dear,—never to be at peace with those fiends the Refugees, whose thefts, murders, and treasons have filled the cup of wo; but show the world that we prefer war, with all its direful calamities, to giving those fell destroyers of the human species a residence among us. We have crimsoned the earth with our blood to purchase peace,—therefore are determined to enjoy harmony, uninterrupted with the contaminating breath of a Tory.

The Society of Cincinnati, which was then being formed, was bitterly denounced. While the armies of the North, engaged in the late rebellion, are repeating, but on a grander scale, the action of the soldiers of the Revolution in 1783, the fears of the *Chronicle* in 1784, which represented a large class, will be noticed with interest and curiosity:

The institution of Cincinnati is concerted to establish a complete and perpetual *personal* distinction between the numerous military dignitaries of their corporation and the whole remaining body of the people, who will be styled Plebeians through the community. * * * * * * If the Order of Cincinnati should appear to be fraught with danger to the exalted rights of human nature, tending rapidly to the introduction of an American nobility, as has been publicly affirmed, and not gainsaid,—such a military nobility, as plagued and domineered over Europe for centuries,—or if it tends to introduce even the mildest nobility, since nobility itself is reprobated by these confederated republican states, is it not the duty of legislators, governors, and magistrates, *and their* ELECTORS, by all judicious and proper means in their power, to prevent such an institution from acquiring any degree of strength or influence in this free commonwealth?

Cambridge, by a formal vote at a town meeting in 1784, indorsed these remarks of the *Chronicle* by instructing their representative in General Court to use his endeavors to have the Society of Cincinnati suppressed. Those few venerable gentlemen, with Hamilton Fish at their head, who meet once a year in the City of New York, on each fourth of July, to elect officers of the Society of Cincinnati, will wipe their glasses and read the above paragraph with a sigh for the ribbons and orders of this much-feared "American Nobility." Where are the ribbons of the Veterans of 1812, a handful of men, poor enough in pocket, who yearly parade the streets of New York? Are they the tape that tie up their annual petitions to the Legislature for relief?

The *Chronicle* and the country bravely survived these two measures. After 1783, and in the interval to 1789, the people were in a state of transmutation, and shaping themselves and their views for the political divisions subsequent to that period. The *Chronicle* was an organ of the Republican Party, fiery against England, and strongly in favor of France. In 1793 the paper was issued twice a week.

The Alien and Sedition laws of 1798 created a prodigious excitement throughout the states. The Sedition Law, restricting the liberty of press and of speech especially, aroused the opposition party, and caused great indignation in all newspaper offices. There were about two hundred papers published in the country at that time. It was calculated that of these twenty or twenty-five were not only opposed to the leading measures of the administration of John Adams, but were edited and controlled by aliens. These laws affected them. It was asserted that Jefferson and Madison, but especially the former, sustained these writers. In Virginia and Kentucky the Legislatures declared these laws to be gross infractions of the Constitution, and appealed to the other states to unite in opposition to them.

The *Chronicle* powerfully opposed these obnoxious laws, and was prosecuted under the provisions of the Sedition Act, in the Federal Circuit Court. When the resolutions of the Legislature of Virginia, denying the constitutionality of these laws, were adopted, they were transmitted to Massachusetts as to other states. The Legislature of Massachusetts, in reply, affirmed the constitutionality of the acts and disapproved of the Virginia resolutions. On this point the irrepressible conflict arose between the North and South which culminated with the surrender of Lee under the apple-tree at Appomattox

Court House in 1865. In noticing these proceedings in Massachusetts and Virginia, the *Chronicle*, on the 18th of February, 1799, said:

<blockquote>

HISTORICAL FACTS.

A correspondent observes, that, on the last Wednesday in May, 1798, the Commonwealth of Massachusetts was a "*free, sovereign, and independent State*, in all matters not specially committed to the Continental Government;" and, in proof of it, appeals to the affidavits of about two hundred respectable witnesses, who made oath to the fact, as well as to the opinion that the Commonwealth "ought to be" so, in order to the admission of the witnesses to a seat in the Legislature of the Commonwealth.

A question being started by the Legislature of Virginia, whether the sovereignty of the individual states was not invaded by certain acts of Congress, which the state of Virginia deems unconstitutional; a majority of the same witnesses, quoted in the preceding paragraph, disclaim for themselves, as members of the Legislature of Massachusetts, and deny to all other States in the Union, *any right to decide on the constitutionality of any acts of Congress.*

As it is difficult for common capacities to conceive of a *sovereignty* so situated *that the sovereign shall have no right to decide on any invasion of his constitutional powers*, it is hoped, for the convenience of those tender consciences, who may hereafter be called upon to swear allegiance to the State, that some gentleman, skilled in Federal logic, will show how the oath of allegiance is to be understood, that every man may be so guarded and informed, as not to invite the Deity to witness a falsehood.

</blockquote>

Another paragraph complimentary to a member of the Legislature for favoring the Virginia resolutions appeared on the same day. These articles were considered as libels on the Legislature of Massachusetts, and Abijah Adams, the book-keeper of the *Chronicle* office—Thomas Adams, the editor, being confined to a bed of sickness—was indicted on the plea that he sold the papers, and therefore published the libel. James Sullivan, for the Commonwealth, upheld the doctrine of libels according to the common law of England. Whitman and Blake, for the defendant, asserted that the common law was inconsistent with the Constitution of Massachusetts, and hostile to the nature and genius of the government. Judge Dana, in charging the jury, declared that the common law of England was the birthright of every American. Adams was found guilty of "publishing only." The sentence was thirty days' imprisonment in the county jail, to pay the costs, and to give bonds for good behavior for one year. The *Chronicle* thus announced the event:

<blockquote>
☞ The Patrons of the *Chronicle* may still depend on the regular supply of their papers. The Editor is on the bed of languishment, and the Book-keeper in prison, yet the CAUSE OF LIBERTY will be supported amid these distressing circumstances.
</blockquote>

While in prison, Adams, like M'Dougall in New York, was visited by many of the chief citizens, among whom was the venerable patriot Samuel Adams. The *Chronicle* of April 25, 1799, thus mentions the expiration of the sentence:

<blockquote>
Yesterday, Mr. Abijah Adams was discharged from his imprisonment, after partaking of an *adequate proportion* of his "birthright" by a confinement of thirty days under the operation of the Common Law of England.
</blockquote>

On the 1st of May the *Chronicle* was purchased by James White, and Ebenezer Rhoades was selected as editor and printer. It was Mr. White's purpose to make the paper an impartial organ of public opinion, and, to a certain extent, he succeeded. On the 1st of May, 1800, the paper became the property of Rhoades and the book-keeper Adams, who had been imprisoned for the libel on the Legislature. The new proprietors, on assuming control, proclaimed these sentiments:

> Every departure from truth is pernicious. Impartiality should be a perpetual attribute of the press. Neither *fear* on the one side, nor the *hope of reward* on the other, should intimidate or influence its inquiries. It should neither be bribed to lavish unmerited applause, nor menaced into silence. The usefulness of periodical publications depends upon their steady adherence to rectitude. The moment corrupt or foreign considerations are suffered to bias or stain their pages, they become injurious to the general interests of society.

The *Chronicle*, under these new managers, still kept up the vigor of its comments. It again got into trouble. E. W. Thomas, in his reminiscences, gives the following particulars of this affair:

> In August or September, I wrote "*Sidney*," addressed to President Adams, and sent it to the post-office in Boston, directed to the *Independent Chronicle*, published by Adams and Rhodes, who never knew who was the author. Two days after, I rode into Boston and found that Sidney was published, and made quite a stir "upon *change ;*" and I was not a little flattered to learn that it was attributed to the celebrated Doctor Charles Jarvis, who declared to me he was not the author, nor did he know who was. All of this I could readily believe, as there was but one person, besides myself, in the secret. Mr. Russell came out in the *Centinel* very severe upon the Doctor; and that there should be no mistake as to whom he took for the author, he said, "*The calomel and jalap of the law would soon be administered to him.*" This satisfied me that they had no suspicion of my being the author. The Sedition Law was then in the full tide of successful experiment, and I had no particular desire to come within the reach of its tender mercies, which Matthew Lyon and others were then in the full enjoyment of. Adams and Rhodes were prosecuted for the publication, and Mr. Adams died while the prosecution was pending. My friend to whom I had confided the authorship could not keep a secret, but must tell it to Doctor Ames, and it became known to some few others. The court met soon after, and the judge gave it in charge to the grand jury; and so far as he had been able to get information on the subject, recommended me to their particular attention; but it was too late; the bird had flown; I was then at Newport, on my way to Charleston.

About this time a tragical incident occurred in connection with the *Chronicle*, which produced a painful sensation in New England. After the Revolution, the well-known Benjamin Austin became one of the volunteer contributors of the *Chronicle*. In spite of his other business pursuits as a manufacturer of cordage, he continued to write for the Press. This labor he performed for the mere love of the excitement it gave him, and for the good he accomplished with his pen. In 1798 he defended the policy of John Adams in regard to a war with France. One of his signatures was Honestus. He was assailed by the opposition writers in violent terms. Some idea of the style of a few of the writers may be obtained from a contribution, abusive of Austin, which appeared in the *Mercury:*

> "HONESTUS"—A hungry, lean-faced fellow,
> A mere anatomy, a rope-maker,
> An envious, hollow-eyed, sharp-looking wretch;
> This living dead man, this incessant scribe,
> Forsooth, took on him as a chronicler,
> And, with no face, out-facing federal foes,
> Cries out, They are possessed.

In 1801 Thomas Jefferson appointed Austin as Commissioner of Loans. Other offices, such as selectman and representative, had been acceptably filled by him. Nothing could keep him out of the excitement of politics, and, in the midst of it, the sad event we have alluded to occurred. It had been arranged in 1806 that each party should celebrate the Fourth of July by a festival. The Republicans held theirs on Copp's Hill; the Federalists in Faneuil Hall. After the celebration it was reproachfully reported that the Republicans had not satisfactorily paid for their festival. In retaliation, the *Chronicle*, in stating that "a receipt in full" could be produced, intimated that the Federalists could not show a similar document. Other irritating paragraphs appeared. In this celebration Austin was the most active member of the Anti-Federal committee, and Thomas O. Selfridge of the Federal committee of arrangements. These gentlemen were, therefore, the most prominent in the affair. After a few more offensive paragraphs, warming up to fever heat, the following card appeared in the *Boston Gazette* of August 4, 1806:

AUSTIN POSTED.

BENJAMIN AUSTIN, Loan-Officer, having acknowledged that he has circulated an infamous falsehood concerning my professional conduct, in a certain case, and having refused to give the satisfaction due to a gentleman in similar cases:—I hereby publish said Austin as a COWARD, a LIAR, and a SCOUNDREL; and if the said Austin has the effrontery to deny any part of the charge, he shall be silenced by the most irrefragable proof.   THOMAS O. SELFRIDGE.

P. S. The various editors in the United States are requested to insert the above notice in their journals; and their bills shall be paid to their respective agents in this town.

The rejoinder appeared in a part of the edition of the *Chronicle* on the same morning:

Considering it derogatory to enter into a newspaper controversy with one *T. O. Selfridge*, in reply to his insolent and FALSE publication in the Gazette of this day; if any *gentleman* is desirous to know the facts on which his *impertinence* is founded, any information will be given by me on the subject.
Boston, Aug. 4.   BENJAMIN AUSTIN.

☞ Those who publish Selfridge's statement are requested to insert the above, and they shall be paid on presenting their bills.

The melancholy incident which followed the publication of these short and sharp cards is thus related by Buckingham:

About one o'clock of the day, on which these publications appeared, Charles, a son of Mr. Austin, and Mr. Selfridge met on the side-walk, on the south side of State-street, not far from the corner of Congress-street. No person was near enough to hear any words that might have passed between them. In less than a minute after they met, Selfridge was seen to draw a pistol from his pocket, and discharge it at Austin. Austin instantly struck Selfridge,—or at him,—with a small stick he had in his hand, and fell from the side-path on to the pavement, and, without speaking, expired,—the blood gushing from his mouth. The ball had entered his heart, just below the left pap, and passed through the body. This sad and agonizing event, the judicial proceedings, which followed, and the acquittal of the man, whom the jury of inquest charged with murder, had a deep and painful influence on the after life of Mr. Austin. The expressions of sympathy were many and sincere, even from political adversaries. Whatever provocation might have been given by the bitterness of political controversy, it is certain that none but the most implacably vindictive, could fail to be softened by a knowledge of the agony of this tremendous infliction, and by the suffering it carried into the midst of a family, which his domestic habits and attachments had made the centre of all his affections.

Charles Austin was in the nineteenth year of his age. He was a member of the Senior class of Harvard College. He acquired the rudiments of a collegiate education at Phillips Academy, in Andover, and had frequently received from the instructers in that institution, as well as those at Harvard, testimonials of approbation. The Faculty of the College had assigned to him one of the highest parts in the exercises of the Commencement, that was then soon to follow. His friends looked forward to that day, with pleasing anticipations of a performance, that would justify the estimate they had formed of his talents and principles. He died by the hand of violence, in the midst of his hopes. His funeral was attended by a long procession of citizens of Boston and the neighboring towns. The pall was supported, and the corpse preceded, by the Senior class of Harvard College, and followed, immediately after the relatives, by the President, Professors, and Tutors of that institution.

For many weeks succeeding this tragedy, the *Chronicle* poured out its anathemas on the Federalists, whom it charged with art, intrigue, and deception, and a desire to stifle all investigation of their measures, even by the use of the pistol. The "Reflections" of the editors, and the communications of correspondents, were not adapted to allay excitement. The federal papers of Boston maintained a general silence in relation to the subject; but numerous letters, written from Boston, and published in other places, tended to provoke a continuance of the animadversions of the *Chronicle*.

Among the numerous writers who contributed to the *Chronicle*, there were Thomas Greenleaf, afterward editor of the *New York Journal and Argus*, Perez Morton, afterward Attorney General of Massachusetts, and Dr. Charles Jarvis, an orator of distinction, and a leading member of the Massachusetts Legislature. Samuel Cooper, Thomas Adams, and Isaac Larkin were also moving spirits in the *Chronicle*.

Among the printers in the *Chronicle* office was the Hon. John Prentiss, now living in Keene, N. H., over ninety years of age, and still a writer for the Press; also George Hough, of the *Courier of New Hampshire*. Mr. Prentiss was an apprentice in 1792 in the *Chronicle* office, which was where the *Advertiser* building now stands. He was afterward editor of the *New Hampshire Sentinel* for nearly half a century, beginning, we believe, in 1807.

The *Chronicle*, true to its Democratic sentiments, zealously advocated and supported the war with England in 1812–15. The publication of the paper was continued by Rhoades and Adams till the death of the latter, and then by Rhoades till 1819, when it became the property of Davis C. Ballard and Edmund Wright, Jr., publishers of the *Boston Patriot*, with which paper it was united. In 1832 the *Patriot* was merged with the *Daily Advertiser*.

The *Boston Gazette*, the contemporary of the *Independent Chronicle*, through the anxious years of the war, the exciting period of the formation of the government, the framing of its financial policy, the adoption of the Constitution, and the resulting organization of parties, continued to be published by Edes and Sons. It had lost much of its vigor, as we have said, by circumstances beyond its control. Its publishers were patriotic printers, but had not the mental capacity to keep up the intellectual fire and spirit of its earlier days, when a club of vigorous writers contributed to its columns, one or two of whom had gone over to the *Chronicle*. But occasionally, when an odious act was enacted by the Legislature, like the " two thirds of a penny" tax on every newspaper and almanac in 1785, the old fire would burst out and light up the public mind in opposition to the measure. This modernized Stamp Act, from the pressure of public opinion, was modified, and advertisements alone were taxed. This second importation of shackles for the Press from England met with the same determined opposition, and the *Gazette* thus evaded the penalties of the law, and showed the folly of the measure :

> The sixteenth article of our Bill of Rights says "The Liberty of the Press is essential to the security of Freedom in a State : It ought not therefore to be restrained in this commonwealth."
>
> While the papers of the other states are crowded with advertisements, (free of duty) those of this state are almost destitute thereof ; which justly occasions the oppressed printers of those shackled presses to make their separate complaints, as many do, owing to their being prohibited advertising in their own papers their own Books and Stationery without incurring a penalty therefor. We, for the same reason that our brother Typographers use, forbear publishing that *Bibles, Testaments, Psalters, Spelling-Books, Primers, Almanacks, &c.* besides *Stationery and all kinds of Blanks*, may be had at No. 42, Cornhill.
>
> The duty on advertisements also prevents our publishing that we have lately reprinted an excellent moral Discourse, entitled, "The Shortness and Afflictions of Human Life illustrated," for the price of said book being but *eight pence*, it will take away the profits of too many ; and perhaps encourage government to continue this burthen."

About this time the editors of the *Centinel* were threatened with personal violence in consequence of some strictures on a club called the *Sans Souci*, in Boston. Edes, true to his instincts, although politically and professionally opposed to the *Centinel*, had the *esprit du corps* to speak thus on the subject :

> The attack made upon the printers of the *Centinel* on Saturday last, by a number of *well-known* persons, ought to excite the serious attention of all those, who duly regard the bulwark of our liberties, THE FREEDOM OF THE PRESS. If a printer, for advertising that he intends to publish a certain book for the information, or merely the amusement or innocent diversion of his fellow-citizens, is to be beset and abused by a set of club-men, because the title-page does not happen to hit *their* taste, we may take a farewell of our independence, which we have gloriously obtained, not without great expense of our treasure, and the loss of some of our best blood. A wound in so tender a point must surely prove fatal ! Should

the government appoint licensers of the Press, it would give just cause of offence. What right, then, has any set of men to forbid the printing a book, till it has had *their* imprimatur, or to punish a printer with club-law, for advertising it? The institution of a society under the name of *Sans Souci*, or *Free and Easy*, has raised the apprehensions as well as curiosity of many men of sober sentiments in this community, and such a manner of defending it does not tend to diminish their apprehensions. But since this mode has been taken for its defence, it concerns the PUBLIC to inquire into its nature and design;—that, if it be innocent, it may have the common protection; but if it tends to promote GAMING, IDLENESS, and DISSIPATION, it may be, as it ought, discountenanced and suppressed.

The *Gazette*, after 1794, was published by Benjamin Edes alone. The paper had, for a variety of reasons, run into strong opposition to the Constitution of 1787 and the Federal Party. Although John Adams was one of the early writers for the *Gazette*, and gave that paper much of its influence in producing the Revolution, it denounced him as a monarchist and an aristocrat. It also opposed Jay's treaty with England, then an exciting topic, and very unpopular with a large class. Without the force of the *Chronicle*, it fell off in influence, in public favor, in dignity of character, and in subscribers. Its rise, its power and usefulness, and its fall, like that of Zenger's *Journal*, presents a bright as well as a melancholy aspect, the two phases often seen in the history of journalism all over the world. On the 1st of January, 1797, the venerable editor of the *Gazette* appealed to his fellow-citizens, and, in doing so, made a few truthful allusions to his career as a journalist:

The aged editor of the GAZETTE to the PUBLIC.

A few years since, the misfortunes and necessities of my family induced me to throw myself on the benevolence of that Public, to which, as an editor of a paper, I have for upwards of forty-one years been a faithful servant, as far as my abilities and the purity of my principles would enable me. I wish not to boast, but a consciousness of the integrity of my motives, and the conspicuous part, which I took in those perilous times, when not only LIBERTY but LIFE, were suspended on the issue, justify me, at this late period of my existence, in GLORYING in those duties, which as a citizen I was called on to perform. The Boston Gazette was both the Herald and the Centinel, in the days of OTIS, HANCOCK, the ADAMSES, WARREN, &c. while contending against Britain! when their declaratory act was expressive of the disposition of that arrogant nation, when they assumed a right to "tax us in all cases whatsoever!" when the streets of Boston were crimsoned with the blood of our slaughtered citizens! At these all-trying periods, did you, my fellow-citizens, ever find the Boston Gazette deficient in a manly and energetic remonstrance against these horrid and cruel impositions? Did an OTIS at that time seek in vain to declare his principles through this channel?—or did WARREN *unnerve himself* or *the cause of freedom*, by strains of *submission*, through this conveyance?—No, fellow-citizens; the Gazette of Edes & Gill, was always subservient to the cause of Freedom, and this was the CLARION, which announced through the continent the sentiments of your Patriots. Soon expecting to quit this world, for the mansions of those, where honesty and integrity will be rewarded, by the Supreme Ruler of the Universe, I shall submit the following simple statement of my determination and situation, and then resign myself to that fate which Providence may allot me in my retirement—conscious, however, that I have served my country with faithfulness, and the most disinterested zeal, I cannot but observe with regret, that thousands have become enriched by a *base speculation* on those services which have impoverished me and many others.

☞ The aged Editor of the Gazette presents the compliments of the Season to his generous Benefactors, and invites all those who have any demands on him to call and *receive their dues:* He likewise requests those of his Customers, who are two, three, and more years in debt, to discharge their arrears, as he finds it impossible to live upon the wind, and promises equally uncertain. By the indulgence of Providence he is determined to complete the 42d year of publication, which will end the last of March ensuing, (and which is longer than any Printer in the United States ever did before, only one excepted) after which time he shall discontinue its publication, unless he meets with greater encouragement than he has had for more than two years past. The former number of subscribers to the Gazette (in times which tried men's souls, and *bodies* too) were upwards of Two Thousand; near three fourths of which are no more. But being now reduced to 400, and not advertisements enough Weekly to procure Paper, he is necessitated to relinquish publishing it any longer than the Time before mentioned.

BENJAMIN EDES.

This produced no effect. His services as a fearless editor in the interests of the country were to obtain no recognition. Those of his colaborers who survived the Revolution had reached high distinction. John Adams had been Vice-President of the nation, and John Hancock Governor of Massachusetts. Others, like Warren, and Quincy, and Otis, had become immortal. What was to become of poor Edes? Like poor Zenger's son at the "dawn of American Liberty," he reached poverty and destitution. On the 17th of September, 1798, Edes issued his farewell address, full of pathos, patriotism, and poverty, which we give in full, as a document too interesting and touching not to be preserved in history:

☞ The EDITORS FARE WELL.

The Editor of the *Boston Gazette*, after repeated attempts to prosecute his professional occupation, *in the declining period of his life*, is at length obliged to relinquish his exertions, and to retire to those melancholy paths of *domestic embarrassments*, to which misfortune has consigned him.

While thus passing the gloomy valley of *old age* and *infirmity*, his consolation still rests on that STAFF, which can support a mind conscious of its own rectitude; and though he often feels the thorns and briers on the road, goading him in his passage, yet he patiently suffers under these afflictions, hoping that ere long he shall arrive at that peaceful abode, "where the weary are at rest."

During upwards of forty-three years of hard labor in that "ART WHICH SUPPORTS ALL ARTS," he has uniformly attempted to vindicate the RIGHTS OF HIS COUNTRY. He *early* made himself conspicuous as the *scourge* of *tyrants*—His press was the asylum of the distressed—through *that medium* an injured people could ever express their wrongs, or plan measures for their deliverance. At that AFFLICTING CRISIS, when America lay groaning under the innumerable tortures of a relentless nation, the Boston Gazette was employed as the HERALD to sound the alarm through the most remote parts of the Continent.

The Patriots of our Country, at those "*times which tried men's souls*," were constantly assembled within the confines of his office, and their manuscripts were displayed as with a TELEGRAPH, in legible characters, within the columns of his periodical publications.

ADAMS, HANCOCK, WARREN, with a train of co-patriots, were his chosen intimates; under their guidance and direction, he stood on the WATCH TOWER, and, like a faithful Soldier in the cause of Freedom, ever held himself ready, and willing, to *fall* or *rise* with the *ruin* or *happiness* of his country.

But, alas! the cause of LIBERTY is not always the channel of preferment or pecuniary reward. The little property which he acquired has long since fell a sacrifice;—the *paper-evidences* of his services were soon consumed by their rapid depreciation, and the cares of a numerous family were too powerful to be resisted, though he fed them with property at *four shillings and sixpence in the pound*, which he faithfully and industriously earned at *twenty shillings*.

However, it is beneath a patriot to mourn his own misfortunes. The INDEPENDENCE of America being obtained, he enjoys the pleasing contemplation, that the *same virtuous sentiments* which led to the *acquisition* will not cease to operate for its *continuance*—That his fellow-citizens will ever revere the FIRST PRINCIPLES of the Revolution ; and it is his earnest prayer to Heaven, that the RISING GENERATION will remember the exertions of THEIR FATHERS, in opposing the lawless attempts of BRITAIN for their subjugation.

Let the citizens of America REVERENCE THEMSELVES. Let them strive to maintain the REPUBLICAN PRINCIPLES of their own Constitution ; and while practising these duties, we may trust to the GUARDIAN ANGEL, which has conducted us through dangers, the most alarming and distressing.

And now, my Fellow Citizens, I bid you FAREWELL ! MAINTAIN YOUR VIRTUE—CHERISH YOUR LIBERTIES—and may THE ALMIGHTY protect and defend you. B. EDES.

Boston, Sept. 17, 1798—*and in the Forty-fourth Year of the Independence of the* BOSTON GAZETTE.

Then, at the age of seventy-five, this once influential journalist passed from affluence and high position, with a few old type, and an elderly daughter as an assistant, to the attic of an old wooden building in Boston, there to eke out five years more of life on a miserable pittance earned at case in a small job-office in the Athens of America !

The fate of the contemporary of the *Gazette*, one of the other spirited organs of the Revolution, the *Massachusetts Spy*, was quite different. Amidst all difficulties it stood erect. After the war, Thomas enlarged and improved the *Spy*. Again changing his motto, as a thing of course with him, and now going beyond " the English undefiled," he dipped into Latin, and adopted *Noscere res humanas est Hominis* as his guide. He published in his columns Robertson's History of America, and Gordon's History of the Revolution, complete. Other useful matter, of a similar character, he gave from time to time. News also appeared in full. Thomas was clearly a man of progress.

The *Spy* was suspended in 1786 in consequence of the State Stamp Act. The revival of an act, made so odious before the Revolution, by a Legislature of a free people, became as unpopular as the original law of 1765, and as obnoxious as the Alien and Sedition laws of 1798. Many of the papers published in that state were suspended, and the editors of Massachusetts felt the oppression, and acted with the same spirit that prompted the following curious article, which appeared in the *Spy* of March 30, 1786 :

Extra Information. Real !

THE MASSACHUSETTS SPY (which it is acknowledged has been of very essential service to the cause of the United States, and to this Commonwealth in particular, before, at, and since the late Revolution) is now languishing with a *dangerous Wound* given *it* by the *Legislature* of *Massachusetts*, on the second day of July last. Humble and united application has been made for a particular kind of *Court Plaister*, which could speedily have wrought a *Cure ;* but as that *Power*, only, who gave the *Wound*, could apply the *Remedy* with effect, it could not be obtained ! The wound grows worse daily—*Mortification* has taken place, and in all probability will soon prove fatal to the existence of that *Old Publick Servant!*—"Alas, POOR SPY!"

Gentle Reader, if thou hast a benevolent heart, thy compassion will be moved, when thou art informed that the *Wound* given was as unjust as it was unmerited—it was given at a time when this faithful Servant of the Publick, after having fought the battles of its country, was sounding forth her Praise—endeavoring to clear her from the Aspersions thrown upon her by her enemies, and diligently watching their motions.

Generous Reader, the services rendered by the SPY to the Publick, were not for the sake of sordid gain, but from *Principle:*—The *only Reward* for *fifteen years* hard duty was this inhuman attack upon its existence! and the existence of all its near Relations, the whole *Family of Gazettes* in this Commonwealth.

On the 2d of April, 1788, the *Spy* came out again, and was happy. It thus felicitated itself:

The Printer has the happiness of once more presenting to the Publick, the MASSACHUSETTS SPY, or the WORCESTER GAZETTE, which at length is restored to its *Constitutional Liberty*, (thanks to our present Legislature,) after a *suspension* of *two years*. Heaven grant that the FREEDOM of the PRESS, on which depends the FREEDOM of the PEOPLE, may, in the United States, ever be guarded with a watchful eye, and defended from Shackles of every *form* and *shape*, until the trump of the celestial messenger shall announce the final dissolution of all things.

While the country was in a transition state, passing from dependence to independence, the *Spy*, like other papers and individuals of intelligence and influence, had its crude ideas on the character which the nation and the people should assume. While it favored the adoption of the Constitution, it strongly advocated the use of titles. Thomas spoke of the President as "His Highness the President General" and "His Highness George Washington." If we recollect rightly, the Constitution of Massachusetts alone, of all State Constitutions, still bestows the title of "His Excellency the Governor" on its chief magistrate, and "His Honor" has been the prefix to the title of Mayor of New York till 1869, when A. Oakey Hall, the incumbent of the office, directed that the title should be dropped. The Senate of the United States had previously directed that "Hon." should not be prefixed to the names of senators. This, however, is a matter of choice with those who choose to use the title. It was sanctioned by no law. "My honorable friend" from Kamtschatka, or the "honorable senator" from Timbuctoo, appeared in speeches. They were mere phrases of courtesy, and oftener of irony.

The *Spy* was published by Isaiah Thomas and Leonard Worcester in 1792, and by Isaiah Thomas, Jr., after 1801. Worcester became a well-known clergyman in 1798, and was settled in Peacham, Vermont, where he preached for half a century.

The energy and enterprise of the elder Thomas continued through life. He opened book-stores, and, like Franklin, started printing-offices and newspapers in half a dozen places. In 1810 he wrote the History of Printing, an elaborate and valuable publication, which

Munsell, of Albany, intends reprinting for an antiquarian society. After that he founded the American Antiquarian Society. In 1812 he was made a justice of the Court of Sessions. Several degrees were conferred upon him by colleges, and he was a member, or an honorary member, of many societies and institutions. He made several donations of value in land, books, and buildings to the town and country in which he thrived. Thus, in striking contrast, Benjamin Edes of the *Gazette*, and Isaiah Thomas of the *Spy*, the two great journalists of the Revolution, passed away—one in poverty at the age of eighty, and the other in affluence at the age of eighty-two, full of years and full of patriotism.

The *Spy*, in 1814, became the property of William Manning. It passed in 1823 into the hands of John Milton Earle, and now, with a new motto—new to those who read the paper of 1801—and the coat of arms of the state for its device, it is published by J. D. Baldwin and Co. It is the second oldest paper in the state. Its daily issue is called the *Worcester Daily Spy;* its weekly the *Massachusetts Spy*. Its editor was a member of the Fortieth Congress, and its politics are Republican. In 1867 the establishment was moved into a new edifice, the *Spy* Building, erected expressly for its use on Main Street, Worcester. One of Hoe's new double cylinder presses was purchased, and the paper enlarged and improved. All these signs, in face of the increasing facilities for circulating the metropolitan papers over the state, are healthy, and speak well for the present management of the *Spy*.

On the day the *Spy* was one hundred years old, July 17, 1870, its present proprietors celebrated the event with a dinner. Its present editor then said:

> The SPY having completed the hundredth year of its age, the proprietors had invited the gentlemen present to dine with them and assist in a celebration. When the SPY was started, an hundred years ago, there were six other papers in Massachusetts ; but they all disappeared before the beginning of the present century. The Boston Newsletter, the first paper printed in America, might be living now, if it had not become a malignant tory and fallen under the influence of the royalists, at the beginning of the revolution. Its first number was printed in 1704. For a long time it had no competitor; it became strong and prosperous; but, when the revolution approached, it took the way to death ; and, instead of living to hold its centennial celebration nearly seventy years ago, it died of toryism, as soon as the British army left Boston. The Spy was living yet, because it received life from the ideas that created the revolution and the nation, and preserved this life. It was established by a patriot whose integrity could not be corrupted.

Ex-editor Earle, "the founder of the daily Spy," made some remarks.

> He spoke of the circumstances under which the publication of the Daily was begun, in 1845. It seemed to him that the size of the city and its business and commercial interests warranted such an enterprise. He had published and edited the Massachusetts Weekly Spy since 1823, and during that time it had been well supported by the people ; but when the question of a daily was brought up, many

discouraging objections were made, especially by business men. On the morning of July 31st, 1845, twenty-five years ago, the first number was issued. One reason urged by merchants against starting the daily, was, that the cost of advertising would be increased. To meet this, he adopted the policy of inserting in the Daily, without charge, the advertisements sent in for the Weekly; and when their customers came, inquiring for articles advertised in the Daily, they began to see that it was greatly for their interest to advertise in the Daily. Then he left out of the Daily their advertisements sent for the Weekly. The result was, that, in a short time, they cared much less for the Weekly than for the Daily.

Another newspaper which survived the Revolution, and stands in peculiar contrast with its unsuccessful contemporaries, is the *Salem Gazette*. Our sketch of this paper in a preceding chapter left it suspended under the Massachusetts Stamp Act of 1785. It was revived in October, 1786, by John Dabney and Thomas C. Cushing. They purchased the materials of the old *Gazette* of Samuel Hall. Cushing had been an apprentice of Hall's. He had also published the *American Recorder* in Charlestown, Massachusetts. The resuscitated paper was first called the *Salem Mercury;* then the *American Eagle;* and then, on the 1st of January, 1790, the *Salem Gazette*. On the 1st of June, 1796, it was issued semi-weekly. Timothy Pickering used to relate that his uncle, John Pickering, was greatly exercised in his mind by this symptom of modern degeneracy. "The paper never had been published but once a week," he said, "and that was often enough; it was nonsense to disturb people's minds by sending newspapers amongst them twice a week, to take their attention from the duties they had to perform."

William Carlton joined Mr. Cushing in 1794, and remained till 1797. In 1800 Mr. Carlton commenced the publication of the *Salem Register*, which has continued in existence, and is now nearly seventy-two years of age. Warwick Palfray, who succeeded to the paper in 1805, was an apprentice with Mr. Carlton. Of Chapman and Palfray, the present proprietors of the *Register*, the latter was son, and the former an apprentice of Warwick Palfray. With the year 1823, the publication of the *Observer* was commenced by William Ives, whose vigorous age, like that of Mr. Chapman, tends to prove the healthfulness of the printing business. Ives served his apprenticeship in the *Gazette* office with Cushing, and his paper has always been thoroughly respectable and creditable to all who have been concerned in its management.

The Boston *Journal*, in November, 1871, published the following paragraph of the present octogenarian editor of the *Register:*

One of the most remarkable instances of a vigorous, green old age, has recently been brought to our notice in the person of the venerable John Chapman, of the *Salem Register*, now nearly eighty years of age. Mr. Chapman began his journalistic life as a boy in the office of the *Essex Register*, when Judge Story wrote the famous motto for that paper:—

"Here shall the Press the people's right maintain,
Unawed by influence and unbribed by gain.

> Here patriot Truth her glorious precepts draw,
> Pledged to Religion, Liberty and Law."

During the past fifty-six years, at half-past twelve o'clock every Sunday night, the city watchman patrolling the street in front of his residence has aroused him, and he has risen, and going to his office assisted in making up the matter for his paper and mailing for his subscribers. During all these years he has never missed a single night, with the exception of the time he was sick with the scarlet fever, and that was some twenty years since, which was the only occasion he was ever ill enough to have a physician. He may often be found at the case lending a helping hand in setting type for his paper. His step is today as firm and elastic as when half a century ago he plodded through the wintry streets of Salem.

The *Gazette* was published by Mr. Cushing from October, 1786, to January, 1823. He then transferred the establishment to Caleb Cushing and Ferdinand Andrews. On the 1st of April, 1825, Caleb Foote bought Cushing's share in the concern. In October, 1826, Andrews sold his share to William Brown, and removed to Lancaster, where he published a paper for several years. He afterwards assisted in the establishment of the *Boston Traveller*. Brown, in 1833, sold out to the present senior proprietor, and the junior partner became interested in the paper in 1854.

The *Gazette* office has been in one building, where the paper is now printed, for over seventy years. Nathaniel Silsbee was in the habit, toward the close of the last century, of resorting, when a boy, to the office to accompany a juvenile friend, who was a carrier of the paper, on his weekly rounds. Among the contributors to this venerable journal was the Rev. William Bentley, one of the fathers of Unitarianism in America. Weekly he furnished articles for the *Gazette*, and afterward for the *Register*, for thirty years. He was a great linguist, reading with ease more than twenty different languages.

The *Gazette*, in speaking of itself in 1868, said :

When the *Gazette* was established, four years had elapsed since the first formal demonstration of opposition to the novel claims of the British Parliament to the entire control and government of the Colonies, and to an authority to impose taxes on and legislate for them in all cases, without their voice or consent. The stamp act had been passed in 1765 ; and in 1766 the Massachusetts House of Representatives had issued an address to all the Colonies, calling upon them to rally their energies, and stand in the breach against parliamentary taxation. The controversy was going on between the General Court and Governor Bernard, the former having been arbitrarily removed from Boston to Cambridge, by order of the latter. The first *Gazette* contained an account of a town meeting, called to support the Salem Representatives in their opposition to the measures of the royal governor.

Throughout the Colony, traders had been compelled to sign agreements to discontinue the importation of British goods ; and their customers had equally obligated themselves, to refrain, as much as possible, from the use of all articles which were superfluous and unnecessary. Nothing can be more curious, as an indication of the spirt of the times, than the agreements, published in the *Gazette*, of the traders of Salem, Marblehead and Beverly, for the non-importation of British goods ; the charges often made against them of violating their agreement, and their defences against the same.

The *Gazette* bristled with personal cards and controversies, and with resolutions of the various towns, small and large, to discourage extravagance and the use of all superfluities, especially of foreign production; to encourage industry and frugality, and to promote manufactures. Spinning and weaving parties were held on Boston common, and took the place of pic-nics with the women and girls of all the country places, while the men planted liberty poles and trees.

* * * * * * * * * * * *

In those years when the contest was fiercest against the "oppressions of Britain" the advertising columns of the *Gazette* were constantly disfigured by such advertisements as "a strong likely negro boy for sale;"—"Run away, a negro man named Pharo, of a very light complexion, something scarred in the face;"—"To be sold, a likely negro man, talks broken French and a little English;"—"To be sold, a likely strong negro girl, about 17 years of age;"—"To be sold, a healthy strong negro boy, very ingenious in the farming business;"—"To be sold, a strong, healthy likely negro boy, about 9 years of age; also, a very likely healthy negro girl, about 6 years old." In 1776 several slaves were brought into Salem, who were found on board a British prize ship from Jamaica, and they were publicly advertised to be sold; but the Legislature forbade the sale, and ordered them to be set at liberty—voting at the same time that "the selling and enslaving the human species is a direct violation of the natural rights alike vested in all men by their Creator, and utterly inconsistent with the avowed principles on which this and the other United States have carried their struggle for liberty even to the last appeal.

Nothing is more striking than the gradual change in the tone of the newspaper from professions of loyalty and devotion to the British crown, to preparations for war, the raising of troops, providing of munitions, &c. By 1774 the people were industriously collecting arms for themselves, wherever and from whomsoever they could obtain them.

The *Gazette* contained an account of the capture of Ticonderoga "by the American forces without the loss of a man. Colonel Easton demanded, in the name of the American Congress, an instant surrender of the fort." Colonel Ethan Allen was left commander of the fort, but there is nothing said of his having demanded its surrender "in the name of Jehovah and the Continental Congress."

One of the earliest newspaper expresses, if not the first of these enterprises, was regularly run for Samuel Hall in the early days of the *Gazette*. Colonel Pickering is the authority for stating that he run the express from Boston to Salem the day before the publication of the *Gazette*, in order to furnish the latest news for its readers. The distance run was fifteen miles! But it was a special express.

There is an incident connected with the *Gazette* worth relating. There was a sharp political contest in the Essex District in 1802. Jacob Crowninshield was the Republican candidate for Congress, and Timothy Pickering, who had been Secretary of State in the cabinet of the elder Adams, was the Federal candidate. The friends of each party became much excited. The *Gazette* and *Register* entered the fight with zeal, and each candidate was violently assailed. One Saturday evening early in November, Joseph Story, afterward Judge of the Supreme Court of the United States, and Captain Crowninshield, called on Editor Cushing at his house, and requested a private interview. They stated that they came on unpleasant business. Story said that he had been placed before the community in an injurious point of view; that he was a young man, come into town to gain an honorable livelihood; that he had a right to express his political sentiments; that he had no objection to having his arguments fairly combated, but that he would not submit to be arraigned before the public in the manner he had been. Captain Crowninshield was more emphatic, and stated that many of the articles in the *Gazette* were highly injurious, and that the editor had been in the habit of making personal reflections on him and his family that he did not like. He concluded by saying that if Cushing persisted in such a course he would shoot him at sight. When this interview became known there was increased excitement in the community, and Cushing was urged to publish a statement of the affair. In his reply to Story and Crowninshield he said:

> That it was my desire, and had been my uniform endeavor to keep my paper free from undue personalities—that I considered public characters and public conduct as proper subjects of animadversion—that such was the present state of parties, and irritation of the public mind, that possibly (for I would not be my own judge) I might have admitted expressions not strictly within the bounds prescribed to myself—that I could not say how I should conduct my paper in future, but should still be governed by the same regard to decency, and endeavor to give no just cause of offence—that threats, however, would have no effect upon me in that respect, but if they meant to address my reason and sense of propriety, on that ground I was willing to hear them. With respect to the asperity of language used in my paper, I observed, if there had been such, it was excited by that of the opposite paper—that the candidates for office in my paper against Captain Jacob Crowninshield had been treated with a degree of indelicacy and abuse in the *Register*, which had not been exercised in return against him. I told them that it had been impossible for me, from appearances, not to view them in connection with the paper in which these things appeared. Here they disavowed all connection with the *Register*, otherwise than that of being its customers, except that Mr. Story acknowledged himself to be one of its writers. They observed at length, that, as to what was past, they had no more to say; their only object was, that I should refrain in future from personalities towards them and their friends. They left it to me to divulge the meeting or not, as I pleased; it would not be done by them. I informed them that I felt a disposition not to make it known.

Editor Cushing was not shot, but Captain Crowninshield was elected to Congress.

The *Gazette*, according to its own photographic view, recorded the troubles arising from the inefficiency of the Old Confederation, and the dangers, dissensions, and distresses consequent to the struggle for liberty. The attempt of the mob in Hampshire County, instigated by the demagogue Parson Ely, to prevent the regular course of justice, and shut up the courts; Shay's rebellion, commencing in Hampshire, and spreading into Worcester, Middlesex, Bristol, and Berkshire, leaving the whole eastern sea-board untouched; the bitter contest between the adherents of Hancock and Bowdoin, as candidates for governor; the tour of Washington through the Northern States, and his reception in Salem by that model speech of welcome by good Quaker Selectman Northey: "Friend Washington, we are glad to see thee, and, in behalf of the inhabitants, bid thee a hearty welcome to Salem."

There, too, are to be found the debates on the adoption of a Federal Constitution; the election and inauguration of Washington; the organization of the national government; the civic feasts, and the roasting of whole oxen in celebration, by the sober and orderly citizens of Massachusetts; of the successes of our allies, the French, at the beginning of the French Revolution; the enthusiastic reception of Genet, Adet, and Fouchet, and their intrigues; the organization of the Federal and Republican parties; the ratification of Jay's British treaty, and the popular commotion against it; the troubles and war with France; the days of the "Black Cockade;" the building of a navy by the voluntary contributions of the people, including the generous gift of the frigate Essex by the patriotic citizens of Salem; the glorious victories of Truxtun and our other naval heroes; the Alien and Sedition laws, standing army, loans, and the "civil revolution," when Jefferson routed and overthrew John Adams, "the Duke of Braintree," as he was called. There, too, is the history of the first settlement of Ohio, and of the founding of every state in the Union except the original thirteen; the narratives of the defeat, by the savages, of Harmer and St. Clair, and the victory by Wayne; Jefferson's embargo, and the War of 1812–15, called "Madison's War;" the Hartford Convention; the Gerrymander—

"A monster of such frightful mien
As to be hated needs but to be seen;"

the cessation of the bitterness of political strife; the "era of good feelings," and consequent unanimous election of Monroe to the presidency; the renewal of party virulence in the contest between Andrew Jackson and John Quincy Adams, and so on to the end of the chapter.

CHAPTER XII.

THE FIRST DAILY NEWSPAPERS.

THE AMERICAN DAILY ADVERTISER OF PHILADELPHIA.—NATIONAL SEAT OF GOVERNMENT.—THE DAILY ADVERTISER OF NEW YORK.—JUNIUS AND THE FEDERALIST. — INTERESTING INCIDENTS. — OLD LANG'S GAZETTE. — AULD LANG SYNE. — SHIPPING NEWS AND NEWS-BOATS. — THE UNITED STATES GAZETTE AND NORTH AMERICAN OF PHILADELPHIA.—NEWSPAPER ENTERPRISE.—THE IMPARTIAL INTELLIGENCER.

THE first daily newspaper published in the United States was the *American Daily Advertiser*. It was issued in Philadelphia in 1784, by Benjamin Franklin Bache, afterwards of the *Aurora*. When the seat of national government was in Philadelphia, it shared the confidence and support of Jefferson with the *National Gazette*. It was strong in its opposition to the Federal section of the administration of Washington, and to all the measures originating with Hamilton. Zachariah Poulson became its proprietor and publisher in 1802, and it was known as *Poulson's Advertiser*, and we believe he continued its publisher till October 28, 1839, when the establishment was sold to Brace and Newbold, the publishers of a new paper called the *North American*. The name after that was the *North American and Daily Advertiser*. The *Advertiser* came from the *Pennsylvania Packet*, published by Dunlap and Claypole. Its character was like that of Poulson, its proprietor, very slow and very respectable. Poulson died in Philadelphia July 30, 1844.

The *New York Daily Advertiser*, the second real journal in the United States, was published in 1785. It was commenced on the 1st of March by Francis Childs & Co. It had a little unpleasantness with the *Journal*. Colonel Oswald, of the latter, charged the *Advertiser* with a design to injure the Widow Holt, of the *Journal*, and quite a newspaper quarrel grew out of the affair.

On the 24th of April, 1789, when Washington arrived at New York from Mount Vernon to enter upon the duties of President, after the adoption of the Federal Constitution, he was received at Elizabethtown, and escorted thence to the city by a procession of boats. In the account of the affair, it is stated that the schooner Columbia, Captain Philip Freneau, eight days from Charleston, came up the bay with the aquatic procession. Shortly after this event Freneau became the editor of the *Advertiser*, and continued in that capacity till the removal of the seat of government to Philadelphia. It was supposed that the articles against the *Journal* were written by him.

John Pintard, so well known in New York, where he was born in 1759, and where he died in 1844, was another writer for the *Advertiser*. Pintard was a strong Federalist, but he and Freneau were close and intimate friends. On all public occasions, and in all public improvements, Pintard was favorably conspicuous. Many of the valuable and useful institutions of the metropolis were suggested by him.

The first paper printed in Maine was the *Falmouth Gazette and Weekly Advertiser*, on the 1st of January, 1785. It was published by Thomas B. Wait and Benjamin Titcomb. In 1786, when Portland was incorporated and made out of Falmouth, this paper was printed by Wait, and called the *Cumberland Gazette*. Titcomb shortly after commenced the publication of the *Gazette of Maine*. It was discontinued in 1796. The *Eastern Star* was established in Hallowell in that year. Elijah Russell, in 1798, issued a paper in Fryeburg, where Daniel Webster taught school a few years later. This paper was known as *Russell's Echo, or the North Star*—a queer combination of names. Its proprietor had previously printed a paper in Concord, N. H.

There was a daily paper issued in Portland in 1829, called the *Daily Courier*. It was edited by Seba Smith, Jr., the original Jack Downing, of Downingsville. The *Courier* was commenced on the 13th of October. On the 5th of January, 1831, the *Daily Evening Advertiser*, the second daily paper in Portland, was published by John and William E. Edwards. It was in this office that James and Erastus Brooks, of the *New York Express*, started as journalists. The *Advertiser* afterwards published a morning edition, which was discontinued in 1869. In an obituary notice of William Bartlett Sewall, who died in Kennebunk in 1869, it was stated that he became editor of the *Advertiser* in 1833, and held that position for several years.

One of those veteran newspapers, that seem to live through all time without growing beyond an influence acquired in their youth, is published in Northampton, Massachusetts. It is the *Hampshire Gazette*. William Butler issued the first number on the 6th of September, 1786. It is an historical paper. In the midst of the excitement growing out of Shay's Rebellion, when meetings were held at which the supposed grievances of the people were strongly depicted, it became necessary to establish a paper to convey information to the people in the interest of the government, and to stem the current of popular insubordination. The *Hampshire Gazette* was the paper thus established. Among the writers for its columns were Caleb Strong, afterwards governor of the state, the Rev. Joseph Lyman, and Major Hawley. It became the duty of patriotism in the infancy of the republic to crush at once the schemes of the demagogues then floating with the *débris* of the Revolution throughout the country, taking advantage of the scarcity of money and the heavy taxes to excite the people to revolt, and it was only by means of newspapers that this could be effectually accomplished. Open insurrections and rebellions, it is true, are physically suppressed by military power, but the only way to reach the minds of the people, and unite sections and communities in the bitterness of their supposed troubles, is through the newspaper, which penetrates to the hearths, and heads, and hearts of every family, and silently and effectively accomplishes its object.

After the suppression of Shay, and Day, and Parson, and their associates, the *Gazette* continued in existence, and became a permanent institution. It was owned by William A. Hawley in 1852, and was the third oldest paper in Massachusetts, the *Salem Gazette* and *Worcester Spy* being its seniors.

With the settlement of the country newspapers began to spread with the population. It is one of the characteristics of America that the newspaper keeps up with the migration of the people. In the progress of the Pacific Railroad, the *Frontier Index*, as we have stated, moved on toward the setting sun, keeping a little ahead of the rails and the locomotive. On the 29th of July, 1786, the *Pittsburg* (Penn.) *Gazette*, the first newspaper printed west of the Alleghany Mountains, appeared, and in 1796 the *Post* was issued, and now there are ten or eleven daily papers printed, three or four of which are in German. The *Oracle of Dauphin* was issued in Harrisburg in 1791. It was the first newspaper in that place. John Wyeth was its editor. The late chief justice of Pennsylvania, Ellis Lewis, and Senator Simon Cameron, were apprentices of Mr. Wyeth. The first paper printed in Kentucky was commenced by John Bradford, in Lexington, also in 1786. Another was soon after issued in Frankfort.

If, in the estimation of many, the letters of Junius, published in the *Public Advertiser* of London in 1765, gave an impulse to the power and influence of the Press in England such as it never before enjoyed, what has been the effect of the Federalist, published in the *Independent Journal* in New York in 1787, on the power and influence of the Press of America? We have seen in these sketches the necessity of the Press in preparing the people for a revolution, and in sustaining the authorities through that eventful struggle. It is true that our independence could not have been achieved by the

Press alone, but mental force was as necessary to success as physical force. It has been so in all great revolutions, and in all important movements affecting the people. On one occasion a Hungarian officer was asked if Kossuth had any military capacity or experience. "Not exactly," replied the officer, "but he was our lip warrior." "Lip warrior?" we asked. "Yes," continued the Hungarian; "when our men were discouraged and needed a little urging, Kossuth would appeal to them with his eloquence, or make a prayer as no other man could, and our soldiers would go to work again with renewed ardor and enthusiasm." So with Junius. So, too, with the power of the newspapers in the Revolution of 1776 and the Rebellion of 1861, and so with the influence of the communications of Hamilton, Madison, and Jay, known as the Federalist, in accomplishing the adoption of the Constitution in 1789, under which we have become a great and powerful nation.

The first number of the Federalist was published in the *Independent Journal* on the 27th of October, 1787. This paper was printed by J. & A. M'Lean, in Hanover Square, New York, near where the *Journal of Commerce* is now printed. The remaining numbers were published in that and the other papers of that day. They were afterwards collected, and printed in two volumes under this title:

THE FEDERALIST: A COLLECTION OF ESSAYS, WRITTEN IN FAVOR OF THE NEW CONSTITUTION, AS AGREED UPON BY THE FEDERAL CONVENTION, SEPT. 17, 1787, IN TWO VOLUMES, VOLUME I. NEW YORK. PRINTED & SOLD BY J & A MCLEAN. NO 41 HANOVER SQUARE, 1788.

The preface, written by Hamilton, thus introduces the letters, giving the reasons for their republication:

It is supposed that a collection of the papers which have made their appearance in the Gazettes of this City, under the Title of the Federalist, may not be without effect in assisting the public judgement on the momentous question of the Constitution for the United States, now under the consideration of the people of America. A desire to throw full light upon so interesting a subject has led, in a great measure unavoidably, to a more copious discussion than was at first intended. And the undertaking not being yet completed, it is judged advisable to divide the collection into two Volumes, of which the ensuing Numbers constitute the first. The second Volume will follow as speedily as the Editor can get it ready for publication.

In this more compact form the Federalist was sent to several State Conventions before which the Constitution was then pending. These communications were anonymous when originally published, and the authorship of several of the essays has been a matter of controversy as late as 1864, but it can be so no longer. Madison, in December, 1787, in writing to Edmund Randolph in regard to the Federalist, was reticent as to the names of those concerned with him in their production. He said:

* * * * * * You will probably discover marks of different pens. I am not at liberty to give you any other key, than, that I am in myself for a few numbers; and that one, besides myself, was a member of the Convention.

About the year 1850, Colonel Alexander Hamilton purchased at an old book-stand in Nassau Street, then opposite the office of the *New York Herald*, kept by John M'Cabe, and much frequented by such men as Washington Irving, an old copy of the Federalist, for which he paid seventy-five cents. After looking over it with great interest and curiosity, Colonel Hamilton crossed the street and walked into the editorial rooms of the *Herald*. "Well, this is very singular," said Colonel Hamilton. "Here is a copy of the Federalist that I have just bought that has the initial letter of each writer of each essay over each one, and the initials seem to be in the handwriting of my father."

It had probably been marked by the elder Hamilton for some friend into whose library it passed, and out of which, in the whirligig of time, it had slipped in some auction, and thence on to the dusty old book-shelves of John M'Cabe; and after a lapse of fifty or sixty years, a son of one of the distinguished writers finds the old copy, with its additional evidence of authorship, in one of the narrow byways of the metropolis.

According to Rives's Life and Times of James Madison, the Federalist appeared in the *New York Daily Advertiser*. It is probable that Madison had saved the essays as they appeared in that paper. But the first essay was published in the *Independent Journal*, and after that they appeared in all the papers. Mr. Hamilton left a memorandum in the law-office of a friend on the eve of his fatal duel with Burr by which it appeared that he wrote sixty-five out of the eighty-five essays. Mr. Madison wrote, in the original edition of 1788, the names of the authors, and by this it seems he wrote twenty-nine. It is claimed that Jay wrote six. There is a mistake somewhere, but it is of very little consequence. This distinguished trio accomplished the great object they had at heart, and that is their reward as well as our gain.

The M'Leans, in consequence, probably, of the name of *Independent Journal* conflicting with Holt's *Journal Revived*, which opposed Washington's administration, changed the title of their paper to that of the *New York Gazette* in 1788. It was afterwards published by John Lang, Lang and Turner, Lang, Turner, and Co., Lang's Sons, and Alexander M'Call. The *Gazette* evidently never aspired to be a commanding journal. Its most important and interesting matter was its shipping intelligence, to which its managers paid great attention. There was no other marked feature in the paper. There is an anecdote illustrative of the character of its chief editor which we must record. It is told by Dr. Francis:

> The scholastic discussions which occurred on the question of the commencement of the present century, awaked some attention among the mathematicians

and astronomers abroad, and of many among us. The learned and pious Dr. Kunze, after much investigation, addressed a communication on the vexed question to Mr. Lang. He had adverted to the Gregorian style in his letter, and had mentioned Pope Gregory. The faithful *Gazette* printed the article Tom Gregory: the venerable Dr. hastened to his friend, and remonstrated on the injury he had done him, and requested the erratum to specify instead of Tom Gregory, Pope Gregory XIII. Again an alteration was made, and the *Gazette* requested its readers, for Tom Gregory, to read Pope Tom Gregory XIII. One more attempt at correction was made, when the compositor had its typography so changed as to read Tom Gregory, the Pope. The learned divine, with heavy heart, at a final interview with the erudite editor, begged him to make no further improvements, as he dreaded the loss of all the reputation his years of devotion to the subject had secured him.

Auguste Villemot had a similar experience. "When I wrote in *L'Indépendance Belge*," said he, "the compositors, if I spoke of the *repertoire classique* of the French comedy, never failed to print the *repertoire elastique*. One day I went to Brussels expressly to touch the compositor's hearts; they promised me that no error should again occur. The following week I spoke of a man with an *elastique* conscience; they printed it *classique* conscience. *Ultra petita!*"

The credit of originating the collection of shipping news by boats in New York Harbor is given to the elder Lang. He was fond of boating, and would frequently go down the bay, accompanied by an old colored servant. On returning home on one occasion, he passed a ship just arrived. He hailed her, obtained her name, and where she was from, and these facts appeared in the next morning's *Gazette*. Those interested in her were surprised to see her arrival thus announced, and before they knew that she had made her appearance. Tradition gives this as the origin of the news-boat service which has since become so necessary, and now we see the steam news-yacht *Herald*, like a water-witch, running around Sandy Hook, and away out to sea, for the latest arrivals and "the freshest foreign advices."

The *Gazette* lived till 1840, when the subscription-list was purchased by the *Journal of Commerce*, and the *Gazette* ceased to exist. Its list had been run down to a few names, and the paper seemed to breathe with only one newspaper lung, its few advertisements, for a number of years before it finally expired. John Lang, the last editor, had previously died, March 17, 1836, in New York City.

The Langs had over the door of their publication-office a bust of Franklin as a sign, a very good figure-head for a printing-office. But Halleck, in "Croaker," in the *Evening Post*, finding that Franklin's bust was carved from a block of wood, wickedly wrote—

> "Take Franklin's bust from off thy door,
> And place thy own head there."

In the latter days of "Old Lang's *Gazette*," as it was familiarly called, there was a famous restaurant in Water Street, kept by a portly gentleman named George W. Browne. Over one of his departments a still more portly gentleman, named Charles Ridabock, presided. He was a wag whom every body liked, and whom every body called Alderman Ridabock, for he always carried an extensive corporation with him. One day, when the *Journal of Commerce* swallowed the *Gazette* for lunch instead of getting a more nourishing one at Browne's, the alderman "set up for himself," and opened a restaurant in the basement of the old Tontine Coffee-house, which since then, we are pleased to say, has been fixed up and painted. Hudson's News-room was on the first floor, and was the centre of news at that time. Merchants, sea-captains, editors, brokers and bankers, resorting there, extensively patronized the alderman. On the sale of the *lars et penates* of Lang's *Gazette*, the genial Ridabock purchased the old bust of Franklin. He had it regilded, the old specs cleaned, and the whole appropriately and conspicuously labeled

OLD LANG'S SIGN.

It was then mounted over his door, and the old scenes of Wall, Water, Front, Pearl, and Broad Streets were thus ever "brought to mind."

The *Herald of Freedom and Federal Advertiser*, published by Freeman and Andrews, made its appearance in Boston on the 15th of September, 1788. It was issued twice a week. It was only remarkable for its advocacy of Hancock for governor in opposition to Bowdoin, and for the fact that it was engaged in the first libel-suit tried in Massachusetts after the Revolution. This occurred in 1791 for a savage attack on a member of the Legislature. The case was decided in favor of the newspaper. Harrison Gray Otis, one of the most brilliant men of his day, was counsel for the editor. The name of the paper was subsequently changed to that of the *Argus*, which was published by Edward Eveleth Powars, previously of the *Chronicle*.

The *United States Gazette* was started in New York in 1789 by John Fenno, of Boston. Its original name was *Gazette of the United States*. It was first issued in New York, because the seat of the national government was then in that city. When Congress removed to Philadelphia in 1790, the *Gazette* went with that body. In 1792 it was the special organ of Alexander Hamilton, the Secretary of the Treasury, and his friends, and was furious on the Jacobins of that day. Thomas Jefferson, in a letter to a friend in Paris, thus spoke of this paper and its opposition:

<small>The Tory paper, Fenno's, rarely admits any thing which defends the present form of government in opposition to his desire of subverting it, to make way for a king, Lords and Commons. There are high names here in favor of this doctrine.</small>

Adams, Jay, Hamilton, Knox and many of the Cincinnati. The second says nothing; the third is open. Both are dangerous. They pant after union with England, as the power which is to support their projects, and are most deteimined Anti-Gallicans.

Fenno died of yellow fever in 1798, in the same year with Bache of the *Aurora*. Mary Eliza Fenno, daughter of the editor of the *Gazette*, married Gulian C. Verplanck, of New York, in 1811. Verplanck, so well known in literary circles in that city, died there in 1870. William Cullen Bryant, in a eulogy on Verplanck, said that he had seen an exquisite miniature of Mrs. Verplanck, by Malbone, "taken in her early girlhood, when about fifteen years old—beautiful as an angel, with light chestnut hair and a soft blue eye, in the look of which is a touch of sadness, as if caused by some dim presentiment of her early death. I remember hearing Miss Sedgwick say that she should always think the better of Verplanck for having been the husband of Eliza Fenno."

Fenno was succeeded by his son, John Ward Fenno, in the management of the *Gazette*. It was subsequently conducted, at different periods, by Caleb P. Wayne, Elihu Chauncey, Enos Bronson, and Joseph R. Chandler. Bronson once, in an affidavit, reproachfully called Cheetham, of the *American Citizen*, "an Englishman and a hatter." Cheetham had a brother in business as a hatter in Chatham Street, New York. Bronson was a brisk journalist, boasting at one time of "seven prosecutions commenced within twelve months." He had more enterprise than any of his contemporaries. There was a paper published a short time in Philadelphia in 1820 styled the *Mirror and United States Gazette*, but it should not be confounded with Fenno's, and Bronson's, and Chandler's paper. But what became of the *United States Gazette*?

When the newspapers of New York experienced a revival in 1844, '45, and '46, the journals of Philadelphia partook of the excitement. Expensive and extensive expresses were run with European news from Boston and Halifax. They extended to the Quaker City. Governor William B. Dinsmore and Colonel E. S. Sandford, of Adams's Express Line, were ardently active in these enterprises. If they had not been in the express business, they would have made splendid journalists.

The most spiritedly managed newspaper in Philadelphia at that time was the *North American*. It was first issued in 1839, as already stated, absorbing the old *Advertiser* in that year. It afterward passed into the hands of Childs and Fry, taking in the *Commercial Herald* in 1840, and thence to the management of George R. Graham, well known as the publisher of *Graham's Magazine*, and Alexander Cummings, who subsequently published the *Evening Bulletin* of

Philadelphia, and spent $200,000 in establishing the *New York World* on religious principles. On account of political differences between the publishers, the *North American*, standing firmly on the Whig platform, became the property of Graham and Judge R. T. Conrad, and then of Graham and Morton M'Michael. Both Conrad and M'Michael have been chief magistrates of Philadelphia. Conrad edited the *Daily Intelligencer* in 1832, and then the *Philadelphia Gazette*, with which the *Intelligencer* was united. Condy Ragout, the economist, was associated with him on the *Gazette*.

It was the *North American* that inspired the other journals of Philadelphia to great efforts, and helped to infuse more energy in the operations and enterprise of the *Tribune* of New York. The amiable George H. Hart, an old partner of Chandler's in the *United States Gazette*, made frequent visits to New York in the news competition of this period; but so largely increased had the expenses of the papers become by this fresh energy in their management, that the venerable Chandler felt constrained to retire from journalism, and in 1847 he disposed of his entire establishment to the proprietors of the *North American* for $45,000, and the two names and the two papers were merged in one. This closed the career of the *United States Gazette*. The intellectual power of the new concern was increased by the addition of Dr. Robert M. Bird, the author of Gladiator and the Broker of Bogota, and G. G. Foster, afterward the well-known "City Items" of the *New York Tribune*, and author of New York by Gaslight.

The *North American* is now owned and nominally edited by Morton M'Michael. It is made up of many papers and of the following material:

1st. *The Pennsylvania Packet, or the General Advertiser*, established in 1771.
2d. *The American Daily Advertiser*, 1784.
3d. *Gazette of the United States*, 1789.
4th. *Evening Advertiser*, 1793.
5th. *United States Gazette*, 1804.
6th. *True American*, 1820.
7th. *Commercial Chronicle*, 1820.
8th. *The Union*, 1820.
9th. *The North American*, 1839.
10th. *Commercial Herald*, 1840.

Thus the *North American and United States Gazette* of the present day has absorbed no less than nine other papers, and if the good qualities of these nine are concentrated in one, that journal ought to be an excellent one. The *North American* can claim to be, by purchase, the oldest daily paper, morning and evening, published in the United States, although its own age dates back to 1839 only, and its name and that of the original journal of the United States are entirely different.

The *Impartial Intelligencer* was established in Greenfield, Massachusetts, on the 1st of February, 1792, by Thomas Dickman. Six months subsequently this name was abandoned, and the paper became the *Greenfield Gazette*. Its publication was continued with various changes in name till 1841, when it was united with the *Courier*, and was thenceforward known as the *Gazette and Courier*, and is still published. It was passed over to John Denio, who had been apprentice to Dickman, by purchase, in 1801. He went to Albany in 1827, where he published the *Morning Chronicle* for several years. Buckingham, and many other prominent printers and journalists, commenced as apprentices in the office of the *Gazette*.

CHAPTER XIII.//
SEVERAL NOTABLE JOURNALS.

THE NATIONAL GAZETTE OF PHILADELPHIA. — ORGAN OF THOMAS JEFFERSON.—THE CELEBRATED FRENEAU. — NEWSPAPERS IN NEW JERSEY.—THE MASSACHUSETTS MERCURY AND NEW ENGLAND PALLADIUM. — SHIPPING NEWS AND HARRY BLAKE. — INCIDENTS IN HIS LIFE. — NOAH WEBSTER AND THE NEW YORK COMMERCIAL ADVERTISER. — COLONEL WILLIAM L. STONE.

ONE of the remarkable journalists that the creation of parties produced in this country was Philip Freneau. We have already mentioned him in these pages. In October, 1791, he started the *National Gazette* in Philadelphia, while he was a clerk in the State Department under Jefferson, a position which he obtained through the influence of Madison, who had been a classmate of his at Nassau College. Ten years previously he was connected, as a writer, with the *Freeman's Journal*. Three or four years of his time were spent on that paper. Other publications afterward received his contributions in numerous sharp paragraphs and satirical verses on the men, manners, and measures of that momentous period of our history. After being a sea-captain, he edited the *Daily Advertiser* of New York. When the national government went to Philadelphia he accompanied Jefferson, and became famous as the editor of one of the leading organs of the rising Democratic Party.

The *National Gazette* was a Democratic organ in every sense of the word. It violently assailed the measures of Hamilton and his adherents in the cabinet of Washington; it was vituperative on Adams, and boldly attacked Washington personally whenever he showed any leaning to the Federal side. The course of Freneau created trouble in the political family of the President. It would have been strange if it had failed to do this. Indeed, it was believed that the policy of the *Gazette* was inspired by Jefferson. Washington was of this opinion. Freneau at one time, on oath, made a statement that Jefferson did not suggest or furnish any of the contents of the paper at that period. This did not shake the belief of Washington, who repeatedly brought the matter up in cabinet meetings. The President had even requested Jefferson to administer some rebuke to Freneau for his conduct. In his *Anas*, Jefferson stated that, at a cabinet council, Washington remarked:

That rascal, Freneau, sent him three copies of his paper every day, as if he thought he (Washington) would become the distributor of them; that he could see in this nothing but an impudent design to insult him: he ended in a high tone.

On another occasion, speaking of the President, Jefferson said:

He adverted to a piece in Freneau's paper of yesterday; he said he despised their attacks on him, personally, but that there had never been an act of the government, not meaning in the executive line only, but in every line, which that paper had not abused. He was evidently sore and warm, and I took his intention to be, that I should interpose in some way with Freneau, perhaps withdraw his appointment as translating clerk in my office. But I will not do it. His paper has saved our Constitution, which was galloping fast into monarchy, and has been checked by no one means so powerfully as by that paper. It is well and universally known that it has been that paper which has checked the career of the monocrats.

According to Griswold, it was acknowledged by Freneau, in his old age, to Dr. John W. Francis, in New York, that Jefferson wrote or dictated the most offensive articles in the *Gazette* against Washington and his Federal friends. On one occasion he showed a file of that paper to Dr. James Meade, in which the alleged contributions of Jefferson were marked.

Shortly after the Presidential election of 1792, when John Adams and George Clinton were the candidates for Vice-President, the *Gazette* published a paragraph which we annex, and which was in full accordance with the views of Jefferson, as indicated in the above memoranda from his *Anas:*

The mask is at last torn from the monarchical party, who have, but with too much success, imposed themselves upon the public for the sincere friends of our republican constitution. Whatever may be the event of the competition for the Vice-Presidency, it has been the happy occasion of ascertaining the two following important truths:—first, that the name of Federalist has been assumed by men who approve the constitution merely as "a promising essay towards a well-ordered government;" that is to say, as a step towards a government of kings, lords, and commons. Secondly, that the spirit of the people continues firmly republican, and if the monarchical features of the party had been sooner held up to the public view, would have universally marked the division between two candidates (equally unassailed in their private characters) one of whom is as much attached to the equal principles of liberty entertained by the great mass of his fellow-citizens, as the other is devoted to the hereditary titles, orders, and balances, which they abhor as an insult to the rights and dignity of man.

Freneau was severe on Hamilton. He was so frequent in his attacks that Hamilton finally came out in reply, in which he charged that the *National Gazette* had been established for the special use of the Secretary of State. In the controversy, Jefferson assigned as a reason for sustaining Freneau the desire he had to have the news from the Continent of Europe translated from the *Leyden Gazette,* instead of having it come frittered through the English press to the American readers: all Jefferson did was to furnish the *Leyden Gazette* to Freneau!

The *National Gazette* continued to be the organ of the Republican

Party, pouring its hot shot into the Federal camp whenever a proclamation was issued or any opportunity offered, and was only eclipsed in violence by the *Aurora*. Soon after the appearance of the yellow fever in Philadelphia in October, 1793, the *Gazette* said:

With the present number (208) concludes the second volume, and second year's publication of the *National Gazette*. Having just imported, on his own account, a considerable quantity of new and elegant printing types from Europe, it is the editor's intention to resume the publication of this paper in a short time, and previously to the meeting of Congress on the second day of December next.

The publication of the paper was never resumed. It had accomplished its work. Freneau afterward contemplated publishing a paper in New York, and both Jefferson and Madison gave him letters to parties in that city, commending him for his "extensive information and sound discretion." The publication of the paper in New York was deferred. In May, 1795, he issued the *Jersey Chronicle* at Mount Pleasant, N. J., in which he continued to oppose the Federalists. He set the *Time-Piece* agoing in New York in March, 1797. Matthew L. Davis afterward became its editor. It passed from his management into the hands of an Irishman, named John D'Oley Burke, the author of a play called "Bunker Hill, or the Death of Warren." Burke was arrested in 1798, under the Alien and Sedition laws. In 1808 he was killed in a duel.

Meanwhile Freneau again "went down to the sea in ships," and commanded a merchant vessel for several years. With his active brain there was no rest, and, for want of other mental stimulant, he published and republished his poems. In the War of 1812–15 he celebrated our victories as the lamented Halpine, better known as Miles O'Reilly, did those of the rebellion of 1861–5, in characteristic song and sentiment.

In 1832, Freneau, in the eightieth year of his age, perished in a snow-storm near Freehold, New Jersey. On the 29th of August, 1871, Miss Catharine L. Freneau, his daughter, died near Newtown, L. I., aged 70. No doubt she has left papers belonging to her father of considerable historical value.

Newspapers have not made their mark in New Jersey as in many of the old states. Situated between New York and Philadelphia, it has been placed in a position to enjoy the news facilities of those two cities. All the expresses of the New York journals from Washington had to pass over its territory. The *State Gazette* and *True American* of Trenton, and the *Daily Advertiser* of Newark, are now the leading papers of the state. The *State Gazette* was established in 1792. It is at present edited by E. R. Borden. The *Newark Advertiser*, which was the old Whig organ, has been the most enterprising sheet in the state. It was the first daily paper there. Its first number was issued on the 1st of March, 1832. It would run expresses from New York with important news, and make other efforts at first-class journalism. William B. Kenney is its proprietor and chief editor. He was appointed minister to Sardinia by President Fillmore. While absent on this diplomatic mission the *Advertiser* was managed by a son of its proprietor. The *True American* is edited by Judge David Noar, and is the Democratic organ in that state. The *Evening Courier* is the extreme radical Republican organ in Newark, and perhaps in the state. The *Daily Journal*, published in Newark, is a leading Democratic paper. It is said that its ablest articles were written by the late ex-Senator James W. Wall.

On New Year's Day, 1793, Alexander Young and Samuel Etheridge issued a tri-weekly paper in Boston, which they named *The Massachusetts Mercury*. In the course of a year the junior partner retired, and Thomas Minns came into the establishment. "Conscious that the low ribaldry and personal defamation which frequently disgrace European publications, and sometimes contaminate the purer effusions of the American Press, have a most certain tendency to depreciate its worth, obstruct its utility, and to sap the foundation of every thing dear and valuable to mankind, the editors of the *Mercury* will ever strive, with the most cautious attention, to avoid the rocks on which but too many of their contemporaries have been shattered." They also endeavored to make the *Mercury* "immutably impartial;" but it became a little excited over a controversy on the organization of the *Illuminati* in Europe, in which the Freemasons in this country became a party. The Rev. Dr. Morse preached a sermon on the subject, which was published in the *Mercury*. Dr. Josiah Bartlett, of Charleston, replied on behalf of the Masons.

Warren Dutton was the chief editor of the *Mercury* in 1801, when the name of *New England Palladium* was appended to the original title. Among its contributors was Fisher Ames, who did so much toward the ratification of the Federal Constitution in Massachusetts. Ames, in an essay on newspapers in 1801, strongly opposed descriptions of murders in the public prints. He was desirous of having a higher class of information given.

Another controversy sprung up in 1808, on the writings of William Godwin and the works of Noah Webster, who was then publishing the Columbian Dictionary. Webster contended for the rights of America in literature, as in commerce and manufactures. All these questions have been solved, and passed into history, and have had their influence on the public mind.

Notwithstanding its "immutable impartiality," the *Palladium*, like all its predecessors, in the midst of so many exciting questions, and of changes of editors and writers, did not always please its readers, and it began to lose the influence and patronage it had received. Its commercial reports, although comparatively meagre, aided materially in its prosperity. These were not affected by politics, or religion, or morals. It was in advance of its contemporaries in this department. Shipping news seemed to have been one of the chief features with the press in Boston, and afterward with the press in all the sea-port towns of the United States. Major Russell, of the *Gazette*, was in the habit of boarding the vessels himself for such news. He paid more attention to this branch of intelligence than many of his rivals. The *Palladium* became well known for the fullness of its marine department. It was under the management of Henry Ingraham Blake, a small, active man, a journeyman printer, who preferred running around the wharves, boarding vessels, and visiting merchants' offices, picking up items of shipping news here and there, to standing all day in an office at case.

Harry Blake, as he was familiarly called, was as much of a genius in his branch of journalism as the most accomplished writer was in his department. Indeed, it requires a man of peculiar tact to collect and arrange shipping news intelligently and economically for a newspaper and the merchant. It has always been difficult to find competent persons to manage such a department with accuracy and knowledge. There is no poetry about it. It is made up of hard facts. There are only two or three attached to the Press of the present day that at all comprehend its value and importance. The *Journal of Commerce* and *Herald*, of New York, have always made a feature of marine news. They have spent large sums of money for this purpose. It has always been a feature with the *Boston Advertiser*, which it inherited when it absorbed the *Palladium* and *Gazette*. Harry Blake made it an indispensable department of the *Palladium*. He knew all about the mercantile marine of Boston. Not a ship, not a vessel, indeed, belonging to that port, that he did not know her history, from her launch till she ceased to float. He knew her owner's name, her captain's name, when she was due at any port, could almost point out on the map where she ought to be on any given day. Wonderful genius was Harry Blake!

It was the early habit in Boston for each paper to collect its own shipping news. Its marine reporter would spend much of his time in looking over log-books, gathering facts from sea-captains, or from late letters just received by merchants. On the establishment of the Merchants' News-room in the old State House by the indefatigable Topliffs, much of the shipping intelligence of the port of Boston was collected by Samuel Topliff, who kept a small row-boat for the purpose of boarding vessels. Such news was immediately placed on his books. Thence it passed, through the reporters, into the papers. But Harry Blake depended upon no one individual for his news. He would travel miles for a solitary fact, and lose a night's sleep for a mere item. In the worst weather he was on duty. He had a quick, nervous way of doing business. He would ask a captain a hundred questions. But for his knowledge, enabling him to put the right questions to the right persons, much interesting information would have been lost. If short of paper, he would dot the latitude and longitude of vessels met at sea on his finger nails, trusting the rest of the intelligence to a tenacious memory. Sometimes he would collect a mass of news on a small piece of paper that, in its stenographic character, would throw the chirography of the elder Napoleon or Jules Janin into the shade. It was, however, as clear as old English to Blake. He put his own news in type. No compositor was necessary for him. It was a curiosity to see him at work at his case. His motion was see-saw, mumbling to himself some words, intelligible only to Blake or Neptune, with an occasional look at an old scrap of paper, or at his finger-nails, for the degrees of latitude and longitude—the most beautiful figures of rhetoric to him.

It is related that on one Tuesday afternoon he saw a ship coming up the Boston Harbor under full sail, with every inch of canvas spread. He was standing on the end of Long Wharf, opposite which the ship rounded to and dropped anchor. Harry Blake hailed her. "Ship ahoy! What's your name?" "The Hero, Captain Fox, from Liverpool," was the answer. "When did you sail?" "Sunday before last!" came thundering from the stentorian lungs of her commander. "Good gracious!" exclaimed Harry, "only two weeks from Liverpool?" Much excited, he ran up the wharf, up State Street, telling every one he met of the Flying Dutchman, and back again to the end of the pier before he became calm enough to get the news brought so rapidly across the Atlantic by this wonderful clipper.

After a long service on the *Palladium*, and then on the *Courier*, he was induced to go to New York, where he undertook to arrange the shipping news for the *Journal of Commerce*, and afterward for the *New York Express*. He failed on both papers. New York, with her extensive range of short piers, her immense commerce, her mode of collecting news of this sort so entirely different from that he had been accustomed to, bewildered an already worn-out and overtasked man. He, therefore, utterly failed, and he returned to Boston discomfited, disheartened, emphatically disgusted with the metropolis. His usefulness was gone, and he died shortly after his return home.

The end of the *Palladium* was near. In 1828 Young and Minns retired, and G. V. H. Forbes, of *Zion's Herald*, took charge of it. In another year it was passed over to E. Kingman. Then it became a part of the *Centinel*, and was finally merged with the *Advertiser*. On their retirement, Young and Minns were, like Major Russell, the recipient of a banquet from the editors and printers of Boston. They both died in the same year—1834.

We recollect Mr. Young very well in 1830. He then lived in Oliver Street, and was very tenacious of his rights to an old pear-tree that bore fruit on the edge of his yard. It was very old—as old, perhaps, as the famous Stuyvesant Pear-tree on the Third Avenue, New York. Such trees were not common in Boston. To get some of the pears before they were ripe was an enterprise of the boys who lived in Milk Street, and whose father's yards extended to the court leading to Mr. Young's yard. But the old gentleman was too much for the boys. There he stood guard, with his white hair streaming in the breeze, watching over that tree. Not a pear could they get. When the fruit was ripe he had it carefully picked, divided into as many lots as there were houses on the court, and sent to each neighbor a full basket, with his compliments to parents and children. Such was the character of the old publisher whose newspaper we have briefly sketched on these pages.

One of the sons of Mr. Young became a distinguished Unitarian clergyman in Boston; another was a teacher in one of the large schools in that city; and a grandson now very creditably occupies a professor's chair at Harvard.

Noah Webster, the lexicographer of America, was a lawyer in 1793, and had an office in Hartford, Connecticut. Washington's administration was then violently assailed by the *Aurora*, *National Gazette*, and other organs of the Republican Party, and by the partisans of France. Jefferson was organizing the opposition elements, and Hamilton was endeavoring to strengthen the Federal party. Newspapers were established on each side as the chief means of accomplishing the objects each party had in view. Noah Webster was considered, in this state of affairs, the man to aid the Federalists journalistically in New York. He was, therefore, induced to remove to that city and take charge of a Federal organ.

On the 9th of December, 1793, he issued the first number of a daily paper, which was named the *Minerva*. According to its imprint, it appeared "every day, Sundays excepted, at four o'clock, or earlier if the arrival of the mail will permit." On its title was inscribed its purposes and objects—its trade-mark. It was the "Patroness of Peace, Commerce, and the Liberal Arts." Mr. Webster, on entering his journalistic career, announced that his paper would be the "Friend of Government, of Freedom, of Virtue, and every

Species of Improvement." Later, in reply to complaints from his readers, he published an address, in which he said:

> I have defended the administration of the national government because I believe it to have been incorrupt and according to the Spirit of the Constitution. I have advocated the Constitution because, if not perfect, it is probably the best we can obtain, and because experience teaches us, it has secured to us important rights and great public prosperity. * * * * I have cautioned my fellow-citizens against all foreign intrigues, because I am aware of the fatal dissensions they would introduce into our councils, and because I hold it proper for us to attach ourselves to no foreign nation whatever, and be in spirit and truth *Americans*.

One of the first numbers of the *Minerva* contained an article on slavery, "intended to demonstrate that the labor of slaves in any country is less productive than that of freemen."

With the *Minerva* was connected a semi-weekly paper called the *Herald*. This was the first weekly, or semi-weekly, or tri-weekly paper arranged for country circulation, and made up without re-composition. Nearly every daily paper has now its weekly edition, prepared in this way, although the telegraph is beginning to drive them out of existence.

The names of *Minerva* and *Herald* were shortly changed to those of *Commercial Advertiser* and *New York Spectator*, and these names have continued for over three quarters of a century, and the principles of the establishment have been those of the Federal, National Republican, Whig, and the present Republican parties. While Mr. Webster was editor, the paper was published by George Bunce & Co. They were superseded by Hopkins, Webb & Co., in May, 1796. On the 1st of July, 1799, Mr. Webster dissolved partnership with Mr. Hopkins, and published the paper in the name of his nephew, Ebenezer Belden, and the firm was E. Belden & Co. till 1803, when he retired in favor of Zachariah Lewis. Noah Webster was a remarkable man. He was "somewhat above the ordinary height, slender, with gray eyes and a keen aspect; remarkable for neatness in dress, and characterized by an erect walk, a broad hat, and a long cue." Mr. Webster died in New Haven in May, 1843, aged 85.

On the 13th of January, 1813, Mr. Lewis announced that he had associated with him Mr. Francis Hall, who had then been with him in the office for about two years. Mr. Lewis continued to occupy the chief editorial chair until April 11, 1820, when he retired in favor of Colonel W. L. Stone, at that time editor of the *Albany Daily Advertiser*. The firm was now changed to Francis Hall & Co. Colonel Stone, in his salutatory, defining his plan of conducting the paper politically, took occasion to hint to those editors who "regret the transfer of this paper because the sacred interests of Virtue, Morality, and Religion may suffer by the change," that "they will so much the more expose to ridicule their own inconsistencies, and slander and insult the printed licentiousness and hypocrisy of their conduct. For their honest fears we thank them, hoping that we may always be induced to exemplify toward them that great Christian example of returning good for evil."

John Inman, a brother of the well-known artist, and called "the erudite and classic Inman," and Robert C. Sands, one of the most brilliant writers of his day, were editors of the *Commercial Advertiser*. Sands became connected with the paper in 1827, and remained till his death in 1833. Much of the reputation of the paper is due to these two writers.

Fitz Greene Halleck relates an anecdote of Colonel Stone, the chief editor of the paper, and James G. Percival, the poet. In 1826, Percival had visited New York in reference to the publication of his poems, the third volume of Clio, which afterwards appeared. On Percival's return to New Haven, Mr. Halleck says:

Mr. William L. Stone, then the editor of the *Commercial Advertiser*, opened a correspondence with him referring to the desired volume, and offering his services in obtaining a publisher, carrying the work through the press, &c., and for a time had reason to hope that his request would be granted; but after a delay of some weeks, PERCIVAL wrote him that circumstances had put it out of his power to devote himself to poetry, and had compelled him to accept employment in that most degrading and disgraceful of all occupations—the editorship of a party newspaper. As Mr. STONE had long and honorably held that position, and cherished it dearly as a source not only of power and profit, but of social pleasure, the *mal apropos* ingenuousness of the sensitive poet amused us all exceedingly, and no one more so than Mr. STONE himself.

Mr. Percival subsequently became connected with Noah Webster in superintending the printing of the first quarto edition of the American Dictionary.

Colonel Stone, having acquired considerable reputation for his Biography of Red Jacket and his Life of Brant, was in 1839 appointed Commissioner to England and Holland, to search for documents in the archives and museums of those countries to illustrate the history of New York, but he was rejected by the State Senate.

The following letter from Mrs. Stone, describing the last moments of Colonel Stone, is interesting:

SARATOGA SPRINGS, Aug. 20, 1844.
GERADUS CLARK Esq.
Dear Sir: I have the honor to acknowledge your communication of the 21st together with the list of the resolutions passed by the Board of Education on the occasion of my husbands death.
* * * * * * * * * *
He suffered greatly during his illness, physically and mentally. His mental depression was doubtless the result of his disease. But the sense which he had of his unworthiness and the depth of his humility, were most touching. He was constantly praying that he might not be deceived—that there should be no mistake —that his repentance might be genuine. "Oh" he would say in the midst of all his mental distress "if it be my Heavenly Father's discipline to fit me for heaven, and I may have the very lowest place at his footstool, I shall rejoice in it all." *
* * * *

One day, he said, "I may go suddenly, and not be able to say any thing to bear testimony to my belief." He then repeated in a very audible and impressive manner the creed as it is in the book of Common Prayer—adding "should my impression be realized, remember this my dying testimony—this I solemnly believe." He had his reason till the last, though he dropped away very suddenly and unexpectedly to us all. But at the closing struggle, a beam of heavenly light overspread all his features, and the expression upon his face was that of unutterable— unutterable happiness. There was also an expression of holy triumph, which seemed to say "I have escaped the tempter forever."

* * * * * * * * * * * * *

With great respect,

S. P. STONE.

Colonel Stone was very particular in the use of words. He was, indeed, a hypercritic. This incident, therefore, is curious. In a paper read before the Historical Society of New York in 1844, by John R. Bartlett, Esq., on American Provincialisms, he said, in speaking of the term "cocked hat,"

About two years ago there was a severe storm in this section of country, the mails were all stopped, and the *New York Commercial Advertiser* on the day of the departure of the steamer for England, apologized for the paucity of its news by saying that the storm had been so heavy as to knock all the mails into a cocked hat. Upon this the *London Spectator* remarked that the news from America, by that arrival, was very light, which was accounted for by the *New York Commercial Advertiser* in a very strange way. That paper stated that there had been a heavy storm there, and that all the mails were knocked into a cocked hat, a singular position of things, which it was impossible to define.

On the death of Colonel Stone, his interest was purchased by John B. Hall. Nothing else of interest occurred till the retirement of Francis Hall on the 1st of January, 1863, when William H. Hurlbut became its editor. Then Thurlow Weed, still affected with the *cacoëthes scribendi*, took up the editorial pen of the *Commercial Advertiser*. But, breaking down in health, compelled to go to Europe, then to pass a winter in South Carolina, he abandoned journalism, and left that paper entirely in the hands of Hugh Hastings, who had become interested in the concern. Hastings had been an editor in Albany, where, among other papers, he managed the *Knickerbocker*. Since his arrival in New York he has been in an irrepressible conflict with Horace Greeley and James Brooks. The latter carried the matter into Congress, of which he is a member. Hastings has modernized the Commercial Advertiser, and made it a lively, spirited paper of the new school.

The *Commercial Advertiser* is the oldest daily newspaper in the metropolis. Of the hundreds of daily papers started in New York, from the time of *Bradford's Gazette* in 1725 to the *Journal of Commerce* in 1827, there are now only two survivors—the *Evening Post* and the *Commercial Advertiser*. So passes away the glory of journalism.

CHAPTER XIV.

THE PRESS AT THE WEST.

THE CENTINEL OF THE NORTHWESTERN TERRITORY.—THE FIRST JOURNALIST OF THE NORTHWEST.—NEWSPAPERS IN CINCINNATI.—THE GAZETTE.—CHARLES HAMMOND.—THE FIRST DAILY PAPER.—INTRODUCTION OF STEAM.—SYMMES'S HOLE.—HORSE EXPRESSES.—E. S. THOMAS.—NEWSPAPERS IN CHICAGO.—WONDERFUL PROSPERITY OF JOURNALISM IN OHIO, ILLINOIS, AND INDIANA.—THE OHIO STATESMAN.—THE ST. LOUIS REPUBLICAN.—SALE OF THE MISSOURI DEMOCRAT.—THE EARLY DAYS OF THURLOW WEED AND WILLIAM L. STONE.—REMINISCENCES OF NEWSPAPERS.

THE introduction of newspapers in the new settlements of America was at first slow, and as difficult, in the latter part of the eighteenth and in the early part of the nineteenth, as the introduction of printing seemed to have been in the fifteenth century. Sometimes type and ink could not be obtained. Then paper and a press were scarce articles. After these materials were gathered, subscribers were as rare as Diogenes found honest men to be. But all this has since been changed. Steam-boats and railroads have annihilated all these difficulties and troubles, and now the progress of journalism is rapid, and encouraging, and remunerative.

The Post-office and the Press were almost as intimately connected in their relations at the West as at the East when Campbell, the Postmaster of Boston, started the *News-Letter*. On the 9th of November, 1793, the *Centinel of the Northwestern Territory*, somewhat of a high-sounding title, was founded in Cincinnati by William Maxwell, who was the second postmaster of that town. This was the first newspaper and the first printing-office established north of the Ohio River, or in what was then called the Northwest. The *Centinel* was subsequently removed to Chillicothe.

It has been stated that Nathaniel Willis, in establishing the *Sciota Gazette* at Chillicothe, was the pioneer journalist of the Northwest. Willis, it will be remembered, was one of the publishers of the *Chronicle* in Boston during the Revolution. After leaving that concern he went to Virginia, and started a paper there in 1793. Then he published a paper at Shepardstown, and another at Martinsburg, familiar places during the Rebellion of 1861–5. The latter paper was called the *Potomac Guardian*. It was after this period that Mr. Willis drifted into the Northwest with his printing material, and it was not till 1796 that he issued the *Sciota Gazette* as the organ of the Territorial government. It is therefore quite evident that William Maxwell must enjoy the title of Father of the Press of the Northwest.

In 1799, another paper, the third in that wild region, was established. Its title was the *Western Spy and Hamilton Gazette*. The name of this paper was changed in 1823 to that of the *National Republican and Ohio Political Register*. In November of that year the *Independent Press and Freeman's Advocate* was united with the *Republican*. This paper has had among its editors Sol. Smith, since so well known as the actor and manager in St. Louis and elsewhere. His valedictory was characteristic. Stating to his patrons that, "with big tears rolling down his cheeks, and conflicting emotions struggling within his bosom, through the vicissitudes of fate he is constrained to take leave of them," he mentions various persons and parties of whom he must take particular farewell. Under the plea that editors are "lawful game," he gives the conductors of the *Gazette, Republican, and Advertiser* some hard hits, and then says :

To Cincinnati Bankers.—I have done you some service—I have opened the people's eyes respecting your praiseworthy exertions to benefit community, and there are not now ten in the city who would not rejoice to see you *exalted* high as your actions have merited.

To the Honorable City Council.—Wear crape on your left arms three weeks in remembrance of me.

Tattlers.—I am such a universal favorite with you that I will not attempt to stop your compassionate tears—let them flow freely—my good creatures.

Editors throughout the U. S.—You must endeavor to elect a President without my assistance.

Sol. Smith died, we believe, in 1869.

On the 9th of December, 1804, the *Liberty Hall and Cincinnati Mercury* appeared, and was published for eleven years, when it was united with the *Gazette*, which had been started into life in 1806. The *Gazette* was one of the most remarkable papers at the West. Its first great reputation was acquired while under the editorial management of Charles Hammond. Judge Bouvier declared it to have been one of the best-edited papers in the Western country. It was originally a weekly. One of its most active proprietors was Ephraim Morgan, who left Springfield, Mass., in the early part of this century, and learned to be a printer in the office of the *Western Spy*, of which he became part owner in 1813. On the reappearance of the *Gazette*, which was suspended for a time, Morgan, in 1815, sold his interest in the *Spy*, and purchased a share of the *Gazette*. About that time, or in 1819, that paper was published as a semi-weekly— the first in Cincinnati.

The West now began to show rapid material development. The Cincinnati press gave us the particulars of the first steam-boat on the Western waters. The General Pike, one hundred feet keel and twenty-six feet beam, was launched at Cincinnati in the winter of 1819. Her cabin was forty feet long and twenty-five broad. She had fourteen state-rooms and twenty-one side berths, and could accommodate eighty-six passengers.

It was in the *Gazette*, somewhere about 1820, we believe, that Captain John Clewes Symmes presented his curious theory of the formation of the earth and other planets, and "Symmes's Hole" was as famous then as the more recent astronomical discovery by Secretary Boutwell of the "Hole in the Sky," which he demonstrated with so much clearness on the celebrated impeachment trial of Andrew Johnson.

Isaac C. Burnet, brother of Judge Jacob Burnet, was editor of the *Gazette* in 1822, and had been such for several years. He sold his interest to Benjamin F. Powers, a brother of Hiram Powers, the sculptor. Powers continued as editor till 1825, when Charles Hammond took his place. Hiram Powers, in a conversation with the Rev. Dr. Bellows, in Florence, in 1868, in giving an account of his life before he went to Italy, said that he "was born in Woodstock, in Vermont. His father was a half blacksmith and a half ox-yoke maker. He lost all the property he had by becoming surety for a friend, and his family came near starving to death, subsisting a whole winter on milk and potatoes. Finally one of his sons picked up education enough to teach school, and migrated to Cincinnati, then a town of 14,000 inhabitants, where he started a newspaper."

There was an effort made to establish a daily paper in Cincinnati in 1826. It was the *Commercial Register*. Morgan Neville was its editor. It lived six months. In 1828 its original publisher revived it, with Edward Harrison as editor. This second effort expired in three months. One year previously, the *Gazette*, with a list of one hundred and sixty-four subscribers, made its appearance as a daily paper. This was on the 25th of June, 1827. In 1834, twenty years after its introduction by the *London Times*, the *Gazette* introduced the steam power-press in the Northwest. Stephen S. L'Hommedieu, another of the owners of the *Gazette*, should have the credit of this piece of enterprise. This press, it is said, has since been doing good service in the office of the *Dayton* (Ohio) *Journal*.

Charles Hammond, as we have stated, gave the *Gazette* its first reputation. This was in the early days of Western journalism. His style was strong and vigorous, and sometimes rather rough. He was thoroughly anti-slavery, and opposed the institution on the "other side of the line" amid all the changes in the ownership and management of the paper. His was the master mind in that establishment. He was assisted as editor by William D. Gallagher from

1839 to 1849. Subsequent to Hammond came Judge John C. Wright in the editorial chair of the *Gazette*. He had been a member of Congress from that district. After Wright, and in 1853, Colonel William Schouler, previously of the *Lowell Courier and Journal*, and of the *Boston Atlas*, assumed control of the paper. It had a circulation of 1800 daily, 6000 weekly, and 400 semi-weekly at that time. Some new energy was afterwards infused into the concern. Joseph Glenn and one or two others took the establishment in hand, and Cincinnati grew in newspaper readers. More attention was paid to news. More vigor was thrown into its original articles. We are told that as much was paid in telegraph tolls in 1868 as the entire receipts of the establishment were in 1853. Its aggregate circulation reached 78,000. Its daily circulation was as high as 44,000, although it has since fallen below that figure. The war excitement, of course, had much to do with this prosperity.

The establishment is now owned by an association of six active men. Its capital stock is $100,000. Its dividend in 1865 was 100 per cent.; in 1866, 50 per cent.; in 1867, 80 per cent. These dividends were exclusive of salaries paid to the proprietors. What is the cause of this marvelous prosperity? Of course the war had its effect, and enterprise its influence; but the real basis was in the wonderful growth of the West in railroads and population. In 1853 there were 80,000 inhabitants in Cincinnati. In 1870 there were 216,000. This great growth is indicated more clearly by the returns of the Cincinnati journals of the receipts from sales alone for the year ending December 31, 1869, as follows:

Enquirer	$172,387	Volksblatt	$ 97,065
Gazette	216,947	Times	127,000
Commercial	251,847	Volksfreund	70,008

Such remarkable facts as these are to be seen in the statistics of every large Western city. All the newspapers had to do, in this state of things, was to keep pace in enterprise with this increase in means and people.

William T. Coggeshall, in speaking of the Cincinnati press, gives the following striking facts:

On the 3d of December 1835, there was published entire in the *Gazette*; "THE CENTINEL OF THE NORTHWESTERN TERRITORY, Vol, 1, No. 10, issued by William Maxwell at the corner of Front and Sycamore streets, January 11th, 1794," almost 42 years previous. This paper occupied four columns and a quarter of the *Gazette*, in which there were *twenty-eight* such columns; therefore the *Centinel* of 1794 only contained about one seventh as much matter as the *Gazette* of 1835. The *Centinel*, gave news from France dated Sept 10th—from Portland, Me., Nov. 11th—from Baltimore Nov. 22d. It was announced in an advertisement that two packet boats would leave Cincinnati for Pittsburgh and return every *four weeks alternately*. Cincinnati was then *four weeks* distant from Pittsburgh—in 1835 it was about *seven* days, and in 1850 it was about 48 hours, by steam, and not *over* fifteen minutes by *telegraph*. In the *Gazette* of Dec. 3rd, 1835, was news from New Orleans as late as Nov. 12th and from New York as late as Nov. 19th. Papers are now received from New York on the third day after their publication, and the readers of Cincinnati daily journals are by telegraph furnished every morning with important New York, Baltimore, Boston, Philadelphia and Washington items, up to ten o'clock on the night previous.

There was another paper of note in Cincinnati called the *Inquisitor and Cincinnati Advertiser*. It was started on the 23d of June, 1818, by Cooke, Powers, and Penny. In 1819, G. F. Hopkins, of New York, took the place of Cooke and Penny. He was a friend of De Witt Clinton, and, full of that statesman's ideas, advocated internal improvements with vigor. It was through his efforts that grants were obtained for the Ohio, Erie, and Miami Canals. James M. Mason succeeded Hopkins and Powers, and during his *régime* Moses Dawson became notorious as an editor. He purchased the paper, and changed its name to that of the *Advertiser*. In 1825 the political status of the newspapers in Cincinnati became defined. The *Gazette*, under Hammond, was Whig, and the *Advertiser*, under Dawson, was Democratic. These journals became bitter foes, and the warfare between Hammond and Dawson was a relentless one. Oceans of ink were wasted in the conflict.

Another attractive paper in Cincinnati is the *Commercial*. It was established in 1845 by Greeley Curtis, although for J. W. S. Browne, now of Memphis, Tennessee, this honor is claimed. These were succeeded by Potter, who in turn was succeeded by Murat Halsted, who is a thoroughly enterprising journalist. In a recent libel-suit its daily circulation was sworn to be 20,000. It cleared, in 1867, a profit of $100,000. This paper was conducted with much tact, ability, and courage. Its correspondence from Washington and elsewhere indicates a true idea of journalism. One of its correspondents at the national capital was placed under arrest, in 1870, for the premature publication of the treaty made by the Joint High Commission of England and the United States.

The *Enquirer*, the well-known Democratic organ in Cincinnati, is a paying concern, with an excellent daily and weekly circulation.

Among the early editors of Cincinnati was E. S. Thomas, a nephew of Isaiah Thomas, in whose office in Worcester he served his apprenticeship. The former edited the *City Gazette* in Charleston, S. C., from 1809 till 1817. He established the *Commercial Daily Advertiser* in Cincinnati early in 1829, and was a supporter of Andrew Jackson till toward the close of his final term. Then he nominated John M'Lean for that office. This political movement proving a failure, he retired from the *Advertiser*. In 1835 he commenced the publication of the *Daily Evening Post* in the same city, which supported William Henry Harrison for the presidency. In December, 1839, this paper was suspended for want of support.

The most interesting literary labor performed by Mr. Thomas was his "Sixty-five Years of Reminiscences." He died in Cincinnati on the 22d of October, 1845.

Frederick W. Thomas, son of the aforesaid E. S. Thomas, and author of Clinton Bradshaw, established the *Democratic Intelligencer* in 1834. It was in favor of Judge M'Lean for the presidency. It lived six months. Thomas's popular song—

> "'Tis said that absence conquers love,
>   But, O! believe it not!
> I've tried, alas! its power to prove,
>   But thou art not forgot—"

was originally published in the *American* of Cincinnati in July, 1838.

The *Times* is an afternoon paper of Cincinnati. Its owner, one of the original proprietors, Calvin W. Starbuck, died in 1870, leaving a property worth three quarters of a million of dollars made by journalism. He refused, a few years ago, $225,000 for his newspaper establishment. Starbuck, with two other printers, started the *Times* in 1841 on a borrowed capital of $200. His associates soon became discouraged, when Mr. S. assumed the whole control, and made the daily and weekly editions two of the wonderful successes of the West.

The *Times* had an opposition paper to contend with in 1868. The *Cincinnati Chronicle*, as an evening paper, was issued in that year, with a capital of $150,000. There was a *Chronicle* printed in Cincinnati a number of years, about 1840, which was edited by E. D. Mansfield, afterward known as the "Veteran Observer" of the *New York Times*. Henry J. Raymond was its New York correspondent shortly after he took up his residence in that city. But this *en passant*. The originators of the new *Chronicle* made an effort to purchase the *Times* before issuing their paper, but refused to comply with Mr. Starbuck's terms. On his death the *Times*, material and good will, was appraised at $200,000. It was afterwards sold at auction for $138,550 to the *Chronicle*, and the two papers merged in one. The *Chronicle* is now the only evening paper published in Cincinnati. It is Republican in politics, and in favor of a protective tariff.

The first notable piece of enterprise on the part of the Cincinnati papers, after the steam power-press, was the running of an express with the President's Message. This was done by the *Gazette* in 1835. It was sixty hours from Washington. Here is a reminiscence:

John H. Wood, when publisher of the *Crisis* in 1825, had "stolen a march" on his cotemporaries by getting several hundred copies of the Message printed in Washington, and having them forwarded by mail, so that they arrived ready for distribution as early as the *Advertiser* and the *Gazette* received their "copy." The Message was issued from the *Crisis* office in *forty-five* minutes after its reception. When the compositors at other printing-offices had just received their "takes," the "extra Crisis" was being "cried" about the streets. On the following year,

Mr. Dawson, of the *Advertiser*, determined not to be behind hand again, through the intervention of a friend had extras printed in Washington and forwarded by mail, but again Wood "stole a march" upon him. Hearing of Mr. Dawson's plan, he made arrangements to have a copy of the Message sent one day in advance of the mail as far as Wheeling. It was brought to Cincinnati by the first boat, and before the "*Advertiser extras*" reached the city, the "extra Crisis" had been extensively sold through the streets. In 1835 the express was managed for the *Gazette* by Mr. Wood. The Message was issued at the *Gazette* office before other copies were received in the city. The expense of this express was nearly $200, still Richard L'Hommedieu was so well pleased with the success of the enterprise, that with characteristic liberality he gave an oyster supper to all the persons concerned, who could be collected at Columbus.

The *Ohio Repository*, which was established in Canton, Stark County, in 1814, is still published. It was started by John Saxton, who continued to work as compositor and writer from that time till his death, early in 1871. He was always a Whig and modern Republican. When news reached the office of the *Repository*, in September, 1870, of the victory of the Germans at Sedan, Saxton copied from his files of more than half a century previous an account of the defeat of the French at Waterloo, and the surrender of Napoleon I. to the Germans and English in 1815, and placed it with that of the surrender of Sedan and Napoleon III. in parallel columns.

The *Ohio Statesman* was once a power in Ohio. It was a wing of the Democracy in the West. What the *Patriot* was in New England, the *Argus* in New York, and the *Enquirer* in Virginia, the *Statesman* was in the Northwest. Samuel Medary, its publisher, was a well-known man in 1837-8-9. The *Statesman* had the public printing to help it along. In those days of party papers it was thought impossible to print a paper without this pap from the public treasury. The *Statesman* for a time was under the management of Charles C. Hazewell. C. C. H. is an extraordinary man; his experience as a political writer is great; his historical knowledge wonderful; his memory marvelous. While he had charge of the *Statesman* he published one number of the *Western Review*. This number contained nearly three hundred pages of original matter. He wrote every article and every line. It was equal in quality and quantity to any number of the *North American Review*. Hazewell, like Greeley, always needed a good business manager to carry him through. Steam-engines, whether on a man's shoulders or on a railroad, must have engineers. Hazewell is now connected with the *Boston Traveller*. Samuel Sullivan Cox, member of Congress in 1871-2 from New York, and known as "Sunset Cox," was owner and editor of the *Statesman* in 1853 and '54.

Indiana followed Ohio. The first paper was published in that state in 1808. It appeared in Vincennes. Since then newspapers have increased in that as in other states. In May, 1870, the journalists of Indiana held their twenty-first semi-annual meeting in Indianapolis. Various topics connected with the profession, such as "The Personalities of Journalism," "The Uses and Abuses of Advertising," "The true Relation of a Paper to its Party," were discussed; and there was also a poem by Benjamin F. Taylor, and an address by Mr. Fishback, of *The Indianapolis Daily Journal.* Indiana had in 1840 the famous Chapman. He was editor of the Indianapolis *State Sentinel* in that year, and in the notable campaign resulting in the election of General Harrison, he received false reports of the success of the Democracy. He ordered a woodcut of an enormous rooster to be inserted in his paper, and wrote to his brother to "Crow, Chapman, crow!" When the correct returns changed the political aspect, poor Chapman became the target of his opponents. But he survived the attacks, was a successful editor, but was always known as "Crow, Chapman, crow."

Missouri came next. The leading paper in that state seemed to be the St. Louis *Republican.* It was established in 1808. When its first issue appeared St. Louis was a small trading post, and Missouri had not even become an organized territory. The *Republican* was 8 by 13 inches in size. Now it is a blanket sheet. Since the commencement of its publication the Missouri Compromise excitement has thrice swept over the country, in 1820, in 1850, and in 1861, and with what wonderful results! The *Republican* has chronicled the weekly and daily growth of the Great West, starting with St. Louis as a small trading station, till the population extends to the Pacific, and St. Louis has become a great city, the fourth in rank in the Union, with a population of 310,864, and Missouri with a population of 1,721,295, the fifth in rank of the thirty-seven states. The *Republican* is a monster folio sheet, ably edited, and conducted with enterprise. One of its editors, Judge William S. Allen, died in 1868. He was editor of the Newburyport *Herald* in 1835, and went to Missouri in 1837. The *Republican* was purchased in 1838 for $28,000. It is now probably valued at $350,000 to $400,000.

The other leading journal of that state and that section is the *St. Louis Democrat*, Republican in politics, which was recently sold for $456,100. J. B. M'Cullough, at one time editor of the *Cincinnati Enquirer*, is the editor-in-chief. The *Republican* of March 23d, 1872, thus described the sale of the *Democrat:*

In compliance with the order of Judge Madill, of the Circuit Court, the *Missouri Democrat* newspaper, together with all its appurtenances, presses, subscription list, engine, type, cases, leases of office building, good-will, &c., was sold yesterday to George W. Fishback, one of the proprietors, for the sum of $456,100. By the terms of the court's order the bidding was restricted to the partners themselves, viz.: William McKee, owning one-half; George W. Fishback, owning one-third; and D. M. Houser, owning one-sixth. The sale was simply an equitable transaction to adjust and close up a partnership which the partners had failed to settle by their own efforts. The terms of the sale were: One-half cash, one-fourth in three months, and one-fourth in six months. The sale took place in the office of Irwin Z. Smith, one of the counsel of McKee and Houser. The partners were attended by their counsel, S. T. Glover, and H. N. Hitchcock, for Fishback, and Sam Knox and Irwin Z. Smith for McKee and Houser, together with William E. Burr, president of the St. Louis National Bank; A. G. Edwards, United States Assistant-Treasurer, and General J. S. Fullerton, as friend of Fishback; James Richardson, W. H. Benton, and Henry T. Blow, friends of McKee; and Constantine Maguire, Thomas Walsh, and ex-Collector Harris, friends of Houser. Mr. Theophile Papin acted as auctioneer. The first bid was made by Mr. Fishback at $100,000, to which Mr. McKee responded with one for $150,000. The third bid was $175,000, and the fourth $200,000, and then the bids were increased of $5,000 up to $330,000, when they dropped first to $1,000, then to $500, and at last to $100. Seventy-five were made at the latter figures, Mr. McKee's last one being $456,000, and Mr. Fishback's last the purchasing price. The sale will be formally completed on Monday, and Mr. Fishback will then take possession of the office and property. This is the first direct public sale of a large and established newspaper that has taken place in this country for many years, and the price paid affords some indication of the cash value of such a journal. It has been held a difficult matter to accurately estimate the worth of such an institution on account of the varied properties that make it up. The actual material in the *Democrat* establishment would be valued at a comparatively small proportion of the price which the journal has just sold for; but this material comprises only a small proportion of the real value of the establishment. The attributes of age, established character, political views, advertising patronage, public influence, and subscription list, all grouped usually under the head of "good will," constitute the substantial elements of value in an established journal. They are of a moral nature, and, to a certain extent, indestructible. The *Democrat* has its own share of the valuable elements, and they represent the larger portion of the handsome price for which the paper was sold. Notwithstanding rumors to the contrary, we understand that the political complexion of the *Democrat* will remain unchanged, and that it will continue to give a cordial support to the administration of President Grant. Mr. Fishback is an experienced and accomplished journalist, who has had a connection with the *Democrat* for nearly eighteen years; he will therefore be perfectly at home in his position as sole proprietor. Mr. McKee and Mr. Houser, in retiring from the profession, will bear with them the cordial good will and esteem, not only of journalists, but of all citizens who have a personal acquaintance with them.

Mr. Henry R. Boss, in a lecture before the Franklin Typographical Society of Chicago on the early newspapers of Illinois, gave the following interesting text:

The first newspaper established in this State was the Illinois *Intelligencer*, printed at Kaskaskia, in 1814 or 1815. The first journal printed in Chicago was the *Democrat*, which was founded in November, 1833. The *Illinois State Journal* was established in 1831, and the *State Register* on February 12, 1836. The latter was originally printed at Vandalia, but removed to Springfield. The total number of newspapers now printed in this State is over 400.

Thus, in Illinois as in Ohio, the progress has been marvelous. Wherever a village is organized and a post-office introduced, a newspaper and a printing-office was sure to follow. Indeed, the *Lanesborough (Minnesota) Herald.* is printed eighteen miles distance from the nearest post-office, and its exchanges are sometimes three weeks old before they reach the editor; and such is the mania for news and intelligence in that teeming region, that Colorado, it is stated, has now as many daily papers as New Hampshire.

One of the Chicago correspondents, in mentioning the newspapers of that city after the Rebellion, said:

The newspapers of this city flourished during the war, and reached large circulations. The *Tribune* took the lead, and its daily issues were sometimes 45,000. The *Journal* probably printed about half that number, and the *Times* two-thirds. But now the *Tribune* prints only 18,500, the *Journal* 7,000, and the *Times* 15,000. Of the *Tribune's* issue 9,000 are taken by one newsdealer and distributed over the Northwest. The same firm take some 7,000 of the *Times* daily. A firm here have adopted the English fashion of printing country papers. It prints the inside forms of about fifty weeklies on the same type. They are then sent to their centres for circulation, where the head is put on and the other form printed. And thus papers of all shades of politics—temperance papers, religious and literary papers, are alike, so far as two pages are concerned.

The *Chicago Evening Journal* claims to be "the oldest paper in the Northwest." If so, it must be seventy-five years of age! It is Republican in politics, and has "steadily advocated protection to home industry from unjust competition with foreign capital and labor, and at the same time demanding the reduction of taxation." The West has always been opposed to a protective tariff, and while many papers are strongly Republican, they are as strongly in favor of free trade. Their interests are largely agricultural, and a liberal exchange of products is their idea of prosperity. The Free Trade League, in their address to the public in 1869, said:

> The press of the West is on the side of liberty of trade; but three small newspapers in the great centres of Western life and thought, Chicago, St. Louis and Cincinatti favor "Protection;" while the great journals like the Chicago *Tribune* and *Times*, the St. Louis *Democrat* and *Republican*, the Cincinnati *Commercial*, *Gazette* and *Enquirer*, daily attack the monopolists. The Democrats have a traditional belief in Free Trade, and nowhere outside of Pennsylvania have the agents of the League found a single newspaper or a politician of the Democratic faith favoring "Protection."

The *Chicago Tribune* is one of the chief Republican papers in Illinois. Indeed, it is the organ of that party in that state, but still independent. It was brought into notice and success by Joseph Medill, who was elected Mayor of Chicago in 1871, and Dr. C. H. Ray, in connection with Mr. J. A. Cowles, its business manager. It is owned now by what is called the *Tribune* Company, and is in a vigorous condition, with a great prestige. It is a strong advocate of free trade. The income returns of 1870 show its prosperity: that of Joseph Medill was $20,859; J. A. Cowles, $30,923; William Bross, $17,978; Horace White, $13,917. The paper probably yields an income of $150,000 per year. Horace White is now the governing power of the establishment.

Ex-Governor William Bross, who has been connected with the Chicago Press for over twenty years, in repelling a charge made against him in 1869 by the *Post* of that city, thus alluded to the *Tribune:*

> But, to be more specific, in 1852, when the late Mr. Scripps and myself established the *Democratic Press*, he took charge of the political department—was practically what is now understood by managing editor—the position now occupied by Mr. White in the *Tribune*, and by yourself, as I suppose, in the *Post*. In addition to having charge of the business, I wrote generally both the local and commercial items. When we became able to procure assistants, I wrote articles on

the topography, resources and the present and prospective development of the city and the Northwest, and often political articles as well. In the intervals of the absence or the sickness of Mr. Scripps—often for weeks and even months together—I had the entire charge of the paper. In 1858 the *Press* and *Tribune* were consolidated, and then four editors were recognized as equals in the management of the paper, Dr. Ray, Mr. Medill, Mr. Scripps and myself. You will not deny that you often read your articles to me and corrected or changed them at my suggestion. Of course this thing was mutual all around. For nearly eleven years I think you must admit I have had good reason to suppose that I was "one of the editors of the *Tribune*." No man can truthfully say that I ever claimed anything more than that. If the public have ever given me credit for anything more, I fancy it is due to the fact that the editors of other papers in the city and out of it have held me responsible, not to say abused me, for nearly all the sins they ever saw fit to charge upon the entire establishment with which I was connected.

The managing editor of the *Tribune* for a few years was Sidney Howard Gay, who occupied the same position on the *New York Tribune* during the Rebellion, a gentleman of integrity, and a writer of ability. With his experience and accomplishments as a journalist, he succeeded in making a capital paper of the Western *Tribune*. Mr. Gay is now connected with the *Evening Post*, of New York.

The *Times* is also a prosperous journal. William F. Storey, its chief, paid a tax on an income of $38,000 in 1870. One of his partners did the same on $12,000. There was an episode in the career of the *Times* which might be made into an epic. Instead of one, however, there were several Helens to be avenged in this plot. Storey saw fit to criticise the performance of the Blonde Burlesque Troupe at the Opera-house in that city, which grievously offended Miss Lydia Thompson and her companions. In return, they posted the editor, in words that were plain, throughout the city. Here is a copy of the card:

> An appeal to the public of Chicago. The Times vs. The Blondes.
> A gross and outrageous public insult having been gratuitously offered to the ladies of the Lydia Thompson troupe by the Sunday and daily editions of the Times, we, the undersigned, hereby stigmatize W. F. Storey, its proprietor, as *a liar and a coward* for uttering what he knows to be false in attacking defenceless women.
> LYDIA THOMPSON,
> ELIZA WEATHERSBY,
> PAULINE MARKHAM,
> NETTIE HOPE,
> LINA EDWIN,
> FANNY CLARMONT.
>
> Crosby Opera House, Chicago, Feb. 21, 1870.

This did not satisfy the wrath of these indignant blondes, and they resorted to more severe measures. Miss Thompson and Miss Markham, assisted by two male members of their company, made an assault on Mr. Storey in the public street, near his residence, on the 24th of February, 1870. The reporter of the *Chicago Tribune* received the following statement of the affair from Mr. Storey. He was calm, and laughingly alluded to the encounter:

> My wife called at the *Times* office about five o'clock this afternoon, and we started for my residence on Wabash avenue. When near Peck court I saw a

man and woman come around the corner and approach a carriage which was standing in front of a house two or three doors from mine. When opposite the carriage a man, who I suppose is Mr. Henderson, stepped up in front of me and said, " Is this Mr. Storey ?" I replied, " Yes, sir." He then stepped back, and a woman approached with a small whip in her hand. She struck me, I think, on the shoulders. I did not feel the blow, as I had my overcoat on. I concluded that it was the intention to have me whipped by a woman, and to avoid it I caught this woman by the throat and took the whip from her. Henderson then came up and struck me on the forehead with the but end of a large cowhide. I took it away from him and he drew his revolver. He retreated some distance when two other men grabbed me from behind and pulled my hair. Quite a crowd had collected by this time, and Mr. Alexander and several gentlemen put Henderson and two of the women, Pauline Markham and Lydia Thompson, I believe, into a hack, and they were taken to the Armory by a policeman. The last two men who assaulted me got into another carriage and drove off. There were two hacks standing near my residence. A lady who lives near by told me that she had observed the two hacks standing there about half an hour, and that she saw the men take out and examine their revolvers, seemingly conversing as to what they intended to do. Some one called at my house during the afternoon and asked what hour I usually came to dinner.

According to the same reporter, Miss Thompson, on being conveyed to the police station, was pale with excitement. She related the circumstances of the case, and said that she had no other means of redress; that the law was powerless to protect her, as she could not break future engagements to return to Chicago and sue him for slander; that Mr. Storey had most cruelly and shamefully abused her; also, that he had called her by the most odious epithet that could be applied to a woman, and she could stand it no longer. She was glad at what she had done. The result of this affair was a fine of one hundred dollars imposed on each party engaged in the assault.

There was an effort made in 1865 to establish a paper on an extensive scale in Chicago. The journal was issued, and named the *Republican*. Its first editor was Dr. A. W. Mack. After having been in the Legislature for fourteen or fifteen years, he was appointed colonel of the Seventy-sixth Illinois regiment, and accompanied General Banks to the Red River. Subsequently Charles A. Dana, now of the *New York Sun*, who had just left the War Department, assumed the management of the *Republican*, but Chicago was no place for him. The paper was originally printed on a quarto form, but this has been changed to a folio—the old style of newspapers. The *Chicago Post*, in alluding to the fact, said that men " have no time to fumble and search for the news from sundry obscure, hidden, and diminutive pages. They want it placed before them in fair, large, open sheets, that they may see and comprehend it at a glance, and then attend to other concerns."

Notwithstanding the almost total destruction of nearly every newspaper establishment in Chicago by the terrible conflagration of October, 1870, the *Journal, Tribune, Post, Republican, Mail,* and *Times* were all published on reduced sheets within forty-eight hours, and in less than two months the publication of these journals in their old size, style, typographical beauty, and editorial vigor, was fully resumed. *Apropos* of this fire, the *New York Tribune*, on receiving news of the calamity, thus announced its mechanical and material capacity as a well-arranged newspaper establishment:

> Ever since THE TRIBUNE office was burnt out, in 1845, we have kept always on hand duplicates of every thing needed for the publication of the paper, forming in fact a complete duplicate office. Mr. Thomas N. Rooker, our foreman, yesterday telegraphed, on behalf of the Association, to Mr. Sidney Howard Gay, Managing Editor of *The Chicago Tribune*, placing this office at his instant disposal for the use of *The Chicago Tribune*, or any other Chicago newspaper. At the time of our own great calamity, twenty-six years ago, the prompt aid of neighbors was so efficiently rendered that we did not miss the publication of a single regular issue; nor have we ever missed one since. We have needed, in a quarter of a century, to call, just once, on a neighbor, for press-work; but we have always remembered the aid of 1845, and held ourselves ready to give help wherever it was needed.

What does Robert K. Fleming, the oldest living editor of Illinois, who published the *Kaskaskia Democrat* in 1822, think of all this?

One of the most graphic accounts of the early struggles of newspapers in the West is related by Mr. A. G. Ellis, the originator of the press in Wisconsin. The first newspaper in that state is thus described by him to the Wisconsin Editorial Association in 1859:

> My first acquaintance with the Art Divine was made at Old Herkimer, N.Y., in the year 1816, in the office of the *Herkimer American*, a thorough-going Federal paper, published by Edward P. Seymour. It had been originally set going by one of the Prentices of Cooperstown, and was the editorial establishment at which had been apprenticed Thurlow Weed and William L. Stone. The latter had just left the case, as I entered — was loafing a little in the streets, previous to his departure for Hudson, where he figured a while publishing a fancy paper called *The Lounger*, previous to his going into the *New York Commercial*. The former, Weed, had already reached Albany, leaving in the office of the *American* an old pair of slippers, a tobacco box minus a cover, a brass rule, and an equivocal reputation with the devil.
>
> I staid five years with Seymour, became expert at the case, could work the old Ramage so well at the commencement of the second year that I obtained the post of foreman, as well as devil, and continued to fill the places of apprentice, master, and editor, to the end of my time; Seymour rarely visiting the office, except to receive the moneys once or twice a week for the last two years. He was a good printer, but never wrote a line — a most towering Federalist, and carefully kept the *American* on the Federal tack, except about election time — when, somehow or other, he would every now and then take a sheer off toward the Democratic channel.
>
> I left my old master, with many feelings of regret, in 1820, and went out into the broad world, with but few acquaintances out of the village, and a little short of $100 in my pocket. Without any particular aim or object in view, I involuntarily directed my steps to the place of my nativity, Verona, Oneida Co., New York. Here I found a few who had known me in boyhood; there was a small grammar school at the place; I entered it for half a year; at the end of the term became acquainted with the notorious Eleazer Williams (Dauphin of France!) He was then in charge of a mission under the patronage of Bishop Hobart, of New York, to the Oneida Indians. He gave me a pressing invitation to join him at Oneida Castle, promising me all sorts of fine things in an educational point, (which, by the way, he never fulfilled.) I accepted his overtures, and repaired to the mission. I found him utterly deficient in English, and soon discovered that

he wanted me to teach him the language. A few months after joining him, he made me acquainted with his scheme for removing the New York Indians, from their reservations in New York to the neighborhood of Green Bay.

Among the various pursuits that engaged my attention at Green Bay, that of printing, and newspaper publishing, was never forgotten; but always thought of as my legitimate business, as soon as circumstances would allow. In 1826, Dr. Philleo, of Galena, volunteered a correspondence with me, proposing a copartnership for publishing two papers—one at Green Bay, and the other at Galena; a meeting was agreed upon between us, to be had at Fort Winnebago in May of that year. I kept my appointment, but the Doctor failed of his, which ended the affair with him. I did nothing further in my profession for several years, except to print a thousand lottery tickets, on a scheme for the benefit of sufferers by fire. John P. Arndt, of Green Bay, had lost a store and its contents by fire. He conceived the plan of selling lottery tickets, to reimburse; there was a singular genius in the place who, among a thousand other notions, had a handful of old Brevier, and an ounce or two of printer's ink. On examination, I found sufficient letter to set the necessary matter for a ticket. A bit of pewter furnished the means of a kind of border for the bill; an oak log, sawed off and made smooth of an end, furnished the stone; and by means of a planer instead of a platten, I worked off 1,000 of these tickets, which was, on the whole, a rather fair job, and the first printing ever executed in the State. Latterly I have offered a premium of $20 for one of them; but in vain.

But this was not starting the newspaper: In 1830-'31, I was chosen by Colonel J. C. Stambaugh, United States Indian Agent, to accompany him as Assistant, with a delegation of Menomonee Chiefs to Washington; it was then that their first treaty was made with the Government. I took the opportunity to draw and circulate, pretty extensively in the East, a prospectus for the *Green Bay Intelligencer;* Stambaugh favoring the scheme, and promising efficient aid in procuring the necessary materials to start it forthwith. So confident was I of his aid, and of complete success, that I contracted in April, 1831, at Detroit, for a Ramage press, and sufficient type, paper, etc., to issue a demi-sheet. But Stambaugh spent all his money, besides what was due me for wages in the expedition, before he got round to the Bay, and my hopes were again dashed.

My next move was to contract for surveying the public lands, for the express purpose of raising means to purchase these same printing materials. I wrought in the woods with the compass, during 1832 and part of 1833; the newspaper enterprise had began to be talked of and agitated in the place. Eberts, ambitious of political distinction, took it in his head that a newspaper would be just the thing to bring him into notice, and send him to the Legislature at Detroit. He approached me with his proposition, which I declined. While I was in the woods, in the summer of 1833, he found a partner to his mind, in John V. Suydam, esq.; between them they engaged the identical press and type I had negociated for a year and a half before, and undertook to start the *Green Bay Intelligencer*. I returned, from a small surveying job, late in November of 1833, and learned, for the first time, the proceeedings of Messrs. Suydam and Eberts, in the publishing line. I was shortly after waited on by Mr. Suydam, who soon disclosed the fact, that the issue of the first number was postponed for want of a practical printer. After a few preliminaries, he proposed to me a copartnership with himself, Mr. Eberts having acted only as factor for the purchase of the materials, which had not been paid for. I accepted the proposition, went into the office, and got out the first number of the *Green Bay Intelligencer*, for which I had issued proposals a year and a half before, on the 11th day of December, 1833, in the name of Suydam & Ellis. We published THREE NUMBERS under the copartnership, when Mr. S., not finding it as remunerative as he expected, proposed leaving the concern. I took the undivided responsibility on myself, and went on with it as well as my limited means would allow. The patronage, of course, was very light. In the course of the next summer, Judge Doty and Hon. M. L. Martin were opposing candidates for the Legislature from the Upper District of Michigan, (Wisconsin and Iowa,) and the *Intelligencer* favoring the pretensions of the Judge, Mr. Martin and his friends established another Press—a young man, by the name of Stevenson, printer. The name of the sheet I have forgotten (probably the *Spectator*, edited by Joseph Dickinson.) Some dozen numbers were published; Martin beat

Doty before the people in Brown County; the object of the paper was accomplished, and its publication suspended: I bought the materials of Martin, and added them to the office of the *Intelligencer*.

My paper was continued, with sundry suspensions and intervals, through 1834, and till June, 1835, when I took in as a partner, C. C. P. Arndt, esq., (who afterwards came to his tragic end in the Capitol, at the hands of Vineyard.) In the mean time it had received considerable patronage and assistance in various ways from the PEOPLE, and had come to be considered an institution of old Brown County, and regarded as a Democratic Organ. It was continued by Ellis & Arndt till 1837, when we sold the concern to C. C. Sholes, he being regarded as an unflinching Democrat, and being about that time chosen by democratic suffrages a member of the Legislature. This gentleman soon associated with his brother, C. L. Sholes, and between them it was not long after (notwithstanding their perfect understanding of the claims of the people of the county upon it) suddenly removed to Southport! This ended the publication of the *Intelligencer* at Green Bay. * * * * * *

Arkansas, then almost beyond the confines of civilization, and where Bowie-knives had their origin, was not without the light of the Press. Two weekly newspapers were published there in 1834, when the government was a territorial one. They were called the *Arkansas Gazette*, printed in Little Rock, and the *Helena Herald*, issued in the town of that name.

With emigration the Press always forms a part of the baggage train. Wherever there is a settlement a newspaper appears. Illustrative of this interesting fact, the Lawrence (Kansas) *Tribune* of April 10, 1870, in calling attention to a meeting of the Kansas, Missouri, Iowa, and Nebraska Press Association, said:

> When we came to Kansas, fourteen years ago, there was not a daily newspaper in the Missouri valley; now there are eighteen dailies, wielding large influence. There was not a telegraph, nor a railroad, except a few miles west of St. Louis, and not a railroad connecting the East with St. Louis, except the Chicago and Mississippi (now Chicago, Alton and St. Louis), and that was only finished to Alton. Now the country is gridironed with railroads, and the telegraph, through these presses, tells all this Western country the news of the East and of Europe for last evening before breakfast of this morning. Next summer these Western editors propose to cross the Rocky Mountains as excursionists to Salt Lake and California. Great is the progress of the age, and the press has done a mighty work in accomplishing these results.

And the *Frontier Index*, true to its name, moved westward with the progress of the Pacific Railroad, always keeping about sixty miles ahead of the trains!

CHAPTER XV.
TWO REMARKABLE NEWSPAPERS.

THE PHILADELPHIA AURORA.—BENJAMIN FRANKLIN BACHE AND WILLIAM DUANE.—CURIOUS INCIDENT IN INDIA.—THE ALIEN AND SEDITION LAWS.—TRIALS AND CONVICTIONS OF EDITORS.—SERIOUS RIOTS.—THE NEW YORK EVENING POST. — WILLIAM COLEMAN. — EXTRAORDINARY DUEL. — JOHN RODMAN DRAKE AND FITZ GREENE HALLECK.—WILLIAM CULLEN BRYANT AND WILLIAM LEGGETT.—NEWSPAPER CIRCULATION.—CHARLES HOLT, OF THE BEE AND COLUMBIAN.—THE FATHER OF "GALES AND SEATON."—CONGRESSIONAL REPORTS.—JOSEPH DENNIE, THE LAY PREACHER.

THE newspaper which unquestionably took the lead of all Republican or Democratic journals in the formation and early origin of the party was the *Aurora*, of Philadelphia. On the death of the *National Gazette* it was the special organ of Jefferson and his followers. It was first published and edited by Benjamin Franklin Bache, a nephew of Benjamin Franklin, and formerly of the *Advertiser*. It arrayed itself so strongly against the Federal measures of Washington's administration that its violence was frequently turned on Washington personally. Inspired by Jefferson, Madison, and other leaders of the party, it was a political power. No better illustration of the violence of party feeling which had been generated between the two factions towards the close of the last century can be given than in the following extract from the *Aurora*, which appeared in that paper immediately after the inauguration of John Adams and the departure of George Washington for Mount Vernon on the 5th of March, 1797. It was alleged at the time to have been the production of a "public functionary" and a distinguished member of the Democratic Party. Thus spoke the *Aurora*:

"Lord, now lettest thou thy servant depart in peace, for mine eyes have seen thy salvation," was the pious ejaculation of a man who beheld a flood of happiness rushing in upon mankind. If ever there was a time which would license the reiteration of this exclamation, that time is now arrived; for the man who is the source of all the misfortunes of our country is this day reduced to a level with his fellow-citizens, and is no longer possessed of power to multiply evils upon the United States. If ever there was a period of rejoicing, this is the moment. Every heart in unison with the freedom and happiness of the people, ought to beat high with exultation that the name of Washington from this day ceased to give a currency to political iniquity and to legalized corruption. A new era is now opening upon us—an era which promises much to the people; for public measures must now stand upon their own merits, and nefarious projects can no longer be supported by a name. It is a subject of the greatest astonishment that a single individual should have carried his designs against the public liberty so far as to have put in jeopardy its very existence. Such, however, are the facts; and with these staring us in the face, this day ought to be a jubilee in the United States.

This article was a little too strong for those days. The Spring Garden Butchers, who had been in the army with Washington, made an attack on the office of the *Aurora*, threw its type into the street, and almost demolished the inside of that newspaper establishment.

On the 9th of May, 1798, which was observed as a day of fasting and prayer, there came near being a very serious political riot in Philadelphia, growing out of the violent declamations from pulpits and elsewhere against Jacobins, philosophers, freemasons, and the illuminati. Several Republican quarters were marked for attack. Bache, for the protection of the *Aurora* office, collected and armed all his friends. Others did the same for the protection of their persons and property. These decided arrangements deterred the ringleaders, and very little damage was done. Several windows and lamp-posts were broken, and a statue of Franklin covered with mud. About this time a man named Humphries was convicted of an assault on Bache for political articles in the *Aurora*. It was charged against President Adams that he selected Humphries as a bearer of dispatches to France before the expiration of his sentence for the assault. So run the political excitement in the days of our political fathers.

In the fury of that dreadful plague, the yellow fever, which visited Philadelphia in 1798 for the second time, Bache was a victim to its ravages. The *Aurora* then became the property of his widow, and William Duane assumed its editorial management. It continued to be the violent partisan sheet it had been under Bache, and, indeed, a little more so. Let us see why. Duane was born in this country. His parents were both Irish. Early in life he went to Ireland, and learned the art of printing. Thence he went to India, and started one or two newspapers, one of which he published in Calcutta. There, with his ideas of the liberty of the press, he came in collision with the authorities, and was sent out of the country in a manner so cowardly and outrageous as to rankle in his bosom ever after. The incidents connected with this part of his career are too interesting to omit.

Duane, at the time of our story, was sole proprietor of the *Indian World*, by which he had acquired a handsome fortune. In September, 1794, he advertised his property for sale, with the intention of returning to Philadelphia. It was to be sold on the 1st of January, 1795, and he had engaged passage on board the Hercules, Captain Delano, of Boston, then lying at Calcutta, to sail in the following April. Strange as it may appear, when we take the result of this incident into consideration, Duane was at that time on terms of apparent friendship and good-will with most of the public characters in that part of India, and especially with the officers of the army, who had made the *World* the means of spreading their grievances before the public. Our editor had been particularly noticed by Sir William Jones and Sir John Shore. He had been flattered and honored with their attentions. On the evening of the 26th of December, 1794, a note was left at Duane's country house, written by Captain John Collins, private secretary of Sir John Shore, inviting Duane to the governor general's house on the next day at eight o'clock. The note did not reach Duane till the next morning. He immediately proceeded to the governor general's, expecting to breakfast there. Captain Collins met him in the saloon, and, after the usual salutations, the following conversation occurred:

Captain Collins. I am glad you are so punctual, Mr. Duane.
Mr. Duane. I generally am, sir; I hope the Governor-General is well.
Captain Collins. He is not to be seen, and—
Mr. Duane. I understand I was invited by him.
Captain Collins. Yes, sir; but I am directed by the Governor-General to inform you, that you are to consider yourself as a state prisoner.

He stamped on the floor, and thirty Sepahis, who stood concealed behind the folding doors of an anti-chamber, rushed out, and presented their bayonets to Duane's breast. The doors, being left open by them, discovered Sir John Shore and two others of the Supreme Council sitting on a sofa.

Mr. Duane. I did not think Sir John Shore, or you, sir, (turning to Capt. Collins) could be so base and treacherous as to proceed, or even to think as you do.

Captain Collins. Silence, sir. (To the Sepahis) *Chillow Sepahi:* Drag him along, Sepahis.

Mr. Duane. (To the Sepahis) *Osti babaa-hum beejagga:* Softly, my friends, I shall go along with you. (To Collins) What is to follow next, Collins; the bow-string or scimetar?

Captain Collins. You are insolent, sir. (To the Sepahis) *Chillow joub, soor Masani:* Drag him along, you pig-eating scoundrels.

Mr. Duane. You are performing the part of Grand Vizier, now, my little gentleman, and these are your mutes. Calcutta is become Constantinople, and the Governor-General the Grand Turk.

It is said that much more passed, and during the last utterances Duane was conveyed down stairs, put into his palanquin, and his bearers beaten all the way to Fort William. With a great parade he was there given in charge, with two sentinels placed at the outer door of his quarters, and one, with a drawn bayonet, always by his side, asleep or awake. This was on Saturday. On the following Monday morning a company of royal grenadiers were paraded on the ramparts, and he was marched to the water side, where a company of royal light infantry was ready to receive him in a barge, upon which he was conducted to an armed Indiaman, commanded by Sir Charles Mitchell, and carried to England. No charge was ever lodged against him. When at St. Helena he was not permitted to go ashore, as he was a foreigner. On reaching England he was landed without a single word of information or explanation.

When he thus left India his property amounted to about fifty thousand dollars. On application to one of the first lawyers in England to commence a suit for its recovery, that gentleman, ascertaining that he had only one thousand dollars remaining, returned him his fee of one hundred dollars, and said that although the case was one of the most oppressive in his knowledge, he advised Duane not to waste what he had left in competition with the wealth and power of the East India Company. Several gentlemen interested themselves in his case, and had written from India in his behalf. One wrote to Lord Lucan. That nobleman advised Duane, if he wished to recover his property, to go to Mr. Dundas, and disclose to him all he knew of persons in India! With a feeling of contempt, he picked up his hat and left. Immediately after, he took his departure for Philadelphia. On his arrival in that city he assumed the editorial charge of the *Aurora*, already a strong Democratic and anti-British organ, with bitter feelings towards England and every thing English. It is therefore easily seen why this well-known journal became, above all others at that time, the oracle of that vigorous young party. It is a curious fact that William J. Duane, the son of this early journalist, was the rebellious Secretary of the Treasury in Jackson's cabinet in 1834, when the government deposits were to be removed from the United States Bank.

Such was the heated state of politics in Philadelphia, then the Capitol of the Union, that mob or a personal assault was not a rare occurence. Duane, like his predecessor Bache, came in for his share. The extreme violence of the *Aurora* brought down upon it all the obloquy of the Federalists. It was evident that the Democratic Party was gaining strength. This fact did not tend to soften the feeling of asperity that had been aroused against Duane. It had, indeed, the contrary effect. The Alien and Sedition laws had been in force about a year, and several Democratic editors, as well as others, had come under their penalties. These laws were not in accord with the spirit of the people. Duane and the *Aurora*, and especially Duane, as these laws, in their operation, reminded him of the treatment he received at Calcutta, were strongly opposed to them. It was proposed in Congress to repeal them. To aid this movement, petitions were in circulation.

On the 9th of February, 1799, Duane and several other gentlemen went to St. Mary's Church, in Philadelphia, and posted upon its doors a petition for their repeal, in hopes of obtaining the signatures of the aliens of that congregation. Instead of accomplishing this purpose it resulted in a riot. Many of the audience rushed out of the church, tore down the petition, attacked those who placed them on the doors, knocked them down, and otherwise maltreated them. Dr. Reynolds, of the Duane party, was brought before the courts on the charge of attempted murder, and his companions on a charge of riot and assault on St. Mary's Church. They were acquitted. But this result was the cause of another more serious affair. On the 15th of May a band of thirty men entered the office of the *Aurora*. One section of this party, with pistols in hand, acted as sentinels over printers and pressmen, while another section prevented any interference from others in the office. The remainder then made an assault upon Duane, who appeared to be the special object of their vengeance. He was knocked down and inhumanly beaten. Then, bleeding and senseless, he was dragged down stairs and out into the street, where he was again brutally beaten. His young son, who had thrown himself across the body of his father to protect him from the ruffians, was also badly maltreated. The office of the *Aurora* would have been entirely demolished but for the timely arrival of a party of Democrats who came to the relief of Duane.

Alluding to this conflict between the journalists and the government, ex-President John Tyler, in 1858, said:

> The President, who was supposed to be inimical to France, was assailed by the press, and in all public assemblies, as well as in private circles, with a bitterness of invective rarely if ever surpassed. In a moment of weakness Congress gave way to the adoption of the Sedition law, and the press, so far from being restrained, seemed rather to increase in its bitterness. The government resolved upon prosecutions against the most violent. Judge Cooper was put on trial for libel, in Philadelphia; and Mr. Lyon elsewhere. Nor did Richmond go unscathed: Callender, who edited *The Prospect Before Us*, in a style of abuse never surpassed, and with whom, personally, no one really sympathised, was thrown into jail. The law of libel, it was said, was made to be more potent than the letter of the constitution which guaranteed the freedom of speech and of the press, and the fires of popular indignation blazed brightly and fiercely. I cannot here forego relating an anecdote which I received from the lips of Governor Mahlon Dickerson, of New Jersey, as illustrative of the violence of the times. Stephen Thompson Mason, then a Senator from the State of Virginia, repaired to Philadelphia, attended by the enthusiastic Dickerson, then a young man, to attend the trial of Judge Cooper. They took their seats on the right and left hand of Cooper at the bar, and when the jury returned their verdict of twenty-four hours imprisonment and a fine of $1,000, they each, rising in the court, shook hands most cordially with the prisoner. The next morning Fenno, who published the administration paper, came out with an article of the following tenor:—

> "The republican party is always committing some act of excess—but what occurred in court on yesterday surpassed anything that has yet occurred. Upon the conviction of Cooper, Stephen Thompson Mason, a Senator from Virginia, shook hands with the culprit in the very face of justice."

> Judge Chase, somewhat remarkable for the rotundity of his person and a florid complexion, presided at the trial. The following morning Dickerson prepared and published in Duane's paper—the *Aurora*—the following reply to Mr. Fenno's article:—

> Mr. Fenno is evermore committing great mistakes—but of all the errors into which he has yet fallen, that in his paper of yesterday is the greatest. He states that Stephen Thompson Mason, a Senator from Virginia, shook hands with the culprit in the very face of justice, mistaking the bacon face of old Chase for the face of justice.

There were a number of alien writers on the Press at this time who had become odious and hateful to the Federalists. John O'Ley Burke was one. James Thomson Callender, mentioned above, was another. William Cobbett, who came over in 1792, was employed by the Federalists to oppose them. Callender published the *Richmond Examiner*. "The Prospect Before Us" was not a newspaper, but a pamphlet. For this publication, which was a libel on President Adams, Callender was sentenced to nine months' imprisonment, and to pay a fine of $200. When Jefferson was inaugurated as President, he pardoned Callender and remitted the fine. Shortly after he was refused the office of Postmaster of Richmond by the President. He then turned against Jefferson, and stated that the latter had aided him with money in his previous libelous publications. Jefferson, in reply, said that he had helped him with $50 now and then, as he would have helped any other man.

The "Mr. Lyon" referred to by ex-President Tyler was Colonel Matthew Lyon, who was a representative in Congress from Vermont from 1797 to 1801. It was charged that he had written a letter, in July, 1798, to a printer of a newspaper, published in Windsor, in that state, "containing artful and indirect accusations" against the President of the United States "rejecting men of age, experience, wisdom, and independency of sentiment," and intimating that the chief magistrate exhibited a fondness for "ridiculous pomp, idle parade, and selfish avarice;" and that he, Colonel Lyon, had published parts of a letter, called the Barlow Letter, "abusing in a most virulent manner the President and Senate of the United States" in regard to France. All this, it was avowed, was with the intention "to stir up sedition, and bring the President and government of the United States into contempt." Colonel Lyon was indicted, arrested, and tried in October, 1798, before Judge Paterson, at Vergennes. He was convicted, and sentenced to four months' imprisonment, and to pay a fine of $1000.

Those days of journalism were days of peril to those who fought for a principle, but a revolution was looming up in the future which was to change all this.

Shortly after Duane had taken the management of the *Aurora* an interesting journalistic incident occurred, resulting in a libel-suit, in which Alexander Hamilton was the plaintiff. On the 6th of November, 1799, the *Argus*, of New York, copied from the *Constitutional Telegraph* the following extract of a letter from Philadelphia, dated the 20th of September:

<blockquote>
An effort has recently been made to suppress the *Aurora*, and Alexander Hamilton was at the bottom of it. Mrs. Bache was offered six thousand dollars down, in presence of several persons, in part payment, the valuation to be left to two impartial persons, and the remainder paid immediately on giving up the paper; but she pointedly refused it, and declared she would never dishonor her husband's memory, nor her children's future fame, by such baseness; when she parted with the paper it should be to Republicans only.
</blockquote>

On the 21st of November, David Frothingham, of the *Argus*, was indicted on the complaint of General Hamilton. The case was tried before Judge Radcliff, Richard Harrison, the Recorder, and the Mayor of the city. There was no sworn evidence on either side except that of Mr. C. Colden, assistant attorney, and General Hamilton. It was stated by Colden that, at the instance of a letter from Major General Hamilton, he had called at the office of the *Argus,* and was introduced to Mr. Frothingham as conductor of the business; that, after some conversation, Mr. F. said he expected that he was liable for any publication which appeared in the *Argus,* but repeatedly observed that he saw no criminality in the present instance as it respected him, as the matter in dispute had been copied from another paper. Mr. Colden added that, in pursuance of this declaration, Mr. Frothingham was arrested.

General Hamilton was called on the part of the state to prove that he was innocent of the charge alleged against him. This was objected to by Brockholst Livingston, counsel for the defendant, and the objection admitted by the court. General Hamilton was then asked to explain certain innuendoes in the indictment respecting speculation, etc. This having been done, he was interrogated as to what was generally understood by secret service money. He gave it as his opinion that it meant money appropriated by a government, generally for corrupt purposes, and in support of the government which gave it. On being asked if he considered the *Aurora* as hostile to the government of the United States, he replied in the affirmative.

Mr. Livingston then attempted to prove that Frothingham was not responsible; that his declaration to Colden should not be admitted as evidence against him, and that the attorney should have arrested the editor.

Mr. Hoffman, in reply, contended that every journeyman and apprentice in the printing-office was liable to a prosecution, as having been accessory to the publication of the libel, and that Frothingham, as foreman of the office, was especially so.

Mr. Livingston pertinently replied, and showed up this obnoxious, pernicious, and oppressive doctrine against the freedom of the Press and the rights of labor.

The jury rendered a verdict of guilty, but recommended Frothingham to the mercy of the court. He was fined $100, and sentenced to four months' confinement in Bridewell.

William Duane died in 1835.

There was an *Evening Post* in New York in 1746. There was another in 1794. The latter was published by L. Wayland and Matthew L. Davis, afterwards known as "the Old Boy *in* Specs," "the Spy in Washington," and the "Genevese Traveller." It was in the interest of Aaron Burr, and lived only a year or thereabouts. The third *Evening Post* was published in 1801. These three *Posts* were entirely independent of each other.

The *Evening Post* now in existence first appeared on the 16th of November, 1801. It was a Federal paper when it came into life. Such men as Alexander Hamilton and John Jay aided in its establishment. Indeed, it was considered the organ of Hamilton. It was edited by William Coleman. He was from Massachusetts, where he had been educated as a lawyer. He resided for a time in Greenfield, and wrote for the *Gazette* of that place. He represented the town two years in the Legislature. Soon after, in 1797 or 1798, he moved to New York, where he received the appointment of clerk to the Circuit Court. With other Federalists, he had been removed from office in August, 1801. In November he established the *Post*.

Although Coleman commenced with the determination to keep the *Post* clear of " personal virulence, low sarcasm, and verbal contentions with printers and editors," and with the design " to inculcate just principles in religion" and in politics as well as in morals, yet he found it impossible to do so. The fever of political excitement run too high to carry out any such purpose. He soon became entangled in a paper war with two leading Republican editors and organs—Cheetham, of the *American Citizen*, and Duane, of the *Aurora*. Their shafts flew so rapidly that he was compelled to ward them off and fight. Coleman was evidently equal to the combat. Some of his expressions were strong and emphatic. He called Duane " a low-bred foreigner ;" and, in alluding to Cheetham, he speaks of " the insolent vulgarity of that base wretch." On one occasion Coleman fired a double shot at his opponents :

> "Lie on, Duane, lie on for pay,
> And, Cheetham, lie thou too ;
> More against truth you can not say,
> Than truth can say 'gainst you."

When Philip Hamilton, the eldest son of Alexander Hamilton, fell in a duel at Hoboken in 1801, Coleman, shocked by the occurrence, denounced the practice of dueling as a " horrid custom," and, as " fashion has placed it on a footing which nothing short" of legislative action " can control," demands "strong and pointed legislative interference" to accomplish this desirable end. Shortly after this Coleman received a challenge from Cheetham, of the *American Citizen*, but, after considerable negotiation between the friends of the parties, Judge Brockholst Livingston, in order to prevent the meeting, ordered out a *posse comitatus*, and had the principals arrested. No hostile meeting, therefore, between these two editors took place. This arrest threw some doubt on Coleman's courage, and Captain Thompson, a harbor-master of New York, and a friend of the administration, declared publicly that Coleman would not fight. Thompson was a brother of Jeremiah Thompson, once Collector of the Port, and of Abraham G. Thompson, both well-known and respected citizens. When Captain Thompson made this charge there was great excitement among the political leaders. Washington Morton, Beekman, and others met at David Longworth's, the bookseller, in Park Row, and, after a brief consultation, it was decided that Coleman must challenge Thompson. Washington Morton carried the missive. Cheetham acted as Thompson's second. This was in 1803.

One morning in the summer of that year, Dr. M'Lean, a well-known physician and surgeon, received an anonymous letter, stating that at nine o'clock in the evening of the day of its date, the day he received it, he would find on the south side of the Bowling Green, at the foot of Broadway, a horse and gig. He was requested to take charge of them, and drive to a spot designated on the road running alongside of Potters' Field, where Washington Square is now, and there he would find some friends waiting for him. He complied with the request. He found the horse and gig at the time and place designated. It was a moonlight night. He drove to Potters' Field. On approaching one of the gates he heard pistol-shots. There were four exchanged between the parties. On reaching the spot and looking over the fence, he saw one man holding up another, and other persons at a little distance. The man who was supporting the other called and asked, "Are you Dr. M'Lean?" "Yes," answered the doctor. "Then," said the man, "this gentleman requires your assistance; be good enough to take charge of him, and place him with his friends." Then he gently laid the person he had held on the ground, and disappeared with the others. When the doctor reached the person thus strangely placed in his care, he found it to be Thompson, the harbor-master. He was severely, and, as it afterward proved, fatally wounded. The doctor stanched his wound as well as circumstances would permit, and brought him to his residence in the city. He was placed at the door of his house; the door-bell was rung, his family came, and found him bleeding and near his death. He refused to disclose the name of his antagonist, or give any account of the affair. He simply said he had been honorably treated, and desired that no effort should be made to find or molest his adversary. In two or three days he died, with the secret unrevealed. Coleman attended to his business as usual, and thus ended this extraordinary affair.

Michael Burnham, an excellent business man, had been the publisher, but not a proprietor of the *Post*. About 1804 he was taken in as a partner, and aided materially in the prosperity of the concern. He published a weekly paper in connection with the *Post*, which was called the *New York Herald*. One day, fifty years after this period, an old bound file of Burnham's *Herald* was taken to the office of Bennett's *Herald*, in 1854, for sale. When the owner of the old volume entered the editorial room, Colonel Alexander Hamilton was sitting there in conversation. "What do you want for the file?" asked the editor. "Two dollars," said the owner. "I will take it," replied Mr. Bennett. Turning to Colonel Hamilton, he said, "Don't you wish to go back to old times, colonel?" Colonel Hamilton took the volume and opened it at the very page containing an account, almost a column in length, of the fatal duel between his father and Aaron Burr. Singular coincidence!

There seemed to have been no lack of mental activity at that period of our history, but it took the editors some time to make up their minds what to say on the important topics of the day. This was part of the discipline of the party press. The annual message of Jefferson of 1801 was published in the *Post* on the 12th of December. It was the 17th before any notice was taken of it, and then this was done by "Lucius Crassus" in a communication. No doubt this delay arose from the fact that Hamilton and the leaders of the party had to be consulted previous to breaking ground on so important a matter as commenting on the first message of the chief of the opposing party. Other public matters were treated in the same way. Time was taken for reflection and consideration. But there was, nevertheless, great vigor in Coleman's articles in the *Post*. After the line of argument was decided upon, there was no lack of strength in the use of the English language. While the *Post* was a Federal paper, its editor was styled Field-marshal Coleman of that party. It was, however, opposed to the famous Hartford Convention of 1814. In alluding to this opposition, the *Post* at a later day said:

> When the New England states held their Convention at Hartford, the New York Federalists refused to send delegates, and their refusal was sustained by the *Evening Post*. Mr. Coleman, however, went to Hartford on that occasion, as an observer. We recollect that, some years afterwards, in his journal, he taunted Theodore Dwight, then editor of the *Daily Advertiser*, in this city, with having been the Secretary of the Hartford Convention. Mr. Dwight replied, that his accuser was also a participator in the doings of that body, and spoke of his presence there as the representative of the New York federalists. Against this imputation, Mr. Coleman defended himself with warmth, and in his usual frank and sincere manner, stated with great minuteness the object and circumstances of his visit. From this narrative, his ingenious adversary, who would otherwise have had little to say, contrived, by a skilful selection of expressions and circumstances, to make it a plausible, though by no means a fair case, against him.

The *Post* supported De Witt Clinton for President in 1812, although for a while it was opposed to that gentleman for Governor of New York. But Coleman finally came in to his support, and was friendly to his administration of the state government in the latter part of Clinton's career. Coleman was bitterly inimical to John Quincy Adams, and favored the election of William H. Crawford, of Georgia. One of Coleman's private letters, obtained in some way, and printed in the *National Advocate*, indicated the turning-point in the politics of the *Post*. It was written to Charles Miner, one of the editors of the *True American:*

NEW YORK, Sept. 28, 1816.

Why do you not make a little review of Mr. Stiles's pamphlet against Binns, such a one that we may all republish? Generally speaking, I feel disposed, in common with the leading federalists here, to stand perfectly still, and wait for events to happen, as Jefferson says, we know not when. Something may come from the quarrels of opposite sections of the democratic factions, and I think the most we can do is occasionally to fan the embers. W. COLEMAN.

It was during this period of political revolution, or in the spring of 1819, that the celebrated humorous odes known as the "Croaker pieces" appeared in the *Post*. They were written by John Rodman Drake. One afternoon, about this time, there was a group of young men standing in the vicinity of the Park in New York, just after a shower, admiring a magnificent rainbow. "If I could have my wish," said one, "it would be to lie in the lap of that rainbow and read Tom Campbell." Immediately another of the group stepped forward and exclaimed, "You and I must be acquainted: my name is Drake." "My name," said the other, "is Fitz Greene Halleck." Then and there Croaker took in a partner in the production of those popular satirical odes, and the firm became publicly known as "Croaker and Co." They created a great deal of amusement, and were much sought after, largely increasing the circulation of the paper. The brilliant Drake was in miserable health, and died in 1821, when only twenty-six years of age. Halleck, full of sadness for the loss he had sustained, wrote those touching tributary verses, the first one of which has become "household words," and is familiar in the obituary columns of all the newspapers to this day, and appropriately appeared with the announcement of the death of the writer when he took his departure:

"Green be the turf above thee,
Friend of my better days;
None knew thee but to love thee,
None named thee but to praise."

Halleck wrote "The Recorder," in which, in the columns of the *Post*, he immortalized Richard Riker, so long known as Dicky Riker, who was always very considerate to the prisoners brought before him for sentence. "Well, well, here you are! You have been a bad man, a very bad man; you must suffer some," was often an expression of the good and genial old recorder of blessed memory, in sending a burglar to the States Prison. Halleck's Fanny, a playful satire on the characters of the day, when there was

"Music from Scudder's balcony,"

now no longer, but where stands, in its place, that splendid marble edifice, the *Herald* building, was his last production. Halleck retired from poetry, and became absorbed in the account-books of Jacob Barker and John Jacob Astor, which seem to have been the epic of his existence. After Astor's death the poet went to Guilford, Connecticut, to live and die. Occasionally he would visit New York to meet his old friends and talk over old times. Slightly bent with age, with an umbrella under his arm rain or shine, walking along Broadway, he reminded one as much of the immortal Finn, as Paul Pry, at the old Park Theatre, as of Halleck the poet.

"I have just read Fanny again," said Alderman Stoneall to Halleck one day. "We see nothing from you now. Why don't you write? There are thousands who want to hear from you again."

"Ah! my good friend," replied the poet, with that quiet smile of his, "some one has told me that I am considered quite a poet. If the public think so, I want them to continue in that pleasant conceit. If I write any more I shall spoil that reputation."

In 1826, William Cullen Bryant, now the chief editor of the *Post*, began to write for its columns. In 1828 it advocated Jackson for the presidency, and fell into the support of his administration. It became the favorite of the aristocratic portion, now called the "bloated bondholders," of the Democratic Party in New York. In the summer of 1829 Coleman was cut off by an apoplectic stroke, after a successful editorial career of nearly thirty years.

The character of Coleman was thus summed up by Dr. Francis:

Coleman was a writer of grammatical excellence, though occasionally sadly at fault in force of diction. Under the influence of some perverse conceits, he would labor for months to establish some theoretical doctrine, or elucidate a useless proposition. He would underrate the best services to the Republic, if rendered by a political opponent. Chancellor Livingston found no quarters with him for his instrumentality in the Louisianian purchase. He would ride a hobby to death. It was hardly in the power of mortals ever to alter his opinion when once formed. That yellow fever was as contagious as small pox; that scull cap (the *scutellaria*) was a specific for hydrophobia; that Napoleon wanted the requisites of a military chieftain, were among the crotchets of his brain. The everlasting tractates which he put forth on these and other subjects, would in the present day of editorial prowess scarcely be tolerated by a chronicle depending on public patronage.

After the death of Coleman, William Leggett, who had been an officer in the navy, and a man of courage and brains, became a writer on the *Post*, and remained as co-editor till 1836, when he retired, and established a weekly political sheet called the *Plaindealer*. Mr. Leggett died in 1839, shortly after his appointment as minister to Central America. What his opinions were in regard to the duties and responsibilities of an editor may be gathered from the annexed :

> To discharge fully the duties of a public journalist would be to elevate the vocation to the loftiest summit of human dignity and usefulness. A public journalist, animated with a due sense of the obligations of his responsible trust, and gifted with the faculties, intellectual and physical, for their adequate performance, would well deserve to be a public leader in a more extended signification of the phrase than that in which it is understood. He should have a mind filled with a great variety of human learning, and a ready command of all its stores. He should have a head cool, clear, and sagacious ; a heart warm and benevolent ; a nice sense of justice ; honesty that no temptation could corrupt ; intrepidity that no danger could intimidate ; and independence superior to every consideration of mere interest, enmity, or friendship. He should possess the power of diligent application, and be capable of enduring great fatigue. He should have a temperament so happily mingled, that while he easily kindled at public error or injustice, his indignation should never transgress the bounds of judgment, but, in its strongest expression, show that smoothness and amenity which the language of choler always lacks. He should, in short, be such a man as a contemporary writer described that sturdy Democrat, old Andrew Fletcher of Saltoun—"a gentleman, steady in his principles ; of nice honor ; abundance of learning ; brave as the sword he wears, and bold as a lion ; a sure friend and irreconcilable enemy ; who would lose his life readily to serve his country, and would not do a base thing to save it." This is the *beau ideal* of a conductor of a public newspaper.

Both Bryant and Leggett were poets, the latter having written " Leisure Hours at Sea" while a midshipman in the navy. In a violent political controversy between the *Post* and the *Courier and Enquirer,* the latter called the editors of the former the "chanting cherubs of the *Post,*" a name they retained for years. While Leggett was editor of a paper called the *Critic,* he brought Edwin Forrest into notice. The *Post* continued as a Democratic organ through the administration of Martin Van Buren, and sustained all its financial measures, co-operating, to the election of Harrison in 1840, with the *Albany Argus* and Washington *Globe.*

There was a paper issued in New York about that time called the *Times,* a Democratic morning sheet, in the interest of Nathaniel P. Talmadge and his handful of adherents, who were called Conservative Democrats before they joined the Whig Party. In the controversy between the *Times* and *Post,* the editor of the former, Dr. Holland, sent a challenge to Bryant. Affairs of honor had become less frequent ; dueling had almost ceased to be a mode of settling personal disputes and insults in the Empire State. But it appears that previously there had been a quarrel between Leggett and Holland, in which a strong epithet had been applied to the latter, and that the affair had remained in abeyance. In reply to the challenge, Bryant informed Holland's friend that when Holland had arranged with Leggett his turn would come, but not till then. Nothing farther was heard of the matter.

Indicative of the status of the *Post* with the Democratic Party in 1843, the opposition elements in the State Legislature nominated

Bryant as their candidate for the profitable position of state printer, a place always sought for with avidity by political editors and publishers. The vote stood as follows:

    Edwin Cresswell (Albany Argus) - - - - - - - - 65
    William C. Bryant (Evening Post) - - - - - - 40
    Scattering - - - - - - - - - - - 3

John Bigelow, a young lawyer of New York, purchased an interest in the *Post* in 1848, and added largely to its prosperity by an infusion of youthful vigor and legal advertisements. But what gave the *Post* an important start was the course taken by W. O. Bartlett, now a distinguished lawyer in New York, in increasing its circulation, getting the paper into the hands of the newsboys, and modernizing its business and news arrangements generally. But to return to Bigelow. He had written news paragraphs for the *Plebeian*, thus showing an early taste for journalism. On his appointment as consul to Paris he disposed of his interest in the *Post*, and William Cullen Bryant, with his son-in-law Parke Godwin, carried on the establishment. On the death of William Dayton, our minister to France, and the declination of that office by James Gordon Bennett, of the *Herald*, the President appointed Mr. Bigelow to the place.

The *Post* followed the fortunes of Van Buren through the contest of 1840, and into Free Soilism, and through the famous contest against Cass in 1848 to the final overthrow of the old Democratic Party. It was favorable to Pierce in 1852, supported Lincoln in 1860 and '64, and was in favor of Grant in 1868. Bryant has always plumed himself on his Free-trade notions. He has been as strong and as consistent a Free-trader as Horace Greeley has been as a Protectionist. The friends of Free-trade—such men as Charles O'Conor, Wilson G. Hunt, and David Dudley Field—gave Bryant a public banquet in 1868, in honor of his doctrines, and as a tribute to his persistency in sustaining them through forty years of high and prohibitive tariffs. It is only fair that the New England manufacturers should, in turn, give Greeley a grand banquet for his consistency and earnestness in favor of protective duties.

The *Post* is now a free lance in politics, following out its own views and its own principles in its own way, the result of an experience of nearly three fourths of a century, and of the progress made by the independent Press in its vigorous, self-relying, and energetic journalism.

It is perhaps as important to know what an editor eats as to read what he writes. If Agassiz be correct, that those who live on the coast and eat fish are healthier, and have brighter brains from the phosphorus of such food, our journalists had better live on salmon, Sandwich trout, cod, and shad, and occasionally a shark chowder would not be out of place on the eve of an election. Mr. Bryant has recently written a curious letter on this subject in reference to his own diet, which we give in full. Now similar letters from Horace Greeley and James Gordon Bennett would be of value to young journalists. Indeed, Greeley has written one. Both Mr. Bryant and Mr. Bennett have safely and vigorously passed their seventy-sixth years, and hence their experience is worth more than that of any advice of any physician in the land. Indeed, Mr. Bennett lived till he was nearly seventy-seven, and passed away while these sheets were passing through the press, after a life of very moderate appetites and remarkably regular habits. Annexed is Mr. Bryant's letter:

WHAT MR. BRYANT WEARS AND EATS.

NEW YORK, March 30, 1871.

I promised some time since to give you some account of my habits of life, so far, at least, as regards diet, exercise, and occupation. I am not sure that it will be of any use to you, although the system which I have for many years observed seems to answer my purpose very well. I have reached a pretty advanced period of life, without the usual infirmities of old age, and with my strength, activity, and bodily faculties generally in pretty good preservation. How far this may be the effect of my way of life, adopted long ago, and steadily adhered to, is perhaps uncertain.

I rise early—at this time of year, about 5½; in summer, half an hour, or even an hour, earlier. Immediately, with very little incumbrance of clothing, I begin a series of exercises, for the most part designed to expand the chest, and at the same time call into action all the muscles and articulations of the body. These are performed with dumb-bells—the very lightest—covered with flannel, with a pole, a horizontal bar, and a light chair swung around my head. After a full hour, and sometimes more, passed in this manner, I bathe from head to foot. When at my place in the country, I sometimes shorten my exercises in the chamber, and, going out, occupy myself for half an hour or more in some work which requires brisk exercise. After my bath, if breakfast be not ready, I sit down to my studies until I am called.

My breakfast is a simple one—hominy and milk, or, in place of hominy, brown bread, or oat-meal, or wheaten grits, and, in the season, baked sweet apples. Buckwheat cakes I do not decline, nor any other article of vegetable food, but animal food I never take at breakfast. Tea and coffee I never touch at any time. Sometimes I take up a cup of chocolate, which has no narcotic effect, and agrees with me very well. At breakfast I often eat fruit, either in its natural state or freshly stewed.

After breakfast I occupy myself with my studies for a while, and then, when in town, I walk down to the office of the *Evening Post*, nearly three miles distant, and after about three hours, return, always walking whatever be the weather or the state of the streets. In the country I am engaged in my literary tasks, till a feeling of weariness drives me out in the open air, and I go upon my farm or into the garden and prune the trees, or perform some other work about them which they need and then go back to my books. I do not often drive out, preferring to walk.

In the country I dine early, and it is only at that meal that I take either meat or fish, and of these but a moderate quantity, making my dinner mostly of vegetables. At the meal which is called tea, I take only a little bread and butter, with fruit, if it be on the table. In town, where I dine later, I make but two meals a day. Fruit makes a considerable part of my diet, and I eat it at almost any hour of the day without inconvenience. My drink is water, yet I sometimes, though rarely, take a glass of wine. I am a natural temperance man, finding myself rather confused than exhilarated by wine. I never meddle with tobacco, except to quarrel with its use.

That I may rise early, I, of course, go to bed early; in town, as early as 10; in the country, somewhat earlier. For many years I have avoided in the evening every kind of literary occupation which tasks the faculties, such as composition, even to the writing of letters, for the reason that it excites the nervous system, and prevents sound sleep.

My brother told me, not long since, that he had seen in a Chicago newspaper, and several other Western journals, a paragraph in which it was said that I am in the habit of taking quinine as a stimulant; that I have depended upon the excitement it produces in writing my verses, and that, in consequence of using it in that way, I had become as deaf as a post. As to my deafness, you know that to be false, and the rest of the story is equally so. I abominate all drugs and narcotics, and have always carefully avoided every thing which spurs nature to exertions which it would not otherwise make. Even with my food I do not take the usual condiments, such as pepper, and the like. I am, sir, truly yours,
W. C. BRYANT.

There was a paper called the *Bee* issued in New London, Connecticut, in 1797, by Charles Holt, known as Dr. Holt because of his history of the yellow fever in that place. The *Bee* was a Democratic organ, and, of course, opposed the administration of John Adams. Holt had been fined and imprisoned under the Sedition Act of 1798. After Mr. Holt's punishment he published the *Bee* at Hudson, N. Y., and removed to New York City in 1808.

There were six daily papers published there previous to this date. The population was then 80,000. The names of these papers were

the *New York Gazette*, edited by John Lang.
   Mercantile Advertiser, " Ramsey Crooks.
   American Citizen, " James Cheetham.
   Evening Post, " William Coleman.
   Commercial Advertiser, " Zachariah Lewis.
   Public Advertiser, " John Holt.

Two weekly papers, the *Museum* and the *Weekly Visitor*, were also published there.

In 1808, Charles Holt established the *Columbian* as the organ of the Clintonians, and to supply the place of the *Citizen*, which had lost its prestige with the party. The *Columbian* was a spirited and effective Democratic paper, ardently supporting the measures of Jefferson and Madison. The editor, however, was a warm friend of De Witt Clinton, and in 1812 supported him for President against Madison, in consequence of which the *Columbian* and its editor, in their turn, were ever after proscribed at Tammany Hall, and the *National Advocate* was established as the Tammany organ. After the war the *Columbian* adhered to the fortunes of De Witt Clinton, and supported him for governor of the state, sustaining, also, the canal policy of Governor Clinton against the attacks of Tammany Hall and its new organ. While Clinton was governor, Mr. Holt sold out the *Columbian* to Alden Spooner, of Brooklyn, who for many years published the Long Island *Star*. The *Columbian* finally expired about the year 1821, and the *Statesman*, published by Carter and Prentiss in

Albany, was removed to New York, and became the general favorite of the Clintonians.

The Baltimore *Patriot*, in 1852, in speaking of the Press of New York in the days of the *Columbian,* said :

> From a reliable source, the letter of an observant correspondent, then a journeyman printer in Gotham, we learn that the following was the circulation of the seven daily papers of New York City in May, 1816—thirty-six years ago :
>
> | | | | |
> |---|---|---|---|
> | Mercantile Advertiser | 2250 | Courier (B. Gardiner's) | 920 |
> | Gazette | 1750 | Columbian | 825 |
> | Evening Post | 1600 | National Advocate | 875 |
> | Commercial Advertiser | 1200 | Total | 9420 |

Thus it appears that the circulation of the seven daily papers of New York, in 1816, amounted, in the aggregate, to about 9500. But two out of the list have survived to the present year. These have, of course, strengthened with increasing years, while others have fallen by the wayside, and live only in memory. But behold the change which a lapse of years has produced in the daily press of the commercial emporium ! In 1816, the whole daily circulation was 9420. In 1852, the aggregate circulation of *three* of the New York dailies is more than *one hundred thousand.*

Thurlow Weed, in the Albany *Evening Journal,* made one or two corrections in the above statement, as follows :

> These figures, low as they are, in comparison with the present circulation of New York journals, are too high. We worked at press on *The Courier* at that time, and have a pretty accurate recollection of the number of "tokens wet down" at each office. *The Courier's* circulation is truly stated ; but there were only eight tokens (2000) worked on *The Mercantile.* That was considered an immense circulation. The sheet was about half as large as *The Tribune,* and generally contained from a column and a half to two columns of news. *The Gazette* frequently went to press with only half a column of news (other than commercial) matter. There were no cylinder or power-presses, or even rollers, in those days.

The *Mercantile Advertiser,* which had the largest circulation at that time, was a paper of very little enterprise. Its publishers for years were Butler and Hyer. Elihu Butler was editor some time after Crooks, and did the "scizzoring." Amos Butler, one of the publishers, remained till the paper died. Then, as before and since, newspaper publishers would purchase the subscription-lists of other journals in order to increase their circulation and produce an effect on the advertising public. Butler, for instance, in 1832, offered James Gordon Bennett two dollars each for his subscribers to the New York *Globe* when the latter proposed suspending that paper to assume the management of the *Pennsylvanian* in Philadelphia. Nearly all the old papers of New York disappeared in this way.

The office of the *Advertiser,* in the closing years of its existence, was in Wall Street, adjoining that of the *Courier and Enquirer.* It was a long, narrow, dingy place. It was a rendezvous of a few old merchants and gossips, who daily and solemnly wound up the affairs of the nation and the world. Butler, like Lang, kept a bulletin-board, made like a music-stand, at his front door. On this the genial Dustan, the marine reporter, would daily and hourly post small scraps of news culled from the exchanges and log-books. These items would always appear in the penny papers of the next morning! Sometimes they would be left out of the *Advertiser.* The cheap press would thus derive more advantage than the *Advertiser* from Dustan's labors.

Amos Butler was a short, thick-set man—a respectable old publisher, who, in a nice, neat suit of black, lived to see the new class of papers prosper. Among his last editorial writers were, we believe, Redwood Fisher, and Wakeman H. Dikeman, a gentleman who has been for many years at the head of an important bureau in the office of the Comptroller of the City of New York.

New Hampshire could boast of other papers than those already mentioned. The *Exeter Federal Miscellany* was issued in Exeter by Henry Ranlet in 1789. It was a strong Federalist organ at that time, if the publication of a song early in 1799, of which the following was the closing verse, is any sign of the political status of the paper:

> Midst Faction enkindled, just bursting to flame,
>   See ADAMS, like Atlas, our glory supporting;
> While the foes of our freedom, encrimsoned with shame,
>   Scarce own the mad rabble, whose smiles they've been courting:
>   Then, ADAMS our guide,
>   In him we'll confide,
>   And safe o'er the whirlpools of Faction we'll ride:
>   *And ne'er to the shrine of a tyrant will fall*
>   *While Phœbus his chariot impels round the ball.*

About 1799, Joseph Gales, the father of "Gales and Seaton," was induced to establish the *Register* in Raleigh, N. C. Nathaniel Macon, that fine old gentleman of the old North State, was one of those who enticed him away from the seat of government. Like many other journalists, Gales had a history. He was born near Sheffield, England. He learned the art of printing in Manchester. In Sheffield he published a paper named the *Register.* These three sentences are three cantos of his early life. When the successful editor of the *Sheffield Register,* he became a reformer, an oracle, and a bookseller. One of his apprentices or assistants, obtained through the medium of an advertisement, was a youth named James Montgomery. This young man was quite useful to him, first as a clerk, then as an assistant editor, and finally as his successor, and always his friend. He is now known to fame as Montgomery the Poet. Amid the political excitement of England, an effort was made to arrest Gales for "words spoken in debate," or rather for an article published in the columns of his newspaper. This was in 1792, when the Revolution in France had thrown all the political reformers of the world into a state of frightful excitement and frenzy. Fortunately for Gales, he was absent from home when the king's messenger paid his domicile a visit. He was advised of the affair by friends. Although innocent and honest, he well knew that his fate was sealed if he returned to Sheffield. Sensible of this, he turned his face towards Germany, and then his heart, with wife and children, towards America, and, after a long passage from Hamburg, landed in Philadelphia. Montgomery settled his home affairs and purchased the *Register*, on the foundation of which he published the *Sheffield Iris*. On his long passage across the Atlantic, like Morse inventing his telegraph characters, Gales studied stenographic characters. On going out in the streets of Philadelphia, he found his labors upon the ocean were "bread upon the waters." In the spring of 1793 he obtained employment as printer. One day, Claypole, his employer, asked him, "Can you report? Our Congressional reports do not satisfy me. I would like better ones if I could get them." Like Croghan, later in time, when asked if he could take Fort Erie, Gales modestly replied, "I'll try." Greatly to the astonishment of the public and the delight of Claypole, the next day's proceedings in Congress appeared in the next morning's paper fuller and better than ever before. There was no delay. There was the debate. Miraculous for those days. Wonderful art has stenography proved to be—the camera obscura of speech. It is to the utterance of the human tongue what the photographic art is to expression of the human face—they preserve the present for the future. So Gales prospered. He became the proprietor of the *Independent Gazetteer*, which he conducted till 1799, when it was turned over to Samuel Harrison Smith, who followed the government to Washington, where he established the *National Intelligencer*, in the columns of which Gales the younger, in after years, practiced the stenographic art for a long period in our nation's history, and so usefully for its historians. Gales the elder went to North Carolina, as we have stated, and the *Raleigh Register* loomed up into life, bearing the old name he left behind in England, and with the public printing of the new state of his adoption as a reward for his industry. After years of successful toil he left the *Register* to his son, Weston Gales, and retired to Washington, where his son Joseph had become part proprietor of the *Intelligencer*.

One of the cleverest writers for the newspapers at the close of the last or in the early part of this century was Joseph Dennie, the "Lay Preacher" of the *Farmers' Weekly Museum*, a paper established by Isaiah Thomas in Walpole, N. H., in 1793. Griswold, in alluding to this popular journalist, said:

> Take, for example, the case of Joseph Dennie, the celebrated editor of *The Port-Folio*. Although the writings of Dennie do not vindicate his traditional fame, he was unquestionably a man of fine and peculiar genius, who exercised in various

ways an extraordinary influence upon the mental habits and tastes of our countrymen. A brief obituary in *The Port-Folio*, with a few reminiscences in the pleasant volumes of autobiography by J. T. Buckingham, furnish all that is here given us of this remarkable individual. Not one word is said of his political troubles in Philadelphia; his intimacy with Thomas Moore; his memoir of Moore's early life, prefixed to the first collection of that poet's works ever printed in the United States; his wonderful talents as a *raconteur;* the brilliancy and kindliness of his spoken wit, "which sometimes," according to his friend Ingraham, "kept his friends in laughter and tears till they were startled from the night's enjoyment by breakfast bells;" of the ruin induced by his amiable infirmities; the epitaph for his monument, in which his young friend, John Quincy Adams, described his character; the youthful writers whom he had brought forward; or the curious fact that one of them—the subsequently renowned Nicholas Biddle—was his immediate successor in the editorship of his magazine. Indeed, we have almost nothing of what should have constituted Dennie's biography.

The reputation of Dennie became so wide-spread that the paper was named the *Farmers' Museum, or Lay Preacher's Gazette*. The "sermons" of Dennie were copied regularly in nearly all the newspapers of the country. In 1799 Dennie migrated to Philadelphia, where in 1800 he established the *Port-Folio* in partnership with Asbury Dickens, the father, if we are not mistaken, of the respected Secretary of the United States Senate for many years.

CHAPTER XVI.

THE OFFICIAL ORGANS IN WASHINGTON.

THE FIRST NEWSPAPER IN WASHINGTON.—THE NATIONAL INTELLIGENCER.—GALES AND SEATON.—ORGANS OF THE GOVERNMENT.—CONGRESSIONAL REPORTING.—ADVENT OF JACKSON.—THE TELEGRAPH AND DUFF GREEN.—THE QUARREL OF JACKSON AND CALHOUN.—THE GLOBE.—FRANCIS P. BLAIR AND AMOS KENDALL.—THE SPECTATOR AND CONSTITUTION.—INTRIGUES AND INCIDENTS.—JAMES WATSON WEBB AND DUFF GREEN.—THE UNION.—THOMAS RITCHIE.—INTERESTING REMINISCENCES.—THE MADISONIAN.—THE NEWSPAPERS OF TO-DAY.

ALL governments have their organs. All political parties, all cliques, all religious denominations have their newspapers, through which they communicate with the people. Nearly every senator and member of Congress has a home organ, more vulgarly called a "mouth-piece."

The English government has the *London Gazette*, established in 1665. It still lives, and is the second oldest organ in the world; the *Pekin Gazette*, the official paper of China, being the father of organs. The French government had *Le Moniteur Universal; Journal Officiel de l'Empire Français.* It was started in 1789, but on the 1st of January, 1869, Napoleon abandoned it, as it was private property, and established a new organ, which he called the *Journal Officiel de l'Empire Français.* The empress, it is said, had her organ in *La France.* Both were swept away by Sedan in 1870. The Thiers government at Versailles and the Communist government in Paris had each a *Journal Officiel* in 1871. Austria and Andrassy speak through the *Gazette* of Vienna; Prussia through the *Staats Anzarger* in decrees and judgments, and Bismarck through the *Nord Deutsche Algemeine Zeitung;* Italy and Victor Emanuel through the *Gazetti Officielle* of Florence; Spain and Amadeus through the *Gacêta de Madrid;* the Pope and Antonelli through the *Observatore Romano;* Mexico and Juarez through the *Diario Oficial;* Greece and George through the *Messenger* of Athens; Russia and Alexander through the *Pranitelstoennii Vyestaik;* and Turkey and Abdel Aziz through the *Turkie.*

The present organ of Russia is a new one. The Czar recently became displeased with the *Invalide Russe* of St. Petersburg, and set it aside. This paper was first issued in 1813, to raise a fund for the relief of the wounded soldiers. It is stated that in that and the two following years it gave relief to sixteen hundred and fifty invalids, and at the close of the war in 1815 it handed over to the committee of relief nearly two hundred thousand dollars. Since then it raised an annual income of ten thousand dollars till the Crimean War, when it paid to this fund fifty thousand dollars. It was the organ, especially the military organ, of Nicolas and Nesselrode, and Alexander and Gortschakoff, from 1839 till superseded in 1868. M. Thiers, in the *Corps Legislatif* in 1868, thus spoke of the influence of a newspaper organ in Russia:

Voyez la presse en Autriche : elle est encore bien jeune, cependant elle révèle déjà l'opinion du pays. Et dans un autre pays que vous serez peut-être étonnés d'entendre citer, en Russie, où la presse n'est pas libre, elle commence cependant à avoir la parole, et il s'y produit un phénomène remarquable ; le gouvernement est sage, discret, mesuré, sincère même dans son langage ; et pourtant, si l'on n'entendait que lui, on ne saurait pas la vérité. Mais il y a à Moscou un homme politique de grande intelligence, M. de Katkof, rédacteur de la *Gazette de Moscou* ; et pour avoir une idée exacte de ce qui se passe en Russie, des mouvemens de cette grande puissance et de ses tendances, il faut combiner les dires du gouvernement avec le langage de la *Gazette de Moscou.*

The Ottoman *Moniteur* was edited by M. Blecque, father of the Turkish minister to the United States in 1869. Although printing was introduced in Turkey in 1727, the first newspaper did not make its appearance in that country till 1827, when this same M. Blecque started the *Spectator of the East* at Smyrna. The present official organ of the Sultan has already been mentioned.

These papers are entirely under the control of the governments *de facto*. Nothing appears except by authority. There is an amusing illustration of this in the announcement, said to be taken from the *Moniteur* of France, in March, 1815, on the escape of Napoleon from Elba :

First announcement.—"The monster has escaped from the place of his banishment ; and he has run away from Elba."
2nd. "The Corsican dragoon, (l'ogre) has landed at Cape Juan."
3rd. "The tiger has shown himself at Gap. The troops are advancing on all sides to arrest his progress. He will conclude his miserable adventure by becoming a wanderer among the mountains ; he cannot possibly escape."
4th. "The monster has really advanced as far as Grenoble, we know not to what treachery to ascribe it."
5th. "The tyrant is actually at Lyons. Fear and terror seized all at his appearance."
6th. "The usurper has ventured to approach the capital to within sixty hours' march."
7th. "Bonaparte is advancing by forced marches ; but it is impossible he can reach Paris."
8th. "Napoleon will arrive under the walls of Paris to-morrow."
9th. "The Emperor Napoleon is at Fontainebleau."
10th. "Yesterday evening his Majesty the Emperor made his public entry, and arrived at the Tuilleries—nothing can exceed the universal joy !"

Our government, at first, had no organ. When located in New York and Philadelphia, and during the formation of parties, the papers arranged themselves for and against the acts of Congress as best suited their interests and inclinations. After the adoption of the Constitution the government was independent. Washington had no newspaper to speak for him. The *Aurora* appeared in Philadelphia as the organ of the opposition, and the *National Gazette* as the special organ of Jefferson. Before the city of Washington became the national capital, newspapers had been published there. The *Washington Gazette*, a semi-weekly, was established by Benjamin Moore in 1796. It made its appearance on the 11th of June, and its prospectus announced that the object of the publisher was first "to obtain a living," and, second, "to amuse and inform" his readers.

When the seat of government was removed to Washington in 1800, the *National Intelligencer and Washington Advertiser* was established by Samuel Harrison Smith, and it became the organ of the administration of Thomas Jefferson. Its first issue as a tri-weekly was on the 31st of October. About the same time the *Washington Federalist* was issued. The *National Intelligencer* was a continuation of the *Independent Gazetteer* of Philadelphia. In 1807 Joseph Gales, Jun., entered the office of the *Intelligencer* as a reporter. He became a partner of Smith's in 1810, and in that year the name of *Washington Advertiser* was dropped. Shortly after Smith retired from business, and connected himself with the United States Bank, and was president of a branch of that institution in the national capital for many years. He died in Washington in 1845. In October, 1812, William Winston Seaton became a partner with Gales, and thereafter the firm was known as Gales and Seaton. Seaton had previously been an assistant editor in Richmond, sole editor of the *Petersburg Republican*, and sole editor of the *North Carolina Journal*. He was then connected with the *Raleigh Register*. The *Intelligencer* became the first recognized government organ in the United States. John Randolph was in the habit of styling it the "Court Paper." It was the vigorous champion of Madison's administration throughout the war of 1812 and '15. In the capture of Washington by the British the establishment was partly destroyed by the enemy. This event helped the paper wonderfully with the people. It thence started on a fresh and prosperous career.

The *National Intelligencer* was the reporter of Congress. For thirteen years after Gales became attached to the paper, and for seven years after Seaton joined the establishment, they were its only reporters. Gales had followed in the footsteps of his father, and had acquired a thorough knowledge of stenography. Seaton had also learned the art. One reported the Senate, the other the House. They gave only running reports of the debates at that time, but on important occasions they would take full notes of speeches. If it had not been for the presence of Gales, the great speeches of Hayne and Webster in 1830 would have been lost to posterity. The original notes of Webster's speech, corrected by Webster himself, were retained by Gales, and are now in possession of his family. Most of the annals of the early Congresses would never have been preserved but for the efforts of the editors of the *Intelligencer*. The stenographic notes of the important debates, those that could not be published at the time of their utterance, were filed for future reference and use. There was no public record of them. They would have been lost, like the early proceedings of the British Parliament, if there had not been later action of Congress authorizing Gales and Seaton to write up and publish the "Debates in Congress." In speaking of this action of that body, the *Intelligencer* of September 3, 1853, said:

> It may not be very generally known that the proprietors of the *National Intelligencer* are engaged in a work, under the sanction of the government, which is to embody and preserve the already perishing history of the earlier Congresses. In this undertaking they have thus far succeeded, even beyond their hopes. In prosecution of the work it has been brought down to the date of the twelfth Congress.

What has been the result of this work? The Annals of Congress. With the combined labor, skill, and ability of the Gales, father and son, Seaton, Houston, Sutton, Hayes, and their assistants as reporters, and the files of the *Intelligencer* and *Globe*, we have the debates of the national Congress from its earliest days. So with the Constitutional Convention. If it had not been for the industry and capacity of James Madison, the important and interesting debates on the Federal Constitution would have been lost to the world. The Convention had no official reporter. The *Advertiser*, in reviewing Rives's Life of Madison, said:

> Mr. Madison imposed upon himself the arduous labor of keeping an exact record of everything said and done in that body. He chose a seat in front of the presiding officer, and noted in abbreviations and marks intelligible to himself what was read from the chair or spoken by the delegates, losing not a moment between the adjournment and reässembling of the convention in writing out his notes. He was not absent a single day, "nor," he says, "more than the casual fraction of an hour in any day; so that I could not have lost a single speech unless a very short one." Mr. Madison regarded these reports as a sacred trust for posterity. He firmly withheld them from publication during his lifetime, while any object of contemporary interest or ambition could be served, intending that, at his death, they should pass into the hands of the representatives of the nation, which was done; and by Congress they have been given to the world. No other complete record of the debates of that convention has been preserved. Judge Yates of New York took some crude and desultory notes, which have been printed since his death; but they have little value. The judge left the convention before the sessions were half completed, or its action had begun to take a definite shape. Besides, he had little tact or experience in such labor. The abstract of these debates which Mr. Rives has given is a valuable contribution to the study of our Constitution.

Of the value of the stenographic notes of Gales, the *Budget* of

September, 1853, relates the following historical and interesting facts:

> Forty years ago, the 12th day of January, John Randolph, of Roanoke, made a speech in Congress. It was one of those long, powerful, sarcastic speeches for which he was so distinguished. It was on the war question. On the 18th day of the preceding June, (1812,) war had been declared against Great Britain. Congress adjourned on the 6th of July, and was called together again on the 2d of November, to adopt such measures as the first brief campaign rendered necessary. Among other measures the military committee reported a bill for raising an additional army of twenty thousand men. A debate followed on the bill in the House, extending through twenty days, in which many distinguished men took part, including Calhoun, and Clay, and Kent, and Lowndes, and Macon. On the 12th of January, John Randolph rose and blowed his bugle blast through the day, reviewing the whole war subject, and the relations between this country and the powers of Europe. Like all his speeches, this was extempore. It fell upon the ears of his hearers, and then was wafted away and lost in thin air. Beyond the mere announcement that Mr. Randolph spoke upon the bill, the press of the country gave the public no information, and no one, save those who heard the speech, knew what he had said, or ever expected to know. And now, lo and behold! on the 3d day of this present month of September, 1853, that unwritten speech, uttered forty years ago, appeared at full length, verbatim, as it was spoken, in the *National Intelligencer,* filling seven large, closely printed columns, in small type. Who, at this day, when the actors in those scenes are sleeping with their fathers—when Calhoun, and Clay, and Kent, and Lowndes, and Macon, and Randolph, are all in their graves, who has wrought this literary miracle?

The *Intelligencer* continued to be the recognized organ of the several administrations, with a brief suspension, till the advent of Andrew Jackson in 1828. It then became the oracle of the opposition, and was accepted as the central organ of the Whig Party through the exciting political contests that followed the elevation of the Hero of New Orleans. Some of its articles emanated from the leading statesmen of that party. Webster and Clay, and even Calhoun, wrote for the *Intelligencer.* One of the incidents in connection with this statement is, that Gales, on one occasion, in preparing an editorial when overwhelmed with other duties, hesitated, and could not proceed to his satisfaction. Webster came to his mind. He sent his unfinished article to that distinguished statesman with a short note of explanation. It came back grandly rounded off and complete. It was the leading article of the *Intelligencer* of the next day. Webster had an exalted opinion of its editors. He once remarked to a friend, in speaking of Gales and Seaton: "Those, sir, are two of the wisest and best heads in this country; as to Mr. Gales, he knows more about the history of this government than all the political writers of the day put together."

The brief suspension in its organic position occurred while John Quincy Adams was Secretary of State in Monroe's cabinet. Adams got into a controversy with the *Intelligencer,* and took away the public patronage from Gales and Seaton, transferring it to the *National Journal.* This paper was started in 1822 by Thomas L. M'Kinney, a gentleman of the old school, and a great friend of the

Red Men. He had been Superintendent of the Indian Trade, and afterwards Chief of the Bureau of Indian Affairs. He was author of the "History of the Indian Tribes of North America." In after years he had a quarrel with Colonel Benton, growing out of a treaty made by M'Kinney with the Indians. In 1825 the *Journal* passed to the control of Peter Force, so well known for his "American Archives," "National Calendar," and splendid library.

On the inauguration of General Jackson on the 4th of March, 1829, the *United States Telegraph*, which had been purchased in 1826 by Duff Green, became the organ of the administration, but, according to Colonel Benton, it was more the organ of John C. Calhoun, the Vice-President, than of Andrew Jackson, the President. Duff Green was a warm personal and political friend of Calhoun; the two families were connected; hence this assertion. Colonel Benton states that in the winter of 1830-31, at a presidential levee, Green invited Mr. Duncanson, the owner of a large job printing-office in Washington, to a private interview. There the intrigues of Van Buren were detailed, and a rupture, then impending between Jackson and Calhoun, predicted by Green, who proposed to Duncanson to join the Calhoun section, and take charge of the Frankfort (Ky.) *Argus;* that the Democratic Press throughout the country would be secured; that a correspondence between the President and Vice-President, then in type in the *Telegraph* office, would be published, and Van Buren overthrown, Jackson set aside, and Calhoun be the next President. This announcement startled Duncanson, who, it appeared, was a firm political friend of the President. He threatened to divulge the whole affair if Green attempted to carry it out; but Green was not to be deterred. There was a second interview, at which Green informed Duncanson that the rupture was determined upon. Then Duncanson caused the whole matter to be laid before Jackson; but the President had suspected the movement, and had made arrangements to meet the emergency whenever it came. While this scheme was on foot the *Telegraph* was the organ and advocate of the administration, and in full enjoyment of government patronage. On the eve of the threatened rupture, a copy of the *Frankfort Argus*, the very paper Duncanson was urged to take, containing "a powerful and spirited review of a certain nullification speech in Congress," was shown to the President. It pleased him. "Who wrote it?" asked Jackson. "Francis Preston Blair." Blair was not the editor of the *Argus*. He was a clerk of a court, a bank president, and an owner of a small plantation, with a few slaves. He was sent for. He was devoted to Jackson, and left all these solid realities and went to Washington, and had an interview with the President. The *Globe* was the result.

This is Colonel Benton's statement in brief. But Duff Green denies it in toto, so far as he is concerned. This interesting episode in official journalism induces us to give a part of Green's statement in his own words:

STATEMENT BY DUFF GREEN.

I had sustained Gen. Jackson in 1824. I was then engaged in St. Louis in a lucrative professional career, which brought me to Washington in the winter of 1824–25. It so happened that I was a passenger on the same boat with Gen. Jackson on the Ohio, and was earnestly entreated by him to remove to Washington and become the organ of his party. I then declined. The reader must see, however, that, thus solicited, I had stronger claims upon his friendship when I afterwards purchased the *Telegraph*, and gave to him a support which contributed, as all admit, more than any other press, to build up his popularity and influence.

In the canvas of 1824, Mr. Crawford, Mr. Clay, Mr. Adams, and Gen. Jackson, were candidates. Mr. Van Buren sustained Mr. Crawford, Mr. Benton sustained Mr. Clay. Mr. Calhoun was the candidate for Vice President on both the Adams and the Jackson tickets, and took no part as between them, but it was well understood that all his influence was exerted against Mr. Crawford. In the canvas of 1828 Mr. Calhoun was the candidate for Vice President on the Jackson ticket, and, being at the seat of government, exerted more influence than any other person in the organization and success of the party.

Mr. Van Buren wished to go to England, and it was not until that mission had been given to another, and Gen. Jackson's election was rendered certain, that he declared for Gen. Jackson. He then sent Mr. Hamilton on a pilgrimage to the Hermitage, who went with Gen. Jackson to New Orleans, and during that visit was told that Mr. Crawford had written to Mr. Balsh, of Nashville, that he and his friends would sustain Jackson if he could be assured that Jackson's election would not benefit Calhoun. He also heard that Crawford had written to Balsh, that Calhoun, as a member of Monroe's Cabinet, had advised Mr. Monroe to arrest Gen. Jackson for the invasion of Florida during the Seminole war. Hamilton deemed this information so important that he travelled all the way to Georgia, (and then there were no railroads, and such a journey was no small matter,) to see and consult Crawford. Yea, it was so important that Van Buren and Cambreleng made the same journey.

Mr. Van Buren was appointed Secretary of State, but, being Governor of New York, he sent Mr. Hamilton to Washington as Secretary *pro tem*. The Cabinet, with the exception of Mr. Ingham, were known to be in Van Buren's interest, and a combination, composed of influential office seekers favorable to his election as the successor of General Jackson at the end of his first term, was organized. In one of their consultations Free Tom Moore, who was afterwards appointed Minister to Colombia, told them that he had known me at school, and that no influence of money or patronage could purchase my support. He therefore advised that Kendall, who was then in Washington under an engagement with me as an assistant editor, should be appointed an auditor, with a salary of $3,000, with an understanding that in case I refused to support Van Buren, Kendall should establish a paper for that purpose. This was disclosed to me at the time, before Gen. Jackson's inauguration. I immediately went to General Jackson, told him of the intrigue to make Van Buren his successor, and then proposed that he should select some one else to be his organ, telling him that, although I was then the printer to both houses of Congress, I would give place to any person whom he might select who would pay me the actual cost of my types and materials, without reference to my own personal services, and would return to Missouri and resume my profession.

General Jackson pledged himself to me that the patronage of the government should not be used to promote Van Buren's election, and declared that he should not remain in his Cabinet if he became a candidate. As an earnest of his sincerity, he declared that one of his first official acts would be to order that the printing of the State Department should be done at my office, and Mr. Hamilton, under his instructions, did send me the printing.

A few weeks after Mr. Van Buren came to Washington I met a Mr. Davis, who told me that he was to print the laws, and was going to purchase a press and materials to publish a paper. I went immediately to the State Department, and told Mr. Van Buren what had passed between General Jackson and myself, and that upon the issue of the first number of Davis's paper I would denounce him and his purpose. He endeavored to persuade me that the paper would be an auxiliary. Failing to convince me of this the publication was abandoned; but in the fall of that year, and before the first meeting of Congress after General Jackson's election, Van Buren was nominated for the next term in the New York *Courier and Enquirer*. I have cause to believe that he procured that nomination to be made. He endeavored to persuade me to let it pass without comment. I opposed it, and that opposition led to the subsequent rencontre between Webb and myself.

The temper manifested during the first session of that Congress satisfied Van Buren that he would not get the nomination for that term. It was not until this truth was forced upon him that he and his partisans resolved to place General Jackson again in nomination, and then with a view to create an open rupture between Jackson and Calhoun. Forsyth, the known partisan of Van Buren, who was afterwards rewarded with the State Department, revived the accusation that Calhoun, as a member of Monroe's Cabinet, had advised General Jackson's arrest for the invasion of Florida, previously communicated to General Jackson by Crawford, through Balsh, of Nashville. General Jackson had then refused to notice this charge, but he now made it the basis of the hostile correspondence, because, under that feeling, he was persuaded that Calhoun intended to become a rival candidate for the Presidency. This brings me to Benton's declaration that, in the winter of 1830-31, at a Presidential levee, I invited a Mr. Duncanson, then a job printer in Washington, to call and see me, and endeavored to engage his assistance in a scheme to prevent General Jackson from becoming a candidate for re-election, and to bring forward Mr. Calhoun in his place.

* * * * * * *

It will be seen that Benton charges that I had a conversation with Duncanson in the winter of 1830-31, and refers to that conversation as furnishing the reason why Gen. Jackson brought Blair to Washington; and yet he admits that in the summer of 1830 "he knew what was to happen, and quietly took his measures to meet an inevitable contingency;" thus proving that General Jackson, having in the summer of 1830 resolved to assail Mr. Calhoun, found it necessary to establish the *Globe*, and "quietly" made his arrangements with Blair before the date of the alleged conversation with Duncanson.

* * * * * * *

So far from coming to Washington because he (Blair) was so much devoted to General Jackson and his measures that he might as editor of the *Globe* defend them against me, he came, professing friendship for Mr. Calhoun and for me, avowedly seeking bread for himself and family, not then knowing, as I verily believe, the duty to which he was called; nor do I believe that General Jackson then intended or expected that he would assail me as he afterwards did; for it was not his interest to provoke the hostility of my press, (and no one was wiser in his way than General Jackson,) and, therefore, long after he had established the *Globe*, he sent his private secretary to me, and through him renewed his professions of friendship and confidence. After I had refused to visit him, although thus invited, he tendered me his hand, which I refused to take in the presence of his Cabinet and of both houses of Congress, because, being convinced that he was exerting his influence to establish and sustain the *Globe*, which was then calumniously assailing me, I was resolved that he and the world should know that there was one press which he could not purchase, and one editor whom he could not intimidate, and therefore I bade him defiance, well knowing that I would, in consequence, lose the printing of Congress and of the Departments, then worth $50,000 per annum.

After the establishment of the *Globe*, the *Telegraph* continued under the management of Duff Green, as the special organ of the Calhoun party, till the fall of 1835. The *Washington Mirror*, which had been published some time previous to 1836, was merged with the *Telegraph* in November of that year. Had Green supported

General Jackson with the vigor and energy he did Calhoun, he would have been the organ of that famous administration, and might have become a millionaire in influence and money. His course has been a remarkable one not only in Washington, but wherever he appeared. He was a man of impulse, of keenness, of ability. His ideas were large, and his schemes expansive.

On retiring from the *Telegraph* Duff Green wrote for a paper called the *Reformation*. He left that concern in January, 1838. The *Chronicle* took its place. Subsequently Green made several visits to Europe, engaged in a number of extensive enterprises. On one of these visits he made the acquaintance of Henry Wikoff, since become well known in diplomatic circles as the Chevalier Wikoff, and one of the remarkable men of the age; the two entered into arrangements to start a Free-trade paper in New York. It was issued in 1848, and called the *Republic*. After a sky-rocket existence it failed. Green then returned to his favorite schemes of internal improvement, and his last public appearance was in connection with the Confederate authorities in Richmond. This octogenarian was living, in April, 1871, in Dalton, Georgia.

On the establishment of the *Globe* it became a power with the government. It was not a member of the regular cabinet. It had a cabinet of its own, known as the Kitchen Cabinet. John Van Buren once said that the "old gentleman," meaning Jackson, would frequently, on receiving his daily budget of letters, many of them anonymous, and full of threats against his life, during the intense excitement about the United States Bank, hand them over to Blair with the remark, "Here, Blair, you take this lot. You know what to do with them." Blair evidently did know, for the *Globe*, the next day perhaps, would sparkle and bristle with them in one form and another, much to the "old gentleman's" satisfaction and delight.

Shortly after the establishment of the *Globe*, that colossal printer and patriot, John C. Rives, weighing two hundred and forty pounds, and standing nearly seven feet in his stockings, became the partner of Blair. Amos Kendall, who had left the Frankfort *Argus of Western America*, and had received the appointment of Fourth Auditor of the Treasury, was installed as regular contributor to the paper. Henry A. Wise, of Virginia, in his reminiscences of Washington, thus speaks of the services of Kendall at this period of his life, and after General Jackson had taken possession of the White House:

> Soon after he was a lodger there, that room was the scene of his (General Jackson's) private conferences at night, in which Amos Kendall was his chief scribe, and amanuensis, to write the broadside editorials of the *Globe* under his dictation and instruction, but not with his diction. He was a better thinker than his scribe, his scribe a better writer than he. He would lie down and smoke and dictate his ideas as well as he could express them, and Amos Kendall would write a par-

agraph and read it. That was not the thing; many times the scribe would write and rewrite again and again, and fail to "fetch a compass" of the meaning. At last, by alteration and correction, getting nearer and nearer to it, he would see it, and be himself astonished at its masterly power. General Jackson needed such an amanuensis—intelligent, learned, industrious—as Mr. Kendall was. He could think, but could not write; he knew what nerve to touch, but he was no surgeon skilled in the instrument of dissection. Kendall was.

Neither Blair nor Rives were remarkable for their personal beauty. Rives, a frank, blunt man in speech, used laughingly to say that they were "the ugliest looking pair in the country." On several occasions he has related the story of the jack-knife as originally applied to him and to Blair. Once traveling on a Western steam-boat, a stranger came forward and politely presented him with a large, handsome jack-knife. "What is this for?" asked Mr. Rives. "I was requested to present it to you," modestly replied the stranger. "To me? By whom and what for?" curiously pressed Rives. "I would prefer not to tell you, sir," said the stranger, "but perhaps my personal appearance will best answer your question." Rives looked more closely at his new friend, and saw "the ugliest looking chap in the country." The stranger then, with much dignity and modesty, said, "Sir, that knife was given to me because I was the ugliest looking man in the country. I was to keep it till I discovered one less handsome than I am. I have owned it several years. I have traveled much. I now have the pleasure of presenting it to you." Rives accepted the knife. "I retained it," he said, "till I came to Washington. It now belongs to Blair." These two journalists were not such ugly looking men, after all. They were excellent public characters, independent, benevolent, fearless, and energetic.

One of Mr. Bennett's amusing letters from Washington, written in January, 1839, in describing Mr. Blair, of the *Globe*, said:

Well do I remember Major Noah's description of the first appearance of Blair, and Kendall, and Isaac Hill at Washington. It was called the irruption of the Goths. "We counted," said the Major, "twenty-one editors, all prepared one morning to sally out and visit General Jackson, in February, 1829." Isaac Hill proposed that Noah should lead the troop. "No," said Noah, "I am too fat and in too good condition. If Old Hickory sees me, he will think that editors require no office. Our deputation must be headed by our worst looking—the lean, the halt, the blind." Upon this the Major put Blair, Kendall and Hill at the head of the deputation.

With the simplicity of a tyro in journalism, Blair, one day in 1856, during the Fremont campaign, asked,

"How does Bennett manage the *Herald*? It is really a wonderful paper. I don't see him any where. He don't seem to mix with the politicians, but he appears to know every thing that is going on around him."

"Very easily," answered the gentleman addressed. "He knows the wants of the people. He understands the politicians by experience and instinct. He don't want any office. He attends to his business. He is full of tact and enterprise, and knows how to make a good newspaper."

"Ah!" exclaimed Blair. Thus the Thunderer of the *Globe* learned that it was not as an organ alone that a newspaper became successful and influential.

When the *Globe* came into existence in December, 1830, most of the rich patronage of the government, the public printing and advertisements, slipped out of the hands of Green, and the *Telegraph* was compelled to rely upon the Calhoun section of the party for its support. All this government patronage was enjoyed by the *Globe* for eleven years. It ceased to be the organ of the government on the 3d of March, 1841. It remained for a while longer the chief organ of its party.

On the 4th of March, 1841, the *National Intelligencer* assumed its old position with the inauguration of William Henry Harrison as President. But it was only for a brief space of time. The early death of Harrison threw the Whig Party into confusion. On the accession of John Tyler, with Webster in the State Department, the *Intelligencer*, with the aid of the pen of the Secretary of State and other leaders of the party, maintained its position as their organ for a short period, but the bank vetoes of President Tyler soon caused a division. The *Intelligencer* adhered to the fortunes of Henry Clay and the Whig Party, and a new paper, the *Madisonian*, edited first by Thomas Allen, and afterward by John Jones, became the organ of the President. This was in 1842. This was an era of great political excitement in Washington. Some of the friends of Mr. Clay, not feeling certain of the *Intelligencer* with the existing friendship of its editor for Mr. Webster, established a newspaper in the national capital in December, 1841. It made an effort to live without the support of Congress or any patronage from any of the departments. It was named the *Independent*, and edited by Edward N. Johnston, Joseph Segar, and John H. Pleasants, the latter of whom was afterwards killed in Richmond by Thomas Ritchie, Jr.

The Presidential contest of 1844 opened with the Texas Question. It absorbed all others. But it seemed to have been mutually agreed upon by Clay and Van Buren, as they were thought to be the two opposing candidates, to ignore the "vital" question—vital to their hopes. Each wrote a letter in opposition to annexation. Events, however, crowded upon them too rapidly. Van Buren's letter killed him at the National Convention, and Polk was nominated. Clay was killed at the polls by a defection of the Abolition Whigs and the loss of New York by a vote of 15,000 thrown for James G. Birney. The electoral vote of that state would have made him

President. James K. Polk thus became the chief magistrate of the United States. On the 4th of March, 1845, he was inaugurated.

This election changed the *personnel* of the Democratic Party. The old *régime* went out of office. It was necessary to have a new organ. There are rewards and punishments in politics, as in schools or elsewhere. Now Duff Green was to have his revenge in spite of himself. South Carolina was to be pacified, and her electoral vote secured only on condition that Blair and Rives, and all the old Jackson and Van Buren elements, were removed. It was so arranged and so ordained. The *Nashville Union* had been the efficient home organ of the Polk wing of the democracy. The *Globe* was wholly in the interest of the Van Buren dynasty. The *Richmond Enquirer* was considered a safe paper by the party just indorsed at the polls. It had been instrumental in defeating Van Buren in the Convention. It was therefore deemed judicious and politic to bring an editor from the *Nashville Union*, and another from the *Richmond Enquirer*, to Washington, and with them establish a new paper in the national capital. This was done, and the result of this combination was the *Washington Union*, edited by Thomas Ritchie and John P. Heiss, as the recognized central organ of the Polk administration. When the overthrow of the *Globe* was in contemplation the reports produced an evil effect on the party. It aroused an opposition within the ranks of the democracy. It aroused the Old Hero in his retreat at the Hermitage, and he wrote several long letters to Mr. Blair and others on the subject. Annexed are extracts:

HERMITAGE, Dec. 14, 1844.

* * * * Our mutual friend, Gen. Robert Armstrong, spent a part of yesterday with me, from whom *I confidentially* learned some movements of some of our democratic friends, not of wisdom but of folly, that would at once separate the democratic party and destroy Polk, and would of course drive you from the support of Polk's administration and separate the democratic party. I forthwith wrote Col. Polk upon the subject, and am sure he will view it as I do, a wicked and concerted movement for Mr. Calhoun's and Mr. Tyler's political benefit. It is this, to amalgamate the *Madisonian* and what was the *Spectator*, and make that paper the organ of the government to the exclusion of the *Globe*. I am sure Polk, when he hears it, will feel as indignant at the plot as I do. I will vouch for one thing, and that is that Mr. Calhoun will not be one of Polk's cabinet, nor any aspirant to the Presidency. This is believed to spring from Mr. Rhett's brain, inculcated into the brain of some of our pretended democratic politicians who want to be great men, but will never reach that height.

* * * * * * * *

I am not at liberty to name names, but you will be able by silent watchfulness to discover those concerned, because the amalgamation of the *Madisonian* with Mr. Rhett's paper will be at once attempted to be put in operation to carry out Mr. Tyler's administration, and attempt to become the administration paper under Polk, and the copartnership between you and Mr. Ritchie broached to you by some of your friends and his. I therefore give you this information that you may not be taken by surprise.

* * * * * * * *

ANDREW JACKSON.

Three or four months later he wrote the following to Major Lewis:

HERMITAGE, April 8, 1845.

I find that Mr. Blair and the President have got into some difficulty about the *Globe* (with Mr. Blair as its editor) being the executive organ. This is a difficulty the President has got into where I can see no result but injury to him and no justifiable cause on the President's part for it. He believes Mr. Blair has become unpopular with part of the Democracy—he has opened his ears to bad advisers. Mr. Blair has more popularity with the democratic members of Congress and the democracy of the United States than any editor in them—and by the course adopted (he) will disunite instead of uniting the democracy.

Present me to Mr. Blair, and say to him that I was so sick yesterday and exhausted writing to the President that I could not say half what I wished, but if I have strength I will soon write him again. Blair has taken a proper stand, and I know will never suffer himself to lose character or be degraded. The *Globe* is to be bought by what political clique and to subserve what interest? Is the renegade politician * * * * * * to have an interest? My opinion is, that when the money is wanted it will not be forthcoming. Is Major * * * * * of ———, to be the purchaser? If so, he is here considered broke, and say to Blair, if he sells, to have the cash, or good security that is known and vouched to be good. This difficulty was entirely unexpected to me and has vexed me sorely.

Your Sincere Friend
ANDREW JACKSON.

The *Globe* of the 14th of April, 1845, settled the fact of organship in the following historical card:

The *Globe* office and its appurtenances passed, on Saturday last, into the hands of Mess. Ritchie and Heiss. The *Globe* had its origin in the will of General Jackson, and owes to him and Mr. Van Buren, and their political friends, the success which has attended it through fifteen years of conflict, closed by the late triumph of the democracy, which effaced the disaster of 1840. It has been the misfortune of the *Globe*, in sustaining the strong administration of Gen. Jackson, the uncompromising administration of Mr. Van Buren, and in opposing the abuses of Mr. Tyler's administration, to make enemies of some who united with the democracy in its last struggle. The interest of the cause requires that all who contributed to the election of the present Chief Magistrate should continue to give their support. It is the good fortune of the conductor of the new official organ not to have offended any portion of those whose adhesion to the party is necessary to its safety and success. We have unbounded confidence in the ability, integrity, and patriotism of the man who is now to preside over the establishment, and shall consider ourselves amply compensated for the sacrifice we are now called on to make, if our anticipations of the continued union and success of the democracy shall be realized by the official journal under its new name and new auspices. We cannot express our gratitude to the democracy, to which we owe every thing.

F. P. BLAIR.
JOHN C. RIVES.

The first number of the *Union* was issued May 1, 1845. On seating himself in the official editorial chair Mr. Ritchie wrote these lines:

And though the editor of the *Union* has not been 24 hours in this city, and is about to tread the boards of a new and more conspicuous theatre, without any rehearsal of the character he is about to fill, yet he throws himself at once upon the generosity of his countrymen. He is unaffectedly conscious of his own deficiencies; he has much to learn; he has a new and more extensive alphabet to acquire; he has new characters to study and new duties to perform; he has scarcely twenty acquaintances in the city: but he will strive to avail himself of all the lights that he can obtain, that he may guide his new bark over the wide ocean that is spread before him. He has, above all, to study those great foreign relations which are particularly confided by the theory and the letter of the constitution to the guardianship of the Federal Government. We shall at least do the best we can. Our opponents are pleased already to predict "a splendid failure" in the new enterprise in which we have embarked. It may be so. "Man proposes but Providence disposes," but if an unflagging zeal in the public service can in any degree supply the place of experience or of other qualifications, we shall not be altogether wanting to the task we have assumed.

So the *Globe*, as an organ, ceased to exist; and what is the moral of the preceding intrigues, and ups and downs of politicians and newspapers? All have their sequence, corollary, and compensation in subsequent events:

1st. Duff Green and the *United States Telegraph*, as the organ of the Calhoun section of the Democratic Party, were set aside, and Blair and Rives, with the *Globe*, were substituted as the organ of the Jackson and Van Buren democracy.

2d. Blair and Rives, and the *Globe*, as the organ of the Anti-Texas Van Buren democracy, were set aside, and Ritchie and Heiss, with the *Union*, were made the organ of the Annexation Calhoun democracy on the election of James K. Polk.

3d. The democracy of 1844, with General Cass, were overthrown in 1849 by the defection of Van Buren, resulting in the election of Zachary Taylor, and the destruction, in its turn, of Ritchie and Heiss, and the *Union* as the organ of the government.

The *Globe* and *National Intelligencer* were organs *par excellence*. They made their mark on their age and on politics in an important and exciting period of our history. There are two descriptions of the leading men of these two organs that are sufficiently attractive to insert in full. The first was written by Colonel Claiborne, and is taken from the New Orleans *Delta;* the other by John C. Rives, and is an autobiography. It is taken from the *Globe*. Since the sketches have appeared, Gales and Seaton, and Rives and Amos Kendall, have passed to

"The undiscover'd country, from whose bourne
No traveler returns."

LETTER FROM COL. CLAIBORNE.

RECOLLECTIONS OF THE METROPOLITAN PRESS.

PEARLINGTON, MISSISSIPPI, May 28, 1856.

The following paragraph is going the rounds of the newspapers:

Just look at the luck of Washington City editors. Gales has a country seat; Seaton has a country seat; Blair has Silver Springs; Rives the dueling ground; Kendall has a place near town; Major Heiss owns a fine place; Mr. Ritchie purchased the princely mansion fronting Lafayette Square and the White House, built by Corcoran of the firm of Corcoran and Riggs. General Duff Green has a number of places, including a large interest in the Cumberland Coal Mines.

There is some truth in this, mixed up with a good deal of varnish; but in these few lines the names of the most distinguished men connected with the press in our country are grouped together, and they form too brilliant a galaxy to pass unnoticed.

Mr. Joseph Gales, well known for half a century, as senior editor of the *National Intelligencer*, is an Englishman by birth, nurtured in North Carolina, and is entitled to be placed, every thing considered, at the head of the first class of American editors. His career is an instructive illustration of the vicissitudes of party. During the administrations of Madison and Monroe, the *Intelligencer* was considered, very justly, the bulwark of the Republican organization. It was the stalwart advocate for war with Great Britain, and ably seconded Mr. Clay in his brilliant efforts on the floor of Congress to maintain the honor, rights, and arms of our country. When the British Army captured the seat of Government, they destroyed the office of the *Intelligencer* in revenge. They adopted, it may be presumed, the maxim of Napoleon: "A journalist!" said he, "that means a grumbler, a censurer, a giver of advice, a regent of sovereigns, a tutor of nations! Four hostile newspapers are more to be dreaded than a hundred thousand bayonets!"

And so they burned the printing office of Mr. Gales, and cast his type into the streets.

When the great contest for the presidency ensued, during the closing year of Monroe's administration, and Mr. Adams, Mr. Crawford and Mr. Calhoun, members of his Cabinet, were candidates, and likewise General Jackson and Mr. Clay, the *Intelligencer* took its stand for Mr. Adams, who, ever since his secession from the Federalists in 1807, had been regarded as one of the leaders of the Republican party. During the four years of his administration the *Intelligencer* was the official organ, and it entered with great zeal into the canvas against General Jackson. It subsequently signalised itself by a steady and able support of Mr. Clay, adhering, it must be conceded, in all these stages, to the same great principles it supported—and the Republicans supported—during the presidency of Monroe. It is certainly entitled to the merit of consistency, and there is no leading press, in either hemisphere, conducted with the same dignity, forbearance, and decorum. In this respect it is a model to the newspaper world, while in point of ability it stands in the highest rank. Mr. Gales is now long past the meridian of life. He is a living political autobiography, having known intimately the statesmen, the diplomatists, the belles, and the intrigues of three generations. What amusing memoirs he might write! He is generous and hospitable to a fault. A professed epicure, and fond of a rich cellar, the pleasures of the table, and the facility with which his purse opens to every application, have always kept him comparatively poor. If he has a country seat I never discovered it; but his table is one of the most *recherché* and hospitable in the city, enlivened by his anecdotes and wit, and graced by one of the most accomplished of her sex.

Mr. Seaton is the junior editor, and late Mayor of Washington—an agreeable gentleman, of great public spirit, and fine colloquial powers—a man of business, and thrifty in his circumstances.

Francis P. Blair, better known as "Blair of the *Globe*," commenced his career as an editor at Frankfort, Kentucky. Amos Kendall was at one time his associate. Originally friendly to Mr. Clay, and connected with him by marriage, he subsequently, with the great body of what was then called the New Court Party in Kentucky, attached himself to General Jackson, and followed the fortunes of that great man to Washington, where he established the *Globe*. It speedily became the national organ of the Democratic party and a prevailing influence at the White House. It maintained its ascendency (notwithstanding occasional and violent opposition in the Democratic ranks) to the close of the next Administration. Mr. Blair was constantly consulted by both Jackson and Van Buren. It is certain he never betrayed them, though he had been charged with treachery to Mr. Clay. His paper was ultra from the outset, and gradually became radical, never exhibiting, at any crisis, the slightest hesitation or timidity. It never went for half-way measures. Its tone was bold, dogmatical, and defiant. Its denunciations savage and ferocious. Its sarcasms bit like vipers, and friends and foes alike dreaded its fangs. As a partisan journal it was conducted with eminent ability, and with rare fidelity and courage. It never betrayed its party, or was ungrateful to its friends. On the opposition it made indiscriminate war—it charged at the point of bayonet, and neither submission nor flight arrested its merciless tomahawk. I remember but one exception—it was always tender to Mr. Crittenden, even when flaying alive his bosom friends.

Mr. Blair is considered a remarkable ugly man. I think otherwise. His features are hard, indeed, but his countenance evinces benevolence; nor does it belie him. His manners are bland—his temper mild; and one would never suppose that he could indite the terrible invectives that daily emanated from his prolific and vigorous pen. It was a volcano constantly in eruption, blazing, burning, overwhelming with its lava floods all that ventured to withstand it. Mr. Blair wrote with singular facility. His most powerful leaders were jotted down upon his knee, in the office, on scraps of paper, and passed immediately to the compositor—mental daguerreotypes leaping from a brain of prodigious energy.

During his residence in Washington he accumulated a handsome fortune. He lived in elegant style; and his mansion, consecrated and adorned by household divinities, whom to see was to worship, was constantly crowded with distinguished guests. He has, for several years, been enjoying the *otium cum dignitate* in a beautiful retreat near the metropolis, but I am sorry to perceive has returned to political life, and is wandering after false gods, forsaking the faith of the fathers, and trampling into the dust its holy emblems.

If the *Globe* owed its reputation to Mr. Blair, he is mainly indebted for his fortune to the indomitable energy and financial talent of his partner, Mr. John C. Rives, who was charged with the business concerns of their extensive establishment. Mr. Rives is a huge, burly figure, from Franklin, the roughest county in Virginia. He has a strong and masculine matter-of-fact mind, a shaggy exterior, and very *brusque* manners. Many of your Mississippi readers remember the late Robert Cook, of Lexington, Holmes County, Adjutant General of the state—an ungainly, rough-hewn, awkward man, of noble heart. He and Rives were cousins, and much alike, except that Cook was an Apollo compared with Rives. He is one of the shrewdest of men. His mind was originally purely arithmetical; but the printing office, the best school in the world, poured its radiance into it, and if he does not adorn every thing that he touches, he has the gift of Midas, and turns things into gold. He made a large fortune out of the old *Globe* establishment, and still coins money out of the *Congressional Globe*. He never made but one failure; that was, when he bought the Bladensburg duelling-ground, where Decatur fell, and turned gentleman farmer. In his office he is a colossus, but on his farm he was like Mr. Thomas Affleck, of "our diggins" and other agricultural quacks, a mere theorist, with the shabbiest stock, the meanest fences, and the poorest crops in the country.

Mr. Rives is a man of warm and humane heart. Merit in misfortune finds in him a steady friend. He is one of the few rich men I know who recur with pride to their former poverty; and it is his boast that, after he acquired wealth, and was looking around for a wife, he chose one from the bindery of his own office, where sixty young females were employed; and well may he boast, for, with characteristic good sense, he selected one whose grace, beauty, and virtue would ornament and honor the most elevated sphere.

The career of Amos Kendall is so well known I shall merely glance at it. The son of a plain farmer—a hard-working student at a New England College—tutor in the family of Mr. Clay—a party editor in Kentucky—Postmaster-General and biographer of Andrew Jackson—chief-director of the National Telegraph—now quietly composing memoirs of his times for posthumous publication. He is universally known for his talents as a writer, his capacity or organization and details, his unconquerable industry and ability to labor. When I first saw him, he had a whooping voice, an asthmatic cough, with a stooping frame, and a phthisicy physiognomy, reminding one of Madame Roland's description of the great war Minister, Louvet, "ill-looking, weakly, near sighted, and slovenly—a mere nobody to the crowd." Yet this little whiffet of a man, whom the Hoosiers would not call even an "individual," nothing more than a "remote circumstance," was the Atlas that bore upon his shoulders the weight of Jackson's Administration. He originated, or was consulted in advance upon, every great measure; and what the prompt decision and indomitable will of the illustrious Chief resolved upon, the subtle and discriminating intellect of Kendall elaborated and upheld. His style is both logical and eloquent. He is, besides, a man of dates and figures—one of those persons whose provoking exactitude so often upsets theories with a plain statement. Tristam Burgess of Rhode Island—one of the few men that ever encountered John Randolph successfully—being once thus put down by Kendall, said, "It was very unbecoming in a *fact* to rise up in opposition to his *theory*."

No man, morally, has been more variously estimated than this gentleman. Mr. Clay told me that he reminded him of Maréchal Villars, whom St. Simons, in his memoirs, describes as having but one virtue—he was faithful to his friend. To serve him there was no depth of servility or baseness to which he would not descend—but that friend was himself!

We must excuse his brutality, said S. S. Prentiss to me. A man who lives on the rack of his own horrible temper, eaten up with remorse, and suffering the pangs of a perpetual indigestion, cannot be expected to be much more than a beast.

His enemies allege that he was, like Swift, the greatest libeller of the day, and possessed all the qualifications it requires—a vindictive temper—no admiration of noble qualities—no sympathy with suffering—no conscience; but a clear head—a cold heart—a biting wit—a sarcastic humor—a thorough knowledge of the baser parts of human nature, and a perfect familiarity with everything that is low in language, and vulgar in society.

These, however, are extreme opinions. Many who know Mr. Kendall intimately attribute to him the most exalted public and private virtue, and great generosity of heart. That he has an appreciation of the noble and illustrious is demonstrated by his ardent attachment and unwavering fidelity to General Jackson. That he has great moral courage is evident from the fact that, in no emergency, was he ever known to retreat; but stood, like a savage, with his spear in his hand, and his bow and quiver at his back. We must make allowances for cotemporary praise —and censure. Men and parties are not so formed that there are only gods on one side, and only devils on the other.

Mr. Kendall was once embarrassed in his circumstances, but was relieved by fortunate investments in Western lands. He has a country seat near Washington, but when I saw it many years since, it was a skeleton farm, and, like himself, meagre and emaciated. Like his friend and co-laborer, the Hon. Thomas K. Benton, he is now devoting himself to literary labors for posterity; and by those labors posterity will pass judgment upon his life and character. At present the opinion of the world in regard to him is conflicting, and may be summed up thus:

"Too bad for a blessing—too good for a curse,
I wish, from my soul, thou wert better—or worse!"

These recollections of the leading journalists of Washington, so interesting in details, brought out more facts in regard to the editors and publishers of General Jackson's time from the pen of John C. Rives. These facts, related with great candor and simplicity, we give in *extenso*.

JOHN C. RIVES'S AUTOBIOGRAPHY.
CONDUCTORS OF WASHINGTON NEWSPAPERS.
[From the Washington Globe, June 23, 1856.]

The "Sunday Delta," printed in New Orleans, publishes an article under the head of "*Recollections of the Metropolitan Press*," which attempts, and we think with much success, to portray the characters of five persons who have been conductors of the Washington Press, namely: Joseph Gales, William W. Seaton, Amos Kendall, Francis P. Blair, and the public's humble servant, John C. Rives. The article, it is said,—indeed it is so said at the head of it,—was written by Colonel Claiborne, formerly a member of Congress, from Mississippi, and who, in that day, was considered a man very capable of so mixing facts and factions together as to make the compound very palatable. We think he has drawn the characters of these gentlemen remarkably well, so well that we would readily recognize who sat for them without the mention of their names. He was intimate with all of them, and being an excellent writer withal, is well fitted to draw life-like portraits of them at length.

As Congress is attending to conventions, and we need copy to fill the Globe, we will amuse ourselves, if not our readers, by throwing some lights and shades on the minor points of Colonel Claiborne's pictures. His portraits at length will be hung under, or on, a column by the side of this touching off, that the reader may see the alterations and additions made by us.

Joseph Gales, William W. Seaton, and John C. Rives, are still in the printing line, and are likely to remain there as long as they live. The other two, Amos Kendall and Francis P. Blair, have gone off on other lines—the former on the telegraph line, as a conductor, or non-conductor, we know not which; and the latter into the Free-Soil line, whilom called the "underground railroad" line. Well, that is their business, and no person has a right to object, so long as they do not invade public or private rights. If they think their new avocations, or vocations —we are in doubt which is the more appropriate word, and therefore have written both to let our readers choose—more lucrative, more honorable, or more easy, than lying for the instruction and amusement of non-paying subscribers, it was due to themselves, to their families, and, perhaps, to the public, that they should change their old, and engage in new pursuits. Every man to his liking—there is no disputing on points of taste. We know, of course, how to render these apt sayings into Latin; or rather, how others have done it; but, as our character for learning is established, we will not inflict a dead language on our living, sensible readers.

So much by way of preface; now for using our paint of all colors, but no varnish to gloss it over. In fact, we have none of the latter on hand, and never had.

Joseph Gales is the first on the canvas—perhaps it would have been more appropriate to have written *in this canvass*, and pass sentence, or give our opinions on both the outer and inner man we are about to examine. There is a small mistake in the second line. He is not the "*senior editor*" of the National Intelligencer. His name stands first at the head of the paper, but Seaton is his *senior* by a year or two—not more. Gales looks older; owing, probably, to his having burnt more of the "midnight oil," and lived less in the field than Seaton. We subscribe to every word said of Gales, from the second line, which we have corrected, down to the last sentence, which doubts of his having a country residence. He has had one during the last fifteen years, to our certain knowledge, for we were there and fared there, that long ago. He usually lives there in the summer, and in this city in the winter. His country residence is about two miles from his office, in a dense forest—for this section—and is named Eckington, the name of his birth-place in England, we believe. We have never seen any of its products in market, when we have been there purchasing produce for our farm; but have heard, and believe the report, that all his poor neighbors about it, are well to live off it—in plain language, he pays them for cultivating it, and gives them about all they raise on it.

The next person in the group is William W. Seaton, the *Senior-junior* editor of the Intelligencer, who stands first in years and last in the firm. Only four lines of the sketch are devoted to him; but there is a good deal of him—much more than the distant public know. He is a ready and a very clear writer. Most of the editorial matter that now appears in the Intelligencer is either written or revised by him. He has probably written more for the paper during the last twenty years than Gales; and yet the latter has been credited for all of it, for no other reason, we believe, than because his name is first mentioned in the firm. If he excels Seaton, it is mainly in this: Gales writes on but few subjects, and makes his articles short, believing in the maxim "the least said the soonest mended." Blair used to complain that the political articles in the Intelligencer were so short that he could not get a hold on them.

It is generally believed that the name first mentioned in a newspaper firm is that of the man who possesses all the talent for writing, and the second one is nothing more than a "scissors editor," to clip stories and scraps from other papers to fill it up, and to run to collect money to pay off. That, we regret to say, was the almost universal belief of the public in regard to the Globe, when the names of Francis P. Blair and John C. Rives floated at its head; and as a true chronicler, we are bound to admit that the public were not far wrong in attributing the leading articles to Blair. We wrote on minor subjects, when Blair was too lazy to write on large ones, which was often the case. When he was absent we sometimes essayed to grasp and lay open large subjects; and Blair got credit for writing them, though the style of the articles was not creditable. But the discerning public, said to be far-seeing, and always right in the end, did not then, and probably never will, see their deformity. We always took care not to write about the tariff, because we entertained notions about it not in the least similar to those of any person that ever wrote on that subject. Our machinery for collecting duties on imports would be very simple, and the working of it very economical. It would be to take, *in kind*, one sixth—sixteen and two thirds per cent.—of all the goods imported, and sell them on the wharf at auction, for cash, taking care to *sample* all the liquors, to be sure that all were alike, and if any were better than others, invoiced at the same price, to take the best for the Government! By this mode of collecting the revenue arising from importations, the services of nineteen-twentieths of custom-house officers in the large cities could be dispensed with, and the expenses of collection would not exceed five hundred dollars, instead of about six thousand five hundred dollars a day, now paid under the present system.

We have digressed, and now return to Mr. Seaton, and will finish his picture by saying of him that he is, in our opinion, a good writer, a good speaker, a good companion in good company, and what would be termed a good fellow in any crowd.

Now we come to Amos Kendall—lean and gaunt, (though there is a great deal in him)—to whom his Delta biographer has ascribed two characters—one very good, the other extremely bad. No person, we suppose, who knows Mr. Kendall, doubts his ability and capability as a writer; but nearly all who knew General Jackson will doubt whether Kendall was, as the biographer says, "the Atlas that bore upon his shoulders the weight of Jackson's administration," and "elaborated and upheld" it. We do not *doubt*—we *know* that *he was not*. General Jackson bore all his measures and all his men on his own shoulders. We should like to know—no, we should like to be told by any man of weight, so that we might confute him—who but Jackson took upon himself the veto of the bill rechartering the Bank of the United States; the removal of the Government deposits from it; the "specie circular;" the coercion of the payment of the French indemnity, &c., &c.; or who, of his Cabinet, or outside advisers, assisted him to shoulder them, or supported him when he walked off with them as easily as would an elephant with a mouse upon his back; or who even claimed to follow in his footsteps, until after he had fought and conquered? Again: who "elaborated" his messages on those subjects? We have had as favorable opportunities for knowing who "elaborated" his messages as any man, and saw but two foot-prints in them; one was these words interlined in the handwriting of Amos Kendall: "The blessings of Government, like the dews of heaven, should descend on all alike;" and the other was: "We will ask for nothing but what is right, and submit to nothing that is wrong." These may not be the very words, but we are sure that we have given the sentiments. Mr. Blair has told me that Mr. Van Buren informed him that he interlined the last words quoted; but that they belonged to General Jackson, as he had first used them in speaking to his Cabinet.

We now recollect that three manuscript pages of General Jackson's special message to Congress, dated the 15th January, 1836, relating to our difference with France, in regard to the indemnity due to the United States, were in the handwriting of B. F. Butler, then Attorney General of the United States. The three pages were written on letter paper, in a large running hand, the lines wide apart, and did not make more than about four hundred words. Mr. Butler told us last winter that they were written at the request, or by the direction of General Jackson; and we think he added, on a point of law—perhaps the maritime law in regard to reprisals.

The Cabinet attempted to alter General Jackson's annual message, delivered the 8th of December, 1835, wherein he treated of this subject of the French indemnity; and while we were waiting for the copy, General Jackson heard Major Donelson, his Private Secretary, read the alteration and ordered him to strike it out—every word of it, and put back what he himself had written, and added that we must wait for the alteration of the three copies—one for each branch of Congress, and the rough draft from which we were to print—although it was then past ten o'clock Sunday night, and Congress was to meet the next day, at twelve o'clock, m. We have filed away, so carefully that we cannot find it, both the original and the alteration; and if they should ever be found by posterity, it will not be believed that they are on the same subject. According to our recollection, the Cabinet struck out only seven or eight lines written by General Jackson, and substituted about forty of their own; and the difference between those stricken out and those inserted was greater than, say—chalk and cheese, not having time to select the names of articles more dissimilar. The following, it is believed, are the words which the Cabinet struck out; if not, they are certainly in the same short paragraph in which nearly all the words are "of the same sort:"

"The honor of my country shall never be stained by an apology from me, for the statement of truth and the performance of duty; nor can I give any explanation of my official acts, except such as is due to integrity and justice, and consistent with the principle on which our institutions have been framed."

These are what we would term "words with the bark on." When shall we have another such man? Never! *never!!* And we will add, we hope our country may never have another occasion that will require the services of such a one. We believe, religiously and firmly, that no man ever lived, not excepting General Washington, who would have stemmed the current and buffeted the waves of corruption as General Jackson did for years, without a canoe putting out to render him assistance. He never once called for help, but said to Henry A. Wise and Bailie Peyton, bold men, who called on him to give him some advice, after hearing them patiently: "If you can't go with me, go away and let me alone;" and they straightway went away. Mr. Wise told us last summer he had come to the conclusion that General Jackson was the greatest man that ever lived.

When writing the above about General Jackson's messages, we did not recollect his famous *proclamation*, published in December, 1832, at the time of the troubles between the Federal Government and South Carolina. It may be well to state here, as the public seem to know but little on that subject, that General Jackson wrote it—at least the outlines—and sent it to Mr. Livingston, then Secretary of State, to read, and make such alterations as he thought proper, and then return it to him. Mr. Livingston added a good deal to it. By the time it got back to General Jackson, the public got wind of it, and became very much excited; and while he was reading it, many leading men of the South came in upon him rather abruptly, and wanted to hear what was in it. He then handed it to Mr. Blair, who was present, and said to him in substance: "Here, Mr. Blair, take it and print it; there is much in it that I do not like, but print it as it is; I will not be annoyed about it." Before it was put to press, a crowd besieged the Globe office, and the doors were barred to keep them out. About fifteen hundred of the first copies printed were thrown out of the windows to get clear of the crowd. Mr. Blair heard General Jackson express his opinions freely and fully about the proclamation; and two or three weeks after it was printed, he wrote, and published in the Globe, early in January, 1833, an article explaining it, which General Jackson approved. Our impression is, that he saw the article before it appeared in the Globe. We were so well convinced that the article reflected General Jackson's sentiments, and met his approbation, that we inclosed it in the proclamation, which, together with all General Jackson's messages, is in the corner-stone of Jackson Hall.

General Jackson consulted with his friends as frequently and as fully as any other President ever did, *before* he undertook any measure of great moment, and heard their opinions patiently, whether they coincided with his own or not; but if, *after* hearing them, he was "of the same opinion still," as he usually, if not invariably, was, then it was useless to talk to him—he was inflexible and immovable. We believe he consulted with Mr. Kendall as much as he did with any other man, until December, 1830, when Blair came first here to reside. After that, we think he consulted chiefly with Blair. He advised with Benton, more than with any other, about the Bank of the United States; they were often together in the dead hours of the night, devising ways and means to kill the *monster;* and they brought him down at last, but not until they had disemboweled him by removing the deposits. It required their combined nerve—and they were almost all nerve—to do it.

When General Jackson determined to remove the Government's money from the Bank of the United States, he selected Amos Kendall, then Fourth Auditor of the Treasury Department, to go North, and inform some of the principal State banks, confidentially, what he intended to do, that they might put themselves in a healthy condition to receive it. As soon as Mr. Kendall started North, in July or August, General Jackson left the heat and dust of this city, and the cares of office, and went down to the "RIP RAPS," a fortification built in the middle of the mouth of James river, to prevent the incursions of any enemy—not to him but to the country—from the sea, to harass the people living near that river, and made his abode within its walls, where no one else lived, and had his meals cooked ashore in fortress Monroe, and sent to him, and, we cannot forbear saying, there enjoyed the *otium cum dignitate*—the *ocean* breezes with dignity.

Kendall first sounded the banks in Baltimore, but none there would agree to receive the deposits. He then went to Philadelphia, where he met with no better success—not so good, we think, for there they doggedly refused to have anything to do with either him or them. Then he searched the city of New York, and could find but one bank there willing to receive them—the Bank of America—and that was considered a Whig bank, which, it was thought, was willing to receive them, and keep them for the benefit of the Bank of the United States, and thus keep them out of the hands of the Democrats. But this suspicion, soon afterwards, we believe, proved to be groundless. The principal, if not the only reason, why the State banks refused to receive the Government money was, they feared that the Bank of the United States would bear down upon them, and crush them, if they did. Even the Bank of the Metropolis, at that time the strongest bank in this city, and still the soundest one in it that emits its own notes, was afraid to receive specie on deposit when drawn from the branch of the Bank of the United States in this city, located in sight. We used to draw specie heavily from the latter, and sweat in pushing it on a wheelbarrow to the former, and thought all the time that we were doing wonders; and we never knew any better, until after the bank *broke*, as General Jackson would say, when John Sioussa, a watchman in the Bank of the Metropolis, said to us, "You used to trouble me a great deal. All the specie you wheelbarrowed from the Bank of the United States, I had to wheelbarrow back to it again *quicker!*"

But to return from this rolling excursion and digression. While Kendall was in New York, or Boston, we forget which, and have not his letter to refresh our memory, he wrote to General Jackson that the deposits could not be removed from the Bank of the United States, or words to that effect. That letter was sent to General Jackson, who was still at the Rip Raps. Blair was there, amusing himself shooting porpoises with his rifle at the instant they showed their backs when *curveting*, and was with General Jackson when he opened and read Kendall's letter. He did not read it to Blair, I believe, but told him its contents, and then said, beginning with three words which I will not quote, as they are not necessary to make what he said clearer, "Mr. Blair, the thing can be done, and it *shall* be done: the bank is broke!" To which Mr. Blair replied, "No, General, the bank is not broke, but it *should* be." General Jackson then repeated, "I tell you, Mr. Blair, that the bank *is broke!*" Mr. Blair answered, "It is not broke, General; it is yet too strong for the Government, and, therefore, should be broke." To which the General replied, "I tell you again, Mr. Blair, the bank *is broke*, and I will tell you now how I *know* it. The United States owe interest in Europe on a loan, and I wrote to *Nick* Biddle, who has more than ten times the amount of Government money in his hands, or *ought to have*, to pay it, and thereupon he came on to Washington, and *begged* me to postpone the payment of it for a while. Mr. Blair, I know the Biddles well; they are high-minded, brave men, and served their country, and fought bravely in the last war. If the bank was not broke, *Nick* Biddle would never, never have bowed and knuckled to me. I tell you again, Mr. Blair, for the last time, the bank is *broke*, and I *know* it."

While the Secretary of the Treasury here, and all the *bear* and *bull* brokers throughout the United States, were reading the reports of the bank and of committees of Congress appointed to examine it, and figuring to ascertain how much its stock was worth—and their calculations ranged from twenty-five to one hundred and twenty-five per cent.—General Jackson read *Nick* Biddle, and came to the conclusion that it was not worth a cent; and he was exactly right. After the deposits were removed, the bank published a statement to prove that its stock was worth one hundred and fifteen per cent., and proposed to take all the United States owned at one hundred and eleven, I think; not expecting the General had the power to sell, or would sell, the seven millions of stock belonging to the United States; but he took the "responsibility" of closing with them, and thus saved for the Government near eight millions of dollars. The people made that much by electing a man who could *read men*.

It is due to Mr. Kendall that we should state that we told the anecdote of his *embassy* to the North to a company of six or seven old Jackson men—Kendall among them—elected to attend to the erection of Mills's equestrian statue of Jackson, all trying to plant a little pedestal for themselves to commemorate the fact that they had lived when Jackson lived, and had gone for him and all his measures *from the start, and all the time;* and he (Kendall) denied writing such a letter as I had described. He admitted that he had written to General Jackson and informed him that some of *his* friends North (he named two) had said the deposits could not, or should not, be removed; but utterly denied that he had faltered at any time. We think we *had* the letter which he wrote to General Jackson in our possession, but never read it. We do not know where it is now, nor whether it is anywhere. No matter.

Next comes our old partner and friend, Francis P. Blair. We had a clerkship in the Treasury Department, which we received without making application for it; and, after keeping it nearly three years, resigned it the 11th April, 1832, and went into the Globe office as clerk and manager, at the same salary. About two years afterwards we became a partner; and, in the year 1849, finding the business of the office would not support both, as the wages of workmen had been raised twenty per cent. since we agreed to print the debates at the present prices, we purchased his interest, and became sole proprietor.

Blair and we have now dissolved our political relations, but have not parted our friendly ties, and it is not at all probable that we ever shall, as we have never had a word of difference during the quarter of a century we have known each other. Our political relations were dissolved by his following the political fortunes — perhaps we should have said, *misfortunes* — of Mr. Van Buren, who, he thought, had been wronged by the Democratic party. We thought with him on that point, but never once thought of following him when we could do him no good by so doing, and would probably do ourself and family a permanent pecuniary injury. We thought as highly of Mr. Van Buren, we believe, as Mr. Blair did, until he accepted the Buffalo nomination for the Presidency in opposition to the regular Democratic nominee. He taught us the necessity of making and sticking to party nominations, and he could not undo his teaching. The idea of leaving the Democratic party because we could not have our own way, never entered our head. That party has sometimes entered upon measures which we did not approve, but, in the main, we have approved its course. No two honest men think alike on every subject. The old homestead, though rough, unsightly, and somewhat dilapidated, take it all in all, is the safest building, we believe, that we have ever seen. No man that has ever left it has ever been permitted to take his seat at the first table anywhere else.

We never blamed Mr. Van Buren for being a Free-Soiler. Having been raised in the North, we could not expect that he could be anything else at heart. And we cannot believe now, that he would keep the negro question constantly before the public, as it has been lately, if he thought it would endanger the Union; nor do we believe that Blair would; and we *know* that we would not run the risk of dissolving it for all the negroes and half the whites in the United States. It is likely that we would be better off if the ten we own would leave us; but we will not part with them "upon compulsion," having purchased them all at their own request, with money earned by the sweat of our own brow. If any white man should attempt to take them off, he would run the risk of having a smart scuffle with us. But we do not believe that there is one white man in a hundred who desires to meddle with slavery in the States. All the noise about negroes is made, in our opinion, with the object, and for the purpose, of trying to make great men out of very small ones, made of poor stuff. "*That* can't be *did*."

The character of Blair drawn by Colonel Claiborne is, we think, a very just one. It was not his nature to be "savage and ferocious," but he thought his duty to his party sometimes — yea, oftentimes — required that he should use the tomahawk and the scalping knife — and he did. It gave him pain to do so. Often, when he was about attacking a man, whom he respected personally, but abhorred politically, he said to us, "It gives me pain to attack that man; but he is restive and kicking in the traces, and complaining that the collar is too small for him, and chafes him. We must whip him in, or whip him out at once, before he gets a little drove to go off with him."

Those whom he considered "not worthy of his steel," he committed to our tender mercies, to squeeze to death by damning them "with faint praise," which was our way of killing them. We have defended a man against a charge of weakness never made against him, though he was, mentally, much stronger than we; another against a charge of stealing, who was much honester than we were supposed to be, and when no such charge had been laid at his door, winding up his character by saying, that if he had had the least opportunity to steal, our conscience would not have permitted us to say a single word in his favor; and so on. Our awkward defense to a man was almost as fatal as Blair's Toledo blade, which was rarely in the scabbard for seventeen years, and was so frequently thrust into some one, that the blood rarely dried on it. He often expected to be called to account for what he wrote, and made up his mind to settle it, if deemed necessary, in a desperate way. In one case with a desperate man, who wrote to him that he would challenge him if he did not take back a charge made, he asked us if we would stand by him, and we replied—reluctantly of course—we would. He then reiterated the charge, and the man acknowledged that he had been guilty as charged, but excused himself by saying that he was very young when he committed the offense. That man afterwards fell in a duel fought with another. We have on file the correspondence which passed between him and Blair.

What Colonel Claiborne has said of him as to his "singular facility" in writing is true; "and pity 'tis, 'tis true." Both his leaders and followers were written with a lead pencil, after night, in a great hurry, and we had to keep two boys to run to him for copy. We have known him to send one of the boys after the other to overtake him, and get the last word on the last sheet sent off. He rarely, it ever, wrote an article by daylight.

He does not care for money. Several times, while we were partners, we attempted to tell him how we were getting along in money matters, and he as often replied that he did not desire to know, and changed the subject. A year or two after we dissolved partnership, he asked us how much he was worth? and we answered, about one hundred and twenty-five thousand dollars, besides his property in this city, and where he lives. He replied, "That is more than any man should own—one hundred thousand dollars is enough." Four or five years ago we told him that the way he was going on spending his money, he would run through it all in ten years; to which he replied, "I don't care; that is as long as I expect to live; and my children are well to do, and doing well."

We will finish Blair's picture by portraying his personal appearance, and stating what he has said in the Globe of others who looked like him. He is about five feet ten inches high, and would be full six feet, if his brain were on the top of his head, instead of being in a *poll* behind it. He looks like a skeleton, lacks but little of being one, and weighed last spring, when dressed in thick winter clothing, one hundred and seven pounds, all told; about eighty-five of which, we suppose, was bone, and the other twenty-two pounds, made up of gristle, nerve, and brain—flesh he has none. His face is narrow, and of the hatchet kind, according with his meat-ax disposition when writing about his enemies. His complexion is fair, his hair sandy, and his eyes blue—his countenance remarkably mild, so firm that he can look any man in the face steadily, without winking. We thought him very homely until we became well acquainted with him and got used to his looks. But we still think he is as homely as one man in ten thousand, not excepting ourself—as far as he goes. Having less face than most men, he is, of course, not so ugly as many. Notwithstanding his emaciated looks, he had *the face* and effrontery to call the late Judge White, when he ran for the Presidency against Mr. Van Buren, *Calvin Edson*—the name of a man who was shown in theatres and menageries, years ago, to prove that a man could survive after losing all his flesh. He called the late George Poindexter, then President of the Senate of the United States, who was very thin and crooked, "the devil's darning-needle;" all of which he published in the Globe several times. We must stop writing about Blair, (who, no doubt, will think we have now written enough about him,) as we are behind time, and must devote a few minutes to ourself, the last picture in the group.

As we have just finished Blair by describing his personal appearance, our own first obtrudes itself; and we wish to get that off our mind. We must admit, as charged, "a shaggy exterior and very *brusque* manners." Well! we are able to bear all. Who cares? We don't. Nature has compensated us—we believe in compensation—for our lack of outside polish, by putting good work inside. The time has been when we would have been glad to be handsome; but we now see that beauty would have materially injured, if not entirely ruined us. If we had been handsome, we would have married while young, and would not have had a dollar wherewith to purchase furniture; but, being as we were, we lived single until we had made money enough to support a wife, and take care of any reasonable number of responsibilities that might befall us, and then married a girl of twenty-five, who suited us to a t, as she brought us no money to throw up to us, if we should happen to run through ours, and hers too; but every thing else necessary to render married life agreeable. We now look back upon our cotemporaries who were handsome, and see them with wigs on their heads, false teeth in their mouths, and paint and paste on their faces, to hide the marks of age, while we defy the tooth of time, dreading none of its effects, except decrepitude and death. We are six feet, five inches high; weigh two hundred and forty pounds, when in good humor, which is usually the case with us; but how much we weigh when mad, we do not know, never being weighed when in that condition; are belligerent, though somewhat bellicose in body; too timid to attack any body, but not afraid of being attacked by any one.

Our biographer gives us credit for "financial talent." All our art in that line lies in sticking to a good business, keeping but one iron in the fire, and living within an income. We plead not guilty to the charge that we now "coin money out of the *Congressional Globe.*" Since we made the contract with Congress, in the year 1846, to publish its proceedings at a certain rate per session, they have increased about one third; the wages of printers have been raised thirty-six and two thirds per cent.; the wages of reporters, twelve and a half per cent.; and the price of paper about sixteen per cent.; and it is now very hard for us to "raise the wind." The wages of printers in this city are thirty per cent. higher than they are in the cities north and west of here, and we pay six dollars a page for the mere reporting the debates; yet the *Congressional Globe* is sold to Congress for less than the first edition of any book is sold for by any bookseller in the world; estimating according to the number of words. We have pointed out this fact before, and no person has denied it; thought if it were not true, there are many who have seen it who would jump to expose the fallacy. We hardly know how we get along now. Perhaps we do so in the way the Irishman said he did, "by doing a large losing business." There should be no joking on so serious a subject—we know that we have gotten along thus far by selling the back numbers of the *Congressional Globe* and *Appendix.* But some of our back numbers are exhausted, and the usual sales will not reimburse us the cost of a reprint in less than twenty years, at the prices at which they are now sold; and, therefore, we do not expect any return of profit to us in our lifetime; but go on buoyed up with the hope that our children may reap some profit from the talents which we are now burying on old musty volumes.

It is not true, as asserted, that we have on our farm, "the shabbiest stock, the meanest fences, and the poorest crops in the country." On the contrary, all our stock are fat, and our fences and crops are good; but we spend about two thousand dollars a year more than we get off the farm, to keep them so; which is only five hundred dollars a year more than we calculated to lose on it when we purchased it. Our principal object for purchasing a farm in the country was to get our children out of the city.

Other journals, organs of course, were printed in Washington. The *Spectator* was one. It was mixed up in the intrigues to shuffle off the *Globe,* and was under the influence of Senator Rhett. It had taken the place of the *Telegraph* as the organ of the South Carolina section only. Martin and Heart were the publishers. Dr. Martin was a smart writer, and his articles always attracted attention. Virgil Maxcy was one of the editors. Martin afterwards went to Paris. William A. Harris then contributed his brains to those of Heart in the management of the paper, changing its name to the *Constitution.*

There were published in Washington, in 1845, five newspapers:
The *Union,* official Democratic organ—Ritchie and Heiss.
The *Globe,* ex-Democratic organ—Blair and Rives.
The *Constitution,* Calhoun organ—Harris and Heart.
United States Journal, Independent Democracy—Fisk and Dow.

National Intelligencer, Whig organ—Gales and Seaton.

Subsequently Heart, of the *Constitution*, joined the *Charleston (S. C.) Mercury*, and Harris was sent as *chargé d'affaires* to Buenos Ayres, and the *Constitution* closed its career. On Harris's return from South America he became connected with the *Union*.

In 1846, a paper called the *Daily Times* was issued by H. H. Robinson as an independent Democratic organ. It occupied the place vacated by the *United States Journal* in the winter of that year.

While the Mexican War was the order of the day, Thomas Ritchie, the editor of the *Union*, was brought before the Senate for the publication of a communication signed Vindicator, which was very severe on the conduct of that body for neglecting to carry out some of the military plans of the government in connection with the war. One of the paragraphs of the communication was as follows:

> In the Senate, on yesterday, the Mexicans achieved another victory. The bill for organizing ten regiments of regular troops having been submitted, with its amendments, to a committee of conference of the two houses, that committee unanimously agreed on a report which was submitted to them for their approval. The House of Representatives at once adopted the report by a very large majority. In the Senate it was, in its most important feature, rejected by a majority of six. When the result was ascertained, a distinguished Senator from Georgia exhibited the most marked tokens of exultation. It is the same Senator who urges a withdrawal of our army from the Mexican territory.

This appeared on the 9th of February, 1847. On the 13th Senator Yulee introduced two resolutions:

1st. For the expulsion of the editor of the *Union* from the privilege of the floor, for a libel upon the Senate.

2d. For the expulsion of the *Union* reporters from the reporter's gallery of the Senate, for an alleged partial report of the debate in the Senate on the previous Monday.

These resolutions gave rise to an important debate, in which Mesrs. Calhoun, Webster, Butler, Westcott, Yulee, Mangum, Mason, Clayton, Cass, Bright, and Archer took part, and in which the next presidential election, the rights of the Press and of the Senate, were fully discussed. It was in this debate, which lasted two days, that Senator Westcott, of Florida, the only man of the passing generation who continues to wear a queue, said:

> If the people of this country knew one twentieth part of the corruptions, the peculent, the reeking corruptions of the government, they would descend in a body upon this city, create a revolution in less than twenty-four hours, and fall upon the President, heads of Departments, Congress, whigs and democrats, and turn them head over heels into the Potomac River.

It seemed from this discussion that the troubles of the Democratic Party entered into the feelings of the senators as much as the rights of the Senate or the liberty of the Press did, the friends of Calhoun, who were opposed to the war, uniting with the Whigs against President Polk and the *Union* as his organ on this point, although the

Union was placed in power by the States-Rights wing of the democracy. On the second day the vote was taken on the first resolution, the second having been withdrawn, resulting in twenty-seven yeas and twenty-one nays.

Thus, without the vigor, and violence, and thunder, and threats of the *Globe*, during the fearless and fiery administration of Jackson, the editor of the *Union* quietly submitted to this mild and harmless tyranny of the Senate, and, as an organ, it was powerless and useless.

The *Globe* was not dead. It had merely given up its official position with the executive. It now sought other pastures. It became the publisher of the Congressional Debates. Blair and Rives, in 1846, were awarded the contract for the publication of these debates. In 1849 Blair sold his interest to Rives, who continued the publication of the *Globe* till his death. It is now published by his sons. In the contest in the Fortieth Congress for a renewal of this contract, the following facts appeared in the report of the Senate committee on the subject:

ACTUAL COST FOR THIRTY-NINTH CONGRESS.
Daily Globe	$82,521
Congressional Globe	209,178
Total	$291,699

ESTIMATED COST OF SAME WORK BY RIVES AND BAILEY.
Daily Globe	$116,351
Congressional Globe	273,104
Total	$389,455

ESTIMATED COST BY JOSEPH T. CROWELL.
Daily	$101,590
Congressional	159,559
Total	$261,149

ESTIMATED COST BY CONGRESSIONAL PRINTER.
Daily	$120,610
Congressional	155,885
Total	$276,495

It was decided to make a contract with Rives and Bailey for two years from March 4, 1869, because they had performed their work "well and satisfactorily." Yet the *Globe* is not a faithful reporter of Congressional debates. We will give an instance. On the 10th of February, 1869, there was a "scene" in joint convention of the two houses for the counting of the Electoral Vote. The correspondent of the *Boston Advertiser* of February 11, 1869, thus describes the affair:

> The scenes of yesterday in the joint convention for counting the electoral vote have been the subject of universal comment today. . . . The *Globe* report of to-day reveals enough to make every good citizen blush, but some of the worst language used by Mr. Butler is omitted, and scores of bitter and excited remarks made by other members are left out, perhaps because the official reporters in the wild confusion failed to distinguish the speakers. . . . . . .

Mr. BUTLER—Will the gentleman allow me ——
Mr. BINGHAM—No, sir.
Mr. BUTLER—I only want to say that you are not using my words in the connection in which I said them.
Mr. BINGHAM—The gentleman's remarks do not appear in the *Globe* this morning, but I find the gentleman's speech reported by the official representatives of the press of the country. I am glad that the gentleman takes back his words.
Mr. BUTLER—I take back nothing.
Mr. BINGHAM—Then I ask the House to compel you to take back your revolutionary resolution.

The omissions in the reports, as indicated in the above extract, are of frequent occurrence in scenes of this character. While the credit of the nation may be saved some damage by these omissions, the accuracy of the reports in the *Globe* is seriously affected. One of the chiefs of the *Globe* staff of stenographers for some time was Robert Sutton, a very accomplished and experienced reporter, who made his début in Washington under the auspices of James Gordon Bennett, of the *New York Herald*, when he introduced fuller reports of the debates in Congress in his paper. The entire staff are faithful and skillful. All these omissions are caused by members themselves, who require them of the publishers of the *Globe*. Many of the speeches which appear in that sheet are never delivered in Congress. Hence such a publication can not be a faithful reporter if what is spoken in debate is afterwards forbidden publication.

The editor of the *Globe* in its glory, Francis P. Blair, was a brilliant graduate of the Transylvania University, Kentucky, and the publisher, John C. Rives, a graduate, with all the honors, of a first-class printing-office. After Blair had sold out to his partner he retired to Silver Springs to prepare his two boys, Montgomery and Francis Preston, Jr., one for the bench and a seat in Lincoln's cabinet, which he occupied in 1861, and the other for the bar, for the House of Representatives, the army, and for the Senate, where he is now.

There was another change in the organship in 1848. Charles W. Fenton had started a paper in Washington in April, 1847, in which the nomination of General Taylor for the presidency was suggested shortly after the battle of Buena Vista, but the paper did not amount to much. On the inauguration of that gallant old soldier another paper was established as his organ. It was named the *Republic*. General Taylor did not recognize the *National Intelligencer*. It was a Webster organ, and Webster had said that Taylor's nomination was one "not fit to be made." John M. Clayton was Secretary of State, and he was in favor of a new paper for the new dynasty. Colonel Alexander Bullitt, of the New Orleans *Picayune*, and John O. Sargent, of the New York *Courier and Enquirer*, were installed as its editors. These selections were considered excellent, but, whatever these writers may have been in the editorial rooms of the *Picayune* and *Courier and Enquirer*, they were neither vigorous nor strong enough for the leading paper of their party in the national capital. Besides "the cohesive power of public plunder," it required boldness and brains to keep the lesser lights of a party in order, and under a good state of discipline. These editors did not possess the requisite qualities for this work. They needed audacity. They lacked the journalistic confidence of the nation. The result of this failure was a change. On the death of President Taylor and the elevation of Vice-President Fillmore, with Daniel Webster in the State Department, the old Bourbon organ, the *National Intelligencer*, was restored to favor. But it was the last of the dynasty. It finally went out of power and influence. New blood, new journals, fresh brains, and more energy, were rapidly coming up all over the country.

On the other side the same signs of organic decay were seen. The organs of the Democratic Party lived longer, but they daily became weaker. When Franklin Pierce entered Washington as President in 1853, the *Union* was restored as the chief organ of the party, with the *Star* as a tender. The *Union* was now owned by General Robert Armstrong, of the *Nashville Union*. Judge A. O. P. Nicholson, and Caleb Cushing, Attorney General, were constant contributors to its columns. General Armstrong was an old personal friend of General Jackson's, and was at the battle of New Orleans with him. He was a genial gentleman of the old school. While American consul at Liverpool in 1846–7, he rendered great service to the nation on the Oregon Question—the Fifty-four Forty or Fight era of our history. One day at the Astor House, surrounded with hungry office-seekers, although just landed from England, he was met by a young friend and congratulated on his return to lead an army through Mexico, and that so many recruits were already with him. "No, no, my young friend," replied the hale old soldier, "we have troops enough in Mexico to accomplish our purpose there. If not, I will again wheel into line with musket to shoulder, if necessary. These gentlemen," added he, smiling, and looking around him, "are not desirous of going to Mexico, but are, they tell me, particular friends of the President."

The little *Star*, the junior organ, was originally edited by Charles W. Denison, but it soon after changed hands, and was owned and edited for many years by that original and energetic journalist, W. D. Wallach. He was an active man, always around, elbowing through crowds at the hotels and elsewhere, and making his appearance at his office at the right time full of gossip for his columns. Not to be outdone by the larger and more pretentious sheets, he claimed and got his share of the government patronage. Not to be eclipsed by them in social comforts, he too purchased a farm and much stock near Washington, to which he retired, a star among the Jerseys, the Chesters, and the Bhramas, till his death, which occurred at Culpepper, Va., December 1, 1871.

The *Union* continued through another administration. James Buchanan entered the executive mansion in 1857. He made the *Union* his organ, but he insisted on a new editor. John Appleton, who had edited the *Portland Argus*, and who had been in the State Department and in London with the President, was the one selected. The *Union* newspaper, like the Union under Buchanan, became entangled in its political affinities and associations. Cornelius Wendell, a printer of Albany, who was connected with the *Union*, felt constrained, in consequence of his old connections with Thurlow Weed, to abandon the concern, and the paper grew weaker as the term of Buchanan's administration approached its end. With the first hostile gun at Fort Sumter, the old Democratic Party, which started into life with Jefferson in 1789, tumbled to pieces, and ceased to be a power. New organs of public opinion sprung into existence. New papers in the form of the Independent Press, new men for political leaders, new sets of carpet-baggers, and new parties, made their *entrée*, on the reconstruction of the nation, with fresh ideas and fresh vigor, and have taken their place in the world of action. These new elements are to control the destinies of the United States for the next fifty years. Old party hacks of all sorts, men as well as newspapers, have passed away. The *Telegraphs*, the *Globes*, the *Unions*, the *Intelligencers*, the *Spectators*, the *Constitutions*, the *Republics*, the *Madisonians*, as official organs, are gone.

The *Intelligencer* clung to life with tenacity. Joseph Gales died in 1860. William Winston Seaton, the surviving editor, continued the publication of the paper three or four years longer, and into the heart of the rebellion. In a funeral note, written by him in January, 1865, he thus closed his editorial career:

> The parting with my old paper is painful in the extreme. But the untoward circumstances of the times had reduced it to the point of extinction, and no alternative was left me but to see it expire or to transfer it to some younger men, who thought that, by withdrawing it from the arena of politics and converting it into a news and business sheet, they could make it pay. I would, I confess, have preferred for it the dignity of death; but justice to a few friends around me, who have enabled me to sustain it during three years of vainly hoping for peace and better times, compelled me to part with it. Pride and hope induced me to srruggle on against the difficulties which beset me, at the sacrifice of every thing I possessed; but I was at last obliged to succumb. The loss of two-thirds of my entire circulation by the secession of the South I could have borne; the proscription of the government I could have borne singly; but the weight of the two united was too much for me, and, receiving no compensating support in the North, I was forced to yield. In the high character of the friends like yourself, who have stood by the old journal in its adversity and cheered its editors by their approval and support,

I find a consolation which I would not exchange for better fortune, although I end fifty-two years of labor with nothing.

On the death of Mr. Seaton in 1866, the paper passed into the hands of Snow, Coyle & Co. Coyle had been a clerk in the establishment. He made an effort to keep it in existence. With half a million of bad debts on its books, and its prestige gone, how was it to survive? Millions of the public money had passed into the establishment, but open house and generous hospitality had swallowed all. There was another change. Alexander Delmar, the statistician, revived it in 1869, and united a paper called the *Express* with the old concern. The *Express* was an evening paper, started as a neutral sheet in 1866, but became a self-styled organ of Andrew Johnson. The *Intelligencer*, thus revived, lived a short time longer, and finally disappeared as a Washington paper. Its remains were carried to New York. The subjoined card appeared in the *New York Sun* on the 14th of April, 1871:

To the Editor of the Sun.

In this morning's SUN appears a statement to the effect that the *National Intelligencer* ceased to be published three years ago. The *Daily Intelligencer* was published in Washington until January 10, 1870; then merged into the weekly, and the latter removed to this city, where it is now published as a journal of national and commercial intelligence and revenue reform. One of the present proprietors purchased the property for cash on the 30th November, 1869, and has owned it wholly or in part ever since. The absence of a legitimate commercial basis for the support of newspapers in Washington was the reason for the removal. It is gratifying to be able to say that the change has resulted beneficially. With the exception of two brief intervals of time—first in August, 1814, when the British troops under Gen. Ross entered and occupied the publishing office; the other in June, 1869—the paper has a continuous file from November, 1800, to date, a period of over 70 years.

THE NATIONAL INTELLIGENCER PUBLISHING COMPANY, 176 Broadway.

Where is it now?

The *National Era* became known as an important organ of the Abolition Party in Washington City in 1847. Its editor, Dr. Gamaliel Bailey, had been editor of the *Methodist Protestant* in Baltimore in 1836, and afterwards, with James G. Birney, started the *Philanthropist*, an anti-slavery paper, in Cincinnati. The printing-office and press of the latter were several times destroyed by mobs, but the publication of the paper was continued till 1847, when it was merged with the *National Era*. That office also passed the ordeal of mob violence. It was managed with considerable enterprise till the death of its editor and proprietor. It was the recognized organ of the Anti-slavery Party at the national capital when it was considered almost an act of temerity to have such an organ in that centre of Southern fire-eaters during the sessions of Congress. It was in the *Era* that Mrs. Harriet Beecher Stowe published her celebrated romance, "Uncle Tom's Cabin." It was commenced in 1851, and published as a serial tale. It was finished in 1852, and was then republished in book form by Jewett, of Boston. It was estimated that up to the period of the breaking out of the rebellion in the spring of 1861, that half a million copies of this tale were sold in the United States, half a million in Great Britain, and half a million on the Continent of Europe. It was translated into all languages, and dramatized every where. It had a run of hundreds of nights in the theatres on the Bowery and Chatham Street, New York City, where the "huge fisted" Democracy, with their families, "most do congregate;" and while Little Topsey nightly produced a most profound effect in tears and applause upon the masses in the theatres, the polls at the elections in the metropolis invariably showed the curious anomaly of annually increased majorities against the Abolition Party!

The colored people of Washington have produced a new paper called the *New Era*, which fully represents their interests. It is edited by Frederick Douglass and the Rev. Stella Martin, both colored men.

There are now published in the national capital seven newspapers:

Names.	Politics.	Editors.
Daily Patriot,	Democratic,	Noah L. Jeffrees.
The Chronicle,	Republican,	John M. Morris. Myron Fox.
The National Republican,	Republican,	Wm. J. Murtagh.
The Star,	Independent,	Crosby S. Noyes.
The Morning News.		
The New National Era,	Republican,	Frederick Douglass. Stella Martin.
The Capital,	Independent,	Donn Piatt.
The Herald.		
The National Standard.		
The Gazette,		T. B. Florence.
Congressional Globe,		Rives and Bailey.

The *Chronicle*, a paper owned for some time by John W. Forney, occupied some attention. Its editor had been an editor in Philadelphia, a working Democratic politician in Pennsylvania, an ardent political friend of James Buchanan, and Secretary to the Senate. After he joined the Republican Party he was equally prominent as a working politician on that side. He sold the *Chronicle* in 1870, and fell back on the *Philadelphia Press*, which he owns. In 1871 he was appointed Collector of the Port of Philadephia by President Grant, a place he has since resigned.

When the *Chronicle* passed from the hands of Mr. Forney, its new proprietor defined its position after this manner:

No person in any way connected with the Executive Department of the Government; no advocate of San Domingo; no aspirant for the Presidency, or for any office in the gift of the President; no person connected with any railroad project, or with any other special project, has furnished one dollar to purchase the *Chronicle*, or now owns an interest of one dollar in it. The present owner of this journal is absolutely untrammelled.

The *Patriot* was established early in 1870 as a Democratic organ. James E. Harvey was its first editor. He had been, before the rebellion, the leading Washington correspondent of the Philadelphia *North American* and *New York Tribune*, and minister to Portugal after the inauguration of President Lincoln.

There are none of the old names represented in the above list; none of the old fire of the *Globe;* none of the old dignity of the *Intelligencer*. None of the papers in Washington now speak as "I am, sir, an oracle." Now the Independent Press of the nation, the Associated Presses north, east, west, and south, are the recognized organs. May they always be the Voice of the People.

CHAPTER XVII.
THE DEMOCRATIC TRIUMVIRATE.

THE CHARLESTON COURIER.—JAMES GORDON BENNETT'S ADVENT AS A JOURNALIST.—THE MORNING CHRONICLE OF NEW YORK.—WASHINGTON IRVING.—SINGULAR DUEL.—HARRY CROSWELL AND THE HUDSON BALANCE.—LIBEL ON JEFFERSON.—OPINIONS OF ALEXANDER HAMILTON.—THE RICHMOND ENQUIRER AND THOMAS RITCHIE.—ANDREW JACKSON ON RITCHIE.—THE NEWSPAPER TRIUMVIRATE.—THE NEW HAMPSHIRE PATRIOT AND ISAAC HILL.—"ORIGIN" OF THE WAR ON THE UNITED STATES BANK.—THE ALBANY REGISTER AND SOLOMON SOUTHWICK.—MOBBING THE OFFICE OF THE BALTIMORE REPUBLICAN.—THE ALBANY ARGUS AND THE REGENCY.—EDWIN CROSWELL.—JUDGE KENT ON NEWSPAPERS.

WE leave the newspapers of Washington to look after the journals in other sections of the country. New organs of political parties, and of the governing commercial and material interests of the nation, were making their call upon public attention.

Quite an important newspaper was issued in Charleston, South Carolina, in the first year of this century. Loring Andrews, of Hingham, Massachusetts, who had previously published the *Herald of Freedom* in Boston, the *Western Star* in Stockbridge, Massachusetts, and the *Centinel* in Albany, New York, established the *Charleston Courier* in 1800. In 1807 he died, but the *Courier* continued in existence, and became an influential commercial newspaper in that section of the country. It was never a violent political journal, but it was the most enterprising paper in Charleston. A. Willington & Co. were for many years its proprietors and publishers, and it was edited, prior to the Rebellion, by Richard Yeadon, who made himself singularly notorious by addressing Edward Everett as the "Great Laudator," in speaking of the famous lecturer on Washington for the preservation of Mount Vernon.

James Gordon Bennett commenced his career as a journalist in the office of the *Courier*. Willington and Bennett met in New York, where arrangements were made for the latter's removal to Charleston. This was in 1823, forty-nine years ago. It was the custom of Willington, at that time, to board the vessels on their arrival at Charleston from Havana with a small row-boat, *à la* Topliff of the Boston News-rooms, and get the latest Havana papers. On taking them to the *Courier* office, they would pass into the hands of Mr. Bennett, who would translate the news from them. Through the

Cadiz packets, which ran regularly to Havana, news from Europe would thus sometimes reach America before it arrived at New York by the old London, Havre, and Liverpool ships. In this way the *Courier* would frequently obtain important advantages over its less enterprising contemporaries. This was during the famous Duc d'Angoulême excitement. In Yeadon's summer trips to New York in 1850–1, or thereabouts, he would, with the usual weakness of editors, boast of the *Courier*, and claimed, with great unction, that it was in that office where Bennett took his first lessons in journalism —that it was, indeed, Bennett's newspaper cradle.

Willington's news-boat arrangement, we believe, embraced nearly the whole scope and extent of the enterprise of the *Courier*, but it was useful and instrumental in building up that establishment. Its power and influence, however, like the power and influence of hundreds of other leading journals at the South, disappeared in the cloud of the Rebellion, and other journals, with other editors, with exceptions here and there, are taking their place. There has been, as the natural consequence of the war, a new infusion of newspaper talent in the Southern States, which will ultimately leaven the entire press of that section, and make it more comprehensive in its character, and homogeneous with the journals of the North, East, and West.

Mr. Willington's daughter, we think, married William Young, for many years editor of the *Albion*, the acknowledged English organ in New York, edited, till lately, by Kinahan Cornwallis, a well-known writer and political economist.

When the *American Citizen* denounced Aaron Burr for his desertion of the Democratic Party, the friends of Burr established a paper in New York to neutralize the attacks of Cheatham. The new paper was called the *Morning Chronicle*, and was first published in 1802. It was edited by Dr. Peter Irving, a man of much literary ability and erudition, but not equal, as a political journalist, to his opponent. Washington Irving first made his appearance in the *Morning Chronicle* of New York as a writer over the signature of Jonathan Oldstyle, as Charles Dickens did in the *Morning Chronicle* of London over the signature of Boz.

The publisher of the *Chronicle* was William A. Davis, brother of Matthew L. Davis. The Van Nesses, the Swartwouts, Matthew L. Davis, and other leading friends of Burr, were contributors to its columns. There was a semi-weekly, entitled the *Chronicle Express*, connected with the daily issue.

The *Citizen* charged Burr with intriguing with the Federalists for the defeat of Jefferson for the presidency. The *Chronicle*, not so keen, was still sharp enough to draw blood. In its efforts to bol-

ster up the character of Burr, it bitterly attacked the Clintons and
Livingstons, accusing them of a desire to absorb all the offices and
all the spoils of party. With the *Chronicle* Burr was a saint. The
old Manhattan Bank entered the arena against Burr, and, in the
heat of this remarkable political contest, the bank managers refused
to re-elect as director Colonel John Swartwout, one of Burr's personal and political friends. Brockholst Livingston was chosen in
his stead. The contest was a warm one, and, in a political conversation growing out of the campaign, De Witt Clinton called Swartwout "a liar, a scoundrel, and a villain." Colonel S. immediately
demanded an apology, or a recantation of this offensive language.
Mr. Clinton stated that Swartwout had charged him with selfish and
unworthy motives in his opposition to Burr, and the epithets were
simply a strong denial of that charge; if Colonel S. would withdraw
his charge, Mr. Clinton would take back what he had said, and not
otherwise. This led to a duel. It was believed by many at that
time that there was a plan on foot to draw Colonel Hamilton into
a personal conflict for the purpose of getting him out of the way,
and that this affair was a part of the conspiracy. Five shots were
exchanged by Clinton and Swartwout, during which the latter was
twice wounded. There were three shots without injury to either
party. "Is your principal satisfied?" asked Richard Riker, acting
as Clinton's second, after each fire. "He is not," replied Swartwout's second. The fourth shot was then exchanged, and Swartwout received Clinton's ball in the calf of his leg.

"Is your principal satisfied now?" again demanded Riker.

"He is not," reiterated Swartwout's second.

The fifth shot was then exchanged, and Clinton's ball again lodged
in Swartwout's leg.

"Is your principal now satisfied?" once more demanded the amiable and accommodating Riker.

There was a moment's consultation with Swartwout while the surgeons were probing the wounds, and, in spite of their protests, he
declared he was not satisfied. Clinton, who was shooting at a man
against whom he entertained no personal enmity, then said, " Well,
well, he may go to the devil, for I will fight no more," and, with his
friends, immediately left the field.

It is thought that a letter from Albany, which was published in
the *Chronicle* in February, 1804, describing the deliberations of a secret meeting of a number of Federalists, where Colonel Hamilton
spoke strongly in opposition to Burr, and which led to his defeat for
governor, was the beginning of the scheme to draw Hamilton into
the duel which ended in his death.

The *Chronicle* continued to be published, notwithstanding the political death of Burr in the physical death of Hamilton, till the summer of 1805, when it was merged in the *Poughkeepsie Journal*, edited by Isaac Mitchell. The *Journal*, under the inspiration of Secretary Tillotson, assailed Clinton and Spencer. The *Plebeian*, edited by Jesse Buel, was also severe on Clinton. On the other hand, Cheatham's *Citizen* and the *Albany Register* came out equally strong for Governor Lewis in the political fight of the state.

The *Albany Register* was edited by John Barber, assisted by his brother-in-law, Solomon Southwick. The latter was represented as a young man of elegant and prepossessing manners and appearance. He was the son of the old editor of the *Newport Mercury*. He became a prominent, indeed, a leading politician in New York. It seems that, after the affair between Clinton and Swartwout, the political feeling against Burr increased in intensity. The *Register*, the organ of the party, after some hesitation, denounced him as a traitor to the Democratic Party. This was followed up by nearly all of the Democratic journals. Southwick was chosen clerk of the Assembly in opposition to the Federalist candidate.

The *Register*, in the time of the Clintons, Burr, Lewis, and Spencer, occupied the same position in Albany that the *Argus* afterwards did in the time of Van Buren, Marcy, and Wright. In the quarrel between Governor Lewis and De Witt Clinton, it was said that Chancellor Lansing, who had received the nomination of the Republican Party in 1804, declined it because of the threatened opposition of Clinton and Spencer on his refusing to pledge himself "to a particular course of conduct in the administration of the government of the state." According to the chancellor, De Witt Clinton, Judge Taylor, Solomon Southwick, and one other, had been seen coming from the office of the editor of the *Register* on the eve of the announcement of his nomination, which announcement was not only very singular, but very exceptionable in its character. The article in question, indicating to him the coming pressure, if elected, induced him to decline the nomination, and thus free himself of the trammels of these distinguished politicians.

This was in 1807. Southwick became the chief editor of the *Register* in 1808. It continued to be the organ of the Clintonians, and endeavored to bring about the nomination of Vice-President George Clinton, instead of Madison, for the presidency in 1809. It was the opening of the quarrel with the Richmond Junta or Virginia Dynasty, which helped defeat De Witt Clinton in 1813.

Southwick, who was now a journalist of commanding influence in New York politics as the accredited organ of the Democratic Party, like many editors of that and every other period, was an office-seeker. In 1809 he was appointed Sheriff of the City and County of Albany.

In 1811 he was President of the Mechanics' Bank of Albany. He was also printer to the state. Then he was made Regent of the University. After these honors there was a change politically and journalistically. In opposing the election of Governor Tompkins, he created an opposition which led to the establishment of a new paper. He was then charged with corruption in connection with the organization of a monster bank in New York, called the Bank of America. He was acquitted, but his influence was shattered. The new journal was the *Argus*. This was Southwick's great mistake as a party editor. Success had spoiled him for such a position. He was on the wane from that time. No mere party editor could dictate to party. The first prop knocked from under him was the withdrawal of the state printing; and although he received the appointment of Postmaster of Albany in 1815, he felt constrained to retire from the editorial chair of the *Register* in 1818, after having become inimical to De Witt Clinton, his oldest and warmest political friend. He established the *Plough-Boy* in 1821, and then the *National Democrat*, both of which were short lived. In 1822 he was removed from the Post-office for cause, and became a candidate for governor. He was signally defeated at the election, and thus closed the career of this brilliant and blundering party journalist. In this election Judge Yates received 128,493 votes, and Editor Southwick 2910. On the next election Yates was not even nominated. In alluding to this fact, he laughingly said that he was the most popular man in the state: at one election he was chosen governor almost unanimously, and at the next election he was unanimously elected to stay at home!

In 1828 Southwick was again a candidate for governor, representing the Anti-masonic party, becoming editor, at the same time, of the *National Observer*, the organ of that new party. He died in 1839, aged sixty-six years.

Israel W. Clark, the new editor of the *Register*, had formerly published the *Watch-Tower*, a Democratic paper, at Cooperstown. The *Register* was the organ of Governor Clinton, and now made strong efforts to recover the state printing. The *Argus*, the new paper, was the organ of Judge Spencer, who had separated from the Clinton section of the party. New editorial talent was introduced in the *Register* in 1819. Nathaniel H. Carter, of New Hampshire, now assumed, in part, the editorial management of that paper. He took the entire charge in 1820, and changed the name to that of the *New York Statesman*. One of his admirers thus described Carter:

> Nathaniel Carter is vividly impressed on my recollection: he had very considerable literary taste; was many years editor of the *New York Statesman;* and after his visit in Europe, published his letters on his tour in two large volumes.

His merit was only equalled by his modesty. He was strongly devoted to Dewitt Clinton and the Érie Canal; with becoming feeling he cherished much regard for his eastern brethren, and was the first I think who introduced his personal friend, our constitutional expositor, Daniel Webster, to the Bread and Cheese Lunch, founded by J. Fenimore Cooper; where sometimes met, in familiar disquisitions, such minds as those of Chief Justice Jones, P. A. Jay, Henry Storrs, Prof. Renwick, John Anthon, Charles King, John Duer, and others of a like intellectual calibre. Carter was of a feeble frame, struggling with pulmonary annoyance, from which he died early. He was little initiated in the trickery of political discussion. His heart was filled with the kindliest feelings of which nature is susceptible.

The current events connected with journalism and politics were so peculiarly interwoven that it is difficult to state them *seriatim*. Sometimes we are compelled to run ahead chronologically, and then return to prior incidents and occurrences. Thus an important event, in a newspaper point of view, happened early in 1804. The *Hudson Balance*, a leading Federal paper, edited by Harry Croswell, assailed Mr. Jefferson with great vigor and violence. The attack was considered so strong and severe that Croswell was indicted by the grand jury of Columbia County for libel. The case came before Chief Justice Lewis in the February term of the Superior Court. Alexander Hamilton, Richard Harrison, and Wm. N. Van Ness, who was afterwards Burr's second when Hamilton was shot, appeared for the journalist; Attorney General Spencer and Lawyer Caines for the prosecution. On the trial Croswell offered to prove the truth of the charges of the alleged libel. The court, as in the case of Zenger in 1735, and in accordance with the English common law doctrine, rejected the evidence, and declared that the only question for the jury to decide was the fact whether or not the alleged libel had been published by the defendant Croswell, and that the question of libel or no libel was to be determined by the court alone. The distinguished counsel then endeavored to obtain a new trial, but the court decided that it could not depart from the fixed rule of common law. To the Press this was an important case. It is related that the effort of Alexander Hamilton in this trial eclipsed that of Andrew Hamilton of 1735. In one case, Andrew Hamilton obtained a great triumph for the freedom of the Press in the early part of last century. In the other case, Alexander Hamilton, by showing, with wonderful eloquence and power, that the maxim "greater the truth, greater the libel," was of modern date in England; that it was at war with the genius of the civil institutions of this country; that it was an outrage on human rights, common justice, and common sense, produced a profound impression on the public mind. It affected the Legislature. The subject was taken up at the next session, a bill introduced, and the matter thoroughly ventilated in the sessions of 1804-5. In the session of 1805, the bill authorizing the truth to be given in evidence when the matter, written or printed, was published "with good motives and for justifiable ends," became a law. It constituted the jury in this, as in all other criminal cases, judges of the law and of the fact. The law of libel was then placed on a surer and fairer foundation, and the principle thus enunciated was afterwards incorporated in the constitutions of 1821, 1845, and 1865, and became a fundamental law of the state.

But what of the Democratic Triumvirate?

The *Richmond Enquirer* is one of the ancient and honorable journals now published. Its history is almost the history of the old Democratic Party. On the 9th of May, 1804, it was first issued on a small semi-weekly sheet by Ritchie and Worsley. Its editor was Thomas Ritchie, the senior proprietor, who became well known in the course of time as Father Ritchie, and the *Enquirer* was deemed a power in the political circles of the country. The *Examiner* had, for several years previously, been the leading Republican paper of Richmond. It had been edited by Merewether Jones, a warm opponent of the Alien and Sedition laws, who maintained the tri-color against the black cockade in that eventful period. Skelton Jones succeeded him, and he published the paper with W. W. Worsley as business partner. James Thompson Callender wrote for this paper. Then the concern grew weak and died. Its material was purchased by Thomas Ritchie and Worsley, and the *Enquirer*, with five hundred subscribers, was issued in its place.

When the *Enquirer* was started Jefferson was President, and the paper, like the old *Virginia Gazette* at Williamsburg, was established under his auspices. Its origin was part of the plan of the organization of the Democratic Party. Its platform was made up of the resolutions of '98 and '99. In his first article the editor said :

He fondly hopes that whenever necessity or inclination shall induce him to abandon his present pursuit, he may be able to lay his hand upon his heart and indulge the consolatory reflection that he has not dishonored the high prerogatives of the press or his own personal character.

The *Enquirer* came under the influence of party and public patronage from its first number. Its initial number published the laws of the United States. This was the President's indorsement. Its circulation was considered large. It was the organ of the Virginia Democracy, and looked upon Virginia as the only nursery in the country for statesmen and presidents. In this view of the mission of Virginia, and after that state had furnished Washington, Jefferson, Madison, and Monroe, the *Enquirer* pooh-poohed at the name of Andrew Jackson, when it was suggested by Aaron Burr in 1817, and Ritchie came out strongly and violently against the Old Hero in the contest of 1824, asserting that his election "would be a curse upon our country." It seems that Ritchie filled the same niche in the mind of Jackson that Freneau, of the *National Gazette*, did in the mind of Washington. The two editors were denounced in similar terms. Jackson once said, "I see that I am attacked in Congress by Cocke, Whitman, and Williams, aided by that infamous press, the *Richmond Enquirer*. If such a corrupt press as the *Richmond Enquirer* were to approbate my conduct, I should think, in some unguarded moment, I had committed some great moral impropriety." The *Globe*, to smooth over the matter, and keep the party lines in order, afterwards explained Jackson's reasons for these strong expressions: they were merely intended in the Pickwickian sense. The explanation was satisfactory to Ritchie at the time. But General Jackson never had the highest confidence in Ritchie. In a letter to Francis P. Blair, written on the 14th of December, 1844, he thus spoke of the Virginia journalist:

> It is true Mr. Ritchie is an experienced editor, but sometimes goes off at half-cock before he sees the whole ground, and does the party great injury before he sees his error, and then has great difficulty to get back into the right track again. Witness his course on my removal of the deposits, and how much injury he did us before he got into the right track again. Another *faux pas* he made when he went off with Rives and the conservatives, and advocated for the safe keeping of the public revenue special deposits in the state banks, as if where the directory were corrupt there could be any more security in special deposits in corrupt banks than in general deposits, and it was some time before the great absurdity could be beat out of his mind.

Most of Ritchie's editorials were, in his early career, written in the first person, and in this way the paper and editor became synonymous terms. Not satisfied with the *Enquirer* alone, its editor dabbled in another Richmond paper called the *Compiler*, which he edited for several years.

The *Enquirer*, like the *Albany Argus*, made and unmade politicians and statesmen in its own state, and, during Jackson's and Van Buren's administrations, the rank and file of the party were regularly, despotically, and systematically controlled and guided by Ritchie of the *Enquirer*, Blair of the *Globe*, and Croswell of the *Argus*—the American Triumvirate of party journalists, who in turn were moved as puppets by the master spirits of the Democratic Party in the Kitchen Cabinet, the Richmond Junta, and the Albany Regency.

Among the contributors to the *Enquirer* was William Wirt. This distinguished man wrote under the signature of "The British Spy" for the *Richmond Argus* in 1802, and under the *nomme de plume* of "The Old Bachelor" in the *Richmond Enquirer* in 1812. It was some time after this period that Wirt became the Anti-masonic candidate for the presidency.

It was Ritchie's habit to place at the end of many of his articles and short paragraphs the wise saying, *nous verrons*. Whenever he wished to impress his readers with the fact that something was to happen in politics which he could not fully divulge, this mysterious phrase would surely be brought into service. They were, in the *Enquirer*, the wink of the politician, or the shrug of the Frenchman's shoulder. He believed in repetition. Other expressions would be often used. In the tariff excitement, which led to nullification in South Carolina in 1832, he was dubbed with various titles: Thomas Nous Verrons, Momentous Crisis Ritchie, Old Nous Verrons, Obeta Principiis Ritchie. "With an attenuated frame, thin and wan, and apparently wasted to a shadow, Ritchie could undergo," said a friend of his, "immense mental exertion and bodily fatigue; and though his dress was such as to have thrown ordinary mortals into consumption, he rarely was troubled with cold. He almost invariably wore a white Marseilles vest, and thin pumps and silk stockings, and we have often seen him thus clad, in snow and mire, in the depth of winter, wending his way homewards with a handful of papers, excerpts, and *copy*, with his white cambric handkerchief twisted around them, and without an overcoat, while all others were wrapped in furs and flannels as heavy as could be worn."

The *Enquirer* of July 24, 1854, in speaking of its old editor, gave the following modest, curious, and interesting account of Mr. Ritchie's *status* in Richmond and in Virginia:

> Mr. Ritchie was secretary to almost all the public meetings held in Richmond during his residence there, was present at all the Legislative caucuses where Presidents and Governors and Senators were made and unmade, acted and consulted with the managers, was advised and counseled with by them, and without his knowledge and concurrence, few moves were made on the political board. In times of high political excitement in the Legislature, while he would be sitting at the clerks' table taking notes of the debates, we have seen the leaders of the party, fearing their own judgment and totally at fault, vacillating and uncertain, come to him for the cue, and obtaining it in a few hurried words, we have seen them return to their positions, and then, with a boldness and intrepidity not before felt, proclaim their course, and sound the bugle, giving the rallying notes which were certain to be taken up and passed from mouth to mouth, till the whole party would stand in solid phalanx not to be broken or shaken. If any man wavered then, woe to his future prospects for advancement in Virginia. If he resisted, his political death was sealed forever.
>
> Mr. Ritchie was manager at all the public balls, and was the perfect gentleman in his attentions to the ladies—was one of the Committee of Arrangements for all public dinners—had something to do in the preparation of the toasts—presided on these occasions with dignity and propriety—and would proclaim, when the company became a little uproarious, that "order was Heaven's first law." He welcomed public guests at public entertainments, and gave them a cheerful and a cordial greeting. He was a member of pleasant clubs, and none so jovial and gay as he. When with old cronies at a round table, he would pass a few hours the liveliest, merriest, noisiest, youngest, though perhaps the oldest, of the set. He was ever attentive to strangers who visited the city—would call upon and receive their calls with punctilious respect; and it was remarkable to notice the curiosity with which he was looked at and enquired for by them.
>
> These civilities and duties and amusements Mr. Ritchie performed and enjoyed in his hours of relaxation; never, however, in all his pleasures, in his gayest moods, stepping beyond the bounds of temperance and moderation. But in his hours of study, or business or composition, he rarely permitted himself to be interrupted. At such times, it was his habit to retire to an upper apartment of his

residence, where, in a dressing gown and slippers, free from all restraint and ceremony, he could think, and cull and pour forth those lucubrations which were the mental food for thousands. How truly did Mr. Jefferson describe him in his letter to John Adams, of the 9th of July, 1819, when speaking doubtingly of the authenticity of the Mecklenburg Declaration of Independence, he said,

"If this paper be really taken from the *Raleigh Register* as quoted, I wonder it should have escaped Ritchie, who culls what is good from every paper as the bee from every flower."

The *Enquirer* did its share toward the defeat of Van Buren's renomination for the presidency in 1844. The Texas Question was then the fighting question of the politicians, especially of the Southern Democracy, and, in consequence of Van Buren's letter in opposition to annexation, the Democratic leaders of the South were determined to throw him overboard. Ritchie canvassed Virginia on the subject. To satisfy Van Buren that "indications of public sentiment precluded the possibility of his receiving the vote of that state," Ritchie sent to Van Buren all the letters he had received from all the influential men in the state, written by most of those who were known to Van Buren to have previously been his warmest friends. The whole package was returned without a line, and without being franked by the ex-President, although he had that privilege. This settled the case. Polk was nominated and elected.

In May, 1845, Ritchie left the *Enquirer*, after forty-one years of service, and went to Washington to take the chief editorial management of the *Union* as the official organ of President Polk. It was evident that the capital was no place for him. Out of Virginia, and out of the *Enquirer*, at his age, and coming after Blair and the *Globe*, he was without power, without vigor, and without influence.

Anterior to his retirement from the *Enquirer* in 1843, two sons, William F. and Thomas Ritchie, Jr., were associated in the management of the paper. William F. Ritchie became its editor on the departure of his father for the national capital.

There was an influential Whig paper printed in Richmond called the *Whig*. It was founded by John H. Pleasants in 1826, and he was one of its chief writers and managers. He had also been an editor in Washington, and was a warm partisan of Henry Clay. While the *Enquirer* was the organ of the democracy, the *Whig* was the oracle of the opposition. They frequently had verbal fights together. On one occasion, however, words ended in blows. This was while Pleasants was editor of the *News*. No affair in the annals of journalism exceeded the desperate personal conflict which took place in Richmond in February, 1846, between Thomas Ritchie, Jr., and Pleasants. They met on the 23d of that month in a field, armed with swords and pistols. Each advanced on the other, firing as they advanced. On coming together they drew their swords. Then a savage conflict took place. Pleasants received four pistol-shot wounds and one gash from Ritchie's sword, and died two days after the frightful combat. Ritchie was slightly wounded. He was arrested, tried, and acquitted. He died in May, 1854.

The *Enquirer* lived through the Rebellion, and is living now. But few papers have succeeded in retaining, for so long a period as nearly sixty years, their power and influence with their party as the *Enquirer* had done prior to the Rebellion. Said the editor on the morning of its fiftieth anniversary, "Men in the highest positions and of the greatest ability have contributed to its columns and courted its power." True of the *Enquirer*, and true, too, of most of the leading journals of all faiths and all parties since the formation of the government. But these party papers have not been so much the *vox populi* as the voice of the politicians.

William W. Worsley, the junior member of the *Enquirer* firm when that paper was started, retired from the concern in 1805, and afterwards, joining the fortunes of Henry Clay, went to Lexington, Kentucky. There, in company with Thomas S. Smith, he established the *Reporter* as the home organ of the statesman of Ashland.

The *New Hampshire Patriot*, which has been a noted political paper, as much so in New England as the *Richmond Enquirer* was in the South, was established in October, 1808, under the title of the *American Patriot*, by William Hoit. In April, 1809, the concern was purchased by Isaac Hill, who had learned the art of printing in the office of the *Amherst Cabinet*.

The *Patriot*, under its new name and its new manager, advocated the Democratic side with unsurpassed zeal, attacking his opponents with unsparing severity. New Hampshire was an old Federal state. It veered round in 1804-'5, when Langdon was elected Governor, and the electoral vote given to Jefferson for President. With political fluctuations from that time to 1815, the Federal Party finally succumbed. The *Patriot* then became powerful and influential, except in 1823, when Levi Woodbury was elected Governor by a combination of Democrats and Federalists against the regular Democratic candidate and the opposition of the *Patriot*. In the following year, too, New Hampshire gave her electoral vote to John Quincy Adams against the wishes of the *Patriot*, which supported William H. Crawford for the presidency, although the Adams electoral ticket was published at the head of that paper as the regular nomination.

The *Patriot* attained, under the management of Isaac Hill, a very large circulation throughout New England. The old Federal families and their heirs opposed the paper in every way, but with the democracy its progress and popularity were great. His political friends showed their confidence in him by taking his paper and electing him to the State Senate, in spite of a tremendous opposition.

The *Patriot* having been a zealous supporter of General Jackson for the presidency in 1828, the President nominated the editor to the office of Second Comptroller of the Treasury. While in this office in 1829, Mr. Hill disposed of his interest in the *Patriot* to Mr. Barton and Horatio Hill, his brother. Owing to the hostility of Tyler, Iredell, and a few other Jackson senators to the appointment of editors to office, Hill was rejected by the Senate. The democracy of New Hampshire resolved to punish the senators for this insult, and they therefore, through the Legislature, elected the rejected comptroller to the United States Senate for six years from March 4, 1831. Taking his seat in the Senate, he sat side by side with Webster, Clay, Benton, Tyler, and those Democratic senators who had combined to reject him to a minor office. But he was out of place in the Senate. He was compelled to prepare his speeches and read them from manuscript. This, in presence of such brilliant men as occupied seats in that body at that time, did not give much influence to Senator Hill.

There is a curious story connected with the political life of Mr. Hill that was firmly believed by his friends to be historically correct. It is that he set the ball in motion for the war with the United States Bank. The President of the United States Branch Bank at Portsmouth, N. H., was Jeremiah Mason, an old Federalist, and a man of fearless independence. Mason regarded Hill and his friends as little better than so many hungry wild beasts, and treated them on all occasions with the most contemptuous indifference. In revenge, Hill requested from Mr. Biddle the removal of Mason from the Portsmouth Branch. This Mr. Biddle refused to do. The result is well known. The war upon the bank commenced; General Jackson engaged in it with all the violence and animosity which characterized his conflicts with his personal enemies on the frontiers of civilization; his party imitated his example, and were met by the Whigs as Greek joins Greek at "the tug of war." A bill rechartering the bank passed both houses of Congress in the summer of 1832, and was vetoed by General Jackson. The excitement was intense. Many leading supporters of Jackson abandoned him—among them James Watson Webb, of the New York *Courier and Enquirer*—and became his bitterest opponents; but the President was sustained by the people, and the bank was destroyed.

After a service of five years in the Senate, Mr. Hill resigned in 1836, having been elected Governor of New Hampshire in March of that year. He was twice re-elected, and then retired to private life for a time.

In 1840 he returned to public service by accepting the office of sub-treasurer at Boston from President Van Buren. The Sub-treasury Act having been repealed in 1841 by the Whigs, the office fell from under Mr. Hill, and he returned to New Hampshire. In that year he issued *Hill's New Hampshire Patriot*, in opposition to the old establishment, and published it, in connection with his two eldest sons, until 1848. He opposed, during this period, a majority of his political friends in their hostility to railroad and other corporations, holding that the prosperity of New Hampshire depended on the encouragement of such enterprises. About 1846–7 the democracy of that state began to appreciate and encourage internal improvement. *Hill's Patriot* was then united with the old concern.

Mr. Hill died in Washington in 1851, in his sixty-third year.

The war of 1812–15, between England and the United States, arrayed the newspapers of that period in strong antagonism to each other and the parties they represented. "Free Trade and Sailor's Rights" became the motto of all those in favor of the war. Those who opposed it were more or less allied to the feelings and sentiment influencing and controlling the proceedings of the Hartford Convention. The popular sentiment of New England was against the war. That in other places was divided. In Baltimore, for instance, the feeling became so intense as to lead to serious riots. Lossing, in his Field-Book, thus describes one of these popular outbreaks:

> There was a violent opposition newspaper in Baltimore called the *Federal Republican*, edited by a young man only twenty-six years of age. Baltimore was then a flourishing commercial city, and this paper was the organ of the mercantile interest, which had suffered from the restricted commercial measures, and was now prostrated by the impending war. The *Republican* denounced the declaration of war, and, in defiance of intimations that had been made in Congress that when the declaration was once made all opposition to the war must cease, the editor announced his determination to speak as freely against the administration and its measures as before, thereby reversing the policy of his party in 1798 in the matter of the Alien and Sedition Laws. "We mean," he said, "to represent, in as strong colors as we are capable, that the war is unnecessary, inexpedient, and entered into from partial, personal, and, as we believe, motives bearing upon their front marks of undisguised foreign influence which cannot be mistaken." This announcement was made on Saturday, June 20, and on Monday evening the 22d a mob, headed by a French apothecary, proceeded to the office of that paper and demolished it. Having thus commenced violence, they proceeded to the wharves and dismantled some vessels and committed some other heinous acts. The publisher of the *Federal Republican* determined to re-establish the office. The lower portion of the house of one of the proprietors was used for the purpose. The paper was printed in Georgetown, but published then in Baltimore after a silence of five weeks. According to expectation, the publishing office was attacked. The magistrates of the city seemed to have used no means to quell the riot in June, and were not expected to do so now. General Henry Lee, then a resident of Baltimore, furnished the proprietors with a regular plan of defense, and offered to superintend the execution of it. General Lingan, another soldier of the Revolution, and also a Federalist, joined him, and about twenty others made up the defensive party. They were well armed and provisioned for a siege. On the evening of the 26th of July, the evening of the day on which the revived newspaper appeared, the mob assembled. After assailing the building with stones for some time, they forced open the door, and when ascending the

stairs they were fired upon. One of the ringleaders was killed and several were wounded. After much solicitude, two magistrates, by virtue of their authority, ordered out two companies of militia, under General Stricker, to quell the mob. A single troop of horse soon appeared, and at about daylight the Mayor and General Stricker appeared. A truce was obtained, and it was agreed that the defenders, some of whom were hurt, and who were all charged with murder, should be conducted to prison to answer that charge. They were promised not only personal safety, but protection of the premises by a military guard. On their way to prison the band played the rogue's march. The mob immediately sacked the house. Only a few more of the military could be persuaded to come out, and the mob had its own way to a great extent. At night they gathered around the prison, and the turnkey was so terrified that he allowed them to enter. The prisoners extinguished their lights and rushed out. They mingled with the mob, and thus several escaped. Some were dreadfully beaten, and three were tortured by the furious men. General Lee was made a cripple for life, and General Lingan, then seventy years of age, distinguished for his services in the field during the old war for independence, expired in the hands of the mob. * * * * The riot was at length quelled, and the city magistrates, on investigation, placed the entire blame on the publishers of the obnoxious newspaper.

On the 1st of September funeral honors were paid to General Lingan at Georgetown. George Washington Parke Custis delivered the oration. There was a great procession, and every respect was paid to the memory of the unfortunate soldier. Alexander Hanson, the editor of the *Federal Republican*, was subsequently elected to Congress.

The Democratic organs in Albany became powerful instruments in the hands of the politicians in carrying out their schemes. The Federalists saw this, and the necessity of more vigor on their part was apparent. With this object in view they induced Henry Croswell, of the *Hudson Balance*, to remove to Albany. Croswell was a man of energy, and a political writer of ability and power. He had managed the *Balance* with skill and courage for many years, and had acquired notoriety and fame in the celebrated libel suit for an attack on Jefferson in 1804. It was therefore deemed a judicious act to bring him forward as the organ of the Federalists in the state capital. For this purpose he started the *Balance and New York Journal*.

Another partisan sheet was issued in Albany in 1812 by Judge Spencer and his friends. It was published by a printer named Brown, and was named the *Albany Republican*, but was known as "the Brown Republican." It was established in opposition to the *Register*, and to counteract the impressions made by the articles of Southwick. The later political name of "Black Republican" was given to the present Republican Party as one of reproach, just before the Rebellion, by Major Heiss, of the Washington *Union*, and the well-known George N. Sanders. They took the idea from the French. "If the Republicans of France are red," said Sanders, "ours must be black."

The *Albany Argus*, which for nearly half a century was one of the newspaper triumvirate of the Democratic Party, first appeared on the 26th of January, 1813. It was the state organ of that party, and was issued only a few months earlier than the *National Advocate*, which was established in New York City as the organ of the Tammany Hall section of the democracy. The leaders in Albany, dissatisfied with the course of the *Register*, especially in regard to the election of Governor Tompkins, issued the *Argus* in opposition to Southwick, and made Jesse Buel, previously of the *Ulster Plebeian*, its ostensible editor. Buel was a careful and discreet man; not brilliant, but judicious and safe, and, therefore, well adapted for the position of a party editor. When strong and powerful articles were wanted, thundering editorial leaders to arouse the rank and file, one of the distinguished chiefs of the party would furnish the electricity.

The prospectus issued for the new paper was signed by John Taylor and over ninety other Democrats. It said that "of the unfortunate divisions in the Republican Party it is not our intention to speak; these divisions are seriously felt and deeply deplored." There was no other allusion to the defection of Southwick, but the chief reason assigned for the establishment of the new organ was the necessity of having a paper that would support the war. The *Argus* at once received the patronage of the national government, and in two years its editor was chosen state printer; and since then, this state printing has been the favorite bone of the politicians to throw to the Cerberus of the Press to snap at and pick while they are engaged in their operations. Some journalistic Hercules will ere long make his appearance in those places where party papers are thus influenced and controlled.

The *Argus*, now the official organ of the state as well as of the Democratic Party, assumed an importance among the journals of the nation. In 1821, Buel, having acquired a competency from the profits of the state printing, disposed of the establishment to Moses J. Cantine, a brother-in-law of Martin Van Buren, and Isaac Q. Leake. The new firm were made state printers. In March, 1823, Cantine died. Martin Van Buren, then senator, wrote the following characteristic letter to Jesse Hoyt on this occurrence:

Jan'y 31, 1823.

My Dear Sir—I am overwhelmed with the account of poor Cantine's death. I knew that nothing from me can be necessary to secure your zealous attention to Mrs. Cantine's interest, if any thing can be done for her. I have written to Mr. Hoes to be at Albany; you will find him a most useful man. I have also written to Mr. Buel, which letter I want you to see. Among you all you must do the best you can. If any thing can be done for Mrs. C. I hope and believe *no republican* will oppose it. Mr. Hoes and myself are responsible to Mr. Buel for $1500 of the last payment. If nothing better can be done, *no person ought at least to be appointed who had not previously purchased the establishment*—and *under no circumstances ought any one to be appointed who is not a sound, practicable, and, above all, discreet republican.* Without a paper thus edited at Albany we may hang our *harps on the willows. With it, the party can survive a thousand such convulsions as those which agitate and probably alarm most of those around you.* Make my sincere thanks to Mr. Duer and Mr. Sutherland for their kind letters, and tell them I will write them soon.   In haste, yours truly,

M. VAN BUREN.

On the death of Cantine the surviving partner associated himself with Edwin Croswell, a young man, son of Mackay Croswell, of the *Catskill Reviewer*. The Croswells had published the *Catskill Recorder*, which is still living, as early as 1802. Edwin Croswell went to Albany to attend the funeral of his friend, Judge Cantine, and while there he was urged by Benjamin F. Butler, Judge Duer, and others, to remain, and aid Leake on the *Argus*. He did so, and during the Legislative session of 1823 he furnished the *Argus* semi-weekly condensed reports of the transactions of the two houses. He also contributed political articles for the editorial columns that were considered smart and able. In the latter part of 1823 Leake retired, and Obadiah Van Benthuysen, a printer, purchased his interest, leaving Edwin Croswell sole editor on the first day of 1824.

The *Argus* was not issued daily till October 8, 1824. It had been a semi-weekly only. With the daily there was a weekly and a semi-weekly. The paper had now reached a marked position in politics. Such men as Martin Van Buren, William L. Marcy, Silas Wright, John A. Dix, Azariah Flagg, and Roger Skinner contributed to its columns. These, with other prominent men of the party, formed the famous Albany Regency. They regulated the politics of the state. These men had reduced politics to a science. They, with the Kitchen Cabinet in Washington and the Junta in Richmond, were the wire-pullers of that great party, *Imperium in imperio*. They had able supporters in the *Nashville* (Tenn.) *Union, Charleston* (S. C.) *Mercury, Boston Post, Concord* (N. H.) *Patriot, Columbus* (Ohio) *Statesman*, and the *Hartford* (Conn.) *Times*. When the *Globe, Argus*, and *Enquirer* spoke, there was an echo from every corner of the nation. They made cabinet officers and custom-house weighers, presidents and tide-waiters, editors and envoys. They regulated state Legislatures and dictated state policies. They were the father confessors to the democracy of the country. Where and what are these papers and politicians now?

The first shock to their power came in the terrible financial revulsion of 1837. Martin Van Buren, one of the Regency, was elected President in 1836. The financial crash came in the following spring. Van Buren was too weak a man to control events, and the tide turned against the triumvirate. William H. Seward was elected Governor in 1838. Then the Hard Cider campaign came on, and William Henry Harrison was elected President in 1840. With this political revolution the *Argus* lost the state printing, when, in

January, 1840, that profitable patronage fell into the hands of Thurlow Weed, of the *Albany Evening Journal*, another remarkable political newspaper of that day. Weed was thereupon dubbed with the title of State Barber by the *New York Herald*. He kept "the slate" for Governor Seward, and all office-seekers looked upon him as the power behind the throne. The real bone of contention with these party editors was the state printing. The Democrats held the Legislature in 1842. A bill was passed depriving the use of the office of state printer. Seward vetoed it, but the bill passed nevertheless; but no effort was then made, neither at the extra session the same year, to appoint a successor. In the early part of the session of 1843 another bill was passed. In the mean time Croswell had admitted a partner into the *Argus* establishment named Van Dyck, of Orange County. When the question came up whose name should be used by the Democratic members, Van Dyck demanded that his name should be inserted alone, declaring, "I will be sole state printer, with the entire control of the press, or nothing." Edwin and Sherman Croswell owned three fourths, and Van Dyck only one fourth of the *Argus*. This course of the latter was strange, if not extraordinary. The Croswells endeavored to arrange matters, but, as the junior would have the whole or none, he retired from the *Argus*. Edwin Croswell was then elected state printer, receiving a majority of 26 votes in legislative caucus over William C. Bryant, of the New York *Evening Post*, and a majority of 56 in joint ballot over Horace Greeley, of the *New York Tribune*.

The success of Croswell divided the democracy into Hard and Soft Shells. Van Dyck's course and the vote for Bryant indicated the same sort of trouble that in 1812–13 led to the establishment of the *Argus*. With exceptions here and there, the old leaders had become inimical to the old organ, and threw their influence in favor of a new paper, which had been started in Albany, called the *Atlas*. The conflict between the two factions increased in intensity and interest till 1846, when another struggle for the patronage of the state took place. Silas Wright was Governor. The Soft Shells, or Radicals, had a majority in the Legislature; but the Whigs joined the Hard Shells. The Democratic legislative caucus selected William Cassidy, of the *Atlas*, for state printer. This movement was defeated by the passage of a law giving the publication of the legal notices to the paper that would publish them at the lowest rate. Croswell offered to publish them without cost to the state. Thus the *Atlas* was defeated, and the *Argus* obtained the honor without the profit, and it held on to this position till 1854, when the printing, with full pay, was restored to Thurlow Weed and the *Evening Journal*. There was a good deal of bitter feeling exhibited during these troubles, resulting, on one occasion in 1847, in a regular street-fight between Edwin Croswell and Peter Cagger, who was afterwards accidentally killed in Central Park.

But the democracy split into two factions. The Soft Shells, known also as Barn-Burners, Free-Soilers, and Radicals, had become, by the defection of Van Buren, a formidable party. In the election of 1848 they polled 120,497 votes for Van Buren to 114,319 Hard Shell or Hunker votes for Cass, thus defeating the regular Democratic candidate for the presidency, and electing Taylor to that office. Edwin Croswell shortly after this abandoned the editorial chair of the *Argus*, and went to New York, and connected himself with ocean steam navigation in association with George Law and others. He lived a number of years in the metropolis, somewhat of an invalid physically, but mentally as bright as ever. One night, several years ago, in riding home from the theatre in a crowded Broadway omnibus, he politely offered his lap for a seat to a standing passenger. In a cramped position, with the weight of the passenger impeding the free circulation of blood, it was found, on arriving at the end of his ride, that his lower limbs were paralyzed. He never fully recovered. He died in 1870.

Sherman Croswell remained on the *Argus*. It continued to be the organ of the Hard Shells till the close of 1854. It expected some assistance from the Pierce administration, but Marcy refused to fully recognize either the *Atlas* or *Argus*. His friends endeavored to purchase the latter in that year. The Know Nothings also talked of buying it, but it is doubtful if the Croswells would have sold it to that party. On the 2d of January, 1855, the establishment was finally disposed of to the Soft Shells. Its power and strength, however, departed with the Croswells. It lingered along till another fight for the state printing, which took place in 1858, when, to settle the matter, and prevent this patronage from remaining in the hands of Thurlow Weed, of the *Journal*, the two Democratic organs, till now kept separately for a political purpose, were united under the title of the *Albany Atlas and Argus* for a time, and then under that of the *Argus* alone. This final act of consolidation was brought about by the sale of Mr. Johnson's interest in the *Argus* to his partner, Mr. Comstock, and the sale by Mr. Van Dyck of his share of the *Atlas* to Mr. Cassidy. By this arrangement the united concern appeared on the 18th of February, 1856.

The *Argus* is again the state printer. It received the appointment in 1869, when the contract with the *Evening Journal* ceased. Happy *Argus!* Unhappy *Journal!*

How can we better close this chapter than by giving a lecture of Judge Kent, of New York, before the Young Men's Association at

Albany, in February, 1854, on the Press of that city thirty years previously?

I said NEWSPAPERS, but, I believe, we had but one—the old *Albany Gazette*, which was quiet as the times, and gentle as the manners were of yore. You would look, in vain, in it for the skill and power of the existing Gladiators of Literature ; for the eloquent invective, the tart reply, the stinging personality, the dexterous argument, and the brilliant repartee of modern Journals. These things would have startled the gentle newsmongers of forty years ago. Nor was it crowded with intelligence from all Christendom, watching by the hour the negotiations of the Russian and the Turk, kindling and extinguishing insurrections, changing or enlarging the boundaries of the republic, examining everything, disturbing everything, and controlling everything.

Not such was our good *Gazette*. But it gave us all we wanted to know in reasonable times, and homeopathic quantities ;—the deaths and the marriages ; the accidents of storm, and flood and fire ; advices from Europe two or three months old, and all the simple annals of a primitive and quiet neighborhood. Occasionally a political essay from Junius, Publius, Cato, or some other Roman Patriot, would disclose to us something rotten in the state of the Republic ; and, before the Spring election, the address of some Federal meeting would declare to us that if Liberty was not absolutely gone, she was packing up her effects for her final departure. We took all this very calmly ; and the annual crisis of Constitutional danger, which has become chronic in our politics, passed off very lightly in good old times. But the *Gazette* was a sensible and useful paper, and is remembered with respect by the fast diminishing number of its former readers. Nor do they forget the place of its publication, the book store, under the old elm tree at the corner of Pearl street, where the visitor was sure of courteous and affable reception, and where the gentle Quidnuncs and elderly Politicians of former days used to love to congregate. I have heard discussions and suggestions there, which, if they reached the ears of the Arch-Duke Charles and the Emperor Napoleon, might have had an important influence on the conduct of their campaigns. But I believe they never reached so far.

The *Gazette* disappeared with the times, of which it was the product and reflection. It gave way to hardier and more skilful journals, as untutored labor yields to scientific skill. It left an unblemished name. It had hurt no man's feelings ; it had injured no man's reputation : it might, like the good Athenian, claim for its epitaph, that no citizen had worn morning on its account. Light lie the earth on its ashes !

I remember the rise, and somewhat of the progress of the modern school of Journalists in Albany ; and did time permit, might attempt some sketches of such of the writers as are departed,—of the bold character, glowing pen, and ardent temperament of SOLOMON SOUTHWICK, the editor of the *Register ;* of HARRY CROSWELL, the witty and fearless manager of the *Balance*, then a Federal paper ; of JESSE BUEL, the discreet and skillful conductor of the dominant Democratic Journal ; and, if personal feeling were permitted, would place a humble chaplet on the tomb of CARTER, of the *Statesman*, accomplished in various learning and warmed with gentle sensibility, which shrank from the fierceness of political strife.

It were indiscreet to go further, though the temptation is irresistible to allude to a surviving writer, whose pen lent occasional and powerful assistance to the *Statesman*—one who supports with unabated strength the inherited right of a splendid name—who stands foremost in our forensic ranks—who sports with labor, professional, political and legislative, under which other men sink, and whose writing was recognized, like an electric gleam, among the political productions of the day. The contests of 1817 and '20 were of no ordinary character. The political Divinities, as in the wars of Troy, were seen mingling in the combat, and Jupiter himself, from his Olympian throne, dispersed his thunders.

The *Albany Advertiser*, Colonel W. L. Stone's old journal, was edited in 1838 by James Gordon Brooks, when he got into some trouble with the Van Rensselaers, the owners of the paper, and resigned his position in consequence. He was belligerent, and posted John S. Van Rensselaer on this occasion. He edited the *New Era*, in New York, in 1839. He had previously been an editor in the metropolis on the *Courier and Enquirer*. This was in 1828–29, although Griswold states that Brooks removed to New York in 1823, "where he was for several years an editor of the *Morning Courier*, one of the most able and influential journals in this country." There was a difference of opinion in the establishment of the *Courier and Enquirer* in 1829 in regard to the control of that journal at that time. The following extract of a letter seems to settle this point in history:

ALBANY, 20th July, 1829.

Messrs. Tylee & Webb:

Your note of the 16th inst. did not reach me till late on Friday night last.

* * * * * * *

Your statement that Mr. James G. Brooks and Mr. James Lawson possess no control over the course of the *Courier and Enquirer* shall be duly attended to when I consult my political friends here and elsewhere. Your assurance settles finally the question of proprietorship. I have written to Messrs. Brooks & Lawson on the subject. By the same mail which conveys this to you, I have informed them of the course I mean to pursue in relation to this matter.

I am, &c., &c.,
JAMES G. BENNETT.

Rufus King succeeded Brooks on the *Advertiser*, and was editor in 1839, and until he went to Rome on a diplomatic mission.

CHAPTER XVIII.
THE NATIONAL ADVOCATE AND ENQUIRER.

TROUBLES OF POLITICIANS.—HENRY WHEATON.—MAJOR NOAH.—WASHINGTON CORRESPONDENCE AND JAMES GORDON BENNETT.—THE DUEL BETWEEN BARTON AND GRAHAM.—INGATHERING OF THE JEWS ON GRAND ISLAND.—THE CITY OF ARARAT.—NOAH'S PROCESSION AND ORATION.—NEWSPAPER EDITOR IN GENERAL.

ORGANS of political parties had to be changed. There would be differences of opinion among leaders difficult to reconcile, and new organs were necessary to meet the emergency and satisfy contending factions. Sometimes an editor would feel less like submitting to party dictation, and would rebel. Often there would be more office-seekers than offices. This would lead to heart-burnings, and jealousies, and troubles of all kinds. Newspapers were an outlet to these personal grievances.

There seems to have been a necessity for a new organ in the Democratic Party in New York City after the death of Cheetham and the *Citizen*. Tammany Hall was dissatisfied with the *Columbian* and Irving, and repudiated both. It set up another paper, the *National Advocate*. It was established in 1813, and was first edited by Henry Wheaton, who became, in after years, a distinguished diplomat and publicist as our minister to Denmark and Prussia, and as the author of Elements of International Law.

Wheaton was a native of Rhode Island, and educated a lawyer. After he graduated he visited Europe, where he remained from 1802 to 1806, in the midst and height of Napoleon's career, a close student of the important events of that eventful period. On his return he commenced the practice of law in Providence, which he abandoned in 1812, to remove to New York. In 1813 he established himself in that city as the editor of the *National Advocate*. "In this capacity," said Edward Everett, "he proved himself an able and enlightened champion of Mr. Madison's administration. The great questions of our violated neutral rights were discussed with the pen, not only of a jurist, but of a gentleman and a scholar. Mr. Wheaton's long residence abroad had given him peculiar opportunities for understanding the controversies of the day. The new liabilities and duties created by the war, then recently declared, were elucidated by him with the learning of an accomplished publicist and the zeal of a sincere patriot. Several topics of international law were discussed in the columns of the *Advocate* with an ability which foreshadowed his future eminence in this department. Among these was a vindication, on the authority of Vattel and Bynkershoeck, of the right of expatriation, in answer to Mr. Gouverneur Morris, an eminent statesman and diplomatist of the Federal Party. Questions of maritime law were of course among those which most frequently presented themselves. In the *Advocate* first appeared the opinion of his friend, Mr. Justice Story, then recently elevated to the bench of the Supreme Court of the United States, affirming the illegality of the trade under enemy's licenses, which had been extensively resorted to for the supply of the British armies in Spain. Mr. Wheaton, as a journalist, enjoyed the entire confidence of the administration, and his columns were sometimes the vehicle of semi-official expositions of its policy. In the autumn of 1814 he received the appointment of Division Judge Advocate of the Army, his nomination to that office being unanimously confirmed by the Senate. The year following he retired from the editorship of the *Advocate* on being appointed one of the Justices of the Marine Court of New York, a tribunal of limited jurisdiction, and now shorn of much of its former consideration, but which has been presided over by some of the most eminent men at the New York bar." In this position, in that of the editor of the *Advocate* at that peculiar juncture in our history, and as a reporter of the United States Supreme Court for a number of years, Wheaton laid the foundation of that knowledge and experience which have given the world his great and valuable work on International Law.

Wheaton was succeeded in the editorial management of the *Advocate* by Mordecai Manasseh Noah, who had been editor in 1810 of the *City Gazette*, in Charleston, S. C. Noah had also been, in 1811, American Consul at Riga, and afterwards at Tunis, with some sort of mission to Algiers. On his way to Tunis he was captured by the English. On his recall in 1816 he became one of the editors and proprietors of this Democratic organ. Wheaton, Gulian C. Verplanck, and others aided him with contributions. When De Witt Clinton was nominated for Governor in 1817, a number of the Tammanyites, or Bucktails, as they were then called, refused to support him on the ground that he had been the Peace Party candidate for the presidency in 1812. Wheaton, the *Advocate*, and a few members of Tammany Hall, threw away their votes and their influence on General Peter B. Porter. Their vote was only 1419, against 43,310 for Clinton. In 1823 Noah claimed to be the only Democratic editor in New York, entirely ignoring the *American*, edited by Charles King, and, as such, demanded a part of the state printing.

He had already received the appointment of sheriff of the city and county of New York, but, in a quarrel with the leaders of the party, he subsequently lost that office. When it was proposed to make him sheriff, objections were raised against him because he was a Jew, and that it would not be right for a Jew to hang a Christian. "Pretty Christians," replied Noah, "to require hanging at all."

Noah continued to act as editor of the *Advocate* till 1825, when Henry Eckford, the celebrated ship-builder, and afterwards chief naval architect to the Sultan of Turkey; Jacob Barker, till lately an active banker in New Orleans at the age of ninety; John Targee, and others, became the secret proprietors of the paper. Noah and Eckford could not agree. So Noah left. Thomas Snowden, afterwards publisher of the *Courier and Enquirer*, was then placed in charge of the mechanical and business part of the *Advocate* as nominal owner, and James Gordon Bennett installed as editor. Mr. Bennett managed the paper for two years, but, on the approach of the next presidential campaign, Eckford, having made up his mind to support the re-election of John Quincy Adams, to which Mr. Bennett was not inclined, he retired in 1827, and Samuel S. Conant, of Vermont, purchased an interest in the concern with Snowden, and assumed the editorial management of the paper, and he continued in that capacity for some time after the *Advocate* and *Statesman* were united as one paper, and called the *Morning Herald*, an arrangement effected by the diplomacy and skill of Thomas B. Wakeman, so well known in connection with the American Institute. He was the mutual friend of all parties, and great in bringing individuals of different interests and opinions together in harmony.

Noah was a true Israelite. About this time, or in 1825, he originated a magnificent scheme of bringing together the scattered tribes of Israel, and forming a settlement of them on Grand Island, in Niagara River, on our northern frontier, since made more famous by the rebels of Canada. He believed that the Indians were the descendants of the lost tribes, and he proposed founding a city on that island as a nucleus for the ingathering of the Hebrew people, including the wild children of America. It appears that the peculiar characteristics of the Red Men, their features, hair, customs, laws, religious ceremonies, and tribal organizations, impressed him with the belief that they came from the Jewish race. Noah may have been right. That they came from the East there is scarcely a doubt. Catlin, the famous traveler among the Indians, said, over thirty years ago, that he believed that they came originally from the East, perhaps driven by storms in canoes across the Pacific and Behring's Straits; and that those who had never come in contact with the whites till he saw them had the tradition of the dove and the olive leaf. Noah carried out his scheme so far as to have a grand procession in full regalia, with a band of music, in Buffalo, in September, 1825. In a splendid costume of a judge of Israel, in crimson and ermine, he delivered an able oration, in which he gave an interesting sketch of the Jews. The corner stone of the new city was then laid with appropriate ceremonies, and the site, in commemoration of the event, and of the elder Noah as the head of his people after the flood, was called Ararat. This extraordinary and droll affair created quite a sensation at the time, especially in religious circles. Noah said that America was the asylum of the Jews. It is manifest that the Hebrew people are increasing rapidly in the large cities of the United States, particularly in New York, where there are nearly forty synagogues, some of them the handsomest edifices in the metropolis, but there are no signs of the ingathering of the lost tribes at the modern city of Ararat. If Major Noah were alive now, he would think that the Indians, instead of making pilgrimages to Grand Island as the New Jerusalem, were in a fair way, as the sons of Abraham, and Isaac, and Jacob, of again being led into captivity, not by Psalmanezer, king of Assyria, but by Sheridan, the dashing cavalry officer of America.

When Noah quarreled with Eckford, he started a paper of his own in 1826, which he called the *National Advocate*. Enjoined in this at the instance of Eckford and Snowden, he changed its name to *Noah's New York National Advocate*. Again enjoined, he named his journal the *New York Enquirer*. This paper was merged with the *Morning Courier* in the spring of 1829. Noah went with the *Enquirer* into the editorial rooms of the new *Morning Courier and New York Enquirer*, where he remained till 1832 as an associate editor with James Watson Webb, James Lawson, James Gordon Bennett, Prosper M. Wetmore, and James Gordon Brooks; and for services to the party, Major Noah, with Amos Kendall, who had been editor of the *Frankfort (Ky.) Argus*, were rewarded each with an office. Noah was appointed Surveyor of the Port of New York, and Kendall Fourth Auditor of the Treasury. Noah was rejected by the Senate by 25 to 23, but subsequently, in the whirligig of politics, he was confirmed. Kendall was confirmed by the casting vote of the Vice-President. Noah, fearing a removal, soon after this resigned his office.

The *Enquirer* introduced a new feature in 1827. In that year James Gordon Bennett was its Washington correspondent, in which he inaugurated a new system of newspaper correspondence, and in which, in March, 1827, he brought forward Martin Van Buren for the first time as the candidate for the presidency to succeed General Jackson. Afterward this political movement was urged in the *Courier and Enquirer*. Van Buren himself inspired this movement in his favor. Washington letter-writing had been, to this time, in its infancy. Members of Congress, in writing occasional letters to their home organs, were the principal correspondents. There were a few regular letter-writers. The change which took place in that important department of journalism is thus amusingly related by Mr. Bennett:

> We happen to know a good deal of this business of letter-writing from Washington, for we were the first to give it its present light and amusing character in a series of letters published in the *New York Enquirer* in the years 1827 and '8. Before that period a Washington letter-writer simply gave the dull details of both houses, the abstracts of reports, or a few sketches of the speakers. In the letters I furnished the *New York Enquirer* in those years, then conducted by Mr. Noah, I changed the whole tone, temper, and style of Washington correspondence. Before my day, the late Mr. Carter had spent a winter or two at Washington, and gave a dull recital of what he had seen and heard, in the *Statesman* newspaper. In Philadelphia, Walsh, sitting in his easy-chair, wrote long, labored letters to himself, heavy, flat, stupid, and disagreeable.
>
> It was in the winter and spring of 1828 that I wrote the series which appeared in the *Enquirer*. No one knew by whom they were written, either here or in Washington, but they were generally attributed to G. C. Verplanck. I remember very well how the idea of writing them originated in my own mind. In the library of Congress I spent much of my time, poring over Jefferson's collection of old pamphlets, which no one, before or since, has perhaps looked into. Sometimes I would take a peep at the new publications of the day, and among them I found the recent publication of Horace Walpole's famous letters and correspondence, written during the reign of George II., and describing, in witty and agreeable badinage, the intrigues, politics, incidents, and explosions of that singular court. These letters were highly amusing, graphic, and interesting. I said to myself one day, "Why not try a few letters on a similar plan from this city, to be published in New York, describing, eulogizing, or satirizing the court of John Q. Adams?" I did so. All the political, gay, fashionable, witty, beautiful characters that appeared in Washington during that winter, were sketched off at random, without being personal or offensive to any of the parties—indeed, they were mostly all complimentary and pleasing to the parties.
>
> These letters were published and became quite popular. They were copied throughout the whole country.

The *Enquirer* had supported De Witt Clinton against Judge Rochester for Governor of New York in 1826, although Judge Rochester was the regular Democratic candidate, on the plea that Rochester was an Adams man, while Clinton was for Jackson. It was suspected at the time that this was done under the influence of Martin Van Buren. In 1827 the *Enquirer* came out for Jackson. It was in that year that Mr. Bennett left the *National Advocate* and joined the *Enquirer*, and wrote for that paper till 1829, after the election of Jackson.

One of the incidents peculiar to the editorial profession of that period occurred in 1828. William Graham was one of the writers for the *Enquirer*. He was a fine-looking man, and of attractive manners. He was born in Catskill, the son of a New York merchant. He was educated at Cambridge, England. It is stated that he was "the intimate friend and forensic rival of Thomas Noon Talfourd." Also, that he once acted as amanuensis to Ugo Foscolo, with whom he afterwards engaged in a bloodless duel. Subsequently he edited the *Literary Museum*, and then, recrossing the Atlantic, he became editorially connected with the *New York Enquirer*. He wrote sketches of society in New York for that paper under the signature of Howard. In one of these essays he made what was supposed to be a personal allusion to the family of Edward Livingston. The matter was taken up by Dr. Barton, who was afterwards Secretary of Legation at Paris. In some personal observations with Dr. Barton on the subject at Niblo's Coffee-house, then on the corner of Pine and William Streets, Mr. Graham struck that gentleman. He was immediately challenged. It was accepted. In a letter to the editor of the *Evening Post*, written the evening before the duel, Graham said :

> I admit that I am in the wrong; that by giving him (Barton) a blow, I have forced him into the position of challenger. I will not hear of any settlement short of some abject and craven submission from him. After he is perfectly satisfied I may perhaps apologize—that is, in case I am fatally wounded.

William Newman, a compositor on the *Enquirer*, engaged a Whitehall boat which conveyed the parties to Hoboken. On that classic ground of the *duello* they met, and Graham was instantly killed. This affair created a good deal of excitement, as all such affairs did, and led to the enactment, by the Legislature of New York, of a strong anti-dueling law, the chief points of which were ten years' imprisonment in the States Prison for fighting, and seven years for sending a challenge.

Noah, in 1834, in company with a printer named Gill, established the *New York Evening Star*. It became a Whig organ, and supported William Henry Harrison for the presidency in 1840. In 1841 he was appointed one of the Judges of the Court of Sessions by Governor Seward, and while on the bench he prosecuted his old associate, Mr. Bennett, of the *Herald*, for libel, one of the reporters of that paper having been too free in his sketches of the proceedings of that court, especially in his personal descriptions.

On the death of Mr. Gill in 1841, the *Star* was sold, and united with the *Commercial Advertiser*. For some time Major Noah was editor of the *New York Sun* and of the *Morning Star*. In 1842, President Tyler, through Paul R. George, selected Major Noah to edit an official organ in New York, called the *Union*. It was a failure. In 1843 Noah commenced the publication of a paper which he named *Noah's Weekly Messenger*. In a short time it was united with the *Sunday Times*. Noah seemed to have a desire to edit all the papers. He was mentally active. He wrote for several at the same time. One day, in 1846 we believe, although he had abused Mr. Bennett without stint, even originating the ridiculous hue and cry of black-mail, he proposed to that editor, on the eve of his departure for Europe, to take editorial charge of the *Herald* in his absence. He thought he could keep up its character better than any other man. "The *Herald*," he said, "had become a great and influential paper. Such it should remain." The interview between Noah's friend and Mr. Bennett did not last long, and Noah did not edit the *Herald*.

Noah was the author of "Travels in Europe and Northern Africa," the "Howard Papers on Domestic Economy," several treatises on the "Prophecies of the Bible," and the "History and Destiny of the Hebrews." He translated the "Book of Jasher." Of his plays we may mention "Paul and Alexis, or the Wandering Boys;" "She would be a Soldier, or the Plains of Chippewa;" "The Castle of Sorento;" "Ali Pacha, or the Signet Ring;" "Marion, or the Hero of Lake George;" "Yusef Caramali, or the Siege of Tripoli;" "Nathalie, or the Frontier Maid;" "The Grecian Captive;" "The Siege of Daramatta;" and "Ambition;" rather a formidable list for an active journalist to produce. All these plays were performed at the several theatres in New York.

Noah was not a journalist in the modern acceptation of the term. He was a sharp newspaper paragraphist. His political squibs were good and pointed. In these short articles he shone more conspicuously than in longer or more pretentious editorial leaders. He was not a journalist to compete with others who had more comprehensive ideas of a newspaper. When, with a capacity for thinking and writing, it was necessary to have tact and energy to obtain the earliest news, Noah could not compete with the enterprising and vigorous journals of even his own period. Hence he was never successful.

Major Noah died March 22d, 1851, while editing the *Times and Messenger*, at the age of sixty-six.

CHAPTER XIX.
THE RELIGIOUS PRESS.

THE FIRST RELIGIOUS NEWSPAPERS.—THE CHILLICOTHE RECORDER OF JOHN ANDREWS, AND THE BOSTON RECORDER OF NATHANIEL WILLIS.—AUTOBIOGRAPHY OF A JOURNALIST.—THE NEW YORK OBSERVER.—THE WATCHMAN AND REFLECTOR.—ZION'S HERALD.—THE CHRISTIAN ADVOCATE.—THE EVANGELIST.—THE INDEPENDENT.—HENRY WARD BEECHER AND WENDELL PHILLIPS AS THE LEADING JOURNALISTS.—ORGANS OF CHURCHES.—CHARACTER OF THE RELIGIOUS PRESS.—ITS UPS AND DOWNS.—ARCHBISHOP HUGHES.—NEWSPAPERS FOR CHILDREN.

WHEN and where was the first religious newspaper published in the United States? When and where in any part of the world?

After the success of an important enterprise; after an invention in mechanics or a discovery in science have become a public benefit; after finding an available candidate for the presidency, numerous claimants spring up seeking the reward of the sewing machine, or the glory of the telegraph, or the honor of ether, or the office for first naming Taylor or Grant for the White House. So with lesser matters.

Several years ago there was a controversy on the origin of religious newspapers. Who first conceived the idea of one? Who published the first one? Morse, of the *New York Observer*, put in his claim for the idea. Willis, of the *Boston Recorder*, filed his *caveat* as the inventor. In 1858, when Mr. Willis was in his seventy-ninth year, he published his reminiscences. It is not often that such an autobiography is given to the public. Its value just now is that it enables us to solve one of the questions of the age:

AUTOBIOGRAPHY OF A JOURNALIST.
BOSTON, Oct. 10, 1858.

It has been suggested to me that my long and successful experience in establishing newspapers, without the advantages of talents, or education, or money, would, if committed to paper, be useful to others who may hereafter control the mighty power of the press. I will therefore attempt to give a narrative.

My father was a practical printer. He printed and published the *Independent Chronicle*, a Whig paper, in Boston, from June, 1776, to January, 1784. I was born in Boston, June 6, 1780. My father removed to Virginia, leaving me in Boston till I was seven years of age, when he, being engaged in printing a newspaper in Winchester, sent for me, and I was immediately set to work in folding newspapers and setting types. He removed to Martinsburg in 1790, and commenced the *Potomak Guardian*, upon which paper I was kept at work until April, 1796. He then removed to Chillicothe, and set up the *Sciota Gazette*, the first paper in Ohio, and I returned to Boston, and commenced an apprenticeship in the office of the *Chronicle*, in the same room in Court street in which my father had worked, and where Benjamin Franklin had worked before him.

Soon after I went to Virginia, my father married for his second wife a daughter of a slaveholder, and she had one of her father's slaves for a servant. Though I was then but eight years of age, I well recollect the cruel operation of the system of slavery. It is not only debasing and brutalizing as regards the slaves. but genders habits of oppression in the masters and mistresses towards all over whom they have power. I felt its effects from my step-mother. It was the cause of my leaving Virginia for Boston.

This was a time of great political excitement; I was in my sixteenth year, and partook of the feelings of the time. Benjamin Austin was a popular political writer in the *Chronicle*, and his articles were put in type by me. I was dependent on my industry, and had no expectation of pecuniary means of establishment in business. After I had served out my apprenticeship and worked two years as a journeyman, application was made to me to go to Portland, and set up a Republican paper in opposition to the Federal party, which then ruled the District (now state) of Maine.

Mr. Austin recommended me as reliable for my politics and industry, and I commenced the *Eastern Argus* in September, 1803. A lawyer named Joseph Bartlett was to have been the editor, but the party doubted his faithfulness, and I went on with the paper with the assurance of pecuniary and literary help from leading political characters. Bartlett forsook the party, and was nominated for Congress in opposition to Richard Cutts, the Republican candidate. T. G. T., Esq., wrote some severe articles in the *Argus* against Bartlett. I objected to publishing them because they were libellous; but Mr. T. assured me I "should not be hurt a hair of my head."

Cutts was elected to Congress, and Bartlett sued me for damages in the libels. The lawyers were all under Federal influence ; the case went through the courts against me, and I was arrested on an execution for $2000 damages. Being unable to pay I was conducted to prison. I endeavored to get released under the Poor Debtor's law after thirty days; but was twice defeated by lawyers' quibbles about citations, and kept a prisoner for ninety days. Having given bonds for the liberty of the yard, which was the whole town in daytime, a false charge of "making an escape" was set up and sustained by the court—my bondsmen were made liable, and had to pay $4000, the amount of the bond, instead of $2000, the amount of the execution. The author of the libels, who promised I "should not be hurt a hair of my head," was dishonorable enough to tell me I must pay these damages; but a reference decided that he should pay, while I was left to pay my own expenses in attending the courts, and, several years after, the lawyer he engaged in the trials.

I was in debt $1300 for money loaned me by politicians to sustain the *Argus*, and I made an appeal in the paper to delinquent subscribers to pay arrearages and enable me to rise above my embarrassments. This was successful, and I was able to extinguish those debts and release my office and household furniture from attachment. A kind Providence sustained me under my afflictions, and I learned that politicians are not only ungrateful, but supremely selfish. They used me as the cat's-paw, but took good care to keep all the chestnuts for their own eating. The political character of the district was changed, and they gained their object in turning the Federalists out of office.

In November, 1807, Mr. Benjamin Radford, a near neighbor, invited me to go with him and hear the Rev. Edward Payson preach a Thanksgiving sermon. I had not attended church for many months, but spent my Sabbaths in roving about the fields and in reading newspapers. I expected Mr. Payson would preach a political sermon, as he had some time previous delivered a Federal address. The sermon agreeably disappointed me; it was truly patriotic and eloquent. Mr. Radford then invited me to go with him to church on the next Sabbath. I went and was much interested, and became a constant hearer. There was a revival there in the ensuing winter. I trust that the Holy Spirit led me to see that there is an eternity; that it was my duty to attend to the concerns of my soul— that the Bible is the Word of God—that Christ is the only Saviour, and that it is "by grace we are saved, through faith, and not of ourselves—it is the gift of God, not of works, lest any man should boast."

It was the custom of the Republicans to have a ball on the evening of the 4th of March, to celebrate the anniversary of Mr. Jefferson's election. I had always attended, and I was expected to attend this time. There was to be a lecture in the church on that evening. It was a trying question for me to decide which I should go to. I feared if I went to the ball I should dance off all my religious impressions. I decided that *I would not go to the ball*, but would go to the lecture. I think that was the turning point in my salvation ; if I had grieved the Holy Spirit at that time, he might have forsaken me for ever.

One very busy day in the *Argus* office, I felt so much distressed in mind that I could not work. I went to my desk and wrote a prayer. Immediately I felt relief, and resumed my work. I have kept that prayer till now. I now began to moderate the severity of party spirit in the *Argus*, and extracted from other papers short articles on religious subjects, mostly on Methodist revivals. I was asked why I published such things. I replied that the Federalists claimed all the religion and morality in the country as being on their side, and I wished to prove that it is not so. I became interested in Doddridge's " Rise and Progress of Religion in the Soul," especially the chapter on family prayer. I printed an edition of that chapter, and circulated them as tracts. Christians would ask me how I could print the *Argus* now. I was trying to serve two masters ; that would not do. I was in perplexity.

I went to see Mr. Payson about it. He said, " I cannot advise you on that subject. Make it a subject of prayer—God will direct you." On parting with him, he repeated the text : " There is no man that hath left house, or brethren, or sisters, or father, or mother, or wife, or children, or lands, for my sake, and the Gospel's, but he shall receive a hundred fold now in this time, houses, and brethren, and sisters, and mothers, and lands, with persecutions ; and in the world to come eternal life."—Mark x., 29, 30. *This is the best advice I could have had.*

The leading politicians now found fault with the *Argus*, saying, " Your paper is milk and water ; you are priest-ridden, or turning Federalist." I replied, " No, I am willing to support the Republican cause so long as I can with truth and fairness, but I have done with personalities and misrepresentations." They said, " You must be as spirited as the Federalists are, or we must set up another paper." I replied, " I will save you all that trouble. I will sell the *Argus* to a man that will suit you."

Mr. Francis Douglas was then employed in my office, first as clerk and then as partner. I sold the *Argus* to him for $4000. It was the hard times of the embargo and war with England, and I ultimately relinquished one-half that sum to secure the rest.

While waiting for better times, I first collected what debts I could, and then opened a grocery store. I would not sell rum ; then my neighbors predicted that I should fail. A year after I found that I was losing money (about $1000 short), and concluded to sell out and give up the business. In 1808, when the politicians were disposed to abandon the *Argus*, on account of the little religion there was in it, I should have made it a religious paper if I had received the encouragement and aid of Christians. Verily, " the children of this world are wiser in their own generation than the children of light."

In May, 1808, I was admitted a member of the 2d Church, of which Rev. Mr. Payson was the junior pastor. I had been sometime thinking of the practicability of setting up *a religious newspaper in Portland*. I conversed with Mr. Payson, Dea. Coe, Dea. Lincoln, Dr. Mitchell, of North Yarmouth, an influential Christian, and many others. They all thought it a good thing, but the times were so hard that it could not succeed now.

Rev. Dr. Jenks has written to me, that at a meeting of the Maine Missionary Society in Bath, in 1810, where he then resided, " I well recollect then and there you mentioned the subject of a religious newspaper to the ministers and others assembled, and asked their advice and approbation."

In 1812 I removed to Boston, bought a new press and types, and opened an office at 76 State street. I printed a variety of religious books and tracts, and sold them as best I could. Dr. Morse employed me to print several editions of a pamphlet entitled " American Unitarianism," which made a considerable stir among the clergy, and led to the Unitarian controversy. I printed also the first edition of " Park street Lectures," by Dr. Griffin.

The subject of a *religious newspaper* still rested heavily on my mind. I talked with Christians in Boston often about it. Many, though they liked the plan, objected to it as impracticable, especially in the hard times occasioned by the war. Deacon Jeremiah Evarts at one time agreed to aid in it, but finally withdrew. Dr. Griffin said he never heard of such a thing as religion in a newspaper; it would do in a magazine. I said I had some experience in newspaper publishing, and believed such a thing could be done, if Christians would encourage it.

In 1814 I had an interview with Dr. Morse on the subject of a religious newspaper. He encouraged it, and said he had a son pursuing his studies in Connecticut, who would make a good editor. He was very sanguine that a large subscription could be obtained. He declined any pecuniary responsibility, but said that the subscribers would pay in advance, if his son was editor. I suppose, like any other kind father, he was desirous of securing a competent support for his son, without risk of loss.

In 1815 the Prospectus of the *Recorder* was written. I printed it, and we circulated them and got what subscribers we could. Mr. Sidney Morse refused any pecuniary responsibility, and no contract was entered into which could bind him. The first number of the *Recorder* was dated January 3, 1816. Mr. Morse's name was not in it, but mine stands as publisher at my office in State street, Boston.

A large edition was printed at his request, in expectation that they would be wanted. After I had printed four numbers, in order to bring him to terms, I said to Mr. Morse that it was a waste of paper to print so many—the income did not half pay the expenses, and that I was unwilling to bear the whole pecuniary responsibility of the paper, and that I should give it up unless there was some contract or agreement made in respect to the expenses of the paper and the editorship. Then, without consulting me on the subject, he engaged Mr. Ezra Lincoln to print the paper, and Mr. D. J. Burr to keep the books and receive the money. About three months after, Mr. Burr told me that Mr. Morse was desirous of relinquishing the paper to me, and if I would assume the expenses already incurred, and engage to pay him one dollar for every new subscriber until the close of the year, he would continue to edit it, and then if either of us withdrew, he should relinquish all claim to the other. I agreed to this, and resumed the printing and publishing. In the *Recorder* of April 1, 1817, Mr. Morse announced that he should withdraw from the editorship, and gave as his reason for doing so that "the profits of the publication are *wholly inadequate* to his support," and I paid him, I think, about $100 for his services.

This history shows Mr. Morse's entire exemption from all expenses in the enterprise, and its being borne by me in all the changes which took place, owing to the unwillingness of others to run any risk in the doubtful experiment—and its ultimate success by my industry and perseverance of twenty-eight years' continuance, aided by the editorial services of Rev. R. S. Storrs and others in succeeding years. With Mr. Storrs's help the *Recorder* rose from the lowest depression, and was prosperous.

During the various changes above alluded to, I was favored with much "advice from outsiders," well-meant and from the best of motives, no doubt, but not always judicious. I was advised to admit the Unitarian controversy into the *Recorder*, but I declined, because the paper was intended as a vehicle of intelligence, which would be excluded so far as long discussions were admitted. Then the *Telegraph* was set up for that purpose. After an unsuccessful trial of about one year, I was advised to annex the *Telegraph* and its editor [Gerard Hallock] to the *Recorder*. This being done, he became half proprietor. In a few months after, an experienced editor from Portland was recommended as the best in the country. He bought out his predecessor at a cost of $7500; but he had too much a mind of his own to suit his advisers, and "he must be removed at any rate." This could only be done by my buying him out at a cost of $6000, which I had to borrow to get the whole establishment into my hands again. Then I was strongly advised to take a very talented editor upon a salary of $1500 a year, which change "would at once double the number of subscribers;" but it resulted in reducing the number in a few months, until I could bear it no longer, and took the business into my own hands, and paid for communications. This was the most profitable method—it yielded the largest dividend.

There was a class of men in olden time who laid heavy burdens on men's shoulders, grievous to be borne; but they would not touch them with one of their fingers.

I had a large and growing family to support and educate, and had to act as compositor, pressman, and clerk, and use all possible economy and diligence, for it was a struggle for life, against the competition of the New York *Observer* and a number of other religious papers, which started up soon after—until my health failed in 1843, and I was obliged to relieve myself by committing the *Recorder* to younger and stronger hands.

I have been thus particular in the history of the *Recorder*, because Mr. Morse has often asserted that he is the founder of the first religious newspaper in the world. The simple question is: *Where was it founded? who did the work and paid the expenses? who would have been responsible in case of a lawsuit for libel or debt?* The first number of the paper answers these questions: "*The Recorder, published by Nathaniel Willis, at No.* 76 *State street, Boston.*"

Mr. Morse and myself had no personal difficulty. We set out together on a difficult and doubtful enterprise. Though I had the heaviest burden to carry, he soon got discouraged and stopped, while I kept on till the object was accomplished.

The city of New York was then a better location than Boston for a religious newspaper to begin, because of the extensive back country, and the New York *Observer* has been able to call to its aid a large body of able assistants, which has made it one of the best religious papers in the country.

Two or three other publications have been named as predecessors of the *Recorder;* but they could with no propriety be called *newspapers*.

Prince's Christian History was an octavo pamphlet or book, printed in Boston at the time of the revivals under Mr. Whitefield's preaching, and consisted mostly of letters from the towns where he had been laboring.

The *Herald of Gospel Liberty* was printed at Portsmouth, N. H., in the quarto form, for Rev. Elias Smith, as I suppose, and contained letters from those places where he had been preaching in his efforts to get up the Freewill Baptist or Christian denomination. It was a circular rather than a newspaper.

The *Christian Remembrancer*, of Philadelphia, was in the quarto form, mostly religious selections, like a scrap-book—while a proper newspaper is in the folio form, and contains secular news, foreign and domestic, and advertisements.

The *Youth's Companion* commenced in 1826. Mr. Asa Rand was my partner at that time. We had a regular children's department in the *Recorder*. We found all the children and youth were interested in it. This suggested the idea of a child's paper. We issued proposals for the *Youth's Companion*, and the number of subscribers which came in induced us to commence it in June, 1827. I had the care of the *Companion*, while Mr. Rand had the care of the *Recorder*, until Mr. Rand withdrew in 1830, when I had the care of both papers until 1844; then the *Recorder* was sold to Rev. Martin Moore. I retained the *Companion* until 1857, when it was sold to Olmstead & Co., by whom it is now published, my name being retained as senior editor.

All three of my papers are now living, and are doing well for their proprietors.

I think that I ought in justice to say, that in all my trials I had one very efficient helper. Before I commenced the *Argus* in Portland I married a lady, who, by her industry, economy, self-denial, and sympathy, made a home, where I found rest and encouragement to battle with the cares, frowns, and selfishness of men. In eighteen years she presented me with nine children, who all lived to adult age, and who owe much to her memory for her love and care. We set out in our Christian course together; but she was taken to her rest and reward in 1844.

I have had severe domestic trials, but I have had a conscience void of offence to support me under them.

Young men who aspire to the press as a profession, let an old man advise you to depend on industry, integrity, perseverance, self-reliance, and the blessing of God, rather than the promises of men. By these I have succeeded with the advantage of an education which only a printing-office affords.

I have paid my debts, and by prudence, and by gathering up the fragments, I have a competence which will carry me to the edge of the Jordan.

NATHANIEL WILLIS, in my 79th year.

Mr. Willis died in May, 1870, at the age of ninety, and religiously adhered to this statement.

Au contraire, a son of Mr. Morse produced in 1872, shortly after the death of his father, the evidence in favor of the Morse claim to the paternity of the *Recorder*. It is our duty to give that too:

To the Editors of the Evening Post:

In your issue of the 16th of January, under the title of the "Parentage of the Religious Press," you publish a letter from Richard Storrs Willis, in which he claims for his father, the late Nathaniel Willis, the honor of being the originator and founder of the Boston *Recorder*. Mr. Willis is mistaken. He undoubtedly believes that the claims of his father to that distinction are just. I am also the son of a recently-deceased father, however, and claim that he was the first inventor, editor, and proprietor of the plan of connecting religion and journalism as embodied in the Boston *Recorder*. The facts are plainly set forth by legal documents and printed papers, and the slightest examination leaves no doubt on the subject. The first volume of the *Recorder* lies before me as I write. The name of Nathaniel Willis appears as publisher of the numbers for January 3, 10, and 17. In the number for January 24 no name appears as printer, but my father says that Mr. Willis printed four numbers, and this must, therefore, be one of them. From January 31 to April 10 we find that Ezra Lincoln published the *Recorder*. From April 10 to May 1 David J. Burr published and Ezra Lincoln printed the paper. From this last date David J. Burr published and Nathaniel Willis printed the *Recorder* until June 19, when Mr. Willis became both printer and publisher. What do these facts show? Let my father, Sidney Edwards Morse, in his own words, tell the story:

The Boston *Recorder*, the prototype of that numerous class of periodicals called "religious newspapers," now established in every part of Protestant Christendom, was commenced in January, 1816. Application was made to me—then a student in the law-school at Litchfield, in Connecticut—to become the editor of the proposed paper. I declined, on the ground that I was incompetent, without a proper training, to discharge the duties of the place. When this application was made to me I was only twenty-one years old. I had, however, been for several years a writer for the Boston *Centinel* of articles which had been extensively copied into other papers throughout the country. A series of twelve anonymous articles, which I wrote in 1812-13, was copied from the *Centinel* into every other Federal newspaper in Boston. This was known to the gentlemen who proposed the establishment of a new paper, and hence, probably, the application to me. The reply was, that Mr. Evarts, editor of the *Panoplist*, would be the senior editor of the new paper, and would train me. I then consented, with the understanding, however, that my father should not incur pecuniary responsibility. This point, it was supposed, was effectually secured by the agreement of Mr. Nathaniel Willis to print and publish the new paper for me, at fixed prices for paper, printing, and clerk-hire, all the receipts from subscribers and advertisers to be retained by him until his bill should be fully paid, but neither I nor my father to be responsible in case of a deficiency. Mr. Willis was induced to make this agreement by the expectation of securing to himself steady occupation as a printer.

In October, 1815, after consulting with my father and Mr. Evarts, and availing myself of their suggestions, I wrote and issued the prospectus of the *Recorder*, a weekly newspaper, on an original plan, to be commenced on the first Wednesday in January, 1816. Mr. Willis estimated that nine hundred and fifty subscribers would pay his bill, if the edition should consist of only one thousand copies. When the day for commencing the publication arrived there were only five hundred subscribers, and Mr. Evarts gave me notice that he could not occupy the post of senior editor. I also wished to retire, but my father said that I must go on as sole editor. At the end of three weeks there had been few additions to the list, and Mr. Willis gave me notice that the fourth number was the last that he would print under the existing arrangement.

When I reported to my father that Mr. Willis declined printing the paper any longer, and that I too wished to abandon it, he said that the paper should not be abandoned; that he would now, himself, become personally responsible for all expenses, and would employ another printer and publisher. Accordingly, he engaged Mr. Ezra Lincoln to print the *Recorder* for three months, and then went to work in his energetic way to get subscribers. In about two months the list advanced, under my father's efforts, from five hundred to eight hundred. Mr. David J. Burr desired to enter into partnership with me in the *Recorder*. I consented, throwing upon him half the pecuniary responsibility, and all the mercantile cares; and when the contract with Mr. Lincoln expired, as Mr. Willis and his friend desired that he should be taken back as printer, Mr. Burr and I consented, and entered into a written contract with him. My partnership with Mr. Burr, after continuing less than three months, was dissolved, in consequence of his return from Boston to Richmond. My father continued his exertions, and before the end of June the list of subscribers had advanced to eleven hundred, which was more than sufficient to pay all the expenses of paper, printing, rent, and clerk-hire.

This statement rests solely upon the word of my father, and I therefore submit the three following documents, the originals of which can be seen on application to me:

First, An indenture between Sidney Edwards Morse and David J. Burr, dated March 22, 1816, the preamble to which reads thus: "That whereas said Morse is the editor and *proprietor* of a certain paper published weekly in said Boston, entitled the *Recorder*, which was commenced on the first week in January last, and it is agreed that said Burr shall become a joint and equal proprietor of said paper," etc.

Second, An indenture between Nathaniel Willis, Sidney Edwards Morse, and David J. Burr, bearing date 30th April, 1816, "Witnesseth that the said Willis does hereby engage and undertake on his part to print for the said Morse & Burr a certain weekly newspaper called the *Recorder*, of which the said Morse & Burr are proprietors, on the following terms," etc.

Third, The original note of which the accompanying engraving is from a photographic copy.

This alone seems to settle at once and forever the question as to original proprietorship of the *Recorder*, a question which has agitated the religious press of our country for more than twenty years. In the heat of the controversy, and during the life of Nathaniel Willis, he claimed that the paper was founded by himself in January, 1816, and that he was its original proprietor, and that he employed my father to edit it; while my father asserted that he founded the paper, and employed Mr. Willis to print it. In 1849 Mr. Willis asserted that Mr. Morse never paid him any money for printing the paper, and challenged my father to produce a receipt. Strange to say, after the lapse of more than fifty years, recently, in emptying some loose papers from an old barrel, the accompanying receipt was found, written wholly by Mr. Willis himself, and signed by him, acknowledging the payment by my father and the receipt by Mr. Willis of money "for printing the *Recorder*."

The discovery of this little paper, after the lapse of more than half a century, seems very much like a direct interposition of Providence for the vindication of an innocent and upright man from the false charge of attempting to rob another of his just fame.

Respectfully, G. LIVINGSTON MORSE.

These archæologic developments are entertaining. It appears that Willis was the original publisher, and Morse the original editor of this paper. They both insist on being the Father of the *Boston Recorder* and the Father of Religious Journalism. If the dispute could be carried before Solomon, how would he determine the case? The *Boston Post*, in deciding the controversy in regard to the two claimants to the discovery of Ether, that the monument in the public garden in that city was erected to Either, became our Solomon in the case of the *Recorder*.

But there is another Father of Religious Journalism in Ohio. To give full credit to Willis and Morse, how shall we dispose of this interesting fact which we copy from the *Historical Magazine?*

THE FIRST RELIGIOUS NEWSPAPER IN THE UNITED STATES.

The Gymnasium and Library Association of this city (in Chillicothe, Ohio), in acknowledging the receipt of a donation of the bound volumes entire of the "Recorder," a newspaper "devoted to Theology, Literature, and all matters of Local or National interest," which was published in this city, by John Andrews, from 1814 to 1817 inclusive, states that this is the first religious newspaper ever published in this country or in the world. Is this so? and if not, when, where, and by whom was the first paper of that character published? E. P. S.

Chillicothe, Ohio, July 18, 1857.

No answer appeared in the *Magazine* publishing this note. But the *Presbyterian Banner*, now published at Pittsburg, claims to be the successor and continuation of the *Recorder* of the Rev. John Andrews. Of all these statements there are three clear points:

1st. Nathaniel Willis first conceived the idea of a religious newspaper.

2d. John Andrews first published a religious newspaper.

3d. Sidney Edwards Morse first edited the *Boston Recorder*.

The *Recorder* now forms a part of the *Congregationalist*. They were published for some time on one sheet, the passing years of one being noted from its origin on one page, and those of the other on another page. Thus the *Congregationalist* is thirty-three years, and the *Recorder* fifty-six years old. In 1871 they were issued separately from the same office.

"That great eight-page paper, *The Watchman and Reflector*," as its advertisement for 1869 announced, was established in Boston in 1819, and is, therefore, half a century old. It is the organ of the Baptists. It claims a circulation of 21,000 copies, which gives it a large reading congregation—an audience thirty times larger than ever crowded into the most capacious Baptist church to listen to the eloquence of the most learned Baptist clergyman in the country—an indication, assuredly, of the advantage of a religious newspaper in its weekly service. In addition to its religious matter it presents the features of a very respectable weekly newspaper.

The *New York Observer* was the third or fourth religious newspaper issued in the United States. After Mr. Sidney E. Morse left the *Recorder* he went to New York, and, in connection with his elder brother, Richard C. Morse, started the *Observer* in 1820. They were sons of the Rev. Jedediah Morse, D.D., of Charlestown, Mass., author of the Atlas that carried the children of the first part of this century through the geography of the world. They were brothers of Professor Samuel F. B. Morse, of artistic and telegraphic fame. The *Observer* was managed by them with great success, its circulation running up as high as sixty thousand, till 1858, when the chief management devolved on a son of Sidney E. Morse. In May, 1868, Richard sailed for Europe for the benefit of his health. In a few months after, while at Kissingen, Germany, he died, in the 73d year of his age. Sidney E. Morse, aged 77 years, died in New York in December, 1871.

The Methodists felt the necessity of having an organ. They established *Zion's Herald*. It is published in Boston, and was commenced by the Rev. Dr. Adam Wilson, who died in Waterville, Maine, in 1871. It has lived a long and prosperous life, and is the leading organ of its Church.

The *Christian Register*, one of the oracles of the Unitarians, was brought out in 1821. It celebrated its semi-centennial in Boston on the 20th of April, 1871. William H. Reed, son of its first editor, read a sketch of its history on that occasion. He said:

> The history was to a great degree the history of its founder. During the few years which succeeded his graduation at Cambridge, he had a wide opportunity for the observation of the condition of religious opinion in various parts of the country. The Unitarian controversy began about 15 years before the establishment of the *Register*. As the reflection from Calvinistic theology grew wider, Mr. Reed became convinced that a weekly journal would be of great service as an organ for the exposition of Unitarian doctrine and the candid discussion of disputed points in theology. He received immediate encouragement, and the first number was issued and sent to 300 subscribers on the 20th of April, 1821. It was printed by John Cotton, and the second number was issued on the 31st of August, after an interval of four months, during which many subscribers were obtained. His chief advisers in the earlier years of the *Christian Register* were Dr. Channing, Dr. Ware, Professor Norton, and other gentlemen of equal position outside of the ministerial profession. Among those who contributed to its columns were President Kirkland, Dr. Noah Worcester, Judge Story, Dr. Greenwood, Dr. Bancroft, President Sparks, and Mr. Edward Everett. In 1826 Mr. Reed relinquished the editorial care of the journal, placing it under the charge of a committee of the government of the Unitarian Association, and the editors the following year were the Rev. Henry Ware, Jr., the Rev. Jas. Walker, the Rev. Saml. Barrett, the Rev. E. S. Gannett, and Lewis Tappan. In 1827 it reverted again to the charge of Mr. Reed. In 1833 the size of the paper was increased about one-third, there having been two previous enlargements in 1824 and 1825. It was enlarged again in 1836. Subsequent to that time it was edited successfully by the Hon. Sidney Willard, the Rev. Chandler Robbins, Rufus A. Johnson, Dr. Barrett, Dr. Lothrop, Dr. George E. Ellis, Hon. Charles W. Upham, the Rev. Dr. Morison, the Rev. N. S. Folsom, Dr. E. Peabody, Dr. A. P. Peabody, the Rev. F. D. Huntington, the Rev. T. B. Fox, the Rev. Mr. Mothe, and the Rev. Dr. S. W. Bush, the present editor. In 1836 the name of the paper was changed to "The Christian Register and Boston Observer," but in 1846 it was changed back again to the present and first title. At the close of 1865 a corporation was formed, to whose care the paper was transferred soon after.

There were present at this dinner, among others, Mr. Olmsted, of the Baptist *Watchman*, Mr. Donahoe, of the Catholic *Pilot*, and Mr. Atwood, of the *Universalist*. The Rev. Edward Everett Hale presided, and, in the course of some remarks, said that the *Register* was the first weekly religious journal in Boston whose editor was not cooped up by any written creed, by any covenant of men, by any traditions of the Middle Ages, nor by any theology of Geneva.

The *Register* is now published by an association, and, as a curiosity, in connection of religion with mammon, one share of the establishment was sold at auction, with other stocks and bonds, in Boston, on the 12th of November, 1870, and brought $13. The *Register* is now edited by the Rev. Thomas J. Mumford.

The other leading organ of the followers of Servetus is the *Liberal Christian*, of which the Rev. Dr. Henry W. Bellows, of New York, is the editor.

The *Christian Intelligencer*, the organ of the Dutch Reformed Church in New York, was first issued in 1830. The Collegiate

Church, as it is called, is a large, influential, and wealthy body, and its organ an interesting weekly publication for the plain and unpretending members of that religious denomination.

The *Evangelist*, published in New York by Henry T. Field, is forty years old. The original idea of its publication was in the purpose of a number of young men to establish an educational, temperance, and anti-slavery organ in the metropolis, or, in its own. words, "expressly to promote revivals and missions, temperance and other reforms." Joshua Leavitt was then its chief editor. He is now connected with the *Independent*. Now that Mr. S. W. Benedict is dead, only one of the young men, William E. Dodge, remains. Its principal editor is one of "the Field family," so well known in law, religion, politics, and telegraphs, and he has occupied that position for seventeen or eighteen years.

The *Evangelist* is a well-managed religious paper, of a conservative character, and may be considered an independent organ of the United Presbyterian Church. It has been in favor of the union of the old and new schools, and of sponging out the disagreeable lines of demarcation between them. In February, 1870, it absorbed the *American Presbyterian* of Philadelphia.

In recently speaking of the course of the *Independent*, and the verdict of the seven clergymen of the West who held an inquest on the soul of that concern, it brought out an article from its contemporary, spiced with capsicum, not obtained at any corner grocery, of which the following is a grain :

* * * Take a man who can neither write, nor preach, nor keep his temper, nor mind his own business ; thrill his bosom day by day with a twenty years' dyspepsia ; flush his brain with the hallucination that his bookkeeping mind is competent to religious journalism ; put a pen in his hand wherewith to write himself down a Pecksniff ; set him like a dog in his kennel to make a pastime of snapping at the respectable people of the neighborhood, and then, gentle reader, you have a specimen copy of the *Evangelist*.

The *Evangelist* received this *Independent* description of its character with becoming grace, in the full belief of the justice of the verdict of the seven Western clergymen.

The *Independent*, thus brought before us, was started twenty-one years ago as an organ of the Congregationalists. Several dry-goods merchants, S. B. Chittenden; S. B. & J. Hunt, and Bowen and M'Namee, furnished the means for its organization. Originally it was edited by the Rev. Drs. Storrs, Bacon, and Thompson. On their retirement Henry Ward Beecher became its editor. Then he retired. Joshua Leavitt, Oliver Johnson, and Theodore Tilton, in their turn, assumed the editorial duties. Its business manager is Henry C. Bowen, the other originators having retired. It will be recollected that, when he was told that his radical notions would affect the business of Bowen and M'Namee, he replied that he "sold silk goods, and not his principles." After disposing of all he had of the former, he left his old business, and carried his stock of principles into the new concern—the *Independent*. The paper was inspired for some time by Tilton, young, fresh, and as ardent as a Northern sun could make him.

One or two years before Tilton became a writer for the *Independent*, there were three young gentlemen of "natural parts" in the metropolis who were intimate friends, and who were then in a state of mental chrysalis. Two were accomplished reporters on the *New York Herald*, and the other came near being an equally accomplished member of the efficient staff of that paper. One shortly after became the editor of the *Metropolitan Record*, established as the organ of Archbishop Hughes; the second became Assistant District Attorney of the United States in New York during the Rebellion, where he was constrained to keep his official eye on his quondam associate of the *Record*, which had slipped from the fatherly care of the astute prelate into an extreme Democratic advocate; and the third, after mentally balancing on the high fence that separates the *Herald* and *Independent*, followed the instincts of his nature, and became one of the leaders of the radical political and Woman's Rights Party, and its chief organ and adviser till he reached the *Golden Age* of his existence.

The *Independent* is conducted with energy. Its writers have been of such a character as to command attention. Henry Ward Beecher gave it a strong push forward. Bowen, having been an active dry-goods merchant, obtained considerable support and character for the paper by his dry-goods and other commercial reports. Its independent tone attracted attention. Thus it started, and thus it has thrived; and although Beecher left the editorial management in not a tranquil state of mind, we see by the recent annual auction sale of pews at Plymouth Church that Bowen has paid the highest premium and secured one of the best pews in that sanctuary.

The most interesting chapter, in a religious point of view, in the history of the *Independent*, is unquestionably the solemn inquest we have mentioned, which was held in Chicago on the soul of the establishment. Seven learned doctors—the Rev. Edward Beecher, T. M. Post, A. L. Chapin, J. M. Sturtevant, John P. Gulliver, G. F. Magoun, and S. C. Bartlett, having found Henry C. Bowen in the Western metropolis—for this country, like Rhode Island, Siam, and Japan, has two great cities, each of which is called a metropolis—proceeded to sit in consultation on his body as the embodiment of the soul of the *Independent*. The conference lasted nearly two days, and resulted, according to these learned divines, in a pledge from

Bowen that thereafter the *Independent* "should be both the organ and the champion of those truths commonly known as evangelical." As we have quoted the *Independent* in regard to the *Evangelist*, it is only fair to quote the *Evangelist* in speaking of this inquest and pledge.

> This understanding and pledge, they now affirm, has been violated by keeping at the head of the paper one who, "in his religious opinions, whatever his private views may be, has never given the public occasion to suspect the existence in his mind of any defined system, or of any well considered convictions;" who, "in his denials of the foundation principles of the Christian system, that have sometimes been very positive and energetic, exhibits an unconsciousness that he was even on debatable ground, which in the editor of a great religious newspaper is at once painful and ludicrous." This negative influence of the "editor-in-chief" opens the door to all loose opinions, when associated with the very positive and decided convictions of the "managing editor," Mr. Oliver Johnson, of whom they say that "outside of the *Independent* office he makes no secret of opinions which, whether justly or unjustly, would be pronounced by evangelical Christians generally not only unevangelical, but infidel." With these associate editors a corps of contributors was announced, in which orthodox divines were brought in on a platform of the broadest liberality, and "in loving partnership with a platoon of that school of the Boston abolitionists, whose denunciations had for years been about equally divided between Southern slavery and evangelical Christianity!"
>
> Such is the case as drawn out at great length by these Western brethren. As to the facts, we take it for granted that they are stated correctly. They require but a brief comment, and this we make with a desire to do justice to both parties.
>
> In the first place, we concede to Mr. Bowen entire good faith. We do not doubt that in his conferences with the ministers at Chicago he spoke as he felt, and that he did then frankly and sincerely desire to conform his paper to their wishes.
>
> Why, then, was it not done? *Simply because it was impossible*—that is, without making a total revolution in the paper. The editor had no sympathy with the attempt. All who know him know that he does not disguise his sentiments or his sympathies, and that he does not pretend to be orthodox or "evangelical" in the ordinary sense. He may indeed claim to be in some vague, general sense, which means any thing or nothing, but as the word was understood by these Chicago divines, and as understood by the churches of New England, he would be the first to repel it with scorn. His manliness revolted at the idea of standing in such a position, of advocating opinions which he did not believe. Hence that memorable "editorial soliloquy" in which he made a bold declaration of independence, and hurled defiance at those who would restrain him of his liberty.

These paragraphs show the animus of the religious press toward each other. We give these as the freshest specimens. Is it not manifest to the millions of readers of newspapers in the country that in vigor of expression the religious press is fully equal to the lay and pagan press of the nation? Is this owing to the bracing air of the country? It must be so. It is robust Christianity; and it has always been so. In the early years of the *Christian Register*, its historian says, religious discussions were marked with "much bitterness and asperity."

The few papers we have thus prominently brought forward are only a small portion of the religious press of the country. Since 1814–16, when the two *Recorders* made their appearance as wonderful innovators on the religious customs of the people, this class of journals have sprung into existence in endless numbers in every direction, and pinned to every faith. Some have reached long lives, as those we have mentioned. Others, like hundreds and hundreds of secular papers, have been strangled in infancy by the public. The Rev. Clement C. Babb, in closing the sixteenth year of his editorial labor on the *Christian Herald*, of Cincinnati, makes what would seem a remarkakle statement—that nearly one half of the religious papers on the exchange list of that paper in 1852 have since died for want of support, and that only two or three of the survivors are either owned or edited by those who had the management of them in that year. The Rev. De Witt C. Talmage, in a lecture delivered in the Brooklyn Tabernacle in 1871, the subject of which he announced as the "Lying Newspapers," stated that "when a paper becomes positively religious, it is almost—not quite—certain to become bankrupt, so that there are to-day, I suppose, not more than five self-supporting religious newspapers in this country." But the failure of one does not prevent the starting of others, for almost every week we see a new one announced.

When Henry Ward Beecher left the *Independent*, he became an editor of the *Christian Union*, a paper which had been edited by the Rev. Crammond Kennedy. It is published by J. B. Ford & Co., who have issued Mr. Beecher's sermons in weekly pamphlets, and who have since published his "Life of Christ." It is probable that there is not another man in the United States who is so much heard and read as Henry W. Beecher, unless the other man be Wendell Phillips. These two preachers, publicists, and journalists are emphatically the greatest of their kind in the country. They use the pulpit, the lecture-room, the stump, the newspaper, in the fullest sense. No question comes before the public that is not immediately seized upon by one or both of these men. Every journal at the North throws open its columns to them. Even the leading papers of New York, full of their own vigorous mental resources, will not only do this, but they will send their best stenographers to report what these orators utter. In addition to this, these leading editors will review the speeches, or sermons, or communications of these two master-spirits of the forum in article after article, thus increasing their notoriety, power, and influence with every article. Wendell Phillips, full of tact, in writing his communications for the *Anti-Slavery Standard* or any other publication, whether it be to abuse Samuel Bowles, of the *Springfield Republican*, or flay Ulysses S. Grant, of the Executive Mansion, makes them short, sententious, and severe, so that every paper can easily find room for them and copy them, and every one who runs reads them. These appeals, embracing popular subjects, are spread broadcast in all the papers. "We have two special dangers to fear," Mr. Phillips would fulminate, "a drunken mob and a moneyed aristocracy. The laws of some of the states were made in the gambling hells of gold speculators rather than in State Houses." Mr. P. would draw a picture of a manufacturing town where the daily paper and the preacher in the pulpit were owned and controlled by a single great corporation. "Put your ear down close to the columns of the *Daily Advertiser*, and you will hear the rustle of cotton, or the chink of bank dollars. If you doubt this, go read its editorials in the light of State Street, and you will read them with anointed eyes." So sharp and vigorous are his remarks that they are published, praised, criticised, abused, and read from Maine to Texas. Editorially he is as much read as the *New York Herald*, for not only that paper, but all others, spreads what he says over the length and breadth of the land. He is a contributor, *nolens volens*, of nearly every paper. All he has to do is to write to be read. Where James Gordon Bennett has half a million readers for one of his articles, Wendell Phillips has one or two millions! While Phillips indulges in politics, Beecher is equally successful with his religious notions. They appear in newspapers and pamphlets, every where to the right of us and to the left of us. Are not these two men, therefore, the two great editors of the United States—the two journalists, *par excellence*, of America?

The organs of the Catholics, of the Episcopalians, of the Jews, of the Mormons, of the Spiritualists, of the Swedenborgians, are numerous, and able and influential, with thousands of readers and believers. Of the Catholics the *Shamrock* was the first. Then the *Truth Teller* was commenced in New York in 1829 or '30 by William Denman. But Archbishop Hughes has stated that the first really Catholic paper was the *Catholic Miscellany*, founded in Charleston by Bishop England. Now there are the *Metropolitan Record*, the *Tablet*, the *Freeman's Journal*, and the *Pilot*, as strong in politics as in religion. Of the Episcopalians there are the *Church Journal*, always a little belligerent in Church matters, and the *Protestant Churchman*.

These are only a few of the many. With the Jews the *Jewish Messenger* and the *Hebrew News*. Within thirty years no less than ten periodicals have been started in different parts of the world in defense of Judaism alone. They have faith in their religion, and are never known as Jews in politics. The million and a half of Spiritualists in the United States have their organs, of which the *Spiritualist* is the chief. Every faith and belief in the country finds utterance and relief in an organ of some sort.

When the *Metropolitan Record* was established as the organ of the Catholic Church in New York, it was the custom of Archbishop Hughes to dictate an article or a sermon to be stenographically taken down by its editor or reporter for the benefit of his Church and people. Sitting at ease in his study, the late archbishop, twirling a valuable ring on his finger, the gift of the pope or a cardinal, as if unwinding his thoughts, would talk off his discourse as glibly as if engaged in common conversation. On one occasion he suddenly stopped and said, "Please turn to—" naming a word six or seven lines back. "Mark out after that word. Now we will go on." Then he would proceed as smoothly and as accurately with the fresh expression as if there had been no break or interruption in his line of argument. Organs are thus frequently supplied from the best brains of the nation. Nearly all the leading clergymen of the country write for the papers; Tyng, Beecher, and many others, have stepped outside of the religious press to write for the *Ledger*.

Several efforts have been made to establish daily religious newspapers. The *World* was originally begun as such. When the *Tribune* and *Times* appeared, nothing offensive to the religious and moral sentiment of the community was published. The *Sun* was purchased, at one time, for this purpose. All these efforts failed. It is stated that the Marquis of Bute lately bought the *London Sun* in order to have a daily religious paper in the metropolis of England. The religious people of New York do not appear deterred by the non-success of previous efforts, for they have established another cheap paper with a Christian code for its management. This is its announcement:

THE NEW-YORK DAILY WITNESS.

A CHRISTIAN, ONE CENT, AFTERNOON NEWSPAPER, WILL BE ISSUED FROM NO. 162 NASSAU-ST., NEXT BUILDING TO THE TRIBUNE, UP ONE STAIR, ON SATURDAY, 1ST JULY, 1871.

It will insert no advertisements of liquors, theatres, lotteries, or any thing inconsistent with its character, but it will present a good medium for all unobjectionable advertisements, which will be inserted at the low rate of two cents per word, or ten cents per line, agate measure. Advertisements of "Wants," such as situations, boarders, &c., will be inserted at one cent per word, none being reckoned less than fifteen words. The paper will give the news of the day and much excellent family reading beside. All who wish to see such a paper established are requested to support it at its commencement by purchasing it from newsboys, and sending their advertisements to the office, 162 Nassau-st.

The power and influence of the press in religion has, since the establishment of the two *Recorders*, and the commencement of the annual reports of the religious gatherings in New York, inaugurated amid violent and bitter opposition by the *Herald*, become an acknowledged fact. The reports of the *Herald*, the repeated remarks of Henry Ward Beecher, the large increase of religious papers every where, testify to this in the strongest manner; and in October, 1869, at the Episcopal Diocesan Convention held in New York, the Right

Rev. Bishop Potter, in his annual address, referred to the great powers to reach the world as the pulpit and the press.

Impressed still more forcibly with the value of newspapers in spreading the Gospel, the Evangelical Press Association of the Reformed Dutch Church of New York City, in May, 1870, took into consideration the propriety of using the press for religious purposes. Such an association also exists in Massachusetts. Its object is asserted to be the publication in secular papers, as advertisements, of religious tracts, in which various seasonable topics could be discussed. The *New York Herald* has devoted, for the last three years, one and two pages of its paper every Monday to reports of sermons preached the day before in the principal pulpits of New York, Boston, Philadelphia, and Washington, and has even had important religious services in Rome, Paris, and London telegraphed by ocean cable for its readers.

What is called the religious press of the country, after it became an institution, and was confirmed as such by the people, entered the political arena, and aided the cause of the Republican Party and the abolition of slavery with all its gigantic moral power. Starting with only five hundred subscribers, as the *Boston Recorder* did, the religious press now numbers millions of readers. The circulation of the several organs of the religious sects in the United States ranges from one thousand to seventy-five thousand copies, and perhaps as high as one hundred thousand. The *Christian Advocate*, established many years as the chief organ of the Methodists, nets an annual profit of $30,000. These publications are in every city in the Union. Mingling with politicians of all shades, the conductors of these papers could not avoid acquiring some of the habits of their peculiar associates. It is not fair to suppose that intercourse of this sort could elevate a press otherwise devoted to religion and purity in public and private morals. It is apparent that a portion of the religious press became somewhat vitiated in its contact with scheming politicians, and that the rough and dirty Pool of Politics was not the soft and sight-giving Pool of Siloam to the editors of these publications. One illustration we have given in the tilt between the *Independent* and *Evangelist*. We have another in the acrimonious contest between the *New York Observer* and *Evangelist*, growing out of that singularly solemn scene at the death-bed of Albert D. Richardson, of the *Tribune*, at the Astor House. The *Evangelist* claims to be the organ of the "United Presbyterian Church" of the United States, while the *Observer*, which denounced "the Astor House scandal," asserts that it reaches "more Presbyterian ministers and people than any other religious newspaper." Yet these two papers, with these great claims to circulation and influence, abuse each other in the strongest terms, entirely losing sight of that meekness of spirit and Christian love which their simple and single-minded readers expect to find inculcated in their columns. It is true that the *Observer* has an advantage over its more liberal contemporary in the dual form of its paper, one half belonging to the " Religious Department," and the other to the " Secular Department ;" and if the pious press will abuse each other, it would not be a bad plan for the *Evangelist* and all other religious papers, wishing to indulge in this sort of luxury, to have a " Secular Department" also. Those of the subscribers of the *Observer* who keep the Sabbath retain one part of that paper for Sunday reading, and the other part for the remainder of the week.

There is another class of religious papers, of which the first was the *Youth's Companion*, established in 1826 by Nathaniel Willis. They are devoted to the entertainment and religious instruction of children. They also give items of interesting news. The *Companion* is now published by Perry Mason & Co., and is an eight page paper, handsomely printed and well filled. There is another, called the *Well Spring*. Another, the *Child's Paper*, of beautiful typography, and with a circulation of 100,000 copies. The Methodists print a Sunday-school paper named the *Advocate*, which had a circulation of 105,000 in 1858, and of 370,000 in 1871. These are religious newspapers for the young. They are cheap, and are within the reach of every child. But in some instances the subscription price is very unfairly arranged in consequence of the premium mania among newspaper proprietors. One paper is $1 50 per annum to a single subscriber. If two names are sent, forty cents are deducted. If three subscribers are obtained, one dollar is taken off. Now if the publisher can afford three copies for three dollars and fifty cents, why don't he reduce his single subscription to one third of this amount? The reason is patent enough, but the single subscribers are the victims and sufferers. The premium system will, however, cure itself in time in the efforts of newspaper publishers to outbid each other in offering pianos, houses, horses, carriages, watches, farms, diamonds, steam-boats, and railroads to subscribers.

There were two hundred and seventy-seven religious periodicals published in the United States in 1860. Three hundred and thirty or forty are issued now. There are probably 100,000,000 copies printed annually.

CHAPTER XX.
SOME OF THE REPRESENTATIVE NEWSPAPERS.

INKLING OF AN INDEPENDENT PRESS. — JUDGE BOUVIER AND THE AMERICAN TELEGRAPH.—NILES'S REGISTER.—THE HARTFORD TIMES.—JOHN M. NILES AND GIDEON WELLES. — CURIOUS FIGHT FOR A POST-OFFICE. — THOMAS H. BENTON AND DUFF GREEN IN MISSOURI.—WILLIAM COBBETT. —THE PORCUPINE. — THE NEW YORK AMERICAN AND CHARLES KING. — THE PROVIDENCE JOURNAL.—WONDERFUL CHANGE OF BASE ON THE TARIFF QUESTION.—THE NEW YORK ALBION.—ORGANS IN OTHER COUNTRIES. —THE POETS AS JOURNALISTS.—FASHIONABLE JOURNALISM.—THE LOUISVILLE JOURNAL.—GEORGE D. PRENTICE AND JOHN GREENLEAF WHITTIER. —THE WITS OF NEWSPAPERS. — THE FIRST PAPER WEST OF ALBANY. — JOHN I. MUMFORD.—FANNY WRIGHT.—RICHARD COBDEN'S OPINION.

AMONG the ornaments of the profession of journalism may be ranked Judge John Bouvier. He was born in the south of France, but became a citizen of the United States in 1812. On arriving at this distinction he opened a printing-office, and in 1814 began the publication of a weekly newspaper called the *American Telegraph*. The first number appeared in Brownsville, Pennsylvania, where Bouvier was town clerk and secretary of a fire-engine company, on the 9th of November of that year, with the motto "Justice, Laws, and Liberty." At that early period Judge Bouvier had an inkling of the Independent Press. He promised, in his prospectus, to "discountenance all factions and factious men, under what plausible name soever they may be shielded," and would not "crouch to any man or set of men, and neglect the duty which every editor in the union owes to the public."

After publishing the *Telegraph* four years, Judge B. removed to Uniontown, where he united his paper with the *Genius of Liberty*, and continued the publication of both papers in one with the two names united, under the firm of Bouvier and Austin. It was too early for an Independent Press; the new paper was "conducted on the principles of pure democracy." Thus Judge B. continued till 1820, when, like Henry Wheaton, he abandoned journalism for the legal profession, and removed to Philadelphia, where, in 1836, he became Recorder, and in 1838 an Associate Judge of the Court of Criminal Sessions. While thus engaged, and finding, from early experience, the need of a well-"arranged digest of that legal information which every student," and, indeed, every lawyer should have, he undertook the great labor of preparing a Law Dictionary, which was published in two volumes, and afterwards the Institutes of American Law, which appeared in four volumes. These six volumes were indorsed by such jurists as Judge Story and Chancellor Kent. They were published by Childs and Peterson. Mr. Childs, of this firm, is now the proprietor of the Philadelphia *Public Ledger*, and husband of a granddaughter of Judge Bouvier, the author of these valuable law-books and the early journalist.

The Judge was a man of great industry and activity of intellect. It is claimed that Nathan Hale introduced the regular editorial articles, the daily comments on public matters in 1814. Not to be far in the rear, we find that Judge Bouvier, early in 1815, began his comments on public affairs in the *American Telegraph*, especially on matters in Europe in connection with the return of Napoleon from Elba.

The independence of the Press was talked about in 1816. Judge Bouvier, in the *Telegraph*, on the 29th of May of that year, published the following article:

INDEPENDENCE OF THE PRESS.

It has been usual, of late, for a few disappointed men in this state, who are subject to, and under the protection of a certain great man in Philadelphia, to publish long essays under this head, in which the printers of the state generally are charged with corruption, and Mr. Duane, their patron, is lauded as the very pink of purity. They declare that they themselves are not only independent of the state government, which they charge with having corrupted the press, but also of Duane himself. Let us see how their declarations agree with facts.

We received a letter a few weeks since from Mr. Duane, stating that, as we disagreed with him upon some particulars, he would no longer exchange papers with us; Mr. Duane having a right to dispose of his paper as he pleases, we should have said nothing on this subject had the matter ended here, but since that period several of his satellites have also discontinued to exchange papers with us, in consequence, no doubt, of orders received by them from head-quarters. This is the way these gentlemen show their independence.

Like most papers of that time, elaborate communications were the editorials of the day.

The most valuable newspaper in its day, as we all find it to be in our researches for historical facts, was *Niles's Weekly Register*. It was established in Baltimore on the 7th of September, 1811, by Hezekiah Niles, an editor of the Baltimore *Evening Post*. William Ogden Niles became associated with his father in 1827. The elder Niles retired in 1836. The *Register* was then conducted by the son till 1848, when its publication was stopped. It was a complete and accurate record of events from 1811 till 1848. Its motto was "The Past—the Present—for the Future." No library is perfect without a set. Its size was convenient to handle for reference. Odd volumes can occasionally be picked up at old book-stores, but all the numbers complete would now be impossible to buy. We have known of a set selling as high as $300.

The *Hartford Times*, which has been a leading party paper in that state for years, and which is still considered an organ of the Democracy in New England, is a journal that deserves a niche. It was established as a weekly paper in 1817, and its first daily issue was in 1839. Its editorial corps has given to two administrations each a cabinet minister—John M. Niles and Gideon Welles. Its founder and principal proprietor was Alfred E. Burr.

Mr. Niles, who had been a printer in the office of the *Courant*, and a writer of books for boys, became editor and foreman of the *Times* in 1817. He continued in this capacity for three or four years. In 1820 he was made judge of the Hartford County Court. In 1826 he was sent to the Legislature. He was appointed postmaster of Hartford in 1829. The *Times*, during this period, had been in favor of the administration of James Monroe, John Quincy Adams, and Andrew Jackson. In connection with the appointment of Niles as postmaster, there is an incident which is professional and interesting. In the excitement growing out of the political campaign ending in the election of Jackson in 1828, the *Times* was ostensibly edited by Major Benjamin Hammett Norton. Niles continued one of the publishers, and was probably the master spirit of the concern, but Norton bore the public honors. On the election of Jackson, Norton, who felt that he should have some of the loaves and fishes, immediately proceeded to Washington, and demanded the office of postmaster at Hartford for his services. It was given to him. On his return home with the commission in his hat, Niles was astonished. Office was his weak point. Norton had circumvented him. Thereupon he joined in the rush to Washington, and presented himself at the executive mansion as the real Simon Pure editor of the *Times*. He informed General Jackson that Norton was only an *attaché* of the office. He was, like Simon Pure, fortified with affidavits. The result was the announcement in the official gazette of the appointment of Niles, vice Norton removed. Poor Norton! What was to be done with him? It was arranged that he should go into the Boston Custom-house with the same pay that Niles would receive in Hartford. He was appeased. John Randolph, of Roanoke, gave him fame by applying the epithet "Jacksonia—Nortonizatia" in one of his famous speeches.

After this Norton got deeply interested in Texas, and in 1837 and '38 he was a banker in Wall Street, New York City, having an office in or near the Tontine Building. In 1847 and '48 he edited a paper in Boston called the *Sentinel*, in which he favored the election of Zachary Taylor for the presidency. In return he was appointed American consul at Picton, N. S., where he remained till his death in 1869. He was a fine-looking gentleman, and treated every body with kindness and consideration. He was much respected while consul in Nova Scotia.

The *Times*, on the appointment of Niles to the post-office, was the organ of the Democratic Party in Connecticut. It was now under the guidance of Gideon Welles, the author, it was alleged, of most of the articles which gave the Hartford Post-office first to Norton, and then to Niles. Welles was considered a vigorous writer for a party paper during the administration of Andrew Jackson, and during the fight with the Nullifiers in 1832. Martin Van Buren gave him some office when he was President. In 1861 he was called to the cabinet of Abraham Lincoln as Secretary of the Navy, where he remained during the more serious fight with the Rebellion. Since his retirement from office he has been engaged in reminiscences, adding his mite to the history of the world. His first contribution was in November or December, 1869, when he wrote a pretty severe letter to his successor in office, Mr. Robeson, refusing to surrender some papers which the latter said belonged to the archives of the Navy Department. Other papers on the relief of Fort Sumter and Fort Pickens, and on the capture of New Orleans, have also been given by him, through the *Galaxy*, to the country.

In 1835 Niles was appointed United States senator from Connecticut, and in 1839 he was the unsuccessful Democratic candidate for governor of his native state. In May, 1840, and for the closing months of Van Buren's administration, he succeeded Amos Kendall as Postmaster General. In 1842 he was again sent to the United States Senate for a full term. It is fair to suppose that while in the cabinet and in the Senate he ceased to be editor of the *Times*.

There was one act on the part of the *Times* that gave it a good deal of character. It opposed, under the editorial guidance of Alfred E. Burr, the repeal of the Missouri Compromise in 1853-4, while nearly all the other organs of the Democratic Party favored that unwise measure. Subsequent events showing the correctness of the judgment of the *Times*, the opinions of that paper have since been treated with more respect and consideration by its political opponents.

The *Times* is now edited by W. O. Burr, a son of one of the original proprietors, and it occupies the same position, in a political and party point of view, in Connecticut that the *Boston Post* does in Massachusetts, and the *Albany Argus* and *New York World* in New York. It has always evinced talent in its leading articles, and is not deficient in enterprise for a provincial paper.

It was proposed by William Cobbett to issue his *Weekly Political Register*, to begin June 21, 1816, from No. 19 Wall Street, New York City. It was to consist "partly of Mr. Cobbett's essays which had been published in England, with the addition of notes; but chiefly of matter from the same pen, wholly new, sent out from England in manuscript." Henry Cobbett and G. S. Oldfield were the agents in New York. Cobbett became so notorious on this side of the Atlantic by his writings when here that it was thought that his *Political Register* would find numerous readers. He was known as Peter Porcupine. Carey's *United States Recorder* of January 24, 1798, gave the following *morceau* under the head of

PORCUPINIAD.

PETER PORCUPINE has at length difcovered that cookery is his forte; and, ftill defirous of ferving a ROYAL MASTER, has volunteered to fupply the table of his INFERNAL MAJESTY with delicacies from this fublunary world of ours.

This generous offer was made yefterday, in language equally polite, elegant, and claffical.

But let the Porcupine fpeak for himfelf. He thus addreffes the printers of the *New-York Gazette:*

Send me a file of your papers, you trimming rafcals, and you fhall fee what pretty creatures I'll make of you. I'll COOK you up in a DISH fit for the DEVIL. WM. COBBETT.

We are yet to learn whether or not Beelzebub will accept of this eleemofynary treat from his good friend COBBET: But of Porcupine's qualifications for fuperintending the infernal kitchen, not the leaft doubt can be entertained; for every man of tafte will readily admit that the OLIOS and OLLA PODRIDAS which this arch cook has hitherto ferved up to the fovereign people of America, where calculated only for a HELLISH APPETITE.

The enterprise of the reprint of the *Register* in New York did not amount to much. The pleasantest description of this conspicuous publicist appeared in Miss Mitford's Recollections of a Literary Life. It is a picture of William Cobbett as a host:

He had at that time a large house at Botley, with a lawn and gardens sweeping down to the Bursleden River, which divided his (Mr. Cobbett's) territories from the beautiful grounds of the old friend where he had been originally studying, the great squire of the place. His own house—large, high, massive, red, and square, and perched on a considerable eminence—always struck me as being not unlike its proprietor. It was filled at that time almost to overflowing. Lord Cochrane was there; then in the very height of his warlike fame, and as unlike the common notion of a warrior as could be. A gentle, quiet, mild young man, was this burner of French fleets and cutter-out of Spanish vessels, as one should see in a summer day. He lay about under the trees reading Selden on the Dominion of the Seas, and letting the children (and children always know with whom they may take liberties) play all sorts of tricks with him at their pleasure. His ship's surgeon was also a visitor, and a young midshipman, and sometimes an elderly lieutenant, and a Newfoundland dog; fine sailor-like creatures all. Then there was a very learned clergyman, a great friend of Mr. Gifford of the Quarterly, with his wife and daughter, exceedingly clever persons. Two literary gentlemen from London and ourselves completed the actual party; but there was a large fluctuating series of guests for the hour or guests for the day, of almost all ranks and descriptions, from the earl and his countess to the farmer and his dame. The house had room for all, and the hearts of the owners would have had room for three times the number. I never saw hospitality more genuine, more simple, or more thoroughly successful in the great end of hospitality—the putting every body completely at ease. There was not the slightest attempt at finery, or display, or gentility. They called it a farm-house, and every thing was in accordance with the largest idea of a great English yeoman of the old time. Every thing was excellent—every thing abundant—all served with the greatest nicety by trim waiting damsels; and every thing went on with such quiet regularity that of the large circle of guests not one could find himself in the way. I need not say a word more in praise of the good-wife, very lately dead, to whom this admirable order was mainly due. She was a sweet motherly woman, realizing our notion of one of Scott's most charming characters, Ailie Dinmont, in her simplicity, her kindness, and her devotion to her husband and her children. At this time William Cobbett was at the height of his political reputation; but of politics we heard little, and should, I think, have heard nothing, but for an occasional red-hot patriot, who would introduce the subject, which our host would fain put aside, and get rid of as speedily as possible. There was something of Dandie Dinmont about him, with his unfailing good humor and good spirits, his heartiness, his love of field-sports, and his liking for a foray. He was a tall, stout man, fair and sunburnt, with a bright smile, and an air compounded of the soldier and the farmer, to which his habit of wearing an eternal red waistcoat contributed not a little. He was, I think, the most athletic and vigorous person that I had ever known. Nothing could tire him. At home in the morning, he would begin his active day by mowing his own lawn; beating his gardener, Robinson, the best mower, except himself, in the parish, at that fatiguing work. For early rising, indeed, he had an absolute passion; and some of the poetry that we trace in his writings, whenever he speaks of scenery or of rural objects, broke out in his method of training his children into his own matutinal habits. The boy who was first down stairs was called the Lark for the day, and had, amongst other indulgences, the pretty privilege of making his mother's nosegay and that of any lady visitors. Nor was this the only trace of poetical feeling that he displayed; whenever he described a place, were it only to say where such a covey lay, or such a hare was found sitting, you could see it, so graphic, so vivid, so true was the picture. He showed the same taste in the purchase of his beautiful farm at Botley, Fairthorn—even in the pretty name. To be sure, he did not give the name; but I always thought that it unconsciously influenced his choice in the purchase. The beauty of the situation certainly did. The fields lay along the Bursleden River, and might have been shown to a foreigner as a specimen of the richest and loveliest English scenery. In the cultivation of his garden, too, he displayed the same taste. Few persons excelled him in the management of vegetables, fruits, and flowers. His green Indian corn, his Carolina beans, his water-melons, could hardly have been exceeded at New York. His wall-fruit was equally splendid; and much as flowers have been studied since that day, I never saw a more glowing or a more fragrant autumn garden than that at Botley, with its pyramids of hollyhocks, and its masses of China-asters, of cloves, of mignonette, and of variegated geranium. The chances of life soon parted us, as, without grave faults on either side, people do lose sight of one another; but I shall always look back with pleasure and regret to that visit.

Thomas Hart Benton, so well known in the opposite characters of bitter opponent and warm partisan of Andrew Jackson, and as United States senator from Missouri, edited the *St. Louis Enquirer* in 1816–17. It was the organ of the dominant party of that period. Selected, with David Barton, as one of the first senators from that new state in 1820, partly because of the active part he took in the famous controversy of that exciting time, he disposed of the *Enquirer* and theoretical statesmanship, and became a practical statesman for thirty years in the national capital. In 1824 the *Enquirer* passed into the possession of Duff Green; and while Benton was making an effort to get the Missouri Legislature to pass resolutions in favor of Henry Clay for the presidency, Duff Green was organizing the Jackson Party in that state. These facts are interesting, in view of the attitude of these two journalists toward General Jackson after his inauguration as President in 1829.

The American Cyclopædia, in giving a sketch of Colonel Benton, said:

He now removed to Missouri, and took up his abode in the City of St. Louis in 1815. There he devoted himself anew to his profession. Soon, however, engaging in the politics of the day, he was led to the establishment of a newspaper entitled *The Missouri Argus*. In this position he was involved in many disputes and contentions. Duels were usual at that time, and he had his share of them, with their unhappy consequences. In one of them, which was forced upon him, he killed his opponent, Mr. Lucas—an event he deeply regretted, and all the private papers relating to which he has destroyed. His journal took a strong and vigorous stand in favor of the admission of Missouri, notwithstanding her slavery Constitution, and when the angry controversy was terminated he was rewarded for his labors by being chosen one of the first senators from the new state. It is from this period, 1820, that his political history and the great influence he has exerted upon public affairs may be said to date. A man in the early prime of life, possessed of a commanding intellect, of large and liberal culture, an assiduous student, industrious, temperate, resolute, and endowed with a memory whose tenacity was marvelous, he soon placed himself in the front rank of those who shaped the councils of the nation.

The Cyclopædia is wrong in the name of the paper. It was the *Enquirer*, and not the *Argus*. In reply to Colonel Benton's article in Thirty Years in the Senate, on the establishment of the Washington *Globe*, Duff Green thus speaks of Benton's early journalistic career in Missouri:

I first knew Col. Benton in St. Louis, in 1817, where, as editor of the St. Louis *Enquirer*, he made himself useful to Gen. Clarke and the dominant party. He was the relative and partisan of Mr. Clay. He took an active part in the Missouri controversy, and was rewarded with a seat in the United States Senate. In 1823 he went to St. Charles, then the seat of government, with resolutions nominating Mr. Clay for the presidency, intending to bring them to Washington as so much political capital. These resolutions I defeated by opposing them in caucus, where I denounced Mr. Benton, and compelled him to leave the seat of government in haste, by declaring that if he remained until the Senate met on the next day I would institute a legislative inquiry into his conduct. In 1824 I purchased from the person to whom he had sold it the St. Louis *Enquirer*, organized a party in support of Gen. Jackson, and carried the popular vote of one district for him, in spite of Col. Benton, who came back to Missouri and made extraordinary efforts for Mr. Clay. It so happened that one of Mr. Clay's half brothers was the clerk of one of the counties which gave a majority for Gen. Jackson, and by his refusal to make the return, and an intrigue in the Legislature, the entire vote of the state was given to Mr. Clay, regardless of the popular will.

The *New York American*, an evening paper, was established by Charles King, son of Rufus King, and Johnston Verplanck, in 1819. It was at first a Tammany, or Bucktail paper, and acted with the Van Buren Democracy in opposition to De Witt Clinton. In 1823 the *American* advocated John Quincy Adams for the presidency, while Van Buren and Tammany Hall, with the *National Advocate*, went for William H. Crawford, after Van Buren and Hamilton's pilgrimage to Georgia, and this movement severed the connection between the *American* and the Democratic Party.

These movements resulted in the establishment of a new paper, named the *New York Patriot*, and edited by Charles K. Gardener, one of the Assistant Postmaster Generals, and an aid of General

Brown during the war. It was believed that Henry Wheaton and John C. Calhoun were both instrumental in the organization of this new political organ in the city of New York. It was the policy of the *Patriot* not to favor any candidate for the presidency, but to oppose the elevation of Crawford to the chief magistracy of the Union. The presidential electors for the State of New York were then chosen by the Legislature, and fears were entertained that the choice would be favorable to the Georgia statesman. Something needed to be done to prevent this. Hammond speaks of this scheme in these words:

> With a view to guard against such a result, it was urged that the electors ought to be chosen by the people. "If the majority of the people are for Mr. Crawford," said his opponents, "we cheerfully acquiesce in their determination; if not, let their will be carried into execution." This plan was formed by a citizen of Albany, whose name has never been mentioned, but who communicated it to Mr. Wheaton, of New York, and immediately the *New York Patriot* took strong ground in favor of the measure.

It is not our intention to go into the political history of New York, but simply to show the reasons for changes in the management and in the politics of newspapers, and for the establishment of new party organs. We all know that Mr. Crawford never became President.

The *American* was thenceforward a Whig and National Republican paper. In 1845 it was united with the *Courier and Enquirer*, on the 16th of February of that year. Its editor then became associate editor with James Watson Webb and Henry J. Raymond till his appointment as President of Columbia College. Mr. King died in Europe six or seven years ago.

Verplanck was a man of superior attainments. He was known as one of the Bucktail bards. He died in 1829. The *American* was remarkable for its neatness, taste, elegance, and dignity, and its pretentions to high breeding and culture were patent to mankind. Its short paragraphs were always well-pointed and epigrammatic.

The *New York Albion*, an organ of English opinion, was established on the 22d of June, 1822. Its originator was Dr. John S. Bartlett. Daniel Fanshaw was the printer. It acquired an influential position, and was a useful paper to the British population of the United States. Peter Simple, Midshipman Easy, Japhet in Search of his Father, were first introduced to the American public through the columns of the *Albion*. This was at a time when these novels, republished by the Harpers and others, were considered too expensive for general circulation. After Dr. Bartlett had successfully managed the *Albion* for many years, he sold the establishment to William Young on the 6th of May, 1848. It then passed into the hands of W. H. Morrell, and was afterwards sold to Kinahan Cornwallis. It is now published by Piercy Wilson. Other English organs appeared in New York. One, the *Anglo-American*, was quite ably conducted by Dr. Pattison, but there was not room for two papers of the same order in the metropolis.

These organs seem necessary in the estimation of many statesmen. *El Noticioso de Ambos Mundos* in 1840, and *El Cronista* since then, have spoken for Spain. The French have had one in New York for many years—the *Courier des Etats Unis*. It has always been ably conducted. It was established in 1828. One of its editors, Frederick Gaillardet, was decorated with the *legion d'honneur* by Louis Philippe. *Galignani's Messenger* has been considered the English organ in Paris since 1814. *Le Nord*, published for years in Brussels—the "Printing-House Square" of the Continent—was the organ of Russia in Western Europe. Napoleon III. purchased the *Morning Chronicle*, of London, and during the last years of its life its editorials, written by H. D. Delille, were inspired by him. It is a noteworthy fact that he kept a scrap-book, in which were filed all the articles of the London *Times* relative to France, on the side of which he made his notes and comments. Many years ago Isaac C. Pray edited an American paper in the English metropolis. There is now published in London and Paris the *American Register*, which is an independent organ of the American people in Europe. It is edited by John J. Ryan, a very accomplished and experienced journalist. He has been connected with the English, French, and American Press, and was for many years on the staff of the *New York Herald*, where he showed both ability and skill of a high order. The *American Register* must be of great service to Americans and to the interests of the United States in Europe. Our country is very little understood on the other side of the Atlantic even now. It will be the mission of the *Register* to educate Europe in American politics, finance, commerce, and society.

Samuel Woodworth and others attempted a neat weekly paper in 1823, and named it the *New York Weekly Mirror*. Woodworth is well known to fame as the author of

> "The old oaken bucket, the iron bound bucket,
> The moss-covered bucket which hung in the well."

The *Mirror* afterwards became the property of George P. Morris and Nathaniel P. Willis. It seemed to have been the *rendezvous* of poets. Morris's lines of

> "Woodman, spare that tree!
> Touch not a single bough!"

are as well known as the "Old Oaken Bucket." Willis, Hoffman, Cooper, Sigourney, Fay, Nack, Halleck, Leggett, Whittier, Verplanck, Irving, Sands, Neal, and a dozen others, contributed to its columns. Willis's "Pencilings by the Way," which gave him so much notoriety on his first visit to Europe, also gave a good many subscribers to the *Mirror*. These "pencilings" excited a good deal of criticism when they first appeared. These poets afterwards published a daily paper called the *Evening Mirror*.

Morris and Willis's *Weekly Mirror* was chiefly sustained by the subscriptions of the fashionable and literary women of the nation. It was the organ of the "Upper Ten," a term originating with Willis. The *Mirror* has been succeeded by the *Home Journal*, now edited by Morris Phillips, a perfect Count d'Orsay in fashionable literature. This paper, established by Morris and Willis, and edited by them while they lived, is not unlike the *Morning Post* of London, although there is another paper, started in 1870, called *Our Society*, that disputes the palm with the *Home Journal* in the gossip of the *boudoir* and *salon*, not only in New York, but in all parts of the republic, and especially at the watering-places and sea-side. They are perfectly *au fait* in all fashionable parlance and movements.

When newspapers were subscription papers, pure and simple, with limited circulation, subscribers believed that they held a power over the editor in the potent order of "stop my paper!" This threat had had its effect in its day, but by the present system of publication editors are ignorant and independent of individual subscribers. Managers of theatres, merchants, actors, snobs, ship-owners, politicians, would resort to this order with the utmost complacency. Of this class of patrons the laurel wreath belongs to a French *savant*, and the interview with the indignant Gaul was described by General Morris, of the *Mirror*, in 1835, soon after the first railroad *furore* in the United States.

"We were sitting in our elbow-chair," said General M., ruminating on the decided advantages of virtue over vice, when a little withered Frenchman, with a cowhide as long as himself, and twice as heavy, rushed into our presence.

"Sair!" and he stopped to breathe.

"Well, sir?"

"*Monsieur!*" he stopped again to take breath.

"*Diable Monsieur!*" and he flourished his instrument over his head.

"Really, my friend," said we, smiling, for he was not an object to be frightened about, "when you have perfectly finished amusing yourself with that weapon, we should like to be the master of our own leisure."

"No, sair: I have come to horsewhip you wis dis cowhide!"

We took a pistol from a drawer, cocked it, and aimed it at his head.

"Pardon, sair," said the Frenchman; "I will first give you some little explanation, Monsieur, *if* you have write dis article?"

We looked it over, and acknowledged ourself the author. It was a few lines referring to the great improvements in railroads, and intimating that this mode of traveling would one day supersede every other.

"You have write dat in your papair?"

"Yes, sir."

"Well, den, sair, 'stop your dem papair.' I have live *quaranteneuf ans*. I have devote all my life to ride *de ballon!—c'est ma grande passion. Bien, Monsieur!* I shall look to find every one wis his littel balloon—to ride horseback in de air—to go round de world in one summair, and make me rich like Monsieur *Astair*, wis de big hotel. Well, Monsieur, now you put piece in your dem papair to say dat de *railroad*, Monsieur, de littel railroad, supercede—*voila 'supersed.'* Dat is what you say—supersede every thing else. Monsieur, begar, I have de honnair to inform you dat de railroad nevair supersede de balloon—nevair! and also, Monsieur, *ventre bleu!* 'stop your dem papair!'"

This ridiculous practice, so aptly illustrated in the indignation of this enthusiastic follower of Montgolfier, was effectively killed by the establishment of the Independent Press in 1835. Subscribers, like those to the London Press, are not now known. They buy the paper when they want it; they stop it when they please: the editor and proprietor are wholly oblivious of the fact. This is as it should be. No sensible reader of a newspaper could wish it otherwise.

It is not often that an editor lives to see the golden anniversary of the journal he ushered into existence. On the 3d of January, 1870, William E. Richmond published in the *Providence Journal* a brief sketch of the early career of that paper, which completed its fiftieth year on that day. Mr. Richmond was its first editor. It is curious enough in its historical statements, and interesting enough in its political data to insert entire:

SOME NOTES ON THE EARLY HISTORY OF THE JOURNAL.

To the Editor of the Journal:

Your desire to know the early history of the Providence *Journal*, now within a few days of its semi-centennial existence, is perfectly natural.

Under your control and management, that paper has obtained a scope and power of usefulness in this state and country, which can scarcely be overrated. I can not pretend, after the lapse of half a century, to remember all the preliminaries of its establishment. Between the conclusion of the war of 1812 and the commencement of the year 1820, an opinion arose and prevailed, with increasing strength among business men, that a new paper was required by the public interests. The business of the community had been greatly modified by the events and consequences of the war. Capital to a large amount had been withdrawn from commerce, and invested in manufactures. The publishers and managers of the newspapers then in circulation had taken up the erroneous idea that the success of manufactures would be injurious to commerce, and destructive to navigation.

It resulted, therefore, that these new enterprises were viewed with jealousy, distrust, and aversion by a portion of the business community, and received no countenance or support from the current newspapers. Nor should it be forgotten that those papers, in their competition for patronage, had gradually fallen under the control of individuals. But the men who had thus embarked their property and their destiny in a new undertaking were not to be disheartened by trifles.

In the course of the year 1819, the project of a new paper devoted to the interests of productive industry was matured, and its *personnel* engaged, the first number to appear the following January. You will naturally desire to know the names of the principal founders of this new institution. First and foremost were Samuel and John Slater, who having, in their native country, learned the cotton-spinning business from Arkwright, came here and made their first establishments, at Pawtucket and Slatersville ; David Wilkinson, one of the greatest mechanics the world has ever produced ; Timothy Greene and Sons—the oldest son Samuel, who died a short time since, was very industrious in the dissemination of the paper and always indefatigable in its support ; Benjamin Aborn and George Jackson, his partner, who were not only manufacturers, but deeply engaged in commerce ; Amasa and William H. Mason, then withdrawing from foreign commerce, to invest their capital in manufactures in Connecticut ; the Coventry Manufacturing Company, consisting of James Burrill, William Anthony, Samuel Arnold, William Valentine, Richard Anthony, Joseph Harris, Richard Jackson, and Nathan W. Jackson; William Sprague, the elder, a stalwart farmer, bold and strong-minded, who conceived the idea of creating a market for the products of his farm by building and stocking a cotton-mill ; who was his own factotum, and on his return from the town at night, could detail to his clerk in their turn, and each with all essential particulars, one hundred business transactions ; his two sons, Amasa, meditative and thoughtful, and always revolving great enterprises in his mind, and William, afterwards governor of the state and senator of the United States, who were then superintendents in the mill ; James, Christopher, and William Rhodes, who were also very industrious and efficient in the establishment of "The Rhode Island Society for the Encouragement of Domestic Industry." These and many others, supported by the sympathy of thousands of the residents on our many water-courses, were the founders of the *Manufacturers' and Farmers' Journal*, which was started as a semi-weekly paper.

It was well understood in the early years of the *Journal* that the paper was to have no concern in party politics. This rule was so strictly observed, that during the excitement occasioned by the Missouri Compromise, that subject was not mentioned in the paper, excepting in the report of Congressional proceedings, although many articles condemnatory of the compromise were furnished by the editor for the *American*, edited by Prof. William G. Goddard. It was afterwards deemed no infraction of this rule to advocate the formation of a written constitution of the state.

In and about the year 1820, although there were as many newspapers as the community required, there was no systematic and well-managed journalism. A printer and publisher, for the purpose of extending his business, put forth proposals and issued a subscription for a new paper. If the number of subscribers were, in his opinion, sufficient to pay the expense, he engaged a person to edit and supervise the paper. At that time literary labor of this description was so meanly compensated, that no lawyer, physician, or schoolmaster would undertake the business for merely the monetary remuneration. In the case of the first editor of the *Journal*, there was no demand or stipulation for pay. That person saw the necessity of a sacrifice by some one for the advancement of great public interests, and he consented to a temporary supervision of the *Journal*. A reference to the early files of that paper, now in the editorial library, will enable you to estimate the amount of labor bestowed. It was almost exclusively in the night season that the *Journal* was edited, as a relaxation from the daily labors of another profession ; and it was understood from the beginning, that so soon as the *Journal* could be considered as securely established, another editor should be procured. At the end of the first year the name of the editor was omitted from the imprint in consequence of the increase of professional business, but he continued for several years thereafter an informal oversight of, and contribution to its columns, for which, and for all previous labors, he received the sum of five hundred dollars.

Simultaneously with the establishment of the *Journal*, a general discussion of what was then called *the Tariff Question* broke out along the sea-board of the country, from the Portland *Argus* southerly to the Richmond *Enquirer*. Judge Story, Mr. Lowell, of Boston, Rev. Lyman Beecher, Matthew Cary, William Duane, Hezekiah Niles, the veteran editor of the Richmond *Enquirer*, occasionally Gales and Seaton, of the *National Intelligencer*, Henry Wheaton, and others of great name and consideration in the country, laid themselves out freely in this contest. At the beginning of the discussion, a large majority of the Democratic party, then predominant in the country and in nearly every state, were in favor of protection to domestic industry, in consequence of their political hostility to Great Britain, while as large a majority of the Federal party, then in the last years of its existence, were in favor of unrestricted commerce. The effects of the discussion soon became apparent in the rapid change among individuals of opinion and position. The slave power had already obtained pre-eminence and dictatorship over the Democratic party, and virtually ruled and directed all the measures of the government. The normal instincts of that party soon led it to perceive the danger to itself of the establishment in the country of an organized system of free and well-paid labor; and although its principal leader, Mr. Calhoun, had already, in 1816, concurred with Mr. Burrill, of this state, and Mr. Clay, of Kentucky, in the establishment of a square-yard duty on cotton cloth, in apprehension of the rivalship with our Southern staple, of India cotton, that gentleman now reversed his policy, *toto cœlo*, and declared his utter hostility to every form of legislative protection. He was followed implicitly by the whole of the ruling southern population. Nor less signal was the change of opinion and position on the other hand. At the opening of the discussion, Boston and its dependent cities were nearly unanimous in opposition to a protective tariff. Webster, Choate, Story, Otis, indeed all their great orators, all their capitalists, all their merchants, great and small, all their traders, all their bankers, and all their money-changers of every description, were frantic in their opposition. Meetings were held, committees appointed, reports received, speeches made by their great orators, and remonstrances adopted and forwarded to Congress. In 1823-4, another demonstration in opposition to protection was made in the same quarter, with greatly diminished intensity; but in 1827-8, *mirabile dictu!* all the aforesaid orators, merchants, capitalists, traders, bankers, and money-changers came out with equal unanimity and ardor in favor of the tariff of 1828. I refer you again to the contemporaneous files of the *Journal* for the part which that paper maintained in these discussions.

It is not necessary for me, at this time, to portray in detail the wonderful impetus which the tariff of 1828 gave to the industry of the country. As a general thing, it advanced the textile fabrics in number and finish, it laid the foundation of the cotton-printing, and it greatly extended the domestic market for raw cotton. It finally brought into existence new mill manufactures and handicraft trades, numerous and useful, and up to that time unknown in the country. These new undertakings, sympathizing with the ordinary business of the country, produced new subdivisions of labor, a call for new laborers and advanced compensation for every description of labor. With increased compensation, the laborer felt a new ability to purchase and enjoy the comforts and luxuries of life. Our commerce soon began to feel the effects of increasing consumption, the importation of foreign comforts and luxuries, and its new prosperity at once exploded the solemn croakings of the anti-tariff party.

Immediately after the adjournment of the session of 1827-28, the anti-tariff parties, north and south, dispatched two agents to England to open correspondence with the ministry and leading mercantile firms of that country, for the purpose of devising measures by which the object of the tariff of 1828 might be defeated. If we may believe the newspaper statements, these men were received with welcome in ministerial and mercantile circles. The idea of a secret league between the British government and the Southern malcontents, and the terms on which it could be established, was deliberately considered.

On the part of the malcontents, it was demanded that the Southern States, in case of separation from the Union, should be received into union with Great

Britain, and should be allowed a certain number of peerages and a certain number of seats in the English House of Commons. To this was to be added the full protection of slavery, as then established by law, in the Southern States. The response of the ministry to these propositions was, that the required seats in the two houses of Parliament might be granted, but that no ministry in Great Britain could maintain a stipulation for the protection of American slavery, and it was finally concluded that, in place of formal stipulations, a perpetual although informal friendship should exist between the parties, to be manifested by either as opportunity might allow. The hurried acknowledgment of Southern rebels as belligerents in 1861, and the subsequent destruction of the American mercantile navy, on the high seas, by pirates equipped and sent forth by permission of the English government, *Perfidia plusquam Punica*, was only a public expression of the policy that in the intervening years had actuated that government.

And all these years, from 1820 to 1870, the *Journal* has been steadfast to the principles of its establishment. Through thick and thin, through faint-heartedness and compromise, through National Republicanism and Whigism, through Polk, Fillmore, Pierce, and Buchanan, it has been unwavering and effective in its support of legislative protection for home industry. Need I say any thing in reply to the oft exploded sophistry which is now urged upon us as if it had never before been urged? The light of history dissipates that sophistry through all the ages. Is there a nation on earth that is richer by exchanging its raw material for the manufactured articles of another nation?

Our ancestors in England, nine centuries ago, consigned their fleeces of wool to the merchants of the Low Countries for the purchase of manufactured goods of all descriptions. In process of time, the returns of these transactions became proverbial as "Flemish accounts," and Parliament interfered, prohibiting the exportation of wool. They not only did this, but they enacted a law that every person deceased should be buried in wool. This course of legislation in regard to raw materials and manufactured articles became general, and was persistently continued to the present day. It has enriched England, notwithstanding her immense waste of productive power in forests and uncultivated farms and pleasure-grounds. There is no other nation of thirty millions so rich as she. Every nation that follows the same policy is rich, every nation which neglects that policy is poor. The idea of free trade is utopian. How can any movement or transaction be free which pays a tax? Where is the government which demands no tax?

The unvarying support, at times very able and effective, given by the *Journal* to the principles on which it was established fifty years ago, have deservedly attracted to it the confidence and support of the business community, while in science, literature, and general information, the labors of an efficient staff, of varied and extensive attainments, are duly appreciated by the cultivated classes.

In the adaptation of the different ingredients composing a newspaper consists the art of a journalist, and his power to please the community. Scholarship alone can not do it—it must add to scholastic attainments the gradual acquisitions of time and experience, and when these components are symmetrically and gracefully united, the art of journalism is attained. With sincere good wishes for your continued prosperity, and that of the *journal* you so ably conduct,

I am yours truly, WILLIAM E. RICHMOND.

The *Journal*, on its semi-centennial, published a *fac-simile* "of the first page of the first issue" of that paper. It was filled with its Prospectus under the head of "Proposals," and a leading article of several columns in length entitled "Introductory Observations." It was then called the *Manufacturers' and Farmers' Journal and Providence and Pawtucket Advertiser.* Its device was a spread eagle standing on an anchor, holding a ribbon in its beak, on which was inscribed the motto, "Encourage National Industry." On one side were agricultural implements; on the other, parts of a ship. Its publishers were Miller & Hutchens.

Since that period the paper has gone through the usual changes and vicissitudes of an American journal. In the early history of newspapers in this country, the changes in names, publishers, and editors were frequent. In some establishments the remains of a dozen papers may be found. The *Journal*, in a sketch of its own progress, gives these details:

On the 1st of July, 1840, Henry B. Anthony was admitted a partner, and the paper was published under the name of Knowles, Vose, & Anthony, till the death of Mr. Vose in 1848, when it was continued by the surviving partners, under the name of Knowles & Anthony; and on the 1st of January, 1863, on the admission of Geo. W. Danielson as a partner, the name was changed to Knowles, Anthony & Danielson, by whom it has, since that time, been published. The editors of the *Journal* have been William E. Richmond, Thomas Rivers, Benjamin F. Hallett, Lewis Gaylord Clarke, George Paine, John B. Snow, Thomas H. Webb, Henry B. Anthony, James B. Angell, George W. Danielson. Of the past editors, Mr. Richmond, Mr. Clarke, and Mr. Angell survive. In 1824, the *Independent Inquirer*, a weekly paper, which had been started the year before, was transferred to the *Journal*, and its name changed to the *Rhode Island Country Journal*, under which it is still published. On the 1st of July, 1829, the *Daily Journal* was started. On the 26th of January, 1863, the *Evening Bulletin* was started.

The mechanical history of the *Journal* illustrates the progress of the art of printing. It was first printed on the old-fashioned handpress, which was thought to do rapid work at 240 impressions an hour. It would require three days, working all the time, night and day, for that press to work off its present daily editions. The first improvement was a machine roller in place of balls for inking the type, and this, in 1836, was succeeded by an Adams press of primitive construction, which performed the marvelous work of 800 impressions an hour, and, it was thought, carried the art of printing to its ultimate capability. In 1845 the old Adams press gave way to a new one of improved construction under the same patent. This served for eleven years, when a steam-engine and a cylinder press of Hoe's patent were introduced, and in 1862 a second press of the same construction, but of double capacity, was added.

Of all the great agencies of civilization, in none has the advance been more wonderful than in journalism. Long after the *Journal* was established, the New York and Boston papers did not together circulate a hundred copies in Providence. For external news the mails were depended upon, and little attention was paid to local information. Day after day the Providence papers came out without an item of news that had not been read the day before by the few who took the New York papers. The *Journal* was among the earliest papers that exhibited spirit and enterprise in the collection of news. Mr. Jackson, more than thirty years ago, organized expresses for the collection of election returns, and Samuel A. Coy, of Westerly, who first took charge of them for Washington and Kent counties, still appears in the *Journal* office regularly, on the night of an election, with the papers distributed among his various pockets, never losing one, but never knowing at first in which pocket he has put them, and bearing his seventy-nine years as though he were a boy. Many times the *Journal* run expresses from Boston to obtain election news, and Richard Haughton, of the Boston *Atlas*, the most enterprising newspaper man of his day in New England, always supplied it with the results of his own labor and expenditure. The *Journal* relates an instance of the enterprise of Haughton :

> At an important election he expressed the State of Virginia, to the wonder of the whole country, and especially to that of the sleepy denizens of the "Old Dominion," chartering a steam-boat, the John W. Richmond, from New York to Providence, where he gave the news to the *Journal*, and then to Boston by a special train.

This was not an election in Virginia, but that of 1840 in Pennsylvania, when it appeared that the hopes of the Whig Party depended on the result in that state. The *Journal* horse expresses repeatedly made the distance from Boston inside of four hours with election news, and with foreign news by the Cunarders, which was always expressed when the ship arrived after the closing of Saturday's mail, and in time for Monday's paper.

In 1841 the *Journal* organized a system of early news by which it gained great credit. The only mail from New York arrived in the early morning by way of Stonington. The news, including a letter from Washington, was set up in New York, and the type sent in boxes, reaching the *Journal* in time to be put upon the press for the morning edition, thus giving its readers the advantage of full twenty-four hours for every thing which came from New York, and anticipating the New York papers themselves. When the day line between Boston and New York was first established by way of the Long Island and Norwich and Worcester railroads, the *Journal* regularly expressed the New York morning papers from Danielsonville, and at first people would visit the office to see the marvel of a New York paper in Providence the day that it was printed. These recitals show the expedients which were resorted to, at that not very remote period, to obtain the intelligence of what was going on in the world. In 1848, in time for the presidential election, Providence was placed in telegraphic communication, and although, for a considerable time, the new arrangements were of a very imperfect character, it was, from the beginning, such an improvement over the existing modes that these fell rapidly into disuse, and now, instead of giving the news from New York twenty-four hours old, every daily paper can print the proceedings of the British Parliament the morning after the adjournment.

One of the editors of the *Journal*, Henry B. Anthony, has been Governor of the state, and is now in the United States Senate. He is President *pro tem.* of that body in the absence of Vice-President Colfax.

The *Daily National Gazette* was established in Philadelphia in 1820, taking the name of Freneau's well-known paper, which existed in that city in the latter part of last century. It was published by Robert Walsh and William Fry. This journal assumed a high tone in literature and politics, and was dignified, and rather pretentious in its articles on national and other matters. Mr. Walsh, we believe, made some reputation as one of the earliest Washington and Paris correspondents of the American Press. Walsh, we believe, when in Europe, prior to the establishment of the *Gazette*, published an article in the *Edinburg Review* on the "True Causes of the Military Power of France," and also a pamphlet on the "Genius and Dispositions of the French Government." These productions appeared in 1809 and 1812, and produced a great sensation at the time. They were powerful expositions in the interest of the Federal party, and were so popular with the enemies of France that they were translated in several languages, and circulated throughout the world. The *National Gazette* ceased to exist on the 1st of January, 1842.

There were no daily papers west of Albany, in the State of New York, till 1826. The Rochester *Daily Advertiser* was established in that year. Its first number was issued on the 25th of October. Some of the early reminiscences of journalism in that section of the nation were related by the Hon. H. C. Frisbee, in a speech in 1871, at a banquet given by the present proprietor of the *Fredonia Censor*. Mr. F. said:

After satisfying himself that he could obtain assistance, he hired a broken-down establishment for sale at Buffalo, brought it to Fredonia, and in 1821 issued *The New York Censor*. There was at that time a paper at Erie and one at Pittsburg — none other west of Fredonia. *The Gazette* died soon afterward. He commenced with fifty subscribers and no advertisements, continued seventeen years, and sold to E. & J. Winchester. About four years thereafter Mr. M'Kinstry purchased the office, and has since controlled it. Mr. K., in due time, took unto himself a fair maiden of the village for his wife, and has raised up a Jr. M'Kinstry, who in turn has secured a permanent attachment, and followed up the programme with still another and revised edition. He liked this partnership of father and son in any business. It signified good order and permanency. In 1821 there were no stage-roads west of Buffalo. To get beyond that point you must go by water, and pay heavy tolls at every point, or travel on horseback or on foot. In fact, a Buffalonian was known from home by the peculiar manner in which he carried his hands, as if taking toll — could always tell him. Nothing ever got by without paying, and that was why even the cholera stopped in Buffalo, and failed to reach Fredonia—we wouldn't pay any toll. The mails from Buffalo to Erie were then carried on horseback once a week, and by a woman at that. In 1823 a tri-weekly stage was opened—a great triumph of the age.

There was a paper called the *Telegraph* issued in New York in 1826, and edited by John M. Mumford. Its publication was stopped shortly after, and its editor went to Europe. On his return he started the *Standard*, which for a time was the organ of the Jackson Democracy. On one occasion, to give the *Standard* a little advantage over its opponents, General Jackson intrusted an advance copy of one of his annual messages to its editor. Its contents were prematurely divulged. Subsequently this important state paper was sent to the postmasters or collectors of the port for distribution to all the papers. In 1830, the *New York Herald*, a paper that had been started nine months previously by Alanson Nash, who, in personal appearance, was Webster's Dromio, was sold to Mumford and united with the *Standard*.

The celebrated Fanny Wright, who flourished as a lecturer before the present race of Woman's Rights advocates were born, entered the field of journalism in 1829. With George H. Purser and others she established the *Sentinel* in New York, and then the *Man*, to inculcate their peculiar religious, political, and social doctrines. It has been claimed that the *Man* was the first penny paper issued in this country, but this claim is not well founded.

The *Louisville Journal*, another paper of note, was established in 1831, with George D. Prentice, the poet, as editor. In 1828 he edited the *New England Weekly Review*. The *Journal* was remarkable for its short editorial squibs, full of point and wit. They hit right and left. They were sharp and smart. There were only a few journalists capable of throwing off these stinging paragraphs at sight. It not only required "mother wit," but a thorough knowledge of men and politics. Major Noah, James Gordon Bennett, Colonel Charles G. Greene, Thurlow Weed, and George D. Prentice were adepts at this sort of journalism. Two lines would often accomplish more than a column of argument. They were the flash of lightning to the long roll of thunder. In the early days of the London Press, Coleridge, Lamb, Swift, and Johnson would indulge in these small shots, which always left a laugh and a sting. Coleridge was remarkably successful in them. The English Press, like most of the party papers of this country, afterwards ran into long editorial articles: words without wit. The *London Times* has published daily, for years, three or four ponderous articles of a column each in length, many of them splendidly written, and are masterly essays. Such a thing as a short paragraph is rarely, if ever, seen in that paper. All the snap of English politics is to be found in

Punch and *Fun* only. The *Louisville Journal, Boston Post, New York Evening Star*, and *New York Herald* revived the short paragraphs, and these papers would sparkle with them. These epigrammatic editorials, "shooting folly as it flies," are always telling and effective.

When the *Morning Star* and the *Telegraph* were established in London a few years ago as the Cheap Press of that metropolis, they neglected to reintroduce the short paragraphs. Richard Cobden was much interested in these papers. When he was in the United States a short time before his death, he spoke of these new journals on a visit to the *Herald* establishment in New York. Their circulation had then run up to above that of the *Times*, but their influence and advertisements were not equal to their circulation. "What we want in London," said Mr. Cobden, "are a few smart paragraphists. They are the most effective editorials. Our cheap papers must adopt them."

This specimen of a news paragraph was written by Prentice and published in the *Journal* in July, 1835. It is an account, *in nuce*, of an affray between several editors of Lexington, Kentucky:

> Mr. Trotter, without provocation, attempted to shoot Mr. Clark in the street; the parties exchanged shots twice without effect; Mr. O'Hara, a friend of Mr. Trotter, made an attack in the mean time upon Mr. Bryant, the associate of Mr. Clark; Mr. Bryant gave Mr. O'Hara an effectual cudgeling, and then laid his cane over the head and shoulders of Mr. Trotter till the latter cried for quarters, and there the matter ended, Mr. Clark retiring to reload his pistols, Mr. Bryant to procure a new cane, and Messrs. Trotter and O'Hara to get their heads mended.

The *Journal* was noted for its satire and abuse. No political opponent was spared by Prentice. The opposition editors in Louisville were continually exchanging shots either with the pen or pistol—the former leading to the latter. There are numerous instances of these personal rencounters on record. William E. Hughes, of the *Democrat*, once sent his card to the editor of the *Journal*. "Tell Mr. Hughes," said Mr. Prentice, "that I will be down as soon as I load my pistols." In 1858, Reuben Durrett, editor of the *Courier*, published a paragraph for several days, strongly insinuating that the conductor of the *Journal* had fallen from a gang-plank under peculiar circumstances. Mr. Prentice stated in his paper that if the paragraph again appeared he would hold the editor of the *Courier* personally responsible. The paragraph appeared. Mr. Prentice called upon Mr. Durrett. They exchanged two shots, and each editor had to be placed under the care of surgeons.

The *Journal* was a loyal sheet during the Rebellion. Charles G. Shanks, at one time connected with that paper, thus relates an incident connected with the *Journal* and the Rebellion:

> When the news of the Bull Run fight reached Louisville, the intensest excitement prevailed, and the rebel population paraded the streets swearing vengeance

against all loyal men who came in contact with them. The *Journal* office had long been floating a United States flag from a staff on the roof, but the staff being too short for the flag, a carpenter had been sent for early in the day to put up a longer one. He arrived at the time quite a threatening demonstration was being made in front. The *Courier* office, which was on the opposite side of the same street, was intensely rebel, and it was bruited about that a Confederate flag would be hoisted upon it during the day. The crowd between the two offices was clamorous for the raising of one flag and the lowering of the other. At this juncture, Mr. Prentice was informed by an excited employé from the counting-room that somebody was on the roof pulling down the flag. The old man's eyes flashed fire.

"Then, by G—," said he, "go up there and throw the scoundrel down among the mob."

Up rushed the willing employé. The flag was already half-masted, and the carpenter, intent mainly on earning his wages, though not insensible to the cries of the admiring crowd beneath, was busily engaged in untying it from the halyards. To his infinite disgust, however, before his work was completed, he found himself hurled back by a strong hand, which in the next breath flirted the flag again to the peak and tied the halyards in an insoluble knot to the staff. The honest carpenter was then lustily kicked down the skylight, and thrust the rest of the way down two pair of stairs to the street door, where he received an energetic parting salute, and found himself landed among his late admirers, without having a single chance to receive or tender an explanation. This bold stroke touched the generous impulses of the mob, if they had any, and all demonstrations against the *Journal* and its flag ceased. The crowd, in fact, turned its ridicule on the unoffending carpenter, who with difficulty made his way to his shop with unbroken bones.

The Southern subscribers of the *Journal* withdrew in large numbers when they saw the course of the paper on the question of coercion. He did not spare them, as the following specimen shows:

TO THE EDITOR.

UNIV. VIRGINIA, May 17, 1861.

PRENTICE:

Stop my paper; I can't afford to read abbolition journals these times: the atmosphere of old Virginia will not admit of such filthy sheets as yours has grown to be. Yours, etc., GEORGE LAKE.

LOUISVILLE, May 24, 1861.

LAKE:

I think it a great pity that a young man should go to a university to graduate a traitor and a blackguard—and so ignorant as to spell abolition with two *b*'s.

G. D. P.

The *Journal*, under the fostering influence of its old editor, has been the means of developing a good deal of the fresh poetic genius of the West, many of the sweetest productions of that fertile region first appearing in the columns of that paper.

It was the custom of Prentice to rise early in the morning and begin at once the labors of the day. He would first overhaul the exchanges, looking over every paper, tearing out any suggestive article or witticism, rarely using the scissors for this purpose. He would be prepared by ten o'clock for his amanuensis. Then he would throw off his editorials and sparks of wit for the next morning's journal.

Mr. Prentice died in 1870, aged 67 years. He had been an invalid during the later years of his life.

The *Courier* and *Journal* were united in 1868, and now published under that double name. It is edited by Henry Watterson, and its old reputation for wit and humor "hangs round it still." One of the correspondents of the *Cincinnati Commercial* in 1871 interviewed the new editor, and developed the following information:

Going up two flights of stairs, I knocked at the door of Mr. Henry Watterson's room, and was told to come in. Mr. Watterson is the head and front of the *Courier-Journal*. He is part owner, managing editor, editor-in-chief, and all that sort of thing. In short, he is the *Courier-Journal*. He was bent over a voluminous pile of manuscript, working like a Trojan, for he lives and flourishes by work. I came near saying that he grows fat by work, but this would not be strictly true, as he is lean and slender. In stature he is small, not weighing, I should think, over a hundred and twenty-five pounds. He has the misfortune to be entirely blind in one eye, and partially so in the other. To see the work that he gets through with in a day, half blind as he is, is enough to make most men with good eyes ashamed.

I had an interesting conversation with Mr. Watterson about the newspaper business, past and present, in Louisville. "I claim to have done some very hard and ungrateful work," said he, "since I came to Louisville. When I came here I found the press of the city as thoroughly infected with the prevailing malady of Southern journalism as it well could be. It either puffed every body and every thing beyond reason, or it blackguarded every body and every thing. Each of the offices was stocked with the riff-raffs of dead-beats and drunkards."

"They were not all dead-beats and drunkards, were they, Mr. Watterson?"

"Oh no. Of course there were exceptions. I am speaking of them in the main. It was the time-honored habit of most of them to get drunk every day. There was one on the press then who is on the press now who was sober all the year round."

"Who is that?"

"Walter Haldeman. He is one of the best men in the newspaper business any where. He deserves a great deal from the commerce of Louisville, and much more from the Democratic party than he has ever got."

"What sort of a set of journalists have you in Louisville now?" I inquired. "I don't mean the *Courier-Journal* particularly, but all the papers."

"We have got a good set—an excellent set. There is not a drunkard on the press of Louisville, so far as I know. On our paper we have got a lot of young fellows, boys picked up at random, and out of the composing-room. They are all sober, and they, together with those at work on other papers in the city, would compare with the employés of any bank institution or members of any learned profession in the country. They don't wear swallow-tailed coats and spend their time and money in drinking saloons and gambling dens."

John Greenleaf Whittier, the poet, it is said, was the editor of a Boston paper in 1829, and that it had a small circulation. It is also said that he was associated with George D. Prentice and Gideon Welles in the editorial management of the *New England Review* in 1830. In an interview, one or two years ago, with a correspondent of the *Commercial*, he thus corrects one or two of these *on dits*:

Mr. Whittier said many things pleasant and interesting for me to recall, but I do not know that I should be pardonable in making his friendly private talk public. One or two things I may be allowed to repeat, in my own language, however. I spoke to him of a paragraph I had seen in the newspapers some time ago, stating that he intended to write his recollections of my old friend, Mr. George D. Prentice, for a proposed volume of his poems. Mr. Whittier said he had himself seen such a paragraph, but that it was a mistake; he had never really known Mr. Prentice, and had never seen him. He then related to me, with a good deal of genial humor, the history of his succession to Mr. Prentice long ago as editor of the *New England Review*, at Hartford. As this may be said to have been the beginning of Mr. Whittier's public literary life, his account was very interesting to me. He said that he was spending a year at school in the academy at Haverhill, and while there happened to see a copy of the *New England Review*, edited by Mr. Prentice, which had struck him with its brightness and sprightliness as distinguished from the ordinary newspapers of the time, and, feeling interested in it, he had ventured to send its editor two or three of his "compositions," as he called them, which, to his great astonishment, had been published with commendatory remarks. They had induced him to send other contributions, and so he continued to do until his year at the Haverhill Academy had come to an end, when he returned to his father's farm. Here one day, a short time afterward, while he was at work in the field, hoeing, perhaps, a letter was brought him from the publishers of the Hartford paper, saying that they had been requested by Mr. Prentice to invite him to become editor of the paper during Mr. Prentice's absence in Kentucky, whither he had gone to write a campaign life of Henry Clay. "I could not have been more utterly astonished," said Mr. Whittier, "if I had been told that I was appointed prime minister to the Great Khan of Tartary." Then he described the struggle between his boyish ambition and his sense of experience and unfitness. He felt entirely unprepared—knew nothing about public affairs, but could not bring himself to think the opportunity was one to be put by, and so his ambition got the better of his timidity, and, having accepted the call, he finally set off for Hartford to take possession. This was then a long journey, he said; even to go to Boston was not a slight undertaking. Mr. Whittier then described, pleasantly, his interview with his publishers, "not letting on," he said, how little he knew of editorial duties and political affairs, but they did not "find him out," and so he continued for two years as editor of the *Review*. His greatest trial, he told me, was when the leading party men came to see him and discuss the political course of the paper. Then he found his policy was to maintain a judicious silence, allowing them to do all the talking, which was quite successful, and left him in their good graces at the end of each interview. What was especially charming to me in the poet's account of this little far-gone experience was the pleasant way in which he seemed to realize his boyish feeling again in its recital. Mr. Whittier spoke kindly of Mr. Prentice, always having regarded him, he said, as a man of good and generous impulses, and, during the recent war of the Rebellion, a true Union man, but, perhaps, unfortunately placed.

Not remaining long in any one place, we find Whittier a member of the State Legislature representing his own town. After this, or in 1836, he is chosen Secretary of the American Anti-Slavery Society, and links his fate to that cause till the emancipation of slaves in the United States. About 1837 he was editor of the *Freeman*, an abolition paper published in Philadelphia. Again changing his location, he settles in Amesbury, Massachusetts, in 1840, and that village has been his residence from that year. In nearly all this time he has been engaged in throwing off his poetic sketches for the admiration of the world—"Mogg Megore," "The Bridal of Pennacook," "New Wife and the Old," "Mary Garvin," "and Maud Muller."

"For all sad words of tongue or pen,
The saddest are these: 'It might have been!'"

Still having faith in the Newspaper Press, on which he commenced his career, many of these attractive little poetic sketches found their way to the public eye and heart through the *National Era* of Washington, which printed so much to live, and yet could not itself survive the general fate of newspapers. Whittier's effusions now find vent in the *Atlantic Monthly*, and other publications of the day.

Whittier still occasionally leaves the field of poetry to dabble in politics. It was not long since that he wrote a long article for the *Amesbury Villager*, urging upon Grant the selection of Charles Sumner for the State Department. Most of our poets have been, or are, editors and reporters. Percival, Bryant, Poe, Prentiss, Wallis, Whittier, English, Gaylord Clark, Lewis Gaylord Clark, Freneau, Drake, Fitz Green Halleck, Leggett, Willis, Arnold, Pike, Park Benjamin, Dawes, Halpine, have all been connected with the Newspaper Press. Nearly every one of these whose names we have mentioned have been political editors, engaged, during their lives, in mixing in equal proportions the muse of Parnassus with the mud of politics.

The Charleston (S. C.) *City Gazette* was a paper of some note in its day. It was prominent in the early part of this century. E. S. Thomas owned and edited it for a time. Then Major M. M. Noah had the management of its columns. This was in 1810. After Noah it was conducted by William Gilmore Simms, the Southern poet, and author of Guy Rivers and other reputable work in literature. It was the first journal in South Carolina that opposed the principle of nullification.

The *Old Colony Memorial* celebrated its fiftieth anniversary on the 2d of May, 1872. Its present proprietor, George F. Andrews, gave a banquet in honor of the event. On the 10th of December, 1822, seven months after the commencement of its publication, John Adams thus alluded to the paper in a letter to Elkanah Watson:

I hope you received the *Old Colony Memorial*, a newspaper instituted at Plymouth, and edited by William Thomas, Esquire—a paper which deserves to be read and encouraged by all America.

Among other writers for the *Memorial* was Daniel Webster. Adams no doubt was a contributor.

CHAPTER XXI.
SPECIAL OR CLASS JOURNALISM.

THE AGRICULTURAL PRESS.—THE FIRST ORGAN OF THE FARMERS.—NUMBER OF AGRICULTURAL NEWSPAPERS.—THE COMMERCIAL AND FINANCIAL PRESS.—THE COMMERCIAL BULLETIN.—ITS CHARACTER AND VALUE.—THE SUNDAY PRESS.—WHAT IS IT?—THE SPORTING PRESS.—WHAT IT HAS DONE FOR SPORT AND STOCK, THE TURF AND THE FIELD.—THE TELEGRAPH ORGANS.—OUR SOCIETY, ETC.

SPECIAL journalism is so rapidly increasing in the United States that it deserves special notice. Newspapers of this character give the freshest and fullest information on the particular interest they represent, and are therefore newspapers. They are the religious, the medical, the scientific, the agricultural, the sporting, the financial, the railroad, the commercial, the shipping, the telegraph, the mining, the art, the musical, the yachting, the Sunday, the army, and the navy press. What a field of operations!

Special or class journalism originated in England. Such papers are common there. They are published, too, in France. They are of recent date in this country, but they are successful, and prosperous, and increasing. Some of them are splendid specimens of typography. We are inclined to think that this sort of journalism originated in the needs of the agricultural interests, and afterwards in the commercial and financial circulars that were years ago issued by merchants, and then expanded into *Bicknell's Bank-note Reporter* and *Sylvester's Prices Current*. The first of these trade circulars appeared half a century ago, and since then *Commercial Lists* have been issued weekly and semi-weekly every where. The *Banker's Circular*, printed in London in 1836-7-8, and longer, was devoted to financial intelligence, and became an oracle in money centres. Newspapers in the United States, in that period of commercial distraction, extensively copied the leading articles of the *Circular*, signed H. B., and his views were deemed of value by the operators and bankers of Wall Street.

Out of the old *Prices Current* and *Bankers' Circulars* have sprung innumerable sheets as the special organs of special classes. We now have the *Commercial Bulletin*, the *Dry Goods Reporter*, the *Tobacco Leaf*, the *Wool Circular*, the *Cotton Buyer*, the *Architectural Review and Builders' Journal*, the *Scalpel*, the *Art Review*, the *Scientific American*, the *Phrenological Journal*, the *Hide and Leather Reporter*, the *Stockholder*, the *Mining Journal*, the *Nautical Gazette*, the *Army and Navy Journal*, the *Musical Review*, and others, handsomely printed sheets, and conducted with ability.

The vast railroad interests have the *Railroad Reporter*, and the extensive telegraph enterprises the *Telegrapher, a Journal of Electrical Progress*, and the *Journal of the Telegraph*. The first is ably edited by J. N. Ashley, an old journalist and an experienced operator, and F. L. Pope, a skillful operator and telegraph engineer. It is the independent promoter of all telegraph inventions, lines, improvements, and operators. The second was for some time admirably conducted by J. D. Reid, long identified with the telegraph interests, and is the acknowledged organ of the Western Union Company. These are the only publications devoted to telegraphy in the country.

Our Society, previously mentioned, printed on tinted paper in New York, is filled exclusively with announcements of parties, balls, engagements, Germans, marriages, receptions, *bals masques*, and has a circulation of fourteen or fifteen thousand. It is the *Court Journal* of the American metropolis. This new idea in journalism originated in New York in 1863 and '4, in a neat little paper called the *Playbill*, an *entr' acte* luxury, and sold every evening at the several theatres in that city. It was then abandoned as too personal. The details of these fashionable movements, not so full as in *Our Society*, are now a conspicuous feature of modern journalism in the United States.

THE AGRICULTURAL PRESS.

Two or three years after the appearance of the first religious newspaper, the pioneer agricultural publication was issued in Baltimore. On the 2d of April, 1818, the *American Farmer* was established by John S. Skinner, so well known in connection with the farm and the turf and their charming surroundings. After thirty-five years of devoted service to the science of agriculture he retired, and in 1851 he died full of honors, and with his name inscribed on every farm and in every stable.

Solomon Southwick, so long the autocrat of the political press in Albany, established the *Plough-Boy* in that city in 1821, and published it for a few years. Some have ascribed the origin of this useful branch of newspaper literature to Mr. Southwick, while others, without reference to the claims of Skinner, have given the credit to Thomas Green Fessenden, who, with T. W. Shepard, established the *New England Farmer* in August, 1822. The only evidence of Fessenden's priority in geoponical literature is in the fact that, after he graduated at Dartmouth College, he wrote for the well known *Farm-*

ers' *Weekly Museum*, published at Walpole, N. H., in 1796. That paper, however, was not devoted to agriculture. It received its name from the farming region where it was published. It was a literary paper, with political tendencies, and was full of wit and humor. It was a famous paper in its day. Fessenden was the "Simon Spunkey" of the concern, Joseph Dennie the "Lay Preacher," and Royal Tyler the "Colon and Spondee." But in 1803 the publishers of the *Museum*, in an appeal to the public for future support, stated that "the interest of the farmer shall claim our notice in the publication of useful agricultural hints, inventions, and improvements." It is probable from these three facts, 1st, that Fessenden wrote for the *Museum;* 2d, that that paper was called the *Farmers' Weekly Museum;* and, 3d, that its publishers promised agricultural intelligence in 1803, that the statement obtained credence that Fessenden was the originator of this valuable class of newspapers.

The *New England Farmer* was published in quarto form from the beginning till within a few years. Shortly after its first appearance the interest of Shepard passed into the hands of John B. Russell. It was in a few years sold to Joseph Breck, who in 1846 transferred it to Luther Tucker, of Albany, N. Y. It was changed by Tucker to the *Horticulturist*. It was managed with a great deal of skill and ability by Fessenden. Without the practical knowledge of farming, he beame a teacher to the practical farmer. He edited the *Farmer* from its first number till 1837, when he died. He was buried in Mount Auburn, where his friends erected a monument with the following inscription to his memory:

THOMAS GREEN FESSENDEN,
died Nov. 11, 1837.
aged 65.

This monument is erected by the Massachusetts Society for Promoting Agriculture, by the Horticultural Society of Massachusetts, and individuals, as a testimony of respect for the talents and acquirements of the deceased, and his labors in promoting the objects of the above institutions.

The *New England Farmer* was revived in Boston, and is now published in folio form by R. P. Eaton & Co., with Simon Brown as its agricultural editor.

The *Southern Agriculturist* was published in Charleston, S. C., in 1828, by John D. Legaré, and in 1830 Luther Tucker issued the first number of the *Genesee Farmer* in Rochester, N. Y. Samuel Fleet, in the same year, published the *New York Farmer and Horticultural Repository*. In 1833, Edward Ruffin, "the white-haired rebel" who fired the first shot on the American flag at Fort Sumter in 1861, started an agricultural publication at Shellbanks, Virginia. The *Maine Farmer* also appeared in 1833. In 1834, Jesse Buel, who had been editor of the *Albany Argus*, preferring good potatoes to bad politics, established the *Cultivator*, and became a Mentor to the farmers of the rich and luxuriant Genesee Valley. Like Grant, he was an inveterate smoker. He and his clay pipe were always together. In the same year Miner and Challis issued a *Quarterly Journal of Agriculture*. Hovey's *Magazine of Horticulture* appeared in 1835.

The *Boston Cultivator* was the next in order. In 1839, William Buckminster, who, like Fessenden, had been educated a lawyer, became one of its proprietors and its editor. In October, 1841, Mr. Buckminster established another agricultural paper in Boston, over which he had entire control. This he called the *Massachusetts Ploughman*. In 1846 he took his eldest son, William J. Buckminster, as associate in the management of the concern. In 1862 he sold the establishment to Hugh W. Greene. Next year it became the property of George Noyes. It is now the official organ of the New England Agricultural Society. Its name was spelt *Plowman* for a short time after it passed from the hands of Buckminster, but its title was soon restored to its original orthography. The *Cultivator* continues to be published by Otis Brewer, its original publisher.

Another leading publication of this class is the *American Agriculturist*. It was started in 1842, and designed mainly as a rural paper. It has since swallowed several other papers of the same sort, and has become an extensively circulated publication. It is a monthly, and can not, therefore, be much of a newspaper, except in its own peculiar line, but its enterprise is a sufficient reason for including it in this summary. It is now published by Orange Judd & Co. Apart from its agricultural value, it has, we hope, accomplished some good for the rural population in preventing them from being too much swindled by all sorts of bogus schemes, by its timely exposure of the cheats, humbugs, and swindles of the day. It claims to have a circulation of one hundred and sixty thousand copies.

Then there is the *Rural New Yorker*, the *Prairie Farmer*, the *Mirror and Farmer*, the *Dixie Farmer*, the *Farmers' Home Journal*, the *Ohio Farmer*, the *Country Gentleman*, the *Farmers' Chronicle*, the *Western Rural*, the *Wisconsin Farmer*, the *Iowa Homestead and Horticulturist*, *Colman's Rural World and Valley Farmer*, the *Journal of Agriculture*, and the *California Farmer*, all weekly publications. Some of these are older and many are younger than several of those we have more particularly mentioned. There is a German agricultural paper published in America. It is issued in New York, and called Gerhard's *Deutsche Amerikanische Farmer Zeitung*. H. Nichols Zerchow is its editor. There are a number of papers published with "Rural" and "Farmer" attached to their titles which are not devoted to agricultural matters. There are now issued in the United States twenty-one weekly and thirty-five monthly and semi-monthly newspapers and periodicals entirely in the interests of the farmer and stock-breeder. It is probable that as many more have been started, and, after a short life of usefulness, "perished by the wayside" of journalism.

The Agricultural Press has done much to make farming a favorite pursuit. It has done much to make it an attractive one to the wealthy classes as well as to the laborer in the field. See what has been accomplished in the creation of the numerous agricultural colleges throughout the country, and in keeping the young farmers at home on the lands of their fathers. The *American Farmer*, the *Country Gentleman*, the *Ploughman*, the *Agriculturist*, the *New England Farmer*, are household words throughout the rural districts. These papers are teachers. They are the business educators of the farmers. They bring to their notice all the improvements in tools and tillage. They tell the lovers of good cows all about the best breeds. They elevate the farm, and make the labor thereon a learned profession. Our farmers are no longer mere drudges. Art, and science, and taste, and the resulting increased wealth, are the work of these newspapers. All this is to be seen in the reaping machines, improved farms, mowing machines, splendid barns, tedders, better breeds of cattle, better horses, superior butter, drained lands, more grass, outside of the mansion; and music, and books, and beauty, and comfort, and happiness inside of the farm-house.

It has been a task to accomplish this result. Old farmers would not be convinced that there was any value in book or newspaper farming. They believed in the old dung-hill; they were ignorant of the compost-heap. Old prejudices are hard to overthrow. With many they are not yet overthrown. Half a century ago, when the *American Farmer* first made its appearance, the rural population carried on their farms as their ancestors had done for generations before. There was no progress, except in raising more potatoes and more corn for the increase of population. It was "living from hand to mouth." Twenty-five years ago there was visible improvement. Agricultural papers had become established facts, and their circulation reached twenty thousand. After this the progress was wonderful. Now one paper alone claims a subscription list of one hundred and sixty thousand, and has probably half a million of readers. It is not an exaggeration, in our opinion, to set the average weekly circulation of all the agricultural press at half a million, and its readers at three millions. Besides this extraordinary exhibit, in the space of fifty years, in this one class of journals, nearly every weekly paper, political, religious, or literary, since Joseph Tinker Buckingham introduced "Geoponics" in the *Boston Courier*, has had a

"Farmers' Department." What is the result? It is to be seen along every railroad, on the banks of every river, in the vicinity of every city, through every town—in a word, every where; and the United States have become the greatest and most progressive agricultural nation of the world. No stronger illustration of this fact is needed than the mere statement that in 1847 there were forty-three agricultural patents granted in this country, while in 1866 the number was one thousand seven hundred and seventy-eight!

THE COMMERCIAL PRESS.

Commercial newspapers form a valuable class. They devote great industry, much research, considerable enterprise, to the development of the mercantile, financial, material, and commercial interests of the country. It is only a little more than half a century that journalists commenced the publication of market reports. If we look back to such papers as the *Boston Centinel*, *New York Gazette*, *New York Commercial Advertiser*, or any of the leading journals of fifty years ago, we find scarcely a reference to commerce or finance. The *New York Gazette* of March 4, 1739, gave the quotations for flour, rum, sugar, tea, molasses, wheat, corn, and stated that of cotton wool, turpentine, and "indico" there were none in market. Enos Bronson, the active editor of the *United States Gazette* of Philadelphia, was the first in this country to introduce commercial matters in his paper on any thing like a comprehensive scale. In 1806 he devoted several columns to Prices Current, as the detailed quotations of prices were called. In the *Columbian Centinel* of Boston, on the 7th of January, 1818, all we see is a table like the following, "corrected by two brokers," which is a curiosity when placed in juxtaposition with the daily stock sales reported in the papers of 1872. There were no remarks, and no other market reports. The *Centinel* was the Thunderer of New England:

PRICES OF STOCKS.
CORRECTED BY TWO BROKERS WEEKLY.

Massachusetts Five per Cents, int. off	97 to 98
U. S. new Six per Cents	106¼ to 106½
" Seven per Cents	109½ to 110
" Threes	70 offered.
" old and deferred	100 to 100½
" new Treasury Notes	4 to 5 adv.
" Sevens	6 to 7 "
Massachusetts Bank	106 to —
Union Bank	106 to —
Boston Bank, per share of 75	85 to —
State Bank, " of 60	65½ to —
New England Bank, per share of 75	85½ to 86
Manufacturers' and Merchants' Bank, per share of 50	51½ to 52
United States Bank	151 to 151½
Drafts on London, 30 days	2 to 2½ adv.

Drafts on London, 60 days	- - - - -	2 to	2½ adv.
Mississippi Stock	- - - - - -	86 to	86¼
Spanish Dollars	- - - - - - -	3 to	3½ adv.
Doubloons	- - - - - - -	$16 each.	

Once a week perhaps a dozen lines were given to show the current prices of flour and a few leading staples. Such reports of the money and produce markets as are now daily published in all the leading papers in all the cities in the country would have startled the whole journalistic and commercial community. When the *New York Herald* initiated the money articles, meagre as they necessarily were at first, the thunders of Wall Street were brought down upon the head of its editor. Now, no journal with any pretensions can live in a commercial community without its daily financial review and its full report of the previous day's operations in these two great money centres—Wall Street and State Street.

According to our researches, the *Boston Prices Current and Marine Intelligencer, Commercial and Mercantile*, the publication of which was begun on the 5th of September, 1795, was the first regular and legitimate commercial paper issued in this country. In 1798 it embraced politics. In 1800 its name was changed to that of the *Boston Gazette*, and became a general newspaper. The second successful attempt to establish a special market reporter or commercial organ was made at the extreme Southwest. On the 27th of July, 1822, the *New Orleans Prices Current* was issued in that emporium. James G. Watts and George H. Hart announced their intention to issue a *Commercial Chronicle* in Philadelphia in 1820, but as it did not appear, the *New Orleans Prices Current* must be considered the pioneer. It struggled and lived, and is alive to-day, always a handsome sheet, and always a valuable one, and is a record of the commerce of the Mississippi Valley for half a century. Then others started, like the *New York Shipping List and Prices Current*, and *Hudson's Shipping List and Prices Current*, and now they are as common as they are necessary. The first Prices Current appeared in Cincinnati in 1835. They have gradually swelled in importance and usefulness, and are consulted and filed away as valuable guides to the merchants, producers, and traders of the country.

Since that period another class of commercial newspapers has been brought into existence more comprehensive in its character. In 1859 the *Commercial Bulletin* was established in Boston. Curtis Guild, one of its proprietors, was educated a merchant, but took to newspapers. He became a clerk in the office of the *Boston Journal*, and afterwards in that of the *Traveller*, and then became one of the proprietors in the latter concern. He turned his hand and his head to every thing connected with the Press. In his travels at the West he found that Boston was very little known. New York met him wherever he went. New York stared him in the face every where. If he desired to see a newspaper, a New York paper was brought to him—never a Boston paper. If he wished to know how to get from Chicago to Boston, he was directed by hotel-keepers, railroad conductors, and steam-boats to go to New York, where he could find a conveyance to Boston. New York was all over the Union—New York oysters, New York fashions, New York newspapers, New York ideas, and the Hub nowhere. Imagine the sensation of a Bostonian under these circumstances. It occurred to him that a commercial newspaper, not to be confined in its circulation to Boston, but to be spread throughout the West in every hotel and in every merchant's counting-room, would greatly tend to bring the New England metropolis to the notice of the people of that wealthy section. Boston has always considered New York her rival. She has never publicly acknowledged her superiority. If one walks through the mercantile streets of the two cities, and sees the same merchants' signs, and finds them identically the same, the ardent admirer of Boston is indignant if he is told that these are the signs of the decay of that ancient town. With these impressions, Mr. Guild felt, on one of his midnight rides, that there was an opening for a commercial paper in Boston with special reference to the spread of information of New England notions over the mighty West. He brought all his experience and energy to bear on this point, and, acting individually and independently, he went to work, and, amid many struggles, he brought out the *Commercial Bulletin* in 1859; and now, thanks to his foresight and energy, he has a prosperous and valuable newspaper in full operation, which is really a valuable institution to the material interests of New England. He entered the Board of Trade. He wrote up the mills of that section of the country. He had his paper on file in three hundred hotel reading-rooms at the West and Northwest. He made his paper attractive in matter and typography. In this way he has made a specialty in journalism. The *Bulletin* is a large folio sheet of nine long columns to the page, and we noticed in one number an entire page devoted to manufactures, seven of which were advertisements, and two filled with interesting news items relative to factories in all the states—the erection of new ones, improvements in old ones, the destruction of some, and the enlargement of others.

The success of the *Bulletin* has led to the establishment of similar papers elsewhere. *Journals of Commerce, Commercial and Financial Chronicles, Economists' and Dry Goods Reporters*, are springing up in all large commercial centres, and thus, with the space given in the regular daily newspapers to commerce and finance, the wealth of this great nation is no longer hid from public view and public appreciation.

THE SUNDAY PRESS.

There were no Sunday papers prior to 1825. One hundred years after the first newspaper was started in New York the *Sunday Courier* was issued in that city. Although the *Galaxy* made its appearance in religious Boston on Sunday mornings as early as 1834–5, there was a strong public sentiment against them in the Northern States. There is a mistaken notion outside of newspaper offices about the work done on this class of papers. The *New Orleans Picayune*, for instance, is published on Sunday, but not on Monday mornings. This arrangement gives the editors, printers, and other *employés* rest on the Sabbath. It is for the edition issued on Monday that the work has to be done on Sunday; but as the paper seen in the streets on that day is the offending sheet, the time of labor preparing it for publication is not taken into consideration by the religious public.

There are Sunday papers, *per se*, issued on that day only. Then there are the Sunday editions of the daily press, like the *New York Herald*, *New York Times*, and *New York World*. The *New York Herald* publishes a paper every day. There is no break in that establishment, and it is the only one in America out of which a paper is issued daily throughout the year. The *Augsburg Gazette* is published every day in Germany. The *New York Tribune* attempted to issue a Sunday edition during the Rebellion, but the remonstrances of several of its subscribers stopped its issue after the first attempt. There are now Sunday papers in Boston and Philadelphia as well as in New York. Several of the papers formerly issued in New York on Sunday are now published on Saturday, but they are circulated and sold with the others on Sunday. It was a part of the management of the *New York Journal of Commerce* to have no work done in that establishment between twelve o'clock Saturday night and twelve o'clock Sunday night. This was probably the only daily city newspaper in the country having such a rule of conduct.

The first Sunday newspaper that we have any record of, as we have said, was the *Sunday Courier*. It was published by Joseph C. Melcher, at the Tontine Coffee-house, on the corner of Wall and Water Streets, New York City. It made its first appearance in 1825. Thomas Snowden, afterwards of the *National Advocate* and *Courier and Enquirer*, was engaged in the enterprise. Very curiously, it was edited by a theological student named William Hill.

The *Telegraph* was the next paper of this class. It did not long survive its birth.

The *Sunday Morning News* was the next in order. Samuel Jenks Smith was its publisher and editor. It came out shortly after the cholera panic of 1832. John Howard Payne, of "Home, Sweet Home," who had edited a little paper called the *Thespian* when he was fourteen years old, was an associate of Smith's.

> " 'Mid pleasures and palaces though we may roam,
> Be it ever so humble, there's no place like home."

In the Reminiscences of Henry Crabb Robinson there is an allusion to Payne. "Mary Lamb has begged me," said Robinson, under date of Paris, August 20, 1822, "to give her a day or two. She comes to Paris this evening, and stays here a week. Her only male friend is a Mr. Payne, whom she praises exceedingly for his kindness to Charles. He is the author of 'Brutus,' and has a fine face." So much for Payne.

Although a stout, fresh, healthy-looking man, Smith became consumptive, sold his establishment in 1838, and sailed for Europe. He died at sea. Warren Draper, who had been connected with the *Shipping List and Prices Current*, and afterwards started a paper called the *Evening Herald* to annoy James Gordon Bennett, edited the *News* after the retirement of Smith. Charles M'Lacklin, of the *Evening Mirror*, and George G. Foster, the "City Items" of the *Tribune*, were also writers for the *News*. It finally passed into the hands of Russell Jarvis, of the Philadelphia *Public Ledger*. Its day of publication was changed from Sunday to Saturday. Then it died.

Another *Sunday Courier* was established in 1834. It was issued by John Tryon, who afterwards became known as a reporter on the *Express*, and as a writer of notices, bills, and advertisements for the extensive circus companies and menageries of Colonel Welsh and Colonel Mann. James Gordon Bennett owned the *Courier* at one time, and we have read many of his short and sharp paragraphs in the old file of that paper.

In 1838, two printers, Anson Herrick, of the *Express*, and Jesse A. Fell, of the *Daily Whig*, started the *Sunday Morning Atlas*. They had no money. They were not supplied with an overplus of industry. But a paper issued once a week they thought they could manage without injury to their health. The *News* was selling at sixpence a copy. These two disciples of Faust calculated that if they could publish a paper at three cents they would obtain a large circulation, and make the concern a success with advertisements. The editorials were supplied gratuitously for a week or two by Samuel J. Burr (one of the editors of the *Daily Whig*), Worthington G. Snethen (formerly of John Gibson's *True American*, of New Orleans), and Frederick West, who issued the first penny paper in Philadelphia called the *Transcript*, afterwards merged with the *Public Ledger*. On the issue of the third number, West, with a limited credit of $50 per week obtained of Dudley Persse, of the firm of Campbell and Persse, for paper, became editor and a partner in the *Atlas*. West was a happy man. He was a clever little Englishman, ready to assist any one with poetry or pennies. Shortly after, Fell fell out of the concern, and John F. Ropes was roped in, and then the firm was Herrick, West, and Ropes. Herrick and Ropes became politicians, and published a daily paper for a short time, to the depletion of their bank account. Then the former was elected an alderman of the metropolis, and the latter held a sinecure in the Custom-house. Herrick was afterwards elected to Congress, and, for obvious reasons, was called a deacon. He died a few years since. The *Atlas*, we believe, is now published by his son.

The *Sunday Visitor* was started in 1839. Its name was changed to *Sunday Mercury* in 1840. Paige and Nichols were the brains of this establishment. Paige was the writer of the peculiar and original sermons of Dow Junior, which attracted pretty much the same sort of attention then as Artemus Ward's epistles have since that period. Nichols was an Englishman, with English tastes. His tone was strongly concentrated on theatricals. Machine poetry was a feature in the *Mercury*.

The first penny Sunday paper was *The Packet*. John M. Moore, who seemed to vie in cheap papers and low-priced advertisements, was the originator. It did not live long. It was too cheap. It was Moore and Hooper who endeavored to obtain a large advertising patronage at low rates—one cent a line—but the price was too low.

Thaddeus W. Meighan, an industrious writer, started *The Star* in January, 1842. This was the second penny paper of this class. Its price was afterwards raised to two cents. It lived about eighteen months.

Two actors, named Anderson and Conway, bought out the *Sunday Globe* in 1843. It was a star engagement only.

Then Mike Walsh and Enoch E. Camp produced the *Sunday Knickerbocker*. After its one pot of ale it died.

George Wilkes then established the *Life in New York*. No one knew life in the metropolis more thoroughly than Wilkes, but it ceased to be, and its editor confined himself, with Enoch E. Camp, to the *National Police Gazette*, now published by ex-Chief of Police George W. Matsell.

These publications attracted considerable attention, and a large aggregate circulation was the result. The *Herald* of the 29th of July, 1844, thus noticed them:

> During the last few years a new class of newspapers—partly literary, partly gossipping, partly silly, partly smart, partly stupid, partly namby-pamby—have grown up from the lowest and most sickly state to a point of some consideration in certain portions of society not much beyond the limits of the city. We allude to the Sunday Newspaper Press. About fifteen years ago we recollect starting our-

self one of the first Sunday newspapers in this city, the *Sunday Courier*, which lasted several months, and contained some very curious articles. But the project was rather premature, and we declined prosecuting it in order to engage in other avocations. The present Sunday Press has sprung into existence during the last six years, the first paper of the class being the *Atlas*, which originated in 1838, if we recollect right.

The third *Sunday Courier* was born in 1845. It was edited by Thomas L. Nichols, afterwards known as a "Water-cure Physician," and the husband of Mrs. Gove, who created a sensation in New York at one time by her lectures. Nichols had been a reporter on the *Herald*, and edited a lively little paper in Buffalo called the *Buffalonian*, where he got into difficulty, and suffered some from libel suits.

The *Sunday Age*, in which Grattan, the actor, and Thaddeus W. Meighan were interested, came into life, but soon disappeared from the foot-lights.

The *Sunday Times* was next established by John Dillon and John M. Moore. John Hooper, the advertising agent, also became connected with the paper. They published a small evening paper called the *Tattler*. William J. Snelling, of Boston, wrote for the *Times*. Major M. M. Noah, as we have already said, united his *Weekly Messenger* with the *Times*, and he became the responsible editor of the newly-arranged concern. This occurred in 1845. The *Times and Messenger* is now published, in 1872, by E. G. Howard & Co. Colonel Jo. S. Du Solle, once of Philadelphia, and Fanny Hobart, write for its columns.

The *Sunday Dispatch* made its *début* in 1846. Amor J. Williamson and William Burns were the publishers and editors. When the latter died, the establishment became the property of Williamson. He made it a sort of tender to the Whig and Republican parties, and its proprietor was elected to municipal offices, and died a wealthy man.

The fourth *Sunday Courier* made its appearance in 1848. It was published by Smith, Adams, & Smith. Harry Franco Briggs and John E. Durivage were its editors. The latter was at one time a reporter on the *Herald*, and had been connected with a brother, F. A. Durivage, with the Boston press. He had also been an *attaché* of the *New Orleans Picayune*. It is stated that he edited the first daily paper established in California. He was a nephew of Edward Everett.

Other Sunday papers were published. The *Sunday Bulletin, Sunday Galaxy, Sunday Chronicle and Sporting Register, Sunday Reflector, Sunday News or Extra, Sunday Era, Sunday Age*, and *Sunday Leader*, are among the names of those that made their entrée and exit. Of all these papers, the only ones now in existence are the *Courier, Times and Messenger, Atlas*, and *Dispatch*.

The *Leader* suddenly died in December. It was a bright, ably-edited Democratic organ. Its last editor was J. C. Goldsmith. Mayor A. Oakey Hall largely supplied it with wit. The *Dispatch* was the antithesis of the *Leader* in politics. These papers have found politics, when properly mixed with poetry, to pay better than when they confined themselves to literature and local news only.

THE SPORTING PRESS.

Bell's Life in London, established many years ago, gives one an idea of a sporting paper. It is an authority in all matters connected with the race-course, the ring, the hunt, and the stream. Its word on these subjects is law. Its editor is the Coke, the Blackstone of the sporting world. When a paper to represent a particular class or interest is established, there is a good deal of satisfaction in finding it an authority—in finding that it is up to the mark, and worth its subscription price. Such is the reputation of *Bell's Life*.

Have we any paper of this kind in the United States?

In the days of Colonel William Johnson, "the man with the white hat," and of John C. Stevens, who did so much for the race-course and for yachting in years gone by, the public were but meagerly supplied with information of the turf and the field. The monarchs of the Union Course were a little exclusive at first, but Stevens, when he comprehended the value of the press, expanded a little, and the fast trotters became more popular, and more numerous, and better known. When such matches as that of Eclipse and Henry created an excitement which extended from the Penobscot to the Mississippi, more attention was paid to such matters.

William T. Porter, a printer in New York, whose tastes and instincts all run in the right direction for the enterprise, then established the *Spirit of the Times*. This was in 1831. It was the *Bell's Life* of America. It was the first weekly sporting paper published in the United States. It was acceptably managed and edited by Porter till 1853 or thereabouts. He became widely known throughout the country as a judge of horses and stock of all sorts. His opinion was sought by every one interested in sporting, from catching a trout with a fly, and shooting a canvas-back on the Delaware, to the capture of a buffalo on the prairies. "The Tall Son of York," as he was familiarly called, became the most genial of companions, and suffered immensely thereby, but he made the *Spirit of the Times* an oracle in the sporting world. Owing to some differences, Colonel Porter left the old concern in 1853 or '54, and, in company with George Wilkes, established what was known for some time as *Porter's Spirit of the Times*, and which continued to keep up the character of sporting journalism. Colonel Porter died in 1858, when the paper passed into the hands of Mr. Wilkes. It is now called *The Spirit of the Times: the American Gentleman's Newspaper.* When the war broke out in 1861 its present editor run into politics, and mixed the rebellion and the race-course in fair proportions in his columns.

One of the curious incidents of life in New York is related, in connection with the *Spirit of the Times*, by Mr. Raymond, of the *Daily Times*, as having come under his observation:

> While walking down Broadway one afternoon, before I had begun to earn much money, I fell into the wake of a tall, handsome, splendidly-dressed young man, displaying himself, in all the luxury of white kids and diamond studs, to the general admiration. I fancied him one of the nabobs of the town, and fell into a train of wondering thought as to how he had probably reached his present height of dazzling splendor. Of course, I could not wholly forbear contrasting my own position with his, though without any feelings of special envy. The next day Mr. Greeley asked me to go to the office of *Porter's Spirit of the Times*, then in Barclay Street, and get him a copy of the paper. While waiting at the desk, the door opened, and my magnificent friend of the day before, all accoutred as he was, sailed in. He walked into the back part of the office, took off, folded, and put away his white gloves, hung up his hat and coat, put on an ink-stained linen jacket, and set himself busily to work writing wrappers. I felt decidedly encouraged as to the prospects of New York life!

Another paper of this class, called the *New York Clipper*, was started in New York about 1853. It is also an authority. It is owned and edited by Frank Queen. It has been quite prosperous, and recently its proprietor erected a fine building in Centre Street, an ornament to that noted thoroughfare, for the transaction of his increasing business. The *Clipper* is a large quarto, handsomely made up and printed. It has the additional title of *the Oldest American Sporting and Theatrical Journal*, but the *Spirit of the Times* is more than twenty years its senior. When such men as Tom Hyer and John C. Heenan prepared for a fight in the ring, the stakes were deposited at the office of the *Clipper*.

The *Turf, Field, and Farm* is yet another publication devoted to the kindred subjects of its title. It makes its weekly appearance in the metropolis, and is also successful. This is not surprising, for there is so much wealth and time now expended in horses that there is every desire to know all about them.

These papers indulge in learned and edifying articles on racing, angling, base-ball, cricket, la crosse, yachting, skating, shooting, rowing—indeed, in all outdoor sports. They give an impulse to open-air enjoyments, and do a great deal towards improving the *physique* of the human family, and towards throwing away the physic of the family physician.

There are other publications in the Union devoted more or less to horses, and hunting, and fishing, but these take the lead, and are specialties in this kind of journalism. John S. Skinner, as far in the rear as 1818, published a *Turf Magazine* in Baltimore, and paid attention to the breed of horses. The *Western Stock Journal* is a paper now printed at the West devoted to the improvement of all sorts of animals. No country surpasses this in attention to this subject. Our daily papers are also interested in all matters connected with the turf, field, and water-courses—the prize ring, the race-course, pigeon shooting, buffalo hunting, mains, and similar sports—but they do not confine themselves to these matters. Occasionally, it is true, a sporting paper takes higher flights—*Wilkes's Spirit of the Times*, for instance—and makes suggestions to politicians, statesmen, and generals, and sometimes brings down such game with a shot or two.

The interest exhibited in the success of these papers is also to be seen in the improvement of our horses, in our game-laws, in the introduction of fish-ways on rivers and streams where factories had driven away or destroyed the trout, shad, salmon, black bass, and alewives, and in all farm animals. When Dexters sell for $30,000 apiece, and Flatbush mares for $20,000, and the value of horses that make their magnificent appearance in Central Park, on Bellevue Avenue, and on the Brighton Road in one day, for pleasure alone, is estimated at a million of dollars, need there be any surprise at the erection of handsome stone edifices for publication offices of sporting papers?

These class papers have their value. Their circulation is not, comparatively, large; it is necessarily limited to the particular interest it represents; but these papers unquestionably give more information on the subjects they treat than the general newspaper can. It may be impossible for a daily paper to embrace within its space all the movements of the day—science, fashion, politics, history, philosophy, literature, theatres, art, music, sporting, yachting, inventions, discoveries, religion, law, poetry, agriculture, trade, finance, morals, education—all in full and complete. News on all these points are given, but the elaborate and scientific details go into the class papers, where each particular interest can learn all that has been developed on the subject, and frequently illustrated with superior engravings of plans, machinery, horses, cows, models, instruments, and diagrams.

CHAPTER XXII.
THE BLANKET SHEETS OF NEW YORK.

THE MORNING COURIER AND NEW YORK ENQUIRER. — JAMES WATSON WEBB. — NEWSPAPER ENTERPRISE.—SIZE OF THE SHEETS.—THE CILLEY DUEL.—THE WOODS RIOT.—THE MARSHALL DUEL.—SENTENCE OF COLONEL WEBB.—WILLIAM L. MARCY AND JAMES GORDON BENNETT.—THE MACKENZIE PAMPHLET.—WEBB AND NAPOLEON.—THE JOURNAL OF COMMERCE. — ITS ORIGIN. — HALE AND HALLOCK. — NEWS SCHOONERS AND PONY EXPRESSES.—ABOLITION RIOTS IN NEW YORK.—ORIGIN OF THE ASSOCIATED PRESS.—THE BOGUS LINCOLN PROCLAMATION.—SUSPENSION OF NEW YORK PAPERS.

THE " blanket sheets" made their appearance in the city of New York in 1827. The *Morning Courier* and *Journal of Commerce* were established in that year, and became leading metropolitan journals. They did not come under the cognomen of " blanket sheets" for several years after that period, but this is the title they enjoy in journalistic annals. They made some noise in Gotham in their day. They were commercial and political papers. They pretended to look after the interests of the mercantile classes. They acquired their influence mostly, however, from their politics, negative and positive. In their early days, one was Democratic, the other Abolition. In their later life, the Democrat became a Whig, and the Abolition a Democratic organ.

THE COURIER AND ENQUIRER.

First in order is the *Morning Courier*. It was established in May, 1827. In the following December it passed into the possession of James Watson Webb, a brother-in-law of its originator. Webb had been an officer in the army, a graduate of West Point, and was young and fresh in the fields of journalism. Thirty-four years after this event, in speaking of his *début* as an editor, he said:

We left the army a mere boy, to take charge of a political press at the commencement of the political campaign which terminated in the election of Andrew Jackson to the presidency in 1828, and, in a party point of view, we possessed not a solitary qualification for the position. We brought into political life the one leading characteristic of the army, a determination on all occasions to speak not only the truth, but the whole truth, and in practicing upon this, to the mere politician, ridiculous theory, we, of course, became in a short time a target at which our political friends were as fond of firing as were our political opponents; and to this we may justly attribute the somewhat well-known fact that we have been considerably the best-abused personage connected with the American Press. Jackson had not been inaugurated a month before we openly condemned some of his acts; and when he abandoned a protective tariff and a Bank of the United States, we abandoned him; and we then made proclamation, and have ever adhered to our declaration, that doing battle under the motto of "Principles, not Men," we should never recognize any allegiance to party except so far as adherence to its forms might be necessary to carry out the great principles which we seek to establish.

The *Enquirer*, as we have stated, was merged with the *Courier* in the spring of 1829. Webb, Noah, and Bennett were in Albany seeking some of the public printing, and, to arrange the pending differences of that time, the latter suggested to Webb the purchase of the *Enquirer*. This idea was carried into effect, and the united papers appeared under the title of the *Morning Courier and New York Enquirer*. The *Courier* started free of party influence. It was established by the father-in-law of its first editor as a business or profession. But in those exciting times neutrality or independence in politics seemed impossible. Hence it became a political paper; and when it came into the hands of Webb, in spite, or in consequence of his inexperience, it assumed a more decided political character. Webb was young and ardent. He was a man of impulse. Excitement to the verge of a fight, and even actual hostilities, suited his temperament. If his rights were at all interfered or trifled with, from a theatrical criticism to a political opinion, there must be an atonement in some way, either in a riot at the Park Theatre or a duel at Bladensburg. Such a man, with sound judgment and strong persistency, would make a splendid journalist.

The *Courier and Enquirer*, by which name it is now known to fame, continued a Democratic organ and an influential Jackson paper till 1832. It was published in 1830 by James Watson Webb, Daniel E. Tylee, and James Lawson; in 1831 by Webb, Tylee, and James Gordon Bennett. It left the Democratic Party in 1832, early in the great fight on the United States Bank question. All sorts of stories have been told in explanation of this change in the politics of the *Courier and Enquirer*, and the well-known Silas E. Burrows, a public-spirited and enterprising merchant, abandoned Jackson, and came out in favor of Nicholas Biddle and the Bank at the same time. The paper was then published by James W. Webb & Co. The Democrats, led by Churchill C. Cambreleng in Congress, made every effort to throw some suspicion on Colonel Webb's motives for his advocacy of Biddle and the Bank. James Gordon Bennett disposed of his interest in the paper when the revolution in its political sentiments was decided upon.

Colonel Webb, in his valedictory in June, 1861, when the *Courier and Enquirer* was united with the *World*, stated that "from the time we became proprietor of the *Morning Courier* in December, 1827, until now, he who now writes has been the sole and only responsible editor of the *Morning Courier,* and of the *Morning Courier and New York Enquirer;*" yet he has been assisted by several leading and distinguished journalists: by James Gordon Brooks, known as "Florio;" James Gordon Bennett, of the *Herald;* James Kirke Paulding; Charles King, afterwards President of Columbia College; John O. Sargent, afterwards editor of the Washington *Republic,* and known as Taylor's organ; Henry Jarvis Raymond, of the *New York Times;* Hoskins, Daniels, Spaulding, Smith, George H. Andrews, and half a dozen others. Some of the most powerful articles on nullification which appeared in the *Courier and Enquirer* were written by James K. Paulding, the novelist, and afterwards Secretary of the Navy.

The paper mostly in competition with the *Courier and Enquirer* was the *Journal of Commerce*—not politically, for the *Courier* was now a decided Whig, and the *Journal* at this time wished to be considered as decidedly neutral. It was for the support of the commercial classes that these papers fought and struggled. They enlarged their respective journals to an enormous size in competition for the advertisements of the merchants; they started news schooners and pony expresses; they spent money, and worked with a will. The news schooners of the *Courier and Enquirer* were the pilot-boats Thomas H. Smith and Eclipse, hired for the purpose. Then a superior clipper was built, and called the Courier and Enquirer. The *Journal of Commerce* had two schooners, one the Evening Edition, and the other the Journal of Commerce. Sometimes these five swift sailers would be together from fifty to a hundred miles at sea from Sandy Hook, in the exciting pursuit of ships and foreign news. These races were almost equal to those of the fast yachts of the New York Squadron in the fall of 1871 with the Livonia. News instead of silver cups were the prizes. This enterprise of these two journals, costing each paper $15,000 to $20,000 per year, was commenced in 1831, and was continued till 1834, when the schooners were disposed of, and small row-boats resumed their position in the harbor.

These "blanket sheets" were equally enterprising with their pony expresses from Washington, which they established to convey their dispatches from the national capital. Many interesting incidents occurred in their contests for news. Neither was persistent in its enterprise. One established a news schooner because the other did. The circulation of these papers was considered large at that time; it was about four thousand to four thousand five hundred each— nothing compared with the circulation of the journals of to-day. If that of the *Herald,* for instance, should rise or fall five thousand any day from any particular excitement, or in the absence of important news, it would not be noticed. But this circulation commanded the advertisements of that day; and the enterprise of the *Courier* and *Journal*, as they both started in the same year, were to them what Bonner's extraordinary advertisements and literary enterprise thirty-five years later are to the *Ledger*.

Among the incidents related of the enterprise of these journals was one affecting the *Journal of Commerce*. In one period of their competition the *Courier and Enquirer* happened to be most fortunate in getting foreign news. Advices from the other parts of the world than Europe came so rarely and were of such small interest, that the news from Europe was always distinguished as "foreign news." Much to Webb's surprise, he found, when he felt sure that he was ahead, that the *Journal of Commerce* also had the news. How was this? After being disappointed in his hopes once or twice in the exclusiveness of his news, he, like a true graduate of West Point, thought he could resort to a little strategy. About that time the Ajax, we believe, was due from Europe with later news. One morning the *Courier and Enquirer* appeared with a postscript, announcing the arrival of their news schooner with the news by the Ajax, which had reached the offing the night before. The "news" was given. It appeared in a few copies only. These were left by the regular carrier in the regular way at the doors of the subscribers' stores nearest the newspaper offices. One was "borrowed." Immediately the others were gathered up and destroyed, and the regular *Courier and Enquirer*, without the "news," delivered to their subscribers. That morning the *Journal of Commerce* published the "news by the Ajax" exclusively.

"Ho! ho! Your neighbor is ahead of you this morning," exclaimed the *Courier* subscribers, rushing into the office.

"Ahead? No! How?" asked the astonished clerks.

"Haven't you seen the *Journal*? It's got the Ajax's news! Beaten this time, my fine fellows. They are too much for you. You had better look out for your laurels," said the considerate friends of the *Courier*.

But these consolatory remarks did not seem to affect the occupants of that establishment as such remarks sometimes do. They looked as if the *Courier* could survive the defeat. After a few congratulations the cat was seen in the meal-tub, and the *attachés* of the *Journal of Commerce* were not very hilarious about Wall Street that day.

The *Courier and Enquirer* and *Journal of Commerce* organized their daily pony expresses from Washington in 1835. This enterprise went into effect for the session of Congress of 1835–6. It was a successful one for these journals. It was not continued, however, and was, therefore, only of temporary advantage. Amos Kendall, then Postmaster General, set up an opposition. Quite an interesting trial before the Court of Sessions of New York grew out of the pony express of the *Courier*. One of the packages of that paper was tampered with by some one, and Messrs. Day and Beach, of the *Sun*, were prosecuted by Colonel Webb for using his news. Although it was shown that they knew the contents of the package, it was not proved that they broke the seal of the parcel which had been brought from Washington by express.

There was a tragical episode in the career of the *Courier and Enquirer* in the winter of 1838. The Washington correspondent of that journal, the well-known Matthew L. Davis, who wrote over the *nomme de plume* of "The Spy in Washington," made a charge of corruption against some member of Congress. The matter was brought before the House, and Mr. Davis was summoned before the Speaker. The charge led to an excited debate, in which one of the members was savagely severe on all newspapers, newspaper editors, and newspaper letter-writers. In this debate, Jonathan Cilley, one of the members from Maine, was particularly severe on the character of Colonel James Watson Webb, of the *Courier and Enquirer*. On reaching the attention of that gentleman, he immediately started for the national capital to obtain satisfaction. Those who were connected with the press and politics in that year will never forget the excitement the appearance of Webb in Washington, and the subsequent tragical scene near that city, produced throughout the country. We will let Matthew L. Davis tell the story, as he did in the following letter to the *Courier and Enquirer*:

WASHINGTON, 24th of Feb., 1838.

To the Editor of the Courier and Enquirer:

It is with great reluctance that I notice, in my letters, the contests or collisions of gentlemen, but cases do occur which seem to be imperative in their character, and one has recently occurred which I can not pass unnoticed.

It is within your knowledge that Mr. Cilley, of Maine, on the floor of the House, made an attack on Col. J. W. Webb. That gentleman arrived here a few days since, and through Mr. Graves, of Kentucky, called upon Mr. Cilley, in courteous terms, for an explanation of his language.

On Mr. Graves presenting the communication of Col. Webb to Mr. Cilley, he demurred as to receiving it, but took time to consider. Shortly after Mr. Cilley declined to receive it, and assumed the ground, in conversation with Mr. Graves, that he did not hold himself responsible for language used in debate, etc., that he intended no discourtesy to Mr. Graves, and, as Mr. Graves understood him, made no objections to Col. Webb's character or standing as a gentleman.

On separating, Mr. Graves addressed a note to Mr. Cilley, requesting him to commit to writing the substance of their conversation, which, as he understood it, he repeated in his note. Mr. Cilley replied, admitting all the points except that which refers to Col. Webb's character or standing, and which he neither admits nor denies. Mr. Graves considered this equivocal, if not impeaching his own statement of the conversation, as contained in his note to Mr. Cilley, and so writes him requiring further explanation.

Mr. Cilley adhered to the course he had adopted, and adds, that he can not permit himself to be catechized on that point, whereupon Mr. Graves, through

Mr. Wise, demanded satisfaction, which demand Mr. Cilley agreed to grant, and proposed to meet this day with rifles, provided the distance of one hundred yards is also accepted. Mr. Graves joins issue; and the parties went out this morning, with their respective friends, to a place unknown to me, for the purpose of terminating the affair with rifles.

While I am writing, I am interrupted by a gentleman entering my room, and informing me that the body of Mr. Cilley has just been conveyed to his lodgings; that he fell, and expired immediately after, on the third fire; and that Mr. Graves has returned unhurt.

The city has been filled with rumors respecting Col. Webb, arising no doubt, out of the fact that he had determined to prevent the fight between Mr. Cilley and Mr. Graves; but he was kept in ignorance as to the time and place; and had no suspicion that they would meet to-day, or for some days to come, until about ten o'clock this morning; when, accompanied by two friends, each of them armed, he proceeded to Bladensburgh in search of the hostile party, with a fixed resolution that Mr. Cilley should permit him to take the place of Mr. Graves. In this decision his friends would have sustained him, at all hazards, regardless of all consequences. Not finding the combatants, Mr. Webb returned to Washington, and having received information that led to the conclusion that they might be found in another direction, with the same friends he renewed the attempt to discover the place of meeting; but this was alike unsuccessful. Returning to this city, they made a third attempt with the like result; and I think most fortunately, for no man can tell what would have been the termination of such a meeting, supported, as Col. Webb was, by two chivalric and resolute friends.

These movements, however, during the morning, produced rumors that Col. Webb was himself embarked in the conflict. They were without foundation. Col. Webb has neither given nor received any challenge, except in the case of Mr. Cilley, since his arrival in Washington. THE SPY IN WASHINGTON.

Matthew L. Davis, "The Old Boy in Specs" as well as "The Spy in Washington," was for a number of years the New York correspondent of the *London Times*, and wrote over the signature of "A Genevese Traveller." He resigned his position in 1848 in consequence of his advanced age. He commenced life as a journalist in the last century, and was always the friend of Aaron Burr. He was his literary executor and biographer. Affairs of honor he was accustomed to, and was mixed up with several in his early career.

Colonel Webb imported a new English printing-press in the spring of 1838. It did not work well. English white paper was necessary to its success. Our flimsy cotton rag paper would roll and clog the machinery. The press was therefore soon abandoned, and the *Courier* fell back on Hoe's inventions. Walker, of the *Daily Advertiser*, had previously imported an English press which was more successful.

One essential point with the *Courier* and *Journal* seemed to be size. One must be the largest! The size of each page of the *New York Gazette*, *Daily Advertiser*, the *Philadelphia Aurora*, and *Relf's Gazette*, the old class of journals, was about the same as those of the *World*, *Times*, *Herald*, and *Tribune* are now. They did not, however, publish double, triple, or quadruple sheets. We speak of the size of each page. It was the ambition of the proprietors of the *Courier* and *Journal*, in their competition, to be large—to cover more white paper than was ever before covered. They were folio sheets. If one enlarged and boasted of more superficial inches, the other would immediately bend its energies to add an inch to its size, and make its paper as inconveniently large as possible. Hence the name of "blanket sheets" which Bennett, of the *Herald*, gave them. In September, 1850, the *Courier* plumed itself on being sixty-eight square inches larger than the *London Times*. It went into a long arithmetical calculation to show how far ahead of the Thunderer it had become. Thus Webb took a copy of the two papers of that period, and counted the number of letters in each, with this result:

In the *London Times*:

	Columns.	Lines in a Column.	Ems in a Line.	Total.
Nonpareil	23½	250	32	188,000
Minion	19	232	28	123,424
Brevier	5½	192	24	25,344
Total ems in the *Times*				336,768

The *Courier and Enquirer* used no Brevier, its largest type being Minion; and the advertisements were set in Agate, which is one size smaller than the Nonpareil used by the *Times*. The following statement shows the number of ems in each kind of type used:

In the *New York Courier and Enquirer*:

	Columns.	Lines in a Column.	Ems in a Line.	Total.
Agate	34½	539	34	632,247
Nonpareil	2	368	28	20,608
Minion	7½	328	25	64,500
Total ems in *Courier and Enquirer*				714,355
Total ems in *London Times*				336,768
Excess in *Courier*				377,587

It will be seen that the number of ems in a single copy of the *Courier and Enquirer* was more than twice as great as the number in a single copy of the *London Times*. Occasionally, however, the *Times* published a double-sheet supplement, filled entirely with advertisements in Nonpareil, each column of which contained 8000 ems. The total number of ems in both the *Times* and its double supplement on such occasions was—

In the *Times*	336,768
In the Supplement	384,000
Total	720,768
In the *Courier and Enquirer*	714,355
Excess in *Times*	6,413

So the *London Times*, with one of its double advertising supplements, which it rarely issued, contained only 6413 *ems* more than a single copy of the ordinary daily issue of the *Courier and Enquirer*, which is an excess of but little over a *third* of one of its advertising columns!

Was it reasonable to suppose that the *Journal of Commerce* would permit this? Were Hale and Hallock to be outdone by James Watson Webb? Not if there were rags enough in Italy and America for the paper-mills. In October, 1850, the *Journal* was enlarged, but, owing to circumstances beyond their control, a copy of that paper measured only 1820 square inches, 61 inches less than the *Courier*. Would this do? Of course not. Therefore on the 1st of March, 1853, the grand climax was reached: the *Journal of Commerce* announced itself the "largest daily paper in the world." It measured 16⅓ feet, or 2057¼ square inches — 76¼ square inches larger than the *Courier*. Happy journalists! It must have been a wet blanket for Col. Webb on that morning. What a difference in size these mammoth sheets of 1850-53 present when compared with Harris's *Publick Occurrences* of 1690, and the Boston *News-Letter* of 1704. Let us see the figures in contrast:

  Boston News-Letter, 1704 - - - - 192 square inches.
  Courier and Enquirer, 1850 - - - 1881 " "
  Journal of Commerce, 1853 - - - - 2057 " "

When the World's Fair was announced to be held in the Crystal Palace in London, among other productions of mankind to be placed on exhibition were newspapers. Many American journals were represented, and the English newspaper critics rather sneered at our specimen sheets. Very few of our papers were then printed as well as they are now. Our advertising columns were disfigured with all sorts of pictures and head-lines. Some of them looked as deplorably as the advertisement pages of the Paris papers, or the side of an old fence covered with placards, with their curious and confounding cross-readings. On that occasion the *Courier and Enquirer* appeared in full costume: a specimen number was published for that Universal Exhibition, and here are the dimensions as they appeared in that paper on the 1st of January, 1851. This specimen was in no spirit of competition with the *Journal of Commerce*. It was merely a broadside at John Bull, to show that conceited and portly old fellow what a Yankee newspaper publisher could do. The *Courier* said:

 This edition of the *Courier and Enquirer* will challenge general attention on account of its size. We believe it is the largest newspaper sheet ever published in the world. The ordinary edition of the daily *Courier and Enquirer* is considerably larger, judged by any standard, than any other daily published either in Europe or in the United States—containing more than twice as many *ems*, and 332 more square inches, than a copy of the *London Times*. But this edition, as will be seen by a slight calculation, transcends any edition of the *Times* or of any other daily newspaper ever published.

 This copy of the *Courier and Enquirer* contains eight pages, of eleven columns each, the total number of *ems* in which may be thus estimated:

	Columns.	Lines in a Column.	Ems in a Line.	Total.
Agate	62¼	539	34	1,145,375
Nonpareil	2	368	28	20,608
Minion	23¼	328	25	192,700
Total ems in *Courier and Enquirer*				1,358,683
Total in *Times and Supplement*				720,768
Excess				637,915

The present number, therefore, of this paper contains nearly TWICE as many *ems* as the *Times* in its double supplement.

These mammoth sheets were merely curiosities in the mechanical department of newspaper literature. They were useless for general use and circulation, and any one would suppose that one experiment would satisfy both the publisher and the public of this fact. But not so. In 1859, George Roberts, formerly of the *Boston Times*, came to New York, and started an enterprise that was to cover the "blanket sheets" and all other papers under its immense pages. On the 4th of July it made its appearance, with the stunning title of *The Illuminated Quadruple Constellation*. It was certainly a curiosity. Nothing of the sort had ever appeared before. Nothing of the sort has appeared since. We never saw even a second number of the *Constellation*. This first number was evidently sufficient for this century, for it appears by the following advertisement that Roberts only intends publishing it once in a hundred years. It was not a daily, nor a weekly, nor a monthly, but a century paper. The next number is to appear on the 4th of July, 1959. But here is the announcement:

THE GREAT WONDER OF THE AGE!
THE MASTERDON OF NEWSPAPERS!
PUBLISHED ONCE IN 100 YEARS!

The subscriber feels great pride in presenting herewith to the American people
THE LARGEST SHEET OF PAPER EVER MADE AND PRINTED?
To which he has affixed the title of
"THE ILLUMINATED QUADRUPLE CONSTELLATION."
Being one sheet 70x100 inches!
Beyond all question it will be pronounced the greatest newspaper curiosity that will be seen for a hundred years. This immense paper contains more matter than six numbers of Harper's Monthly, or fifteen numbers of the New York Ledger, or Harper's Weekly.
A limited edition of
ONLY 28,000 COPIES
has been printed, and it is impossible to issue more of them, as the different pages have all been distributed. It contains
EIGHT MAMMOTH PAGES,
thirteen columns to a page. Each column FORTY-EIGHT INCHES in length. The paper is of superior quality, of great strength and durability, so as to be capable of standing great usage, weighing 300 pounds to the ream, and costing $60 a ream —being twelve times more than a ream of the Herald, Times, or Tribune costs. The weight of paper required for the limited edition of 28,000 copies is equal to that required for over 200,000 copies of the Times and Herald. It has taken eight weeks of unceasing labor of nearly forty persons to produce this
MASTODON PAPER!

We can wait without impatience for the next number. But, in a mechanical and typographical point of view, these two specimens—that of the *Courier and Enquirer* for the World's Fair, and the *Illuminated Constellation*—were certainly wonderful curiosities in journalism.

The *Courier and Enquirer* was always a demonstrative paper. Its first illustration of this fact was in suggesting the nomination of Martin Van Buren for the presidency in 1829, to succeed General Jackson at the expiration of his first term. The *Telegraph*, then the organ of Jackson, denounced the movement in such a way as to lead to the famous encounter between Colonel Webb and Duff Green on the steps of the Capitol. This affair, one of the sensations of that exciting era in politics, was thus described by the two parties interested. Annexed is the

STATEMENT OF COL. JAMES WATSON WEBB.

WASHINGTON CITY, Thursday, May 6, 1830, 2 p.m.

I arrived here at 11 o'clock, having taken the 5 o'clock stage from Baltimore with a view of being here in time to inflict upon Duff Green, on his arrival at the Capitol, the personal chastisement which I promised him and which he so richly merited. I reached the Capitol at half past 11, and having ascertained that he was not in either house of congress, took up my position in the rotunda, selected that as the theatre of his disgrace and not, as he on a former occasion selected a committee room of the senate, when he pulled the nose of an assistant editor of the —— ——. This being the day on which an interesting race was to be contested on the Washington Course, many of the members were leaving the house, and those who knew me were naturally attracted by my position. They at once saw my object and urgently recommended me to select some other place to punish Green. I complied with all their wishes, and determined to punish him in front of the building. I accordingly repaired to the library, which, as you well know, commands a view of the approach to the Capitol by the Pennsylvania Avenue, and leisurely waited for the arrival of Green. At about 1 o'clock I saw him enter the gate opposite the west front, and immediately left the library to meet him, previous to his entrance into the building, and thereby avoid the charge of assaulting, within the Capitol, an officer of Congress. On my arrival at the foot of the stairs, however, (Green had passed the wide brick walk in front of the door, and was entering the building,) I immediately exclaimed, "Well met. I was seeking you!" He retreated backwards a few paces, which carried him some distance from the door, drawing, at the same time, from the right hand pocket of his pantaloons, a pistol, about eight inches long, with percussion lock and half cap, and having a mahogany stock. His retreat, the drawing of the pistol, and its being cocked and levelled at me were the work of a moment, and owing to my distance from him, when he discovered me, I could not close with and disarm him. After looking at him in silence some seconds, I placed under my arm the walking cane which I used, and leaned against the south jamb of the door, addressing him in the following terms, which are still fresh in my recollection:

"You poor, contemptible, cowardly puppy, do you not feel that you are a coward, and that every drop of blood that courses through your veins is of the same kind of hue as your complexion? There you stand, secured from punishment by a weapon which you dare not use, and virtually proclaiming that you only presume to assail private character, because you think it will not add to your infamy by being known as an assailant! Contemptible and degraded as you are, throw aside your pistol, and I pledge you my honor, I will not injure you. I will throw away my cane, and only pull your nose and box your ears."

He refused to do so, alleging that he would never descend to my level. He then requested me to proceed and let him pass. I told him that I would not, but that he should pass me as I then stood, or stand and hear me abuse him. He did not dare to pass, fearing that I should take the pistol from him. After some moments, however, I told him I would return up stairs, and proclaim to every member of congress his cowardly conduct. We accordingly proceeded to the house of representatives, where I related all that had passed, and from thence hastened to commit it to paper, while the expressions I used to him were still fresh in my memory.

I have already, and will again prove him a wilful and malicious slanderer. He now stands branded as a coward. Can he remain where he is? No. He is a disgrace to the station he fills, and must sink into the oblivion from which he was accidently brought forth. JAS. WATSON WEBB.

The editor of the *Telegraph* wrote to a friend in New York giving his version of the meeting. Colonel Webb was called the "senior editor" of the *Courier* at that time, and hence that phrase in General Green's letter. The *Herald* alluded to in this communication was a paper of that name edited by Alanson Nash, and which was afterwards merged with the *Standard:*

GENERAL DUFF GREEN'S STATEMENT.

WASHINGTON, May 7, 1830.

Dear Sir. Your "senior editor" is here. I yesterday, passing up to the Capitol, met him at the west front. I had been advised by a letter from New York that he was on his way for the purpose of carrying into execution his threat of "personal chastisement;" and a friend had given me a pocket pistol. When I met him, I halted on the platform; he raised his cane; I then drew my pistol. He then, for the first time, spoke and said: "throw away your pistol and I will throw away my cane, and give you a damned whipping." To this I replied: "I do not intend to be whipped by you, nor will I put myself in a position to invite attack from you." He then said: "are you not a coward to draw a pistol on an unarmed man?" To this I replied, "I have not time to waste with you, so you must march out of my path." He said, "I will not." I told him "You shall," and cocked my pistol and presented it, saying at the same time "march on, march." He said "I will go back." "Very well," said I; "you may go backward or forward as you like, but march out of my path." He then turned through the door, and run up a flight of steps into the rotunda, and from thence passed into the hall of the house of representatives. When I entered the house, he was giving his version of the transaction to judge Wayne of Georgia. I understand that he brags of his triumph and declares that I am down! I had no other desire from the first, than to vindicate my character and defend my person from his assaults. It would be a source of regret to me to be under the necessity of doing him personal injury. If he is satisfied with the issue, I will have no cause of complaint—and my only object is to guard against misrepresentation. If he should publish, as in all probability he will, another account of this affair than that which I transmit, I trust that you will do me the justice to insert this in your paper; and also request the editors of the *Herald* to do the same.

Your friend, D. GREEN.

After this and other excitements had somewhat calmed down, the Abolition Riots broke out in New York. These occurred in 1834. The *Courier* took a most decided stand against the Abolitionists and agitators. On the arrival of George Thompson, the English Radical, in that year, it fanned the fire of the opposition with great vigor. Here is one of its articles:

No man not blind to future consequences, to all former examples, and to all the lessons of past experience, can hesitate a moment in foreseeing that the triumph of the Abolitionists is a thousand times more likely to be consummated by the extermination of the masters, their wives and their children, than by the freedom and consequent happiness of the slaves.

As the enemies then of social order, of the rights of property, of the lives of hundreds of thousands of our brethren of the race of white men, their wives and their children, and as the vilifiers and sappers of our social institutions, laws and Constitution, we say, therefore, that the preachers and expounders of such doctrines are justly amenable to the laws of the land, as common and notorious disturbers of the public peace, enemies to the rights of property, and traitors to the country.

What renders the conduct of these *instigators of treason, robbery and massacre* still more outrageous and indefensible, is the fact of their having imported more than one organ of mischief from England to assist in sowing the live coals of ruin and desolation over a large portion of this prosperous land. Not content with the agency of the wretched libeller of his country, the exclusive "*friend of all the human race,*" they have associated in their righteous race an imported incendiary, " who left his country for his country's good ;" this apostle of the old pussy-cats of Glasgow ; this tool of Tappanism, has hitherto escaped the Bridewell, transportation, or some other species of modern martyrdom, is a proof either that our laws are defective, our magistrates neglectful, or our people the best natured in the world.

We hope and trust that his next attempt in this city will end in a transfer to the Penitentiary, as a common disturber and enemy to society, and would earnestly recommend to the superintendent of that society a solitary probation, lest he might corrupt the morals of his pupils.

Another sensation sprung up in the midst of the Abolition excitement. The Woods were singing at the Park Theatre. They formed the principal part of a celebrated English Opera troupe. Joseph Wood and his wife were considered the best English vocalists that ever appeared here. They were, of course, very popular and very successful. Wood was vain and conceited. He had had some difficulty with Mrs. Conduit, a popular vocalist of the Park stock company. One day he took exception to a criticism in regard to his treatment of this lady which had appeared in the *Courier and Enquirer*, and that evening, meeting Dr. Hart, the critic of that paper, in the lobby of the theatre, applied some epithet to the paper, and spit in the doctor's face. It turned out that Wood spit in the face of the public, for the fact was known immediately all over town, and very quickly resented. The *Courier and Enquirer* took the matter up in its accustomed manner. On the evening of the 27th of May, 1836, the Woods were announced to appear in Guy Mannering. The house was full. Very few ladies were there that night. On the appearance of the Woods the greatest tumult prevailed. They were driven from the house, and did not sing again in New York for years.

On one occasion arrangements had been made to mob the office of the *Courier*. What was done? Webb brought his West Point education into practice ; he turned his building into a fortress ; armed his printers, editors, clerks, pressmen, and friends, and quietly awaited the assault. The mob marched down Wall Street prepared to make the attack and demolish the establishment. They halted. All was as still as a church in the *Courier* office. Its windows presented an ominous silence. The mob was packed in a narrow street in front. Some one informed one of the leaders of the preparations made by Webb. There was a brief consultation. "Fall into line!" was heard among the crowd. "Forward—march," said a man, recognized as the chief. In ten minutes Wall Street was as quiet as Greenwood. Not a soul was to be seen.

The Hon. Thomas F. Marshall, the eloquent member of Congress for Kentucky, and who became famous as a temperance orator in 1842, became involved in a personal difficulty with General Webb, and in a speech before the Court of Oyer and Terminer in New York, made some allusion to General W., leading to a challenge and a duel, which took place in Delaware in June of that year, resulting in a shot in Webb's leg, which disabled him for some time. The Grand Jury of New York indicted Webb for the offense of "leaving the state with the intention of receiving or giving a challenge." In his special plea before the Court of Sessions, General Webb made this statement:

> * * While I do not pretend to deny that I left this state for the express purpose of fighting a duel with the Hon. Thomas F. Marshall, there are those who will bear witness that I utterly refused to sanction any arrangement which would give to our meeting a sanguinary appearance. With me it was strictly a point of honor; and my declining to fight at four or eight paces, my repeated refusals to suffer the meeting to take place on a Sunday, and my solemn determination that under no circumstances would I take the life of my antagonist, can leave no doubt on the minds of honorable men that I was not actuated by any feeling of malice towards him, but that I simply acted in accordance with the dictates of that public opinion which I had not the moral courage to contemn—that public opinion which is alike arbitrary and unjust, and which, while it forever disgraces all who shrink from these personal rencounters, at the same time gravely censure all who engage in them. It was with me but a choice of evils. I selected what I deemed the least; and solemnly resolving that in no contingency would I take the life of my adversary, I had a right to suppose that a law which had never been enforced against others would not be revived against me.
>
> I need not tell you that from the duel I alone am the sufferer; while, had I been actuated by the same feelings as my antagonist, whose boast it is that he sought my life, he might long since have been the tenant of the silent tomb, and I a wanderer from my home, and the object of execration and denunciation by that very society which compelled the meeting. * * * * * *

Having thus pleaded guilty, Col. Webb, it was supposed, would have been sentenced to imprisonment, but he was discharged, on account of some informality in the indictment, by Recorder Tallmadge. In November he was again indicted, when he entered the same plea, and was then sentenced to imprisonment in the State Prison for two years. When the clerk of the court asked Col. Webb what he had to say why judgment should not be pronounced against him, he said,

> I might say much against the policy, the justice, and the constitutionality of the law under which I have been indicted. I might say still more in relation to the unjust persecution by which that indictment was originally got up; but I feel satisfied that, much as I might say, it would have no influence on the minds of this court, or alter your judgment. I shall therefore simply content myself with submitting to your decision without any further remark, satisfied as I am that whatever of odium there is in the matter attaches to my persecutors, and not to me.

The Recorder, in passing sentence, concluded as follows:

> The punishment provided for this offense, and I allude to it particularly, as there has been some misunderstanding out of doors in relation to it—the extent to which the Court can sentence for an offense of this nature is limited to seven years; at the same time, the Court can not sentence for a less term than two years. The sentence of the Court therefore is, that you, James Watson Webb, be imprisoned in the State Prison at Sing Sing for a term of two years.

Many petitions for his pardon were signed, and before the time arrived for his departure for Sing Sing he received a full pardon from Governor Seward.

In a speech to his constituents, Mr. Marshall thus alluded to this affair of honor:

> In conclusion, the only really plausible charge urged against him was in relation to his long absence, during the late session, from his legislative duties. In this matter he threw himself upon the mercy and liberal spirit of his people. He had joined the Washingtonian Society. He was invited to New York, and he wished to see that magnificent city before he left Washington. He had been grossly abused by the celebrated Colonel Webb, editor of the *New York Courier*, for his active exertions to repeal the Bankrupt Law. Whilst he was in New York, this editor daily continued his detraction and slander; and in his last article of outrageous attacks, held him up before his constituents as a recreant knight, ready to inflict injury, but destitute of the courage to resent insult or vindicate character. Forbearance now ceased to be a virtue. He called Col. Webb to the field, and only regrets that he was but partially punished for his unprovoked, vindictive, and unprincipled abuse of private reputation. Col. Webb had promised to fight him in six hours, but delayed the matter three weeks. He could not return to Washington City whilst the affair was in progress, for in the District of Columbia the giving or receiving a challenge was a Penitentiary offense. If, under all these circumstances of wanton aggression on the part of Col. Webb, he had not called him out, there was not a Presbyterian lady in his district who would not have whipped him with her garter, in scorn and contempt, from her presence.

The *Courier and Enquirer* had a great advantage over its contemporaries in 1843. All the notices of proceedings in bankruptcy under the Bankrupt Act of 1842 were ordered to be printed in that paper, because it had the largest circulation. All the small papers were ignored in this award. The daily circulation of the *Courier* was then 5000, and its weekly circulation 3000. The *Sun* had 19,000 daily and 3000 weekly; the *Herald* 13,000 daily and 14,000 weekly.

The publication of the Mackenzie pamphlet was an episode in political journalism in the metropolis. So many private letters, bringing to light so much rich and curious material, called forth personal explanations of a still more curious character; and those who had newspapers under their control endeavored to make their epistolary productions clearer to the public and more interesting in filling the gaps in political history. Thus General Webb, of the *Courier and Enquirer*, on the 25th of September, 1845, in publishing some of the letters from the Mackenzie pamphlet, said, in explanation of the course of his paper in regard to the nomination of Governor Marcy,

> In 1832 we had not as yet abandoned the support of General Jackson, because

he had not then quite forsaken every principle upon which he was elected to the presidency. But, being the friend of William L. Marcy, and entertaining the most sovereign contempt for the Albany Regency, we placed Mr. Marcy's name at the head of our columns for Governor, in defiance of the intrigues of the Regency to defeat his nomination. The editor of the *Argus*, and similar tools and creatures of party, urged upon Senator Marcy to authorize them to declare that he had not connived at or sanctioned our course. He refused to do so.

The *Courier and Enquirer* then published a letter from the pamphlet from Senator Marcy to Jesse Hoyt, written June 3d, 1832, in which he mentions the efforts made to get him to withdraw. He said,

"The result was that I am not to persist in declining now, but am to be let alone if it can be done. * * * * * * Webb has not modified and published your articles."

Then follows another letter from Senator Marcy to Jesse Hoyt, taken from the same page of the pamphlet. This is the epistle:

WASHINGTON, Saturday.

DEAR SIR,—I have this morning received a note from Webb, and I learn from the tenor of it that you had written to him on the subject which engaged us in two or three conversations. I find that our opinions of him were perfectly correct. Attacked as he is on all sides, he is willing to do something for others as well as himself. I find my intimation to you is well founded that Bennett had been too sanguine in the matter referred to, and had understood from me more than I intended to convey. Webb has undoubtedly every disposition to put things right, and he ought to be permitted to do so to a certain extent in his own way. I have had full conversations with you, and from them you can make to him such suggestions as will apprise him of my views. He may think I ought to write to him—and so I should perhaps—but I have two reasons for not doing so; the one is, that if I should go over the whole matter as I did with you in conversation, it would make a prodigiously long letter, and I am too much engaged to afford the time to write it; but the second is, I have declined to write to all editors on the subject (except one which I explained to you). This resolution was early taken to preserve my position—to keep silent. He will appreciate my motives, and, I hope, approve of the course.

The key to the above is given by James Gordon Bennett in the *Herald* of the 26th of September, 1845. It is a nice bit of autobiography:

The reference made to Bennett in the above letter of Senator Marcy, now Secretary of War at Washington, requires some correction. I positively and unequivocally deny that I had ever been "too sanguine" in the case referred to, or that I "had understood more" than Mr. Marcy "had intended to convey." This matter had reference to his nomination for Governor in 1832.

In 1832, during the session of Congress, I was at Washington as one of the editors of the *Courier and Enquirer*, enjoying the confidence of the party and all concerned, and corresponding with that journal. Mr. Marcy was then a member of the Senate. I had frequent personal intercourse with him on politics alone. We never discussed piety, as Mr. Butler does in his letters, or finance, on the plan of John Van Buren. We were both men of business—practical politicians—stuck to the thing in hand, and never troubled ourselves either about the stated preaching of the Gospel, or whether Lawrence was likely to run like the cholera; nay, we didn't even trouble ourselves about the price of stocks or the chances of an election bet. During that session I used to see Mr. Marcy almost every day. In the course of conversation one day, during a walk up Pennsylvania Avenue, to which he invited me, I found that the senator had something heavy, very heavy indeed, on his mind which he wished to disclose. He called me out of his room, and we walked along the street, and during that walk I discovered, after a good deal of backing and filling in the way of language, and in a style something similar to that in which Cæsar refused the crown in Shakspeare's play of Julius Cæsar, that the heavy business on the heart of the senator was a desire to be brought forth in the columns of the *Courier and Enquirer* as a candidate for the gubernatorial chair of New York, in anticipation of the Convention of the party to be held in Herkimer in the fall. We discussed the matter in all its aspects for several weeks. I considered it in every point of view, and I concluded that it would be a famous movement for the *Courier and Enquirer*, and particularly for my friend Webb to take up, as he was in rather an awkward predicament in relation to the party, growing out of the disclosure about the $52,000 affair of the United States Bank, which had been previously brought out by Cambreleng. In this state of the case, I commenced a series of private letters addressed to Mr. Webb, stating all the views of the case—Senator Marcy's opinions, the position of Webb himself, and the admirable movement it would be in enabling the *Courier and Enquirer* to checkmate the *Argus* and "the Regency" on their own ground. I suppose I wrote twenty or thirty letters on this subject, disclosing and explaining the position of affairs. These letters contained a variety of the views communicated to me for that special purpose by Senator Marcy himself. If Mr. Webb were to look among his old papers he would find these letters; and as they will justify the course he took, and show distinctly that the charge made by Senator Marcy in his private letter to Jesse Hoyt that "Bennett had been too sanguine, and had understood more than he intended," was altogether incorrect. I deny having been "too sanguine;" I deny that I had understood and communicated more to Mr. Webb than Marcy intended to convey. Indeed, almost every day, or every other day, at that time, Senator Marcy used to meet me in the Capitol and at his own room, and there he would disclose to me all the information which he had received from the regency camp at Albany, in order that I might be enabled to apprise Mr. Webb of the facts, and qualify him to complete the checkmate which we intended to give him. In all this business Senator Marcy wished to stand still between the two contending *cliques*, while I was to work the wires in Washington, and Mr. Webb was to fire off the big gun in New York. Senator Marcy and I in Washington used to laugh and chuckle most amusingly over the movements by which, through the *Courier and Enquirer*, we accomplished ultimately his nomination, checkmated his personal foes at Albany, and elected him triumphantly Governor of this state for the first time. Before the summer was over, however, Mr. Webb bolted from the Democratic Party on the United States Bank question, and came out against the re-election of General Jackson, including also the election of the very man, William L. Marcy, whom he had so much contributed to bring before the public. I stuck to the movement, and left the *Courier and Enquirer* on account of this bolting. Two months before November I made an estimate of the votes of every county in the state, and elected Marcy by ten thousand five hundred. Matthew L. Davis made an estimate at the same time, which was published in the *Courier*, electing his antagonist by nineteen thousand four hundred. Marcy was elected by nine thousand seven hundred, being within a few hundred of the estimate I made before the election.

Such is a true and correct statement of that piece of simple political intrigue by which Senator Marcy was made Governor Marcy, and in which I participated, like a political sinner as I was, as one of the electric wires between Washington and Albany. Every thing I did was after consultation with Marcy; and although I prompted many things, yet he concurred in them, and I did nothing that he did not sanction. It was, therefore, very unhandsome in him to have been, as it now appears, writing letters to Jesse Hoyt censuring me privately for the very thing which he approved and concurred in to myself personally at Washington.

Mr. Bennett never forgave Mr. Marcy for his conduct to him in this affair. He held him as a Scotch terrier would a rat through the remainder of his political life, and one day, somewhere about 1852 or '53, after he became Secretary of State under President Pierce, the genial Richard Schell called on Mr. Bennett with an invitation to call on Secretary Marcy, then stopping at the Irving House. "No," said Mr. Bennett, "I have no desire to see Mr. Marcy. I am already acquainted with him. I helped make him Governor of this state; I do not intend to aid in any way to make him President of the United States. That's his present object." Secretary Marcy was then making his arrangements to secure the nomination which afterwards fell to Mr. Buchanan, resulting in the election of the latter in 1857.

On the 12th of November, 1846, the Whig Young Men's Committee of New York City passed a series of resolutions reading the *Courier and Enquirer* out of the party for its opposition to John Young, the regular nominee of the party for Governor of New York, and for being "mainly instrumental in defeating a Whig Lieutenant Governor, two members of Congress, the Sheriff, and County Clerk in our city, and creating a feeling between the Whigs of different sections of our state prejudicial to the success of the Whig Party," and that "the *Courier and Enquirer* has no longer the confidence of the Whig Party of this city."

Mr. Henry J. Raymond, who had left the *Tribune* and joined the *Courier and Enquirer* in 1843, infused a good deal of spirit in the editorial management of the latter journal. One of his strong points of character was controversy. It was his *forte*. He delighted in a verbal fight. His tilt with Horace Greeley on Fourierism, with Archbishop Hughes, with Mr. Chase, M. C. from Tennessee, and with others, showed this. He was quick and smart in repartee. His mind was keen and bright. What he most lacked was persistency in journalism. In March, 1845, he had a controversy with Nathaniel P. Willis while on the *Courier and Enquirer*. It became quite personal. Willis was then editor of the *Evening Mirror*. He was soon placed on the defensive, and to repel Raymond's assaults he felt constrained to give copies of social invitations from several of the nobility of Europe, and from distinguished ladies and gentlemen in the United States. The controversy was an exciting and amusing one, but there was no violation of the public peace.

Mr. Raymond made an effort to turn the *Courier and Enquirer* on the track of the new class of journals. Thomas Snowden, a heavy, phlegmatic printer of the old *Advocate* and of the old school, was the business manager of the concern at that time, and could not appreciate the energy and enterprise of the new spirit in the establishment. Every effort made in this direction brought forth a groan of despair from the ancient Snowden. "That little Raymond," Snowden would say, "will not rest contented till he has turned the *Courier and Enquirer* into a two-cent paper."

On the election of General Taylor to the presidency, General Webb was appointed minister to Austria; but, in the language of a friend of the editor,

General Webb in Brazil. 361

Public feeling in America ran very high at that moment against Austria on account of her conduct towards Hungary, and the Democratic party opposed General Webb's nomination as a preparatory step to the suspension of diplomatic intercourse with Austria, and on that ground were sustained by many of Webb's personal and political friends. His nomination was defeated, and it was the avowed intention of the Senate to reject in like manner any other nomination for the same post. General Cass, the Democratic candidate for the presidency, originated the movement against the nomination, and against sending any minister to Vienna, but in so doing took especial occasion to declare, in the most pointed and direct terms, that he did so from no personal objection to General Webb, with whom, on the contrary, he declared that, despite political differences, he had for many years been on terms of the most intimate friendship, and for whom he had the highest personal regard, as well as a high opinion of his unquestionable talents, and his entire qualification for the post to which he had been appointed.

Webb had, however, started on his mission, and met his rejection in Vienna. In his absence the *Courier and Enquirer* was placed under the editorial management of Mr. Raymond. After General Webb's return Mr. Raymond retired from the establishment. This was early in 1851, in consequence of a difference of opinion with the editor-in-chief on the great compromise measures of the previous year. The *Times* was brought out in the fall of that year.

On the 1st of July, 1861, the *Morning Courier and New York Enquirer* was united with the *World*, under the title of *The World and Courier and Enquirer*. Since then the latter name has been dropped, and the *Courier and Enquirer* passed to the Greenwood of journalism.

General Webb was appointed minister to Brazil by President Lincoln, and confirmed as such, and, with an occasional excitement with the British minister, with Admiral Davis on the Paraguayan difficulty, and with the Brazilian foreign minister, he passed a very agreeable time. In a recent letter to Secretary Seward, in speaking of his affair with Admiral Davis, he said, "One thing is certain: we can not both be right, and one of us should be severely censured, if not recalled." As General Webb was at home about the time this was published, and afterwards returned to Brazil, the government let the matter drop till it afterwards turned up in Congress.

Although at the head of no newspaper, Webb has never ceased to be, in one way or another, engaged in some affair which has kept his name before the public. The last one was in relation to the withdrawal of the French troops from Mexico. The *New York Times* gave a history of General Webb's connection with this matter. It had been generally believed that the abandonment of Mexico by France was caused by Secretary Seward's demand, made in December, 1865. But it appears that as early as 1863, in an interview with Louis Napoleon, the promise was given to General Webb that the French troops should be recalled if France was not threatened by the United States; and that at a breakfast at St. Cloud in November, 1865, the emperor made an arrangement with General Webb that the Imperial troops should be withdrawn, and this arrangement was to be communicated to the President in person, and without the circumlocution of the State Department, or the American embassy in Paris. The *New York Herald, au contraire*, published a letter from the Chevalier Wikoff, in which he claimed to have arranged the matter with Napoleon. These two diplomats were both personal friends of the Emperor in his days of exile and imprisonment. General Webb became acquainted with him at the Washington Hotel, in New York, in 1834, and the Chevalier Wikoff when Louis Napoleon was in prison at Ham. But in a recent biography of Webb the following important letter from Napoleon to General Webb is printed, which seems to entitle the latter to most of the credit of this achievement:

THE EMPEROR TO GENERAL WEBB.

PARIS, March 22d, 1863.

MY DEAR GENERAL,—I received your letter of March 8, and the interesting note inclosed therein, which, after perusal, I burned immediately, according to your wishes, and without mentioning the subject to any one. The questions you treat of are very important and very delicate; still, I will answer them in all frankness.

You are greatly mistaken if you believe that any motive of ambition or cupidity has led me into Mexico. Engaged in this enterprise by Spain, and led by the doings of Juarez, I reluctantly sent, first, 2000 men; afterwards, the national honor being compromised, my troops were increased to 8000; finally, the repulse at Puebla having engaged our military honor, I sent over 35,000 men. It is, therefore, much against my inclination that I am compelled to wage war at such a distance from France; and it is in no way for the purpose of taking possession of the mines of the Sonora that my soldiers are fighting. But, now that the French flag is in Mexico, it is difficult for me to foretell what may happen; at all events, my intention is to withdraw as soon as honor and the interests now engaged allow me.

It would be wrong in the United States, therefore, to make my being there a subject of dispute; for a *menace* would then change all my plans, which now are *disinterested*. As regards the war which desolates your country, I profoundly regret it, for I do not see how and when it will end, and it is not the interest of France that the United States should be weakened by a struggle without any good results possible. In a country as sensible as America, it is not by arms that domestic quarrels should be settled, but by votes, meetings, and assemblies. In Europe, too, we have many causes of disturbance—many grave questions to solve. For this purpose, France needs the alliance of England; hence my efforts have always been directed toward maintaining the ties of good understanding, often in spite of the ill will of the English government.

I have now sincerely explained my position to you, and in that way, you see, I reciprocate the perfect frankness of your communication. Be always persuaded, my dear general, of my interest in your country, as well as my friendship and the high esteem which I profess for your character.

With these sentiments, I remain yours very affectionately, NAPOLEON.

THE JOURNAL OF COMMERCE.

The *Journal of Commerce* was the second of this class of newspapers. It was established in New York City on the 1st of September, 1827, under the auspices of Arthur Tappan. It was first edited by William Maxwell, of Norfolk, Virginia. Mr. Maxwell, with the Monroes, Madisons, Barbours, Faulkners, and M'Dowells, was in favor of the abolition of slavery in Virginia at that period, and the subject was strongly advocated in the Convention of that state. The measure was defeated then by Nat. Turner's insurrection, and the appearance of Abolitionism in the North, and especially in New England, with such men as William Lloyd Garrison at the head of the movement in Boston, and the Tappans in New York. Maxwell came to New York with this idea on his brain, and assumed the editorial management of the *Journal of Commerce*. Arthur Tappan, and his brother Lewis, were extensive dry-goods merchants in Pearl Street, in the middle of the district of the great fire of 1835, full of piety and philanthropy. They aided the *Journal of Commerce* to the extent of thirty thousand dollars, a large sum in those days to invest in the luxury of a newspaper or an idea. Arthur Tappan then became fatigued with spending money, and disposed of his interest in the concern. It passed into the hands of Lewis Tappan, David Hale, and Horace Bushnell, afterwards the well-known theologian. It was then purchased by Hale and Hallock, the former of whom had been connected with the paper from its origin. Abolitionism now began to assume a serious phase. Mobs, riots, tar, feathers, and hanging in effigy were frequently spoken of in connection therewith. The agitation of Lloyd Garrison in Boston, and the affair of Nat. Turner in Virginia, changed the whole aspect of the question, and emancipation in Virginia was postponed till 1859–61, when it culminated in the hanging of John Brown and the firing on the Stars and Stripes at Fort Sumter.

David Hale and Gerard Hallock, both of Boston, became proprietors of the *Journal of Commerce* in the fall of 1828. Hale managed the business part of the establishment and the commercial department of the paper. Hallock had the editorial management, and guided the general policy of the journal. The former retained his place till his death early in 1849, and the latter was the responsible editor till September 1, 1861, when he retired to New Haven, Connecticut, where he died on the 4th of January, 1866.

Hallock was the originator of the *Boston Telegraph*, which was started on the 1st of January, 1824, and edited that paper till its union with the *Boston Recorder* in 1825, which he edited till 1827. He then became part proprietor of the *New York Observer*, and remained as such for one year. He did not know, however, what journalism was till he took hold of the *Journal of Commerce* in 1828. He was a painstaking, well-meaning, conscientious editor; a man of intelligence, a careful writer, an accomplished linguist, but not a brilliant man. He did not wish to injure any man's feelings, but he always deemed it necessary to do his duty. Although the *Journal of Commerce* came into existence as an Abolition paper, it ran into strong conservatism. It endeavored to save the Union in 1850, when Castle Garden was the seat of government, and Washington the Executive Mansion. It was the organ of the Southern Aid Society in 1860, and Hallock retired to private life rather than accept the situation of 1861. He was a genial gentleman, honest and honorable ; fair and firm in all transactions, and a valuable citizen. With his wealth he did all the good he could in accordance with his views. It is said that he built and almost supported a church in New Haven. He was a man of frugal and simple habits ; fatherly in his family, and fatherly in his manners ; plain and modest in his dress and deportment, positive and decided in his convictions. In a word, he was a man to be respected.

Hale was a tall, slim, brusque, vigorous man, with a loud manner and a loud voice. He was energetic ; felt sure that success depended on attending to his business ; was not afraid of any one ; had two religions, in both of which he was orthodox. One religion was as a member of the old Tabernacle Church in Broadway, where all the splendid oratorios of the New York Sacred Music Society were given ; where Herz gave his monster concerts, and Leopold de Meyer wore his big plaid pants ; where Ole Bull, Vieux Temps, and Sivori played so exquisitely on the violin and the people's feelings ; where so many mass meetings were held on so many popular subjects, and where they had stated preaching morning, afternoon, and evening of each Sunday throughout the year. When the church was sold, Hale bought it to save it ; and, if he had felt disposed, he could have realized a handsome fortune by the operation, but he bought it for the Church. Hale's other religion was opposition to Webb and the *Courier and Enquirer;* to beat that concern in getting news whenever that was possible, and obtain all the yearly advertisers he could from that paper. He went on 'Change every day to gather what he could there for his evening editions, which were a feature of the *Journal of Commerce* at that time, and added many names to its subscription-list in the neighboring towns and cities before the telegraphic wires were stretched over the country. We have seen crowds, in Topliff's News-room in Boston, disagreeably elbowing each other around the file of the *Journal of Commerce*, on the arrival of the New York mail, for the brief one and two line item in these late editions. We have seen Hale mount a chair in his office in New York, and read off to the crowds of merchants, with the voice of Stentor, some fresh news just received. Newspapers were then a curious institution, and Hale was fully up to the mark as a journalist to 1835-40, but he never went beyond that notch of time.

Hale and Hallock inaugurated the famous news schooners in 1829-30. Much interest was manifested in this country in the affairs of France, then on the eve of the Revolution of July, 1830. To obtain the news from Europe, these "old fogy" journalists, in the words of the *Journal*, bought and equipped a small, swift schooner, called her the *Journal of Commerce*, and sent her to cruise at sea, intercept packet ships, and bring in the latest intelligence. This was the first news-boat of any size in America. Small row-boats had been used to board shipping in the harbor by the *Journal* as well as other papers, but no one had, up to this time, sent a news-boat to sea. The enterprise was regarded by others as ridiculous and ruinously expensive, but the result proved the wisdom of Hale and Hallock. The Semaphoric Telegraph would report the *Journal of Commerce* in the offing, and business would be at once suspended to await her arrival. Crowds would then surround the office, as in the days of modern war bulletins, and the news would soon appear in an Extra. This was the commencement of the New York *Extras*. The success was such that the firm built and equipped another schooner, of 90 tons, calling her *The Evening Edition*, and thus had two swift vessels constantly cruising for news. An association of other papers was then formed, and a pilot-boat hired to compete with the *Journal of Commerce* squadron. The association subsequently fitted out a small vessel, and the business of news-boats continued for some time a fixed fact with New York dailies.

These successes on water had given such strength and prestige to the establishment that Hale and Hallock determined to introduce their system on the land. Accordingly, in 1833, they established a horse express from Philadelphia to New York, with eight relays, and by this means published the proceedings of Congress and all other Southern news one day in advance of their contemporaries. The other papers established an opposition express, and the government then commenced it, and ran the express from Philadelphia to New York; whereupon the proprietors of the *Journal of Commerce* extended their relays to Washington, so that they regularly beat the government express twenty-four hours. In one instance the Norfolk *Beacon* (published 229 miles southeast of Washington) copied the Washington news on two successive days from the *New York Journal of Commerce*, which it received by sea, before it had any advices from the capital. The *Journal* express employed 24 horses, and often made the whole distance of 227 miles inside of 20 hours.

The *Journal of Commerce* claims that these news-boats and expresses were the origin of the whole system of expressing and telegraphing which has since been brought to so much perfection by the New York Associated Press and the enterprising independent journals of the country. After five or six years' enterprise of this sort, however, the New York papers became somewhat tired of the expense, and combined their forces, and finally relapsed to the small row-boats for the collection of ship-news and foreign intelligence. When, in 1837 and 1838, the new class of papers came into noticeable existence, the *Herald* and the *Sun*, for instance, the Wall Street papers had fallen into great apathy. The *Herald* then, as it acquired means, began to accomplish wonders in the acquisition of news, and it succeeded in making its mark on the public mind as the pioneer of modern journalism. The editors and proprietors of the old class of papers first endeavored to crush out these fresh additions to journalism by abuse. They opened their batteries upon the *Herald*, but that establishment was an iron-clad. It continued on its pathway, increasing its enterprise with its increased resources. The "penny press" were spoken of with contempt. Sneer followed success, and more success succeeded sneer. All of the small cheap papers, and especially the *Herald*, were ignored by the "respectable sixpennies." There was no public recognition!

Amidst this state of things, what was to be the result? It was evident that the Cheap Press were making inroads upon the old class, slowly it was true, but surely. Hale and Hallock, with some of the foresight they had shown when they took hold of the *Journal of Commerce* in 1828, came to the rescue.

One forenoon, after the *Herald* had published some exclusive news, a knock was heard at the door of the editorial rooms of that paper. "Come in!" answered the editor. The tall, gaunt figure of David Hale entered. One of the magnates of Wall Street journalism was actually in the office of a despised penny paper! But Hale was a practical man. He saw the handwriting plainly enough. There was very little circumlocution about him.

"I have called," said he, "to talk about news with you. Have you any objection?"

"None," replied the penny editor. "Am always pleased to talk on that subject."

"We propose to join the *Herald* in getting news," continued Mr. Hale. "Have you any objection to that?"

This led to a brief conversation on newspaper enterprise, pony expresses, and news-boats. This conversation on the establishment of the telegraph led to the organization of the New York Associated Press. This interview was the origin of that institution. Out of this conversation grew up an *entente cordiale* in news between the old *Journal of Commerce* and the young *Herald* which was of great service to the former during the war with Mexico, and in its competition with the *Courier and Enquirer.* When the *Associated Press* was organized, Gerard Hallock became its president, and remained as such till he retired from the Press; respected by every member of that body.

It has already been said that these two representative "blanket sheets" were constantly in opposition. It was particularly so during the Abolition Riots in New York in 1833 and '34. The contents of the *Courier and Enquirer* and *Journal of Commerce* in 1833 and 1860 present a curious contrast. But the same wonderful changes in sentiment are every where visible. Nevertheless, the extracts we make are either curiosities in newspaper literature, or they exhibit wonderful progress in human freedom.

Many old citizens will remember these Abolition Riots. Then a handful of men and women, mostly of the latter sex in Boston, headed by Mr. Joshua Leavitt in New York, and William Lloyd Garrison in Boston, set the Anti-slavery ball in motion. New York was then comparatively a small place. It contained a population of less than a quarter of a million. Its fences and walls, on the 1st of October, 1833, were placarded with a very simple announcement. But it aroused Gotham. It read as follows:

The friends of immediate abolition of slavery in the United States are requested to meet at Clinton Hall on Wednesday evening, 2d October, at half past seven o'clock, to form a New York City Anti-slavery Society.

Committee: Joshua Leavitt, John Rankin, William Goodell, William Green, Jr., Lewis Tappan.

This apparently harmless call was immediately followed by another, more full of meaning, which appeared throughout the city on the same day. Here it is:

NOTICE.
TO ALL PERSONS FROM THE SOUTH.

All persons interested in the object of a meeting called by J. Leavitt, W. Goodell, W. Greene, Jr., J. Rankin, and L. Tappan, at Clinton Hall, this evening, at seven o'clock, are requested to attend at the same hour and place.

MANY SOUTHERNERS.

N.B.—*All* citizens who may feel disposed to manifest the *true* feeling of the State on this subject are requested to attend.

These two calls proved to be sparks in a powder magazine. There was an explosion, the noise of which was heard all over the Union for the next thirty years. The movement of Leavitt and Tappan was denounced by the newspapers, and strong appeals made to the people to crush it in its infancy. Our two "blanket sheets" entered the arena with great vigor, one for and the other against these new philanthropists.

The trustees of Clinton Hall became alarmed, and refused their rooms to the Abolitionists. Other public halls could not be obtained. Immense crowds gathered in Nassau Street and vicinity, and then adjourned to Tammany Hall. Amidst this excitement, the Abolitionists quietly met at the old Chatham Street Chapel, which had been the old Chatham Theatre, only a stone's throw from Tammany. There they organized the "Anti-slavery Society of New York." In thirty minutes the thing was done, and the fifty-three individuals composing the meeting voted to adjourn. Meanwhile the crowd outside swelled in numbers. They had scented the Abolitionists to the chapel and stormed the place. But all but one man had vanished through the back doors leading into another street as the mob carried the citadel. That man was Isaac T. Hopper, who refused to leave except by the front door, and the crowd let him pass. Hopper was a well-known Quaker philanthropist in New York. He was the image of Napoleon after he became emperor and stout. Joseph Bonaparte once called upon Hopper when in New York, and said that he never saw a more striking resemblance between two men. Hopper, it seems in this affair, was like Napoleon in another point: he did not know fear. The steps of the Chatham Street Chapel were his Lodi.

After this night of wild excitement what did the "blanket sheets" say? On the morning of the 3d of October, 1833, the *Journal of Commerce*, in speaking of the affair, held forth as follows:

> These "many Southerners" were probably a handful of "Northern fanatics," who, not content with enjoying their own opinions, and uttering them when and where they pleased, were anxious to prevent others from enjoying the same privilege. But, whether Northern or Southern, they have mistaken the genius of our institutions if they imagine a cause, be it ever so bad, can be permanently injured by such disgraceful proceedings. "The blood of the martyrs," it is said, "is the seed of the Church;" and persecution in *any* form, or against any set of opinions, is very apt to produce reaction. In this country there is no such thing as putting down error by physical force, or any thing equivalent thereto. If Fanny Wright and Robert Dale Owen, in their late mission to New York, had met with this kind of opposition, instead of being permitted to belch out their poison at pleasure, it is more than probable they would have found, both for themselves and their doctrines, a permanent lodgment among us. As it was, they soon exhausted their resources, and betook themselves to other shores, followed by the pity and disgust of almost our whole population. Let us not be understood as alluding to this case for the sake of invidious comparison, but only for the purpose of illustration. The immediate Emancipationists, though embracing but a small part of our population, enroll among their numbers many gentlemen of exalted worth, and who, whatever may be their errors on this subject, will be remembered and honored long after the tongues of their traducers shall be silent in the grave.
>
> But it is not upon this ground merely that we condemn the proceedings of last evening. Though the individuals referred to were men of the feeblest intellect and of the most worthless character, we would still maintain that they had as good a right to assemble and make speeches, free from interruption and insult, as any of their opposers. What sort of toleration is that which bears with those who agree with us in opinion? Just such as may be found in Spain, or Turkey, or in the dominions of the Czar. The essence of toleration is to bear with those who differ from us, and with opinions which we hold in utter abhorrence. There

are plenty of men in this country, and plenty of editors, who are stanch advocates of toleration on paper, but the moment you touch a subject in which *they* feel deeply, their liberality has vanished into smoke. Toleration is very good when it applies to themselves, but when it is called for in favor of others, and when *they* are the persons to exercise it, that alters the case materially. It is no longer your bull that has killed one of my oxen.

We said that *common interest* required that public meetings should not be interrupted. For it is as easy to interrupt a Colonization meeting as an Abolition meeting. A very few persons suffice to accomplish the object. They have only to make more noise than the speaker, and the work is done. And what enterprise, good or bad, has not its opposers? No one. Let, then, the principle be established, that any bevy of gentlemen or vagabonds may invade the peace of a meeting, the design of which they disapprove (or profess to disapprove, for the sake of having a *row*), and what will be the consequence? Why, that all public meetings will be at the mercy of the evil-minded. There is no line of distinction which can be drawn. We say, then, that all parties, on all subjects, are interested in putting down the disgraceful practice.

We are happy to believe that whoever else is implicated in the transactions of last evening, the Colonization Society is not. The *Commercial Advertiser*, which is more the organ of that society than any other paper in this city, foresaw the interruption, and entered its protest against it.

After all, it appears that the immediate Emancipationists outgeneraled their opposers; for while the latter were besieging Clinton Hall, or wasting wind at Tammany Hall, the former were quietly adopting their Constitution at Chatham Street Chapel. They had but just adjourned, we understand, when the din of the invading army, as it approached from Tammany Hall, fell upon their ears; and before the audience was fairly out of the chapel, the flood poured in through the gates, as if they would take it by storm. But lo! they were too late; the Antislavery Society had been formed, the Constitution adopted, and the meeting adjourned! So they had nothing to do but go home.

"The King of France, with twenty thousand men,
Marched up the hill, and then marched down again."

The *Courier and Enquirer*, in opposition, denounced the *Journal of Commerce* as the "principal organ of Fanaticism and Hypocrisy," and "the advocate of every measure calculated, directly or indirectly, to cast a stigma on the character of our country, our people, our wives, our mothers, sisters, and daughters," and following up the subject, the *Courier* said:

There can no longer be any doubt of the objects of these fanatics, nor of the tendency of their proceedings; and it becomes the duty of every good citizen to frown upon them, as dangerous to the harmony of the country, and hazardous to the property and lives of our Southern brethren. What, then, is to be done? Are we tamely to look on, and see this most dangerous species of fanaticism extending itself through society, until at length it acquires a foothold among us sufficient to induce those partaking of it to array themselves openly, as they now are secretly, against the Constitution of the United States? Or shall we, by promptly and fearlessly crushing this many-headed hydra in the bud, expose the weakness, as well as the folly, madness, and mischief of these bold and dangerous men? We confess this latter course appears to us the most proper, and, under all the circumstances, the only one which can with safety be pursued.

Thus the crusade against slavery opened. This was "the small cloud no bigger than a man's hand." Then the excitement became more intense, and spread over the entire country. The Washington *Telegraph*, edited by Duff Green, the organ of John C. Calhoun, took up the subject, and set the South on fire by its inflammatory appeals. Other newspapers embraced the idea. Fifty thousand dollars reward were offered in New Orleans for the body of Arthur Tappan, and another reward for Lewis Tappan. Abolition editors were indicted by Southern grand juries. Trade between the North and South entered largely into the contest, and so the ball of agitation rolled on.

One afternoon in July, 1834, as Lewis Tappan was sitting in his store in Pearl Street, a colored waiter from the City Hotel touched him on the shoulder, and said, in a quick under-tone,

"Mr. Tappan, your house will be mobbed to-night."

"How do you know?" asked Tappan.

"I hear the gentlemen talk so at dinner," replied the negro, and he disappeared.

Mr. Tappan left his store earlier than usual on that day, engaged a carriage, and proposed to his family to take a short ride in the country. The carriage was driven up the Bowery and out to Harlem, where the husband, wife, and children took supper. They passed the night at the hotel. The first paper opened on the next morning showed the correctness of the negro waiter's information. There was the fact in large capitals:

GREAT RIOT—LEWIS TAPPAN'S HOUSE SACKED.

New York had its riot week then as in 1863. It was one of commotion, excitement, and fear. The Chatham Street Chapel, the Bowery Theatre, Dr. S. H. Cox's church and house, Zion's (colored) Church, the Rev. Mr. Ludlow's church, St. Philip's (colored) Church, African Baptist Church, Arthur and Lewis Tappan's houses, were mobbed and sacked. Windows and doors were smashed; bonfires of furniture, with church organs and parlor pianos thrown in to increase the conflagration, lighted up the city, and it was some time before order reigned in the metropolis. Now all has passed into history, and only three daily newspapers published in that exciting period are in existence; and the *Journal of Commerce*, said Hallock, in 1861, " is now the only paper of its class in the city, all the other large dailies, five or six in number, which were in existence when its publication commenced, as well as all which have since been started, being now defunct, or metamorphosed into some new form of physical existence."

There were assistant editors, of course, on the *Journal of Commerce*, as on other papers. In its early days, Richard Haughton, afterwards of the *Boston Atlas*, was one of these. One of his duties was to collate the election returns. These figures, so interesting to politicians and to office-seekers when they result in majorities on the right side, are very difficult to arrange clearly and intelligently. Sometimes they are a Chinese puzzle. One must understand the science not to make stupid blunders. Haughton understood them. Bennett, of the *Herald*, thoroughly comprehended them. So did Greeley, of the *Tribune*. Others, in attempting to give election returns, would often get them terribly confused. When Haughton left the *Journal of Commerce* to take charge of the *Atlas*, who was to look after this peculiar department in that office? Hale told Hallock he must perform this task. "I don't understand such things; I never did, and I never could," said Hallock. "Well," replied Hale, "we must have them, and you must try your hand at them." Hallock, patient and obliging man, did try, and succeeded. Some of the Union merchants, in giving some silver plate to him one day for his services to the country as a journalist, included in their compliments one for the accuracy of his election returns.

Hallock slept on his arms. His family resided in New Haven. On Friday afternoon he would go home. On Monday morning he would return. It was a regular swing of the pendulum backwards and forwards. The remainder of the week was spent in his office. Next to his editorial room was a nice, neatly-furnished bedroom. There he slept. He would take his meals at the restaurants—to-day at George W. Browne's, to-morrow at Alderman Ridabock's. In the early days of the *Journal* he would run to fires. No fire occurred at night in New York that was not chronicled in his paper the next morning. Once he nearly lost his life in this sort of enterprise. In running through one of the narrow, dark streets, when the city was not lighted, as the almanacs had arranged for the moon to shine, he was precipitated into a freshly-excavated cellar of considerable depth. With some difficulty he extricated himself. "And didn't you miss that fire?" asked a friend, when he was telling the incident. "Oh no," said he; "I sat down on the curb-stone to rub myself, and, seeing the light of the fire brighten up, I started for it again. It was in the *Journal* the next morning." Our respect for the practical journalist was immensely increased by the incident.

When the *Journal of Commerce* was started in 1827 it was 35 by 24 inches in size. When it reached its growth on the 1st of March, 1853, it was 35 by $58\frac{3}{4}$ inches. Imagine a folio sheet of the latter size to hold out at arm's length to read. Nast and Leitch sometimes represent such sheets in *Punch* and *Harper's*. It is painful, even now, to think of the effort. In 1828 the circulation of the paper was 850. In 1853 it had increased to 4500. It also had 800 yearly advertisers in that year, as many as its entire circulation in 1828. Its circulation is now about 5000. This is considered large for a paper of this class. It depends for its revenue on the commercial classes—on its "yearly advertisers"—who are not quite yet prepared for the prices demanded by the new class of papers—the

Independent Press. These advertisers paid $32 per year each in 1850. Some advertised largely and greedily, others modestly and moderately, leaving a fair average for the newspaper proprietor. This unfair system was changed in the *Journal* in 1853. Then the yearly advertiser was limited to ten lines per day for $32 per annum, or one cent per line per day. With the increased cost of every thing since 1861, this price is now much higher, but not relatively higher than the rates in the new class of papers.

There is an incident which will illustrate this point, and the difference in the two classes of journals in this respect. One of the large steam-ship lines in New York advertised in nearly all the papers—in the *Journal of Commerce*, and in the *New York Herald*. Sixty dollars was paid the former, and one thousand dollars the latter, for the same service for twelve months. When viewed together by the steam-ship company, these bills appeared somewhat incongruous to their minds. "There must be some mistake in that bill," said Mr. Cunard, the manager of the line, to the chief of the advertisement bureau of the *Herald*. "Not at all," replied the chief; "our bill is correct." "How?" said Mr. Cunard. "Look at that," showing the *Journal* bill. "Nine hundred and forty dollars difference for the same advertisement, and no mistake? Impossible!" And the steam-ship manager took his hat. "I will tell you what we'll do," said the amiable and accommodating man of the *Herald*. "We will advertise at the same rate that the *Journal of Commerce* charges you." "That is what I thought," interrupted the active man of steam. "Stop a moment," continued the journalistic clerk. "Our rates are to be the same as those of the *Journal*. The circulation of that paper is 4500—we'll call it 5000. Ours is 100,000. Sixty dollars for 5000 is $1200 for 100,000 circulation. Is it not? Our regular rates are, therefore, in fact, $200 per year less. Then, where the *Journal* has three readers, the *Herald* has five. Again: cut your advertisement from one copy of the *Herald*, weigh it, multiply that by 100,000, and then by 365 daily publications, and the cost of the white paper alone on which it is printed will astound you in a small way. Then again—" "Enough!" exclaimed the practical merchant. "I am satisfied." On returning to his office he ordered the bills to be paid, and the advertisements of this popular and well-managed steam-ship line continued daily in the *Herald* and *Journal of Commerce*.

On the 1st of September, 1861, owing to political circumstances growing out of the Rebellion, and a desire to retire from active business, now interfered with by government, Gerard Hallock sold his interest in the paper. After this the *Journal* was published by David M. Stone, who for the previous twelve years had been at the head of the commercial department of the paper, and William C. Prime, author of "Owl-Creek Letters," "The Old House by the River," "Travels in the Holy Land," "Tent Life in Egypt," "Boat Life in Egypt and Nubia," "Later Years," etc., William H. Hallock, and David A. Hale, representing the heirs of David Hale, deceased. On taking leave of the press and the public in 1861, after a journalistic life of nearly forty years, Gerard Hallock said:

> Accordingly, although we have denounced secession again and again as a dangerous heresy, unauthorized by the Constitution, and never justifiable unless revolution is justifiable, because of heavy oppression, and because redress can be obtained in no other way, yet so industrious has been the tongue of slander, through the press and otherwise, that I suppose one half the population of New York honestly believe that the *Journal of Commerce* is a secession paper, and that I am an advocate of that heresy. Accordingly, I have received anonymous letters by the dozen, threatening personal violence and the destruction of my office. Volunteer committees have waited upon numbers of our subscribers, urging and sometimes significantly *advising* them to stop taking the *Journal of Commerce*. Anonymous letters and circulars have been served upon advertisers, warning them that if they continue to advertise in the *Journal of Commerce*, their own business will suffer in consequence. The ultra-War Press, whose name is legion, has been set upon us, or has set itself upon us, and continued the onset for weeks and months, with a ferocity that knew no bounds. The U. S. Grand Jury has presented us, or half presented us, just at the close of their session, asking no instructions from the judge, and expressly stating that they desired none, preferring to let the matter go over to the next term of the court. Lastly, on the strength of that presentment, the Postmaster General has refused to our paper the common right of transmission in the mails. Had the Grand Jury waited for instructions, the judge, whatever might be his prejudices, would have been compelled to tell them that we had violated no law, and therefore that they had nothing to do in the case. But by leaving the matter in abeyance for two months, there would be time for the poison to work in the community, without the possibility of our administering an effectual remedy, and also a chance for the Postmaster General to apply the screws to an old enemy of Abolitionism, and sectionalism generally. Had this last form of oppression been omitted, all the others would have failed of their object; for, in spite of them all, our circulation in the aggregate has been steadily increasing, and we have more subscribers to-day in the non-seceded states than we had on the 1st of January last in the whole Union. But I can not contend with the government, and have no disposition to do so. I believe the exclusion of the *Journal of Commerce* from the mails is sanctioned by no law, but that it is in violation of law and of the Constitution. But as neither the law nor the Constitution was available against the edict of the government, or one branch of it, I concluded to save my partners by disposing of my interest in the establishment, and retiring from its direction, thus atoning for the sins of the ultra-war papers, whose testimony in regard to the *Journal of Commerce* the Postmaster General doubtless received as true. Had it not been for my partners, or some of them, I might have preferred to leave the dead body of the *Journal of Commerce* unburied, as an illustration of the measure of liberty now enjoyed by the press in this free country.

But the *Journal of Commerce* did not escape trouble by the retirement of its senior editor. In 1864 a bogus proclamation of President Lincoln, calling for half a million more troops, was imposed upon several of the newspapers of the metropolis. The *Journal* was one of the innocent victims. Its office was seized, and the publication of the paper suspended by order of the government in the most arbitrary manner. The history of this outrageous affair, so entirely new since the Alien and Sedition laws, is so important that we give a sketch of the proceedings in the case as it appeared in the *Journal of Commerce* of March 26, 1870:

THE BOGUS PROCLAMATION.

The forged proclamation issued in the name of the late President Lincoln was published at a critical period of the war, and in a time of great excitement. It is quite natural, therefore, that later writers, who endeavor in good faith to give its true history, should fall into serious errors by copying statements which were originally made without a full knowledge of the facts. Within the last few months several such accounts have appeared, each of them containing grave inaccuracies, and calculated to perpetuate the earlier erroneous impressions. Mr. Maverick, in his Life of Raymond, has inadvertently spoken of that invention as having imposed upon the editors of this paper, and within a day or two a contemporary has alluded to the sharpness of the *Times* and *Tribune* in suspecting the hoax and refusing to publish it. It should be known that no one in any way connected with the editorial department of the *Journal of Commerce* ever saw the proclamation until it was printed, and that no copy was ever left at the *Tribune* office, so that the editors of that paper had no opportunity to suspect or reject it. The fact that the *Tribune* had no copy was one reason, if not the governing motive, for making the inquiry as to its authenticity of the agency of the Associated Press, which resulted in excluding it from several other papers.

We propose to make a contribution to the history of this case. Where we make positive statements we speak of facts within our own knowledge or which are undisputed: some explanations we supply from incidents brought out in the investigation at the time, but without vouching in all cases for their absolute correctness.

The proclamation was invented by Joseph Howard, now editor and publisher of the New York Daily *Star*, but then a prominent Republican, being one of the Kings County Republican Committee, and a communicant in Rev. Henry Ward Beecher's church in Brooklyn. The copies presented for publication were written on a book of manifold paper which had been abstracted from the office of the Associated Press, and this work was executed by F. A. Mallison, formerly employed in such service, whose hand was familiar to the papers.

Copies were sent to all of the morning papers in this city accustomed to receive the dispatches of the Associated Press, but, as no printed envelopes could be obtained, the loose pages were folded and delivered without any wrapper. The boy who was sent was not very familiar with the night entrance to the several offices. He pounded for a long time on the wrong door of the *Tribune* building, and failed to obtain access; hence that paper had no copy of the document. The *Daily News*, not a member of the Association, had but recently been entitled to buy the news, and when the copy was laid on its counter the person in attendance asked why it was not sent in an envelope. The boy prevaricated, and hastily left. Having his suspicions aroused, the receiver sent down to the *Times* office to see if it was a Press dispatch. He was answered in the affirmative; but attention being thus called to the production itself, suspicion was aroused in the *Times* office, and a message sent across the street to see if the *Tribune* had it, and what was thought of it there. The answer returned was that the *Tribune* knew nothing about it. We have always believed that if the *Tribune's* copy had been delivered, all the papers receiving it in time would have printed it. After the answer came from the *Tribune* a question was sent over to the office of the Associated Press, when it was ascertained that the pretended dispatch was not genuine. The *Times* then suppressed the document, but apprised no other paper of its discovery save the *News*, which had made the first inquiry.

The *World* received and printed it without question. The *Sun*, which had a very large edition, and always went to press early, had made up its form, and could not get it in, if its editors had been disposed to print it.

The *Herald* received it as genuine, stereotyped it in its form, and went on printing it. After about twenty-five thousand copies had been struck off, a messenger sent for an early copy of the paper called at the *Herald* press-room with the *Times* and *Tribune* in his hand. On being questioned as to whether the proclamation had reached those papers in time for their first edition, he expressed surprise, and a search revealed the fact that those papers did not contain it. The *Herald* immediately struck it from the paper and recast the form. Only a few copies with the insertion had been sent out, and the remainder were consigned to the flames or the paper-mill.

The messenger had been instructed to deliver the copy to the *Journal of Commerce* last of all, and he subsequently testified that doubts had been expressed if it would pass muster at this office, no similar attempt at imposition ever having been successful in this quarter. It was half past three o'clock in the morning before the conspirators ventured to send it. Not only had the night editor in charge and all his force left for home, but all the compositors save those employed in manipulating the forms had been dismissed. The proof-reader lingered a moment on the outside step of the entrance at No. 93 Wall Street to talk with the copy-holder, who had just been discharged for inattention and general incompetency. The boy was making some plea in the hope of being restored, after which the proof-reader turned down the street toward his Brooklyn home, and the copy-holder started in the opposite direction. As the latter passed the corner he heard a pounding on the door of No. 91, which led to the business office, but did not connect with the upper stories. He called to know what was wanted, when a boy who was knocking came down the short steps and handed him the proclamation, saying that it was a very important dispatch from the Associated Press. He remarked that it was too late for the paper, but he would take it in, and thus receiving it from the other boy, he rushed with it up the stairs to the printing office. But for his officiousness the *Journal of Commerce* would have missed it as the *Tribune* did, and precisely for the same reason. Pausing a moment at the first landing, where there was a gas-light, to see what the news could be, his eye caught the words "a day of fasting," and he dashed up to the imposing table, where the foreman, with three assistants, was just taking off the form, with the words, "You'll have to wait; here's a holiday for you!"

On being questioned, he said he had received the dispatch "from an Associated Press boy at the foot of the stairs." As most of these messengers were intimate with the boys of the office, the foreman had no question of this statement, but he hesitated because the hour was so late and his workmen gone. His orders were that, after the form was closed and the editor gone, he should stop the press for nothing but the news of a battle or an official order. Of the latter the *Journal of Commerce* had published gratuitously enormous quantities about drafts, enlistments, etc., a large proportion of which came from Washington at a late hour in the night.

This proclamation was written on several pages of thin tissue paper. Looking at the foot of the last page the foreman saw the signature "Abraham Lincoln," and the countersign of Wm. H. Seward. Reluctantly he yielded to what he supposed to be the necessities of the case, and giving each of his assistants part of the copy, he set up part with his own hand. No proof was taken, each compositor setting his own part as carefully as possible, and thus the whole of it was read by no one in the office until it came from the press.

The writer of this was the first at the editor's office next morning. By a singular coincidence, the paper had failed to reach his hand that morning at his house for the only time during the whole year. There was an excited crowd on the streets and around the publication room. Hastily glancing at the page of the paper, we called for the copy. It was presented at once, and bore every internal evidence, both in paper and handwriting, of its genuineness as a Press dispatch, but we placed on the bulletin at once our suspicion of its authenticity.

A telegram of inquiry to the State Department at Washington was not answered until the next evening! But the moment we ascertained that the copy did not come from the office of the Association, we denounced it at once as a forgery, and forwarded at our own expense by the Cunard line a contradiction to be circulated by telegraph in Europe. The forged proclamation was printed on Wednesday morning, the 18th of May, 1864. The *Herald* was not molested for the few copies it had issued; but orders came immediately from the President to arrest the editors and proprietors of the *Journal of Commerce* and the *World*, lock them up in Fort Lafayette, and suppress their papers. Major General Dix, then in command of this military department, in a correspondence which reflected much credit upon him, endeavored in vain to secure the modification of this order by representing that the parties to be punished were the victims of the fraud and not its perpetrators, and could not have been guilty of any disrespect to the national authority. The offices named were seized, and a portion of the designated persons arrested. The military were searching for the remainder, and a boat with steam up was waiting off the Battery to take them down the bay, when about three o'clock Thursday morning the President countermanded the order of arrest, but the troops still kept possession of the printing establishments that had been seized. In addition to the telegrams actually sent by General Dix to Washington, we have heard it asserted by undoubted authority that this distinguished officer wrote a still more creditable letter, declining to execute the military decree, and tendering his resignation if the service were insisted upon; but he was overruled in his judgment of what his sense of justice and a proper self-respect required, and, retaining the letter in his desk, he executed his disagreeable mission in the open violation of law and the sacred rights so solemnly guaranteed by the Constitution.

Mr. Howard, the author of the forgery, was arrested on Thursday, the 19th of May, and, making a full confession, was on Friday sent to Fort Lafayette. Mr. Mallison, the instrument, was arrested a day after, and on Saturday was sent to the fort. The newspaper offices were vacated by the military on Saturday afternoon, and resumed the publication of their issues on Monday morning. The guilty perpetrators of the forgery, having strong friends among the leading men of the dominant party, were soon after discharged from custody without punishment.

The Governor of this state called the District Attorney's attention to the violation of both "the state and national laws" in the attempt of the authorities to punish the victims instead of the authors of the wrong, and Major General Dix, with several inferior officers, were arrested, and on July 9th had a hearing before Judge Russell. Judge Pierrepont, General Cochrane, Wm. M. Evarts, and other eminent counsel, were heard, and Judge Russell held these officers subject to indictment by the Grand Jury. The editors who had suffered so unjustly, however, did not urge the prosecution, and no further action was ever taken.

After the newspapers were suspended the government discovered that it had been precipitate, and made efforts to withdraw from the untoward dilemma in which it had placed itself against the advice of Major General Dix, who at one time was on the point of sending in his resignation rather than carry out the orders of the authorities at Washington. The friends of the administration endeavored to induce the editors of the *Journal of Commerce* to petition the Secretary of War to release that paper from arrest and suspension, but Mr. Stone positively and properly refused to do so. "I'll ask no such favor," said Stone, in his vehement manner and tone, to the mild but firm General Dix. "I have wittingly committed no offence, and the *Journal of Commerce* shall never appear again if it must be on such conditions. Let the government right its own wrong."

The most extraordinary part of this extraordinary affair was the actual promulgation, a few weeks after these arbitrary proceedings, of a *bona fide* proclamation almost of the same purport of the bogus document! Modern usurpation could not go farther than this. It was as much as the people would permit under the peculiar condition of the country at the time, and for America in 1864 it was an extreme measure, and tolerated only in the supposed exigencies of the government.

Shortly after the death of Mr. Gerard Hallock in 1869, his son William H. Hallock retired from the concern and went to Europe. On his return he made an effort to establish a cheap evening paper in New York. It was started, and called the *Republic;* but young Hallock having received his newspaper education in the office of one of the old class journals, he was not equal to the new state of things introduced by modern journalism and the telegraph. After losing $30,000 he gracefully succumbed to fate, and the *Republic* is no more.

Since then Mr. William C. Prime has withdrawn from the *Journal of Commerce* to indulge in books, art, lectures, travel, and numismatics, leaving that paper entirely under the editorial management of David M. Stone, who seems fond of his position, and hugely enjoys himself as presiding officer of that distinguished *illuminati*, the New York Associated Press.

CHAPTER XXIII.
SOME OF THE BOSTON NEWSPAPERS.

THE BOSTON DAILY ADVERTISER.—HORATIO BIGLOW AND NATHAN HALE. —THE FIRST DAILY NEWSPAPER.—EDITORIAL ARTICLES.—THE EVENING TRAVELLER. — THE BOSTON COURIER. — JOSEPH TINKER BUCKINGHAM.— THE TRANSCRIPT.—THE LIBERATOR.—WILLIAM LLOYD GARRISON.—OLD FILES OF NEWSPAPERS. — THE BOSTON POST. — CHARLES G. GREENE. — THE ATLAS.—RICHARD HAUGHTON AND JOHN H. EASTBURN.—THE MERCANTILE JOURNAL.—THE HERALD. — THE LAST NEWSPAPER ENTERPRISE. —THE GLOBE.

NEW ENGLAND could always boast of her newspapers. She is the mother of them in America. They were always well edited; always neatly printed; always felt an *amore propre* that was of service to them; always believed in New England; and always had faith in Boston. Augusta, Concord, Montpellier, Hartford, and Providence are nice cities, and respected as capitals in their respective states, but Boston above all in the estimation of every New Englander. She being the Hub, the others are the spokes, and so they revolve. The newspapers of Boston, therefore, are the newspapers *par excellence* of New England. The *Springfield Republican* and *Worcester Spy*, and one or two other journals in the rural districts, are influential, and as potent, probably, as the metropolitan papers, but not in the same districts and in the same way. These journals have an individuality and an enterprise of their own that has kept them in power with their readers. Our pages indicate the prominent part the papers of New England have performed in history, from the *News-Letter* to the *Globe*.

The first prominent daily paper issued in New England was the *Boston Daily Advertiser*, the publication of which was commenced on the 3d of March, 1813. There was a daily paper begun in that city on the 6th of October, 1796, by Alexander Martin, and edited by John O'Ley Burk, one of the "United Irishmen." It lived about six months. It was called the *Polar Star and Boston Daily Advertiser*. Another was attempted on the 1st of January, 1798, by Caleb P. Wayne, who was afterwards editor of the *United States Gazette* of Philadelphia. This second daily paper of Boston was named the *Federal Gazette and Daily Advertiser*. It lived three months. The third attempt at a daily paper in the capital of Massachusetts was a success. It was published by William W. Clapp, afterwards of the *Saturday Evening Gazette*, and edited by Horatio Biglow. Its editor, on the previous January, printed a prospectus, of which the following is an extract:

> Whilst every other city on the continent is teeming with diaries, we will not, by unnecessary apology, anticipate the charge of presumption in offering to the patronage of the citizens of Boston the plan of a Daily Commercial and Political Gazette, nor betray, by the wariness of precaution, a diffidence to that candor and liberality which has ever characterized the inhabitants of this ancient and respectable metropolis. We might, however, find a sufficient justification in the features of the times, which are of so extraordinary an aspect and so varying a hue, that whilst every interest is absorbed in political anxiety, every hour gives a different complexion to the chameleon-like object of our solicitude. By delaying the impression of our paper till the arrival of the Southern mail, we shall be able to insert an abstract of congressional debates, and so communicate the earliest intelligence of any portentous movement in the cabinet or camp. The frequency of publication will prevent the accumulation of important matter, and leave us ample room for the favors of our advertising friends.

It was the intention then to name the new paper the *Morning Post and Daily Advertiser, a Commercial and Political Journal*. On the 3d of March, however, the first number appeared as the *Boston Daily Advertiser*. This was the principal head-line. On the second number the name of *Repertory* was added to the sub-head only. The editor, in the initial sheet, said:

> It is about six weeks since the editor of this paper first announced the design of it to the public. The liberal encouragement he has already received, and an arrangement with the proprietor of the *Repertory*, have enabled him to commence the publication sooner than he could have anticipated. He has, in one respect, departed from his original intention. In compliance with the wish of his advertising friends, the *Daily Advertiser* will be issued at an early hour, without regard to the arrival of the morning post, and forwarded to distant subscribers by the mail of the day.
>
> * * * * * * * *
>
> In instituting the comparison, he has no wish to derogate from the merits, or the ability, or the utility of the Federal papers of this town. No one can be more ready to do justice to their character, and no one can more highly appreciate their services. He would be unwilling to think that his support must detract from theirs—he only asks for a share of public patronage. Besides monthly, weekly, and semi-weekly publications, EIGHT daily papers are circulated in *New York*, and the little city of *Alexandria*, with not half the population of *Salem*, is provided with TWO. It were an unworthy supposition that *Boston*, with all its wealth and liberality, is incompetent to the maintenance of ONE.

Biglow conducted the paper till the 6th of April, 1814. He then went to New York, where he edited the *American Monthly Magazine and Critical Review* in 1817. Nathan Hale, a nephew of "the patriot spy of the Revolution," after whom he was named, assumed the editorial management of the *Advertiser* on the 7th of April, 1814. Mr. Clapp continued to be the publisher. Its sub-head was then *Repertory and Daily Advertiser*. It was once more changed, and *Repertory* was dropped.

Mr. Hale entered upon his duties with a full appreciation of the responsibilities of an editor. On the 7th of April he said:

The great variety of duties which fall at once upon the present editor of this paper, on his entering somewhat suddenly upon his new engagements, might perhaps excuse him in the omission of the customary formality of an introductory address.

* * * * * * * *

Many of these readers rely solely for information upon the amount afforded by a single paper. Thus the intellectual appetites of thousands of readers, through which nourishment or poison is to be afforded to their political, moral, and sometimes religious principles, by which arguments are to be supplied for their daily discussion, facts for their history, and an impetus to all their mental exercise, are dependent for their periodical supply upon the frail understanding of a single editor.

* * * * * * * *

One of the peculiar traits of national character alluded to above is the insatiable appetite which exists in all classes of people in this country for news. It is a thirst so universal that it has given rise to a general and habitual form of salutation on the meeting of friends and strangers, *What's the news?* This is an inquiry of such universal interest that he who can answer it is always welcome, while he who brings the second report of an event, although it be much more full and correct in its details, is listened to with indifference. From this diseased state of the public taste arises a very great obstacle to the suitable performance of the editorial duties. The most correct rumors are seldom the most rapid in their flight; and while the editor is waiting for the arrival of a true statement of any affair, his readers are satisfied with the distorted representation that had gone forward. If he would keep pace with the curiosity and anticipations of a great part of his readers, he must deal more in crude reports and loose conjectures than in well-authenticated facts and the materials of history.

The new editor, with these views, was the first to introduce the regular editorial articles as a feature in journalism. Edward Everett, in some remarks before the Massachusetts Historical Society on the 12th of February, 1863, relative to Mr. Hale, observed:

It was said of the *Daily Advertiser* by a distinguished contemporary journalist, the founder and editor of the *Boston Courier*, that the *Advertiser* was the first journal which systematically introduced the editorial discussion of political topics, that branch of journalism having been before left to correspondents, the most celebrated of whom are the authors of the Federalist and Junius. I have not the means of verifying the accuracy of this remark, but certain it is that the columns of the *Daily Advertiser*, for forty years, contained, as a standing feature, an editorial comment on passing affairs at home and abroad; and not less so, that such comment, prepared as it was by Mr. Hale, in a manner to exercise a marked influence on public opinion, could be the achievement of no ordinary mind.

Managers of newspapers, for a long period in this country, were not generally writers. They were printers whose expectations were that their pages would be filled with advertisements, tales, news extracts, and gratuitous contributions from politicians and a few public spirited writers. They were mostly controlled by the leading politicians of the day, who would assist them with their pens and purses. The introduction of regular comments on passing events from the responsible editor of the paper was therefore a great feature in the history of the *Advertiser*, and an immense step forward in the progress and improvement in journalism.

Other papers had previously editorial articles, but they were rare. All public matters were discussed in communications. Our early editors were known as Publius, Tacitus, Fabius, Massachusettensis,

Laco, Zeno, Jonathan Oldstyle, Tullius, Honestus, Curtius, Solon, Busy Body, Federalist, Old South, Junius, Socrates, Veritas, Cato, Brutus, Poor Richard, Miles Juveniles, Thucydides, Spy, Senator, Scrutator. They wrote for the papers before the Hales, Weeds, Bennetts, Webbs, Hallocks, Raymonds, Greenes, Marbles, Danas, Greeleys, Brookses, Blairs, and Bryants became journalists. When this editorial feature was introduced in the *Advertiser*, it was the first step towards the Independent Press. The editorial comments of this paper had, as a national result, a large influence on the affairs of New England, and in the development of the resources of Massachusetts. There were other writers for the *Advertiser*, but Mr. Hale was so tenacious of his prerogatives that, if Edward Everett, or Daniel Webster, or Alexander H. Everett wrote for the paper, their productions, it is said, appeared as communications.

There was some journalistic enterprise in Mr. Hale. It is mentioned that he was the first to introduce steam power-presses in New England, as Walter, of the London *Times*, was the first to introduce them in Old England. With William Tudor and a few others, Mr. Hale was also one of the founders of the *North American Review* in 1815, and of the *Christian Examiner* at a later period.

With the change of base in the protective policy of the nation from the South to the North, Mr. Hale wrote, in 1828, a pamphlet on that policy, which became the basis of the protective tariffs of the United States from that day to this. He also entered largely into the system of internal improvements, which has done so much for this country. He was the first president of the Boston and Worcester Railroad, the first railway in New England, and over which the first locomotive in that section of the land drew a train of cars.

The *Advertiser* has absorbed a number of newspapers which were prominent and influential in their day, as these pages testify, but which could not outlive their peculiarity and specialty. Our researches develop the curious fact that of all the numerous papers which have been started into existence in the United States, and produced a sensation for a time, very few have continued in prosperity long after the demise of their founders and energetic conductors; and of those which have survived half a century are not now famous for any particular brilliancy, or energy, or enterprise. Our readers will recognize in such names as the *Boston Repertory*, the *Independent Chronicle and Boston Patriot*, the *Columbian Centinel*, the *New England Palladium*, the *Commercial Gazette*, and the *Centinel and Gazette*, journals that, in years gone by, had an influence, and made their mark in public circles. Well, all these papers now constitute the *Boston Daily Advertiser* of 1872.

The *Advertiser* is now called the "respectable daily" of Boston, and the organ of Harvard College. It never admits any thing offensive to State Street, or Beacon Street, or the illuminati of old Harvard. In old times it never sought an advertisement or a subscriber by personal application, because such a mode of doing business was not dignified. All this may have been true. All may be true now. What of it? Is it a sin for a newspaper to have a character of its own? But these statements are not all correct now. There is young blood in the concern. There is more enterprise in the establishment. There is a daily column of news items that, "in general," spice the solid and well-written leaders. Its money-market and marine news reports have always been reliable. It shows its respect for Harvard by publishing all the Latin rhyme the students may send in.

The office of the *Advertiser*, in a splendid new building, now stands in Court Street, on the spot where Benjamin Franklin began his career as printer and journalist in the early part of last century.

There was a paper printed on the corner of Cornhill and Court Street, Boston, forty-seven years ago, that was interesting and entertaining, and a valuable guide to the traveler. It had a peculiarly plain head-line for its title, which was the *American Traveller*. Its editor was Royal L. Porter. The first number was issued on the 1st of January, 1825. There was another paper previously published, which was an affinity to the *Traveller*, called the *Stage Register*. It was like the railroad guide of to-day—filled with two and three columns of advertisements of stage lines in the United States, as our newspapers are now filled with advertisements of railroad lines —of the departures of the numerous trains to every section and corner of the Union.

These two publications very properly came together and were united, and the same sort of advertisements, with the old familiar cut of the stage-coach, four-in-hand, dashing over the dusty roads, appeared in the *American Traveller*, and no better name could have been selected for a paper with such a class of advertisements. With the increasing steam-boat lines, and the railroads just beginning to come into use, the *Stage Register* was becoming a misnomer: it was not up to the spirit of the age.

We recollect in the *American Traveller* the publication of a correspondence from along the Hudson and elsewhere, among the first of the kind, descriptive of the routes, scenery, country, over the signature of F. H. These letters, a novelty then, were written by Freeman Hunt, afterwards the successful manager of *Hunt's Merchants' Magazine*, a very valuable and useful financial and commercial publication.

On the 1st of April, 1845, the *Boston Evening Traveller*, a daily paper, took the place of the *American Traveller* in one sense, and the latter became the semi-weekly issue of the new enterprise, and the old *Stage Register* was transformed into the *Weekly Traveller*. The first editor of the *American Traveller*, Royal L. Porter, died in 1834, ten years before this change was contemplated. Others had the management of the establishment then. Ferdinand Andrews and the Rev. George Punchard were the originators of the *Evening Traveller*. R. Worthington, the present senior proprietor, joined them in June, 1845. Andrews had been connected with the *Salem Gazette*, and published the *Landmark* in that ancient town of commerce and wealth. It was in that paper that the famous sketch of Deacon Giles's Distillery, by the Rev. Dr. Geo. B. Cheever, appeared, creating a sensation in Church, court, and country from Maine to Mississippi, and making the Deacon and the Dominie notorious every where and forever.

When the *Traveller* was issued as a daily, all the papers then published in Boston, with the exception of the *Mail* and *Times*, were sixpenny sheets, and too respectable to be sold in the streets by the newsboys. The *Traveller* was started as a two-cent paper, and not sold in the streets at first, because of the prevailing dignity of the Press in modern Athens. But all things, as well as leaves, have their time to change. On the nomination of General Taylor for the presidency, Daniel Webster did not enter the campaign with his usual enthusiasm. It was, however, announced one day in August, 1848, that it was the intention of the Constitutional Expounder to have a talk with his neighbors at Marshfield on the political aspects of the country. Worthington immediately engaged Dr. James W. Stone, the stenographer, and started for that charming and classic spot. Webster delivered his great speech, in which he uttered, in his most emphatic and impressive manner, these memorable but useless words, that the nomination of General Taylor was one "not fit to be made. No, my friends, not fit to be made." Worthington, with Stone and his short-hand notes, returned by express to Boston, and had the speech ready in an *Extra Traveller* for sale early the next morning. The Athenians were delighted. This piece of newspaper enterprise was a success, and was the introduction of that paper to the ragged and rugged newsboys of Boston. Webster's speech sold all day in that city. It was sent specially to the *New York Herald*, and thus spread over the Union, to the delight of the Democrats and the disgust of the Taylor Whigs. But Old Zach was elected.

There was another bit of enterprise that gave the *Traveller* a fresh impetus in the right direction. When the news of the flight of

Louis Philippe reached Boston, also in 1848, it was issued in an extra from that office early in the afternoon, and so extensive was the demand for the news that the presses were occupied till late in the evening in meeting the wants of the news-seekers. These extras were also sold by the newsboys, and this put the finishing touch to the respectability of selling papers in the public thoroughfares.

Those staring placards of the leading points of news which are now so attractive in front of each newspaper office in Boston originated in that city with the *Traveller;* and when the irrepressible Curtis Guild, of the *Commercial Bulletin*, then in the office of the *Journal*, placed a spreading one in front of that establishment, Colonel Rogers, one of its proprietors, tóre it down with his umbrella in utter disgust, remarking that "the *Journal* had not yet come to that!" Those in front of the *Journal* office were afterwards among the most readable and sensational long before the colonel died.

The *Traveller* is to-day one of the leading successful papers of Boston. With other features it has two persistent ones: an elaborate weekly review of the events of the world, liberally sprinkled with puns, and pepper, and attic salt, prepared by that "learned printer" with a prodigious memory, Charles C. Hazewell; and the weekly publication of Henry Ward Beecher's sermons, which are so useful to the clergy at large in all parts of the country.

The *Boston Courier*, for a long time one of the chief Whig papers of Boston, was established on the 2d of March, 1824. It was edited till 1848 by Joseph Tinker Buckingham, one of the best-known editors of New England. He had also editorial charge of the *New England Galaxy* and *New England Magazine*. In addition to his editorial labors, Mr. Buckingham has given the public and the profession his "Reminiscences," which ranks with "Thomas's History of Printing" in this country. He learned the art of printing newspapers in the office of the *Greenfield Gazette*. In 1805 he published the *Polyanthus*. In 1809 he established the *Ordeal*.

The New England *Galaxy*, the publication of which was commenced by Buckingham in 1820, has been edited by a number of writers at different periods. Theophilus Parsons, author of "Deus Homo" and "The Infinite and the Finite," and for many years Professor of Law in Harvard College, was one. About 1833 it was under the management of William J. Snelling, a very erratic, but brilliant and powerful writer at that time. When he had charge of the *Galaxy* he made a desperate war upon the gamblers of Boston. He had his office ornamented with the paraphernalia of an extensive gambling establishment. All sorts of threats were made against him by the gamblers. It was the sensation of that day. So many stories were related of him that people visited his office in numbers to see it, and its wonderful and bold editor. He was always found, at that time, in a miniature fortress, selling his own paper over the counter. He was to be seen on Sunday mornings in his shirt sleeves, walking to and fro, evidently ready for any emergency. We believe no attack was made upon him; the matter became a nine days' wonder, and after that Snelling edited, for a brief period, a paper called the *Censor*, in New York. Several young journalists, such as Isaac C. Pray and A. L. Stimson, took charge of the *Galaxy* in 1838, and managed it till they sought "other fields and pastures green."

But the *Courier* was the paper that gave him his fame as a journalist. It was spiritedly conducted, and became a very influential sheet with the Whig Party. His views were sound and his opinions respected by the party leaders of his day. No editor stood higher in public esteem in New England.

One feature of the *Courier* was the information it gave to farmers every Saturday morning under the head of "Geoponics." It was very useful and valuable, and materially assisted in making farming attractive. Some idea of the character of the man may be gathered from the anecdote related by Colonel Ropes, of the New York *Sunday Atlas*, once a compositor in the office of the *Courier*. One day, the assistant foreman of the office, William Sweet, in making up a crowded paper, and not supposing Mr. Buckingham to be near, exclaimed with an oath, "I wonder what the old gentleman wants all this Geoponical matter in to-day for." Mr. Buckingham, who always went up and down stairs with a light, soft step, entered the printing-office at that moment, and politely lifting his specs, quietly remarked, "And why not, Mr. Sweet?" Geoponics always went in after that, much to the delight and edification of the farming interest of Massachusetts and elsewhere.

On the 24th of June, 1840, the four hundredth anniversary of the invention of printing was celebrated in Boston. On this interesting occasion, Editor Buckingham, of the *Courier*, presided. There was a procession and a banquet. The procession was formed into line at the State House, and marched, under the command of Colonel Charles G. Greene, of the *Post*, to the "Old Cradle of Liberty." There were some specimen toasts at the dinner. Here are a few of them :

The Press.—The magnificent, tremendous, universal power of the Press, second only in effluency to the Archangel's trumpet that is to revivify the uncounted millions of the dead.

Newspapers.—The intellectual spring into which every body dips his bucket, whilst few thank the fountain for its supply.

The old fellowship between Faustus and the Devil.—When the Press became emancipated, the Partnership was dissolved. The Free Press tells the truth and shames the devil.

The Printers' Devil.—A harmless *familiar*, to whom many an author has been indebted for reputation as a wit and novelist, and never gave the devil his due.

Buckingham was a strong and vigorous writer, and many recollections of him to-day are that he was very bitter and very personal in his editorials. But he was evidently a careful journalist, for in writing to James Gordon Bennett to secure letters from him from New York for the *Galaxy*, he said,

The proposed sketches ought to be free from personalities, at least such as might give offense to the respectable citizens of New York.

One of the most fascinating writers for the *Courier* was Louisa Maria Child. Her charming letters from New York were fine specimens of newspaper correspondence. She immortalized Ole Bull in these letters on his first visit to the United States. She was one of the leading editors of the *Anti-Slavery Standard* in 1842.

The *Courier* is now a weekly paper. It has till lately been edited by George Lunt. It became a conservative organ, and amid so much radicalism it fell from grace and ceased to be a daily. Before Mr. Lunt it was edited by Samuel Kettell, who, with Frederick S. Hill, wrote the "Six Degrees of Crime," which was produced with some success in 1832, or thereabouts, at the Tremont Theatre. W. L. Brigham is its present chief editor.

The *Boston Transcript*, the family paper, the paper for the teatable before late dinners became a business and social necessity, was established in July, 1830, by Dutton and Wentworth, two excellent printers and pleasant gentlemen. They were the state printers. Mr. Dutton was foreman of Wells & Lilly's printing-office when James Gordon Bennett was proof-reader there in 1819–1820. The *Transcript* was remarkable for its neat typographical appearance. It was small, always clean, and was a general favorite in the family circle. It was lively, without any large pretensions to enterprise, carefully edited, and profitably patronized.

The first editor of the *Transcript* was Lynde M. Walter. He performed the duties of his office with taste and tact till 1840. He died July 24, 1842. Dr. Joseph Palmer was editor *pro tem.* during Mr. Walter's illness. Dr. Palmer afterwards edited the *Centinel and Gazette*, and died in 1871, while commercial editor of the *Daily Advertiser*. On the death of Mr. Walter, his sister, Miss Cornelia M. Walter, assumed editorial charge of the *Transcript*, and managed the intellectual department of the paper to the satisfaction of every one. Subsequently Epes Sargent was its editor for a number of years.

The *Transcript* is now edited by D. M. Haskell, and is published by Henry W. Dutton & Son. They have, like the proprietors of the

Post, Advertiser, Journal, and *Herald,* erected a splendid building for their establishment, which is one of the ornaments of Boston.

The *Transcript* has had, like other journals, many volunteer contributions. We recollect those of Nathaniel J. Bowditch, signed "Gleaner," which were of great interest to the real-estate owners of Boston.

The Boston *Liberator* was one of the remarkable papers of its day. All the world recognized it as the organ of Abolitionism in the United States. It was better known as Garrison's *Liberator*. Its publication was commenced on the first of January, 1831, and for thirty-four years it fulminated against the institution of slavery in spite of persecution, tar and feathers, denunciation, rewards for its editor's head, threatened assassination, hanging in effigy, assaults, and mobs, from which the bold editor barely escaped with his life. William Lloyd Garrison was the master-spirit of the paper. What manner of man he was may be seen in an extract of a letter he wrote to John Neal, editor of *The Yankee,* and which appeared in that paper on the 20th of August, 1828, nearly two years and a half before the issue of the *Liberator*. This is the extract:

> I have only to repeat, without vanity, what I declared publicly to another opponent—a political one—(and I think he will never forget me) that, if my life be spared, my name shall one day be known so extensively as to render private inquiry unnecessary; and known, too, in a praiseworthy manner. I speak in the spirit of prophecy—not of vainglory—with a strong pulse, a flashing eye, and a glow of the heart. The task may be yours to write my biography.
>
> WM. LLOYD GARRISON.

The same idea was embraced in an article in the first number of the *Liberator*. He then said:

> It is pretended that I am retarding the cause of emancipation by the coarseness of my invectives and the precipitancy of my measures. The charge is not true. On this question my influence, humble as it is, is felt at this moment to a considerable extent, and shall be felt in coming years, not perniciously, but beneficially; not as a curse, but as a blessing; and posterity will bear testimony that I was right.

Immediate emancipation was the principle on which Garrison conducted the *Liberator*. Such was the effect produced by the circulation of this paper that the Legislature of Mississippi, by special enactment, offered a reward of $5000 for the arrest of and prosecution of any person who should be detected in the circulation of the *Liberator* in that state. Several other states adopted the same policy of suppression. The *Emancipator,* issued in New York, was indicted in Alabama, and Governor Gayle, of that state, actually sent on a requisition to Governor Marcy, of New York, for the surrender of R. J. Williams, its publisher. Mr. Williams was not considered a fugitive from justice by the Governor of New York.

The *Liberator* was managed with great energy and boldness from its commencement till the emancipation of the four million of slaves in the United States was an accomplished fact. Then, in 1865, with its work done, the *Liberator* ceased to exist. The spirit of prophecy, which was so strong with Garrison in 1828, was unabated in 1871, for on the 17th of May of that year, at a convention of the Middlesex County Woman Suffrage Association, Mr. Garrison, in reviewing his work since forty years ago, when he first spoke in Charlestown in the anti-slavery cause, said that he had lived to see every slave set free, and was still working in the same cause—the cause of liberty; and in offering a series of resolutions, of which the chief one is annexed, he evidently felt that the woman suffrage movement would be as fully successful as that which led to the abolition of slavery :

> *Resolved*, That in simply recommending that "the petitioners have leave to withdraw," the committee have virtually confessed that no valid reasons can be adduced against the claim to equal and impartial suffrage, and without regard to the natural distinctions of birth ; and, no matter how adroitly postponed or evaded, that claim must be asserted and demanded until the woman of Massachusetts shall stand on the same political platform with the man, and as fully entitled to vote and to be voted for in every municipal state and national election.

The friends of Garrison, in Europe and America, in consideration of his services towards emancipation, subscribed the sum of $31,000, which they presented to him in 1868.

There are few complete files of the *Liberator* in the country—not more than four or five. One was lately presented to the Public Library of Portland. This, indeed, is incomplete. The volumes of 1831 and 1832 are entirely wanting. Otherwise, however, the set is nearly perfect. Newspaper files are important to every library. There are very few complete sets of any of the older papers. Those in the library in Washington are probably the most perfect. All the daily papers of New York are preserved, and many are from the date of the first issue. The London *Gazette*, we have seen it stated, is complete from 1665, and the British Royal *Calendar* from 1772. The London *Times* is filed from 1796. The *Almanac de Gotha* is from 1776. It was first issued in 1771. All the files of Washington papers are complete. The library of the *New York Herald* is rich in newspaper data. So is that of the Boston *Athenæum*. Some of the old public libraries and Historical Societies are well supplied ; but the new institutions, such as the Public Library in Boston, are lacking in this valuable historical department. Time is requisite to secure old volumes of newspapers. Now and then they are offered for sale. The *Worcester Spy*, from 1791 to 1866, was recently sold for $500. The Common Council of New York paid $2000 for a file of the *Herald* from 1841 for the City Library. The New York Historical Society has a complete file of the *Boston News-Letter* from 1704 to 1775, the only one extant on this side of the Atlantic. Other sets of newspapers are mentioned in our sketches. Three copies of each journal printed in England have been regularly transmitted to the Stamp-office in London for preservation. On the expiration of each year a complete file of each newspaper has been deposited in the British Museum, and kept for reference.

The *Daily Morning Post* is a famous paper of Boston. It is famous for "all sorts" of things. Its first number was issued November 9, 1831. Beals and Greene were the publishers. Charles Gordon Greene was the editor, and he still remains at his post, hale, happy, and humorous. It has always been a Democratic paper. It is to the democracy of New England what the *Argus* has been in New York, the *Statesman* in Ohio, the *Enquirer* in Virginia. In Jackson's time it was mixed up with "blanks, paper, and twine," and other similar political clap-trap and banter. Its career has been an honorable one throughout. Nathaniel G. Greene, a brother of the editor, of fine literary taste and culture, and for a long time Postmaster of Boston, wrote for the *Post*. He was clearly a man of letters. Charles G. Greene, the editor, has been Naval Officer of the port of Boston, and would handsomely and ably fill any office, although he fills that of editor the best of any. One of the charges against the *Post*, in circulation in State Street, in the persistent minority of the democracy in Massachusetts, was that the leaders of that party purposely kept its size down to the precise number requisite to fill the federal offices in the Old Bay State. This slander has only once been refuted, and that was when Marcus Morton was elected governor by a majority of one.

The *Post* is celebrated for its wit, fun, and *bonhomie*. It originated the column of smart sayings that are now to be seen in every paper, to the utter annihilation of comic journalism in the United States. "All Sorts," "Odds and Ends," "Happenings," "Flashes," all had their origin in that paper. When Park Benjamin resided in New York and wrote letters to Boston, he promised some one a "first-rate notice in the Boston Morning *Post*," and the phrase became a standard one in newspaper offices.

The genial good humor of its editor never deserted him. After a very exciting political campaign, and when his party were completely routed at the polls, he naïvely announced the result the next morning by requesting the drivers of the carriages bringing the fortunate Whigs to the office of the *Post* to collect their bets to head the horses down Water Street, to prevent confusion, and not block up the thoroughfare. There was always a joke in the paper, always a sparkle of wit, always a smile for each reader, always a ray of sunshine for the defeated Democrat of Massachusetts.

The proprietors, in their annual announcement for 1870, thus expressed this characteristic of the paper:

> To infuse good humor and kindly feelings is an object we diligently seek; and when we can soften asperity by forbearance, we shall feel that something has been done to promote that genial fellowship which gives society its richest blessing. Thanking our old friends for past favors, we solicit their continuance, and also their efforts to bring others into our subscription-lists, that all may see whether we preach the true doctrine of '76—the only doctrine that can hold the "stars" in our political firmament.

The *Post* has remained in the hands of Beals and Greene from its commencement. Sons of the original proprietors are enthusiastically engaged on the paper. Its editorial management is now in the hands of Charles G. Greene, and Nathaniel H. Greene, his son. The establishment is in a splendid granite building of its own, opposite the new Post-office in Boston—where one is the Post-office, and the other the office of the *Post.* They vie with each other in architectural beauty, and are ornaments to that part of Boston. There are probably as many *belles lettres* in one as in the other; and as for "blanks, paper, and twine," they are all on the other side of the line.

The organ of the Whig Party in New England, in its days of vigor, was the *Boston Atlas*. It was established by John H. Eastburn on the 2d of July, 1832. Mr. Eastburn was long and favorably known as the City Printer of Boston. He did his work promptly and neatly. He had been in the employment of Major Ben. Russell, of the *Centinel*, and he imbibed some notions of a newspaper from that veteran, who so much resembled Zachary Taylor in his personal appearance. Eastburn reversed the order of things, and carried the *Atlas* as vigorously on his shoulders as a man could with one hundred and fifty subscribers to start with. He was originally aided in the intellectual part of his enterprise by John T. Austin, Henry H. Fuller, Elisha Fuller, and Robert C. Winthrop. Indeed the *Atlas* brought Winthrop before the public. These gentlemen, too, would prop up the *Atlas* by getting subscribers for it. Austin at one time, in the early struggles of the paper, took a subscription paper from door to door in State Street, and returned to the happy Eastburn a list of one hundred and thirty-seven subscribers. Daniel Webster also contributed to the thunder of the *Atlas*. One day Eastburn was standing in his doorway at the head of State Street—a custom of his—and he has stood there for over fifty years, with a beaming smile for every one, when the Godlike, as the Bostonians were wont to call Webster, came down the street, and, seeing Eastburn, stopped for a chat with him. Very soon the walk on the opposite side of the street, under the eaves of the old State House, filled with people, gathered out of curiosity to see Webster in a familiar street conversation. "Mr. Webster," said Mr. Eastburn, "if you remain here any longer I shall have to send for the police to clear the street." "Why so?" asked the great Expounder, turning round to see what the matter was. "Stopping to chat with me, sir, has crowded that sidewalk, you see." Mr. Webster, as his eye caught sight of the large gathering, gracefully raised his hat and passed down the street, and every head was instantly uncovered in response. Webster was then in the height of his fame and popularity. He had not delivered his 7th of March speech.

Eastburn imported Major Haughton from New York, where he had been employed in the office of the *Journal of Commerce*, making up election returns, and performing other duties. He gave him $800 per annum to manage the editorial part of the paper. He had previously employed Richard Hildreth to write certain articles. With Eastburn and Haughton newspaper enterprise of the right kind began to dawn on Boston. Haughton was not much of a writer, but he knew how to make others write. He was a good manager, and wonderful on figures when returns came in from the polls. It was the *Atlas* that originally established the horse and railroad expresses from every town in Massachusetts to bring in the results for publication on the morning after election. There were very few railroads then. The whistle of the locomotive was not heard every five minutes as now. Most of the work had to be done by horses. Yet it was done, and many will recollect that, on the first attempt, it was nine o'clock in the forenoon before the edition was issued. That part of State Street near the *Atlas* office was crowded for hours by people waiting for the news.

Eastburn, having the city printing on his hands, felt constrained to dispose of his interest in the *Atlas* to Haughton, who then carried on the establishment alone. He continued his enterprise, and run expresses on all important occasions. Once, in 1840, when Pennsylvania went for Harrison by a majority of only 343 in an aggregate popular vote of 287,693 votes, an express conveying this important political intelligence was run from Philadelphia to the *Atlas* office. The presidential election was not then held throughout the United States on one and the same day. That year it occurred in Pennsylvania on the 30th of October, and in New York, in Massachusetts, indeed in all the New England States, on the 2d, 3d, and 4th of November. In that excited and uproarious Hard-Cider Campaign,

"For Tippecanoe and Tyler too,"

the influence of the result in Pennsylvania was deemed of the deepest importance. Hence the express, and

"Van, Van, was a used-up man."

It was a great success politically as well as journalistically, and gave quite an impulse to the *Atlas* at that period with the Whig Party. It was Haughton who withdrew Webster from this contest for the presidency and substituted Harrison. With his foresight it became necessary for the Whigs of New England to abandon their idol. Webster at first could not see the necessity of the movement. But Haughton was equal to the emergency. He prepared a leading article indicating this course, and had it put in type. In the evening, with a proof-sheet in his hand, he rung the door-bell of Mr. Webster's house in Summer Street. Imagine the interview. Mr. W. read the article, and it appeared in the *Atlas* the next morning. Webster was no longer a candidate for the presidency. Expediency set him aside. Harrison was the next president.

Colonel Schouler, one of the successors of Major Haughton, thus speaks of him and of this incident with Webster:

> The man who best grasped the whole question, had the courage to act, and knew when, where, and how to strike, was Richard Haughton, the editor of the Boston *Atlas*. He was a warm and devoted friend of Mr. Webster, and had supported him with all his strength in the preceding canvass. He saw there was no chance for Mr. Webster's nomination at the Harrisburg Convention, that the race would be between Mr. Clay and General Harrison, and that a great part of Mr. Clay's strength in the Convention would be found in states that never had given, and never would give, a Whig majority. Many of Mr. Webster's friends in Boston, and Mr. Webster himself, held that his chance for the nomination was good. Major Haughton knew better; and, as he preferred General Harrison to Mr. Clay, and a Whig national triumph to either of them, he decided to take his part in advance. His object was to unite the friends of Mr. Webster and of Scott with the friends of Harrison, and thus insure the defeat of Mr. Clay at Harrisburg—not that he disliked Clay, but he believed that with Mr. Clay as the Whig candidate the Whigs would be beaten.
>
> Major Haughton was in the prime of life—about forty years old—of medium stature, with a handsome, gentlemanly face and figure; he wore gold-bowed spectacles, and had dark curly hair; the expression of his countenance was pleasant, and he was, in fact, a genial, warm-hearted man. He was born in Connecticut, and was a graduate of Yale; had been connected with the New York *Journal of Commerce* as assistant editor and Washington correspondent before he assumed the editorial chair of the *Atlas*. He possessed that rare quality in a leader of attaching himself to young men of the best talents, of infusing a portion of his own spirit and enthusiasm into them, and making them subservient to his purpose. He encouraged them to write for his paper, and in this way formed around him a body-guard of the young and aspiring men of the party. The "*Atlas* Clique" became a by-word, and now, almost every day, some of the old members of "the clique" pass up and down our streets, and are numbered among our best merchants and lawyers. Major Haughton was not a ready writer himself, but he could direct others how to write. Nature had made him just what he was—a splendid *editor* of a party newspaper, wise, intelligent, and bold. When the time came to speak out, he did not hesitate.
>
> Major Haughton was appointed in the spring of 1840 on a confidential commission abroad; a day or two afterwards he was struck with apoplexy, and died in his room in the Tremont House, literally in the arms of Alfred T. Turner, Esq., the honored and respected City Auditor of Boston, who was then a young man employed in the *Atlas* office. Major Haughton lived and died a bachelor. His last words were, "I am going to the Eternal City."

Few of our active Whigs, now living, have forgotten the leading editorial articles which appeared in the *Atlas* in the fall of 1838, upon the presidential question. They were bold, well-considered, and to the point. They were written in part by Richard Hildreth, who was then attached to the *Atlas*, and who afterwards gained a more lasting renown as the author of one of our best histories of the United States. He died a few years ago in Italy, and his remains lie buried in the Protestant grave-yard in Florence, near those of Theodore Parker.

The position taken by the *Atlas* was that General Harrison must and ought to be the Whig candidate for the presidency. He represented the Democratic element of the party, as Mr. Clay and Mr. Webster did the Aristocratic and Conservative elements, and without this infusion of democracy into the party—this "descending from the forum and taking the people by the hand"—we could not succeed. We could have a respectable party, but never a successful one, and success was a legitimate aim of any party.

After Haughton came William Hayden, who possessed neither the tact nor the enterprise of his predecessor. He was a respectable editor, but not a pushing one. He afterwards became City Auditor, an office he filled for a number of years. Dr. Thomas M. Brewer was an associate editor with Hayden. About this period there were fourteen daily papers printed in Modern Athens. One of the waifs of the present day floating through the newspapers gives the best idea of the number of the Press of that city at that time. It is this:

> In 1846 there were fourteen daily papers in Boston, and now (1871), after a lapse of twenty-five years, the number has decreased to eight. Some of the old fourteen were short-lived affairs, but most of them might have maintained their existence to the present time by judicious management. The following were the names of the papers and their editors: *American Traveller*, F. Andrews and G. Punchard; *American Eagle*, George W. Tyler; *Courier*, Buckingham and Foster; *Advertiser*, Nathan Hale; *Journal*, Sleeper and Rogers; *Whig*, Richard J. Atwell; *Post*, Greene and Beals; *Transcript*, Dutton and Wentworth; *Atlas*, Hayden and Brewer; *Bee*, C. J. Howland; *Mail*, J. W. Bradley; *Star*, Streeter and Corliss; *Sun*, Smith and Byram.

William Schouler became part proprietor of the *Atlas* in 1847. Schouler for six years previously edited the *Lowell Courier and Journal*, and after his connection with the *Atlas* he edited the Cincinnati *Gazette*.

But where is the *Atlas* now?

There were too many papers in Boston. Some step was necessary to reduce the number. To do this, an enterprise was started that promised immensely for journalism in that city. Haughton was dead. Hayden, and Schouler, and Brewer had retired. There were several papers struggling for supremacy and bread, such as the *Atlas*, the *Bee*, and the *Traveller*.

The new project would reduce this number in two ways, it was expected—by absorption and annihilation. It was proposed to unite the *Atlas*, *Bee*, and *Traveller* in one association, based on the plan of the New York *Tribune*, and with Samuel Bowles, of the *Springfield Republican*, as editor in chief, and Richard Worthington, of the *Traveller*, as business manager, to publish a great journal worthy of the Hub and New England. The design was carried into effect in 1857, and on the 13th day of April the first number of the *Boston*

Daily Traveller was issued. It was made up like the *Tribune*, its ideas were of the *Tribune* character, and it looked like a spoiled copy of the *Tribune*. It was amusing to see Horace Greeley look over the first number. With all the reputation of Bowles, with all his journalistic ability, and with all the business capacity of Worthington, acquired in the *Advertiser* office and with the *Traveller*, the enterprise failed.

Why? Simply because Bowles's newspaper aspirations had reached the highest standard of excellence and expensiveness without the means or the field to carry them into effect. Simply because Worthington, who understood the capacity of Boston in a journalistic point of view, knew that there was not money enough in all the newspapers of that city combined to carry on the new paper to a paying success on the plan adopted. Simply because, with two such antagonistic interests in its management, no enterprise could succeed. It therefore failed, and Bowles, full of vigor and full of vim, fell back on his first love, the *Springfield Republican*, by which he had made a fortune and a reputation; and Worthington, full of faith, fell back on his early hope, the old *Traveller*, where he has since made fame and fortune by his tact and pluck, and prints, every evening, a first-rate paper, with the latest news, at four cents per copy.

So the *Atlas*, renowned from the earliest days of the Whig Party for its power as a journal in New England, passed away; but its founder, John H. Eastburn, full of years, full of anecdote, full of money, full of genial good humor, round and rotund, still stands, on pleasant days, in his doorway at the head of State Street.

One of the most prosperous papers in Boston is the *Boston Daily Journal*. It was established in 1833. Its original publishers were Ford and Damrell. Its editor was John S. Sleeper. It struggled along for several years with indifferent success. Indeed, in 1837, its financial condition was such that Mr. Damrell deemed it his duty to withdraw from the concern. In 1841 the paper passed into the hands of Sleeper, Dix, and Rogers. One or two of these three owners infused some life and energy into the establishment, which soon began to tell upon the best side of its financial exhibit and in its reading columns.

Sleeper was the editor. He was called Captain Sleeper. He wrote a series of sea tales over the signature of Hawser Martingale, which increased the circulation of the *Journal*, and added interest to its pages. Boston has always been a famous sea-port town. Its boys are full of love for ships and the sea, and for those who go "down to the sea in ships." These tales suited them, and made the paper publishing them the popular journal with them. So the boys and the paper grew up together as warm friends. It was the *Mercantile Journal* with them.

But Sleeper was not a man of enterprise in the modern sense of that word. Hawser Martingale was not an express rider. It took a hurricane to call him on deck. Rogers and Dix had the vim of the establishment. When one of its present editors, Mr. Stockwell, was a reporter, he once suggested to Captain Sleeper that he could run out to Brighton and make a brief report of a speech that Daniel Webster was to deliver in that town. Captain Sleeper, pushing his spectacles back over his forehead, said, "Well, no, I guess not, Mr. Stockwell; somebody will send us in something about it within two or three days."

It had one of those necessary appendages to a prosperous journal, an energetic business manager, in Charles O. Rogers, a son of the publisher of the *National Ægis*, in which office he took his first lessons in the art of printing and in the science of journalism. After years of tact and labor, he did so much towards building up the paper that he became the chief owner of the establishment; and when he died in 1869, it was found that, in leaving a property valued at a million and a half of dollars, he deserved the reputation he had obtained for skill and ability.

In 1852 a *California Journal* was issued, and boasted of the largest circulation of that edition of any of the kind in the country, and these California editions were a feature in those days of the Sullivans, and Gregorys, and other Pacific news agents. It was when the Atlantic furnished the Pacific with its newspapers—when the *New York Herald* sent out 10,000 copies by each monthly steamer, the *New York Tribune* nearly as many, and the *New Orleans Delta* 8000. San Francisco and the mines were then merely colonies of New England, New York, and the West.

The *Journal* is now managed by an association. Its chief editor is Stephen N. Stockwell, who has been connected with the paper for a quarter of a century or more. He commenced as a phonographic reporter, and through his skill, energy, and ability he kept the *Journal* up to the highest point of excellence in all important speeches and trials, not allowing the New York papers to have any advantage in his own bailiwick, when he had his own way. Webster and Choate praised him. This was the ribbon of the *legion d'honneur* to a stenographer of Boston. One of the other editors was James A. Dix, who twenty-five years ago looked after the marine news department—an important department in all commercial newspapers, and deemed especially so in Boston, where Harry Blake achieved renown in this peculiar journalistic science. Yet another editor, W. W. Clapp, son of the Clapp who started the *Daily Adver-*

tiser, and whose fame comes from the *Saturday Evening Gazette*, in the title of which, years and years ago, it repeated, and, therefore, had faith in the prediction, of circling the world with the electric wire. It published weekly, long before the introduction of the telegraph, a neat little portrait of the first telegraph operator, Puck. It pinned its faith to its motto, "I'll put a girdle around about the earth in forty minutes." Such a man ought to make a journalist of the modern type, and in this telegraphic age.

There are other papers of talent and tact in Boston. Several are of recent origin. The *Herald* has done well since the days of the sedate William B. English. Ex-Postmaster Bailey managed it skillfully and made a fortune. Its present conductors keep up its character and reputation. Then there are the *News* and *Times*, and on the 4th of March, 1872, the *Globe* was inaugurated. It is a double sheet, made up in the style, somewhat, of the New York papers, with a touch here and there of Boston in its general appearance. It is the only "double sheet" printed in that city. It will need vigor, independence, and money to make it what it should be.

CHAPTER XXIV.
ANTI-MASONRY AND NULLIFICATION.

THURLOW WEED AND THE ALBANY EVENING JOURNAL.—THE ANTI-MASONIC PARTY.—WHO WROTE THE JUNIUS LETTERS?—THE ROORBACK HOAX.—THE NASHVILLE UNION.—THE CHARLESTON (S. C.) MERCURY.—THE CHIEF ORGAN OF THE NULLIFIERS AND SECESSIONISTS.—MORE DUELS.—NICE POINTS OF HONOR.—THE CODE.—THE "INDEPENDENCE" OF THE PRESS.

NEARLY all the leading journals of this period, being party papers, were established in the midst of great political excitements, or for the purpose of creating a political division, or to represent a new faction. The *Albany Evening Journal* came into existence in this way as the organ of the Anti-Masons in the Empire State. Another paper, named the *Albany Journal*, as an organ of this party, was issued in 1825 by a son of Hezekiah Niles, of *Niles's Register*, but it passed out of existence before the *Evening Journal* made its appearance. Solomon Southwick, a name known to our readers for his brilliant and disastrous journalistic career, published the *National Monitor* in 1828 and '9, in the interest of the Anti-Masons, and became their candidate for governor in 1828. But it was not till 1830 that the Anti-Masonic party became formidable as a national as well as a state organization, and it was in that year that the *Evening Journal* was established, absorbing the *Monitor* in its publication. Thurlow Weed and Henry Dana Ward were the publishers of the new paper.

Thurlow Weed was editor of the *Norwich* (N.Y.) *Journal* in 1817. Shortly after he issued an opposition paper, named the *Republican Agriculturist*, in the interest of De Witt Clinton. In 1825 he became a member of the Legislature, where he met William H. Seward, and attached himself, in those days of political excitement, to the Anti-Masonic party. In 1830 he appeared in Albany as editor of the *Evening Journal*, the leading organ of that party.

It has been stated that he was a drummer-boy in 1812. No doubt, if he had occupied that position, he would have performed his part at *réveille;* and when ridiculed for this by his opponents, he could have answered, as the rich merchant, William Gray, retorted, when told that he had been nothing but a drummer-boy, "What! a drummer-boy! and did you ever hear me drum?" asked Mr. Gray. "Yes,

I have," confidently answered his would-be tormentor. "Well, well, didn't I drum well?" retorted the independent merchant. But Weed had not been a drummer-boy in the War of 1812, but he had been a cabin-boy on board of a splendid North River sloop, where he undoubtedly acquired the rudiments of Salt River navigation, so necessary, sometimes, in political life.

Of the two hundred and eleven papers published in New York in 1830, when the *Evening Journal* was established, thirty-two were Anti-Masonic organs. The *Journal* made the thirty-third. This party obtained its popular existence in 1827 with the mysterious disappearance of William Morgan in the previous year, after he had threatened to publish a pamphlet disclosing the secrets of masonry. It grew in popular favor with the increase of popular excitement caused by that curious event. It was, like the Know Nothing party, a political sensation, to bring all the elements in opposition to the Democracy into one party, and could only exist for a time and for a special purpose. It became an organized state party in 1830, and nominated Francis Granger, who had previously been on the Adams ticket, for governor, and gave him 120,361 votes against 128,842, which the Democrats polled for E. T. Throop. Such men as William H. Seward, John C. Spencer, Albert H. Tracy, and Millard Fillmore were Anti-Masonic members of the Legislature at this period of our political history. William Wirt, the distinguished lawyer of Virginia, was the national representative of the party, and obtained the electoral vote of Vermont in 1832. John C. Spencer, with his original and brilliant mind, wrote for the *Journal*, and aided in its becoming a leading and influential paper. This was the real beginning of the political career of Thurlow Weed and William H. Seward, electing the latter Governor of New York in 1838, and culminating with the administration of Andrew Johnson and a trip around the world.

After Weed assumed the editorial management of the *Evening Journal* he never held office, but devoted all his energies to the labor of putting others in and out of office—a sort of Warwick. His intimacy with William H. Seward commenced in the Legislature in 1830, when both were members, one in the Senate and the other in the House. Then came into existence the well-known firm of Seward and Weed. After the latter had secured the services of Horace Greeley, in 1839–40, to edit the *Log Cabin*, in the famous and hilarious campaign for William Henry Harrison, the name of the firm was changed to Seward, Weed, & Co., which was dissolved by mutual consent in 1856 by the retirement of the junior partner. No two men ever worked so well and harmoniously together, one before and the other behind the scenes, from 1830, when one was state senator and the other an editor, as Seward and Weed.

It is a singular fact that Mr. Weed has never held any other office since 1830 than that of state printer. He has had plenty of offices and opportunities within his grasp. It is fair to suppose that he might have been governor, senator, and vice-president. These nominations were offered to him and refused. When talked of for the United States Senate, he said:

> Looking back through the long vista of time that has elapsed—nearly forty years—since a responsible and delicate political duty devolved upon us, it is much less a matter of surprise that we are surrounded, in our own party, with enemies, than that, amidst the disappointments and jealousies incident to the experience of all parties, we retain so much of its regard. When it is *supposed* that an individual exercises influence in the councils and conventions of his party—where, of necessity, the aspirations of hundreds are disappointed—nothing but an abiding faith among the people, in that individual's judgment and unselfishness, can sustain him. All men err, but if a politician, whom the people trusts, *endeavors* to do right, they find it out and stand by him.

The *Evening Journal*, in the warmly-contested presidential campaign of 1844, published what purported to be an extract of a tour through the South in 1836 by a traveler named Roorback. It pretended to describe scenes in the Southwest. Among other things, it stated that a party of slaves had been torn from the places where they were born and sold at auction. "Forty-three of these unfortunate beings had been purchased, I was informed," said the account, "of the Hon. J. K. Polk, the present Speaker of the House of Representatives, the marks of the branding-iron, with the initials of his name, on their shoulders distinguishing them from the rest."

It appeared that an extract from Featherstonhaugh's Tour in 1834 was made, and the above extract incorporated with his description of what he saw, and the whole accredited to another traveler, who was called Roorback. The story went the rounds of the Whig Press, in order to defeat the chances of Polk's election to the presidency. The extract was alleged to have been made from "Roorback's Tour through the Western and Southern States in 1835." The statement produced a great sensation, but the affair was soon exposed by the *Albany Argus*, and the *Journal* made an effort to relieve itself of any responsibility in the hoax in the following manner:

> The *Albany Argus* of this morning charges the *Evening Journal* with fabricating from the whole cloth the extract published in this paper on Monday last from "Roorback's Tour through the Southern and Western States in 1836." This charge is utterly and unqualifiedly false. The extract in question was taken, precisely as it appeared in the *Journal*, from an exchange paper, and was published by us without a doubt of its genuineness.

The hoax had its origin, it was stated, in this way: Some one made the interpolation in the extract, and sent it to the editor of the *Ithaca Chronicle*, a Whig paper, to see if the manager of that paper, "moral and religious as he was allowed to be, would not, equally with others, publish any falsehood, however gross, if he could thereby effect a political object!" Wholly ignorant of the fraud, the editor published the extract. It was then transferred to the *Albany Patriot*. Thence it made its appearance in the *Evening Journal*, and became a feature of the campaign. With Thurlow Weed's indorsement, it had wide-spread circulation before the truth of the story could be told.

The *New York Herald* made Weed the subject of many newspaper squibs; that he kept the slate of Governor Seward, containing the names of all the office-seekers of the Whig Party, and dubbed him State Barber. These squibs made a Warwick of him, and influential with that class of politicians, and gave the *Evening Journal*, outside of Albany, a name and a fame it would not have otherwise obtained. Although closely allied with Mr. Seward in his crusade against slavery, Mr. Weed was not fanatical on the "irrepressible conflict" of the two races. When Helper's famous work was published, his name appeared as aiding in its publication. This is what he said on the subject:

WASHINGTON, Dec. 7, 1859.

DEAR SIR,—Our brief conversation this morning confirmed an impression long resting on my mind that the sentiments and opinions of Republican editors are greatly misunderstood. This misapprehension results, I suppose, from the circumstance that we are only known to the Southern people through journals politically interested in misrepresenting us. The opinions we express upon existing questions go to the South garbled and perverted.

During the forty years of my editorial life, though ever opposed in sentiment and sympathy to slavery, I have never cherished a feeling or uttered a sentiment intended to affect injuriously the property, the rights, or the safety of the citizens of the slaveholding States.

In the lifetime of the Whig Party my affinities and associations were stronger with Southern than with Northern statesmen. Clay, Mangum, Williams (N. C.), Preston, Clayton, Crittenden, etc., of the early, with Bell, Botts, Stanly, Rayner, Morehead, etc., of the later schools, were the men whom I "delighted to honor." But during all that period I was just as persistently stigmatized as an Abolitionist by the Democratic Press as are Republicans at the present day.

I read Mr. Helper's book hastily soon after its appearance. As the work of a Southern man, addressed to Southern people, I thought it calculated to assist in forming public sentiment upon the relative value and effect of free and slave labor. Not finding for several months refutation or denials of its general accuracy, when called upon for aid to publish a large edition of a "Compend," I contributed $100. Had I known, as is now asserted, that this "Compend" would counsel a severance of the business, social, and religious relations existing between slaveholding and non-slaveholding citizens, or that the book itself, as is also asserted, invites or countenances servile insurrection, I certainly should have withheld both my approval and my money, for my opposition to slavery rejects all such teachings.

Evidence too clear and conclusive to admit of doubt or denial satisfies me that the slavery agitation, which we all deplore, owes its existence to the repeal of the Missouri Compromise, followed by a determination to extend slavery into Kansas. But I would not return aggression for aggression, nor attempt to right a wrong by doing wrong. With slavery, as it exists in the States, we have no right to interfere. Northern men who invade a Southern State either to run off slaves or excite insurrection, deserve the punishment they receive. Our common safety depends upon maintaining the "supremacy of the laws." To preserve the Union we must obey the Constitution. Very truly yours, THURLOW WEED.

With others, Weed has taken a deep and abiding interest in the authorship of Junius's Letters. Since their publication in the *Public Advertiser* of London, they have been considered of so much importance to journalism and the freedom of the Press every where, that any new light shed on their authorship is read with pleasure. We therefore append Weed's testimony in clearing up this wonderful mystery:

JUNIUS—THE FRANCIS PAPERS.

In the spring of 1862 an intimate friend of Mr. John Taylor, the author of *Junius Identified*, informed me to the effect that that gentleman was preparing for the press some papers of Sir Philip Francis, which would be conclusive as to the authorship of the celebrated letters ; and a letter dated from London, May 12, in the same year, from Mr. Thurlow Weed to the Albany (U. S.) *Evening Journal*, stated that "before the present year expires all doubt or question as to the authorship of the 'Junius Letters' will be removed." Since then both Mr. Taylor and his friend have died, and, although the subject is still of much interest, I have neither seen nor heard any thing further relative to either Mr. Taylor's *Francis Papers* or the evidence (which, perhaps, may be the same) to which Mr. Weed alluded. Perhaps the editor or some reader of "N. & Q." will be kind enough to say in what position the matter now stands.   ERIC.
VILLE MARIE, Canada.

[The late Mr. Joseph Parkes, who had purchased *The Francis Papers*, and also the original "Letters of Junius addressed to Woodfall," had been for some years preparing for publication a *Life of Sir Philip Francis*, and in which, in his opinion, would be found conclusive evidence of the identity of "Francis and Junius." The work was, however, far from complete at the time of Mr. Parkes's death ; and although we believe the whole of the papers have since been submitted to the examination of one eminently qualified to do justice to them, we are not aware that there is any prospect of their being published just at present.]

The American consul at Frankfort, in Germany, inclosed the foregoing items to me. The note of the editor of the "N. & Q.," appended to the communication of "Eric," furnishes the information sought for by that inquiry.

In 1862, the late Mr. Joseph Parkes, a gentleman of large and various information, informed me that he had been for several years devoting his intervals of exemption from official duties (as Tax Commissioner) to a Life of Sir Philip Francis, and that his researches would result in disproving the confident assertion of "Junius," in one of his private letters to Woodfall, "that he was the sole depositary of his own secret," and that it would *"die with him."*

The subject was one which had interested me much at a period when "Junius" was read more generally and with greater interest than exists now. The question as to who "Junius" was engaged the attention of authors and editors. I had, forty years ago, entered with much zeal into that controversy. Finding me thus sympathetic and familiar with the subject, Mr. Parkes invited me to his apartments at Staple Inn, Holburn, and submitted his manuscripts to my perusal. There I passed many charmed hours. The materials for his work were not only ample, but conclusive. They established beyond a doubt, or a cavil, or a peradventure, that Sir Philip Francis was the author of the *Letters of Junius*.

Twice during these readings, in company with Mr. Parkes, I visited the then venerable and since departed John Taylor, author of *Junius Identified*, first published nearly fifty years ago. Mr. Taylor had intended to avail himself of subsequent and cumulative evidence, but, on account of his advanced age, had cheerfully committed the whole question to Mr. Parkes. These breakfast conversations with Mr. Taylor were exceedingly interesting. His bachelor life, like that of Charles Lamb, was solaced by an aged maiden sister. He had formerly known most of the literary celebrities of the last years of the past and the first years of the present century, and gave us pleasant recollections of their personal characters and habits.

Only a few weeks before the sudden death of Mr. Parkes he informed me that he expected to get his life of Sir Philip Francis to press the then ensuing autumn, and, in pursuance of a previous understanding, I was to arrange for its republica-

tion here. Since his death I have heard nothing further about it. The researches had all been accomplished, and the work had progressed so far toward its completion that no difficulty existed, nor was any such delay necessary. I had expected and hoped that Miss Bessie Parkes, the gifted daughter of my old and cherished friend (already a distinguished and disciplined writer), would complete and publish the unfinished work of her honored father—a work on which he had bestowed years of toil, and to the publication of which he looked forward with confidence, in an appreciative and approving popular sense of its value, for his reward.
T. W.

Mr. Weed finally severed his connection with the *Evening Journal* in 1862, and traveled in Europe for the government and for his health. On his return in 1867, he edited the *Commercial Advertiser* for a while, but was soon after compelled to retire from that concern in consequence of continued ill health and increasing years; and now, at the age of seventy-five or six, he is engaged in writing his reminiscences of politicians and statesmen. Mr. Weed is a genial man, full of anecdotes, with a homely, rural manner that is rather captivating, and a heart full of generous impulses. When it was known that his old political antagonist, Edwin Croswell, of the *Argus*, had met with misfortune, he quietly and unostentatiously obtained a large subscription from old political friends and enemies, which he had conveyed to Mr. C. in a manner so touching and agreeable as to annihilate all previous animosities, and in this way the path to the grave of that once powerful journalist was made smooth and pleasant.

The *Nashville Union* was established March 30, 1835. It was printed by George James Harris in 1837, and edited by Samuel M'Laughlin. Mr. Harris had been foreman in the office of the *Boston Post*, and afterwards publisher of the New Bedford *Gazette*. It was not long after his appearance in Nashville that he became involved in a difficulty with Ephraim H. Foster, Jr., son of Senator Foster, of Tennessee, growing out of the editorials of the *Union* against the senator. Harris received a pistol-shot on this occasion which passed through his right arm, through his right breast, up through the passage between the two lower jaws, coming out of the left cheek. In spite of the desperate nature of these wounds, Harris recovered, and was sent on a Tobacco Mission to Austria by President Tyler, and afterwards made a Purser of the Navy by President Polk in the year 1844. After this encounter between Harris and Foster, Major John P. Heiss, who had served his time with General Simon Cameron, of Pennsylvania, became one of the publishers of the *Union*. M'Laughlin continued its editor till the elevation of Mr. Polk to the presidency, when he was appointed Register of the Land Office in Washington, and Heiss became the publisher of the official organ—the *Union*. Thus the President liberally provided for the *attachés* of his home organ, even transferring its name to the national capital. The title of the paper is now the *Nashville Union and American.*

The *Charleston* (S. C.) *Mercury*, always ably edited, always neatly printed, always an oracle, was one of the marked papers of the nation in the editorial rooms of other journals, and in the opinion of politicians north, east, west, and south. Why? It was the chief organ of the Nullifiers of South Carolina in 1832, and of the ultra Secessionists of the South, culminating in the events of 1861–5. It was, through its long life, a paper of remarkable ability, and not surpassed by any other Southern newspaper in the support of its peculiar political views. It paid more attention to its political hobby than to news, and on the one idea of the necessity of slavery to the planting interest it was speciously brilliant and tenacious. All the Haynes, the M'Duffies, the Barnwells, the Rhetts, the Calhouns, the Hammonds, the Hamiltons, the Tabers, contributed to its columns. It gave the key-note to the other newspapers of the South on the vital interests of that section from the nullification of 1832 to the terrible climax in the rebellion of 1861–5.

The *Mercury* belonged to the chivalric school of journalism. It believed in the code of honor. The argument of the pistol at ten paces was, in all personal grievances, the last resort. Some of the affairs have been serious and tragical, while others resulted harmlessly and humorously. There was one in 1856, the details of which will be read with interest and edification even in 1872, and even after the greater duel between the North and South has settled and reconstructed the long-pent-up troubles of our brethren of the South.

There was a meeting in September, 1856, resulting fatally, between W. R. Taber, Jr., one of the editors of the *Mercury*, and Edward Magrath, brother of Judge A. G. Magrath. The history of the affair is detailed by Mr. John Cunningham, one of the seconds, and is a very curious narrative. Apart from its connection with journalism, it is peculiarly instructive in the nice points and precise punctilio in matters affecting personal interviews of this kind on the field. After a few preliminary observations, Mr. Cunningham said:

The duel occurred on the afternoon of Monday, the 29th of September. I had left Charleston for Virginia on the evening of the 16th, and returned to it on Saturday morning, the 27th. In the mean time, the first two articles, signed "A Nullifier," against Judge A. G. Magrath, had appeared in the *Mercury*—the third was on Monday. I first saw and read them on the day of my return. Mr. Taber and I met in the forenoon of that day, when he showed me the challenges from Mr. Ed. Magrath to himself and Mr. Heart as editors of the *Mercury*, announced his intention to become the first responsible party, and desired me immediately to take charge of the matter as his friend. Expressing at once my hearty readiness ever to serve him, and acknowledging the claims which in every way he had upon me, I yet earnestly requested him, in the fullness of our intimacy as friends, to excuse me, as I was myself a candidate for Congress, from counseling him in a difficulty pertaining to one of my opponents, and with whom I had had obliging relations. To this he assented, upon the agreement that I would serve him on the field in the event of a hostile meeting. In the course of that forenoon a few of us were in the *Mercury* office, and the whole matter was freely conversed upon, preliminary to the momentarily expected coming in of one or more advising friends, whose counsels had been requested. Mr. Taber was not only much annoyed by the insulting language contained in the challenge, but evidently was aroused by an impression that an imputation had been thrown out that he would avoid responsibility. He announced his fixed purpose to fight, and to do so apart from all considerations affecting the position of Mr. Edmund Rhett as the author and publisher of the articles. I urged him, if such was his intent, to state fully in his note of acceptance his own case and position. Previous to the full assembling of his friends I left him, and proceeded to Sullivan's Island, where I was residing during the yellow-fever season, by the one o'clock ferry-boat. On parting with him, I said, in substance, and in accordance with my whole previous conversations with him, that upon one point I would give him positive advice, that on that point my opinion was absolute, and it was that Mr. Ed. Magrath's hostile note should be returned to him through the hand of whoever was to bear his correspondence, because of its clearly offensive language, inadmissible in such connection under every rule and courtesy recognized in such cases, and that an intimation should be given to Mr. Magrath that none but a respectful cartel would be entertained. I expressed the opinion that a gentleman was not bound to treat as insult any offensive language in a challenge, but, on the contrary, that it was his duty, on account of it, to return the note containing a demand thus couched. I charged him not to delay, neglect, or disregard this his first duty and true step. * * * *

The first exchange of shots took place a few minutes after half past 4 P.M. I did not then ask Mr. James Conner, the acting friend of Ed. Magrath, Esq., who was the challenging party, whether his principal was satisfied. This inquiry would have conformed to the usual practice, and there is no limitation, established either by written codes or the custom of gentlemen, upon the number of shots which the party seeking satisfaction may require. But, regarding the meeting as in the nature of a cross demand, and the claims of Mr. Taber to redress for the insulting language of the challenge, I only intimated to Mr. Conner that we were ready to load in continuation of the duel, but at the same time I suggested that if propositions for settlement were to be made, or their terms discussed, it had better be then. In response, Mr. Conner proposed, as the terms of adjustment, that Mr. Taber should repudiate or disclaim the articles signed "A Nullifier," and apologize for their publication. * * * * * *

I rejected his proposition, and a second exchange of shots took place within ten or fifteen minutes after the first. At this stage I deemed the attitude of parties to each other to be changed, and entertained the conviction that the affair should, if possible, and consistent with honorable obligations, be settled. The double exchange of shots had at least met all the technical requirement of their cross demands. I have long held, and it has been known to many, and although without the authority of precedent, that an exchange of shots would be deemed, *ipso facto,* satisfaction on a mere point of honor, and where there was no direct wrong or insult between the parties. With these views I addressed myself, and I aver it before God and man, with all my mind and heart, to the adjustment of the difficulty. Looking to an adjustment, Mr. Conner and I earnestly discussed all the facts and possible terms. We differed, each evidently looking at the whole case from variant points of view; he deeming Mr. Taber to have been throughout a wanton aggressor upon the brother (Judge A. G. Magrath) of his principal, and that he was bound to disclaim and apologize for such, his assumed aggressions, and I, that Mr. Taber had assumed no connection with the articles of "A Nullifier;" that as editor of the *Mercury* he had the right to publish them, they being in relation to a candidate for political position and office; that he was on the ground, and had been called there only in the character of editor of the *Mercury;* that as such *he was there maintaining the liberty and independence of the Press;* that as such he had had insult, in addition to the challenge, put upon him; that, therefore, he could not comply with the terms required, and that no terms could be acceded to by him which were not coupled with a disclaimer by Mr. Ed. Magrath of the offensive language of his challenge. * * * * * *

I told Mr. Conner that I spoke no longer as a mere second, but as a man, and

that I had but urged my real convictions. Up to this time we had acted and conferred only together and alone. Finding that we could not agree, and when we were about to separate, I expressed a wish, as I had observed that he consulted with some invited gentlemen on the ground, to know who were his advising friends, and to explain to and confer with them on my views. He replied that they were Messrs. J. B. Campbell, J. J. Pettigrew, and J. H. Wilson, and went from me to present my request to them. He returned, declining to accede to it—I presume by their concurrence or direction. At this moment Dr. Bellinger advanced to us and expressed a desire to intervene between the parties. He urged that as there had been two exchanges of shots, and each party had had sufficient chances at each other, the difficulty should be adjusted and terminated. His intervention was cordially accepted; and as I understood Dr. Bellinger to make, by his remarks, the proposition that there should be a mutual declaration of satisfaction, in view of two exchanges of shots, I intimated my assent to it. * * * * * * *
The basis of the discussion on both sides was as I have previously stated. At length I succeeded, as I thought, in turning their views in the direction of the written propositions which I made on the field. At least, finding discussion would be uselessly prolonged, I offered those propositions as the best and all that I could do; and with the concurrence of Mr. Conner, I reduced them on the spot into writing, and to the effect that, as simultaneous declarations, Mr. Taber disclaim the intent, as editor of the *Mercury*, to have made by the publication of the articles an attack on the private character of Judge Magrath, and Mr. Ed. Magrath disclaim the intent to insult Mr. Taber by the language of his challenge. I would here state that in every previous instance where terms of adjustment were proposed by either side, Mr. Conner and Dr. Bellinger insisted that those on the part of Mr. Taber should be the condition of those on the part of Mr. Magrath. To this I steadily objected, on the ground that gentlemen seeking to place themselves in their true positions should declare those positions independently of, yet simultaneously with each other, and the other mode was either distrustful or humiliating.

Mr. Conner carried my propositions to his group of friends for advisement. After a time Mr. Conner returned to me, bringing, as the *sine qua non* of their acceptance, the proposition that Mr. Taber should also express regret for the publication of the articles. Mild and harmless as it may seem, it was too palpable to me that it amounted not only to an identification of Mr. Taber with the whole responsibility for those articles, but as a disclaimer of and apology for them. It would have been a stultification of him as an editor, and a humiliation of him as a man, and so I stated to Mr. Conner. I not only rejected it, but regarded it as the index to the whole meaning of that hostile meeting. It must rest on the head of those or him who made it.

I then inquired of Mr. Conner whether I must proceed to load for another shot, and he bowed his head in assent and requirement.

Near an hour had been consumed after the second shot in discussion, and the third shot took place with its fatal result.

* * * * * * * * *

It is material to note the following:

1. That Mr. Heart, co-editor of the *Mercury*, had also been challenged, and had accepted.

2. That satisfaction in behalf of the *Mercury*, although to be deemed a unity, was to be rendered by Mr. Taber or Mr. Heart, or both; and that, if rendered complete, in entirety, by Mr. Taber, Mr. Heart should not be called upon; if not, Mr. Heart could be.

3. That Mr. Heart's meeting had been appointed at the same ground, at a time immediately following that of Mr. Taber, and that he was actually at the place long before the third shot, waiting to respond in satisfaction.

I can now give my reasons for not withdrawing Mr. Taber, and not declining a third shot.

1. I was satisfied that Mr. Taber would not have been willing.

2. I would have assumed a responsibility contrary to all precedent, in face of the demand of the challenging party. I might have assumed it in despite of these considerations, but for the reason,

3. That if Mr. Taber had been withdrawn, the other party could have insisted, on the pretext of a failure of satisfaction on the part of the *Mercury*, upon Mr.

Heart taking his place and making it complete. If Mr. Heart, in such event, had fallen, what would have been the position of my friend and myself? Mr. Taber had assumed to render satisfaction in full, and nothing but the admission of his opponent or the decree of an intervention could have availed.

It is but justice to Mr. Edmund Rhett, Jr., who promptly avowed himself the author of the article signed "A Nullifier," and who instantly endeavored to prevent the duel by challenging Judge Magrath with that object, to state that Mr. Taber's meeting with Mr. Ed. Magrath took place on grounds entirely distinct from his, had no reference to his position, and could not have been arrested by his action. I therefore refused to permit him to be on the field, and would not have suffered his interference. He was, however, near it, ready to interpose and assume all responsibility, in the event Judge Magrath had appeared and intervened.

Thus the death of Mr. Taber prevented two other duels between parties already on the ground, and "the liberty and independence of the Press" was vindicated!

Now we have another affair which occurred only three months after that between Messrs. Taber and Magrath, and in which a member of the Rhett family challenged the editor of the *Charleston* (S. C.) *Standard* for a communication furnished by one of the actors in the previous tragedy, and, in a word, for precisely the same reason. These two journalistic affairs were so curious in their causes and effects as to make us sometimes wonder at the eccentricities of man. We give the correspondence between Alfred Rhett and L. W. Spratt, of the *Standard:*

THE INSULT AND THE DEMAND FOR REPARATION.

Tuesday Evening, Jan. 6, 1857.

SIR,—You thought proper to publish in your paper of the 27th of November a communication, in which I was gratuitously and unjustly assailed by Dr. Bellinger, who, in the very piece, declared that he was not responsible under the laws of honor, and argued *that editors of newspapers were more accountable for what they published than the writers of their articles.* In deference to the prevailing sentiment of the community against further strife, and in hope that you also would forbear additional wrong, I let this pass, and published an explanation and defense, in which I denied the facts as false inferences alleged against me. You also published in a subsequent communication, on the 1st of January, from the same irresponsible source, a reiteration of the offensive and insulting imputations previously made against me, with additional remarks more offensive than any already published, and this in the teeth of my published statement. You have thus made yourself responsible for the articles, and have left me no other alternative than to meet the responsibility you have assumed. I am under the necessity of requesting that you make a suitable amende to me for the injury you have done me. Your obedient servant, ALFRED RHETT.

L. W. SPRATT, Esq.

WHAT IS WANTED?

CHARLESTON, Jan. 7, 1857.

SIR,—Your note of the 6th instant was handed to me by Mr. ———, and has received the earliest attention consistent with my engagements. It does not appear, from the tenor of your note, what atonement it is in my power to render you. If it will consist in disclaiming any purpose on my part of wounding your feelings, or of injuring your character, you will confer a favor by stating the terms in which such a disclaimer would be agreeable, and I can scarcely apprehend the possibility of not being able to make it in accordance with your wishes.

Respectfully yours, L. W. SPRATT.

ALFRED RHETT, Esq.

THE ATONEMENT REQUIRED.

CHARLESTON, Jan. 8, 1857.

SIR,—I take pleasure in expressing my gratification at your disposition to disclaim any purpose of wounding my feelings or injuring my character by the publication of the communications alluded to in my note. You desire me to state what atonement or disclaimer would be agreeable. I can but presume that your reflection has shown you that, in publishing the articles of Dr. Bellinger, in view of his declared non-amenability, and of my being a private citizen, and of the fact that I had not assailed him through your columns, you have inflicted, in fact, a wound upon my feelings and an injury upon my character, and that you have become unavoidably responsible for this wrong. Your candor will therefore, no doubt, induce you to perceive the wrong, and to express regret for the consequences which have ensued from your acts.

Respectfully yours, ALFRED RHETT.
To L. W. SPRATT, Esq.

THE AMENDE.

CHARLESTON, Jan. 8, 1857.

SIR,—Your note of to-day has been received. In permitting the appearance, in the columns of the *Standard*, of the articles referred to, I certainly had no intention to injure or to offend any one; and I readily acknowledge my regret that any wound was thereby occasioned to your feelings, or any injury to your character. Respectfully yours, L. W. SPRATT.
ALFRED RHETT, Esq.

SATISFACTORY.

CHARLESTON, Jan. 8, 1857.

L. W. SPRATT, ESQ.—SIR,—It gives me pleasure to state that your note of to-day has been received, and is satisfactory.

Very respectfully, ALFRED RHETT.

But the days of duels are rapidly passing away, and the days of the *Mercury* have been numbered. Its career is at an end. It ceased to exist in November, 1868. Ninety-one volumes of the paper had been published, fuller of the brilliant sophistries of the South than can be found any where else. Messrs. R. B. Rhett, Jr., and Brother, with Roswell T. Logan for an assistant, were its last editors and conductors. Why its publication should have been suspended is a mystery, when we take into view the following announcements, which appeared in the *Mercury* in August, 1868, and which seemed to be standing notices in that remarkable paper:

THE CHARLESTON MERCURY HAS NOW A LARGER BONA FIDE COUNTRY CIRCULATION THAN ANY OTHER PAPER PUBLISHED IN CHARLESTON.
THE CHARLESTON MERCURY HAS THE LARGEST NUMBER OF PERMANENT ANNUAL AND SEMI-ANNUAL SUBSCRIBERS OF ANY JOURNAL IN SOUTH CAROLINA.

What are reminiscences? The records of the past. The *Mercury* of March 26, 1832, contained this notice:

MARK!

Monday, March 19, 1832.

The Senate of the U. States, by a vote of 23 to 18, *five majority*, adopted Mr. Clay's proposition to remodel and aggravate the tariff.

ARE WE READY?

TOCSIN.

In his valedictory in 1868, Editor Rhett, in lamentations over the result of the fruitless efforts of the leaders of the South, declared his intention "to take his place among her ruined children—better so than to be the proudest and most honored of her successful enemies—and to wait, hoping, praying, expecting the bright coming of her final deliverance, the independence and prosperity of the South."

Sic transit gloria mundi.

THE FIFTH EPOCH.

1832—1835.

JOURNALISM IN A TRANSITION STATE.
CHAPTER XXV.
THE BEGINNING OF THE NEWSPAPER REVOLUTION.

SIZE OF NEWSPAPERS IN 1832.—WASTE OF SPACE.—SMALLER PAPERS.—THE NEW YORK GLOBE.—JAMES GORDON BENNETT.—THE PENNSYLVANIAN.—THE HOYT, VAN BUREN, AND BENNETT CORRESPONDENCE.—BLAIR'S OPINION OF BENNETT.—OPPOSITION OF POLITICIANS. — INCOMING OF THE INDEPENDENT PRESS.—SEWARD, WEED, AND GREELEY.

IT was now necessary to have a revolution in the Press. Those in existence were too large, and too much under the influence and control of politics. Something new was needed. Something fresh and vigorous.

Newspapers, beginning with the *News-Letter* in 1704, on sheets 8 by 12 inches in size, run up, with the *Journal of Commerce* and *Courier and Enquirer* in 1827, to 24 by 35 inches; and these comparatively large papers, in their competition, as we have shown, increased their dimensions to 35 by 58¾ inches in 1853. Size seemed to have absorbed most of the other qualities that make up a first-class journal. Such large folio sheets, when we consider their form, circulation, and advertising patronage, were beyond the legitimate requirements of newspapers at that time. Space for advertisements in the "blanket sheets" was not only sold at very low rates, but was thrown away. Their publishers were compelled to allow as many lines as a grasping advertiser chose to take for $32 per year or $40, including the daily paper. Many advertisements would appear day after day till long after they had accomplished their object. One or more pages would thus frequently become old or stereotyped matter, continually staring the reader in the face, and appearing worse even than a thrice-told tale. It was admitted that these stale business notices seriously damaged the fresh advertisements, and the newspapers generally, as a matter of course, with nothing but politics besides, and without a new idea, became heavy and uninteresting when compared with the vigorous sheets of the present day.

It was necessary to change all this. But how? It required time, money, courage, tact, persistency, talent, industry, and enterprise to effect a revolution. Were they to be had? All these elements, barring the main one—money, began to develop themselves in 1832 or a little earlier. Smaller and cheaper, and more independent papers, with fresh matter, fresh arrangements, and fresh ideas, began to be thought of and projected. With what result?

On the 29th of October, 1832, about the time Emile de Girardin was making arrangements to start *La Presse*, at half price, in Paris, there was issued in New York City an evening paper called the *New York Globe*. Its size was 12 by 17—half that of the ten dollar papers, or "respectable sixpennies" then in existence. Its price was eight dollars, which was also a reduction in the right direction, but not sufficient. Its prospectus, as it appeared in the first number, intelligently tells its own story, and is a concise and curious history in itself:

TO THE PUBLIC.

I publish this evening, at No. 20 William Street, the first number of a new daily journal called the *New York Globe*, price eight dollars a year. Early arrangements will be made to issue a weekly and a semi-weekly paper from the same office.

Since my withdrawal in August last from the *Courier and Enquirer*, I have been taking measures for the establishment of a new paper, but unavoidable obstacles have hitherto prevented its appearance. I am now in the field, sword in hand, with unfurled banner, resolved to aid the great cause of Jackson and Democracy—the Union of the States, and the rights of the States. My politics are well known. I was one of the first in this state to put the names of Jackson and Van Buren before the people in 1827—I fought through the great conflict of 1828, and again in June, 1829, I was the first to bring the name of our venerable President up for a re-election. I have always supported the principles and nominations of the Democratic Party, and shall continue in that course. Opposed to nullification, I adhere to Jefferson's doctrines of State Rights—*equal legislation—economy in public expenditures—reduction of unnecessary taxes—and the advancement of human liberty and human happiness.*

Up to the next election, politics will be the staple article of the *Globe ;* but *after that event I shall give it all the variety which makes a daily paper the welcome visiter of the tea-table or counting-room.* And if industry, experience, and resolution are any warrant for success, I entertain no doubt that, in less than *two years*, I shall count, without affidavits, at least *five thousand* good subscribers to the *New York Globe.*

A word on the size of my paper. *For years past the public has been cloyed with immense sheets—bunglingly made up—without concert of action or individuality of character—the reservoirs of crude thoughts from different persons who were continually knocking their heads against each other, without knocking any thing remarkably good out of them.* I have avoided this inconvenience. I shall give my readers the cream of foreign and domestic events. My sheet is moderate in size, but neat and manageable, printed on fine paper and with beautiful type. When an overflow of patronage shall demand more room, as it soon will, I may enlarge a little, but I shall avoid, as I would a pestilence, those enormous sheets—the pine barrens of intelligence and taste, which have been undoubtedly sent into the world as a punishment for its growing wickedness.

In taking my position as the editor of a daily paper in this community, I am no new recruit—no undisciplined soldier. I have acted in this capacity for twelve years past, eight of which I have been associated with the *National Advocate*, the *New York Enquirer*, and latterly the *Courier and Enquirer*, all of this city. I have hitherto labored for the reputation and profit of others; I am now embarked on my own account—on my own responsibility. In coming before this community I do not feel therefore as a stranger thrown among new faces. Though personally unknown to many newspaper readers, I stand before them as an acquaintance—a friend—an intimate. I feel myself connected with New York by that captivating species of relationship—that delightful community of thought and sentiment which exists between an industrious and moral editor, and a numerous and encouraging body of readers. With these remarks I commit my bark to the breeze.   JAMES GORDON BENNETT.

New York, October 29, 1832.

This paper failed. More correctly speaking, it was suspended. The idea, not the name, remained. It was the beginning of the "small papers," the pioneer of the "Penny Press," the precursor of the "Independent Press," but it did not then succeed. Why? In its general scope it was a political journal, yet its contents indicated a more comprehensive purpose, and exhibited touches of that peculiarity and originality which afterwards so fully characterized the leading journal of the Independent Press of the country. It was, indeed, the prospectus of this new class of journalism. But why did it fail? Simply because, locally and politically, it was started one year too early. It was, however, the intellectual entering wedge. When the New York Hotel, in Broadway, near Eighth Street, was finished, it was leased to Captain Jo. Comstock. He was known to fame, liked by every one, and knew how to keep a first-class hotel, but he succumbed after losing largely in the enterprise. Within six months his *chef de cuisine* was placed in charge, and he made a fortune in a few years, retiring with a stable full of race-horses. Hiram Cranston, of Rockaway, succeeded him, made another fortune, and drove four-in-hand through Central Park. "Will you tell me, captain," inquired a sanguine friend of Comstock one day, "why you gave up the New York Hotel?" "Certainly," replied the portly and pleasant captain; "I opened the house just one year too early." Such was the case. It was opened too soon. If he had delayed that event twelve short months he would have been in full possession when the tide of the metropolis, which had just set up Broadway, was "at its flood," and he would have been led "on to fortune." So it was with the *Globe*. It was started too soon: as in all revolutions and change, however, there had to be a beginning. It was what the public wanted, but it was hampered with party politics, and its proprietor, although he knew how to edit and manage a newspaper, was unable, without capital, to perfect his plans and bide his time. With the *Globe* as with the New York Hotel, the "up town movement" in journalism had not commenced, but it was close upon the heels of that interesting event.

Apart from all other causes and considerations, the political element was vehemently opposed to new papers, and especially to new papers with ideas and opinions of their own. Every newspaper writer and every printer in the United States had been educated for half a century in the belief that no journal of any respectability could be established without the consent of politicians and the pecuniary aid of party. It was particularly so during Jackson's second term and Van Buren's administration. It was so, indeed, with both parties. "To the victor belongs the spoils" was the motto of the Albany Regency, and it had been fully adopted in Washington. "Under which king, Benzonian? Speak or die!" Thus with the *Globe*. When it showed any symptoms of independence it was deemed necessary to stop its supplies and crush it out. When its editor afterwards took charge of the *Pennsylvanian*, another political paper, in Philadelphia, fortunately for improved and enterprising journalism, the same occurred there. All the correspondence of Martin Van Buren, James Gordon Bennett, Jesse Hoyt, Abijah Mann, Jr., and others, show this feeling in the strongest light. In one of his notes to Jesse Hoyt, written in 1829, Mr. Bennett makes the following curious disclosures on this point:

ALBANY, 20th July, 1829.

DEAR SIR,—Since I arrived here I have seen our friends in the *Argus* office and *State* department—I mean Major Flagg, Mr. Wright, and Mr. Croswell. They are very friendly, but they say they have heard little of our local matters in New York consequent on the sale of *the Enquirer*, with the exception of a passing remark from Mr. Cambreleng as he passed through here a few weeks ago. * * * They told me to-day that if the party had the control of the political course of the *Courier and Enquirer*, it would be more eligible than a new paper. This they think could be done by placing an editor there *under the auspices of the General Committee—an editor who would take care of* the interests *of the party and its friends*. They are afraid that *the political patronage is not sufficient for the support of a new paper*, and they are of opinion that a journal which now enjoys all such patronage as the *Courier and Enquirer ought to give up* its columns to a political editor appointed by the General Committee.

How would such a plan work now with such journals as the *Times, Tribune, Herald*, or with the *Evening Post*, each with an editor selected by a political clique in Albany or Washington, or a General Committee?

Again, writing from Philadelphia on the 13th of June, 1833, he said:

DEAR HOYT,—* * * * * * *

John Mumford has been aided to the extent of $40,000. With a fourth of that sum I would have done twice as much—soberly and with some decency too.

I should be sorry to be compelled to believe that my friends in New York should bestow their friendship more effectually upon a ——— fellow than me, who certainly *has* some pretensions to decency.

I am sorry to speak harshly of any body, but really I think there is something like ingratitude in the way I have been treated.

I want no favor that I can not repay.

I want no aid that is not perfectly safe.

Yours, etc., J. GORDON BENNETT.

The John Mumford mentioned in this letter was editor of the *New York Standard*, which was, at that time, supported almost entirely by the party, and it received all sorts of aid and comfort from Washington.

Another letter was sent, five or six weeks later, of which the following is a copy:

PHILADELPHIA, July 27th, 1833.

DEAR HOYT,—I have written to Van Buren to-day about the old affair. I must have a loan of $2500 for a couple of years from some quarter. I can't get on without it; and if the common friends of our cause—those I have been working for for eight years—can not do it, I must look for it somewhere else. My business here is doing very well, and the money would be perfectly safe in two years. You see already the effect produced in Pennsylvania—we can have the state; but, if our friends won't lay aside their heartlessness, why, we'll go to the devil—that is all.

There is no man who will go further with friends than I will—who will sacrifice more—who will work harder. You know it very well.

I must be perfectly independent of the little sections in this city, who would hurry me into their small courses, at the risk of the main object.

Kendall leaves Washington to-morrow on his tour of Bank inspection. Let me hear from you. Yours, etc., JAS. GORDON BENNETT.

The italics are ours, as indicative of the spirit which governed the writer as an editor at that time, and which has characterized the *Herald* since its first issue. But here is the sequel:

MR. HOYT TO MR. BENNETT.

August 16, 1833.

MY DEAR SIR,—I have not answered yours of the 3d for various reasons. Among other reasons, I was quite too much provoked with you. It appears, at the moment I was trying to favor you, the *Pennsylvanian* was taking such a course as calculated to thwart all my efforts. There are but very few of our people, comparatively, that see your paper, and they have to look for its character to the party papers here. And what does the *Post* and *Standard* say of it? I am not going to set myself up as the judge to decide who and which is the aggressor, but I admit that an intelligent newspaper, edited any where in this country, ought to have known that the *Northern Banner* and the *Doylestown Democrat* are papers substantially hostile to the administration; but, because it was not known to some of our "corps editorial," it was no reason why you should quarrel with all of us—by which I mean all the prominent Jackson papers, from the *Argus* down. There is a wonderful coincidence between the course the *Pennsylvanian* threatens to take and that taken by the *Courier and Enquirer* when it first began to secede from the Jackson ranks. It began, you will recollect, by assailing what was called the "Money Changers." You are about to commence "No. 1, New York Stock Jobbing, etc., etc., and certain expresses in the fall of 1832." This has all been published in the opposition papers, and they did not make much of it, and, therefore, I should doubt whether a *bona fide* Jackson paper could do better with it. If this was intended for Mumford, I could tell you reasons for letting him alone; if for Mr. Hone, there are similar reasons; but as he is no friend of mine, I speak only from general principles—there is nothing to be gained by it; it mends nobody's principles, or improves the morals of any one, but rather helps your enemies in their efforts to satisfy others that you are not "a reliable man," as the phrase is. The *Post*, this afternoon, no doubt will call you hard names for associating "vinegar" with the complacent countenance of my excellent and amiable—ay, amiable friend Croswell. Dr. Holland, of the *Standard*, will rewrite the same idea for to-morrow morning. All this is quite ridiculous on all sides, but you will perceive it is the worst for you here, because the people read but one side, and that is the side against you.

I suppose you think it is time to have the moral of my tale, and it is this, that I can get no one to join me in rendering any aid, and my means alone are wholly inadequate to render you any relief, and what I have written you is but the essence of the arguments that have met me at every turn.

You have heard me talk to Webb by the hour of the folly of his being on the face of the record a friend of Mr. Van Buren's, and, at the same time, attacking his most firm and consistent friend, viz., the editor of the *Argus;* and you stand in almost the same attitude, and there are many here who believe that your friendship will end as Mr. Webb's has. I will do you the justice to say that I believe no such thing, but at the same time I will exercise the frankness to say that the course of your paper lays you open to the suspicion. I know enough of affairs to know that you had high authority for the ground you have taken on the Deposit Question, and I thought you managed the subject well for the meridian you are in. I was told by a person a day or two since that you would be aided from another quarter; I could not learn how. But you ought not to expect my friend at the North to do any thing, not that he has an indisposition to do what is right, or that he would not serve a friend, but he is in the attitude that requires the most fastidious reserve. The people are jealous of the public press, and the moment it is attempted to be controlled, its usefulness is not only destroyed, but he who would gain public favor through its columns is quite sure to fail. I am satisfied the press has lost some portion of its hold upon public confidence; recent developments have had a tendency to satisfy the people that its conductors, or many of them at least, are as negotiable as a promissory note. This impression can only be removed by a firm adherence to principle in adversity as well as prosperity. I can, my dear sir, only say, as I have before said to you, be patient, "love them who persecute you." You have a great field before you, and it is impossible but you will succeed if you are, as I think you to be, honest, intelligent, and industrious. Yours truly, J. HOYT.

In reply to this letter Mr. Bennett said:

PHILADELPHIA, August 16th, 1833.

DEAR HOYT,—Your letter amuses me. The only point of consequence is that conveying the refusal. This is the best evidence of *the deadly hostility which you all have entertained towards me.* It explains, too, the course of the *Standard* and *Post* in their aggressions upon me ever since I came to Philadelphia. The name for such a feeling in the breasts of those I have only served and aided at my own cost and my own sacrifice puzzles me beyond example. I can account for it in no other way than the simple fact *that I happen to have been born in another country.* I must put up with it as well as I can. * * * * * * The assaults of the *Post* and *Standard* I shall put down like the grass that grows. I shall carry the war into Africa, and "cursed be he who cries hold, enough." Neither Mr. Van Buren and the *Argus*, nor any of their true friends, will or can have any fellow feeling with the men—the stockjobbers—who for the last two years have been trying to destroy my character and reputation. * * * * * * I will endeavor to do the best I can to get along. I will go among my personal friends, who are unshackled as to politics or banks, and who will leave me free to act as a man of honor and principle. So, my dear Hoyt, do not lose your sleep on my account. I am certain of YOUR friendship, whatever the others may say or do. I fear nothing in the shape of man, devil, or newspaper; I can row my own boat, and if the *Post* and *Standard* don't get out of my way, they must sink me—that is all. If I adhere to the same principles, and run hereafter as I have done heretofore, *and which I mean to do,* recollect it is not so much that "I love my persecutors" as that *I regard my own honor* and reputation. Your lighting up poor Webb like a fat tallow candle at one end, and holding him out as a beacon-light to frighten me, only makes me smile. Webb is a gentleman in private life, a good-hearted fellow, honorable in all his private transactions as I have found him, but in politics and newspapers a perfect child—a boy. You will never find the *Pennsylvanian* going the career of the *C. & E.* That suspicion answers as a good excuse to those who have resolved beforehand to do me all the injury they can, but it will answer for nothing else. I am, dear Hoyt, yours truly,

JAMES GORDON BENNETT.

The war was indeed carried into Africa, and vigorously continued for more than a quarter of a century. The result is before the journalistic world. Mifflin, Parry, and Bennett, as publishers of the

Pennsylvanian, dissolved partnership in December, 1833, and Mr. Bennett gave up the editorial management of that and all other party papers forever. He returned to the metropolis, and made arrangements, under great difficulties and obstacles, for the publication of the *New York Herald* on purely journalistic principles, which have made it a wonderful and permanent success.

After the excitement is over, and most of the characters have passed away, what does one of the chief actors in these political scenes say of the play? In a conversation with a correspondent of the *Herald* in 1870, Mr. Blair, the old editor of the Washington *Globe*, thus oddly and pleasantly speaks of Mr. Bennett and his course in that sensational period of our political history:

> I knew Mr. Bennett during the administration of Jackson, while I was editing the *Globe*. Mr. Bennett had a desire to join his fortunes with mine in the *Globe* enterprise; but I told him two such great men as he and I would be too great a weight for such a small vessel as the *Globe*, and that we might swamp it. I advised him to go to Philadelphia, which he would find to be a Bœotia. There he would find a splendid field for his talents and genius. He went there and established a paper, but at one time the weight of Jackson's administration was thrown against it and it was crushed. A few years ago, when I visited Mr. Bennett, he reminded me of this circumstance, and I said to him, "It is the best thing that ever happened you, and you ought to thank General Jackson and me for it; for was it not the cause of driving you to New York, where you started the *Herald*, and have built up the greatest newspaper enterprise? Now, sir, you are higher than the highest senator on earth." I have followed Mr. Bennett's course with a great deal of interest, and we have always been good friends, though sometimes he gives me a rap in his paper.

Such was the position of the Press throughout the country at this period of its history. It was bound to party. It was fettered in every way. It was the slave of the two political oligarchies. It was necessary, in the estimation of the Albany Regency, that every paper should have "an editor who would take care of the interests of the party and its friends." If any further evidence of this sort is wanted, our readers will find it in the "Recollections of a Busy Life" of Horace Greeley, published in 1868, in which he describes, with refreshing *naïveté*, the famous political firm of Seward, Weed, and Greeley, and the causes of its dissolution, which, we are happy to say, made the *Tribune*, although still a party paper, a more independent and a more successful journal. Seward and Weed finally retired to private life in 1869, leaving Greeley alone in his glory as a journalist, and as a political traveler reading the unreliable guide-posts on the road to the White House.

This political element, which was afterwards joined by the financial and religious elements, was powerful in 1832, and for a number of years after in its opposition to the Cheap Cash Press. The crusade against it, the moral war of 1840, the threats, the personal assaults, the attempts at assassination, and the libel suits which rapidly followed each other, were episodes of no small proportions in the history of modern journalism. But time, with energy and perseverance, creating a revolution with the reading public, swept away all this rubbish and all these obstacles. In 1833 and '34 the "Penny Press" was an accomplished faćt, and in 1835 the "Independent Press" was organized, and has since become a permanent and overshadowing institution in America.

CHAPTER XXVI.
THE PENNY PRESS.

WHERE DID IT ORIGINATE?—THE CENT OF PHILADELPHIA.—THE MORNING POST OF NEW YORK.—DR. HORATIO D. SHEPARD AND HORACE GREELEY. — THE NEW YORK SUN. — SPEECH OF THE ORIGINATOR. — THE MOON HOAX.—RICHARD ADAMS LOCKE.—ENTERPRISE OF THE SUN.—OPINION OF A "BLANKET SHEET" ON THE CHEAP PRESS. — THE CITIZEN AND MILES O'REILLY.

THE Penny Press of America dates from 1833. There were small and cheap papers published in Boston and Philadelphia before and about that time. The *Bostonian* was one. The *Cent*, in Philadelphia, was another. The latter was issued by Christopher C. Cornwell in 1830. These and all similar adventures were not permanent. Most of them were issued by printers when they had nothing else to do. Still they belonged to the class of cheap papers. The idea came from the *Illustrated Penny Magazine*, issued in London in 1830, which was imported and sold in large quantities in New York and other cities, thus creating a taste for cheap literature in this country.

There were low-priced papers in England as early as 1706. The *Orange Postman* was established then, and sold for one cent. It was the Father of the Penny Press. Newspapers in this country run into subscription papers at a fixed price per year, and delivered to subscribers by mail or by regularly paid carriers employed by the newspaper publishers. Before the time of L'Estrange, in London, in 1665, there were newsboys and newswomen, as in New York, Boston, Philadelphia, and Chicago now. They were condemned by L'Estrange in the *Intelligencer*. He, indeed, refused to employ them to sell his paper. In New York, newspapers were sold in places where the people mostly congregated in 1765; but the Press became, in the course of time, "blanket sheets" and "respectable sixpennies," mammoth folios of ridiculous dignity and limited circulation. Stone, and Webb, and Bryant, and Hale, and Hallock, and others, all over the country, following in the footsteps of L'Estrange, would only sell their "wares" over the counter, or deliver them by their regular carriers; and as late as 1850, as sensible and as practical a journalist as he was considered to be, Gerard Hallock boasted of an "increase of daily circulation of five hundred" in one year, which were ordered, he said with much unction, "without solicitation in a single instance." This, too, when the entire circulation of the *Journal of Commerce* was only 4500, in a city with a population of over half a million of active people. While the *Sun, Herald, Tribune*, and *Times*, established five to fifteen years later than the *Journal of Commerce*, run their circulation up to twenty, thirty, forty, and sixty thousand each in the same year, and to a much higher figure since then, the *Journal of Commerce*, on its old system of credit and carriers, is probably very little higher now than in 1850. But it is the last of the blanket sheets—the only paper of its class in existence in the metropolis.

The *Morning Post* was the first penny paper of any pretensions in the United States. It was started on New-Year's Day, 1833, as a two-cent paper, by Dr. Horatio David Shepard, with Horace Greeley and Francis V. Story as partners, printers, and publishers. With two hundred dollars capital, and a credit so doubtful that it would pass only at one place for $40 for type, the *Post* was issued, but the price was too high, in the unprepared state of the public mind, for the article offered for sale. According to Greeley's recollections of the enterprise, its capital and credit in brains was no larger than in money. Its circulation reached two or three hundred. After one week's trial, with the exhaustion of the capital, the original idea of Dr. Shepard, his dream of the previous year 1832 was attempted, and the price reduced to one cent; but it was too late. The concern was in debt; it had no mental resources to fall back upon, and, after the expiration of twenty-one days from the issue of the first number, the *Morning Post* ceased to exist.

This experiment, however, was the seed of the Cheap Press. It had taken root. On Tuesday, the 3d of September, in the same year 1833, the first number of the *Sun* was issued by Benjamin H. Day, a printer, who had previously been connected with the *Free Enquirer*, the organ of Frances Wright and Robert Dale Owen. It became a permanent institution. Its motto with its first number was "E Pluribus Unum," which was displayed on a modest-looking spread eagle. "It shines for all" afterwards became its brilliant emblem. Its prospectus was brief and business-like:

PUBLISHED DAILY,

AT 222 WILLIAM STREET - - - - - - - BENJ. H. DAY, PRINTER.

The object of this paper is to lay before the public, at a price within the means of every one, ALL THE NEWS OF THE DAY, and at the same time afford an advantageous medium for advertising. The sheet will be enlarged as soon as the increase of advertisements requires it, the price remaining the same.

Yearly advertisers (without the paper), Thirty Dollars per annum. Casual advertising at the usual prices charged by the city papers.

☞ Subscriptions will be received, if paid in advance, at the rate of three dollars per annum.

The origin of the *Sun* has been told several times, and differently each time. It is probable that Mr. Day can give the truest version of its start in the world. In a speech at a dinner in 1851 to Colonel R. M. Hoe, the inventor of the famous "lightning press," the originator of this pioneer penny paper said :

> It is true I originated the *Sun*, the first penny newspaper in America, and, as far as I have known, the first in the world. But I have always considered the circumstance as more the result of accident than any superior sagacity of mine. It was in 1832 that I projected the enterprise, during the first cholera, when my business as a job printer scarcely afforded a living. I must say I had very little faith in its success at that time, and from various causes it was put off. In August, 1833, I finally made up my mind to venture the experiment, and I issued the first number of the *Sun* September 3. It is not necessary to speak of the wonderful success of the paper. At the end of three years, the difficulty of striking off the large edition on a double cylinder press in the time usually allowed to daily newspapers was very great. In 1835 I introduced steam power, now so necessary an appendage to almost every newspaper office. At that time all the Napier presses in the city were turned by crank-men, and as the *Sun* was the only daily newspaper of large circulation, so it seemed to be the only establishment where steam was really indispensable. But even this great aid to the speed of the Napier machines did not keep up with the increasing circulation of the *Sun*. Constant and vexatious complaints of the late delivery of the paper could not be avoided up to the time that I left the establishment, and I suppose these complaints continued until my friend here, the worthy guest in honor of whom we have assembled this evening, came forward with his great invention of setting types upon a cylinder, the success of which, I doubt not, has brought gladness to the hearts of a multitude of newspaper men. Mr. President, it is really not in my power to express sufficient admiration of the energy and genius which has brought about so stupendous an improvement, and I trust some more able voice than mine will do more justice to the merits of Colonel Hoe's wonderful invention, from which, I doubt not, will date an important era in the art of printing.

One cent continued to be its price per copy for thirty years, or till the recent rebellion, when, every thing advancing to so high a point, the *Sun* was doubled in price, and it will probably never again be a penny paper. Its first editor was named Benton. Not fully coming up to the mark, George W. Wisner was engaged. He was an improvement. He was limited to local matters, and, in accordance with the spirit of the Penny Press in its infancy, he relied largely on police reports and the coarse humor of the police courts for interesting matter for his columns. Wisner, according to the traditions of the printing-offices, was an intelligent, reliable man. After a year or two he removed to the West, where he became a prominent citizen of one of the new cities of America.

The *Sun*, its first number, with a circulation of three hundred, was made up of twelve columns, each ten inches long. Of these, four columns were of advertisements ; one column embraced a "New York Bank-note Table," with "Barker's Ex." quoted "uncer.," which was, we believe, the late venerable Jacob Barker's Bank ; there was one column of poetry, "A Noon Scene," which scene was laid in the country, on the meadows and in the woods, and not in Wall Street, among the excited bulls and bears of that day and that hour; two columns were given to anecdotes and a short story; a quarter of a column to the arrivals and clearances of vessels on the previous day, and the remainder was devoted to police and miscellaneous items.

Two lines indicated that Mexico was in as disturbed a condition as she is now, and that the troops of Montezuma had to leave San Luis Potosi in consequence of the cholera. One item stated that New York City was "nearly full of strangers from all parts of this country and Europe." There were four advertisements of "situations" and "servants" wanted. Now the *Herald* has a page or two of such advertisements. Mail-stages then run between Boston and Lynn, and one was robbed of $13,000. One thousand dollars reward was offered in the *Sun* for the thieves and money. Another paragraph described the indignation of the passengers on one of the Hartford steamers, compelling the captain to land the obnoxious Rev. Ephraim K. Avery, of Sarah Maria Cornell notoriety, at Middletown. J. Bleecker & Sons then sold real estate at auction. Another generation of the same family, A. J. Bleecker & Sons, now do the same thing, and largely too. The steam-boat Benjamin Franklin, Captain E. S. Bunker, then carried passengers "round the Point" between Providence and New York; the Commerce, Captain R. H. Fitch, run between Albany and New York; and the "splendid low-pressure steam-boat Water Witch, Captain Vanderbilt," did the same, and "through by daylight," between Hartford and New York: passage one dollar. Where are Bunker and Fitch now? Where is Vanderbilt? On "low pressure" or "high pressure?"

What recollections these old papers bring up to one's mind! What a picture of the past! Then E. K. Collins advertised "the very fast-sailing coppered ship Nashville." Were the "lines" of the swift ocean steamers Pacific and Baltic, with their nine days' run across the Atlantic, then on his mind? The sixth annual fair of the American Institute was announced for the 15th of October, to be held at Masonic Hall, then opposite the old City Hospital, just above the City Hall Park, on Broadway. Of the ten managers mentioned not one is probably left, but the Institute still lives, with Horace Greeley as one of its bright lights. John A. Dix was then Secretary of State of New York, as appears by an advertisement giving notice of the annual state election.

Such was the first number of the first permanently established penny paper in New York or in the United States. It was evident that the publisher was not a journalist in the present acceptation of that comprehensive term. But he made no promises, and made no improvements except in fuller reports of local events and in the size of his paper, which was increased to make room for the business notices of the new class of advertisers created by this new class of journals. There were no editorials of any kind in the early numbers; no opinion given; no financial reports or stock sales; no commercial reviews or market items. But this paper lived to assist in the great revolution of the Press in this country and in France, and ultimately throughout the world; and it still lives. It helped to make newspaper readers. With increase of means it became more enterprising. When two months old it boasted of a daily circulation of two thousand, and of eight thousand on the 1st of January, 1835.

Shortly after this period, when the paper was under the management of Benjamin H. Day, Moses Yale Beach, and Richard Adams Locke, there was a curious psychological and legal episode in its history. It then became the property of Moses Yale Beach, who was a connection of its originator, and had been the clerk of the establishment; and by him and his sons it was skillfully, energetically, and successfully managed from 1837 to 1860, when it was purchased for the round sum of $100,000 in gold by a wealthy religious young gentleman of Philadelphia, who entered the field of journalism for the purpose of making a daily newspaper useful as a daily lay preacher to the poorer classes of the metropolis for their moral and religious education and reformation. In this laudable object he was assisted by the experience and ability of William C. Conant as editor. On the failure of this praiseworthy experiment, after a trial, we believe, of twelve months, the establishment reverted to Moses S. Beach, who had previously succeeded his father. Assisted by his younger brother Joseph, he carried on the paper till late in 1868, when it was again sold, and Charles A. Dana and his associates, of one wing of the Republican Party in New York, became the purchasers. They paid, it is said, $175,000 in paper for the establishment, its name, its subscribers, its advertisers, its good will, and its reputation. Its cheapness sent it extensively among the mechanics of the metropolis, each with a vote, and hence it was considered of great value to a party to secure its columns, its influence, and its support. Its circulation was large, running up, at one time, as high as 65,000 daily, and in the number of sheets printed it was ahead of every other New York journal except the *Herald*.

The Beaches did not pretend to great intellectual superiority. They were enterprising in getting news, and run all sorts of expresses. It was the effort and ambition of the *Sun* at one time to beat the *Herald* in the acquisition of late intelligence; and the rivalry between the two establishments was great, and sometimes amusing and expensive. Tact, sometimes, was superior to money. On one occasion two expresses were arranged to bring the European news from Boston to New York—one to run over the Norwich and Worcester road for the *Sun*, and the other to run over the Providence and Stonington road for the *Herald*. The Cunard steamer made a longer passage than usual, and was not telegraphed at Boston till early Saturday morning. The *Herald* was not then published on Sundays, and the *Sun* never issued a regular edition on that day. If the expresses were run they would reach New York about midnight on Saturday. What was to be done? The agent of the *Herald* determined not to run his express, but he was anxious for the *Sun* to enjoy the luxury. So he made his arrangements, with locomotive fired up, to start the moment the news reached his hands. The wide-awake agent of the *Sun* was not to be beaten. He was watchful. The moment the Cunarder touched the wharf at East Boston he started with the news for the Worcester dépôt. John Gilpin's time was beaten through the streets of Boston as easily as Bonner's team now beats all others on Harlem Lane. On the panting and puffing locomotive jumped the indefatigable man of the *Sun*, and with one shrill whistle he was off for New York. The agent of the *Herald*, as soon as his plucky companion was out of sight and going off at the rate of a mile a minute, had his locomotive run into the engine-house and cooled off. He then went down to the office of the *Mail*, published in State Street by Purdy and Bradley, and quietly got out the news and had it printed on extra sheets, with the *New York Herald* head. He took several thousand by one train that afternoon, and sent as many by a messenger by the other regular line. They reached New York about six o'clock the next morning, and the extras were immediately sold to the newsboys. Meanwhile the *Sun* express had made splendid time from city to city, and there was great commotion in the *Sun* office. All was bright and watchful, but quiet at the *Herald* establishment. There was no news there. "The *Herald* is beaten!" gleefully exclaimed the happy fellows in the *Sun* building. But, to their bewilderment, about six o'clock they heard the cry, "'Ere's the Extra 'Erald! Important news from Europe!" under their very windows. It was too late: the *Sun* was eclipsed that morning.

Thousands and thousands of dollars were spent in these delightful contests. Some of this money was apparently thrown away, but none was in reality wasted. It assisted in the great development of newspaper enterprise, which has become a leading characteristic of the American Press. When the *Sun* "beat" its news rival, its rays on the next day were gorgeous indeed; but frequently the *Sun* did not "shine for all;" then the glad tidings were heralded by its neighbor. Justice, however, requires us to say that the *Sun* and the Beaches did surprisingly well, and did not hide their light under a bushel.

We have wandered a little from the regular order of events. Let us return to our lambs. What is very curious in newspaper annals, a hoax, a spurt in intellectual enterprise, did as much for the *Sun* as any of its other or later efforts. It was the only really brilliant thing that emanated from its brain in its early days, and it gave the paper its real start in life, and a world-wide notoriety. It was the famous "Moon Hoax." This was in 1835. It purported to be an account of some wonderful discoveries of Sir John F. W. Herschel, made at the Cape of Good Hope, taken from a "Supplement of the *Edinburg Philosophical Journal*." It was a great success. Every body was moon-struck. Indeed, it seemed as if the man in the moon was seen at last and fully described. According to this account, Herschel's new telescope developed every thing in the moon. It was apparently one of the most remarkable discoveries made since the creation of the world, and the placing of "the lesser light to rule the night" in "the firmament of the heaven." One paper, the *New York Daily Advertiser*, a "respectable sixpenny," said that "Sir John has added a stock of knowledge to the present age that will immortalize his name, and place it high on the page of science." Another paper, the *Albany Advertiser*, read "with unspeakable emotions of pleasure and astonishment an article from the last *Edinburg Scientific Journal* containing an account of the recent discoveries of Sir John Herschel at the Cape of Good Hope." Others claimed to have received the news as early as the "small cheap paper" did, and would publish it immediately. *Savans* in science, and the learned pundits of newspapers in religion and in politics, were all deceived. Who deceived them? Who wrote the account?

There was a bright, intelligent young Englishman connected with the Press at that time named Richard Adams Locke. He was pleasant and genial, modest and unpretentious. He had been a reporter on the *Courier and Enquirer*. He had become the editor of the *Sun*, and was afterwards editor of the *New Era* with Joseph Price. One day he made these wonderful "Discoveries in the Moon," and wrote out the details. Appending the name of the *Edinburg Philosophical Journal* as authority, he published the account as a piece of interesting news. That morning he waked up famous. Nothing in fiction exceeded the interest these pretended discoveries created in the public mind for a few days, when the *New York Herald* pricked the bubble.

This extraordinary production, in its effect on the public, has since been equaled by "The Man without a Country," written by the Rev. Edward Everett Hale, and published in the *Atlantic Monthly*, with this difference : one was intended as a hoax, while the other, prepared in the midst of our rebellion, was intended to show the utter despair of a human being without a country; but the two accounts were written with so much skill, and were so full of imaginary truth, with incidents so graphically described, that in both instances the world read and believed. When the moon is explored, the truth of Locke's description of its inhabitants and topography will be fully tested. Hale's description has already passed the ordeal. There are cases as sad in reality as Philip Nolan's was in imagination.

When Samuel Swartwout, the bluff old Collector of the Port of New York in the exciting days of Jackson's and Van Buren's administrations, suddenly left for Europe in the Great Western in 1838 as a "stupendous defaulter" to the government, he became a "man without a country." He had assisted every body, bought lands in Texas, speculated, and was a general friend to mankind. But he slipped, and was an exile. He wandered upon the face of Europe, and, with the pride of position crushed within him, "there were none so poor as to do him reverence." One day a citizen of New York, a friend of the collector in his palmy days, then traveling in Europe, met Swartwout on a steamer on the Rhine. Mournfully and thoughtfully he was sitting alone, his giant figure bowed down with sadness, and shame, and sorrow. Approaching him, the gentleman, as of old, held out his hand. Swartwout looked up, and in a moment was in tears. "You don't know what it is to be an exile," said Swartwout. "Not to be able to return home is terrible, sir— terrible. No one can realize the feeling in imagination." After a brief conversation, Swartwout added, "If I were at home I could in time arrange my affairs with the government." On the return of this gentleman to New York, he talked the matter over with Swartwout's old friends and the government, and it was finally arranged that he should return. Texas became a state, her lands increased in value, and the result was, as we have seen it stated, that not a cent was lost by this "stupendous defaulter," who for so many months suffered the mental pangs of "a man without a country."

Several months after the appearance of Mr. Hale's narrative in the *Atlantic Monthly*, and when the fate of Philip Nolan had excited the commiseration of every one, a parcel was received at the office of the *New York Herald* from Mazatlan, Mexico. On opening it, Mr. Bennett found a letter from General Don Domingo Gorcuiria, once of the famous Cuban Junta, afterwards with William Walker, "the gray-eyed man of destiny," in Nicaragua, and in his renewed efforts to obtain the independence of Cuba in 1870, was captured by the Spaniards, and, after a mock trial, garroted in Havana. This note stated that the writer had read the sketch of the "Man without a Country" with unalloyed interest; that shortly after, in looking over the archives of Mazatlan, his eye fell upon a list of thirty *filibusteros*, names of men who had, in 1806, we believe, attached themselves to Aaron Burr's well-known expedition, and that, on the arrest of Burr and the fracture of his schemes, had drifted into Mexico, where they had fallen into the hands of the authorities. To Gorcuiria's astonishment, the name of Philip Nolan headed the list. He had the document copied and forwarded to Mr. Bennett, of the *Herald*, as a curiosity. Our impression is that it was afterwards sent to the editor of the *Atlantic Monthly*. It is not unlikely that the discoveries in the moon made in 1835 by Locke will yet be as fully verified as the existence of Hale's hero has been by the patriotic Gorcuiria.

But this is a digression. Our chapter is on the Penny Press. The success of the *Sun* "fired the hearts" of several enterprising and intelligent printers. Swain, Abell, Simmons, Stanley, Lynde, Lincoln, Evans, Drane, Anderson, Smith, and others, felt the influence of Day's enterprise. Other penny papers were started in Boston, Baltimore, and Philadelphia, as well as in New York. Some thrived for a while and died. Three or four lived, and made large fortunes for their indefatigable projectors and proprietors.

Shortly after the appearance of the *Sun*, the *New York Daily Bee* was established by John Lemuel Kingsley, but it did not long survive the perils of the early Penny Press. It was revived, however, by the same publisher in 1836, but again succumbed. We believe Mr. Kingsley afterwards turned his attention to improved modes of stereotyping newspaper forms, which in a few years began to be a *desideratum* to journalists of the new and more energetic class.

The *New York Transcript* came next in chronological order. Three excellent and clever compositors, Wm. J. Stanley, Willoughby Lynde, and Billings Hayward, were its publishers. It made its appearance in 1834, and in one year it had a circulation as large as that of the *Sun*. William H. Attree, then a compositor with Conner & Cooke, type-founders, became its police reporter, Willoughby Lynde its paragraphist as well as one of its printers, and Dr. Greene its editor. Attree was full of broad, coarse humor, and gave graphic local reports. The paper promised to eclipse the *Sun;* but Attree went to Texas, and Lynde died, and the vitality of the concern was gone. On the 24th of July, 1839, the *Transcript* was dead, and for a quarter of a century after this, Billings Hayward, one of its proprietors, was employed in the composition rooms of the *Herald* instead of taking his daily drive over the Bloomingdale Road and through the Central Park as one of the journalistic millionaires of New York.

The *Man* appeared next. It was published by George H. Evans in 1834. It was more directly the organ of the mechanics than any of its predecessors. They were simply local news reporters. Evans's aspirations were higher. He had published the *Working-man's Advocate* for several years, and was radically progressive in his ideas, but had not quite reached the point of perfection of Prudhomme. Both Lynde and Stanley, of the *Transcript,* had been connected with him as printers and publishers of the *Advocate;* and they had also published an evening paper, the *New York Daily Sentinel,* in 1830, '31, and '32, a paper which had previously been edited and published by James Gordon Brooks and Edward V. Sparhawk. Evans carried it on alone in 1833. In 1834 he started the *Man,* with the *Working-man's Advocate* as its weekly issue. It became a radical political paper, and was published a year or two.

Thus the Cheap Press sprung into existence, and since 1833 over a hundred one and two cent daily papers have been started in New York City alone. Where are they now? These cheap papers did not make any decided impression on the public mind, or excite the jealousy or attract the attention of the larger papers till 1835. The establishment of the *Herald* in that year began a new era in their career. On the 29th of June, 1835, one of the "blanket sheets," the *Journal of Commerce,* always the most liberal of that class of papers, with commendable fairness and honesty thus truthfully and philosophically described the Penny Press of that day:

PENNY PAPERS.

It is but three or four years since the first Penny Paper was established. Now there are half a dozen or more of them in this city, with an aggregate circulation of twenty or thirty thousand, and perhaps more. These issues exceed those of the large papers, and, for aught we see, they are conducted with as much talent, and *in point of moral character we think candidly they are superior to their sixpenny contemporaries.* By observing the course of these papers, we have been led to regard them as quite an accession to the moral and intellectual machinery among us. The number of newspaper readers is probably doubled by their influence, and they circulate as pioneers among those classes who have suffered greatly from want of general intelligence. Let all classes of the community but read, and they will think, and almost, of course, will become less entirely the dupes of designing individuals. There is hardly any thing which his Holiness of Rome has more reason to be afraid of than the Penny Papers. Those who have read them will, as a natural consequence, come more or less to the commission of the execrable offense of forming opinions for themselves. But for the subserviency which, from the nature of their circulation, they are compelled to exercise towards Trades Unions and such like humbug affairs, we see not why the effect of the little papers should not be almost wholly good. They are less partisan in politics than the large papers, and more decidedly American, with one or two exceptions. The manner in which their pecuniary affairs are conducted shows how much may come of small details. They are circulated on the London plan, the editors and publishers doing no more than to complete the manufacture of the papers, when they are sold to the newsmen or carriers at 67 cents per 100. The carriers distribute the papers, and on Saturday collect from each subscriber six cents, so that for each call their net income to the carriers is but one third of a cent. We wish our penny associates all success, hoping that they will grow wise, good, and great, until they make every sixpenny paper ashamed that tells a lie, or betrays its country for the sake of party, or does any other base thing.

There was only one paper, we think, that was ever regularly published in New York at a cheaper rate than these Penny Papers; that paper was the *Citizen*. It was the organ of the Citizens' Association, at the head of which is Peter Cooper. It was the object and purpose of this association to reform the abuses of the public authorities of the metropolis. Its members were rich and public-spirited, and what they had in view was commendable and praiseworthy. No doubt the city needed, and always will need, looking after, as the frightful exposures of the *Times* in 1871 fully proved. But none of the newspapers in existence at that time were of any use to these reformers. None of the editors would trust them. In order to enlighten the people under these circumstances, and show where the trouble was, they published the *Citizen*, and had it distributed gratuitously. When Hercules undertook his stupendous jobs, he had no newspaper to help him; but Hercules did not live in New York, and printing had not been discovered. Peter Cooper, the modern Hercules, and his associates, needed an organ. But Americans have an idea that if any thing is worth having, it is worth paying for; hence no one would read a paper that was regularly served to them for nothing. The *Citizen* was too cheap. It, therefore, had no influence. It was used for wrapping-paper. After a while, and after the war, Charles G. Halpine, so familiarly known as Miles O'Reilly, was induced to take hold of the concern and write for the paper. Speaking of the enterprise to a friend, he said it was a free paper—given away—or rather thrown away. "What do you think of the plan? What shall I do with it?" asked Miles. "Don't give away another copy. Don't throw away your brains, my dear boy. Sell your paper, if you only sell three copies, and you will have three readers at any rate," was the reply. Two cents per copy were afterwards charged for the *Citizen*, and Miles O'Reilly's contributions made it known and read. Thomas M'Elrath, formerly of the *Tribune*, managed its business affairs for a while for the brilliant Halpine, who was as innocent and as ignorant as a babe in such matters. It was afterwards, with the *Round Table*, owned by Robert B. Roosevelt, M. C. from New York.

Many of the papers issued after the *Sun*, such as the *Herald*, *Tribune*, *Times*, and *World* in New York, began at one cent; but as they expanded and increased in circulation, enterprise, and ability, they advanced their price and their value. These journals thus passed the transition state, and became permanent and powerful institutions. They have educated the present race of journalists, and as these modern men of the Press increase in number and ability the old party papers cease to exist, and more able, more independent, and more influential journals take their place. This process, which really commenced in 1829 and '30, is still going on in all parts of the country.

In the origin of the Cheap Press its owners were mostly printers. They were practical men. They had worked in the old party newspaper offices, and had had their joke and their moral over the articles they had put in type. This was their journalistic experience. They had no very comprehensive ideas of newspapers. New ideas did not often appear where they worked. They knew that local news was always interesting. Village gossip had taught them this. They saw in the coffee-houses, bar-rooms, theatres, hotels, boarding-houses, and streets that politics and local affairs were the staples of conversation. Politics had sustained the old Party Press and had become a tyranny. It was not, therefore, considered safe, in a business point of view, to meddle with the exciting element. So the Cheap Press commenced with local matters, with small-talk, with items from exchange papers, and with advertisements. Beyond these, in their early life, they had no enterprise. Want of money, too, made all things difficult. But journalists with brains and boldness were making their appearance, and meanwhile the small papers were performing their part in the revolution. Young writers and reporters, with active minds, educated as newspaper politicians and statesmen, began to get restive on the old party papers and under selfish dictation. They were seeking a change and a chance for expansion, and we have seen the result in the establishment of the Independent Press in 1835, and, with enlarged views and more comprehensive ideas, becoming, in the future, the great palladium of the people.

The Penny Paper, therefore, marks an important epoch in journalism ; and thus the *News-Letter* as the pioneer of newspapers in America, the *Sun* as the pioneer of the Penny Press, and the *Herald* as the pioneer of the Independent Press, form remarkable eras in the intellectual development of the United States, and are a study for the philosopher and historian.

THE SIXTH EPOCH.

1835—1872.

THE INDEPENDENT PRESS.
CHAPTER XXVII.
THE NEW YORK HERALD.

JAMES GORDON BENNETT, SENIOR. — HOW HE STARTED THE HERALD. — IT CAME WITH STEAM-BOATS AND RAILROADS.—ORIGIN OF THE MONEY ARTICLES.—NEWS AGENCIES AND NEWS COMPANIES.—OCEAN STEAM NAVIGATION.—THE EXTRADITION TREATY.—THE CASH SYSTEM.—SAM. HOUSTON AND TEXAS. — AMOS KENDALL AND NICHOLAS BIDDLE. — PERSONAL ASSAULTS.—ILLUSTRATIONS AND WAR MAPS.—THE RELIGIOUS ANNIVERSARY MEETINGS.—OPPOSITION OF THE CLERGY.—HARBOR NEWS ARRANGEMENTS.—VISIT TO EUROPE.—EUROPEAN CORRESPONDENCE.—THE HARRISON HARD-CIDER CAMPAIGN.

" Is it true that five hundred dollars started the *New York Herald ?*"

This question has often been asked. It is evident that this capital alone could not have accomplished such a result. But five hundred dollars, in the condition of the Press at that time, with the tact, experience, ability, and vigor of previous years of persistent industry and application, achieved this important work. With all these mental and physical elements in full strength, however, it would now require a cash capital of five hundred thousand dollars to establish a newspaper that could successfully compete with the leading journals which are published to-day in the metropolis. Indeed, without any extra effort in the expenditure of money in newspaper enterprise, such a capital as that even would hardly suffice for the purpose of fairly and hopefully entering the lists in New York City against the wealthy and well-organized journals in full prosperity there. One paper of that city, which ranks as the fourth or fifth in circulation and advertisements, sunk over two hundred thousand dollars in reaching a permanent position ; and in regard to the value of a leading newspaper, several offers have been made for the purchase of the *Herald*, ranging from one to two millions of dollars.

The question, therefore, at the beginning of this chapter was a pertinent one.

With a nominal cash capital of five hundred dollars the *New York Herald* was established, and the Independent Press inaugurated. But the real capital of the concern was in the brains of its founder. With twelve or fifteen years of active application and close observation in manners, politics, and society in New York, Albany, and Washington, and in the newspaper offices of the *Charleston* (S. C.) *Courier*, the *National Advocate*, the *Sunday Courier*, the *New York Enquirer*, the *Morning Courier and Enquirer*, the *New York Globe*, and the *Pennsylvanian*, as reporter, correspondent, assistant editor, editor, and owner, he was prepared for such a paper as the *New York Herald*. Journalism had become a science with him, and this science he applied in building up the greatest newspaper establishment in the world.

On Wednesday morning, the 6th of May, 1835, the initial number of the *Morning Herald* was issued by James Gordon Bennett & Co. from the basement room of No. 20 Wall Street, New York. Autobiographically the editor, in 1845, thus described the process through which he passed in reaching this point in his career. This sketch was brought out by the publication of the Mackenzie pamphlet containing the famous Jesse Hoyt correspondence:

I commenced my connection with the newspaper press of New York in the year 1824. From that period to 1827 or 1828 I had no particular predilection or fancy for political matters. I wrote, and reported, and furnished articles for several papers with which I was connected, but it was not till 1828 or 1829 that I became intimately associated with the movements of the Van Buren or Jackson Party of that day, and that connection was effected without any violation of principle—without any improper conduct—without any thing disreputable to myself as a man of independence and honorable feeling. The letters published by Mackenzie refer to two periods of my life—the first embracing my connection with the Van Buren Party in 1829, when I was negotiating an arrangement with Webb in relation to a position with the *Courier and Enquirer*. I consulted and compared notes, and looked on all these matters with Hoyt and his associates, nor was there any thing improper or unbecoming in any of these sayings and doings. I became connected with the *Courier* during that year, 1829, and my connection with it continued till 1832, when I abandoned it in consequence of its abandonment of General Jackson and his administration. I then removed to Philadelphia, purchased an interest in the *Pennsylvanian* there, and commenced a movement for the purpose of elevating Mr. Van Buren to the succession after General Jackson's second term. In all these movements and matters I was open, aboveboard, frank, without any reservation or equivocation. In my newspaper operations in Philadelphia I wanted a loan of some money, and I very naturally turned my attention to the friends I had left in New York, whose cause I was advocating, and who sympathized with my movements. Hence the correspondence that took place between Jesse Hoyt and myself, and hence, after a time, the issue of it as there seen, which ended without effecting any thing at all. My own personal friends, however, supplied me with the funds, which were repaid at the proper time, and I still went on supporting Mr. Van Buren and his cause in Pennsylvania. It is, of course, very easily explained why Mr. Van Buren and his friends, knowing that they had treated me very badly, could not conceive how I could entertain any feeling of friendship for them, and they very meanly and seeretly went to work to create a difficulty with me in Philadelphia, and ultimately to produce an explosion between my partners and myself, which ended my connection with that paper, and also my connection with the Van Buren Party.

When I first entered Tammany Hall, I entered it as an enthusiast studying human nature, as a young man would enter a new country, full of interest, and deriving advantage from every movement and every sight. I kept a diary during the whole period of my connection with that party, and the sentiments therein recorded, just as they occurred to me, still remain, and are the very sentiments which I entertain at this moment. I found out the hollow-heartedness and humbuggery of these political associations and political men; but yet I was so fascinated with the hairbreadth escapes and adventures that I could not disconnect myself from it until the revulsion took place between me and my partners in Philadelphia. After that period I regained my liberty and independence completely; and a fortunate thing it was for my prosperity that Van Buren and his men did behave so meanly and so contemptibly towards me in the year 1833. I then returned to New York, started the *Herald* with the knowledge I had of men and matters throughout the country, and have been successful ever since.

What was the condition of journalism in New York City and in the United States at this period, when a new era was to open for newspapers and newspaper enterprise?

There were seven large morning papers called "sixpenny sheets;" four evening papers of the same character and price; and four small cheap papers, known as the "Penny Press," issued in the metropolis on the 1st of May, 1835. We append their names:

SIXPENNY MORNING PAPERS.

New York Gazette and General Advertiser	John Lang & Co.
Mercantile Advertiser and New York Advocate	Amos Butler & Co.
New York Daily Advertiser	Dwight, Townsend & Co.
Morning Courier and New York Enquirer	James Watson Webb.
New York Journal of Commerce	Hale & Hallock.
The New York Times	Holland, Sanford & Davies.
Business Reporter and Merchants' and Mechanics' Advertiser	H. L. Barnum.

SIXPENNY EVENING PAPERS.

New York Commercial Advertiser	Francis Hall & Co.
The Evening Post	Bryant, Leggett & Co.
New York American	Charles King.
The Evening Star	Noah & Gill.

SMALL DAILY OR PENNY PAPERS.

The Sun	Day & Wisner.
The Transcript	Hayward, Lynde & Stanley.
The Man	George H. Evans.
The Jeffersonian	Childs & Devoe.

What was the circulation of these fifteen papers at that time? What was the circulation of the daily and weekly Press? Here is the answer:

NUMBER AND CIRCULATION OF NEWSPAPERS IN NEW YORK CITY IN 1834-5.

Class.	Number.	Copies Printed.
Daily	15	9,300,000
Semi-weekly	11	1,716,000
Weekly	31	2,840,000
Copies printed in one year—1834-5		13,856,000
Number of copies of all newspapers printed in the United States in the same period		95,000,000

The population of New York in 1835 was 270,089. The population of the United States was, in round numbers, 15,000,000.

Only one paper in 1835 circulated 6000 copies daily. All the others were far below 5000, and running down to 500. It was estimated that the average daily circulation of the "sixpenny sheets" was 1700 only.

Let us look at the situation then.

Steam-boats, comparatively few in number, were running on several of our rivers, and there were only two short railroads, one in New York, and the other in South Carolina. It was not till 1828 that the first locomotive was introduced in this country, and then only on a coal-mine track. Major Horatio Allen acted as engineer on this occasion on the Lackawanna coal-mine road. No other attempt was made till 1831, when a locomotive called the John Bull, and an engineer named John Hampden, were imported from England, and run with a small train from Albany to Schenectady over the Mohawk and Hudson Railroad. Twelve passengers, including Thurlow Weed, who represented the Press, were conveyed on this first steam passenger train. Newspapers till this time had to rely upon the old stages, coaches, and post-riders for the distribution of their papers. This mode, slow and slack, was described a short time since by E. P. Walton, formerly editor of the *Montpellier* (Vt.) *Watchman*. He said:

> The post-riders sent out by the printers of Vermont to distribute their newspapers were the pioneers of the mail routes. I remember a time when there was but *one mail route through Central Vermont*, while the counties of Washington, Orange, Caledonia, Orleans, Lamoille, and part of Franklin, Chittenden, Addison, and Windsor were supplied by post-riders from the office of *The Vermont Watchman*. In February, 1784, seven years before Vermont was admitted to the Union, the General Assembly established five post-offices, located at Bennington, Rutland, Brattleboro, Windsor, and Newbury. Anthony Haswell, of *The Vermont Gazette*, Bennington, was appointed Postmaster General, and the newspaper postmen were the mail-carriers. In July, 1787, a post-rider was sent once a week from Bennington to Lansingburg and Albany, N. Y., and in January, 1788, Daniel Marsh advertised that he had established himself as "post-rider from Clarendon to Onion River, to ride once a fortnight." At Clarendon, Mr. Marsh, of course, connected with the rider from Bennington bringing *The Vermont Gazette*. It is worthy of remark that "the price of the papers as far north as Brandon" was "*four bushels of wheat per year;* one bushel of which to be lodged at the time of subscribing, or as soon after as possible." Mr. Marsh delivered papers as far north as Jericho, where the price ought to have been nearly double that at Brandon. But the farmers could not afford it. Governor Chittenden on one occasion had 700 bushels of wheat on hand, not a bushel of which would he sell, even for hard cash, as he had reserved it to supply the people at a time of need.

Over two years elapsed after the opening of the two railroads mentioned before another road was opened to newspapers and traffic. In 1833–4 regular steam trains were run from Charleston, S. C., to Hamburg, on the Savannah River, and on this road the point we make was clearly demonstrated. In speaking of these trains, the directors of the road, on the 6th of May, 1834, stated that "the company now sends an express daily from one commercial city to another, distant 136 miles, in twelve hours, and that in the daytime. *The daily papers of this city* (Charleston) *are sent by this conveyance, but merchants' letters, of the utmost importance to them in business, are not less than two days* going under contract." Other railroads soon after opened rapid communications between certain points: the Boston and Providence, the Boston and Lowell, and the Boston and Worcester in 1835; the Utica and Schenectady in 1836; the Providence and Stonington, and Baltimore and Wilmington in 1837; the Worcester and Springfield in 1839. After this the progress was rapid, but this was the condition of the country and the Press in 1835, when the *New York Herald* was started and the Independent Press inaugurated. The Postmaster General reported that the mails were carried by steam-boats and over railroads,

           In 1840   -   -   -   -   -   -   3,889,053 miles.
           In 1859   -   -   -   -   -   -   31,838,346   "

Thus this new class of papers came into existence with steamboats and railroads. With these great and rapidly developing physical forces as powerful assistants as distributors of news, the *Morning Herald*, as it was then called, made its appearance.

The first issue of the *Herald* was neatly printed on sheets ten by fourteen inches in size. Twelve columns of reading matter and four columns of advertisements filled this number. There was a population within the radii of the city at that time of two hundred and seventy thousand, with fifteen daily newspapers printed inside of the metropolitan limits. Now, with a population of a million, there are only eighteen daily papers published there.

The editor introduced the first number with the following unique announcement of his purposes and intentions. It was his declaration of independence and the platform of his journalistic principles. The italics are ours:

> James Gordon Bennett & Co. commence this morning the publication of the MORNING HERALD, a new daily paper, price $3 per year, or six cents per week, advertising at the ordinary rates. It is issued from the publishing office, No. 20 Wall Street, and also from the printing-office, No. 34 Ann Street, 3d story, at both of which places orders will be thankfully received.
> The next number will be issued on Monday morning—this brief suspension necessarily taking place in order to give the publishers time and opportunity to arrange the routes of carriers, organize a general system of distribution for the city, and allow subscribers and patrons to furnish correctly their names and residences. It will then be resumed and regularly continued.
> In the commencement of an enterprise of the present kind it is not necessary to say much. "We know," says the fair Ophelia, "what we are, but know not what we may be." Pledges and promises, in these enlightened times, are not exactly so current in the world as Safety-Fund Notes, or even the U. S. Bank bills. We have had an experience of nearly fifteen years in conducting newspapers. On that score we can not surely fail in knowing at least how to build up a reputation and establishment of our own. In *débûts* of this kind many talk of principle—political principle—party principle, as a sort of steel-trap to catch the public. *We mean to be perfectly understood on this point,* and therefore openly *dis-*

claim all steel-traps, all principle, as it is called—all party—all politics. Our only guide shall be good, sound, practical common sense, applicable to the business and bosoms of men engaged in every-day life. *We shall support no party—be the organ of no faction or* COTERIE, *and care nothing for any election or any candidate from president down to a constable.* We shall endeavor to record facts on every public and proper subject, stripped of verbiage and coloring, with comments when suitable, just, independent, fearless, and good-tempered. If the *Herald* wants the mere expansion which many journals possess, we shall try to make it up in industry, good taste, brevity, variety, point, piquancy, and cheapness. It is equally intended for the great masses of the community—the merchant, mechanic, working people—the private family as well as the public hotel—the journeyman and his employer—the clerk and his principal. There are in this city at least 150,000 persons who glance over one or more newspapers every day. Only 42,000 daily sheets are issued to supply them. We have plenty of room, therefore, without jostling neighbors, rivals, or friends, *to pick up at least twenty or thirty thousand for the* HERALD, and leave something for others who come after us. By furnishing a daily morning paper at the low price of $3 a year, which may be taken for any shorter period (for a week) at the same rate, and making it at the same time equal to any of the high-priced papers for intelligence, good taste, sagacity, and industry, there is not a person in the city, male or female, that may not be able to say, "Well, I have got a paper of my own which will tell me all about what's doing in the world. I'm busy now, but I'll put it in my pocket, and read it at my leisure."

With these few words as "grace before meat," we commit ourselves and our cause to the public, with perfect confidence in our own capacity to publish a paper that will seldom pall on the appetite, provided we receive moderate encouragement to unfold our resources and purposes in the columns of the MORNING HERALD.

On the 11th of May, after the short suspension mentioned, the second number of the *Morning Herald* appeared. The editor then promised to "give a correct picture of the world—in Wall Street—in the Exchange—in the Police-office—at the Theatre—in the Opera—in short, wherever human nature and real life best displays their freaks and vagaries." This promise, like the famous order of General Scott to turn Cerro Gordo in his Mexican campaign, has been fully carried out.

Thus originated the *New York Herald*.

All the brain-work of the new paper was performed by its editor. The leading articles, the police reports, the literary intelligence, the pungent paragraphs, the news from abroad and from home, the account-books, the bills, the clerks' duties in the office, were all written, prepared, arranged, made out, and performed by Mr. Bennett. The columns of the little sheet were filled with the peculiar points, and hits, and predictions which have ever since characterized the *Herald*. In one of the first numbers, for instance, he said,

The New York and Erie Railroad is to break ground in a few days. We hope they will break nothing else.

Since that paragraph was written the Erie Railroad has done a vast deal more than simply breaking ground for its roadway, as Jay Gould, J. Fisk, Jr., and the English shareholders can amply testify. Such paragraphs were frequent and prophetic.

Many of the advertisements, even, were written by the editor for the advertisers. He did not indorse them, as in the olden time, when the editor of a newspaper was printer and publisher as well as writer. Then the advertisements would read, "I want a cook-maid for a merchant." "If any one will sell a free estate, within thirty miles of London, with or without a house, to the value of £100 the year, or thereabouts, I can help to a customer." "A fair house in Eastcheap, next to the Flower-de-liz, now in the tenure of a smith, with a fair yard, laid with freestone, and a vault underneath, with a cellar under the shop done with the same stone, is to be sold: I have the disposal of it." "Mr. D. Rose, chirurgeon and man-midwife, lives at the first brick house on the right hand in Gunyard, Houndsditch, near Aldgate, London. I have known him these twenty years." It would scarcely do nowadays for the editor of the *Herald* to undertake, with the present pressure of advertisements, to write them, and indorse them too, in the above free and easy style.

While engaged in organizing his establishment, he did not lose sight of Wall Street, the financial centre of the nation. On the 11th of May, in his second number, he introduced an entirely new feature in American journalism—the Money Articles; and these articles, thus originated and for many years written by Mr. Bennett, became famous throughout the commercial and financial circles of Europe and the United States, and the public, those with money to invest, as well as the bulls and bears, have derived great benefit in having the financial affairs of the world daily spread before them. These money articles were irregularly given in the *Herald* till the 13th of June, 1835, when they became an institution, and daily made their appearance, growing in length and importance with time, experience, and events. Mr. Bennett had made political economy a study, and was peculiarly fitted for the task of intelligently describing the transactions and operations in the financial world. On one or two occasions he delivered public lectures on this interesting science in the old chapel of the Reformed Dutch Church which stood on the corner of Ann and Nassau Streets, New York City.

But the first Wall Street Report—what was it? Here it is, taken from the *Herald* of Monday, May 11, 1835:

MONEY MARKET.

Stocks are somewhat shaken since the late arrivals. The winding up of three or four U. S. Branch Banks makes dealers pause as to the future operations of the money market. On Saturday railroads started two or three per cent.

New York, Philadelphia, Baltimore, Boston, are all on the *qui vive* about stocks. Speculation in this article was never so flourishing. The rise is greatest in fancy stocks or new banks, such as Morris Canal—Baltimore Canton Company—Kentucky Northern Bank—and especially certain railroads.

What is the cause of these movements? How long will they last? Who will be losers? Who the winners?

This uncommon rise in the stock market is not produced by accident. A secret confederacy of our large capitalists in the commercial cities, availing themselves of the political and commercial events of the times, could easily produce the speculation that has astonished the world during the last three months. It is a universal law of trade that if an article is made scarce it will rise, if plenty it will fall. A dozen large capitalists, controlling twenty or thirty principal banks in the chief cities, can make money plenty or scarce just as they choose. When money is scarce stocks of all kinds fall. The confederates buy in at low prices; loan money to the merchants also at 2 or 3 per cent. per month. This is one operation. The next movement is to set on foot the machinery to raise stocks, which can be effected by permitting the banks to loan money liberally to the merchants at large. Stocks then will begin to rise slowly at first, but faster and faster as the speculators lead the way. When the confederates have got rid of all their fancy stocks at high prices to merchants, small dealers, or any body not in the secret, then they begin secretly to prepare for a fall. This is done by a general and simultaneous curtailment of discounts by the Banks, which soon knocks down stocks, ruins thousands, and raises the value of money to 2 or 3 per cent. per month, thus furnishing always, either falling or rising, the knowing ones an opportunity to make at least 30 per cent. on their capital all the year round.

This is truth, and we seriously advise young merchants and dealers to be careful. Who can tell but at this very moment two dozen large moneyed men in our commercial cities have not already appointed the very week, day, even the hour, when a new movement will commence, which will knock down stocks 20 to 40 per cent. a month? When the April weather is particularly sweet and soft, look out for a storm the next day.

There were no stock sales given till the 14th of May. On the previous day there had been a fall of 2 to 4 per cent. on some description of fancy stocks in Wall Street, "the railroads especially." We append the sales of that day for the operators of to-day to look over and compare with the stock and bond sales nowadays. What a change in names, and kinds, and amounts! Harlem Railroad then extended to Harlem River only. But here is the Wall Street curiosity:

SALES AT THE STOCK EXCHANGE, MAY 13, 1835.

25	shares	United States Bank	112¼
160	"	Union Bank	122
40	"	Union Bank	121¾
50	"	Butchers' and Drovers' Bank	126
100	"	Delaware and Hudson	112½
450	"	Delaware and Hudson	112½
200	"	Delaware and Hudson	112½
310	"	Harlem Railroad Company	106
550	"	Harlem Railroad Company	105½
100	"	Harlem Railroad Company	105¼
200	"	Harlem Railroad Company	104¼
51	"	Dry Dock Bank	150
50	"	Dry Dock Bank	149½
100	"	Ohio Life and Trust Company	126¾
450	"	Ohio Life and Trust Company	126
150	"	Ohio Life and Trust Company	125¾
50	"	Ocean Insurance Company	150
10	"	American Marine	150
20	"	American Marine	149½
30	"	Jersey Railroad	120
50	"	State Marine Insurance Company	87
150	"	Jackson Marine	110
40	"	Washington Marine Insurance	96¾

300 shares	Farmers' Loan						time	122½
110	"	East River Insurance						99
25	"	Manhattan Gas Company						129¾
50	"	Manhattan Gas Company				on time	130
150	"	Mohawk Railroad Company					126
500	"	Utica and Schenectady Railroad			opening	128
350	"	Utica and Schenectady Railroad			opening	128¼
250	"	Jamaica Railroad						119

On the 23d of July, 1835, the *Herald* stated that it was "the only paper in the city which gives authentic and correct daily reports of Wall Street operations, stocks, and the money market."

This was the beginning. Approaching the financial crisis of 1837 these money articles became more interesting and valuable, and in going through that terrible revulsion the greatest opposition was manifested in financial circles to their publication; but Mr. Bennett persevered, and made them one of the chief features of the *Herald.* They were entirely written by him till 1838. All the facts he gathered in person by daily visits to Wall Street. After that period, other duties claiming his attention, he employed an assistant, and sent him to the street for facts, and on these facts, thus collected and detailed to him, he daily dictated the articles for several years. By this personal superintendence he gradually educated those who afterwards wrote the articles. He never speculated, never bought a share of any thing to sell again, and never allowed himself to be influenced in any way in the tone or matter of his Wall Street Reports. It is well known that the course of the *Herald* in regard to operations in Wall Street led to many threats and two or three personal assaults, one or two with Webb of the *Courier and Enquirer*. But in the course of time, these money articles, more and more appreciated, gave the *Herald* a high character, and compelled all the other journals to devote some attention to this important subject, and now no newspaper is without its financial department and its financial editor. Mr. Thomas Clarke, who was afterwards Treasurer of the first Morse Telegraph Company between Boston and New York, one day saw an advertisement for the back files of the *New York Herald.* He had purchased and saved the paper daily from its first number. His attic was "full of them, and in his wife's way at every house-cleaning." He called upon the advertiser and said he had the desired article. This was in 1845 or '46. "What do you ask for them?" asked the advertiser. "I don't exactly know, but I should say sixpence a copy would be about right," replied Mr. Clarke. "Send them down, and I will give you a check for the amount," said the advertiser. Clarke was astounded. He went home, counted the papers, had them carted to the gentleman's office, and received about $200 cash. "Now," said Mr. Clarke to the purchaser, "I would like to know what you want of those papers at two or three times their original cost?" "We have purchased them," answered the advertiser, "for a Hamburg banker. He sent over to us to buy a complete file of the *Herald* for its money articles, and we are glad to have secured them so easily."

The articles became quite celebrated, and several claimed their authorship. On the death of Theron Rudd, it was stated in the obituary notices that he was "the originator of the famous money articles of the *New York Herald.*" Mr. Rudd had been one of the editors of the *New Era*, and was never in any way or shape connected with the *Herald*, and never wrote the money articles of that paper. Bankers, and brokers, and financial writers have claimed the credit of not only writing, but of originating them. This belongs exclusively to Mr. Bennett. Very curiously, on the day when the above was written, the *Herald* of February 20, 1869, was received, containing an editorial article on speculations in Wall Street, from which we make the following very appropriate extract:

> There is particularly one instrumentality in some cases, we fear, accessory to the swindling of the sharpers. This is the financial column. The financial editors of the several journals are much howled over on the street, and the opinion prevails that in order to set this or that stock all right in public estimation it is only necessary to hand a certain number of shares to the gentlemen whose duty it is to write for the various papers respectively a true history of the daily occurrences in that financial centre. It is assumed, either on general principles or on special experiences, that these gentlemen, caring more for their own interests than for the interests of the public, will not hesitate to deceive the readers they are employed to enlighten in order that they may pocket part of the money thus extorted from they know not whom. In such hands the financial report becomes a dangerous machine; but it must not be in such hands, for it is capable of being a great benefit to the public. *The daily financial report was begun by us when we started the Herald. We made it personally.* Getting through that part of our varied labors that could be done at an early hour, we went to Wall Street, saw for ourselves what was in progress there, and returned with our report sketched out in fragmentary fly leaves of letters or other handy scraps of paper. We told the truth, for we were in the interest of the public; and the truth of that locality was not complimentary in those days any more than it would be now. War was made upon us right and left by the men whose little games were spoiled whenever the public came to know what they were at; and, strangest of all things for a war originating in that quarter, it was a "moral war." We lived through it, however.
> Compelled to delegate our labor in the preparation of a financial report, we have always meant and still mean to keep that report as honest as it was in its origin; to constitute it a legitimate and exact record of what is honestly done in Wall Street, and an exposure—a laying bare to the eyes of the public of what is dishonestly done there. We will compound none of the villainies with the fellows who trade on public credulity to abuse public confidence. *One journal shall tell what Wall Street really is and what is done there.*

On the 30th of May, the increased demand for the *Herald* induced its proprietor to advertise for twelve to twenty more carriers. He then made arrangements to extend its circulation in Newark, Paterson, Albany, Troy, Hudson, Poughkeepsie, Providence, and Philadelphia, as suburbs of New York, thus introducing a new plan of distributing papers, which has since grown up to be an immense business. This mode of distribution led to the formation, 1st, of large individual agencies like Stringer, Burgess & Townsend, Wm. Taylor, Redding & Co., Wm. Zeiber, Alexander Williams & Co., and, 2d, of incorporated associations, which have swelled into immense companies, and are now known as the American News Company, New England News Company, New York News Company, Western News Company, and St. Louis Book and News Company. Through these establishments millions of *Tribunes, Heralds, Ledgers, Harpers, Frank Leslies, True Flags, Godeys, Atlantic Monthlys, Every Saturdays, Worlds, Suns, Travellers*, annually pass to subscribers and readers in every corner of the Union, and all with the most clock-like regularity and certainty.

There is an account, in the *Herald* of June 30, 1835, of the arrival of an English police officer—" a second Vidocq"—in pursuit of a runaway from the British dominions with a large sum of money. The robber was captured, but could not be detained. There was then no treaty with England for the extradition of such characters. In a conversation with this English Vidocq, he was asked,

" Is there no mode of satisfying the demands of justice ?"

" None that I know of," answered John Bull.

" Could not a treaty be agreed upon between the United States and Great Britain, by which the Police Department of one nation might aid and assist the Police Department of the other in ferreting out rogues and discovering cheats ?"

The English detective paused a moment, and said, " It might."

"Why, then, can't it be done? Why should not the Vidocqs and old Hayses of each country reciprocate each other's courtesies?"

" There is no reason why they should not," replied the officer.

"Will Mr. Forsyth, the Secretary of State, at Washington," continued the *Herald*, "please put on his spectacles and read this article, from beginning to end, twice over?" But no effect was produced at that time on Mr. Forsyth or any other statesman in Washington. When Lord Ashburton, however, came over in 1842 on a special mission to settle the Northeastern Boundary dispute, he and Mr. Webster put their heads together, " read this article over twice," and made the Extradition Treaty, the more comprehensive provisions of which have since been incorporated, with highly beneficial results, in treaties with nearly all the nations of the world. So much for auxiliary newspaper statesmanship.

On the 12th of August, 1835, the office, type, presses, books, and papers of the *Herald* were destroyed by fire. All disappeared in flames. Owing to this calamity, there was a suspension of the publication of the paper for nineteen days. On the 31st of August it reappeared. It was now called *The Herald*, and owned, edited, and published by James Gordon Bennett alone. This was its second epoch. Its editor thus heralded his reappearance :

We are again in the field, larger, livelier, better, prettier, saucier, and more independent than ever. The Ann Street conflagration consumed types, presses, manuscripts, paper, some bad poetry, subscription books—all the outward material appearance of the *Herald*, but its soul was saved—its spirit as exuberant as ever. From the past we augur well for the future. In the first six weeks of its existence, the *Herald* reached nearly the extraordinary circulation of seven thousand per day, and a corresponding amount of advertising patronage. We started then to reach a daily issue of twenty thousand in a period of six or nine months —*we restart now to rise to twenty-five thousand daily circulation before we stop.* This is no astronomical dream—no Herschel discovery in the moon. It can be done, and if industry, attention, resolution, and perseverance can accomplish the feat under the encouraging smiles of a kind public, the *Herald* shall do it. We are organizing on a better footing than formerly—have it entirely under our own control, and have arranged our carriers and routes in such a way that, as we think, a week will make us go like a piece of ingenious clock-work.

In other respects we trust we shall please the public. Avoiding the dirt of party politics, we shall yet freely and candidly express our opinion on every public question and public man. We mean also to procure intelligent correspondents in London, Paris, and Washington, and measures are already adopted for that purpose. *In every species of news the Herald will be one of the earliest of the early.* Our Wall Street reports, which were so highly approved by every business man in the city, and copied extensively throughout the country, we shall enlarge and improve to a considerable extent. The former *Herald*, from its large circulation among business people down town (being larger in that respect than any paper in the city), had a very rapid increase of advertising patronage. We expect that the renovated *Herald* will far outstrip its predecessor. Our position at 202 Broadway is admirably central—more so than even in Wall Street. Several merchants and auctioneers are preparing to advertise in the *Herald*. They are beginning to find out that a brief advertisement in our sheet is seen and read by six times as many as it would be in the dull prosaics of the *Courier and Enquirer*.

On the whole, and " to conclude," as Dogberry did not say, we bid our former kind friends and patrons a hearty, a cheerful, and pleasant good morning ; and we hope that while we give them a regular call to have a little chat over their coffee and muffins, we may often see them at 202 Broadway when they have any small thing to do, cheap and good, in the advertising line, or any hint or curious piece of information to communicate to the public, barring always discoveries in astronomy, which our friends of the *Sun* monopolize.

Thus started the *Herald* on its second race, and from this start it has become, under the sole guidance of one man, the establishment it is to-day. It took hold of every subject interesting to the people. Its advertising columns, as well as its news and editorial columns, showed the vitality of the concern. It had its daily hits at the Abolitionists as well as at Fanny Wright and Robert Dale Owen. It enlightened the public on morals, religion, politics, as it has since more comprehensively done.

Among the novel advertisements we find the following in the *Herald* of August 31, 1835. It is curious after reading Greeley's American Conflict, and looking at the social condition of Charleston on the close of Grant's first term :

SUPPRESSED NEWSPAPERS, ETC., AT CHARLESTON.

Those persons who are desirous of examining the character of the publications issued by the American Anti-Slavery Society, and forming a correct judgment of them, can receive copies gratuitously on application at the society's office, No.

144 Nassau Street. Those destroyed at Charleston were principally the newspaper called the *Emancipator* for August; together with the *Anti-Slavery Record* No. 7, and *Slaves' Friend* No. 3. It is possible that there were a few of the newspaper entitled *Human Rights* for July. It is deemed proper to say that no publications have been sent into the Slave States, within the knowledge of the committee, except to respectable free citizens; and that nothing will be found in them contrary to the Constitution and laws of the United States, or inconsistent with the character of good citizens, or designed to excite insurrection among the Southern slaves.

They address, not the slave, but his master. And in employing the Press and the U. S. Mail to address the understanding and conscience of their fellow-citizens who hold slaves, they conceive that they are but exercising one of the most sacred rights which the Constitution has solemnly guaranteed to every citizen. At the same time they declare that they by no means intend to press their publications upon any gentlemen who signify that it is not their wish to receive them. Those who are not disposed to pay the postage, and read or circulate our publications, are requested to return the copy first received, with their name and post-office address legibly written upon them.

By order of the committee, R. G. WILLIAMS,
Pub. Agent Am. A. S. Society.

"One of the grandest enterprises which the year 1835 has brought forth," said the *Herald*, in October of that year, was that proposed by one of the old packet captains, Nathaniel Cobb, of the old Black Ball Line. It was a line of steam-ships to run between New York and Liverpool. Application was made to the Legislature for a charter, and the passage across the Atlantic was to be reduced to fourteen days. The *Herald* urged the scheme upon the public with great spirit, but the English anticipated America by sending over the Sirius and Great Western early in the spring of 1838. Successfully navigating the Atlantic with steam was then, in the estimation of Dionysius Lardner, as much a problem as the laying of a telegraph cable from Ireland to Newfoundland was, with many men of science, in 1865.

Indicative of the progress thus made early in the revolution in journalism, the *Herald*, on the 31st of October, 1835, stated that the aggregate circulation of the *Courier and Enquirer, Journal of Commerce, Gazette, Daily Advertiser, Times,* and *Mercantile Advertiser*, the "respectable sixpenny papers," on the previous day was twelve thousand and five hundred, while that of the three "penny papers," the *Sun, Transcript,* and *Herald*, was twenty-eight thousand and five hundred. With this fact in view, Mr. Bennett made the following prediction on the 10th of the next month:

Penny papers are rapidly increasing throughout the country. Yesterday we received a new one from Mobile, Alabama, called the *Transcript*. In all the large cities there exists not a doubt but the large papers will sink down in a few years to mere Prices Current and Shipping Lists. They are good for nothing else. All the wit, the humor, the business, the life of society are found in the penny papers.

These small papers, independent of politics, and cheap in price, were thus rapidly taking the place of the large partisan sheets. They were starting up every where. The *Times, Herald, Mail* in

Boston, the *Sun* and *Clipper* in Baltimore, the *Transcript, Sun,* and *Public Ledger* in Philadelphia, were established. Politicians endeavored to take advantage of this novelty in journalism, but there was no permanency to a political penny paper *per se.* It lived only while the party contributions lasted. Hence, of the long lists of small papers commenced all over the country, the names of two or three only remain. Large sums of money were wasted by politicians in these enterprises, but the result shows that they could not control the principle underlying the independent character of this new class of papers.

On the 10th of March, 1836, Mr. Bennett, fully appreciating his new position in journalism, and with that instinct and foresight in public matters for which he has been remarkable, enlarged his paper, and in announcing the fact and his future intentions, which have been so amply carried out, said,

* * * * * * * * *

In a city of this kind there is no limit to enterprise, no bounds to the results of industry, capacity, and talent. I began the *Herald* last year without capital and without friends. Every body laughed and jeered at the idea of my succeeding. "Bennett, you are a fool"—"Bennett, you are a blockhead." By effort, economy, and determination I have got a firm footing, mastered all opposition, *and begin this day a new movement in newspaper enterprise which will astonish some persons before I shall have completed it.* The public are with me. They feel my independence—they acknowledge my honesty—and, better than all, they crowd in their advertisements. Without the aid of $52,725 from any bank, I am now in a position to carry rapidly all my own ideas of newspaper enterprise into effect. I never deal or dealt in stocks—never bought or sold a dollar's worth, although I have studied that science for years. Hence my Wall Street reports are relied upon, because the public believe I have no private reason to deceive them.

This statement is thus confirmed by a paragraph which appeared in the *New York Times* on the 30th of March, 1871, thirty-five years after the above extract was published in the *Herald:*

We find it stated in the *Chicago Times* that Mr. James Gordon Bennett, the editor and proprietor of the *Herald*, is worth a fortune of ten millions of dollars. How true this may be the public have no precise means of knowing, but there can be no doubt that Mr. Bennett is a very rich man. The profits of the *Herald* alone must be half a million yearly, which would make the value of that establishment somewhere from four to five millions; and it is certain that Mr. Bennett must have large investments elsewhere, both in real estate and other property. This handsome competence has all been accumulated in the management of a newspaper, for it is believed that the editor of the *Herald* has never strayed from his proper occupation to engage in outside speculations of any sort. He has never been connected with jobs either in state or national politics; he has never sworn allegiance to any party; and he has built up the great newspaper which he controls solely by his own genius, courage, and pertinacity. As a newspaper writer, he is perhaps more truly a man of genius than any other who has risen to distinction in this country. His mind is characterized by originality of thought and wit in equal proportions; and he has always appreciated the value of news. These elements—independence, originality, wit, courage, and news—have made the success of the *Herald;* and this success there is now nobody to dispute.

The "cash system" in the publication of newspapers was introduced by Mr. Bennett on the establishment of the *Herald*, and it has saved hundreds of thousands of dollars, nay, millions, to the Press of this country who have adopted the same system. The most reckless credit was in vogue till then. Horace Greeley, in the brief period of the publication of the *New Yorker* in 1835, lost $10,000 in bad debts for subscriptions alone. The *Courier and Enquirer* probably lost, during its career of forty years, half a million dollars in unpaid subscriptions and advertisements. One of the Western papers lately offered $30,000 of such debts for $30 cash. Thomas Ritchie, of the *Richmond Enquirer*, after publishing his paper for forty years, stated that the debts due him on his books amounted to $150,000. Other instances are given in these pages. It is probable that the average loss of all the papers conducted on the credit system has been fully twenty-five per cent. Inaugurating the cash system, which Mr. Bennett has persisted in, the *Herald* loses nothing. There are no bad debts. Not an advertisement is inserted for a longer period than agreed upon and paid for. Not a paper leaves the office beyond its term of subscription. The business of the establishment is, therefore, not only greatly simplified, but there is no loss; and on each Saturday night Mr. Bennett knows precisely where he financially stands. This cash system is now very generally adopted. Charles King, of the *New York American*, a paper which belonged to the strictly aristocratic and financial circles of the metropolis, was the first of the old class of journals to see the handwriting on the wall. In April, 1843, he made the following announcement:

CASH PRICES.
TO THE READERS OF THE NEW YORK AMERICAN.

In conformity with the times, and with the urgent request of many of our old subscribers, we have determined, on and after the first day of May next, to reduce the price of the *New York American*, and to issue it for CASH only.

The paper will be continued on its old footing as to size, and it will be conducted as heretofore, with all the ability and undivided attention of its editor. * *
* * * * * *

The terms on which the *New York American* will be issued on and after the 1st of May, 1843, will be, for the daily paper, TWO CENTS each copy, or Twelve Cents per week, to be paid to the carriers; or SIX DOLLARS per annum, to be paid in advance at the office.

Ten persons (residing out of the city) clubbing together, and ordering not less than ten copies of the daily paper sent to *one* address, will receive the same for FIVE DOLLARS per annum each copy, so long as the number does not go below ten.

Newsmen in large cities will be supplied on accommodating terms.
* * * * * * * * *
Newsboys will be supplied at the usual rate.

Those who were acquainted with the history of the Metropolitan Press were greatly astonished on reading this announcement. Its editor was a son of Rufus King, was brother to James G. King, of Prime, Ward & King, the bankers of that period, and was considered an elegant gentleman of the old school. Such papers as the *American, Courier and Enquirer, Evening Post,* and *Commercial Advertiser* had always treated the *Sun, Herald, Transcript, New Era,* and *Plebeian* with the utmost contempt. One and two cent papers and the ragged newsboys were with them synonymous terms with vulgarity and scurrility. But revolutions in newspapers as well as in nations will take place. The world moves on. Hence the above manifesto. It came too late, however, to save the *American.* Mr. King was a scholar and a finished writer, but he was not a man with broad enough views and sufficient enterprise to make a successful newspaper. He was too slow. He could write a good editorial article and a neat paragraph, but he did not know how to make a good newspaper. After a short struggle with the energetic Penny Press the *American* crept into the office of the *Courier and Enquirer,* and Mr. King became associate editor with Colonel Webb till called to preside over the destinies of Columbia College.

The independence of Texas was a subject of great interest in 1836, and the *Herald* became one of its strongest advocates. All its hopes and predictions were verified by the brilliant victory of General Sam. Houston at San Jacinto. When Houston was in New York in 1833-4 on his way to Texas, he met the future editor of the *Herald* on the street. They were old acquaintances in Washington. "How are you, Bennett?" said the general. "You are the man I want to see. I am going to Texas, and I want you to go with me, start a paper there, and we'll build up a great republic. Will you go?" It happened to be the case at that time that Mr. Bennett's business engagements detained him in New York. Houston went to Texas and made a republic at San Jacinto, and Bennett remained at home and made the *Herald* at New York. In 1851, when Dr. Anson Jones, the last President of the Republic of Texas, was in New York, he called at the office of the *Herald.* The above incident was mentioned to him. "Ah!" said he, "Texas was the place for Houston, and New York for Bennett; Texas would have been too small for Bennett."

On the 17th of August, 1836, the price of the *Herald* was raised to two cents. Such was the *furore* of the public for the paper at that time, in consequence of its originality, its vim, its contents, so rare and so far above the dull monotony of the larger papers, that the newsboys and news dealers charged two cents per copy every where. Mr. Bennett, therefore, made a financial calculation, with the following result, of how much the public were paying, and how much he was getting of their money. His summing up of the case was curious:

Daily circulation of the *Herald*	20,000
Receipts per day, at one cent, 33 per cent. off	$133.34
Receipts per day, at two cents, 25 per cent. off	300.00
Difference in my favor per day	166.66
Difference, clear, a week	999.96

"With this sum," continues the arithmetical editor, "I shall be enabled to carry into effect prodigious improvements, and to make the *Herald* the greatest, best, and most profitable paper that ever appeared in this country."

While the *Herald* was expanding, the editor's enthusiasm and independence pushed him into personal difficulties with some of his contemporaries. While many abused him in round terms in the columns of their journals, Colonel James Watson Webb, of the *Courier and Enquirer*, and Dr. P. S. Townsend, of the *Evening Star*, came in direct personal collision with Mr. Bennett in Wall Street. Those with Colonel Webb grew out of alleged stock speculations of the colonel in connection with Henry Lynch, and the allusions in the *Herald* to the United States Bank. These scenes produced great excitement at the time. But no threats, assaults, torpedoes, or intimidations of any kind affected the editor of the *Herald*. He had marked out his line of policy, and persistently pursued it to the end.

In November, 1836, a desperate assault was made on Mr. Bennett in his office by Thomas Hamblin, manager of the Bowery Theatre. There had been a difficulty and a separation between Hamblin and his wife. Theatrically, the matter was made a public one. The *Herald* espoused the cause of Mrs. Hamblin. When the Bowery Theatre was destroyed by fire, an effort was made to give Hamblin a complimentary benefit. This the *Herald* opposed in the strongest terms in a series of effective articles. They produced such an impression on the public mind that the benefit was a comparative failure. Shortly after there was a dinner-party of a dozen of Hamblin's friends at the rooms of Jared W. Bell, near the *Herald* office. Bell was the publisher of the *New Era*. While at this dinner it was arranged, in the excitement of the occasion, to assault Mr. Bennett in his office. It was asserted that it was the intention of Mr. Hamblin and some of his friends to break the right arm of the editor. Whether or not this be true, it was evident that the manager intended some mischief. He was a large and powerful man. Accompanied by three or four friends, he entered the newspaper office through a back passage unawares, and commenced a furious assault on the editor. The police and others interfered, and prevented serious consequences. This affair was afterwards more thoroughly elucidated in the following letter from an ex-editor of the *New Era:*

JOSEPH PRICE TO THE EDITOR OF THE HERALD.

New Times Office, 17th November, 1837.

My dear Sir,—I was anxious to respond to your *appel* of this morning respecting the dinner at Mr. Bell's, but my associate in the *New Times* objects to its being mentioned in the paper, and as we each exercise a positive veto upon any production of either, I can not enforce its publication, and write directly to you instead of the other channel.

I have no hesitation in saying to you, however, that, to the best of my recollection, it was Mr. Hamblin who demonstrated to General Morris the anatomical experiment to which you refer. I have seen Mr. H. this morning, and he admits the fact. They were both of them very much excited on the occasion, but I am convinced that the subsequent affair would never have taken place if Mr. Blythe had not arrived. Mr. Bell and myself acted as pacificators.

Mr. Hamblin expressed his wishes to me most earnestly, about half an hour ago, that the subject should not be again alluded to, and, under the circumstances, I think it would be the preferable course. General Morris expresses his regret at every stage of the business, and deprecates most emphatically any revival of the affair. Very truly yours, Joseph Price.

James Gordon Bennett, Esq.

There were lawsuits, and cards, and explanations, and correspondence subsequent to this desperate affair, and finally the whole matter was settled by time, which is so potent in sponging off the animosities of life.

The *Weekly Herald* was issued in December, 1836, and with it was inaugurated the summaries of news which the editor afterwards introduced in his daily issue, to the great advantage of the active business public, who desired to have all the news, every morning, comprehensively epitomized, to read at a glance, leaving the details to be read at more leisure moments. Nearly all the newspapers have since adopted this plan, and the *Herald* has abandoned it. This was not the beginning of weekly newspapers, but it gave impulse to that kind of publication which has since become so extensive and widely circulated. Then an edition of three thousand was considered large. Out of this acorn has grown the *Ledger*, with its three hundred thousand circulation, the *New York Weekly*, the *Weekly Tribune, Leslie's* and *Harpers' Weekly Illustrated* papers, with their enormous issue. Weekly publications of mere news, however, have since lost their position, in consequence of the telegraph, and have ceased to command large circulations. When news was conveyed from one point to another by steam, thousands of newspaper readers in the interior towns willingly waited for the arrival of their weekly paper, but in this telegraphic age the daily newspaper has taken the place of the weekly, and the more political, agricultural, religious, literary, and illustrated hebdomadaries have taken the place of the news weeklies.

More extensive arrangements were made in 1837. News-boats were purchased and ship-news establishments organized. This increased the war between the small papers and the blanket sheets. "Have you noticed the *Herald* lately?" asked a merchant one morning of a Wall-Street editor in the Tontine Restaurant. "Yes," said the editor, "I see that Bennett is making an effort." "Well," continued the merchant, "my opinion is that this *Herald* is bound to shine. If it goes on as it has begun, his paper will be the newspaper of New York. Mark that!" "Nonsense," answered the editor; "you will see how we will beat him. Wait and see." Of all the large papers then in existence, seven in number, the *Journal of Commerce* and *Express* are the only ones remaining, and the latter has adapted itself to the new class of journals.

The Canadian Rebellion of 1838 brought out the journalistic resources of the *Herald*. On this exciting occasion, while the news was given promptly, a new feature in newspapers was introduced, or reintroduced, which has since, in the war with Mexico, in the wars in Europe, and in the late Rebellion, been carried out extensively and advantageously to the public, the press, and the art of engraving. The "seat of war" was then on Navy Island, just below the Falls of Niagara. The *Herald*, on the 5th of January, 1838, published a very clear map of that strategic point of the rebels. That was the beginning of the "war maps" in this age, which have done so much in the last thirty years to illustrate the most important events in the world, and to give the public, at a very cheap rate, a vast deal of useful geographical knowledge.

With the organization of the ship-news establishment and the aid of the Sandy Hook pilot-boats, the *Herald* began its real career as a great newspaper. These were the early days of news excitement among the new class of journals of New York. Nearly all of the European news received then by sailing packets first appeared in the *Herald*. Its fleet of pilot-boats became known as the Teaser, the Celeste, the Tom Boxer, but the Teaser was the famous name in every newspaper office. The packet ships were boarded off Montauk Point, where the messengers would land and proceed to New York by locomotive. They would arrive at the *Herald* office covered with perspiration and glory. "News-boats, nay, steam-boats I can afford to get to pick up news," said Bennett, Sr., in 1837. News-boats he had in 1838, and steam news yachts were introduced by Mr. Bennett, Jr., in 1868.

The crusade of the other journals against the Cheap Press became more intense in 1838. The *Herald* had enlarged its commercial reports, and devoted more space to the material interests of the country. Its commercial advertisements were increasing. It had extended its correspondence to important points. It had enlarged its facilities for obtaining news from Albany and Washington. It commenced to give important speeches of such men as Henry Clay, Daniel Webster, and John C. Calhoun, in full, issuing double sheets to accomplish this purpose—the first double sheet making its appearance on the 15th of March, 1838. It then gave the evidence in the famous Phœnix Bank case exclusively, which finally forced the other papers into the same line of enterprise. It printed daily slips of news, which were gratuitously sent by Amos Kendall's express mail to the newspapers in the interior one mail in advance of their regular transmission in the regular issue of the *Herald*. These slips were equal in value to the telegraphic news dispatches of the present day, and all the papers of the country which exchanged with the *Herald* were thus daily placed in the earliest possession of news. Hundreds of instances of the advantageous effect of this enterprise were to be seen in the Press all over the land.

It is probable that Mr. Bennett was better acquainted with the public and private movements affecting the great contest between General Jackson and the United States Bank than any other editor in the country. He was one of the editors of the New York *Courier and Enquirer* at the beginning of that memorable conflict, and left that paper when General Webb abandoned the Democratic Party on the Bank Question. He was then editor of the *Pennsylvanian* during the exciting scenes preceding the removal of the deposits in the fall of 1833, and was in constant correspondence with Secretaries Ingham, M'Lane, and Duane, and Amos Kendall, whose special duty it was to "sound the State Banks" on the subject, and in social relations with Nicholas Biddle, the president of the mother bank. The events of that important period, so full of excitement and imaginary peril to the nation, have passed into history, and most of the leading actors engaged in the struggle have passed to that bourne where politics have ceased to trouble them. It was an era in which the participants and eye-witnesses now living will never forget. Here is one of Amos Kendall's letters to Mr. Bennett on the removal of the deposits. It shows the character of the writer, and the enthusiasm with which he performed his part of the work:

AMOS KENDALL TO JAMES GORDON BENNETT.

BALTIMORE, 31st July, 1833.

DEAR SIR,—I felt a strong inclination to drop you a line when you announced that the deposits would not be removed, and I can give no good reason, perhaps, why I did not follow its bent. I was sorry to see the article, although I have no doubt you have the information in a shape much more authentic than the usual *on dits* of the day. I do not wish to know through what channel it comes, because it might make me think less of some one of my fellow-men than I now do; but he who originated it knew that the President had come to no such decision. If there are men who expect to take the government out of the President's hands, and, in confidence of their power to do so, caused this communication to be made, they may find themselves mistaken, as many a wise man has been before. It would have been at least prudent to have examined a little more carefully the foundation of their own power before they caused their desires to be announced. Andrew Jackson, and nobody else, is President of the United States, and, whatever others may say, the course of his administration can not be fixed on so important a point contrary to his opinions, wishes, and will.

Do not misunderstand me. I do not blame you. What mysterious channel of communication exists between the Treasury and the Bank, I know not; but sure it is that the directors of the U. S. Bank know what is passing in that department better than the President does. Do not think I suspect the secretary. Though very wrong in some of his opinions, and I fear too timid for the times, I believe him to be an honest and honorable man—too honest to guard with sufficient caution against some who have sought to draw forth his opinions for sinister purposes.

They talk of a Kitchen Cabinet, etc. There are a few of us who have always agreed with the President in relation to the Bank and other essential points of policy, and therefore they charge us with having an influence over him! Fools!! They can not beat the President out of his long-cherished opinions, and his firmness they charge to our influence! How complimentary to the President! If they could do what they say we prevent, the President would, in truth, be what he is falsely represented to be—a man without independent opinion or action.

But he is always Andrew Jackson. So highly do I think of his capacity, patriotism, and virtue, that I value myself more highly since finding that my views on so many subjects correspond with his. Yes, and I will risk all of fortune, of hope, even life itself, in aiding him to carry his great designs into effect. Who would not be proud to aid a man so bold, so good, so devoted to liberty and his country?

But I am turning enthusiast.

I came here on Sunday evening, and have been cautiously sounding the State Banks. The prospect is that I shall accomplish more than I expected. There will be no difficulty in making arrangements here, unless it be in choosing between several sound institutions.

Probably I shall not leave here until Saturday. Your city will be for me the most difficult point. I shall want your most prudent counsels when I get there.

With high respect, your friend, AMOS KENDALL.

J. G. BENNETT, Esq.

No two men were more abused and vilified, during this stupendous politico-financial contest, than Andrew Jackson and Nicholas Biddle. No political campaign was ever more violently and ruthlessly fought in this country than the one on the rechartering of the United States Bank. The Whig Press were unstinted in their attacks on the President of the United States, and the Democratic Press were for the utter annihilation of the President of the United States Bank. They bore these assaults with wonderful equanimity. There is an interesting anecdote of the temper of Jackson while under this terrible fire from the Whig Press. It was related in the *Pennsylvanian:*

A revolution in Poland occurred about the time that Jackson was waging a war with the United States Bank in this country. The Emperor Nicholas treated the unfortunate Poles with extraordinary severity, and was terribly and justly scored for it by the Press of this country. About the same time the Whig Press was heaping all sorts of abuse upon General Jackson for opposing the recharter of the United States Bank.

The Russian minister, then at Washington, was greatly annoyed by the abuse of his emperor and master. He determined to appeal to the government to have the evil remedied, and collected from the miscellaneous press a numerous array of articles bearing down very strongly on Nicholas, showed them to the Secretary of State, and demanded that this abuse should cease, or he would hold the government responsible, and the peaceful relations of the two nations would be interrupted. The Secretary of State in vain attempted to explain to him the freedom of the Press, and that the American government had no more power over it upon such subjects than Nicholas himself. The Russian minister regarded this as a mere subterfuge, and grew very angry.

He finally concluded to appeal to General Jackson himself upon the subject, and, producing his collection of newspaper denunciations, laid his grievances before the old hero. General Jackson heard him patiently, and after he was through, pleasantly complimented him on his industry in searching the papers ; but, said he, " Look over them again, and if you do not find that I am called tyrant, rascal, fool, and all sorts of foul names, ten times for every mention of Nicholas's name, I will have the thing stopped at once." This sort of reasoning threw a new flood of light upon the mind of the Russian minister. He then comprehended what the freedom of the Press meant in this country, and really perceived that Jackson could not be expected to stop the Press from abusing Nicholas, when it was every day boldly assailing him. He accordingly dropped the subject.

There was this difference in this Bank War in the position of the two presidents. Jackson took the responsibility of his acts, and in history they speak for themselves. Biddle, without the gigantic political power of his great antagonist, was obliged to assume the responsibility of not only his own acts, but those of his board of directors, whether right or wrong. There is no doubt that he has been misjudged and misrepresented in consequence of the peculiar position in which he was placed, regardless of his own mature financial and commercial views. Of course he was a Whig in principle and a decided Bank man ; but the enormous speculations in cotton, and the fearful expansions and contractions of credits were not his act alone, but, as the head of the United States Bank, controlled by directors, as well as by a president, he had to bear all the discredit, as well as all the honor that the people chose to mete out to him in those days of political phrensy and excitement. All the Biddles were highly honorable men ; Jackson, in the height of the war, publicly and frankly admitted this ; and nothing more clearly indicates the feelings of Nicholas Biddle, in his position as chief of the great institution which Jackson crushed as a national bank, than the following note, which he wrote to Mr. Bennett in 1839, after the exciting financial conflict had ceased :

NICHOLAS BIDDLE TO JAMES GORDON BENNETT.

PHILADELPHIA, March 29, 1839.

DEAR SIR,—You have often expressed an interest in my proceedings, and I therefore inclose a copy of some correspondence in the Bank. Being anxious that the measure may be understood on both sides of the water, I could wish you to treat it as a matter entirely personal—as the ordinary case of a servant worn out who wishes to retire. Such, I assure you, is the fact. My health is beginning to break under the severe work to which I am condemned, and I wish exercise and quiet ; for the salary of $8000 a year is really no compensation for the labor. If, therefore, you thought well of it, I could wish that you would present that view of the subject. To mention the fact, express, if you feel, regret on public grounds, but that, after such severe labor, you are not surprised at my retiring. This will prevent the exaggeration and the misconstruction to which every thing connected with the Bank is exposed.

And now, if I get fair possession of my leisure, I shall be glad to see you at your next visit, and in the mean while remain very truly yours,   N. BIDDLE.

JAMES GORDON BENNETT, Esq., New York.

N.B.—I can not procure the copy of the letters in time, but you will see them in our papers. They are merely my letter asking for repose after 20 years' service, now that the wars were over, and the kind answer of the directors.

The follies of the times were illustrated in the *Herald* in 1838. This was the beginning of the pictorial papers. A map of the burnt district and a view of the old Merchants' Exchange were given in 1835. The scenes at the polls and in Wall Street were graphically pictured in 1838. These, with war maps of Canada, were the earliest illustrations. Wood engraving was then in a very imperfect state in New York. There were very few engravers. Its contemporaries ridiculed these efforts of the *Herald*. The famous Boz Ball, at the Park Theatre, was described with twelve excellent illustrations. On the funeral ceremonies of General Jackson in New York in June, 1845, that paper gave a pictorial view of the procession, occupying one page. It was admirably done, considering the state of the art of wood engraving, but the *Albany Evening Journal*, and others, endeavored to demolish this enterprise of the *Herald* by the statement that this picture had already done duty at Victoria's coronation, General Harrison's funeral, and the Croton Water Celebration! The engraver came to the rescue with the following note on the subject:

NEW YORK, June 28, 1845.
JAMES GORDON BENNETT, ESQ., *Editor of the Herald:*

SIR,—I perceive that several of the city papers, and some out of it, from motives best understood by their editors, have indulged in some unjust remarks respecting the wood-cuts which appeared in your columns illustrating the funeral of General Jackson. As the engraver who executed them, I consider it due to you as well as myself to say fully and explicitly that they never appeared before in any newspaper, magazine, or book published in this country or any other, but that they were executed at my place of business, in Nassau Street, nor were they ever out of my possession until they appeared in the *Herald*. One editor, in his knowledge, has even gone so far as to say that they originally appeared in the *London Illustrated News* at the time of the coronation of Queen Victoria, seven or eight years ago, when any one that knows any thing at all of the progress of wood engraving is aware that that pictorial has been published but about three years! I reiterate, the *Herald* is the only paper the cuts ever appeared in, nor were they completely finished until after the funeral procession had taken place. One editor having remarked that they were the work of no "native" rather sneeringly, allow me to say that I was born in this city, where I hope to remain, and execute, with satisfaction, all orders the public may place in my hands.

Your most obedient servant, THOMAS W. STRONG,
Publisher and Wood Engraver.

When the little steamer Sirius crossed the Atlantic and anchored off the Battery, in New York Harbor, early on the beautiful morning of April 23d, 1838, followed a few hours after by the Great Western, not only New York, but the whole country, was thrown into a delirium of excitement. All the newspapers partook of the popular sensation. It was only equaled by the laying of the Atlantic Cable in 1866. The *New York Herald* was buoyant on the topic. Its editor immediately seized the opportunity to enlarge his enterprise. On the 1st of May he left New York, on the return trip of the Sirius, to make extensive arrangements for correspondence from the news centres of Europe. Very few letters had previously appeared in any of the American papers from the other side of the Atlantic. Robert Walsh, of the *National Gazette*, and Nathaniel Carter, of the *Statesman*, had been correspondents. Nathaniel P. Willis, the poet, had written to the *New York Mirror;* James Brooks, now of the *Express*, sent his notes afoot to the *Portland Advertiser*. O. P. Q. had become well-known by his letters to the *New York Daily Advertiser*. R. Shelton M'Kenzie, now of the *Philadelphia Press*, had sent some pleasant gossipy correspondence to Noah's *Evening Star*. But there had been no organized European correspondence, such as the leading Press—the New York *Times, Tribune, Herald,* and *World*—now receives at an enormous annual expense. Europe was not then known in detail. Mr. Bennett, as we have stated, was a passenger on the Sirius on her first return trip in May, 1838, to initiate this enterprise, and thus, with the solution of the problem of successful steam navigation on the Atlantic by the arrival of this pioneer ocean steamer, this important department of a newspaper was to be perfected. Now, Europe and European politics are much better known in the offices of the New York *Herald*, Philadelphia *Press*, Chicago *Tribune*, Boston *Traveller*, and New Orleans *Picayune*, than American affairs are in that of the London *Times*, or the *Journal des Débats* of Paris, or the *Independance Belge* of Brussels. With the increase of steamship lines the European arrangements of the *Herald* were improved and enlarged, the celebrated Dionysius Lardner at one time having charge of the bureau in Paris.

The Atlantic steamers, the Sirius, Great Western, Royal William, Liverpool, and British Queen, gave the New York papers opportunities to exhibit their enterprise in their own harbor. News schooners were of little use with steam-ships. They became obsolete. Swift row-boats and light sail-boats were the best. These little skimmers of the sea could meet the steamers below Quarantine, and while the inspection of the Health Officer was going on, these would run to the city and have the news issued in extras before a passenger landed. Scenes of great excitement would occur on these occasions. No Oxford, or Cambridge, or Harvard, or Gale regatta excelled the contests of the ship-news collectors of New York. One of the scenes is thus described in the *Herald* of May 18th, 1840:

The way in which we walk into the whole combined Press of New York, in newspaper enterprise and energy, is, as they say in the West, "a caution." We will here describe our last effort—that on the arrival of the British Queen, as performed by our beautiful boat, the Fanny Ellsler, on Saturday morning.

On Friday night last, at 12, Commodore Martin, our high admiral, was quietly asleep on a delicious hard board, in the log cabin or boat-house of Dr. Doane, at the Quarantine Ground, Staten Island. On each side of him were his men, also in the same state of tranquillity. At the wharf, under the window, lay our beautiful new boat, called the Fanny Ellsler—cool and quiet, yet trembling on the top of the moonlit waves like a bird ready to shoot into the eternal blue of the heavens at a moment.

They were waiting for the arrival of the British Queen, momentarily expected.

On a sudden, at half past 12, the voice of a big gun was heard booming up the harbor like the voice of distant thunder. The cry was raised outside the log cabin, "The Queen is coming," "the Queen is coming." Martin—half asleep, half dreaming—was on his feet in an instant ; rubbing his eyes and clapping his hat on his head, he looked down the harbor towards the Narrows. A big bright blue light went up to heaven and almost dazzled the brilliant moon. "Rouse, boys, rouse ! the Queen is coming ; there's her blue light."

In another moment, Martin, with his two men, were in the Fanny Ellsler—sail set, oars splashing, and dashing over the bright wave down to the Narrows. The moonlight was most brilliant, and the shores of Staten and Long Islands were almost as bright as day. As the lovely Fanny skimmed like a swan over the silvery wave, another boat, clumsy and heavy, like a tub, came sneaking and swearing after her. It was the news-boat of the Wall-Street Press, called the "Dot-and-go-one."

The beautiful Fanny kept her watery way, and in ten minutes time was, as a certain prince now is, under the lee of the magnificent British Queen.

"Steam-ship ahoy !" cried Martin.

"Ay, ay," responded the gallant Captain Roberts.

"The Fanny Ellsler," roared Martin.

"The what ?"

"The Herald," responded Martin.

"Oh—stop her," cried Captain Roberts to his engineer—"throw him a line."

Martin clinched the line, and in an instant was on the deck of the Queen.

"Martin, is that you ?" said Captain Roberts. "How in the devil do you always beat ?"

"By working harder than my competitors—the way you beat, captain—where's your private bag ?"

"Here are your papers," replied the captain.

By this time the news-boat of the Wall-Street Press, "Dot-and-go-one," came alongside, after a great deal of puffing and blowing. In a few minutes the steamer was at the Quarantine Ground. Here she stopped for the physician. Martin, with the private bag for the consignees, jumped aboard the Fanny Ellsler, and started for the city, "Dot-and-go-one" having started a little ahead ; but it was no go.

"Rouse up, Fanny," cried Martin, coaxing his boat — "courage, Fanny — stir up, my angel of a skiff !"

In a few minutes Fanny, skimming over the bright blue waters, and seeming to feel the words of her commander, passed "Dot-and-go-one" almost without an effort, and with a sort of gentle smile on the figure-head which adorns her prow.

Martin whistled and gayly cheered his lovely skiff—"Skim along, Fanny—skim along, my lovely angel ! Don't you see the big bright moon and the seven stars looking down upon you, and betting a thousand acres of the blue heaven that you will beat ? Skim along, Fanny—skim along, love !"

Fanny did skim along. She shot past the Wall Street tub, and reached Whitehall at half past two o'clock on Saturday morning.

Martin jumped ashore, rushed up Broadway, down to 21 Ann Street, and found the lights burning brightly at the *Herald* office. In five minutes all the editors, writers, printers, pressmen were in motion. The immense daily edition of the *Herald* was about one fourth worked off when the news arrived. The press was stopped—the announcement made : this was the second edition. In two hours it was stopped again, and three columns of news put in and sent by the various mails : this was the third edition. In another two hours six columns were put in : this was the fourth edition—also sent by the mails. By this means we sent the news all over the country—New England, Canada, the South and West, one day in advance of every other paper in New York.

This is the way in which we are producing a revolution in the New York Press. The Fanny Ellsler is a beauty of a skiff. If you want to see her, go to Whitehall at sunrise any morning, or to the Park this evening.

It was in the spring of 1839 that the *Herald* undertook to report the proceedings of the religious anniversary meetings annually held in New York City. These large religious societies had met in that city for years, but their doings, so far as the public were concerned, were only to be found in their annual reports, printed by the societies, of limited circulation, and which gave the public only the financial exhibit of each. Editorial articles in the few religious newspapers of the day, and a brief paragraph or two of the proceedings of the most prominent of the societies, appeared in the secular journals. Nothing of the audiences, nothing of the spirit of these meetings, could be found any where. Millions of dollars had been contributed and expended, and only a few knew what good the money had accomplished. Opening the columns of a widely-circulated daily paper to this new matter for public perusal and public thought was a novel and useful enterprise. But, strangely enough, it excited the jealousy of the clergy, the religious Press, and the opposition of the old class of inactive journals. The *Herald* was denounced from rostrum, pulpit, and editorial chair. All tended to the accomplishment of the great purpose in view. Year after year the proceedings of these religious meetings were fully and faithfully reported. They aided so materially in attracting crowds to the meetings, and in increasing the contributions, that they in a few years became wonderfully popular, and all the newspapers entered the lists in competition, and instead of the proceedings being known by only those who could get into the buildings where the meetings were held, they were spread before hundreds of thousands scattered throughout the country. In this *coup de journal* the editor of the *Herald* was frightfully abused by men and women, who afterwards bitterly complained if reporters were not sent to the meetings of the societies to which they belonged. So goes the world. The revolution thus effected in the Press is probably one of the most remarkable in its history, and Mr. Bennett, no doubt, in the enjoyment of his *otium cum dignitate*, often thought of the great contests he had had with the clergy and the lay members of the mammoth religious societies, and laughed over the many amusing and edifying scenes of Anniversary Week in New York ; and the fact that he finally saw the success and popularity of his plan of reporting these peculiar meetings must have been one of the gratifications of his professional career.

Spreading the leading sermons, preached on Sunday to a few hundreds in the churches, before a large audience of thousands, was a part of the plan. This idea was carried into effect in 1844, but the reports did not appear till Tuesday. Now the *Herald* of each Monday devotes one and two pages to the important sermons preached on the previous day, not only in New York, but in Boston, Philadelphia, Washington, Cincinnati, and even in Dublin and in London! Thus Archbishop M'Closky, or Henry Ward Beecher, or Mr. Spurgeon preaches a sermon to one or two thousand people. The next morning these preachers appear before another audience of half a million—not of Catholics or Congregationalists alone, but to an audience of Jew and Gentile, Episcopalian and Unitarian, Universalist and Orthodox, infidel and believer, of all shades of opinions—to an audience, indeed, that would crowd all the cathedrals of the world if they were thrown into one vast edifice or amphitheatre. The *New York Times* and several other papers have adopted this plan of giving sermons, and the cause of religion gains thereby. Such men as Beecher and Hepworth are charmed to have their sermons thus published. They are delighted to have their ideas thus spread before the world. One day, said the *Congregationalist*, an orthodox clergyman was asked what religious newspaper he took. "None," he replied. "Then how do you keep posted on Church matters?" continued his friend. "By reading the religious intelligence in the *Herald*," was his reply.

The Rev. David Mitchell, in a recent discourse in New York, thus spoke of the Press and Pulpit:

> Several newspapers, but more prominently than any other the *New York Herald*, treated their readers on Monday mornings to synopses of many of the sermons of the previous day. It was such a new and striking feature that even the *Saturday Review* had an editorial on it, commending the practice to the Press of Great Britain. Some time ago a strong point was made by one Robertson, in Glasgow, who had been charged by the Session for breaking the Sabbath in that he had followed his usual avocation of compositor on that day. Robertson retaliated that some of the clergy sent their manuscript of sermons on Sunday nights to be noticed the following day. In this highly favored city of New York the clergy did not need to resort to such practices. Reporters were every where photographing our preachers. No one can read these reports without feeling that the preacher's occupation is not gone. It is an acknowledgment on the part of the Press of the power and value of pulpit instruction.

But here and there a clergyman with a high reputation objects to this increase in the size of his audience. There are contrasts in all phases of life. One of the reporters of the *Herald*, several years ago, visited the Calvary Church, on the Fourth Avenue, to report a sermon of Dr. Hawks. When Dr. H. rose he saw the reporter, with his note-book before him, ready for service. He stopped, beckoned to the stenographer, and said that he did not wish his sermon reported; that he wrote it for his own audience, and not for the newspapers; and if the reporter attempted to take notes, he should refuse to preach. There were eight hundred persons present. The *Herald* at that time had three hundred thousand daily readers!

That hilarious, noisy, Hard-Cider campaign, resulting in the overthrow of the Democracy after the financial revulsion of 1837, was carried on in the early days of the Cheap Press, and was the first presidential election after the starting of the *Herald*. Then its editor, in assisting Harrison into the White House in 1840, wrote out popular descriptions of Harrison's military operations, and especially of the siege of Fort Meigs, which produced considerable effect on the public mind in that bubbling, uproarious age of politics, and swelled the vote for Tippecanoe and Tyler, and sent Van Buren into retirement at Kinderhook, which was probably a dividend due the latter for what he refused to do for the editor in 1832 and '3.

CHAPTER XXVIII.
MORE OF THE NEW YORK HERALD.

THE GREAT MORAL WAR.—TREMENDOUS STRUGGLE BETWEEN THE OLD AND NEW CLASS OF JOURNALS.—THE CURIOUS RESULT.—JOHN HOWARD PAYNE.—ATTEMPTED ASSASSINATION.—AN INFERNAL MACHINE.—NEW MODE OF ADVERTISING.—INTERESTING INCIDENTS.—THE MEXICAN WAR.—OVERLAND EXPRESSES.—LIBEL SUITS.—THE POLICY OF THE HERALD.—OBITUARY NOTICES.—CURIOUS INCIDENT WITH SIR HENRY BULWER.—STYLE OF EDITORIALS.—THE GREAT REBELLION.—THE HERALD WAR CORRESPONDENTS.—NEWS FROM THE SOUTH.—LETTER FROM SECRETARY STANTON.—THE FRENCH MISSION.—WHAT DID PIERCE, BUCHANAN, AND LINCOLN DO?—JAMES GORDON BENNETT, JR.—WONDERFUL ENTERPRISE IN EUROPE AND AFRICA.—THE ANGLO-ABYSSINIAN EXPEDITION.—THE NEWS STEAM YACHTS.—THE HERALD EXPLORING EXPEDITIONS IN AFRICA.

ONE of the most remarkable of all newspaper wars broke out in May, 1840. It was declared by the Wall-Street Press, aided by a few disappointed small papers of New York, and several of the leading Whig papers in Albany, Boston, Philadelphia, and Baltimore, against the *New York Herald*. Nearly every paper in the country, Whig, Democratic, and neutral, became engaged on one side or the other before there was a truce. Several novelists, magazine writers, lecturers, and newspapers of England were pressed into the service. It was an extraordinary intellectual combat. Nothing like it has ever occurred in the history of literature or journalism.

Anterior to the establishment of the *Herald* in 1835, most of the papers were party prints. Their policy was dictated by party. They were sustained by party, or crushed by party. There was scarcely an exception till the *Herald* appeared. Its editor had served his time on party papers. He had gained his knowledge of politicians in the offices of political newspapers. The Democratic leaders had endeavored to use him as they had all other journalists. He had become disgusted with the manufacture of candidates and of great men. With his experience he determined to set up a party of his own—the people's party—and with this in view he started the *Herald*. Very curiously, the issue and success of this independent paper aroused four powerful interests against its editor: the politicians, the clergy, the stock brokers, and the managers of the old newspapers. His political and financial articles and squibs in 1835, '6, and '7 led to a skirmish or two in the latter year. His continued boldness and success in 1838 and '9 brought on the general war of 1840.

It was organized by the *Courier and Enquirer*, but it opened with a shot from the *Signal*, a small evening paper edited by Park Benjamin, and published in New York.

According to the reports current at the time, Park Benjamin, under the inspiration of General Webb, arranged the preliminary details of the campaign. After the *Signal* gun the *Courier and Enquirer*, the *Journal of Commerce*, the *Evening Star*, the *American*, the *Express*, the *Evening Post*, and the *Commercial Advertiser* wheeled into line, and discharged broadsides that would have utterly annihilated any other establishment. The war lasted several months, and in that time the attacks were vehement, virulent, violent, vigorous, and incessant. Advertisers were first coaxed, and then threatened, to induce them to withdraw their patronage. Hotel proprietors were called upon to exclude the *Herald*, and all connected with it, from their houses. Subscribers and readers were denounced as impious and immoral if they read the paper. No stone was left unturned to crush out journal and editor. Some of the incidents connected with this "moral war," as it was called, were very amusing and very instructive.

"You must take the *Herald* off your files," said a couple of merchants to the manager of Gilpin's Exchange Reading-room in New York.

The manager looked up with some surprise.

"You must, or we will withdraw our names," repeated the subscribers.

Much embarrassed with this interference, in the absence of Mr. Gilpin, the manager felt constrained to obey these potential characters, and removed the *Herald*. Shortly after a gentleman came up, and, missing the paper, asked, "Where's the *Herald*?" Another and another appeared, till a dozen gathered around the empty file. The manager told his story: "Well," said these gentlemen, "if you don't restore the *Herald* at once, we will withdraw our names. We will not be dictated to by Webb, or Noah, or any other man or set of men what we shall read."

So the *Herald* went back on to the files again.

Mr. Edward K. Collins, the enterprising merchant of New York, who afterwards established the famous line of ocean steamers bearing his name, was sitting at his desk in South Street one bright, beautiful day early in June, in 1840, when three well-known politicians and merchants entered his office.

"We have called, Mr. Collins," said this self-constituted committee, "in regard to your advertisements in the *Herald*. You are aware, Mr. Collins—"

"Yes, yes," replied Mr. Collins, in his quick, decided tone, "yes,

yes, I understand. Charles," calling to a clerk in another room, "how many advertisements have we in the *Herald* this morning?"

"Three, sir," answered the polite Charles.

"Three—yes, yes. Well, Charles, put in three more to-morrow morning." Then turning to the committee, he said, "That is my answer, gentlemen. Good morning."

This same committee called upon Mr. John I. Boyd, an old and much-respected merchant, a quiet gentleman who minded his own business and never meddled with the affairs of his neighbors. After explaining to Mr. Boyd the bad character of the *Herald*, a paper which he had read from its first number, they asked him to withdraw his advertisements. Mr. Boyd patiently heard them through, and said, "Gentlemen, when I find I can not attend to my own business, I will send for you to aid me." They left.

Such efforts as these were made every where, and in every nook and corner. The managers of theatres were threatened with the vengeance of the other papers if they advertised in the *Herald*. These were Simpson, of the Park Theatre, Niblo, of Niblo's Garden, Mitchell, of the Olympic, Thorne, of the Chatham, Dinneford, of the Franklin, Hamblin, of the Bowery, and one or two others. Of all these Hamblin was the only one to withdraw, and partly from old grievances of his own. Some of the incidents which occurred with these managers in this affair were very droll and funny. One will suffice. The *New York Corsair* of July 2d, 1840, related the particulars of this one so neatly that we are induced to give it in full:

MR. SNOWDEN, PRINTER OF THE COURIER, *vs.* MR. THORNE, MANAGER OF THE CHATHAM.

The following ludicrous story is going the rounds of the city, and creating considerable laughter at the expense of Mr. Snowden, of the *Courier and Enquirer*. We do not vouch for its truth, but if true, Mr. Snowden has no fair reason to object to people's merriment; and if not, he owes it to himself to come out with a public contradiction. Mr. Snowden, through his connection with the *Courier*, has monopolized the printing of the whole, or nearly the whole, of the large theatrical show-bills, which, it is said—we trust without foundation—that he levies as a sort of black mail by refusing to notice any theatrical establishment in the city whereof the managers had not given him all the printing. However this may be, a few days since Mr. Thorne, of the Chatham Theatre, went into Wall street to transact some business with Mr. Snowden, when the latter asked him if he had given up advertising in the *Herald*. "I have not," replied Mr. T. "Then," said Mr. Snowden, "you must do so at once." "Must do so! By what compulsion must I?" inquired the manager. "By my compulsion, and that of the public Press," answered Mr. Snowden; "for, if you don't withdraw your advertisement from the *Herald*, the *Courier* won't notice the Chatham, and I won't print your show-bills!" "Well," said Mr. Thorne, "I presume you will give me a day of grace to consider." "Why, I don't mind," answered Mr. Snowden. So the manager made him a polite bow and vanished.

Mr. Thorne might then be seen wending his way along Wall Street in what an immoral sixpenny paper might call "a devil of a pucker"—or else in a devil of a passion. His hands and arms were thrust almost up to the elbows in his breeches pockets; his hat was jammed over his eyes, and he kicked the paving-stones before him in such a fashion that it was very evident he was meditating the pleasure he would derive from kicking something else, which would have a less awful effect on his corns. Nor is his paroxysm to be wondered at, for his republican spirit rebelled at the idea of being dictated to. At the same time, he knew he could not do without the show-bills, and labored under the impression that Snowden was the only man in the city who could print them. Suddenly, however, and just as he was in a fair way for exploding with internal combustion, he remembered having heard of Applegate's Mammoth Printing-press in Ann Street. So away he posted, and asked Mr. A. if he could print bills of such and such size. "Certainly, sir, and four times the size, if necessary," replied that individual. "My dear boy," returned Thorne, heaving a long, long sigh, "you were born to be my deliverer." And then, having ascertained that his "deliverer" could do any sort of printing under the sun, and at prices that no one could grumble at, he made an arrangement with him for the printing of the Chatham bills from that day forward, through all time, and went his way rejoicing.

The next day Mr. Thorne went down to Mr. Snowden's. "Well, Mr. T.," said Mr. S., looking pretty big, as he mostly does, "have you made up your mind about that little matter?" "I have," said Mr. T. "And I suppose you intend to withdraw your advertisement from the *Herald?*" "No, I'm hanged if I do." "Then I won't do your printing for you." "Can't be helped—I must go elsewhere." This going elsewhere, however, was just the thing of all others that Mr. Snowden didn't want, for he profited about thirty dollars a week by the job; so, after frowning a little, and fidgeting a great deal, and biting his upper lip, and looking as if he was wishing himself in the moon, he endeavored to calm down his agitated countenance into an air of excessive patronage, and said, "Well, had it been any one else, he should never have another type stuck for him in my office; but seeing that it's you that's in it, Mr. Thorne, I'll go on with the printing." "You must not do any such outrage to your feelings on my account," returned Thorne, "especially as I have already made an arrangement with Applegate!" And, having thus delivered himself, he made himself scarce, for he didn't chance to have his smelling-bottle about him, and he perceived that poor Mr. Snowden was deeply affected, and might stand in want of some such delicate attentions.

Remarks.—This spirit of dictation will never be submitted to in such a community as ours. It is not probable that Mr. Thorne set any amazing value upon his advertisements in the *Herald*, but he did upon his own liberty to do as he pleased—and acted accordingly. We need scarcely add that he acted like a man.

Thus this remarkable war went on in the newspapers, in society, in the theatres, on the railroads, in hotels, in bank parlors, in public reading-rooms, on steam-boats, and on the street corners. All sorts of influences were brought to bear against the *New York Herald*. The incidents already narrated show the inside efforts to accomplish the prime object in view. The vituperation of the press was terrible. The strongest language was used to bring Mr. Bennett and his paper down to the lowest level. We will add a few of the epithets used on this occasion:

BY PARK BENJAMIN, IN THE SIGNAL.

"Scoundrel pen," "Obscene vagabond," "Infamous blasphemer," "Loathsome and leprous slanderer and libeller," "Wretch," "Profligate adventurer," "Nuisance," "Venomous reptile," "Accursed sting," "Notorious bane and curse," "Filthy sheet," "Pestilential scoundrel," "Vagabond," "Habitual scoffer," "Witless balderdash," "Instinct of brutes," "Mass of trash," "Ghoul-like propensity," "Murdered reputation," "Fiendish lies," "Venal wretch," "Instrument of mischief," "Cursed," "Daring Infidel," "Monstrous lies," "Infamous Scotchman," "Foreign vagabond," "Polluted wretch," "Habitual liar," "Licentious," "Prince of darkness," "Infamous journal," "Veteran blackguard," "Contemptible libeller," "Lying slang and abuse," "Scurrilous," "Caitiff," "Monster," "Foul jaws," "Black-hearted," "Dirt," "Ass," "Gallows," "Rogue," "Ribaldry."

BY M. M. NOAH, IN THE EVENING STAR.

"Rascal," "Rogue," "Cheat," "Licentious," "Infamous," "Lies," "Vile,"

"Nuisance," "Outrage," "Common bandit," "Dungeon," "Scaffold," "Prowling," "Pollution," "Demoralize," "Contaminate," "Slander," "Libel," "Vicious," "Depraved appetite," "Drummed out," "Not live an hour," "False," "Inquisition," "Torture," "Villain," "Turkey-buzzard," "Falsehood," "Humbug."

BY JAMES WATSON WEBB, IN THE COURIER AND ENQUIRER.

"Unprincipled conductor," "Grossly slanderous," "Vulgar attacks," "Pollute our sheet," "Wretch," "Blasphemy," "Obscenity," "Cell at Sing Sing," "Personally offensive," "Fulsome praise," "Disgusting attacks," "Dastardly assaults," "Reckless depravity," "Unprincipled adventurer," "Moral pestilence," "Infamous," "Lowest species of scurrility," "Disgusting obscenity," "Revolting blasphemy," "Slanderous abuse," "Moral leprosy," "Insidious poison," "Gloat," "Disreputable sheet," "Disgusting organ," "Worthless sheet," "Horror and disgust," "Ribald vehicle," "Vile sheet."

Such epithets as these run through the many articles published in the papers which had combined against the *Herald*. These are specimens, and we give them to show the strong animus of the fight. With such a crusade against him, the wonder is how the *Herald* or its conductor survived. How did he meet them? Amusingly and philosophically. Not the slightest evidence of ill temper during the entire "war" appeared in the *Herald*. One day, in publishing some European news in advance of his contemporaries, he would, in a humorous article, put in his enterprise in answer to their attacks. Then he announced his marriage. Another day he would make a contract with Hoe & Co. for a new cylinder press. Then the death of one of the "allies," the old *Gazette*, for want of patronage, was heralded. The enlargement of the *Herald* was the next reply. So on. Sandwiched with such practical answers, he would throw in his small shot—sharp hits at Major Noah, Colonel Webb, Park Benjamin, Charles King, David Hale, and Colonel Stone. He knew their weak points. When the battle raged the fiercest, he summed up the material and intellectual strength on each side in the following curious manner. This appeared on the 3d of June, 1840:

THE FORCE IN THE FIELD.

It may be interesting to many of our readers to know the exact circulation of the Press, as compared with our own, which the Wall Street Holy Allies bring into the field to put down the *Herald*. We shall here state them from undoubted data in our possession:

THE HOLY ALLIES. Name.	Circulation.	THE HERALD. Circulation.
Evening Star	2,200	
Evening Signal	600	Daily,
American	700	Weekly, and 51,000
Courier and Enquirer	4,200	Extra,
Journal of Commerce	3,100	
Express	2,800	
Sun	21,000	
News	450	
Mercury	1,500	
Aggregate circulation,	36,550	
		51,000
		36,550
Herald circulation over the Allies		14,450

The engineers, sappers and miners, which attend both camps, may be estimated as follows:

HOLY ALLIES.		HERALD.	
Description.	Horse Power.	Description.	Horse Power.
Lies	10	Energy	20
Impudence	15	Sobriety	20
Ignorance	20	Moral Courage	25
Hatred	15	Intellect	20
Jealousy	15	Wit	20
Cash	—	Poetry	20
Credit	—	Virtue	20
Virtue	—	Cash	20
Horse Power	75	Horse Power	165

This is sufficient reason for "Tray, Blanche, and Sweetheart to snarl" at us; but it gives us not only the means to counteract the poison, but to place us immeasurably on the "vantage ground." Accordingly, the accession of patronage of every kind, since the war began, has been greater than we ever knew. Subscribers and advertisers pour in from all quarters. The miserable attempt to dictate to the community against their own senses is a miserable failure.

Active hostilities, so far as the public were concerned, ceased after a few months. None of the "allies" ever recovered their lost ground. Many of them went out of existence. Only two or three are left in the newspaper world. The *Herald* continued on its career of prosperity, and is now the richest establishment in the country. Its class, the cash independent newspapers, have become the ruling power in the land. But what is the sequel, personally, of this formidable effort to crush a newspaper? Major Noah, of the *Star*, had commenced two libel suits in 1841-2 against the *Herald*. He was one of the judges of the Court of Sessions. When the cases came up in Oyer and Terminer on the 9th of February, 1842, John A. Morrell, Esq., said that

Judge Noah had arrived in New York the day before, and he had written to and received an answer from him in relation to a *nolle prosequi* being entered on each of the indictments; Judge Noah had replied that he was perfectly willing the matter should take that course, as far as he was concerned, and that Judge Noah was now in court, connected with the application.

Judge NOAH. As far as I am individually concerned, I am perfectly willing that a *nolle prosequi* should be entered in these cases. Indeed, from the first I had no feeling or interest in this matter. It was first brought on, as I understood, at the request of one of the petit jurors—he made the complaint; and, so far as I am concerned, I am willing to have it settled thus. The whole affair has undoubtedly arisen out of a long editorial quarrel, in which violent attacks were made on both sides, and perhaps I ought to say that I think that the balance of aggression was on my side. * * * * * *

District Attorney WHITING then stated to the jury the circumstances under which the indictments were found, which, he remarked, were rather extraordinary. * * * * And we have now, gentlemen, the singular spectacle of one of the very parties complaining, one of the judges said to be libeled, coming into court asking for a *nolle prosequi* to be entered, confessing that he also has libeled others considerably, and perhaps at that business he has done the most. I have no disposition to find fault or quarrel with this opinion of the judge; he ought to know best; and, at the same time, I do not wish it to be understood that I have any feeling or interest in pressing this matter; rather the reverse. I have no wish that Mr. Bennett should be punished for this matter, or that it should be thought that the District Attorney is opposed to one of the judges—to have a person punished for an alleged offense, when one of the judges confesses he has committed the most of those offenses, and that perhaps he began the battle, and there is still a balance of abuse due to him yet. * * * * * *

Judge Noah, in 1846, notwithstanding his violent articles and actions against the *Herald* and its editor, even originating the ridiculous charge of "black mail," applied to Mr. Bennett, on the eve of his departure for Europe, through a mutual friend, for the management of the *Herald* in the editor's absence. It is useless to say that the proposition met with no favor. But, in face of this confession in court, and this application to renew the editorial connection which had existed between these two journalists twenty years previously, what prompted him to enter on the crusade against the *Herald* in 1840?

Another point indicating the same curious change in sentiment, but in a stronger light, when we consider the peculiar personal relations of the parties, is in the opinion expressed in 1851 or 1852 by General Webb.

One day an *attaché* of the *Herald* was introduced to General W. in the office of the *Courier and Enquirer*. It was shortly after his return from Austria. "Of the *Herald?*" said Webb. "Yes, general," replied the *attaché*, "your favorite paper, I believe." "Well, well," continued Webb, "Mr. Bennett deserves the highest credit for the energy and skill he has shown in building up his paper. Wherever I happened to be in Europe, and asked for an American newspaper, the *Herald* was invariably brought to me—never my own paper."

Another instance, in these subsequent relations, was in the personal application of David Hale to Mr. Bennett, after the enterprise of the latter had so distinctly made its mark, to unite the news arrangements of the *Journal of Commerce* with those of the *Herald*, leading to years of *entente cordiale* between those establishments.

There is yet another case in point exhibiting the marvelous *finale* of this unparalleled and unprecedented war against the *Herald*. On one occasion, when the *Herald* had published some important news exclusively, Park Benjamin drove up to a gentleman then connected with the *Herald*, and, after a few other remarks, said, "The *Herald* is a great paper this morning. Seeing you, I could not resist the impulse of giving you my opinion of the wonderful enterprise and ability of Mr. Bennett as a journalist. It is really marvelous; and if the *Herald* goes on at this rate, it will completely revolutionize the Press of the country."

It required time for the logic of events to work out this result. Such an organization as that in opposition to the *Herald* could not be dissolved at once. *Amour propre* forbid it. General Webb, Charles King, and Colonel Stone kept up the fire for some time.

In 1842, these editors, in the *Courier and Enquirer*, *American*, and *Commercial Advertiser*, severely criticised the result of the libel-suits of Major Noah. But gradually the asperities of bitter war wore off, and in the intercourse of the Associated Press there was almost always pleasant feelings and a few *bon mots*. Before this period, however, the epitaphs of the *Signal*, the *Evening Star*, the *American*, the *News*, and many others, had been prepared for the cemetery, and since then these mortuary inscriptions have become dust and blown away. We now rescue their names from oblivion.

No great newspaper can always be praised. Its conduct can not please every one. Abuse is the lapidary of journalism. If its old opponents subside or die, others rise up full of criticism and fight. Murillo and Shakspeare had their critics. Opinion is not infallible. Successful enterprise begets envy. Attractive subjects are always sought by magazine writers. Hence neither the *Herald*, nor any other leading and successful newspaper, is to sip honey from every flower. After the close of the general war on the *Herald* in this country, the *Foreign Quarterly* and *Westminster Review* took up the subject of the Press in America, and the *Herald* was the principal object of attack. This was in 1842 and '43. It seemed as if, in the extensive field of operations in the war of 1840, the fact of the cessation of hostilities around headquarters had not reached the outskirts, and a regiment here and there still kept up the fight. The *Foreign Quarterly* followed in the wake of Charles Dickens, and denounced the newspapers of the United States in the strongest terms, and without stint; but the *Westminster Review* occupied a more liberal and independent position, and carefully examined files of the *Herald* to understand its character. After this investigation the *Review* gave the *Herald* the credit of much enterprise in the early publication of important news, of the excellence and copiousness of its commercial intelligence, and correctly stated that the reason of the enmity against the paper arose from its cheapness and consequent "circulation of more than twice the number of copies issued of any other daily paper."

In the articles in the *Foreign Quarterly* in 1843, and in the review of the *Herald* in the *North American Review* in 1866, extracts were given to show the character of the Press of the United States. Those from the *Herald*, amusing, slashing, piquant, incisive, and full of wit and sarcasm, having their point for local effect, like the neat paragraphs and hits in *Punch*, were understood and appreciated by the two or three hundred thousand readers at the time of their publication, but no more comprehended by these reviewers than are the mere local hits of *Charivari* in Paris, or of *Punch* in London, of last month, would be understood or appreciated in

Alaska, if those funny papers ever reach that sealed country. Any one carefully reading those articles from the *Herald*, especially about the Pope and Van Buren, must see the point, and smile even now. But, taken out of their time and place, and inserted separately in a review for a special purpose, is like taking a single ejaculation from a fervent prayer, and accusing its utterer of profanity.

"Art preservative of all art" gives a very neat and true idea of the value of a newspaper conducted by men of taste and culture. They have it in their power to do more than any other class or profession in developing the genius of a nation in art or in song, in politics or in trade. How many men and women of mind and merit have been encouraged, brought out, assisted, developed, by newspapers. Indeed, editors are the grand Board of Examination of the world, and give out their rewards of merit to each candidate as he or she passes the ordeal before this universal school committee. Often has this fact occurred to us, been seen and appreciated by artists and statesmen, actors and students, artisans and scholars, and here is an instance, one of a thousand, in a note from John Howard Payne to the editor of the *Herald*, which speaks well for the generous impulses of the author of "Home, Sweet Home."

WASHINGTON, July 22, 1849.

MY DEAR SIR,—I venture to ask a favor from you, and I trust it is not of a nature which a gallant and generous man can quarrel with, as it is to serve a lady, and one of worth, and who can be substantially benefited by some help from the Press. To come to the point. I wish to get you to insert the annexed paragraph—or something to the same effect in your own words—about Miss F——'s pictures; but I only wish it in case you can give the notice as editorial, because it is only in that shape that it can do service. You may take my word for her fully meriting the best that any one may say. I have got a number of sitters for her here, thus enabling her to raise for herself friends, money, and reputation. She has been invited as an inmate to the house of Mr. R——, where they are all charmed with her and her works. I think a proper lift, now, in New York, may gain her, on her return thither, a fair start to a regular and permanent course of profitable employ.   * * * * * *

Ever faithfully yours, JOHN HOWARD PAYNE.

The *Herald* was not destined to live in peace. With the Native American excitement in New York in 1844, the editor of that paper was severely handled by Archbishop Hughes, the distinguished Catholic prelate of the Metropolitan District. The School Question had been agitated, and created no little excitement in Protestant and Catholic circles, and the *Journal of Commerce, Commercial Advertiser*, and *Herald* entered into the sensational controversy with some enthusiasm. But the popular course of Mr. Bennett aroused the controversial archbishop. In a series of letters, addressed to Colonel Stone, of the *Commercial Advertiser*, he denounced Mr. Bennett, by name, in no measured terms. It was almost an excommunication from the Church. The editor replied good-naturedly, speaking of the early days of the archbishop as a gardener raising cabbages, but still keeping the main question, relative to the Bible and the School, always and strongly in view. These letters provoked discussion, and aided in the increase of the circulation of the *Herald*. They produced no other effect. Yet in 1865, the *Daily News*, twenty-one years after they were written, and when all the surrounding circumstances were forgotten, republished them in all their length and breadth, to punish the *Herald* for a few hits at the Hon. Benjamin Wood!

The most diabolical attempt to destroy the *Herald* was made in 1852. It was not by any combination of newspapers to write Mr. Bennett out of journalism, or by any effort of any prelate to send him to perdition through a series of letters. It was to have been done by an infernal machine, or torpedo, ingeniously contrived, so that the editor might be his own executioner.

On the 18th of October, 1852, between 8 and 9 o'clock in the evening, a parcel was left at the office of the *Herald* by a short, stout man, muffled in a cloak, who drove to the office door in a hack. The parcel was cylindrical in form, six inches in length, wrapped in common brown paper, tied with green ribbon, and securely sealed with red wax, bearing the impression of a cent. It bore this direction:

For
JAMES GORDON BENNETT,
PROPRIETOR AND EDITOR,
Office N.W. Corner of Fulton and Nassau Streets.
Private, and with Care.

This address had been clipped from a copy of the *Herald* and pasted on a piece of white paper, which was secured to the outer envelope with sealing-wax impressed with an American half dime. The "private, with care," were badly printed with a pen. Over the direction, and on the brown paper, were these words:

Native Silver and Copper Ore from the Cuba Mountains, with Letter inside the Box.

Tied to the parcel was an enameled card with this inscription:

SENOR V. ALCAZOR,
of Cuba.
For Mr. Bennett,
who will call on his Return to the City.

When this outside wrapper was taken off by Mr. Bennett, a small pasteboard box appeared, resembling those used by shirt-dealers for collars. On the side of the box was a strip of foolscap paper, on which was printed with a pen, in red ink, these words:

SPECIMENS AND PRIVATE DOCUMENTS,
FROM THE INTERIOR OF HAVANA.
FOR MR. BENNETT (only).
SHOULD HE BE OUT OF TOWN, KEEP FOR HIM.
Island of Cuba, September, 1852.

This box was handed to Mr. Bennett, in a few minutes after its receipt, by one of his clerks. He made two attempts to take off the lid. Not succeeding, he passed it to an assistant editor by whose desk Mr. Bennett was standing. This gentleman then attempted to pry off the cover with a pair of scissors. In doing so, some black powder fell on to a sheet of white paper on his desk. It looked more like gunpowder than silver or copper ore. Throwing some of it into the grate, it exploded. There were no more efforts made that night to open the box. It was a suspected article.

The next morning the mysterious box was placed in the hands of Alfred E. Baker, afterwards Fire Marshal, James Leonard, afterwards Inspector of Police, and Robert Bowyer, three of the best detective officers of New York. They put it in a pail of water and gave it a few days' soaking. It was then carefully examined. It proved to be an ingeniously constructed torpedo. There was a circular piece of pine wood, half an inch thick, inside, supported by four light pegs fastened in the bottom. About three quarters of an inch above this was a similar one, but less in circumference. This was fastened to the bottom of the box by two pieces of strong cord running through holes in the lower wood. Then to the lid, or cover, was secured a round bunch of lucifer matches, the igniting part resting on a groove in the upper surface of the middle wheel, or partition. This groove was covered with sand-paper. The lid, with the bunch of matches glued to it, was tied down by the cords passing inside. In attempting to remove the lid, the expectation was that it would have to be taken off by turning it around. In doing this, the friction end of the matches would be rubbed over the sand-paper and instantly ignite. The box was filled with fine rifle and fulminating powder. Fortunately for Mr. Bennett and his assistant editor, the cords which secured the cover were a little loose, and hence, in the effort to remove it, the end of the matches was lifted from the sand-paper. This saved their lives. The machine was a diabolically contrived affair, and the escape of these gentlemen was a miraculous one. Although the name of the constructor and sender of this infernal machine was known, yet there was not sufficient proof to warrant his arrest, and this occurrence, like many others, became only an episode in the epoch of journalism. But infernal machines produced no effect on the course of the *Herald*. Its editor went on as if no torpedo had been within an ace of blowing him to atoms.

Mr. Bennett introduced a new style of writing. It was fresh, original, clear. It was the French style, with an infusion of the dash and vigor of the young Republic. Our journalists had previously aped that of modern England—solid, argumentative, heavy. They were the solemn communications of "Honestus," "Scævola," "Americus," "Publius," "Scipio," written by veteran politicians and retired statesmen; the antiquated philosophy of one age turned into editorial articles for the next. To comprehend one, the series must be read. But Mr. Bennett changed all this in the *Herald*. He made each article and each paragraph tell its own story. Style in the English papers had become fixed in the Addison, Junius, Swift, Bolingbroke standard. "Style is it that you want?" asked Lord Oxford. "Oh, go and look in the newspapers for style."

"Why do you read the *New York Herald?*" asked a gentleman of one of the European ministers in Washington. "I never see you with any other American paper."

"Because I understand its articles," replied the diplomat.

The French journalist largely adopts this method in writing for the public. Thus, while the French journal is not a newspaper in its details of news and in its enterprise, it is thoroughly one in its editorials. Mr. Bennett, in the *Herald*, combined these two great journalistic qualities, and hence his marvelous success.

In order to fully comprehend the party journals of the day, it was necessary to know the ins and outs, and the platforms and policies of parties. No one leader in a party newspaper was clear in itself to the reader not conversant with the party politics of the country. It was like an extract from a book without context or sequence.

One day the *Herald* published a very strong article on a prize-fight that had just taken place near New York. It happened that, on the day of publication, Tom Hyer, the handsome pugilist, visited the office. It was thought that he came on account of that article, but he made no allusion to it till asked if he had read it, and what he thought of its tone. "Well," said Hyer, "I suppose you meant to be hard on the boys, but you made a mistake. Why, do you know," continued he, "that you newspapers can't use words strong enough to make the boys mad? Did you ever hear them talk when angry with each other? Can you publish the slang and the oaths they use? They use strong language. They mean business. No paper can publish what they say. Your article is milk and water. The boys won't notice it." Thomas Hyer was correct. Such is style with this class of the community.

The advertisements in the *Herald* increased with its enterprise and its circulation. It had been the custom of all newspapers in the United States to illustrate the business notices of their patrons with pictures representing the character of the advertisements—of ships, race-horses, houses, stage-coaches, railroad trains, dogs, birds, runaway apprentices and slaves with packs on their backs, wagons, steam-boats, cattle, and the Muses. Typographically, the plan was not a good one. In a business point of view, it was unfair to those not represented pictorially. The *Herald* in 1847 omitted all cuts and all display. All advertisements were printed in the same style, but neatly and systematically arranged. They gave a thorough business appearance to the paper. Since then no pictures have appeared. There has been no typographic splurge for one to the injury of another. The new plan worked well from its initiation, and the public and the advertisers were alike pleased. Mr. Bennett made a study of this important part of his paper. He saw that it should be entirely independent of the news and editorial departments. There should be no favoritism. There should be no dependence on politicians, cliques, or individuals. In this way the *Herald* would be valuable for three reasons: 1st, its news; 2d, the independence of its editorials; and, 3d, its advertisements, forming an interesting and attractive feature of the paper.

The Secretary of the Navy in 1845 wrote the following note to the *Herald*:

NAVY DEPARTMENT, July 23, 1845.

SIR,—You will be pleased to copy in your paper, from the *Union*, the advertisement from the Bureau of Yards and Docks, inviting proposals for executing the work, etc., at the Navy Yard, Memphis, Tennessee.

I am respectfully yours, G. BANCROFT.
The Publisher of the *New York Herald*.

This advertisement was refused insertion for several reasons. One was because the Post-office Department had acted unfairly in not giving the "list of letters remaining in the New York Post-office" to the paper having the largest circulation, according to law, and because the government chose to fix its own prices for the payment of such a service, regardless of position, readers, or circulation, outside of party circles. Mr. Bennett held to the opinion that it was not just to the cooks and chambermaids of New York that they should be compelled to pay more than the United States government for their advertisements. When the Secretary of the Treasury afterwards sent an advertisement to the *Herald*, that paper, on the 30th of November, 1847, said:

Mr. Walker, Secretary of the Treasury, has published a long advertisement from his department in the *Washington Union*, giving directions to a number of newspapers to copy it, and send their bills for payment to Washington. Among the papers to whom these directions are addressed is the *New York Herald*. We thank Mr. Walker for his kind intentions in offering us a little Treasury pap, but we beg leave to decline the dose. It is not worth our while to do any of the advertising of the Treasury Department, or any other department of the government, and we now, once and for all, declare publicly that we will have nothing to do with any printing or advertising from the departments.

This was followed by fresh innovations on the old system of advertising. Early in 1847 no advertisements were taken for over two weeks' insertion. This was still further improved upon. On the 30th of December of that year the *Herald* contained this announcement:

On the first of January we shall begin a new system of taking in advertisements of persons publishing in the columns of the *Herald*. On and after that day, no advertisements will be taken for more than one day, or for one insertion, payment to be made at the delivery of it over the counter.

This system has been adhered to ever since. It was announced at the same time that no editorial notices of advertisements would be given, thus placing all advertisers on an equality, and showing no preference to any class, company, association, corporation, interest, or individual. What is the result? The *Herald* has published as many as sixty solid columns of advertisements in one sheet. This excellent plan is now becoming the plan of many of the leading journals, and its beneficial results in the *Herald* will cause it to be generally adopted in the course of a few years.

On the 21st of June, 1861, the *London Times* contained this announcement:

Our impression of this day will be found to consist of twenty-four pages, the extraordinary pressure of advertisements having compelled us to add an extra sheet to our already ample dimensions. Fifty years ago the average number of advertisements in a single impression was about a hundred and fifty; to-day, no less than *four thousand* advertisements will make known the wants of the community throughout the length and breadth of the empire. We have long discontinued the heading of "Supplement" to the second sheet of the *Times*, and have only adopted the title of "Extra Sheet" in this instance to attract the notice of our readers to this, the largest production that has ever issued from the Daily Press. We trust it will not be too large for "a constant reader" to get through within the compass of this, the longest day in the year.

This was the wonderful result after a prosperous and unexampled existence in England of sixty-six years. It mentions its condition fifty years previously, and contrasts its size and the number of advertisements with that period. But what do we see in America? On the 13th of April, 1869, the *New York Herald* appeared as a quadruple sheet from the same cause, a pressure of advertisements, and the fact is thus chronicled by the Seneca (Kansas) *Courier* of the 22d of the same month:

The *New York Herald* of April 13 is now before us, and in many respects is the greatest newspaper in the world. It is certainly the most enterprising and largest in the United States. The copy now before us is a quadruple sheet, forty-six by sixty-eight inches, containing eight columns of editorial, thirty-eight columns of news, and fifty columns of advertisements—in all, ninety-six columns. The cost of type-setting alone is enormous, the *Herald* being the only paper in the world that sets every portion new every day—advertisements and all. To print the single issue now before us requires the setting up of 360,000 ems Agate, 343,000 ems Nonpareil, and 46,550 ems Minion—849,550 ems in all—and the consumption of over eleven tons of paper. The type-setting and proof-reading alone cost full $600 for a single day. Enormous as these figures are, they give but little idea of the aggregate expense of publication. Ocean telegrams at $2 20 per word; telegrams from all parts of the American continent; correspondents in all parts of the world; a corps of editors at the home office, and two distinct corps of correspondents at Washington, have all to be paid at highest rates. It is thus easily seen why every body reads the *Herald*.

If the *Herald* were alluding to this result, it could only go back thirty-four years to its first number, in order to make any comparison indicative of its marvelous success—more extraordinary and astonishing than that of the *London Times*, if we take the difference in time and population into consideration. Other journals in the United States—in Philadelphia and in Boston, and at the West, in Chicago, St. Louis, Cincinnati, and San Francisco, show results equally wonderful when we look at the size of the respective places of publication.

The advertisements of the *Herald* are a feature. They are fresh every day. It is intended, by its system, that they should be. Its proprietor would prefer to have every business notice freshly written daily. On this plan the advertisements form the most interesting and practical "city news." They are the hopes, the thoughts, the joys, the plans, the shames, the losses, the mishaps, the fortunes, the pleasures, the miseries, the politics, and the religion of the people. Each advertiser is therefore a reporter—a sort of "penny-a-liner," he paying the penny. What a picture of the metropolis one day's advertisements in the *Herald* presents to mankind!

On the 7th of May, 1871, the day after its thirty-sixth anniversary, there was a quadruple sheet, and its regular "directory for advertisers" showed the following different kinds or classes of advertisers:

DIRECTORY FOR ADVERTISERS.

AMUSEMENTS—FOURTEENTH PAGE—Fourth, fifth, and sixth columns.
ASTROLOGY—SECOND PAGE—Fourth column.
BILLIARDS—FOURTH PAGE—Fifth column.
BOARD AND LODGING WANTED—SIXTEENTH PAGE—Fifth column.
BOARDERS WANTED—SIXTEENTH PAGE—Second, third, fourth, and fifth columns.
BROOKLYN BOARD—SIXTEENTH PAGE—Fifth column.
BROOKLYN REAL ESTATE FOR SALE—FOURTH PAGE—First and second columns.
BUSINESS OPPORTUNITIES—FIFTEENTH PAGE—Sixth column.
BUSINESS NOTICES—NINTH PAGE—Sixth column.
CITY REAL ESTATE FOR SALE—FOURTH PAGE—First column.
CLERKS AND SALESMEN—FIFTEENTH PAGE—Third column.
CLOTHING—SIXTEENTH PAGE—Sixth column.
COACHMEN AND GARDENERS—FIFTEENTH PAGE—Third and Fourth columns.
COAL AND WOOD—FOURTEENTH PAGE—Second column.
COASTWISE STEAM-SHIPS—FIFTEENTH PAGE—Fifth column.
COPARTNERSHIPS—FIFTEENTH PAGE—Sixth column.
COUNTRY BOARD—SIXTEENTH PAGE—Fifth and sixth columns.
DANCING ACADEMIES—FOURTEENTH PAGE—Third column.
DENTISTRY—FOURTEENTH PAGE—Third column.

DRY GOODS—First Page—Second, third, fourth, fifth, and sixth columns, and Second Page—First, second, third, and fourth columns.
DWELLING HOUSES TO LET, FURNISHED AND UNFURNISHED—Third Page—First and second columns.
EUROPEAN STEAM-SHIPS—Fifteenth Page—Fifth column.
EUROPE—Fourteenth Page—Third column.
EYES AND EARS—Second Page—Sixth column.
EXCURSIONS—Fifteenth Page—Sixth column.
FINANCIAL—First Page—Second column.
FINE ARTS—Fourteenth Page—Second column.
FOR SALE—Second Page—Fourth column.
FURNISHED ROOMS AND APARTMENTS TO LET—Third Page—Second, third, and fourth columns.
FURNITURE—Fourth Page—Sixth column.
FRENCH ADVERTISEMENTS—Fifteenth Page—Fourth column.
HELP WANTED—MALES—Fifteenth Page—Fourth column.
HELP WANTED—FEMALES—Fifteenth Page—Second and third columns.
HORSES, CARRIAGES, Etc.—Third Page—Fourth, fifth, and sixth columns.
HOTELS—Sixteenth Page—Fifth column.
HOUSES, ROOMS, Etc., WANTED—Second Page—Sixth column.
INSTRUCTION—Second Page—Sixth column.
JERSEY CITY, HOBOKEN, HUDSON CITY, AND BERGEN REAL ESTATE FOR SALE—Fourth Page—Second column.
LEGAL NOTICES—Fourteenth Page—Third column.
LOAN OFFICES—Third Page—Sixth column.
LOST AND FOUND—First Page—First column.
MACHINERY—Second Page—Fourth column.
MARBLE MANTELS—Fourteenth Page—Third column.
MATRIMONIAL—Fourteenth Page—Third column.
MEDICAL—Fourteenth Page—Third column.
MILLINERY AND DRESSMAKING—Second Page—Fourth column.
MILITARY—Fifteenth Page—Fourth column.
MISCELLANEOUS ADVERTISEMENTS.—Twelfth Page—Fifth and sixth columns.
MISCELLANEOUS—Fourteenth Page—Second column.
MUSICAL—Fourteenth Page—Third column.
NEW PUBLICATIONS—Fourteenth Page—Second column.
PERSONAL—First Page—First column.
PIANO-FORTES—Fourteenth Page—Fourth column.
PROPOSALS—Sixteenth Page—Sixth column.
PROPERTY OUT OF THE CITY FOR SALE OR TO RENT—Fourth Page—Second, third, and fourth columns.
REAL ESTATE TO EXCHANGE—Fourth Page—Fourth and fifth columns.
REAL ESTATE WANTED—Fourth Page—Fifth column.
RELIGIOUS NOTICES—Second Page—Sixth column.
REMOVALS—Fourth Page—Fifth column.
RESTAURANTS—Fourteenth Page—Second column.
REWARDS—First Page—First and second columns.
SALES AT AUCTION—Sixteenth Page—First and second columns.
SITUATIONS WANTED—FEMALES—Fifteenth Page—First and second columns.
SITUATIONS WANTED—MALES—Fifteenth Page—Third column.
SPECIAL NOTICES—Second Page—Fifth and sixth columns.
SPORTING DOGS, BIRDS, Etc.—Third Page—Fourth column.
STALLIONS—Third Page—Fourth column.
SUMMER RESORTS—Sixteenth Page—Sixth column.
THE TRADES—Fifteenth Page—Fourth column.
THE TURF—Third Page—Fifth column.
TO LET FOR BUSINESS PURPOSES—Third Page—First column.
TRAVELERS' GUIDE—Fifteenth Page—Sixth column.
UNFURNISHED ROOMS AND APARTMENTS TO LET—Third Page—Fourth column.

WANTED TO PURCHASE—Fourteenth Page—Third column.
WINES, LIQUORS, Etc.—Fourteenth Page—Second column.
YACHTS, STEAM-BOATS, Etc.—Fourteenth Page—Third column.

All advertisements are curious. Each one has its story. In looking over old files of newspapers, advertisements are read with more interest than any other part of the paper. They are pictures of the times—*Meissoniers* in printing ink. The most curious column of this part of the *Herald* are the "personal" advertisements. Will these attract as much attention a century hence as the few business notices of the *News-Letter*, *Spy*, and *Courant* of the last century? Take the "personals" of the *Herald* of any day, and they will set one to thinking. So will similar advertisements in the *London Times*. We have taken at random the following notices under this head that appeared in the *Herald* of April 21, 1871:

PERSONAL.

ANY INFORMATION OF MISS ELLEN AGNETTE JOHANNESsen, who came to New York City in 1852 from Gromstad, Norway. She is the daughter of P. Johannessen, schoolmaster of Gromstad in 1843. Information of her will be thankfully received and reasonably rewarded by addressing G. M. JOHANNESSEN, Post-office, Jackson, Tenn.

A.—LAURA—COUPE—HAVE SECURED THE BOX FOR THE Grande Duchesse Ball at the Central Park Garden next Tuesday evening. Get the ladies ready and come up.   LAWRENCE.

ALBANY—FRIDAY AFTERNOON, 14TH.—THE LADY FROM the East, taking a drawing-room car West, raised the window and received the Herald with writing on to notice "Personals" certain date. Your acquaintance would be dearly prized. The gentleman earnestly entreats you to send address and grant a correspondence. Address HOMER HIGHLAND, Box 230, New York Herald Office.

AND THINE EYES ARE NOT HIDDEN. YES!
    VIS-A-VIS.

A. H. HUMPHREY ARRIVED IN TOWN YESTERDAY, IT IS PRE- sumed sick. Any one knowing of his whereabouts will confer a favor on his friends by addressing G. S. HUMPHREY, 547 Broadway.

BEN—SECURE FIVE PARQUET SEATS FOR NEWCOMB & ARlington's Minstrel matinee Saturday. Will be over at 1.
    BROOKLYN.

IN THE GOODS OF MALTILDA DERINZY, DECEASED.—IF WILliam Richards Derinzy, Esq., formerly of Clobernon Hall, in the county of Wexford, then of Fredericksburg, in the State or Province of Virginia, in the United States of America, and lastly supposed to have resided about the years 1846 and 1847 in Brooklyn, New York, in said States, apply to the undersigned, he will hear of something to his advantage. Dated this 24th day of March, 1871. TENCH & REYNOLDS, Solicitors, 57 Lower Dominick Street, Dublin.

INFORMATION WANTED—OF ANNE GEAR. SHE IS SUPPOSED to be in the neighborhood of Poughkeepsie, N. Y., or Danville, Conn. She is 14 years and 6 months old. Any information of her will be thankfully received by her father, T. J. GEAR, at 592 Third Avenue, New York City.

INFORMATION WANTED—BY JOSEPH H. DEERY, NO. 10 WHITE Street, New York, of John Smith, or J. Arlington Smith, native of Kells, Ireland. He had served in some New York volunteer company during the war.

When last heard from was studying medicine in New York. His brother William has died in the South, leaving a considerable amount of money.

INFORMATION WANTED—OF CHRISTOPHER DELMAR, OF THE parish of Miltown, county Westmeath, Ireland, by his sister Mary. When last heard from was in Chicago, Ill. Any information concerning him will be thankfully received by MARY DELMAR, at 43 West Thirty-fourth Street, New York. N. B.—All expenses will be paid.

IF THE HACKMAN WHO TOOK TWO TRUNKS FROM IN FRONT of the Summit Hotel, in the Bowery, on Friday, the 14th inst., will send his address to Box 424 Rahway, N. J., he will be liberally rewarded.

MAUD—WILL NOT BE PRUDENT FOR ME TO WRITE. I want to see you ever so much.   LITTLE FRIEND.

STRAYED—ON MONDAY MORNING LAST, AFTER LEAVING the cars at Yonkers, "Old Man Banquo." His eyesight being bad, it is feared that he has met with foul play while examining the lines of a paper boat. Any information regarding him will be thankfully received by his disconsolate chum, Captain HARRIS, People's Line.

VENUS.—FRIDAY, AT 3; SATURDAY, AT 11 AND 3.
                                        JUPITER.

WILL THE LADY IN BROWN DRESS THAT LEFT STAGE AT Canal Street about 6 P. M. on Wednesday, and went to Brandreth House, and afterwards noticed gentleman passing through the hall and down stairs, please send address, in strict confidence, to S. T. H., Herald office?

WANTED TO ADOPT—A GOOD HEALTHY CHILD, FROM nine months to five years old, where it will find a good home. Must have blue eyes. Address ALDEN, Herald office.

WILL—PLEASE CALL AT STATION A, SPRING STREET, FOR letter addressed to yourself.   M. D., New Haven.

I "LIKE BIRDIE."

401.—9 A. M.

These personal advertisements in newspapers of large and comprehensive circulation have been of great value in various ways. Friends and separated families living at the North and South during the rebellion of 1861–65 communicated their welfare, sickness, and movements to each other through this medium in the *New York Herald*. These were copied in the Southern papers. The same mode was adopted during the war between France and Germany in 1870–71. The French exiles in London communicated to their friends and relatives in Paris and elsewhere through the London *Times*. "We are safe," in the *Herald* of 1865, and "*Tout va bien,*" in the *Times* of 1870, were each an item of intelligence giving great joy around two or three firesides in those critical periods of the world's history.

During the siege of Paris the *Times* was sent into that city by carrier pigeons! That paper of the 31st of January, 1871, described the wonderful way this was accomplished:

Attempts to establish a ready communication between the beleaguered inhabitants in Paris and their relatives and friends beyond the German lines have given rise to many contrivances which are not unlikely to make a new era in the history both of æronautics and photography. Among them may be mentioned the ingenious device by which the matter of two whole pages of the *Times* has been transmitted from London to Paris. This has been accomplished by photography. Those pages of the paper which contained communications to relatives in Paris were photographed with great care by the London Stereoscopic and Photographic Company on pieces of thin and almost transparent paper about an inch and a half in length by an inch in width. On these impressions there could be seen by the naked eye only two legible words, "The *Times*," and six narrow brown bands, representing the six columns of printed matter forming a page of the newspaper. Under the microscope, however, the brown spaces became legible, and every line of the newspaper was found to have been distinctly copied, and with the greatest clearness. The photographs were sent to Bordeaux for transmission thence by carrier-pigeon to Paris. When received there they were magnified by the aid of the magic lantern to a large size, and thrown upon a screen. A staff of clerks immediately transcribed the messages and sent them off to the places indicated by the advertisers. The success of this experiment gives rise to the hope that the new art of compressing printed matter into a small compass will not stop here. If a page of the *Times* can be compressed into a space little larger than that occupied by a postage-stamp, the matter of an octavo volume might be made to cover not more than two of its own pages, and a library could be reduced to the dimensions of the smallest Prayer-book. What a relief it would be to the learned persons who frequent the Library of the British Museum if, instead of having to make fatiguing journeys from letter A to letter B of the ponderous catalogue of books, they had its many hundred volumes reduced to a space a yard square, over which a microscope could be hurriedly passed. Such suggestions are now occupying the thoughts of photographers.

Other incidents of a very interesting character have occurred in connection with these personal advertisements. Many lost relatives and friends have been found by means of these brief notices. Wandering children have been restored to their parents through information thus conveyed. Divided households have been united by one line under this head: "All is forgiven. Come home." Estates in Europe have reached rightful heirs by a short "personal" in the *Herald*.

One morning a young Scot called on Mr. Bennett at his office to relate what an advertisement had accomplished for him. He left Scotland several years previously, and, after various attempts to obtain a situation, he had settled down as an assistant in the engine-room of one of the steamers on Lake Erie. One day, on reading a copy of the *Herald* taken by the captain of the steamer, he saw his own name in an advertisement. It informed him that, by calling at the office of a lawyer in New York, he would hear of something to his advantage. He started for that city, and made his appearance before the lawyer and proved his identity, and "now," said the young Scot, "you are the second person I have called upon; and what do you suppose the lawyer wanted of me? Of course you can't tell. Well, yesterday I felt that I was only worth my daily wages. To-day I am a rich man. An uncle of mine has died in Scotland, and I am heir to all his property. It amounts to £175,000—one estate in Scotland and one in England. If the advertisement had not been put in the *Herald* I should probably have continued a fireman on board of a steam-boat." He called to tell Mr. Bennett the incident, and to invite him to visit him at his "new-found home."

Another incident will suffice to show the value of a newspaper and its advertisements, if incidents were necessary for this purpose.

Several years ago, in the spring of 1852, a boy in rags and dirt, in search of his mother, was sent to the office of the *Herald* as a sort of National Intelligencer Office by a benevolent captain of one of the North River steamers.

"How can we find your mother, and where did you come from?" asked one of the clerks.

"I don't know where she is," sobbed the little fellow. "I left home five years ago to live on an uncle's farm in Ohio. He has almost worked and starved me to death. So I left him, and have walked part of the way home. Several conductors and the captain of the steam-boat have been kind to give me free rides. My mother has moved, and I don't know where to find her. On my way here I lost what little baggage I had."

The clerks and the boys of the *Herald* immediately became interested in the lad. They took him under their protection, provided him with his meals and lodging, and had the following advertisement inserted in the *Herald*.

INFORMATION WANTED OF MRS. E—— C——, WHO IS SUPposed to be at present in this city, and married a second time to some person whose name is unknown. Her son Milton has returned to the city from Ohio, where he was sent about five years ago, and is anxious to find his mother, or his uncles Albert and Franklin, who are also in the city. Any information of the above persons will be received at the desk of the Herald office, and the residence of the boy, M—— C——, who is friendless and destitute, in the absence of any knowledge of his mother, be given.

"Now," said the clerks, "the advertisement will go in to-morrow morning. You must remain in the office, so that you will not miss your mother if she comes."

The next morning he was there. About 8 o'clock a lady entered, and, looking around, saw the lad and recognized him at once. The recognition was mutual. With the exclamations "Mother!" "My boy!" they were soon in each other's arms. Of clerks, boys, and strangers present there was not a dry eye.

The mother was full of gratitude, and, leaving, said she would take him to her home, clean him up, and bring him back in order to show his benefactors what a splendid boy he was. She did so.

"Have you ever received any return for the large expenditure in time and money in erecting your Institute?" asked a gentleman one day of Mr. Peter Cooper, in a Fourth Avenue car.

"Oh yes," replied that gentleman, "several. It is only the other day, in one of these cars, a young man in uniform came to me and said, 'Mr. Cooper, I have been desirous of speaking to you, but a want of confidence in myself has deterred me till now. I was a poor boy, without any prospects, when your Institute opened. I applied for admission, learned engineering, the rebellion broke out, and now I am an assistant engineer. But for you, Mr. Cooper, what would have become of me!'"

"That," said Mr. Cooper, "was a gratifying return, and I have felt happier ever since that interview in the car. One or two incidents of this kind are sufficient compensation to me."

On a smaller scale, in a pecuniary point of view, the *attachés* of the *Herald*, in the scene of the reunion of mother and son, felt themselves more than compensated for the trouble they had taken with the stray boy; and "one or two incidents of this kind" show that the advertisements of a paper are not the least important part of such an institution.

The relations of Mexico and Texas with the United States began to assume an importance in 1844, and news from those republics was read with no little interest. To meet the demand for such intelligence, Mr. Bennett arranged an overland express from New Orleans, and announced the fact on the 26th of December of that year. The arrangements went into operation in January, 1845. It was the first express of the kind ever run. It beat the great Southern mail from New Orleans to New York from one to four days. Obstructions of all sorts were thrown in the way of the success of this express by the Post-office authorities. It was arranged by the *Herald* and the New Orleans *Crescent City*, and run each way. So inimical became the government to this enterprise that Mr. O'Callaghan, one of the proprietors of the *Crescent City*, was arrested in Georgia by order of Postmaster General Wicliffe for a violation of Post-office laws! The Post-office authorities deemed the act of beating the time made by the mails an illegal one! Another attempt was made by the *Herald* in May to improve on its previous arrangements. When the war with Mexico broke out in the spring of 1846, these expresses became a necessity. Then, in connection with the *Baltimore Sun* and the *Philadelphia Ledger*, arrangements were made to run one every week, or every day, or on the receipt at New Orleans of important news from the seat of war. These arrangements lasted during the war. The *Herald* announced, on the 10th of April, 1847, that four expresses from different parts of the country had reached that office in the previous twenty-four hours. On the 11th of the same month it published the following paragraph:

THE CAPTURE OF VERA CRUZ AND THE CASTLE OF SAN JUAN D'ULUA.

Our special and extraordinary express, which we had arranged for some time past on the Southern line between Philadelphia and New Orleans, arrived at Philadelphia yesterday morning at 8 o'clock, when the news which it brought was transmitted to our office by telegraph.

The *Herald* of the 13th of April said that if its express from Mobile to Montgomery had not been run, the intelligence of the capture of Vera Cruz would not have been made public till Monday, whereas it was published on Saturday morning.

The *Journal of Commerce*, the *Sun*, and *Tribune* joined the *Herald* in this great enterprise, culminating in the receipt of the news of the operations in the vicinity of the Halls of the Montezumas. It was thus announced on the 21st of October, 1847 :

> Our readers will be pleased to see in this morning's *Herald* the long-looked-for intelligence from the city of Mexico. It reached New Orleans on the 13th inst., and was brought by the special overland express for the *New York Herald* and other papers. Owing to its importance, however, our special messenger was instructed to bring the intelligence to the government at Washington, and it will at once have general circulation throughout the country. This we thought due to the public.

These expresses were almost the last of their kind. The magnetic telegraph wires were being rapidly stretched over the country, and horses, and locomotives, and carrier pigeons were as rapidly going out of use. They are now only necessary to run to telegraph stations.

The discovery of gold in California immediately after the close of the war with Mexico gave an enormous impulse to newspapers and the country. The *Herald* had its share in this wonderful development. One of its correspondents was Thomas O. Larkin, who resided on the west coast of Mexico as navy agent and United States consul at Monterey. Early in 1848 he sent to the office of the *Herald* a small pinch of gold-dust, equal in quantity to a moderate pinch of snuff, with a statement that it was from freshly-discovered mines in California. This gold and this information came overland by the way of Mazatlan. All newspaper offices had been for a number of years more or less afflicted with wonderful discoveries of rich deposits of gold in Georgia, Virginia, and North Carolina ; so much so, indeed, that editors looked with suspicion upon all such description of intelligence. Although every confidence was placed in any statement that Mr. Larkin would make, the sample of gold from California was carefully laid on the table. After the lapse of weeks other letters came from Mr. L., confirming his first reports, with a little more enthusiasm thrown into his statements of the magnificent Dorado that had been found. Thereupon the modest pinch of gold was brought forward and again examined. It was the only specimen that had been received from California.

"Let us see," said Mr. Bennett, "if this be gold. If it be the pure article, and Mr. Larkin's statements prove correct, we are on the eve of one of the most extraordinary events of the age."

The pinch of dust was sent to an experienced assayer, with the following result :

REPORT OF AN ASSAY OF CALIFORNIA GOLD-DUST RECENTLY RECEIVED BY JAS. G. BENNETT FROM MR. T. O. LARKIN, U. STATES CONSUL AT MONTEREY.

NEW YORK, Dec. 8, 1848.

MR. BENNETT:

SIR,—I have assayed the portion of gold-dust, or metal, from California, which you sent me, and the result shows that it is fully equal to any found in our Southern gold mines.

I return you 10¾ grains out of the 12 which I have tested, the value of which is 45 cents. It is 21½ carats fine—within half a carat of the quality of English sovereigns or American eagles, and is almost ready to go to the Mint.

The finest gold metal we get is from Africa, which is 22½ to 23 carats fine. In Virginia we have mines where the quality of the gold is much inferior, some of it as low as 19 carats, and in Georgia the mines produce it nearly 22 carats fine.

The gold of California which I have now assayed is fully equal to that of any, and much superior to some produced from the mines in our Southern States.

Yours respectfully, JOHN WARWICK,
Smelter and Refiner, 17 John Street.

This analysis was published. The letters had previously appeared, and created a commotion in the community. There were no steamers then on the Atlantic or the Pacific to convey passengers to this veritable Dorado. Other means had to be adopted to get there. The first batch of gold-hunters were so eager to become millionaires that they chartered a bark, the John Benson, which left New York in December, 1848, for Chagres. After untold troubles and difficulties, these pioneers, about sixty in number, reached the mines and went to work. Among these energetic men was Jem Grant, the well-known *Herald* barber of Ann Street, who not only became an alderman in San Francisco, but a millionaire, without shaving any one in that state.

Libel suits were a feature of the *Herald*. As its editor grew rich these suits increased. They were, in many instances, frivolous cases, made out of police reports, and instituted by speculating lawyers, who carried them on for a share of the damages obtained. Mr. Bennett employed abundance of counsel, and fought these cases, in the general interest of the Press, as long as the law would permit. He did more, by this mode, in stopping these vexatious suits than by all the changes in the law of libel. There was one case, known as the Opera libel suit, that lasted for years, which must have cost $10,000 or $15,000, and became really a *cause célèbre*. The first verdict in this case was $10,000 in 1855. There were new trials, and the final verdict was $6000, which appeared to be the value of an adverse criticism.

The general policy of the *Herald* was based on these six points, which it has powerfully and persistently kept in view from its first issue:

First. The Constitution and prosperity of the United States under all circumstances.

Second. The growth and prosperity of the City of New York.

Third. To give all the news, freshly, fully, and faithfully, from all parts of the world.

Fourth. To comment clearly, freely, and independently on the events of the world as they daily developed themselves.

Fifth. To sustain every enterprise that would elevate the human race, and unite all the nations in commerce and civilization.

Sixth. To make the *Herald* a cosmopolitan journal *par excellence*.

On these cardinal virtues the *Herald* has become great with the greatness of the nation, and prosperous with the prosperity of the metropolis. It was and continues to be an excellent platform. All the energies of its editor were bent on subserving these points. His efforts were appreciated in advertisements, subscriptions, news, attentions, and influence in abundance. On the 1st of January, 1855, a large, mysterious-looking box was sent to the St. Nicholas Hotel for Mr. Bennett. He looked at it attentively for a few moments, and declined receiving it. That looks like another infernal machine on a large scale. He could not decipher the signature of the note accompanying the handsome box. But the hotel-keeper assured him that it was all right by bringing down one of the firm of Ball, Black & Co., from whose establishment it came. It was then opened, and found to contain a splendid service of silver plate, consisting of ten pieces, each with an appropriate inscription. This is the chief one:

PRESENTED
TO
JAMES GORDON BENNETT
AS A
TESTIMONIAL

To the Editor of the truly National Newspaper of the American Republic; the firm and unwavering Supporter of the Constitution; the Opponent of the Spoils System of Government; the ready and effective Advocate of the Rights of the People.

New York City, January, 1855.

On the milk pitcher—the inscription should have been engraved on the hot-water pitcher—were these words:

PRESENTED TO
JAMES GORDON BENNETT,
THE MOST ABUSED
EDITOR IN AMERICA.

The *Herald* has been accused of inconsistency in its editorial course—that it would contradict to-day what it said yesterday.

What is a daily newspaper but a reflex of the previous day? Is the world to-day what it was half a century ago? Is there not change every where? Look at the United States as they were on the 13th of April, 1861, and then as they were on the same day in 1865. *Au jour le jour*, the motto of Girardin, is it not a bad one for a newspaper? But the *Herald* itself, in 1868, gave the best answer to this silly charge :

> If we saw a party pursuing a course calculated to involve the country in civil war, we should oppose it with all our might ; but if war should come in spite of our efforts, and the integrity of the country were threatened, we should go with the very party we had opposed to save the life of the nation. And this, in fact, as is well known, has been our course. The Radical Press was consistent in forcing civil war and then carrying it out, and the Copperhead Press was consistent in opposing the interests of the republic after war commenced. Which was most consistent as regards the welfare of the country, they or we, under the circumstances? Every right-thinking person will say the *Herald* was consistent in the proper sense of the word, and the Party Press inconsistent.

It is impossible, in a work like this, to give all the important points of a leading newspaper like the *Herald*. Its treatment of local as well as national events were of consequence to the people, and many reforms were made and many abuses stopped by its influence, and the influence of other journals acting in common with it. On the election of General Pierce to the presidency in 1852, General Scott ascribed his defeat to three causes :

1st. The opposition of the *New York Herald*.

2d. The mutiny of Mr. Webster and his friends.

3d. The coldness of Mr. Fillmore and his friends.

The *Herald* killed the Taylor cabinet by its exposé of Crawford's Galphinism. It destroyed the American Art Union with a few articles and squibs. It has built up as well as pulled down. No good cause was without its support ; no bad cause without its denunciation.

The introduction of the telegraph was its great theme. Morse had no greater friend and supporter than the *Herald*. It felt that with the electric wire a new impulse would be given to the country and to the Press. It liberally used the wires from the first flash over them. It has spent hundreds of thousands of dollars in tolls. One of the probabilities of the future is that the *Herald*, as well as all others, will have all its news come by telegraph—that the mails will be as obsolete as stage-coaches. But the *Herald* has been beaten even by telegraph. The *Tribune*, in the early part of the Franco-German war, in its splendid descriptions of the battles of Gravelotte and Sedan, completely eclipsed its rival, and obtained great credit for its success and energy. This competition is the soul of enterprise. It makes such papers as the *Herald*, *Times*, *Sun*, *World*, and *Tribune* the great journals of the world. One defeat leads to a dozen victories, and the public gain by the spirited contest.

There are abundance of incidents connected with newspaper offices. The *Herald*, for instance, in 1850, published a letter from the English minister at Washington, of which the following is an extract:

SIR HENRY L. BULWER TO FREDERICK CHATFIELD.

WASHINGTON, Feb. 26th, 1850.

DEAR SIR,—I have received your communications up to the 3d of January inclusive. I was glad to hear of your arrangement with the Governor of Honduras, and I trust that you will thus have settled the question of claims before the order for evacuating Tigre Island arrives. * * * * * *
Neither do I think that this government has at the present moment the views you seem inclined to credit it for. *It is, however, a weak government*, and, being suspected by the popular party, is ever afraid of seeming in favor of any policy that is unpopular. Thus, though its intentions may be trusted, *its course can not be relied upon.* * * * * * *

I am again, dear sir, yours respectfully, H. L. B.

How was this letter obtained? How was it received? It was a grievous offense in diplomacy for a foreign minister to speak in this way of a friendly government, still Sir Henry did not receive his passports from General Taylor as Catacazy did from General Grant. But how did this letter fall into the columns of the *Herald?* A gentleman traveling from the interior of Honduras to Omoa, on his way to Havana, found by the road-side portions of a mail which had been examined and rifled by robbers. He gathered up some of the letters, among which was the above free and easy note. It was carried to Havana and shown to a number of Spanish merchants, and obtained by the correspondent of the *Herald* in that city. It created a sensation in diplomatic circles in Washington and London. Clayton was speechless for a day. What did Bulwer say? Soon after its publication that wily diplomat visited New York, and stopped at the Union Place Hotel. Editor Bennett boarded at the same popular house. Bulwer's rooms were next to Bennett's. When Bulwer ascertained this fact, he went to the proprietor of the hotel, and said, "My rooms, I find, adjoin those of Mr. Bennett, of the *Herald*. Now Bennett is a queer man; he lately, in some mysterious way, got hold of a letter of mine written to Central America. It may possibly happen that he will spirit away some of my instructions from my government, and I therefore wish to lock them up in your safe!" Bulwer, from his own experience in such matters in Madrid, had become suspicious, and this did not satisfy him. In a day or two he had these precious documents sent to the office of the British consul!

There is no one feature in journalism that has surprised the public more than the marvelous promptness with which elaborate biographical sketches of the distinguished dead are published. There need be no astonishment. All well-arranged newspaper offices have such matters carefully prepared. "In the midst of life we are in death." The "obituary" library of the *Herald* is quite full. When Burton, the comedian and manager, was on his death-bed in New York several years ago, a sketch of his life and career as an actor was prepared in that office, and was ready for publication. Indeed, it came near being prematurely published. In some way the fact became known to Burton. He sent a request to the editor that he might read his own obituary notice before he died, and if there were any mistakes in the statements he would correct them! The sketch was sent to him in proof, and he carefully read it, making one or two verbal corrections, and returned it to the editor with his thanks. He died a day or two after this singular occurrence, evidently satisfied with his record. It has happened several times that statesmen and other distinguished men have had the pleasure of reading very flattering notices of themselves by false reports of their deaths reaching newspaper offices late at night. Lord Brougham enjoyed this felicity, and he was charmed to find that he still lived, after so many splendid eulogiums had been passed upon his character.

There were constant improvements in the art of making newspapers in the *Herald* establishment. Mr. Bennett devoted his whole time and thought to journalism. He was a walking newspaper. After he started the *Herald* the success of his journal was the aim of his life. Early and late he attended to his business. No political office had any attraction for him: to increase his circulation; to improve and fill his advertising columns; to obtain the best correspondents; to get the news to his office before any of his contemporaries had it, were his ambition. To accomplish these points he would spare no expense.

The Rebellion of 1861–5 gave him his best opportunity to show what could be done in journalistic enterprise. Anticipating trouble at the South, he had dispatched half a dozen correspondents to the infected districts, and when the signal gun was fired at Fort Sumter, these correspondents were still at the South, and surrounded by excited crowds, ready to hang them on the first tree. The accounts of their narrow escapes were intensely graphic. With the organization of the first army the *Herald* corps of army and navy correspondents were organized. With every division marched a young representative of that establishment. At every fight one of its correspondents was an eye-witness. There was a *Herald* tent and a *Herald* wagon with each army corps. Other journals of New York, Cincinnati, Boston, Philadelphia, Chicago, Baltimore, St. Louis, were also extensively represented, but the *Herald* is taken as an illustration of the newspaper enterprise of the nation. Horses and servants were supplied to these correspondents. Their outfits were perfect. Occasionally a representative of the paper was made a prisoner. His wants were looked after while in the hands of the rebels. Of the details of a battle no efforts were spared to get the news to New York. Horses, steam, and electricity were freely used. No history of the war will be complete with the incidents connected with these war correspondents omitted. What did all this enterprise cost the *Herald* during the years 1861, '62, '63, '64, and '65? Half a million of dollars! Yet the investment was a splendidly remunerative one.

Newspapers passed through the lines of the several armies. No effort was spared on either side to obtain them. While nearly every one sought these papers to obtain a general idea of the state of public feeling then bubbling up in hate on either side, the soldier of tact and the journalist of experience studied them for the material resources of each in the pending conflict. While Banks proclaimed the necessity of calling out a quarter of a million of men at once to the field, and Sherman was declared insane because he asked for two hundred thousand men for the invasion of the South, most of the leading men of both sides sought to lessen the power and resources of each section, and felt sure of the superiority of his own government. Out of this doubt the newspaper was the guide.

With the breaking out of the war a Southern bureau or department was established in the office of the *Herald*. It was the duty of the chief of this bureau to collect and file away all information, of whatever character, that came from the South. Of the instructions issued to correspondents, the principal one was to obtain rebel newspapers. Neither trouble nor expense were to be spared in their acquisition. Contrabands and deserters, abandoned camps and villages, were searched for them. Many were obtained, and are now in the office library of that journal. The chief of this bureau compiled from these papers lists or rosters of the military forces of the Secessionists. Occasionally these, in an incomplete form, would be published, but finally a very full roster of the whole rebel army made its appearance in the *Herald*. When a copy of the paper, with this wonderful array of names and figures, reached Richmond, it created a veritable commotion in the War Office in that capital. Several of the clerks, accused of furnishing the information, were placed under arrest. On the evening of its appearance in New York, one of the *attachés* of the *Herald* rode in a Fourth Avenue car with Mr. Geo. M. Snow, of the *Tribune*, as a fellow-passenger.

"If any thing were wanting," said Snow to the aforesaid *attaché*, "to show the intimacy between the rebels in Richmond and the office of the *Herald* in New York, the list of the rebel army, as published this morning, is that thing."

"What do you mean?" asked the *Herald attaché*.

"What do I mean? That roster of the rebel army could only have been obtained from the rebel War Office. That is quite enough, I should think," replied Snow, with a touch of professional jealousy.

"Why, Snow, you don't mean to say that the *Herald* obtained that list direct from the War Department in Richmond? That information was wholly made up from advertisements and local news paragraphs of the Southern newspapers which were run through our lines."

"Nonsense," said Snow. "Don't you suppose that the *Tribune* and *Times* could have done the same thing?"

"Let us know," said the *Tribune* of the 9th of June, 1862, "from what source, and through what channels, the *Herald* has twice procured for publication the alleged muster-rolls of the rebel armies. Let us see by what means the *Herald* has been repeatedly supplied with rebel newspapers."

It is fair to suppose that the *Herald* did not tell the *Tribune* how these papers were obtained.

On one occasion a Union prisoner was released from Libby, where several *Herald* correspondents were confined. This soldier, on his arrival in New York, called at the *Herald*, cut off one of his hollow military buttons, and presented it to the editor. "You will find a letter in that," said he. On taking it apart, a letter was found, written on tissue paper, describing affairs in Richmond, which made three quarters of a column in the *Herald*. No one knew how that intelligence reached that office.

The course of the *Herald* through this stupendous struggle was a wise and patriotic one. It was appreciated by the people, by the executive, by the army, and by the navy. The following letter from Secretary Stanton to the editor of that journal indicated the value he placed upon the newspaper as one of the most available and influential means of putting the vital points of the war clearly before the masses:

WASHINGTON, May 2, 1862.

DEAR SIR,—I take the liberty to inclose to you some observations respecting the present state of things as they appear to me. The great question involved in the rebellion has always seemed to me in a great measure a commercial question, and the history of the Federal Union shows that the commercial interest was one of the strongest inducements to the formation of the government. We have experienced the misfortune of the dissolution of the Union in our *commercial* interests most sensibly (using that word in its most general sense), and have proved the wisdom of the framers of the Constitution by our loss in the destruction of their work—a wise and liberal system of domestic and foreign commerce. To the re-establishment of commercial relations I look, under Providence, for the restoration of the government, and that work I regard, in a great measure, accomplished by the opening of the ports occupied by our forces. Of course I consider the destruction of the enemy at Yorktown and Corinth as necessary conditions.

Holding these views, I think the public mind should be directed to this state of the question, and therefore venture to submit it to you.
Yours truly, EDWIN M. STANTON.

But this was only one of the many indications, pointing to the same view, of the importance of journals in the administration of the government.

The French mission! How much has been said of this political bauble! When Franklin Pierce was elected President, after a spirited campaign, in which the *Herald* accomplished so much with the people, it was asserted that Mr. Bennett was seeking the French mission as a reward for his services. We know what General Scott thought of this campaign. Here is General Pierce's opinion:

CONCORD, N. H., Nov. 30, 1852.

MY DEAR SIR,—Your obliging letter of October 25 should have been answered before.

Nothing could have been more kind and considerate, under the circumstances, than the letters both of Mr. Bennett and yourself.

It is quite unnecessary for me to say that I have not been insensible to the vast influence of the *Herald* throughout the late canvass. Will you assure Mr. B., when you write him, that I appreciate both the motive and the ability, and at the same time present to him my sincere acknowledgments?

I am, very respectfully, your friend and servant, FRANK. PIERCE.

This was Mr. Bennett's reward. He did not want even that. Well, when James Buchanan was elected, the same story was put in circulation. What did the new President confer on the *Herald?* Mr. Buchanan wrote a very complimentary letter to Mr. Bennett, and that was all. Not so much even as that was expected. Meanwhile the editor made one or two visits to Europe as minister plenipotentiary from that sovereign power, the *New York Herald.* When Abraham Lincoln was elected President for the second term, what did he do? What was his opinion of a leading journalist? He unreservedly offered this great prize—the French mission—to Mr. Bennett, and with what result? It was respectfully and positively declined. In his letter to the President the editor said his editorial mission was high enough and honorable enough for him; that he could do more good in the *Herald* than in France, and did not want office. Thus ended all the talk and gossip of the French mission.

After all these struggles and all these triumphs, full of years and full of honors, James Gordon Bennett, Sr., somewhere about the year 1866, inducted James Gordon Bennett, Jr., into the mysteries of journalism. Impulsive like his father, as energetic and as fearless, he assumed the management of the *Herald* with great vigor and skill. One of his first *coups* was the Prusso-Austrian war. The cable transmitted the whole of the King of Prussia's important speech after the battle of Sadowa and peace with Austria, costing in tolls $7000 in gold.

But one of his most wonderful achievements was in the Anglo-Abyssinian Expedition of 1868. He sent H. M. Stanley, a name now famous, as a special correspondent with General Napier on that memorable and victorious march, and was the means, through his agents, of not only giving the result of that important military movement to the *Herald* first of all, but of supplying the English government, the English Press, and the English people with the news in advance of their own dispatches. The *Times* and other papers in London handsomely acknowledged their indebtedness to the American journal for this news of the victory of their own army in the heart of Africa!

The London *Spectator* of the 7th of March, 1868, thus spoke of this enterprise:

If old John Walter were alive, what would he say? Here is the *Times*, which for half a century has beaten every journal in Europe in energy and enterprise, actually publishing the latest news of a British expedition per favor of a London correspondent of the *New York Herald*. According to a message received by that gentleman on Wednesday, and apparently ten days later than the latest official intelligence, General Napier reached Antalo on February 15, was to meet the "Prince" of Tigré on the 20th, and was then to press on to Magdala, fifteen marches off.

There is nothing in the history of journalism equal to this achievement.

The steam news yachts, splendid little water locomotives, were introduced in 1867. They overshadowed the news schooners of 1834 enormously. With these steamers the *Herald* has perfected its marine department. With them, too, the *Herald* has been of infinite service to the commercial community of New York. These steamers meet in-bound ships some distance at sea. They enable the *Herald* to boast of its enterprise. When the Grand Duke Alexis visited New York, that paper annoyed its contemporaries and made the imperial family of Russia happy with the announcement of his safe arrival, the steam yacht *Herald* having boarded the frigate Svetland at midnight several miles from Sandy Hook.

This is not all. The *Herald* has become a geographical explorer. In the universal interest felt for the safety of Dr. Livingstone, the African traveler, Mr. Bennett, the younger, organized, in 1870, an expedition, at his own cost, to proceed in search of that distinguished man, to "interview" him on the bank of some newly-discovered river in Africa, or perhaps at the "source of the Nile." The *Herald*, in December, 1871, published the first dispatches from Mr. Stanley, the chief of this expedition. But in the summer of 1872 it startled every one with the extraordinary announcement of the discovery of Livingstone alive at Ujiji. If the achievement in Abyssinia was a wonder in journalism, what should this exploit be called? The fact astonished the world, and journalists have every where awarded the meed of praise to the editor of that paper for his sagacity and marvelous enterprise. Not to stop here, the proprietor of the *Herald* fitted out another expedition, in December, 1871, to go up the Nile in search of Sir Samuel Baker. The chief correspondent of this expedition, ignorant of the viceroy's views, paid a visit to Nubar Pacha, minister of foreign affairs, and was very cordially received.

"I assured him," said the correspondent, "that I desired to visit the equatorial region, and deliver a firman from his excellency."

"*Soyez tranquille! soyez tranquille! je vous donnerai tous qu'il faut,*" continued his excellency. "You will find a rude country there. You go to explore?"

"I go as a correspondent of the *New York Herald*—not so much an explorer as a journalist—to ascertain Sir Samuel Baker's fate, and to look at the country with newspaper eyes."

"It is a rare spirit of progress," said the Talleyrand of the East, "which dominates your American Press. It is the go-ahead in your people. I tell you frankly that none but an American journalist would receive the support of the viceroy's government in going to the equatorial basin, and no American will receive greater assistance from his highness than a representative of the *New York Herald*. Americans have energy, and do not come here to harass the government; besides, they have no selfish interests."

What next?

The *New York Herald* is the history of journalism in the United States since 1835. There are now eighteen daily papers printed in the city of New York. With three exceptions, these have been established since 1833, and in the success of those now in existence how many failures have occurred in that city, and what vast sums of money have been lost in these efforts! Since that year one hundred and eleven daily papers have been started in the metropolis. Here is a list of their names:

THE CHEAP PRESS OF NEW YORK.
NAMES OF DAILY PAPERS ORIGINATING IN THE METROPOLIS SINCE 1833.

Morning Post - 1833	Democrat - 1836
Sun - 1833	New Era - 1836
Jeffersonian - 1834	Rough Hewer - 1836
Man - 1834	Daily Whig - 1837
Democratic Chronicle - 1834	Evening Chronicle - 1837
Transcript - 1834	New Times - 1837
Morning Star - 1834	Examiner - 1837
Daily Bee - 1834	Morning Chronicle - 1838
Herald - 1835	Daily Conservative - 1838
True Sun - 1835	Censor - 1838
Serpent - 1835	Daily News - 1838
The Light - 1835	New York Chronicle - 1838
Morning Star - 1836	Times and Commercial Intelligencer - 1838
Express - 1836	
Union - 1836	Corsair - 1839

Planet	1839	American Flag	1845
Evening Signal	1839	Independent Press	1445
Reformer	1839	The Irishman	1845
Evening Tattler	1839	Human Rights	1845
Morning Dispatch	1839	The Woman	1845
New Era	1839	Constitution	1845
Hudson's Express	1839	The Crisis	1845
New York Whig	1839	Humorist	1845
Evening Times	1840	Splinificator	1845
Democratic Press	1840	Citizen and True Sun	1845
True Sun	1841	Subterranean	1845
Tribune	1841	The Olio	1845
Aurora	1842	Irishman's Advocate	1845
Morning Chronicle and Penny-a-line Advertiser	1842	Workingman's Advocate	1845
		American Advocate	1845
Plebeian	1842	The Globe	1847
Morning Post	1842	Day-Book	1849
Washingtonian Daily News	1842	National Democrat	1850
Morning Star	1842	Daily Times	1851
Union	1842	True National Democrat	1852
Evening Herald	1842	The Citizen	1855
Native American Democrat	1842	Daily News	1855
True Sun	1843	State Register	1857
Arena	1843	The World	1859
Cynosure and Chronicle	1843	Evening Gazette	1866
American Republican	1843	Evening News	1867
Republic	1844	Evening Telegram	1867
Evening Mirror	1844	Democrat	1867
National Reform	1844	Evening Mail	1867
Morning News	1844	Star	1867
Democrat	1844	The City	1868
American Ensign	1844	Evening Republic	1869
Citizen and American Republican	1844	Evening Free Press	1869
People's Rights	1844	Standard	1870
Ladies' Morning Star	1844	Evening Commonwealth	1870
Penny Daily Gazette	1844	Evening Globe	1870
Evening Gazette	1845	Evening Leader	1871
Major Downing's Advocate	1845	Morning Ray	1871
The Mechanic	1845	Daily Witness	1871
Sachem	1845	Daily Register	1871
Advertiser	1845		

Two of these papers, the *True Sun* and the *New York Star*, were started by the operatives of the old *Sun*—the *True Sun* by the printers on a strike, and the *Star* by the *employés* of the *Sun*, when that paper was sold to Charles A. Dana. The *True Sun* did not remain long in existence, but the *Star*, it is said, has been quite successful as a local paper, and lately swallowed the *New York Democrat*.

It will be noticed that there are repetitions of names in the above list. The names represent new papers in almost all, if not in all cases. Some are given from memory, where the date is not fixed accurately enough to add to the name. Some of the dates published may not be strictly correct. These hundred papers, more or less, have come in competition with the survivors, and have shown some enterprise, have heaped a good deal of abuse on their more successful neighbors, and have spent a vast amount of money. It is not probable that the list, formidable as it is, embraces the names of all the papers started in the metropolis since 1833. It is doubtless true that of many of these journals not a copy is in existence.

What has become of the hundreds of editors and writers of these papers—Morris, Willis, Park Benjamin, Winchester, Mike Walsh, Snelling, Rufus Dawes, Carr, Burr, Rudd, Slocum, Locke, of the Moon Hoax, Snethen, West, Griswold, Hastings Weld, Nichols, Noah, Pomeroy, Duff Green, Wikoff, Price, Camp, Halpine, Ryan, Fitz James O'Brien, Arnold, Wilkins—where are they?

Several of these papers were absorbed in others, and in this way their names passed out of sight. The *Plebeian*, for instance, swallowed the *Union*, the *American Advocate*, the *Aurora*, the *Arena*, and one or two others. Is it astonishing, with the remains of so many papers, that the *Plebeian* long survived? Then the *Morning News* swallowed the *Plebeian!*

The *Evening Express*, early in May, 1871, in mentioning the failure of several of its contemporaries included in the above list, made the following remarks:

Three daily New York city newspapers, two evening and one morning, have died within a month, and more must be on their last legs. None of the dead journals had a long life, but they lived long enough to lose at least three or four handsome fortunes. Take away government and official patronage, and forty per cent. of all the journals of the country would die. It takes long years of labor and large investments in capital to establish or maintain a successful journal; but especially is this true of this city, where the expenditures are enormous, if a live newspaper is printed, with telegrams from Europe and at home. The *Express* is not among the oldest of the living city journals, but since it was established in 1836 it has seen the oldest die out, as the old *Mercantile Gazette* [*Advertiser?*], the old New York *Gazette*, the New York *Daily Advertiser*, the New York *Evening Star* of Mr. Noah, the New York *American* of Mr. King, the New York *Evening Mirror*, the New York *Courier and Enquirer*, the New York *Statesman*, etc., etc. These of the dead past, existing before the *Express* was established. Since then, in this city alone, over sixty daily papers have started and died, after losing at least twenty millions of dollars. There is no business more precarious than journalism, unless it is mercantile business, in which it has been proved that in a long course of years from ninety-three to ninety-five per cent. fail in business.

The *employés* of the *Herald* have two associations: one called the *New York Herald* Club, which is social and convivial in its character, and celebrates the anniversary of the establishment on the 6th of May by a grand banquet at the Astor, Metropolitan, or Delmonico's; the other is styled the Pension and Annuity Fund Association, charitable and benevolent in its organization, and accomplishes much good. This association was established in 1869, and to give it a start, Mr. Bennett presented $10,000 to the fund. Small weekly payments are made by the *employés*, and then in sickness they are cared for, and in death their wives and children are provided with sufficient means for support and education. It is a praiseworthy institution.

The Founder of the *Herald* died on the 1st of June, 1872, in the seventy-seventh year of his age. No journalist surpassed him in his profession. No journalist was more abused or more praised, during his public career, than he. But on his death the Newspaper Press every where paid him unusual but deserved honors. The New York Associated Press, which embraces the leading journals of the metropolis, thus spoke of him:

> *Resolved*, That his long and eventful connection with the Newspaper Press of the country in a career of unexampled success and prosperity was the result of his great foresight, energy, and industry; that in all these qualities the example of Mr. Bennett inspired the greatest enterprise in journalism in the United States and throughout the world, and must, therefore, for all time, leave their impressions for good in the diffusion of knowledge and the advancement of the Press.

The funeral of the late proprietor of the *Herald* was a large and impressive one. Courts were adjourned and flags displayed at half-mast. In no other instance was journalism so fully recognized as an important public institution as on this occasion. Among the pall-bearers were Horace Greeley, David M. Stone, Erastus Brooks, George W. Childs, Charles A. Dana, Robert Bonner, Major Bundy, George Jones, and Hugh Hastings.

The *Herald* is now owned by James Gordon Bennett, Jr. It is still a "one-man" power. It is therefore probable that, like the London *Times*, it will outlive all other papers in its usefulness and enterprise. It is a remarkable fact that none of the famous journals have survived more than one generation as leading papers. Their enterprise, and ability, and fame would pass away with their originators. Look at the instances recorded on these pages; and even the London *Times* begins to show signs of decline. But it is in its third generation. The *New York Herald* seems more vigorous than ever. It has just started on its second generation, full of brains, full of tact, and full of money. Has not its new conductor a splendid opportunity? Let us compare the *Herald* of to-day with the *Herald* of 1835. What a difference! Will not the *Herald* of 1909, compared with the *Herald* of 1872, show as marked a change? *Nous verrons.*

CHAPTER XXIX.
NEWSPAPERS IN NEW ORLEANS AND MOBILE.

THE INITIAL PAPERS OF THE CRESCENT CITY. — JOURNALISM IN FRENCH AND ENGLISH.—NEW ORLEANS BEE.—THE PICAYUNE.—GEORGE WILKINS KENDALL.— WAR CORRESPONDENCE FROM MEXICO.—DECLINE OF JOURNALISM IN NEW ORLEANS.— ITS CAUSE. — NEWSPAPER ARCHITECTURE.— THE FIRST PAPER IN MOBILE.—NEWSPAPERS IN THAT CITY.—JOHN FORSYTH.

NEW ORLEANS is a news centre. It has always been an important place for journalism. It is situated just above the Delta, at the mouth of the Mississippi, which, on the authority of Sir Charles Lyell, has taken one hundred thousand years to form. Nearly all the commerce of the Mississippi Valley, to the extent of millions, has made that city its principal *entrepôt*. Most of the news from Mexico came through that port. When Texas attracted the eyes of the world, our intelligence from the Lone Star Republic reached us by the way of New Orleans. It has ever been a converging southern centre of commerce, news, fashion, sport, and politics. There Jackson and Farragut immortalized themselves and their country.

The first paper published in that section appeared in 1803, and was called the *Moniteur*, when the great Southwest belonged to France. It was printed by Fontaine. The first paper issued there, after the purchase of the territory of Napoleon, was the *Louisiana Courier*, in 1806, when that quarter of the continent was almost as little known as California was in 1846, or as Alaska is at the present day, and the *Courier*, or a paper of that name, was printed in New Orleans in French and English as late as 1848. French was the language spoken there at that early period. English slowly crept in with the spread of the Anglo-Saxon race. Newspapers were at first printed entirely in French, but subsequently in French and English. Nothing is more slowly accomplished than changing the language of a people. All the laws were printed in French, and it was only after the cession of the territory to the United States that American ideas began to migrate there, take root, spread, and bear fruit in pure Anglo-Saxon. Newspapers appeared as the teachers.

The *New Orleans Bee*, established in 1826, and still living, has been printed in both languages till 1872. One half of the sheet bore the title as above, in English; the other half was printed under the head of *L'Abeille de la Nouvelle Orléans*. It is now printed exclusively in the French language. It is a large paper, and is conducted with spirit. In October, 1871, the *Bee*, then in its forty-fifth year, gave some interesting facts connected with the progress of journalism in the Crescent City, which are curious and full of philosophy. Notwithstanding the large aggregate increase of newspapers in the United States since 1847, the facts presented in New Orleans are to be seen in the statistics of the Press in other cities, even in the North, but only in the numbers of newspapers, and not in their circulation:

The marked decline of two great industrial interests in the United States—those of ship-building and gold-mining—afford the clearest evidence of the economic disorders that afflict the country, and in New Orleans we have another undeniable proof of the existence of those disorders in the decline of journalism.

In 1847 the following papers were published here daily: The *Tropic*, the *Jeffersonian*, the *Courier*, the *Bee*, the *Bulletin*, the *Picayune*, the *Delta*, the *Crescent*, and the *Evening Mercury*. Now there are published daily the *Bulletin*, the *Bee*, the *Picayune*, the *Republican*, and the *Times*. Thus, in 1847, there were nine daily papers printed in the city against five in 1871.

It might be supposed that the circulation of the five papers now published is greater than, or at least as great as, that of the nine published in 1847. Having been connected with the newspapers of 1847, with opportunities of knowing the issues of the journals then published, and with like opportunities at present, we feel warranted in saying that the circulation is certainly not greater than that of 1847, and it is very doubtful if it is so large.

With the growth of the city the demand for newspapers should have largely increased, instead of declining or remaining stationary. According to the United States census, the population of New Orleans in 1850 was 116,375. This only included the First, Second, and Third Districts. In 1852, the city of Lafayette, now Fourth District, was added, and Algiers and Jefferson City have been annexed since. The population of the two last-named suburbs in 1850 we have not the means of ascertaining, but that of Lafayette was 14,190. We think 135,000 is a full estimate of the inhabitants of the present area of the city at that time. And, referring to Lafayette, we are reminded that a daily paper, the name of which has escaped our memory, was also in existence there in 1847, which made the tenth daily printed at that time in the territory which is contained within the present limits of the city. The enumeration of inhabitants for 1870 is 191,000. No intelligent person, who has observed the growth of the city, regards that enumeration as correct. By such persons the number is believed to be nearer to 250,000 than it is to 200,000. But take it as the United States Marshal has returned it, at 191,000, and the increase of newspaper circulation should have been in the proportion of 135 to 191. But there are other reasons besides an increase of population for an increased newspaper circulation. By emancipation thousands of colored people, formerly living with their owners, have become independent householders, providing for their own wants and indulging their own tastes. Numbers of these colored people have acquired a knowledge of letters since the war began, and among the whites themselves the reading class has been greatly enlarged since 1847 by the establishment of public schools and free denominational schools. For these reasons, it is not too much to suppose that the reading capacity of the people between 1847 and 1870 doubled; yet, we repeat, there is no increase in the demand for journalism.

Why? In 1847, and for many years after, it was in the power of every sober and industrious head of a family—mechanic, clerk, drayman, and laborer, as well as the merchant, the capitalist, and the professional man, to pay for a daily paper. Now a whole neighborhood borrow a paper from the corner grocery. Publishers are compelled to charge twice as much as they did in 1847, and the people have scarcely half the ability to pay that they had then. Why? again, and the answer opens a wide survey for the reformer. It is because the masses, however industrious, economical, and sober they may be, can barely earn a subsistence. They can indulge in no luxuries, and the newspaper, once deemed a necessity to an American citizen, has become a luxury, which can only be enjoyed by the sufferance of the man from whom he buys his tea and sugar. After he pays interest upon public debts, and after paying the enormous tax of a universal credit system, which is the inevitable result of public debts and paper currency, and which swells the cost of government as well as the cost of goods, he has nothing left except a pittance to feed and clothe himself and his family. And journalism is not an exceptional sufferer. Every branch of legitimate business suffers by laws or systems that impoverish the masses.

While the fact exists of the Franco-American papers in Louisiana, it is worthy of note that at another extreme border of the United States newspapers have to be printed in these two languages to meet the wants of our citizens there. *L'Union Canadienne* is published in Vergennes, Vermont, because of the irruption of the French Canadians in that locality. Another paper is printed in Burlington, Vermont, called *L'Idée Nouvelle*, with its matter in French and English in alternate columns. It is an annexation paper. There are three journals of this sort now printed in the Green Mountain State. There is a paper, the *North Star*, the most northern newspaper printed in the United States, published at Caribou, Maine. Its office is near the French and Swedish settlements, and departments in both languages are introduced.

Newspapers in German, French, Spanish, Welsh, Italian, Cherokee, Danish, Croatian, Chinese, Dutch, and Swedish are published in the United States. There are not less than four hundred foreign newspapers issued in this country. Those in German are numerous, with large circulation. It is estimated that over sixty thousand copies of these German newspapers find their way to Germany and circulate there, gradually sowing the seed of more liberal ideas among the Germans at home. Some of the German authors have, in consequence of this cheap circulation, at their own firesides, of their productions republished by these American-German papers, protested against their introduction in the German states. If Bismarck was less of a Republican, he would take this protest as an excuse for stopping this circulation of republican ideas inside of the North German Confederation.

The *Picayune*, printed entirely in English, has long been a representative paper in the Crescent City. It was originally a cheap, independent paper there, like the Penny Press at the North, and began a new era in journalism at the Southwest. It sold for a picayune a copy. Hence its name.

In the midst of the first cholera year in New York in 1832, Mr. Joseph Elliott, for many years the superintendent of the mechanical and publishing department of the *Herald*, was passing up Broadway, and met Mr. George Wilkins Kendall hurrying down that thoroughfare.

"What's your hurry, George?" asked Elliott.

"Oh, Joe, is that you? I'm off for New Orleans. You will die of cholera if you remain here. Come with me."

The two compositors parted—Elliott to go into the *Sun* office, and afterwards, in 1837, into the *Herald* office, where he has since remained, and Kendall, with his note-book full of jokes, to arrive in New Orleans, where, also in 1837, in company with Lumsden, he started the *Picayune*. With Kendall's short, humorous paragraphs, and genial tone and pleasant manners, the paper at once became attractive and popular, and has continued to be so ever since that period.

The *Picayune* first appeared on the 25th of January, 1837. It needed a good manager, as the *Tribune* and many other papers did in their early struggles, and the *Picayune* found one in Colonel A. M. Holbrook, who took charge of the establishment in June, 1839, and has had control of the concern from that month and year to the present time. The names of Lumsden & Kendall, and Lumsden, Kendall & Co., have since passed out of sight, and that of A. M. Holbrook alone now stands at the head of the paper.

The *Picayune* has had a great many contributors. Among others, and in addition to Kendall, there were Colonel S. F. Wilson, previously of the *True Delta* of that city and of the *Mobile Register*, Matthew C. Field, brother of J. M. Field, of the *St. Louis Reveille*, and Judge Alexander C. Bullitt, who was once connected with the *New Orleans Bee*, and afterwards with the Washington *Republic*. It was Bullitt, while editor of the *Bee*, who found it necessary to fight a duel before breakfast one August morning in 1839 with editor Wagner, of the *Louisianian*, in which neither was hurt. These were all accomplished writers and journalists. They are now no more. Colonel Wilson, just before his death in 1869, took the hand of Colonel Holbrook in his, and said, "You are the last of us!"

Of all the editorial corps of the *Picayune*, Kendall was probably the most widely known in connection with that paper. He never lost a joke, or a bit of wit, or scrap of humor, or a ray of sunshine. He had a keen appreciation of these pleasant, healthy elements of life and happiness. If a bright thought was uttered in his presence, he would "take a note of it" and "turn down a leaf." If a spark of wit flitted across his vision, Kendall would rescue it from oblivion. If any humor was in circulation in any social circle where he happened to be, he would treasure it up for future use. He became a Treasury of Wit. If the god of Wit and Humor had been in New Orleans when Kendall lived there, he would have crowned him with the brightest and gayest of flowers.

Kendall gave great character to the *Picayune* with his accounts of the Santa Fé expedition and during the Mexican War. He took the field with our troops, and his letters descriptive of the battles in that republic were among the first of the kind in this country. They were excellent, and some of them very graphic. The enterprise was new to American journalism, and was indulged in at that time only by the *New York Herald*, and New Orleans *Picayune* and *Delta*. Kendall's letters, with their "plunging fire," were copied every where, and made the reputation of many a gallant officer and soldier, whose name and fame would have been smothered in the musty reports of the War Department. When peace came he conceived the idea of publishing his war correspondence in a book, and for this purpose he made two or three visits to Paris to have the illustrations properly executed. They were elegant specimens of battle scenes— Horace Vernets on paper. Kendall spent large sums of money in having them truthfully and artistically done.

The great military reputation which Jefferson Davis and Braxton Bragg enjoyed with the people came from the war correspondents of the *Picayune*, and *Herald*, and *Delta* in the Mexican War. The repulse of a tremendous charge of Mexicans at Buena Vista by the Mississippi Rifle Regiment, commanded by Colonel Davis, which he did by suddenly placing his regiment in the form of a V, brought his name prominently and favorably before the public. This piece of tactics on the field of battle was previously and successfully performed in India by Sir Colin Campbell. Who would have ever known Braxton Bragg beyond and above hundreds of other deserving and meritorious officers but for the phrase put into the mouth of General Taylor on the approach of a large mass of Mexicans near Bragg's Battery? "A little more grape, Captain Bragg," is as famous a command in military annals as "Up! guards, and at them," of Wellington at Waterloo, and neither ever appeared in official reports.

Kendall purchased an extensive plantation in Texas, and became a landed proprietor on a princely scale—a farmer, a planter, a cattle-fancier, a stock-raiser, not in small numbers, but in herds whose tramp across the fields would make Texas tremble. There he passed many of the later years of his life with the admiration of a Rosa Bonheur for his fine animals and splendid flocks. He died a few years ago, and the pleasant recollections of the man, and what he did for journalism in the Southwest, are all that remain for the public and for those who knew him in those days of sunshine.

One of the encouraging features of the Newspaper Press is its architecture. In every city in the Union some of the handsomest and most costly buildings are those erected by journalists for their business purposes. Of the first to put up such an edifice were the proprietors of the *Picayune*. In 1850 their old establishment was destroyed by fire. In the same year they had a new, four-story granite building erected, a description of which occupied two columns of the paper. They were proud of it, just as the *Sun, Times, Herald, Ledger, Post, Advertiser, Journal, Transcript*, are proud of their still grander edifices erected twenty years later in several Northern cities.

Several excellent newspapers have been published in Mobile. It is not a very large city in population. The last census gives her thirty-two thousand inhabitants. This number will not afford a very liberal support to many papers, but three or four daily newspapers have been published there at the same time. Mobile is an important market for the transhipment of cotton, and this fact aids the Press there. The first paper appeared shortly after the evacuation of the place by the Spaniards, about 1814. We are ignorant of its name. There was a paper called the *Gazette* issued in that city in July, 1817.

The *Register* is now the oldest paper. It was established in December, 1821. It has lately been published by W. D. Mann, and edited by John Forsyth. The latter started a penny paper in Mobile, on the cash system, in January, 1842, the first of that class in that city. It was named the *Ledger*, and was selected to publish the laws of the United States in March of the same year. Forsyth afterwards, in 1850, edited the *Columbus* (Georgia) *Times*. There were two old-class papers published there then, the *Register*, Democratic, by Sanford & Wilson, and the *Advertiser*, Whig, by C. C. Langdon, once mayor of the city. The *Register* has lately been published every morning except Monday, and every evening except Sunday. Early in 1872 the establishment was modernized, and is now published by an association.

The father of the present chief editor, John Forsyth, Sr., of Georgia, was once minister to Spain. After his return from Madrid he was made Secretary of State in 1834, in the cabinet of General Jackson. The editor, John Forsyth, Jr., was one of the Peace Commissioners sent to Washington on the eve of the late rebellion.

The *Advertiser*, mentioned above, was established in 1833. It issued, in November, 1852, an afternoon edition, called the *Evening News*. Another paper, named the *Tribune*, was founded in 1842, and still another, a State Rights organ, with the title of *Mercury* flying at its head, was established on the 12th of August, 1857. There was a penny paper, the *Transcript*, published for a time.

CHAPTER XXX.
FEMALE JOURNALISTS.

THE LADIES' MAGAZINE.—THE LOWELL OFFERING.—EARLY FEMALE PERIODICAL WRITERS.—SARAH JOSEPHA HALE.—THE WOMAN'S RIGHTS MOVEMENT.—THE REVOLUTION.—THE SOROSIS.—WOMAN'S JOURNAL.—WOODHULL & CLAFLIN'S WEEKLY.—THE TRUE WOMAN.—FREE LOVE.—FEMALE SUFFRAGE.—THE TROUBLES OF THE REFORMERS.

THE first daily newspaper printed in the English language was published by a woman. Elizabeth Mallet began the publication of the *Daily Courant* in London in March, 1702, and it was issued to "spare the public at least half the impertinences which the ordinary papers contain." But the *Courant* was not intended as a woman's paper.

Mrs. Sarah Josepha Hale was probably the first to establish a magazine in this country wholly devoted to the tastes and interests of women. It was not a newspaper in any sense. It was a magazine. It can scarcely, therefore, come within the scope of a compilation like this. But, as Mrs. Hale was the first of female periodical writers, it is fair to begin with her enterprise. In 1827, in connection with a Boston publisher, she established the *Ladies' Magazine* in that city. It was afterwards united with *Godey's Lady's Book* of Philadelphia, of which Mrs. Hale became the editor, and is still the editor in 1872, although in her 85th year, 45 of which have been devoted to that periodical. Mrs. Hale has, therefore, long been before the public. She wrote Northwood, Woman's Record, and Household Receipt-books. The publication of the *Ladies' Magazine* led to others, such as the *Ladies' Companion*, issued in New York by W. W. Snowden, *Graham's Magazine*, in Philadelphia, by C. R. Graham, the *Artist*, *Peterson's Magazine*, the *Gem*, the *Passion Flower*, by the accomplished daughters of Captain Samuel G. Reid, and numerous others. These were illustrated with steel and colored engravings and fashion plates, some of which were very creditably executed. This art, indeed, received its first important impulse in America from these publications. Since then, however, our national banking institutions and the national government have given it an impulse beyond all others in furnishing choice historical engravings, some of the finest specimens the world has ever seen, for millions of greenbacks and National Bank bills. But the first impulse and encouragement came from these magazines.

The *Lowell Offering*, originating with the factory girls of Lowell in 1840, was another development of female writers in the United States in periodical literature. It was filled with the productions of factory girls or "female operatives" exclusively. This was before the foreign element crowded the native talent out of the mills at Lowell and elsewhere. Madame Demorest's *Magazine*, on the plan of *le Mode*, *le Follet*, and the *Bazar*, was established several years ago in New York, and is almost entirely absorbed with the fashions for ladies at home and abroad, with handsome colored plates and engravings. But, as we have said, these were not strictly newspapers: some gave the latest news of the fashions; they were, however, literary and fashionable publications of the light, gossamer order; they led ultimately, however, to newspapers and periodicals more devoted to the wants, desires, interests, dreams, eccentricities, and æsthetics generally of women here and around the world.

The more modern class of publications for women are above fashion, above the small-talk of the ballroom, or the gossip and envy of the reception-rooms of the *modistes*. Some of these papers are edited by strong-minded women, seeking a higher sphere for female labor, and the right of women to vote, to buy and sell stocks in Wall Street, to fulminate from the pulpit, to visit sick-rooms as physicians as well as nurses, to a right to surrender their seats in railway cars to tired old gentlemen, to labor on farms, in digging canals, in grading railroad beds, in running locomotives, to serve in the army and navy, in Congress, on school committees, to run with the fire-engines, to be newspaper carriers, governors of states, policemen, diplomats, hod-carriers, ward politicians, and drivers of garbage-carts. There is now the *Woman's Journal* and the *Revolution* to urge these social changes on the world. They have taken the place of the old lecturers, and talk to the millions. They are active and persistent workers, full of poetry and poverty, boldness and beauty, independence and impudence, pouts and persuasiveness, in pushing their plan of reform before the monster public.

Women, under peculiar circumstances, have managed newspapers long before our day. Mrs. Franklin, for instance, carried on the *Newport Mercury* for a while in the middle of the last century, and Mrs. Holt managed the *New York Gazette* some time after the death of her husband. When Lynde M. Walter, of the *Boston Transcript*, departed this life in 1842, his sister, Miss Cornelia M. Walter, supplied his place as editor of that paper. Mrs. M. Elizabeth Green has managed the *Quincy* (Mass.) *Patriot* since the death of her husband. Miss Piney W. Forsythe succeeded her father as proprietor and editor of the *Liberty* (Miss.) *Advocate* in 1868. She is assisted by two sisters who were brought up as practical printers. She lately declined to attend a convention of Mississippi editors for fear her male contemporaries would stare at her. Mrs. Jane G. Swishelm, of Pittsburg, Pennsylvania, one of the oldest of female journalists, is still attached to a newspaper in that smoky place, and has made no little noise in the world; and is not Fanny Wright known to fame as a political newspaper writer and lecturer in New York, with the Tammany Hall leaders of 1829–'30–'31? Who has forgotten Mrs. Bloomer? Over the world, wherever short petticoats were worn by one sex and admired by the other, her name is enshrined; and that agreeable and affable Polish woman, Madame Ernestine Rose, became well known several years ago as a spirited contributor to the Press.

There are now quite a number of female managers and publishers of newspapers in the United States. They do not push themselves forward or make themselves very conspicuous in their profession. They are not propagandists; they are simply getting a living, and making what money they can without ostentation. Iowa has three lady editors: Mrs. Mary L. Morey, of the Jefferson *Era*, Mrs. Mary Hartshorn, of the Corydon *Monitor*, and Mrs. Mary Reed, of the Wright County *Register*. But, apart from these, the modern female journalists are smart and demonstrative. They start for the amelioration of woman. All else must subserve that point. Woman is a wretched slave, with nothing to wear. The *Revolution* was established for her emancipation, and edited, for some time, by Susan B. Anthony. In May, 1870, she disposed of her interest to Laura C. Bullard, of Brooklyn, who then became its editor. The paper is owned in shares. Theodore Tilton, of the *Golden Age*, it is said, is one of the shareholders. The *Revolution* has been the leading organ of the Sorosis, or Woman's Rights Party, from its inception. Some idea of the scope of its principles and doctrines may be gathered from the following neatly-worded extract from that paper:

> Multitudes of our noblest girls are perishing for something to do. The hope of marriage, all we offer girls, is not enough to feed an immortal mind; and if that goal is never reached, what then? The more fire and genius a girl has, with no outlets for her powers, the more complete is her misery when all these forces are turned back upon herself. The pent-up fires, that might have glowed with living words of eloquence in courts of justice, in the pulpit, or on the stage, are to-day consuming their victims in idiot and insane asylums, in domestic discontent and disgust, in peevish wailings about, in the vain pursuit of pleasure and fashion, longing for that peace that is found only in action.

Another paper was issued in New York in 1869 by the female bankers and brokers of Broad Street. It is called *Woodhull & Claflin's Weekly*. It was a sixteen-page paper, and dealt in finance and fashion, stock-jobbing and strong-minded women, sporting and sorosis, politics and president-making, supporting a woman even for the executive mansion. This periodical is edited by Victoria C.

Woodhull and Tennie C. Claflin, two sisters who seem capable of accomplishing what they undertake. "Upward and Onward" is the motto of these editors in crinoline. Their course and comments on men and corporations are particularly peculiarly bold.

All that glitters is not any better gold with the female than with the male journalists and reformers of this prosperous country. There are heart-burnings and troubles even among those who are thus seeking the amelioration of their sex and race. It is probable, however, that rascal man is at the bottom of an occasional unpleasantness with these reformers. Indeed, the *New York Sun*, a paper constantly and actively engaged in social excavations, in ventilating one of these troubles in 1869, published the following paragraph:

> It was stated in the *Revolution* not long ago, that after a formal invitation had been extended to Mrs. Elizabeth Cady Stanton to attend the recent Woman's Rights Convention in Boston, the invitation was as formally withdrawn. This excited surprise with the public, who regard Mrs. Stanton as the most conspicuous lady identified with the so-called women's cause. We are informed that the reason for this withdrawal was the following rather amusing state of facts:
>
> Mrs. Stanton, through the columns of the *Revolution*, has taken occasion now and then to point her sharp pen at Mr. Wendell Phillips's inconsistency in confining his advocacy of universal suffrage exclusively to masculine negroes, seemingly overlooking the claims of white women to a place on his broad platform. Taking umbrage at this, Mr. Phillips declared that he would not attend the Boston Convention if Mrs. Stanton did. So the committee recalled their invitation to her. Just at this juncture came another hitch in the proceedings. Strange to say, a feud has for some time existed between Mr. Phillips and Mr. William Lloyd Garrison; and Garrison declared that he would not attend the Convention if Phillips did. The upshot of this phase of the affair was, that Phillips fell to the rear and Garrison came to the front, and, in company with Senator Wilson, played a leading part in the assemblage.
>
> We hope there is some mistake about this. If there is not, we would say to these eminent reformers, in the language of a distinguished public character, "Let us have peace."

Still later, in May, 1871, there was more discord among these organs in developing their peculiar views. Stephen Pearl Andrews, in *Woodhull & Claflin's Weekly*, which is the organ of the free lovers, made the annexed statement:

> The Steinway Hall Convention—the Boston wing of the movement—felt called upon to hedge against the imputation of meaning just what many of the women sitting, then and there, on the platform, do really mean and intend, and what the logic of the whole movement really means, and resolved against free love, confessing surely, negatively, that that is now the issue, since the suffrage question is disposed of. The Apollo Hall Convention—the more enterprising and progressive, the more logical and consistent wing of the movement—planted itself, on the contrary, boldly and unhesitatingly upon the ground of absolute emancipation—"the right of private judgment in matters of conscience" ultimated in morals. The resolutions offered by Mrs. Paulina Wright Davis, the President of the meeting, cover the whole ground, go the whole length, and are as conclusive on the subject as a demonstration of Euclid. They will bear continued study as an epitomized ethical code, and will shine brighter and brighter the more they are rubbed.
>
> * * * * * * * * *
>
> This large and enthusiastic woman's meeting has, then, put the movement on a new basis. It has propounded three new, and startling, and pregnant propositions:

First: That it is no longer the suffrage question, but the social question entire, and the complete social enfranchisement of the sexes, which are to be discussed and vindicated on this platform.

Second: That a new government, adapted to the wants of the whole world, but continuing for the present in America, has to be inaugurated, and may be requisite at a very early day, to complete the political revolution in behalf of woman's rights.

Third: That from now, henceforth, the inquisitorial impertinence of an investigation in the personal characters of women who are able and willing to co-operate in the movement, an investigation to which men are not called upon to submit, shall be completely and definitely set aside and ended.

T. W. Higginson, in the *Woman's Journal*, the organ of woman's suffrage, spoke on that subject in the following manner:

Our strength thus far has been in the weak logic of our opponents. But men do not adopt a change merely because there is nothing to be said against it; there must be good reasons for it. Those reasons will be mainly determined, at last, by the instincts and preferences of sensible and high-minded women. It is useless to overlook the fact that the overwhelming majority, even of such women, are still indifferent or opposed. It is harder to reach them than to reach men, but they must be reached. There is no other way to make substantial progress. Mere denunciation, and ridicule, and childish threats will never do it. I have no doubt that a time will come when women will vote, equally with men, in all the states of this Union. But it is certain that it will not be done in 60 days, and I should be glad to have some guarantee that it will be done in sixty years. Facts are abundant, so are arguments; the want is of something less easy to supply. Reason as we may, the community will predict the results of our agitation from its tone; and every thing that lowers the tone will perceptibly postpone the results.

Messrs. Andrews and Higginson, it thus appears, are the male *attachés* to this great movement of the female revolutionary party. Other men are interested in its progress. The active spirits in the contemplated reform in our social system begin to suspect some of their male co-operators, and seem to think that the politicians are endeavoring to use the women in the accomplishment of some of their schemes. Man is a selfish being. The *Revolution* is very emphatic on this point. There is evidently danger of a counter revolution—the Communists in crinoline against the Versaillists. This is the latest manifesto of the *Revolution:*

In spite of resolutions recently passed at Apollo Hall, we are convinced that the mass of the good, earnest women of the country will only allow themselves to rank as followers of those who, by purity of life, nobility of purpose, and elevation of character, have won their right to wield the sceptre of an exalted and conspicuous station. Our reform has heretofore been led by noble captains, who gravitated to the positions they held through force of intellect and moral worth. A nobler band of women never trod the earth, and it is in vain now to ask those who have been educated in the school of the past to swear allegiance to a different order of leaders in the present. They have pinned their faith to women who have every requisite to enable them to speak with authority, and without fuss, noise, or tumult, they will, we believe, quietly refuse to lower their standard of leadership or muddle their ideas of right.

The true growth of this reform must be in the hearts and minds of good and honest people. We can not afford to sacrifice one iota of integrity. The eternal law of justice is the eternal law of rectitude. No matter how often the ark of our faith is carried into the wilderness, we believe it will always return to the one straight path. The devout workers, in a religious spirit, look to this reform for the regeneration of society; they believe the moral forces women will bring into politics are urgently needed. Moral reform lies at the root of political reform. The ballot is only a means to an end. Political and social purity, liberty and order, protection and safety for all classes, work and wages, mental and material benefits, march hand in hand. The ballot for women is not the enemy, but the ally, of morality—Christian morality. We owe it to ourselves as women to adopt different and better methods of political action than those made odious by male tricksters. The world is waiting for an example of the moral power of the sex exerted on public affairs, and we feel assured it will not wait in vain.

The imprint of the *Woman's Journal* in 1871 is as follows:

THE WOMAN'S JOURNAL,
— AND —
THE WOMAN'S ADVOCATE.
CONSOLIDATED AUGUST 13, 1870.

A Weekly Newspaper, published every Saturday, in BOSTON and CHICAGO, devoted to the interests of Woman, to her educational, industrial, legal, and political Equality, and especially to her right of Suffrage.

MARY A. LIVERMORE, EDITOR.
JULIA WARD HOWE, LUCY STONE, HENRY B. BLACKWELL, and T. W. HIGGINSON, *Associate Editors*.

These editors, happily, do not appear desirous of hiding their light or their faces under a bushel. They have their reception days. On the 26th of August, 1871, they published this announcement:

CALL AND SEE US!

The editors of the *Woman's Journal* are at home to callers on Mondays, from 10 A.M. till 2 P.M. At that time, some, if not all the editors, will be in the office of the *Journal*, 3 Tremont Place, to receive whoever may call. Come and see us!

Inducements to subscribers for the *Journal* are, with one exception, of chromos and engravings of women—and why not?

SPECIAL PREMIUMS.

For ONE new subscriber, we will give Prang's beautiful chromo, "Grace Darling, or the Rescue," price $2 50.
For TWO new subscribers, we will give Prang's steel engraving, "Our Woman Warriors," worth $5 00.

The *Journal* is a handsomely printed folio of eight pages. Its reading matter is mostly of woman's movements. Among its advertisements we notice those of "Mercy B. Jackson, M.D.," "Woman's Medical College of Pennsylvania," "Emily Ruggles & Co., Real Estate Brokers," "Sarah A. Colby, M.D.," "The St. Louis Ladies' Magazine," by Margaret L. Johnson, "Woman's Medical College of the New York Infirmary," of which Dr. Emily Blackwell is the Secretary, "E. G. Stevens & Daughter, Conveyancers," and "Thrift School for Girls." So in the last century did women indulge in trade and professions. The Newport (R. I.) *Mercury* of 1758 contained an advertisement of Mary Tate offering "all sorts of blacksmith tools" for sale, and "Sarah Osborn, Schoolmistress in Newport," was ready to receive pupils, as women have always been before and since. Abigail Davidson announced in the *Boston Gazette* of March 12, 1770, that she had just "imported in Captain Paddock, from London," all kinds of vegetable and flower-seeds, trees, and berry bushes, which she would sell "at the very lowest Prices, by Wholesale or Retail, for Cash."

This new class of publications forms a part of the general system of newspapers. The contents of the *Woman's Journal* and the *Revolution* embrace the news and the details of the extraordinary social movement that now absorbs the attention of many women. The establishment of these organs recognizes the necessity of the Press in all social upheavals and revolutions. Whatever may be the accomplishments of woman in the sublime art of talking, it is manifest that they think the pen and Press important and essential auxiliaries to the tongue. Once the tongue was mightier than the sword. But the female propagandists meet with distinguished and able opponents among their own sex. There is a paper published in Baltimore, called the *True Woman*, which opposes the notions, and actions, and doctrines advocated by such prints as the *Revolution*, and its supporters petition Congress not to be deceived by the fascinations and blandishments of the Sorosis. The *True Woman* is edited by Mrs. Charlotte E. M'Kay, and the principles governing her policy are to make woman more womanly, to elevate her, and make her, in every way, good and noble.

Our large cities are now the centres of numerous female writers and reporters. They are attached to the Newspaper Press, and several of them to the editors. They consider themselves journalists in every sense of the word, as the following invitation, headed with the monogram N. Y. P. C., clearly indicates:

NEW YORK, November 12th, 1869.
A number of ladies and gentlemen of the Press will dine at Delmonico's on Saturday, November 27th, at 5 P.M. You are invited to participate. Tickets, not transferable, may be obtained on application, inclosing three dollars, to Mr. S. S. Packard, 937 Broadway. Any one procuring a ticket may purchase another for a friend. One hundred and ninety-six tickets only will be sold, and in the order in which they are paid for. Whether able to attend or not, please send in a sentiment.

OLIVER JOHNSON.	ALICE CARY.
MARY L. BOOTH.	S. S. PACKARD.
J. W. SIMONTON.	JEANNIE C. CROLY.
JNO. RUSSELL YOUNG.	THOS. W. KNOX.
AMOS J. CUMMINGS.	MARY CLEMMER AMES.
MARY KYLE DALLAS.	WHITELAW REID.
JAMES PARTON.	LUCIA G. CALHOUN.
SHIRLEY DACE.	FREDERICK CREIGHTON.
CHAS. E. WILBOUR.	

These and many others are theatrical and musical critics, fashion reporters, book reviewers, Washington correspondents, interviewers, and writers of social sketches and on social subjects. Some report yacht races. Some are attendants at Jerome Park Course. They form quite a *coterie* in New York City. They are bright, influential, many of them beautiful, talented, experienced, and useful. Some of them are Bohemians in crinoline. They can frequently do what men can not accomplish. These female journalists, pure and bright, are the growth of the last fifteen years in America. They are now to be seen every where—in every large city where influential papers are printed.

CHAPTER XXXI.
THE CHEAP PRESS IN PHILADELPHIA AND BALTIMORE.

THE PUBLIC LEDGER OF PHILADELPHIA.—THE SUN OF BALTIMORE.—SWAIN, ABELL, AND SIMMONS.—THEIR WONDERFUL SUCCESS.—THE WAY GEORGE W. CHILDS PURCHASED THE LEDGER.—HIS MANAGEMENT OF THE PAPER.—"THE PEN IS MIGHTIER THAN THE SWORD."—THE LEDGER ALMANAC.

ALL great enterprises are originally problems. It is a curious study to ascertain how they commence; how large concerns are initiated; how vast schemes and establishments grow from the acorn planted and watered by energetic men. It is not always that the wonderful success of an enterprise is apparent in the infancy of the scheme. It is so largely controlled and governed by circumstances that its final success is as often a marvel to its originators as to the public. When Commodore Vanderbilt, then a smart young Staten Islander and Whitehall boatman, rowed the celebrated William Gibbons from Staten Island to New York in a gale of wind, he had not then dreamed of owning entire railroads, of presenting steam frigates to his country, and having a bronze statue, costing half a million of dollars, and illustrating the material progress of the nation, erected in the most conspicuous part of the metropolis to his honor. When Alexander T. Stewart first opened a small store on Broadway, with a stock of lace insertings and scallop trimmings worth about $5000, he did not imagine that he was to be the Dry Goods King of America, a Secretary of the Treasury of the United States, or a giver of millions in charity to his fellow-men and women. When Alvin Adams accidentally and unavoidably met an old friend in Brattle Street, Boston, and arranged with him to start a small parcel express on the Worcester Railroad in 1838 or '39, he had not the slightest idea of the magnitude, the value, and the importance that the express business of the United States would reach in a quarter of a century from that time. When Samuel F. B. Morse, in 1844, offered to sell his whole right and title in the Magnetic Telegraph to the United States for the sum of $100,000, no one then conceived that the wires stretched over the United States alone in thirty years thereafter would represent a capital of $50,000,000, and that the whole world would be connected by submarine cables. So with William M. Swain in starting the *Public Ledger* of Philadelphia. When he received $12 per week as foreman of the printing department of the *New York Sun,* he never dreamed of owning a penny newspaper of his own that would enable him to leave, in less than the span of a generation, over $3,000,000 on the pages of his ledger to his family when he departed from this world. But such instances, it appears, are common in this country. Within a quarter of a century, one could easily count the millionaires on their fingers, and now we find them too numerous to notice. Nearly all the large concerns of the last thirty or forty years were originally based on bread and butter, with occasionally the extra luxury of a cigar. Almost all of our vast enterprises have grown up, not on any original expectation of such enormous results as they now exhibit, but in the marvelous and coincident development of the country in gold, cotton, grain, manufactures, oils, coal, printing, brains, silver, railroads, photography, emigration, science, steam, electricity, wool, iron, and copper, combining to bring out the astonishing capacity of our people in emergencies and in their remarkable adaptation to circumstances, no matter how complicated, in the management of extensive business schemes and projects ; and in these national strides the progress and expansion of the newspaper keeps *pari passu* with the most advanced industry and enterprise.

When the Penny Press was established in New York in 1833 and '34, there were three printers, named W. M. Swain, A. S. Abell, and Azariah H. Simmons, who did not believe much in cheap papers, but who worked as compositors in the offices where they were published, and were satisfied with their board and clothes for the work they performed at the case. When the *Sun* was started in New York in 1832, Swain could not be persuaded to join in the enterprise. Solemn and solid in the utterances of his views, as he was considered to be by his associates, he nearly discouraged Mr. Day from issuing the first number of that paper. But when the concern passed into the hands of Moses Y. Beach, he became the foreman of the composition room at $12 per week. Overtasking himself, he was confined to his house with sickness for several weeks. On returning to his duty, a difficulty occurred in regard to his pay while absent, and he resigned his situation in disgust. It was then that he began to have faith in the Cheap Press, and to think of starting a penny paper of his own. He considered New York fully supplied with the article in the *Sun, Transcript,* and *Herald.* There was no chance in the metropolis for him. Having won Abell and Simmons over to his convictions, this trio of typos proceeded to Philadelphia, and afterwards to Baltimore, and established the *Public Ledger* in the former, and the *Sun* in the latter city. But we have now to speak of the *Ledger.* Its first number was issued on the 25th of March, 1836. Each page was nine by thirteen and a half inches in size. Its type were set up by these three compositors; its editorials were written by Russell Jarvis, who had received his journalistic education under Duff Green, of the *United States Telegraph*.

The *Ledger* was not the first penny paper issued in Philadelphia. The *Daily Transcript* had made its appearance a few days earlier, in March, 1836. The *Cent*, too, had been issued, for a brief time, in 1830. The *Transcript* was edited by Frederick West, an amiable young English poet, who afterwards became a reporter and writer on the *New York Herald*, and then an editor of the *Sunday Atlas*. Shortly after the establishment of the *Ledger* it united with the *Transcript*, and the name was changed to that of *Public Ledger and Daily Transcript*. All of the cheap papers were made up and arranged on the plan of the originals in New York. Journalism in the metropolis, then as now, was the pattern for the country. In the first editorial article in the *Ledger* in 1836, this was manifested in this way:

> In the cities of New York and Brooklyn, containing a population of 300,000, the daily circulation of the penny papers is not less than seventy thousand. This is nearly sufficient to place a newspaper in the hands of every man in the two cities, and even of every boy old enough to read. These papers are to be found in every street, lane, and alley; in every hotel, tavern, counting-house, shop, etc. Almost every porter and drayman, while not engaged in his occupation, may be seen with a penny paper in his hands.

This is as true in 1872 as in 1836, but in a more enlarged sense and in a greater degree. Indeed, this class of papers, now grown to be a mighty power in the land, have created readers, educated the masses in the politics and resources of the country, and made almost every man a reader, a thinker, a politician, and a statesman. The Declaration of Independence had previously made them sovereigns. The *Ledger*, like all newspapers, and especially those of that time, was compelled to struggle for its existence in its early days. It resorted to sensations. It abused the old United States Bank in the warm days of the "Bank War." It came out for abolition, and its office was twice mobbed. It had that chronic distemper of journalism—libel suits. Indeed, it went through all the vicissitudes of a finally successful newspaper. Its circulation run up and down with the exciting events of the day. In 1844, during the frightful riots in Philadelphia growing out of the Native American excitement, the *Ledger*, in condemning the violence and excesses of the mob, run against popular sentiment, and came near being annihilated. The *Sun*, edited by Lewis C. Levin, one of the leaders of the Native American movement, and afterwards elected to Congress by that party, was a vigorous supporter of the principles of the new political organization, and the *Spirit of the Times*, edited by John S. Du Solle, now a journalist in New York, was as vigorous in opposition. The result was, that between the fulminations of these two sheets the *Ledger* was near coming to the ground. But these papers lacked the judgment necessary in the management of a journal when such a tremendous excitement has subsided. Without the excitement, the *Sun* and *Spirit of the Times* were nothing. Swain succeeded in carefully carrying the *Ledger* over the precipice, while his contemporaries, for want of their natural food, lost the thousands of readers that they had taken from the *Ledger*. This was the crisis in the fate of that paper. It now became an established institution.

There was one curious feature in the management of the *Ledger*. Its chief editor lived in New York. He was often met in the streets of that city. He was a short, dark-complexioned man, with quick movements and a pugnacious mind. He would write editorials as they built ships in Maine, by the yard or mile, and cut them off at any length to suit the latest order. How could this editor manage his editorial articles for a daily paper in Philadelphia when he resided in New York? It was a problem, but he seemed to have worked it out, for he accomplished this wonderful task for upwards of fifteen years, to the satisfaction, we are sure, of the proprietors of the *Ledger*. But it appears that the paper was a purely business concern for some time. Swain, who was the master-spirit of the establishment, made the paper a people's paper, yet he never had a very comprehensive idea of what a journal *par excellence* should be. There was no deficiency of enterprise in Swain so far as the needs of his paper, in his opinion, required. He had enough for his purpose, as our records may show, and he finally increased the circulation of the *Ledger* to 60,000, subject to the usual fluctuations, caused by the appearance of other cheap papers and local events. This was the desired point gained. It gave him the lists of post-office letters to advertise. This officially indorsed his circulation and filled his columns with other advertisements; and then his opponents, which had started up all along from 1836 to 1869, the *Sun*, as a Temperance as well as a Native American organ, the *Daily Focus*, edited for a time by Charles J. Peterson, afterwards of the *Evening Bulletin*, the *Chronicle*, the *Spirit of the Times*, the *Daily News*, the *World*, edited by Russell Jarvis, the old editor of the *Ledger*, and others, left the field to him. Sometimes his attention, too strongly fixed on immediate cash returns, interfered with his enterprise, and the *Ledger* occasionally made its appearance without any other intelligence or reading matter than advertisements, which filled the entire paper.

On one occasion a gentleman called upon Swain with an advertisement for the benefit of a poor widow. Telling the sad story of the widow's troubles, he asked, "How much will you insert this advertisement for, under such circumstances?" "At our regular rates, sir; business is business, and charity is charity," replied Mr. Swain. "But," said the gentleman, "the widow is poor, and every dollar saved—" "Business is business, I repeat, sir," interrupted Mr. Swain; "I regulate my own charities as well as my own business." "Then you will make no reduction?" "Not a cent, sir." Very reluctantly, the gentleman paid two dollars for the insertion of the advertisement, and when on the point of leaving, Mr. Swain said, in taking a ten-dollar note out of his pocket, "Have the kindness to give this to the poor widow."

An incident similar in character to this occurred in 1869, in the office of the *Boston Journal*. One of the Committee on the Humboldt Centennial Celebration, a clergyman, carried an advertisement to that office and asked to have it inserted for half price. "That is not the way we do business," said the gentlemanly proprietor of the *Journal*. "But all the others do so," replied the descendant of John Knox. "That may be, sir, but we do not mix our business with our charities." "Then, sir," asked the clergyman, "will you give us the half in money?" "No, sir," said the journalist, "not in that way." When copies of the eulogy of Professor Agassiz on Humboldt, delivered on that occasion, were given to the Press, the order was that none should be given to the *Journal!*

> Alas! for the rarity
> Of Christian charity
> Under the sun!

The *Ledger* prospered. Its enterprise was often well considered, and often successful. Whenever there was an excitement in the city or in the country it would exhibit its energy. It paid attention to European news, and would run expresses to obtain the latest papers. It co-operated with the *New York Herald* in the famous pony expresses which were run between Montgomery and Mobile during the Mexican War, by which the news and details of all the battles and victories, from Palo Alto and Resaca de la Palma to the triumphant entry of General Scott into the halls of the Montezumas, were received by these journals in advance of the authorities in Washington.

When the magnetic telegraph became a realization, Mr. Swain became largely interested in it, and was at one time president of the Washington line. Instead of carrying his journalistic experience, with its enlarged views, into the management of the telegraph, he introduced the mere business details of his office—the advertising experience as acquired at his counter, at so much per line—into the organization of the business of the telegraph. It did not work well.

It was too narrow. He was penny-wise only. But he saw the error, not, however, till the telegraph management became involved in complicities with the Press and with the public, requiring a radical change in the system to extricate the telegraph companies from their difficulties; and this peculiarity was noticed throughout Swain's career. He was not a man of new ideas nor of great progress. He had no faith in the success of the Atlantic cable. He believed it impossible to transmit a message across the ocean. But he worked hard in all his enterprises. It is stated by Mr. Childs that it was the custom of Mr. Swain "for more than twenty years to examine the proofs of the paper, from the first paragraph to the last, to make sure that nothing improper should be admitted into its columns."

Mr. Swain was an obstinate man. He persisted in keeping the price of the *Ledger* at one cent during the rebellion, when every thing else had advanced one and two hundred per cent. He lost $100,000 in doing so. When Mr. Childs became proprietor of the *Ledger* he advanced the price to two cents, and on the 10th of December, 1864, he gave these reasons for the increase:

> Less than three years ago, white paper could be purchased for nine cents per pound, while that on which the *Ledger* is now printed costs twenty-six and a half cents per pound. Here is an increased cost in the principal item in the production of a newspaper of nearly threefold. The pay of compositors when the *Ledger* was commenced was at the rate of twenty-five cents per thousand ems; it is now forty-five cents a thousand ems, or an increase of nearly twofold in this item. The cost of presswork (besides the immense expense of modern printing machines), and all the other principal items of labor and materials required in the production of a newspaper, have been augmented in like proportion. But it is in the heavy increase in the price of paper that the ruling standard of prices bears most heavily on the printing business. The sheet of white paper on which the *Ledger* is printed costs two and one third times the price the proprietor receives for the printed copy; or, in other words, he has to pay for three sheets of white paper as much as he receives for seven printed sheets.

Hence the rise in the subscription price of newspapers every where, and hence the disappearance of the original Penny Press. Thus the *Ledger* passed along under the management of Mr. Swain till 1864. Mr. Simmons died in 1855. Mr. Abell had charge of the *Baltimore Sun*, which these three printers had established on the 17th of May, 1837. The management of the *Ledger* had therefore entirely devolved on Mr. Swain, and, with these facts in view, he saw that his ideas were in conflict with surrounding circumstances. He had reached the end of his journalistic mission. So, in December, 1864, he disposed of the whole establishment, and retired from the publication of a daily newspaper after twenty-eight years of labor, during which time he accumulated the large property we have mentioned. But Mr. Abell, the survivor of the two, still manages the *Sun*, and has just purchased "Guilford," the M'Donald estate near Baltimore, for $475,000.

One of the exceptions to the general rule mentioned in the opening of this chapter is to be found in the new proprietor of the *Ledger*. After the death of Simmons, and after the effort of Swain to maintain a penny paper in spite of high prices, the *Public Ledger* became the property of George W. Childs, well known as the "Philadelphia Publisher." When fourteen years of age, in the year 1843, he went to Philadelphia, and begun his business career as a lad in a book-store. After a brief and bright apprenticeship of four years he opened an establishment of his own, and for this purpose he hired an office in the old *Ledger* Building, where he retailed newspapers. He was smart, industrious, and a young man of destiny, in which he seemed to place the utmost reliance. On completing his arrangements for the opening of his little store for the sale of periodical literature, young Childs, in speaking of his prospects, said to the colossal Swain, "I have made up my mind, Mr. Swain, to own the *Ledger* one of these days." "Have you? Well, well, my young friend, you will be an old man before you accomplish that, I guess," replied Swain. Childs went to work. With tact, courage, perseverance, and skill, he became a publisher of books; then one of the firm of Robert E. Peterson & Co.; then Childs & Peterson; then one of the house of J. B. Lippincott & Co. He brought out Dr. Kane's Arctic Explorations, Bouvier's Law Dictionary, Fletcher's interesting work on Brazil and the Brazilians, Allibone's Dictionary of Authors, Sharswood's Blackstone's Commentaries, the American National Almanac, Mrs. Hannah M. Paterson's Familiar Astronomy, Parson Brownlow's Book, Lossing's Civil War, and other works, which had very extensive and profitable sales every where. In 1863 he assumed the publication and editorship of the *American Literary Gazette and Publishers' Chronicle*, which has become the organ of the booksellers of the United States, and is a valuable periodical to the trade, and an interesting one to the public. It seems likely to rival, if not eclipse, *The Bookseller*, which has made its monthly appearance in London for many years. The Christmas numbers of the *Literary Gazette* for 1869, '70, and '71, as specimens of typography, with their illustrated covers and illustrated advertisements, were wonderful productions, which would have profoundly astonished Schœffer had he appeared at that merry season in Chestnut Street, Philadelphia. The *Literary Gazette* is now known as the *Weekly Trade Circular*, and is published by F. Leypoldt, New York.

Having acquired wealth and wisdom in these sixteen years of experience in selling newspapers and publishing books, Mr. Childs became ripe for the predestined position of a newspaper proprietor. In all this time, in reading the *New York Herald* and *Public Ledger*, in looking over the law-books of Judge Bouvier and Judge Sharswood; in his active researches through the fascinating details of Kane's explorations; in studying the progress of Don Pedro as described by Fletcher; in making the acquaintance of the authors of the world under the guidance of Dr. Allibone; in pondering on the material glory of the United States as developed in the American Almanac; and in carefully looking over his bank account, he came to the conclusion that he was prepared for the great object of his life. One fine day, therefore, neat and natty in dress, and confident in manner, he called upon Mr. Swain. It was no novelty to call upon that gentleman. He had been in the habit of doing so for years. Socially he had often met him; but on this occasion he had a great purpose in his visit—something on his mind. "Mr. Swain," said Mr. Childs, "do you recollect the 'threat' I made, and which you laughed at, sixteen years ago, that I intended one day to be proprietor of the *Ledger?*" "Why, yes," replied the millionaire journalist. "I recollect a chubby little fellow hiring an office of me, and boasting that he would own the *Ledger*, and me too, I suppose he would have added, if I hadn't pooh-poohed the conceit out of him." "Then you think you did that? But you are mistaken. It has remained in my head ever since, and I have made it my special business to call upon you to-day to carry out my purpose, if I can. If I can not now, I'll wait. I am yet young. But I want the *Ledger*, and I will give—" "Stop, stop," interrupted Swain; "you are too fast. What am I to do? It takes two, at least, to make a bargain. Let us see—"

What was the result? On the 3d of December, 1864, Mr. Childs became proprietor of the Philadelphia *Ledger*, and Mr. Swain, who left New York in 1836, resigning a situation worth $12 per week, had become trebly a millionaire, retired, but not altogether from newspapers, for he said a short time after the sale of the *Ledger*, and his remark sounded like the expiring neigh of an old war-horse on the field of battle, "I have given up the *Ledger*, but I don't wish you to think that I am entirely out of the business. I still retain the *Dollar Weekly*, simply to keep off the rust, you know." In his valedictory Mr. Swain said:

* * * * * * * * *

When the *Ledger* commenced its publication (March, 1836), the united editions of all the daily newspapers of Philadelphia was between 7000 and 8000 copies per day. Now (December 3, 1864) the editions of the morning and evening journals of this city, English and German, are not far from 175,000 copies per day, and the daily newspaper is an indispensable part of every man's instruction and information. The one cent, or penny paper, as it is called, has made hundreds of thousands of readers, and in making these readers it has advanced the interests of every other newspaper in the city, as well as enlarged the information of the people, and contributed to the enterprise and prosperity of the city.

It was claimed for the *Ledger*, among other things, and justly too, no doubt, that it aided materially in the union of the city in one municipality; in the introduction of city railroads; in urging the present convenient system of street numberings, so important to a large city; in concentrating the public buildings to enable the people to save time in the transaction of their business; and in the introduction of the steam fire-engines, with the fire-alarm and police, telegraphs.

Mr. Swain did not long survive his separation from his pet child. His iron constitution succumbed to the ravages of labor and time, and in 1867 he passed away, after thirty years of active and constant mental and physical application and labor.

What did Mr. Childs do with the *Ledger* when it came into his possession? It needed a little recuperation. It needed, with the growth of the city, a wider and more comprehensive grasp of intellect in its management. It was well organized. Indeed, it was considered a model establishment. But all enterprises had made rapid progress in this century. Newspapers can not stand still. It was with the *Ledger* as with all other journals. It required young blood and fresh intellect. These were immediately infused into the concern by its new proprietor. The reading columns showed more industry. They exhibited more power and greater variety. One of the most splendid buildings in Philadelphia was erected for its editors, clerks, machinery, compositors, and customers, and now the *Ledger* Building is not only a great ornament to that city, but one of numerous monuments to journalism that are springing up all over the country. It contains 64,812 square feet of space, and is lighted by 354 windows. It is more than a mile around the apartments above the ground. Meanwhile the circulation of the paper kept equal steps with the general spread of the establishment. It run up to 70 and 75,000, and 82,000 in 1872, and as there are 70,000 houses in Philadelphia, there is one copy of the *Ledger* for each house, and a few for strangers at the hotels. Its annual advertising patronage reaches $400,000 to $500,000. With this income its proprietor can accomplish much good. The price of the paper is now, as we have said, two cents a copy.

The *Ledger* has been a carefully conducted paper. It was not liable to be deceived. But in October, 1866, it was the means of throwing the community into a state of intense excitement. On the 11th of that month it published a dispatch from Washington relative to the supposed designs of President Johnson, which were to eclipse the famous factions of the British Parliament by Pride, and the dispersion of the French Council of Five Hundred by Napoleon. This dispatch was prepared in Washington by Henry M. Flint, whose fertile imagination was greatly exercised during the war, and embraced what purported to be a summary of five questions which had been submitted to the attorney general by the chief magistrate. These questions were in substance as follow:

1st. Is the present Congress a legal one?

2d. Would the President be justified in sending his next annual message to an unconstitutional assemblage?

3d. Has a Congress like the present a right to exclude representatives from ten states?

4th. Is the President required to enforce those provisions of the Constitution which give to each state an equal right to representation?

5th. What steps should the President take to secure the assemblage of a Constitutional Congress?

This dispatch was considered of such importance that the editor of the *Ledger* gave it to the agent of the Associated Press, and it appeared in nearly every paper in the United States on the same morning. It is unnecessary to say that it produced a profound sensation. The *New York Tribune* gave it extra head-lines, displayed as follows:

STARTLING QUESTION OF MR. JOHNSON TO THE ATTORNEY GENERAL.

AN OFFICIAL DECLARATION OF THE ILLEGALITY OF CONGRESS DEMANDED.

INTIMATION OF HIS PURPOSE TO RECOGNIZE A REBEL CONGRESS AND FORCE THE ADMISSION OF THE REBEL STATES.

Startling the journalists, it aroused Wall Street and the whole country, and the premium on gold advanced three or four per cent. There was a general alarm. But, thanks to the telegraph, the false character of the dispatch was soon ascertained, and it resulted in no disastrous consequences. The proprietor of the *Ledger* very properly and characteristically had the matter immediately and thoroughly investigated, and thus preserved the high character his paper had acquired for correctness and fairness. It was an episode which, fortunately, has not often occurred with the Press, the only other instance during the rebellion being that of the "bogus" proclamation of President Lincoln, which led to the unfair and unjust suspension of two New York papers, as already described in these pages.

The seal and motto of Mr. Childs in all his publications is the device of a broken sword, and a quill pen *à travers*, with the legend, "The pen is mightier than the sword," under the device. It is a capital design and an appropriate motto for a journalist. On the

6th of June, 1869, the Duke of Cambridge, the commander-in-chief of the English army, presided at a dinner in aid of the Newspaper Press Fund in London. In his remarks the duke said:

> Professionally I am placed at the head of one of the great services of the state not connected with any politics, and who may be supposed not to take that great interest in the institutions of the country which every citizen of a state ought to take. Now I am come here this evening to prove, as far as lies in my power, that the army and the other institutions do take interest in these matters. The fact of the head of one of these professions coming here to-night is an earnest and visible proof that such a view is no mere matter of phrases and words, but is a fact and a reality.

Honi soit qui mal y pense and *Dieu et Mon Droit* look very pretty and sound very valiantly on the English coat of arms, but a place will now have to be made for "The pen is mightier than the sword," since the royal family have been so remarkably convinced of the fact as to have one of its members, the man of the sword, preside at a Press dinner. Additionally to this evidence in favor of the pen, one day in March, 1872, President Grant, leaving his victorious sword in the White House at Washington, visited Philadelphia, and, while there with his family, was the guest of editor Childs, of the *Ledger*, who gave one of his splendid entertainments to the chief magistrate of the nation, which was a brilliant affair in every respect.

Among the good things Mr. Childs has done in his bailiwick has been the establishment of the Printers' Cemetery at Woodlands, the giving of a handsome sum for a fund for the widows and orphans of printers, and the insurance on the lives of ten of his leading *employés* for the benefit of their families. Once a year, on a national birthday like the Fourth of July, or on a universal birthday like Christmas, he brings all the newsboys of Philadelphia, with big patches on their jackets and big hearts under them, together at a feast, making them feel as if some one of them, in the future, would loom up as the proprietor of an influential newspaper, or as a member of Congress, or as occupant of the White House. *Instar omnium.* Thus the newspaper in proper hands, and out of its own abundance, becomes a great almoner, a great educator, and a great elevator. The *Public Ledger* may yet wield a greater power than ever. With a growing city the influential journalist can do much good and accomplish important results, and his work is never finished.

The *Dollar Weekly*, which Mr. Swain clung to till the last, is now the property of Mr. Childs, and is published under the name of the *Home Weekly*, and Mr. C. brings out native talent by offering premiums for the best stories. American intellect is in this way developed by such publishers as Bonner, Childs, Bennett, and Greeley.

Such writers as Coleridge, Swift, Addison, and Dickens were brought out by the *Chronicle*, the *Post*, and other papers of London, and our journals are to develop and make the literature of America.

There is an Almanac issued from the *Ledger* office that is quite valuable. It is sixty pages in size, and filled with useful matter of reference. Ninety thousand copies are published annually, and a copy is given gratuitously to each subscriber of the *Ledger*.

CHAPTER XXXII.

THE EXPRESS NEWSPAPER AND THE EXPRESS LINES.

THE NEW YORK EXPRESS.—WILLIS HALL AND JAMES BROOKS.—THE EXPRESS LINES.—HARNDEN, ADAMS, DINSMORE, AND SANFORD.—IMPORTANCE OF THE EXPRESSES TO NEWSPAPER PUBLISHERS.

ONE beautiful soft morning late in the spring of 1836, while the brokers, bankers, merchants, shipmasters, and gossips were talking over the affairs of the day in the vestibule of Hudson's News Rooms, in the Old Tontine Building in Wall Street, New York, Willis Hall, Esq., with his rotund body, glowing face, and shaggy eyebrows, was seen ascending the steps of that building, accompanied by a man with a long nose, a long face, dark features, and a very large head, with an enormous bell-crowned hat thereon. They entered the private office of the Hudsons, who had, the previous year, established an Exchange News Room, and had in successful operation at that time a *Shipping List*, on the plan of *Lloyds*, and a *Prices Current*. The great fire, which had, a few months before, laid waste acres of buildings in front of the Tontine, did not touch that ancient and plain edifice.

"Who is that rosy-cheeked, pleasant-looking man, with the heavy eyebrows?" asked a gentleman standing in the vestibule.

"That man? Why, that is Willis Hall, one of the magnates of the Whig Party," answered a by-stander, who seemed to pride himself on his superior knowledge and acquaintance with distinguished men.

"Well, my friend, since you are so well acquainted here, who is the gentleman with him—he with the big hat and swarthy face?" asked the gentleman.

"The man with the big hat? Was he with Hall? Some politician, no doubt," replied the other. Another by-stander volunteered the information.

"That man," said he, "is James Brooks."

"James Brooks? You are mistaken," said gentleman No. 1. "I know James Brooks. He was one of the editors of the *Courier and Enquirer*, and is now, I believe, editor of the *Albany Advertiser*. You are mistaken, my friend."

"But I am right. This James Brooks is not that James Brooks. This James Brooks is of the *Portland Advertiser*, and the writer of the letters from Europe published in that paper and copied all over the country. Why, my dear sir, I know all about him. He traveled over Europe on foot—he never rode ; he walked over England, Ireland, Scotland, up the Rhine, over the Alps, into the crater, and wrote letters. Willis is not a circumstance to him, sir ; Willis used Cologne and the stage-coaches. I don't mean Willis Hall, but N. P. Willis. Your James Brooks is James G. Brooks, a smart man, a smart editor, and a smart poet. You see, sir, I know all about these men."

This settled the matter, especially when Hall and Brooks came out of the office and passed up Wall Street.

"That's the man," said the walking directory. " I know him, sir. That's the man. What an enormous hat! Is that the latest Paris fashion, do you suppose ?"

With these remarks the conversation between these two strangers ended. But the result of this visit of Hall and Brooks to the old Tontine was the establishment of the *New York Express*, now known as the *Evening Express*. Its first number appeared on the 20th of June, 1836, and its proprietors then announced that "the political character of the *Express*" would " be decidedly Whig." *Hudson's Prices Current and Shipping List* were merged with the *Express*, and all appeared as one publication. On the 1st of November, 1836, the *Express* was united with the old *Daily Advertiser*, an organ of the followers of the Hartford Convention, which had been published by Theodore Dwight, William B. Townsend, and John A. Walker. Dwight was the secretary of the Hartford Convention, and wrote a history of that remarkable convocation of New England opponents of the War of 1812.

The *Express* has been remarkable for its politics, its numerous editions, and its strangers' lists. It started as a Whig paper, and adhered to the fortunes of Henry Clay as long as that statesman lived. On the appearance of Know-Nothingism James Brooks went to Europe, leaving the paper under the management of his brother, the junior editor, Erastus Brooks. The *Express* then became one of the organs of the new party, and Erastus Brooks was elected state senator in New York. When that meteoric party went out of existence the *Express* drifted into the ranks of the democracy, and James Brooks, the senior editor, was elected to Congress from one of the metropolitan districts, and is now a leading Democratic member of that body.

The numerous daily editions of the *Express*, containing the spirit of the morning and evening papers, the latest telegrams to the Associated Press, and the arrivals at the hotels, gradually destroyed its regular morning issue, till it was decided to make the paper an evening one exclusively, and the original *New York Morning Express* thus disappeared in 1864 or thereabouts. The strangers' list, or the daily arrivals at the several hotels, has always been a feature of the *Express*. It has ever been considered useful to merchants constantly on the watch for customers, and the *Herald* one time, from envy probably, called that paper the *Drummers' Gazette*.

The *Express* has a character of its own. It is made up not like any other paper. Its editorials seem hurriedly written, and have a sort of homely vigor about them. Every thing about the paper looks as if it had been thrown together in great haste. Its "Spirit of the Press" is always fairly given. It will take news wherever and whenever it can get it, but it has little or no individual enterprise outside of the Associated Press. It has never spent very large sums of money in this way. Whenever attacked, it fights stoutly and persistently, and its editors possess the merit of courage in their editorial course. James Brooks has had the Know-Nothing policy of the *Express* violently attacked in Congress because of his zealous democracy now. One of its contributors for many years was a son of the well-known Theodore Dwight. He was a small man physically, with bright black eyes and an active intellect; he was always a fluent writer. On one occasion the *Express* was severe in its remarks on the famous Empire Club, of which Isaiah Rynders and John S. Austin were the master spirits. One of the members of the Club called at the office of the *Express* to seek satisfaction for its strictures. He met Mr. Dwight, and with eye full of fire and fight, said,

"I am a member of the Empire Club. Are you the editor of this paper?"

"Have the kindness to be seated," mildly answered Mr. Dwight; "I will send for him."

Calling a messenger-boy, he dispatched him for James O'Brien, the manager of the engine-room of the establishment. O'Brien, standing nearly seven feet in his shoes, and with breadth of shoulders in proportion, soon made his appearance.

"Mr. O'Brien," said Mr. Dwight, with a twinkle in his eye, "this gentleman is a member of the Empire Club, and desires to see the editor. Will you please receive his message?"

The member from the Empire Club thought discretion the better part of valor, and prudently retired.

The circulation of the paper is largely confined to the numerous railway cars and steam-boats running to and from and within the limits of the city, where a numerous class engaged in business in the metropolis do all their reading. It has outlived a number of evening papers. Within the last four or five years it has had to compete with many new evening journals, and its circulation has probably suffered a little in consequence, although, with all well-managed papers, an increased number of journals in a city like New York is not without its advantages. The *Gazette*, the *Mail*, the *Globe*, the *Republic*, the *Free Press*, the *Telegram*, the *Leader*, the *Commonwealth*, have been started since 1865, but only the *Telegram* and *Mail* are left to compete with the *Express*, the old *Post*, and the older *Commercial Advertiser*. These new papers are a spirited class, and may yet somewhat affect the morning journals, with their telegrams from all parts of the world.

The *Express* was the first paper of that name, pure and simple, in the United States. With the establishment of this paper and the Cheap Press, a great necessity was met in the organization of the express lines. There was no connection between these lines and the *Express* newspaper. There was only a coincidence. The express lines were originated more in the spirit of the *Sun* and *Herald*. These papers were sold to news agents in other cities, and delivered by special express messengers, while the *Express* was established on the old system of credit and mail subscriptions, and did not come into the new plan, originating with the *Sun*, *Transcript*, and *Herald*, till years after, when circumstances forced the change upon the proprietors. But the express lines were commenced shortly after the *Express* was started. Harnden, then Adams, then Dinsmore, then Sanford, then Wells, then Fargo, appeared at the head of this new enterprise, one of the business marvels of this country. Harnden and Adams made their appearance on the Providence and Worcester railroads in 1838. The Harndens, two brothers, had been conductors, and had often been requested to carry small parcels for immediate delivery at the other end of their routes. Passengers by the steam-boat lines would be importuned by merchants in Boston and New York to carry letters and money parcels. These facts suggested the express business, which is now so extensive throughout the United States. Harnden and Adams extended their lines to Philadelphia. In 1841 a line between Albany and New York was established. Now, in 1872, lines run from the metropolis to the rest of the world. They became useful in bringing the latest papers to the newspaper offices. Stimson, the clever historian of this wonderful enterprise, in speaking of this part of the business, states that "the newspaper editors who conducted the New York Press in 1841, '42, '43, and '44, will remember, as long as they live, we presume, a sandy-haired, rosy-cheeked, bright blue-eyed lad, who used to rush into their sanctums once or twice a day with the 'latest news from Boston,' and desire them to give credit to Adams & Co.'s Express. That was John Hoey."

Well, he performed his part admirably, and is now a millionaire and a happy man. William F. Harnden, Alvin Adams, William B. Dinsmore, and Edwards S. Sanford performed the more arduous part of running locomotive expresses with the latest news from Europe. Dinsmore, and Sanford, and Adams have many a time covered themselves with coal-dust and glory in running a mile a minute on a locomotive for the New York and Philadelphia journals. Dinsmore, black with coal-dust, and brilliant in wit and good humor, once made the run from Boston to New York in seven hours and thirty minutes, the quickest at that time on record. Those were sparkling days in journalism. Sanford will relate incidents by the volume in his genial, pleasant way, of the competition between Adams and Harnden. Those were times of lively enterprise among the newspapers. They were days to remember. Adams and Dinsmore, with their magnificent farms, and herds of Alderney and Guernsey cows, now eclipse the farmers on the field as they did the old stage-coaches on the roads. Sanford became the right-hand man of Secretary Stanton during the rebellion, and military supervisor of telegraphs. Harnden was gathered to his fathers many years ago.

These express lines are of great importance to the Press as newspaper carriers. They deliver the *Suns*, *Heralds*, *Tribunes*, *Times*, *Worlds*, *Ledgers*, *Travellers*, and *Telegrams* of the various cities along the railroads of the United States as the carriers in a particular city delivers them along the streets of that city. News agencies, such as Zeiber in Philadelphia, Jones in Albany, and Williams in Boston, branched out and extended into colossal news companies as a part of the spirit, and energy, and necessity of the age. Huge parcels of *Heralds*, and *Tribunes*, and *Times* have been conveyed in bulk to these agencies by these express lines, and distributed every where. Along our railroads, news agents on the early morning trains throw out parcels at every cross-road and at every dépôt. With the extension of railroads and express lines the circulation of city journals becomes greater, and will become larger every year. Thus these tri-enterprises work together for the general good. But in the course of time the pneumatic parcel-tubes will be laid, and then the rapidity of the delivery of newspapers to distant points will be second only to the telegraph in speed and importance in our intellectual development and journalistic progress. *En avant!*

CHAPTER XXXIII.
THE NEW YORK TRIBUNE.

HORACE GREELEY. — WHAT HE HAS DONE IN JOURNALISM. — THE DAILY TRIBUNE. — THE WEEKLY TRIBUNE. — INDUCEMENTS TO SUBSCRIBERS. — ASSOCIATED OWNERSHIP. — CIRCULATION AND ADVERTISEMENTS. — THE ISMS OF THE TRIBUNE. — CONTESTS WITH THE HERALD. — THE GREAT HALIFAX EXPRESS. — THE ATLANTIC OCEAN EXPRESS. — THE FIRM OF SEWARD, WEED, AND GREELEY. — ITS DISSOLUTION. — GREELEY BEFORE A PARLIAMENTARY COMMITTEE. — HIS SLAP AT THE HERALD. — WHAT IT COSTS TO PUBLISH THE TRIBUNE. — MANAGING EDITORS. — INTERVIEWING AND ITS ADVANTAGES. — THE INITIAL EDITORS. — GREELEY'S PENMANSHIP. — THIRTY YEARS IN THE TRIBUNE. — ASPIRATIONS FOR THE PRESIDENCY. — NEWSPAPER ALMANACS.

ANOTHER remarkable newspaper is the *New York Tribune*. If James Gordon Bennett and the *New York Herald* are synonymous terms, *Horace Greeley* and the *New York Tribune* are equally so. If, in writing of these men and of these institutions, we become somewhat mixed in the use of names, the matter will be clear to the reader whether we mention Greeley for the *Tribune*, or the *Herald* when we have to say a word of Bennett. It is the same with Richard the Third, or Hamlet, or King Lear, and Shakspeare.

Horace Greeley, when he set up some of the type of the first regular penny paper in America for Dr. Shepard; when he failed in a literary enterprise like the *New Yorker;* when he wrote letters from Albany, in 1838, to the *New York Daily Whig*, and let himself out at a cheap rate to Thurlow Weed and the Albany politicians to make a splurge with the *Log Cabin* during the Hard-cider campaign for Harrison, "and Tyler too," in 1840, he was learning the business of newspaper maker. He was serving his apprenticeship with the usual reward. There is a similarity in the early lives of Horace Greeley and Benjamin Franklin worthy of notice. Indeed, Whittier calls Greeley our "later Franklin." They were printers' apprentices; they entered Philadelphia and New York with packs on their backs and nothing in their pockets; they struggled, and prospered, and were cheated; they gave a great deal of advice to young men; they started newspapers and run into politics; they became great philanthropists; they sought offices and wrote autobiographies; and if Franklin did not use electricity as a means of getting news for the *Pennsylvania Gazette*, he dealt largely and usefully in the article for the benefit of the rest of mankind.

The *Tribune* was considered by a few a political necessity. All of the Whig papers at that time were the high-priced "blanket sheets," with limited ideas and circulation. Horace Greeley thought that a cheap Whig paper, to counteract the influence of the Democratic tendencies of the Cheap Press then in existence, would succeed. With a small borrowed capital in money, with some reputation for industry and ability, which the leading politicians of that day thought to use, and with the aid and comfort of a few sincere friends, the *Tribune* was ushered into the world. It was commenced as a one-cent paper. This journalistic event took place on the 10th of April, 1841. Important date in the life of a newspaper, if not in the life of Washington. *Vide* Irving's Biography of the *Pater Patria*.

The *Tribune* started with a moral character. Announcing his intention to publish a cheap daily paper, he issued a prospectus full of this excellent idea. In our researches among the dusty and delightful records of journalism, from the days of Butler and Campbell to those of Pomeroy and Dana, we find these epics of our history very instructive and very suggestive. Sometimes they are deceptive. But they point a moral in any view, and Horace Greeley, personally, has endeavored, after his peculiar fashion, to adhere to his original moral idea. For a long time all theatrical advertisements were carefully excluded. No "immoral or degrading police reports" appeared. If descriptions of panel-houses and bagnios have since been published, they were to illustrate a needed reform in the police arrangements of the metropolis. If the advertisements of theatres are now admitted, it is because the people will go to such places, and they are the news of the day. But here is the announcement of the coming *Tribune*:

NEW YORK TRIBUNE.

On Saturday, the 10th of April instant, the subscriber will publish the first number of a New Morning Journal of Politics, Literature, and General Intelligence.

The *Tribune*, as its name imports, will labor to advance the interests of the People, and to promote their Moral, Social, and Political well-being. The immoral and degrading Police Reports, Advertisements, and other matter which have been allowed to disgrace the columns of our leading Penny Papers, will be carefully excluded from this, and no exertion spared to render it worthy of the hearty approval of the virtuous and refined, and a welcome visitant at the family fireside.

Earnestly believing that the political revolution which has called William Henry Harrison to the Chief Magistracy of the Nation was a triumph of Right, Reason, and Public Good over Error and Sinister Ambition, the *Tribune* will give to the New Administration a frank and candid, but manly and independent support, judging it always by its acts, and commending those only so far as they shall seem calculated to subserve the great end of all government—the welfare of the People.

The *Tribune* will be published every morning on a fair royal sheet (size of the *Log Cabin* and *Evening Signal*), and transmitted to its city subscribers at the low

price of *one cent* per copy. Mail subscribers $4 per annum. It will contain the news by the morning's Southern Mail, which is contained in no other Penny Paper. Subscriptions are respectfully solicited by
HORACE GREELEY, 30 Ann Street.

Thus, in 1841, Greeley became a temporary convert to the idea that he protested against in 1832, when Dr. Shepard endeavored to enlist him in the publication of a penny paper. But the *Tribune* was sold for a penny only to give it a start, and in this way Greeley returned to the fact that a good newspaper could not be published for one cent.

The *Tribune* lacked a business man to manage its affairs. It had poverty and conspiracy, like all papers established in those days, to contend with; and, what is interesting in a psychological point of view, Park Benjamin, the leading spirit in the great conspiracy to crush out the *New York Herald*, thus describes in the *Evening Signal* the small effort made by a rival to destroy the *Tribune* in its cradle:

> The publisher of the *Sun* has, during the last few days, got up a conspiracy to crush the *New York Tribune*. The *Tribune* was, from its inception, very successful, and, in many instances, persons in the habit of taking the *Sun* stopped that paper, wisely preferring a sheet which gives twice the amount of reading matter, and always contains the latest intelligence. This fact afforded sufficient evidence to Beach, as it did to all others who were cognizant of the circumstances, that the *Tribune* would, before the lapse of many weeks, supplant the *Sun*. To prevent this, and, if possible, to destroy the circulation of the *Tribune* altogether, an attempt was made to bribe the carriers to give up their routes; fortunately, this succeeded only in the cases of two men, who were likewise carriers of the *Sun*. In the next place, all the newsmen were threatened with being deprived of the *Sun* if, in any instance, they were found selling the *Tribune*. But these efforts were not enough to satisfy Beach. He instigated boys in his office, or others, to whip the boys engaged in selling the *Tribune*. No sooner was this fact ascertained at the office of the *Tribune* than young men were sent to defend the sale of that paper. They had not been on their stations long before a boy from the *Sun* office approached and began to flog the lad with the *Tribune;* retributory measures were instantly resorted to; but, before a just chastisement was inflicted, Beach himself, and a man in his employ, came out to sustain their youthful emissary.

The *Tribune*, like some of its predecessors, survived these assaults and persecutions, but, as we have said, it lacked a business manager to aid its editor in perfecting his plans and to reap the advantages of surrounding circumstances. Thomas M'Elrath was the needed man. Educated a lawyer, and having been a book publisher, active and intelligent, he took hold of the business details of the establishment with energy. It is but justice to Mr. M'Elrath to say that a large portion of the success of the *Tribune* was due to his skill in the early management of these details. On the 31st of July, 1841, he commenced his career on that paper.

There were nine cheap cash papers and seven "sixpenny sheets" printed in New York City in the following year. There were also five Sunday and six Saturday papers. Annexed is a list of the papers, with their estimated circulation:

NEW YORK PAPERS IN NOVEMBER, 1842.

Cash Papers.		Wall-street Papers.	
Herald, 2 cents	15,000	*Courier and Enquirer*	7,000
Sun, 1 cent	20,000	*Journal of Commerce*	7,500
Aurora, 2 cents	5,000	*Express*	6,000
Morning Post, 2 cents	3,000	*American*	1,800
Plebeian, 2 cents	2,000	*Commercial Advertiser*	5,000
Chronicle, 1 cent	5,000	*Evening Post*	2,500
Tribune, 1½ cent	9,500	*Standard*	400
Union, 2 cents	1,000		
Tattler, 1 cent	2,000		
	62,500		30,200

Sunday Papers.		Saturday Papers.	
Atlas	3,500	*Brother Jonathan*	5,000
Times	1,500	*New World*	8,000
Mercury	3,000	*Spirit of the Times*	1,500
News	500	*Whip*	4,000
Sunday Herald	9,000	*Flash*	1,500
		Rake	1,000
	17,500		21,000

The *Tribune* has always béen remarkable for its peculiar *penchant* for isms of all sorts. It committed itself to Fourierism in the autumn of 1841; and in the communications of Albert Brisbane, an enthusiastic pupil of Charles Fourier, in the controversy of Horace Greeley in the *Tribune* and Henry J. Raymond in the *Courier and Enquirer*, and in the showers of ridicule from the *Herald*, the paper became widely known, and its editor famous. In every thing new and ultra, the *Tribune* was its champion. It was an early advocate of woman's rights, and its course was strongly indorsed by Mrs. Julia Ward Howe in the Woman's Rights Convention, held in Worcester, Massachusetts, in December, 1869. Mrs. Howe advocated the establishment of a newspaper devoted to their cause, and spoke of the corruption in city governments. She referred to the attacks on Henry Ward Beecher and Mr. Frothingham in New York, and said that the enemies of the *Tribune* and the friends of violence, the lovers of scandal, naturally flashed their noisy artillery at so glittering a mark.

It is fair to suppose that the editor of the *Tribune* was sincere, and believed all he said. But novelty was attractive to him, and this was his idea of progress, and success and progress were necessary to the happiness of the world. On one occasion, when absent, a strange affair was reported which the editor in charge thought to be too absurd to publish. On Mr. Greeley's return to the city he bitterly complained of the omission. "It was too ridiculous to publish," said the editor *pro tem*. "Too ridiculous to publish! Nonsense. Nothing is too ridiculous. I can not leave town without something going wrong. You will crucify me—yes, you will crucify me with such management." The strong desire for novelty which found vent in this emphatic expression was thus translated by Greeley on the 25th of April, 1859, in one of those periodical articles which appear in the leading journals of the metropolis :

> Doubtless many of our readers have heard of the *Isms* of *The Tribune*, its disorganizing doctrines, its numerous hobbies, and its frequent changes from one of these to another. And yet, as one mind has presided over its issues from the outset, so one golden thread of purpose may be traced through them all, under every variety of circumstance and condition. That purpose is the elevation of the masses through the diffusion and inculcation of intelligence, freedom, industry, skill, virtue, and the consequent abolition or limitation of ignorance, slavery, idleness, pauperism, and vice. To accord a generous welcome to every novel suggestion, every unselfish effort, tending to the great end thus meditated, whether that suggestion contemplate the more perfect development and diversification of our material industry through protection to American labor, or improved facilities of intercourse with our brethren across the continent by a railroad to the Pacific, or the present limitation and ultimate abolition of human chattelhood, or the securing to every man the unchallenged possession and use of a patch of the earth's surface whereon to live and support his family by the freedom of the public lands, or the diminution of human wretchedness and debasement through a war of extermination on intemperance and its accessories, is, as it has been, our unshaken purpose, our unshrinking aim.

The *Tribune*, in the progress of time and events, became the organ of the extreme National Republicans, the extreme Whigs, the extreme Republicans, and of Horace Greeley. It had two strong national ideas: a high protective tariff, and the abolition of slavery; and one social idea—Fourierism. Commencing political life as an ardent admirer of Henry Clay, and then of William H. Seward, the *Tribune* has kept on the opposition track to democracy till it is now the special organ of Horace Greeley. It is perhaps best for the interests of the people, if a newspaper is to be organ of any party or any person, that that party and that person should be its own responsible editor, and with the *Tribune* there is a Greeley Party. There is more honesty in this policy.

Apart from the *Herald*, no paper has been more individual in its course than the *Tribune*. No other paper is so well known. Its influence, however, has been attained by its weekly rather than by the daily edition. It could never reach a large circulation in the city of New York. It could not, therefore, obtain a large paying advertising patronage in that city. It was not adapted to the political and commercial atmosphere of the metropolis. But with the *Weekly Tribune* great results were obtained. Its subscription price was put down to the lowest rate. It was advertised every where. It instituted all kinds of premiums, from a strawberry plant and a gold pencil to a steel engraved portrait of Horace Greeley for the largest number of subscribers. It established the club system now so prevalent with struggling newspapers. Its editor became a public lecturer to spread himself, his opinions, and his paper. When he issued the *New Yorker* in 1834, in his appeal to the public he said:

THE PUBLISHER'S ADDRESS.

There is one disadvantage attending our *début* which is seldom encountered in the outset of periodicals aspiring to general popularity and patronage. Ours is not blazoned through the land as "The Cheapest Periodical in the World," "The Largest Paper ever Published," or any of the captivating clap-traps wherewith enterprising gentlemen possessed of a convenient stock of assurance are wont to usher in their successive experiments on the gullibility of the public. No likenesses of eminent and favorite authors will embellish our title while they disdain to write for our columns. No "distinguished literary and fashionable characters" have been dragged in to bolster up a rigmarole of preposterous and charlatan pretensions. And, indeed, so serious is this deficiency, that the first (we may say the only) objection which has been started by our most judicious friends in the discussion of our plans and prospects has inevitably been this: "You do not indulge sufficiently in high-sounding pretensions. You can not succeed without humbug." Our answer has constantly been, "We shall try," and in the spirit of this determination we respectfully solicit of our fellow-citizens the extension of that share of patronage which they shall deem warranted by our performances rather than our promise.

The circulation of the *Weekly Tribune* run up to 200,000, and its issue contained a page of advertisements. Those inserted in 1872 have to pay two, three, and five dollars per line for each insertion! This was the result of a system, not like that developed in the above prospectus for the acquisition of readers and patronage for the *New Yorker*. Times have changed, and this large circulation of the *Tribune* has been the result, largely, of such announcements as the following, which appeared in 1868:

GREELEY'S HISTORY OF THE WAR.

The *Tribune* also proposes to send "The American Conflict," by Horace Greeley, in 2 volumes of 648 and 782 pages respectively, to clubs on terms stated below. This history has received from all quarters the highest commendation for accuracy of statement and fullness of detail. It is substantially bound, and must be deemed a valuable addition to any library. These volumes should be placed in every School District library in the land, and each school contains scholars who can, with a few hours of attention, raise a *Tribune* Club and secure the history. Almost any one who wishes can now obtain it by giving a few hours to procuring subscriptions for the *Tribune* among his friends and neighbors, and we hope many will be incited to do so. The work will be promptly forwarded, prepaid, by express or by mail, on receipt of the required subscriptions.

Apropos of the American Conflict, there is a fact connected with its sale which exhibits the fickleness of public favor, and the want of stability in any one man's power and influence in a republic. On the appearance of this History of the Rebellion, the demand for it was really enormous. Thousands of copies were sold, and the agents for the sale of the work were disposing of them with great rapidity, when the scene which occurred at Richmond, where Horace Greeley appeared to sign the bail-bond for Jefferson Davis, was described and published in the papers. Immediately the sale of the American Conflict stopped. No one would purchase a copy. The publishers had $50,000 worth returned to them from the agents scattered over the country. Such a collapse was never before known in literature. Greeley himself describes it as something very remarkable. Since then, however, the sale of the work has recommenced.

These facts are eccentric and instructive in the history of journalism, and are worth the space they occupy. They show that all wares need publicity. Newspapers, which are so necessary to the public as advertising mediums, are first compelled to go through the same process, and in this way the whole country has become a nation of advertisers and newspaper readers. We are, indeed, the Republic of Letters. One of the chief reliances of the *Tribune* has been the heated political campaigns that periodically pass over this happy land. Greeley's wonderful success in his first effort with the *Log Cabin* in 1840 was the experience upon which he works. Thus, in 1867, on the eve of a great political fight, the following manifest was issued. It will be seen that Greeley calculated on obtaining half a million of subscribers in the excitement of that campaign:

> In view of the momentous issues of our presidential struggle now opening, we have resolved to offer the *Weekly Tribune* for 1868 to clubs of fifty or more for *one dollar per annum*—that is to say, for fifty dollars we will send, *to one address,* fifty copies of the *Weekly Tribune* for one year, and any larger number at the same rate.
>
> No newspaper so large and complete as the *Weekly Tribune* was ever before offered at so low a price. Even when our currency was at par with gold, no such paper *but* the *Tribune* was offered at that price, and the *Tribune* then cost us far less than it now does. But the next election must be carried for liberty and loyalty, and we mean to do our part toward effecting that consummation.
>
> We believe that the circulation of half a million copies of the *Weekly Tribune* during the coming year would be more effectual in influencing and confirming voters than five times their cost spent in the ordinary way just before election.

But the great effort, personal and journalistic, was made in 1869. In that year an inducement of a peculiar kind was advertised every where, posted every where, and sent every where. It was, in spite of the protestation of the *New Yorker*, the offer of a portrait of the chief editor of the paper:

> The publishers of the *New York Tribune* having received many inquiries from time to time for a good likeness of the editor, have made an arrangement with Messrs. Derby & Miller to furnish copies of Ritchie's engraving, from a photograph by Brady, which will be sent to such subscribers to the *Tribune* as wish it on the conditions below. This is much the best likeness of Mr. Greeley that has been engraved. The print sells for one dollar. Each subscriber who sends us ten dollars for the *Daily*, four dollars for the *Semi-weekly*, or two dollars for the *Weekly Tribune*, the paper to be sent by mail, and who requests the engraving at the time of subscribing, will have a copy carefully mailed, post-paid, to his address. One will likewise be sent to any person who forwards a club of ten or more semi-weeklies at our club rates, and asks for the portrait at the time of remitting. We do not propose this as a premium, but to gratify the many friends of the *Tribune* who feel a desire to possess a good likeness of its founder.

But the circulation of the *Weekly Tribune* would fluctuate with the political excitements and sensations, notwithstanding these efforts—increasing immensely on an exciting national political campaign, and decreasing with the subsidence of the excitement and the expiration of the term of subscription.

It is a common thing with newspaper proprietors to exalt their circulation. We continually see at the head of newspapers that "our circulation exceeds that of any other paper." This is praising our own wares to sell. With most of the newspapers it is to obtain advertisements. In 1847, when the circulation of the *Tribune* was considered large, both of its daily and weekly editions, it got into a controversy with the *Herald* on the subject. To settle the point, it challenged the *Herald* to an investigation. The challenge was accepted. James G. Wilson, the ex-publisher of the *New York Daily Whig*, and Daniel H. Megie, of the paper-house of Campbell & Persse, were selected as the committee of examination. Annexed was the result:

The undersigned, having been designated by the publishers of the *New York Herald* and *New York Tribune*, respectively, to examine jointly and report for publication the actual circulation of these two journals, have made the scrutiny required, and now report, that the average circulation of the two papers during the four weeks preceding the agreement which originated this investigation was as follows:

New York Herald.		New York Tribune.	
Average Daily circulation	16,711	Average Daily circulation	11,455
" Weekly circulation	11,455	" Weekly circulation	15,780
" Presidential circulation	780	" Semi-weekly circulation	960
Total	28,946	Total	28,195

The quantity of paper used by each establishment during the four weeks above specified was as follows: By the *New York Herald*, 975 reams for the *Daily*, 95½ reams for the *Weekly*, and 5 reams for the *Presidential*. By the *New York Tribune*, 573 reams for the *Daily*, 131¾ reams for the *Weekly*, and 16 reams for the *Semi-weekly*.

We therefore decide that the *Herald* has the larger average circulation.

JAMES G. WILSON.
DANIEL H. MEGIE.

The two hundred dollars pending on this result was paid by the *Tribune*, by mutual agreement, to two orphan asylums, and the lesson learned by the *Tribune* in newspaper book-keeping, as Wilson and M'Elrath both admitted, after the inspection of the *Herald* books, was fully worth the two hundred dollars. In this investigation the *Tribune* relied upon its large weekly circulation, and the *Herald* upon its large daily circulation, to gain the victory. But the result, published in both papers, was a splendid advertisement at that time, although a daily issue of sixteen thousand would not now be considered at all attractive to a shrewd advertiser, in face of one hundred and forty-five thousand copies which the *Herald* has printed in one day, nor would fifteen thousand for the *Weekly Tribune* amount to much against a circulation of two hundred thousand which it afterwards obtained.

After the *Herald* had gained its great reputation as a newspaper, and had frequently anticipated its contemporaries in the acquisition of news, especially from Europe, the *Tribune*, *Sun*, and *Journal of Commerce*, of New York, combining with the leading papers in Boston, Philadelphia, Baltimore, and Washington, made one or two prodigious efforts to destroy the prestige of their single-handed contemporary. Intimations of these efforts developed themselves mysteriously. The *Herald*, in common with the other journals of New York, published the following advertisement on the 6th of February, 1846 :

LETTERS FOR EUROPE.

A vessel of extraordinary speed, with choice sailing-master and picked crew, will leave New York for Liverpool on Monday, the 9th inst., at 12 o'clock, and returning, will leave Liverpool on or about the 26th or 27th inst. Letter-bags will remain open until Monday morning at 10 o'clock.

This escaped general observation on the first day of its insertion. But in the excitement in the community on the Oregon Question, the fact of the dispatch of a vessel of "extraordinary speed" soon spread throughout the newspaper offices, reading-rooms, hotels, and business circles. What could it mean? Some thought it was a special government express, with an Oregon treaty quietly made with the British minister at Washington. Some, that it was a stock or cotton speculation. Others, that the vessel was to be sent by Sir Richard Packenham with important dispatches relative to Oregon, Mexico, and Texas. No name appearing with the advertisement, and no place indicated where letters could be deposited, tended to increase the mystery. It was ascertained, however, that the vessel was one of the famous pilot-boats of New York. Implicit faith was placed in her speed, for she was advertised to leave New York on the 9th, and Liverpool, on her return trip, on the 26th or 27th of the same month. Once a pilot-boat, in pursuit of a defaulter to the government, crossed the Atlantic in eighteen days, including three days' detention in a storm. The new enterprise was arranged to beat that time; but

"The best laid schemes of mice and men
   Gang aft aglee."

The "vessel of extraordinary speed" was the pilot-boat William J. Romer. She was engaged by the *New York Tribune, Journal of Commerce, Courier and Enquirer, Sun*, Philadelphia *North American*, and several papers in other cities, for the purpose of getting news from Europe in advance of the *Herald*, and putting a stop to the unpleasant boasting of that paper on the arrival of each packet-ship from England. It was deemed especially necessary to accomplish this object at this particular time, when many believed in a war between the United States and Great Britian on the Oregon Question. The enterprise was a splendid one, and deserved success for its boldness, and originality, and cost. The *Herald* had, by the assistance of the New York pilots, its own news-boats, and its expresses from Boston, anticipated its contemporaries so many times that they saw the necessity of one or two great efforts to counteract the effect of their neighbor's enterprise.

The name of the parties who chartered the Romer was so closely kept a secret that the public, for some time after her departure, believed that she was dispatched by either our own authorities at Washington or by the British minister. The pilot-boat was cleared at the Custom-house by J. H. Braine, interested in trade with the British Provinces, and the important correspondence between Mr. Packenham and Mr. Buchanan came out just at that time. These circumstances assisted in keeping the real parties in the enterprise out of sight. It was only the peculiarly smiling face of Mr. M'Elrath, as if he was satisfied with some arrangement of his own, and the patronizing manner of the *North American,* that betrayed the origin of this brilliant effort.

The Romer left New York on Monday, the 9th of February, under the command of Captain M'Guire. One or two days after her departure the *Boston Transcript* contained the following paragraph:

> It is rumored that the Portland folks are going to beat the *New York Herald* in the foreign news by the Cambria, now six days out from Liverpool. The *modus operandi* is to have an agent board the steamer off Halifax, cross overland by horses to Annapolis, join the steamer Kennebec and run to Portland, and from thence by railroad to Boston. We are inclined to believe this operation will cost more than it will come to.

About the time of the appearance of this paragraph, private information was received at the office of the *Herald* of this extensive arrangement. One morning the mail brought a letter from Bangor to Mr. Bennett, asking the suggestive question, "Are you stocking the road for an express from Halifax?" Such a question, so soon after the departure of the Romer, was a small problem to solve. Seeking information, the editor of the *Herald* ascertained the extent of the opposition, and laid his plans accordingly. The *Herald* had arranged an ordinary express to start from Boston on the arrival of the Cambria, running over the Worcester and Norwich roads to Allyn's Point, thence across the Sound to Greenport, and thence over the Long Island road to New York.

The expected steamer was commanded by Captain Judkins, a thorough sailor, an energetic navigator, and not partial to what are called "beats." The Cunarders, at that time, ran to Boston only. There was no opposition. Sufficient time was taken to discharge passengers and cargo, and take in coal, at Halifax. They never hurried. Thirty-six hours were occupied in making the run to Boston. The "Holy Alliance," as the *Tribune* and its associates were called, had taken all these facts into their calculations. So, it appears, had the *Herald.*

It became important to notify the agents of the steamer at Halifax of the impending struggle, and inform Captain Judkins, immediately on his arrival, that when he reached Boston he would find that his news had preceded him. Human nature is pretty much the same in England as in the United States. The *Herald*, in this view, published numerous paragraphs on the great race, and sent them to Halifax to be shown to Captain Judkins as soon as the pilot stepped on board the Cambria.

"Is an express to beat me to Boston?" asked Captain Judkins. "I'll see about that."

There was never greater activity displayed at Halifax. No Cunarder ever remained so short a time in port; and the Cambria made the run to Boston in thirty hours! It was fair to suppose that the "Holy Alliance," entering on such a costly enterprise, would have all its arrangements for speed and success complete from Halifax to New York. It would be unjust to suppose otherwise. Time and space between these two points were therefore to be fully considered by the *Herald*. What did that establishment do under these circumstances? No plans existed east of Boston. The only imperfection in the *Herald* arrangements was in the steamer engaged to connect the Norwich with the Long Island Railroad. She was slow. The only hope of the *Herald* was in making a very quick run from Boston. If it beat, it would be an Austerlitz, a Marengo, and a Jena rolled into one magnificent victory. If defeated, its opponents would call it a Leipsic, if not a Waterloo. If this great overland express was a success, Napoleon Bennett would be sent to Elba. If the Romer anticipated the packet-ship, he would go to St. Helena.

Eh bien! To prevent one and accomplish the other of these contingencies, a fast steamer was necessary to carry the *Herald* messenger across Long Island Sound. There was one steamer, called the Traveler, and owned by Commodore Vanderbilt, suitable for this purpose. The *Herald* called on the Commodore, and told the story of the plans of the opposing journalists, and of the importance of the coming news.

"What can I do?" asked the Commodore. "If I can aid you, I will; I like your pluck."

"We want the Traveler," said the *Herald*, "to run across the Sound, land one messenger at Greenport, and then come through the Sound to New York with another messenger."

"Well, well, let me see;" and, turning to a young man, said, "Write out an order for the Traveler for Mr. Bennett."

Signing the order, the Commodore passed it to the *Herald*, and said, "There's the boat. Keep her till your express arrives. Now go ahead. Good morning."

"One word more, Commodore. Will you send one of your smartest captains in her, with orders to keep up the fires and not sleep?"

"Yes; I'll send two."

The Traveler, with Captains Scott and Lefevre, was immediately dispatched to Allyn's Point to await the arrival of the news. Mr. Joseph Elliott, of the *Herald*, went in her, prepared to catch Mr. Bigelow in his arms as he jumped from the locomotive to the steamer. The *Boston Transcript* of February 20th, 1846, gives the result of this spirited journalistic affair as follows :

THE EXPRESSES FOR NEW YORK WITH THE CAMBRIA'S NEWS.

Mr. L. Bigelow left the Worcester *dépôt* on the locomotive Jupiter on Wednesday evening at 11 o'clock; arrived in Worcester in 1 hour and 13 minutes; from thence to Allyn's Point in 2 hours; took the crack steamer Traveler, for Greenport, which place was reached in 1 hour and 40 minutes. Here Mr. Bigelow took the locomotive Jacob Little, and run to Brooklyn in 2½ hours, arriving in New York at half past 7 o'clock, in 8½ hours from Boston. This, we believe, is the quickest time ever made between the two cities, and was run exclusively for Mr. Bennett of the *New York Herald*, beating the *Tribune* combination express 5½ hours. The latter was run *via* Worcester, Hartford, and New Haven, and arrived at 1 P.M. Thursday.

The scene around the *Herald* office was one of great excitement. The Oregon Question, for a time, was overshadowed by the result of the great race. Mr. Bennett immediately had the news from Europe prepared and thousands of *Extra Heralds* printed; and as the express horse of the "Holy Alliance," covered with perspiration, passed down Nassau Street to the office of the *Journal of Commerce*, the newsboys with the *Extras* swarmed after him. Among the crowd of spectators in front of the *Herald* Building was Colonel James Watson Webb, much amused with the scene before him. He had refused to join in the overland express.

The account of this extraordinary express in the *Tribune* differs somewhat from the above in point of time on the road, but not as to the result. We republish it from that paper :

The Portland *Bulletin* has been unintentionally led into the gross error of believing the audacious fabrication that Bennett's express came through to this city in *seven* hours and five minutes from Boston, beating ours *five* or *six* hours ! That express left Boston at 11 P.M. of Wednesday, and arrived here 20 minutes past 9 on Thursday—actual time on the road, over ten hours. The *Bulletin* further says that our express was *sixteen* hours on the road. No such thing. We lost some fifteen minutes at the ferry on the east side of Boston. Then a very short time (instead of an hour and a half, as it is reported by the express) in finding our agent in Boston ; then an hour in firing up an engine and getting away from Boston, where all should have been ready for us, but was not. The locomotive was over two hours in making the run to Worcester—42 miles—though the *Herald* runner who came through on the arrival of the Cambria some time after, was carried over it in about half the time, with not one fourth the delay we encountered at the *dépôt* in Boston. (We could *guess* how all this was brought about, but it would answer no purpose now.) At Worcester, Mr. Twitchell [now member of Congress from Massachusetts] (whom our agent on this end had only been able to find on Tuesday, having been kept two days on the route to Boston by a storm, and then finding Mr. Twitchell absent in New Hampshire) was found in bed, but got up and put off, intending to ride but one stage. At its end, however, he found the rider he had hired sick, and had to come along himself. At one stopping-place he found his horse amiss, and had to buy one before he could proceed. When he reached Hartford (toward morning) there was no engine fired up, no one ready, and another hour was lost *there*. At New Haven our rider was asleep, and much time was lost in finding him and getting off. Thus we lost in delays, which *we* could not foresee or prevent, over *three hours* this side of Boston Ferry—the Cambria having arrived two or three days earlier than she was expected, before our arrangements could be perfected, and on the only night of the week that the rival express could have beaten even *our* bad time—the Long Island Railroad being obstructed with snow both before and afterwards. The *Herald* express came in at 20 minutes past 9; our express was here at 15 minutes past 12, or *less than three* hours afterwards. Such are the facts. The express for the *United States Gazette* crossed the ferry to Jersey City at 10½ instead of 11½, as we misstated recently.

The editor of the *Herald* did not go to Elba after this affair. But the pilot-boat William J. Romer had sailed for Cork, and was expected to leave that port on the 26th of February, in less than a week after the arrival of this express, on her return. It was believed by the proprietors of this enterprise that the pilot-boat would make a shorter passage across the Atlantic than any of the famous packet-ships of that period, and the only ocean steamers then running were the Cunarders, making monthly trips to Boston. The Romer run light, carrying only two mysterious messengers, with glazed caps on their heads and carpet-bags in their hands, besides the regular officers and crew. These mysterious messengers were Gale, assistant foreman of the *Tribune*, and Brogan, ship-news collector of the *Sun*.

Now that the great overland express had been run, the hopes of the enterprising journalists who had chartered the Romer were centred in her. It was at this period in the history of the metropolitan Press that the *Herald* enjoyed almost a monopoly of the news from Europe. It was to demolish this that these extended and expensive arrangements were made. All the pilots of New York acted as news collectors for the *Herald*; all the packet-ship captains freely gave their news to that paper; there was zeal and industry in the office of the *Herald*. There were high hopes in the offices of the *Tribune, Sun, Journal of Commerce*, and *North American* in the success of this effort against their amiable neighbor to break up this exclusiveness in the European news. There were also hopes in the *Herald* office. Meanwhile the gallant pilot-boat and her gallant crew were dashing across the Atlantic.

One morning one of the news collectors of the *Herald* brought in the report of the St. Patrick, Captain Proale, which had just arrived from Liverpool. She had spoken the Romer on the 1st of March standing east. This intelligence was sent to the *Tribune*, with the compliments of Mr. Bennett. On the 11th of April the Adirondack, Captain Hackstaff, arrived at New York. She not only reported the arrival of the Romer at Cork on the 6th of March, but of her sailing for New York on the 12th of that month. The Adirondack sailed on the 13th, and her news appeared in the *Herald*. It was deemed an act of courtesy to advise the editors of the *Tribune* of this fact also.

"We are certainly obliged to Mr. Bennett," said Mr. M'Elrath, with his accustomed suavity, "but isn't he mistaken about our connection with the Romer?"

"I don't know about that," replied the messenger. "He thought you would like to know of her arrival, and especially of her departure, as the foreman of your office is on board."

Shortly after the Romer arrived, and the two mysterious men, with the same glazed caps on their heads, and the same carpet bags in their hands, but filled with old English papers, safely landed, and were soon in the bosom of their families. Thus ended the great news combination against the *Herald*. But, if the *Tribune* failed in these two wonderful efforts at enterprise, that paper now and then would flash up brightly and brilliantly, and astonish its neighbors with an account of a great battle here and there, sometimes at Slievegamon, and, better still, at Gravelotte and Sedan.

These were, after all, pleasant incidents in the life of an editor. What journalist does not look back upon these exciting events with pleasure? They were especially exhilarating when "our" express came in ahead, and a defeat only tended to make one more energetic in future efforts. The enterprise thus exhibited by the New York Press, at an immense outlay of money, brains, and time, has diffused itself all over the country, making the American Press the most active, mentally and physically, of the world. But the days of "pony expresses" and special engines, when messengers would arrive black with smoke and beaming with pride, have passed away, and telegrams have taken their place. Yet the energy and the enterprise remain, and newspapers continue to improve, rapidly approaching that elevated position they are destined to reach.

The *Tribune* has always been a political paper. It has always been a party paper, in one sense of the word. It is now an independent party paper, and instead of being controlled by a few political leaders, its editor has acquired sufficient experience in many ways, which he is candid enough to disclose now and then, to manage his own course and the policy of his own paper, even if it elects the very men who have cheated him. But the *Tribune* has been a violent party paper, and has uttered a large amount of prime nonsense in its day. When it became known in 1844 that James K. Polk was elected President, it said:

Each morning convincing proofs present themselves of the horrid effects of

Locofocoism in the election of Mr. Polk. Yesterday it was a countermanding of $8000 worth of stores; to-day the *Pittsburg Gazette* says that two Scotch gentlemen who arrived in that city last June, with a capital of £12,000, which they wished to invest in building a large factory for the manufacture of woolen fabrics, left for Scotland when they learned that the Anti-Tariff champion was elected. They will return to the rough hills of Scotland, build a factory, and pour their goods into this country when Polk and his break-down party shall consummate their political iniquity. These are the small first-fruits of Polk's election, the younglings of the flock—mere hints of the confusion and difficulties which will rush down in an overwhelming flood after the Polk machine gets well in motion.

Any one would suppose, after reading the above, that the country would long since have gone to the dogs in consequence of the election of Polk. What is the fact? Since then the country has doubled, nay, trebled itself in wealth, and the name of Polk is now only seen by those who occasionally look over the public documents of that ancient period.

The idea of association in newspapers in the United States originated in the *Tribune* office. It was carried into effect in 1846. It is now quite common for newspapers to be owned in this way, or as incorporated institutions. The *Tribune*, at that time, was managed by Greeley in the editorial department, and M'Elrath in the business department. Greeley could never keep any money, and M'Elrath was full of plans to make more than he had. About this time the writer of its financial articles, George M. Snow, formerly of Boston, full of the idea of incorporated companies and the financial schemes of Wall Street, proposed to Greeley and M'Elrath to make the *Tribune* a stock concern, and divide it into one hundred shares of one thousand dollars each, Greeley and M'Elrath to retain a majority of the stock, and the remainder to be distributed among the principal *employés* of the establishment. Each one was to be placed on a salary, from its chief editor to its office-boy. When Charles A. Dana received the appointment of managing editor, he took ten shares in the concern. In this way its financial writer, its literary editor, its chief reporter, its foreman of the press-rooms, its cashier, and its foreman of the composition rooms, became joint owners with its projectors and original proprietors. This plan was attractive to Greeley, because it partook somewhat of his socialistic idea of co-operative labor, and to M'Elrath, because one hundred thousand dollars were, at that time, a very large sum in a newspaper point of view. Greeley and M'Elrath owned a majority of the shares; the residue were owned by five assistant editors and five other assistants, who had been, for the longest time, connected with the business and mechanical departments of the paper. In 1851, in speaking of the prosperity of the *Tribune*, the editor thus alluded to the success of the associated ownership of that paper:

The course of the *Tribune* is still onward. Commenced individually by him who has continued to be its chief editor, the number of its proprietors has since been gradually increased to twelve, including all those responsibly connected with its conduct, editorial, financial, or mechanical. These purpose and hope in time to make still further application of the general principle that the workman should be his own employer and director, and should receive the full reward of his labor. The quickened sense of responsibility, and the more thorough devotion of mind and muscle to the appointed work which this system induces, will be found to overbalance any incidental disadvantages, if its application be wisely made, so that the new idea and the old habits may be gradually and safely harmonized.

One hundred thousand dollars for a successful metropolitan journal in 1846, considered a large sum, became, in twenty years, a mere *bagatelle* in estimating the value of a prosperous newspaper. In 1866 the *Morning Call* was sold in San Francisco for $105,000 in gold, when that precious article was worth 123½ in Wall Street. Indeed, the *Tribune* is worth $1,000,000, and now annually pays its entire value in 1846 for intellectual labor alone. The shares of the *Tribune* advanced in value, with the general prosperity of the Press and the country, till they reached $3500, and a few have been sold as high as $6500, and even $10,000. In the changes of shareholders, prices would, of course, fluctuate in accordance with circumstances. Those held by Greeley have considerably diminished in number, while M'Elrath has felt himself constrained to part with all of his and leave the concern. Yet Greeley, who now owns only one tenth of the establishment, is really the life of the concern; and although he is generally defeated for all other offices, he is annually and unanimously chosen editor-in-chief of the *Tribune*, with the pay of a cabinet officer. When there became a little unpleasantness between Greeley and his chief assistant, Charles A. Dana, the latter sold his shares to Dr. J. C. Ayer, of Lowell. Among the shareholders in 1870 were Horace Greeley; Samuel Sinclair, its business manager; the late Albert D. Richardson; the family of Stephen T. Clark, its late financial writer, and formerly of the *Express;* Bayard Taylor; Theodore Tilton, lately of the *Independent*, now of the *Golden Age;* Oliver Johnson, of the *Anti-Slavery Standard;* Thomas N. Rooker, foreman of the *Tribune* composing rooms; Dr. J. C. Ayer, of Lowell; and Solon Robinson, the author of *The Farm*, and other agricultural works.

The plan of association in newspapers is French in its origin. It grew out of the socialistic ideas of that country, and is a part of the system of a division of labor, and to bring into active use the savings of men of small means. Emile de Girardin introduced the plan in the ownership and management of the *Presse*, of Paris. The *Siècle*, of Paris, recently gave a very clear idea of the plan in its call of a meeting of its shareholders, which we insert:

Avis aux actionnaires du Siècle.

Le directeur gérant de la société du journal le *Siècle* a l'honneur de prévenir MM. les actionnaires que l'assemblée générale annuelle aura lieu le samedi 13 mars 1869, au siége de la société, rue Chauchat, 14, à quatre heures précises du soir.

Cette assemblée aura pour objet :

1°. D'entendre le rapport du directeur gérant sur la situation morale et matérielle de l'entreprise ;
2°. D'entendre le rapport du conseil de surveillance ;
3°. D'approuver les comptes de la gérance ;
4°. De procéder à la révision des statuts.

Aux termes de l'art. 71 de l'acte de société, l'assemblée générale ne pourra délibérer que dans le cas où les actionnaires délibérants représenteront les deux tiers des actions émises. Dans le cas contraire, l'assemblée générale s'ajournera a quinzaine, et, dans l'intervalle, il sera fait de nouvelles convocations indiquant les motifs de l'ajournement.

L'assemblée générale ainsi convoquée pourra délibérer valablement quel que soit le nombre des actions représentées par les actionnaires présents.

Pour assister à l'assemblée il faut être porteur de dix actions, qui devront être déposées, au moins trois jours avant la réunion, entre les mains du caissier dé l'administration, qui en délivrera un récépissé signé par le directeur gérant.

Ceux de MM. les actionnaires qui ne seraient pas propriétaires de dix actions sont priés d'envoyer leurs titres à l'administration, avec une lettre autorisant à les représenter l'un de MM. les membres du conseil de surveillance.

Aux termes de l'art. 69 de l'acte de société "MM. les actionnaires absents ou empêchés pourront se faire représenter par un mandataire spécial, pris parmi les actionnaires ; la femme séparée de biens pourra se faire représenter par son mari ; les mineurs émancipés pourront être présents aux délibérations et y auront voix délibérative."

Women and children, it appears, were shareholders in the *Siècle;* and, of course, they will become shareholders as heirs, if not as purchasers—as in the case of the London *Times*, on the death of the elder Walter in 1846—in other journals hereafter ; and it will not surprise us to see shares in newspapers publicly sold, as shares are now sold in railroads, banks, telegraph and express lines. Why not? Indeed, in 1869, a share in the *Christian Register* was disposed of at auction in Boston with shares in other incorporated concerns. In the spring of 1869 it was reported that Mr. Bennett would sell the *Herald* establishment. Ten gentlemen of wealth met, talked over the matter as if they were organizing a railway company, and each agreed to subscribe $200,000, making a total of $2,000,000, for the purpose of making the purchase. They selected a gentleman to make the offer to Mr. Bennett. What was his answer? "Two millions of dollars for the *Herald?* What shall I do with the money? More important yet, what shall I do with myself? The *Herald* now pays me more than the interest on the sum offered. I can not eat any more than I now do. I can not wear any more clothes. No! no! I will not sell." So the *Herald*, like the New York *Ledger*, remains among the few newspapers thus owned, the exclusive property of one man.

This co-operative system. in labor has largely spread to other trades and business. Always fascinating in theory, it frequently fails in practice. There was a Printer's Association in Boston organized in 1865.

The only condition of membership was the payment of a weekly instalment of two dollars by each member until sufficient funds to buy an office was accumulated. It was at first intended that the association should number fifty members, the first twenty-five subscribers to select the remainder by ballot from among the later applicants; but the number was finally confined to the original twenty-five signers. The first payment of the original instalment was made in November, 1866, and regular weekly payments were made from that time forward. The capital stock was fixed at $4000, and it was not intended to begin work until that sum was paid up.

In 1867 the *New York Shipping List*, an old publication, was purchased, and the office was opened by the association in May of that year.

At the close of the second fiscal year—May, 1869—the association gave full and remunerative employment to twenty-eight compositors and pressmen. At the end of that year the association also declared a dividend of fifty per cent. The capital stock was increased to $15,000—twenty-five shares of $600 each—and the dividend went in part payment. A second dividend was declared January 1st, 1870, and half yearly afterward. It is thought by the president and the manager that the stock inventory at the end of 1869 will show a value of not less than $20,000.

Somewhere about 1850, Horace Greeley, in giving "Hints to Volunteer Correspondents," suggested a course which would now strike the mind of a true journalist as rather queer. He laid down this law:

When you want an article inserted to subserve some purpose other than the public good, you should offer to pay for it. It is not just that you should solicit the use of columns not your own, to promote your own or your friend's private interests, without offering to pay for them. The fact that you are a subscriber gives you no right in this respect; if the paper is not worth its price, don't take it. True, you may often crowd an article in, through the editor's complacency, that you ought to pay for; but he sets you down as a sponge and a sneak forthwith, and is not often out of the way. If you wish to use the columns of any journal to promote your own or some other person's private interest, offer to pay therefor; there is no other honest way.

If Mr. Greeley would send such persons to the advertisement desk, his course would be the wisest for the *Tribune* and for its readers. No matter outside of the advertisement columns should be paid for. When an editor talks about his space, and his time, and that he publishes a paper for his bread and butter, he tells his readers what they already know; but to admit matter in his news and editorial columns which is paid for is simply treating his readers dishonestly. Newspapers have two sorts of revenue: one comes from subscribers, and the other from advertisements. The former, in reading the contents of the news and editorial columns, do not expect to find, under the implied indorsement of the editor, all sorts of schemes for the making of money. They know what the advertisements are, and are influenced by them without imposition. Newspapers like the *Tribune* are now, we hope, beyond permitting their columns to be used in any other than in the most legitimate way.

When the editor of the *Tribune* visited Europe in 1851, he made his appearance in England during one of the agitations for the repeal of the stamp duty on newspapers and the duty on advertisements in that kingdom. Eight members of the House of Commons had been selected as a committee to take evidence on the subject. Richard Cobden and Milnor Gibson were on this committee. Nearly all of the leading editors and newspaper managers of Great Britain had been examined, and had fully given their views on this subject, resulting in important concessions to the Press. While this committee was holding its sessions, Greeley arrived in London, and was called before them, and the following facts and opinions were elicited from him. Their report was published on the 16th of September, 1851, and we think the evidence of the editor of the *Tribune*, with its points and peculiarities, should be given almost *in extenso*, as an interesting part of this incomplete history of the American Press:

THE AMERICAN PRESS BEFORE A PARLIAMENTARY COMMITTEE.

On Wednesday, September 16, 1851, the parliamentary paper giving the minutes of evidence taken before the Select Committee on Newspaper Stamps was published. The following extracts will place before our readers the statements of an American publisher relative to the Press in the United States.

Mr. Horace Greeley called in and examined:

Chairman—(Mr. Milner Gibson). Are you able to give the committee any information with respect to the Press in the United States, and whether the absence of a stamp in the United States is productive of any bad effects, in your opinion?

Mr. Greeley. I will readily answer your question. We could not comprehend the operation of the stamp; it would be impracticable, under our institutions, every way. I can state something with regard to what the Press is doing in our country, but I can not imagine the application of the stamp at all; it would require an entire revolution in the habits and feelings of the people generally.

Question. You are the publisher of a newspaper, are you not?

Answer. I am.

* * * * * * * * *

Ques. Can you give the committee any idea of the number of the New York daily papers that are published?

Ans. The number of daily papers that are published in New York are fifteen in all, in the city.

Ques. How many morning and how many evening papers are there?

Ans. Ten morning and five evening papers. Some of the morning papers are also published in the evening; we publish two evening editions, like the *Times*, and other papers. There are five distinctive evening papers.

Ques. Can you inform the committee what the aggregate circulation of those daily papers is?

Ans. There are five of them cheap ones, at 1*d.* or ½*d.*, whose aggregate circulation is a little over 100,000 copies per day; the other ten are sold dearer—that is, at ten dollars per annum, a little more than 1½*d.* each, not 2*d.* a copy. Of those ten I should say that the average circulation is about 3000—being 30,000 of the dearer papers, the commercial sheets, and 100,000 of the cheap journals.

Ques. The aggregate is 130,000 papers daily?

Ans. Yes.

Ques. What proportion of these, at a rough guess, should you say are consumed by the 700,000 inhabitants of New York, and what proportion do you suppose are sent to remote distances?

Ans. About 60,000 are circulated in the city and its suburbs, and about 45,000 are sent away.

* * * * * * * * *

Ques. You stated that the weekly newspapers cost a penny, or two cents?

Ans. Yes, when sent to clubs of twenty or more subscribers; we charge more for a single copy of, a weekly than of a daily paper, because the advertisements form a great part of the contents of the daily journal. The charge is two dollars a year for a single copy of a weekly paper; that will be twopence each number; but to the clubs it is reduced to one dollar a year—twenty copies for twenty dollars. The object is to get a wider circulation in the different villages by making them cheap. A large number of city papers are taken, so as to come to about one penny each to a subscriber, and a halfpenny for his postage.

Ques. You do not report, in your papers, the proceedings of the Congress in the way in which they report here the proceedings in Parliament?

Ans. No, except in the Washington journals, in which they report them very fully—I think quite as fully as they are reported here. We have a telegraph report occasionally of a speech by some distinguished statesman, such as Mr. Clay or Mr. Calhoun, or any of the leading men; they are reported fully; but the mass of the speeches are not, except that they are sketched in a telegraphic report, occupying about two columns a day, but stretching sometimes to four or five.

Ques. Your Newspaper Press is of a more local character than the Press in this country, is it not?

Ans. It is, I presume, more local than the London journals, because its circulation is more circumscribed by the fact that the local journals are so abundant.

Ques. You go to considerable expense in obtaining news for your papers from various parts of the world, do you not?

Ans. Yes; but mainly it is by telegraphing from different parts of the country. The leading journals have correspondents; but the great item of expense is telegraphing, and sending off boats sometimes. When steam-ships do not touch at Halifax, we sometimes send off boats to intercept them.

Ques. You have correspondents in different places, who telegraph up to you any occurrences that may be interesting?

Ans. Yes, all over the country—a net-work.

Ques. You employ those correspondents to pay constant attention to such things?

Ans. Yes; but telegraphing is done mainly by an association called the Associated Press of New York.

Ques. Do you complain of piracy in the United States; for instance, of one publisher, who has not himself been at the expense of obtaining news, copying immediately from another?

Ans. It is sometimes talked of, for effect's sake; yet, on the whole, I would rather that those who do not take it should copy than not. We have six or seven journals in the city, which form a combination, and spend, perhaps, $100,000 a year in telegraphing; and the evening journals all copy from us, and we rather like it.

Ques. Have you any protection, in the nature of copyright, to your news?

Ans. Not the least; the moment it is out any body can take it, and they do take it and issue it.

Ques. There is no precaution at all taken against piracy?

Ans. No; we only take this precaution: we have, for instance, a very important piece of information, which has cost us $1000. We will suppose that two journals take charge of the foreign news, and two journals take charge of another part of the news, and the journals having charge of it, when they send the news round to the others, say, "This is not to be issued till four [or five] o'clock," and no journal of the combination will let a copy go out of the office till the hour named; it is in the hands of the carriers, but it is not allowed to go out till the hour named, and thus nobody can get it.

Ques. Supposing it were something of great interest, there would be a continued demand for your paper if you were the only one who could communicate it; and, for a given period, that demand would continue, and you would keep striking off your copies to supply it. Is there nothing to entitle you, having incurred the first expense of obtaining that news, to issue it for any period?

Ans. Not for a moment—any body may print it—but the public are apt to take the paper which has the first news.

Ques. They give the preference to the parties who have obtained the news first, and in practice piracy does not inflict injury upon you?

Ans. I would choose that they should print it rather than not; they can not sell as we could. The fact that certain journals have the earliest news soon becomes notorious, and almost every one wants his newspaper with his breakfast, delivered between the hours of five and half past seven. They take the morning papers to read with their breakfast; and those who take the news after we issue it can not have it in time to deliver it to a very large number in a suitable morning season, and we regard it as of no consequence.

Ques. Does the interest of the intelligence evaporate so soon?

Ans. Not that; but a subscriber must have the paper that gives him his news in the morning before he goes to his work.

Ques. You retard the publication of news sometimes?

Ans. Yes; when we have important intelligence.

Ques. Is not that an inconvenience to the public?

Ans. We get them out in our regular way, but we do not let a copy go out of the hands of our confidential agents till the hour, say, of five o'clock in the morning.

Ques. At what rate can you print the *New York Tribune?*

Ans. Our press will work but 10,000 an hour; there is one faster, an eight-cylinder, which will work 20,000, they say; I call it 18,000.

Ques. Do you believe that there is a press at work in New York which will print 18,000 copies an hour?

Ans. Yes; I have seen it at work, and it will throw off as fast as men can feed sheets upon it.

Ques. Have you seen the press that is used for the *Times?*

Ans. Yes.

Ques. Do you consider that the press at New York prints with more rapidity than the one at the *Times* office?

Ans. Yes; the press at the *Times* is fed on what I would call a drum or vertical cylinder; we feed on horizontal cylinders, directly on and around our greater or type cylinder. One man stands over the top, and another below, and so on, feeding, and the four cylinders are fed on each side of the large cylinder, on which the form revolves, and they feed the four paper cylinders, one above the other, on each side of the large cylinder; the sheets are laid over and over on the face as fast as the great cylinder can be turned, and every time it makes one revolution it has printed eight journals.

Ques. Is that machinery used by the proprietor of a penny paper?

Ans. Yes; a halfpenny newspaper—the *Sun.*

Ques. Must not that require the use of considerable capital?

Ans. Yes; the *Sun* concern is worth a quarter of a million of dollars; £50,000 were given for it.

Ques. Do you speak of copyright and plant?

Ans. There was very little property besides. It was sold for a quarter of a million of dollars, and it was very cheap.

Ques. Fifty thousand pounds for a halfpenny paper?

Ans. Yes.

Ques. What is the circulation?

Ans. Fifty thousand; but the circulation is a very light matter; there is no profit upon that; but the advertising would be, I suppose, £60, or $300 a day.

Ques. Could you furnish the committee with some statistical information as to the Newspaper Press of America?

Ans. Yes, when our census returns are published. I should say that the whole number of journals printed in the United States is about 3000 now. If you count, for instance, one daily, with its weekly and semi-weekly, all as one paper, the number is 2500 journals published.

Ques. Are there 2500 with distinct and separate titles?

Ans. Yes, distinct establishments; of which about 2000 are devoted to general intelligence and politics, and the others are devoted to science, religion, and education.

Ques. And they are published at all intervals, from once a day to once a month?

Ans. Yes, some twice or thrice a day.

Ques. Your principal profit is derived from advertisements, is it not?

Ans. Yes, on daily papers.

Ques. With reference to the *Sun* paper, you stated, in your last examination, that the circulation was large, but that the profit derived therefrom was from the advertising?

Ans. The profit is nothing on the circulation. I will state how, in our country, there being no duty on the advertisements, the prices are very much less for advertising. The prices range from 25 cents up to any amount—that is to say, 25 cents is the lowest; for instance, the advertisement of a religious meeting, or any public gathering, will be some 25 cents, or 1*s.* of the money of this country; the consequence is, that the amount of their advertisements is enormous. Every religious meeting, or meeting to take place of any religious society, benevolent or philanthropic, is advertised in all the journals, and forms a very large proportion of our receipts, though the receipts, in each case, are very small. We regard those as a portion of the news of the day; and advertising which possesses a public interest is done at a less price than advertisements intended for the pecuniary profit of the advertiser. Now an advertisement duty would destroy new papers. Its operation is this: your duty is the same on an advertisement in a journal where it is worth ten times as much, for instance in a journal of 50,000 circulation, as in a journal with 2000, although the value of the article is twenty times as much in the one case as in the other: the duty operates precisely as though you were to lay a tax of 1*s.* a day on every day's labor that a man were to do; on a man's labor which is worth, say 2*s.*, it would be destructive, while by that man who earns 20*s.* it would be very lightly felt. It would entirely destroy new papers. An advertisement is worth but a certain amount, and the public soon get an idea what it is worth; you put a duty on advertising, and you prevent any advertisement coming to a new establishment. To those people who advertise in the *Sun* and our well-established journals, they could afford in charge a price to include the duty, and do very well; but in a new concern the advertisements would not be worth the amount of the duty, and the consequence would be it would be utterly withheld. Now the advertisements are one main source of the value of daily papers, and thousands of business men take them in mainly for those advertisements. For instance, at one time, in New York, our auctioneers were appointed by law, and were, of course, party politicians, and one journal which was high in the confidence of the party in power obtained, not a law, but an understanding, that all the auctioneers appointed should advertise in that journal. Now, though that journal has ceased to be of that party, and the auctioneers are no longer appointed by the state, yet that journal has almost a monopoly of the auctioneers' business, because at a certain time all the auctioneers were obliged to advertise in that paper; consequently, all the men who buy and sell at auction were obliged to take the paper; and now, although the necessity has gone away, yet still every advertiser by auction must advertise in that journal, because he knows that purchasers are looking there, and every purchaser by auction must take that journal in, because he knows that the advertisements by auction will be there, without regard to the goodness of the paper, but simply because of its containing those advertisements; all the great dry goods interest, with the corresponding interests, must take that paper, and they continue to take it; and precisely in that way the advertising duty is an enormous help to any paper which has the most circulation: it tends to throw the advertising always on the greatest concern; and the persons who take, as I know men in this town do take, one journal mainly for its advertisements, must take the *Times*, because every thing is advertised there; consequently they do take it—advertisers must advertise in it for the same reason. If we had a duty on advertisements now, I will say not only that it would be impossible to build a new concern up in New York against the competition of the older ones, but it would be impossible to preserve the weaker papers from being swallowed up by the stronger ones.

* * * * * * *

Ques. It is clear, then, that the effect of the stamp and advertisement duty is to lessen the amount of the receipt from the duty on paper?

Ans. Enormously. I see that the circulation in London is but 60,000 against 130,000 in New York City, while the tendency is more to concentrate on London than on New York. Not a tenth part of the daily papers of the United States are printed in New York City.

Ques. Do you consider that there are upwards of a million daily papers issuing from the Daily Press in the United States?

Ans. I should say about a million; I can not say upwards. I think there are about 250 daily journals published in the United States.

Ques. You would consider that there are a million of daily papers issuing from the Press of the United States?

Ans. I think very nearly that.

Ques. You stated that there are fifteen daily papers in New York; how many are there in Boston?

Ans. Twelve, I think.

Ques. What is the population of Boston?

Ans. Boston contains about 140,000 inhabitants, but Massachusetts is much more compactly peopled and better supplied with railways. All the towns in Massachusetts and New England take more or less of the Boston daily papers.

Ques. What number of daily papers are published in Philadelphia?

Ans. Philadelphia has ten, I think; they are not so many in number, but one or two have a much larger circulation.

Ques. How many in Baltimore?

Ans. Six.

Ques. How many in New Orleans, should you think?

Ans. Ten or twelve, I think.

Ques. At what amount of population of a town in America do they generally begin to have a daily paper; they first of all begin with a weekly paper, do they not?

Ans. Yes. With regard to newspapers the general rule is this, that each county will have one. In all the free states, if a county has a population of 20,000, it has two—one of each party. The general average is about one local journal in the agricultural counties for 10,000 inhabitants. A county containing 50,000 has five journals, which are generally weekly papers; and when a town grows to have as many as 15,000 inhabitants, or thereabouts, then it has a daily paper. Sometimes that is the case when it has as few as 10,000. It depends more on the business of the place, but 15,000 may be stated as the average at which a daily paper commences. At 20,000 they have two, and so on. In central towns, like Buffalo, Rochester, Troy, and such towns, they have from three to five daily journals, each of which prints a semi-weekly or a weekly journal.

Ques. Have those papers much circulation outside the towns in which they are published?

Ans. The county is the general limit, though some pervade a judicial district including five or six counties.

Ques. They do not penetrate into counties and towns in which other papers are published?

Ans. Not as a rule; but the Buffalo papers will have a circulation round Lake Erie, which is a country easily reached by them.

Ques. Would the New York papers, for instance, have much circulation at Charleston?

Ans. The *New York Herald*, I think, which is considered the journal the most friendly to Southern interests, has a considerable circulation there.

Ques. Independently of peculiar reasons, they would not circulate in the more distant states?

Ans. To a certain extent, the leading political journal of one party would be taken by the leading politicians in other states; and, if it is a business journal, there is one I know particularly that has a very large circulation among the pork buyers and the grain buyers throughout the free Western States, having relations with New York; they want fuller reports of the markets than those the telegraph brings them.

Ques. Substantially the newspaper of any of those states finds the bulk of its readers within its own state?

Ans. Yes; the Washington papers are an exception.

Ques. The New Orleans papers would have but little circulation in New York, for instance?

Ans. No.

Ques. When a person proposes to publish a paper at New York, is he required to go to any office to register himself?

Ans. No, not at all.

Ques. Is he required by law to give any security that he will not insert libels or seditious matter?
Ans. No.
Ques. He merely publishes a paper at his own will and pleasure, without consulting any public authority?
Ans. Yes.
Ques. If he should libel any body in his paper, he would be liable to an action at law, would he not?
Ans. To two actions, civil and criminal.
Ques. Then a newspaper publisher is not subject to any liability more than other persons?
Ans. No more than one starting a blacksmith's shop.
Ques. They do not presume, in the United States, that because a man is going to print news in a paper he is going to libel?
Ans. No, nor do they presume that his libeling would amount to much, unless he is a responsible character.
Ques. Are there not many actions brought in America for libel?
Ans. Very few indeed, unless founded on police reports, such as the report of a man being arrested on the charge of swindling, or the like of that.
Ques. Are you not permitted by the law of America to publish the police reports?
Ans. No; it is not regarded as lawful even to say that John Jones was arrested for swindling; it is not a privileged publication; he might show a damage in that case and convict you, even though it was the fact that he was so arrested for swindling, unless you could prove that he was actually a swindler; that rule is derived from your courts.
Ques. From what you have stated with regard to the circulation of the daily Press in New York, it appears that a very large proportion of the adult population must be customers for them there?
Ans. Yes, I think three fourths of all the families take in a daily paper of some kind.
Ques. The purchasers of the daily papers must consist of a different class from those in England—mechanics must purchase them?
Ans. Every mechanic takes a paper, or nearly every one.
Ques. At what time does he buy his paper?
Ans. He subscribes at an office. The carrier of a paper is the owner of a certain ward of the city; it is a property of his own; on the *Sun* I have known one sold for seven hundred dollars; that is, the privilege of buying the papers at the office at seventy cents a hundred, and serving them to subscribers, and getting one dollar a hundred for them. In every particular ward of the city the carrier has a property in the right to receive the journals for the ward, and to distribute them in that ward.
Ques. Then the working class receive their papers regularly through the carrier in the morning?
Ans. Yes.
Ques. What time are they delivered in the morning?
Ans. Between six and seven, as a rule.
Ques. Do these people generally get them before they leave home for their work?
Ans. Yes, and you are complained of if you do not furnish a man with his newspaper at his breakfast; he wants to read it between six and seven usually.
Ques. Then a shipbuilder, or a cooper, or a joiner, takes in his daily paper in the morning, and reads it at his breakfast time?
Ans. Yes, and he may take it with him to read at his dinner, between twelve and one; but the rule is that he wants his paper at his breakfast.
Ques. After he has finished his breakfast or dinner, he may be found reading the daily newspaper, just as the people of the upper classes do in England?
Ans. Yes, if they do.
Ques. And that is quite common, is it not?
Ans. Almost universal, I think. There is a very poor class, a good many foreigners, who do not know how to read, but no native, I think.
Ques. Do the agricultural laborers read much?

Ans. Yes; they take our weekly papers, which they receive through the post generally.

Ques. Is there any sending of papers from one person to another person—a person having bought a paper and read it, does he send it to a friend by post?

Ans. There has been a little of that. It is often done when there is a marriage or a death, or some piece of information that you want your friend to know in another country.

Ques. It is not done for the purpose of economy, and to share the expenses of the paper between different persons?

Ans. No; they are so cheap that it is not worth while.

Ques. The transmission by post would be nearly as expensive as the cost of the paper, would it not?

Ans. Quite so, as they send them in separately, and the post-offices do not like to receive them in that way.

Ques. The working people in New York are not in the habit of resorting to public houses to read the newspapers, are they?

Ans. Yes, they are, but not to read the papers.

Ques. They resort to public houses to drink spirits, or any thing else?

Ans. A good many of them do; it is not the general practice, but still there are quite a class who do so.

Ques. The newspaper is not the attraction to the public house?

Ans. No; I think a very small proportion of our reading class go there at all; those that I have seen there are mainly the foreign population—those who do not read.

Ques. Are there any papers published in New York, or in other parts, which may be said to be of an obscene or immoral character?

Ans. We call the *New York Herald* a very bad paper—those who do not like it; but that is not the cheapest.

Ques. Have you heard of a paper called the *Town*, published in this country, with pictures of a certain character in it—an unstamped publication?—have you any publications in the United States of that character?

Ans. Not daily papers. There are weekly papers got up from time to time, called the *Scorpion*, the *Flash*, the *Whip*, and so on, whose purpose is to extort money from parties who can be threatened with exposure of immoral practices, or for visiting infamous houses.

Ques. Will you look at that paper (the *Town* being handed to the witness)?

Ans. There was a class of weekly papers got up there that were printed for two or three months. I do not know of any one being continued any considerable time; if one dies another is got up, and that goes down.

Ques. They do not last, do they?

Ans. No; and I suppose they do not here; but the cheap daily papers, the very cheapest, are, as a whole, I think, quite as discreet in their conduct and conversation as other journals. They do not embody the same amount of talent; they devote themselves mainly to news. They are not party journals; they are nominally independent—that is, of no party. They are not given to harsh language with regard to public men; they are very moderate.

Ques. Is scurrility or personality common to the publications in the United States?

Ans. It is not common; it is much less frequent than it was; but it is not absolutely unknown.

Ques. What do you call a newspaper? Where do you draw the line between what comes under the postage rate and what is liable to a higher rate?

Ans. The rule has been that every thing printed as often as once a week was a newspaper; the others are generally regarded as magazines and periodicals.

Ques. Has there ever been any proposition made in the United States with a view to control the Press? for instance, that it should be liable to a stamp duty, and give security in the same manner as is required in France?

Ans. I have heard a suggestion that it might be well to charge one cent on a copy, and let it go free through the post, but not by any number of persons. Some have said that it would improve the character of the Press, but it was never seriously taken up. I have seen it in newspapers as a suggestion.

Ques. What is the circulation of the *New York Herald?*

Ans. I think 25,000.
Ques. Has its circulation been increased during the last few years, or otherwise?
Ans. I think it has rather increased, not diminished.
Ques. Is that an influential paper in America?
Ans. I think not.
Ques. It has a higher reputation probably in Europe than at home?
Ans. A certain class of journals in this country find it their interest or pleasure to quote it a good deal.
Ques. As the demand is extensive, is the remuneration for the services of literary men who are employed on the Press good?
Ans. The prices of literary labor are more moderate than in this country. The highest salary, I think, that would be commanded by any one connected with the Press would be £1000—the highest that could be thought of; I have not heard of higher than £600.
Ques. What would be about the ordinary remuneration?
Ans. In our own concern it is, besides the principal editor, £300 down to £100. I think that is the usual range.
Ques. Are your leading men in America, in point of literary ability, employed from time to time upon the Press as an occupation?
Ans. It is beginning to be so, but it has not been the custom. There have been leading men connected with the Press, but the Press has not been usually conducted by the most powerful men. With a few exceptions, the leading political journals are conducted ably, and this is becoming more general; and, with a wider diffusion of the circulation, the Press is more able to pay for it.
Ques. Is it a profession apart?
Ans. No; usually the men have been brought up to the bar, to the pulpit, as printers, and so on. They are not originally literary men.
Ques. Your extensive circulation of those cheap papers is based, to some extent, upon the fact that your whole population can read?
Ans. Yes.
Ques. I presume that the non-reading class in the United States is a limited one?
Ans. Yes, except in the slave states.
Ques. Do not you consider that newspaper reading is calculated to keep up a habit of reading?
Ans. I think it is worth all the schools in the country. I think it creates a taste for reading in every child's mind, and it increases his interest in his lessons; he is attracted to study from the habit of always seeing a newspaper and hearing it read, I think.
Ques. Supposing that you had your schools as now, but that your Newspaper Press were reduced within the limits of the Press in England, do not you think that the habit of reading acquired at school would be frequently laid aside?
Ans. I think that the habit would not be acquired, and that often reading would fall into disuse.
Ques. Does not the habit of reading create a demand for newspapers, rather than the supply of newspapers create a habit of reading?
Ans. I should rather say that the capacity that is obtained in the schools creates a demand for newspapers.
Ques. The greater number of persons who read in the United States accounts for the greater number of newspapers that are published, does it not?
Ans. There is no class in the free states who do not know how to read except the immigrant class.
Ques. But in proportion to the number of persons who can read will be the number of papers supplied?
Ans. Yes.
Ques. But the means of obtaining cheap newspapers enables people to keep up their reading, does it not?
Ans. Yes.
Ques. Must not the contents of a newspaper have a great effect upon the character of the population, and give a more practical turn to their minds?
Ans. I should think the difference in intelligence would be very great between a population first educated in schools, and then acquiring the habit of reading journals, and an uneducated non-reading.

Ques. If a man is taught to read first, and afterward applies his mind to the reading of newspapers, would not his knowledge assume a much more practical form than if that man read any thing else?

Ans. Every man must be practical. I think that the capacity to invent or to improve a machine, for instance, is very greatly aided by newspaper reading—by the education afforded by newspapers.

Ques. Having observed both countries, can you state whether the Press has greater influence on public opinion in the United States than in England, or the reverse?

Ans. I think it has more influence with us. I do not know that any class is despotically governed by it, but the influence is more universal. Every one reads it and talks about it with us, and more weight is laid upon intelligence than on editorials; the paper which brings the quickest news is the one looked to.

Ques. The leading article has not so much influence as it has in England?

Ans. No; the telegraphic dispatch is the great point.

Ques. Observing our newspapers, and comparing them with the American papers, do you find that we make much less use of the electric telegraph for transmittting news to newspapers than in America?

Ans. Not a hundredth part as much as we do.

Ques. That is a considerable item of expense there, is it not?

Ans. Enormous; but it is cheaper with us than with you.

Ques. An impression prevails in this country that our Newspaper Press incurs a great deal more expense to expedite news than you do in New York; are you of that opinion?

Ans. I do not know what your expense is; I should say that $100,000 a year are paid by our association of the six leading daily papers, besides what each gets separately for itself.

Ques. Twenty thousand pounds sterling a year are paid by your association, consisting of six papers, for what you get in common?

Ans. Yes; we telegraph a great deal in the United States. For instance, the Scientific Association held its annual meeting in Cincinnati this year, and we had telegraphic reports from that place, though we, and I presume other journals, had special reporters to report the proceedings at length. So we have reports every day 1000 miles—from New Orleans daily, and St. Louis, and other places.

After this evidence before Cobden, and Gibson, and Ewart, and Rich, of the British Parliament, there are a few points given to James Parton and John Russell Young which we must add to make the thing more complete.

Soon after Parton's article appeared in the *North American Review*, Greeley met him, and criticised his published statements. It happened to be during a strike of the New York Street-railway Conductors for higher wages. "I believe my general view is true," answered Parton; "to-day I can learn more about this street-railway excitement from the *Herald* than from any other paper." "Well," explained Greeley, "I don't want to encourage these lawless proceedings." "Exactly," returned Parton; "I could not ask a better case in point. But the true theory is, not to serve one side or another upon any question—merely to give *all* the news." In Parton's article he remarked, "An editorial is a man speaking to men, but the news is Providence speaking to men."

"Mr. Greeley," said John Russell Young, "would be the greatest journalist in the world if he did not aim to be one of the leading politicians in America. Very often does he sacrifice himself to his prejudices. I remember on one occasion asking him to let me report a speech of Governor Seymour in full, as a matter of news for the *Tribune*. 'Yes,' he said, 'I will print Governor Seymour's speech when the *World* will print those of our side.'"

Horace Greeley, as we have said, became an enthusiastic admirer of William H. Seward. To the fortunes of that politician he was intimately connected for twenty years. When he first assumed the position of political editor in 1834, having started the *Constitution* in that year, Seward was for the first time a candidate for the office of Governor of New York. He worked so zealously for that politician, in conjunction with Thurlow Weed, of the *Albany Evening Journal*, doing the rough work without much, if any compensation, that the trio became known as the firm of Seward, Weed, and Greeley. Twenty years of such labor without reward, and in the midst of disappointed political aspirations, finally led to a rupture, which is thus naively described by the junior member of the concern in his notice of the dissolution of the partnership :

HORACE GREELEY TO WILLIAM H. SEWARD.

NEW YORK, Saturday evening, November 11, 1854.

GOVERNOR SEWARD,—The election is over, and its results sufficiently ascertained. It seems to me a fitting time to announce to you the dissolution of the political firm of Seward, Weed, and Greeley, by the withdrawal of the junior partner—said withdrawal to take effect on the morning after the first Tuesday in February next. And as it may seem a great presumption in me to assume that any such firm exists, especially since the public was advised, rather more than a year ago, by an editorial rescript in the *Evening Journal*, formally reading me out of the Whig Party, that I was esteemed no longer either useful or ornamental in the concern, you will, I am sure, indulge me in some reminiscences which seem to befit the occasion.

I was a poor young printer and editor of a literary journal—a very active and bitter Whig in a small way, but not seeking to be known out of my own Ward Committee;—when, after the great political revulsion of 1837, I was one day called to the City Hotel, where two strangers introduced themselves as Thurlow Weed and Lewis Benedict, of Albany. They told me that a cheap campaign paper of a peculiar stamp at Albany had been resolved on, and that I had been selected to edit it. The announcement might well be deemed flattering by one who had never even sought the notice of the great, and who was not known as a partisan writer, and I eagerly embraced their proposals. They asked me to fix my salary for the year; I named $1000, which they agreed to; and I did the work required to the best of my ability. It was work that made no figure and created no sensation ; but I loved it, and I did it well. When it was done, you were governor, dispensing offices worth $3000 to $20,000 per year to your friends and compatriots, and I returned to my garret and my crust, and my desperate battle with pecuniary obligations heaped upon me by bad partners in business and the disastrous events of 1837. I believe it did not then occur to me that some one of these abundant places might have been offered to me without injustice ; I now think it should have occurred to you. If it did occur to me, I was not the man to ask you for it ; I think that should not have been necessary. I only remember that no friend at Albany inquired as to my pecuniary circumstances; that your friend (but not mine), Robert C. Wetmore, was one of the chief dispensers of your patronage here ; and that such devoted compatriots as A. H. Wells and John Hooks were lifted by you out of pauperism into independence, as I am glad I was not ; and yet an inquiry from you as to my needs and means at that time would have been timely, and held ever in grateful remembrance.

In the Harrison campaign of 1840, I was again designated to edit a campaign paper. I published it as well, and ought to have made something by it, in spite of its extremely low price ; my extreme poverty was the main reason why I did not. It compelled me to hire press-work, mailing, etc., done by the job, and high charges for extra work nearly ate me up. At the close, I was still without property and in debt, but this paper had rather improved my position.

Now came the great scramble of the swell mob of coon minstrels and cider-suckers at Washington—I not being counted in. Several regiments of them went on from this city; but no one of the whole crowd—though I say it who should not—had done so much toward General Harrison's nomination and election as yours respectfully. I asked nothing, expected nothing; but you, Governor Seward, ought to have asked that I be postmaster of New York. Your asking would have been in vain, but it would have been an act of grace neither wasted nor undeserved.

I soon after started the *Tribune*, because I was urged to do so by certain of your friends, and because such a paper was needed here. I was promised certain pecuniary aid in so doing; it might have been given me without cost or risk to any one. All I ever had was a loan by piecemeal of $1000 from James Coggeshall, God bless his honored memory! I did not ask for this, and I think it is the one sole case in which I ever received a pecuniary favor from a political associate. I am very thankful that he did not die till it was fully repaid.

And let me here honor one grateful recollection. When the Whig Party under your rule had offices to give, my name was never thought of; but when, in 1842–'3, we were hopelessly out of power, I was honored by the party nomination for state printer. When we came again to have a state printer to *elect* as well as nominate, the place went to Weed, as it ought. Yet it is worth something to know that there was once a time when it was not deemed too great a sacrifice to recognize me as belonging to your household. If a new office had not since been created on purpose to give its valuable patronage to H. J. Raymond, and enable St. John to show forth his *Times* as the organ of the Whig state administration, I should have been still more grateful.

In 1848 your star again rose, and my warmest hopes were realized in your election to the Senate. I was no longer needy, and had no more claim than desire to be recognized by General Taylor. I think I had some claim to forbearance from you. What I received thereupon was a most humiliating lecture in the shape of a decision in the libel case of Redfield and Pringle, and an obligation to publish it in my own and the other journal of our supposed firm. I thought, and still think, this lecture needlessly cruel and mortifying. The plaintiffs, after using my columns to the extent of their needs or desires, stopped writing, and called on me for the name of their assailant. I proffered it to them—a thoroughly responsible name. They refused to accept it unless it should prove to be one of the four or five first men in Batavia—when they had known from the first who it was, and that it was neither of them. They would not accept that which they had demanded; they sued me, instead, for money, and money you were at liberty to give them to your heart's content—I do not think you *were* at liberty to humiliate me in the eyes of my own and your public as you did. I think you exalted your own judicial sternness and fearlessness unduly at my expense. I think you had a better occasion for the display of these qualities when Webb threw himself untimely upon you for a pardon which he had done all a man could do to demerit. (His paper is paying you for it now.)

I have publicly set forth my view of your and our duty with respect to fusion, Nebraska, and party designations. I will not repeat any of that. I have referred also to Weed's reading me out of the Whig Party—my crime being, in this as in some other things, that of doing to-day what more politic persons will not be ready to do till to-morrow.

Let me speak of the late canvass. I was once sent to Congress for ninety days merely to enable Jim Brooks to secure a seat therein for four years. I think I never hinted to any human being that I would have liked to be put forward for any place; but James W. White (you hardly know how good and true a man he is) started my name for Congress, and Brooks's packed delegation thought I could help him through, so I was put on behind him. But this last spring, after the Nebraska Question had created a new state of things at the North, one or two personal friends, of no political consideration, suggested my name as a candidate for governor, and I did not discourage them. Soon the persons who were afterward mainly instrumental in nominating Clark came about me and asked if I could secure the Know-Nothing vote. I told them I neither could nor would touch it; on the contrary, I loathed and repelled it. Thereupon they turned upon Clark.

I said nothing, did nothing. A hundred people asked me who should be run for governor. I sometimes indicated Patterson; I never hinted at my own name.

But by-and-by Weed came down, and called me to him to tell me why he could not support me for governor. (I had never asked nor counted on his support.) I am sure Weed did not mean to humiliate me, but he did it. The upshot of his discourse (very cautiously stated) was this: If I were a candidate for governor, I should beat, not myself only, but you. Perhaps that was true; but, as I had in no manner solicited his or your support, I thought this might have been said to my friends rather than to me. I suspect it is true that I could not have been elected governor as a Whig; but, had he and you been favorable, there *would* have been a party in the state ere this which could and would have elected me to any post without injuring itself or endangering your re-election.

It was in vain that I urged that I had in no manner asked a nomination. At length I was nettled by his language—well intended, but *very* cutting as addressed by him to me—to say, in substance, " Well, then, make Patterson governor, and try my name for lieutenant. To lose this place is a matter of no importance, and we can see whether I am really so odious."

I should have hated to serve as lieutenant governor, but I should have gloried in running for the post. I want to have my enemies all upon me at once; I am tired of fighting them piecemeal; and, though I should have been beaten in the canvass, I know that my running would have helped the ticket and helped my paper.

It was thought best to let the matter take another course. No other name could have been put on the ticket so bitterly humbling to me as that which was selected. The nomination was given to Raymond, the fight left to me. And, Governor Seward, *I have made it*, though it be conceited in me to say so. What little fight there has been I have stirred up. Even Weed has not been (I speak of his paper) hearty in this contest, while the journal of the Whig lieutenant governor has taken care of its own interests and let the canvass take care of itself, as it early declared it would do. That journal has (because of its milk-and-water course) some twenty thousand subscribers in this city and its suburbs, and of these twenty thousand I venture to say more voted for Ullmann and Scroggs than for Clark and Raymond; the *Tribune* (also because of its character) has but eight thousand subscribers within the same radius, and I venture to say that of its habitual readers nine tenths voted for Clark and Raymond—very few for Ullmann and Scroggs. I had to bear the brunt of the contest, and take a terrible responsibility in order to prevent the Whigs uniting upon James W. Barker in order to defeat Fernando Wood. Had Barker been elected here, neither you nor I could walk these streets without being hooted, and Know-Nothingism would have swept like a prairie-fire. I stopped Barker's election at the cost of incurring the deadliest enmity of the defeated gang, and I have been rebuked for it by the lieutenant governor's paper. At the critical moment he came out against John Wheeler in favor of Charles H. Marshall (who would have been your deadliest enemy in the House); and even your colonel general's paper, which was even with me in insisting that Wheeler should be returned, wheeled about at the last moment and went in for Marshall, the *Tribune* alone clinging to Wheeler to the last. I rejoice that they who turned so suddenly were not able to turn all their readers.

Governor Seward, I know that some of your most cherished friends think me a great obstacle to your advancement—that John Schoolcraft, for one, insists that you and Weed shall not be identified with me. I trust, after a time, you will not be. I trust I shall never be found in opposition to you; I have no farther wish but to glide out of the newspaper world as quietly and as speedily as possible, join my family in Europe, and, if possible, stay there quite a time—long enough to cool my fevered brain and renovate my overtasked energies. All I ask is that we shall be counted even on the morning after the first Tuesday in February, as aforesaid, and that I may thereafter take such course as seems best without reference to the past.

You have done me acts of valued kindness in the line of your profession; let me close with the assurance that these will ever be gratefully remembered by
      Yours,   HORACE GREELEY.

This was written immediately after the campaign of 1854, but not published till the summer of 1860, when it appeared in the *Tribune*, brought to light by the repeated assaults made upon Greeley by James Watson Webb in the *Courier and Enquirer*, and Henry J. Raymond, of the *New York Times*, warm personal friends of Seward, who, it seems, had been to Auburn, and had had full access to this refreshing political autobiography of the editor of the *Tribune*.

There was great excitement in the journalistic and political circles of the country in the winter of 1856 and 1857, in consequence of some extraordinary developments made in Washington affecting these Siamese classes. O. B. Matteson, a member of Congress from New York, figured prominently in the scenes. Twenty or thirty other members of Congress were mixed up in the affair. Among other statements, it was charged that Horace Greeley was implicated in the Des Moines Improvement Company to the extent of a check for one thousand dollars which had been mysteriously deposited with him, and which, as a conscientious editor, he could not consistently retain. When the charge was made the editor of the *Tribune* was in Iowa, and there he met it with the following card:

To the Editor of the Iowa City Republican:

* * * * * * * *

I went to Washington at the opening of the long session of the present Congress, December 1, 1855, and remained there, with brief intervals of absence, until about the middle of April last. During all this time I can not remember that I once heard of this Des Moines Company; and I am very sure that neither this nor any railroad or other company or claimant employed me to do any service, or paid me one farthing on any account whatever. In a single instance only did an old and esteemed friend ask me to aid him in securing for his claim the favorable attention of Congress, which I thought it deserved; but he, on my explaining to him my position, and the annoyance and embarrassment to which any connection with measures involving pecuniary interests would inevitably subject me, dropped the subject, and never renewed it.

* * * * * * * *

As I was leaving Washington for the last time up to this present, on or about the 1st of July last, a friend handed me a draft for one thousand dollars, drawn on the treasurer, in New York, of the Des Moines Company, which he asked me to take with me and use to pay a draft which he said would probably be drawn on me by an agent employed by said company. I took this draft, accordingly, home with me, and held it until I was apprised, nearly four weeks thereafter, that a draft on me, answering to this one, was coming on from Washington. I immediately, and for the first time in my life, visited the office of the Des Moines Company, and found therein an old and valued friend, Mr. Alvah Hunt, formerly treasurer of our state, and now treasurer of this Des Moines Company. I said to him, "Mr. Hunt, do you know of a draft for one thousand dollars on your company, payable to my order?" He answered, "Yes, I understand it." I rejoined, "Do you know that I have no interest in said draft?" He said, "Yes, I know all about it." "Then," said I, "shall I accept and pay the draft against it?" He said, "Certainly," and I presented the draft in my hands, which he paid, and with the proceeds I paid the one thousand dollars draft drawn from Washington on me. That draft is now in my possession.

These are the facts in the case, to which, immediately on the story being started that I had been employed by this company, I made affidavit in due form of law, and transmitted the same to the investigating committee of the Iowa Senate, corroborated by the statement of Alvah Hunt aforesaid, that I never was interested in nor employed by said Des Moines Company, and never was paid nor promised by it one farthing for any service whatever. I believe other leading members of the company, familiar with the facts, addressed similar statements to members of the Iowa Senate. At all events, my affidavit and the statement of Treasurer Hunt were forwarded to Hon. J. B. Grinnell of that Senate, and by him handed to the committee of investigation. And yet, in full view of these facts, the secret archives of that committee are drawn upon at pleasure for garbled evidence to bolster up a charge which its responsible authors know to be a wanton calumny. * * * * * Yours, HORACE GREELEY.

IOWA CITY, February 4, 1857.

The *Tribune* always threw its whole strength into any political fight it engaged in. On the Kansas Question, for example, it was all Kansas. Its columns, day after day and week after week, were filled with articles on this question. There was no space for any other subject. Some time after this had become a "dead issue," a stranger entered the office of the *Tribune* and spent several hours in looking over the files of that paper. He appeared a perplexed and bewildered man. One of the *attachés* of the establishment finally asked him what he was seeking. "It is an advertisement," answered the man. "Perhaps," said the polite clerk, "I can find it for you, if you can give me a clew as to the time. Perhaps you can tell what was in the paper when the advertisement appeared." "Oh yes, yes," said the stranger, hopefully brightening up. "I believe there was—yes, I feel sure there was something in it about Kansas."

Immediately after the inauguration of President Lincoln in 1861, it became the talk in newspaper circles that the *Tribune* would be depleted of its writers in consequence of the necessity of the new administration for suitable men to send abroad as ministers, *chargé d'affaires*, and consuls, and it was apparent in Washington that very few diplomats could be found outside of that establishment. It was announced that James E. Harvey, the chief of the *Tribune* bureau in the national capital, would go as minister to Portugal, James S. Pike as minister to the Hague, and several other writers and correspondents to different points as consuls, custom-house officers, and internal revenue assessors and collectors. It is true that Harvey, and Pike, and Cleveland, and several other fortunate office-holders under the new *régime* were interested in the *Tribune*, but this is the way Greeley, on the 3d of October, 1866, disposed of the matter, and spiked the big gun of one of its neighbors:

JOURNALISM—OFFICE.

The *World* says:

The *Tribune* has found neither time nor space, as yet, to give a column or two to a list of the attachés and ex-attachés of the *Tribune* who have received, or begged, or now hold federal appointments, ranging from first-class consulships to almost any class clerkships. The *Tribune*, probably, has not had a correspondent in Washington for years who did not hold a nominal clerkship to a Congressional committee, or enjoy some other sinecure.

So far as we can recollect, Mr. James S. Harvey, minister to Portugal, is the only person ever connected with the *Tribune* who now holds any office under the federal government, save that we understand that Mr. M'Elrath, formerly publisher of the *Tribune*, has very recently been appointed to a place in the Custom-house. We need hardly say that neither of these appointments was suggested or prompted by us, though we esteem Mr. M'Elrath a very fit and worthy man. He was once before in some revenue place—perhaps the same that he now holds—until we won him away from it by offering him a better salary than the government gave him.

As a very large proportion of those Republicans who write well have, at some time or other, written for the *Tribune*, we really can not say how many "attachés and ex-attachés of the *Tribune*" have either had, or wished they had, some sort of office. It would not be possible for us to make a list of them. We might pretty accurately name those who have *held* office; but as to those who sought it ineffectually, their griefs generally lie buried in their own bosoms. All we can say is, that we have paid fairly for the services they rendered us, and they have fairly earned the money we paid them, so that we consider the account fairly balanced. If any one ever made his connection (past or present) with the *Tribune* a claim to office, he was guilty of a very gross impertinence, for which he had neither authority nor excuse.

As to our correspondents at Washington, we have paid them fully for their services, and have been fairly entitled to their whole time. If any of them ever sold a part of it to the government, he defrauded us, and deserved the severest reprehension. No appointment of any correspondent of the *Tribune* to any "clerkship" or other office at Washington was either sought, desired, or acquiesced in by us, and, if any such infidelity to our service has existed, it must have been very rare. Let our correspondents take notice that we shall henceforth consider the acceptance of any government employment or stipend a sufficient reason for their dismissal from our employment.

Other newspapers were represented abroad. Editors make splendid diplomats. James Watson Webb, of the *Courier and Enquirer*, who had been *chargé* to Austria, was appointed minister to Brazil. John Bigelow, of the *Evening Post*, received the appointment of minister to France after that office was declined by James Gordon Bennett, of the *Herald*. Allen A. Hall, of the old *Nashville Whig*, was minister to Bolivia; Edward Jay Morris, of the Philadelphia *Inquirer*, minister to Turkey; and Rufus King, formerly editor of the *Albany Daily Advertiser*, represented this blessed nation at Rome. Charles Hale, of the *Boston Advertiser*, was consul general to Egypt, where he pleasantly mingled Oriental with Occidental hospitality. These appointments were made by President Lincoln, and none of these distinguished journalists have either disgraced their profession or their country while dressed in the plain republican diplomatic costume, so neatly arranged by that eminent statesman, William L. Marcy. Still, Greeley was right not to have too many offices thrust upon his shoulders at one time.

One of the newspapers, in noticing the political campaign in Pennsylvania in 1871, thus spoke of some of the candidates:

Both parties in Pennsylvania are honoring their editors in the political campaign this fall. For instance, there is Dr. E. L. Acker, editor of the Norristown *Register*, nominated by the Democrats of Montgomery and Lehigh for Congress; John H. Oliver, Esq., former editor of the Lehigh *Register*, nominated by the Republicans for Congress in the same district; Hon. J. Lawrence Getz, formerly editor of the Reading *Gazette*, nominated by the Democrats of Berks County for Congress; Hon. H. S. Evans, editor of the *Village Record*, nominated by the Republicans of Chester, Delaware, and Montgomery counties for state senator; Thomas V. Cooper, Esq., editor of the Media *American*, nominated by the Republicans of Delaware County for Assembly; J. Irvin Steele, editor of the Ashland *Advocate*, nominated by the Democrats of Schuylkill County for Assembly; P. Gray Meek, Esq., editor of the Bellefonte *Watchman*, nominated by the Democrats of Centre County for Assembly; and Thomas Chalfont, Esq., editor of the Danville *Intelligencer*, nominated by the Democrats of Montour County for Assembly.

Since the indignant and very proper denial of Greeley in regard to political office, he has been elected to Congress; and in the canvass of 1869 for a portion of the state officers of New York, he was the unsuccessful candidate for the office of comptroller. Twice efforts have been made to send him to the United States Senate. On the first occasion, during Greeley's absence at the West, Charles A. Dana, then managing editor of the *Tribune*, personally went to Albany, and, with that energy for which he is remarkable, sought, by all the legitimate means in his power, to have his chief editor made a national senator by the Legislature. Once or twice he has been talked of for postmaster general. When General Grant came into office, it was his intention to have made Greeley minister to England instead of J. Lathrop Motley, but the President changed his mind after a personal interview, and the editor of the *Tribune* was afterwards appointed chief government commissioner of the Pacific Railroad, which important position he resigned in favor of General Hiram Walbridge, a warm personal friend of his, and Greeley's candidate for collector of the port of New York.

In 1871, when Greeley made his tour through the Southern States, after a special visit to Texas, he became, to use a French term, an "officious" candidate for the presidency. Before the Rebellion Greeley was anxious to live in a country where he could travel from one end to the other with as much safety as he could travel in Europe or New England. It was then deemed unsafe for an anti-slavery man to travel south of Mason & Dixon's line. The editor of the *Tribune* has lived long enough to enjoy this privilege. His trip through the South was a triumphal march, but whether or not to the White House remains to be seen. Writers, and reporters, and editors of newspapers—Adams, Madison, Colfax—have been elevated to the presidency and vice-presidency; and those offices may hereafter be bestowed by the people as often on the journalistic as on the military heroes of the nation, and, perhaps, with more political safety.

There was one incident connected with the *Tribune* that created a good deal of excitement, and which seriously affected its editor at the time of its occurrence. While the rebel army, under Beauregard, and the Union army, under M'Dowell, were encamped opposite each other in front of Washington in the early part of the summer of 1861, the *Tribune*, impatient as all others at the North were at the apparent unnecessary delay of a forward movement, almost daily urged an immediate advance of M'Dowell. "On to Richmond." This was the cry, and it was uttered with such persistent energy, that finally the movement was made, resulting in the disgraceful affair at Bull Run and a panic throughout the North. It was necessary that some one should suffer for this deplorable military *fiasco*, and it was thought that Greeley was the one to shoulder the entire responsibility of the movement and its result. He therefore was compelled to take it in all its unpopular proportions and weight. On the 25th of July, 1861, he came out in the *Tribune* with a rejoinder to the numerous attacks made upon him:

JUST ONCE.

An individual's griefs or wrongs may be of little account to others; but when the gravest public interests are imperiled through personal attacks and the coarsest imputations of base motives, the assailed, however humble, owes duties to others which can not be disregarded. I propose here to refute months of persistent and envenomed defamation by the statement of a few facts.

I am charged with having opposed the selection of Governor Seward for a place in President Lincoln's cabinet. That is utterly, absolutely false, the President himself being my witness. I might call many others, but one such is sufficient.

I am charged with what is called "opposing the administration" because of that selection, and various paragraphs which have from time to time appeared in the *Tribune* are quoted to sustain this inculpation. The simple fact that not one of those paragraphs was either written or in any wise suggested or prompted by me suffices for that charge. It is true—I have no desire to conceal or belittle it —that my ideas as to the general conduct of the war for the Union are those repeatedly expressed by myself and others through the *Tribune*, and of course are not those on which the conduct of that war has been based. It is true that I hold and have urged that this war can not, must not, be a long one; that it must be prosecuted with the utmost energy, promptness, and vigor, or it will prove a failure; that every week's flying of the secession flag defiantly within a day's walk of Washington renders the suppression of the revolt more difficult, if not doubtful. *It is true that I think a government that begins the work of putting down a rebellion by forming "camps of instruction," or any thing of that sort, is likely to make a very long job of it. It is true that I think our obvious policy, under the circumstances, would have been to be courteous and long-suffering towards foreign powers, but resolute and ready in our dealings with armed rebels; and it seems to me that the opposite course has been taken. But the watchword, "Forward to Richmond," is not mine, nor any thing of like import. I wish to evade no responsibility, but to repel a personal aspersion. So with regard to the late article urging a change in the cabinet. While I know that some of the best material in the country enters into the composition of that cabinet, I yet feel that changes might be made therein with advantage to the public service. Yet I did not write, and I did not intend to have published, the article calling for a change of cabinet,* which only appears through a misapprehension. I shrunk from printing it in part because any good effect it might have was likely to be neutralized by the very course which had been taken—that of assailing me as its supposed author.

I have no desire in the premises but that what is best for the country shall be done. If the public judge that this great end—an energetic and successful prosecution of the war—will be most surely subserved by retaining the cabinet as it is, I acquiesce in that decision. The end being secured, the means are to me utterly indifferent.

I wish to be distinctly understood as not seeking to be relieved from any responsibility for urging the advance of the Union grand army into Virginia, though *the precise phrase,* "*Forward to Richmond!*" *is not mine, and I would have preferred not to iterate it.* I thought that army, one hundred thousand strong, might have been in the rebel capital on or before the 20th instant, while I felt that there were urgent reasons why it should be there if possible. And now, if any one imagine that I, or any one connected with the *Tribune*, ever commanded or imagined such strategy as the launching of barely thirty thousand of the one hundred thousand Union volunteers within fifty miles of Washington against ninety thousand rebels enveloped in a labyrinth of strong intrenchments and unreconnoitred masked batteries, then demonstration would be lost on his closed ear. But I will not dwell on this. *If I am needed as a scape-goat for all the military blunders of the last month, so be it. Individuals must die that the nation may live. If I can serve her best in that capacity, I do not shrink from the ordeal.*

Henceforth I bar all criticism in these columns on army movements, past or future, unless somebody should undertake to prove that General Patterson is a wise and brave commander. He seems to have none to speak his praises; so, if there is any thing to be said in his behalf, I will make an exception in his favor. Other than this, the subject is closed and sealed. Correspondents and reporters may state facts, but must forbear comments. I know that there is truth that yet needs be uttered on this subject, but *this paper has done its full share—all that it ought, and perhaps more than it could afford to do—and henceforth stands back for others. Only I beg it to be understood—once for all—that if less than half the Union armies directly at hand are hurled against all the rebel forces that could be concentrated—more than double their number—on ground specially chosen and strongly fortified by the traitors, the Tribune does not approve and should not be held responsible for such madness. Say what you will of the past, but remember this for the future, though we keep silence.*

Henceforth it shall be the *Tribune's* sole vocation to rouse and animate the American people for the terrible ordeal which has befallen them. The great republic eminently needs the utmost exertions of every loyal heart and hand. We have tried to serve her by exposing breakers ahead and around her; henceforth be it ours to strengthen, in all possible ways, the hands of those whose unenviable duty it is to pilot her through them. If more good is thus to be done, let us not repine that some truth must be withheld for a calmer moment, and for less troubled ears.

The journal which is made the conduit of the most violent of these personal assaults on me attributes the course of the *Tribune* to resentment "against those who have ever committed the inexpiable offense of thwarting Mr. Greeley's raging and unsatiated thirst for office."

I think this justifies me in saying that there is no office in the gift of the government or of the people which I either hope, wish, or expect ever to hold. I certainly shall not parade myself as declining places that are not offered for my acceptance; but I am sure the President has always known that I desired no office at his hands; and this, not through any violation of my rule above stated, but through the report of mutual and influential friends, who at various times volunteered to ask me if I would take any place whatever under the government, and were uniformly and conclusively assured that I would not.

Now let the wolves howl on. I do not believe they can goad me into another personal notice of their ravings. HORACE GREELEY.
July 24, 1861.

No one who lived in New York City in the summer of 1863 will ever forget the terrible "draft riots" which threatened so much damage to the metropolis. The war between the Communists of Paris and the Versailles government exceeded them a thousand fold in the horrible scenes enacted in the streets of the French capital; but the citizens of New York were unused to such scenes, notwithstanding the many riots that have occurred there, and in the helpless condition of the city in the summer of 1863, in consequence of the absence of the state troops in Pennsylvania, there was a terror in the uncertainty of the hour more than in the reality of the disturbance or the destruction of property. One of the objects of attack, in the programme of the mob, was the *Tribune* establishment. One of the patrolmen engaged in suppressing the riot, in speaking of a pictorial illustration of the scene, thus accurately described the affair in Printing-House Square on that memorable occasion:

> Late in the afternoon of July 13, 1863, a number of the police force belonging to the lower precincts were held in reserve at the City Hall for the preservation of peace in the lower part of the city. A report reached us that the mob were murdering the negroes down in the First Precinct. We turned out to "nip this in the bud," and after scouring part of the First and Second Wards, we started to return to the City Hall. The Twenty-sixth Precinct men, led by Captain T. Thorn, came up Nassau Street. I think we numbered 32 men. When we got in sight of the *Tribune* office, we could see books and papers flying from the office into the street. As it had been reported all the afternoon that the *Tribune* was to be destroyed, we concluded, from the appearance of things, that the mob had commenced their work. Captain Thorn, without halting his men, shouted, "Boys, they have attacked the *Tribune*. Keep together, boys. Steady! Let them feel your clubs. Forward, double quick—march." The rush to the south corner of Spruce Street was more than double quick. Here we encountered the mob, and every rioter who could not get out of the way went down. The scene was an exciting one for some minutes. Every man of that little party realized the fact that his life depended on the sudden effect of the onslaught. There were not less than 5000 rioters and only about 32 of us. We were equal to the emergency. I think in about four minutes we drove them out of the office, and stamped out the fire with our feet that they had kindled to burn it down. There were not more than eight or ten of us got into the office. The others followed up the attack and drove the mob toward Frankfort Street and across the square into the Park. This scene was all enacted in about ten minutes, when we were re-enforced by the men of the other lower precincts. Then it was we drove the mob across the Park. The painting referred to represents the flying rioters, met by Inspector Carpenter and his force in the Park in front of the City Hall, and it is a good representation of that incident.

There were five thousand men and boys in front of the *Tribune* office at the time mentioned, but not more than a hundred, if so many, were actually engaged in the attack on the building; the others were spectators. But in the eyes of the policemen and the law the entire crowd were rioters, and treated as such. Newspaper reporters who were there were looked upon as a part of the mob, because they were unknown. Still, the conduct of the police as it marched up Nassau Street, and in the assault on the rioters, was splendidly courageous, and the *Tribune* building was thus saved from destruction by fire, and the city the cost of rebuilding that establishment.

Another scene connected with the *Tribune* during these disturbances was the reported retreat of its editor to Windust's restaurant, and seeking safety, some said, "under a table," and others asserted "in a huge refrigerator." After these reports had become almost historic by repetition, Mr. Greeley denounced the story of his "hiding" as false, and gave the following graphic and emphatic account of the circumstances:

> On the 13th of July, 1863 (the first day of the Draft Riots in our city), the editor of the *Tribune* was visited in his office about midday by a devoted friend, who urged and entreated him to accompany the said friend to his home, a few miles distant. That friend assured him that he knew that the life of said editor was to be taken forthwith—that it had been plotted and settled that he should be an

early and certain victim of the ruffian mob then howling about the *Tribune* office, and inciting each other to the assault, which they actually made at dusk that night, when they smashed the windows, furniture, etc., and set fire to the building, but were promptly routed and expelled by the police. Riot, arson, and pillage were then rife in different sections of our city, of which the rebel mob appeared to have undisputed possession. The editor (who writes this) informed his friend that nothing would induce him to leave the city—that he was where he had a right to be, and where he should remain. That friend, after exhausting remonstrance and entreaty, left him to his fate, not expecting to see him again. About five P.M. of that day, the editor, having finished his work at the office, went over to Windust's eating-house for his dinner, passing through the howling mob for nearly the entire distance, and recognized by several of them. Two friends accompanied him, but not at his invitation or suggestion. Neither of the three was armed. At Windust's dinner was ordered and eaten exactly as on other days, but in the largest room in the house, without a shadow of concealment or hiding of any kind. Dinner finished, the editor took a carriage and drove to his lodging, where he resumed writing for the *Tribune*, and continued it through the evening, sending down his copy to the office, and being visited thence by friends who informed him of the mob's assault, and the narrow escape of the building and contents from destruction. Remaining all night at his lodging, he returned next morning to the office (now being armed), saw from a window the mob howling in its front hastily repair to the City Hall Park, there to listen to a harangue from Horatio Seymour, and remained there nearly to the close of the day (Tuesday), when he was finally induced to leave by the representation of the good and true soldier who commanded it as fortress, that he would prefer that the mob should not be provided with the extra inducement for assault which the known presence of Mr. Greeley in the building would afford. He returned to the office the next morning, though the first hackman to whom he applied refused to let him enter his carriage; and he was in the office nearly throughout each day of that memorable week up to Friday evening, when he (as usual) took the Harlem cars for his home at Chappaqua, where he spent the Saturday, as he has done nearly every Saturday, save in winter, for the last fifteen years. And whoever asserts that he, at any time that week, "was hiding under Windust's table," is a branded liar and villain, as Mr. Windust, Mr. William A. Hall, and other surviving and most credible witnesses will gladly attest.

One of the chief troubles of the *Tribune* has been its "managing editors," a title lately introduced in the offices of the Metropolitan Press. It is a French idea: in Paris they are called *Directeur gerant;* but we borrowed the title direct from the London *Times*. If a journal has an editor, and editor-in-chief, it is fair to suppose that he is also its managing editor. What is a manager but one having control of the institution managed? Now, besides these editors-in-chief, the leading journals of New York have managing editors, who not only make an effort to manage the chief editor, but frequently manage to get into hot water. The *Tribune* has had four managing editors: 1st, Charles A. Dana; 2d, Sidney Howard Gay; 3d, John Russell Young; 4th, Whitelaw Reid. It is almost unnecessary to speak of the two first, because they are already well known; one is the present editor and shining light of the *Sun*, and the other has been "managing editor" of the Chicago *Tribune*, and is now an assistant editor of the New York *Evening Post;* but of the third this history would be more incomplete than it is if his name is not mentioned. There appears to be a strong and strange desire on the part of some journalists to double and treble themselves. John R.

Forney, for a number of years the chief Democratic politician of Pennsylvania, afterwards secretary of the United States Senate, and lately collector of the customs at Philadelphia, in one of his letters spoke of his "two papers—both daily," thereby inductively claiming his share of influence with the public. These two papers were the Washington *Chronicle* and Philadelphia *Press*. This idea was original with Daniel de Foe, who, at one time, in the early part of last century, wrote for six or seven flourishing newspapers in that interesting period of English history. It is related of Lord Brougham that he would write a powerful article for the London *Times* on one day, and reply to it yet more powerfully in the *Chronicle* of the next morning. Thus this distinguished statesman clearly had "two papers—both daily," at his command. Swain, Abell & Simmons were not content with the Philadelphia *Ledger;* they established the Baltimore *Sun*, and Swain was very desirous of starting a paper in New York. James Gordon Bennett, with all his shrewdness, contemplated in 1840, in the fullness of his early enterprise, when the Cunard steamers commenced their trips, establishing a paper in Boston in connection with the *New York Herald*. So they run. John Russell Young, of the *Tribune*, had this mania. He became a leading journalist in one jump. He was not satisfied with being "managing editor" of the *Tribune*. So, if we believe the record, he published "three papers—all daily:" the *Tribune* in New York, and the *Star* and *Post* in Philadelphia; and in his efforts to make the trio successful, he came in collision with Simonton, the general agent of the Associated Press, who, *en passant*, is not only the manager of this influential association of newspapers all over the country, but owns and edits one or two in California. When this collision between Simonton and Young occurred, the New York *Sun* came to the rescue, and appeared one balmy April morning in 1869 with a shower of brilliant letters written by Young, full of electric sparks and politics, and indicating, in the estimation of the *Sun*, a wrong use of the news belonging to the Associated Press. The result was a veritable sensation in Printing-House Square. The *Tribune*, on the 1st of May, 1869, in reply, over the initials of H. G., said:

* * * * * * * * *

The charges on which Mr. Young stands arraigned by the *Sun* on the strength of these letters are substantially these :

1. Having an exaggerated conceit of his own abilities and qualifications for journalism, with a corresponding defective appreciation of the merits of his present or recent associates.

2. Abusing his position on the *Tribune*, and his influence as a journalist, to promote his private ends, and especially to procure loans or subsidies for his or his friends' Philadelphia venture or ventures.

3. Betraying the confidence reposed in him by this establishment to transmit surreptitiously the dispatches of the Associated Press to his Philadelphia journal or journals not entitled to receive them.

With the first of these imputations the public has no proper business; the second, we are confident, is false and unfounded; the third, we trust, will prove equally so; but this involves the interests of others whose right to a searching investigation is unquestionable, no matter what they must think of the means whereby it has been rendered necessary. We call, therefore, upon our partners in the Associated Press to institute forthwith a rigorous scrutiny, before some impartial arbiter or tribunal, of the charges against Mr. Young with regard to the dispatches of the association, proposing to take no part in that scrutiny unless we are made the party defendant, but insisting that Mr. Young, or whoever may be suspected or implicated, shall not be stabbed in the back, but shall have the fullest opportunity for explanation and defense. We need not add that we consider the offense alleged a very grave one, especially if the offender be one honored and trusted as Mr. Young has been. But, pending such scrutiny, we beg that it be understood that Mr. Young has not been removed, nor suspended, nor in any manner condemned by us, as has been mistakenly asserted by the *Sun* and telegraphed all over the country. It is not our custom to pass judgment on any one on the strength of a mere indictment, especially when the finding of it was plainly impelled by envy, malice, and blighted aspirations.

Shortly after this Mr. Young's connection with the *Tribune* ceased, and subsequently he established the *Standard*, a two-cent paper, in New York. Mr. Young is now said to be the Paris correspondent of the *New York Herald*. He is a brilliant writer, and Mr. Greeley considers him an accomplished journalist. Greeley stands by his friends with splendid tenacity. He would not desert Young. He clung to Seward and Weed. Illustrative of this fact, we subjoin an account of an interview between Mr. G. and a reporter of the *Sun*, which appeared in print on the 11th of December, 1869. One of the writers and shareholders of the *Tribune*, Albert D. Richardson, had been shot in that office by Daniel M'Farland for alleged improper intimacy with Mrs. M'Farland, and just before the death of the unfortunate man at the Astor House, the Rev. Henry Ward Beecher had performed the ceremony of marriage between Richardson and Mrs. M'Farland. Mr. Beecher, in one of his statements, said that he did this at the request of his "old friend Greeley." But here is the account of the interview:

Reporter. There must be some misunderstanding; for Mr. Beecher most assuredly told me, in his own house, that you *did* ask him, or, at least, he was led to understand that you so asked him.

Mr. Greeley. Whom did Mr. Beecher name as representing me in this request, or in leading him to understand that I made it?

Reporter. Mrs. Calhoun.

Mr. Greeley. I can explain that. I was not well acquainted, or personally intimate with Mr. Richardson, nor did I know Mrs. M'Farland, but Mrs. Calhoun said she knew all about them. So I wrote a letter of introduction for her to Mr. Beecher, telling him that she would explain her business, and I presume she did; but I knew very little, next to nothing, about the matter, and *I certainly never asked Mr. Beecher or any body else to marry them, or any body else, in the whole course of my life.* I have other things to think about besides getting people married. Besides, why didn't you ask Mr. Beecher to show you the letter I wrote to him introducing Mrs. Calhoun? If he told you all the rest, he would have been willing enough, I should think, to show you the letter, if you had asked him for it.

Reporter. Well, all I can say is, Mr. Greeley, that Mr. Beecher certainly must have imagined and believed, from what he told me, that it was your wish that the marriage should be consummated, or he would never have promised Mrs. Calhoun, even conditionally, to solemnize it. He certainly said that he considered Mrs. Calhoun as your representative.

Mr. Greeley. I have not the slightest doubt that Mrs. Calhoun told Mr. Beecher the truth—that you may be sure of. You may depend what she said was true, every word of it; but I gave her no authority to represent me; nobody *can* represent me.

Reporter. There you are right, Mr. Greeley. No one can adequately represent so wonderful a man. (Mutual bows.)

Mr. Greeley. But I tell you what it is, sir, there are plenty of people who can *mis*represent me, and they are doing it just about all the time.

Reporter. How?

Mr. Greeley. In the newspapers—in the *Herald*, the *Sunday Mercury*—all the papers. They have all told lies about me, and the people believe them, because they want to, or because they don't know any better—just as in the Jeff. Davis case. Why, they have all garbled the evidence in this matter regarding the Sinclairs.

Reporter. In what respects?

Mr. Greeley. Why, they have suppressed in their published reports all the material facts in the testimony. What if Mr. Richardson and Mrs. M'Farland did occupy the same room, or about the same room, as they call it, don't they know well enough that Mr. Richardson was a wounded and feeble man? But, no, it don't suit the papers to publish THAT. If all the testimony was published, the Sinclairs would be all right; but, no, they must garble it to suit their d—d petty malice. No; the Sinclairs and all the rest of us must be identified with this Free-love crowd. By G—d (bringing his venerable fist upon the desk), there's no such crowd, at least not around the *Tribune* office. The whole thing has been got up by the enemies of the *Tribune*.

Reporter. I do not exactly understand.

Mr. Greeley. There is the *World*, for instance, talking about the morality of the *Tribune*, when it hasn't any of its own. Why, if it hadn't been that the parties were in some way or other connected with the *Tribune*, there wouldn't have been a mother's son of the whole lot but would have thought it all right that Mrs. M'Farland should be called Mrs. Richardson; for, after all, it was only the matter of a name.

Reporter. Only the matter of a name, Mr. Greeley?

Mr. Greeley. Yes, whether a woman should be called Richardson, or whether she should be called M'Farland—nothing more. Because, as Mr. Beecher says, it was understood that the marriage was not to be consummated unless Richardson was about to die. In that case nobody could be hurt by the marriage. It was only a matter of benefiting the children.

Reporter (innocently). Whose children? M'Farland's?

Mr. Greeley. No; they had a protector—at least they had their father. But Richardson's children I mean. It was to leave *his* children with a parent—it was for Richardson's children that the thing was done. Mind, I don't back out of it (emphatically); not a bit of it. I think it was rightly done—that this woman should be called Mrs. Richardson, not Mrs. M'Farland.

These interviews, if correctly reported, are of as much value to the public as to those whose conversations are given. But in this case there was evidently a misunderstanding, as the editor of the *Tribune* was constrained to send a correction to the *Sun*. In giving the conversation and the correction, we do so to point a moral, and show a little of the animus of the Metropolitan Press in matters appertaining to themselves:

TO THE EDITOR OF THE SUN:

SIR,—I thought I might be allowed to keep silence with regard to the circumstances preceding and attending the murder of my late associate and friend, Albert D. Richardson; but one of your reporters, who called on me on Friday, and concealed from me the fact of his connection with the *Sun*, has given an account of our interview so full of errors that I can not leave them wholly unnoticed.

Passing over many, I desire to assure your readers that no name of the Supreme

Being was used by me in that conversation, whether profanely or otherwise; that I said nothing of the morality or immorality of the *World*, unless an allusion to its animus in this matter can be tortured into that; that I did not say "I will have to testify" on the trial of M'Farland (that being a matter over which I have no control). I did not say, "I don't want to hurt Mac;" did not—but I must stop correcting somewhere, and will stop here.

What I *did* say with regard to the main point in controversy was substantially this—that this marriage on a death-bed, besides giving the woman a legal right to be a mother to Richardson's young and doubly orphaned children, was operative mainly in giving her a right, throughout her black and bitter future, to be called by the name of him who for her sake was so foully murdered, rather than that of his stealthy, cowardly assassin; and this small mitigation of her immeasurable woes I regarded as humane and just. That *is* my opinion, and I propose to stand by it.   Yours,   HORACE GREELEY.

Interviews with distinguished individuals is now quite a feature in New York journalism. It was commenced by the *New York Herald* in 1859, at the time of the celebrated John Brown raid at Harper's Ferry. Among others implicated in that affair was the well-known Gerrit Smith. One of the special reporters of the *Herald* was dispatched to his residence at Peterborough, where he had a long interview with that distinguished philanthropist. This was published in full, in conversational style, and produced a sensation. It was the origin of "interviewing." Interviews were had on the eve of the rebellion, in 1860, with leading rebels at their homes; one, in particular, between Alexander H. Stephens, and Robert Toombs, and a special correspondent of the *Herald*, with entertaining and instructive results. After the war they were continued with leading statesmen, army and navy officers, and politicians, giving these prominent men an excellent opportunity to communicate with the people, and enabling the journalist to lay a vast deal of thought and intelligence before his readers. This feature in news was extended to Europe, Asia, and Africa. Thus Napoleon, Bismarck, Antonelli, General Grant, the Catholic Cardinal-Bishop of London, Count Membrea, the Premier of Italy, the Prime Minister of Egypt, Von Beust, the Chancellor of Austria, one of the Rajahs of India, General Sherman, Cyrus W. Field, General Butler, Commodore Vanderbilt, the Emperor of Brazil, at home and in Egypt, Secretary Boutwell, Mayor Hall, ex-President Johnson, among others, were interviewed. Meeting the Emperor of Brazil in Cairo in November, 1871, one of the correspondents of the *Herald* said to him:

Correspondent. I see a copy of *Galignani*, containing an interview with Mr. Seward, from the *New York Herald*, on your table. Has your majesty read it?

Dom Pedro. I did, with interest. Mr. Seward has been a great traveler, and seems to have thoroughly improved his opportunities for observation. I shall not be able to go so far as he has done. By the way, I suppose I am now being "interviewed," which, I believe, is the term.

Correspondent. Yes, your majesty; but I will with pleasure submit my manuscript to your secretary if there should be any thing you may wish expunged.

Dom Pedro. Thank you; but perhaps it will not matter. I have been in a constant state of "interview" all my life, and consequently say nothing I am not willing to have made public. It is rather novel, though, to find a correspondent of the *New York Herald* under the shadow of the Pyramids.

Correspondent. They are very enterprising men, the *Herald* correspondents, and go every where.

Dom Pedro. Well, you are an enterprising people, and deserve the great prosperity you enjoy. There are many Americans in Brazil, and when Mr. William Garrison fairly commences his steam-ship line we expect more. But he is compelled to build his ships in England. That is bad. Your shipping interest is of more importance than the revenue gained by taxation, which, after all, you are so rich you do not need. But I must ask you to excuse me now, as I am engaged to receive the Prince Heretier at this hour. I wish you good morning.

The public were never before brought so near to the views of these statesmen, and politicians, and merchant princes. Napoleon talked with a correspondent one day at Wilhelmshöhe, and by means of the cable it appeared in the *New York Herald* the next morning, and his views were known to the civilized world in forty-eight hours! Other papers adopted the idea. Every body of any note, or who had been guilty of any crime or extraordinary act, was immediately called upon by a reporter. State-houses and state prisons were visited by representatives of the Press for notorious subjects. Interviewing, indeed, became a journalistic mania, till at last, as the above conversation with Mr. Greeley shows, the climax was capped ; for when a reporter of one newspaper interviewed the chief editor of another in the same block, and within three doors of each other's offices, the sublimity and the perfection of the idea is reached, and nothing more need be said.

But these interviews are useful—useful to the individuals interviewed, and useful to the public. If it is considered necessary for the ministers of England and France to have seats in Parliament and in the *Corps Legislatif* that they may "rise to explain," how much more necessary, in this age of universal suffrage, and when the whole world is a Congress, becomes the relative position of statesman and journalist, in order that in any crisis in a nation the statesman may have direct communication with the people without delay or circumlocution. The interviews that have taken place, and the conversations that have already been published, have been the means of dissipating many erroneous impressions on the public mind, and made doubtful questions of state policy clear and satisfactory to the people. Thus the executive powers of the world are placed in more intimate relations with the governed classes, and the result can not but be beneficial for the general peace of mankind. But interviewing can be carried too far.

Some odd stories are told of Greeley, a few of which are true, but the larger number are manufactured by rival journals, disappointed politicians, wits, and Bohemians. But Greeley's effort at originality sometimes gets him into trouble. He is fond of writing over his initials. There are half a dozen editors in the United States who rush into print over their initials whenever they are attacked by other journalists, or whenever asked for their advice. Greeley is one of these. H. G. is often seen in the *Tribune* when an editorial article without these initials would answer the emergency as well. But H. G. are *ex cathedra*. Thurlow Weed, James Brooks, and Erastus Brooks belong to the initial class of journalists. It has, perhaps, been more necessary for the brothers Brooks to indulge in this style to prevent mistakes in their political *status*. Alexander H. Stephens, ex-Vice President of the Southern Confederacy, signs his editorials in the *Atlanta* (Ga.) *Sun* A. H. S. to avoid complications. Mr. Stephens, too, has a copyright of his own: his articles are so long that no other paper can find room for them. Ritchie, of the *Richmond Enquirer*, for some time wrote in the first person. So did Bennett of the *Herald*.

Amusing anecdotes are related of the editor of the *Tribune*. He was once invited to lecture in Sandwich, Illinois. In reply to the invitation, he is reported to have said:

DEAR SIR,—I am overworked and growing old. I shall be 60 next Feb. 3. On the whole, it seems I must decline to lecture henceforth, except in this immediate vicinity, if I do at all. I can not promise to visit Illinois on that errand—certainly not now. Yours, HORACE GREELEY.
M. B. CASTLE, Sandwich, Ill.

This letter, plain enough as above given, appeared in hieroglyphics to the lecture committee of the town of Sandwich. They finally succeeded, as the story runs, with the aid of several experts, in deciphering its contents to their evident satisfaction, as the annexed reply will show:

SANDWICH, Ill., May 12.
HORACE GREELEY.—DEAR SIR,—Your acceptance to lecture before our association next winter came to hand this morning. Your penmanship not being the plainest, it took some time to translate it; but we succeeded, and would say your time, "3d of February," and terms, "$60," are entirely satisfactory. As you suggest, we may be able to get you other engagements in this immediate vicinity; if so, we will advise you. Yours, respectfully, M. B. CASTLE.

Yet Horace Greeley is a better penman than either Rufus Choate or Napoleon I. Any one who will compare Greeley's notes with the specimen of Napoleon's chirography in the Lyceum at the Brooklyn Navy Yard will readily admit this to be a fact. Choate's penmanship was positively shocking. On one occasion he delivered an address at Dartmouth College, we believe, and two reporters from New York—one from the *Tribune* and the other from the *Herald*—were in attendance. Finding that Mr. C. had prepared his address, they arranged to take his manuscript after he had finished its delivery, and assist each other in making an extra copy for one of the two journals. So they formed a part of the audience, and congratulated themselves on saving the labor that taking stenographic notes of the oration would involve. The last word of the peroration had scarcely reached the ear of the most distant hearer before the manuscript was in the hands of the reporters. They looked over the pages of Choate's brilliant eloquence; they turned the pages upside down, then sideways, then cornerways, then all sorts of ways, and gazed at each other in blank astonishment. Not a word could they decipher. They sought the orator.

"Why, Mr. Choate," said one of the reporters, "we can not make out a word of your manuscript. What shall we do?"

"Can not read it! That's unfortunate," replied Mr. Choate. "It seems plain to me; but I can not aid you, for I start immediately in an opposite direction to New York. But let me see; I guess I can help you. An old clerk of mine lives about twelve miles from here. He can read it," and off went Mr. Choate.

The two reporters hired a team and drove over to the residence of the clerk. He read, and they took stenographic notes, and succeeded in reaching New York in time to write out their reports for their respective journals. These reporters, ever after, in asking for manuscript, first carefully inspected the chirography.

But, according to the *Printer's Circular*, there is a worse writer than either Choate, or Greeley, or Napoleon. There was a banquet to the International Typographical Union in June, 1870; among the toasts on that occasion was the following:

George M. Bloss, of the Cincinnati *Enquirer*, the worst writer in the country.

It was stated that Mr. Bloss responded in "a few happy remarks;" it is therefore fair to suppose that he acknowledged the truth of the toast.

What does it cost to publish a first-class journal? The *Tribune* answered this question very fully in 1867:

RECEIPTS OF THE TRIBUNE FROM SUBSCRIPTIONS, SALES, AND ADVERTISING.

1865—$816,537 02.   1866—$909,417 89.

EXPENDITURES.

	1865.		1866.
Printing-paper	$315,162 61	Printing-paper	$418,199 62
Pressmen, repairing presses, etc.	35,255 07	Pressmen, repairing presses, etc.	46,398 08
Ink	8,420 00	Ink	9,927 50
Glue and molasses, for rollers	869 46	Glue and molasses, for rollers	943 67
Compositors	73,769 71	Compositors	86,609 14
Editorial expenses	51,884 05	Editorial expenses	81,775 40
Correspondence	41,073 76	Correspondence	49,300 57
News by telegraph	22,044 76	News by telegraph	58,776 04
Harbor news	1,875 20	Harbor news	2,112 34
Publishing office, salaries	19,720 72	Publishing office, salaries	22,841 65
Advertising	7,080 48	Advertising	17,219 07
Mailing, counting, and packing papers	35,088 36	Mailing, counting, and packing papers	35,005 60
Carried forward	$612,244 18	Carried forward	$829,108 68

Brought forward	$612,244 18	Brought forward	$829,108 68
Postage	6,184 23	Postage	11,963 74
Printing and stationery	2,463 16	Printing and stationery	6,198 06
Libel suits	1,390 51	Libel suits	876 65
U. S. tax on advertising receipts	8,376 45	U. S. tax on advertising receipts	10,082 19
Gas-light	5,077 15	Gas-light	5,862 50
Expense account, including plumbing, gas-fixtures, carpenter-work, etc.	10,371 48	Expense account, including plumbing, gas-fixtures, carpenter-work, etc.	18,816 57
Total	$646,107 16	Donation to Freedmen's Aid Union	1,000 00
Receipts over expenditures	170,429 86	Donation to Union State Committee	1,000 00
		Donation to Portland Sufferers	250 00
		Total	$885,158 39
		Receipts over expenditures	24,259 50

There is a general notoriety attached to the *Tribune* and its editor. He has made mistakes, and he has made fortunate hits. He was in favor of secession early in 1861; he was curiously mixed up with the peace negotiations at Niagara Falls with George N. Sanders and others during the rebellion; he put his name on the bail-bond of Jefferson Davis after the war was over—his reasons why and wherefore were given at the time. If the Southern States wished to go out of the Union, and could not be retained, let them go. If the rebellion could not be suppressed, why not come to terms with the rebels? If the government would not bring Davis to trial for his treason, why should he be kept locked up in a fortress? All cogent to his mind.

On the 10th of April, 1871, the *Tribune* was thirty years old. It was the close of a full journalistic generation. On that day the founder of the paper gave a succinct and edifying history of his labors and achievements. It is as follows:

The *Daily Tribune* was first issued on the 10th of April, 1841; it has therefore completed its thirtieth, and to-day enters upon its thirty-first year. It was originally a small folio sheet, employing, perhaps, twenty persons in its production; it is now one of the largest journals issued in any part of the world, containing ten to fifteen times as much as at first, and embodying in each issue the labor of four to five hundred persons as writers, printers, etc., etc. Its daily contents, apart from advertisements, would make a fair 12mo volume, such as sells from the bookstores for $1 25 to $1 50; and when we are compelled to issue a supplement, its editorials, correspondence, dispatches, and reports (which seldom leave room for any but a mere shred of selections) equal in quantity an average octavo. The total cost of its production for the first week was $525; it is now nearly $20,000 per week, with a constant, irresistible tendency to increase.

Other journals have been established by a large outlay of capital, and many years of patient, faithful effort: the *Tribune* started on a very small capital, to which little has ever been added except through the abundance and liberality of its patrons. They enabled it to pay its way almost from the outset; and, though years have intervened, especially during our great Civil War, when, through a sudden and rapid advance in the cost of paper and other materials, our expenses somewhat exceeded our income, yet, taking the average of these thirty years, our efforts have been amply, generously rewarded, and the means incessantly required to purchase expensive machinery, and make improvements on every hand, have been derived exclusively from the regular receipts of the establishment. Rendering an earnest and zealous, though by no means an indiscriminate support, for the former half of its existence to the Whig, and through the latter half to the Republican Party, the *Tribune* has asked no favor of either, and no odds of any man but that he should pay for whatever he chose to order, whether in the shape of subscriptions or advertisements. Holding that a journal can help no party while it requires to be helped itself, we hope so to deserve and retain the good will of the general public that we may be as independent in the future as we have been in the past.

So long as slavery cursed our country, this journal was its decided and open, though not reckless adversary; now that slavery is dead, we insist that the spirit of caste, of inequality, of contempt for the rights of the colored races, shall be buried in its grave. The only reason for their existence having vanished, it is logical and just that they should vanish also. Since the substance no longer exists, the shadow should promptly disappear.

The protection, looking to the development of our home industry, by duties on imports, discriminating with intent to uphold and fortify weak and exposed departments thereof, has ever been, in our view, the most essential and beneficent feature of a true national policy. Our country has always increased rapidly in production, in wealth, in population, and in general comfort, when protection was in the ascendant, while it has been cursed with stagnation, paralysis, commercial revulsions, and wide-spread bankruptcies under the sway of relative free trade. This journal stood for protection under the lead of Henry Clay, Daniel Webster, Walter Forward, George Evans, Thomas Corwin, and their compeers; it stands for protection to-day as heartily as it did then, and for identical reasons. It asks no Free-trader to forego his economic views in order to be a Republican; it insists that no Protectionist shall be bullied out of his convictions in deference to the harmony of the party. It asks no more than it concedes, and will be satisfied with no less. If the Republican Party shall ever be broken up on the Tariff Question, it will take care that the responsibility is placed where it belongs.

The editor of the *Tribune* was also its publisher and sole proprietor when it first commended itself to public attention. He long ago ceased to be publisher, and is now but one among twenty proprietors. As the work required has grown, it has been divided, and in part assigned to others, but the chief direction and supervision of its columns has been continued in his hands, and is likely to remain there so long as his strength shall endure. Half his life has been devoted to this journal, the former half having been mainly given to preparation for its conduct; and now few remain who held kindred positions in this city on the 10th of April, 1841. His only editorial assistant then, though several years his junior, was, after a brilliant independent career, suddenly called away in 1869, leaving behind him few equals in general ability; and of those who aided in the issue of our No. 1, but two are known to be still living, and are among our co-proprietors, still rendering daily service in the establishment, and rejoicing in the possession of health and unfailing strength. Ten years more, and these three will probably have followed their associates already departed. But the *Tribune*, we fondly trust, will survive and flourish after we shall have severally deceased, being sustained by the beneficence of its aims, the liberality of its spirit, and the generous appreciation of an intelligent and discerning people.

The *Tribune* and the *Cincinnati Commercial*, in May, 1871, published the treaty of Washington, arranging our differences with England, before the seal of secrecy had been removed by the Senate. All the facts connected with this document were generally known, but the full text of the treaty, it was supposed, were still sacred in the executive sessions chamber when these two enterprising papers gave it to whom it belonged—the public. But the dignity of the Senate was insulted, and two correspondents were therefore arrested, and, for refusing to divulge from whom they received the document, they were placed in durance. There was a fuss in the Senate, a few ridiculously solemn proceedings, and that is about all. There was a similar case in which the correspondent of the *New York Herald* was concerned in 1847–8. The treaty of Guadalupe-Hidalgo, which ended our war with Mexico in 1847, was published in the *Herald* before the seal of secrecy was removed. There was an excitement over that affair as in 1871. The correspondent was arrested; he refused to divulge the name of the person who gave him the copy, and he was placed in the custody of the sergeant-at-arms of the Senate. When the term of that Congress expired his term of arrest expired also, the Senate having had no legal power beyond that point. Jay's treaty with England in 1794 was " prematurely " published in the Philadelphia *Aurora* shortly after it was received by the State Department. In time, diplomatic matters will cease to be clothed in the mystery and deception that now surround them. The people will then be the Senate, sitting *en permanence* on all affairs of state, with the newspapers as the reporters of its proceedings.

The editor of the *Tribune* was one of the candidates for the presidency in the bitter campaign of 1872. In the following letter, which appeared in the Lexington (Mo.) *Caucasian*, he mildly told his correspondent, who is a Free-trader, that " I am not the man you need :"

NEW YORK, Oct. 18, 1871.
DEAR SIR,—I have yours of the 14th inst. I have no doubt that the policy you suggest is that which your party ought to adopt. They should have taken up Salmon P. Chase in 1868; then, as the result of that contest, the return of genuine peace and thrift would have been promoted. That policy gave you more last year in Missouri than could have been achieved by a party triumph. You only err as to the proper candidate. *I* am not the man you need. Your party is mostly Free-trade, and I am a ferocious Protectionist. I have no doubt that I might be nominated and elected by your help, but it would place us all in a false position. If I, who am adversely interested, can see this, I am sure your good sense will, on reflection, realize it. You must take some man like Gratz Brown, or Trumbull, or General Cox, late Secretary of the Interior, and thus help to pacify and reunite our country anew. Yours, HORACE GREELEY.

But in Cincinnati in May, 1872, and in Baltimore in July of that year, the opposition elements united on the editor of the *Tribune*, and made him their presidential candidate in spite of their Free-trade notions, and in spite of his being " a ferocious Protectionist." Shortly after the nomination was made at Cincinnati the following card appeared in the *Tribune:*

The *Tribune* has ceased to be a party organ, but the unexpected nomination of its editor at Cincinnati seems to involve it in a new embarrassment. All must be aware that the position of a journalist who is at the same time a candidate is at best irksome and difficult—that he is fettered in action and restrained in criticism by the knowledge that whatever he may say or do is closely scanned by thousands eager to find in it what may be so interpreted as to annoy or perplex those who are supporting him as a candidate, and to whom his shackled condition will not permit him to be serviceable. The undersigned, therefore, withdraws absolutely from the conduct of the *Tribune*, and will henceforth, until further notice, exercise no control or supervision over its columns. HORACE GREELEY. May 15, 1872.

The *Tribune* issues an almanac. In 1841 Greeley commenced the publication of a Politician's Register, containing a compilation of the votes of the several states in 1836, 1838, and 1840. This was found to be both valuable and useful to our nation of politicians. Edwin Williams, the well-known statistician, had previously collected and published such returns, but put in this compact form as Greeley published them, was an excellent enterprise. This little pamphlet was afterward enlarged and improved; calendars, calculations, and other interesting facts were added, and the publication was called the Whig Almanac. It went by this name till 1856, when the title was changed to that of the Tribune Almanac, by which name it has since been known. It has a full astronomical department, gives all the election returns, important political movements and platforms, short essays on the topics of the day, and statistics of value, and has become, in its way, as much of an institution as the *Tribune* itself.

The issue of almanacs from newspaper offices is a very old idea. Indeed, they precede newspapers in the history of printing. John Foster printed one in Boston in 1678. William Bradford's first piece of work in Philadelphia was a sheet almanac in 1687. This appeared seventeen years before the *News-Letter* was published, and thirty-eight years before Bradford issued the first newspaper in New York. Benjamin Franklin originated Poor Richard's Almanac, and James Franklin, the "nephew of his uncle," inserted the following advertisement in his *Newport* (R. I.) *Mercury* of Dec. 19, 1758, of the curious contents of this almanac for the following year:

Juſt Publiſhed,
And to be SOLD by

James Franklin,

At the PRINTING OFFICE,

Poor Richard's Almanack

For the YEAR 1759,
CONTAINING,

BESIDES the uſual Calculations, a plain and eaſy Proceſs for making HARD-SOAP, in which certain unerring Rules are laid down for the Workman to know the Strength of his Lees.—How to make Aſhes from green Vegetables far ſuperior to Wood aſhes; very advantageous to Soap-makers, who will find one Buſhel of Aſhes, thus prepared, worth four Buſhels of common Wood-aſhes, the Duſt of the Vegetables being thereby almoſt formed into Pot-afh.—Some very ufeful and approved Prefcriptions in Farriery; particularly, how to cure a Horfe when foundered; of the Pole-Evil, when broke, or not broke; and of the Botts.—How to deftroy Moths, Bugs and Fleas, at a very trifling Expence, and without any Inconveniency.—The Advantages of Fortitude. —True Happinefs, where to be found.—Man's Dependance on his Creator.—Of Reputation:—The Pride of Science, and Self-fufficiency expofed—The abfurdity of Parfimony and extravagance. How to recover and preferve Health.—A very neceffary and interefting Defcription of Love.—Rules for taking a wife; well worth the Attention of all that would fecure Happinefs in a married State.—Of Contentment.—Rules for taking a Hufband; calculated to promote the Happinefs of the Fair Sex.—Of Friendfhip; fhewing the Expediency of Reconciliation with Enemies, and the Danger of defpifing even the meaneft.—A fafe and fure Remedy for Convulfions, that fo frequently prove fatal to Children in breeding their Teeth.—Of Ridicule.—Of folid Glory; or the Way to become truly Great and Eftimable.—An effential Point in Generalfhip, explained and recommended by one of the greateft Warriors of Antiquity; highly deferving the Perufal of all who are defigned for the profeffion of Arms.—And a Letter of the celebrated Cicero to his Son Marcus, fill'd with noble and juft Sentiments.—With wife Sayings, &c. &c. &c.

Here is an advertisement of another almanac of the last century, the contents of which were more like those of a modern stamp. Edes & Gill, publishers of the *Boston Gazette,* issued one from their office in 1770. There were no election returns then, no republic, no political platform except a "Liberty Song" and a few inklings of the approaching Revolution, no yacht clubs, no yearly quotations of stock sales. These old newspaper publishers gave what they had, and Edes & Gill made out this interesting list:

EDES & GILL'S

North-American ALMANACK,

AND

Maffachufetts REGISTER,

For the Year 1770.

Being the Second after BISSEXTILE or LEAP-YEAR. Calculated for the Meridian of BOSTON,

Latt. 42 Deg. 25 Min. North.

CONTAINING,

A Profpective View of the Town of Bofton the Capital of New-England; and of the Landing of ———— Troops in the Year 1768, in Confequence of Letters from Gov. Bernard, the Commiffioners, &c. to the Britifh Miniftry—Eclipfes— Extract from the Life of Publius Clodius Britano Americanus, continued——A Lift of the Importers and Refolves of the Merchants &c. of Bofton—A Table in Sterling, Halifax, Maffachufetts L. M. & O. T. Virginia, Pennfylvania, and New-York Currencies—Courts in Maffachufetts-Bay, New-Hampfhire, Connecticut and Rhode-Ifland——Judgment of the Weather, Suns and Moon's Rifing and Setting, Time of High Water, Feafts and Fafts of the Church of England, &c.— A Lift of the Hon. His Majefty's Council, and the Honorable Houfe of Reprefentatives——Judges of the Superior and Inferior Courts, Judges of Probate, Regifters of Deeds, High Sheriffs and their Deputies—Officers of the Admiralty and Cuftom-Houfe—Notaries Public—Poft-Office—Juftices of the Peace thro'out the Province, and for each County—Barrifters at Law—Prefident, Overfeers, &c. of Harvard College——Minifters, Churches and Religious Affemblies thro' the Province—Officers of the 14th & 29th Regiments in Bofton—Officers of the

Ancient and Honorable Artillery Company, with the Names of the Captains of ſaid Company, from its Incorporation—Officers of the Troop of Horſe Guards—Officers of the Boſton Regiment—Field Officers of the ſeveral Regiments through the Province—Officers of Caſtle William, and the Batteries in Boſton—Coroners—Officers of the Town of Boſton—Fire-Engine Men—Liſt of Commiſſioners and other Officers of the Revenue, WITH THEIR SALARIES!—Liberty Song—Parody Parodiz'd—A New Song, to the Tune of the Britiſh Grenadier, by a SON OF LIBERTY—Public Roads, with the beſt Stages or Houſes to put up at—Quakers Yearly Meetings in New-England—Difference of the Time of High Water at ſeveral Places on the Continent, &c.

Now read the advertisements in the newspapers of December and January, 1871-2 and of 1872-3, of the World Almanac, the Public Ledger Almanac, the Atlantic Monthly Almanac, the New York Herald Almanac, the Evening Journal Almanac, in contrast with these of the ancient publications. These announcements are each a column or more in length. The Herald Almanac is 240 pages in size, and filled with all sorts of information that every body is constantly seeking to know. Then the *New York Observer* issues its Year-Book, which is also an almanac and a book of reference in all religious matters; it contains 200 pages. These are all newspaper almanacs, and are splendidly printed.

About Christmas, annually, the number of these publications on sale in London and Paris is really fabulous; but they are so funny, so useful, so grotesque, so valuable, so edifying, amusing, and attractive in contents and illustrations as to circulate largely and freely. Father Time, with his scythe, is represented in all manner of laughable and instructive forms and shapes, wholly regardless of the later introduction of the splendid mowing machines and reapers in the harvests of the world. Many of the curious almanacs are issued from the offices of the illustrated and comic papers, and are sent to the United States and sold in large numbers and at high prices.

The shares of the *Tribune* are now distributed, it is believed, as follows:

Horace Greeley, chief editor	10 shares.
Samuel Sinclair, publisher	24 "
Dr. J. C. Ayer, Lowell	16 "
Estate of Stephen Clarke, late financial editor	13 "
Mrs. Greeley, wife of chief editor	5 "
George Ripley, literary editor	5 "
Bayard Taylor, ex-editor	5 "
Thomas N. Rooker, foreman	5 "
Estate of A. D. Richardson	5 "
Solon Robinson, ex-editor	2 "
Fitzpatrick, pressman	2 "
O'Rourke, engineer	2 "
Runkle	2 "
Theodore Tilton	1 "
Oliver Johnson	1 "
Whitelaw Reid, managing editor	1 "
J. F. Cleveland, editor of Almanac	1 "
Total	100 shares.

Thus the *Tribune* and Greeley have prospered journalistically from 1841 to 1872, a long and eventful period in the history of a newspaper and of the nation. The *Tribune* is a leader. It has become so by the efforts of one man. Assistance, of course, he has had, and in abundance, and the establishment has gained much from other minds; but the strong, individual character of Greeley has placed the paper where it is. It is a great paper, and if its founder and manager was less of a politician, and more free of crotchets and isms, the *Tribune* would be a powerful rival of any competitor. It will continue to be a leading paper of the country, and its editor-in-chief may yet be chief magistrate of the republic. The shareholders have faith enough in it to propose a new building in 1872–3, an idea they have had since 1867. The project, we are told, is now to be carried into effect in a way to surpass any newspaper building in America. If this be done, it will require half a million of dollars, or thereabouts, for the new printing palace. We shall hope to see the work begun and finished. Then that already renowned square, with the *Times, Staats Zeitung, Sun,* and *Tribune* buildings, of magnificent architectural proportions, and the colossal bronze statues of Benjamin Franklin and Horace Greeley, one opposite the *Times* office, and the other in front of the *Staats Zeitung* establishment, one with the *Pennsylvania Gazette* of 1732 in hand, and the other holding out the *New York Tribune* of 1872 to the people as they pass, will be one of the attractive spots of the metropolis.

CHAPTER XXXIV.
ALL SORTS OF POLITICAL PAPERS.

THE FIRST NEWSPAPER IN TENNESSEE.—THE KNOXVILLE WHIG.—PARSON BROWNLOW AND ANDREW JOHNSON.—THE ALBANY REGISTER.—THE PLEBEIAN, NEW ERA, MORNING NEWS, GLOBE, AND AURORA.—SLAMM, BANG & CO.—THE REPUBLIC.—CHEVALIER WIKOFF AND DUFF GREEN.—THE ALBANY ATLAS.—THE WAR OF THE ROSES.—THE SPRINGFIELD REPUBLICAN.—SAMUEL BOWLES.—ARREST IN NEW YORK.—CONTROVERSY WITH DAVID DUDLEY FIELD.—THE FIRST JOURNAL IN THE OIL REGIONS.

ONE of the sons of New England, named Roulstone, a printer of Massachusetts, opened a printing-office in Knoxville, Tennessee, in 1793, and issued therefrom the *Knoxville Gazette*, the first newspaper in that state.

The *Knoxville Whig*, published in East Tennessee since 1839, has been a remarkable paper, politically considered. It was published by William G. Brownlow, known as the "Fighting Parson," for more than a quarter of a century. Its name and that of its editor is on the page of newspaper history. The *Whig* has been a vigorous political journal, and nothing else. Newspapers, in a Northern point of view, were rare in the South. Some idea of the character of the editor of the *Whig* may be obtained from the following appeal to his constituents in 1845:

TO THE VOTERS OF THE FIRST CONGRESSIONAL DISTRICT OF EAST TENNESSEE.

FELLOW-CITIZENS,—Having been nominated for Congress in this district by a meeting of the Whigs of Greenville, during the late term of the Circuit Court; and having received various calls, by letter and from esteemed friends in person, in every portion of this large district, to permit my name to be run for that important trust, I take this method of responding to all concerned.

I have repeatedly said, both on the stump and through the columns of my widely-circulated paper, that I would never declare myself a candidate for any office within the gift of the people, as office was not my aim, but the good of my country. * * * * * * *

If elected, as I am told I will be, there will be peace and a final cessation of all hostilities here, because I will then abandon my editorial pursuits forever, and devote my time and talents to the interests of the people. In that event, too, "a consummation most devoutly to be wished for," I request all aged men, cripples and idiots, widows and orphans, who are entitled to pensions, or whose fathers and husbands are entitled to receive them, to meet me at the courts in each county in this district before I go on to Washington, and I will arrange their papers and procure them pensions, and even back pay, where they are entitled to it, as many are. I will take the same trouble to serve Democrats that I would Whigs, and all without fee or reward, as I consider the eight dollars per day, paid me by the government, sufficient to compensate me for thus serving my constituents!

The Locofoco candidate, Mr. Johnson, hopes to succeed, because he is a *tailor* by trade, and of humble pretensions! Why, I am a *house carpenter*, and served a regular apprenticeship at the business in Western Virginia, and am, therefore, entitled to as much credit for taking the stand I have in the world as he is! True, he can urge that I am a man of more consequence in the world than he is, and I am more extensively known and spoken of by all parties, but it is because I am a more meritorious man, and more worthy of public consideration. And as a proof of what it is feared the people think, Johnson and his particular friends are now weary, and evidently fear the result. I will have them in greater trouble before the first of August.

And now, having been at the trouble and expense of publishing this circular, in which I barely announce my determination to suffer my name to be run for this office, I hope all friendly to the cause of sound principles, and to the best interests of this thieving section of the country, will be at the trouble to circulate it among the free and independent voters of the district. Those who are not free and independent—who are side-lined and driven by party leaders, had better not get hold of it, for they will commit it to the flames. In some three weeks from this I promise the public a circular of interest, one in which I will make the fur fly and the wounded pigeons flutter! WM. G. BROWNLOW.

JONESBORO', June 25, 1845.

The two characters in this manifesto are Senator Brownlow and ex-President Johnson. They were thus prominent in Tennessee in 1845. The rebellion of 1861 brought them more conspicuously before the people, and gave them a national character.

Mr. Brownlow retired from the *Whig* in 1869. On leaving his editorial chair he issued the following card:

Having founded the *Whig* in the spring of 1839, I have been its chief editor and publisher for a term extending through thirty years—first at Elizabethton, next at Jonesboro', and for the last twenty years at Knoxville. Declining health and other engagements render it impracticable for me longer to look after the business interests of the office. I have therefore sold my entire interest in the *Whig*, and henceforth I own no part of any newspaper establishment in this state or elsewhere. The publication of the *Whig* will be continued under a new organization, but by whom it will be published and edited I am unable to say. I have the assurance, however, that it will be continued as a Republican journal, advocating the principles and policy of the Republican Party, and rendering a cordial support to President Grant and his administration.

* * * * * * * *

W. G. BROWNLOW.

KNOXVILLE, Tenn., September 14, 1869.

The "unpleasantness" between the ex-president and the ex-editor has neither been harmonized nor arranged. The ex-president, in speeches, has claimed that he contributed $1500 towards the capital of the *Whig*. The ex-editor retorts that the money came from the funds of the government, and were paid by the sub-treasurer at Cincinnati. But transitory are the things of this life. The *Whig*, having lost its master-mind, was absorbed in 1871 by the Knoxville *Press and Herald*, and ex-editor and ex-parson Brownlow is now only a senator.

The administration of John Tyler produced a flood of papers. They started on the wave of politics every where, but especially in Philadelphia, New York, and Boston. Numbers of those in existence, a little shaky in their condition, hoisted the Tyler flag in order to obtain support from the custom-houses and post-offices. The

Democratic papers, of course, favored the President because of his financial policy, and in the hope of breaking up the Whig Party. Other papers were established by the opposition to break down Tyler. They are nearly all dead now.

One of the Democratic organs in New York, the *Plebeian*, was a noticeable sheet. It was started about 1842–'3, and succeeded the *New Era*. Its editors were Levi D. Slamm, a very genial Locofoco, and Alexander Ming, Jr., with several assistants in and out of office. It was a sledge-hammer in journalism and politics, and the *Herald*, in speaking of it, gave its editors the title of Slamm, Bang & Co., and as such they were ever after known in local politics. Slamm, on leaving the Press, became a purser in the navy.

The *New Era, Morning News, Democrat, Globe, Union*, and *Aurora* were of the same class in New York, and the *Times* in Boston. The *New Era* was a pretentious Democratic sheet, commenced in October, 1836, by Jared D. Bell, and edited by Joseph Price and Richard Adams Locke. The *News*, started in August, 1844, was edited by Parke Godwin, son-in-law of William Cullen Bryant, and afterwards associated with him in the management of the *Evening Post*. John L. O'Sullivan, who had been connected with Langtree in the publication of the *Democratic Review*, was also editor of the *News*. He was sent as minister to Portugal, where he wore the black dress-coat and white cravat at court receptions, in obedience to the famous dress instructions of Secretary Marcy. Samuel J. Tilden was also one of its editors. The *News* was the organ of Bryant, Sedgwick, and the *Evening Post* clique. The *Plebeian*, which had previously united with the *New Era, Democrat, Aurora*, and other papers, was in turn grafted with the *News* in May, 1845.

The *Globe* was published in New York in 1845, and was the organ of Secretary Walker, of the Treasury Department, in Polk's administration. Another *Globe*, a daily sheet, an organ of Tammany Hall, was started in 1847 by Casper C. Childs. It had, in the course of its existence, a number of editors and writers, who either passed from the editorial rooms into fat offices, or slipped off into oblivion, where many a journalist has gone before them. The paper was sustained by party contributions and party pap. It was suspended in April, 1851, and never revived. Samuel J. Bayard was one of its editors. He had been editor of the Cincinnati *Republican* as far back as 1829, and succeeded Elijah Hayward, who had received the appointment of Commissioner of the General Land Office from General Jackson.

The small Democratic papers were nearly all published in the vicinity of Tammany Hall, and, with the *Sun* and *Transcript*, were the first to make the square now known as "Printing-House Square," a name borrowed from the London *Times*, famous as a centre of journalism. This historic square, where the organs of the unwashed and unterrified Democracy, of the Huge-paws and the Sledge-hammers, of the Subterraneans and Hard-fisted, loomed up so fitfully and frightfully, from the days of Van Buren to the end of Polk's administration, is now occupied by the *Times, Sun, Tribune*, and other lights in journalism, literature, and politics.

One of the opposition elements then coming up in politics established the *True American* in December, 1843. It was the organ of the American Republican, or Native American Party, which elected James Harper as mayor of the metropolis. It lived but a short time. Then there were the *American Republican* and the *American Ensign* attached to the same party. The *Gazette*, Free-trade organ, was established in the same year. But the paper that attracted the most attention for a few months was the *Republic*, which was issued early in 1844 by Henry Wikoff, now so well known as the Chevalier Wikoff. It started under the most pretentious auspices as a Free-trade organ. It was edited by the famous Duff Green, with a staff of editors and reporters imported by the Chevalier Wikoff direct from London and Paris. It was journalistically fortunate to publish the first news, received by special express, of the explosion of the monster gun on board the Princeton, which killed so many leading politicians in Washington. After Wikoff had sunk about $70,000 the paper passed into the hands of the Clay Whigs, and was edited by John O. and Epes Sargent. It was about one year in existence. The *Herald* extensively and gratuitously advertised the paper and its editors in April and May of 1844 by the publication of the brilliant Wikoff and Fanny Ellsler correspondence.

Editors and politicians are on the stage to-day and off to-morrow, and, in the rapid changes of scenes and actors, it is difficult to keep all the characters in sight. There was, for instance, a division in the Whig Party in New York in 1850. The political interests of the Seward and Silver-Gray Whigs were carefully looked after by the *Evening Journal* and *State Register*, the former the organ of William H. Seward, and the latter the organ of Millard Fillmore. Seward had other newspaper affiliations scattered over the state, but President Fillmore had only the *Commercial Advertiser*, of Buffalo, of any note, to uphold the cause of the conservative Whig policy of the actual head of that wing of the party. Dr. Thomas M. Foote was Fillmore's chief editor. He had been for many years connected with the *Advertiser*, and had, therefore, considerable experience; but his paper was not located in Albany. He was afterwards appointed *chargé d'affaires* to New Granada. The *Register*, after Fillmore's reign, became the organ of the Know-Nothings, and was edited by

Joseph A. Scoville, in the interest of George Law, the millionaire, an aspirant for the presidency, and dubbed the "Live Oak" candidate by the *New York Herald*. The paper and office was removed to the metropolis, where it died.

The *Albany Atlas* was the offspring of a quarrel in the Democratic Party and for a number of years made itself felt as a power in the political affairs of New York. It was originally established by Cornelius Wendell and George Vance, who had been compositors in the office of the *Argus*. They issued it as an auxiliary to the *Argus*, and it was for a while a mere local organ.

William C. Bouck was elected governor in 1842. On reaching the capital in the month of December preceding the assembling of the Legislature in 1843, the governor elect repaired to the state departments for information for his forthcoming message. All the facts connected with the canals, banks, and finances generally were to be obtained from the comptroller. Azariah C. Flagg was at the head of that department. The comptroller was anxious to ascertain the policy Governor Bouck intended to pursue in relation to the canals. The governor said that he had no special policy to suggest different from that of the Democratic Party under Throop and Marcy. This did not satisfy Flagg. He desired to know whether the governor would recommend a continuance of the system that had reduced the state securities to eighty cents on the dollar, or go with the comptroller, and stop the works altogether. The two gentlemen could not agree. The governor elect then paid a visit to Edwin Croswell, of the *Argus*, and he advised him what to do. It is affirmed that Governor B.'s first message was amply supervised by Croswell.

The state officers were then Samuel Young, Secretary of State; Azariah C. Flagg, Comptroller; George P. Barker, Attorney General; and Thomas Farrington, Treasurer. Such men as Henry W. Strong, John B. Scott, Robert Denniston, Michael Hoffman, Arphaxad Loomis, Levi S. Chatfield, John A. Dix, John L. O'Sullivan, Conrad Swackhammer, Sanford E. Church, and George R. Davis, were members of the Legislature. They had enunciated the "policy of '42," and were determined to carry it out. These statements are necessary, as leading to the course of the *Atlas* from that day. On this occasion the *Atlas* was brought into requisition. Its proprietor was then James M. French; William Cassidy was his assistant. All the state officers above named, together with their friends in and out of the Legislature, threw the weight of their influence toward making the *Atlas* the successful rival to the *Argus*. The patronage of Flagg's department, the banking and the canal, in job printing and advertising, was immense; this was exclusively given to the *Atlas*.

The administration became divided. On the one side stood Governor Bouck, Lieutenant Governor Dickinson, nearly all the canal commissioners, with Edwin Croswell, of the *Argus;* on the other were the state officers, the speaker of the House, and other enemies of the canals, with the *Atlas*. Its columns teemed with bitter effusions from the pens of Colonel Young, General Barker, Mr. Hoffman, Mr. Flagg, and others. Mr. Hoffman commenced a series of articles advocating the expediency and necessity of a new Constitution; the *Atlas* was the leading organ in placing that writer's views before the people. Although the Whigs and leading Hunkers did not openly or violently oppose the calling of a Constitutional Convention, still they were lukewarm, and the result showed that there was in the state a vote of nearly thirty-four thousand against calling it. The act authorizing the Convention was passed in the early part of the session of 1846, and upon ratifying the new Constitution about ninety-two thousand votes went against it, nearly three times the number opposed to the call. This result gave the *Atlas* greater prominence.

In the mean time, the term of office of state printer expired, and the time had arrived when the Barnburners thought they had the power to make the promised reward for Mr. French, in return for the great sacrifices he had already made in sustaining the *Atlas*. Mr. Croswell had enjoyed the princely patronage of state printer during many years, except the short time Thurlow Weed held it, and would have been willing to yield to any fair political opponent; but he keenly felt the blows which the Barnburners had inflicted upon him and his friends. He put his power to the test in order to defeat French or Cassidy. Henry H. Van Dyck was then a partner with Croswell in the *Argus*, who was ambitious to become state printer. He would not allow his name to be used in copartnership with Croswell's; but with regard to state printer he was determined to be, as he said at the time, "*aut Cæsar, aut nullus.*" Croswell conquered, and Van Dyck ingloriously left the *Argus* office. The whole combined force of the Barnburners had thus been defeated and outgeneraled by a single man. They had cherished the hope that the proprietor of the *Atlas* would become state printer, and that it would then assume a position of strength, and eventually demolish its indomitable antagonist at the capital.

Mr. French then became discouraged. He had spent a large fortune, inherited from his father, in sustaining the *Atlas*. The establishment was in debt, and those payments must be met, or the concern would sink. Silas Wright was then Governor; Flagg, Comptroller; John Van Buren, Attorney General; Farrington, Treasurer. The paper was on the point of being abandoned. It lived from hand to mouth, and on contributions collected for its indispensable weekly payments. The largest creditors were advised of the state of things, a majority of whom agreed to settle for fifty per cent. A stock concern was then proposed, and Mr. Flagg, Dr. Crain, of Herkimer, Dr. Beekman, of Kinderhook, John A. Dix, of New York, James S. Wadsworth, of Livingston, Dean Richmond, of Buffalo, and a few others, were solicited to deposit certain assessed amounts. John Van Buren, though brother-in-law of French, did not subscribe a dollar. This arrangement being perfected, the aforesaid fifty per cent. paid, Mr. French withdrew, and Mr. Van Dyck, then a clerk in Mr. Flagg's office, and afterwards sub-treasurer in New York under Lincoln and Johnson, was transferred to the *Atlas*. This was in 1846.

About this period the Wilmot Proviso was thrust into the lower house of Congress as a means and for the purpose of distracting the national democracy. In October, 1847, a Democratic State Convention was held at Syracuse, called for the object of nominating candidates for comptroller and other state officers. The Hunkers and Barnburners had then become visibly divided on the Proviso Question. Neither faction could confidently rely upon a majority in that body. There were a dozen contested seats, and it became evident that the section which could control and admit the contending delegates would have the Convention. Several days were consumed in settling the claims. The first question taken showed a Hunker majority, though the vote was a close one. John Van Buren was ousted, claiming to represent one of the Albany districts. Two or three of the Barnburners were voted in, and all the rest rejected. Among the leading Hunkers, James T. Brady and Horatio Seymour bore the most conspicuous part. Not a single Barnburner would consent to serve as an officer of the Convention after Robert H. Morris, of New York, was made president. A thorough Hunker ticket was nominated, upon which was placed Orville Hungerford for comptroller. David Dudley Field did not desert the Convention, as scores of other Free-soilers did, but remained a silent member, for the purpose of distraction, until near the close of the business. He then arose and submitted the following resolution :

Resolved, That while the democracy of New York, represented in this Convention, will faithfully adhere to all the compromises of the Constitution and maintain all the reserved rights of the states, they declare—since the crisis has arrived when the question must be met—their uncompromising hostility to the extension of slavery into territory now free which may hereafter be acquired by any action of the United States.

The Hunkers, having the majority, promptly laid this missile on the table. It was introduced for mischievous purposes, and it produced the intended effect, which was a rupture in the Convention, and a scattering of the Democratic hosts. This was food for the *Atlas*. Van Dyck, returning from the Convention, placed Field's abolition resolution over the editorial columns as the corner-stone of the Barnburner faith, accompanied with the expression, impious as it was, "The stone which the builders rejected, the same shall become the head of the corner." This gave new vigor to that sheet; it became at once the leading Abolition print in the North. The Buffalo platform, and the nomination of Martin Van Buren to effect the defeat of General Cass in 1848, gave the *Atlas* still greater prominence, as it outstripped all other publications in advocating the Free-soil plank of that platform and in the support of Van Buren. Its columns teemed with excoriating articles from the ablest abolition pens in the state. Among these contributors were Gerrit Smith, Preston King, Benjamin Welch, Charles S. Benton, Charles B. Sedgwick, Dudley Burwell, William Jay, Erastus D. Culver, James W. Nye, William Barstow, and Henry B. Stanton. Subscriptions rolled in abundantly; the columns and dimensions of the paper were enlarged; contributions toward the support of the *Atlas* came in abolition torrents. The paper was Free-soil, and nothing else. It supported for office such men as Charles Francis Adams and Seth M. Gates. It continued to prosper during the contest of 1848, and claimed the support of the Abolitionists, Free-soilers, and Barnburners, without associating at all with the democracy, down to 1852, keeping floating at its flag-staff the celebrated anti-slavery "corner-stone," with William Cassidy as editor. But the leading Abolitionists found that they had made a mistake. They became convinced that all the love the *Atlas* ever had for slave emancipation was to keep up an excitement against General Cass as long as he was prominently a presidential candidate, and no longer. After the nominations in 1852 of Seymour for governor and Pierce for president, the *Atlas* threw aside its abolitionism. The celebrated "corner-stone" was silently dropped, and the paper came out and supported the national nominees in 1852, and in less than three months after the election of Pierce it became apparent why the abolition guns of the *Atlas* had been spiked. It was then evident that Pierce had made an alliance with the Free-soil Barnburners of New York. The cases of Bronson, of New York, and Reynolds, of Albany, were specimens of administrative harmony produced by means of the *Atlas*. Thus, from the 4th of March, 1853, till after the fall election of 1855, that paper was daily praising Pierce.

The proprietor and the editor then took opposite grounds. One day the columns of the *Atlas* teemed with vindictiveness against Pierce, Marcy, and the entire national administration; these articles were written by Van Dyck. The subsequent issue contained extraordinary laudations and high praises of the same public functionaries. The public was highly delighted with this singular harmony, and every one saw in it a crisis in the affairs of that concern. Van Dyck, who held the title, offered the establishment for sale. The *Argus* offered to purchase. It was finally arranged that the two papers should be amalgamated, with Cassidy and Comstock as editors and proprietors. The united paper was called the *Argus and Atlas*.

The *Springfield* (Mass.) *Republican* is a representative paper. It is one of the most influential provincial journals in the United States. Its vigor of management, and its central position in Massachusetts, gives it this power over other journals published in the interior.

The *Republican* was established in 1847. Samuel Bowles & Co. are the publishers. It has always had an excellent staff of writers. Such as Timothy Titcomb have contributed to its columns. Its chief proprietor is an energetic journalist, and looks keenly and shrewdly after the interest of his paper. It is said that he has a desire to expand his journalism in New York. Several years ago he combined a number of papers in Boston, and issued a paper somewhat after the style of the *Tribune*. There were high anticipations of its success among the Republican journalists and friends of the editor. When the first number reached New York, Horace Greeley asked another journalist,

"What do you think of Bowles's new paper in Boston? Will it succeed?"

"I am afraid not," was the reply. "It is too much like the *Tribune*. The only difference is in the size of the type. There is not enough originality in its make-up."

It did not live long, for other reasons, however. Its internal organization was not cohesively arranged. The treasury was not equal to the enterprise, and Boston had not yet been educated up to the financial expenditures of the leading New York papers.

The *Republican* is an eight-page paper, called a double sheet, neatly printed and spiritedly edited. It has an opinion of its own, and utters it whenever it chooses to do so. It has for its device, with the head-line, a cut of a Napier cylinder press capable of printing three thousand sheets per hour. Where the old style of papers inserted their mottoes, the *Republican* has "R. Hoe & Co." If that firm be its motto, the device should be changed to a ten-cylinder lightning press, or newspaper advertisers will think that the concern has not kept up in progress with its great and enterprising motto-firm and press-builders.

The *Republican* is emphatically a New England institution. Its editor's platform is laid down in these words:

To picture the progress of the varied and busy life of New England as to represent its inquisitive and active thought on all questions that concern the comfort and the elevation of society; to make, indeed, a part of that life and that thought—this is the scope and aim of the *Springfield Republican* newspaper. Confessedly it has become the most representative and comprehensive of New England journals; as a record of its news, for home use or foreign enlightenment; as an exponent of its best thought, most intelligent, candid, and advanced on questions of political and religious liberty and progress, of social order and development, and of literary and art culture; and it is the ambition and effort of its conductors to maintain and extend this leadership, to still more elevate and widen the character of the paper, and to vary and enlarge its interest and usefulness for all classes of our people.

The *Republican*, in 1868, published an article reflecting on the conduct and character of Colonel James Fisk, Jr. Shortly after, Mr. Bowles visited New York. One evening he was arrested at the Fifth Avenue Hotel, at the instance of Colonel Fisk, and incarcerated for one night in Ludlow-Street Jail on a suit for libel. The whole affair was a gross outrage on the rights of a citizen and the freedom of the Press. On the return of Mr. Bowles to Springfield he received the following invitation, signed by fifty of the first citizens of Boston:

To SAMUEL BOWLES, ESQ.:—The undersigned, desirous of testifying our respect for your character as a man, and for your course as an independent editor, request you to do us the honor of dining with us at such early date as suits your convenience. ALEX. H. BULLOCK, WILLIAM CLAFFIN, N. P. BANKS, CHARLES G. GREENE, and others.

BOSTON, December 24, 1868.

Editor Bowles, in reply, very appropriately said:

SPRINGFIELD, December 28, 1868.

* * * I can not feel that I have done or suffered so much more than many of my brethren for the cause of independent journalism as to justify me in so far violating my conviction of the desirability of maintaining the impersonality of the Press as a great means of its growth, its power, and its independence. Besides, no dinner, with speeches and presence, however brilliant or attractive, could add force or influence to the brief word you have written. When gentlemen of so widely different associations as yourselves, representing opposing political parties, and all the leading interests and professions of society, unite to speak for the integrity and independence of journalism, there is cause for rejoicing and hope for us all.

The corruptions in politics and the corruptions in business affairs have become offensive and startling within the last few years, and the moral sense of the community seems at times to have become blunted by the successful display and repetition of practices that violate every principle of fair dealing and integrity, and put the control of government and the value of many kinds of property at the mercy of political adventurers and ruthless stock gamblers. The Press really seems to be the best, if not the only instrument with which honest men can fight these enemies of order and integrity in government and security in property. * * * American journalism is now but in its feeble infancy; but we have more to fear at present from its good nature, from its subserviency, from its indifference, from its fear to encounter prosecution and loss of patronage by the exposure of the wrong and the exposition of the right. A courageous independence and integrity of purpose, coupled with a fearless expression of truth as to all public individuals, corporations, and parties, are the features in its character to me most encouraged now. * * * * *

My own observation is that the Press rarely does injustice to a thoroughly honest man or cause. It may be deceived with regard to a private individual, and misrepresent him for a time ; but with reference to public men and measures, its knowledge is more intimate and complete than that of any other agency possibly can be ; and I know that it withholds unjustly to the public one hundred times where it speaks wrongly once of the individual. Certainly, nine out of ten of all libel-suits against the Press are brought by adventurers, and speculators, and scoundrels, whose contrivances to rob the public have been exposed. * * *

SAMUEL BOWLES.

But roses have their thorns ; and under the head of "retributive," Wendell Phillips, in the *Anti-Slavery Standard*, thus resumes specie payments with the editor of the *Republican:*

> The New York journals are wasting a great deal of indignation on Mr. Fisk for the course he took in the matter of Mr. Samuel Bowles, of the *Springfield Republican*. When we remember the abuse and insolence lavished by Mr. Bowles, from his coward's castle, on every true man for the last fifteen years, we think such an offender has nothing to complain of. He has only been paid in his own coin. The combatants seem about equally matched; though, to be sure, Mr. Fisk, a new beginner, can not expect fully to equal Mr. Bowles, who is a veteran in this fine art.
>
> If Mr. Bowles had recalled George Thomson's faithful dealing with him when that gentleman and his friends were mobbed in Springfield seventeen years ago, and the scores of times since that he has done his utmost to poison the mind of Western Massachusetts against the best men in the state, he might have used his prison hours in profitable, if penitential meditations—a much better employment than whimpering.
>
> The *Springfield Republican*, like the *Boston Advertiser*, has belonged, in times past, to a class of journals noted for abusing those men whose personal unpopularity made it safe, and sometimes profitable, to abuse them. For once it has miscalculated.
>
> W. P.

There was a long correspondence, in December, 1870, and January, 1871, between David Dudley Field, a distinguished lawyer of New York City, and Samuel Bowles, growing out of an attack on the professional integrity, or, rather, the professional rights of the lawyer. The "attack" was contained in a letter from New York which was published in the *Republican*. This is an extract :

> David Dudley Field, though hardly old enough to be called a veteran, is one of the ablest lawyers in New York, and has by far the largest practice. His receipts as counsel for the Erie Railroad Company alone are understood to have exceeded $200,000 in a single year, and his regular income is enormous. His connection with Fisk and Gould secures him the favor of Barnard and the other ring judges, though it has destroyed his reputation as a high-toned lawyer with the public, while the bar always disliked him for his avarice and meanness. David Dudley Field is a strong Free-trade advocate, and often presides at the meetings of the Reform Club. He is an authority on international law, and was also the chief codifier of the present Code of Procedure of the State of New York. His reputation as a lawyer is based upon his knowledge of legal technicality, and once, during a conversation with the late James T. Brady, the latter dubbed him "the king of pettifoggers," which title has stuck to Field ever since.

The lawyer, in a brief note, "took exceptions" to this statement. The editor, in reply, regretted the peculiar wording of the letter, but justified its sentiments. This led to a long discussion, which filled a moderate-sized pamphlet, or a page of the *Tribune*, on the respective rights of lawyers and clients, and editors and critics. Mr. Field, who is evidently opposed to anonymous journalism, in his second letter said :

I am amazed and indignant. Do you not mistake your own position as well as mine? What gives you, sitting in private and writing anonymously, authority to render "judgment" upon me? I am not disputing your right, as a collector of news, to publish any facts concerning any body; but you have, certainly, no greater right to publish your opinions respecting the character or conduct of a private person than you would to publish them to his face in a private company; and you must know that you would not have ventured to say what is contained in that paragraph to my face in any company whatever. It seems to be imagined in some quarters that as soon as one can get the control of types and write anonymously, he may publish whatever he pleases about whomsoever he will. For many of the conductors of the public press I have great respect, as for intelligent, cultivated, large-hearted men; but there are others, as you must know, who are "hostes humani generis," and who evidently fancy that as soon as they can fill the columns of a newspaper they may put off the character of a gentleman and take on that of ruffians. Such, I hope, is not your opinion; it certainly is not mine. So much for your position.

Mr. Bowles, in reply, assumed this position for the journalist:

Of course I can not accept the limitations which you put upon journalism. The gathering and publication of facts is but one part of its vocation. To express opinions is a higher and larger share of its duties. The conduct of public men before the public is the legitimate subject for their discussion. The lawyer before the court, as the minister in his pulpit, the executive in his chair of state, and the legislator in his hall of assembly—all these are alike public men, and their conduct in their public vocations the proper theme of both journalistic report and discussion. Nor is such arraignment the province of the Press alone. Without invading the sanctities of private character, or the courtesies of personal life, reason and the habits of civilization give to every man the right to arraign and discuss the public or professional conduct of his fellow-men. The politician on the stump discusses his fellow-politicians; the minister in his pulpit summons his fellows for inconsistency, or unreason, or infidelity; so the lawyer arraigns his fellow-lawyers in court or in public gathering; and each, too, crosses the line of his own profession, and disputes the conduct of men of the other professions. There is no court more thoroughly established than this of public opinion, and no right more finally settled, or more largely improved, than this of the free discussion of the public and professional conduct of all our fellow-men; and I am surprised to find you disputing it.

Neither the lawyer nor the editor, in their columns of argument pro and con, convinced the other; and, so far as the opinions of these two gentlemen affect the public mind, it still remains in doubt whether a lawyer has a right to make any one with sufficient money his client, or the editor the right to hold the lawyer up to public gaze for the crimes and conduct of his client. It is probable that a lawyer with a notoriously bad client will suffer in public estimation, and the editor's criticism be sustained. Such will always be the *vox populi*.

The *Republican* has a large circulation for an interior publication. It claims 25,000. No paper out of Boston has so large a circulation in New England.

"The first daily paper in the oil regions." This is the proud boast of the *Titusville Morning Herald*, and is kept as a standing notice where other papers insert their motto. The *Herald* was established on the 14th of June, 1865. It already claims the largest circulation of any daily newspaper in Pennsylvania outside of Philadelphia and Pittsburg, and that it is the largest daily newspaper in the same commonwealth with the same two exceptions. If this be so, the oil regions have bubbled up to some purpose, and is another of the marvelous instances of the fabulous growth of a populous and wealthy community in the United States. The *Herald* is a large-sized single-sheet paper, pretty well filled with advertisements, and full of news received by telegraph and otherwise. It publishes a monthly statistical review of the petroleum business of that oleaginous section.

CHAPTER XXXV.
CHEAP LITERATURE.

NOVELS MADE INTO NEWS AND SOLD BY NEWS-BOYS.—THE BROTHER JONATHAN AND NEW WORLD.—THE BOSTON NOTION.—COMPETITION FOR THE LAST NOVEL BY THE LAST STEAMER.—DICKENS'S AMERICAN NOTES AND THE QUEEN'S SPEECH.

ABOUT the time the Atlantic began to be traversed by steam-ships, several large papers, published weekly, were established in New York and Boston. They were entitled the Boston *Notion*, and the *New World* and *Brother Jonathan*, of New York. They were literary sheets, and made news of literature. Park Benjamin, an associate of Horace Greeley and Henry J. Raymond on the *New Yorker* in 1838, Rufus Wilmot Griswold, George Roberts, and Jonas Winchester, were the publishers. John Neal, Louis Fitzgerald Tasistro, Griswold, and Benjamin were the chief editors; but they impressed Bulwer, James, Dickens, Ainsworth, Lever, Sheridan Knowles, Lover, and all the writers of note, into their service *nolens volens*. They made war, by their enterprise, on the Harpers and other large book publishers, and brought literature into the market at reduced prices. They were a sensation in New York. What the *New York Herald*, New York *Sun*, Boston *Times*, and Philadelphia *Ledger* endeavored to do with the political, commercial, criminal, financial, and marine movements of the day, these energetic *litterateurs* and publishers attempted to accomplish with Bulwer's Zanoni, Dickens's American Notes, and Knowles's Love-Chase. Zanoni was published by the Harpers, the *New World*, and *Brother Jonathan* in the spring of 1842. It sold for $12\frac{1}{2}$ cents, and in some instances at $6\frac{1}{4}$ cents. The Harpers and a few other booksellers would issue such works as these, taking their own time, and charging $1 and $1 50 for a copy. Although there was no copyright law, these book publishers had as much of a monopoly as if Bulwer, James, and Dickens wrote exclusively for them.

These weekly sheets, by the enterprise of their proprietors, changed all this. They made the same arrangements to get early copies of the last novel by the coming steamers as the *Herald* or *Tribune* made to obtain the latest London *Times* or *Liverpool Mail*. An entire novel would be published on the day of its reception. They would give Bulwer's Night and Morning, complete, in an extra, as the *Herald* would an important speech of O'Connell, or Peel, or Palmerston, or the Queen. Such a feat was considered a marvel in typography. These novels, plays, and romances, in monster folios and double sheets, were sold in the streets by the news-boys at ten and twelve and a half cents each. On the 11th of December, 1839, the *Herald* received by the steamer Liverpool an advance copy of Sheridan Knowles's play of Love-Chase, which was published entire in that paper, and sold with the news of the day for two cents! Ann and Nassau Streets, where the *New World* and *Brother Jonathan* were published, were scenes of wild and extraordinary excitement on the arrival of a steam-ship with a fresh novel. "'Rival of the Britannia. 'Ere's Dickens's Notes—only ten cents." These papers obtained large circulations by this sort of enterprise. It was, however, too sensational to last. They were too dependent on foreign brains. Immense quantities were sent all over the country, especially to the Southern States; and as other matter than novels and plays was published, some of which was considered objectionable and contraband in a Southern political and social point of view, there was trouble and difficulty with the authorities in that section of the country. One of the Boston papers, for instance, contained the following paragraph in November, 1842:

The agent of the *New World* at Charleston, S. C., writes a piteous letter, in which he states that he had been held to bail in the sum of $1000, on the complaint of the South Carolina Association, for having sold a certain number of our journal containing a discourse by the late William Ellery Channing on Emancipation in the West Indies.

Newspaper dealers and agents at the South are now free from such troubles. Any publication or individual can circulate in the South, from Horace Greeley and Benjamin F. Butler to the *Anti-Slavery Standard* and Wendell Phillips.

These monster weekly papers commenced, in a simple way, the system and style of advertising that is at the present time so widely and extensively carried out in this country by Bonner and others. It was a moderate beginning. Instead of the entire columns and pages occupied in typographical display which is now indulged in, Jonas Winchester, of the *New World*, headed the advertisement of the number issued on the 4th of February, 1843, as follows:

THE NEW WORLD.—A GREAT NUMBER.—TWO SPLENDID ENGRAVINGS.

This issue contained Sheridan Knowles's "thrilling tale" of My Grandfather's Dream, and Lamon Blanchard's My Dream at Hop Lodge.

One number of the *Boston Notion* was thus announced:

Another rich Number.—The Boston Notion, L. F. Tasistro, Editor. This journal, so justly celebrated for its high-toned literary criticisms and racy articles, is fast gaining the largest circulation of any weekly in this country.

So great and sharp was the competition among these large literary news sheets that the *Herald* uttered the following predictions relative to them in March, 1843 :

> The terrible contest and competition now going on among the publishers of cheap literature will produce two or three results : 1st, the ruin of all the publishers ; 2d, the fortunes of all the vendors in the large cities ; and, 3d, the spread of literary taste among the people. All these results are positive and certain.

These predictions have been fully verified. In 1845 the *New World* was absorbed by the *Emporium*, and Park Benjamin became an editor in Baltimore in 1846. He was the father of cheap literature in the United States. The *Boston Notion* ceased to exist, and its publisher opened a first-class hotel in New York, and its editor became chief translator in the State Department at Washington, and afterwards, becoming partially blind, he astonished every one with his extraordinary memory in reciting entire plays of Shakspeare. John Neal, who was chief editor of the *Brother Jonathan* in 1843, still lives, with his brain as active as ever, in Portland, Maine, mixed up in railroads and literature.

This cheap literature circulated through the mails at low rates of postage, going, even when printed on extra sheets, as regular newspapers. This was an additional advantage the weekly-paper publisher enjoyed over the old book publishers ; but in April, 1843, instructions were issued from the Post-office Department to charge pamphlet postage on all the cheap publications of the day issued as extras. The postage on the extras of the *New World* and *Brother Jonathan* was two and a half cents a sheet. On the following July these publications were shut out of Canada, in accordance with the provisions of the copyright law, by the restrictions of the authorities of that province, through the efforts, it was asserted at the time, of Bulwer, Dickens, James, and other English authors.

These official acts were serious blows to the cheap publications, but the taste of the public for the productions of first-class writers had spread and become standard, and was seen afterwards in the improved class of literary papers issued in the United States.

CHAPTER XXXVI.
NEWSPAPERS ON THE PACIFIC.

THE FLUMGUDGEON GAZETTE, OF OREGON. — STEVENSON'S EXPEDITION. — TYPE AND PRESSES GO WITH THE TROOPS. — THE DISCOVERY OF GOLD. — SPECIMENS SENT TO THE NEW YORK HERALD. — TREMENDOUS GOLD EXCITEMENT. — HOW NEWSPAPERS IN CALIFORNIA ORIGINATED. — EASTERN JOURNALS IN THE MINES. — HOW EARLY NEWS FROM CALIFORNIA WAS OBTAINED. — THE PRESENT. — THE FUTURE.

THE Pacific slope will not long be in the rear of the Atlantic slope in the number and wealth of its newspapers; indeed, the journalists in that part of the world even think that they are now up to the mark in point of ability and enterprise. Many of the papers published in San Francisco are handsome specimens of typography, and in talent and energy they stand well in the ranks.

The first paper printed on the coast of the Pacific made its appearance before the war with Mexico, before the invasion of California, and before Marshall and Sutter discovered gold where the former was building a mill for the latter in January, 1848. Many years previously to those events Astor and Gray had made the Columbia River known, and there was an excitement in 1830 in New England and New York, among the young men, to migrate to Oregon and develop that region of the Northwest. Oregon, therefore, was not a *terra incognita* when the Texas Question came up to vex the politicians in 1844, and a newspaper was printed there about that time. This pioneer in journalism in that part of the continent was rescued from oblivion when its proprietor, in after years, became an applicant for the public printing in California. One of his amiable *confrères* in San Francisco gives the following facts in regard to the

FIRST AMERICAN NEWSPAPER PUBLISHED ON THE PACIFIC COAST OF NORTH AMERICA.

If it be any farther argument in favor of the editor of the *Western American* obtaining the public printing, we would add, for information of legislators, that the first American newspaper ever published on this coast was issued by him at Oregon City in the spring of 1844.

The title of the paper was the *Flumgudgeon Gazette, or Bumble-Bee Budget*, edited by the Long-tailed Coon, a sort of Pike County *Punch* affair. The motto read, "Devoted to scratching and stinging the Follies of the Age."

It was tri-weekly, some eight or ten numbers being issued, continuing during the session of the Legislative Council of the Territory. The paper made quite a stir in those parts, and kept the members on their p's and q's all the time. It was burlesquing, comical, and humorously critical upon the honorable body, which, like the California Legislatures, was a compound mixture of Hoosierism and Yankee, without the addition, as with us, of the Chivalry, Greasers, and Sour-Krout.

Governor P. H. Burnett got hold of several copies, and may possibly have them now among his papers. Mr. Springer, a German limner, drew in crayon the person of the editor at the head of each sheet. Mr. S. is now living on the banks of the Rio Guadalupe, just in the edge of the Pueblo de San José, where he keeps a public house, the best of liquors, and our friends will be doing us a favor by calling at his casa for a drink on passing.

This original sheet, more a copy of *Punch* than of the *Weekly News-Letter* in its title, made its appearance in 1844. Only a quarter of a century later, in 1870, there were thirty-four daily, one hundred and eighty-eight weekly, and six monthly publications in California and Oregon alone! There are, besides, numerous publications in Washington, Colorado, Utah, New Mexico, Arizona, Dakotah, Montana—all west of the Mississippi, and all started since the *Flumgudgeon* flashed upon the world and disappeared.

Newspaper brains and material went out to the Pacific with Stevenson's Expedition in 1846. Graduates of the *New York Herald*, such as John Nugent, William C. Hamilton, Edward Connor, E. Gould Buffum, migrated to the Dorado of the West, and the *Alta California* and the *San Francisco Herald* came into existence. Graduates of the *New York Tribune* and *New York Times* afterwards went out to that golden shore, and the *San Francisco Bulletin* and many other daily papers were established, some to live, and many to die. On the 7th of July, 1846, the following paragraph appeared in the *New York Herald*:

We are informed, upon good authority, that, in company with the new regiments to be commanded by Colonel Stevenson, a gentleman of this city will go with a press and type to establish a newspaper in California.

On the next day the *Herald* said:

Among other articles to go, there will be one or two printing-presses, accompanied by men to operate them and men of talent to conduct them. We are happy to say that the idea of establishing a government paper is not entertained by Colonel Stevenson, but that the paper, when established, will be perfectly independent.

This was the beginning of real journalism on the Pacific. Out of the brains and material carried to that region by this military expedition have grown the newspapers of California and the Pacific. There are now twenty-seven daily papers published in that state, and one advertising agency in New York in 1870 announced that it would receive advertisements for 163 newspapers in California, 26 newspapers in Oregon, 12 newspapers in Washington Territory, 8 newspapers in Montana, 6 newspapers in Idaho, 4 newspapers in Dakotah, 6 newspapers in Wyoming, 11 newspapers in Nevada, 7 newspapers in Utah, 2 newspapers in Arizona, 3 newspapers in New Mexico, 15 newspapers in Colorado, 1 newspaper in Indian Territory, 40 newspapers in Nebraska; and among these there is a *News-Letter* in San Francisco, and, in recollection of the pioneer of Boston, it seems quite appropriate that its name should be perpetuated on the other side of the continent. Alaska is not included in the above list, but a paper is published there called the *Times*.

When Vice-president Colfax visited California a few years ago, his old associates of the case and stick, who had migrated to the Pacific to assist in printing these papers, presented him with a rule made of the mere dust of that state—the golden rule—suitably inscribed, which he always proudly carries, and proudly exhibits as one of the neatest gifts he ever received.

As already mentioned on page 478, the first specimen of gold-dust sent from California to the Atlantic was a pinch of the rare article, in the shape of small scales, inclosed in a letter from Thomas Larkin, long the United States Naval Agent at Monterey and Mazatlan, to James Gordon Bennett, of the *New York Herald*. Wonderful discoveries of precious metals in North Carolina, Georgia, and other parts of the United States had been made known at various times to the *Herald*, and announcements of these discoveries were largely mixed up with cupidity. It was first thought these discoveries in California were of a similar character; but on the publication in that paper of the analysis of the tiny specimen, a great popular excitement began, and as news arrived overland from California of additional developments and discoveries, it increased till there was a perfect stampede to the Pacific. There were no steamers then; the Isthmus of Panama was crossed with difficulty, and the passage up the coast an uncertain adventure. Small parties crossed overland through Mexico. The Pacific Mail Steam-ship Company had been organized, but the steamers were not then on the line. It was difficult to hold in the ardent lovers of gold who wished to go at once to the new Dorado. Fernando Wood had, curiously enough, dispatched the bark John W. Cater around the Cape with an assorted cargo; but the first vessel to leave New York with gold-hunters was the John Benson, which sailed for Chagres with sixty passengers, including Jem Grant, the well-known *Herald* barber, the pioneers of that immense throng of gold-seekers that afterwards left the Atlantic and Middle States to people the shores of the Pacific, and where Jem Grant became an alderman and a millionaire. The three regiments composing Colonel Stevenson's expedition, of course, preceded all these, but when they took their departure from New York no one dreamed of the wealth so soon to be discovered and developed in California.

Obtaining the latest news from the mines was the feature of New-York journalism till the steamers commenced their regular trips.

All other matters, in Europe or elsewhere, were subordinate in interest to the freshest advices from California. News came at uncertain times, sometimes by the way of Panama, but oftener by individuals, who came overland by the way of Mazatlan and the City of Mexico. These individuals were interviewed and facts "pumped" out of them. There were no newspapers to take news from. For some time the intelligence was verbal. The *Herald* was remarkably successful in getting the much-sought-for news in this way. Watchfulness and industry thus had their reward.

After the discovery of gold and the rush of gold-hunters from the Atlantic States, the miners were largely supplied with news from home by California editions of the *New York Tribune*, the *New York Herald*, the *Boston Journal*, the *New Orleans Delta*, and a few others. These sheets were made up expressly for that region, and every steamer for the Isthmus from New York and New Orleans would carry forty, fifty, and sixty thousand copies of these journals. The *Boston Journal* and *New York Herald* would each send ten thousand copies by each steamer.

Scenes on the arrival of these papers at San Francisco, as they have been described, were full of fun and sentiment. One month and six weeks without tidings from home wound up the feelings of the miners to the highest point of tension, and when the steamers arrived they found vent in all sorts of ways. Some idea of this "pent-up Utica" is developed in the enthusiasm of a party of miners, who had not seen a female form for months, who danced with the wildest glee for hours around a cast-off crinoline which had mysteriously come into their possession, and which they had suspended on a pole, so that they could the more fully enjoy the sight. Once or twice, by the way of Vera Cruz, the City of Mexico, and Mazatlan, a single copy of the *New York Herald* would reach San Francisco in advance of the steamers. Fabulous sums have been paid for these journalistic waifs; and they would be so thoroughly read as to be completely deprived of all signs of printing-ink. They would be worn to a dirty white paper. On occasions, as has already been stated, the owners of the papers would mount tables, chairs, rocks, and stumps, and read the contents to the assembled crowds of deeply-excited and attentive listeners.

The Grass Valley *National*, in 1865, thus described a scene which its editor witnessed in 1850, which fully illustrates what we have said on the subject:

Arriving in Sacramento from across the Plains, we could not help but wonder (although it was a natural consequence of the immense immigration) at the myriads of people who thronged the streets. Ahead of us on J Street we saw a crowd dividing, as if to make way for something authoritative to pass, and soon we beheld a burly personage of about forty years, with a grizzly head, and a face full of energy, striding onward, looking neither to the right nor the left, and bearing on his arm an enormous basket containing papers. As he went, he exclaimed at the top of his voice, "Here's the California *True Delta*, the greatest paper ever published in the United States of America, or in any part of the civilized world. Any body that has money can throw a dollar into that basket and take a copy, and any poor man may take a copy for nothing." Paper after paper disappeared, and dollar after dollar jingled in the basket. All this time the burly vender disdained to look around to see whether payment was correctly made or not, or how things were going. As unconcerned as if money were a mere matter of moonshine, and it was totally indifferent to him whether he made $1000, or $50, or $10, he moved serenely on, making a broad lane as he went, and stepping to the music of the silver coins which played in his basket. Attracted by the originality of this exceedingly eccentric proceeding, we followed in the track of this marvelous disseminator of intelligence until he got rid of his last paper, and saw him go back in the direction from whence he came, with nothing in his basket but a huge pile of silver, which he paid no attention to whatever, although every man that he passed had an opportunity to take out a handful if he chose. Still curious to see more of this unique way of doing business, we followed on until our hero arrived at a huge building, into a large room of which he entered, as if he were at home, and, opening a drawer, tumbled the contents of his basket into it as though he had been emptying out of it potatoes or onions. The place was a grand *dépôt* for Atlantic newspapers, and the character described one of the notabilities of that primal period of California history.

News agents, such as Gregory, who had been a gardener on Staten Island, and Sullivan, who had been an active news-boy in New York, were the *avant coureurs* in this pursuit. Afterwards Adams's Express Company, and then Wells & Fargo, energetically and skillfully managed the carrying business of that remote section; but, on the establishment of enterprising newspapers in California, and the extension of the telegraph lines to the Golden Gate, this enormous circulation of the Eastern journals fell off to almost nothing, and the newspaper business there assumed the same natural position as in other parts of the country. Telegrams from New York, reaching San Francisco, and published almost simultaneously, the difference in time considered, with their delivery to the New York offices, shut out newspapers which were twenty-five, or even seven days *en route*. But it is not improbable in the future, in the marvelous progress of events, and the wonderful strides of science, to have parcels of newspapers daily distributed all over the Union by pneumatic tubes, and delivered, too, on the morning of publication! Then the leading papers of the metropolis may again largely circulate in distant cities, where they have been suppressed by telegraphic news dispatches. San Francisco, New Orleans, Oregon, Washington City, Detroit, Chicago, Nashville, Salt Lake City, will then be, in a newspaper point of view, extended streets, and wards, and districts of the metropolis, as the New-England villages and cities are now to the city of Boston by their network of railways.

CHAPTER XXXVII.
THE TELEGRAPHIC ERA.

VARIOUS MODES OF TRANSMITTING INTELLIGENCE FOR NEWSPAPERS.—CARRIER PIGEONS AND BALLOONS.—INTRODUCTION OF THE TELEGRAPH.—ITS STRUGGLES. — OPINION OF A WALL-STREET MILLIONAIRE. — NOMINATION OF SILAS WRIGHT.—INFLUENCE OF THE TELEGRAPH ON THE PRESS.—CURIOUS PREDICTION OF LAMARTINE.—THE BATTLES IN MEXICO.—MARVELOUS PROGRESS.—THE BATTLES IN EUROPE.—AFFAIRS OF THE WORLD DAILY ELECTROTYPED FOR THE JOURNALIST.—THE LIGHTNING EXPRESS LINES.

MORSE has been a benefactor of the Press. This, it is true, is not the opinion of every publisher, narrowly, perhaps meanly, looking after the financial affairs of his establishment, nor of every journalist desirous of an influence beyond the limits of the city where his paper is published, especially when he reads an announcement that "the *Elmira* (N. Y.) *Advertiser* publishes telegraph news fifteen hours in advance of the receipt of the New York dailies." But newspaper statistics prove our position. Morse has undoubtedly struck, as with lightning, many newspapers off the lists of journalism, yet he has added many others, and increased newspaper enterprise and newspaper readers by the thousands. He has placed an electric force in every printing-office in the land.

When the *News-Letter* was the only paper printed in America, it had but three hundred weekly circulation. When the *Gazette* and *Mercury* in Boston, the *Mercury* in Philadelphia, and the *Gazette* in New York were added to the number, all within the period of twenty years of the first issue of the *News-Letter*, and with only a small increase in population, the weekly circulation of these five papers reached an aggregate of two or three thousand copies. The colonists had acquired more taste for newspapers by their periodical appearance, and this taste had increased with the increase of papers, and the facilities for acquiring news and spreading it before the people. It is probable that the circulation of the *New York Herald* or the New York *Sun* is as large to-day as the united circulation of all the New York papers, daily and weekly, issued in 1844, when the telegraph was first practically introduced in this country. Other cities present the same fact. This circulation is, perhaps, not so comprehensive in a national point of view; but the facilities for obtaining news from every quarter of the globe are now so easy and extensive, that nearly every one acquainted with the alphabet reads the papers, and every one in New York, or London, or Paris, or Berlin feels as much interest in the affairs of the rest of the world as they previously did in events nearer home. Village gossips are magnified into world gossips.

> "No pent-up Utica contracts our powers,
> The whole boundless universe is ours."

Intellectual vitality and physical energy are constantly at work devising means to annihilate space. Fast horses in the time of Reeside, the great mail contractor in the days of mail-coaches; carrier pigeons, with their tissue-paper dispatches prepared in cipher; swift locomotives and steam-boats on our public highways, and telegraphic lines in this electric age, have been the progressive steps in developing the physical forces of the world. While canals, railroads, steam-ships, telegraphs, have occupied the minds of active and acquisitive business men, these same enterprises have entered extensively into the dreams and calculations of journalists, as necessary parts of the machinery of well-organized newspaper establishments. Means of swift communication have always been a study in the offices of leading journals. Horses, pilot-boats, pigeons, steam-boats, locomotives, and semaphore telegraphs had become common carriers of news previous to 1844.

Of all these means of communication between distant points anterior to the magnetic telegraph, none surpassed the carrier pigeon for speed. Next to light and electricity, these beautiful birds are the most rapid in their flights. They were used in 1249 in the crusade of Louis IX. In the midst of the battle of Mansourah, a pigeon was dispatched by the Saracens, in great alarm, to Cairo. This pigeon carried this message under its wing:

At the moment of starting this bird the enemy attacked Mansourah; a terrible battle is being fought between the Christians and Mussulmans.

This threw that city into a state of great commotion. Another pigeon was sent off late in the afternoon announcing the total defeat of the French. Since then, carrier pigeons have been more or less used by journalists, speculators, and governments. They are swift flyers, and can go long distances without intermission. Their speed ranges from forty to seventy-five miles an hour. They have been known to fly, in a few instances, at the rate of one hundred miles an hour. Nothing practical but the telegraph can exceed this velocity. Cannon balls move at the rate of 1200 miles per hour; eagles fly 145 miles; swallows, 185 miles; and the ice-yachts Quick Step, Flying Cloud, and Icicle run over the frozen surface of the Hudson at the rate of a mile a minute; but neither cannon balls, nor eagles, nor swallows, nor ice-yachts can be employed as news messengers. Locomotive engines can run one hundred miles in sixty minutes, but they very rarely accomplish this rate of speed, and in all the newspaper expresses on railroads, all hinderances considered, rarely averaged over thirty-five miles per hour. But pigeons were not reliable on distances exceeding four or five hundred miles.

The Belgians are fond of pigeon races from the southern provinces of France. Our best birds come from Antwerp. There were over ten thousand trained pigeons in Belgium in 1870, when the war between France and Germany commenced, and they were declared contraband of war for fear that they would be made military couriers through the air. They were employed, in connection with balloons, to convey intelligence between the Gambetta government at Bordeaux and the Favre government in Paris. On one occasion, during the siege of the French capital in 1870, a carrier pigeon carried into that city a newspaper $4\frac{3}{4}$ inches square, with 226 dispatches microscopically photographed upon it, embracing the news of the day from all parts of the world. This paper had to be read by the aid of a powerful microscope and the magic lantern.

There are many curious incidents and anecdotes related of the pigeon as a news-carrier. One is of an Antwerp journalist, who sent a reporter with two carrier pigeons to Brussels in 1846 to await the king's speech, and send it to Antwerp by these birds. On his arrival at Brussels, the reporter gave the pigeons in charge to a waiter at the hotel and ordered breakfast. He was kept waiting for some time, but a delicious fricassee atoned for the delay. After breakfast he paid his bill and called for his pigeons. "Pigeons!" ejaculated the waiter; "why, you have eaten them!"

But with this extraordinary bird there were great difficulties in its use and management, and it could be employed only on occasions when events were anticipated. On unlooked-for emergencies in unexpected places the pigeon was of no value. Something else was needed to satisfy the craving, grasping mind of a modern journalist.

Telegraphs by signs, arms, flags, and signal-fires on hill-tops had been tried. Ships at sea and in action, yacht squadrons and military movements, are now more or less regulated by the use of signal flags. Quite a conversation can be carried on in this way. But only short distances are overcome by such means as these. Others had to be devised for newspapers. It was contemplated by the *Herald* to bring balloons into requisition for the transmission of news. This was during a mania for aerial flights, and when several distinguished æronauts believed that the air could be navigated. The subject was thoroughly investigated. All that the experience of Durant, Wise, Clayton, La Mountain, Green, Godard, Lauriat, and Lowe, the well-known balloonists, could give on the matter was thoroughly examined and sifted. It was wisely decided that regular balloon expresses were an impossibility; that the practical navigation of the air was out of the range of probable events. This conclusion has since been amply sustained by the use of balloons during the siege of Paris in 1870. They were very convenient and serviceable in carrying dispatches out of the city. Fifty-four balloons left Paris from September 23, 1870, to January 28, 1871. They carried 2,500,000 letters outward. But none dropped from the clouds into that devoted capital; and carrier pigeons proved to be the only reliable aerial news messengers yet discovered.

After all the experiments, the study, and investigation, and after the employment of all the means and appliances known to be within the reach of man, the great *desideratum*, in the form of the magnetic telegraph, was discovered and put into practical operation by Morse. It is of no consequence to us when electricity was first known as an agent of communication if it could not be brought into practical use. The point was the power to transmit a message instantaneously from one city to another. News of a disastrous event happening in Chicago at midnight, and published in New York and London the next morning to arouse the sympathy and sublime generosity of the people and millionaires of those cities, was the fact to be accomplished. Morse did this, and thus he became a benefactor, not to the Press alone, but to the human race. Let monuments to his honor, therefore, rise in Central Park and Pennsylvania Avenue. Let them rise, as Webster said of the obelisk on Bunker Hill, "and meet the sun in his coming."

The *Sun*, and *Herald*, and *Tribune* seized upon this wonderful piece of machinery with great eagerness. The *Herald* predicted its success from its first flash. It recommended it to the public in every way; it urged it upon the Press; but journalists were not so wealthy then as now; they were struggling on limited resources.

With some difficulty, and after Morse had offered to sell his whole patent right, represented to-day in this country alone by $50,000,000 of capital, for the sum of $100,000, Congress, amid the jeers of some of its members, appropriated $30,000 for the construction of an experimental line between Washington and Baltimore. This line was opened early in 1844, and it was no easy matter to draw public attention to this pioneer line. Except with the two or three telegraph operators, and the two or three owners of the patent right, there was no interest or excitement about the marvelous instrument. It was not till the nomination of Silas Wright for the vice-presidency by the National Democratic Convention at Baltimore in May of that year that the value of this new and wonderful means of communication was made manifest to the world. The *Herald* of June 4th, 1844, thus placed on record this important realization of the dream and hope of Morse. It is, indeed, the record of the first definite pulsation of the real nervous system of the world:

ANNIHILATION OF SPACE.

What has become of space? The magnetic telegraph at Washington has totally annihilated what there was left of it by steam locomotives and steam-ships. We give a certified copy of ten minutes' conversation between Mr. Wright at Washington and Colonel Young at Baltimore in relation to the nomination of Mr. Wright. This shows what can be done.

CONVERSATION.

WASHINGTON. Important! Mr. Wright is here, and says, Say to the New York delegation that he can not accept the nomination.

Again: Mr. Wright is here, and will support Mr. Polk cheerfully, but can not accept the nomination for Vice-president.

BALTIMORE. Messrs. Page, Young, Fine, Ballard, and Church are here, and have received Mr. Wright's communication, and hope he will reconsider it.

WASHINGTON. Under no circumstances can Mr. Wright accept the nomination, and refers to his two former answers.

BALTIMORE. Shall Mr. Fine say any thing to the Convention?

WASHINGTON. Yes; what Mr. Wright has already said.

Again: Mr. Wright has well considered, and begs his previous answers may be satisfactory.

ALFRED VAIL,
Assistant Superintendent of the Electro-Magnetic Telegraph for the United States.
May 29, 1844.

It should be borne in mind that the distance from Baltimore to Washington is thirty-six miles.

This was its start—its first impulse; but, with this positive and unequivocal result in the presence of the assembled wisdom of the governing party of the nation, Morse still met with serious obstacles. Faith was yet needed. With the complete success of the line between the national capital and Baltimore, only a few men felt its influence and stepped forward in its behalf. Seven months subsequently the *Herald* published the following suggestive paragraph in its favor, in order to draw the attention of Congress to the fact it expressed:

Professor Morse offers to sell his right to the magnetic telegraph to the government, as he prefers that government should possess it, although he thinks he could make more money by selling it to individuals.

Another notice appeared in the same paper a few weeks later, on the 29th of March, which now reads strangely enough when we look at the innumerable telegraph lines spread over the surface of the globe in 1872. It was intended as a "puff"—a "first-rate notice." It reads more like a paragraph in favor of an exhibition of a useless automatic chess-player like Maelzel's:

MORSE'S TELEGRAPH.

The rooms for the exhibition of the electric telegraph present one of the most attractive and interesting lounges in this city. Just step up stairs at 563 Broadway, and be delighted, instructed, and astonished by the working of this magical means of communication.

All things, however, must have a beginning, and these were the incipient steps of the telegraph. Morse, in this way, was compelled to bring his extraordinary invention before the people. While he was thus engaged, another ingenious man was at work—the Talbot to our Daguerre—in developing the power of electricity for the public good. The *Herald* of the 5th of June, 1845, announced the equally astonishing invention of House's printing telegraph:

> We understand that a magnetic printing telegraph is shortly to be introduced to the world which is superior to any now in use. Instead of making lines, each to designate a letter, it makes the full letter itself, and with astonishing rapidity. This new discovery will be of great value, for it can be managed by any one without difficulty.

When the war with Mexico opened in May, 1846, with the dashing battles of Palo Alto and Resaca de la Palma, the tidings of these engagements were telegraphed from Washington, and were the first to electrify the people of the United States. With these brilliant conflicts on the Rio Grande the Telegraphic Era of the Press really began. What a commencement! What a revolution!

On the 23d of May, 1846, two years after the experimental line was opened, the *Herald* thus announced the progress—the slow progress, indeed—of its early days; but on this impulse, on the eve of the startling news from the Rio Grande, the hopes of the enterprising journalist were enthusiastically centred:

> THE MAGNETIC TELEGRAPH AND THE PRESS.
>
> We now publish regularly, in our morning edition, the Southern news received in Washington up to six o'clock the previous evening, together with the Congressional news of that day. Our dispatches are sent from Washington to Baltimore by telegraph, and thence to Wilmington by special steam and horse express, from which point they are telegraphed to Jersey City. In a few days we shall have an uninterrupted communication by telegraph from Washington to New York, and then we shall be able to give the Southern news in full, together with a more particular report of the Congressional proceedings, simultaneously with the Washington papers.

Now what will be the effect of the universal extension of the telegraph on the Press? Will it make newspapers greater intellectual powers than they were previous to 1844? What has been the effect thus far? Will not the common property in news compel journalists to employ better, brighter, broader brains? With the events of the world hourly placed before the conductor of a leading newspaper, will he not have to be a man of greater and more comprehensive grasp of intellect than has yet been seen? With dispatches from every quarter and nation of the earth continually pouring into the editor's office, the face of the globe becomes to him a vast field of battle—the desperate battle of life, and he is placed like a Napoleon, surrounded by his staff, to decide at once what is to be done, and to act. But there are other views and facts to be taken into consideration.

It is proposed to place the telegraph lines under the control of government. This has been done in Europe. What will be the effect of such management? Will it not place the newspaper publisher in the material position he occupied before the introduction of the telegraph? Space is annihilated, and the daily transactions of the world can be seen at a glance. What else? When the telegraph lines of the nation are all under the care of a Secretary of the Telegraph Department, our leading journalists, in mind and money, will receive nothing by mail—their special messengers will be electric sparks. So far as events in other states and cities are concerned, the post-office will cease to exist. All newspaper correspondence will be dropped into telegraph boxes, as they have hitherto been dropped into the letter-boxes of the post-offices. Instead of penny postage we shall have a penny telegram agitation; instead of hundreds of different rates of toll, there will be a uniform rate throughout each country, without regard to distance. In England the rate is one shilling sterling for every twenty words, and sixpence for every additional ten words. Then the morning paper of enterprise will convey to its readers at their breakfast tables the occurrences of the previous day in Europe, Asia, Africa, and America, not in such brief and often unintelligible dispatches as are now seen, but in regular correspondence, describing events fully and amply to the latest moment of the previous night in Pekin and Paris, St. Petersburg and San Francisco, London and Liberia, Canton and Cincinnati, Vienna and Valparaiso, Berlin and Baltimore, Warsaw and Washington, the Five Points and the Fifth Avenue. The newspaper reader will have a fresh photograph of the world twice a day, taken by electricity, and spread before him in all its amplification morning and evening. Journalism will then be perfect. Lamartine, as far back as 1831, imagined this position of the newspaper. It was a poet's dream then, as Puck was Shakspeare's dream three centuries earlier. In a note to the editor of the *Revue Européane*, declining to write for that publication, Lamartine made this prediction, which is rapidly becoming *un fait accompli*:

Do not perceive in these words a superb disdain of what is termed journalism. Far from it; I have too intimate a knowledge of my epoch to repeat this absurd nonsense, this impertinent inanity against the Periodical Press. I know too well the work Providence has committed to it. Before this century shall run out journalism will be the whole Press—the whole human thought. Since that prodigious multiplication which art has given to speech—multiplication to be multiplied a thousand-fold yet—mankind will write their books day by day, hour by hour, page by page. *Thought will be spread abroad in the world with the rapidity of light;* instantly conceived, instantly written, instantly understood at the extremities of the earth—it will spread from pole to pole. Sudden, instant, burning with the fervor of soul which made it burst forth, it will be the reign of the human soul in all its plenitude. It will not have time to ripen—to accumulate in a book; the book will arrive too late. The only book possible from to-day is a newspaper.

The President, in his message on the 4th of December, 1871, recommended the purchase of the existing telegraph lines, and attaching them to the Post-office Department. The Postmaster General, on the same day, in urging this important matter upon the attention of Congress and the country, gave the following interesting particulars of the operation of the telegraphs in Europe, especially on news and newspapers:

The postal telegraph is by far the most important subject now inviting consideration in connection with the transmission and interchange of intelligence. The governments of the continental countries of Europe have, with few exceptions, claimed and exercised for years past the right of controlling and managing the electric telegraph, and in every instance with a degree of success commensurate with the care and attention bestowed upon their respective administrations. In Sweden, Norway, Russia, Bavaria, Italy, Turkey, Greece, and Spain, great advantages have been gained by making the telegraph a part of the public postal system; while in Switzerland, Belgium, the Netherlands, Prussia, and France, where modern appliances and improvements have been more thoroughly utilized, the policy of governmental control has been fully vindicated. It remained for Great Britain to give a practical test of the public system as compared with the management of corporations and companies of private stockholders. After a protracted and most laborious investigation, Parliament passed, on the 31st of July, 1868, "An act to enable her Majesty's Postmaster General to acquire, work, and maintain electric telegraphs," which was followed on the 9th of August, 1869, by an act providing the money necessary to purchase the undertakings of the several telegraph companies in Great Britain and Ireland. On the 5th of February, 1870, the transfers were effected, and the work of the postal telegraph began. At first, serious difficulties were encountered by reason of the delay in passing the money bill, and the inadequate preparations to accommodate the immense increase of business which immediately followed the large reduction of rates. These difficulties, however, were soon overcome, and, thanks to the indefatigable and intelligent labors of Hon. Frank Ives Scudamore, second secretary, and his assistants, the advocates of the measure can already boast of its triumphant success. The charges established in the beginning were uniform throughout the United Kingdom, without regard to distance, and were fixed at the maximum permitted by law, that is to say, one shilling (24 cents) for the first twenty words or part of twenty words, and threepence (six cents) for each additional five words or part of five words, exclusive of signature and address. Referring to an elaborate report of Mr. Scudamore, it appears that the average cost of inland messages was about one shilling one penny (26 cents) against an average cost prior to the transfer of one shilling sevenpence (38 cents), showing a reduction in price of nearly one third. In the first week after the transfer, the number of messages (exclusive of news and Press messages) forwarded from all stations was 128,872; in the week ending 31st March, the number had risen to 160,775. The average weekly number in 13 weeks, to 30th of June, was 177,410; the average number in 13 weeks, to 30th of September, was 200,787; and the average number in 13 weeks, to 31st of December, was 203,572. In the week ending on the 31st of December, which is usually considered the worst week in the year for telegraphic work, the number was 144,041, or nearly 16,000 in excess of the number of the first week.

In addition to the foregoing, ample provision was made for the Press and news work. The companies, before the transfer, sent news to 306 subscribers in 144 towns only in the United Kingdom; the postal telegraph sent news to 1106 subscribers in 365 towns. The companies sent news to 173 newspapers only; the postal telegraph sent news to 467 newspapers, showing an increase of 221 in the number of towns to which news was sent, an increase of 800 in the total number of subscribers for news, and an increase of 294 in the number of newspapers taking news. There was, moreover, a vast increase in the quantity of news transmitted. The companies sent, during the session of Parliament, nearly 6000 words of news daily; during the remainder of the year they sent nearly 4000 words daily. The postal telegraph sent, during the session of Parliament, in behalf of the news associations, nearly 20,000 words of news daily; and during the remainder of the year, nearly 15,000 words daily. The postal telegraph also transmitted from 15,000 to 20,000 words daily for the ordinary newspaper correspondents; and seven newspapers rented special wires during the night at the uniform rate of £500, instead of rates ranging from £750 to £1000 as before. Two other wires were about to be rented to newspaper proprietors at the close of the year, and many more could have been rented if the department could have spared them. There has been doubtless a still further increase of messages during the current year.

These facts, all tending, with overwhelming force, in one direction, demonstrate conclusively the utility of the postal telegraph for both government and people.

Some may hesitate to adopt it in this country because of the great extent of our territory, the paucity of our population in some large sections, and the great expense involved in extinguishing the rights of telegraph companies. The first two are the same objections that were urged for many years against all ameliorations of our postal service; nevertheless, postages have been cheapened and made uniform, and, at the same time, the postal system has been maintained and improved. Rightly viewed, the extent of the country is a strong argument in favor of a postal telegraph, and the additional facilities and uniform rates it will afford. It is only in countries of large extent that the value of instantaneous, or nearly instantaneous, communication can be appreciated. Who that desires to convey or acquire any information would hesitate between sending a telegram from New York to California in seven minutes for twenty cents, and sending a letter in seven days for three cents?

It is not forty years since Morse, lying in his narrow berth on board the packet-ship Sully, half seas over from Europe, first conceived the idea of the telegraph. Now, more than half of the business of the world is transacted through its agency, and most of the news of the universe is transmitted over its wires. The first thirty-six miles of wire were put up in the United States in 1844, and in 1872 there are over 180,000 miles in this country, 450,000 miles stretched over Europe, 14,000 in India, and 10,000 in Australia. There are 30,000 miles of submarine cables in operation. It is 24,000 miles around the world. Hence there are lines enough now in use to encircle the entire globe nearly thirty times!

With these connections with the rest of the world, we are dependent on our daily telegraphic dispatches. It would be a *dies non* if there was a suspension of news between the rising and setting of the sun. All business would stop in the absence of the regular telegrams. We must hear from London and Paris morning and evening. All movements in Europe are watched by our business men. When Bismarck sneezes the vibration is felt from Berlin to Pekin; the crust of the earth and the bed of the sea are tremulous with the electric currents of the busy, restless movements of the human race; and if Captain Hall penetrates the "open sea" and attaches a wire to the north pole, Prescott and other scientific operators will have much more to say about auroral disturbances and perturbations than has yet been recorded in any of their interesting publications, and Craig, and Reuter, and Havas, and Bullier, and Simonton, and Hasson, and other news agents will hold a jubilee around the statue of Morse in the Central Park, while Dodworth's Band plays the Electric Quick Step.

Operations in Wall Street and State Street is to-day governed by the transactions of this morning in London, Paris, and Frankfort.

Millions of dollars daily hang upon the click of the telegraphic instrument. With the difference of time in our favor, our business begins as that on the other side of the Atlantic closes. While the bulls and bears of Europe are walking home to dinner, ours are walking down from breakfast. Gold is paid in any part of Europe by the Rothschilds on telegraphic dispatch from Belmont in New York. When gold rises up to 160 in New York, and Wall Street is in a frenzy, it is knocked down to 130 in an instant by a single flash of lightning from Washington.

"Mr. Little," said a journalist to that great operator of Wall Street in 1846—a Vanderbilt and Drew in a single pair of breeches in those days—"we want to build a telegraph line from Boston to New York; will you aid us by subscribing for some of the stock?"

"A telegraph from Boston! Nonsense! Money thrown away. Wouldn't trust it. Won't subscribe a dollar," was the prompt and abrupt reply of Jacob Little. His mind was made up.

"But it will be built, Mr. Little. Mr. Bennett, Colonel Webb, Greeley and M'Elrath, and Mr. Beach have subscribed, but not enough to complete the work. We thought that it would be just in your line."

"Pooh! pooh! I wouldn't trust it, I tell you. I will give you $100 to help you along, but not as a subscription to any stock."

"That will be of no use, Mr. Little. I see you do not comprehend the matter. You will live long enough to do all your business by telegraph. When that time comes, have the kindness to think of this interview."

"I tell you, my young friend," replied Mr. Little, "that I would not sell a dollar's worth of stock on a telegraphic dispatch. I would not trust it. There is no safety in those wires, nor in those posts. Any body can tamper with them, and any body can destroy them."

Several years after this conversation, after Mr. Little had lost millions in Wall Street, and only a few months before his death, he met the same journalist on a beautiful Sunday morning in one of the Fourth Avenue cars. Some of the lustre of his bright eyes was gone; some of the elasticity of his quick, nervous manner had disappeared; he was in a philosophic mood—meditative and reflective. He was not then a millionaire. He had been five times one, but had lost enough, he said, in one day, "to buy the whole of Union Square and every body in it!"

On stepping into the car he took his seat by the side of the journalist, and related to him an incident that had occurred the previous night at a little party given by his son. One of those enterprising clothes-dealers called "hall thieves" had been into his house and made a clean sweep, carrying off every hat, cap, and coat deposited there. Suddenly said he, "Do you recollect the interview you had with me about the telegraph several years ago?"

"I do," said the man of newspapers, "most clearly."

"Well, sir, that was the great mistake of my life. Strange that I should have had such an idea of the value of the telegraph; but I hadn't a particle of faith in it—not a particle."

"You were not alone, Mr. Little; I found many connected with the Press, even, whose business was telegraphic, who had the same erroneous idea."

"Yes, yes," continued Mr. Little; "but it's too late—too late—too late." Then, as if to change the topic, he said,

"Do you see that man walking on the sidewalk?"

I looked, and saw a portly man evidently on his way to church. "Yes," said I.

"That is —— ——. That man, sir, would have gone to the dogs in 18— if I had not advanced him $70,000 when he could not get a cent—no, sir, not a cent any where else to save him from suspension. He would not now lend me $5. What do you think of that?"

The car had reached the Astor House, and we parted. In a few months after, Jacob Little left the whirl of Wall Street never to return. He was a wonderful man in his day—abrupt in manner, but honorable in business. Vanderbilts, Jeromes, Drews, Fisks, Goulds, have since made their mark, and millions are now counted where thousands were counted before. Telegraphs are projected to every nook and corner of the earth. Every large establishment in Europe and America has its own private wire connecting the city warehouse with the country factory; every leading editor ties his residence to his printing-office with an electric string. Beautiful articles of furniture may be seen in Fifth Avenue palaces, looking like a *bijou* of an *escritoire*, or some musical instrument. Suddenly a bell rings, as if by magic. It is rung by electricity. Some one goes to this mysterious piece of furniture and lifts its cover. It is a telegraphic instrument.

"Here is a message from the office."

"What is it?"

"Three friends have just arrived from Europe. They will dine with us to-day. We shall be home at five P.M."

Some wonderful journalistic achievements have been accomplished and others contemplated by telegraph. The first feat was in sending an abstract of Henry Clay's speech on the war with Mexico, which he delivered in Lexington, Kentucky, on the 13th of November, 1847. It was expressed to Cincinnati, and thence telegraphed to the *New York Herald*. This effort cost $500. It was considered an instance of great enterprise. There were then only 3000 miles of wire in the United States. There was no line south of Charleston; none west of Cincinnati; none east of Portland. The next was reporting one of John C. Calhoun's famous speeches in full. This also appeared in the *Herald.* Calhoun was a telegraphic orator. His speeches had to be given as he spoke them: the matter was fully condensed when uttered. It was contemplated by Robert Bonner, of the *New York Ledger,* if the first Atlantic cable had been successful, to have a short original story telegraphed by Charles Dickens for the *Ledger.* After the success of the second cable, and at the conclusion of the triangular contest in 1866 between Prussia, Austria, and Italy, the important speech of the King of Prussia was telegraphed to the *New York Herald* at a cost of $7000. This dispatch was published by two or three other New York papers, and they paid their share of the tolls. On the appearance of Mrs. Harriet Beecher Stowe's defense of her very curious statement relative to Lord Byron, the *Pall Mall Gazette* of London had a column of the defense telegraphed from New York, a remarkable instance of telegraphic enterprise in an English journal. Since then, the war between France and Germany in 1870 has still farther developed the resistless enterprise of the Press and the unmeasured capacity and importance of the telegraph. The *Tribune, Herald, World,* and *Times* have had long and graphic reports of the sharp and decisive battles of Gravelotte and Sedan, the surrender of Napoleon, the operations around Paris, the Commune war, interviews with Napoleon, Bismarck, Von Buest, and Antonelli, obtained and telegraphed regardless of personal labor, personal risk, and lavish expenditure of money. The interest and anxiety created by the Chicago fire throughout the world was, in a measure, owing to the telegraph, and the London correspondent of the *New York Tribune,* writing on the 21st of October, 1871, gave the following particulars:

Nothing could be a better proof, if any proof were needed, of English interest in Chicago, than the extraordinary efforts of the London Press to get early and full accounts. A sharp lookout was kept for the Silesia at Plymouth, and for the Java at Queenstown, bringing, respectively, New York papers of the 10th and 11th. The Silesia arrived at 8 o'clock yesterday morning, and the Java (Queenstown being half a day's sail nearer New York) late in the same afternoon. The Silesia's papers were in season to be forwarded by train to London, but the Queenstown dispatches had to be telegraphed. The Postal Telegraph being seldom equal to an emergency without special preparation, an agent had been sent from London to facilitate the transmission of dispatches both to London and other parts of the kingdom. The newspaper reporters went off in a steam-tug to intercept the Java, caught her some distance out at sea, got papers, and this morning we have from three to six columns in each of the leading journals, partly by telegraph and partly from the papers which came by the Plymouth train. All this is very different from the sleepy way in which such things were once managed. The use of the inland telegraph, I must add, must become far more common than it now is, and will be limited only by the ability or inclination of the post-office to transact the business which its customers want done. Mr. Scudamore's idea that the newspapers "want too much news" may some day take its place among the fossil curiosities of the department. He must get the consent of Parliament to raise the rates if he expects to check the new enthusiasm of the British Press. They put a clause into the bill which transferred the telegraphs to government, fixing the tariff for Press dispatches at one shilling (24 cts.) for a hundred words from any part of the United Kingdom. The actual cost of these very showy-looking dispatches is therefore about $5 a column.

Our newspaper telegraphic enterprise is marvelous. It appears that the Press news telegrams alone which passed over the wires in the United States in 1866 were greater than the entire telegraphic correspondence of the whole of Continental Europe in the same year. Here are the figures:

STATEMENT SHOWING THE NUMBER OF TELEGRAMS IN CONTINENTAL EUROPE AND OF PRESS TELEGRAMS IN THE UNITED STATES IN ONE YEAR.

Total number of messages transmitted in Continental Europe for 1866 - - 12,902,538	Total number of messages furnished to the newspapers of the United States for 1866 - - - - - - 14,715,181
Gross receipts for above $11,597,682 71	Gross receipts for above - $521,509
Average cost of telegrams 81 cents.	Average cost of Press telegrams - - - - - - 3½ cents.

Improvements are being continually introduced in telegraphy. Accuracy and rapidity are the points now sought to be reached. The highest rate of speed attained in telegraphic communication by the Morse instrument was accomplished between Boston and Providence in May, 1868. Twenty-seven hundred and thirty-one words were transmitted in one hour without a break, and legibly and correctly copied. This was equal to forty-five or forty-six words per minute. On short lines sixty or seventy words per minute have been transmitted. This has been the progress—the expansion. Since then, automatic telegraphic instruments have been invented by Humiston and Little in the United States, and Wheatstone in England. That of Little, which is said to be superior, is capable of transmitting through perforated paper one thousand to fifteen hundred words per minute! When this is in full operation, and each individual can prepare and send his own messages, will not the Post-office Department give place to a Telegraph Department, and the title of our Post-master General be changed to that of Telegraph-master General? Will not autographic correspondence entirely cease?

What reflections must have passed through the mind of the inventor of such a marvelous instrument of civilization and progress as he sat in his study at Poughkeepsie and looked over the result of his inspiration in the narrow berth on board the Sully in 1832! "No pent-up Utica" to his thought then. Artist as he was, he could not picture on his own mind the reality of his wonderful, yet simple discovery; but if he had lived a year or two longer he would have seen the enterprising newspaper of the metropolis filled every morning, with every line of its contents, excepting a portion of its editorials, some of its city news, and a part of its advertisements, made up of telegrams from the surrounding world—from the remotest corner on the surface of the earth, to the nearest neighboring village, ward, or street!

CHAPTER XXXVIII.
THE NEW YORK ASSOCIATED PRESS.

ITS ORIGIN.—ITS NECESSITY.—ITS OBJECT.—ITS OPERATIONS.—WAR WITH THE TELEGRAPH COMPANIES.—ATTEMPT AT MONOPOLY.—LEASE OF THE NEWFOUNDLAND LINE.—INTERCEPTING STEAMERS OFF HALIFAX AND CAPE RACE.—WILL THE ASSOCIATION BE A PERMANENT INSTITUTION?

THE Associated Press belongs to the telegraphic era.

But what is the Associated Press? Is it not a monster monopoly? Does it not cripple the enterprise of individual journals? Is it a permanent institution?

These are common questions with newspaper editors and publishers. They are problems that perplex the journalist. Most of the general news of the world is gathered by the agents of the Associated Press, and its title is known all over the globe. There are news associations in Europe. These were established by individuals, and were considered useful auxiliaries, and encouraged by the absence of enterprise in newspaper proprietors until they became institutions and somewhat dictatorial. Reuter was the first; Havas and Bullier followed. Reuter is now king of news in Europe, and wears a ribbon from one of the German powers for special telegrams during the Franco-German war. He is, besides, a telegraph contractor, and lays cables. He is an electric power.

It is the common belief that news associations were the result of the introduction of the telegraph. This is correct so far as the present extensive organizations are concerned; but organizations existed before 1844 on a limited and local scale. There were associated arrangements with several of the New York papers prior to 1840 for the collection of shipping news. There was one, at the head of which was the *Courier and Enquirer*, which run pony expresses from Washington. There were three in existence in New York City in 1837-'8. Captain Bancker was at the head of one for the *Courier and Enquirer* and *Journal of Commerce;* Captain Hurley had charge of another for the *Express, Mercantile Advertiser*, and *Gazette;* Captain Cisco was at the head of the third for the *Commercial Advertiser, Evening Star*, and *American*. These were for marine news. The *Herald* had its independent establishment. Captain Hamil commanded the news-boat for that journal. There was no unity then between the "Sixpenny" and the "Penny Press." The *Sun* afterwards set up an enterprise of its own for important arrivals only, one of the men with "a glazed cap," Captain Brogan, in charge.

The New York papers had passed through their period of enterprise when the *Courier and Enquirer* run horse expresses and news schooners in competition with the *Journal of Commerce*. Those days of spirit and dash, when James Watson Webb was in his glory, had subsided, only to be aroused by the Cheap Press coming vigorously into existence. All "pony" expresses had been stopped, and the newspapers had fallen back on row-boats for the gathering of shipping intelligence. The news schooners Evening Edition, Courier and Enquirer, and Journal of Commerce were laid up "in ordinary" or had become pilot-boats. With the establishment of the *Herald* this journalistic energy revived. It opened a new era with the American Press. With the increase of this class of papers, full of tact and spirit, with the extension of railroads, the introduction of ocean steamers, the spread of express lines, and the inauguration of the magnetic telegraph, the competition of journalists to keep step with these new forces in the field became lively, comprehensive, and costly. We all see and appreciate the splendid result.

The *Herald* had its row-boats for marine news under the command of such men as Robert Hamil, Robert Martin, William Bassett, Robert Silvey, and John Hall, and they did well. They were a new race of ship-news reporters. Besides these, the pilot-boats, a dozen in number, clippers in every sense, favored the *Herald*, and that paper, as a matter of course, continually eclipsed the older papers of New York in news from every quarter of the globe, for most of the intelligence from other parts of the world, outside the United States, had to pass Sandy Hook. The "blanket sheets," the old Wall-Street Press, were constantly "beaten" in European news. Added to these exploits, the *Herald* began its expresses from Boston in 1841-'2 with the advices brought by the Cunard steamers. The *Sun* soon followed in competition. Expresses were also run from Albany with the annual messages of the governors. When the war opened with Mexico, accounts of the several battles were expressed in advance of the government dispatches. All this enterprise produced a great effect. The *Herald* and *Sun*, of New York, and *Ledger*, of Philadelphia, began to make their mark. The despised "Penny Press" were multiplying, and the "blanket sheets" rapidly losing what reputation they had previously acquired. They swelled in size only till many collapsed. The *Herald* was alone in its enterprise. So was the *Sun*. But with the progress of events combinations began to be formed in consequence of the persistent success of the *Herald*, and because of the enormous expense attending these operations.

The first combination was in 1846, during the Oregon excitement, resulting in dispatching a pilot-boat across the Atlantic especially for news, and in two expresses—one from Halifax and one from Boston—costing the combined papers $5000 for the pilot-boat, $4000 for the Halifax express, and $1000 for the Boston express—very large sums to spend for news in those days. These were arranged for the purpose of achieving decisive victories over the *Herald*. Our pages give the details and the result. This was the first news combination after the establishment of the Cheap Press. The struggle went on especially between the *Sun*, *Tribune*, and *Herald*. In the heat of the fight, the telegraph came in as a mediator and regulator.

When the first battles were fought on the Rio Grande, the magnetic telegraph extended from Washington to Wilmington, Delaware, and soon after to Jersey City. Efforts were made to reach the southern telegraph office first. Sometimes the *Herald* would succeed, and sometimes the *Sun*. Frequently the messengers of these journals would enter the office together. The exclusive use of the wires could not be given to either. They were therefore allowed fifteen minutes each. Not many lines of news could be transmitted in that brief space of time over poor lines, with miserable insulation and inexperienced operators. The result was not favorable to the enterprise of these journals. They spent a good deal of money, but gained very little advantage over each other. It was in consequence of this difficulty that the *New York Herald*, in connection with the Philadelphia *Public Ledger* and the *Baltimore Sun*, established the successful express between Montgomery and Mobile.

But the telegraph lines became more extended. Wherever the wires were stretched the same trouble manifested itself. The few wires could not send all the dispatches at once. Meanwhile the enterprise of the Cheap Press expanded, and the few remaining "blanket sheets" were aroused to the reality of their situation as newspapers. They found that the tether they gave the "penny papers" was a long one.

Other expresses were run. Other plans were maturing for a ruinous competition. It was at this juncture that the interview, already mentioned, took place between David Hale, of the *Journal of Commerce*, and James Gordon Bennett, of the *Herald*.

In looking over the ground, it was manifest that the telegraph lines were not equal to the emergency. They did not expand rapidly enough. They could not transmit all the dispatches of the newspapers if the journals acted independently of each other. It was apparent that, with the business of the public, the capacity of the telegraph was not equal to the transmission of single dispatches of one day's news to one paper alone. It became absolutely necessary, therefore, to enjoy the benefit of this miraculous invention, for the newspapers to form an association, in order that their individual competition should not destroy the early usefulness of this wonderful means of communication. The result was, that representatives from the *Journal of Commerce, Courier and Enquirer, Tribune, Herald, Sun*, and *Express*, met at the office of the *Sun*, and formed, 1st, the Harbor News Association, and, 2d, the New York Associated Press. It was a Congress of the Republic of News. The amiable and venerable Gerard Hallock, of the *Journal of Commerce*, was elected president. This was in 1848-'9. On the establishment of the *Times* in 1851, that paper became a member. On the establishment of the *World* in 1859, that paper became a participant in the news privileges, and afterwards a full member on its union with the *Courier and Enquirer*. These journals, so recalcitrating to each other in their columns, so full of rivalry in their business affairs, so incongruous in their political opinions, thus came together, and their representatives met monthly for years thereafter harmoniously and happily, maturing plans for their mutual interests and prosperity. It is said that there has been an occasional flurry within the past few years, but under the calm guidance of Editor Hallock there was never a ripple.

It was no part of the plan of the original organization of this association to do any more than obtain news for its original six or seven members. No paper published beyond the limits of the metropolis was included in the early plan of the organization. Its extensive ramifications and affiliations since then have been the result of its superior enterprise, its surpassing geographical position, and its supreme advantages. Newspapers in other parts of the country desired to avail themselves of its arrangements, and out of this combination have grown up the New England Association, the New York State Association, the Western Association, the Southern Association, and one or two others, but all working together as one, and is thus generally known as the Associated Press.

One of the first expensive undertakings of the New York Association was the purchase of the steamer Naushon, of Boston, for the collection of shipping news off Sandy Hook. She cost $30,000. Her name was changed to that of the News-boy. She was kept in service about six months and then sold. Afterwards the yacht Wanderer, of Sir John Harvey, of Nova Scotia, was purchased to cruise off Halifax for the European steamers.

All the details of the business of the Association are intrusted to a general agent. There is an executive committee, to whom all matters in dispute, all extensive arrangements, and all business that a general agent could not conclusively arrange, are referred for decision; but the general agent is the executive officer of the institution. Three gentlemen, at different periods, have filled this important office and performed its arduous duties, namely,

1st. Alexander Jones.
2d. D. H. Craig.
3d. J. W. Simonton.

The first, Dr. Jones, undertook the management of the news in the infancy of the Association, and when the telegraph lines were few in number. He was an indefatigable worker. In the "Historical Sketch of the Electric Telegraph" prepared by him, he mentions the first news telegram from the metropolis in this way:

> It was early in the autumn of 1846 when the writer of this handed in his first message for the Newspaper Press at No. 10 Wall Street. It contained a brief account of the launch of the United States sloop-of-war Albany at the Navy Yard, Brooklyn, and was directed to the *Washington Union*.

Dr. Jones was succeeded in 1851 by D. H. Craig. Mr. Craig had been an independent news collector in 1844-5, and a successful one in flying carrier pigeons, under great difficulties and obstacles, from the Cunard steamers as they approached Boston. He sold his news to any one who would purchase—Jacob Little or James Gordon Bennett—and he attracted the attention of the executive committee in 1849 or thereabouts, and was appointed the local agent of the Association at Halifax, to look especially after the European news. He remained there for a year or two, and exhibited great tact and perseverance in expressing and telegraphing the news to Boston and New York, in spite of impediments of no mean proportions; and in the general management of his agency he was remarkably efficient and prompt—so much so, indeed, that he was called to New York in 1851 to become the general agent, and assist in arranging the details and carrying out the news plans of the Association, now rapidly increasing, and becoming huge and comprehensive with the extension of the telegraph lines to all parts of the Union.

The Association had its thorny paths as well as its smooth roads to pass over. Opposition came from independent news agencies, from disappointed journalists, and from inexperienced as well as grasping telegraph managers. New telegraph lines had to be encouraged, rival interests had to be conciliated, and local quarrels had to be adjusted. Assisting in the arrangement of these matters, the general agent did not increase the number of his personal friends; but amid all the trials he fought the battles mildly, pleasantly, and gentlemanly in conversation, but savagely, bitterly, and ruthlessly on paper. His correspondence was always a full-charged galvanic battery. His epistolary style did not please every one; it was strong and decided, and offended; but he was a faithful worker, a prompt news collector, an excellent executive officer, always on duty, and wrapped up in the interests of the New York Associated Press.

Among the embarrassments of Morse in the infancy of the telegraph system was the necessity of placing his patent in the hands of so many individuals acting independently of each other. Short sections of lines connecting cities and towns were owned or controlled by single individuals. The line between Portland and Boston was in the hands of one man. While Mr. Craig was the local agent of the Association at Halifax there was a bitter feud between him and the manager of this section of the telegraph. Serious charges were made to the executive committee of the Association against the agent by the telegraph manager, and his discharge from service suggested for the harmonious working of the two interests. The charges not having been sustained, the executive committee declined acceding to the request of the manager, and Mr. Craig continued the agent at Halifax. But the implacable telegraph manager was not satisfied. One evening the executive committee, who were then in the habit of personally receiving the European news coming over the wires from Halifax, were notified, as usual, that the steamer was off Halifax. On entering the telegraph office, they were notified by an official telegram from Portland that no more news for the New York Press should pass over the line from that city to Boston if sent by Mr. Craig—not a word should pass that night! Here were sixty miles of telegraph wire thus placed entirely under the control of one man, and it was at his option, as he thought, whether or not the coming news from Europe should be given to the people of the United States in the next morning's papers. The great danger of placing such a mighty instrument for good or evil in the power of one individual thus unmistakably manifested itself to the executive committee, and they therefore had a duty to perform beyond their own immediate interests or those of the Press. They at once decidedly refused to dismiss Mr. Craig. They asserted the right of the Press and the public to use the telegraph as a common carrier of news; that no telegraph manager or company could dictate as to the employment of agents; and that respectable parties were responsible for the character of the news sent and published, and not the telegraph manager. But, in asserting and maintaining this right, it was no part of the intention of the executive committee to be deprived of the approaching news; it was telegraphed from Halifax to Portland; thence run by locomotive engine to Boston; thence telegraphed to New York and other sections of the country, and published the next morning in all the papers in the United States; and this arrangement was continued till a new line, worked under the House system, was constructed between the two blockaded points.

Subsequently, in the multiplication of telegraph lines, a certain class of telegraph owners conceived a vast plan of placing the whole telegraphic system of the country in the hands of one company; collect news, and retail it out to any one—broker or banker, speculator or newspaper—who would purchase at the rates to be fixed by the telegraph managers. Some progress had been made in this scheme before the executive committee became satisfied of its existence. It was then ascertained that all the wires to the coast except the Newfoundland line had been secured by the American and other telegraph companies. The Newfoundland line was almost too big to touch. There was no time to be thrown away. One of the committee met an active director in this line:

"Mr. Field," asked the journalist, "will the Newfoundland Telegraph Company lease their line to the Press for five years?"

After a moment's thought, Mr. Field, whose brain is always driven by a powerful steam-engine, answered,

"Are you serious?"

"Never more so," said the journalist.

"I will call a meeting of the directors and let you know."

"When?—to-morrow?"

"No; this evening."

"Splendid. You are a man worth talking to. Then we shall have an answer to-morrow," enthusiastically responded the newspaper man.

That evening Peter Cooper, Marshall O. Roberts, Moses B. Taylor, David Dudley Field, and Cyrus W. Field met and decided that they would lease the Newfoundland line to the New York Press, for the use of the public and Press, for a term of five years, or till the Atlantic Cable was laid and in operation.

Mr. Field met the executive committee the next morning and said,

"You can have the line for five years, at so much per annum, the line to be restored to the company in as good order as it is now in at the expiration of that period, or when the Atlantic Cable is laid. How will that do?"

"We will take it."

Thus the New York Press, to protect itself, its associates in all parts of the country, and the public from a huge monopoly then looming up before them, assumed the responsibility of the management and keeping in order of a telegraph line strung along nine hundred miles of a frightfully bleak and exposed coast, and in doing so it accomplished the great object it had in view, although at a large extra expense in money, time, and labor.

"The Newfoundland line leased to the New York Press? Nonsense! I don't believe a word of it," said one of the most persistent promoters of the contemplated combination.

But he was ocularly satisfied of the truth of the statement; and in this way, and by this arrangement, the backbone of the threatened monopoly was broken. Those interested in the telegraph saw the danger. One or two of those in the scheme retired, and new officers were elected. Such men as Professor Morse, Colonel E. S. Sanford, and Cambridge Livingston took an active interest in the matter, and the result was a proposition, inspired by Colonel Sanford, for a Telegraph Committee and a Press Committee to meet in consultation on the twin interests.

On the night of a monster torch-light procession of the unterrified democracy of the metropolis, marshalled under the renowned Captain Isaiah Rynders, illuminating and enlivening that grand city with its bengola lights, its Roman candles, its music, its rockets, its cheers, its Drummond lights, and its enthusiasm, there met, on an early November evening in 1860, at a room at Delmonico's, on the corner of Chambers Street and Broadway, Amos Kendall, Edwards S. Sanford, Cambridge Livingston, and Zenas Barnum on the part of the telegraph companies, and the executive committee on the part of the Associated Press. These gentlemen, comprehending the situation, at this and three or four subsequent meetings concluded a treaty and a contract by which the rights of the public, of the telegraph, and of the Press were fully recognized. On the basis of this arrangement the harmony and efficiency of these three great interests were secured; and in accomplishing this happy result too much credit can not be given to Colonel Sanford for the efforts he made to preserve the *entente cordiale* between the telegraph and the Press.

To make this Newfoundland line efficiently useful to the Press, it was necessary to extend the arrangements at Cape Race so that the European steamers passing that point could be intercepted. Obtaining the news off that cape shortened the time between Europe and New York from forty to sixty hours. On the great circle, a majority of the steamers would pass within sight of that station. The first attempt to get news in this way was previous to this time, and when the Collins steamers commenced their trips. Tin cans were prepared with small flag-poles. The news parcels were placed in these in Liverpool, and when the steamers arrived off the Cape the pursers would throw them overboard. If the news-boat was not in sight, a gun would be fired in the daytime and in foggy weather, and a rocket or two sent up in the night. Captain Ezra Nye, of the Pacific, successfully initiated the enterprise off Halifax. On his second trip, not seeing the news-boat, he threw Halifax into a state of great excitement by running almost into that harbor, firing guns all the way up. His news reached New York forty-eight hours in advance of the arrival of his steamer. After this there were intercepted off Cape Race,

In 1859, 13 steamers.	In 1861, 34 steamers.
" 1860, 31 "	" 1862, 46 "

Fifteen or twenty steamers outward bound were also intercepted, and two days' later news from all parts of the United States placed on board for Europe. Arrangements such as these displayed the marvelous energy of the Press of the country.

But nothing is permanent in this ever-shifting world of ours. When the ocean cable was laid and in working order, these tin cans and flag-poles, these guns and rockets, ceased to be of value; and with these changes others came. The Press-telegraph embroglio, so nicely adjusted in 1860 at Delmonico's and at the Astor House, has experienced some of the perturbations of the day, and a portion of the Press and the present telegraph managers have had their doubts and differences, their trials and troubles, their heart-burnings and heave-offerings. The Associated Press has another general agent, and Mr. Craig is now devoting his experience and energy in developing the power of Little's Automatic Telegraph, capable, it is asserted, of transmitting sixty thousand words per hour. Editor David M. Stone, of the *Journal of Commerce*, is the present president of the Associated Press, his much-respected predecessor, Gerard Hallock, having been gathered to his fathers. James W. Simonton, once connected with the *New York Times*, once a correspondent in Washington, and now a proprietor and editor of the *San Francisco Bulletin*, and a proprietor, we believe, of the *Morning Call*, of that magnificent city with a Golden Gate, is the general agent. It is a vast machine, with its local agents in every nook and corner of the United States, and its correspondents scattered over the wide, wide world. It serves two hundred daily papers with telegraphic news, and pays over $200,000 yearly for cable telegrams alone.

Is this extensive news organization to last forever? It was not, probably, expected or intended by its originators to make it a permanent institution. It was an expedient. It originated in the necessities of the time—in the want of capacity of the telegraph lines. It came into life when horses, and steamers, and carrier pigeons ceased to be available; it will go out of existence as soon as the network of electric wires and cables are capable of transmitting easily, and without delay, the news correspondence of the Press and the business dispatches of the public. Already an independent combination has been formed. In January, 1870, several new and cheap papers in Boston, New York, and Philadelphia, shut out of existing arrangements, organized the American Press Association. This organization met in Boston in July, 1870. Its president is Joseph Howard, of the *New York Star*. The principal journals in this association are the *Evening Mail*, *New Yorker Journal*, and *Daily News*, of New York; the *Day* and *Bulletin*, of Philadelphia; the *Star*, of Providence; the *Eagle*, of Brooklyn; the *Times*, of Boston; and the *News*, of Washington. Its general agent is John Hasson. News is furnished to eighty-four daily papers in the United States.

There is also the New York News Association. Other local organizations are in existence. Others will be formed. Special telegrams will be received by individual papers that will neither be paid for nor used by others; and this disintegration, thus commenced, will go on till each leading journal will have its own special dispatches from its own correspondents stationed in all parts of the world, transmitted for its own exclusive use and benefit. There will be news associations to sell news to any one who will purchase, but they will be comparatively small concerns, and overshadowed by the great newspaper establishments in the news centres of the Union.

CHAPTER XXXIX.
THE NEW YORK TIMES.

How it originated.—Negotiations on the Ice.—The Tilsit Raft of the Times.—Henry J. Raymond its Editor.—His Ability as a Reporter.—His early Career in Politics.—Why he was called "Little Villain" by Horace Greeley.—Trouble with James Watson Webb.—Threatened Duel with Thomas Francis Meagher.—Sharp Controversy with Archbishop Hughes.—The Elbows of the Mincio.—The Draft Riots.—Fortifying Newspaper Offices.—Manners in Journalism.—Sudden Death of Mr. Raymond.—Henry Ward Beecher's Eulogy.—The new Management of the Times.—The Gold Speculations of 1869.—The War on the Tammany Ring.—Its great and important Result.

The *Times* originated on the Hudson. In a walk across the ice at Albany, in the winter of 1850–'51, it was arranged by several gentlemen to establish a new journal in the metropolis.

The *Tribune* had boasted of its large profits. Ninety thousand dollars it claimed to have divided the previous year among its stockholders. "That boast," said Greeley, "started the *Times*." Henry J. Raymond was then Speaker of the Assembly. George Jones, a publisher, E. B. Wesley, a banker, with two or three leading politicians, furnished the money for the new enterprise. One hundred and ten thousand dollars were subscribed for the undertaking, and such was the feeling created at the time by the large dividends of the *Tribune*, and the acknowledged prosperity of the *Herald*, that two or three times that amount were offered. The first number of the *Times* appeared on the 18th of September, 1851. It was a one-cent paper.

Its editor, Henry J. Raymond, had been connected with the Press for a little over ten years. While at Burlington College he wrote for the *New Yorker* over the *nomme de plume* of Fantome. On graduating, and while studying law in New York, he became a constant contributor to that paper, receiving from Horace Greeley, its editor, a salary of eight dollars per week. He also wrote news letters to the *Cincinnati Chronicle* at five dollars per week. When the *Tribune* was started in the spring of 1841, he was installed its assistant editor and chief reporter at ten dollars per week. He remained with Greeley till 1843. He then determined to be a journalist, and bent all his energies to accomplish this great end. Although not a stenographer, he was an accomplished reporter, and was unquestionably the swiftest writer connected with the Press. He held his own with such stenographers as Robert Sutton and James A. Houston, the two best reporters in the country at that period. But with marvelous rapidity in writing Raymond displayed great tact. If the *Herald*, or any other newspaper, succeeded by any especial method in accomplishing an important result, it was not despised by him.

On one occasion, when Daniel Webster was to speak in Boston, several reporters were sent from New York to report his speech. Raymond attended for the *Tribune*. There were no telegraphs then. On his return, instead of losing time, he engaged a stateroom, where he wrote out his long-hand notes. While the reporters were in Boston, types, cases, and printers were quietly placed on board the Sound steamer, and as rapidly as Raymond wrote out the speech the printers put it in type. On their arrival at New York the speech was in type and ready for the press, and appeared the same morning in a late edition of the *Tribune*, much to the mortification of the other reporters and the surprise of the other journalists.

Mr. Raymond was also a very accurate reporter. Mr. Webster always preferred him to any other to take down his speeches. When he intended making one any where, he sent for Mr. Raymond to be present.

"Why does Mr. Webster prefer your reporting to others?" asked a journalist one day of Mr. Raymond; "I am told that you are not a stenographer."

"Well," replied Mr. Raymond, "I once asked that question myself of Mr. Webster, and he said I always reported him correctly, and that I never spoiled his quotations. Webster, you know," continued Raymond, "is very apt in his quotations. They are full of meaning. His most beautiful and telling illustrations were from old classic authors. I disliked to see these beautiful images broken by execrable Latin, and I therefore took pains to have them correct. Mr. Webster appreciates this. Hence he sends for me, I suppose."

The most wonderful incident in reporting occurred after Mr. Raymond became attached to the *Courier and Enquirer*. Mr. Webster made an important speech in the Senate. Raymond was present. All the other papers were represented. Looking at the clock, it just occurred to him that the distinguished senator would finish about the hour of the closing of the mail. He therefore prepared himself. Webster began his speech. Raymond took every word down in long-hand. The other reporters, of course, in short-hand. Webster, it is true, was a slow, deliberate speaker, but as the average speed of an orator's tongue is six uttered to one carefully written word, our readers can imagine the rapidity of Raymond's writing. Webster finished. It was nearly mail-time. It would be utterly impossible to write out the speech for that mail, and that was the mail to carry the speech. Raymond looked at his notes, and again at the clock. Rolling all up in an envelope, inclosing a private note to the foreman of the office of the *Courier and Enquirer*, he dropped the parcel into the Editors' Bag. It reached the office in Wall Street, the copy was distributed among the compositors, and the whole speech appeared in the next edition of the *Courier and Enquirer*, to the dismay of the other papers and the chagrin of the reporters. Its accuracy received the fullest indorsement of Mr. Webster.

The wonderful rapidity of Raymond as a writer, and the marvelous amount of mental labor he could perform, are related in many incidents. His biography of Daniel Webster is cited as a striking instance. Charles S. Halpine, of the *Citizen*, was a wonder in this quality. The same can be said of William Cobbett. But it was not persistent, daily, constant with either Raymond or Halpine. Other instances of these extraordinary powers in writers are mentioned in history and biography. Dr. Francis said:

> To a suggestion that I might instance the late Wm. Cobbett as associated with the Periodical Press of this country, I see no impropriety; unquestionably a minute record would necessarily include his *Porcupine, Gazette*, and his *Weekly Register;* the one the offspring of his juvenile life, the other of his ripened years. I had some personal acquaintance with him at the time of his last residence in New York. Haslitt has, in his attractive manner, described him to the life. He was deemed the best talker of his day, and his forcible pen has given us indubitable proofs of his powers in literary composition. It was not unusual with him to make a morning visit at the printing-office at an early hour, to take his seat at the desk, and, after some half dozen lines were written, throw off the MS. with a rapidity that engaged eleven compositors at once in setting up. Thus a whole sheet of the *Register* might be completed ere he desisted from his undertaking. I think that in his quickness he surpassed even the lamented William Leggett, of the *Evening Post.* The circumstance is certainly a psychological fact, and yet may not be deemed more curious than that Priestley should have made his reply to Lind, quite a voluminous pamphlet, in twenty-four hours, or that Hodgkinson, the actor, was able to peruse crosswise the entire five columns of a newspaper, and within two hours recite it thus by memory.

With experience thus acquired, with first-rate journalistic ability, and with a knowledge of politics which he had obtained in the offices of the *Tribune* and *Courier and Enquirer*, and as Speaker of the Assembly, he assumed the entire editorial management of the *Times*. In the spring of 1851 he went to Europe, sending home the prospectus of the new paper, which he wrote, under the mild influence of Neptune, on board the steamer on her outward trip. The *Times*, by the tone of this announcement, was to be a modestly model newspaper.

On the 18th of September, 1851, the *Times*, in accordance with the programme thus prepared, was issued. Is not a prospectus a peculiarly interesting document to an editor? It is doubtless written more thoughtfully, more carefully, more hopefully than any other paper emanating from the writer. His future is wrapped up in it. Vitality pervades every line. Sometimes it is rather sluggish vitality; nevertheless, what is in the writer at the time is there. Announcements of this character, too, mark the progress of journalism, and in those we have given, if simply strung along chronologically, without remarks or explanations, would form very interesting historical chapters.

The introductory article of the *Times* embraces the points of the policy that was to govern its editor. Mr. Raymond, in his initial number, said :

> We publish to-day the first number of the *New York Daily Times, and we intend to issue it every morning* (Sundays excepted) *for an indefinite number of years to come.* As a newspaper, presenting all the news of the day from all parts of the world, we intend to make the *Times* as good as the best of those now issued in the City of New York; and in all the higher utilities of the Press, as a public instructor in all departments of action and of thought, we hope to make it decidedly superior to existing journals of the same class. * * * We shall seek, in all our discussions and inculcations, to promote the best interests of the society in which we live ; to aid the advancement of all beneficent undertakings, and to promote in every way, and to the utmost of our ability, the welfare of our fellow-men.
>
> Upon all topics—political, social, moral, and religious—we intend that the paper shall speak for itself, and we only ask that it may be judged accordingly. We shall be *conservative* in all cases where we think conservatism essential to the public good, and we shall be *radical* in every thing which may seem to us to require radical treatment and radical reform. We do not believe that *every thing* in society is either exactly right or exactly wrong ; what is good we desire to preserve and improve ; what is evil, to exterminate and reform.
>
> We shall endeavor so to conduct all our discussions of public affairs as to leave no one in doubt as to the principles we espouse or the measures we advocate ; and while we design to be decided and explicit in all our positions, we shall, at the same time, seek to be temperate and measured in all our language. *We do not mean to write as if we were in a passion* unless that shall really be the case, and we shall *make it a point to get into a passion as rarely as possible.* There are very few things in this world which it is worth while to get angry about, and they are just the things that anger will not improve. In controversies with other journals, with individuals, or with parties, we shall engage only when, in our opinion, some important public interest can be promoted thereby, and even then we shall endeavor to rely more upon fair argument than upon misrepresentation or abusive language.

It was a fortunate period for the appearance of a new journal. Those in existence had created a larger circle of readers than they could easily and promptly supply with the machinery in use. Then there was a middle class of readers—a class of quiet, domestic, fireside, conservative readers that needed an organ. The *Times*, by its respectability of tone and matter, obtained a large number of this class. They liked neither the *Tribune* nor the *Herald.* There was a portion of even this class that were disappointed in the *Times*. They wanted a paper more religious in its tone. This class has always met with disappointment. But it was on these middle men and women that the *Times* based its support. Shortly after the appearance of the paper Kossuth arrived, and landed on that "lovely but exposed isle," as the Hungarian patriot called Staten Island, on a cold December day, in acknowledging the receipt of a warm overcoat from an enthusiastic tailor. Raymond entered largely into the Hungarian sensation, which culminated in a splendid Press dinner to Kossuth and the organization of a Press Club in New York, which ate a weekly dinner at the Astor House for a year or two after that notable event. On this excitement the *Times* gained laurels and subscribers, and the Hungarians dollars and sympathy, which, we are sorry to say, did not avail them much.

"I must work hard for five years," said Raymond on the issue of the first number, "to put this bantling on a solid footing." It made its mark in one year. It was then doubled in size and price. Its original proprietors were Henry J. Raymond, George Jones, E. B. Morgan, D. B. St. John, and E. B. Wesley. At one time the *Times* was published under the firm of Raymond, Harper & Co., one of the Harpers having purchased Mr. St. John's shares. Harper shortly retired, and the publishers were Raymond, Wesley & Co. Wesley afterwards sold his shares to Leonard W. Jerome, the well-known financier, who had been a journalist in Rochester. With these changes the firm became Henry J. Raymond & Co., and under this style the *Times* was published till some time subsequent to the death of Raymond.

It had its struggles in its first years, as all other papers have had. When the *Herald* was started the greatest combined efforts were made to crush it. When the *Tribune* came into existence the *Sun* endeavored to kill it outright. When the *Times* made its appearance, the managers of the *Tribune*, in turn, made an effort to prevent its circulation. The *Tribune* carriers were forbidden to carry or touch the *Times*, under penalty of losing their routes. Something of the same feeling still exists. It is a mistaken notion, however, on the part of the existing papers, to prevent the increase of newspapers. If we place the statistics of journalism in the metropolis under our eye, it will be found that the increase of newspapers increase the number of newspaper readers. One paper only in New York City would be a stupid affair. The real policy of the *New York Herald* has been, so far as it can be known outside of the office, to show its feeling in regard to new papers by improving the quality of its own columns, and the books of that establishment will unquestionably exhibit an increase of circulation and an increase in advertisements with the issue of every new journal; and when the other papers heap abuse, Ossa upon Pelion, on the *Herald*, its editor smilingly remarks, "What nonsense! All this only helps me. If they want to kill off the *Herald*, why don't they make a better paper?"

Mr. Raymond occupied his niche in journalism, if not in politics. He loved the two professions. In becoming one of the leading and responsible journalists of the country, he should have given up politics. He did not do so, and that was his error. He therefore had two loves, and he would have been satisfied with either " were the other dear charmer away." If he had ceased to be a politician and devoted all his time to the *Times*, he would have made it a greater and more powerful journal; yet, with this adverse influence, the position of the *Times* on the day of his death was third, if not second, in the country.

Such is the inevitable logic of events that no editor can make his mark in this country without a controversy with some one or with some party. Take the newspapers of America, from the *News-Letter*, when Campbell got into trouble with Brooker and the Franklins in 1720-5, to the time of the *Tribune* in New York, and you will find them filled with explanatory cards. "Just once," and a hundred more. Historically considered, these cards are valuable; they are signed; they mean what they say; they are like the business notes of a merchant. No one is to suppose that Raymond is to be an exception. One of the most interesting of his cards is subjoined, because it brings him out in his dual character of editor and politician. It speaks for itself:

A CARD.

I find, in the telegraphic correspondence of some of the New York papers of this morning, a statement that "the following communication was read by the President of the Whig National Convention prior to taking a recess" on Monday afternoon:

To the President of the Whig Convention:
SIR,—As I have been assailed, without the privilege of a reply, may I ask of you to say to the Convention that the dispatch in relation to H.J.Raymond was opened on the floor of this hall by me in the presence of Moses H.Grinnell and George Ashmun. After reading it, I placed it in the hands of Mr. Grinnell, with authority to use it as he thought proper, and that I gave such authority at his request. In regard to the charge of personal hostility to Mr. Raymond, it is merely a matter of inference, arising from the fact that during my absence in Europe he was guilty of a breach of trust, and made the *Courier and Enquirer* measurably an abolition paper, and, in consequence, was compelled to leave it.   J. WATSON WEBB.

Although no such paper as this was read, or, so far as I know, received in Convention at all, the fact that it has been foisted into the published reports of its proceedings renders it proper that I should take some notice of its contents.

During Mr.Webb's absence in Europe, from November, 1849, until September, 1850, the *Courier and Enquirer* was under my conduct and control—subject to no restrictions, so far as I was made aware, except that it was to be conducted according to my best judgment.

Without discussing here the question whether it was or was not "made" during that time "measurably an abolition paper," I desire now merely to say that Mr. Webb, soon after his return, expressed to me the most unqualified approbation of the course it had pursued, and the manner in which it had been conducted; that he subsequently made the same declarations to other persons, accompanied by the assertion that, had he been at home, its course would not have been different in any respect; that as lately as in January, 1851, Mr.Webb sought to secure what influence the position I then held as Speaker of the Assembly of the State of New York was supposed to give, in order to be made the Whig candidate for United States Senator before the Legislature of the State of New York; and that he urged his application upon the express plea that it was of the utmost importance to the friends of Mr. Seward that he should have an abler associate to aid him in the Senate than Governor Fish would be. It was not until more than three months after this endeavor, and more than seven months after his return from

Europe, that Mr. Webb first intimated to me, or, so far as I know, to any one else, that the paper had not been properly managed during his absence. Whether his failure to be elected senator had any thing to do with this tardy discovery, it is not necessary that I should express an opinion. I refer to the fact that the application was made, simply because it shows that he desired to avail himself at that time of the favor of Mr. Seward's political friends, and that he did not then regard with special dislike the "measurably abolition" character which the *Courier and Enquirer* was supposed to have acquired during the time it was under my control.

As to the statement that, in consequence of this "breach of trust," I was "compelled to leave" the *Courier and Enquirer*, I have only to say that I hold an affidavit in which Mr. Webb swears that, on or about the 7th of May, 1851, I "withdrew from the position of associate editor of the *Courier and Enquirer* without the consent, and in opposition to the will and wish" of said Webb.

HENRY J. RAYMOND.

In 1852 Mr. Raymond was sent as a substitute to the Whig National Convention at Baltimore, where he made an impression as a public speaker. Honors crowding upon him, he received in 1853, from Horace Greeley, the title of "Little Villain." Why did Greeley apply this epithet to his old and esteemed associate? It was required by law, in 1853, to publish the weekly statements of all the metropolitan banks in some one newspaper. These statements occupied two or three columns, and had to be paid for by the banks at the regular advertising rates of the paper publishing them. They also contained valuable financial information for the public. They were therefore sought for by all the newspaper publishers. All the papers would have published them as news, but only one paper could receive pay for the service. Mr. D. B. St. John, who had been a shareholder in the *Times*, was Superintendent of the Bank Department. He selected the *Times*. In his official note to that paper, he desired proof-slips to be sent to other journals of the city. Some delay occurring in the receipt of the slips at the office of the *Tribune*, the editor of that paper wrote the following characteristic note to the Bank Superintendent:

MR. GREELEY TO MR. ST. JOHN.

NEW YORK, August 8, 1853.

MR. ST. JOHN,—I desire most respectfully to inform you of the manner in which your directions respecting the bank returns were complied with at the *Times* office.

Those returns were handed in during Monday (yesterday), and were all, or nearly all, in the *Times* office before dark. We sent there, from time to time, during the evening, and at length got a few of them; at 12½ (midnight) we obtained what our foreman was told were the last. They were *not* the last, however, and this morning our paper comes out with an imperfect list, and the *Times* with a full account and the editorial, which you have doubtless read with great satisfaction.

Mr. St. John, I feel deeply wronged in this matter; and even if you are a partner in the *Times*, and share in the profits of this operation, I think *you may live to repent of it.* I have asked you for no advertising. I asked nothing that I did not deem my right. Heap public money on your partners or favorites as you can, but it is *not* right to use the power of your office to supply them with public legal information to my damage. *I will try this question out.*

Yours,   HORACE GREELEY.

D. B. ST. JOHN.

The superintendent wrote a reply to the editor of the *Tribune*. After denying any pecuniary or personal interest in the matter, he said he would request the editor of the *Times* to furnish the slips in season for the *Tribune*, but "not because of the threat contained in" Mr. Greeley's note. More letters passed on the subject, and as they contain interesting and pungent matter affecting the Press and Greeley's patent of nobility to Raymond, we give them here:

MR. GREELEY TO MR. ST. JOHN.

NEW YORK, August 11, 1853.

Mr. ST. JOHN,—You have from the first persisted in misunderstanding or misrepresenting me. I did not ask you *to request* the *Times* to furnish slips, but to *make it a condition* of giving it to any paper that it should seasonably give slips containing the condensed information to all the papers that wanted them. If you had done this, all would have been right, and any paper in the city would have gladly taken the job on that condition. By doing this, you would have *secured* the publication in *all* the papers, while only one would be paid for it; and if the publication be worth any thing, the wider its publication the better. You have all along tried to understand me as asking something else than what I did ask, and I am now satisfied that the law was passed expressly to favor the *Times* at the expense of its rivals. As *I don't like this, and don't mean to forget it,* I thought it but candid and honest to tell you so. And I believe that, though you are not *now* a partner of the *Times,* you were when this bill was concocted and pushed through the Legislature. I don't think this was fair.

Yours, HORACE GREELEY

D. B. ST. JOHN, Esq., Bank Department, Albany.

MR. ST. JOHN TO MR. GREELEY.

Bank Department, ALBANY, August 13, 1853.

HORACE GREELEY, Esq.,—I have your letter of the 11th. If I have heretofore been so unfortunate as to not understand you, I certainly can not misunderstand your last communication.

You no doubt intended it as a direct personal insult, and as such I regard it. At the same time, I pronounce the charge you make, that I had a personal or pecuniary interest in the *Times* at the time the law you refer to was passed by the Legislature, as utterly and totally false. I go farther and say, as to the intimation or insinuation that I had any thing to do with concocting the bill or getting it passed by the Legislature, that it is entirely and totally false. I never saw the bill until after it became a law. When Mr. Smith, the Chairman of the Bank Committee, told me, a short time prior to the passage of the law, that he intended to get such a bill through the Legislature, I dissented from his views, and told him frankly that I thought it was a law that would create much dissatisfaction in New York. To my knowledge, I never had a word of conversation with any person connected with the *Times,* prior to the passage of the law, in relation to the selection of that or any other paper; and when you say that the law was got up and passed expressly to help the *Times* at the expense of its rivals, you say what I believe is untrue; and I state distinctly that I never had any knowledge or suspicion of any such thing, I never advocated the passage of the law, nor was I instrumental in any way or shape in getting the bill through the Legislature.

If the selection of the *Times* has given you offense, be it so; but I still insist that it is no excuse for your personal insults and abuse.

Yours, D. B. ST. JOHN.

MR. GREELEY TO MR. ST. JOHN.

NEW YORK, August 16, 1853.

Mr. D. B. ST. JOHN,—What share you had in getting up the bank law, which has subjected me to gross injustice and needless insult, I only professed to infer from the facts which appear on the surface. There was no occasion for your passion on the subject. I take your denial with reasonable abatement, because your previous letter denied with equal particularity and emphasis that you were a partner in the *Times*, whereas a letter from an Albany friend of the same date informed me that you *had* been a partner in that paper, and had sold out to a Mr. Harper.

All this is immaterial. The essential case is this: Months ago, before I was aware of the purpose for which this law was evidently got up by *somebody*, and when I supposed the *Tribune* as likely to be selected for this service as any other paper, I wrote requesting you to make it a condition of your selection of a paper that said paper should *agree*, as a matter of justice to the residue of the New York Press, to furnish them slips of this intelligence. I did not solicit this patronage, but I probably told you that I, if selected, would willingly do this, and that any other paper would do it if made a condition of the selection by you. I dare you to submit to Mr. Weed, or any other person qualified to judge in the premises, whether this was not a reasonable and proper request, which you ought to have complied with. You have chosen to misrepresent, to quibble about it, and to (in effect) refuse it. The consequence is, that I and others are put to a serious expense to collect these returns, which the official paper might give us without expense or trouble. I have a most insolent and scoundrelly letter from your favorite, Raymond, offering to send me these returns at his own convenience if I will credit them to the *Times* (not the Bank Department, of which only have I asked them), and talking of his willingness to *grant favors* to those who prove worthy of them, but not to be "*kicked into benevolence,*" etc. *All this insolence of this little villain is founded on your injustice.* I have not written to him; I have asked no favor of him; and I shall not answer him. I am sorry to find one of his falsehoods copied into your letter—that which speaks of my being offended at your selection of the *Times to print the advertisements!* You both know a great deal better—that I have never asked you for advertising of any sort, but solely for the information to publish without charge. Have I not reason to despise alike the author and propagator of this unfounded imputation?

Indignantly,   HORACE GREELEY.

D. B. ST. JOHN, ESQ.

"Little Villain" adhered to Raymond through life. Epithets always stick. Old Hickory, for instance, to Jackson; Little Giant to Douglas; Rough and Ready to Taylor; Old Bullion to Benton; the Little Magician to Van Buren; Old Poins to Poindexter; Little Corporal to Napoleon. Raymond first published the above correspondence, and he said soon after, "Well, I suppose I must accept the title, as I first gave it publicity."

In 1854 Raymond was elected Lieutenant Governor of New York. In 1856 he wrote the "Address to the People" which was adopted by the Republican Party at its first National Convention, held in Pittsburg, Pennsylvania. These political honors made the *Times* more antagonistic to the *Tribune*. The chief editors of these two journals were equally desirous of political offices in addition to their journalistic positions. More favors were showered upon Raymond than upon Greeley, and the latter looked upon the fact as one of ingratitude in every way and sense.

Our modern journalists are not yet wholly exempt from the "code of honor." Occasionally an editor is annoyed with a challenge. It is not two years ago that an editor of a Spanish paper felt constrained to exchange shots with an opponent. These pages will relate many instances of this kind that have occurred since the institution of the Press in this country, but as years roll on and civilization advances they become less frequent. They never occur nowadays in England. In France, on the contrary, they are of weekly occurrence among the fraternity. Time is rapidly obliterating this code from our books. But it was Mr. Raymond's experience to go through a correspondence which fortunately did not end in coffee and pistols. It came on the *tapis* in this way. The following article appeared in the *Times* on the 28th of November, 1856:

A REGULAR IRISH REBELLION.

The whole Irish (cis-Atlantic) race is flying to arms. The blood of the O'Dowdys and the O'Mulligans is up. The soul of the Celt is roused and eager for revenge. The *Times's* squib about Irish servant-girls has stirred the heart of Irishdom to its profoundest depths. Scores of epistolary fulminations from the "illigant bould boys" who espouse the battle of the Bridgets lumber our waste basket. Our old friend of the *Irish American* was first in the field with his proclamation; but that thrice valiant hero, his brother of the *Irish News*, Thomas Francis Meagher, lags not far behind, and makes up in fury what he lacks in time. He wields adjectives and epithets as ferociously as he wielded his pike at that famous Irish battle—we forget the name of it—where he delivered his country from the Saxon tyrant, and bound his victorious brow with wreaths which not even his flight from Australia has availed to wither. "Mean," "cowardly," "neither high-minded nor gentlemanly," are some of the sweet phrases he scatters behind him, while he talks, meanwhile, lamentingly about "irresponsibility," and mourns over the days, departed long ago, when he could, at discretion, fight without breaking the law, or run away without breaking his parole. Poor man! Perhaps he may feel better when he gets over his passion; we hope he will have nothing worse to reflect upon than the consciousness of having made an ass of himself.

Thomas Francis Meagher, the well-known Irish orator, and an editor too, immediately on reading this paragraph sent a hostile note to the editor of the *Times*, resulting in the following correspondence:

MR. MEAGHER TO MR. RAYMOND.

Irish News Office, No. 29 Ann Street, November 28, 1856.

SIR,—I inclose an article which appeared in the *New York Daily Times* of this morning. I notice an expression in it which I have underlined.

You will gratify me by stating whether by that observation you mean to charge that I, at any time, broke my parole.

A direct answer will oblige your obedient servant,

THOMAS FRANCIS MEAGHER.

Lieutenant Governor RAYMOND, Editor of the *New York Daily Times*.

MR. RAYMOND'S REPLY.

NEW YORK, Friday, November 28, 1856.

SIR,—In reply to your note, which has just been handed to me by Mr. Clason, I have merely to say, that, as the expression you have underscored in the paragraph cut from the *Daily Times* speaks only of your being able to "run away *without* breaking your parole," I am unable to see how it affords any ground whatever for the question you ask.

I am your obedient servant, HENRY J. RAYMOND.

T. F. MEAGHER, Esq.

MR. A. W. CLASON TO MR. RAYMOND.

Friday, November 28, 1856.

DEAR SIR,—I have called twice to see you since we parted.

Mr. Meagher requests me to return your letter to him received through me. I inclose it. That letter is rejected by Mr. Meagher as an answer. Therefore I occupy the position I did this morning on handing you his note.

I beg an early answer to the letter I had the honor of bearing.

Most respectfully, your obedient servant, A. W. CLASON.

H. J. RAYMOND, Esq.

MR. RAYMOND TO MR. CLASON.

NEW YORK, Saturday, November 29, 1856.

DEAR SIR,—Your note of yesterday, with its inclosure, was handed to me this morning.

Mr. Meagher had asked whether an expression which he quoted from the *Daily Times* was intended to charge him with having broken his parole. In reply, I directed his attention to the fact that the language quoted expressly excludes the idea of his having done so.

Until I am favored with some reason for Mr. Meagher's "rejection" of this answer, I must decline giving him any other.

Very respectfully, your obedient servant, HENRY J. RAYMOND.
A. W. CLASON, Esq.

MR. CLASON TO MR. RAYMOND.

Saturday, November 29, 1856.

DEAR SIR,—In your letter to Mr. Meagher you point to the expression in the *Times* and exclude the right of inquiry into its meaning. In other words, you assume that a phrase which is susceptible of double meaning and an offensive interpretation does not need a disclaimer of intended offense. To this assumption I can not subscribe. An imputation of dishonor can be conveyed by indirection.

Mr. Meagher has a right to know whether any imputation upon his honor was intended to be conveyed by the expression in the *Times*, and, moreover, that the disclaimer shall be as public as the phrase which necessitated it.

Very respectfully, your obedient servant, A. W. CLASON.
H. J. RAYMOND, Esq.

MR. RAYMOND TO MR. CLASON.

NEW YORK, December 1, 1856.

A. W. Clason, Esq.:

DEAR SIR,—Your note, bearing date November 29, did not reach me until late last evening.

My letter to Mr. Meagher was not designed to "exclude the right of inquiry" into the meaning of the expression to which he had taken exception, but rather to express my own decided conviction that its terms were so explicit as to leave no room for such inquiry.

I assumed that the language employed was the best evidence of the intent with which I had employed it, and that it indicated clearly enough—what was the fact —that I did not intend by its use to charge Mr. Meagher with having broken his parole. I did not intend then to express any opinion whatever on the subject, nor do I intend to do so now.

You are at liberty, if you see fit, to present this note to Mr. Meagher; and he is at liberty to consider it a reply to his letter, and to publish it in the *Times*, or elsewhere, at his discretion.

Your obedient servant, HENRY J. RAYMOND.

At the date of the above Mr. Meagher was out of town. When he returned, in pursuance of a suggestion from Mr. Clason that the communication should be made direct to Mr. Meagher, the following note was sent:

MR. RAYMOND TO MR. MEAGHER.

NEW YORK, December 4, 1856.

SIR,—Referring to your note of November 28, I can say with pleasure that I did not intend by the expression you quote to charge that you had at any time broken your parole. The language of the article does not seem to me to import any opinion on that subject; it certainly was not intended to express any such opinion. Your obedient servant, H. J. RAYMOND.
T. F. MEAGHER, Esq.

Two days after this note of Mr. Raymond to Mr. Meagher, on the 6th of December, the following paragraph was inserted in the *Times:*

A PERSONAL EXPLANATION.

We have received a note from Mr. T. F. Meagher, inquiring whether, by an expression used in a recent paragraph in the *Times*, we intended to charge that he had at any time "broken his parole?" *Certainly not*. We did not suppose that the language used *conveyed any such meaning*, or, indeed, expressed any opinion upon that point. Although the paragraph in which it occurred was written under the provocation of a very offensive personal article in Mr. Meagher's paper, *The Irish News*, it was not intended to transcend the ordinary limits and proprieties of newspaper controversy, or to cast any reproach upon the personal character of Mr. Meagher.

This did not quite end the matter, for the *Times* afterwards gave a full account of the escape of Meagher from Australia, and this closed the affair.

If Raymond had one *forte* in which he felt at home, and was always ready to indulge in, it was a controversy. With Greeley on Fourierism, it was conceded that he came off with flying colors. Afterwards he got into a serious one with Archbishop Hughes. Now, if the editor of the *Times* was fond of a controversy, the Archbishop of New York was more so. He seemed perfectly delighted when engaged in one. *Vide* the bitter personal one with James Gordon Bennett, of the *Herald*, and then on the School Question in New York. This affair with Raymond grew out of an article written by the archbishop on the Catholic Press, and the publication of a reply in the *Times* signed Equitas, and purporting to come from a Catholic clergyman. It seems that Mr. Raymond had been imposed upon as to the authorship of the communication, but Archbishop Hughes endeavored to impress upon the public mind that Raymond was the real author of Equitas, and that he was endeavoring to shuffle out of the responsibility. The controversy became very personal, the archbishop using the columns of the *Herald* and *Tribune*, and Mr. Raymond those of the *Times*, in three-column communications. They seemed well matched—perfect terriers in mental grip. Specimens of the style of each of these intellectual gladiators are annexed:

Archbishop Hughes closes his communication of July 20, 1857:

Forger, you do not fabricate as adroitly as an unprincipled editor of the *Times* might be expected to do. The first sermon preached by the archbishop on his return from Rome was in honor of the solemn definition by our holy father the Pope, of the Immaculate Conception. It was not a written, nor even a well-prepared sermon, but it was taken down by a reporter of the *New York Herald*, and, through the circulation of that paper, found its way, uncorrected as it was, into the Eternal City. Imperfect as it was, it was deemed worthy of translation, and of being deposited among other similar documents in the archives of Rome. The archbishop, at the same time, announced the purpose of constructing a new church in honor of the Immaculate Conception. And then, forger, you are equally unfortunate in your allusion to Archbishop Bedini. You say that Archbishop Hughes turned his back on the nuncio of Pius IX. while the said nuncio was being assailed by the Press, hooted and stoned by the mob, and burned in effigy in a hundred cities and villages, during a period in which he most needed "his" (the archbishop's) support.

Now it so happens that as long as the nuncio honored the archbishop with his presence and society, he was treated, both in New York and elsewhere, with all the courtesy, and not a few of the honors, to which a distinguished foreigner visiting the United States on lawful business would be entitled. But the Archbishop of New York, during his tour with the nuncio, contracted a violent cold, which threatened the most serious consequences, as it was thought by his physicians that his lungs were, or would be soon, deeply affected. They advised his going to Cuba; but, previous to his departure, no personal insult had been offered to the amiable and learned nuncio Bedini.

Rome, therefore, has no complaint against the archbishop for having neglected to honor the definition of the Immaculate Conception, nor for having turned his back on the nuncio of Pius IX.

* * * * * * * *

The writer of this can state on the highest authority that the Archbishop of New York has not the slightest idea of asking for a coadjutor, and that there is not the slightest probability of one being appointed during his life, except at his own request. Then, as to resignation, he will take that into serious reflection about the year 1879, if his life should be prolonged to that remote period. It may not be amiss, however, to state, that if St. Peter, in the person of Pius IX. or his successor, should wish his resignation at any time, he will descend the steps of his archiepiscopal throne with a more willing and a lighter heart than he had when he mounted them for the first time. As to administrators and all that, if the forger were not as ignorant as he is malicious, he should know that they can have no place in the Catholic Church. It does not recognize "standing committees" to play bishops in the vacancy of a Catholic see.

* * * * * * * *

Oh, forger! ambitious as you suppose the archbishop to be, he would not have the courage to see the bishops who are to take charge of his diocese bowing and burning incense before him, and, especially, upholding his train or kissing his ring. This would be too much.

* * * * * * * *

+ JOHN, Archbishop of New York.

Editor Raymond, not at all alarmed, it would seem, closed his reply to the above on the 20th of August, two or three days after his return from Europe, as follows:

The object of this paragraph was to convince the public that you had discovered the author of "Equitas." Who he was you do not disclose; but, after a long and wholly needless apology for using private and confidential letters for such a purpose, you close your second epistle with the following threat:

"*This matter, however, is somewhat serious. If it should turn out to be as the experts think it is, the consequences will place Mr. Raymond in a position that will disarm his worst enemies of every sentiment except pity. Mr. Raymond is now absent, and it would be ungenerous to press this matter further until he shall be on the spot to answer for himself.*"

Mr. Raymond is at last on the spot to answer for himself; and he now demands at the hands of Archbishop Hughes a distinct explanation of these conveniently vague, but evidently serious insinuations. The impression sought to be conveyed to the public is, that "Equitas" was either myself, or some one writing with my knowledge and connivance; that when called upon for the author I resorted to the pretense of having supposed it to come from Rev. Dr. M'Elroy, and of having corresponded with him upon the subject, and sent the correspondence to Archbishop Hughes as a means of evading the demand; that I resorted to all this machinery because I was afraid to write or publish any thing against the archbishop upon my own responsibility; and that he has now in his hands the documents which will *prove* all this to the satisfaction of "experts" and of the public. You think it would be "*ungenerous*" to do more in my absence than to *publish* these slanders; you content yourself, therefore, with infusing them into the public mind, giving them the weight of your official influence and authority, and withholding all evidence of their truth on account of my absence from the country. This is the generosity of an archbishop! This is the justice and the courtesy of a prelate who permits himself to talk of the "instincts of a gentleman," and who professes to have been instructed concerning plausible treachery by "mutual friends." Permit me to remind you that the manuscripts by which you threaten to overwhelm me were placed in your hands by myself, and that I have from the beginning been quite as anxious as you could be to detect the authorship of "Equitas." You pretend to have done so; you will oblige me, then, by placing before the public whatever discoveries you may have made. So far as I am concerned, you are at full liberty to use any private letter, or any confidential communication that may ever have been made to you upon any subject; and I shall be especially happy to aid you in submitting these papers, or any others that I can furnish, to any jury of "experts" you may select—provided, only, it be not made up of such "mutual friends" as the one upon whom you rely for your impressions of my character.

You will have no difficulty, sir, I trust, in perceiving the necessity of responding to this demand, and of either establishing or retracting the menacing insinuations which you have placed before the public. I am fully prepared to meet the disastrous consequences of the threatened revelations; and you must be aware that your failure to make them will put you in a position that will not leave room even for pity, either to your friends or foes. I trust, moreover, that this letter may have at least the effect of disabusing your mind of the strange impression it seems to have received, that I am under any necessity of speaking my opinions in regard to you by stealth, or that I have any hesitation in doing it openly, and upon my own responsibility.   I am, sir, your obedient servant,

HENRY J. RAYMOND.

Mr. Raymond refused the nomination for Governor of New York in 1857. His thoughts were then on the *Times*. He had made arrangements for the erection of the building now occupied by that establishment. It was one of the first of the kind erected in the metropolis. They are now almost as common as newspapers or hotels. The *Herald* and *Tribune* then had large establishments, but they were a sort of patchwork. When the old Brick Church property was on the market, and Horace Holden interested in its sale, it was proposed that the proprietors of the *Herald, Tribune,* and *Times* should purchase the entire site and erect a block of buildings thereon for the use of their respective establishments—to make a Printing-house Row. That scheme fell through. The proprietors of the *Times* then entered into negotiations which resulted in the purchase of one end of the site, where the *Times* establishment now stands, an architectural ornament to the city.

There is an amusing incident affecting the *Times* that has been as adhesive to Raymond as the *sobriquet* given him by Greeley. In 1859, during the Italian War, a remarkable article appeared in the *Times* on the war, as it was intended to be, but it really embraced three or four topics. Such a literary curiosity would have been immortalized by Disraeli. We append it in full, in order that it may not be wholly lost in the bound volumes of a newspaper, and shelved in the Historical Rooms:

THE DEFENSIVE SQUARE OF AUSTRIAN ITALY.

When the Austrians were beaten at Magenta, a sudden conviction seems to have seized upon their leaders that, if they could once put their forces in safety beyond the lines of the Chiese and the Mincio, they would be able to make head against the courage and skill of France. The extraordinary speed with which the French troops were moved across the Alps to the succor of Turin and of the Piedmontese provinces seems to have paralyzed for a moment the energy of the Savoyards, and the skillful movements by which the Sardinian troops were brought into relations with the village insurrections of the Lombard people combined to make the Austrian authorities understand the impossibility of holding their ground against a disorganized and revolutionary people. The Austrians, following up the strategic plans of Marshal Radetsky in 1848, abandoned with an unwise haste their first lines of defense upon the Mincio, and threw themselves beyond the river, in the empty hope of beating back the allied troops.

The result of this mad enterprise has been their complete imprisonment within their famous strategic square.

The square is closed to the north by the last spur of the Alps on the shores of the Lago di Garda; to the west it is defended by the Mincio, which leaves the Lake of Garda at Peschiera, waters the plains of Mantua, and joins the Po at fifteen leagues' distance from its springs at Governolo, after opening a real lake, on the banks of which lie the fortresses of Mantua; to the south the strategic square is defended by the line of the River Po, which flows beneath the walls of Cremona, and draws to itself all the torrents flowing from the Alps; to the east the boundary of the Austrian defences is formed by the Adige, which descends from the mountains of Switzerland, and flows on a parallel line with the Po, after passing by Trent, Roveredo, Verona, and Legnago. The strength of a position so fortified by nature and by art does not need to be developed. It borrows strategic importance from the numerous breaks of the ground, which—if we may be pardoned for the expression—seem but to have formed the successive steps in the natural defense of Austrian Italy.

But if nature has done much for the "strategic square," art has done more.

Austria has neglected nothing which might assure her dominion over the waters of the Danube. She has done all in her power *to favor the development of Europe, which is the pacific development of England.* She has dealt with edged tools—boldly, but not, we feel sure, in utter vanity.

In 1848 Peschiera was captured by the Sardinians under King Charles Albert; but there can be no doubt that the French bore away from the first fight of Magenta very questionable compliments. At this time the Sardinians, under the Duke of Genoa, were ready to defend the famous Quadrilateral. To-day the Quadrilateral has ceased to exist.

The fortress of Peschiera lies on an isle near the scene of the late conflict.

A broad road has been made by Austria in the direction of the Alps, to unite the regions of the Vorarlberg and the Tyrol with Lombardy by the pass of the Stelvio. This road passes through the Valtelline, runs around the Lake of Como, and ends at Bergamo. It may serve as well for the retreat of the beaten Austrians into the Tyrol as for the advance of the victorious Austrians upon Italy. Two railways pass also by this central point of the Austrian position. One of these railways unites Lombardy with Vienna by circling around the crescent of the North Adriatic; the other, leaving Botzen, in the Tyrol, skirts the Lago di Garda, touches Trent, Roveredo, and Verona, and by a branch road reaches Mantua, and thus unites the two main angles of the famous square. The New York *Herald,* in giving yesterday a pretended map of this square, carefully omitted the bridge-head of Legnago, and thus converted the square into a triangle. The strength of Peschiera and Legnago is out of all proportion to the besieging force. The main merit of Peschiera is that this fortress lies on an island, and was captured by the Duke of Genoa in 1848. At this time the Sardinians crossed the Mincio after several hours' hard fighting; and *if we follow the windings of the Mincio, we shall find countless elbows formed in the elbows of the regular army* at places like Salianza, Molini, and Borghetto. These places make up the base of the allied army. The line of the Mincio is the base of the new campaign we are about to open.

Almost at the southern end of the River Mincio lies the strong fortress of Mantua, the only Gibraltar of Austria in Italy, guaranteed by the treaties of 1815. Mantua, as we have said, lies on a lake of the River Mincio. In spite of the labors spent upon it, Mantua still holds the next rank to Verona. It is a post of danger for the army shut between its walls rather than for the enemy without. After a battle of several hours' duration, the Sardinians at Goito gave way; and if we follow up the course of the Mincio, *we shall find innumerable elbows formed by the sympathy of youth.* Defended by Wurmser in 1797, Austria surrendered to Napoleon III. in 1859. Notwithstanding the toil spent by Austria on the spot, *we should have learned that we are protected by a foreign fleet suddenly coming up on our question of citizenship. A canal cuts Mantua in two; but we may rely on the most cordial cabinet minister of the new power in England.*

Mantua is protected in the centre by five detached forts: the Citadel, Pradella, Castle of Faith, St. George, and Migliaretto, which commands Cremona, Borgo Forte, and Governolo.

A canal divides Mantua, and makes a small port in the lake, communicating by five fortified roadways with the land.

At Roverbello are machines for flooding the whole region, and in the upper lake floats an Austrian squadron. The region between Mantua and the Po is impracticable for an army. *'Tis a marsh full of fevers. On this side the square seems impregnable. But how with the line from Mantua to Legnago?* Legnago is no stronger than Peschiera, but it has the double advantage of a bridge over the Adige, and of dikes ready to inundate the whole Adriatic region. The fourth face of the square links Verona to Legnago. This is the best defensive line of Austria in Italy. At Verona the last features of the opposition lingered. The Adige is swift and deep at Verona; it can only be passed at Cerpi and Bussolengo in the face of a thousand perils. *Paris is strong in her circle of fortifications.*

All the credit of this extraordinary production, all the fame it has acquired, is unreservedly given to Mr. Raymond. He is not entitled to it at all. When it appeared he was in Europe, on that very field of battle, in the vicinity of these "elbows of the Mincio" described so topographically, and was wholly ignorant of the sensation the article had produced at home for weeks after it appeared in the *Times*. After that number of the paper had reached Paris, and after the laugh had subsided, Mr. Raymond returned to that gay city, and was quietly walking along the Place de la Bourse, when a friend met him facetiously and spoke of the "elbows of the Mincio" and the "sympathy of youth."

"What do you mean?" asked Raymond, who had witnessed the battles of Solferino and Magenta, and could see no joke in the aforesaid elbows.

"Why, Mr. Raymond, haven't you seen the *Times?*"

"No, not wholly; I have just returned from Italy," replied the editor.

"Well, well, my dear friend, I'll not say another word. Reserve yourself. Go to the reading-room and carefully read the editorials of the *Times*. I have the date. Read that paper; it will pay you for the trouble. *Au revoir.*"

Mr. Raymond's curiosity was aroused. Off he posted to the reading-room; he examined the files; he read article after article; finally he read one that seemed a little confused; he read it again, and it became more cloudy; he read it for the third time, and then he saw the cause of that sparkle in the eye and that peculiar wreath around the mouth of the friend who had stopped him on the Place de la Bourse.

How was such an article written? How did it get into the paper? Two simple questions. On the day before its appearance, a distinguished literary gentleman of New York took his departure for Europe. Several of his friends ate breakfast with him that morning, and accompanied him to the steamer. They had a very pleasant time; they enjoyed themselves. One of these gentlemen had been selected by the editor of the *Times, ad interim,* to write three articles on three different subjects. On the return of the party from the steamer, this gentleman proceeded to the *Times* editorial rooms to comply with his instructions. He wrote a few lines on one of the chosen subjects, and then reflected. Resuming his pen, he continued his article with one of the other subjects. Again reflecting over the parting scenes of the morning, he again resumed his article with the third subject on his mind, and finished it, evidently to his own satisfaction. When the proof-sheet came to the proof-reader he was puzzled. "Is it in pi?" asked he. He looked at the manuscript; the printers had clearly followed copy. "It must be all right," he said, and it appeared the next morning, and threw New York into convulsions.

"Why didn't you leave it out," asked the managing editor of the foreman on the day of its publication.

"Because the writer, two days before, remonstrated with me for altering one of his articles, and gave me strict orders never again to change a word, but insert the articles precisely as he wrote them."

Newspaper work did not suffice for Mr. Raymond. On his return from Europe in 1860, he took an active part in the campaign resulting in the election of Abraham Lincoln. In 1861 he was again elected to the State Legislature, and again chosen Speaker of the Assembly. Always weakening his journalistic power in his efforts to gain political position, he entered earnestly in politics in 1863. He was a candidate in that year for the United States Senate. William M. Evarts and Governor Morgan were also before the Legislature for the same office. The superior tactics of the latter secured the prize.

Mr. Raymond wrote the Baltimore resolutions of 1864, and was elected Chairman of the Republican National Committee. In that year he was sent to Congress from New York City, and became a strong conservative Republican in the councils of the nation. He wrote the "Life of Abraham Lincoln" in 1865, afterwards enlarging it to the more pretentious title of "Life, Public Services, and State Papers of Abraham Lincoln."

One of Raymond's qualities was pluck. It is an excellent quality in an editor. Moral courage, especially, is a necessary element in a journalist. When the metropolis was in partial possession of the mob in the draft riots of 1864, the newspaper offices were threatened with demolition. That of the *Tribune* was attacked, and efforts made to set the building on fire, as we have described. Immediately after this attack, it was thought prudent to place the offices of the *Times* and *Tribune* on a war footing. They were accordingly fortified. The two establishments were on opposite corners, both facing Printing-house Square and the Park, an area capable of holding ten thousand persons. Printing-house Square can be approached across the Park, down Chatham and Centre Streets, up Park Row, Nassau, Spruce, and Frankfort Streets. Expecting the mob to approach from the upper part of the city, the editor of the *Times* had two pieces of artillery of a new invention, a sort of *mitrailleuse*, capable of one hundred discharges per hour, placed in position in front of his office, so as to rake Chatham and Centre Streets. Leonard W. Jerome had command of one of these cannon, and Raymond the other, with the necessary assistants — both remarkably cool men in emergencies. Scouts were out in all directions, and every thing was in readiness for instant action. On each night of the riot, in order to show that the *Times* was prepared, the entire establishment was brilliantly illuminated. In the midst of the fears and anxieties of that dreadful riot, the *Times* presented a remarkable sight. The *Tribune* fortified its establishment inside. It had its windows barricaded with bales of printing paper, as Guy Mannering had his mansion with books. Who the Dominie Sampson was we did not see. Loop-holes were made for Minie rifles, and apertures through which to throw hand-grenades upon the mob, if Raymond's artillery did not succeed in repelling the rioters. Major General Wool aided the *Tribune* with men and material, and a young naval officer was on duty to direct operations in Fort Greeley. These preparations, fortunately, answered the purpose; there was no farther demonstration in that quarter. In a day or two the riots ceased, and the journalists laid aside the weapons of war, and resumed the pen, which again was proved to be "mightier than the sword."

The policy of President Johnson attracted the attention of Mr. Raymond, and he became one of its active supporters in 1866, preparing the address adopted at the National Convention held in Philadelphia on the 14th of August. The struggle between the radical portion of the Republican Party and the President had become very bitter; and in the failure of Johnson, those who pinned their faith to him failed also. But, previous to the retirement of the President, the editor of the *Times* was appointed minister to Austria. This honor he very properly declined. This political *fiasco* with the President induced the editor of the *Times* to abandon politics professionally, and he publicly stated his determination. He resigned the position of Chairman of the National Committee. It was his purpose thereafter to devote his time and thoughts entirely to the *Times*.

It was one purpose of Mr. Raymond to preserve the dignity and decorum of the Press. If he was abused he would never make use of his columns to abuse his antagonist in reply. Perhaps the best illustration of his policy on this point in the management of a newspaper is to be found in the following article that appeared in the *Times* on the 15th of April, 1868:

GOOD MANNERS IN JOURNALISM.

The *Tribune* headed a leading editorial article a day or two ago, "Governor Seymour as a Liar," and proceeded to vindicate the epithet by showing that, in a political speech in Connecticut, Governor Seymour had largely overstated the annual expenses of the government. The *World* came to the governor's defense, and tried to show that the statements he had made were substantially correct; whereupon the *Tribune* replies statistically, and then adds that the editor of the *World* is a liar as well as the governor. And in yesterday's issue the *Tribune* undertakes to vindicate not only the truth of its statement, but the gentlemanly character and perfect propriety of its language, "taking issue," as it says, with the code that assumes that it is "rude and ungentlemanly" to call a man a liar, and insisting that "it is only the liar who proves himself to be no gentleman."

We do not propose to discuss the morality of lying, or the manners of men guilty of it. But as the editor of the *Tribune* is to preside at the dinner to be given to Mr. Dickens on behalf of the Press of the United States, and thus becomes in a certain sense a representative of American newspapers, we deem it worth while to dissent from his theory of journalistic manners. We do not think it either "gentlemanly" or proper for a newspaper to call Governor Seymour or any other man a "liar," because we do not think the use of such epithets proper any where. Mr. Greeley would not use them in conversation. He would not use them in personal intercourse, nor would he invite a man who did use them to social relations with himself or his family.

The fact that language of this sort is used only by the coarsest, lowest, and most ignorant people, is a sufficient reason why it should not be used by newspapers. If Mr. Greeley will go into the grog-shops of the Five Points, he will hear it on every side of him. If he goes into the houses of the respectable, virtuous, and cultivated, he will not hear it at all. This fact alone is entitled to a good deal of weight as to the propriety of its use in the columns of respectable newspapers. Mr. Greeley would scarcely care to imitate, from choice and as a matter of taste, the language of low sailors in Cherry Street, rather than the language of civilized people in respectable quarters of the town. He would not do it in personal intercourse; why should he do it in the columns of the *Tribune?* He has the same excuse for it in the one case as in the other. The language itself is stronger; it is more direct; it corresponds more accurately, perhaps, with the feeling of the moment, and only expresses the truth; why, then, says Mr. Greeley, should it not be used? Simply because it is indecent. It shocks the taste, the sense of propriety of every man. It is coarse, brutal, and it is used only by coarse and brutal people; and the reason why they use it is because it corresponds with the coarseness and brutality of their natures.

Mr. Greeley has probably chanced, at some time of his life, to be present at a sharp personal dispute between very low, coarse ruffians, or between degraded, voluble, and enraged women, whose main object at the moment was to express their opinions of each other—to give each other "a piece of their minds." He has had on such occasions a chance to see his theories as to the use of language put into practice. The epithets which he thinks so just and proper were fully appreciated and vigorously used, and were doubly re-enforced by the use of various adjectives and other expletives, all falling strictly in the line of the *Tribune's* argument, and adding decided weight to the naked, unadorned epithets themselves. As a matter of personal taste, we do not believe Mr. Greeley enjoys hearing men calling each other liars, or d—d liars, or any of the other epithets, more or less ornamented with theological adjectives, which come so easily into use at such encounters, and which, upon careful inquiry, may prove to be literally just and true. Why, then, does he put them into his newspaper? And why, on his theory of epithets, does he not "go the whole figure," and use them "mixed" as well as "straight?" Why not head his editorial " *Governor Seymour as a d—d liar*," or make it even stronger than this, if he thinks the case deserves it? He would find it just as easy to vindicate the one, on the score of taste, as the other.

We do not deny that there is a certain public appetite which relishes this style of discussion. But there is also a public appetite for a still lower and a still coarser style. There are people who relish obscenity and profanity, just as there are people who enjoy prize-fights, dog-fights, or cock-fights, or any other low and brutalizing exhibition; but it is not always proper or decent to pander to such tastes, and the number of American newspapers which adopt it as their standard of manners and propriety is much less than it once was.

We see no reason why the language of a newspaper should be very different from the language of decent society, from the language used by gentlemen in their daily intercourse. Mr. Greeley, if he were conversing with Governor Seymour on the expenses of the government, would not call him a "liar," even if the governor should put them higher than he did himself. He would scarcely style his neighbor at table a "villain," even if he ate mustard with his beef, while he himself did not. He would not feel called upon to say, in every society, every thing that he thought true about every body present, nor would he quite relish the frankness and candor of every one who should apply to him, in straightforward and unmistakable English, every epithet which he might think he deserved. Why should he assert, or act upon, a different theory of manners and decorum in the editorial conduct of a newspaper?

It seems that Horace Greeley thought differently. Webster, and Worcester, and Johnson, in their dictionaries, embraced these expressive expletives; they were a part of the English language; they were strong and emphatic, and meant what they said. So Editor Greeley believed in their use when he desired to say that any one was guilty of telling a falsehood. So Cambronne, of the Old Guard, believed, when he gave expression to his contempt for the English in the utterance of a single word, found only in Bailey's Dictionary, when called upon to surrender at Waterloo. But here is the opinion of the editor of the *Tribune* on this subject, as it appeared on the 18th of April, 1868, in reply to his mild-mannered neighbor, the journalistic Chesterfield:

> The *New York Times* favored us with a column lecture on manners and professional courtesies *apropos* of the *Tribune* and Governor Seymour, wherein it compared the matter at issue between us to the diversity of taste between two gentlemen, one of whom should prefer to eat his beef with mustard, the other without. We received the rebuke with due meekness, and only ventured, at its close, to propound the question, "Is it true or is it false that our government is now spending $300,000,000 per annum, apart from payments on account of the national debt, and that $150,000,000 of this is the cost of holding the South in subjugation by means of a great standing army?" Hereupon the *Times* favors us with another column of moralities and courtesies, but never a word of answer to our questions. It appears to have no choice between beef *with* mustard and beef without.
>
> * * * * * *
>
> We would have the *Times* use such terms as most forcibly express its ideas. We especially beg it not to be "mealy-mouthed" in speaking of the *Tribune*. So far from deeming it "unfortunate" *for us* that other journals should be abusive, we insist that no one is ever harmed by any bad language but his own.

But politics had taken possession of Raymond. In spite of his best intentions, he could not keep out of the pool. He entered the presidential campaign of 1868 not as an independent journalist, and he was Chairman of the Republican Committee in New York till a few days before his death; and on the eve of that sudden and sad event—indeed, the last known of him alive—was in attendance at a political meeting. He died June 18, 1869.

On the afternoon previous to his death, he had been to Greenwood with his daughter to select a family burial-place, for the purpose of having the remains of his youngest son Walter, named after the editor of the London *Times*, transferred thither. Meeting Mr. Joseph H. Medill, founder of the Chicago *Tribune*, Mr. Raymond entered into conversation with him, in the course of which Mr. M. referred to a letter which he had just received from Chicago announcing the death of a friend there by apoplexy. Mr. Raymond remarked, "Well, after all, that is the kind of death I would myself prefer to die. I have always had a dread of a lingering death from paralysis, or a nervous disorder, or some kindred slow disease. Sudden death is far preferable."

This incident recalls the expressed wish of James Otis, one of the brilliant and ardent writers for the Revolutionary Press of Boston from 1766 to 1776, that when his time should come he might be struck by a flash of lightning. One day, standing in the doorway of his house, a single thunderbolt from a small passing cloud struck and instantly killed him.

Among those present at the funeral of Mr. Raymond was the Rev. Henry Ward Beecher. He delivered the funeral address, which was characteristic. After a few introductory remarks, he said:

His was the career of the journalist, and he spoke from a pulpit whence his words were echoed and re-echoed throughout the world. The lawyer speaks within the narrow sphere of the court-room; the senator and representative within the legislative walls; the minister preaches from the pulpit, and his words are confined within the walls of his church, and he rarely speaks beyond it; but he spoke from a pulpit that has no limit—the Press. Thence comes forth a louder voice than that of all the others—the voice of one who speaks, who cries in the wilderness; for all across this populous land, across the territory from the Atlantic to the Pacific Ocean, the Daily Press speaks to all the people. This is the great, the all-important civilizer. There is no power for good that can compare with the Daily Press; no pulpit like it for disseminating knowledge among men. And among those who have been the builders of this great moral agency, this great agency of civilization—not the founders, but the finishers of the institution—stood Mr. Raymond pre-eminent. Aside from the general ability with which he conducted the Press, it is gratifying to remark here how singularly free his whole public career has been from bitterness; how nobly and persistently he refused to lend his paper to passionate discussions; how he never lent himself to passionate invective, and never permitted his paper to be the medium in this respect for others; how sagacious reasoning and a high moral strength breathed in his words; and now that he has departed from among us, it is gratifying to look back on his career, and to say that the work he was engaged in, of giving a higher, a nobler, and a purer moral sentiment to the Press, covers a multitude of imperfections. This was the work he was engaged in; this is the work he did. I have it in my heart to say here that instability of character in his conduct of the Press was charged against him. I have heard it said that he was weak, and never believed in the principles or things he advocated; but I recall a time when the nation shivered like an aspen leaf; I recall a time when a man was worth an army—those days when what was needed most was open, manly, patriotic courage. And you and I should never forget to be grateful for the example he set to those brave men who at once pressed to the front through his appeals. He let his voice ring out clear, and without variability, and without weakness or changing, to the very end, and the great conflict for national life was brought to a successful, a glorious, and blessed termination. If this be instability and variability, oh that there had been more of such men among us. The services he rendered the country then should enshrine his memory in our hearts and make his name dear to all. I still thank him, and I am glad, my friends, to make mention and to bear testimony to his fidelity in this great struggle, which, to be consistent in at all times and under all circumstances, required greatness of soul. My friends, it is painful to speak of one who was so short a time ago among us; of one who has been stricken down by press of work in our midst; of one the next ten years of whose life, had he lived, should have been worth more than twenty of the past—fallen from the wrong he has done to himself. He so taxed his mental and physical resources—he so unduly taxed his life—that he was suddenly and prematurely cut down in his vigor. Because he did not live within the bounds of moderation, he left himself an easy captive to death.

* * * * * * * *

And now, my friends, he who is departed, his name will not be forgotten. His name will be cherished so long as his work lives and is remembered; but in the great thundering city, like as in the ocean, like one who has fallen overboard, the cry rings out, the simple fact is known, the ship moves on, the waves encircle him, and then all the ripples that showed the spot where he fell are rubbed out, and the ocean flows on and is no fuller than before. So, in this great city, life follows life. A prominent man dies in our midst; it is the voice on the ocean—a "man overboard;" but the next moment the great multitude will forget him and pass on. And thus the matter of importance to-day will be insignificant to-morrow. And you who are to-day in the springtime of life will pass away even like the noise of thunder that breaks over our heads and passes away. God grant that the scene of this solemn occasion may sink into your hearts, and make your life one that you can lay down here and take it up again, even beyond the grave, by beginning now a nobler, a manlier, and a purer life, which may God in his infinite blessing grant.

The course of the *Times*, subsequent to the death of its chief founder and chief editor, is of interest to the public and to journalism. Mr. George Jones, who had been the business partner and cherished friend of Mr. Raymond from the origin of the *Times*, assumed the entire management of the concern, and placed its old *attachés* over its several departments. It was thought necessary, however, to obtain the services of an experienced journalist to take Mr. Raymond's place. Mr. John Bigelow, formerly of the *Evening Post*, and more recently minister to France, was selected; but, as he had never managed a paper of the modern school, and as he had imbibed some peculiar notions on journalism that belonged even anterior to the present *Evening Post*, he did not make a brilliant success, and he resigned his position.

While Mr. Bigelow was editor-in-chief, one of the most important features connected with the famous gold speculation in New York in September, 1869, was the connection of the *Times* with the affair, innocently and guilelessly, but in such a way as to produce an effect, and show the great care necessary in the management of a leading organ of public opinion. It will be recollected that the names of

President Grant, Mrs. Grant, General Butterfield, A. R. Corbin, the brother-in-law of the President, Jay Gould, and James Fisk, Jr., were mixed up in the operations in Wall Street on this memorable occasion. Gold run up from 130 to 160 almost in as many minutes, and back again to the old price in a flash of the telegraph. Numerous failures and lawsuits were the result. It was stated that the transactions reached $300,000,000—of course, on honor and on paper. The speculation was so extraordinary in its character that Congress ordered an investigation, and took an immense amount of evidence, which will make a volume exceeding in interest any work of fiction extant. Jay Gould's testimony affecting the *New York Times* was as follows:

Question. You stated something in another part of your testimony concerning an editorial that was being prepared. Did you have any thing to do with the preparation of that editorial, and if so, what?
Answer. Mr. Corbin prepared an editorial, submitted it to me, and wanted my views of it. He said it embodied the policy of the administration. I looked it over very carefully, and it agreed with my views. Then he wanted me to get it in the papers. Mr. Bigelow was then the editor of the *Times*. I gave it to James M'Henry, and he had it put in.
Ques. Did it appear as it was prepared, or as you saw it?
Ans. It was changed slightly, but not substantially. This article said that the government would not sell gold while the crops were being moved.
Ques. Do you know whether the news of the fact that the Treasury was going to sell reached any body in New York before it was officially announced?
Ans. I guess every body knew it pretty nearly.
Ques. Do you know the fact that it did get to New York and was known before the official announcement of it?
Ans. I only know it from evidences of observation, which are very difficult to describe.
Ques. Repeating the same question, do you say yes or no?
Ans. I should not want to say either very positively.
Ques. From your knowledge of the transactions of that day, do you believe that it was known in New York that the Secretary of the Treasury had ordered the sale of gold before the official announcement of the fact?
Ans. Certainly.
Ques. How long before?
Ans. I think it was known an hour in advance.
Ques. What made gold break down?
Ans. It broke down because I was selling, and had been selling all the morning.
Ques. Did the Treasury order cause gold to break down?
Ans. No, sir.
Ques. Did it break before the order came?
Ans. Certainly.
Ques. Did it break before the order was known to be issued?
Ans. No; the announcement of the order had no effect on gold at all. Gold had been sold all the morning, and I expected the order would come.
Ques. How did you become satisfied in your own mind that the government was going to sell gold?
Ans. An editorial came out in the *New York Times* that morning which went on to state that parties interested in gold used very freely the name of the highest potentate in the land, his brother-in-law, the Secretary of the Treasury, etc. I understood that that editorial was written for the purpose of being telegraphed to Washington to frighten the officials down here, and that it would probably have the effect it did. I did not want any further information to come to me anyhow. That editorial led me to believe that the government would sell, and I acted accordingly. I sold all the morning.

The Chairman of the Congressional Committee, in his report, after stating the schemes of the speculators in part, said :

They therefore sought by a stratagem to make an impression to that effect on the public mind through the Press, and in this they came near being successful, as will presently appear. On the 15th of August, Mr. John Bigelow, editor of the *New York Times*, had an interview with the President, during which the financial condition and prospects of the country were discussed. The statements in two editorial articles, which appeared in the *Times* of August 6 and 7, were understood to represent the President's views, if they were not directly inspired by him. On the 19th of August the President again passed through New York, and immediately thereafter the conspirators sought to use the columns of the *Times* for the publication of an article which should appear to be a semi-official declaration of the financial policy of the administration, but which should have the effect to raise the price of gold, and thus aid their speculation. At the suggestion of Jay Gould, Mr. Corbin, on the 23d day of August, had completed an article (the manuscript text of which, in his own hand-writing, is in possession of the committee) in which it was declared to be the policy of the administration to advance the price of gold, and in which the transportation theory of Gould and Fisk was strongly advocated. This article was headed "Grant's Financial Policy." It was agreed that it should be published as a leading editorial, for only in that form could the purposes of its authors be accomplished. This delicate business was to be managed by Mr. Gould ; and, lest his personal application to the editor of the *Times* should carry with it a flavor of Wall Street, he secured the services of Mr. James M'Henry, a prominent English capitalist and personal friend of Mr. Bigelow, who called at the *Times* office and presented the article as the expression of a person in the intimate confidence of the President, and whose utterances were the faithful pictures of the President's mind. The article was put in type, and double leaded for a leading editorial ; but, on reading it over, suspicions were aroused, and the financial editor, Mr. Norvell, was sent for. He testified : "Not knowing where the article came from, yet, from whatever source it originated, I suspected there might be, from the statements of the last paragraph, a sinister purpose to bull gold, so the double leads were taken out, the tail of the article stricken off, and the article, as it appears, published on the 25th ; the intention, I have no doubt, was that it should appear just as much semi-official as the other article of the 6th of August, which Mr. Bigelow himself wrote after his interview with the President." The article as it was written, and the amended article as published, appear in parallel columns of Mr. Norvell's testimony. A comparison of the doctrines of the two will show how cunning was the fraud attempted.

On the 30th of August Mr. Gould addressed a letter to the Secretary of the Treasury, with the manifest purpose of drawing out a denial or admission that the article in the *Times* correctly reflected the financial policy of the administration for the next three or four months. This letter is made a part of Mr. Boutwell's testimony. The brief and formal reply of the secretary gave Gould no clew to the purposes of the government.

On the retirement of Mr. Bigelow, the position of managing editor was given to Mr. George Sheppard. He retired after a brief period, and after a short and sharp controversy with a contemporary. Mr. Jones then appointed Mr. L. J. Jennings as editor in chief, and that gentleman still holds that important position. Mr. Jennings had been connected with the *London Times*, and was for some time the correspondent of that paper in the United States.

The *New York Times*, towards the close of 1870, began to criticise, freely and independently, the financial management of the metropolis by the political leaders, who had formed a "ring" for the purpose of controlling the local government of New York. This combination was styled the "Tammany Ring." The *Times* was general in its remarks at first, as the comptroller had refused its reporters all access to his books. In addition to this annoyance, some threats had been uttered against that journal. In March, 1871, one of the city papers published the following paragraph:

> We are informed that negotiations are in progress for the sale of the *New York Times* to a company, in which Mr. Peter Cooper, Moses Taylor, Cyrus W. Field, A. Oakey Hall, James Fisk, Jr., Jay Gould, Peter B. Sweeny, and William M. Tweed are to be the principal stockholders. The present managers of the establishment will leave as soon as the purchase is concluded. The intention of those who propose to buy is to run the paper for the present ostensibly in the Republican interest; but as soon as the Hon. A. O'Hall has completed his term as mayor, he will become the editor, and then the political character of the concern will doubtless be changed. We learn, also, that the first overtures for this transaction were made by George Jones, through a third party, to Mr. Sweeny, about six months ago, but that the plan has not been entertained until recently.

This was too much for the manager of the *Times* to read with patience and resignation. He had too much spirit to submit to such a statement. On the 28th of March, the following manifesto, in reply, appeared in the *Times:*

> The above statement appears in a journal which is said to be controlled by the Tammany Ring.
> It is my duty to say that the assertion that I have ever offered to dispose of my property in the *Times* to Mr. Sweeny, or any body connected with him, or that I have ever entered into negotiations for that purpose, or am ever likely to do so, directly or indirectly, is a fabrication from beginning to end. I am aware that Mr. Nathaniel Sands, Secretary of the Citizens' Association, has been for some time actively engaged in the effort to purchase or otherwise silence this journal, in the interest of his Tammany employers. But, believing that the course which the *Times* is pursuing is that which the interests of the great body of the public demand, and that it would be a base betrayal of the public to turn aside from that course until an honest government and an incorruptible judiciary are restored to the community, no money that could be offered should induce me to dispose of a single share of my property to the Tammany faction, or to any man associated with it, or, indeed, to any person or party whatever, until this struggle is fought out. I have the same confidence in the integrity and firmness of my fellow-proprietors, and believe that they will decline to sell their honor to a corrupt clique at the instigation of "Republicans" who are as unprincipled as their employers.
> Rather than prove false to the public in the present crisis, I would, if necessity by any possibility arose, immediately start another journal to denounce those frauds upon the people which are so great a scandal to the city, and I should carry with me in this renewal of our present labors the colleagues who have already stood by me through a long and arduous contest. Even if the *Times* could be silenced by some fresh abuse of judicial authority, as I believe it can not be, it would not cause a week's cessation of the exposures which we are now making of the frauds committed by the "Ring." I have from the first number of the *Times* taken too active a part in its management, and feel far too deep a solicitude for its good name, to dishonor it by making it the advocate of mendacity and corruption. I pledge myself to persevere in the present contest, under all and any circumstances that may arise, through good report and evil report, in success or in failure; and even though the "Ring" and its friends offered me for my interest in the property as many millions of dollars as they annually plunder from the city funds, it would not change my purpose. This determination is, I have every reason to believe, fully shared by my co-proprietors, and by the staff who act with me in the paper. GEORGE JONES.

It was clear from this that although Mr. Jones was determined not to abate one jot or tittle the exposures he had commenced of the corruptions of the Tammany leaders, yet he was not certain of always having the *Times* ready to spread these corruptions before the people. But this point was settled on the 19th of July, 1871, and was thus announced:

> The shares in the *New York Times* attached to the Raymond estate, representing about one third of the property, were yesterday purchased by Mr. E. B. Morgan, of Aurora, Cayuga County. Mr. Morgan was an original stockholder, and has been for some time past one of the managing partners of the paper, in conjunction with Mr. George Jones, another of the original proprietors. These two gentlemen now hold eighty-two out of the hundred shares of stock in their own hands. It has been repeatedly asserted that the Raymond shares were likely to fall into the possession of the New York "Ring," and it is in order to assure our friends of the groundlessness of all such statements that we make known the actual facts. The price paid in ready money for the shares in question was $375,000. Down to the time of Mr. Raymond's death, the shares had never sold for more than $6000 each. Mr. Morgan has now paid upward of $11,000 each for thirty-four of them, and this transaction is the most conclusive answer which could be furnished to the absurd rumors sometimes circulated to the effect that the course taken by the *New York Times* toward the Tammany leaders had depreciated the value of the property.
>
> The public may feel assured that the *Times* will not swerve from the policy which it has long pursued, but that it will hereafter be more persistent than ever in its efforts to bring about those political reforms which the people require and expect.

The *Times* thus placed entirely under the control of two gentlemen of decided character and energy, the war against the "Tammany Ring" was carried on with the utmost vigor, and the end was the utter annihilation of the immense power the leaders of the "Ring" had acquired in the metropolis. The particulars of this extraordinary affair are too fresh on the public mind to need repeating here. There has been nothing equal to the result thus obtained in the history of journalism. The developments of the stupendous corruptions in the city government made by the *Times* aroused the indignation of the people through the length and breadth of the land. The gigantic increase of the public debt; the enormous wealth acquired in two or three years by a few men in office; the way the State Legislature was influenced, corrupted, and controlled, were fully exposed in the *Times*. It was boldly and fearlessly done by that paper, and Messrs. Jones and Morgan deserve well of their country. The only similar instance on record is that of the London *Times* in exposing, regardless of all risk, a well-laid plan for defrauding the bankers of Europe of immense sums of money by a "ring" of skillful and expert forgers. This exposure led to a vexatious and costly libel suit. The merchants and bankers of London, in appreciation of the great and important service thus rendered them, subscribed a large sum to reimburse the journalists for the costs incurred. The proprietor of the London *Times* very properly refused the money. He had simply done his duty to the public. The subscribers to the fund thereupon decided to appropriate the amount in a testimonial to that influential journal. It was divided into four parts: one paid for a mural slab inserted in the principal room of the Exchange in London, bearing a suitable inscription; another was paid for a similar slab, and placed in the office of the *Times;* the remaining two parts established two scholarships, always to be known as the *Times* scholarships, at Oxford and Cambridge; and thus journalism, in its highest state of usefulness and value in the community, was fully and appropriately recognized and rewarded.

If the merchants and bankers of the English metropolis thus appreciated the service rendered by the London *Times*, how should the taxpayers of the American metropolis recognize that rendered by the *New York Times* to them, and, indeed, to the entire community? Is it not made clear by these statements that the Press is the real palladium of the rights and interests of the public? that the Press is, in fact, no longer the Fourth Estate, but the first and the highest in the land? that, with a free and independent Press, there is safety for the people from the corruptions and machinations of political leaders and office-holders?

The effect of the developments made in the *Times* was seen at the polls throughout the state at the November elections. Instead of electing every candidate by overwhelming majorities, as had been the usual custom of the metropolis, only two or three of the Tammany nominations succeeded; and the change in the popular vote on the state ticket, which was divested as far as possible of the corrupt influence, is an indication of this power of the newspaper when properly wielded.

	Tammany.	Anti-Tammany.
Vote in New York City, 1870	86,668	34,391
" " " 1871	83,326	54,137
Vote in New York State, 1870	399,532	366,436
" " " 1871	368,204	387,107

This is a revolution of 23,000 votes in the city, and nearly 52,000 in the state. But the revolution in the metropolis was much more thorough than these figures indicate. On the local tickets the popular vote was as follows:

	Tammany.	Anti-Tammany.
For Judge of Supreme Court	45,916	89,127
" " Superior Court	56,885	80,424
" Register	54,448	82,565

The Tammany majority in the city in 1870 was 52,277. The Anti-Tammany majority in 1871 was, on the Supreme Court ticket, 43,211. Popular change in one year, 95,488 votes—one of the most wonderful political revolutions on record!

In its annual announcement for 1872 the *Times* said:

This journal is now thoroughly identified with the greatest political necessity of the hour—uncompromising warfare against all forms of corruption, whether in national or local government. For years past the *Times* has been exposing the demoralizing schemes of self-interested politicians, and its recent warfare upon the Tammany Democrats has been received with universal approval. * * * * They purpose that the *Times* shall continue to keep clear of all narrow and unworthy influences and cliques, and aim to represent the great body of the public as distinguished from personal factions. It occupies a perfectly independent position, and is free to speak the truth on all subjects and about all men. Its greatly-increased circulation throughout the country adds to its power and influence. It will continue to be a faithful exponent of Republican principles, and advocate with untiring energy every cause which tends to further the welfare of the people.

This is twenty years' history of the *New York Times*.

CHAPTER XL.

THE NEW YORK LEDGER.

ITS ORIGIN.—ITS FIRST NAME.—WHY BONNER BOUGHT IT.—HOW HE BROUGHT IT INTO NOTICE.—MRS. SIGOURNEY THE FIRST CONTRIBUTOR.—WHO WRITES FOR THE LEDGER?—BONNER'S ADVERTISEMENTS.—HOW HE MANAGED THE HERALD.—HIS SYSTEM.—ANXIETY OF HIS PASTOR.—NOVELS BY TELEGRAPH. — INTERESTING INCIDENT. — CORRESPONDENCE WITH GENERAL GRANT AND HENRY WARD BEECHER.—HIS HORSES.—HIS COUNTRY SEAT AND THE FEVER AND AGUE.—CIRCULATION.

WHAT is in a name? Is that of the *New York Ledger* a suitable one for such a paper? The *Public Ledger* of Philadelphia is appropriately named, because it keeps the public posted in the affairs of the world. The *Herald* is a good name for a newspaper as the harbinger of the tidings of the day to every one. The *Times* is excellent, because it is "the embodiment of the times." The *Journal of Commerce* and the *Commercial Bulletin* are capital titles for purely commercial sheets. The *Daily Advertiser* is good for a paper devoted to business notices. The *Post* is not a bad name if, as with the *Ledger*, all are correctly posted therein. The *Intelligencer* is not an inappropriate name; nor is the *Sun* for a morning paper; nor are the *Dispatch*, the *Express*, the *Telegram*, in bad taste. The *News* is the name for a paper that always gives the latest intelligence. Such names as the *Tribune*, the *World*, the *Opinion*, the *Record*, the *Nation*, the *Commonwealth*, are after the style of the French. There are the *Opinion Nationale*, the *Monde*, the *France*, the *Peuple*, published in Paris.

It is only since the Revolution of '76 that new names have been given to newspapers. The old titles of *Gazette*, *News-Letter*, and *Mercury*, which run through previous generations, were only varied by the names of the places where they were printed, and the artistic devices which adorned the first page. Now, in addition to the *Herald*, *Journal*, *Tribune*, *Times*, *Sun*, *World*, *Traveller*, and *Star*, which are in the nineteenth century, we find such curious names as the following list exhibits:

Iowa Hawkeye.	*The Daily Lever.*
The Billet Doux.	*The Artery.*
Corn-stalk Fiddle.	*Our Society.*
St. Louis Picket Guard.	*Nashville Orthopolitan.*
Presque Isle Sunrise.	*The Coon-skinner.*
The Election Bell.	*The Eye of Mississippi.*

The Mutual Alliance.
The Gimlet.
Anti-monopolist.
Mountain Warrior.
Territorial Enterprise.
Seaside Oracle.
Round Table.
Hickory-nut.
The Live Giraffe.
Kettle-drum.
Helping Hand.
Warning Words.
Evening Caterwaul.
Established Fact.
Pontiac Bill-poster.
Frontier Index.
Wabashaw, or *Red-headed Herald.*
Iberia (La.) *Sugar-bowl.*
Tattler.
Run and Read.
Aurora.
The Sand-piper.
Examiner.
The Bazoo.
Truth-teller.
Transcript.
Boston Notion.
Arcturus.
Corsair.

Bartram's Cheek.
Copperhead.
The Moonly Voice.
The Paper.
Tidal Wave.
Citizen.
Billiard Cue.
Cosmopolite.
Head Light.
Hawkeye.
Lean Wolf.
Town and Stage.
Rough-hewer.
Interior.
Ultra Ku-klux.
Common Sense.
Evening Signal.
Planet.
Autograph and Remarker.
Plaindealer.
Day-book.
Plebeian.
The Yankee.
Calumet.
Picayune.
Subterranean.
Iron Age.
Log Cabin.

Some of these names indicated the object of the publication. Some were merely campaign papers, intended only for a presidential election. The *Log Cabin,* Whig, for instance, in 1840; and the *Corn-stalk Fiddle,* also Whig, and the *Coon-skinner,* Democratic, in 1842.

But it is the *New York Ledger* that we have to speak of here. Its inappropriate name led us off on this digression. *Mais revenons.*

The *New York Ledger* was originally called the *Merchants' Ledger.* It was devoted to mercantile affairs previous to 1851, largely, we believe, to the dry goods interest, and had less than three thousand circulation. Our researches produced an unpresuming and unimpressive advertisement of the paper as it appeared before its name and character were modified or changed—an advertisement as unlike the recent monster ones of Bonner as the "tall and pillared Alleghany" is unlike the Observatory Hill in Central Park.

It was originally started by an ex-merchant, who conceived the idea of making a paper that would interest country merchants. It was purchased by Robert Bonner in 1851. Bonner at that time owned a small printing-office, in which he set up the type of the *Ledger,* and of one or two other small papers. He had been a practical printer in the office of the *Hartford Courant,* and a proof-reader of the *Evening Mirror.* It appears that the first proprietor of the *Ledger* had invented a printing-press which he thought would super-

sede Hoe's lightning machines, and wished to devote his whole time
and attention to its development, for with success there was a fortune. With an eye to the main chance, Bonner did not like to lose
the weekly job of setting the type of the *Ledger*, and this, as much
as any other reason, induced him to purchase the paper. "There
is a tide," it seems, with printers as well as with politicians and other
patriots.

This is the way Bonner became a newspaper proprietor and the
owner of Dexter.

Having secured the establishment, he scarcely knew what to do
with it ; but, not being desirous of publishing a purely class paper
of limited circulation, he gradually dropped its mercantile features,
and substituted family reading matter for the quotations of flour, and
bank-note tables and reports. This increased the circulation somewhat, which encouraged the new proprietor, who was a man of common sense and tact. It then occurred to him that he might branch
out a little. He therefore, in 1853, engaged Mrs. Sigourney to write
for his paper, and she continued to be a contributor till the day of
her death. She was the first to "write for the *Ledger*." Two years
later, or in 1855, feeling still more encouraged, he made arrangements with Fanny Fern, who had acquired quite a reputation in her
peculiar style. Then the new journalistic star made a brilliant dash
in publishing her famous "one hundred dollars a column" story.
This created a sensation, caused the news-dealers to seek the paper, and the *New York Ledger* began its prosperous career.

Stronger and stronger intellectually and financially, Mr. Bonner
expanded his literary enterprises till he embraced all the leading
writers of the day : Everett, Bancroft, Bryant, Beecher, Bennett, Greeley, Raymond, Dickens, Fitz-Greene Halleck, Mrs. Southworth, Mrs.
Harriet Beecher Stowe, Alice Cary, and George D. Prentice. No
less than twelve college presidents, and a dozen bishops, clergymen,
and deacons, wrote regularly for the *Ledger*.

After Fanny Fern's "one hundred dollars a column" story had
produced its effect on the public mind, Mr. Bonner was prepared
with another literary wonder. About this time an immense effort
was being made to purchase Mount Vernon by public subscription.
Edward Everett, full of patriotism and brains, lent his powerful aid
to this object, and he visited every part of the country, delivering
his famous lecture on Washington to swell up the sum to the necessary amount. It is said that he uttered this eulogy on Washington over two hundred times without changing a word or altering a
line. It was considered one of the most finished and masterly productions of the age. It was at this period "in the affairs of men"
that Mr. Bonner made an offer of $10,000 to Mr. Everett for a series

of short articles to be called the "Mount Vernon Papers." After some hesitation, Mr. Everett accepted the offer, and devoted the money to the Mount Vernon Fund; and he continued ever after, till his death, a constant contributor to the *Ledger*, and a warm friend of its proprietor. It was the most brilliant success of all of Bonner's efforts.

Meanwhile it became necessary to let the public know of these wonderful intellectual feats of Bonner. How was this to be done? Only by making use of the other papers. Then began the system of advertising that became continental in practice and world-wide in fame. Single columns would at first be occupied; then half a page; then an entire page; then all the available space any leading newspaper would let him have, with what appeared a reckless disregard to cost, economy, or common sense. The repetition system of advertisements, which has since become so common, originated with Bonner in the *New York Herald*. One day he desired to have his advertisement displayed. Mr. Bennett objected to any display; he had very sensibly discarded pictures and displayed advertisements in the *Herald*, and Mr. Bonner must come under the rule.

"What are your rules?" asked the indomitable Bonner.

On being informed what they were, he had his notices repeated *ad infinitum*. This was objected to after one or two insertions.

"What do you want now?" again asked the irrepressible Bonner.

"Not so much display," replied the sagacious proprietor of the *Herald*.

"Very well," said Bonner; and he had published one sentence, announcing a new story, and ordered it to be repeated to fill an entire column, all to be "run in," professionally speaking, with no blank lines — all, indeed, in one solid paragraph. What was the result? It was the most conspicuous advertisement in the *Herald* that morning.

"How do you like that?" asked Bonner the next day. Mr. Bennett laughed and said,

"Well, I guess we had better let you have your own way hereafter."

The proprietor of the *Ledger* has paid as high as $27,000 for one week's advertising; he has paid $150,000 in one year; yet, strange to say, not an advertisement is inserted in the *Ledger*, and no money will obtain the insertion of one. He once paid the *Herald* $2000 for a single advertisement, and Mr. Bennett was compelled to issue a quadruple sheet to accommodate his enterprising neighbor. This was in 1858, and was the first sheet of this size ever issued in America. It was a *Ledger-Herald*, or *vice versa*. When this advertisement appeared, the good pastor of the church where Mr. Bonner and family attended became very much agitated. On looking over the *Herald* that morning at his breakfast-table, he said to his wife,

"I must call upon Mr. Bonner immediately after breakfast; I am really anxious about him."

"Why, what is the matter? Is he sick?"

"I don't know that he is sick," replied the kind-hearted clergyman, "but I think he must be insane. Just look at the *Herald;* it is Bonner on every page. If he has paid for that he will be ruined. Give me my hat."

Mr. Bonner was surprised at an early call from his spiritual adviser.

"I have called," said the clergyman, "to talk with you about the advertisement, or, rather, series of advertisements which appeared in the *Herald* this morning. May I ask if you paid the regular rates for them?"

"I gave my check for $2000 for a single insertion," coolly answered Bonner.

The clergyman, with a deep sigh, wiped his forehead with his handkerchief.

"Two thousand dollars! two thousand dollars!"

After a moment's reflection, as if overcome with the magnitude of the sum thus recklessly thrown away, he said,

"Mr. Bonner, I have called upon you as a friend: You know that I am one. I felt that there was something wrong. What a waste of money! Two thousand dollars for one publication of one advertisement? Would not a single square, like that, for instance," pointing out a ten-line advertisement—"would not that, at a cost of three or four dollars, have answered your purpose as well as all that display and costly space?"

Much amused at the perplexity of his amiable pastor, Mr. Bonner, in reply, said,

"I see how it strikes you, my good friend. But if I had put in the single square you mention, would you have taken the trouble to call upon me to remonstrate? Would you have even noticed my advertisement from any of the others in the paper?"

"Why, no, I don't think I should have noticed the matter at all."

"Then," said Mr. Bonner, triumphantly, "you have demonstrated the correctness of my policy. Every other reader of the *Herald* is as much astonished as you are. This is the secret of advertising. Eureka!"

Alive to the intellectual needs of his paper, he conceived the idea of having the three lions of the Daily Press in New York—Bennett, Greeley, and Raymond—write for the *Ledger*. He accomplished this, and the public were astonished with advertisements in all the papers that they would each contribute an original article; and they did, and the productions appeared in the same number of the *Ledger*. This gave him considerable *éclat*, and created a sensation. Then he induced twelve distinguished clergymen to write twelve stories. Afterwards he obtained as many contributions from twelve presidents of colleges. Then Horace Greeley's Autobiography was a feature. Norwood, a novel, by Henry Ward Beecher, costing $20,000, had its famous run. The Life of General Grant, by his father, Jesse Grant, not only sold thousands of the *Ledger*, but obtained as many votes for the general for the presidency. Its peculiar incidents and style made it a first-class campaign document. It took with the masses. After this manner Bonner met the wants, and tastes, and feelings of the different classes of the reading community.

When the first Atlantic cable was being laid by the Niagara and Agamemnon, it was contemplated by Bonner to have a short original story, written by Charles Dickens, sent by telegraph across the ocean to the *Ledger*, like a regular news dispatch to the *Herald* or *Times*. The failure of that cable prevented the scheme from being carried into effect; but a story was written about that time by Dickens for which Bonner paid $5000. It was this idea that no doubt suggested to the *Pall Mall Gazette*, of London, the costly telegram of the introductory chapter of Mrs. Harriet Beecher Stowe's rejoinder in the famous Byron slander.

If the *Ledger* has not yet produced any new writers, it has been the means of developing the talents and genius of many on both sides of the Atlantic. Sylvanus Cobb has been its most prolific contributor. He was employed on *Gleason's Pictorial* before he wrote for the *Ledger*. "The Gunmaker of Moscow," written by him, had a "great run," as they say on the play-bills. Mrs. Southworth's "Island Princess" and "Hidden Hand" were also popular, and increased the circulation of the paper. Leon Lewis, and his wife, Harriet Lewis, are both employed exclusively on the *Ledger*. She wrote "The Double Life," and he produced "Kit Carson's Last Trail," the best Indian story, it is averred, since the days of Fenimore Cooper. How ample the editorial basket must be to hold the discarded manuscripts of such an establishment!

Among the recent writers are Miss Dupuy, Mrs. Dallas, Mrs. Ethel Lynn Beers, John G. Saxe, James Parton, Professor Wm. Henry Peck, and Judge Clarke. Immense sums are paid for the reading matter of the paper. If any thing is worth publishing, it is worth paying for. Of course, the revenue is commensurate. The income tax returns, that fickle barometer of the wealth of America, place Mr. Bonner high on the scale of millionaires.

One feature in the character of the proprietor of the *Ledger* is his originality. It has enabled him to give his paper a position of its own. When he appears in public, whether behind Dexter and Peerless, or in an advertisement offering the *Ledger* or his country seat for sale, he attracts attention. Worn down with fatigue, he purchased a farm near the metropolis, where he intended to recuperate, and give himself and family the advantages of fresh air. After residing there for two or three seasons, the following advertisement made its appearance in the papers:

A COUNTRY SEAT FOR SALE WHERE THERE IS FEVER AND AGUE.

I hereby offer for sale my country residence at West Morrisania, near Melrose Station, where I have lived for the past three summers, but do not think I could live much longer. I have heard that people looking for a place to purchase could never find one where they have chills and fever; they always have it about a mile, a mile and a half, or two miles off, but never right there, at the place that is for sale. Now I offer for sale a curiosity—something rare—the precise, exact spot where the fever and ague is. I will warrant it to be there. Three of my children have it; my gardener has it; my groom has the sure premonitory symptoms; and I have a sufficient inkling of it myself. Any doctor, with a large family, who has a specific for fever and ague, would find this a most eligible situation. The neighborhood is full of the disease, and if he could keep it out of his own family it would give him a reputation which would insure his fortune. Besides the fever and ague, the estate consists of a fine double house, with all modern conveniences and improvements, such as hot and cold water, furnace, range, etc., and about two acres of land, with a pretty fair barn, and some good box-stalls for good horses. It is really a beautiful place; the grounds are handsomely laid out, and covered with trees and shrubbery of the choicest kind. These trees afford not only a delightful shade, but a nice harbor for musquitoes. The musquitoes, thus far, have not been so much affected by the fever and ague as to prevent their biting—in fact, it is a good place for musquitoes. I bought it for my wife, and shall leave it to please my whole family. Terms, cash. I am afraid any security on it would get the fever and ague and become shaky. Those wishing to purchase will please apply immediately. I want to get away from it as fast as Dexter can carry me. ROBERT BONNER.

Ledger Office, No. 90 Beekman Street, September 18, 1867.

P.S.—The town authorities have begun to make alterations in the street adjoining, and if they drain the place as well as they do the pockets of the landholders, it may become healthy.

When President Grant got into trouble with the gold-dealers of Wall and Broad Streets, in the memorable gold-gambling operations of September, 1869, Bonner came to the rescue, and caused any amount of envy and jealousy in the other newspaper offices of New York by the following correspondence, which appeared in almost every journal in the land:

EDITOR BONNER TO PRESIDENT GRANT.

Office of the *Ledger*, corner of Spruce and William Streets,
NEW YORK, October 11, 1869.

MY DEAR GENERAL,—As I stated to you immediately after your election that there was no office which I desired either for myself or any friend, I have had no occasion to write to you in regard to such matters. There is a matter now, however, that concerns you personally, and in which I feel that I discern your interest so plainly that I take the liberty to write to you with reference to it. I do this with less hesitation, because you did me the honor, after your election, to confide to me pretty fully your views. In the present disturbed state of the public mind concerning the recent gold combination, is it not the quickest and surest way to set at rest the great excitement and uneasiness which prevail for you to make a

brief denial over your own signature of all foreknowledge of that combination, in order to relieve yourself entirely from all responsibility for the acts of others? Of course, those who know you personally do not require such a disclaimer; but the great public, whose minds are liable to be warped by the determined and persistent efforts to injure you, will be, it seems to me, at once satisfied and quieted by such a statement.   Sincerely yours,   ROBERT BONNER.
President GRANT.

PRESIDENT GRANT TO EDITOR BONNER.

WASHINGTON, D.C., October 13, 1869.
Robert Bonner, Esq.:
DEAR SIR,—Your favor of the 11th inst. is received. I have never thought of contradicting statements or insinuations made against me by irresponsible parties, as those are alluded to in your letter; but as you have written to me on the subject in so kind a spirit, I will say that I had no more to do with the late gold excitement in New York City than yourself, or any other innocent party, except that I ordered the sale of gold to break the ring engaged, as I thought, in a most disreputable transaction. If the speculators had been successful, you would never have heard of any one connected with the administration as being connected with the transaction.   Yours truly,   U. S. GRANT.

P.S.—I have written this in great haste, and without exercising judgment as to the propriety of writing it, but I submit it to your judgment.   U. S. G.

So, too, with the *cause célèbre* of M'Farland and Richardson. Bonner saw that his *protégé*, Henry Ward Beecher, had made a mistake, and he therefore saved him by giving the Plymouth pastor an opportunity to free himself by open confession. This was neatly done in this way, and it "went the rounds" of the Press. Bonner took infinite pleasure in doing these kind acts.

MR. BONNER TO MR. BEECHER.

Office of the *Ledger*, NEW YORK, December 11, 1869.
MY DEAR MR. BEECHER,—According to the corrected report in the *Tribune* of your remarks at the Astor House, you seem to charge M'Farland with the only offense which is a scriptural ground for divorce. His friends most emphatically deny the truth of such a charge. From many years' intimate acquaintance with you, I know you to be incapable of an act of intentional injustice towards any one, especially towards a man about to be tried for his life. If, in the haste and excitement of the occasion, you took this statement without time to investigate it, on mere hearsay evidence, and without any legal proof to sustain it, is it not a plain matter of duty on your part towards the accused to come out and say so publicly? I never saw M'Farland in my life—never expect to see him; but I know that you would be as unwilling as I to be the cause of any unjust prejudice against him at the time of his trial. I know, in common with your other friends, that if you have been misled in regard to any one circumstance, it is owing to the warmth and readiness of your sympathy for suffering, however caused, even if by a man's own sins.   Your friend,   ROBERT BONNER.

MR. BEECHER'S REPLY

BROOKLYN, December 11, 1869.
MY DEAR MR. BONNER,—I took every statement of every kind respecting the affair of which you write me "without time to investigate." The man was dying. Was that a time for sifting evidence? What was to be done must be done quickly. I asked only such things as should determine whether I had a right to go forward. It was for my own sake, therefore, that I hastily inquired, and not to inculpate or to exculpate any one.

But as you now call my attention to the fact that what I did for my own justification is hanging over M'Farland to his injury, and tends to forestall a verdict against him, I agree with you that I ought not to let it remain uncorrected. I should be as unwilling to do an act of injustice towards him as towards any one else. Concurring, therefore, with you, that it is now due to M'Farland for me to state that I know of no legal proof against him on that point, I do so unhesitatingly. At the time that I stated what I did, I thought of its relation only to other parties. I did not dream of its bearing upon M'Farland.

I am truly yours,   HENRY WARD BEECHER.

This journalist, who has accomplished so much, has another hobby besides the *Ledger*. He rides two. The second is the horse. No man has spent so much money, nor devoted so much study to this noble animal as Bonner. It is estimated that the horses in his stables are worth $150,000. He would not take that money for them. They are the fastest in the country. They are splendid in every point of view. No other man better understands the diseases of the animal, especially of the feet, so important to keep in order in a horse. No veterinary surgeon can excel him in this knowledge. He was lately asked which he enjoyed the most, the *Ledger* or Dexter?

"That is difficult to answer," he said. "One is business, the other pleasure: I enjoy both. Some people are silly enough to think that I bought Dexter as an advertisement. I bought him because I wanted to beat Commodore Vanderbilt and to have the fastest horse in the world."

"But you do some things partly as an advertisement?" interrogated his friend.

"I never engaged a writer, or bought any thing, or did any thing as an advertisement. What I have done has been natural to me, and because I wanted to do them, but never was the impelling motive the notoriety that was likely to follow. When I want advertisements I pay for them as advertisements."

Whether these matters of pleasure and taste, as affecting his business, were the impelling motives or not, it is manifest that what such a man does invariably attracts general attention, and tends to the same result as if he really did buy Dexter or write to the President as a means to notoriety. It is clear, however, that if the *Ledger* was not a good paper, and worth its subscription price, all the Dexters in Christendom would not make it the great success it has proved to be. It has a circulation of nearly four hundred thousand. This, we believe, is confined almost wholly to the United States and Canada. One news company—the American—takes all, except what are called the mail subscribers, which go direct from the office of publication. That company takes weekly nearly three hundred and fifty thousand copies, and pays cash for them. About fifty thousand are sent by mail. Forty thousand copies go to Boston, twenty five thousand to Philadelphia, twelve thousand to Baltimore, seven thousand to St. Louis, six thousand to Providence, and so on throughout the country.

The *Ledger*, like many other prosperous and wealthy newspaper establishments in New York, Boston, Baltimore, Philadelphia, Chicago, and New Orleans, has a building of its own. It is constructed of marble, and is a palace in appearance, and comfort, and convenience. Its press-room is said to be one of the finest in the country. It has eight drum cylinder presses—four of Hoe's and four of Taylor's—and an Andrews engine.

Thus the *Ledger* stands superior in the periodical and news literature of America, and, with increased wealth, will do much towards developing the fresh, robust, and prolific intellect of the New World. *En avant.*

CHAPTER XLI.
THE PRESS CLUBS AND ASSOCIATIONS.

ORIGIN OF THE PRESS CLUB OF NEW YORK.—KOSSUTH'S RECEPTION AND SPEECH.—THE DICKENS BANQUET.—SPEECHES OF GREELEY, DICKENS, RAYMOND, CURTIS, AND HAWLEY.—THE PRESS SOCIAL ASSOCIATIONS.— WHAT THEY DO.—NO CONNECTION WITH THE NEWS ASSOCIATIONS.

ONE Saturday evening in the month of November, in 1851, there was a gathering of journalists at the Astor House in New York, to see what the Press should do in recognition of Kossuth, who was then flashing over the country like a meteor. Kossuth had been an editor in Hungary. He had been a lawyer, a politician, a patriot, a statesman. He had been fêted by each of these classes and professions. It was therefore considered to be the duty of the Press also to fête him as an editor. These journalists met at the Astor House for this purpose. Three gentlemen, Parke Godwin, of the *Evening Post*, Henry J. Raymond, of the *Times*, and one of the editors of the *Herald*, were selected as a Committee of Arrangements. It was decided to give the distinguished Magyar a dinner.

The banquet took place at the Astor House on the 13th of December, 1851. It was a splendid affair. Speeches were made, and Kossuth, as usual, uttered a brilliant one. The Press were delighted. William Cullen Bryant, of the *Evening Post*, presided. George Bancroft, the historian, made some remarks, concluding with the sentiment,

The American Press—it is responsible for the liberties of mankind.

That part of Kossuth's speech respecting the Press, and its power and influence, we give:

* * * * I address you with joy, because, conscious of the immensity of the power which you wield, it is natural to feel some awe in addressing those in whose hands the success or the failure of our hopes is placed. Still, I equally know that in your hands, gentlemen, the independent republican Press is a weapon, but a weapon to defend truth and justice, and not to offend. It is no screen to hide, no snuffers to extinguish the light, but a torch lit at the fire of immortality, a spark of which is glistening in every man's soul, to prove its divine origin; a torch which you wield loftily and high, to spread light with it to the most lonely regions of humanity. And as the cause of my country is the cause of justice and truth, as it has in no respect to fear light, but rather wants nothing but light to see secured to it the support and protection of every friend of freedom, of every noble-minded man, these are the reasons why I address you with joy, gentlemen—the more with joy, because, though it is sorrowful to see that ill-willed misrepresentations or secret Austrian intrigues, distorting plain, open history to a tissue of falsehood and lies, know how to find their way even to a small, insignificant part

of the American Press, still I am proud and happy to see that the immense majority of the American Press not only proved inaccessible to these venomous intrigues, but, conscious of the noble vocation of an independent Press, and yielding to the generous inclination of freemen, of protecting truth and justice against the dark plots of tyranny, has, without any interference on my part, come forth to protect the sacred cause of Hungary. The independent Press of this great republic has in this very case also proved to the world that even against the mischievous power of calumnies the most efficient protection is the freedom of the Press, and not preventive measures, condemning human intellect to eternal minority. I address you, gentlemen, the more with joy, because through you I have the invaluable benefit to address the whole university of the great, glorious, and free people of the United States. That is a great word, gentlemen, and yet it is literally true. While, eighty years ago, immortal Franklin's own press was almost the only one in the colonies, now there are over three thousand newspapers in the United States, having a circulation of five millions of copies, and amounting in their yearly circulation to the prodigious number of nearly four and a half hundred millions; every grown man in the Union reads on the average two newspapers a week, and one hundred and five copies a year; nearly eighteen copies fall, in the proportion to the population, to every human being in the Union, man, woman, and child. I am told that the journals of New York State alone exceed in number those of all the rest of the world beyond your great Union, and the circulation of the newspapers of this city alone nearly exceeds those of the whole empire of Great Britain. But there is yet one particularly remarkable fact which I can not forbear to mention, gentlemen. I boldly declare that beyond the United States there exists scarcely a practical freedom of the Press—at least in Europe, not except perhaps Norway, of whose condition, in that respect, I am not quite aware. You know, gentlemen, how the Press is fettered throughout the European continent—even, for the present, in France itself, whose great nation, by a strange fate, sees, under a nominally republican but centralized government, all the glorious fruits of their great and victorious revolutions wasting between the blasting fingers of centralized administrative and legislative omnipotence. You know how the independent Press of France is murdered by imprisonment of their editors and by fees; you know how the present government of France feels unable to bear the force of public opinion, so much that in the French republic the very legitimate shout of "*Vive la République*" has almost become a crime. This very circumstance is sufficient to prove that in that glorious land, where the warm and noble heart of the French nation throbs with self-confidence and noble pride, a new revolution is an unavoidable necessity. It is a mournful view which the great French nation now presents, but it is also an efficient warning against the propensities of centralization, inconsistent with freedom, become inconsistent with self-government, and it is also a source of hope for the European continent, because we know that things in France can not endure thus as they are; we know that to become a true republic is a necessity for France, and thus we know also that whoever be the man who in the approaching crisis will be honored by the confidence of the French nation, he will, he must be faithful to that grand principle of fraternity towards the other nations, which, being announced by the French Constitution to the world, raised such encouraging but bitterly disappointed expectations through Europe's oppressed continent. But it is chiefly, almost only Great Britain in Europe which boasts to have a free Press, and to be sure, during my brief stay in England, I joyfully saw that really there is a freedom to print, almost an unlimited one, so far that I saw printed advertisements spread at every corner, and signed by the publishers, stating that Queen Victoria is no lawful queen; that she ought to be sent to the Tower, and all those who rule ought to be hanged. Men laughed, and nobody cared about the foolish extravagancy. And yet I dare say, and I hope the generous people of Great Britain will not feel offended at my stating the fact, that there is no practical freedom of the Press. The freedom of the Press, to be a practical one, must be a common benefit to all, else it is no freedom, but a privilege. It is wanting two ingredients—freedom of printing and freedom of reading. Now there is no freedom of reading there, because there is no possibility for the people at large to do so—because the circulation of newspapers, the indispensable moral food of human intellect, is, by a heavy taxation, checked. The Press is a source of public revenue, and by the incumbrance of stamp and paper duties, made almost inaccessible to the poor. Hence it is that the newspapers in the United States are only one tenth, and in some cases one twentieth the price of English or French papers, and hence, again, is the immense difference in their circulation. In the United States several of the daily papers every morning reaching from thirty to forty thousand readers, whereas the *London Times* is considered to be a monster power because it has a circulation of from twenty-five to thirty thousand copies, of which I was told during my stay in England that the good, generous sense of the people has abated some six thousand copies in consequence of its foul hostility to the just and sacred cause of Hungary. Such being the condition of your Press, gentlemen, it must, of course, be a high source of joyful gratification to me to have the honor to address you, gentlemen, because in addressing you I really address the whole people of the United States—not only a whole people, but a whole intelligent people, gentlemen. That is the highest praise which can upon a people be bestowed, and yet it is no praise—it is the acknowledgment of a real fact. The very immensity of the circulation of your journals proves it to be so, because this immense circulation is not only due to that constitutional right of yours to speak and print freely your opinions; it is not only due to the cheap price which makes your Press a common benefit to all, and not a privilege to the rich, but it is chiefly due to the universality of public instruction, which enables every citizen to read. It is a glorious thing to know that this flourishing young city alone, where streets of splendid buildings proudly stand, where a few years ago the river spread its waves, or the plow tilled, nearly one hundred thousand children receive public education annually. Do you know, gentlemen, where I consider the most glorious monuments of your country? If it be so as I have read it once, it is that fact that when, in the steps of your wandering squatters, your engineers go on to draw geometrical lines, even in the territories where the sound of a human step never yet has mixed with the murmurs by which virginal nature is adoring the Lord—in every place marked to become a township, on every sixteenth square, you place a modest pole, with the glorious mark, "Popular Education Stock." This is your proudest monument. However, be this really the case or not, in every case, in my opinion, it is not your geographical situation, not your material power, not the bold, enterprising spirit of your people which I consider to be the chief guarantee of your country's future, but the universality of education; because an intelligent people never can consent not to be free. You will be always willing to be free, and you are great and powerful enough to be so good as your will. My humble prayers to benefit my country's cause I must so address to the public opinion of the whole intelligent people of the United States. You are the mighty engineers of this sovereign power upon which rest my country's hopes; it must be, therefore, highly gratifying to me to see, not isolated men, but the powerful complete of the great word "PRESS" granting me this important manifestation of generous sentiments and of sympathy; still I address you with fear, gentlemen, because you are aware that since my arrival here I had the great honor and valuable benefit to see my whole time agreeably occupied by the reception of the most noble manifestations of public sympathy, so much that it became entirely impossible for me to be thus prepared to address you, gentlemen, in a language which I but very imperfectly speak, as the great importance of this occasion would have required, and my high regards for yourselves had pointed out as a duty to me. However, I hope you will take this very circumstance for a motive of excuse. You will generously consider that whenever and wherever I publicly speak, it is always chiefly spoken to the Press; and, lowering your expectations to the humility of my abilities, and to the level of the principal difficulties of my situation, you will feel inclined to some kind indulgence for me, were it only out of brotherly generosity for one of your professional colleagues, as I profess to be one. Yes, gentlemen, it is a proud recollection of my life that I commenced my public career in the humble capacity of a journalist. And in that respect I may perhaps be somewhat entitled to your brotherly indulgence, as you, in the happy condition which the institutions of your country insure to you, can have not even an idea of the tortures of a journalist who has to write with fettered hands, and who is more than fettered by an Austrian arbitrary preventive censorship. You have no idea what a torture it is to sit down to your writing-desk, the breast full of the necessity of the moment, the heart full of righteous feelings, the mind full of convictions and of principles, and all this warmed by the lively fire of a patriot's heart, and to see before your eyes the scissors of the censor ready to fall upon your head like the sword of Damocles, lopping your ideas, maiming your arguments, murdering your thoughts; and his pencil before your eyes, ready to blot out, with a single draught, the work of your laborious days and of your sleepless nights; and to know that the people will judge you, not by what you have felt, thought, and written, but by what the censor wills; to know that the ground upon which you stand is not a ground known to you, because limited by rules, but an unknown, slippery ground, the limits of which lie but within the arbitrary pleasure of your censor, doomed by profession to be stupid, and a coward, and a fool; to know all this, and yet not to curse your destiny, not to deny that you know to read and to write, but to go on, day by day, in the torturing work of Sisyphus.—oh! it is the greatest sacrifice which an intelligent man can make to fatherland and humanity. And this is the present condition of the Press, not in Hungary only, but in all countries cursed by Austrian rule. Our past revolution gave freedom to the Press not only in my fatherland, but by indirect influence also to Vienna, Prague, Lemberg—in a word, to the whole empire of Austria. This very circumstance must be sufficient to insure your sympathy to my country's cause, as, on the contrary, the very circumstance that the victory of the Hapsburgian dynasty, achieved by treason and Russian arms, was a watchword to oppress the Press in Hungary, in Austria, in Italy, in Germany, nay, throughout the European continent. The contemplation that the freedom of the Press on the European continent is inconsistent with the preponderance of Russia, and the very existence of the Austrian dynasty, this sworn enemy of freedom and of liberal thought, your generous support will sweep away those tyrants and raise liberty where now foul oppression proudly rules.

Among the speakers were Charles King, formerly of the *New York American,* and then of the *Courier and Enquirer,* Henry J. Raymond, of the *Times,* Parke Godwin, of the *Evening Post,* Charles A. Dana, of the *Tribune,* and Freeman Hunt, of the *Merchants' Magazine.*

Au contraire of these opinions of Kossuth in 1851, we annex the views of Count Von Beust, the present leading statesman of Austria, who so recently and quietly settled the very troubles that Kossuth so elaborately ventilated through the Press of America. In an interview with the Vienna correspondent of the *New York Herald* on the 21st of December, 1869, Count Von Beust said:

The condition of our Press is by no means as satisfactory as it might be. Instead of seriously ventilating important political questions, and arriving at the best means of their solution, as is done by journalism in your and other countries, they adopt the inferior tactics of dealing in vituperations and personalities, and thus forget the real cause at issue. So violently has this "national autonomy" question been brought forward, that it has completely put in the shade the Concordat excitement, and individual dissensions have been mixed up with it in such a manner as to undermine the harmony of the cabinet. Much fault must be attached to the venom of the Press; and, of all reforms, this is the most necessary. Up to 1848 the different nationalities lived peaceably enough together. After the revolution, and with the setting in of the reactionary period, bickerings commenced, which have slowly increased. The clamors of the Magyars of Hungary have much engrossed the attention of his (the count's) predecessors, though none of them had been able to find a remedy. One thing they considered unavoidable, namely, the protection of the German minority, and Count Schmerling's ingenious system of apportionment of franchise and qualifications of voters had answered its purpose most wonderfully. The increasing clamors of the non-German element were not hushed by the catastrophe of 1866; indeed, they became so loud in Hungaria—which, by ancient privileges and the compact mass of the Magyars, was the most entitled to be heard—that, when entering office in Austria after the war, I felt the necessity of grappling with the subject, and determined, as the only means of quieting the country, upon instituting the present dualistic form of government. The ultra Magyar party, going still further in its pretensions, was successfully beaten; the moderados, or address party, willing to obtain reforms by petition, gained the upper hand; the emperor was then crowned at Pesth, and great was the joy and general satisfaction. In doing this I had to revive the former constitution, which had been rather illegally suspended by one of my predecessors. But, then, when the Reichsrath was called in the Tcheckians of Bohemia, Moravia staid away and would have no share in it. Now their affair has become the paramount question, and it is useless to deny that something must be done for them and their grievances. But here again you may see the want of judgment of our public Press, and, I may add, of many of our public men and representatives, who waste time in endless rhodomontades without ever arriving at any tangible or practical result.

Well, this editorial banquet originated the Press Club in New York. It dined every Saturday at the Astor House. Every distinguished stranger was invited to dine with the club. It became an institution with a large portion of the journalists of the metropolis. We don't suppose its dinners, or its speeches, or the intercourse of its members improved the tone of the Press; intellectual and material competition is more effective in that direction. It made the editors of New York better acquainted with each other, and they were brought more closely together; but, like merchants, lawyers, and clergymen —indeed, as in all other professions and trades—they continued to criticise and abuse each other, as they always did and always will.

The dinners of the Press Club were always considered private. It was never mentioned in the newspapers who dined with them, or what they said. Much wit was thus lost to the world. All was always under the beautiful rose that hung over their table—the scent went no farther. But when Charles Dickens was invited to dine with the club in 1868 the occasion was made an exception to the general rule. This banquet took place on the 18th of April of that year, at Delmonico's.

Among the names of the journalists present were Horace Greeley, of the *New York Tribune;* Henry J. Raymond, of the *New York Times;* Samuel Bowles, of the *Springfield Republican;* W. H. Hurlbert, formerly of the *Times* and *World;* George William Curtis, of *Harper's Weekly;* James Parton, of the *North American Review;* M. Halstead, of the *Cincinnati Commercial;* J. T. Fields, of the *Atlantic Monthly;* Charles F. Briggs, of *Putnam's Magazine;* D. G. Croly, of the *New York World;* Oliver Johnson, of the *Independent;* Charles Nordhoff, of the *Evening Post;* John Russell Young, formerly of the *New York Tribune*, and afterwards of the Philadelphia *Post;* John R. G. Hassard, of the *New York Tribune;* C. P. Dewey, of the *Commercial Advertiser;* General Joseph R. Hawley, of the *Hartford Courant;* G.W. Demers, of the *Albany Evening Journal;* the Rev. H. M. Field, of the *Evangelist;* Samuel Sinclair, of the *New York Tribune;* A. J. Schem, of the *New York Tribune;* F. J. Ottarson, of the *New York Tribune;* Colonel T. B. Thorpe and D.W. Judd, of the *Commer-*

cial Advertiser; J. W. Simonton, of the Associated Press ; Augustus Maverick, of the *Evening Post;* S. S. Conant, of the *New York Times;* George Sheppard, of the *New York Times;* W. W. Harding, of the *Philadelphia Inquirer;* A. D. Richardson, of the *New York Tribune;* C. B. Seymour, of the *New York Times;* F. B. Carpenter and Henry E. Sweetser, of the *New York World;* Charles H. Sweetser, of the *Evening Mail;* Thomas M'Elrath, formerly of the *New York Tribune;* J. F. Cleveland, of the *Tribune;* the Hon. William Orton ; Thomas Nast, of *Harper's Weekly;* E. H. Clement, of the *New York Tribune;* Edwin De Leon, of the *New York Citizen;* J. Smith Homans, of the *Bankers' Magazine;* Whitelaw Reid, of the *Cincinnati Gazette*, afterwards of the *New York Tribune;* B. C. Howard, of the *Evening Mail;* W. W. Warden, of the *Philadelphia Inquirer;* William Stuart, formerly dramatic critic of the *New York Tribune;* John Bonner, formerly of the *Herald* and *Harper's Weekly* ; William Young, formerly of the *Albion*.

Our intention, in giving a few extracts of the speeches delivered on that interesting occasion, is to exhibit the tone of the speakers in regard to their own profession, rather than to occupy any of our space in the splendid praise bestowed upon Dickens. These remarks are somewhat autobiographical in character, and therefore form a part of our compilation. Horace Greeley presided. He said:

> It is now a little more than thirty-four years since I, a young printer, recently located in the city of New York, had the audacity to undertake the editing and publishing a weekly newspaper for the first time. Looking around at that day for materials with which to make an engaging appearance before the public, among the London magazines which I purchased for the occasion was the old *Monthly*, containing a story by a then unknown writer—known to us only by the quaint designation of "Boz." That story, entitled, I think, at that time "Delicate Attentions," but, in its present form, entitled "Mr. Watkins Tottle," I selected and published in the first number of the first journal with which my name was connected. Pickwick was then an unchronicled, if not uncreated character. Sam Weller had not yet arisen to increase the mirth of the Anglo-Saxon race. We had not heard, as we have since heard, of the writer of those sketches, whose career then I may claim to have in some sort commenced with my own [great laughter], and the relation of admirer and admired has continued from that day to the present. I am one of not more than twenty of the present company who welcomed him in this country, on an occasion much like this, a quarter of a century ago. When I came to visit Europe, now seventeen years ago, one of my most pleasant experiences there, and one of my pleasantest recollections of Europe, is that of buying in the farthest city I visited—the city of Venice, on the Adriatic—an Italian newspaper, and amusing myself with what I could not read—a translation of "David Copperfield," wherein the dialogue between Ham and Peggotty, with which I was familiar in English, was rendered into very amusing Italian. * * * * Friends and fellow-laborers, as I am to set you an example to-night of a short speech, I will, without further prelude, ask you to join me in this sentiment: "Health and happiness, honor and generous, because just, recompense to our friend and guest, Charles Dickens."

After the applause Mr. Dickens replied. We merely give that part of his speech relating to his connection with the Press :

> I can not do better than take my cue from your distinguished president, and

refer in my first remarks to his remarks in connection with the old, natural association between you and me. When I received an invitation from a private association of working members of the Press of New York to dine with them to-day, I accepted that compliment in grateful remembrance of a calling that was once my own, and in loyal sympathy toward a brotherhood which, in the spirit, I have never quitted. To the wholesome training of severe newspaper work when I was a very young man I constantly refer my first successes, and my sons will hereafter testify of their father that he was always steadily proud of that ladder by which he rose. If it were otherwise, I should have had but a very poor opinion of their father—which, perhaps, upon the whole, I have not. Hence, gentlemen, under any circumstances, this company would have been exceptionally interesting and gratifying to me. But whereas I supposed that, like the fairies' pavilion in the Arabian Nights, it would be but a mere handful, and I find it turn out, like the same elastic pavilion, capable of comprehending a multitude, so much the more proud am I of the honor of being your guest; for you will readily believe that the more widely representative of the Press in America my entertainers are, the more I must feel the good will and the kindly sentiments toward me of that vast institution.

The president then remarked that, as the Press was to "celebrate itself," he called upon Mr. Raymond to respond to the toast of "The New York Press." Mr. R. said:

The Press of New York, from its geographical position, to say nothing else, maintains a *quasi* prominence among the Press of the country. That Press has maintained an independent existence, not only in itself, but through its organization. For many years (if I may say *many* in speaking of the few years during which I have been connected with it) it has had an organization in form as a Press Club; and it is among the most pleasant of my recollections in connection with the Press of New York that, in that form of organization, it has been our good fortune, at various times, to greet as guests and to entertain, with whatever hospitality we were able to extend to them, gentlemen of distinction and position who did us the honor to visit us from the countries of Europe. I remember almost the first of those occasions, when that truly great man, then recently expelled from the office of governor of Hungary—Kossuth, the exile—came to this country, and charmed so many of our people by the sea-shore, and in the depths of the densest wilderness of the West, and in great cities, and every where he went, by the silver voice in which he uttered such sweet words in behalf of liberty and freedom, and by that sad, solemn eye with which, as our eloquent orator, Rufus Choate, has said, "he seemed constantly to be beholding the sad procession of unnamed demigods who had died for their native land." He was one of the most honored guests of the New York Press. Then came to us, and honored us by his presence, as he has honored England and the world by his services, that great statesman whom your people, sir (turning to Mr. Dickens), now honor as they honor or few among their dead or their living—Richard Cobden. Then, too, came to us, and greeted us with the right hand of brotherhood, your great brother in literature, William M. Thackeray. And I may say that, of the many things that touched the hearts of our people, none touched them more nearly, or struck home more closely, than the feeling and eloquent words of the heart in which he spoke to us of his brother in letters, Charles Dickens. We did not need, sir, that he should tell us how much that name was cherished by the lovers of humanity all the world over, wherever the English tongue was spoken or read; but he never said one word in praise of that name that did not meet with as hearty a response here as human words ever brought from human hearts. He told us then what was true then, and what has been growing more and more true ever since, that the writings of that illustrious brother of his in the world of letters had done more than any other event or occurrence, more than any other service which he could call to mind, to make the men of the world feel that they were brothers, that they had common interests, that they were all sons of one father, striving and marching toward one end, and that each deserved and ought to have the love, the sympathy, the cordial good offices and kindly feeling of every other. These, sir, are among the felicities of the New York Press. The Press of other parts of the country have enjoyed them also to a greater or less extent, and I know they have all sympathized with the feelings which pervaded our hearts at our good fortune in meeting such men, and hearing them speak such words of brotherly kindness and love. * * * We are all laboring in a common cause. I think it may be truly said that the Press, the free Press, all over the world, has but one common mission —to elevate humanity. It takes the side of the humble, the lowly, and the poor— always of necessity, a necessity of its own existence—as against those who from mere position and power hold in their hands the destinies of the lowly and the poor, for whom the Press is instituted. We are all of us, more or less directly, more or less exclusively, connected with the movements of governments—governments of various forms—in different parts of the world, and through different agencies and ways, in that common effort to elevate the great mass of our fellow-men, to improve their material condition, and give them a higher ground to stand upon and a stronger foot to go through the weary task that all of us, in some degree, have to undergo before we fulfill our pilgrimage here on earth.

Mr. Greeley now called upon the Weekly Press. He said:

When we speak of the Press of New York, we are too apt—we gentlemen of the daily journals are too apt—to monopolize the phrase as peculiarly, if not exclusively our own. The Daily Press has a certain conspicuous position in the public eye. By means of the telegraph and its connections it seems more directly related to the leading minds of the country than any other portion of the Press; but we must remember that where one man reads a daily journal there are several who read a weekly journal, and that the position of the Daily Press, though important, is certainly not solitary. I propose "The Weekly Press," and I call upon George William Curtis to respond.

Mr. Curtis, in a very neat and professional way, said:

As I now look around upon this cheerful company, I like to think that this pleasant feast is not merely a tribute to an author whose books have made all his readers his friends, but is a fraternal greeting of welcome and farewell from us, who are all in various ways reporters, to our comrade, a late reporter of *The London Morning Chronicle*, who shall here and now, and at no other time, and nowhere else in the world, be nameless. He has ceased, indeed, to write for *The Morning Chronicle*, but he has not ceased to be a reporter. He is a famous story-teller; but I ask this table of experts whether that shows him to be no longer a reporter? He is a great novelist; but what are novelists? They are men commissioned by nature to see human life and the infinite play of human character, and write reports upon them. So a certain Spaniard inspected the grotesque aspect of decaying chivalry, and wrote his famous report, "Don Quixote." So a certain Scotchman beheld the romantic splendor of the Crusader, and called his report "Ivanhoe." So a sad-eyed countryman of ours saw a tragic aspect in early New England life, and called his marvelous report the "Scarlet Letter." And so our nameless friend of *The Morning Chronicle*, with the same commission as that of Cervantes, of Scott, of Hawthorne, observing the various aspects of life in his own time, has written his prodigious series of reports, which have become household words all the year round. They have not only revealed wrongs, but have greatly helped to right them. One he called, for instance, Nicholas Nickleby, and with hilarious indignation Dotheboys Hall was laughed and cried away. Perhaps he called another Oliver Twist, and the cold poor-house was turned inside out, and warmed with the sun of human charity. Upon another I read Bleak House; and, as I turn the pages, the long, bitter winter of the law's delay lies exposed. He turns his eye backward, and it seems to me nobody truly understands the terrible form and spirit of the French Revolution, although he may have read all the historians, if he has not read that wonderful report, The Tale of Two Cities. And still, thank Heaven, the good work goes on. The eye, and the heart, and the hand are untiring. The eager world reads, and reads, and reads; and the reporter's genial magic makes it a great, good-natured Oliver asking for more. If, in the pursuit of his calling, he came to us who loved and honored him, he still faithfully and frankly reported his observations. The old proverb says nobility obliges; but genius obliges still more. Fidelity to his own observation is all that we can ask of any reporter. However grateful he may be for our hospitality, we can not insist that he shall pour our Champagne into his eyes so that he can not see, nor stuff our pudding into his ears so that he can not hear. He was obliged to hear and see, and report many things that were not pleasant nor flattering. It is the fate of all reporters. I do not remember that those very competent observers, Mr. Emerson and Mr. Hawthorne, whom we sent to England, represented that country as altogether a paradise, and John Bull as a saint without blemish. They told a great deal of truth about England, as it seems to me our friend told a great many wholesome and valuable truths about us. Naturally we did not find every part of his report very entertaining ; but neither, I suppose, did Lord Dedlock find Bleak House very amusing, and I am sure that to this day neither Sergeant Buzfuz nor the Lord Chief Justice Stareleigh have ever been able to find the least fun in Pickwick. For my undivided thirty-millionth part of the population I thank the reporter with all my heart, and I do not forget that if his touch, like the ray of a detective's lantern, sparkled for a moment upon some of our defects, the full splendor of its light has been always turned upon the sins and follies of his own country. If I seem to have wandered from my text, Mr. Chairman, it only seems so. The members of the Weekly Press, for whom I have the honor of speaking, pursue literature as a profession, and I know not where we could study the fidelity, the industry, the conscience, the care, and the enthusiasm which are essential to success in our profession more fitly than in the example of the editor of *All the Year Round*. M. Thiers, in a recent speech, says that the world now needs every day a new book written every day. Hence the newspaper. The responsibility of the authors of that book is enormous. The world is governed by public opinion, and nothing moulds that opinion more powerfully than the Press. Its great divisions, as we know them, are two—the literary and the political. The paramount duty of the Literary Press is purity ; of the Political Press, honesty. Our copyright law, as you are aware, Mr. Chairman, inflicts a fine for every repetition of the offense, so that the fine is multiplied as many times as there are copies of the book printed ; so the man who, as a writer for the Press, says what he does not believe, or defends a policy that he does not approve, or panders to a base passion or a mean prejudice for a party purpose, is so many times a traitor to the craft represented at this table as there are copies of his newspaper printed ; and as honest, or even dishonest difference of opinion is entirely compatible with courtesy, as even denunciation is a thousand-fold more stinging and effective when it is not vituperation, decency of manner becomes the Press no less than decency of matter. When the manners of the Press become those of Tombs pettifoggers, or Old Bailey shysters, or the *Eatanswill Gazette*, its influence upon society will be revealed by a coarse and brutal public opinion. While we boast of the tremendous power of the Press, let us remember that the foundations of its power as a truly civilizing influence are, first, purity, then honesty, then sagacity and industry. It may sometimes seem otherwise ; but it is an illusion. A man may build up a great journal as he may amass any other great fortune, and seem to be a shining miracle of prosperity ; but if he have neither love, nor honor, nor troops of friends, his prosperity is a fair orchard bearing only apples of Sodom. It is a curious and interesting fact that, at an official investigation made a few years since in England, a newspaper dealer, in reply to a question of Mr. Cobden's, gave it as the result of twenty years' experience that objectionable newspapers, daily or weekly, were short-lived, while the publications of the highest intellectual and moral quality constantly increased in circulation. It is impossible to determine the limits or the merits of individual agency, but there is no doubt that among the most vigorous forces in the elevation of the character of the Weekly Press had been *Household Words* and *All the Year Round ;* and since the beginning of the publication of *Household Words*, the periodical literature of England has been born again.

The President then called upon General Joseph R. Hawley, of the *Connecticut Courant*, one of the centenarian newspapers, to respond for "the New England Press." General H. said :

It is but a few hours, comparatively, since I received warning that I should be called upon, and as I was obliged to work diligently upon other matters in order to secure the pleasure of being here at all, I had hoped to be "off duty" this evening. I feel somewhat as might a very respectable and very courteous old bachelor if he should kindly consent to hold a small bundle for a few minutes while the lady stepped round the corner, and should then find himself the responsible holder of a strange baby, growing to be a very big elephant on his hands. This chair, just vacated by my side, belongs to the gentleman who should have responded for the New England Press—our excellent friend, Sam. Bowles, of the *Springfield Republican*, the model newspaper of the Provincial Press. But there will be one merit—brevity—in what I shall have to say. One still July afternoon the city items man of the journal upon which I worked, in despair of matter for his column, sat meditatively observing a small boy climbing up to and upon the figure of Madame Justice upon the State-house cupola. Said he, "If that boy should fall he would make about so much"—measuring a "stickful" on his finger. If I were to speak of and not for the New England Press, perhaps I may claim that New England has spoken already, and speaks for herself through her newspaper men every where. The honored chairman [Mr. Greeley] is one of our New England boys; and so also is the gentleman who has just spoken so eloquently upon the right of our distinguished guest. [Mr. Raymond shook his head.] Well, we certainly educated him, and I thought from his versatile and characteristic ability that he must be one of our own Yankees. The venerated senior of the *Post*, whose absence we all regret, went from us, and the able editors of the *World* and the *Journal of Commerce*, and the other eloquent gentleman upon my left [Mr. Curtis], were ours. There is then little necessity that I should continue. But I am right glad and proud to have an opportunity of gratefully acknowledging our indebtedness to Mr. Dickens. Twenty-five years ago, as a school-boy, I hung upon the timbers of a bridge that I might have a fair opportunity to look upon the man whose books were my delight beyond all others, and I could not have dreamed that after such a lapse of time I should have the happiness of thanking him. It is sometimes said that there is something rigid and severe in the traditional New England character, though we have been unable to see it as clearly as some of our critics outside. Whether it be so or not, I do most heartily thank him in behalf of many thousands of Yankee boys who have grown up his devoted readers and admirers, and whom he has for a generation wonderfully delighted and greatly instructed, whom he has taught to look tenderly upon the weaker side of humanity, whom he has taught that it is not unmanly to cry, and certainly not to laugh most heartily. Those who have preceded me have spoken of the debt we owe him. Newspaper men owe no small share of it. What a deal of trouble it saves us, for example, to say of an opponent that he is a Pecksniffian! You anticipate me by seeing at a glance the numberless instances in which a word from Dickens, by a sort of stenographic system of allusions and characterizations well comprehended by a universal public, saves you whole columns of writing.

Out of this club, and in sympathy with the idea originating it, Press Associations have been formed in many cities and in many states. The Press of New Jersey has its annual dinner; the Press of Boston its annual supper; and the Press of the interior of New York enjoy the same sort of pleasure. There is the Maine Press Association; the New England Press Association; and the Western Press Association. There is also the Massachusetts Editors' and Publishers' Association. There is an organization in New Orleans called the Association of American Medical Editors. They throw their "physic to the dogs" the day before their banquet. The members of these associations have their regular meetings, where they talk over the business of their profession, eat the most *recherché* dinners and suppers, plan pleasant excursions to distant parts of the country, and are happier mortals.

These organizations are entirely distinct from what is known as the Associated Press. That is purely a news institution, and has been nearly a quarter of a century in existence; that deals in facts, and not in fricassee; that originated in the introduction of the magnetic telegraph as a news-carrier. The clubs are social gatherings. Besides those formed of editors and proprietors, the reporters have organized separate associations of their own, not only for mutual enjoyment, but for mutual benefit in the event of illness, or accident, or death.

None of these social circles are destined for a long life, but they are useful while they last.

CHAPTER XLII.
THE NEW YORK WORLD.

HOW IT WAS STARTED.—ITS RELIGIOUS CHARACTER.—TWO HUNDRED THOUSAND DOLLARS LOST IN THE ENTERPRISE.—ITS CHANGE OF BASE.—ITS UNION WITH THE COURIER AND ENQUIRER.—THE BOGUS PROCLAMATION.—SUSPENSION OF THE WORLD BY THE GOVERNMENT.—ITS REAPPEARANCE AND MANIFESTO.—REPUDIATION OF SEYMOUR AND BLAIR.—THE LITERARY CHARACTER OF THE PAPER.—ITS ENTERPRISE.—MANTON MARBLE, ITS EDITOR.

THE *New York World* appeared in June, 1860. Why was it started? What has it accomplished?

The *Herald*, *Tribune*, and *Times* were active and had large circulations. The *Journal of Commerce*, the *Courier and Enquirer*, the *News*, the *Sun*, and the *Express* were published every morning; the *Commercial Advertiser*, *Evening Post*, and *Express* appeared every evening. They represented all classes apparently; where was the place for the *World*?

It was at this period that the *Times*, *Herald*, and *Tribune* had become representative papers. The *Herald* had its own community of readers, and the *Tribune* its peculiar class; the *Times* represented the *juste milieu*. It was thought that these famous journals met the wants of the community; and if not, the remaining papers, the staid *Journal of Commerce*, the impulsive *Courier*, the semi-religious *Commercial*, the poetic and free-trade *Post*, the plebeian *Sun*, and the democratic *News* would meet any deficiency. But all the journalists of that day were in error. What was wanted was a daily religious paper—a daily moral paper—to give all the news, to shut out the wretched criminal police reports, to ignore the slander-suits and prurient divorce cases; not to shock the public with the horrid details of murders, but to give the news, such as ought to satisfy any reasonable being—indeed, it was to publish a paper conducted on high moral principles, excluding advertisements of theatres, as the *Tribune* for a time had done; excluding all improper matter, as the *Times* for a time had done; and giving all the news, as the *Herald* always had done.

With this high purpose in view, a large sum of money was subscribed by some of the best men in the metropolis. Alexander Cummings, formerly of the *North American*, and afterwards of the

Evening Bulletin, of Philadelphia, was selected as its manager. He had evidently full powers. He was editor plenipotentiary and journalist extraordinary in this new enterprise. His chief assistant was James R. Spalding, a classmate of Henry J. Raymond, and for some time a writer on the *Courier and Enquirer.* He was a tall, dignified, scholarly editor. Hoe made one of his fastest lightning presses for the new establishment. The splendid new building on the block with the *Times* was leased. One of the largest and most dangerous looking signs ever seen was erected on its roof. Park Row and Beekman Street were excavated for deep vaults for press-room and paper-room. Besides all this, the new concern unwisely became a member of the Associated Press. Editors and reporters were engaged. All the arrangements were made and completed, and one bright morning in 1860 the *World* made its appearance.

It was a dignified and a moral sheet. When we take the religious statistics of New York City into consideration, we find a religious community large enough to support such a paper as the *World* was intended to be, and to support it handsomely—magnificently; but it lacked something; it did not fill the eye of the religious portion of the public; they would look at the *World*, but they would not go to bed without reading the *Herald*, or the *Times*, or the *Tribune.* There was evidently something wrong. What was it? The *World* had all the telegraphic and all the shipping intelligence that the other papers had, and, with its contemporaries, it had the world, physically and mentally, before it—as full of events, as full of news, as full of meat, in a word, as an oyster. But the universal world was Pandora's box to the *New York World.* It refused to give any details of the evils that filled the box, and waited patiently and expensively for the appearance of that sleeping beauty, Hope, which was so snugly and cosily coiled up at the bottom.

Two hundred thousand dollars, it was maintained, were spent in the effort to make the *World* a success. Those who subscribed this money became disgusted. No wonder they did. Alexander Cummings became not only disgusted, but he afterwards became Governor of Wyoming Territory. The *World* changed hands. It then became a secular paper—a worldly *World*, and has not since deviated from its new path. The *Herald*, after this, in speaking of its three contemporaries, called them "the world, the flesh, and the devil."

No better men than the originators of this paper ever lived. They wished to inculcate sound principles and sound morals among the masses. Their intentions were excellent, but difficult to carry out. Colonel Cummings was a journalist of great experience in Philadelphia; he was educated under the wing of the Hon. Simon Cameron; he was shrewd, active, intelligent; every one supposed that, if any one knew the requirements of a first-class paper, he did; but he failed. The *Tribune* was started on high moral grounds; so was the *Times;* but the managers of these papers found that they could not ignore the facts of the day. They live. So it was with the *World;* but its financial supporters, in the fullness of their own integrity and honesty of purpose, would not consent to a change of policy in that paper for all the pecuniary gain in the world. They preferred to sink the two hundred thousand dollars. Their motto was Principles with Principal, or nothing.

On the 1st of July, 1861, the *World* and the *Morning Courier and New York Enquirer* were united, and appeared on that morning under the double name of the two papers. The *Courier and Enquirer* of the 27th of June, 1861, thus announced its partial disappearance from the field of journalism:

TO THE PUBLIC.

On Monday, July 1st, the *Courier and Enquirer* will change its form from folio to the more popular quarto shape. This change of issue we have long had in contemplation, having several years since advanced so far in that direction as to cause a portion of the necessary machinery for such a change to be prepared, but the advice of timid friends dissuaded us. The intended change will not affect our business relations with advertisers in any respect, except that, for the future, their favors will have the important advantage of an immensely increased circulation. Our advertising and publication office will continue, as heretofore, at No. 162 Pearl Street; and in the absence of the senior editor, General Webb, from the country, he will be represented by his son, Mr. Robert S. Webb, who has been actively connected with the *Courier and Enquirer* for the last twelve years, and who has justly won the reputation of being the equal of any associate editor ever employed on the *Courier and Enquirer.*

* * * * * Fashions change, and so do the tastes of the public; and in nothing has this change been more apparent than in regard to newspapers. The folio form of the *Courier and Enquirer* is less attractive than formerly, and a very large majority of the public demand cheap newspapers, which may be purchased at the corners of the streets and upon every thoroughfare of the country. We have long felt the necessity of conforming to this change in public taste, but, in consequence of the number of competitors already in the field, we have hesitated to make an experiment which would necessarily involve a very large outlay of capital, and greatly increased labor in the mechanical department of the paper.

We are happy to announce, however, that we have completed an arrangement with the *World* newspaper, which, while it accomplishes in a single day all that we have desired, secures to the readers of the *Courier and Enquirer,* and all who favor us with their advertisements, every advantage which energy, enterprise, and an enormous outlay of capital could have promised them. In one word, from and after the 1st day of July, the *Courier and Enquirer* and the *World* become one newspaper, and will be published as the *World and Courier and Enquirer* in the form and on the terms and conditions of the *World.*

We need not dwell on the advantages of this union to the readers, and the friends and advertisers of the *Courier and Enquirer.* There is not one of them who would not greatly rejoice to know that we had received an addition of some THIRTY THOUSAND to our subscription list, and it certainly would not be cause of regret to them that the price of subscription to the joint paper is, at the same time, reduced more than a third. And such is precisely the intelligence which we this morning have the pleasure to communicate.

The leading feature of the *Courier and Enquirer* has been its identification with the commercial interests of our city, and for years past the question has been asked, Why can you not combine the benefits of the sale papers and their extended circulation with your peculiar commercial character? We have always admitted the necessity of such a Press, and have repeatedly promised that, when practicable, it should be furnished, and we indulge the hope that that promise is about to be redeemed. Most assuredly there shall be no faltering on our part to render our *commercial* department even more attractive than it heretofore has been, and, to accomplish this object, great additional labor will be expended in condensing in the smallest possible space every species of information which has heretofore rendered this department of our paper so acceptable to every class of readers. We pledge ourselves to the readers of the *Courier and Enquirer*, and to the public at large, that whatever may be the shortcomings of the joint newspaper in other respects, its commercial character shall not only be sustained, but, if possible, improved. We flatter ourselves, however, that, with the combined talent of the two papers, "*The World and Courier and Enquirer*" will in all respects commend itself to the intelligent reader as being at least equal in every department to its enterprising rivals, at the same time that it will sustain and advance the reputation which has been honestly won by the *Courier and Enquirer*, of being *the* leading commercial newspaper in the Union.

Thus passed away one more of the "blanket sheets"—one more of the "respectable sixpenny" papers—one more of the old class of newspapers in the metropolis, to become another of the reviled cheap papers, verifying the prediction of Snowden that "Raymond would not be satisfied till he saw the *Courier and Enquirer* a two-cent paper."

These absorptions of newspapers are not always beneficial to the absorber. Of the papers now in existence, the *Herald*, *Tribune*, *Times*, *Sun*, and *Evening Post* never bought out or took in other papers as a means of success. The *Journal of Commerce*, *Evening Express*, and *Commercial Advertiser* have done so. The old *Gazette* was merged with the *Journal*, the old *Daily Advertiser* with the *Express*, and the *Evening Star* with the *Commercial*. The *World* is now made up of the *Morning Courier*, the *New York Enquirer*, the *New York American*, and *Weekly Argus*, these five in one—the *World and Courier and Enquirer;* but, finally, with a determination to stand alone in its glory, it quietly dropped the latter name, and sensibly adheres to that of *The World* alone.

There was a lamentable episode in the career of the *World*, which occurred in 1864, that gave it a marked position with the conservative portion of the community. It was one of those events that will happen in any age and in any country, and, in fact, was of little real consequence, as it afterwards proved, as the forged proclamation, the cause of the suspension of the *World* and *Journal of Commerce*, at that time merely antedated a few weeks a *bona fide* proclamation of similar purport. The suspension of these journals was "an untoward event," and was a mistake, or rather a blunder, of Secretary Stanton. It is our duty to place on record the letter of the editor of the *World* which he addressed to the President on resuming the publication of his paper. Historically and journalistically it is a communication of importance:

SIR,—"That the king can do no wrong" is the theory of a monarchy. It is the theory of a constitutional republic that its chief magistrate may do wrong. In the former the ministry are responsible for the king's acts. In the latter the President is responsible for the acts of his ministers. Our Constitution admits that the President may err in providing for a judgment upon his doings by the people in regular elections. In providing for his impeachment, it admits that he may be guilty of crimes.

In a government of laws and not of men, the most obscure citizen may without indecorum address himself to the chief magistrate when to the Constitution whence you derive your temporary power, and he the guarantee of his perpetual rights, he has constantly paid his unquestioning loyalty, and when to the laws, which your duty is to care for a faithful execution of, he has rendered entire obedience.

If the matter of his address be that in his person, property, and rights the Constitution has been disregarded and the laws disobeyed; if its appeal to the principles of justice be no more earnest than the solicitude of its regard for truth, and if the manner of his address be no less temperate than firm, he does not need courtly phrases to propitiate an attentive hearing from a magistrate who loves his country, her institutions, and her laws.

In the *World* of last Wednesday morning was published a proclamation, purporting to be signed by your excellency, and countersigned by the Secretary of State, appointing a day of fasting and prayer, and calling into military service, by volunteering and draft, four hundred thousand citizens between the ages of eighteen and forty-five. That proclamation was a forgery, written by a person who, ever since your departure from Springfield to Washington in 1861, has enjoyed private as well as public opportunities for learning to counterfeit the peculiarities of your speech and style, and whose service for years as a city editor of the *New York Times* and upon the *New York Tribune* acquainted him with the entire newspaper machinery of the city, and enabled him to insert his clever forgery into the regular channels by which we receive news at a time when competent inspection of its genuineness was impossible, and suspicion of its authenticity was improbable. The manifold paper, resembling in all respects that upon which we nightly receive from our agents news, and from the government itself orders, announcements, and proclamations, was left with a night clerk about 3 or 4 o'clock in the morning, after the departure of every responsible editor, and was at once passed into the hands of the printers, put in type, and published. No newspaper in the country but would have been deceived as we were.

Our misfortune was complete. At an early hour, however, before the business of the city had fairly begun, it was discovered that we had been imposed upon, and were being made to appear the instruments of a deception of the public. There was no delay in vindicating our character. Our whole machinery for spreading news was set in motion instantly to announce that we had been deceived by a forgery—that your excellency had issued no proclamation. The sale of papers over our counters was stopped. Our bundles to the Scotia, bound for Europe that day, were stopped. The owners' and purser's files were stopped. News-room bundles and files were stopped, and the agent of the line was informed that the proclamation was a forgery. Our printers and pressmen were brought from their homes and beds to put in type and publish the news of our misfortune. Our bulletin-boards were placarded with the offer of reward for the discovery of the forger; and to the agent of the Associated Press I sent a telegram reciting all the facts, for him to transmit at once to nearly every daily paper in the North, from Maine to California. Thus, before the Scotia sailed—before your Secretary of State had officially branded the forgery, the wings which we had given to Truth had enabled her to outstrip every where the falsehood we had unwittingly set on foot, and in many places the truth arrived before the forger had come to tell his tale.

For any injury done to ourselves, to the government, or to the public, this publicity was ample antidote. It, indeed, made injury impossible.

But the insult to your excellency was the greater in proportion to the eminence of your station. Early in the afternoon of Wednesday, therefore, I went with Mr. Wm. C. Prime, the chief editor of the *Journal of Commerce*, which had been deceived precisely as we were, to the head-quarters of the Department of the East, and we laid before the commanding general every clew in our possession which could lead to the discovery of the guilty persons. All the facts above recited were telegraphed at once to you through the Secretary of War by General Dix. I assert our utter blamelessness. I assert, moreover, that I have never known a mind so prejudiced in which acquaintance with these facts would not enforce the conviction of our utter blamelessness.

Here was the absence of an intent to do wrong; here was an antidote for an injury unwittingly assisted, more complete and effectual than the injury itself; here was alacrity in search of the wrong-doer, and assistance rendered to your subordinate to discover the author of the insult done to you.

With these facts set fully before you by the general commanding this department, you reiterated an order for my arrest and imprisonment in Fort Lafayette; for the seizure and occupation of the *World* office by a military guard, and the suppression of its publications. The *Journal of Commerce*, its editors and publishers, were included in the same order.

I believe, though I can not state of my own knowledge, that to the commanding general's assertion of our entire blamelessness it was owing that the order for our arrest and incarceration was rescinded. But the order for the suppression of the *World* was not rescinded. Under your orders, General Dix sent a strong military force to its publication office and editorial rooms, who ejected their occupants, and for two days and three nights held possession there, injuring and abstracting some of their contents, and permitting no one to cross the threshold.

Not until Saturday morning did this occupation cease. Not until to-day has the *World* been free to speak. But to those who have ears to hear its absence has been more eloquent than its columns could ever be.

To characterize these proceedings as unprecedented would be to forget the past history of your administration, and to characterize them as shocking to every mind would be to disregard that principle of human nature from which it arises that men submitting once and again to lawless encroachments of power, with every intermission of a vigilance which should be continual, lose something of the old, free, keen sense of their true nature and real danger.

Charles was doubtless advised to, and applauded for the crimes by which he lost his crown and life; nor can you do any such outrageous, oppressive, and unjust a thing that it will not be applauded by those whose prosperity and power you have created and may destroy. To characterize these proceedings as arbitrary, illegal, and unconstitutional, would seem, if such weighty words have not been emptied of all significance, to befit better an hour at which you have not arrived, and a place where, not public opinion, but the authority of law speaks, after impeachment, trial, conviction, and judgment.

But, sir, the suppression of two daily journals in this metropolis—one the organ of its great commercial public, the other a recognized exponent of the democratic principles which are shared by half, or nearly half your fellow-citizens—did shock the public mind; did amaze every honest and patriotic citizen; did fill with indignation and alarm every pure and loyal breast. There were no indignation meetings; there were no riots; there was no official protest; but do not imagine, sir, that the governor of this state has forgotten to do his duty; do not imagine that the people of this city, or state, or country have ceased to love their liberties, or do not know how to protect their rights. It would be fatal to a tyrant to commit that error here and now. A free people can at need devise means to teach their chief magistrate the same lesson.

To you, sir, who have by heart the Constitution which you swore to "preserve, protect, and defend," it may be an impertinence to cite those natural and chartered rights therein enumerated, among which are these: That the people shall be secure in their persons, houses, papers, and effects, against unreasonable seizures, and that no warrant even shall issue, except upon probable cause, supported by oath, and particularly describing the place to be searched and the persons or things to be seized; that no person shall be deprived of life, liberty, or property without due process of law. Yet these are the most priceless possessions of freemen, and these you took away from me.

Even a captured and guilty criminal, who knew that his crime would be proved, and that the law would assuredly visit upon him condign punishment, might with propriety plead these rights, and demand of the chief magistrate to throw over him these shields. Assaulted by the bayonets of a military commander, he might protest and assert his inalienable right to the orderly processes, the proofs, and the punishment of the law; but has the Saxon tongue any terms left for him to use who, being the victim of crime, has been made also the victim of lawless power?

It is the theory of the law that, after the commission of any crime, all proceedings taken before trial shall be merely preventive; but the proceedings taken against the *World* were of the nature of a summary execution of judgment. Would trial by law have been denied? would the law itself have been set aside for the bayonet? would a process as summary as a drum-head court-martial have been resorted to by you in a peaceful city, far from the boundaries of military occupation, had the presses which consistently applaud your course been, as we were, the victims of this forger? Had the *Tribune* and *Times* published the forgery (and the *Tribune* candidly admits that it might have published it, and was prevented only by mere chance), would you, sir, have suppressed the *Tribune* and *Times* as you have suppressed the *World* and *Journal of Commerce*? You know you would not. If not, why not?

*　*　*　*　*　*　*　*　*

Can it be possible, sir, that for a moment you supposed that journals like ours could afford to be guilty of this forgery? Let the unanimous voice of your own Press answer. Such a trick would hardly have succeeded in Sangamon County, Illinois. For a party which is about to go before the people, and ask them to commit to its hands the administration of affairs—which has been more generous and forbearing to your errors than you have been just to its guides—permit me to say that it was less possible to be true of any one of them than it was of any man, high or low, who suspected them.

And so the end has proved. The confessed and guilty forgers were your own zealous partisans. Joseph Howard, Jr., who has confessed his crime, was a Republican politician and Loyal Leaguer of Brooklyn. Consider, sir, at whose feet he was taught his political education, and in whose cause he spent his political breath. Mr. Howard has been from his very childhood an intimate friend of the Republican clergyman, Henry Ward Beecher, and a member of his Church. He has listened, year in and year out, to the droppings of the Plymouth sanctuary. The stump speeches which there follow prayer and precede the benediction he for years reported in the journal which is your devoted organ in this city. For years he was the city editor of that journal, the *New York Times*; for a long time he was the Washington correspondent of the chief abolition newspaper of the country, the *New York Tribune*; he has been a frequent contributor to the columns of the *Independent*; he journeyed with you from Springfield to Washington; he represents himself a favored visitor at the White House since your residence there.

By a curious felicity, the stylus with which his amanuensis copied on tissue paper the proclamation and signed your name was abstracted from the editorial rooms of the *Tribune*. The party principles upon which you were pledged to administer the government have been the daily meat and drink of this forger. He has denounced as faithfully as you the party by whose defeat you rose to power. He has been the noisy champion of an exclusive loyalty; he has preached in clubhouses and at street corners those politics which stigmatize constitutional opposition to the administration as disloyalty to the government. The stock-brokers who were his confederates will be found to be of the same kidney. They all advocated a paper-money legal tender; they have all countenanced the paper inflation; they have all been heedless of the misery to poor men which such inflations breed; they have all rejoiced at the speculation thus fostered, and by speculation they had hoped to thrive.

*　*　*　*　*　*　*　*

Yet no citizen who regards his duties should ever hesitate at the last to oppose lawless deeds with legal remedies. The law may break down. It will then disclose to a watchful people the point of greatest danger. Courts may fail; judges may be intimidated by threats or bribed by the allurements of power, and those who have sworn to execute the laws may shrink from the fulfillment of their oaths. A craven Congress may sit silent and idly watch the perishing liberties of the people whom they represent, but this can not deter him who, in defending his rights, is determined to do his whole duty, and to whom it is competent at last to

commit the issue to that Power, omnipotent and inscrutable, who presides in events, and sways the destinies of nations and the hearts of men.
MANTON MARBLE.

NEW YORK, May 23, 1864.

Such an event as this, of course, produced a profound sensation. The suspension was undoubtedly the hasty result of impulse, and had to be sustained, if possible, by the Secretary of War. But the government had to succumb to such an arbitrary and unnecessary measure. The Albany *Evening Journal*, the organ of Thurlow Weed and Secretary Seward, in mentioning the circumstance, published a few interesting facts of a precedent which are worth reproducing:

FROM THE ALBANY JOURNAL, MAY, 1864.

Howard, the Brooklyn reporter, is not the first one who issued a bogus missive in war-time in order to affect the stock-market. A remarkable precedent to his case is found in the history of English Criminal Proceedings; and as it may at once interest and afford a guide for the course of our authorities toward the present offender, it may be worth while to refer to it.

The case occurred in 1814, during the great war between France and England. Charles Random de Berenger, Sir Thomas Cochrane, Andrew Cochrane, Johnstone, Richard Gathorne Butt, Ralph Sandom, Alexander M'Rae, John Peter Halloway, and Henry Lyte, subjects of Great Britain, were large operators in the funds. It occurred to them that by forging a document announcing decisive results on the Continent, stocks would suddenly go up, they might sell at a large advance, and make their fortunes. Accordingly, the first-named of their number wrote a letter purporting to have been addressed by a high government official to the British admiral commanding at Deal, announcing the defeat of the French, the death of Napoleon, etc., etc. The document is so curious that we copy it in full:

To the Honorable J. Foley, Port Admiral, Deal, etc.:

DOVER, 1 o'clock A.M., February 14, 1814.

SIR,—I have the honor to acquaint you that the *L'Aigle*, from Calais, Pierre Duquin, master, has this moment landed me near Dover, to proceed to the capital with dispatches of the happiest nature. I have pledged my honor that no harm shall come to the crew of the *L'Aigle*; even with a flag of truce they immediately stood for sea. Should they be taken, I have to entreat you immediately to liberate them. My anxiety will not allow me to say more for your gratification than that the Allies obtained a final victory; that Bonaparte was overtaken by a party of Sachen's Cossacks, who immediately slaid him, and divided his body between them. General Platoff saved Paris from being reduced to ashes. The allied sovereigns are there, and the white cockade is universal; and immediate peace is certain. In the utmost haste, I entreat your consideration, and have the honor to be, sir, your most obedient servant, R. DU BOURG,
Lieut. Colonel and Aid-de-camp to Lord Cathcart.

The news was believed, the funds took a sudden start, and the cunning forgers reaped a golden harvest.

They were subsequently arrested on a charge of conspiracy against the public welfare and the interests of the realm, and tried in the Court of King's Bench. The trial was fully reported, and may be found in the State Library. It lasted two days, and was sharply conducted on both sides. Some of the evidence is very amusing, while the speeches of the counsel were most elaborate and exhaustive. The forgery was proved, and the defendants found guilty.

Cochrane and Butt were sentenced to pay a fine of one thousand pounds each, Holloway to pay a fine of five hundred pounds; all six to be "severally imprisoned in the custody of the marshal of the Marshalsea of our lord and king for twelve calendar months," and Beranger, Cochrane, and Butt to be "set in and upon the pillory opposite the Royal Exchange, in the city of London, for one hour, between the hours of twelve at noon and two in the afternoon;" and that they "be severally committed to the custody of the marshal, and severally imprisoned until their fines be paid."

We have spoken of the two cases as parallel. They are not so, strictly speaking. The offense in the case of Howard is the greater. The English forgers sought to put money in their pockets by *stimulating* the public confidence ; the American forger aimed at a similar result by making it appear that the country was on the verge of ruin. The former played upon the hopes, the latter upon the despair of the people. The one endeavored to compass no public mischief beyond the narrow circle of stock-jobbers ; the other committed an act that might have for its effect, if it did not have for its design, the destruction of the national credit and the overthrow of the government. If Cochrane and his confreres were put in the pillory, what punishment should be meted out to Howard?

It has become chronic with the *World* to be the property of *millionaires*. After it ceased to be the organ of the wealthy religious *coterie* that brought it into existence, numerous reports were in circulation that it belonged to August Belmont, the well-known banker, Mayor Fernando Wood, John Anderson, the wealthy tobacconist, Collector Augustus Schell, Thurlow Weed, Benjamin Wood, and half of the bankers in Wall Street. Then that Thurlow Weed was its editor. Anon it became the property of Samuel L. M. Barlow and the Albany Regency, with a large slice disposed of to Manton Marble, who became its responsible editor. Finally, that the whole concern passed into the hands of Marble. It has been through fire. Starting full of religious sentiments, it became a half-and-half Democratic sheet; then it swallowed two or three Old Whig and Republican organs, and became more Democratic than before, even to the status of what is called a Copperhead organ in silks and satins.

The *World* has tact and energy. Sometimes it is too sensational, which, in a modern point of view, is exaggerated high-pressure enterprise. Such enterprise has to be managed with great skill and boldness to be successful in the end. It needs a safety-valve in its news arrangements. But the *World* has enterprise. It threw away one chance in 1859. It threw away another in 1866. There was an unpleasant feeling in the Associated Press in that year. Its old agent was dismissed. Not being of that mild type of the human race that succumb to any trifling event, this agent organized an opposition news association. Circumstances, inclinations, a glimmer of some bright object in the future, placed the *World* at the head of this new enterprise. It left the old association. It was alone in its glory in the metropolis. Owing to the want of money, or want of courage, or want of confidence, or want of something, it abandoned the newly-arranged association and lost its chance. Opportunity made Napoleon, and Grant, and Bismarck. Opportunity makes a newspaper. It should never be thrown away.

The *World* is a party paper, but at the same time it is an independent organ of public opinion. All party papers are now semi-independent papers. We are happy to record this fact. There is very little of real party dictation in our modern journalism. The *World* is an instance of this. During the presidential campaign of 1868 it became manifest to a portion of the democracy that their nominations for the offices of President and Vice-president were not strong enough to be elected in the face of the enthusiasm for Grant. The *World* boldly and recklessly came out almost on the eve of election day, and demanded the withdrawal of the candidates and the substitution of others in their place. It produced an impression and created a sensation; it showed the independence of the journal favoring such an enterprise in the midst of an exciting political campaign, if it did not exhibit power and influence enough to accomplish its object.

On the 29th of December, 1869, Manton Marble, who commenced his journalistic career on the *Boston Traveller*, continuing it on the *New York Evening Post*, culminated by becoming sole proprietor of the *World*, paying $100,000 for one fourth of the stock. It is probable, therefore, of all the leading daily papers in New York, the *World* and *Herald* are the only two owned by single individuals, and not bound to the depressing influence of a batch of shareholders whose eyes are constantly fixed on dividends.

The *World* has assumed an excellent position as a literary newspaper. Its reviews of books are considered superior to those of many other daily newspapers, and we believe a number of the essays of that journal have been published in a book and met with a large sale; and its conductor is called by some of his contemporaries "the Student Editor."

Newspapers of a political character have for years deemed it necessary to define their position annually in a showy announcement of the future policy of the journal. It has become a custom with the *Times*, *Tribune*, and *World* to do this. It assumes the shape of an appeal for subscriptions and advertisements. In the platform of the *World* for 1872 there are seven planks, with the following introduction:

In the year 1872 General Grant's successor is to be chosen; the Forty-third Congress to be elected.

The people's votes, white and black, North and South, will thus decide the future destiny of the republic, select its rulers, prescribe their course.

How to influence the people's votes?

By the newspaper—for it includes every other agency. It makes known events and facts—among all influences the chief. It assembles the vaster outside audiences which can not gather to the state-house, the pulpit, or the stump. It is the constant interpreter of men's affairs, and of error or truth is the daily seed-sower.

Next November is our political harvest-time. As we sow we shall reap.

The *World's* seed-sowing will be fruitful to the extent that its circulation is widely pushed by those who approve its aim.

It closes with a claim to be the organ of the Democratic Party, and that "the ballot-box is the true battle-field of republics."

CHAPTER XLIII.
THE NEW YORK SUN.

ITS MODERN CHARACTER.—ITS SALE TO CHARLES A. DANA AND ASSOCIATES.—IT IS NO LONGER A PENNY PAPER.—WHO IS EDITOR DANA?—HIS CONNECTION WITH THE TRIBUNE.—ASSISTANT SECRETARY OF WAR.—EDITOR OF THE CHICAGO REPUBLICAN.—EDITOR OF THE NEW YORK SUN.

THE *New York Sun*, no longer the penny paper, now conducted by Charles A. Dana, dates its new existence, under its new management, from January, 1868. It is an entirely new luminary, more ardent in its policy and more brilliant in its sunshine. It is owned in shares by the *Sun* Company.

Mr. Dana is a journalist. The first we know of him was as a member of the famous Brook-Farm Community, composed of such men as Nathaniel Hawthorne, Ralph Waldo Emerson, William E. Channing, A. Bronson Alcott, George Ripley, and Charles A. Dana. Some of these were merely ornamental appendages. Some, like Dana, were the real operatives of the concern. It failed. Emerson, we believe, considered it a success, on the idea, we suppose, of Thoreau, that there is more war in peace than in war itself.

After Brook Farm, Dana wrote for the *Chronotype* in Boston, and then naturally drifted into the *Tribune* office. This happened in 1846 or thereabouts. Ripley, being on the same raft, also floated into that haven at the same time. Dana, being an accomplished linguist, and full of European ideas, facts, and the rights of man, took charge of the foreign department of that paper at $12 per week, and Ripley, who had been a Unitarian clergyman, became its hard-working and scrupulously neat literary editor at $5 per week. So neat was Ripley that he could never allow the smallest scrap of waste paper to remain on the floor between his desk and his nobility. While these two Brook-Farm philosophers were thus engaged, they managed to edit the New American Cyclopædia, a work of ability and value, and now a standard work in American literature. In the course of events, and as brains will tell, Dana became the managing editor of the *Tribune*, and, as such, Greeley held him in high estimation, and felt, at one time, that he was an indispensable adjunct to that establishment.

But it became manifest, in the development of brains in the *Tribune* editorial rooms, that Greeley and Dana, valuable as the latter

was, could not entirely agree on the affairs of the day or the logic
of events. There was a little difficulty, and then a separation. It
became necessary for one to leave the establishment. Dana left.
This happened early in 1862, and had something to do with the
"On to Richmond" movement which resulted so disastrously at
Bull Run. What then? Secretary Stanton, who wrote the famous
Joshua and Lord of Hosts letter to the *Tribune*, took to Dana, and
Dana took to the field. He was appointed Assistant Secretary of
War, and sent to the West to co-operate personally with General
Grant in his operations against the rebels. He filled this position
with ability from August, 1863, to August, 1865. Activity marked his
course during the war. On the suppression of the rebellion it was
thought that a new paper was necessary in Chicago. The Chicago
Tribune, the representative journal there, bright and enterprising as
it was, did not fill the measure of the hopes of those who did not
control the columns of that organ of the Republican Party in that
wealthy and growing metropolis of the West, leading to a split in
the Republican Party respecting the election of Senator Yates. The
Chicago Republican, organized on an extensive scale with a large capital, was therefore started, but not by Mr. Dana. He was editor-in-chief at $7000 a year, and one fifth of the profits of the concern. It
was not a first-class success. Many who believed that Dana was a
journalist were disappointed. Others, who had lived in France,
shrugged their shoulders. None knew the facts in the case. On
making an investigation as to the causes that led to this apparent
failure, it was ascertained that the *Republican* had more than one
head, and no paper can succeed brilliantly with more than one.
That was the real secret of the difficulty. The result was the return of Dana to New York, which was the true field for him, after
receiving $10,000 for surrendering his interest.

Newspapers, meanwhile, were increasing in wealth and influence.
Editors were becoming more independent in their pockets and in the
utterance of their own views. The *Tribune* in New York was daily
becoming less an organ of political leaders. Seward and Weed had
ceased to be a power with Greeley. The *Times* could not be so
fully controlled by mere politicians as they desired. The *Herald*
always uttered the sentiments of its editor. The *World* was largely
democratic. The Republican Party had one set of leaders in Albany and another set in New York. One of these sets, not too
friendly with the *Tribune*, needed an organ. They had abundance
of money, but no journalist. Dana, like Blucher, arrived at this
juncture. It was then arranged that he should establish a new paper, to be called the *Evening Telegraph*. This fact became the talk
of editors and reporters all over the country. There was a long de-

lay. Numerous reports as to the cause were in circulation. It was then ascertained that, owing to the opposition of two or three members of the Associated Press, the new paper could not have the telegraphic news of that institution, and without that news the contemplated paper could not succeed; indeed, it would be folly to bring out the first number. So these newspapers believed, and the Associated Press became an autocrat. But it seems that every great event must have its crisis, and in the crisis of this journalistic event the genius of Dana exhibited itself.

The New York *Sun* was a member in full and good standing in the Association. Its proprietor had paid the dues, and had done his share of the work for its benefit. He would sell his establishment, with all its brains, news arrangements, patrons, and good will, for $175,000. One morning the opposition members of the Associated Press were informed that that concern had changed hands, and that the *Sun* of Moses S. Beach had set, and the *Sun* of Charles A. Dana had risen to "shine for all" who wished for and would pay two cents per ray for its genial and fructifying warmth. In this way the first penny paper of the country, after a prosperous existence of over thirty years with its democratic tendencies, became an independent organ of the Republican Party in the metropolis, and a thorn in the side of the *Tribune*. In a short time the old establishment was removed to Tammany Hall, which Dana had also purchased for $175,000, and where, with its new motto "Excelsior" added to the old one, the *Sun* has continued to make its daily appearance. Of the first number under Mr. Dana's management 43,000 were printed. Since, over 100,000 copies have been sold in one day.

If the policy of the late Emperor of France had been fully foreshadowed in the *Idées Napoléonnes* which he published before the Revolution of 1848, the journalistic policy of the new editor of the *Sun* had been clearly foreshadowed in the *Tribune* before he became an independent newspaper manager. In an article on "The Newspaper Press," written by Dana and published in that paper in 1850, he said :

American journalism, like the American national character, is less conventional, more versatile, various, and flexible than European. A German, French, or English journalist can not put his paper to press without one or more regular long editorials, wrought out with due attention to all the rules of rhetoric, in a style smacking often quite as much of the scholar's study as of the crowded and rapid world in which a real editor has his being. The American is more a *journalist*, that is, a writer who seizes upon the events of the day and holds them up, now in this aspect, now in that, flinging on them the most condensed and lively light. He does not seek to make elaborate essays; his ambition lies not in fine writing; he spends no long hours in polishing the turn of his periods. All that presupposes a certain degree of leisure, and perhaps a kind of taste to which he is a stranger. At any rate, he has too many things to look after, too many subjects to discuss, too large a round of affairs to understand and write about, to cultivate with assiduity the mere perfumeries and pigeon-wings of his profession. From necessity, he had rather be brief and pointed than elegant and classical; his best triumph as a writer is an occasional felicity, which is, after all, often an accident. It is remarkable that the only paragraph writers are Americans. In fact, paragraphs are a natural invention of the more youthful period of journalism, before a great variety of talent, or thorough study and treatment of subjects are required in the editorial columns of newspapers. The tendency seems to be to abandon them as the Press is improved. Take, for instance, a file of any leading London journal of sixty, or even thirty years ago, and you will find these brief, pithy editorials quite frequent, though the same paper has since ceased to use them. And yet a paragraph of two or three brief sentences will often have more force and produce a greater effect on the convictions of its readers than the same idea expanded through two or three columns, though set forth with the richest resources of the language, and illustrated and supported by all the suggestions of wit and learning. Not that the whole warfare of journalism can be accomplished with light weapons; but the editor should have every sort of arms in his arsenal, and know when to strike with the small-sword and when to fire off his big guns. For the rest, this kind of writing requires a genius to do it in perfection. Many a quill-driver will turn off indefinite lengths of correct and even elegant English, not deficient in sense either, who can not achieve a dozen lines such as every body shall read and nobody forget the point of. Well, this sort of writing is peculiarly American. A German or French paper may employ it, but never in its editorial columns, nor on subjects which have a serious importance. Conceive, if you can, of a genuine paragraph among the editorial articles of the London *Times* or the *Journal des Débats*. The thing is impossible; it would be against all the rules; it would infringe on the stately dignity of the journal. The American editor is luckily shackled by no such consideration. On the contrary, he prefers an article of ten lines to one of ten hundred, provided he can thereby hit the nail on the head; and if he has one or two long articles, he seeks to relieve them by several short ones. Thus his solid leader on some question requiring thorough discussion may be preceded by one or two paragraphs on subjects of most immediate importance. By this means, his most elaborate and carefully-reasoned articles are, as it were, combined with matters of universal interest, and gain force and freshness from the connection. And, indeed, he feels himself under no absolute obligation to have a "leader" at all. His first business is to have the news, that being what the public most desires to read, and, accordingly, he does not hesitate to occupy the columns else given to his own disquisitions with the latest and most important intelligence that has reached him, whether it be in the shape of a telegraphic dispatch or the letter of a correspondent.

American journalism is no less remarkable for its variety and comprehensiveness than the German. It has, perhaps, an even greater range of subjects, at the same time that it is superior in a certain living interest with which it treats them. The American regards nothing with indifference, and, even where he does not take sides as a partisan, he carries with him a degree of genuine sympathy in the event and its actors which renders him an excellent observer and reporter. He is no dull analyzer, and sees the thing before he attempts to speculate on its philosophy and consequences. He is the most practical of men, and thus his enthusiasm—of which he has a large stock—concentrates itself upon persons and deeds, and makes him almost a part of the occurrence he describes. His element is action, and his method rapidity; his weakness, if he has one, is a too excitable patriotism, and the habit of forever glorifying his country, its institutions, and its people, as if they stood in need of laudation, as well of rather fiercely, or even gaseously resenting any foreign disrespect to the same, as if his own confidence in their comparative superiority were somewhat shaky. This fault, however, grows out of a certain immaturity of the national character, and, with the rapid rate at which our journalism goes ahead, it ought soon to be free of such impolitic exaggerations.

It is true that our American brevity, speed, and variety are too often accompanied by a superficial apprehension of ideas, and an imperfect knowledge of facts, especially such as have happened at a distance—characteristics more natural to youth than creditable to the energy and pretensions of manhood, and which may well make us regret the penetration of the French, and the thorough information of the Germans; but these are faults which every day helps to diminish, and which must soon be reduced to mere exceptions. Moreover, they are faults which indicate deficient organization in the editing of newspapers quite as much as personal deficiency in the writers. Most of our leading papers have hitherto depended on single individuals, not merely to give the tone to their columns, but also to write almost every thing in the way of editorials. But this has already changed considerably within a few years, and is destined to entire alteration. The time will soon arrive, if it has not arrived already, when the chief editor of a daily paper which aspires to circulation and influence will not presume to treat every topic that may arise, or to venture into every region of thought and science, but will confine himself to a comparatively limited sphere of writing, and leave the rest to the labors of the most numerous and able corps of assistants at his command. Let those, then, who find American journalism less philosophical than the French, and less finished and artistic in its productions than the English, take courage and believe that they will not always have reason for such criticism. Besides, having admitted the charge, we have a right to ask if French, German, and English papers are so uniformly well-informed, and so profound in thought upon American ideas and events, as to be fit standards of perfection in comparison with their contemporaries on this side of the water?

Started on this platform, it began its new career on the first of January, 1868. One year after this event, its spirit showed itself in an advertisement of one of its cheap editions:

The Dollar Sun.
CHAS. A. DANA, Editor.

The cheapest, smartest, and best New York newspaper. Every body likes it. Three editions: DAILY, **$6**; SEMI-WEEKLY, **$2**; and WEEKLY, **$1** a year. ALL THE NEWS at half price. Full reports of markets, agriculture, Farmers' and Fruit-growers' Clubs, and a complete story in every Weekly and Semi-Weekly number. A present of valuable plants and vines to every subscriber; inducements to canvassers unsurpassed. $1000 Life Insurances, Grand Pianos, Mowing Machines, Parlor Organs, Sewing Machines, etc., among the premiums. Specimens and lists free. Send a Dollar and try it.
I. W. ENGLAND, Publisher Sun, New York.

True to his education, the publisher could not resist premium inducements for subscribers. If the *Tribune*, where Dana and England both graduated, increased its weekly circulation by gifts of strawberry plants, and gold pens, and steel engravings of its editor, certainly "valuable plants and vines," added to "life insurances, grand pianos, mowing machines, parlor organs, sewing machines," especially when these are only "among the premiums" offered, ought assuredly to run the *Dollar Sun* high up on the list of successful newspapers, and reach the very zenith of prosperity.

Secretary Boutwell, of the Treasury Department, although he must have known the office was neither to the "taste" nor "inclination" of Mr. Dana, offered him the position of appraiser in the New York Custom-house in 1869, and this is the polite way the editor snubbed the secretary for the offer:

NEW YORK, April 17, 1869.

MY DEAR SIR,—Your unexpected favor of the 14th instant was duly received. It would have been more speedily answered but for the personal request with which it closes. In these days of corruption in high places as well as low places, no upright citizen ought hastily to refuse such a request; but, after due consideration, I find myself constrained to decline this mark of your esteem and confidence. I beg you, however, to believe that this is not done from either of the reasons which you suggest. Having been educated to commercial pursuits, the office is not repugnant to my tastes; and as for serving the government at some sacrifice of my own interest and convenience, I trust that during the past few years I have sufficiently proved my readiness to do it. But I already hold an office of responsibility as the conductor of an independent newspaper, and I am persuaded that to abandon it or neglect it for the functions you offer me would be to leave a superior duty for one of much less importance. Nor is it certain that I can not do more to help you in the pure and efficient administration of the Treasury Department by remaining here and denouncing and exposing political immorality than I could do as appraiser by the most zealous effort to insure the faithful and honest collection of the customs. Very sincerely yours,

CHARLES A. DANA.

Hon. GEORGE S. BOUTWELL, Secretary of the Treasury.

The *Sun* became sensational and personal, and increased in circulation. Judgment of a superior order is requisite to manage a journal on this basis, because there must sometimes be a change in policy in order to accomplish the great intellectual purpose of a newspaper. In this new position of Mr. Dana he did not forget his old *confrère* of the *Tribune*, and when the opportunity came, as it did in the Young *bouleversement*, he published a broadside of letters and comments under the head of "At Last—At Last." Some of the points of this affair we have mentioned in the sketch of the *Tribune*. Managing Editor Young immediately commenced a libel suit against the *Sun*, laying his damages at $100,000. The affidavit on which Mr. Dana was arrested is a curious and interesting development of persons and papers:

SUPREME COURT, KINGS COUNTY.

The Sun Printing and Publishing Association, Charles A. Dana, individually, and as President of said Association, and Thomas Hitchcock, John H. Sherwood, F. A. Conkling, Marshall B. Blake, and F. A. Palmer, as Trustees of said Association.

John Russell Young, being duly sworn, says that he is a resident and householder in the city of Brooklyn. That since the month of May, 1866, he has been and now is the managing editor of the New York *Tribune*, a daily and weekly newspaper, published in the city of New York, and also a stockholder and one of the trustees of the Tribune Association, an association organized under the law of the State of New York, being the owners and having the control of the said newspapers and their publication. That the daily circulation of said *Tribune* is about 50,000 copies, and the weekly is about 200,000 copies. That on the 27th day of April, 1869, the defendants above named were the publishers, owners, and proprietors of the *Sun*, a newspaper by them published, printed, and sold daily, semi-weekly, and weekly in the city of New York, and having a large circulation in the city of Brooklyn and in other places. That on the said 27th day of April, 1869, the defendants above named, contriving and maliciously designing to injure the plaintiff in his good name, fame, and credit, and to bring him into public scandal, infamy, contempt, and disgrace with and among all his neighbors, employers, associates, and other good and worthy citizens, and to harass and oppress this plaintiff, did falsely, wickedly, and maliciously compose and publish, and cause and procure to be published in said newspaper called the *Sun*, so, as aforesaid, owned and published by said defendants, of and concerning this plaintiff, a false, malicious, and defamatory libel, containing the false, scandalous, malicious, defamatory, and libelous matter following, that is to say—[Here appears the article.] Deponent further says that by reason of the said grievances committed by the said defendants the plaintiff has been and still is greatly injured in his good name, fame, credit, and character, and brought into public scandal, infamy, and disgrace with and among all his neighbors, associates, employers, and other good and worthy citizens, and has been and still is greatly harassed and oppressed by reason of said false and malicious libel, and has suffered damages by reason of the premises in the sum of one hundred thousand dollars. Deponent further says that he has commenced an action against said defendants upon said sufficient cause of action, and has issued a summons therein. Deponent further says that he is informed and believes that Charles A. Dana, S. B. Chittenden, Roscoe Conkling, Edward D. Morgan, Charles Gould, A. A. Low, C. E. Detmold, David Dows, George Opdyke, William T. Blodgett, Marshall O. Roberts, A. L. Brown, T. G. Churchill, F. A. Palmer, F. A. Conkling, A. B. Cornell, Cyrus W. Field, Thomas Hitchcock, M. B. Blake, E. D. Smith, T. Murphy, P. M'Martin, are stockholders of said association, holding and owning a majority of the capital stock of said association. And deponent further states that the said article speaks of "how Chase, Cameron, Grow, and Brewster were fleeced," meaning thereby that this deponent obtained certain sums from the Hon. Simon Cameron, Hon. S. P. Chase, the Hon. G. A. Grow, and the Hon. B. H. Brewster, in a corrupt manner, for improper purposes, all of which defendant denies as without the least foundation in truth, and as false and scandalous. And deponent further states that the said article says that "the commodore (meaning deponent) ordered all hands to go a fishing and to bait for Salmon," meaning thereby that the deponent was engaged in a clandestine manner in endeavoring to obtain from the Hon. Salmon P. Chase sums of money to secure his (deponent's) support for his nomination for the office of President of the United States, all of which deponent denies as without the least foundation in truth, and as false and scandalous, he never having directly or indirectly received, or endeavored to receive, or expected to receive any sum of money from the Hon. Salmon P. Chase, or from any friend of the Hon. Salmon P. Chase. And deponent further states that the said article contains the following: "The commodore (meaning deponent), however, reminded Mr. M'Clure that the fourth page of the *Tribune* was all-powerful; that its influence was a valuable consideration, and would prove worth more than the price paid for the *Post*," all of which deponent denies as without the least foundation in truth, and as false and scandalous. And deponent further states that said article contains the following: "Grow struck heavily;" thereby meaning that the Hon. Galusha A. Grow was asked or compelled by corrupt means to pay certain sums of money to this deponent, all of which deponent denies as without the least foundation in truth, and as false and scandalous. And deponent further states that said article contains the following: "It is understood at this time Cameron was bled to the tune of $5000," thereby meaning that the Hon. Simon Cameron was corruptly compelled to pay $5000 to deponent for the influence of the *Post* or the *Tribune*, all of which deponent denies as without the least foundation in truth, and as false and scandalous. And deponent further states that the said article contains the following: "It is also stated that the Hon. Thomas N. Rooker, the veteran foreman of the *Tribune* composing-room, became an eyesore to the commodore (meaning deponent), who resolved to dig him out," thereby meaning that this deponent was endeavoring to have Mr. Rooker removed from the office of foreman, all of which deponent denies as without the least foundation in truth, and as false and scandalous. And deponent further states that said article contains the following:

"PHILADELPHIA, April 21, 1869.

"DEAR SIR,— * * * Since Mr. Young assumed the duties of the position he now holds on the New York *Tribune*, he has repeatedly assured me, up to the time when the troubles commenced on one of his daily newspapers in this city, in August last, that I would be the publisher of the *Tribune*. He said that Mr. Sinclair was an old fogy, like Mr. Brown, the manager of the *Press* in this city, and that the stockholders would soon make a change. In fact, the last time he visited me at my present residence, shortly before the *Morning Post* moved into its new building at Seventh and Jayne Streets, he stated, while sitting at the breakfast table, 'that every thing was working nicely, and that inside of six months I should be publisher of the New York *Tribune*, and keep myself in readiness to leave Philadelphia at short notice.' CHAS. M'CLINTOCK."

Thereby meaning that deponent had promised to Charles M'Clintock the office of publisher of the *Tribune*, which allegation is without the least foundation in truth, and is false and scandalous; and deponent further states that he is desirous of vindicating his good name, fame, credit, and character among his said neighbors, associates, employers, and other good and worthy citizens, and for that pur-

pose prays that an order of arrest may issue against the said defendants and each of them.   JNO. RUSSELL YOUNG.
Sworn before me, April 27, 1869—A. B. TAPPAN, Justice Supreme Court.

With the peculiar state of society and politics in New York, with the tactics of the management of the *Sun*, with the low price of subscription, and with the character and reputation of its chief editor, the *Sun* could not but have a large circulation, and in May, 1870, we find in the *New York Herald* the following advertisement, which is a journalistic curiosity:

TWO AND A HALF MILLIONS A MONTH.

THE NEW YORK SUN
AHEAD OF ALL COMPETITORS.
The circulation of
THE SUN
is many thousands larger
than that of any other daily newspaper.
The aggregate daily editions of
THE SUN
last week were
SIX HUNDRED AND TWENTY-TWO THOUSAND FOUR HUNDRED
(622,400).

The daily circulation of THE SUN for the four weeks of May was as follows:

First week	611,800
Second week	620,100
Third week	614,600
Fourth week	622,400
Total in four weeks	2,468,900

or nearly two millions and a half. This is equal to a daily average of 102,870 (one hundred and two thousand eight hundred and seventy) for the twenty-four days of publication. This simple statement of facts is sufficient evidence of immense and growing popularity of the *Sun*. It demonstrates conclusively that the *Sun* is no servant of a clique or class, but

THE GREAT ORGAN OF THE PEOPLE.

As such it will continue to uphold with all its might that which is good and true, while it will fearlessly expose knavery, corruption, and imbecility in high or low places, wherever their practice imperils public safety or private virtue.

THE SUN IS THE BEST AND MOST READABLE NEWSPAPER published. Its news is the freshest, most interesting and sprightliest current, and no expense is spared to make it just what the great mass of the people require.

As a matter of information for such as may not be aware of the fact, we may mention that the *Sun* sheds its genial beams upon all at the
MODEST PRICE OF TWO CENTS.

The *Sun* has introduced a new feature in one department of that paper. For some time the newspapers of this country gave only the marriages and deaths. European papers published the births. Several years ago this feature was introduced, but not very extensively carried out by our people. American mothers have been opposed to such announcements. But the *Sun* now daily publishes the divorces. They are inserted with the other domestic announcements, and in chronological order. 1st, " Born." 2d, " Married." 3d, " Divorced." 4th, " Died." That journal also gives under these heads all those of prominence in any community that have met with any of these incidents or accidents.

James Grant tells a story of the origin of the custom of requiring payment for the insertion of marriage announcements in the *London Times*. They were published gratuitously in all the English papers till then. So were the announcements of deaths. The same custom prevailed in the United States. It appears to have been the early practice of the *Times*, in announcing a marriage, to state the amount of the bride's dowry—£20,000 or £30,000, whatever it might happen to be. One morning at breakfast Mr. Walter threw out the suggestion that if a man married all that money he might certainly pay a trifling percentage upon it to the printer for acquainting the world with the fact. "These marriage fees would form a nice little pocket-money for me, my dear," added Mrs. Walter, and, as a joke, her husband agreed to try the experiment. The charge at first was but a trifle, and the annual amount probably not much; but Mrs. Walter, at her death, passed this prescriptive right to her daughter, and when, a few years ago, the right was repurchased by the present proprietor, it was assessed at £4000 or £5000.

Our papers formerly published these announcements as interesting items of domestic news. Mr. Bennett, of the *Herald*, first made the change in this country. Now the income from this source alone to that paper is not far from $30,000 per annum. There is rarely less than a column daily of marriage and obituary notices in the *Herald*.

"No cards" has become a familiar announcement in the marriage notices of newspapers. Several years ago, about 1865, a lady and gentleman were married in New York. They were quietly united in the bonds of matrimony. They had many friends and acquaintances. Not wishing any display, and not wishing to have it appear that they had slighted any one, the gentleman, in having the announcement of the marriage inserted in the *Herald*, added "No cards" to the notice. These cabalistic words, on the morning of their publication, puzzled the fashionable world. "No cards! What does that mean?" asked every one. Their inventor was famous for nine days in Gotham. But now a large number of the daily marriage announcements, to the disgust of the card engravers, have these words as the "amen" of the ceremony.

The *Sun*, too, has its platform for 1872. It lays down the issues of the campaign in these six paragraphs:

I. One term of office for the President, and no more; the Constitution to be amended to secure this reform.

II. Both Grantism and Tweedism to be abolished in national affairs by laws for the summary punishment of present-taking and bribe-taking as well as of public robbery.

III. Universal amnesty and restoration of political rights to all persons concerned in the late rebellion.

IV. Reform in the Civil Service, so that appointment to office will no longer depend on party patronage, and can not be used as a means of corrupting the politics of the country and perpetuating unworthy men in high places; and so that the President can not appoint his own relations or those of his wife to any office whatever.

V. Reform of the revenue; reduction in the number of revenue officers and the expenses of collecting duties and taxes; fixed salaries for all revenue officers; the abolition of import duties on all the necessaries of life, and the reduction of other duties to a consistent, rational, and moderate system; the abolition of unconstitutional and superfluous internal taxes, leaving only stamps, tobacco, and distilled spirits as the subjects of such taxation.

VI. Legislation to prevent the levy of blackmail upon clerks and other public officers for party political purposes, and for the summary punishment alike of those who demand and those who pay such contributions.

Consistent with the above, the *Sun* made serious charges against Secretary Robeson, of the Navy Department, and was so persistent in them as to call forth the following summons:

Forty-second Congress U. S., House of Representatives,
Washington, D. C., March 16, 1872.

Sir,—I am instructed to notify you that in pursuance of the terms of the inclosed resolution adopted by the House of Representatives on the 11th instant, the committee appointed in accordance therewith are now ready to receive any communication that you may desire to make in support of the charges appearing in the New York *Sun*, of which you are understood to be the responsible editor, against the Hon. George M. Robeson, Secretary of the Navy.

The committee will be glad either to have you appear before them and make any statements likely to lead to a full discovery of all the facts, or to receive information from you or any of your associates in any way most convenient for you.

The committee will be ready to subpœna any witnesses you may name, and to give a full hearing of the entire case, and have for that purpose adjourned to Thursday next, the 21st instant, at 10 o'clock, A.M., from which time they desire to proceed with the investigation as fast as possible.

I am very respectfully yours,   Henry H. Smith,
Clerk of Select Committee, etc.

How did not the *Sun* meet this letter? That "of course we shall appear before the committee," which is responsible journalism in a few words.

The *Sun* is now entered for the race of newspapers for the next ten years. While it has the advantage in price for circulation, it has the disadvantage in size for news and advertisements. It is at the head of a class of newspapers. Of this class there are the *Star*, the *Witness*, the *Mail*, the *Telegram*, in New York; the *Herald* and the *Times* in Boston; the *Public Ledger* and the *Post* in Philadelphia. They occupy the same position in 1872 to the *Tribune*, the *Herald*, the *Times*, and the *World*, in New York, that the *Herald*, *Tribune*, and *Sun* did in 1842 to the *Courier and Enquirer*, *Journal of Commerce*, and *New York Express*, but only in cheapness. The *Tribune* and *Herald*, in 1842, were the cheap, energetic Press at two cents per copy. The *Courier and Enquirer* and the *Journal of Commerce* were the dear, heavy newspapers at six cents per copy. The *Sun* and *Star*, in 1872, are the two-cent papers, and the *Herald*, *World*, *Tribune*, and *Times* are double that price. But—and there is as much virtue in this but as in an if—the high-priced newspapers of to-day, all things considered, are as cheap as the low-priced journals;

and then the age is an electric one. All are high-strung like the telegraphic wires. So long, therefore, as the *Tribune*, and *Herald*, and their class keep up their enterprise, they are safe from any inroads from their competitors.

In closing our sketch of the *Sun* the subjoined statement of one year's sale of newspapers in the metropolis comes in very appropriately. It is the return of the Assistant Assessor of the gross receipts from the sales of the various New York newspapers in 1869. Each return is in excess of $1250 per quarter allowed by law:

Newspapers.	Quarter ending June 30, 1869.	Sept. 30, 1869.	Total for past 12 Months.	Newspapers.	Quarter ending June 30, 1869.	Sept. 30, 1869.	Total for past 12 Months.
Herald	$204,919	$206,256	$801,327	Irish Republic	$ 6,950	$ 6,850	$ 28,564
World	127,261	146,127	689,040	Methodist	2,885	1,905	21,487
Tribune	102,780	88,950	514,207	Christ. Intelligencer	3,430	3,430	14,760
Times	118,643	100,350	445,211	Wilkes's Spirit	6,854	7,750	25,243
Staats Zeitung	63,750	68,750	217,250	Leader	6,210	6,132	24,702
Sun	49,683	58,315	186,707	Day-Book	6,322	6,987	33,860
Post	23,021	22,423	100,435	Scottish American	5,151	3,524	18,112
Express	24,763	27,822	99,472	Shipping List	4,980	12,925	37,491
News	69,750	70,750	269,000	Army and Navy Journ.	2,830	4,600	15,500
Journal of Commerce	23,000	22,000	99,500	Examiner and Chron.	10,334	1,953	42,166
Belletristiches Journal	21,714	20,920	86,302	Albion	2,880	3,222	10,592
Democrat	23,850	23,506	77,265	Courier	5,927	2,450	18,147
Demokrat	5,000	11,035	26,511	Produc. Price Current	1,538	1,059	5,635
Commerc'l Advertiser	10,317	8,073	41,050	Irish People	2,615	1,235	7,869
Ledger	155,014	163,187	699,828	Handel Zeitung	710	2,933	6,851
Funny Fellow	130,981	116,488	488,595	Emerald	3,721	5,136	27,535
Harper's Weekly and Bazar	113,098	112,649	444,934	Turf, Field, and Farm	5,120	6,310	12,703
Sunday Times		7,687	21,840	Time-Table	13,859	11,042	24,901
Mercury	38,087	36,325	151,907	New Yorker Journal	18,950	20,251	39,201
Observer	13,159	9,141	73,014	Fireside Companion	17,974	27,281	86,714
Hearth and Home	10,339	16,250	52,589	Rural New Yorker	6,835	18,853	135,677
Atlas	7,468	3,015	22,766	Yankee Notions	835	654	3,242
Evangelist	8,575	6,644	37,017	Liberal Christian	1,883	2,750	7,619
Scientific American	20,574	19,742	77,241	Counting-house Monitor	1,900	1,810	5,400
Irish American	11,012	10,125	43,298	Comic Monthly	4,672	2,700	13,523
Dispatch	16,150	14,600	59,744	Telegram	3,558	3,639	10,108

The *New York Citizen* and *Round Table*, consolidated during the last quarter, made a return of $8023.

Within the last six months the *Clipper* and the *Franco-American* removed from the district.

If we look back to 1833, when the *Sun* was started, we find that the total number of copies of all the papers printed in New York City was 6,000,000 to 8,000,000 in that year, valued then at $400,000 or $500,000. The total sales in 1869 reached the enormous sum of 7,000,000. It is probable that, against the 8,000,000 copies issued in 1833, the number in 1869 came up to 150,000,000 to 200,000,000, almost twice as many copies as were issued in the whole country in the year that the first penny paper made its appearance.

It is to be considered, in analyzing this table, that the sums mentioned there do not include the receipts from advertisements except in the returns of the *World*, the proprietor of which, it is mentioned, made a mistake in one or quarters, and returned his total receipts. But this inadvertence is not sufficient to change the wonderful aggregate result of the statement.

CHAPTER XLIV.

THE COMIC PAPERS.

THEIR FAILURE IN THE UNITED STATES AND SUCCESS IN EUROPE.—THE CAUSE.—WIT AND HUMOR HERE AND ELSEWHERE.—MARK TWAIN ON ARTEMUS WARD.—INTERVIEW WITH PETROLEUM V. NASBY.—WHAT ONE HUMORIST SAYS OF ANOTHER.—ABUNDANCE OF WIT IN AMERICA.

Quid rides?
While comic journalism, *per se*, does not thrive in the United States, we have plenty of comic writers and talkers, who have grown fat, made money, set the nation in a roar, and thrown Momus into ecstasies of delight over the fresh, free, funny, and broad humor of our numerous *raconteurs*, and wits, and punsters.

One of the earliest writers in this special department of our literature was the original Joe Strickland, whose productions were short and witty. They were written by George W. Arnold, who kept a lottery office in Broadway, New York, and graced the newspapers in 1826, '27, and '28. The Croaker papers of Drake and Halleck were also full of points. Seba Smith, of Portland, Maine, then wrote the queer and quaint letters of Major Jack Downing, of Downingsville. They had their sensation in their day. Andrew Jackson was in the height of his popularity at that time, and he was the subject of these epistles. Charles Augustus Davis, of New York, was Jack Downing the second. Then Judge Halliburton came out with Sam Slick of Slickville. He was a Nova Scotian, it is true, but his droll sketches and humor belong to the Western Hemisphere. Then Joseph C. Neale, an editor in Philadelphia—not John Neal, of Portland—"not this man, but that"—appeared with his curious "Charcoal Sketches," and created some pleasure and merriment. Then such wits as Prentice, Greene, Bennett, Lewis Gaylord Clarke, John Waters, Kendall, Felix Merry, Henry J. Finn, Oliver Wendell Holmes, Lumsden, Cornelius Matthews, and Briggs came before the footlights of our continental theatre.

There was a lithographer, named Robinson, who lined the curbstones and covered the old fences of New York with his peculiarly characteristic caricatures during Jackson's and Van Buren's administrations, which frequently produced a broad grin on the face of the metropolis in those days. Since that period a number of humorists and wits of purely native growth have become well known throughout the land. Artemus Ward, Mark Twain, John Phœnix, Doesticks, Josh Billings, Bret Harte, Petroleum V. Nasby, who seems to be a descendant of Jack Downing, Leland, Wilkins, Congdon, and Mrs. Partington, in their real names and in *noms des plumes*, have introduced a new order of comic literature, which, for quaintness, and richness, and freshness, is a feature of the times. Still later, Orpheus C. Kerr, Captain Watt A. Lyre, Yuba Dam, Eli Perkins, Oofty Koofty, Will M. Carleton, M. T. Jugg, and Si Slokum have turned up in the fertile soil of the East and West. Humor is a specialty with them; yet none of these writers, nor all of them combined, have been able to establish and keep in prosperous existence a publication like *Punch* for a single year. Our people don't want their wit on a separate dish. These wits and humorists write when the spirit moves them. No one can always be funny. Weekly drafts, like a run upon a bank, tend to exhaust them. Specie payments would cease at the treasury of wit. Nickel would take the place of silver and gold, and we should no longer hear the real ring of the true metal. There must be variety in wit; one style is not sufficient for Americans. Wit, and humor, and fun are spontaneous productions in the United States, and effervesce and bubble up like the oil-wells of Pennsylvania; they are as rich and golden as the mines in California—indeed, no crowd is without its wit, no riot without its jest; there is a laugh in every street. America is filled with Tom Hoods to keep the Niagara in a roar. They find no vent in special publications; their safety-valves are in the regular weekly and daily papers. Each newspaper has one or more. Some of the leading editorial articles sparkle with wit as a duchess does with diamonds.

No single publication, like *Judy, Vanity Fair, Yankee Doodle, Lantern, Puck,* or *Fun,* answer the needs of this country. Wit can not be measured off like tape, or kept on hand for a week; it would spoil in that time. Hence the failure of such papers in New York. Thus, while London generously sustains a publication like *Punch,* Paris laughs over the real hits of *Charivari* and nineteen or twenty other comic papers; while Germany enjoys her lager bier with the *Kladderadatsch* and more than thirty other humorous journals, with a circulation of three hundred thousand copies, Italy eats her maccaroni with her illustrated fun for seasoning, and Spain, with her cheap and slovenly journalism, has her bull-fights, with her comic publications printed in large type, with illustrations done in chalk. Australia, too, has not been able to make her rapid progress in gold and glory without a *Punch,* in imitation of the original in London, and full of smartness and wit. But the United States lives, and breathes, and prospers, builds the longest railroads, and suppresses the biggest rebellions without a *Punch,* or a *Charivari,* or a *Kladderadatsch.*

We have tried all kinds of comic periodicals. *Vanity Fair,* which was started in New York in 1859, probably lived the longest. It was not stopped till 1863. George Arnold wrote over a hundred articles for it, including the M'Arone Letters. *Mrs. Grundy* was issued in July, 1865. Twelve numbers only were published. The *Jolly Joker, Momus, John Donkey,* and, without much exaggeration, fifty others, were issued at different times and at different places with the same result. They came into existence with a laugh, but, poor fellows! how did they make their exit?

It was announced early in 1870 that fifty thousand dollars had been subscribed for the establishment of a new comic paper in New York. After so many failures, the mention of this sum was deemed necessary in order to assure the public that permanency was secured. Shortly after, advertisements appeared of the publication of *Punchinello* by the Punchinello Publishing Company. Its first number promised well. It contained this journalistic pun to start with, divided into four equal parts:

Let Stone, of the *Journal of Commerce,* Wood, of the *News,* Marble, of the *World,* and Brick, of the *Democrat,* put their heads together and make a new conglomerate pavement.

But neither this quadruple pun nor the fund of fifty thousand dollars was sufficient. The competition of the lay papers was too much for even genuine wit or greenbacks. No one can wait a week for a laugh; it must come in daily with our coffee. What has been the fate of the *Punster,* lately issued in Mobile, we have not ascertained. If alive, it has our best wishes. And *Puck,* in St. Louis, how is he?

It is probable that the original comic paper was the *Merrie Mercurie,* which was printed in London in 1700. The world has always been full of wit, but it never came from any other than the wine-press till then. The *Scourge,* not a very funny name, was published in England. It appeared in 1811. George Cruikshanks made his *début,* we believe, on this periodical. Since then, *Figaro, Diogenes, Charivari, Puck, Punchinello, Puppet-show, Asmodeus, Squib, Lion, Town Talk, Fun, Porcupine, Mephistopheles, Chat, Odd Fellow, Balloon, Judy, Banter, Zou-Zou, Punch,* and, indeed, many others, have appeared. *Punch,* the real Comus of all, made its bow on the 17th of July, 1841, and has lived, and laughed, and become rotund on wit, and wisdom, and wine ever since. It is now a universally recognized character. It has developed more wit with pen and pencil, and has accomplished more good, socially and politically, in England than any politician or statesman is willing to accord to its influence.

Charles Philopon is the head of this description of art and literature in France. He established a comic paper in July, 1830, which he called *La Caricature*. This overwhelmed him with lawsuits, and his paper was suppressed. He then started the *Charivari*. What Mark Lemon, the manager of *Punch*, accomplished, after his fashion, in London, Charles Philopon achieved, after his style, in Paris. John Leech was developed and made famous in England, and Amedée de Noé, the celebrated Cham, and Gustave Doré, brought out to shine in France; but these wonderful artists were only a part of the result and use of these comic papers. *La Lune*, of Paris, obtained permission from great men to lampoon them. Victor Hugo seemed delighted with the *pasquinades* on him. In a note to the editor in regard to a caricature of him that was to appear, he said, "I applaud it in advance. You are a legion of charming writers and sparkling artists. I give myself up entire to Mr. Gill, who has so often enchanted me. There is a painter in this caricaturist; there is a thinker in this parodist."

Wit and humor, politics and religon, science and philosophy, are taken in separate doses in Europe. Each has its place. The Episcopal and Catholic churches, Oxford and the Sorbonne, the London *Times* and *Le Journal Officiel* of Paris, *Punch* and *Charivari*, beer and claret, meet the mental, physical, and psychological wants of the people, each in its own way, and in accordance with the recognized rules of society. No joke appears in the London *Times* except by accident. All is solemnly grand there. Is there any wit in the official journal of France? Only the grim humor of Napoleon or Thiers pointed with bayonets. Occasionally a smile creeps over the face of a hearer of Spurgeon in London when an *outré* illustration escapes from the preacher's lips. When an Englishman, or a Frenchman, or a German is in need of wit, he goes to *Punch*, or *Charivari*, or *Kladderadatsch*, or to the theatre, where there is a supply. They want it concentrated. Hence the pecuniary success of these publications on the other side of the Atlantic.

Very different is the love of wit in America. It is not a specialty here; it is every where; it is in the bright, clear atmosphere; we are crammed with wit from the attic down; it blooms in every thing; it is on the field of battle, in the newspaper, on the plantation, in the pulpit, in the court-room, at the polls, in Congress, at the fireside, in the state prison, in the railway car, on steam-boats, at fires, in theatres, on the gold exchange, where men are ruined by scores, in the gambling houses, at the dinner-table, in the kitchen, and even in the sick-room—indeed, the face of America seems always wreathed in smiles at the last *bon mot*.

Our wits lecture on each other. Artemus Ward is a subject for

Mark Twain. He spoke of Artemus in a lecture in Brooklyn in November, 1871, as follows:

> Artemus Ward's real name, as most of you are probably aware, was Charles F. Brown. He was born in Waterford, Me., in 1834. His personal appearance was not like that of most Maine men. He looked like a glove-stretcher; his hair, red, and brushed well forward at the sides, reminded one of a divided flame. His nose rambled on aggressively before him with all the strength and determination of a cow-catcher, while his red mustache, to follow out the simile, seemed not unlike the unfortunate cow.
>
> Ward never had any regular schooling; he was too poor to afford it for one thing, and too lazy to care for it for another. He had an intense, ingrained dislike for work of any kind; he even objected to see other people work, and on one occasion went so far as to submit to the authorities of a certain town an invention to run a tread-mill by steam. Such a notion could not have originated with a hard-hearted man. Ward was a dutiful son, and his first act, when money began to come in on him from his lectures, was to free from incumbrance the old homestead in his native town and settle it upon his aged mother.
>
> His first literary venture was type-setting in the office of the old Boston *Carpet-Bagger*, and for that paper he wrote his first squib. He tried every branch of writing, even going so far as to send to the Smithsonian Institute—at least, so he himself said—an essay entitled "Is Cats to be Trusted?" He soon tired of settled life and poor pay in Boston, and wandered off over the country to better his fortune, obtaining a position in Cleveland as a reporter at $12 per week. It was while in Cleveland that he wrote his first badly-spelled article, signing it "Artemus Ward." He did not think much of it at the time of writing it, but it gave him a start that speedily sent him to the top of the ladder without touching a single rung.
>
> He soon left Cleveland, and, going to New York, assumed the editorship of *Vanity Fair*. Settled employment, however, did not suit him, and he soon started out on his first lecture tour. The success of this new employment, although not great at first, soon exceeded his most sanguine expectations, and he adopted it as a permanent profession. When he went to England his reception was of the nature of an ovation. It is said that for each of his articles contributed to *Punch* he received $600. His panoramic exhibitions in Egyptian Hall were a grand success, drawing, night after night, immense crowds to witness them.
>
> The English climate of cold and fog seemed to have the effect of eating away his life, and, although he struggled hard, he had to relinquish his avocation. When he knew that he must die, his only desire was to get home, but this was denied him. He got as far as Southampton, but his physician peremptorily forbid his attempting the sea voyage, and at Southampton, in the thirty-fourth year of his age, he died.

Our humorists, too, are interviewed. The *Newark* (N.J.) *Courier* successfully performed this operation on Postmaster Nasby, also in November, 1871. The account is quite rich, as those who read it will see:

> *Reporter.* Have you ever been interviewed before, Mr. Nasby?
>
> *Nasby.* No; this is my initiation.
>
> *R.* Mr. Nasby, who is the worst speller, you or Mr. Billings?
>
> *N.* Billings, by all odds. He does it on purpose. Mine is a scientific spelling, founded on phonetic principles, and, consequently, much in advance of the civilization of the age. It is constructed on a uniform principle.
>
> *R.* How long have you been lecturing?
>
> *N.* This is my fifth season.
>
> *R.* Is it your last?
>
> *N.* (laughing). Redpath, of the Boston Lyceum, says, actors, the *demi monde*, and lecturers never reform; so I really can't say.
>
> *R.* Why did you leave your post-office in Kentucky?
>
> *N.* I guess it was because there was some irregularity in the accounts; nothing like being fashionable, my boy.

R. Where have you got your postmaster now?
N. I have taken the "old man" back to the X Roads. We didn't get along well enough in the "Harp of Erin" s'loon, New York.
R. Did you find the people in New York an improvement on the Kentuckians?
N. Not at all; only another kind of cussedness.
R. Have you reconciled Deacon Pogram to Nasby?
N. Yes; they're living now in a state of harmony.
R. I thought you said in the State of Kentucky?
N. You're right; there's quite a difference.
R. Is it true you're "Will M. Carleton," the farm balladist?
N. By no means. He is a young man from Hillsdale, Mich. I brought him out first on the *Blade*, where the four poems of the "Betsy and I" series were published. Then the Harpers lassoed him. He has a brilliant future before him.
R. What do you think of Bret Harte?
N. I like Harte very much. He has decided genius, and socially he is a perfect gentleman.
R. Do you know Nast, Harpers' great pencil satirist?
N. Intimately.
R. Tell me something about Nast.
N. I will, if you will promise not to get off the joke nast-y.
R. Agreed.
N. Nast is a man about thirty-four years of age, and about five feet seven inches in height. He has a keen, sharp eye, and a good German face; has black hair, and is dapper and neat in his person. I think he was born in Breslau, Germany, and came over here when he was about three years of age. His father wanted him to be a jeweler, but he was already betrothed to art. Frank Leslie, I think, brought him out first, at the time he sent him to England to make pictures of the great Heenan-Sayers prize-fight. And then, when the war broke out, the Harpers sent him South to sketch battles. It was in 1862, just after the election, when all the country was clamoring for peace at any price, that he struck the particular vein in which he has since become famous. The picture he drew then, entitled Peace, was grand. It represented a Union soldier's grave, over the tombstone of which was weeping Columbia. At the foot stood a companion to the dead loyalist, stripped of his arms, and shaking hands with a rebel armed to the teeth, and with one foot upon the grave. That picture made his reputation. He was as well known the next day as he is now. It was circulated by the million as a campaign document.
R. How about his domestic life?
N. He lives, I think, in One Hundred and Twenty-fifth Street, New York, in a modest frame house. His wife and his three sons constitute his family. They have no servants. At the end of the lot on which his house stands is a one-story brick building, where he does his work. He has there the quaintest collection of curiosities, chiefly of art, that could be imagined. His wife is a lady of rare intelligence, who assists him greatly in his labors. She is a relative of James Parton. Nast is a man of indomitable courage and rare intelligence. Politically he is a most intense Radical.
R. What is his masterpiece?
N. He has a thousand. The last thing he does is always his best. Nast is a moralist—a man who must have an idea. His pencil is savage and bitter, and cuts like the knout. That cartoon, published a week or so ago, of the "Tammany Tiger Let Loose," and wanting to know "what you were going to do about it," was fearful in its power. He tells in ten strokes of his pencil what it would take volumes to express.
R. How did you become acquainted with Nast?
N. He was the only artist, out of many who tried, who drew for me a picture of "Nasby" that suited my idea of the character. It was at the time I was publishing a volume of my letters entitled "Swinging Round the Circle," and it was through that I met him.
R. Is this character of Nasby simply a brain-child?
N. Yes; I don't believe he ever existed in flesh and blood.
R. When did you first conceive the idea?
N. In 1861 I was in Hancock County, Ohio. I had determined upon a series

of letters the year previous. It was in the spring of 1861 that I wrote my first letter. The subject was secession, and I worked up a mock article about the secession of Crawford County, Ohio. It was in type when the first battle of Bull Run occurred. I didn't think it advisable then, the whole country being in mourning, to publish it, and held the letter till fall. About that time my second letter was written. All the Border States democracy were howling about the great influx of negroes which the war would cause. They said they wouldn't work, and must go to the poor-houses or jails, and thus be a burden to the community. There was one fellow, named Flenner, who lived in the town of Findley. He didn't work himself, and his family were supported by the township, and yet he howled the loudest of them all. I met him one day with a petition against the negroes, which he was getting signed, and made it the basis of a letter, in which I published Mr. Flenner's name. I produced this in the Hancock *Jeffersonian*, which I was running at the time. It had a sudden and a great popularity all over the country, and it was in this gradual manner that Mr. Nasby was born. Poor Flenner, I think he died in one hundred days' service, from inducing gangrene by scratching a sore foot with a nail in order to avoid duty.

R. Did you know Artemus Ward?

N. Knew him well. He and Griswold, the "Fat Contributor," and myself were at different times all employed upon the same paper, the Cleveland *Plaindealer*. That was when J. W. Gray, the best editor in the West at that time, had charge. I went on first as a compositor, and then became a local reporter. Reporters in the country are entirely different from your city chaps. They're of more importance. When A. Ward was in Cleveland he was the greatest man there. Nothing could be done without him. He was making his reputation then, although he commenced in Toledo, and eventually got to New York, and thence to London. The "Fat Contributor" succeeded him.

R. What kind of a man was Artemus Ward?

N. He was a jolly, jovial soul, and a true friend. His great delight was to get a company of good fellows together in his room at his hotel, and make a night of it.

R. I almost forgot to compliment you on your poem.

N. What, did you read it?

R. Yes.

N. All through?

R. All through.

N. And still live?

R. And still respirate.

N. Well, you make the third man who has read it, I guess; you, the proof-reader, and myself, although I can hardly accuse the proof-reader, because there was a fearful lot of blundering in it.

R. I suppose you have met, in your rural editorship, some queer characters?

N. I have, scores of them. I will tell you about an epitaph that I once published. I was sitting in my office one afternoon, when there came in an old lady with a red nose, black gloves, and a large umbrella. She looked at me and sighted, and then advanced to the counter. Says she, "Do you publish death notices, sir?" and she heaved another sight at me. Says I, "We do—ten cents a line," and I hove. Says she, "Will you print poetry to the end of it?" I replied that, if necessary, we do add an auction notice. And then she took a piece of paper out of her pocket, and, adjusting her venerable spectacles, read this in a sort of diseased hurdy-gurdy tone :

"Fare thee well, thou loved and lost one,
 Small George Skinner, fare thee well.
God he gave thee, God he took thee,
 Up in heaven with him to dwell.
Our school marm rid that, sir."

Here the interview ended, both parties retiring in good order.

Horace Greeley even delivers lectures on wit. What he knows about farming gives way to what he knows about wit. His admiration is for the higher order of the article. He wants his wit spelt according to Webster. He denounces the modern humorist who thrives on bad spelling. The editor of the *Tribune* despises a pun, and would strike the Wilmington (N. C.) *Commercial* from his exchange list for the following perpetration on the newspapers of Philadelphia :

As an *Item* of news, and for the benefit of an *Inquirer*, we *Herald* the fact that a man seen one *Day* this week with a *Bullet-in* his hand, and a *Telegraph* on a *Post* in his hat. Putting a *Bee* in his pocket, he *Press*-ed, and saw *Stars* before he reached home. The man was a *North American*. We did not know his *Age*, but the *Ledger* will doubtless *Record* it when he dies.

Mr. Bennett, of the *Herald*, had a keen appreciation of wit, but was utterly opposed to puns. One day, at the dinner-table, in a general conversation on poets, one gentleman expressed great admiration for Beranger. "Yes, yes," said Mr. Bennett, "I admit all you say, but I think Burns has more fire than Beranger." "Why," said a gentleman present, "I thought, Mr. Bennett, you detested puns." "So I do," said Mr. Bennett. "But you just uttered one." "I did!" with a look of surprise. "Why, yes ; you said that Burns had more fire than Beranger." He gracefully submitted that it was without prepense.

These are the reasons why no comic paper prospers in the United States. Our wit finds vent in the daily newspapers. Where wit is so spontaneous a production, it must be gathered at once or it is lost. We do not live on the article. No one can thrive on Champagne alone. We take it with other wines, and with other mental food and drink. Our four or five thousand daily and weekly publications have columns of " Nuts to Crack," " Sunbeams," " Sparks from the Telegraph," " Freshest Gleanings," " Odds and Ends," " News Sprinklings," " Flashes of Fun," " Random Readings," " Mere Mentions," " Humor of the Day," " Quaint Sayings," "Current Notes," " Things in General," " Brevities," " Witticisms," " Notes of the Day," "Jottings," " All Sorts," " Editor's Drawer," " Sparks," " Fun and Folly," " Fact and Fiction," " Twinklings."

These are the daily dishes set before our sovereigns. They are the comic departments of the regular Press. We need not count the names of our wits and humorists on the ends of our fingers. It is not necessary to say, " There is Hood, or Douglas Jerrold, or Hook, or Leitch, or Cruikshanks, or Mark Lemon." They are not here in separate and distinct form, even if we do hear of Bret Harte, and Davenport, and Artemus Ward, and Mark Twain. We are a nation full of such characters, perhaps a little thin here and there, but always in abundance and in good humor. They are present on every festive occasion. Our greatest patriot, during the recent gigantic rebellion, with the cares of state on his shoulders, was overflowing with genial stories, and apt humorous anecdotes, and keen illustrations. We are, in a sentence, like the modern hero who could dive deeper, swim farther, and come out drier than Leonidas, or any other man. Hence wit can not thrive here as a specialty. Hence the failure of the *Carpet Bag, Punch and Judy, Vanity Fair, Charivari, Fun, Picayune, Lantern, Yankee Doodle, Phunny Phellow,* and *Punchinello,* common names on both sides of the Atlantic, with all the brilliant flashes of Brougham and Halpine, or the striking sketches of M'Lellan, Bellew, Nast, and Morgan.

Our wit, as we have said, goes into all the papers. Our actions, our talk, our reading, our journals, our trade, our labor, our politics, our religion, must be spiced with it. All we do has its point. Our Attic salt, indeed, seasons every thing except our cooking. There, as the amiable Frenchman said, we have but one gravy for a hundred dishes.

CHAPTER XLV.

THE PRESS IN CONGRESS.

JOURNALISTS IN THE SENATE AND HOUSE OF REPRESENTATIVES.—NEWSPAPERS.—REPRESENTATIVES IN THE NATIONAL CAPITAL.—THE TWO CONGRESSES.

THERE are two Congresses in the United States. One sits in the national Capitol in Washington periodically, and makes and unmakes laws; the other sits *en permanence* in newspaper offices in every city and important town in the nation. They are both deliberative in their character. They are both potential. One Congress is composed of members elected by the people, but can only be heard by their constituents outside the walls of the Capitol by the aid of the other Congress. The members of the first-named talk to each other, often abuse each other, air their ideas and their vanity, enact laws, impose taxes, and make war. They appear before the great public audience like actors on the stage, perform their part, and disappear. The other Congress is larger in numbers and more independent in character. It talks all the time. It is an incessant babbler. It watches public men and public events. It warns the people of approaching danger. It takes large sums of money from the people, but gives something in return. Instead of imposing taxes, it does all in its power to reduce them. It curbs licentiousness in public places. It is the palladium of the people's rights.

What are these two Congresses called? One is the Senate and House of Representatives, and the other the Press of the United States.

These two important branches of the public service are more largely intermixed than one would suppose without an investigation. But, while one is greatly dependent upon the other in order to reach the public eye and the public mind, the Press happily is entirely independent of Congress. In times past the criticisms of the journalist would frequently cause members of the Senate and House to rise to a "question of privilege," under the mistaken idea that the national Congress was superior to the popular Congress; and sometimes these "questions of privilege" have resulted in "satisfaction elsewhere," or "outside of these walls," as in the case of Cilley and Webb, and Rust and Greeley.

While John Walter, the principal proprietor of the *London Times*, ignores in a deliberate speech his journalistic responsibility in the House of Commons, Henry B. Anthony, of the *Providence Journal*, Horace Greeley, of the *New York Tribune*, Henry J. Raymond, of the *New York Times*, and James Brooks, of the *New York Express*, assert theirs in the Senate and House of Representatives without fear or favor. In 1835, Mr. Roebuck, in his political pamphlets, denounced in no measured terms the nameless writers, mentioning the two master-minds of the London *Times* at that time—Edward Sterling and Thomas Barnes—the two men whose slashing and able articles gave the title of "Thunderer" to that journal. Mr. Roebuck said that he "was in the habit of meeting Mr. Sterling in society, and was not a little amused by the charlatan game he played to hide his editorship of the *Times*. If any one had assumed the fact he would have taken it as an affront. Often has it been whispered in my hearing, 'That is the editor of the *Times*; but hush! he will hear us.' 'Well, and what then?' 'What then? He will abuse us, to be sure.'" When this publication appeared, Captain Sterling sent a message to Mr. Roebuck by his friend, Colonel Campbell, in which he said, "I have never been, technically or morally, connected in any manner with the editorship of the *Times*, not possessing over the course or choice of its politics any power or influence whatever, nor, by consequence, being responsible for its acts," whereupon Mr. Roebuck withdrew the language complained of. Yet, in the face of these statements, there appeared in Carlyle's "Life of John Sterling" two letters which passed between Sir Robert Peel and Edward Sterling in the same year, 1835, in which the latter acknowledges the receipt of a high compliment paid him as editor of the *Times* by that distinguished statesman for disinterested services rendered the government of Sir Robert Peel only a few months previous to this affair with Mr. Roebuck.

What is the connection between these powers in France? Sir Henry Bulwer thus described the manner of editing a leading journal in Paris in the time of Louis Philippe:

> If you went to the French opera and saw a very large and very brilliant box— rather larger and more brilliant than any other—whose would you suppose it to be? The king's? no; a minister's? no; an embassador's? no; a French peer's? a deputy's? Guess again. That box is the *Temps* newspaper's! What! a newspaper have a box at the opera? To be sure; that box is where the newspaper does the greatest part of its business. You see that fat, smooth-faced little gentleman, and that tall, thin, pale figure in spectacles—one was a great man a little time ago, and the other expects to be a great man soon. The editor is giving these statesmen an audience. They tell him their views; he listens. They tell him the strength of their party; he takes a note. They tell him what course they mean to pursue; he proffers advice. The editor is a clever man. This is his way of conducting his journal. He pretends that to influence the politics of the day; and, indeed, to know the politics of the day, he must know the political men of the day. He makes his paper the organ of a party, and he makes himself the head of the party. But how to keep this party together? He used to give dinners—

he now takes an opera box. I do not know any thing that better paints the character of the French, or the stand of France, than the journalist at the head of his political party assembled in a box at the opera.

This is the *status* in each country of the power and influence of the newspaper in the three great nations of the world.

In the Congressional Directory of the Forty-first Congress, published in 1869, and compiled with great care by Ben. Perley Poore, an old journalist, we find some very interesting facts of the intermixture of these two estates in the National Assembly. It is our purpose to take from this catalogue a list of the journalists connected with Congress, and to show what they are and what they have been. It is curious to see, in the mutations of life and trade, in the changes of professions, the effect on the minds of individuals when they are responsible editors and when they are mere politicians.

Here is our array of Congressional journalists. Every Congressional Directory embraces more or less of editors. They have always done much as leaven for the whole body. In the future the Newspaper Press will be more largely represented in the legislative halls of the nation:

THE JOURNALISTIC MEMBERS OF CONGRESS.

CALIFORNIA.—Eugene Casserly, Senator, connected with the Press in New York for five years. He began as a reporter; afterwards, in 1850-1, published a daily paper in San Francisco.

INDIANA.—Jasper Packard, Representative, edited the *Laporte Union* in 1856-7.

IOWA.—Frank W. Palmer, Representative, editor of *Jamestown* (N.Y.) *Journal* in 1848, editor of the *Dubuque Daily Times* in 1858, and editor of the *Iowa State Register* from 1861 to 1868.

KANSAS.—Edmund G. Ross, Senator, was foreman of the *Milwaukee Sentinel*, and became editor of the *Kansas Tribune*, the only Free State paper in that Territory at that time, all the others having been destroyed.

Sidney Clarke, Representative, published the *Southbridge Press* in Massachusetts.

MAINE.—James G. Blaine, Speaker of the House, was editor of the *Portland Advertiser* and *Kennebec Journal*.

MASSACHUSETTS.—Henry Wilson, Senator, edited the *Boston Republican*.

Nathaniel P. Banks, Representative, was a newspaper editor prior to 1849.

Henry L. Dawes, Representative, edited the *Greenville Gazette* and *Adams Transcript*.

MISSOURI.—Carl Schurz, Senator, edited a revolutionary paper in Cologne in 1848. He was the Washington correspondent of the *New York Tribune* in 1865 and 1866; afterwards he was connected with the Press of Detroit and St. Louis.

Joel F. Asper, Representative, edited the *Western Reserve Chronicle* in 1849, and the *Chardon Democrat* in 1850. In 1866 he commenced the publication of the *Chillicothe Spectator*.

NEVADA.—Thomas Fitch, Representative, was local editor of the *Milwaukee Free Democrat* in 1859-60; afterwards edited the *San Francisco Times* and *Placerville Republican*.

NEW YORK.—Henry A. Reeves, Representative, editor of the Greenport (N.Y.) *Republican Watchman* since 1858.

Samuel Sullivan Cox, Representative, owned and edited the Columbus *Ohio Statesman* in 1853-4, and has been a constant contributor to the Press.

James Brooks, Representative, has been a newspaper correspondent in Washington and in Europe, an editor of the *Portland Advertiser*, and is now the chief editor of the *New York Express*.

NORTH CAROLINA.—Joseph C. Abbott, Senator, edited the *Manchester* (N. H.) *American* for five years, and was subsequently editor of the *Boston Atlas*.

David Heaton, Representative, was a contributor to newspapers for more than twelve years.

Alexander H. Jones, Representative, was an editor in the early part of the rebellion.

OHIO.—Peter W. Strader, Representative, passed three years of his life in a printing-office.

William Lawrence, Representative, was a reporter for the *Columbus State Journal*, and afterwards edited the *Logan Gazette* and the *Western Law Monthly*.

William Mungen, Representative, was editor of the *Findlay Democratic Courier*.

Philadelph Van Trump, Representative, was editor of the *Lancaster Gazette and Enquirer*.

PENNSYLVANIA.—Simon Cameron, Senator, was a printer and edited newspapers at Doylestown and Harrisburg.

William D. Kelly, Representative, had been a reader in a printing-office.

J. Lawrence Getz, Representative, edited the *Reading Gazette and Democrat* for twenty-five years.

Henry L. Cake, Representative, published the *Pottsville Mining Record* up to the breaking out of the rebellion.

Richard J. Haldeman, Representative, owned and edited the *Daily and Weekly Patriot and Union* at Harrisburg, Pa., from 1857 to 1860.

RHODE ISLAND.—Henry B. Anthony, Senator, editor of *Providence Journal*.

SOUTH CAROLINA.—B. Frank Whittemore, Representative, edited the *New Era*, the first journal established in South Carolina after the surrender, devoted to Reconstruction, etc.

WISCONSIN.—David Atwood, Representative, is editor of the Madison *State Journal*.

TENNESSEE.—William Gaunaway Brownlow, Senator, edited the *Whig* from 1839 to 1861. This paper was published for ten years in Jonesboro', East Tennessee, and afterwards in Knoxville till it was suppressed by the rebels.

ARIZONA.—Richard C. M'Cormick, Delegate, European correspondent of *New York Courier and Enquirer* in 1854–5; edited the *Young Men's Magazine* in 1859–60; was correspondent of the *New York Evening Post* and *New York Commercial Advertiser* in the first year of the rebellion.

DAKOTAH.—S. L. Spink, Delegate, editor and publisher of the *Prairie Beacon*, in Paris, Ill., in 1860.

MONTANA.—James M. Cavanaugh, Delegate, had been a newspaper editor.

Thus there were eight editors in the Forty-first Senate, and twenty-six in the House of Representatives. The Speaker of the House, it will be seen, had been an editor, and the chief officer of the Senate, Vice-president Schuyler Colfax, established and edited the *St. Joseph Valley Register*, at South Bend, Ind., in 1845, and while conducting that paper he learned the art of printing, or setting type.

There were twenty-four journalists in the Forty-second Congress, and this is about the number of this profession that are intermixed with lawyers, merchants, mechanics, politicians, pugilists, publicans, in the Congresses of the nation.

Notwithstanding that there are four or five thousand newspapers and periodicals in this country devoted to the distribution of news, and in spite of the general interest manifested every where and by every one to know what is done in the Legislature of the country, there are only one hundred and twenty-five newspapers directly and officially represented in the two houses of Congress as correspondents. Those not specially represented are furnished with the information they need by the agents of the several Press Associations and News Agencies, and by the city journals in their vicinity.

THE NEWSPAPER DELEGATION.

NAMES OF THE CORRESPONDENTS IN THE FORTY-SECOND CONGRESS.

New York World	G. W. Adams,
	Miss M. A. Snead,
	J. B. Stillson.
New York Herald	G. O. Seilhamer,
	H. A. Preston,
	Mrs. H. M. Barnard.
New York Tribune	H. J. Ramsdell,
	E. V. Smalley,
	Z. L. White.
New York Sun	U. H. Painter.
New York Times	Justin E. Colburn,
	L. L. Crounse.
New York Independent	Mrs. M. C. Ames,
	D. W. Bartlett.
New York Irish Republic	William Cogswell.
New York Journal of Commerce	W. P. Copeland.
New York Home Journal	Mrs. Mary E. Nealy.
New York Evening Post	W. Scott Smith.
New York Standard	Clifford Warden,
	James R. Young.
New York Evening Mail	R. J. Hinton.
New York Associated Press	D. R. M'Kee,
	A. Devine,
	L. A. Gobright,
	H. G. Hayes,
	James G. Holland.
American Press Association	W. H. Clarke,
	H. M. Irwin,
	J. M. Sarvis.
Southern Associated Press	M. W. Barr.
Baltimore Associated Press	O. K. Harris,
	F. A. Richardson.
Bureau of Correspondence	J. C. Gallagher.
Philadelphia Ledger	D. D. Cone,
	J. C. Proctor.
Dakotah Herald	M. K. Armstrong.
Daily Michigan Herald	William L. Avery.
Chicago Advance	D. W. Bartlett.
Springfield Republican	" "
Republican Press Association	J. E. Beardsley.
Washington Star	R. F. Boiseau.
Cincinnati Gazette	H. V. Boynton.
Chicago Tribune	" "
Pittsburgh Commercial	" "
St. Louis Democrat	" "
Boston Daily Advertiser	H. L. Bridgman.
Philadelphia Press	Mrs. Briggs.
Congressional Globe	D. W. Brown.
Augusta Republican	J. E. Bryant.
Ed. Washington Herald	I. N. Burritt.
Norwalk Gazette	A. H. Byington.
Homestead Champion	Hugh Cameron.
Milwaukee Sentinel	L. C. Carpenter.
Leavenworth Times	W. C. Coffin.

Iowa Gleaner	William Cogswell.
Maryland News	" "
Washington National Standard	" "
Erie Dispatch	Asa B. Cook.
Shelby Republican	S. B. Crew.
Fort Smith New Era	Y. Dell.
Portland Transcript	John Deering.
Aurora (Ill.) Beacon, et al.	Thomas L. De Land.
Washington New Era	C. W. Denison.
Chicago Prairie Farmer	C. R. Dodge.
Ed. Washington New Era	Frederick Douglas.
Congressional Globe	J. K. Edwards.
Philadelphia Presbyterian	J. S. Elliot.
New Northwest	D. A. Fish.
Ed. Washington Gazette	T. B. Florence.
Washington Republican	John P. Foley.
Newark Advertiser	C. H. Folwell.
Washington Sunday Chronicle	D. C. Forney, John W. Forney, Jr.
Ed. Washington Chronicle	Myron Fox.
Baltimore Gazette	R. Geddes.
Congressional Globe	H. J. Gensler.
Middlesex County Journal	John F. Gleason.
Maine Voice	" "
Irish Republic	W. H. Grace.
Boston Journal	O. K. Harris.
Laporte (Ind.) Herald	J. F. Heaton.
Detroit Herald	M. H. Heggins.
Congressional Globe	W. Hincks.
Worcester Spy	R. J. Hinton.
Ed. Washington Chronicle	William W. Holden.
Lancaster Express	S. Houston.
Davenport Gazette	F. H. Impry.
Alabama State Journal	A. C. Jones.
Washington Star	S. H. Kauffmann.
Rutland (Vt.) Herald	L. W. Kennedy.
Washington German Advertiser	Werner Kock.
Chicago Tribune	J. W. Knowlton.
Delaware (Ohio) Gazette	Alfred E. Lee.
Congressional Globe	William Blair Lord.
Pella (Iowa) Blade	Alexander Lynch.
Philadelphia Press	J. MacFarland.
Philadelphia Evening Telegraph	" "
Washington Patriot	W. C. Macbride.
Congressional Globe	J. J. M'Elhone.
San Francisco Bulletin	D. R. M'Kee.
Carson State Register	Alexander M'Kenady.
San Francisco Chronicle	" "
Washington Chronicle	H. C. Merritt.
Albany Evening Journal	R. W. C. Mitchell.
Ed. Washington Chronicle	John M. Morris.
Galveston News	A. P. Morse.
St. Louis Times	J. B. Motley.
Congressional Globe	D. F. Murphy, E. V. Murphy, J. J. Murphy.
Washington Republican	W. J. Murtagh.
Col. German Advertiser	J. F. Myers.
Mobile Herald	J. J. Noah.
Rochester Democrat	S. N. Dexter North.
Troy Times	" "
Utica Herald	" "

Ed. Washington Star	C. S. Noyes.
Washington Patriot	S. V. Noyes.
Sacramento Record	W. O'Brien.
Louisville Courier-Journal	W. G. Overton.
Philadelphia Inquirer	U. H. Painter.
Lawrence (Kan.) Journal	G. W. Partridge.
Indianapolis Journal	E. F. Peck.
Ed. Washington Capital	Donn Piatt.
Atlanta Constitution	Charles A. Pillsbury.
Mobile Register	" "
Savannah News	" "
Boston Journal	Ben. Perley Poore.
Daily Courier (Iowa)	J. P. C. Poulton.
Cincinnati Commercial	H. J. Ramsdell, H. V. Redfield.
Idaho Statesman	J. S. Reynolds.
Minneapolis Tribune	Clinton Rice.
Boston (Mass.) Plowman	C. N. Richards.
San Francisco Alta California	J. Henry Riley.
Boston Evening Traveller	William E. Sawyer.
Boston Journal	G. W. Scribner.
Taunton (Mass.) Gazette	E. Shaw.
Boston Transcript	W. B. Shaw.
Chicago Journal	" "
Cleveland Herald	" "
Toledo Blade	" "
Washington Republican	Arthur Shepherd.
Congressional Globe	T. F. Shuey.
Cleveland Herald	H. M. Slade.
Philadelphia Bulletin	W. Scott Smith.
Concord (N. H.) Statesman	J. E. Snodgrass.
Cleveland (Ohio) Herald	D. W. Stevens.
Topeka State Record	Maria A. Stetson.
Washington Patriot	A. B. Talcott.
Chicago Tribune	G. A. Townsend.
Ohio State Journal	W. J. Vance.
Boston Post	Clifford Warden.
Baltimore Gazette	W. W. Warden.
Boston Post	" "
London (Eng.) Telegraph	L. Q. Washington.
Louisville Ledger	" "
New Orleans Times, et al.	J. R. Wheatley.
Jackson (Miss.) Leader	J. Webster.
Alexandrian (Va.)	A. J. Wedderburn.
Cincinnati Chronicle	E. B. Wright.
Cincinnati Times	" "
Chicago Evening Post	" "
Philadelphia Evening Star	James R. Young.

There are no less than four News Associations represented in the above list. Then there is an enterprise called the Bureau of Correspondence, a European idea, represented by J. C. Gallagher. These furnish many of the lesser journals throughout the country with cheap and condensed dispatches of events in the national capital. Another association was formed in New York in January, 1870, which is called the American Press Association, which intends to furnish news to all those papers not recognized by pre-existing combinations of this sort, and especially in opposition or in competition with what is known as the New York Associated Press. Most of these journals, besides their desks in the galleries of Congress, have their *bureaux*, where they meet, receive news, and prepare their dispatches at all hours of the day and night. Twenty of these offices are in close proximity on Fourteenth Street, and their location is known as Newspaper Row.

There is only one foreign journal recognized in Congress—the *London Telegraph*. L. Q. Washington is its correspondent. The *London Times* and one or two other European journals stationed correspondents in Washington during the rebellion. Many papers are represented in the national capital, but not with desks and seats in the galleries of Congress. Members of Congress, from Colonel Matthew Lyon, of Vermont, in 1798, to the present day, have more or less indulged in newspaper correspondence.

CHAPTER XLVI.

THE ILLUSTRATED PAPERS.

NEWS PICTORIALLY REPORTED AND DESCRIBED.—WOOD-ENGRAVING IN THE UNITED STATES.—HARPER'S FAMILY BIBLE.—THE FIRST ILLUSTRATED NEWSPAPERS.—FRANK LESLIE'S ILLUSTRATED NEWS, HARPER'S WEEKLY, AND HARPER'S BAZAR.—SINCLAIR'S PHOTO-ZINCO.—THE NEW ART.—EXCHANGE OF ENGRAVINGS.—OUR NATIONAL GALLERY.

ILLUSTRATED papers have become a feature. Every newspaper stand is covered with them. Every railroad train is filled with them. They are "object-teaching" to the multitude. They make the battle-fields, the coronations, the corruptions of politicians, the balls, the race-course, the yacht race, the military and naval heroes, Napoleon and William, Bismarck and Von Beust, Farragut and Porter, Grant and Sherman, familiar to every one. They are, in brief, the art gallery of the world. Single admission, ten cents.

When Avery, and Reid, and Horton, and Baker, and one or two others, engraved for the *New York Herald*, the art, for newspaper use and illustration, was but little known in the United States. There was some taste in drawing, but rather rough and slow work in cutting. It was a task to get the smallest and simplest diagram cut. News engravings have to be rapidly executed to be of value. In 1861–'5, during the Rebellion, Waters made half-page maps in one day. Such a piece of work, indeed, to illustrate a brilliant victory, was accomplished on one occasion in one night. News of the battle came at tea-time; the map appeared in the next morning's *Herald*. But the block was in twenty pieces, and twenty engravers worked on it at the same time. Thirty-five years ago there were not as many engravers in the country as worked that night on that one map.

There was an excellent engraver living in New York about thirty or thirty-five years ago, named Adams. He was almost the first engraver-artist in the United States. He was a pleasant, quiet, thoughtful man. It appears that he read the Bible. He was our Doré. In going over the pages of that great book, some of the wonderful events narrated there suggested to him the idea of sketching them on wood. He did so, and cut them himself during his leisure hours. The work was an agreeable one, and he continued it till he had accumulated a large number of beautiful illustrations of the Holy Scriptures. They grew in value, and he purchased an iron safe for them. It had occurred to him during this work that the Bible, fully illustrated, would be a popular publication, and one that would compensate him for his labor of love. Applying to the Harpers, he found they would be delighted to undertake such a work. The interview between the artist and publishers resulted in Harper's Illustrated Family Bible, so well known a quarter of a century ago. When the incident was related to the writer, Mr. Adams's share of the profits of the work had reached the sum of $60,000. These illustrations showed great taste and were well executed, but the art has made such progress since then that they are excelled by some of the exquisite engravings of the present time.

Our illustrated newspapers live on wood-engravings. The two most important ones are Harper's and Frank Leslie's. Before either of these appeared, the Messrs. Beach, of the *New York Sun*, and Barnum, of the Museum, each contributed $20,000 for the establishment of an illustrated weekly in New York City; and Gleason and Ballou, of Boston, had made the attempt to introduce these publications in America. The two latter made fortunes, and Ballou built the St. James's Hotel. Among the artists engaged on *Gleason's Pictorial* was Frank Leslie. Boston, probably, was not large enough for him to swing in freely and safely; New York loomed up before his artistic vision. Ascertaining that Barnum intended to issue an illustrated paper, Leslie started for Iranistan, and arrived there on Thanksgiving day, in 1852, just before dinner. Introducing himself to Barnum, he stated his business. "Why, this is Thanksgiving day, and dinner is almost ready. Never mind; business is business," said Barnum. So he gave up turkey and family, and talked over the project. It ended in the departure of the artist for New York by the train of that evening, and Barnum satisfied himself with a wing of a chicken. In this way Frank Leslie became the managing foreman of the *Illustrated News* of New York, and made his *début* in the metropolis. This paper appeared on the 1st of January, 1853, and its circulation ran up to 70,000 copies. It lived one year.

After the suspension of this publication, or, rather, after it passed over to Gleason, Frank Leslie issued one which is now favorably known as *Frank Leslie's Illustrated Newspaper*. His establishment has grown so extensively that seventy wood-engravers are constantly and actively employed. Illustrated papers in German and Spanish, as well as in English, are issued therefrom. He publishes the *Chimney-corner*, *Ladies' Journal*, *Pleasant Hours*, *Boys' and Girls' Weekly*, and the *Budget of Fun*. The aggregate circulation of his weekly and monthly issues average half a million copies weekly. One hundred thousand copies of the *Chimney-corner* alone are issued. One of the former contributors to Frank Leslie's paper was John J. Ryan, now the *redacteur en chef* of the *American Register* in Paris. The present managing editor is E. G. Squier, so well known for his early researches in the Valley of the Mississippi, and as the author of several interesting works on Central America, where he resided for some time as the *chargé d'affaires* of the United States.

The first number of *Harper's Weekly, a Journal of Civilization,* was issued on the 3d of January, 1857. The intention of the publishers, as indicated by its second title, was to make a high-toned literary weekly paper, especially adapted for the family, and the few engravings that appeared in the earlier numbers were simply story illustrations; but before the expiration of the first year the events of the day began to be pictorially recorded in its pages, and *Harper's Weekly* had fairly taken the field as an illustrated newspaper. Its first editor was Theodore Sedgwick. Among his collaborateurs was Fitz James O'Brien, who contributed a brilliant series of weekly papers under the heading "The Man about Town." On Sedgwick's retirement from the editorial chair in 1858, he was succeeded by John Bonner, an experienced and accomplished journalist, who conducted the *Weekly* for several years with ability and tact. Bonner was followed, in 1864, by Henry M. Alden, the present editor of *Harper's Magazine.* Charles Nordhoff, for several years managing editor of the *Evening Post,* John G. Foster, and W. F. G. Shanks, were also at different times connected with the *Weekly.* The present executive editor is S. S. Conant, for some time managing editor of the *New York Times* under Henry J. Raymond. Since the 1st of January, 1864, the political columns of the *Weekly* have been intrusted to the management of George William Curtis, from whose pen a series of charming and brilliant papers, under the heading of "The Lounger," had been an attractive feature of the *Weekly* from the second year of its establishment. His editorials are distinguished by breadth of view, evident sincerity of opinion, force and clearness of style, and strict and unvarying attention to the amenities of journalism. Mr. Curtis is also the author of a series of papers in *Harper's Bazar* entitled "Manners upon the Road," commenced in the first number of that journal, and still continued weekly. In these papers, under the signature of "An old Bachelor," the author displays a fertility of invention, a grace and freedom of style, a happy facility in the treatment and illustration of every-day topics, the little as well as the great moralities of home and social life, which make these pleasant essays a unique feature of newspaper literature.

The pictorial department of the *Weekly* embraces a wide range of subjects—current events of interest and importance, art and story illustrations, portraiture, the humor and comedy of social life, and foreign and domestic politics. The battle-fields of our own great war, and those of recent European conflicts, were graphically reproduced in its pages. The political cartoons of Thomas Nast constitute one of its most popular features. Nast is a genius. He can not be compared with any other artist, living or dead. With a style peculiarly his own, wide in range of subject, of inexhaustible fertility, and serious as well as playful imagination, he now reminds us of Hogarth, now of Leach. His political cartoons during the late presidential campaign were among the most effective weapons against the Democratic Party, and his masterly attacks on the Tammany Ring, in the pages of the *Weekly*, contributed largely to the overthrow of that corrupt clique.

Since the outbreak of the Rebellion, *Harper's Weekly* has been conducted in harmony with the Republican Party, but it has never assumed a partisan attitude, nor has it lost any of its distinctive features as a literary journal. Some of the best works of Bulwer, Charles Reade, Wilkie Collins, George Eliot, and other eminent English novelists, have been introduced to American readers through its pages, and among its constant contributors are numbered many of the leading authors of our own country. Among its latest features is an important Scientific Department, conducted by Professor Spencer F. Baird, of the Smithsonian Institute.

These illustrated papers are a power in the reform of public abuses. We have alluded to the effect of Nast's inimitable sketches in aiding so materially in the overthrow of the infamous Tammany Ring. Several years ago Frank Leslie undertook a very commendable public duty in exposing, by a series of illustrations, the deplorable condition of hundreds of "swill-fed" cows stalled in and around New York, and supplying the inhabitants of the metropolis with "pure Orange County milk." The effect produced by this pictorial crusade was of the first importance to the health of the community.

Harper's Bazar, a Repository of Fashion, Pleasure, and Instruction, was first issued on the 2d of November, 1867. Designed as a family paper, it was a success from the start. Politics are excluded from its columns. Its literary features comprise serial stories by leading English and American authors, short stories, poems, social and domestic essays, and the "Old Bachelor" papers already alluded to. Besides the fashion and pattern illustrations, giving, from authentic sources, the latest European styles, the *Bazar* contains many beautiful fine-art pictures. It has been from the first under the skillful management of Miss Mary L. Booth.

The *Aldine*, and *Appleton's Journal*, issued in New York, are illustrated, but they scarcely come under the class we have to speak of in our collection; they are literary papers, and their pictures are given to illustrate stories or biography. *Every Saturday*, published in Boston, was an illustrated paper of no mean pretensions till the close of 1871, when it abandoned pictures, by some arrangement made, it was said, with the Harpers of New York. Some of its engravings were very artistically executed. The *Illustrated Christian Weekly* was issued in March, 1871, by the American Tract Society.

It is edited by Lyman Abbott and S. E. Warner, and may be considered the first illustrated paper of a purely religious character.

Wood-engraving has increased so rapidly, and improved so immeasurably beyond all expectations, that as nice work can be done in the United States as in any other country. When we compare *Frank Leslie's Illustrated Paper* and *Harper's Weekly* with the London *Illustrated News*, or *L'Illustration* of Paris, or the *Illustrated News* of Leipsic, we see no reason to find fault with our publications. The paper of the English and French papers is generally superior, which sets off the engravings to advantage. The pictures in the London paper are fine, but stiff; those in *L'Illustration* are more natural, but inferior as engravings. The illustrations in the United States partake of the best characteristics of the two; they are not so stiff as the English, and they are as finely executed as the French. Ours are the *juste milieu* of the art, as far as it has progressed in the world as an auxiliary to the news of the day.

There is a new mode of illustration just brought out in Philadelphia in a publication called *Sinclair's Photo-Zinco*, which gives reproductions of drawings and engravings. This mode could be made of value, we should think, in the interchange of engravings among the illustrated papers of the world. Now the proprietors of these publications sell and exchange electrotypes of the most popular pictures. The London *Illustrated News* sends quite a number of its engravings to Paris, Berlin, and Vienna. Some reach New York. The London *Illustrated Times* takes electrotypes of the engravings originating with *La Monde* and *L'Illustration* of Paris. The expense thus saved must be very great, but the practice, unless very limited, must prove more injurious than profitable to any paper relying much on its own artistic merit for popular favor.

Other papers publish pictures. There is the *Child's Paper*, the *Child's World*, and the *Illustrated Police News*. The *Agriculturist* represents the best breeds of animals, new implements of husbandry, architectural designs for farmers, premium pears, new species of apples and squashes, and bunches of grapes. The *Scientific American* contains finely-engraved models and diagrams of newly invented machinery, and elegantly and attractively done too. The publisher in the rural districts illustrates his paper with pictorial advertisements, which, with the quaint devices at the heads of the papers of a century ago, were the original and pioneer illustrations of the American newspaper. But all the superior work in our wood engravings is the growth of thirty years. Then there were twenty engravers in the United States; now, it is stated by Lossing to the New York Historical Society, there are no less than four hundred. Peter Cooper has done much for this art by having free classes for girls in his Institute, and they become expert and skillful engravers.

CHAPTER XLVII.
THE TRANSIENT PRESS.

NEWSPAPERS IN THE ARMY AND NAVY.—NEWSPAPERS IN COLLEGES.—THE SCHOOLS OF JOURNALISM.—NEWSPAPERS WITH THE TROOPS IN THE FIELD. —AMATEUR JOURNALISM.—THE AVANT COUREURS OF AMERICA.

IF we have a few newspapers each a century old, we also have a few not intended to live a hundred months, or a hundred weeks, or a hundred days in any one place. Additionally to the daily Press, the weekly Press, the religious Press, the special Press, there are clubs, colleges, circles, classes, schools, societies, soldiers, and sailors with their representative prints. Newspapers are published on board of vessels of war; and wherever our troops marched during the Mexican War, as well as in the late Rebellion, newspapers would be printed in camps for circulation in the army, and for home and friends. Newspapers were printed in General Scott's army, and were dated from the advanced posts of the troops as they advanced towards the city of Mexico. They also appeared in General Taylor's army as it moved from the fields of Palo Alto to Monterey and Buena Vista. The *American Flag* was the journal that kept up with the victorious march of Old Rough and Ready.

In the early part of 1846, it was proposed to establish a republic, to be composed of the Mexican states of Tamaulipas, Coahuila, Nuévo Leon, and Chihuahua. This was soon after the first victories of the American troops. To carry out this plan, the publication of a newspaper was commenced in Matamoras, and called the *Republic of the Rio Grande*. The result of the war, of course, killed this political enterprise, but the newspapers went on with the troops.

Our volunteers embraced all trades and professions. Printers and pressmen were as patriotic as any other class. When Mexico was invaded in 1846–7, type, presses, ink, paper, and printers marched with our soldiers. Newspapers were established in every important city and town as they were captured by Generals Taylor, Scott, and Kearney. In this way the *American Pioneer* was published in Monterey, New Leon; the *American Flag* at Matamoras; the *Californian* in Monterey, California; the *Sentinel* in Tampico; the *Eagle* at Vera Cruz; the *American Star* at Jalapa; the *Picket Guard* at Saltillo; and the *Anglo-Saxon* at Chihuahua. They were excellent specimens of brains and business, and aided the military authorities in circulating their orders and proclamations. Wherever a regiment of our army appeared, a newspaper was sure to be issued. The only mistake made at the time was in not printing these papers half in Spanish, in order to have a greater influence on the surrounding population.

These newspapers were edited and printed by what are called "common" or "private soldiers." When the war broke out with Mexico, as when the Rebellion burst upon us, volunteer soldiers poured in from all quarters. One cause of the superior efficiency of our armies in the field, and especially in emergencies, was to be found in the fact that they were composed of carpenters, masons, blacksmiths, printers, joiners, gunsmiths, plumbers, painters, wheelwrights, pressmen—indeed, mechanics of all kinds. They were ready for any thing. Writers and reporters helped to make up the quota from each state. Newspapers were, therefore, easily produced. With a small press and a font of type as part of the baggage-train, a newspaper was improvised on any spot, and some of those thus issued were very creditable productions.

With the Northern armies in the late Rebellion these publications became common. But in this conflict our soldiers found the material ready for use in the captured cities and towns. The *Weekly Junior Register* was issued after the occupation of Franklin, Louisiana, by the army of General Banks. It was dated April 25th, 1863, and printed, as many of those papers were, on the blank side of "paper-hangings." One side was a handsome pattern of house wall-paper, and the other side contained the news of the day. Another was called the *Vicksburg Citizen*, and dated June 30, 1863. This was also printed on house paper—a satin figure on one side, and the reading matter on the other. It was two columns wide, and eighteen inches long.

Newspapers are published at our colleges. One was established at Dartmouth as far back as 1800 under the title of *Gazette*. Daniel Webster wrote for it in 1802-3. Once he asked a friend if he had read the articles signed Icarus in the *Gazette*. Not receiving a reply favorable to the articles, nothing further was said at that time, but several years after Webster acknowledged himself to have been the veritable Icarus. He wrote the Newsboy's Message for the *Gazette* for the 1st of January, 1803. There was a periodical called the *Collegian* published at Harvard in 1830. These college papers may not come under the head of transient, for they live longer than those published by our troops, but it is not expected, from the nature of things, that they are to be permanent institutions. Their editors are changed, at any rate, as often as politicians are changed in and out of office.

Two of the neatest papers published in 1870 were issued, one from Harvard College, called the *Harvard Advocate*, and the other from Yale College, entitled the *College Courant*. Williams College also boasts of its paper—the *Vidette*. The Amherst Agricultural College issues the *Index*. That from the Cornell College is the *Era*. The *Deaf Mute Pelican* is published by the inmates of the Louisiana Institute for the Deaf, Dumb, and Blind. The young ladies of the Marshall (Texas) Female College issue a paper called the *Casket*. These papers are edited by students, and some of the contributions are marked with ability and a show of genius. Now and then the *Advocate* throws off something equal to the following, which appeared in May, 1870:

TO PUPILS IN ELOCUTION.

The human lungs reverberate sometimes with great velocity,
When windy individuals indulge in much verbosity.
They have to twirl the glottis sixty thousand times a minute,
And push and punch the diaphragm as though the deuce was in it.

Chorus.

The pharynx now goes up ;
The larynx, with a slam,
Ejects a note
From out the throat,
Pushed by the diaphragm.

Another class of transient newspapers is what comes under the head of amateur journalism. There is quite a number of this class now published in the United States. These amateur publications, like the *Dew-drop* and the *Hub* of Boston, and the *Rose-bud* of New York, are increasing in all parts of the country. They have formed associations like the Eastern Amateur Association, and are rapidly acquiring a knowledge of older journalism that will be of value to the profession in the future. No doubt some of the writers for these papers will yet be distinguished and influential journalists, instead of learned divines, or skillful physicians, or keen and accomplished lawyers, or merchant princes. These college and amateur papers are a means of educating young men to the profession of journalism. Now scholarships for this purpose have been established in the University of Virginia, over which General Robert E. Lee presided at the time of his death. There a class are to be educated. Twenty-five are to begin the course, and they are to be nominated by typographical societies and editorial recommendation. What the precise course of studies are to fit young men for the printing-office and editorial room is unknown to us ; but the *Courant*, of Yale College, in December, 1871, gave us some idea of the course proposed there :

So much has been said all over the country about the "New School of Journalism at Yale" that it seems time that some clear statement was made in regard to the course of study which has received this unfortunate name. The first idea which suggests itself on hearing of a school of journalism is that of a kind of "business college" to teach penny-a-liners how to write, and it can not but be considered inauspicious that a most dignified branch of study should be announced by that name. The school of political science and history, as we must call it, for want of a better name, will present to most students far more attractions than any other of the graduate courses of study recently established here. The plan, as it now works, is principally as follows :

President Woolsey meets the students once a week at his house, discusses familiarly with them various topics in political science, directs their reading, and interprets the works of Ahrens and Von Mohl. It is hoped that by next year a professor of political economy and international law will be procured to take the chair in the academic department, formerly occupied by President Woolsey, and that he will also give instruction to graduate students. Professor Wheeler meets the class once a week at his room for instruction in history, and, for the present, his teaching is confined to the constitutional history of England and the United States. His meetings with the class are mainly occupied with conversations on the studies which they are pursuing. It is his intention, during the second year, to give out to individual students different historical subjects for investigation, the results of their studies to be embodied in theses which are to be read before the class and freely criticised.

Instruction in English literature will be given by Professor Lounsbury. The plan which he intends to pursue for the present is to begin with Chaucer, and to consist of a critical study of the greatest English authors. This study is to continue through the two years of the course. Can any one imagine a more delightful way of spending a year in study than this? The course is wide, and offers a great variety of learning. The full course for those who wish to take the degree of Ph. D. is two years; but any one can at any time take a part of either of the graduate courses, or can pursue at the same time studies in different courses. It may be as well to mention that the peculiar advantages of this course to those who intend to be editors, and the fact that several "journalists" who recently graduated at Yale are in attendance, is what gave to it its narrow and unmeaning title, " The School of Journalism."

Such an establishment as the *New York Herald*, or *Tribune*, or *Times* is the true college for newspaper students. Professor James Gordon Bennett or Professor Horace Greeley would turn out more real genuine journalists in one year than the Harvards, the Yales, and the Dartmouths could produce in a generation. These old institutions are, indeed, only the primary schools of editors. Journalism is not entirely made up of fine writing; tact is as much a necessary element as talent. Writers of learning, and ability, and brilliancy abound, but journalists are rare. One thorough journalist can keep twenty or thirty men of talent constantly at work carrying out and developing his plans and ideas. Journalists should, of course, be thoroughly educated. College education will not spoil a journalist any more than it does a lawyer or a clergyman. All professional men should be men of culture; they should be hard workers and hard thinkers; they should be cosmopolitan in education and views; and what they need to cultivate more than any other feature are their perceptive faculties. Quickness of thought and quickness of action are essential in newspaper offices. Coolness of purpose and coolness of judgment are valuable elements in an editor. Impartiality is a very important feature to be inculcated. But, after all, great journalists, like distinguished statesmen, brilliant lawyers, skillful physicians, and eminent divines, are naturally so—the genius for the work is in them. It is not to be acquired at a college in Virginia or Massachusetts. The elements are there, so far as books embrace them, unquestionably; but the tact, and the experience, and the genius are not there by any course of study that any faculty may inaugurate or impose upon any set of students that may be brought before them.

One of the most curious instances of our transitory journalism, and which marks the American character in this respect most decidedly, was the publication of a newspaper by an excursion party from Boston to San Francisco over the Pacific Railroad. This party consisted of the Board of Trade of Boston and a few invited guests, embracing about one hundred and fifty ladies and gentlemen. They left that city on the 23d of May, 1870. With the train was a thoroughly equipped printing-office, from which was issued a daily paper during the progress of the party. It was edited by W. R. Steel, of Chicago, who had a force of four compositors and one pressman. All the news of the world was telegraphed to the point where the train stopped each night, and a special dispatch, containing all the local and general news of Boston and the Eastern States, published each morning, together with such gossip and events as had transpired on board the train. The paper was called the *Trans-Continental*, and consisted of four pages, and the quantity of matter it contained was about equal to that of one page of the *New York Herald*. The first number was issued somewhere on the New York Central Road, the second number near Detroit, the third near Chicago, the fourth near Omaha, and the others near Cheyenne, Sacramento, and San Francisco. Copies of the *Trans-Continental* were mailed to their friends daily by the excursionists from whatever point the train happened to be, and the postmaster general ordered that they be transmitted by the first mail, free of postage.

When the air is navigated with balloons, it is fair to suppose that newspapers will be regularly published and distributed from the clouds as the aerial trains pass over the cities and towns. If a class paper in the interest of architecture should be among those thus issued, we shall then learn how the *châteaux en Espagne* are constructed.

CHAPTER XLVIII.
THE WAR CORRESPONDENTS.

WHAT HAVE THEY ACCOMPLISHED?—THEIR LABORS AND DANGERS.—THEIR CAPTURE AND IMPRISONMENT. — JOURNALISTS IN ACTION. — WHAT IS THOUGHT OF THEM.—THEY ARE THE HISTORIANS OF THE GREAT CONFLICTS OF THE WORLD.—THE REBELLION.—THE FRANCO-GERMAN WAR.

THE war correspondent! How much would be lost without him! How many noble deeds and gallant actions have disappeared with the smoke of battle for want of a reporter!

Borrow, in his "Bible in Spain," thus speaks of this class of journalists:

What most extraordinary men are these reporters! Surely, if there be any class of individuals who are entitled to the appellation of cosmopolites, it is these, who pursue their avocations in all countries indifferently, and accommodate themselves at will to the manners of all classes of society. Their fluency of style, as writers, is only surpassed by their facility of language in conversation; and their attainments in classical and polite literature only by their profound knowledge of the world, acquired by an early introduction into its bustling scenes. The activity, energy, and courage which they occasionally display in the pursuit of information are truly remarkable. I saw reporters, during the Three Days at Paris, mingled with *canaille* and *gamins* behind the barriers, while the *mitraille* was flying in all directions, and the desperate *cuirassiers* were dashing their fierce horses against those seemingly feeble bulwarks; there stood they, dotting down their observations in their pocket-books as unconcernedly as if they were reporting the proceedings of a reform meeting in Finsbury Square; while in Spain, several of them accompanied the Carlist and Cristino guerrillas in some of their most desperate raids, exposing themselves to the danger of hostile bullets, the inclemency of the winter, and the fierce heat of the summer's sun.

What the correspondents of the newspapers did in the Mexican War, in the Rebellion, and in the recent conflict between France and Germany, is well described in this extract. Newspaper correspondents in the Rebellion incurred double risks in performing their duty. On the eve of the war, the *Herald*, *Tribune*, and *Times* had several " specials " in the Southern States, feeling the public pulse and describing public sentiment in that disturbed section. When the first gun was heard at Fort Sumter, these gentlemen were immediately denounced as spies and abolitionists. Efforts were made by mobs to hang a *Herald* correspondent in Richmond. One of the agents of the *Tribune* was arrested in Charleston, South Carolina. One of the correspondents of the *Times* barely escaped hanging on a " sour apple-tree " at Harper's Ferry. Glenn and Farrell, both of the *Herald*, one in Charleston and the other at New Orleans, managed, with the greatest courage and adroitness, to reach the Northern line with their heads on their shoulders. It seemed as if that "first gun" turned the South into a lunatic asylum.

Incidents, anecdotes, hairbreadth escapes, sufferings, enough to fill this volume, could be related of the war correspondents of the Northern papers during the years 1861, '62, '63, '64, '65. After the war broke out the journalists in the field assumed new dangers and run new risks. Anderson, of the *Herald*, taken prisoner, was confined in an iron dungeon in Texas, and afterwards, with a bullet-hole through his arm, took notes at Spottsylvania in the thickest of the fight; Osborn, of the same paper, the only correspondent on the iron-clads in action, calmly watched the effect of each impact, and subsequently, as signal officer in the rigging with Farragut, run the gauntlet at New Orleans; Richardson and Browne, of the *Tribune*, and Colburn, of the *World*, captured in running the blockade at Vicksburg, were immured for months in Libby, till they escaped to the Union lines through marsh, and brush, and forest; Cook sat aloft on the flag-ship of Porter, pencil and book in hand, and watched the bombardment of Fort Fisher; Shanks, amid the plunging fire at Lookout, wrote a description of the battle that surpassed Napier's brilliant efforts; Hosmer, in the hottest of the great battle of Gettysburg, was full of fire and facts in his neat and accurate account of that decisive conflict of the war; Cadwallader and Fitzpatrick, of the *Herald*, and Crounse, of the *Times*, were captured by Mosby's band, deprived of watches and note-books, and had their facts published in the rebel papers; Skestfall fell into the hands of Morgan's guerrillas, who also fancied his valuables and notes; Stiner shivered out on picket, days and nights, for the latest rebel newspapers; Conyngham and Doyle made the famous march with Sherman to the sea; Ashley and Carpenter shared with the grand old Army of the Potomac its glory and repulses; Knox, "mit Sigel" in Missouri, described the brilliant battle at Pea Ridge; Chapman, at the "Headquarters of the New York *Herald*" at Cairo and all along the line, looked after maps and plans; Dunn died at his post on the Mississippi; Brady, lost in a canebrake, turned up as editor in Mobile; Hendricks, the indefatigable, always had a description of a battle; Swinton, of the *Times*, with his risks and dangers at Chancellorsville and Fredericksburg, gave graphic pictures of desperately fought battles; Keim, bivouacking with the lamented M'Pherson, was mild and mindful of his duties to the Press and the public.

Others, many others, indeed, could be mentioned who are entitled to all the praise that we could bestow, and all that Borrow has given to his *beau idéals*. If the Press had ribbons and orders to confer for gallant conduct on the field of battle, these correspondents would have their breasts covered with brilliants on state occasions; but their decorations shone in the columns of the papers, where they are imperishable. While the correspondents of the *Tribune* and *Herald* performed their duty splendidly in the recent Franco-German War, they are satisfied with the glory their reports gave them. Their *légion d'honneur* and their iron crosses are in their descriptions of Gravelotte, Sedan, and the siege of Paris. But the Emperor of Germany recognized the services of William Howard Russell, of the *London Times*, by conferring on him the Iron Cross of the second class, with the White Ribbon. What order in *Heraldry* should Stanley, the correspondent with the Abyssinian Expedition, receive after this? These emperors and kings have no idea of the cost of a war to a newspaper. They are made famous in history, and they bestow a paltry ribbon for the service. They are not aware that the New York *Herald* alone spent $500,000 during the American Rebellion, and $100,000 during the short and sharp war between France and Germany, in keeping its corps of correspondents in the field. Half a million for preparing one historical work!

Conyngham, in "Sherman's March through the South," speaks of his instructions, which describe, in a few words, the duties of a journalist in the field:

> The instructions of the *Herald* to its army correspondents were brief, but comprehensive. They were simply these: To obtain the most accurate information by personal observation, and forward it with the utmost dispatch, regardless of expense, labor, or danger. Guided by these concise instructions—with his horse, his revolver, his field-glass, his note-book, blanket, and haversack—the army correspondent of the *New York Herald* started forth to share the vicissitudes and hardships of the camp, the fatigues of the march, and the perils of the battle-field, to contribute his narrative to the history of the great war.

One of the eccentricities of the Rebellion was the harmonious association of the representatives of the Northern Press in the several *corps* of the army. Knox, in his " Camp-fire and Cotton-field," in the opening chapter, said that early in February, 1861, he entered the editorial rooms of the *Herald* to make arrangements to become one of its correspondents. He said:

> I announced my readiness to proceed to any point between the poles, wherever the *Herald* desired a correspondent. The editor-in-chief was busy over a long letter from some point in the South, but his response was promptly given. Half reading, half pausing over the letter, he briefly said,
>
> A long and bloody war is upon us, in which the whole country will be engaged. We shall desire you to take the field—probably in the West. It may be several weeks before we need you, but the war can not be long delayed.

When Knox called at the *Herald* office for his final instructions, he found that

> The managing editor had determined upon a vigorous campaign. Every point of interest was to be covered, so that the operations of our armies would be fully recorded from day to day. The war correspondents had gone to their posts or were just taking their departure. I was instructed to watch the military movements in Missouri, and hastened to St. Louis as fast as steam could bear me.

Knox went to the West and fought with Sigel. Afterwards, joining General Wallace, he proceeded southwest to Memphis. Three newspapers, the *Avalanche, Argus,* and *Appeal,* had enlightened the rebels of that city. The *Appeal,* like the old *Spy, Gazette,* and other prints of the Revolution of '76, became a migratory sheet, and was issued wherever it could safely be published. The *Avalanche* changed its name to that of the *Bulletin,* and became moderate in tone. After the war it resumed its old title. The *Argus* did not change its sentiments so readily, and needed the prick of the pen, if not of the sword. General Wallace therefore issued the following order:

Head-quarters Third Division, Reserved Corps, Army of Tennessee,
MEMPHIS, June 17, 1862.

EDITOR DAILY ARGUS,—As the closing of your office might be injurious to you pecuniarily, I send two gentlemen—Messrs. A. D. Richardson and Thomas W. Knox, both of ample experience—to take charge of the editorial department of your paper. The business management of your office will be left to you.

Very respectfully,   LEWIS WALLACE,
General Third Division, Reserved Corps.

This order was printed at the head of the *Argus.* The eccentricity of this affair was in the peculiar fact that Richardson was a correspondent of the *New York Tribune,* and Knox a correspondent of the *New York Herald.* Notwithstanding this rather extraordinary combination, the *Argus* was a vigorously consistent sheet, and gave general satisfaction to all, save the radical rebels, while under the editorial care of these military historians and gushing journalists.

All correspondents with troops in the field are compelled to do their duty as historians under great difficulties, and frequently amid great danger under fire. But they are always ready. Edmund About, in describing for the *Moniteur du Soir* the defeat of the French at Woerth, mentioned this incident, showing the usefulness of a journalist to a military chieftain in retreat:

* * * * But here come one or two regiments of the line, quite firm, tolerably complete in numbers, rifle on shoulder, and knapsack on back. Behind them Marshal M'Mahon, calm, dignified, almost smiling, and fresh as a rose. I salute him as he passes. He responds without noticing me. One of his aids, M. d'Alzac, names me. Then the old hero stops, and tells quite simply the story of his defeat, thus: "I had only 35,000 men, and found 150,000 in front of me. We have given way before numbers. They have killed or wounded about 5000 men. But we have our revenge. Explain this to the public. But where are you going in that direction?" "To Saverne," I reply. "You will be captured. The Prussians will be there in two hours," says the general. "I have my wife and children there," I answer. "God preserve you. Do not fail to say that the *morale* of the troops is excellent." We shake hands.

This war between France and Germany developed more journalistic enterprise than had ever been seen in Europe. American editors spiritedly and successfully entered the lists. The London *Publishers' Circular* of September, 1870, gave a list of correspondents engaged at the seat of war:

Newspaper correspondents work at the peril of their lives, as the death of the correspondent of the *Times*, Colonel Pemberton, late of the Fusileer Guards, will prove. Of the other correspondents, the *Pall Mall Gazette's* "Azamat Batuk," who is now back at the seat of war, is M. Thiebland. Captain Dashwood, late of the 91st Highlanders, is among the journalists following the campaign. Mr. N. A. Woods, who was in the Crimea for the *Herald*, and did the Atlantic cable for the *Times*, is at the war for the *Scotsman*. The *New York Herald*, it is said, has twenty-four correspondents in the field, and the Paris *Gaulois* twenty-six. A telegram, sent by the *Pall Mall Gazette's* correspondent immediately after Sedan, only reached the editor on Tuesday afternoon. Meanwhile the correspondent had come home with his description in full, and gone back again. Much of Dr. Russell's manuscript, including the portion describing the actual battle of Sedan, had not reached the *Times* in time for publication on Tuesday, though subsequent letters had. Mr. G. A. Sala has been seized in Paris as a Prussian spy, seriously ill-treated and imprisoned. Mr. Sydney Hall, the artist of the *Graphic*, who accompanied the French Army of the Rhine, has again been heard of. He disappeared for some time, and there was subsequently a report that he had been arrested by the Prussians as a spy. He has now written from Nancy announcing his release, and that during his detention he was very well treated by his captors.

What these correspondents have accomplished, through the journals employing them, is strikingly illustrated by Lord Granville, the foreign minister of England, in a speech made in November, 1870. He said :

We have seen the Press of this country speaking *with that freedom which fortunately is our privilege, and which we shall always maintain*, discussing all the conditions of the war—that freedom sometimes necessarily leading to some irritation on the one side or the other—an irritation which is very natural on the part of the belligerents—but with an unswerving purpose, which I am glad to acknowledge, of showing that the great desire of this nation, expressed through the Press, is to promote and accelerate a speedy conclusion to a terrible calamity. (Hear.) *And here I may, perhaps, in passing, remark that the extraordinary energy and exertions of the Press*, of which the country may well be proud, have created, under very great difficulty, what was called *a war literature, unexampled in ability and interest, putting before the public all the various astonishing events which have so rapidly succeeded each other in this tremendous struggle.* (Hear, hear.)

This is a meagre account of the war correspondent and what he has done. No great conflicts like our own Rebellion, or the Franco-German War, were ever so fully, so graphically, so truthfully described. No records of previous wars can surpass those of the years between 1861 and '71. Anterior to these events we spoke of Napier, Thiers, Gibbon, Bancroft. They were compilers from old documents. Now we speak of the *Tribune, Times, World, Herald*. They have been eye-witnesses.

CHAPTER XLIX.
THE REPORTERS OF THE PRESS.
THEIR EARLY STRUGGLES IN REPORTING SPEECHES AND DEBATES. — THE REVOLUTION.—VALUE OF REPORTS.—NUMBER OF REPORTERS.

THE reporter is the amanuensis of the public. Through him statesmen speak to the people; through him Congress is heard; through him orators become celebrated.

There was a time when stenographers and phonographers were scarce in the United States. Joseph Gales was the first reporter, and he was in the first Congress in Philadelphia. Stenographers, fifty years ago, could not have earned twenty dollars a week on any metropolitan journal. No paper of that day would devote the space for a full report of a long speech. There is nothing on record of the great and important speeches in the early history of the country. It was only lately that the early debates in Congress were rescued from oblivion. There is not a speech of Aaron Burr to be found any where. Tradition has made him out a remarkably brilliant orator. There is no proof of the statement on record. It was not till 1837, '38, '39, and '40 that reporters were introduced on our Daily Press. The early troubles in this line of newspaper labor would astonish the present generation to witness.

The *New York Herald* experienced the same spirit of opposition in first reporting the religious anniversaries in New York that the English journals met with in their early attempts at reporting the debates of the British Parliament; but the Press was successful in both instances—only, however, after a severe fight. On the 13th of April, 1738, Sir William Yonge made himself famous in his efforts to have the reporters suppressed. Speaker Onslow, of the House of Commons, complained that there was "an account of their deliberations in the newspapers." Sir William then declared his determination to have the printers punished, and in his speeches predicted the wonderful ability and enterprise that have since been developed in this profession. "They deserve to be punished," he said; "and if you do not either punish them, or take some effectual method of checking them, you may soon expect to see your votes, your proceedings, and your speeches printed and hawked about the streets while we are sitting in this house."

Our clergymen were at first much opposed to having their sermons reported. Now, with more wisdom and tact, and seeing the advantages of larger audiences, many of those with any ability seek publicity. Henry Ward Beecher is a notable instance of this. His sermons are reported phonographically, and published weekly, not only in pamphlets, but in the newspapers of the day. Thus he preaches to half a million of people every week. The Rev. Dr. Hawkes, less of a genius, and with less tact, took the other view, as we have described. Of course, when once in print, his sermons could not very well be repeated from the pulpit. But this did not alarm Mr. Beecher; he was always ready with a fresh sermon.

The *Herald* now devotes a page, and sometimes two pages, every Monday morning, to the leading sermons preached the previous day in the churches in the metropolis and vicinity. Many are abstracts, of course, except when of special interest or importance. These reports are very ably done. The way they are received by the clergymen is in singular contrast with the course of Dr. Hawkes, and of the clergy generally, when the proprietor of that paper commenced the reports of the Religious Anniversaries in New York. Here are two indorsements which appeared in one day:

Church of the Messiah, NEW YORK, November 8, 1869.
To the Editor of the Herald:
I have read your reports of my sermons from Sunday to Sunday, and want to thank you for their general accuracy. In these days, when one is so often reported as saying what he has taken great pains not to say, it is refreshing to see an account which is truthful. You get the gist of the sermon every week, and I hope you will not think me intrusive in thanking you for it.
Yours sincerely, GEORGE H. HEPWORTH.

NEW YORK, November 8, 1869.
To the Editor of the Herald:
Let me thank you for the report of my sermon in this morning's *Herald*. I have sometimes, and, indeed, so frequently, been made to suffer by the reporters, that it is refreshing to fall into the hands of one at once intelligent and appreciative. Will it be too much trouble for you to give my thankful acknowledgments to the gentlemanly reporter who was in my church yesterday?
Respectfully yours, WILLIAM AIKMAN.

The Jewish Rabbinical Convention, held in Philadelphia in November, 1869, closed its labors with a vote of thanks to Mr. Ellinger, editor of the *Jewish Times*, for his valuable services, and to the *New York Herald* for the faithful report of its proceedings. The Jewish Synod, held in Leipsic, acknowledged through the Hebrew organs the services of the *Herald* for spreading its proceedings before the world. That paper also had representatives at the Œcumenical Council at Rome and the Protestant Convention at Worms. Nothing can show the cosmopolitan character of the enterprising Press of the present day more conclusively than these facts. The intimate relations of the Pulpit and Press were recently far more correctly appreciated by a tavern-keeper at a railroad junction than by the late distinguished prelate of Calvary Church. The Rev. Dr. Price, of England, in a sermon lately delivered in London, illustrated this fact in relating his experience in America:

> Stopping on one occasion at a junction, he went to the hotel close by and had an excellent dinner. Afterwards, going into the clerk's office, he entered his name, "Thomas Price, Baptist minister, Aberdare." "Oh, sir," said he, "I guess you're a minister." "I guess so too," said I. "Well," he said, "you have only half to pay. The dinner is eighty cents; if you pay forty you get free of the other forty." "On what principle is that?" said I; and he said, "We give fifty per cent. off to ministers and editors." "Indeed," I said, "I happen to be an editor too." "Editor of what?" "Of *Seren Cymru.*" "Don't know the paper; where is it published?" "In Wales." "I don't know it; but you're an editor, are you?" "Yes, I am." "Well, I guess we are about square, exactly." I said, "I really think that I will come again on those terms." "Come whenever you like, and we will treat you on those terms."

On one occasion Edward Everett delivered an elaborate address before the New York Historical Society. It had been previously prepared, and proof-sheets of it had been sent to the offices of the morning papers. One of the reporters of the *Herald* put these proof-sheets in his note-book, and attended the lecture in the expectation that Mr. Everett would make alterations in the warmth of the moment, and that the *Herald* would therefore have a report of the address as it was actually spoken. It was the habit of Mr. Everett never to read his lectures, but to deliver them from memory. This is a New England habit. As school-boys would say, he "learned his lesson by heart." Well, the reporter closely followed Mr. E., word after word, from beginning to end of his splendid production, and how many changes does the reader suppose the lecturer made in the hour and a half he was engaged in "speaking his piece?" One, only one, and that was merely using the synonym of a single word that was in the original!

The United States are a great field for reporters. We have seen it stated that there are four hundred phonographers in the country. Thirty years ago there were none, and not more than half a dozen stenographers. Where there are so many legislative bodies—twenty or thirty in session every winter; where there are so many public meetings and public speeches; so many lectures, and so many important cases in courts, there is room for accomplished reporters in every state and in every city. Our newspapers, too, devote so much space now to these public matters, that skillful stenographers and phonographers can always command remunerative situations. Many of our courts have lately appointed official stenographers. So accurate are these gentlemen, that their reports are given in evidence in vitally important cases, and accepted by judge and jury. Some of the scenes in Congress, in courts, and in state Legislatures are so graphically and accurately reported that the reader can almost imagine that he has the *dramatis personæ* before him.

CHAPTER L.

THE COPYRIGHT IN NEWS.

WHAT PROTECTION HAS A NEWSPAPER WITH ITS NEWS?—COLONEL THOMAS H. BENTON'S LECTURE.—WEEKLY PAPERS ENTERED AT THE OFFICE OF THE LIBRARIAN.—THE PROPOSED INTERNATIONAL COPYRIGHT TREATY OF 1853. —IMPORTANT LAWSUITS.—THE REAL COPYRIGHT IN NEWS.—WHAT IS IT? —THE NEW COPYRIGHT TREATY.

SEVERAL papers, mostly weekly publications, although we have seen one daily newspaper, regularly appear with this announcement under the head-line :

Entered according to Act of Congress, in the year 1871, in the office of the Librarian at Washington.

This secures the contents of the paper, thus filed, from piracy, and the intention is to confine these contents within the circle of its own circulation. According to Prudhomme, "property is theft," and this copyright law is clearly in opposition to the brilliant idea of this distinguished French philosopher. Colonel Thomas Hart Benton, the senator from Missouri, so far as his public lectures were concerned, was a disbeliever in Prudhomme, much to the annoyance of reporters and publishers. He would not allow his lectures to be reported for the newspapers. He prepared one with great care, and, in order to prevent the reporters from appropriating the flashes of his thunder, he had the lecture copyrighted before uttering a single word. We recollect the supreme disgust of the reporters at the time. The *Nautical Gazette*, the *New York Ledger*, *Harper's Weekly*, and other publications, in having each number copyrighted, only wish to preserve their wares from those who are indifferent to the rights of others. Authors have the same property in their ideas, whether expressed in novels, romances, histories, plays, poems, or lectures, as in reaping machines, telegraph instruments, plows, fire-arms, and printing-presses. Irving, Bancroft, and Emerson's rights are as patent as those of Morse, M'Cormick, or Hoe. Newspapers, it would seem, hardly needed to be copyrighted. With a daily circulation of one hundred thousand, it is fair to suppose that that would practically be a copyright. Not so, however, in all cases. If the *Herald*, or *Tribune*, or *Times* should spend $10,000 for a cable dispatch of an important event in Europe, it could be circulated in half an hour after its issue from another printing-office which would pay but five cents for the copy of the *Herald* or *Times*. There would be difficulties in the way of doing this, yet the sublime feat could be performed by an extensive printing establishment. During the Mexican War, while the *Herald*, and *Sun*, and *Journal of Commerce* were running expresses with intelligence of the battles, another paper in New York regularly stole the news, and unblushingly called the act "ingenuity." Then, however, the circulation of these papers was small compared with the number of copies now issued, and the power of the presses was limited. To-day, for instance, the *Herald* could print one hundred thousand copies in one hour! This constitutes a very effective copyright, so far as that establishment is concerned.

In 1851, in the effort made in England to remove the stamp from the Newspaper Press, it was urged to grant a copyright in news for twelve hours to the journalist having the enterprise, at great cost, to get important dispatches from India, America, and the Continent of Europe. It was stated by F. Knight Hunt, of the Fourth Estate and of the London *Daily News*, that instances had been known when the *Times*, for instance, would receive an important dispatch from Paris, and, while printing it for the railway trains, a penny paper would obtain a copy, and circulate 70,000 to 100,000, and thus completely forestall the *Times* with its own news, and at one fourth the price. There was some protection in the stamp, but that has now ceased to trouble the English journalists, after an existence of one hundred and sixty-eight years. It finally disappeared on the 30th of September, 1870. The *Times* gives this historical sketch of this tax:

> In the year 1712 Queen Anne sent a message to the House of Commons complaining of the publication of "seditious papers and factious rumors, by which means designing men had been able to sink credit, and the innocent had suffered." On February 12 in that year, a committee of the whole house was appointed to consider the best means for stopping the then existing abuse of the liberty of the Press. The evil referred to had existence in the political pamphlets of the period. A tax upon the Press was suggested as the best means of remedying the evil, and, for the purpose of avoiding a storm of opposition, the impost was tacked on to a bill for taxing soaps, parchment, linens, silks, calicoes, etc. The result of the tax was the discontinuance of many of the favorite papers of the period, and the amalgamation of others into one publication. The act passed in June, 1712, came into operation in the month of August following, and continued for thirty-two years. The stamp was red, and the design consisted of the rose, shamrock, and thistle, surmounted with a crown. In the *Spectator* of June 10, 1712, Addison makes reference to this subject, and predicts great mortality among "our weekly historians." He also mentions that a facetious friend had described the said mortality as "the fall of the leaf." The witty Dean Swift, in his "Journal to Stella," under date of August 7, speaks of Grub Street as being dead and gone. According to his report, the new stamps had made sad havoc with the *Observator*, the *Flying Post*, the *Examiner*, and the *Medley*. Twelve years afterwards—namely, in 1724—the House of Commons had under consideration the practices of certain printers who had evaded the operation of the Stamp Act by printing the news upon paper between the two sizes mentioned by the law, and entering them as pamphlets, on

which the duty to be paid was 3s. for each edition. Its deliberations culminated in a resolution to charge 1d. for every sheet of paper "on which any *Journal, Mercury,* or any other newspaper whatever, shall be printed, and for every half sheet thereof the sum of one halfpenny sterling. In 1761 the stamp duty upon newspapers was made 1d., or £4 1s. 8d. for 1000 sheets. The next change in the stamp duty was effected on May 28, 1776, when Lord North advanced the price from 1d. to 1½d. Another alteration was made on August 12, 1789. On this occasion the stamp was increased from 1½d. to 2d. In 1794 the stamp went up to 2½d., and in May, 1797, to 3½d. The highest rate of the stamp was obtained in 1815, when the amount was 4d.

After this date a period of decline ensued. In the reign of William IV. an act was passed for the reduction of stamp duty upon newspapers from four pence to one pence, and one halfpence upon any supplement. This act came into operation on September 15, 1836, from which date the rise of the cheap newspaper era may be dated. The next improvement occurred in 1855, when the compulsory use of the stamp was abolished, save and except as a means of passing the paper through the post. During the last session we had the latest touch of Stamp-act legislation, when it was decided to determine the operation of the old act, and to inaugurate a new order of things more in "accordance with the liberal spirit of the age." It is perhaps necessary to add, now that the impressed stamp is abolished, that the postage rate on all *bona fide* newspapers is reduced to one halfpenny. Packets of newspapers come under the book-post regulations. Newspapers sent abroad must have a postage stamp affixed to them. Should they be required to pass through a foreign country, the additional postage must be paid. Stamped newspapers must be folded so that the whole stamp may be exposed to view; they must be posted within fifteen days of the date of publication, either without cover or in a cover with the ends open, and must contain no inclosure, mark, or writing.

Such laws as the above caused us to rebel in 1776. After the Revolution, when Massachusetts imposed a stamp duty on newspapers and advertisements, several of the newspapers suspended publication till the tax was removed. Thus far our journals have been free and without any protection. None is needed. It is different with authors of books and pamphlets. When Daniel Webster was Secretary of State, he and Sir John Crampton, the British minister, made a draft of a copyright treaty. It was amended and completed by Edward Everett, the successor of Mr. Webster, in December, 1852. The *New York Herald* advocated the confirmation of this treaty by the Senate. The draft of Messrs. Everett and Crampton was liberal in the main, and would probably have met the needs of literary men on both sides of the Atlantic. The points of this proposed treaty were submitted to the editor of the *Herald* at the time. An article was suggested to compel publishers to state whether or not they abridged the works republished. Although not fully up to the complete requirements of all authors, it was considered an excellent international arrangement, and efforts were made to push it to a ratification in the Senate. It was opposed by many of the booksellers, and it was a new idea for that body to discuss. It was a measure, too, out of which little or no political capital could be made. Yet it came near becoming a law.

Our own copyright law is not altogether free from fault and flaw. Occasionally cases come before the courts requiring legal interpretation. The most notable case was the recent one of William Beach Lawrence against Richard Dana. Another case was a theatrical one. In December, 1868, Augustin Daly, the author of "Under the Gaslight," made an application for an injunction to restrain Jarrett & Palmer from bringing out at Niblo's Garden Theatre Boucicault's play "After Dark." The ground of the application was that the play of "Under the Gaslight" was duly copyrighted by the plaintiff, and that in Mr. Boucicault's play, "After Dark," the sensation of the piece, the "railroad scene," was imitated so closely as to make it a violation of the copyright law. Judge Blatchford reviewed the points of resemblance between the two plays, and, supporting the plaintiff's view, granted the injunction requested.

Managers of one theatre have sent reporters to another theatre to take stenographic notes of a new play in order to obtain a copy to produce the piece in a night or two after at their establishment.

Newspapers have been affected by our law in other instances than that of the lecture of Colonel Benton. There was an important case in which the *New York Lancet*, published by James Gordon Bennett, was defendant, and the New York University the plaintiff in the suit, for reporting and publishing the clinical lectures of Professors Mott, Pattison, and others. It was decided in favor of the defendant. This decision, based on the fact that a lecture became public property the moment it was uttered in public, seems inconsistent with the right of Colonel Benton to his lecture, and with the decision of Judge Blatchford in the case of "After Dark" and "Under the Gaslight."

There was lately a decision in England which is of interest and importance to editors, writers, and publishers. There is printed under the head of many of the leading papers in the United States this

Notice.

We can not, under any circumstances, return rejected communications, nor can we undertake to preserve manuscripts.

The decision in England met a case that this notice would embrace. An unsolicited article was sent to *The Echo*, an evening paper in London. It was rejected, and the manuscript not returned. The writer sought to recover its value. The editor testified that he had received, rejected, and destroyed the manuscript, according to the practice of most newspaper publishers. The judge decided that articles so sent were at the disposal of the editor, and that, if he gave notice similar to the above, he had the right to destroy those he declined to accept.

There is another effort now being made to obtain an international copyright law. This, of course, will not affect newspapers. Such a law would have killed the *Brother Jonathan*, and *New World*, and *Boston Notion* in 1840–'43, when they brought out the last novel from England as news and sold it in extras. Our booksellers, before and since that period, have reaped all the benefit of this business of republication. They would purchase a single copy of Domby and Son, Foul Play, or Enoch Arden, and flood the country, at cheap rates, from their printing-offices. Our people, too, have enjoyed this advantage. But there is no protection to native talent in this. It is not like a high tariff to our cotton and woolen manufactures. It is cheaper to buy "Our Mutual Friend" in London and reprint it here than to aid in developing a Dickens in New York.

All this *en passant*. Our newspapers must continue to find their copyright in their superior enterprise, their superior machinery, their superior circulation, and in their superior means of delivering their papers to the public.

CHAPTER LI.
ADVERTISEMENTS.

THE FIRST ADVERTISEMENT.—ANNUAL VALUE OF A COLUMN OF ADVERTISEMENTS.—THE PROFESSIONAL ADVERTISEMENT WRITER.—VARIOUS MODES OF ADVERTISEMENTS.—PLACARDS ON THE FACE OF NATURE.—CURIOUS ADVERTISEMENTS.—THE SPREAD OF RELIGION BY ADVERTISEMENTS.—THE PHILOSOPHY OF THE BUSINESS.—THE ADVERTISING AGENCIES.—THEIR EXPANSION.

THE first advertisement appeared in London in 1648.

Is it true that Walter left one advertising column of the London *Times* to his daughter as her only legacy?

We do not know whether this statement be founded on fact or not, but it is manifest that the interrogator had an imperfect idea of the value of such a gift. One column of the *New York Herald* is worth one hundred dollars per day, or thirty-six thousand dollars per year. On the fifth page of that journal the annual income would be $100,000! This yearly income would not be considered small even by an Astor or a Stewart.

Apart from the necessity of the receipts from advertisements in a large newspaper establishment as a revenue, this class of reading matter has become a most interesting part of newspaper literature. Writers of business notices are as sensational and make as much money as some of the feuilletonists of Paris. There was one Dunan Mousseux lately died in the French capital who devoted himself exclusively to this peculiar kind of business. Talent of no mean order is displayed in the composition of these attractive notices. Mousseux has received as much as one hundred dollars for writing a single advertisement. According to the Paris correspondent of the *London Literary Gazette*, as far back as 1851, a curious specimen of the *mœurs littéraires* of France was exposed before a court of justice in a squabble between two tradesmen :

> Leon Gozlan, well known to the public as a dramatist, received a commission for the *feuilleton* of one of the daily newspapers. He immediately drew up a detailed account of the plot he intended to employ, with descriptions of the principal scenes and incidents. He then charged an advertising agent to carry this document round to the principal tradesmen, and in his name to propose to them (of course for a consideration) to introduce their names and addresses, with puffs on their wares in particular places. His prospectus ran somewhat in this way : Chapter I. Marriage of the hero and heroine. (Here the author can introduce the name and address of the former's tailor and of the latter's milliner, with a glowing

description of the excellence of the garments.) Chapter 20. The husband, having obtained proof of his wife's guilt, rushes upon her with pistols and poison, that she will choose which death she will die. (Names of gunsmith and druggist to come in here.) Chapter 21. She dies, and is to be buried. (Name of undertaker.) 22. Turns out to be only in a trance, and is brought to life by Dr. ———, ——— Street. In short, there was not a single chapter nor a single incident which our ingenious author did not propose to make the vehicle of a puff. Opinions may, perhaps, differ as to the literary value of this line of novel writing, but at least all will agree in admitting that it is a bold and daring advance in the noble art of advertising.

How many are deceived by the first few lines of a business notice in a New York paper! It opens with the announcement of some important event, and ends in offering the reader the cheapest hat or the most perfect sewing machine. No one gets angry over these modern cheats. Some of the advertisement agents of the metropolis are rich, and presidents of banks. Quite a number of women are engaged in the business. The late Mr. Raymond, of the *Times*, relates the fact that, in his early career in New York, he secured what he "deemed a first-class engagement, to write daily a fancy advertisement of some vegetable pills which had just been invented, and which were to be commended to public favor every morning in the daily journals by being ingeniously connected with some leading event of the day, for which service, which cost me, perhaps, ten minutes of daily labor, I received the sum of fifty cents." It was stated in 1868 that an advertisement agent, the first in Germany, made a fortune in Berlin in two years.

Among the curious modes of advertising was one in London of a dog walking along the Strand with a bill suspended from his neck inviting the public to deal with his master, and another bill attached to his tail giving the address of his master. Another fact is mentioned of the proprietors of a diorama in London who advertised their exhibition by inflating small balloons and attaching to them a great number of tickets of admission, which tickets, after the balloons had risen a certain height in the air, were scattered in all directions, the finders of the tickets being entitled to admission to the exhibition at half price on writing on the tickets the places where they had been respectively picked up. The Northwestern Railway Company of England authorized all their station-masters at 180 stations to receive advertisements to insert in certain spaces allotted at the different stations for their exhibition, and they even appointed an agent in the Strand to receive advertisements, and, as an inducement, the railway company stated that 6,000,000 passengers traveled on the road in one year—an advertising circulation which, the company asserted, no newspaper could boast of.

Our people learn the ways of the rest of the world, and introduce foreign fashions in business as in dress. Our railway stations, however, confine their advertisements mostly to railroad business, and hence we rarely see any other notices in *dépôts* than of railroads, steam-boats, and hotels. In our street or horse cars the panel advertising system is in vogue. Wagons were introduced in New York some time ago—somewhere about 1830—by Gosling, to bring his blacking before the people. His turn-out was gorgeous. Barnum sent Tom Thumb's carriage and four Shetland ponies daily through the streets as an advertisement. Advertising vans are quite common. Individuals grotesquely dressed are also employed to perambulate the streets with banners. Illuminations are resorted to for the same purpose.

Some one, in 1869, purchased the right, at a high price, to advertise on the fence around the new post-office site in New York City. Curb-stones are variegated with cards. Cities are placarded with business notices. Theatres for a long time enjoyed a monopoly of street-posters, but all trades have adopted the placard form, and disfigure fences and old buildings with their effusions. It is worth one's while to read the notices thus brought before the people. Some very funny cross readings appeared on a City Hall fence. Religion, the drama, election notices, the opera, buchu, official proclamations, balm of a thousand flowers, and steam-ship lines are mixed, and overlap each other in a most extraordinary manner. Throughout the country, this mania, originating in England to avoid the tax on advertisements in newspapers, has run into a positive nuisance—so much so, indeed, as to call for special legislation to prevent the defacing of nature. On every rock, on every cliff, on every exposed place—sometimes positively dangerous of access—the traveler in the United States will see these business announcements painted in the most artistic manner, in letters from six inches to two feet in length. Along every railroad, on every bridge, on every unoccupied building, on all temporary fences of any size, appears a notice in printing-ink or in oil colors, and in all styles of fancy lettering, of some "ready relief," "instantaneous pain-killer," "hair restorer," "neuralgia cure," or "buy your clothing at the blue store," which stare you in the face in every direction. Splendid wagons, with two horses finely caparisoned, are sometimes seen standing in country roads, while the artist, thus stylishly riding around on this business, is engaged in disfiguring or ornamenting a public bridge. Yet, with all this peculiar mode of making business known, our American newspapers are filled with advertisements, and at what would have been considered, twenty years ago, fabulous prices; and in the American newspaper we see the style and substance of the advertising systems of all other nations, even to the enormous placard system of France, where the *Journal des Débats* frequently presents its readers with advertisements in letters one to two inches long, looking like a large show-bill. The peculiar personal advertisements, which are often so mysterious and curious, are, in part, an importation from Germany by the way of England. In Germany the newspaper announces the birth of a child, or of twins, or an engagement to be married, or any domestic event, in the most affectionate and public manner. One Teuton advertises "the happy delivery of my wife Agnes, born Weishoff, of a healthy girl; I respectfully announce to relatives and friends." Another was made happy by the birth of "twin daughters." Two announce themselves "as married," and "we recommend ourselves to our relatives and friends." Then parents announce "the marriage of their only daughter." Such advertisements are quite common in the Berlin papers, and are now creeping into those published in New York.

With an eye to business, the following advertisements once appeared:

      Here lies
     ADOLPHE B———,
  who died at the age of — years,
  in the possession of all his teeth,
   thanks to the dentifrice wash
    of the house of X. & Cͦ
    No. — —— Street.
    Ten francs a bottle.

On a tombstone erected forty years ago at Montmartre one could read this inscription:

To the memory of M. Jabart, a most excellent husband and father. His inconsolable widow continues to carry on the grocery business in the Rue St. Denis.

This was issued by a Paris hosier for the soul and sole of his customers:

I supplicate you, sir, to look with indulgence upon these few observations; my desire for your eternal welfare has induced me to address you. I beg to direct your attention to the sacred Scriptures, and, at the same time, to the extremely moderate price at which I sell cotton goods, etc.

One of the Kentucky papers thirty-five years ago had:

Ebenezer Jackson takes leave to say that there is no sensible character located in all the states, whether he hangs up his brim in a fine new-painted house or in an independent log hut with the bark on, who will not rejoice like thunder when he hears of the just-arrived and piled up in my store percussion locks and caps, and slap his thigh that the horses will startle at it a mile off!

Another class of special advertisements come under the head of medical notices. Some of these are quite objectionable. They have been a good deal reformed and cut down to comparative decency, but still some of our newspaper columns continue to be disfigured with them in their worst style of expression. This class of notices came to us from England. Efforts have been made in that country to exclude advertisements of this character, and these efforts have met with considerable success, especially with the Provincial Press. One paper, the *Bray Gazette*, in 1865, published with its terms of advertising, "No quack advertisements inserted." The *York Herald* of the same year had the following notice: "All objectionable medical advertisements will be rigorously excluded from this paper so soon as existing contracts have expired." The *London Lancet*, the leading medical periodical of the world, started this movement. It has been stated, in connection with this fact, that the Evangelical Advertising Association of the United States proposed, in 1868, to "intersperse moral and religious truths" among the miscellaneous advertisements of all the leading periodicals. This idea is apparently a novel and original one. The Boston *News-Letter* of May 28, 1711, when that was the only paper in the country, contained three advertisements. One was as follows:

A Guide for the Doubting and Cordial for the fainting Saint, or Directions and Consolations for Afflicted Consciences; being an Answer to above thirty Particular Doubts or Objections, which many Christians are sometimes grievously disgusted with. By the Rev Mr Benjamin Wadsworth, Minister of the Gospel in Boston: And sold by Eleazer Philips at his shop under the Exchange in Kings Street, Boston.

The columns of our modern papers daily show more ingenuity in preparing advertisements for publication. We take a few at random:

WE ARE A LITTLE FAMILY OF THREE PERSONS, LIVING just out of Fifth Avenue. We own the house we dwell in, and have twice as much room as we want. If we knew of some nice people, who could appreciate a cheerful, home-like home, as much unlike a boarding-house as possible, we would invite those people to call at our house and see what arrangement we could make. Address BARKIS, Herald office.

GILFILLAN—"IF EVER I CEASE TO LOVE."—I SUPPOSE YOU are still living, as I have not seen any obituary notice; have neither seen, heard of or from you since I saw you two weeks ago; it is very unkind not to communicate when it can so easily be done. Do so for old friendship sake. C.

THE UNRIVALLED EUROPEAN MEDICAL AND BUSINESS Clairvoyant tells past, present, and future; shows likeness and gives name of future husband. No.—West Forty-first Street, Broadway and Seventh Avenue.

Two Kickers and a Lugger to be Educated to-night at Prof. ——'s Academy, corner Broadway and Thirty-fifth Street.

ARE YOU HAPPY IN MAKING ME MISERABLE?—WHY DO you continue to avoid me? Have you forgotten your solemn promise made me? T. H. E.

TWEED THE DEVIL! Ten cents; in downfall of Tammany Hall; no fall at all.

ABSOLUTE DIVORCES LEGALLY OBTAINED FROM DIFFERent states; desertion, etc., sufficient cause; no publicity; no charge until divorce granted; advice free. ——, Attorney, 180 Broadway.

Adam Smith would be shocked to read that an article worth $12 should sell for $8:

GREAT REDUCTION IN PRICES.
PANTALOONS WORTH $8 FOR $6.
PANTALOONS WORTH $12 FOR $8.
PANTALOONS WORTH $16 FOR $12.

AN INDISPUTABLE FACT.—The political revolution has had a marked effect upon the trade of the city. This is shown by the advance in stocks and the increased demand for K——'s unapproachable hats, and his widely-known establishment, No. —— Broadway, is a scene of decided and gratifying activity. To complete your outfit to the proper point of elegance, you must secure a handsome hat at K——'s.

The Hall case has taken on a new phase, owing to the unfortunate death of one of the jurors; but the excitement attendant on this event is nothing to the excitement exhibited by the visitors to the store No. —— ——, where the American agents of the Great —— Watch Company are selling off the stock of that company at the lowest prices. Gold watches are there sold for $15, and those in silver cases as low as $6.

DEAR CHARLES—SHOULD SUCH A TRIFLE AS A HANDY hat-brush sever love? Come to your ruffled LU-LU.

H—— WILL PAY $500 FOR ARTICLES ON CORRUPTION, ETC., in C. H. Can not find you. Call soon. TRIBUNE.

Has the late attacks on the custom-house in the *New York Tribune* any connection with the last-quoted advertisement?

One of the clerks in the counting-room of the *New York Herald* gives the following as the various ways of spelling the word "situation" that have come under his notice in the receipt of advertisements for that journal:

situation,	scitiation,	sitienching,	sitiation,
sickwatchian,	suation,	citation,	sitiatione,
sittution,	sitooashon,	cituation,	sicthshion,
situatione,	situaetion,	sitution,	sttion,
sictuation,	situertoin,	sitation,	sitwaytion,
sittyoation,	sitatone,	sitooshun,	sitatuon,
situatian,	situason,	setuation,	suition,
setusation,	sutation,	situtain,	situution,
situesion,	sitution,	situasion,	situashin,
sutuation,	situaton,	sittuation,	situeation,
situashon,	situwation,	situashan,	situtain,
situashion,	sitouin,	sitwashon,	sitwation,
sitwishon,	sitieshon,	sitwashan,	stituation,
	scituation.		

Some idea of the magnitude of the advertising of one paper in New York, the *Herald*, may be gathered from the following article, which appeared in that journal on the 28th of September, 1869:

A day or two since our post-office messengers applied for an increase of compensation, alleging, as a reason therefor, their increased labors on account of the heavily enlarged business of the *Herald* with the letter department of the post-office. On examination, we found that the application of our messengers was well founded, for in a single mail received at noon yesterday, and counted in our presence, there were no less than *six hundred and twenty-nine letters in answer to advertisements alone,* which, of course, was exclusive of our usual batch of correspondence from all parts of the world. These letters were in reply to advertisements for a single day, and by a single mail, embracing many of the prominent trades and professions, such as business opportunities, financial matters, instruction, the turf, horses and carriages, boarding and lodging, real estate, dwelling-houses, rooms, etc., to let, sales at auction, amusements, and so on, and, of course, had no reference to responses made personally by parties advertising—all going to show the value of advertising in our columns. It is a noteworthy fact that these letters, in reply to advertisements in the *Herald*, exceed in number that of an entire great Southern mail received at the post-office in this city less than fifty years ago. Who says this is not an age of progress?

The *New York Telegram*, in October, 1871, said:

COSTLY ADVERTISING.

The country papers are making a great ado over the enormous price which is charged by a Chicago paper for a column advertisement for one year, the sum being $22,000. It may be, and we have no doubt is a large amount for such service in Chicago, but it sinks into insignificance compared with the charges of some of the New York papers. The *Herald*, for instance, would charge for a column advertisement on its fifth page for one year $109,500.

Several years ago the *Herald* refused to insert the advertisements of the Maretzek Opera and Barnum's Museum in New York. There was then an association of theatrical managers in existence in that city for mutual protection. These two unfortunate managers called a meeting of their associates to devise means to compel the editor to publish the excluded advertisements. They decided that the announcements of all the theatres must appear in the *Herald*, or none. None appeared. No dictation was the rule in that office. It was estimated that the annual loss to the editor would be $100,000, and that his readers would have to seek other papers for information in regard to these popular places of amusement. But the managers, in withdrawing their advertisements, had conspicuously inserted over their notices in all the other publications, and on their bills and posters, the fact that "This establishment does not advertise in the *New York Herald*." This constant announcement attracted universal attention to that paper, and the independence of its editor in face of this costly crusade against him. It was worth more to him than twice the receipts from the theatrical managers. But in less than one year they were tired of their course, and returned to the *Herald*.

Various estimates have been made of the number of advertisements inserted in the newspapers and periodicals in the United States and England. In 1847 the number in the United States was estimated to have reached 11,000,000. In Great Britain, in 1848, the number was 2,109,179. These figures have probably doubled in England and quadrupled in the United States.

Advertisers are a calculating class. They spend their money, and they take their choice of newspapers. At one period in the life of the *New York Sun* it monopolized the advertisements of "situations wanted" and "help wanted." Several years later these brief domestic notices, each one chronicling a revolution in a household, appeared almost wholly in the *New York Herald*. That paper, on Tuesday mornings, would contain an entire page of such advertisements. What was the cause of this change? The circulation of the *Sun* was even then larger than that of the *Herald*. It was readily explained by a pretty and bright servant-girl: "Why, don't you see that where we want to live the *Herald* is taken in? The *Sun* is a cent paper, and taken by poor people only, who do their own work. Our advertisements there would be of no use to us."

This young woman developed the philosophy of advertising in these three sentences. It is not so much the extent in numbers of the circulation of a newspaper as it is the character of that circulation. The *London Telegraph* circulates three times as many copies as the *London Times*, yet the latter retains its enormous advertising patronage.

This remunerative branch of journalism is now arranged on the most expansive scale by the different advertising agents scattered over the country. It is wonderful to see the perfect system of their arrangements. One agency in New York City has compiled an octavo volume of three hundred pages, giving the names of nearly all the newspapers published in the country, with the names of editors and publishers, and circulation. They receive advertisements for nearly one thousand papers in the United States. Another agent, in Boston, takes another step forward, for he promises editorial notices with the advertisements. We insert this attractive part of his notice:

OUR LOCAL LIST FOR BOSTON ADVERTISERS
COMPOSED OF
22 PAPERS,
IN THE SUBURBAN TOWNS,
offers rates which defy competition.
Advertisements inserted in all the lists of other Agencies.
ADVERTISEMENTS WRITTEN.
Editorial Notices Obtained.
A first copy of paper furnished to advertisers.

Then the "Great Western Improved Newspaper Advertising Company" in St. Louis places its claims before the business community. They have "facilities for securing the insertion of advertisements on a new plan, at low rates, a portion of the space in over two hundred Western and Southern papers belonging to them by contract."

But "our plan" of the *Milwaukee Wisconsin* surpasses any thing that has yet been devised to accomplish the largest publicity of business notices at the lowest prices. If we insert this plan from the *Wisconsin* in full, it will be because of its novelty here, and because it develops the mode of publishing papers at the West and in other parts of the country which is not practiced in New York City. It is an English plan, and is the way many of the provincial papers are published there.

The *Nashville Union* states that five of the journals published in that state get the outer pages of their papers printed in some city outside of Tennessee. These publishers get the paper they use, with one side printed, delivered at their respective offices at about what the white paper would cost them.

The *Wisconsin* programme is the following:

THE
Milwaukee Wisconsin.
NORTHWESTERN LIST
—OF—
NEWSPAPERS.

OUR PLAN OF ADVERTISING.

We call the plan of printing country papers with advertising "OUR PLAN," because we originated and first put it in practice. At the breaking out of the war, when printers had largely gone to the front, we devised the plan of printing one side of the country papers, and using a certain space for advertising purposes, to pay us for the type-setting and press-work, our maximum price to the papers themselves being the cost of the white paper. We have increased our advertising to such an extent that the price to country papers for printed paper is considerably less than the cost of white paper at the mills, besides a saving of $500 to $1000 a year to each paper for type-setting and press-work.

Now if an advertisement should be sent direct to 200 newspapers, four squares in length, the publishers would set the type 200 times. As an advertisement of four squares is about 1000 ems of type-setting, it is evident somebody must pay for 200,000 ems of type-setting. This, at fifty cents per 1000, the usual rate, would amount to $100. Our price for such an advertisement is only $50, or one half the cost of type-setting, counting nothing for the insertion in the papers themselves.

Long before any other house in the world we invented and put in practice this system of co-operative printing and advertising, and are justly entitled to the distinction, if there be any, of calling it "OUR PLAN."

OUR CIRCULATION.

Papers.	Circulation.
6—The Evening Wisconsin, Milwaukee	48,000
2—The Semi-weekly Wisconsin, Milwaukee	5,000
1—The Weekly Wisconsin, Milwaukee	20,000
50 Weekly Papers in Wisconsin	45,000
50 Weekly Papers in Illinois	40,000
25 Weekly Papers in Minnesota	20,000
20 Weekly Papers in Michigan	16,000
20 Weekly Papers in Iowa	16,000
15 Weekly Papers in Indiana	12,000
10 Weekly Papers in Ohio	8,000
20 Weekly Papers in other States	20,000
Circulation per Week	250,000

AN ADVERTISEMENT
INSERTED IN
ALL THE NEWSPAPERS
PRINTED AT THE OFFICE OF THE
Evening Wisconsin
WILL REACH
250,000 Subscribers per Week.

The *New York Tribune* claims to print 300,000 papers per week. The *Tribune's* charge—and a very reasonable one too—is $25 for ten lines one week in this circulation; that is, for $25 they print ten lines 300,000 times, and send it through the mails to the subscribers.

For **$12 50**—just half the sum—the EVENING WISCONSIN prints an advertisement of ten lines and sends it to 250,000 subscribers in a week.

Some of these agencies advertise their own business very extensively. We have seen, for example, an entire page of the *New York Herald* taken up, at a cost of $500 or $600 for a single insertion, with one advertisement of Rowell's Newspaper Directory. Those mild, persuasive, industrious agents of the old school, Hooper, Palmer, Pettingill, Oatman, looked upon these active, energetic innovators with a constituency of a thousand newspapers, these modern canvassers with lists of journals to be measured by the yard, with perfect amazement. No wonder they fell in with such a brilliant association. But is not this new mode, after all, the style of our journalism of to-day? Is it not all on a grand scale?

CHAPTER LII.
THE MOTTOES OF THE PRESS.

ARE THEY THE EDITORS' PLATFORMS OF PRINCIPLES?—SPECIMEN MOTTOES. —THE POPE'S MOTTO FOR JOURNALISTS.

THESE are the curiosities of newspaper literature. They were the platforms of the editors in olden times. They endeavored to convey to the public the principles on which their journals should be conducted by these short sentences, sometimes in English, sometimes in French, but oftener in Latin—*Multum in parvo*. In the early days of American journalism these mottoes were accompanied with all sorts of curious pictorial devices, some of Minerva, some of the figure of Liberty, some with a clock representing the time, some with a printing-press, some with Mercury. Not only have the devices nearly disappeared, but the mottoes have gone and are going with them. Often the opinions of an editor and his adopted motto would present a perfect antithesis on his pages. Many of the mottoes are grand, some of them immensely so. Here are a few specimens:

Constitutional Courant	1765.	Join or die.
Virginia Gazette	1766.	Open to all parties, but influenced by none.
Worcester (Mass.) *Spy*	1771.	Open to all parties, but influenced by none.
Independent Chronicle	1776.	Appeal to heaven : Independence.
Independent Ledger	1778.	All hands with one inflamed and enlightened heart.
Boston Independent Chronicle	1784.	Truth its guide, Liberty its object.
Loudon's New York Diary	1793.	Tout le monde.
The Gazette of the United States,	1800.	"I, from the Orient to the drooping West, Making the wind my post-horse, still unfold The deeds commenced on this ball of earth."
American Telegraph	1814.	Justice, law, and liberty. Prodesse civibus.
The Genius of Liberty and American Telegraph	1818.	Where a government is founded on opinion, it is of the essence of its preservation that opinion be free.
Philadelphia Aurora	1818.	Surgo ut prosim.
Providence Journal	1820.	Encourage national industry.
The Yankee and Boston Lit. Gaz.,	1828.	The greatest happiness of the greatest number.
Niles's Register	1836.	The Past—the Present—for the Future.
Boston Saturday Evening Gazette,	1840.	I'll put a girdle around about the earth in forty minutes.
New York Tribune	1841.	I desire you to understand the true principles of the government. I wish them carried out. I ask nothing more.

Multum in parvo.

New York Chronicle	1842.	God and the elevation of the people.
The North American	1847.	Devoted to truth.
The American Pioneer (Monterey, Mexico)	1847.	Render unto Cæsar the things that are Cæsar's.
New York Courier and Enquirer,	1860.	Principles, not men.
New York Express	1860.	One country, one Constitution, one destiny.
Richmond (Va.) Whig	1864.	The Constitution—State Rights.
New York Express	1868.	The Constitution, the Union, and the Laws.
Council Bluffs Democrat	1868.	The world is governed too much.
Charleston (S. C.) Mercury	1868.	Vindice nullo sponte sua, sine lege, fides nectumque colentui.
Macon (Ga.) American Union	1869.	With malice towards none, with charity for all, but with firmness for the right, as God gives us to see the right.
Atlanta (Ga.) Intelligencer	1869.	Error ceases to be dangerous when reason is left free to combat it.
Quincy (Mass.) Patriot	1869.	Born to no master, of no sect are we.
Bartram's (Mich.) Cheek	1869.	Beauty and business.
New York National Standard	1870.	Justice and equal rights to all.
Woodhull & Claflin's Weekly	1870.	Progress! Free thought! Untrammeled lives!
Charlotte (N. C.) Observer	1870.	Onward—upward.
Lynchburg (Va.) Republican	1870.	Virginia victrix.
Cooperstown (N.Y.) Freeman's Journal	1870.	Principles, not men. Be just, and fear not.
La Crosse (Wis.) Democrat	1870.	Democratic at all times and under all circumstances.
Newport (R. I.) Mercury	1870.	Hope.
Lynchburg Virginian	1870.	The rights of the states and the union of the states.
Marion (S. C.) Crescent	1870.	Non eventu rerum sed fide veritatis stamus.
Charleston (S. C.) Courier	1870.	What is it but a map of busy life.
Atlanta True Georgian	1870.	Wisdom, justice, and moderation.
Richmond (Va.) Whig	1870.	Sic semper tyrannis.
Printers' Circular	1870.	Free and unshackled.
New York Albion	1870.	Cœlum, non animum, mutant qui trans mare currunt.
Mobile Herald	1871.	Free, fearless, and fair.
New Haven Register	1871.	Equal and exact justice to all men, of whatever status or persuasion, religious or political.
New York Independent	1871.	But as we were allowed of God to be put in trust with the Gospel, even so we speak, not as pleasing men, but God, which trieth our hearts.
Wisconsin Chief	1871.	Right on.
New York Republican	1871.	With malice toward none, with charity for all—with firmness in the right, as God gives us to see the right, let us strive to finish the work we are in.
New York Sun	1871.	It shines for all. Excelsior.
Worcester (Mass.) Spy	1871.	The spy should have the eye of Argus: he is honorable if he do but look to the welfare of the commonwealth.
Typographic Messenger	1871.	Vox dicta perit; litera scripta manet.
Our Dumb Animals	1871.	We speak for those who can not speak for themselves.
Congressional Globe	1872.	The world is governed too much.
The Episcopal Register	1872.	Speaking the truth in love.

Pope Pius IX. has given a motto for the Press in general. About three years ago, in 1869, a correspondent of the *Événement Illustré*, traveling in Rome, called on Pio Nono. Another journalist accompanied him. In a letter to the *Illustré*, describing the interview, he said :

<small>When I was received with my companion, the chamberlain plucked me by the sleeve to make me kneel. The Pope, perceiving the movement, spared us the genuflexion, and made us approach the table at which he was sitting. "So, then," his holiness said, "you are two journalists, friends, going together to Naples?" He spoke about Naples, and asked us how we liked Rome, adding that people found themselves very free during their stay. He then took two photographic likenesses of himself, one for each of us, and, with a sly smile, said, "I am going to write something for the journalists," and in a firm hand traced these words :</small>

"Diligite veritatem, filium Dei,"

<small>after which he held out his hand to us. His affability is extreme. He speaks French with as much accent as Rossini, and the impression he produced on me was that of a pleasant and tranquil old man who appears to be but little occupied with external matters.</small>

If the heretical Press of the world will not adopt this excellent motto as their platform, there is no reason why the organs of the Catholic Church should not place it at the head of their papers, and act upon the precept in all its fullness and meaning.

CHAPTER LIII.
THE LAW OF LIBEL.

TRIALS AND RESPONSIBILITIES OF THE PRESS. — WHAT IS THE LAW OF LIBEL?—INTERESTING AND INSTRUCTIVE CASES.—THE EDITORIAL RIGHT TO CRITICISE.—THE SUITS OF J. FENIMORE COOPER, CHARLES READE, AND GEORGE AUGUSTUS SALA.—THE RUSSIAN LAW.—EATING HIS OWN WORDS. —THE EMPEROR OF GERMANY AND THE PRESS.—THE ORGANIC LAW OF THE UNITED STATES.

THE freedom of the Press has been of slow growth if we take the records of our courts as an indication, for the same ruling was adopted in a case of libel in the Supreme Court of New York in 1803 under the Republic, as in 1735 in the same state under a monarchy, and the same ruling has since been held in other courts. Andrew Hamilton in 1735, and Alexander Hamilton in 1803, occupied the same position towards the Press; exhibited the same eloquence, and gained the same points with the people. Our state Constitutions are clear on the rights of the newspaper, but the law of libel is not so clearly defined, and much is still to be done to obtain the desired result for the Press and public.

The first case, that of Zenger, of the *New York Gazette*, in 1735, was a political one, and brought down the whole power and influence of the governor and court on the journalist's head, but the latter signally triumphed. The second case, that of Croswell, of the *Hudson Balance*, in 1803, was also political, and grew out of the bitter feud between Burr and Hamilton. Hildreth thus describes this important action :

While these political intrigues were in progress, a case came on for argument before the Supreme Court of New York, then sitting at Albany, in which the rights and freedom of the Press were deeply involved. Ambrose Spencer, as attorney general, had instituted a prosecution for libel against a Federal printer for having asserted that Jefferson had paid Callender for traducing Washington and Adams. The case had been tried before Chief Justice Lewis, who had held, among other things, that in a criminal trial for libel the truth could not be given in evidence, and that the jury were merely to decide the fact of publication, the question belonging exclusively to the court whether it were a libel or not. These points coming on for a rehearing before the Supreme Court, on a motion for a new trial, Spencer maintained with great zeal the arbitrary doctrines laid down by Lewis. Hamilton, a volunteer in behalf of the liberty of the Press, displayed, on the other side, even more than his wonted eloquence and energy, denouncing the maxim, "the greater the truth the greater the libel," at least in its relation to political publications, as wholly inconsistent with the genius of American institutions. The court, after a long deliberation, was equally divided, Kent and Thompson against Lewis and Livingston. The opinion of the chief justice stood as law;

but Hamilton's eloquence was not lost. A declaratory bill, conforming to the doctrine maintained by him, was introduced into the Assembly, then sitting, by a Federal member. The Republicans shrank from this implied censure on their candidate for governor, and the matter was postponed to the next session. An act, allowing the truth to be given in evidence, was then passed, but was defeated by the Council of Revision, composed of the judges and chancellor. The act, however, with some modifications, became law the next year; and such, either by constitutional provisions, legislative enactment, or the decisions of the courts, is now the law throughout the United States.

This "law throughout the United States" is summed up in this rule for editors and publishers. Blackstone said:

> Every free man has an undoubted right to lay what sentiments he pleases before the public; to forbid this is to destroy the freedom of the press; *but if he publishes what is improper, mischievous, or illegal, he must take the consequences of his own temerity.*

But what is "improper" and "illegal?" Fox obtained the enactment of a law in England in 1792 which left to the jury the right to decide on the character of what was published as well as on the fact of publication; yet Chief Justice Lewis, in the United States, in 1803, refused to admit the first clause of this law. In all decisions since the time of the Hamiltons, there has been so much diversity of opinion that no editor is sure of the "freedom of the Press" till a judge and a jury have decided upon his case. There is as great a variety in the points made by the judges in the several states as there are states in the Union.

We propose to cite a number of cases in this chapter, not mentioned in other pages of this volume, to show the uncertainty of the law of libel in the United States, and the necessity of a revision, and of the enactment of a code for the whole country. These cases will form a *mélange*, but in this shape they may be of use to those who take an interest in the subject. The *New York Herald*, in 1869, gave a brief historical sketch of the most important suits under the laws of libel, which should be placed in a convenient place for reference. We therefore transfer it to our pages:

> It is the boast of this country that in its fundamental laws—federal as well as state—the inviolability of the freedom of speech and of the liberty of the Press is fully guaranteed. It is so by custom and Parliamentary enactment in England; but not even there, the freest country of Europe, is the liberty of the Press made sacred by written constitutional provisions. It is conceded by all that no healthy political life can develop itself among a people where the first requisite for it is wanting—perfect freedom of discussion and criticism by word of mouth, and by the pen through the public Press. Hence we see the demand for a free Press increase in France with every passing year. It is for this reason that regenerated Germany, in the North German Parliament, at Berlin, as well as in the Diets at Munich, Stuttgart, Karlsruhe, and Vienna, measure upon measure has been introduced, discussed, and, in some instances, are emanating from the liberal members, and all tending to enlarge the freedom of the Press, and place it forever after upon solid, secure ground. These measures have of late succeeded most in Vienna, under the liberal guidance of Baron Beust, the present chancellor of the Austro-Hungarian empire, and latterly there was introduced, by Parliamentary enactment, sanctioned by the emperor, trial by jury for all offenses against the Press law. In the other South German states this had obtained for years past,

but in enlightened Prussia it is still denied, and a mere edict of some police official is enough to cause the seizure of a whole edition of a paper containing an offensive article, just as the same thing is done in France. The prince of the politico-satirical journals of Germany, the *Kladderadatsch*, of Berlin, has more than once been the victim of this supervision, and its principal editor has on several occasions paid for his journalistic temerity by several weeks' imprisonment in the Molken Markt, a city prison in Berlin. In Bavaria they managed things in a more liberal way years ago even. The editor of the *Volksbote*, at Munich, was sued for libel on the chief of staff of the Bavarian army during the memorable German War of 1866, and on the case being tried before the jury, the editor was triumphantly acquitted, amid the general applause of the people, it being considered a verdict of condemnation upon the manner in which the Bavarian army had been managed.

Of all such troubles, to which the Continental Press of Europe is even now to some extent subjected, the American people fortunately know but little. From the beginning the liberty of the Press was considered one of the main pillars of the Republican edifice, and its safety from encroachment was not left to legislative whim or caprice, but firmly placed as one of the bulwarks of free, constitutional life. Still, for many years, and even now, this boasted freedom of the Press is exposed to insidious attacks. This is owing to the old traditionary maxims of the common law, which we inherited from England, and to the stiff-necked adhesion of our courts and judges to the authority of adjudicated cases, whether cited from the English or American bench, and whether recent and in consonance with the advanced spirit of the times, or perhaps a generation, or may be even a century old. This complaint refers especially to the system of libel suits against the publishers of newspapers, by means of which every censoriously criticised public officer, or every exposed rogue, seeks to re-establish himself in public esteem by attempting to bleed the publisher or editor, and fill his own pockets at the latter's expense.

PRESENT CONDITION OF THE LAW OF LIBEL.

It is true, however, that we have made some progress over the antiquated ideas of the last century. The theory of libel has been far more liberalized than it was heretofore. The outrageous principle, ascribed by some to Sir Matthew Hale, and for a long time rigidly adhered to in England, that "the greater the truth the greater the libel," is now no longer recognized. In England they have encroached upon this rule by what is called "judge made law," the courts inventing the distinction of privileged communications; and while our courts have followed this lead, we have thrown a further protective shield over the liberty of the Press by enacting in our Constitutions that in actions for libel the truth of the alleged libel may be given in evidence by the defendant, and that the article was published from good motives and for justifiable ends. This sweeping provision, apparently covering every thing in the shape of an action or prosecution for libel, was, however, cropped down, and limited by the courts, in that they decided that in civil suits for damages, based upon the publication of an alleged libel, the truth can not be given in evidence as a justification, except upon notice to the other party, and by laying the foundation for it in a proper plea contained in the answer, and by further exacting of the defendants in such cases that such plea of justification must be as precise as a count in an indictment, and as broad as the original charge, and the proof in support of it must be as positive as that required by the rules of criminal practice on the trial of an indictment. It was only under the imperative provision of the Code of Procedure that the courts relaxed somewhat in their severity, and allowed mitigating circumstances to be given in evidence if the truth could not be proved in justification, as the rigor of the criminal code demanded, and this only in mitigation of damages.

WHAT IS A LIBEL?

How firmly our courts and judges adhere to the old definitions of what constitutes a libel is easily seen by looking into a few of the decisions of our highest courts, even of very recent date. The definition given of the nature of a libel by Alexander Hamilton reads as follows : "A censorious or ridiculous writing, picture, or sign, made with a mischievous and malicious intent towards government, magistrates, or individuals." This declaration was made at a time when the Federalist Party was in power under John Adams, and the popular excitement provoked by the enforcement of the Alien and Sedition Laws ran at its highest tide. It is as concise a statement of what these laws aimed at as ever given, and it must be taken as a political declaration in favor of the Federalist legislation. And yet, in a number of libel suits decided by our former Court of Errors, and again by the present Court of Appeals, this definition is praised as the very acme of legal precision and discernment.

Again, in the well-known literary libel case of J. Fenimore Cooper against the *Commercial Advertiser* for a somewhat severe and perhaps rather savage criticism of the former's "History of the United States Navy," referring especially to its account of the naval engagement on Lake Erie under the late Commodore Perry, the opinion of the court goes still further back into antiquity than the time of Alexander Hamilton, and quotes approvingly the definition of libel elaborated by the Lord Chief Justice Holt, of England, as follows : "Any thing written of another which holds him up to scorn and ridicule, or might reasonably be considered as provoking him to a breach of the peace, is a libel." Under this definition, rigidly construed and enforced, as it was in Chief Justice Holt's day, and under his rule, every police report, and every report of a row or a personal debate in Congress or a state Legislature, or the description of the inkstand thrown about each others' head occasionally by our city fathers, would be adjudged a gross libel, and subject the publisher of the journal to heavy damages. And a still older definition, probably dating back to the days of Sir Edward Coke and the Year-Books, was decided by the Supreme Court of Massachusetts to be the true one, reading as follows : "A malicious publication, expressed in printing or writing, or by sign and pictures, tending either to blacken the memory of one dead or the reputation of one who is alive, and expose him to public hatred, contempt, and ridicule." And as courts, almost as often as not, do rule that in such cases special proof of malice is not needed, as the law presumes its existence, this definition would also cover almost every thing, and would render the publication of a daily journal such as the wants of the time demanded not only highly difficult, but almost utterly impossible.

WHAT OUR LEGISLATURE HAS DONE.

The oppressive condition of the law of libel, owing to the persistency of courts to adhere to old, worn-out, and blown-up traditions, at last influenced the Legislature to exert its power in order to provide a remedy for the evil, and protect the public Press in its efforts to gather the news of the day and spread it before the public with all possible speed. In the session of 1854 the following act was passed, intended to have this effect. It is chapter 130 of the session laws of that year, and the first section reads as follows :

> No reporter, editor, or proprietor of any newspaper shall be liable to any action, civil or criminal, for a fair and true report in such newspaper of any judicial, legislative, or other public official proceedings of any statement, speech, argument, or debate in the course of the same, except upon actual proof of malice.

The second section of this act provides that this privilege shall not extend to libelous comments or remarks added to such reports by the publisher, editor, or reporter. And still the courts would not loosen the chain. The first time that this act was invoked the courts decided that the hanging of a man by the sheriff in Greene County under the sentence of death pronounced over him by a court of competent jurisdiction, and what was said and done while the doomed man was being brought from life to death, was not a public official proceeding, nor a judicial proceeding. It is to be hoped that in the future the courts, whenever called upon to decide as to whether a publication is libelous, will take a more liberal view of the question ; that they will look into the nature of the publication of a modern newspaper, and not apply to the modern lightning Press principles of jurisprudence dug out from musty law reports of centuries ago.

A FEW HISTORIC REMINISCENCES OF THE TRIALS OF THE PRESS IN THE PAST.

One of the most remarkable evidences of the desire of the federal government to limit and restrain the freedom of the Press, and circumscribe its power and influence, has already been referred to. Directly it could not be done, for there stood a constitutional provision prohibiting it in express terms ; but indirectly it was attempted by pretending to restrain the excesses of the Press, and its so-called licentiousness. This it was sought to effect through the Alien and Sedition Laws, where certain publications and criticisms of Federal officers were declared offenses against the United States, and subjected to summary punishment. Many were the editors and printers thrown into prison during the last two years of John Adams's administration, until the result of the presidential election of 1800 opened the doors of their cells, and the first Congress thereafter repealed the law.

The liberty of the Press—its right freely to criticise the official acts of all public officers, was again the subject of long and earnest discussion in Congress preparatory to and during the impeachment trial of Judge James H. Peck, United States District Judge for Missouri. It all came about a newspaper article, and the course of the judge in regard to it. There was an action pending in his court brought by the widow and heirs-at-law of Antoine Soulard against the United States about some old Spanish land grant. In December, 1825, the judge decided the case against the heirs, and they appealed. In March, 1826, Judge Peck published in the *Missouri Republican* an elaborate opinion, to which Luke Edward Lawless, the attorney of the heirs, published a respectful reply, over the signature of "Citizen," in the *Inquirer*. Judge Peck considered this reply an act of contempt of his court, and he had first the editor of the paper arrested, and then Mr. Lawless, who admitted having written the article. After various proceedings, Lawless was sentenced to twenty-four hours of imprisonment, and suspended from practice as an attorney for eighteen months. For this the judge was impeached by the House of Representatives in May, 1830, and the trial commenced before the Senate in December. The leading counsel for the judge, and conducting his defense, was that gifted son and orator of Virginia, William Wirt. The following sentences, quoted from his closing argument, contain all that has ever been said —and never better—on this side of the argument:

> It is said that in punishing this publication as a contempt the judge has invaded the liberty of the Press. What is the liberty of the Press, and in what does it consist? Does it consist in a right to vilify the tribunals of the country, and to bring them into contempt by gross and wanton misrepresentations of their proceedings? Does it consist in a right to obstruct and corrupt the streams of justice by poisoning the public mind with regard to causes in these tribunals before they are heard? Is this a correct idea of the liberty of the Press? If so, the defamer has a charter as free as the winds, provided he resort to the Press for the propagation of his slander, and, under the prostituted sanction of the liberty of the Press, hoary age and virgin innocence lie at his mercy. This is not the idea of the liberty of the Press which prevails in courts of justice, or which exists in any sober or well-regulated mind. The liberty of the Press is among the greatest of blessings, civil and political, so long as it is directed to its proper object—that of disseminating correct and useful information among the people. But this greatest of blessings may become the greatest of curses if it shall be permitted to burst its proper barriers. The liberty of the Press has always been the favorite watchword of those who live by its licentiousness. It has been from time immemorial, is still, and ever will be the perpetual *decantatum* of all libelers. * * * To be useful, the liberty of the Press must be restrained. The principle of restraint was imposed upon every part of creation. By restraint the planets were kept in their orbits. The earth performed its regular evolutions by the restraint of the centrifugal force operating upon it. The vine would shoot into rank luxuriance if not under the restraint of the laws of nature, by which every thing was preserved within its proper bounds. Was not every thing on earth impressed with this principle? And was not the liberty of the Press to be restrained to the performance of its rightful functions of propagating truth for just ends?

This argument proved successful at the time, and, as the result showed, not all the eloquence of M'Duffie, of South Carolina, Storrs, of New York, and Buchanan, of Pennsylvania, arguing for the right of free and unrestrained criticism of all the acts of those in public office, could convince the Senate; for, out of forty-three senators voting, twenty-two pronounced Judge Peck not guilty of "high misdemeanor," as charged. Thus the liberty of the Press was again sought to be hampered by restrictions in the house of its friends, in the Senate of the United States. The proceedings in this city a few years ago, when a judge of our Supreme Court was seeking to punish the editor of a morning paper as for a contempt on account of a law report published in that journal the day before, was undoubtedly patterned after the affair of Judge Peck in Missouri.

Much more numerous than these and similar encroachments upon the freedom of the Press have been other attempts to compel its silence and diminish its usefulness. These were and are resorted to by individuals who claim to have been defamed and libeled, and brought into contempt and ridicule among all good citizens of the community by some publication of and concerning them, and for which defamation of character they generally are willing to receive, as a healing plaster and unfailing antidote, a judgment in their favor of some thousands of dollars. Looking over the records of prominent libel suits in this state, one is unavoidably reminded of some very interesting occurrences of our early and later political history.

There is, for instance, the case of Genet *vs.* Mitchell, reported in 7 Johnson, 120. Monsieur Genet was the minister of the new-born and rather turbulent French Republic to this country under Washington's administration. Every body knows the troubles that the enthusiastic French Republican fell into when he attempted to violate our laws—wage war against England from our shores—and being peremptorily stopped by Washington, venturing to appeal from the government to the people. It was about this time that the defendant Mitchell charged Genet publicly with having betrayed his own government by communicating his private instructions to others. For this an action for libel was brought by the irate Frenchman, which was a little more sensible than calling for "coffee and pistols for two." But he got very little out of it.

Another somewhat historical libel suit was that commenced by Lieutenant Governor Root, in 1824, against King & Verplanck, publishers of the New York *American*, which paper had stated that some day in August, 1824, while presiding over the Senate, Lieutenant Governor Root was so drunk as to be unfit for his place and a disgrace to the station. The evidence for the defense was very voluminous, and tended to prove that the editor acted on good and sufficient information; but under the ruling of the court as to what was necessary to make the proof of justification available and successful, the plaintiff got a verdict of $1400.

The case of Littlejohn against Greeley had its origin in the "philosopher's" habit of growling and scolding at every body who is not of his own mind, and hence calling one day Mr. Littlejohn one of the most corrupt members of the Legislature brought him a summons and complaint for libel, and a small verdict on the result.

J. Fenimore Cooper took umbrage at the way and style in which the *Commercial Advertiser* and the *Tribune* criticised his naval history. He denounced it as defamatory, brought his actions, and recovered small verdicts in both cases.

A rather humorous case was that of Mezzara, an Italian portrait painter in this city. He had finished the portrait of a gentleman, who afterwards refused to take and pay for it. Mezzara sued the refractory customer, obtained a judgment, and, under the execution, the sheriff seized the picture, on which the painter had added to the head of the portrait a pair of ass's ears. This, on the complaint of the original of the picture, was held by the Criminal Court of the city to be a libel.

An interesting reminiscence is offered in the libel case of Jacob Gould against Thurlow Weed, which originated in the Anti-Masonic excitement—the alleged kidnapping and murder of Morgan, who was afterwards said to have been "a good enough Morgan till after the election." Weed edited at that time—1827-'28— the *Anti-Masonic Inquirer* at Rochester, and charged Gould with being in the pay of the Masons while pretending to act on an Anti-Masonic committee. Reading the mass of testimony offered on the trial, and the sage and ponderous reasonings of the judges now by the light of subsequent experience, evokes a hearty smile. But Gould got a verdict of $400.

As Gould was so successful in his libel suit against him, Thurlow Weed may have believed it the best means of healing his own offended honor, and in 1845 or thereabouts he rushed into court himself, and sued Foster & Stimson, of the *Day-book*, for libel, because they asserted that in 1840 he had received $5000 for securing to some one the appointment of Pork Inspector in New York City from Governor Seward. The result of this suit was not overgratifying, as the expenses outran the income.

Mr. Delavan, one of the wealthy temperance men of Albany, got himself into trouble with the brewers and maltsters on "the hill" by publishing in the paper that they used stagnant water in their establishments in the manufacture of beer. No less than three libel suits were commenced against him, two of which only were successful, the third failing on technical grounds.

Another interesting libel suit has just been decided at the General Term of the Supreme Court in the Second Judicial District against the plaintiff, Elnathan L. Sanderson, of Brooklyn, who, on the trial in the Circuit, secured a verdict against Cauldwell & Whitney, of the *Sunday Mercury*, for $5000. Mayor Hall was the attorney for the liberty of the Press, and to his masterly presentation of the case on behalf of the defense, and his exhaustive points, legal, philosophic, humorous, historical, and poetical, obtained a reversal of the verdict and the granting of a new trial. Thus the injured reputation of the plaintiff is not healed yet. In connection with this a little anecdote must be told. On the jury in the court below was a German, a friend of the defendants, and he eagerly voted in the jury-room for the highest amount of damages suggested by the others. This becoming known and talked about, he was asked one day by an acquaintance why he had done so, to which he archly replied, with a peculiar twinkle in his eye, " You see, if the verdict had been for a small sum, they (Cauldwell and Whitney) would have been stuck to pay. The larger the sum came out from the jury, the less likely will they be to get a red penny." This seems to be shrewd, if not correct reasoning.

Still another suit is worth mentioning, which about fourteen years ago convulsed our whole German population from the Battery to Harlem Bridge. It was a suit brought by Gustave Neumann, the editor of the *Staats Zeitung*, against Karl Heingen, editor of the *Pioneer*, then published in this city, now in Boston, for heavy damages on account of a libel which appeared " of and concerning him" in the latter journal. The result was a verdict for six and a half cents damages, which brought out the broad grins of many of our Teutons.

THE LATE REVIVAL OF LIBEL SUITS.

For some years there was quite a lull in these respects, and libel suits were rather few and far between. But lately they have been revived, and at a rate so tremendous that, in comparison with the demands made upon the Press by offended honesty in former years, they were as but a moth upon the smoke-stack of a locomotive. The irresistible and irrepressible James Fisk, Jr., of Erie-Grand-Opera-railroad notoriety, first began to have recourse to this sort of rehabilitation of wounded honor, and he opened with a libel suit for $100,000 against Mr. Bowles, of the Springfield *Republican*, and he quickly followed it up by another against Mr. Greeley, of the *Tribune*, for a like sum; then against Mr. Norvell, of the *Times*, claiming another $100,000, and finally against Mr. Raymond for the snug amount of a round million. Not to be outdone by the railway impetuosity of Mr. Fisk, Mr. John Russell Young has commenced about ten suits in different parts of the country, and two or three of them in this city, and two in Philadelphia, each at the exact figure of $100,000; a trifle less would not satisfy him. The *Evening Mirror*, at Indianapolis, has lately been sued for $30,000 damages for libel by one Talcott; and a case is now pending at Pittsburg, by an ex-member of the Pennsylvania state Legislature, against the Pittsburg *Leader*, which journal had charged him with venality and corruption. Thus the revival of libel suits goes bravely on all over the country. There are now no less than 756 libel suits pending against editors or publishers in this country by personages who claim a plaster of greenbacks for their wounded reputation, and the total amount of damage alleged to be done to these 756 injured plaintiffs sums up to $47,500,000! Who will deny hereafter the power of the Press?

There are other cases and other points than those grouped in the above which should not be omitted. For instance, there is the case of Police Justice House against the *Syracuse Star*, on February 27, 1851. General Nye, afterwards United States senator from Nevada, in his argument for the defense, said:

The public Press, gentlemen, occupies an important position in public affairs, and I venture the assertion that to no one thing at the present day is community so much indebted for the good order of society as the Press. I step over the impartial administration of *justice* (turning towards Justice House)—I step over the stringent statutes which have been enacted—I stand upon the broad and truthful platform of this assertion, that to the Press is the community more indebted for the good order and security it enjoys than to any other one thing, and therefore it becomes important for you to inquire *how* it happens that this is so. In no respect is it more potent than when this power is exercised in reviewing with fairness and candor the acts of public officers. Even the judge upon the bench is not exempt, and should not be exempt, from a fair and full review of his public conduct, and he must not expect to escape the candid scrutiny of a candid Press. It is through the Press—through a fearless and independent Press alone—that his merits and demerits can be brought before those who are to decide upon his qualifications. If, upon a full view, thus furnished, the people see fit to re-elect, they do so. If they deem it safer for the cause of impartial justice that another man be selected, they then adopt that course. In this consists the strength of our system.

* * * * * * * *

While the Press is the great avenue through which the public gain correct information, yet you can not expect that it should always run clear of mistake and misinformation. It may sometimes give a wrong impression of a public act, which is calculated to work an injury to the person against whom it seems to be pointed. And what next? Whenever that is made known, the *Press*, with a magnanimity which does it justice, offers a free column to Justice House, or whoever is accused, and through the same avenue whence this poison oozed out comes the antidote, which runs its round through the same channel and neutralizes its malignity.

This should be the law every where. In France a newspaper manager is compelled by law to insert a correction, or a rectification of any incorrect statement made in his columns affecting any individual. These are often seen under the head of *communiqué*, especially from members of the government.

The suits of James Fenimore Cooper were important, as tending to settle the rights of editors to criticise the literary productions of others. These suits were brought against the *New York Tribune*, the *Commercial Advertiser*, the *Courier and Enquirer*, and Albany *Evening Journal*. Owing to the partisan character of the parties— Mr. Cooper a Democrat, and these newspapers all Whig—and the reputation and popularity of the plaintiff as a writer, the suits created a good deal of conversation and criticism. The distinguished novelist was tenacious of his supposed rights and privileges, as the following letter indicates:

Congress Hall, May 21, 1845.

To the Editor of the Argus:

In passing through Albany this morning, I have seen an article in last night's *Evening Journal* in which Mr. Weed, after once retracting all his libels on me, when published, has seen fit substantially to repeat them. For this article he and I will again appear before a jury. But I will make no remarks here. Mr. Weed says he has always been ready and able to prove the truth of all he has ever said about me. Now I am prepared to show, as an evidence of this personal accuracy, that he has himself admitted publicly in his journal his inability to prove one of his libelous accusations, and I shall give him as early an opportunity as the law will allow to prove some more of them. This admission was entirely disconnected from his retraction.

The pretense that our courts have ever overruled that the truth is not a complete defense in a libel suit in the civil action can only gain credit with the supremely ignorant. Your obedient servant, J. FENIMORE COOPER.

Other authors have felt aggrieved enough to bring suits against editors for unsatisfactory criticisms on their productions. One of these cases, an extraordinary affair, was that of Charles Reade, author of "Griffith Gaunt," in 1870, against the *Round Table* of New York, for its review of that novel. Charles Reade is an Englishman, and resides in England. This was, therefore, an international suit, like that of Napoleon I. against the London *Times*. The novelist claimed $25,000 damages.

The plaintiff, in his declaration, stated "that he is a resident of London, and an author by profession; that the novels written by him have acquired great popularity, so that he has become well known as an author, derives great profit and emolument from his works, and depends upon such income for his livelihood."

The defendants admitted that Charles Reade is an author, and that he published, or caused to be published, "Griffith Gaunt," but whether he composed or wrote it they didn't know, and therefore denied the same. They also denied that they were the publishers or proprietors of the *Round Table*, but that it was owned and published by a corporation called the *Round Table* Association. They denied that there was any malice in the publication of these articles, and that they were published of Mr. Reade as an author, but of the book "Griffith Gaunt." They claimed that, the *Round Table* being a critical and literary paper, and the magazines having been sent to them for a notice, the conductors of the *Round Table* honestly criticised "Griffith Gaunt," as was their duty and privilege. They also claimed, in mitigation of damages in reference to the allegations, that the story was not written by Mr. Reade; that it is identical in all prominent features, and in its plot and distinguishing incidents, with other stories written and published by other persons prior to the publication of "Griffith Gaunt."

The counsel of Mr. Reade introduced George Vandenhoff, the actor and public reader, to read the novel of "Griffith Gaunt" to the jury. It was a novel mode of bringing the descriptive powers of the author to bear upon the twelve jurors who were to decide the case. It was an improvement on the Cooper suits, for in those the author appeared in person as his own counsel; but, in spite of the supposed fascinations of "Griffith Gaunt," the jury vindicated the rights of the Press to criticise and review works of fiction.

George Augustus Sala, another English writer, was more successful in a similar case at home. He brought an action for libel against the publishers of "Modern Men of Letters honestly criticised." The result is chronicled in this way:

In summing up the case to the jury, the Lord Chief Justice said the law, as laid down by Lord Ellenborough, was, that a comment on a literary production, exposing its follies and errors, and holding up the author to ridicule, would not be deemed to be a libel, provided it did not exceed the limits of fair and candid criticism by attacking the writer's character. Although the author might suffer loss from the criticism, the law did not consider him injured, but that it was a loss he ought to sustain, inasmuch as it was only a loss of time and profits to which he was not fairly entitled. If a man sitting in judgment, or, rather, asking the public to sit in judgment on any given work which the writer believed had a mischievous tendency, or if he believed it calculated to pervert or vitiate public taste, and to be injurious to the literature of the country, it had been held by Lord Ellenborough to be privileged. But when a critic, from a cruel and spiteful disposition, or from any sinister and unworthy motives, took the opportunity of criticizing a work in a malevolent or malignant manner, in order to pull a man down from the pedestal upon which his public reputation and fame had placed him, it was not privileged, and such a writer was liable to an action for libel.

Mr. Sala obtained $2500 damages.

The mode of punishing a person convicted of libel in Russia is peculiar—actually compelling him to "eat his own words." It is very graphically described by a traveler who witnessed the scene:

>While I was at Moscow a quarto volume was published in vindication of the liberties of the subject. In this work the Czar was severely scrutinized and freely blamed; the iniquity and venality of the administration of law described in strong language.
>
>Such a book in such a country naturally attracted general notice, and the offender was taken into custody. After being tried in a summary way, his production was determined to be a libel, and the writer condemned to "eat his own words."
>
>I was induced to see this singular sentence put into execution. A scaffold was erected in one of the most public streets of the city; the imperial provost, the magistrate, the physician and surgeon of the Czar, attended; the book was separated from its binding, the margin cut off, and every leaf rolled up into the form of a lottery ticket when taken out of the wheel at Guildhall.
>
>The author was then served with them, leaf by leaf, by the provost—who put them into his mouth, to the no small diversion of the spectators—and was obliged to swallow this unpalatable food on pain of the knout, a punishment more dreaded than death.
>
>When the medical gentlemen were of opinion that he had received enough into his stomach, as much as was at one time consistent with safety, the transgressor was sent back to prison, and the business resumed the two following days. After three very hearty but unpleasant meals, I am convinced, by ocular proof, that every leaf of the book was actually swallowed.

The sketch from the *Herald* mentions a case against the *Volksbote* of Munich in 1866. There was a similar action against the *Zeitung* of Frankfort. The Prussian government was the complainant, and the responsible editor of the *Zeitung* was the defendant. The bill of indictment charged the editor with criticising the merits of General Manteuffel, and drawing his majesty the emperor into a circle of discussion in a way insulting to the dignity of the monarch. According to the journalist's estimate of Manteuffel, he was a great favorite at court, and to this favoritism his elevation over the heads of Von Falkenstein and Von Steinmetz was due. The emperor had a high opinion of Manteuffel, which Moltke and Bismarck could not indorse. Manteuffel was a courtier, not a soldier. This was the treason which the editor uttered in the plainest kind of language. The state attorney conducted the prosecution, and made most of the material at his disposal. The journalist, however, was equal to the task, and contended that he was doing a patriotic duty in the course he pursued. He believed in his right to criticise even the emperor, who is human and is liable to err. The verdict was in favor of the editor, and he was declared free.

There are many cases scattered through the records of the courts where journalists in the United States, without malice, and in the performance of their duty, have made mistakes, and have been prompt to publish suitable corrections, yet they have been prosecuted, and sometimes mulcted in heavy damages in time and money by the peculiar views and feelings of judges and juries before whom the cases were brought. Frequently suits are instituted by worthless characters, and upon the merest pretext, for the purpose of extorting black-mail, and there are plenty of lawyers who are always ready to aid the rascals. Sometimes timid people are disposed to make a compromise rather than submit to the annoyance of a defense. Very often libel suits are instituted from mere malice, and when there is no libel at all, because, under the present law, the prosecutor can punish the defendant by causing him heavy costs, even though the suit goes against himself in the end. The proprietors and editors of newspapers are more subject than any other people to unjust, costly, and annoying suits of this character. We hope the law will be amended so as to make all the costs fall upon the prosecutor if he should fail to substantiate the charge of libel, and to hold him in bonds both to do this and to compensate the defendant in case the charge should prove groundless or merely malicious.

There was an important case against the *Baltimore American* in 1869, where the damages were laid at $10,000. The rights of the Press in this instance were set forth by Judge Dobbin as follows:

Newspapers exercise an overwhelming influence over the world, and they are essential to the welfare of mankind. We could not exist without them. But the public is interested in their always being vigilant, truthful, and discreet; the public are interested in the welfare of newspapers, and it is for the court to consider how much discretion was used in their publication. The testimony, the judge held, showed most conclusively that outrages had been committed upon successive occasions upon the passengers traveling through the city, and he was of the opinion that newspapers had a perfect right to speak and comment upon the occurrences. But why these outrages were not prevented, or the grievances not redressed, the court will not inquire, as it does not intend to reflect upon the officers of the peace then in power. If the newspapers are not protected they are deprived of all benefit to the community, and if they do not speak out in cases where the public are interested, then they fall short of their duty. The public is always ready to condemn violence and say crime should be redressed, and it is, therefore, not out of the duty of a newspaper in the statement of public acts to color highly such acts, so as to describe and point out, as nearly as possible, the probable perpetrators of the outrage; all these things, his honor held, were not only right, but highly meritorious. The counsel for the plaintiff, the court remarked, might argue that the Press had no right to charge innocent parties with a crime, but the court thought that there might be cases in which the innocent might possibly be called to suffer, for the Press has run the risk of injuring the innocent. The court thought this was the justice of the case, and cited a number of cases in point. To entitle the plaintiff to recover in this action, the jury must find that the writings set out in the declaration were published by the defendants of and concerning the plaintiff. But if they shall also find that at, or just previous to the time of said publication, the peace of the city was repeatedly disturbed, and the rights of private persons traveling on their own lawful business between Washington and Philadelphia violently and unlawfully invaded and violated by evil-doers, who were not arrested or punished, as detailed in the evidence, then it was the right and duty of the defendants, as publishers of a public newspaper, to publish the facts which came to their knowledge constituting said crime, and to comment thereon with such severity of rebuke as a flagrant breach of the peace deserves; and such statement and comments, if fairly and *bona fide* made, with a view to the public good, were privileged communications, free from the legal presumption of malice which attends a libelous communication not privileged, and the plaintiff is not entitled to recover.

The jury awarded $250 damages.

In a libel suit against a newspaper in California also, in 1869, the judge ruled that, as an editorial article appeared in the same paper after the one of which complaint was made apologizing for the first, and averring a lack of all malice, the allegations might be considered as proof of the character and intent of the first. The jury, under this ruling, found a verdict for the defendant.

An important decision was made in a libel suit in New Hampshire in 1869, affecting the rights of journalists in protecting the community from heartlessness and cruelty. It was the case of David R. Ambrose against the *Daily Chronicle*, of Portsmouth, N. H. The plaintiff was charged with refusing shelter to a party of smelt fishermen on the occasion of the great snow-storm in 1867, whereby they were subjected to great suffering and narrow escape from death by exposure. Judge Doe made an able charge to the jury, holding that the defendant had a right to publish the truth. The jury rendered a verdict in favor of the journalist.

All public debates in courts, in Congress, in Parliament, in public meetings, and freely reported by the Press, are free from responsibility, so far as the Press are concerned. This is common law; yet, as late as 1868, a case occurred in London in which the *Times* was the defendant. It was Wason *vs.* Walter. The *Times* was sued for damages for the publication of a parliamentary debate containing language injurious to the personal character of the plaintiff, and the case was brought before the Court of Queen's Bench. But it was decided against the plaintiff, the court ruling that the complaint was not actionable. Our papers can not safely, however, publish police reports unless in a most qualified manner. One or two years ago, a Chicago paper published a report of a police case. The aggrieved party in the affair brought a suit for libel against the editors, and obtained a verdict of $7500. The editors of the paper showed that the publication was made against their express directions; that it appeared through the negligence of the reporter and foreman of the office, and that every retraction possible was made after its publication. These pleas ought to have had some effect upon a jury, and no doubt they would have had if the paper in question had exhibited a little better taste in its manner of reporting the trial. Motive was shown there, if not in the original publication.

There is a bill before the Illinois Legislature to meet just such cases as this one. It provides that the newspapers may publish the proceedings or evidence given in courts and before coroner's juries without being subject to damages in libel suits, and that journalists may plead in justification that these matters are published without malice, and that retraction was made.

We will cite two more actions.

One was the celebrated opera libel suit against the *New York Herald*. It grew out of criticisms on the opera. After a prolonged and exciting trial, the jury rendered a verdict of $10,000 against the editor. One of the jury made the remark that the editor was rich and the opera manager poor, and that the former would not feel the loss of the money. On placing this fact before the judge a new trial was granted. The next verdict was $6000.

The other was against the same paper. In the financial revulsion of 1837, that journal originated the idea in this country of publishing the names of commercial failures. Such publications were made in England, and were of great value to the commercial community. Such publications, however, were not known on this side of the Atlantic. The *Herald*, in its effort to do its duty as a public journal, undertook to publish such lists. One of them appeared on the morning of the departure of a packet for England. It contained the name of a very respectable auction and commission house in New York. But this house had not failed. Another merchant, nearly of the same name, and representing another house, had suspended. Here was the cause for action. Notwithstanding that the paper made the necessary correction on the following morning, a criminal suit was immediately instituted, and, after an exciting trial, the editor was convicted, but, instead of imprisonment, was fined $500.

Now what is to be done in face of all these facts?

The Constitutions of the several states have, at divers times, emphatically recognized the liberty of the Press, and one would suppose that these articles and these sections had become the organic law of the land. They are so, indeed; but judges and juries are the final interpreters, and on them depend the result in all libel suits in the country. We append the sections of the several state Constitutions bearing on this important point:

NEW YORK.—The Constitution of New York, 1846, Art. 1, § 8, provides that "every citizen may freely speak, write, and publish his sentiments on all subjects, being responsible for the abuse of the right, and no law shall be passed to restrain the liberty of speech or of the Press. In all criminal prosecutions or indictments for libel the truth may be given in evidence to the jury, and if it shall appear to the jury that the matter charged as libelous is true, and was published with good motives and for justifiable ends, the party shall be acquitted, and the jury shall have the right to determine the law and the fact." The same provision existed in the Constitution of 1821, Art. 7, § 8.

MAINE.—The Constitution of Maine, 1819, provides that "every citizen may freely speak, write, and publish his sentiments on any subject, being responsible for the abuse of this liberty. *No laws shall be passed regulating or restraining the freedom of the Press; and in prosecutions for any publications respecting the official conduct of men in public capacity, or the qualifications of those who are candidates for the suffrages of the people*, or where the matter published is for public information, the truth thereof may be given in evidence, and in all indictments for libel, the jury, after having received the direction of the Court, shall have a right to determine at their discretion the law and the fact."—Art. 1, § 4.

MASSACHUSETTS.—The Constitution of Massachusetts, 1780, provides that "*the liberty of the Press is essential to the security of freedom in a state;* it ought not, therefore, to be restrained in this commonwealth."—Part 1, § 16. Compare with 2 De Lolme, 959, by Stephens.

NEW HAMPSHIRE.—The Constitution of New Hampshire, 1782, provides that "*the liberty of the Press is essential to the security of freedom in a state; it ought, therefore, to be inviolably preserved.*"—Part 1, § 22.

VERMONT.—The Constitution of Vermont, 1793, provides that "*the people have a right to a freedom of speech, and of writing and publishing their sentiments concerning the transactions of government, and therefore the freedom of the Press ought not to be restrained.*"—Chap. 1, Art. 13.

RHODE ISLAND.—The Constitution of R. Island, 1842, provides that, "*the liberty of the Press being essential to the security of freedom in a state, any person may publish his sentiments on any subject, being responsible for the abuse of that liberty; and in all trials for libel, both civil and criminal, the truth, unless published through malicious motives, shall be sufficient defense to the person charged.*"—Art. 1, § 20.

CONNECTICUT.—The Constitution of Connecticut, 1818, provides that "every citizen may freely speak, write, and publish his sentiments on all subjects, being responsible for the abuse of that liberty. *No law shall ever be passed to control or restrain the liberty of speech or of the Press.* In all prosecutions or indictments for libel the truth may be given in evidence, and the jury shall have a right to determine the law and the facts under the direction of the Court."—Art. 1, § 5, 6, 7.

NEW JERSEY.—The Constitution of New Jersey, 1844, provides that "every person may freely speak, write, and publish his sentiments on all subjects, being responsible for the abuse of that right. *No law shall be passed to restrain or abridge the liberty of speech or of the Press.* In all prosecutions or indictments for libel the truth may be given in evidence to the jury, and if it shall appear to the jury that the matter charged as libelous is true, and was published with good motives and for justifiable ends, the party shall be acquitted, and the jury shall have the right to determine the law and the fact."—Art. 1, § 5.

PENNSYLVANIA.—The Constitution of Pennsylvania, 1838, provides that "*the printing-presses shall be free to every person who undertakes to examine the proceedings of the Legislature or any branch of government, and no law shall ever be made to restrain the right thereof.* The free communication of thoughts and opinions is one of the invaluable rights of man, and any citizen may freely speak, write, and print on any subject, being responsible for the abuse of that liberty. *In prosecutions for the publication of papers investigating the official conduct of public officers, or men in a public capacity, or when the matter published is proper for public information,* the truth may be given in evidence; and in all indictments for libel the jury have the right to determine the law and the facts, under the direction of the Court, as in other cases."—Art. 9, § 7.

DELAWARE. — The Constitution of Delaware, 1831, provides that "*the Press shall be free to every person who undertakes to examine the official conduct of men acting in a public capacity*, and any citizen may print on any subject, being responsible for the abuse of that liberty. *In prosecutions for publications investigating the proceedings of officers, or where the matter printed is proper for public information*, the truth thereof may be given in evidence, and in all indictments for libel the jury may determine the facts and the law as in other cases."—Art. 1, § 5.

MARYLAND.—The Declaration of Rights of Maryland, Aug. 14, 1776, provides that "*the liberty of the Press ought to be inviolably preserved.*"—§ 38.

VIRGINIA.—The Declaration of Rights of Virginia, June 12, 1776, confirmed by the Constitution of 1830, Art. 1, provides that "*the freedom of the Press is one of* the great bulwarks of liberty, and can never be restrained but by despotic governments."—§ 12.

NORTH CAROLINA.—The Declaration of Rights of North Carolina, December 18, 1776, provides that "*the freedom of the Press is one of the great bulwarks of liberty, and therefore ought never to be restrained.*"—§ 15.

GEORGIA.—The Constitution of Georgia, 1798, provides that "*the freedom of the Press as heretofore used in this state shall remain inviolate.*"—Art. 4, § 5.

KENTUCKY.—The Constitution of Kentucky, 1799, provides that "*printing-presses shall be free to every person who undertakes to examine the proceedings of the Legislature or any branch of government, and no law shall ever be made to restrain the right thereof.* The free communication of thoughts and opinions is one of the invaluable rights of man, and every citizen may freely speak, write, or print on any subject, being responsible for the abuse of that liberty. *In prosecutions for the publication of papers investigating the official conduct of the officers or men in a public capacity, or where the matter published is proper for public information, the truth thereof may be given in evidence.* And in all indictments for libel the jury shall have the right to determine the law and the facts, under the direction of the Court, as in other cases."—Art. 10, § 7–8.

TENNESSEE.—The Constitution of Tennessee, 1834, provides that "*the printing-presses shall be free to every one who undertakes to examine the proceedings of the Legislature, or of any branch or officer of government, and no law shall be made to restrain the right thereof.* The free communication of thoughts and opinions is one of the invaluable rights of man, and any citizen may freely speak, write, and print on any subject, being responsible for the abuse of that liberty. But *in prosecutions for the publication of papers investigating the official conduct of officers or men in a public capacity, the truth thereof may be given in evidence.* And in all indictments for libel the jury have a right to determine the law and the facts, under the direction of the Court, as in other criminal cases."—Art. 1, § 19.

OHIO.—The Constitution of Ohio, 1802, provides that "*the printing-presses shall be open and free to every citizen who wishes to examine the proceedings of any branch of government, or the conduct of any public officer, and no law shall ever restrain the right thereof.* Every citizen has an indisputable right to speak, write, or print upon any subject as he thinks proper, being liable for the abuse of that liberty. *In prosecutions for any publication respecting the official conduct of men in any public capacity, or where the matter published is proper for public information,* the truth thereof may always be given in evidence, and in all indictments for libel the jury have a right to determine the law and the facts, under the direction of the Court, as in other cases."—Art. 8, § 6.

INDIANA.—The Constitution of Indiana, 1816, provides that "*the printing-presses shall be free to every person who undertakes to examine the proceedings of the Legislature or any branch of government, and no law shall ever be made to restrain the right thereof.* The free communication of thoughts and opinions is one of the invaluable rights of man, and every citizen may freely speak, write, and print on any subject, being responsible for the abuse of that liberty. *In prosecutions for the publication of papers investigating the official conduct of officers or men in a public capacity,* or where the matter published is proper for public information, the truth thereof may be given in evidence, and in all indictments for libel the jury have a right to determine the law and the facts, under the direction of the Court, as in other cases."—Art. 1, § 9–10.

LOUISIANA.—The Constitution of Louisiana, 1812, provides that "*printing-presses shall be free to every person who undertakes to examine the proceedings of the Legislature or any branch of government, and no law shall ever be made to restrain the use thereof.* The free communication of thoughts and opinions is one of the invaluable rights of man, and every citizen may freely speak, write, and print on any subject, being responsible for the abuse of that liberty."—Art. 6, § 21. And the amended Constitution of that state, 1845, provides : " The Press shall be free. Every citizen may freely speak, write, and publish his sentiments on all subjects, being responsible for the abuse of this liberty."—Table 6, Art. 110.

MISSISSIPPI.—The Constitution of Mississippi provides "*that every citizen may freely speak, write, and publish his sentiments on all subjects, being responsible for the abuse of that liberty. No law shall ever be passed to control or restrain the liberty of speech or of the Press.* In all prosecutions or indictments for libel the truth may be given in evidence, and if it shall appear to the jury that the matter charged as libelous is true, and was published with good motives and for justifiable ends, the party shall be acquitted, and the jury shall have the right to determine the law and the fact."—Art. 1, § 6, 7, 8.

ILLINOIS.—The Constitution of Illinois, 1818, provides that "*the printing-presses shall be free to every person who undertakes to examine the proceedings of the General Assembly, or any branch of government, and no law shall ever be made to restrain the right thereof.* The free communication of thoughts and opinions is one of the invaluable rights of man, and every citizen may freely speak, write, or print on any subject, being responsible for the abuse of that liberty. *In prosecutions for the publication of papers investigating the official conduct of officers or men acting in a political capacity, or where the matter published is proper for public information, the truth thereof may be given in evidence;* and in all indictments for libel the jury may have the right of determining both the law and the fact, under the direction of the Court, as in other cases."—Art. 8, § 22, 23.

ALABAMA.—The Constitution of Alabama, 1819, provides that "*every citizen may freely speak, write, or publish his sentiments on all subjects, being responsible for the abuse of that liberty.*"—Art. 1, § 8.

MISSOURI.—The Constitution of Missouri, 1820, provides that "*the free communication of thoughts and opinions is one of the invaluable rights of man,* and that every person may speak, write, or print on any subject, being responsible for the abuse of that liberty; and that in all prosecutions for libel the truth thereof may be given in evidence, and the jury may determine the law and the facts under the direction of the Court."—Art. 1, § 16. And the amended Constitution of the state, 1845, provides that "the free communication of thoughts and opinions is one of the invaluable rights of man, and that every person may freely speak, write, and print on any subject, being responsible for the abuse of that liberty; and in all prosecutions for libel the truth thereof may be given in evidence, and the jury may determine the law and the facts under the direction of the Court."—Art. 2, § 16.

MICHIGAN.—The Constitution of Michigan, 1835, provides that "*every person may freely speak, write, and publish his sentiments* on all subjects, being responsible for the abuse of that right, and no law shall be passed to restrain or abridge the liberty of speech or of the Press. In all prosecutions or indictments for libel the truth may be given in evidence to the jury, and if it shall appear to the jury that the matter charged as libelous is true, and was published with good intentions and for justifiable ends, the party shall be acquitted, and the jury shall have the right to determine the law and the facts."—Art. 1, § 7. See also Art. 6, § 25 of Constitution of 1850.

ARKANSAS.—The Constitution of Arkansas, 1836, provides that "*the printing-press shall be free to every person, and no law shall ever be made to restrain the rights thereof. The free communication of thoughts and opinions is one of the invaluable rights of man,* and every citizen may freely speak, write, and print on any subject, being responsible for the abuse of that liberty. *In prosecutions for the publication of papers investigating the official conduct of officers or men in public capacity,* or where the matter published is proper for public information, the truth thereof may be given in evidence; and in all indictments for libel, the jury have the right to determine the law and the facts."—Art. 2, § 7, 8.

FLORIDA.—The Constitution of Florida, 1838, provides that "*every citizen may freely speak, write, and publish his sentiments on all subjects, being responsible for the abuse of that liberty; and no law shall ever be passed to curtail, abridge, or restrain the liberty of speech or of the Press.*"—Art. 1, § 5.

TEXAS.—The Constitution of Texas, 1845, provides that "*every citizen shall be at liberty to speak, write, or publish his opinions on any subject, being responsible for the abuse of that privilege; and no law shall ever be passed curtailing the liberty of speech or of the Press.*"—Art. 1, § 5.

IOWA.—The Constitution for the State of Iowa of 1846 provides that "every person may speak, write, or publish his sentiments on all subjects, being responsible for the abuse of that right. *No law shall be passed to restrain the liberty of speech or of the Press.* In all prosecutions of indictments for libel the truth may be given in evidence to the jury, and if it appear to the jury that the matter charged as libelous is true, and was published with good motives and for justifiable ends, the party shall be acquitted."—Art. 2, § 7.

CALIFORNIA.—In the Constitution of California, Art. 1, § 9, it is provided that *"every citizen may freely speak, write, and publish his sentiments* on all subjects, being responsible for the abuse of that right ; *and no law shall be passed to restrain or abridge the liberty of speech or of the Press.* In all criminal prosecutions or indictments for libel the truth may be given in evidence to the jury, and if it shall appear to the jury that the matter charged as libelous is true, and was published with good motives and for justifiable ends, then the party shall be acquitted, and the jury shall have the right to determine the law and the fact."

To-day the newspapers are filled with personal allusions, and all sorts of charges are made against individuals and office-holders. Some of them are of a very serious character. These charges are against presidents and politicians, lawyers and lobbyists, clergymen and choirs, counsel and clients, brokers and bankers. Notes of correction are sometimes published. No other notice is taken of many of them. Still, the *Herald* says, there are nearly a thousand suits pending, with $50,000,000 in damages depending on the result.

Let us have a national law of libel—a national code that will benefit alike the Press and the public. That will be a step in the right direction.

CHAPTER LIV.
THE CASH VALUE OF NEWSPAPERS.

VALUES IN THE UNITED STATES.— SALE OF THE BULLETIN IN PHILADELPHIA AT PUBLIC AUCTION.— OFFERS FOR THE NEW YORK HERALD AND TIMES.— MILLIONAIRES IN NEWSPAPERS AND DRY GOODS.

VALUES in the United States are now somewhat fabulous. Stores in New York rent for $50,000 to $100,000 per annum — hotels for the same. One enterprising merchant lives in a palace on the Fifth Avenue costing a million of dollars. Half a million is offered for the country residence of the leading New York editor. One of the brokers who failed in the famous corner on gold in Wall Street, in the fall of 1869, owned a country seat valued at $800,000, and on the improvement of which he was contemplating an expenditure of a million. Another Wall Street financier visits Europe in a steam yacht. Another editor owns pleasure-horses to the value of $150,000, and offers $100,000 for a single animal that can beat the fastest time of the famous Dexter. It is no uncommon occurrence to see $100,000 worth of oil paintings enriching the walls of private residences in the metropolis. Sir Morton Peto, who failed in 1867 for $35,000,000, and James M'Henry, said that operators could not now afford time to talk of thousands — millions were the figures. Newspaper offices are now in buildings costing, including the land, from $100,000 to $1,000,000, and owned, too, by the newspaper proprietors themselves. Thirty years ago one or two of these papers were started on a borrowed capital of $500, and transacted their business in cellars. This array of rich facts was suggested by the sale of a second or third class newspaper — of its rights and its property, the press, the engine and boiler, the type, and the materials, in Philadelphia, on the 1st of February, 1865. The journal was the *Evening Bulletin*. The terms were cash. The sale is thus described in the *Age*:

At the appointed hour for the sale, a large attendance of spectators assembled at the office of the establishment, among them being representatives from nearly every publication in Philadelphia. The terms of the sale were announced, and the bidding commenced. The first bid was made by George W. Childs, Esq., proprietor of the *Public Ledger*, for $50,000. This was followed by a bid of $51,000 from Gibson Peacock, editor, and one of the stockholders of the paper. Mr. John T. Money bid $52,000, followed by Mr. Peacock again with $1000 better. The contest here narrowed down to Messrs. Peacock and Money, who, bidding one thousand each on each successive bid, ran the sum up to $65,000. Here

Mr. Peacock dropped off, and Messrs. Cummings and Chambers, also stockholders in the concern, commenced bidding. The amount was run up to $88,000, when Mr. Money made the last bid by adding an additional thousand, footing up $89,000. Here all competition ceased, and the paper was accordingly "knocked down" at $89,000.

"Who's the purchaser?" inquired Mr. Freeman, the auctioneer.

"Gibson Peacock, sir," responded Mr. Money.

This took every one by surprise, as Messrs. Money and Peacock had, from the first, bid against each other, and the latter had dropped off at $65,000, leading to the belief that this was the extent of his pile.

Newspaper property is peculiar in its value. If the material alone of the *Evening Bulletin* were sold, it would not have brought over $20,000. But the character of the paper, its circulation, its advertising patronage, its reputation, sometimes dependent upon the life and health of one man, were what run the price up to the point indicated; and, as the establishment was bought by its editor, with a full knowledge of its value, it is fair to suppose that the price paid was not too high. Thus a newspaper in Philadelphia, and by no means a leading one in that city, brings almost as much at auction as was paid in the fall of 1869 for the *Journal des Débâts*, one of the oldest and most influential journals in Paris, where newspapers are as necessary as the opera or a glass of absinthe. But we do not give this instance as a complete illustration of the value of newspapers in the United States; it is only a public instance, a forced instance under the hammer. The *Morning Call*, in San Francisco, at private sale, brought over $100,000, and the Cincinnati *Times* $135,000. Two years after the *New York Tribune* was turned into a stock concern at $1000 per share, sales were made at $3500, and $10,000 is now the quotation. One million of dollars have been several times offered for the *New York Herald*, and in the spring of 1869 ten gentlemen subscribed $200,000 each, and two others $100,000 each for the purchase of the *Herald*, and that large sum, $2,200,000, was refused. We have seen it stated that $800,000 had been refused for the *New York Times*. Thirty-four shares were recently sold for $375,000, making the total value of the concern $1,100,000.

None of the valuable newspapers are more than thirty-five years old. Very few journals reach a century in age. More newspapers die than live; yet journalism is becoming permanent as a profession in the United States, although, to the present time, property in newspapers has been uncertain and precarious. Where is the *Globe*, the thunderer of Jackson's administration? Where is the *National Intelligencer*, that controlled the destinies of the great Whig Party? Where is the *Boston Atlas?* the *Courier and Enquirer?* Where are hundreds of journals that made their mark on the public mind within a short space of time? All gone. Where is the power and influence of the *Albany Argus*, and *Richmond Enquirer*, and *Ohio Statesman* to-day? Yet, in the face of hundreds of instances like these of the precarious character of newspaper influence and newspaper property, these large sums are offered and refused for establishments like the *New York Herald* and *New York Times*.

But these values thus set upon newspapers are not unreasonable, after all, when we see the stock values of our railroads and telegraph lines. If the New York Central Railroad can safely represent $100,000,000 in stock, and sell for $25 above par; if the Erie Railroad Company can be swelled to a similar amount in bonds and shares; and if the Western Union Telegraph Company can carry its capital to $42,000,000, it is not a wild investment to pay $2,000,000, or even $5,000,000, for an established journal like the *Herald;* and, in this view, Sir Morton Peto and James M'Henry were certainly not far out of the way in saying that we now talk of millions, and can not waste our time on thousands. Gerard Halleck, one of the proprietors of the New York *Journal of Commerce*, died worth a quarter of a million; Moses Y. Beach, of the *Sun*, left over three hundred thousand dollars; Henry J. Raymond, of the *New York Times*, left nearly half a million; Charles O. Rogers, of the Boston *Journal*, died worth a million and a half; William M. Swain, of the *Philadelphia Ledger*, left three millions; James Gordon Bennett, we see it stated, left five millions; and Charles Starbuck, of the *Cincinnati Times*, died worth three quarters of a million. George Peabody, in government stocks; Cornelius Vanderbilt, in steam-boats and railroads; and Alexander T. Stewart, in silks and calicoes, have made more money, but we must remember that newspapers in this country are yet in their infancy as profitable property.

CHAPTER LV.
THE DUELS OF EDITORS.

ASSAULTS AND ASSASSINATIONS.—THE CODE OF HONOR AMONG JOURNALISTS.—SEVERAL EXTRAORDINARY DUELS.—STATE OF FEELING AT THE SOUTH SINCE THE REBELLION.

ONE would imagine, from the preceding chapter, that editors lived " 'mid pleasures and palaces ;" but what a mistaken idea such a financial exhibit gives to the reader!

There are pleasures, and palaces, and pains, and penalties, and privations connected with the editorial profession as with all others under the sun. The life of a journalist has its fascinations as well as its fatalisms. Assassinations, duels, and assaults have not been infrequent with the editorial corps. Some have been murdered outright, some have been killed in accordance with the code of honor, and many have been violently assaulted for words uttered in their columns.

Many of these peculiar incidents are recorded in their proper places in these sketches where the journals affected by them are mentioned. Others we include in this separate chapter.

Editors have it in their power to settle their differences in their respective journals, as members of Congress have the floor of the Senate or House where they can cool off their heated sentiments. When an editor unfairly reflects on the character and acts of those outside of his office, the law steps in to protect the rights of the injured individual. When a member of Congress stands behind the right of debate, and assails any one not entitled to reply, as in the case of Henry Clay and John Randolph, it has been the custom to resort to the code of honor. Sometimes the two classes become involved, as in the duel of Graves and Cilley, arising from a challenge of Colonel Webb, of the *New York Courier and Enquirer*, to the latter, for words spoken in debate ; and, in connection with this point, we find the subjoined note, in the sixth volume of Calhoun's works, introducing two political essays, entitled " Onslow" and " Patrick Henry," on the powers of the Vice-president as President of the Senate :

The following correspondence grew out of the failure of Mr. Calhoun, as President of the Senate, to call Mr. Randolph, of Virginia, to order during the delivery of his celebrated retrenchment speech, in which he indulged in certain remarks highly offensive to the administration, and especially Mr. J. Q. Adams (the

President) and Mr. Clay, his Secretary of State. The former resorted to the newspapers under the signature of "Patrick Henry," and arraigned the Vice-president (Mr. Calhoun) for neglect of duty, while the latter appealed to the *duello*, and called Mr. Randolph to the field. The letters of "Onslow" (Mr. Calhoun) contain, in a brief space, a clear and forcible exposition of the power of the President of the Senate in questions of order.

Although the friends of Mr. Adams denied that he was the author of "Patrick Henry," yet the incident thus recorded is a very fair illustration of the mode of treating such a matter at the North and South—one by appealing through the Press to the judgment of the public, and the other through the pistol-barrel to the *punctillo* of a barbarous code, carrying the matter to the final tribunal, where the survivor of a fatal duel may never appear.

Where a duel did not result from the comments of editors on the conduct of members of Congress, cowardly assaults were made in two or three instances. In describing the attack made upon Senator Sumner, of Massachusetts, by Mr. Brooks, of South Carolina, General Webb, in a letter to the *Courier and Enquirer* on the 24th of May, 1856, said:

And if any other illustration of the truth of my position may be required than that to which I have referred, let me instance the occurrences of the kind alluded to within the last five months, which have happened here in the capital of the nation, and in which members of the House of Representatives have been the principal actors. I confine the record to them alone.

First, then, William Smith, an ex-Governor of the State of Virginia, and member of the House of Representatives, assailed and beat the editor of the *Evening Star* in December last, in the lobby of the House.

Second, Albert Rusk, a member of the House of Representatives from Arkansas, assailed and beat the editor of the *New York Tribune* in the grounds of the Capitol immediately after leaving the House of Representatives.

The killing of an Irish waiter at Willard's by Congressman Herbert, of California, in addition to the assault on Senator Sumner, was also cited. General Webb then adds that—

Greeley carried a revolver during the latter part of his sojourn here, and then, and then only, even he was no longer molested; and since the brutal assault on Mr. Sumner, two thirds of the anti-Nebraska members of Congress, and all who claim and exercise the right of free speech as distinct from abusive language, or a bullying, threatening manner, have arrived at the conclusion that the time has come when it is a duty they owe alike to themselves and to the country to assert, and, if necessary, to vindicate this great constitutional privilege, and to be in a situation at all times effectually to protect themselves from the bully and assassin.

The *Vicksburg* (Miss.) *Sentinel*, of all the newspapers in the country, appeared to have been the most celebrated in the annals of serious street encounters and fatal duels. It was established as a daily paper in January, 1836, and its editor immediately showed considerable vigor and boldness in his editorial course. Its first editor to make his mark was Dr. James Hagan. He was a small-sized, mild-mannered, amiable man in social intercourse. After completing his medical education in Philadelphia, he went South and became an editor. Summers he would visit the North. In the crisis of 1837-'38 there was quite a controversy in that paper growing out of cotton speculations, which led to one or two duels. In 1838, after several desperate encounters in the streets, Dr. Hagan fought a duel with the editor of the *Vicksburg Whig*.

Subsequently Dr. Hagan went to Europe, and, while traveling in Holland in a car filled with passengers and tobacco-smoke, he opened a window for fresh air. One of the passengers, without uttering a word, immediately shut it. The doctor reopened it, with a request, in English, that it should remain open. The other passenger, not understanding English, again shut the window, and in an emphatic manner. Dr. Hagan for a moment looked at this passenger, and then at the others in the car. Not one spoke English. He then drew his pistol and reopened the window. He had fresh air for the remainder of the trip. But it was amusing, he said, to notice the effective persuasiveness of that weapon.

On his return he became involved in more *rencontres* in the public thoroughfares, but he gave up the practice of constantly carrying arms. In describing one of these he coolly said, it ended by " laying his antagonist to the land." In 1842, an editor of the *Sentinel*, James F. Fall, fought a duel with T. E. Robins, of the Railroad Bank. Neither killed. The affair, however, led to a bitter controversy with the *Whig*. In June, 1843, Dr. Hagan was killed in the street by Daniel W. Adams. Dr. Hagan was not armed, and the parties were entire strangers to each other. On the coroner's inquest, Adams stated that he killed Hagan because of an article in the *Sentinel* reflecting on his father, Judge George Adams, of Jackson, Mississippi.

In May, 1844, there was another meeting connected with this noted journal. Colonel Thomas E. Robins and James M. Downs fought a duel with yagers at fifteen paces. The latter was shot across the breast, but not fatally. There was a street-fight a day or two after between Captain Walter Hickey, the new editor of the *Sentinel*, and Dr. Macklin, the second of Downs in the preceding duel. The attack was from the latter. The parties struck several blows and then resorted to revolvers, by which Macklin received a mortal wound in the abdomen. These affairs originated in a difference between Colonel Robins and the Honorable S. S. Prentiss about real estate, which had been commented upon by the *Sentinel*.

The succeeding editors of this paper were thus disposed of in a newspaper paragraph a few years ago:

Dr. J. S. Fall, an assistant, had a number of fights, in one of which he was badly wounded. James Ryan, editor, was killed by R. E. Hammet, of the *Whig*. Next came Walter Hickey, who had several rows, and was repeatedly wounded; he was soon after himself killed in Texas. John Lavins, another editor, was imprisoned for the violence of his articles. Mr. Jenkins, his successor, was killed in the street by H. A. Crabbe; Crabbe was afterwards murdered in Sonora. F. C. Jones succeeded Jenkins, but soon afterwards drowned himself.

In March, 1843, Melzer Gardner was editor of the Portsmouth (Va.) *Chronicle*. In a political controversy in regard to the employment of black laborers in the Navy Yard, the Norfolk *Herald* and *Chronicle* became quite personal. Gardner had had one personal affair with Barney O'Neil on this question. Shortly after, at a political meeting in Portsmouth, a lawyer, named Mordecai Cook, Jr., made an attack, in a speech, on Gardner. The latter replied in a strong article, reflecting severely on Cook. This led to a meeting of the parties on Ferry Wharf. Cook demanded an apology of Gardner; the latter demanded a retraction from Cook. "I will not retract," said Cook. "Neither will I," said Gardner. Cook then advanced on Gardner with a cane and assaulted him. Gardner drew a revolver. Cook dropped the cane, grasped the revolver, and wrenched it from the hands of Gardner, and, turning it, fired, shooting Gardner through the heart. He expired without uttering a word. Cook walked away, remarking, "Let him lie there; I am satisfied." Another account states that in the struggle the pistol accidentally went off. On the day after the affair the workmen of Portsmouth took the matter up, as the friends of the editor, and after doing considerable injury to O'Neil's house, and ordering him to leave the town in seven days, marched past Cook's house, and in the noise and confusion the servants of Cook rushed to Mrs. Cook with the report that the mob had threatened to tear down the house. She fainted, and soon after she was taken ill, and died the next day.

There was a duel between Mr. J. Hueston, editor of the *Baton Rouge Gazette*, and Mr. Alcée Labranche, member of Congress from Louisiana, in August, 1843. The *Gazette*, a few days previously, contained an editorial reflecting severely on the Congressional delegation elect from Louisiana. Meeting Mr. Hueston in the billiard-room of the St. Charles Exchange after this article appeared, Mr. Labranche made an attack on Mr. Hueston with a cane, knocking him senseless to the floor. On his recovery, the first words he uttered were, "Where is the damned rascal?" Soon after the parties met at "the Oaks," and settled the matter in the most determined manner. The *New Orleans Diamond* of August 20, 1843, described the meeting as a prize-fight would be described:

The distance agreed upon was forty yards, and the weapons selected were double-barreled shot-guns, loaded with ball. The parties fired between the words one and five. They fought four rounds.

First round. Mr. Labranche discharged both barrels at the same time, and before Mr. Hueston had fired a second barrel the time fixed upon expired. Of course he lost a fire.

Second round. Both fired single barrels at intervals. Mr. Labranche's second ball struck the pantaloons of Mr. Hueston, and passed through the knees of them without touching the flesh.

Third round. Mr. Labranche fired both barrels at the same time; the balls passed through the hat of Mr. Hueston about two inches apart.

Fourth round. Mr. Hueston fired first. Mr. Labranche's shot took effect in the left side, on the last rib, and passed out on the other side, ranging low down. He threw his gun forward and fell back at full length on the ground. The wound was pronounced fatal by the physicians in attendance. He expired shortly after, in full possession of his mental faculties.

The parties exhibited on the ground the utmost coolness and fortitude.

Henry Rives Pollard, brother of Edward A. Pollard, of "The Lost Cause," was shot in Richmond, Virginia, on the 24th of November, 1868. On the previous Saturday a report was published in the *Southern Opinion* of the elopement of the daughter of William H. Grant, of that city. About ten o'clock on the morning of the 24th, as Pollard, the editor of the paper, was near his office door, a shot was fired from the upper window of an opposite building. Pollard was instantly killed, eleven buckshot having entered his body, one passing through his heart. On searching the opposite building, James Grant, a brother of the young lady named, was found in one of the rooms. There was a double-barreled gun, with one barrel discharged, in the same room. On the day before the assassination young Grant had called on Pollard and demanded a retraction. Not obtaining this satisfaction, he said he would shoot him at sight. Mr. J. M. Hanna, the assistant editor of the *Opinion*, thus described the shooting of his principal:

At about a quarter before nine o'clock the vehicle was announced as ready to carry us into the city and to the office of the *Opinion*. The presentiment of trouble yet strong on my mind, I said to Mr. Pollard, "Suppose you do not go into town to-day; I can supply the printers." "No," he answered, "I must go in. Besides, I must see that man to-day."

That ride was not more eventful than many other rides we had taken together. Mr. Pollard sat on the front seat with Mr. Redford, the driver; I behind him. Of conversation, save casual remarks, there was none until the vehicle had passed into the city on Main Street. We passed the residence of Rev. Dr. Hoge, and I observed that there was crape on the door. "Who is dead?" inquired Mr. Pollard. "Not Dr. Hoge, I hope." Mr. Redford said the party deceased was a female member of the family, which appeared to relieve greatly the sudden anxiety of Mr. Pollard.

On down Main Street, past the Spotswood, we drew swiftly towards the spot where death lay in wait watching for the coming of the victim.

Sitting behind him, I noticed that Mr. Pollard bowed occasionally to persons on the street. Once, after a salute, he turned to me and said, "There goes a man who I know hates me."

On we were driven—one of us to death. The assassin's eye, peering from the curtained window, is already fastened upon its mark, coming nigher and nigher, charmed with the circle of death. We alight—Mr. Pollard first, I after him.

One eye of the garreted assassin is closing, the other glances along the charged barrel; his forefinger presses the deadly trigger. Providence separates us by a little time and space—a moment—a few feet; another second, there is a flash, a crack, sharp and sudden, a splash of buckshot against the brick wall, and H. Rives Pollard lies dead, stretched at my feet.

Grant was tried on a charge of murder and acquitted.

These affairs are not confined to our native editors. On a beautiful June Sunday in 1869, Señor Jose Ferrer de Canto, editor of *El Cronista*, a Spanish paper printed in New York, and Señor Francisco Porto, a wealthy Cuban, met at Lundy's Lane, in Canada. The Cuban received a pistol ball through both legs at the first fire. Señor Porto was one of the writers for the Cuban organ, *La Revolucion*, and the affair grew out of the rebellion on the "ever-faithful isle," the Queen of the Antilles.

Charles Wallace, editor of the Warrenton (Ga.) *Clipper*, was shot and instantly killed on the 12th of March, 1869. Wallace had applied for admission into the Masonic lodge at Warrenton, and was black-balled by Dr. G. W. Darden, who had promised not to oppose his application. Wallace then attacked Darden through the columns of his paper, denouncing him as a liar and a villain. As Wallace was passing Darden's office, the latter shot him from his window with a rifle, the ball passing through Wallace's head and causing instant death. Wallace was a Democrat and Darden a Republican. Darden surrendered himself to the authorities and was placed in jail. Sheriff Norris, fearing that Darden would not be safe there, called upon the citizens to act as a posse to guard the jail over night; but they declined to act, being overawed by a band of Ku-Klux, numbering about one hundred, who took immediate possession of the town. They then demanded the keys from the sheriff, and, on his refusal to deliver them, became so violent that he was compelled to seek safety in flight, taking the keys with him. The band then returned to the jail. Fearing that Darden had a pistol, the mob built a fire at the door and smoked him out. Dr. Darden asked time to make a will, which was granted. He was then taken out, and, in presence of his wife and children, barbarously murdered, not less than one hundred and fifty pistol balls piercing his body.

The New Orleans *Picayune* of April 6, 1869, thus sketches a journalistic *rencontre* in Louisiana a few days previously:

It appears that some time since the editor of the *Advocate* (Republican), Mr. Swords, inserted an article in his paper reflecting upon Judge Pintado, a Republican, but belonging to a separate wing of the party. In this article the editor stated that Judge Pintado had been seen lurking about the office of the *Pioneer* (the Democratic paper), and that such an office was a fit refuge for such vermin, or words in substance to that effect. The editor of the *Pioneer* (Mr. Duppaty) thereupon demanded a retraction of the article, or satisfaction in accordance with the rules of the code. The editor of the *Advocate* replied that he was opposed to dueling, and would not accept a challenge. Mr. Duppaty then informed him that if the article was not retracted in Saturday morning's issue of the *Advocate* he would shoot him on sight. At about eleven o'clock on last Saturday forenoon, the *Advocate* having appeared without any apology, and while the citizens of the town, apprised of the expected difficulty, were gathered about in groups, Mr. Swords appeared upon the streets armed with a revolver, walking up and down, as if awaiting the coming of Duppaty. Upon being informed, however, that his antagonist had been seen with a double-barreled gun, he retired, and soon reappeared, armed in a similar manner. The parties soon came in sight of each other, and, when at about one hundred yards' distance, commenced firing at the same time, yet, strange to say, although the pieces were loaded with buckshot, neither the principals or any one in the crowd were injured by the discharges. After discharging both barrels of his gun, Mr. Swords drew his revolver and fired once, but, before Mr. Duppaty could use his revolver in return, he was arrested by the sheriff, a brother of Swords, and about the same moment Swords was arrested by a justice of the peace, and the difficulty, for the time, brought to a close. The origin of the difficulty grew out of a split in the Republican ranks, which splits at present seem to furnish material for all the lively disputes now going on in the South.

Mr. Robert W. Hughes, the editor of the *State Journal*, published in Richmond, Virginia, in 1869, had been very severe in his comments on the Conservatives. The extreme bitterness of his articles attracted considerable attention. On the 7th of June the Petersburg (Va.) *Index* noticed one of these articles in the following sharp style:

There is an article in the Friday evening's *State Journal* which, in its vileness and virulence, betrays its parentage. Hell hath no fury like a woman scorned, perhaps, but humanity knows no hatred so bitter, so reckless, so unrelenting as that the traitor feels towards those whom he has betrayed. None but a renegade Virginian, smarting under the sense of his own shameless treachery, and brimming with enmity to all that is better and truer than himself—an Arnold seeking to cloak his baseness by slander of the cause he has sold—could have penned such language in regard to Virginia gentlemen as that which we quote :

"If names could typify the meaning of words, the *mene, mene, tekel, upharsin*, which a bloody and destructive history has pronounced upon the sectional party that has so long ruled and ruined in Virginia is especially expressed in such names as Bocock, Douglass, and Aylett. These are but types of the class who have gone forth to reinvoke the people to courses of treason. It is well for the cause of loyalty, reconstruction, and state regeneration that a class of parricides so notorious, with the mark of Cain upon their foreheads, and the guilt of Cain upon their consciences, have gone out as the champions of a discontented, remonstrant, and incorrigible sectionalism. They know that the ascendency of national ideas and loyal sentiments must consign them to fixed and branded obscurity; and in the spirit of Beelzebub, 'Better to rule in hell than serve in heaven,' they are ready to drag down the Commonwealth into a deeper damnation than that in which she already writhes and perishes."

There is only one journalist in this state who is at the same time sufficiently capable as a writer and utterly degraded enough in character to have indited those lines. He is one of those who lent truculent and almost inhuman bitterness to the Richmond *Examiner* during the war—the man upon whom John M. Daniel chiefly relied for his strongest appeals to the worst passions of our people. He sat at the feet of John B. Floyd, a disciple who forgot all that was good in the lessons of his master, but seized upon the bad with the instinct of natural depravity, cultivating and developing it until he has sunk to a depth which Peter in his denial never knew. His first act after the war was to connect himself with the dirtiest of all the poisonous sheets which have disgraced Richmond since 1864—the Richmond *Republic*—and his undeniable versatility as a writer was there employed to brand as infamous all that he had advocated for six years previous. Since then he has played a part which is, thank God! stranger to Virginia journalism. His venal pen has been sold to the highest bidder to bolster any and every cause whose directors were willing to buy his brains. He has said that his articles were merchandise, and that if sufficiently remunerated he would feel warranted in arguing for polygamy. And the time came when his former friends, finding how valueless were words which the public knew were bought and sold like herrings in the market, ceased to remember his talent in the presence of his want of principle. He is now contributing editorially to the Richmond *State Journal*, which has lost thereby four fifths of its previous claim to respectability. The people of Virginia want no stronger evidence of unreliability in a public print than to know that its sentiments flow from the purchased pen of Robert W. Hughes.

What was the result of such a publication? Satisfaction was immediately demanded of Wm. E. Cameron, the editor of the *Index*. Cameron accepted the challenge, and the parties met at Chester Station, on the Petersburg Railroad; but, before they could exchange a shot, the police made their appearance, and caused a flight of the parties. They passed into North Carolina, where they fought on the 12th of June with pistols. Cameron was hit in the breast at the first fire, the ball striking a rib and glancing. Hughes demanded another fire, but the surgeons declared that Cameron could not deliver another shot, and the affair ended "to the satisfaction of all parties."

While Virginia is not free of affairs of this kind, as the above meeting indicates, there are editors in that state who are opposed to dueling. There has lately been a difficulty between the editors of the Richmond *Whig* and Richmond *Enquirer*, both belligerent journals. The last quarrel of these papers arose from a controversy on the Funding Bill before the Legislature. The *Whig* asserted that the *Enquirer* was the hired organ of the Pennsylvania Central Railroad. The latter retorted that the *Whig* was under the pay of the "Virginia Railroad Ring." It was expected that a duel would have been the result. On the 6th of March, 1872, the *Enquirer* uttered the following sentiments:

> The *Inquirer* of Saturday contained an article in reference to the *Whig* and its editor which, according to our understanding of the use of language, was, as it was intended to be, as insulting as genteel words could make it. To that article the editor of the *Whig* has replied by recrimination, and stating that the charges made against Mr. Moseley were true to the letter, and most of them can be substantiated by testimony. If he considered himsef aggrieved he should have sought redress otherwise than through the columns of the *Whig*. Mr. Moseley doubtless knew what all know who have been at all conversant with my life-long opinions, that I would neither give nor accept a challenge to fight a duel, but he no doubt knew as certainly that I am always ready to resist in a proper manner any attack made upon my character or person, and knowing that, he has chosen to defend himself by cowardly recriminations against charges which he knew to be true and declined to resent.

James C. Southall is the editor of the *Enquirer*, and Alexander Moseley editor of the *Whig*. Both parties were subsequently arrested and held to bail.

These are instances and incidents enough to illustrate our point. It is probable that the details of all the duels, assaults, and assassinations in the journalistic world would fill several volumes like this. But these affairs are closing up in this country. Our journalists find that they can manage their papers without these episodes, and live longer by the peaceful code than by that of the *duello*.

CHAPTER LVI.

THE END.

STATISTICS OF THE PRESS IN THE UNITED STATES.—OUR PROGRESS.—NEWSPAPERS A HALF CENTURY OLD.—NUMBER OF PERIODICALS IN THE WORLD.—THE FUTURE.

How many papers are published in the United States? How many in the world?

Our statistics of American newspapers are mainly correct; those of other nations are an approximation only. Our returns, however, give the reader an idea of the number of journals throughout Christendom. Our pages show the beginning, in 1457, in Germany, and in 1690 in the United States; the progress to the era of the Cheap and Independent Press in 1835, and the wonderful growth of journalism since then to 1872. Is it not all full of incident and promise?

After nearly two hundred years of subserviency to kings, governors, cliques, cabals, Essex Juntas, Kitchen Cabinets, Richmond Juntas, Albany Regencies, Tammany Rings, and Union Leagues, the Press in the United States may now be considered free and independent. They represent the people and the wants of the people. In these two centuries newspapers have passed through their different epochs as creditably as laws, customs, and circumstances would permit.

First. The Colonial Press was one of neutrality. It obeyed the authorities. It was thrust into prison if it did not. It, therefore, published the news when it did not conflict with the opinion of the magistrate. It had no opinions of its own.

Second. The Revolutionary Press was one of action. It subordinated every thing to the one glorious idea. It was full of independence—the independence of the country. But this class of papers could not last beyond that great struggle.

Third. The Party Press was the natural consequence of the Revolution. The nation had to be organized. The transition from dependence to independence created parties. There is always a difference of opinion on the polity and policy of a government, but in the process of organizing the United States there were more crude than ripe opinions. There were plenty of conflicting views in 1783.

These were represented in newspapers, and hence the Party Press, which was almost wholly controlled by politicians and cliques.

Fourth. The Independent Press, which came into existence with the railroad, prospered with the organization of those national news-carriers the express lines, and is becoming the arbiter of nations with the telegraph.

Is there another step forward? What will be the effect of the success of the pneumatic tunnels, when the *Tribune, Times, Herald, Sun,* and *World* of New York are read in San Francisco on the day of publication?

There were 37 newspapers published in the United States on the commencement of the Revolutionary War in 1775: with these began the independence of the Nation. On the 1st of January, 1835, there were 1258 daily, semi-weekly, and weekly newspapers issued: with these commenced the independence of the Press. With all the struggles, failures, and successes of the Press, this was a great result. Here are the figures:

NUMBER OF PAPERS, WITH THEIR ESTIMATED CIRCULATION, IN THE UNITED STATES IN 1835.

States and Territories.	No. of Papers.	Copies circulated during the year.	States and Territories.	No. of Papers.	Copies circulated during the year.
Alabama	20	624,000	Mississippi	15	468,000
Arkansas	3	75,000	Michigan	7	182,600
Connecticut	39	2,448,000	Missouri	17	452,000
Delaware	4	208,000	New Hampshire	27	1,404,000
District of Columbia	6	1,500,000	New York	260	27,636,000
Florida	5	130,000	New Jersey	36	3,346,000
Georgia	31	1,622,400	North Carolina	23	720,000
Indiana	23	837,200	Ohio	145	4,914,000
Illinois	18	561,600	Pennsylvania	200	14,976,000
Kentucky	27	1,249,200	Rhode Island	16	1,612,000
Louisiana	18	2,309,600	South Carolina	24	1,591,000
Maine	52	2,520,000	Tennessee	28	1,114,000
Massachusetts	112	9,984,000	Vermont	26	1,352,000
Maryland	37	3,536,000	Virginia	40	3,089,600
			Total	1258	90,361,000

With the semi-monthly, monthly, and quarterly papers and magazines, the circulation of periodical literature in 1835 must have reached ninety-five million copies. This large number, among less than fifteen millions of people, indicated an intellectual culture and activity never before equaled. On this basis the Independent Political Press of the United States began its splendid career.

Since 1835 the returns made to government have been published, and the figures for the following four decennial periods, with those of 1783 and 1835, will show the progressive steps of journalism on this side of the Atlantic since this nation became a power on earth:

STATISTICS OF THE DAILY AND WEEKLY NEWSPAPERS IN THE UNITED STATES.

States and Territories.	1840. Daily.	1840. Weekly.	1850. Daily.	1850. Weekly.	1860. Daily.	1860. Weekly.	1870. Daily.	1870. Weekly.
Alabama	3	25	6	53	9	82	12	75
Arkansas	—	9	—	9	—	36	3	45
Arizona	—	—	—	—	—	—	—	2
California	—	—	4	3	22	74	27	162
Connecticut	2	31	7	34	14	33	17	53
Colorado	—	—	—	—	—	—	9	13
Delaware	—	6	—	10	—	9	1	13
District of Columbia	3	11	5	13	5	4	8	11
Dakotah	—	—	—	—	—	—	—	2
Florida	—	10	—	10	—	17	—	23
Georgia	5	29	5	40	12	60	13	77
Illinois	3	40	8	88	23	239	26	378
Indiana	—	73	9	97	13	160	22	234
Iowa	—	4	—	27	9	107	18	204
Idaho	—	—	—	—	—	—	—	7
Kansas	—	—	—	—	3	21	10	55
Kentucky	5	33	9	45	4	62	5	74
Louisiana	11	23	11	43	4	64	10	80
Maine	3	33	4	44	7	43	6	59
Maryland	7	35	6	58	6	49	6	93
Massachusetts	10	81	22	141	17	109	19	162
Michigan	6	26	3	49	8	100	12	152
Minnesota	—	—	—	—	4	44	7	76
Missouri	6	29	5	49	15	133	20	211
Mississippi	2	29	—	50	5	63	7	68
Montana	—	—	—	—	—	—	1	8
North Carolina	—	27	—	45	8	53	12	48
Nebraska	—	—	—	—	—	12	1	24
New Hampshire	—	27	—	35	—	18	7	39
Nevada	—	—	—	—	—	—	4	12
New Mexico	—	—	—	1	—	2	—	5
New Jersey	4	32	6	43	15	65	21	86
New York	34	211	51	329	68	336	77	535
Ohio	9	114	26	211	22	256	33	320
Oregon	—	—	—	2	2	12	7	26
Pennsylvania	12	175	24	264	28	285	49	406
Rhode Island	2	14	5	14	5	12	5	17
South Carolina	3	14	7	32	2	30	4	62
Tennessee	2	44	8	38	8	61	14	75
Texas	—	—	—	34	3	69	10	102
Utah	—	—	—	—	—	—	1	2
Vermont	2	28	2	31	2	28	6	44
Virginia	4	47	15	67	15	98	14	79
West Virginia	—	—	—	—	—	—	4	46
Wisconsin	—	6	6	39	14	128	14	146
Washington	—	—	—	—	—	4	—	14
Total	138	1266	254	2048	372	2971	542	4425

These figures, with the exception of those of 1870, are taken from the official census returns. Those of 1870 are from the *Proof-Sheet*. The census returns of that year, embracing all periodicals, give the following very interesting and instructive result :

NUMBER OF PUBLICATIONS, WITH THEIR CIRCULATION AND ANNUAL ISSUE, IN THE UNITED STATES IN 1870.

PERIODS OF ISSUE.

	Number.	Copies annually issued.	Circulation.
Daily	574	806,479,570	2,601,547
Three times a week	107	24,196,380	155,105
Semi-weekly	115	25,708,488	247,197
Weekly	4295	550,921,436	10,594,643
Semi-monthly	96	32,395,680	1,349,820
Monthly	622	67,810,116	5,650,843
Bi-monthly	13	189,900	31,650
Quarterly	49	846,680	211,670
Total	5871	1,508,548,250	20,842,475

CLASSES OF PUBLICATIONS.

	Number.	Copies annually issued.	Circulation.
Advertising	79	4,689,800	293,450
Agricultural and horticultural	93	21,541,904	770,752
Benevolent and secret societies	81	6,518,560	257,080
Commercial and financial	142	31,120,600	690,200
Illustrated, literary, and miscellaneous	503	160,061,408	4,422,235
Nationality, devoted to	20	4,671,000	45,150
Political	4333	1,134,789,082	8,781,220
Religious	407	125,959,496	4,764,358
Sporting	6	3,222,000	73,500
Technical and professional	207	15,974,400	744,530
Total	5871	1,508,548,250	20,842,475

The number of copies of the daily papers printed in 1870 reached, in round numbers, 800,000,000. The issue of the weekly publications amounted to 600,000,000 copies. All other publications printed 100,000,000 copies. The aggregate issue in that year of all the political and literary periodicals of the country was over 1,500,000,000 copies. What an astounding exhibition! Let us look at the comparative results since 1704:

NEWSPAPER AND PERIODICAL CIRCULATION IN THE UNITED STATES.

Years.	Newspapers and Periodicals.	Copies annually printed.	Population.	Years.	Newspapers and Periodicals.	Copies annually printed.	Population.
1704	1	16,000	600,000	1835	1258	90,361,000	14,000,000
1725	4	170,000	1,000,000	1840	1631	195,838,673	17,069,453
1775	37	1,200,000	2,800,000	1850	2526	426,409,978	23,191,876
1810	359	22,321,700	7,239,814	1860	4051	927,951,548	31,445,080
1828	852	68,117,796	12,000,000	1870	5871	1,508,548,250	38,555,753

Newspapers and periodicals increase more rapidly than population—we mean in a greater ratio. This is owing to the increased educational facilities of the people. Newspapers, too, make readers. They are read in preference to all other printed matter. They are the national teachers, every where in circulation, easily and cheaply obtained, and always clear to the comprehension of every one who can read. This enormous circulation is also explained in the fact that many readers purchase several publications. They do not confine themselves to the *Tribune*, or the *World*, or the *Ledger*, or the

Herald, but purchase two, three, or four different daily papers at a time ; neither do they confine themselves to one weekly paper.

Of all the newspapers published in the United States, very few, comparatively, live half a century. While the Press is ever existing, ever increasing in number and power, individual newspapers are begun, thrive for a time, create a sensation, possess an influence, and then disappear. We have made out a list of those newspapers which are now published which have been in existence for fifty years and upwards. There are not more than fifty in the country! Of these, not a dozen are known beyond their own states. Is not this a curious fact? There are seven which have lived over one hundred years. There are only two older than the oldest inhabitant, unless one of Washington's nurses is yet in existence.

HALF-CENTURY NEWSPAPERS.

NAMES OF PAPERS NOW PUBLISHED WHICH HAVE BEEN ESTABLISHED FIFTY YEARS AND UPWARDS.

Name.	When established.
1. *Portsmouth* (N. H.) *Gazette*	October 27, 1756.
2. *Newport* (R. I.) *Mercury*	June 12, 1758.
3. *New London* (Conn.) *Gazette*	November 1, 1763.
4. *Hartford* (Conn.) *Courant*	October 20, 1764.
5. *New Haven* (Conn.) *Journal*	October, 1767.
6. *Salem* (Mass.) *Gazette*	August 5, 1768.
7. *Worcester* (Mass.) *Spy*	July 17, 1770.
8. *Pittsburg* (Pa.) *Gazette*	September, 1786.
9. *Northampton* (Mass.) *Gazette*	September 6, 1786.
10. *Greenfield* (Mass.) *Gazette and Courier*	February 1, 1792.
11. *Pittsburg* (Pa.) *Post*	——— 1792.
12. *Rutland* (Vt.) *Herald*	January 1, 1793.
13. *New York Commercial Advertiser*	December 9, 1793.
14. *Utica* (N.Y.) *Herald and Gazette*	——— 1796.
15. *Newburyport* (Mass.) *Herald*	October, 1797.
16. *Virginia Advertiser*	January 1, 1800.
17. *Charleston* (S. C.) *Courier*	January 1, 1800.
18. *Salem* (Mass.) *Register*	May 12, 1800.
19. *Frederick* (Md.) *Herald*	November 14, 1802.
20. *Eastern* (Me.) *Argus*	September, 1803.
21. *Richmond* (Va.) *Enquirer*	May 9, 1804.
22. *New York Evening Post*	November 16, 1804.
23. *Catskill* (N.Y.) *Recorder and Democrat*	December 16, 1804.
24. *Cincinnati* (Ohio) *Gazette*	——— 1806.
25. *Cooperstown* (N.Y.) *Freeman's Journal*	——— 1808.
26. *St. Louis* (Mo.) *Republican*	——— 1808.
27. *Lynchburg* (Va.) *Virginian*	September 16, 1808.
28. *Albany* (N.Y.) *Argus*	January 26, 1813.
29. *Boston Daily Advertiser*	March 3, 1813.
30. *Canton* (Ohio) *Repository*	——— 1814.
31. *Alexandria* (Va.) *Gazette*	January 3, 1816.
32. *Boston Recorder*	January 3, 1816.
33. *Hartford* (Conn.) *Times*	June 12, 1817.
34. *Zion's Herald*	——— 1818.
35. *Boston Watchman and Reflector*	——— 1819.
36. *New York Observer*	——— 1820.
37. *Providence* (R. I.) *Journal*	January 1, 1820.
38. *Christian* (Mass.) *Register*	April 20, 1821.
39. *Mobile* (Ala.) *Register*	December, 1821.
40. *Old Colony Memorial*	May 2, 1822.

Some statisticians have endeavored to give the returns of newspapers and their circulation throughout the world. Our own estimates and returns form only an approximation. No country can compare with this in this kind of literature or in this sort of enterprise. There were 426,000,000 copies of newspapers and periodicals printed in the United States in 1850. There were only 91,000,000 printed in Great Britain in 1851. We printed as many in 1835. It is estimated that the number of copies printed in Great Britain in 1870 was 350,000,000, and the same in France. The census returns show that over 1,500,000,000 were issued in the United States in the same year. It is probable that the *New York Herald* prints 36,000,000 and the *New York Ledger* 15,000,000 annually. One is a daily, the other a weekly. Others, such as *Harper's Weekly*, the *Public Ledger*, of Philadelphia, the *Sun*, of New York, are about as prolific.

Now let us see how many newspapers and periodicals are printed in the world. Our figures are by no means official; we give them for what they are worth:

NEWSPAPERS AND PERIODICALS IN THE WORLD.
THE ESTIMATE IN 1870.

Great Britain	1456	Norway and Sweden	184
France	1668	Netherlands	174
Prussia	809	Switzerland	394
Austria	650	Egypt	7
Other German States	467	Africa	14
Russia	337	Asia	30
Italy	723	Turkey	8
Spain	306	Other parts of the world	150
Belgium	194	Total	7642
Portugal	26		
Denmark	96	United States	5871

With the same rate of increase in the next ten years as in the past, there will be more newspapers and periodicals printed in the United States than in all the rest of the world combined. Indeed, the *American Newspaper Directory* of 1872 gives the aggregate number of periodical publications in this country at 6432, only 1200 less in that year than in all other parts of the world. Our growth, as a nation, is more rapid; then, with common schools, churches, politicians, theatres, lectures, libraries, and reading-rooms every where, there is a greater demand for cheap literature and cheap reading. Yet, in the face of this marvelous progress, we have been, till quite lately, retarded by mechanical and physical causes.

First. The Press was limited in circulation, prior to 1835, for want of means of transportation. Newspapers were compelled to rely on stage-coaches. Publishers in villages and towns had to deliver their papers by postmen on horseback.

Second. When steam-boats and railways came into use, population increased so rapidly that printers could not sufficiently supply the demand, in consequence of the want of mechanical power in their press-rooms. Napier's double cylinders would print only three thousand sheets per hour.

Third. Hoe having invented the lightning press, the difficulty of supplying the demand was met for a time; but with the increase of railroads and steam-boats, and the spread of Adams's, Harnden's, Wells and Fargo's express lines, the demand for newspapers ran ahead of Hoe's eight-cylinder presses, printing from twelve to fifteen thousand copies per hour, and the ten-cylinder presses, printing eighteen to twenty thousand sheets an hour, were brought forward.

Fourth. Ocean steam-ships, the telegraph, the wars in Europe, and the rebellion again increased the circulation of the newspapers beyond their capacity to print. Then came the grand *desideratum*, the stereotyping process, by which pages of an entire newspaper are duplicated in thirty minutes, and the circulation increased *ad libitum*. Now, with half a dozen of Hoe's ten cylinders, or a dozen of Bullock's presses, one hundred thousand sheets can be printed every hour in any establishment possessing these facilities.

When the Cheap and Independent Press fairly commenced its career, the means of distribution, as we have stated, were limited. Only one paper circulated over 6000 daily in 1835. Only 95,000,000 copies were printed in the whole country in that year. Now the number of copies, in round numbers, is over 1,500,000,000. Our newspaper mails were carried by steam-boats and over railroads,

in 1840 - - - 3,889,053 miles ;
in 1871 - - 60,241,826 miles.

This is the ratio of increase of newspaper circulation and newspaper readers. Several years ago a system of "free delivery" of newspapers was introduced by the Post-office Department in fifty different cities. Look at the result:

COPIES OF NEWSPAPERS DELIVERED.

In 1868 - - 16,910,715. | In 1870 - - 27,867,023.
In 1869 - 21,954,898. | In 1871 - 32,610,353.

Yet the Post-office Department performs but a small part of the service of newspaper carriers for the Press of the country.

These have been the progressive steps of journalism in the United States till the number of newspapers and periodicals is almost equal to those printed in all other parts of the universe, and the aggregate circulation is superior to that of Europe, Asia, and Africa! So in the future, with presses striking off twenty thousand impressions an hour, stereotyping apparatus duplicating, triplicating, quadruplicating forms, type-setting machines driven by steam, the automatic telegraph transmitting five hundred to one thousand words per minute, and the pneumatic dispatch lines, for parcels, to traverse the continent from the Atlantic to the Pacific in the difference of time between the two oceans, the *Sun*, the *Herald*, the *World*, the *Tribune*, the *Times*, in existence to-day, and the *Future*, the *Universe*, the *Cosmopolitan*, the *Pneumatic Dispatch*, and the *Omniscient*, newspapers yet to be established, will have it in their power to lay the events that have occurred to-day on both hemispheres on every breakfast-table and in every counting-room on the continent early to-morrow morning. Where will the pulse of the world be felt then? London? Paris? Berlin? St. Petersburg? San Francisco? New York? Where?

Meanwhile population is increasing, newspaper readers are multiplying, mind is expanding, wealth is augmenting, and the physical forces of the world are developing. Will the newspapers of to-day, the wonderful *Times'*, the marvelous *Heralds*, the brilliant *Suns*, the learned *Tribunes*, perfect wonders compared with the meagre *News-Letters* and miserable *Gazettes* of a hundred and fifty years ago, become, in the progress of this globe, and in their turn, the miserable *Times'* and the meagre *Heralds* to the giant journals of the next century?

It is possible.

ADDENDA.

NEWSPAPERS have postscripts. Why should not books have addenda? Fresh news is constantly pouring into newspaper offices. Fresh facts are as continually pressing upon book publishers.

One of our leading journalists, Horace Greeley, was the candidate of one of the great political parties of the nation, in 1872, for the office of President of the United States. On the 15th of May he issued a card, stating this fact, and withdrawing from the editorial management of the *New York Tribune*. That card will be found on pages 569–70. Well, after a spirited contest, the election took place on the 5th of November. Over six millions of votes were polled. Horace Greeley received nearly one half of this immense number, but Ulysses S. Grant was elected President. This important national result was thus characteristically and semi-officially announced in the *Tribune* of the 7th of November:

A CARD.

The undersigned resumes the editorship of *The Tribune*, which he relinquished on embarking in another line of business six months ago. Henceforth it shall be his endeavor to make this a thoroughly independent journal, treating all parties and political movements with judicial fairness and candor, but courting the favor and deprecating the wrath of no one.

If he can hereafter say any thing that will tend to heartily unite the whole American People on the broad platform of Universal Amnesty and Impartial Suffrage, he will gladly do so. For the present, however, he can best commend that consummation by silence and forbearance. The victors in our late struggle can hardly fail to take the whole subject of Southern rights and wrongs into early and earnest consideration, and to them, for the present, he remits it.

Since he will never again be a candidate for any office, and is not in full accord with either of the great parties which have hitherto divided the country, he will be able and will endeavor to give wider and steadier regard to the progress of Science, Industry, and the Useful Arts than a partisan journal can do; and he will not be provoked to indulgence in those bitter personalities which are the recognized bane of journalism. Sustained by a generous public, he will do his best to make *The Tribune* a power in the broader field it now contemplates, as, when Human Freedom was imperiled, it was in the arena of political partisanship. Respectfully, HORACE GREELEY.

NEW YORK, November 6, 1872.

These intentions, now so painfully recorded—this new departure in political journalism—we all regret to say, were not destined to be carried out by the respected writer of this card. With the saddest of all domestic afflictions added to the most impressively terrible political excitement of our era, the depressed and perturbed brain, overtasked and strained by forty years of constant labor and friction, submitted to Providence, and on Friday evening, the 29th of November, 1872, Horace Greeley ceased to be of this world, and with his death a great journalist passed away.

Since the 18th of June, 1869, three of our leading editors have died: Henry J. Raymond, James Gordon Bennett, and Horace Greeley. They made their mark on this epoch. They made journalism in this country a profession, each in his own way, and after his own style. They established three great newspapers. One founded the Independent Press; the other two were among the last of the active, influential party editors that have flourished in the United States since September 17, 1789. With the death of the founder of the *Tribune*, party journalism pure and simple, managed by accomplished and experienced editors, inaugurated by Jefferson and Hamilton, aided by such writers as Fenno, Bache, Duane, Freneau, Coleman, Cheetham, Ritchie, and Croswell, has ceased to exist, and Independent Journalism becomes a fact impressed on the minds of the people; and it is not likely that any other class can hereafter prosper in this country, and be a power in the United States.

Horace Greeley was an editor clearly of the political school. He was educated in the *Log Cabin*, his primary school, to the *Tribune*—his Harvard College of journalism. His fixed views on public matters made him a leading party editor. It would have been difficult for him, had he lived, to keep pace with the new class of papers without the infusion of fresher, younger, more unbiased intellects. Henry J. Raymond was a pupil of the *Tribune* school, and, with all his efforts to the contrary, he found it impossible to remain out of the political field. Still, these two journalists were more or less independent, even as party organs, because they soared above the mere politicians that controlled the primary elections and nominating conventions of the land. James Gordon Bennett, although a partisan editor for twelve or fifteen years, was never a politician. He never wanted political office, and would never accept of any nomination. He always looked upon the Press as superior to Party. Hence the success of the *Herald* as an independent journal. This success, together with the shabby treatment that Horace Greeley always received from the politicians, as shown so clearly and plaintively in his public card dissolving the partnership of Seward, Weed & Co., would have made the *Tribune* a more independent paper in spite of the life-long tastes of its founder.

But all this now belongs to the past. Only two or three of the old party editors remain in active life. James Watson Webb, Francis P. Blair, and Thurlow Weed have retired from the ranks of journalism. Charles Gordon Greene, of the *Boston Post*, James Brooks, of the New York *Express*, and William Cullen Bryant, of the New

York *Evening Post*, are still at work. All the others known to fame have passed from this world; and we have endeavored, in our poor way, to enroll their names on the pages of history.

Sic Transit Gloria Mundi.

There have been changes in the offices of two other newspapers, sketches of which are given in the preceding pages.

1st. It is announced that R. Barnwell Rhett, Jr., formerly of the Charleston (S. C.) *Mercury*, has become chief editor of the *New Orleans Picayune*, which paper, it appears, is no longer owned by one man, but by an association of shareholders.

2d. The *St. Louis Republican*, for a long time a blanket sheet in size and folio in form, has been changed to the quarto form, after the style of the leading journals of New York City. Also, that the *Republican* is to be located in a splendid new building erected especially for its use, and will be printed on three kinds of presses—Hoe's, Bullock's, and Walter's—the latter the invention of the principal proprietor of the London *Times*.

That we may keep pace with the subjects of our sketches, it may be fair to state that any further additions to our facts will be given in second and third editions.

INDEX.

ABELL, A. S., 510.
Abolition of Slavery, 192, 240, 363, 373, 400, 439.
    Riots, 354, 367, 370.
Abyssinian Expedition, 486, 717.
Adams, Alvin, 505, 521.
    Charles Francis, 581.
    John, 105, 107, 153, 165, 210, 328.
    John Quincy, 155, 220, 229, 272, 284.
Adams's Express Company, 505, 517, 520.
Advertisements, 36, 357, 372, 408, 419, 433, 458, 467, 469, 470, 471, 472, 543, 654, 685, 728, 731, 733 734.
Advertiser, Albany Daily, 192, 280, 517.
    American Daily, 175, 185.
    Boston Daily, 155, 164, 189, 191, 302, 378.
    Boston Independent, 102.
    Boston Weekly, 109.
    Buffalo Commercial, 577.
    Cincinnati Commercial, 199.
    Mobile, 496.
    Newark Daily, 187.
    New Jersey Weekly, 136.
    New York Commercial, 192, 225, 402, 430.
    New York Daily, 175, 219, 430, 518.
    New York Mercantile, 225, 226, 430.
    New York Public, 225.
    Portland Evening, 176, 517.
    Rochester Daily, 322.
Advocate, Christian, 304.
    National, 225, 276, 282, 285, 312.
    Workingmen's, 425.
Agricultural Newspapers, 330.
Agriculturist, 709.
Albion, New York, 263, 313.
Alden, Henry M., 707.
Aldine, New York, 708.
Alien and Sedition Laws, 159, 213, 215, 268, 274.
Allen's, Colonel Ethan, Interview with Rivington, 133.
Almanacs, Old and New, 570, 571.
Alta Californian, 591.
Amateur Journalism, 712.
American, Baltimore, 751.
    Conflict, 527.
    Cyclopædia, The New, 677.
    Herkimer (N.Y.), 207.
    Journalism before the British Parliament, 540.
    Literary Gazette, 511.
    Newspaper Directory, 774.
    New York, 283, 312, 430, 442, 746.
Ames, Fisher, 188.
André, Major, 133.
Andrews, Alexander, British Journalism, 21.
    Rev. John, 295.
    Stephen Pearl, 500.
Anecdotes and Incidents, 212, 220, 221, 239, 474, 475, 481, 508, 511, 512, 519, 525, 527, 532, 535, 553, 565, 582, 604, 619, 633, 654.
Anglo-American, 314.
Anniversaries, New York Religious, 453, 720.
Anthony, Henry B., 320.
Appeals to Subscribers, 57.
Appleton, John, 258.

Appleton's Journal, 708.
Argus, Albany, 222, 266, 275, 399, 579.
    Frankfort (Ky.), 235, 238.
    Greenleaf's, 145.
    New York, 215.
    Portland, 258, 290.
    Richmond, 269.
Armstrong, Robert, 241, 257.
Army and Navy Papers, 710.
Art encouraged, 464.
Assassination of Charles Austin, 163.
    Charles Wallace, 766.
    Henry Rives Pollard, 765.
Assaults—On Benjamin Austin, Jr., by Major Russell, 152.
    Benjamin Franklin Bache, 211.
    Columbia College, N.Y., 122.
    Duff Green by James Watson Webb, 353.
    Editor Jenkins, of Vicksburg Sentinel, 763.
    Editor Washington Star by William Smith, 762.
    Edwin Croswell, 279.
    Federal Republican Office, 274.
    Horace Greeley by Albert Rust, 762.
    James Gordon Bennett by James Watson Webb, 436.
    James Gordon Bennett by Thomas Hamblin, 444.
    James Ryan, of Vicksburg Sentinel, 763.
    Major Benjamin Russell by Samuel Jarvis, 149.
    Melzer Gardner, of Portsmouth (Va.) Chronicle, 764.
    Philadelphia Aurora Office, 211.
    Rivington's Gazetteer Office, 122.
    William Duane, 214.
Associated Press, American, 617, 703.
    New York, 261, 366, 463, 608, 610, 614, 675, 679, 704.
Associations, General, 536, 608, 609, 611, 622, 656, 665.
Atlantic Steamers, 450.
Atlas, Albany, 278, 578, 582.
    Boston, 198, 321, 371, 390, 394.
Aurora, Philadelphia, 153, 175, 182, 187, 191, 210, 215.
Austin, Benjamin, Jr., 105, 161, 163, 234.
Authorities, 24.
Authors, Encouragement of, 515.
Autobiography of A. G. Ellis, 207.
    Benjamin Franklin, 66, 77.
    John C. Rives, 246.
    Nathaniel Willis, 289.

Bache, Benjamin Franklin, 175, 182, 210.
Bailey, Dr. Gamaliel, 259.
Balance, Hudson, 267, 275, 280.
Balloons as News-carriers, 315, 597.
Bankrupt Act of 1842, 357.
Banner, Presbyterian, 296.
Barn-burners, 279, 581.
Bartlett, Dr. John S., 313.

Bartlett, W. O., 223.
Beach, Moses S., 420.
　　Moses Yale, 420.
Bee, New Orleans, 491, 494.
　　New York, 225, 424.
Beecher, Henry Ward, 299, 301, 561, 653, 673.
Benjamin, Park, 457, 459, 462, 524, 589.
Bennett, James Gordon, Sr., 22, 49, 223, 226, 239, 256, 262, 281, 284, 285, 346, 350, 358, 359, 386, 410, 428, 446, 450, 464, 465, 479, 485, 490, 538, 560, 695, 713.
　　James Gordon, Jr., 49, 446, 485, 486, 490.
Bentley, Rev. William, 171.
Benton, Thomas H., 235, 249, 311, 312, 723.
Berkeley, Sir William, 119.
Bible, Proposals to print, 72.
Biddle, Nicholas, 250, 345, 449.
Bigelow, John, 223, 639.
Bigelow, Horatio, 379.
Billings, Josh, 692.
Biographical Sketches, 481.
Bird, Robert M., 183.
Birney, James G., 240, 259.
Black Republicans, 275.
Blair, Francis Preston, 235, 242, 247, 251, 414.
Blake, Henry Ingraham, 189, 190.
Blanket Sheets of New York, 344, 349.
Boarding Steamers off Cape Race, 615.
Bogus Proclamation, 373, 671, 674.
Bonner, Robert, 606, 647, 649, 652.
Boone, Nicholas, of Boston, 33.
Boston Massacre, 106.
　　News-Letter, 54.
　　Newspapers, 378.
　　Notion, 589.
Bourne, Nicholas, of London, 33.
Boutwell, George S., 682.
Bouvier, Judge John, 196, 306.
Bowles, Samuel, 393, 582, 583.
Bradford, Andrew, 60, 75, 78.
　　Thomas, 99.
　　William, 50, 72, 74, 81, 92, 111.
　　William, Jr., 97, 100.
British Journalism, 21.
British Spy, 269.
Brook Farm Community, 677.
Brooker, William, 58.
Brooks, Erastus, 176, 518.
　　James, 176, 517.
　　James Gordon, 280, 346, 425, 517.
Brother Jonathan, 588.
Brownlow, William G., 574.
Bryant, William Cullen, 182, 221, 222, 224, 576, 656.
Buchanan, President James, 485.
Buckingham, Joseph Tinker, 22, 384, 386.
Buel, Jesse, 276, 280.
Buildings, Newspaper, 342, 382, 387, 496, 513, 631, 655.
Bulletin, Boston Commercial, 335.
　　New Orleans, 492.
　　Philadelphia Evening, 182, 758.
　　San Francisco, 591.
Bullitt, Alexander C., 256, 494.
Bulwer, Sir Henry L., 481.
Burke, John D'Oley, 187, 214.
Burr, Aaron, 145, 154, 219, 263, 268.
Burrows, Silas E., 345.
Burton, William E., 482.
Butler, Amos, 226, 430.
Butters, Nathaniel, 33, 57.
Byles, Mather, 76.

Calhoun, John C., 235, 312.
California Gold Excitement, 395, 477.
Call, San Francisco Morning, 616, 759.
Callender, James Thompson, 214, 268.
Cameron, Simon, 177.

Campbell, John, 52, 64.
Cards, Editors', 623.
Carrier Pigeons, 596, 597.
Carriers' Addresses, 99, 711.
Carroll, Charles, of Carrollton, 118.
Carter, Nathaniel H., 266, 280.
Cash System, 441.
Cass, Lewis, 279.
Censor, Royal Organ in Boston, 128.
Censorship, 48, 60, 69.
Centinel, Columbian, 152, 155.
　　Massachusetts, 147.
　　of the Northwestern Territory, 195.
Cent, Philadelphia, 416.
Chandler, Joseph R., 182.
Channing, William Ellery, 149.
Charitable Associations, 489.
Charivari, 690.
Cheap Press in New York, 487, 775.
　　in Philadelphia and Baltimore, 505.
　　Literature, 587, 727.
Cheetham, James, 145, 146, 182, 217, 218.
Childs, George W., 100, 510, 511, 512, 515, 758.
　　Louisa Maria, 386.
Child's Paper, 305.
Choate, Rufus, 565.
Christian Remembrancer, 293.
　　Union, 301.
Chronicle, Boston, 122.
　　Boston Independent, 137, 144, 145, 158, 160, 289.
　　Cincinnati, 200, 618.
　　Cologne, of 1499, 31.
　　Constitutional, 119.
　　New England, 65, 124.
　　New York, 126.
　　New York Morning, 263.
　　Pennsylvania, 123.
　　Portsmouth (N. H.), 752.
　　Washington, 260.
Cincinnati, Society of, 158.
Circulation of the first American Newspaper, 57.
Citizen, American, 145, 217, 225, 263.
　　New York, 426.
Claiborne's, Colonel, Recollections, 243.
Clapp, William W., 379, 395.
Clark, Lewis Gaylord, 79, 320.
　　Willis Gaylord, 79.
Class Journalism, 329.
Clay, Henry, 240, 272.
Clergy, Troubles with, 67, 71, 80, 453, 721.
Clinton, De Witt, 155, 225, 264, 283, 286.
Clubs, Newspaper, 489, 503, 622, 656, 665.
Cobbett, William, 154, 309, 310, 620.
Cobden, Richard, 324.
Cockades, The Black and Tri-colored, 153.
Coggswell, Dr., of Astor Library, 25.
Coleman, William, 146, 217, 221.
College Newspapers, 711.
Collins, Edward K., 457.
Columbia College, Attack on, 122.
Columbian, New York, 225.
Combinations of Newspapers, 610.
Comic Papers, 688.
Commercial, Cincinnati, 198, 214, 219.
Commercial Press, 334.
Compiler, Richmond, 269.
Conant, Samuel S., 284, 707.
Confederation, Articles of, 143.
Congregationalist, Boston, 296.
Congress, Editors and Reporters in, 697.
Congress of the Republic of News, 611.
Conrad, R. T., 183.
Constitution, Federal, 144, 149, 165, 233.
Constitution, Washington, 253.
Cooper, J. Fenimore, 267, 744.
　　Myles, of Columbia College, 122.
Copyright, 589, 723, 725, 726.
Correspondents, Foreign, 314, 322, 451, 518.

Index. 783

Correspondents, War, 482, 483, 493, 606, 715, 717, 719.
    Washington, 239, 285, 701.
Corruptions in Congress, 552.
Cosby, Governor William, 81.
Cost of a first-class Journal, 566.
Country Seats, 243.
Courant, Boston, 40, 61.
    Connecticut, 113, 144, 156, 664.
    Wilmington (Del.), 112.
Courier and Enquirer, New York, 222, 226, 256, 273, 281, 412, 430, 443, 669.
Courier and Journal, Louisville (Ky.), 326.
Courier, Boston, 384.
    Charleston (S. C.), 262.
    Louisiana, 491.
    Lowell, 198.
    Morning, of New York, 281, 344.
    Portland Daily, 176.
Craig, D. H., 612, 613, 616.
Crawford, William H., 220.
Croaker & Co., 220.
Crooks, Ramsey, 225.
Croswell, Edwin, 223, 277, 279, 402, 412, 578.
    Harry, 267, 275.
    Sherman, 279.
Cummings, Alexander, 182, 667.
Curtis, George William, 663, 707.
Cushing, Caleb, 257.
    Thomas, 105.
Custis, George Washington Parke, 275.
Cyclopædia, The New American, 677.

Dana, Charles A., 206, 420, 488, 555, 559, 677, 678, 679.
Daniels, John T., 22.
Davis, Matthew L., 145, 187, 216, 263, 348.
    Jefferson, 527, 567.
Dawson, Moses, 199.
Day, Benjamin H., 417.
Deacon Giles's Distillery, 383.
Debates in Congress, 233.
De Foe, Daniel, 560.
Delta, California True, 594.
    New Orleans, 243, 492, 593.
Democrat, Chicago, 203.
    Kaskaskia, 207.
    St. Louis, 202.
Democratic Organ, The first, 145.
Dennie, Joseph, 228.
Deposits, Removal of the, 250, 273, 447.
Dexter, Lord Timothy, 24.
Diario Oficial, of Mexico, 230.
Diary, or Loudon's Register, 146, 150.
Dickens, Asbury, 229.
    Charles, 651, 660.
Dikeman, Wakeman H., 227.
Dinsmore, William B., 182, 521.
Directory, The first New York, 139.
Dix, John A., 376, 580, 772.
Douglass, Frederick, 260.
Downing, Major Jack, 176, 688.
Draft Riots in New York, 557.
Drake, John Rodman, 220.
Duane, William, 211, 212, 216, 217, 307.
Duels: A. C. Bullitt and Editor Wagner, 494.
    Advocate (La.) Editor and Pioneer Editor, 766.
    Baton Rouge Gazette Editor and Alcée Labranche, 764.
    DeWitt Clinton and John Swartwout, 264.
    Dr. James Hagan and Daniel W. Adams, 763.
    Dr. James Hagan and Editor Vicksburg Whig, 763.
    Editors of El Cronista and La Revolucion, 766.
    Editor Vicksburg Sentinel and T. E. Robins, 763.

Duels: George J. Harris and E. H. Foster, Jr. 402.
    Graves and Cilley, 348, 761.
    James Cheetham and William Coleman, 146.
    James Watson Webb and Thomas H. Marshall, 356.
    John D'Oley Burke's death, 187.
    John H. Pleasants and Thomas Ritchie, Jr., 271.
    Reuben Durrett and George D. Prentice, 324.
    Robert W. Hughes and William E. Cámeron, 768.
    Thomas E. Robins and James M. Downs, 763.
    Walter Hickey and Dr. Macklin, 763.
    William Coleman and Captain Thompson, 218.
    William Graham and Dr. Barton, 287.
    W. R. Taber, Jr., and Edward Magrath, 403.
Dutton, Henry W., 386.
Dwight, Theodore, 219, 518.

Eastburn, John H., 390, 394.
Eckford, Henry, 284.
Edes and Gill, 105, 106, 138, 148, 164, 166.
Editorial articles, Origin of, 219, 380, 381.
Editors: Ancient and Modern, 381.
    as Diplomats, 485, 553, 554, 576, 577.
    Imprisonment of, 70, 80, 112, 160.
    what they should eat, 224.
Effigies in Boston, 123.
Elbows of the Mincio, 631.
Election Returns, 370, 391.
Emancipator, New York, 387, 440.
Emigration to California, 592.
Engraving, 497, 705.
Enquirer: Cincinnati, 198, 199.
    New York, 285, 345.
    Richmond, 241, 268, 768.
    St. Louis, 311.
Enterprise, News, 56, 75, 182, 321, 346, 383, 395, 530.
Epochs of Journalism, 27.
    First—the first American Newspaper, 43.
    Second—the Colonial Press, 51.
    Third—the Revolutionary Press, 102.
    Fourth—the Political Party Press, 141.
    Fifth—the Transition—the Cheap Press, 408.
    Sixth—the Independent—the Telegraphic Press, 428.
Era, Washington National, 259.
Ethnology, 25.
Evangelist, New York, 298, 304.
Evarts, Jeremiah, 292.
Everett, Edward, 282, 380, 722, 725.
Every Saturday, 708.
Examiner, Richmond, 22, 215, 268.
Excitement in the Gold Mines, 593.
Exeter Federal Miscellany, 227.
Expresses, Pony and Steam, 172, 182, 188, 200, 321, 365, 391, 421, 476, 530, 531, 609, 613.
Express Lines, 505, 509, 517, 520, 521, 594.
Express, New York, 176, 190, 446, 517.
    Washington, 259.
Extradition Treaty, 438.

Fanny Fern, 648.
Farmer's Weekly Museum, 228.
Fashions, 64, 80.
Federalist, The, 177.
    Washington, 232.
Federal Party: its Organization, 151.
    its Disruption, 154.
Female Journalists, 497, 498, 503.
Fenno, John, 181, 214.

Field, Cyrus, W., 614.
　David Dudley, 584.
Financial Articles, 434, 437.
Fish, Hamilton, 159.
Fisher, Redwood, 227.
Fleet, Thomas, 80.
Foote, Dr. Thomas M., 577.
Force, Peter, 235.
Foreign Quarterly Review on the American Press, 463.
Forney, John W., 260, 560.
Forrest, Edwin, 222.
Forsyth, John, 496.
Fourierism, 525, 629.
Fourth Estate in England, 21.
Fowle, Daniel, 103, 108, 137.
　Zechariah, 127.
Francis, Dr. John W., 146.
Frank Leslie, 693, 706.
Franklin, Benjamin, 53, 60, 66, 67, 77, 98, 110, 112, 125, 126, 180, 382.
　Ann, 109, 110.
　James, 60, 61, 69, 70, 94, 109, 126.
　James, Jr., 109, 110.
　Printing Presses, 110, 111, 125.
Freeman, Philadelphia, 327.
Free-Soil Barnburners, 581.
Free Trade, 204, 223, 274.
French Mission, 485.
French Press, 21.
Freneau, Philip, 103, 111, 134, 136, 175, 185, 187.

Gacêta de Madrid, Official, 230.
Gaine, Hugh, 103, 150.
Galaxy, New England, 384.
Gales, Joseph, Sr., 227.
　Joseph, Jr., 228, 232, 247, 258.
Gallagher, William D., 197.
Garrison, William Lloyd, 367, 387.
Gay, Sidney Howard, 205, 207, 559.
Gazette, American Literary, 511.
　Arkansas, 209, 328.
　Boston, of 1719, 39, 58, 104.
　Boston, of 1753, 104.
　Boston, of 1755, 105, 107, 144, 152, 164.
　Boston Saturday Evening, 379, 396.
　Cape Fear, 117.
　Charleston, and Country Journal, 119.
　Charleston City, 199, 283.
　Cincinnati, 196.
　Connecticut, 105.
　Constitutional, 136.
　Essex, Salem, and American, 124, 144, 170.
　Falmouth (Me.), 176.
　Georgia, 112.
　Greenfield, 184, 217.
　Hampshire, 176.
　Hugh Gaine's, 150.
　Independent, of Boston, 144.
　Knoxville (Tenn.), 574.
　Lang's, New York, 179, 225, 430.
　Maryland, of 1727, 40, 79, 100, 118, 144.
　Moscow, 231.
　National, 175, 185, 191, 210, 322.
　New Hampshire, of 1756, 40, 108, 137, 144, 155.
　New Jersey, 139.
　New Jersey State, 187.
　New London, 112.
　New York, of 1725, 40, 72, 81, 83, 93.
　New York, of 1759, 111, 121.
　North Carolina, 108.
　Nuremburg, of 1457, 30.
　Oregon Flumgudgeon, 590.
　Oxford, of 1665, 35.
　Pennsylvania, of 1728, 77, 79, 144.
　Pittsburg, 177.
　Providence, 112.

Gazette, Relf's, 78.
　Reprinted London, 50.
　Rhode Island, of 1733, 40, 94.
　Royal American, 133.
　Scioto (Ohio), 195.
　South Carolina and American General, 108, 118.
　South Carolina, of 1731, 40, 96.
　United States, 181.
　Vermont, 140.
　Virginia, of 1736, 40, 96.
　Virginia, of 1766, 120, 268.
　Washington, 232.
Gazetteer, Royal, of New York, 122, 132.
Gazetti Officielle, of Italy, 230.
Genevese Traveller, 216.
German Newspapers, 100, 198.
Gerrymandering, 155.
Girardin, Emile de, 409, 537.
Gleason's Pictorial, 706.
Globe, Boston, 22, 396.
　Congressional, 245, 253.
　New York, 409, 576.
　Washington, 233, 235, 242, 414.
Goddard, William, 123, 135.
Godwin, Parke, 223, 576, 656.
Gold: its Discovery in California, 477, 592.
　the Panic in New York, 639.
Golden Age, 299, 499.
Gordon, William, the historian, 138, 167.
Graham, George R., 182.
　William, 286.
Grant, James, the Newspaper Press, 21.
　President Ulysses S., 653.
Greeley, Horace, 22, 223, 394, 398, 414, 417, 522, 525, 540, 549, 555, 558, 565, 569, 624, 661, 694, 713.
Green, Bartholomew, 51, 54, 63.
　Duff, 235, 238, 241, 243, 311, 353, 369, 577.
　Joseph, 123.
　Samuel, 122.
　Thomas, 122.
Greene, Charles G., 385.
Greenleaf, Thomas, 144.
Gridley, Jeremy, 79.
Griswold, Rufus Wilmot, 587.
Guardian, Potomac, 195, 289.
Guild, Curtis, 335, 384.

Hagen, Dr. James, 762, 763.
Hale, David, 22, 363, 366, 462, 610.
　Nathan, 379.
　Sarah Josepha, 497.
Hall, David, 78.
　Francis, 192.
　Samuel, 110, 124, 126.
Halleck, Fitz Greene, 180, 193, 220, 221.
Hallock, Gerard, 22, 363, 367, 371, 373, 611.
Halpine, Charles J., 187, 426, 620.
Hamblin, Thomas, 444.
Hamilton, Alexander, 122, 143, 175, 178, 181, 186, 215, 217, 219, 264, 267.
　Andrew, 85, 90, 121, 267.
Hammond, Charles, 196.
Hancock, John, 137, 165.
Hard Cider Campaign, 277, 391, 454.
Harnden, William F., 521.
Harper & Brothers, 587, 693.
Harper's Bazar, 707, 708.
Harper's Illustrated Weekly, 707.
Harris, Benjamin, the first American Editor, 39, 44, 49.
Harrison, William Henry, 240, 277.
Hartford Convention, 219.
Harvard College, 382.
Hastings, Hugh, 194.
Hatin, Eugene—the French Press, 21.
Haughton, Richard, 321, 370, 391.
Hazewell, Charles C., 201, 384.

Heiss, Major John P., 402.
Henry, Patrick, 118, 151, 152.
Herald, Boston, 396.
Herald, Boston American, 140.
    Christian, 301.
    Helena (Ark.), 209.
    Minnesota, 203.
    Newburyport, 202.
    New York, 23, 34, 50, 56, 100, 115, 147, 189, 219, 221, 288, 302, 304, 366, 375, 414, 421, 428, 439, 451, 456, 458, 464, 465, 478, 479, 495, 522, 531, 538, 544, 548, 592, 622, 735, 759.
    of Freedom, Boston, 181.
    of Gospel Liberty, 293.
    San Francisco, 591.
    Titusville Morning, 585.
    Zion's, 296.
Hildreth, Richard, 391, 393.
Hill, Isaac, 272.
Hoaxes, 347, 399, 422, 514.
Hoe, Colonel R. M., 418, 460, 648, 775.
Hoey, John, 520.
Holt, John, 103, 105, 121, 144, 225.
Hopper, Isaac T., 368.
Hospitality of Editors, 244.
Houston, General Sam., 443.
Howard, Joseph, 374, 617, 673.
Hoyt, Jesse, 276, 358, 411, 413.
Hughes, Archbishop, 299, 302, 464, 629.
    John, Stamp Commissioner, 98.
Hunt, F. Knight, of Fourth Estate, 21.
Huske, Ellis, Originator of Stamp Act, 96.

Illuminated Quadruple Constellation, 352.
Illustrated Papers, 705.
    Advertisements, 468.
    Frank Leslie's, 706.
    Harper's Weekly, 707.
Illustrations, 450.
Impartial Intelligencer, 184.
    Journalism, 161, 188.
Impending Conflict, Helper's, 400.
Incidents in Advertisements, 474.
Independence, Declaration of, first published, 121.
Independent Advertiser, the first Revolutionary Organ, 102.
    Gazetteer, 228, 232.
    New York, 298, 673.
    Press, 258, 261, 306, 316, 410, 429, 569, 676, 678.
Index, Frontier, 177, 209.
Indian World, Duane's, 211.
Infernal Machines, 465, 466, 479.
Initial Editors, 565.
Inquisitor and Cincinnati Advertiser, 199.
Intelligencer, Christian, 297.
    Green Bay, 208.
    Illinois, 203.
    Impartial, 184.
    National, 22, 228, 232, 259.
Interviewing, 326, 487, 561, 563, 606.
Irving, Dr. Peter, 263.
    Washington, 263.
Israelites at Grand Island, 284.

Jackson, Andrew, 235, 238, 241, 248, 268, 448.
Jacobins, 153, 181, 211.
Jarvis, Dr. Charles, 161, 163.
    Russell, 507, 508.
    Samuel, 149.
Jay, John, 179, 217.
Jefferson, Thomas, 120, 153, 154, 181, 185, 232, 267.
Jeffersonian, New York, 430.
Jenkins, the Original, 65.
Jerome, Leonard W., 622, 635.
Johnson, President Andrew, 575, 635.

Jones, Alexander, 612.
    George, 618, 639, 641, 642.
Journal, Albany Evening, 226, 278, 397, 402, 549, 577, 674.
Journal, Boston Daily, 171, 384, 394, 509, 593.
    Chicago Evening, 204.
    Connecticut, 122.
    Continental, 138.
    Essex, 135.
    Freeman's, 185.
    Home, 315.
    Illinois State, 203.
    Independent, of New York, 177.
    Indianapolis Daily, 202.
    Louisville, 323.
    Maryland, 135.
    National, 234.
    New England Weekly, of 1727, 60, 75.
    New Jersey, 139.
    New York Weekly, of 1733, 81, 103, 121, 144, 152, 179.
    of Commerce, New York, 22, 141, 180, 189, 194, 347, 351, 362, 372, 392, 425, 430, 446.
    Pennsylvania, 97, 144.
    Poughkeepsie, 265.
    Providence (R. I.), 316.
    United States, 253.
    Woman's, 498.
Journalism, American, 679.
Journalistic Diplomats, 360, 361.
Junius, 21, 146, 177, 401.
"Just once," 556.

Kansas Question, 553.
Keimer, Samuel, 77.
Kendall, Amos, 53, 238, 243, 245, 248, 285, 348, 447, 615.
    George Wilkins, 493, 495.
Kent, Judge James, 279.
King, Charles, 267, 283, 312, 346, 442, 659.
    Rufus, 281.
Kneeland, Samuel, 75, 104.
Know-Nothings, 518, 550, 551, 577.
Kossuth, Louis, 178, 621, 656.

Lamartine, Alphonse, 601.
Lang, John, 179.
Lay Preacher's Gazette, 229.
Ledger, Independent, 140.
    New York, 666, 646, 649, 651.
    Pennsylvania, 136.
    Public, of Philadelphia, 22, 100, 505, 507.
Leggett, William, 221, 620.
L'Estrange, Sir Roger, 34.
Lewis, Zachariah, 225.
Lexington, Battle of, 130.
Liability of Publishers, 545.
Libel Suits: Aaron Burr *vs.* James Cheetham, 145.
    Alexander Hamilton *vs.* New York Argus, 215.
    Andrew Hamilton's Speech, 85-90.
    Chas. Reade *vs.* Round Table, 748.
    Colonel Matthew Lyon, M. C. of Vermont, 215.
    D. R. Ambrose *vs.* Portsmouth (N. H.) Chronicle, 752.
    Edward Fry *vs.* Jas. Gordon Bennett, 753.
    E. L. Sanderson *vs.* N. Y. Sunday Mercury, 746.
    George Augustus Sala *vs.* Modern Men of Letters, 749.
    Gov. Cosby *vs.* John Philip Zenger, 82.
    Herald of Freedom, of Boston, 181.
    Jacob Gould *vs.* Thurlow Weed, 746.

Index.

Libel Suits: J. Fenimore Cooper vs. Commercial Advertiser, 744.
    J. Fenimore Cooper vs. Albany Journal, 748.
    J. Fenimore Cooper vs. New York Tribune, 746.
    James Fisk, Jr. vs. Springfield Republican, 747.
    James Thomson Callender, 214.
    John Haggerty vs. James Gordon Bennett, 753.
    John Russell Young vs. Charles A. Dana, 682.
    Judge Peck vs. Missouri Inquirer, 745.
    Lt. Gov. Root vs. New York American, 746.
    Massachusetts vs. Boston Chronicle, 160.
    M. M. Noah vs. James Gordon Bennett, 287, 461.
    Pennsylvania Journal, 98.
    Staats Zeitung vs. Pioneer, 747.
    Thomas Jefferson vs. Hudson Balance, 267.
Libel, the Law of, 267, 741, 743, 745, 750, 753, 757.
Liberal Christian, 297.
Liberator, Boston, 387, 404.
Liberty Hall and Cincinnati Mercury, 196.
Liberty of the Press, 31, 150, 164.
Lincoln, Abraham, 485, 671, 695.
Little, Jacob, 604.
"Little Villain," 624.
Livingston, Edward, 249.
    Judge Brockholst, 217, 264.
Livingstone, Search for, 486.
Locke, Richard Adams, 420, 422.
Log Cabin, 398, 522.
London Gazette, Official, 230.
Loudon, Samuel, 115, 138, 146, 150.
Louis Philippe, King, 153.

Mackenzie, William Lyon, 357.
M'Dougall, Alexander, 111, 112, 121.
M'Elrath, Thomas, 426, 524, 535, 537.
M'Kenzie, R. Shelton, 451.
M'Kinney, Thomas L., 234.
M'Michael, Morton, 183.
Madison, James, 178, 225.
Madisonian, Washington, 240.
Magazine, Historical, 295.
    Hunt's Merchants', 382.
    Madame Demorest's, 498.
Mails, 76, 79, 431, 432, 775.
Managing Editors, 559, 610.
Man, New York, 430.
    without a Country, 422.
Manners in Journalism, 636, 637.
Maps of Battle Fields, 61, 446.
    Burnt Districts, 450.
Marble, Manton, 671, 675, 676.
Marcy, William L., 357.
Marine Reports, 180, 189, 262, 445, 608.
Marriages and Deaths, 56, 75, 684, 685.
Marshall, Thomas F., 356.
Masons, Anti-, 397, 746.
    Free-, 188.
Massachusetts Gazette, 109.
Mather, Cotton, 52, 67.
    Increase, 51, 67.
Maxwell, William, 363.
Mayhew, Jonathan, 102, 105.
Meagher, Thomas Francis, 627.
Medary, Samuel, 201.
Mein, John, 123.
Memorial, Old Colony, 328.
Mercurie, the Bogus English, of 1588, 29.
Mercury, Cape Fear, 126.
    Charleston (S. C.), 254, 277, 403, 407.

Mercury, Massachusetts, 188.
    Newport (R. I.), 95, 109, 111, 118, 144.
    New York, Hugh Gaine's, 103.
    New York, Lewis's, 133.
    New York Sunday, 746.
    Pennsylvania, 136.
    Philadelphia, of 1719, 39, 60, 78.
Merriam, Eben, 116.
Messenger, Jewish, 302.
    Noah's Weekly, 287.
    of Athens, Official, 230.
Metropolitan Record, 299.
Metternich's Opinion, 143.
Mexican War, 495.
Miles O'Reilly, 187, 426.
Mills's Statue of General Jackson, 250.
Minerva, New York, 191.
Minister to France, 485.
Mirror, New York, 314.
    Washington, 237.
Mobile Journals, 491.
Money Articles, 434, 436.
Money lost in Newspapers, 489.
Moniteur, Ottoman, 231.
    Universal; Journal Officiel de l'Empire Français, 230.
Montgomery, James, the Poet, 227.
Monuments to Printers and Printing, 31, 513, 573.
Moon Hoax, 422.
"Moral War" on New York Herald, 456, 460, 461.
Morgan, William, 398.
Morris, George P., 125, 314.
Morse, Samuel F. B., 296, 480, 505, 595, 598.
    Sidney E., 292.
Mother Goose Melodies, 80.
Mottoes and Devices, 105, 119, 128, 129, 130, 152, 170, 396, 480, 514, 582, 738, 740.
Mrs. Grundy, 690.
Mumford, John I., 323, 411, 451.
Mutiny Act of 1768, 111.

Names of Newspapers, 646.
Napoleon, 362.
Nasby, Petroleum V., 692.
Nast, Thomas, 693, 707.
National Era, Grass Valley (Cal.), 593.
    Intelligencer, 22.
    Newspaper Carriers, 521.
    Washington, 259.
Native American Party, 577.
Nautical Gazette, 723.
Neal, John, 387, 587, 688.
Neale, Joseph C., 688.
New Era, New York, 576.
New Orleans Newspapers, 491.
Newport in 1732, 95.
News Agencies, 438, 594.
    Boys, 33, 34, 119, 383, 711.
    Circulars, 29, 52.
    from California, 592.
    from Home, 593.
    Letter, Boston, of 1704, 39, 54, 65.
    Letter, San Francisco, 592.
    London Weekly, of 1622, 33.
    New York, 576.
    Rooms, Topliff's, 189, 364.
    Gilpin's, 457.
    Schooners and Steamers, 180, 346, 365, 446, 486, 530, 608, 611.
    the first, published in America, 45.
Newspapers: Century, 32, 169, 176, 277, 352, 773.
    Circulation of, 57, 199, 204, 226, 305, 357, 371, 417, 420, 440, 507, 512, 519, 525, 529, 543, 595, 679, 684, 687, 736, 770.
    College, 711.
    Contents of the first American, 45.
    Distribution of, 76, 79, 431, 521, 775.

Index.   787

Newspapers: First daily, in America, 35, 175.
    England, 35.
    France, 35, 37.
  First, in the World, 28, 40.
  First Penny, 37.
  Foreign, in the United States, 493.
  French, in the United States, 314, 492, 493.
  German, in the United States, 100, 198.
  Incorporated, 536.
  in the World, 774.
  Largest, in the World, 351, 352.
  Losses of, 442.
  on the Pacific, 590.
  Profits of, 618.
  Religious, 64, 289, 420, 667.
  Spanish, in the United States, 314.
  Suppression of, 48, 373, 439.
  Transient, 710.
Newspaper Press in England, 32.
New World, New York, 588.
New Yorker, 526.
Niles, John M., 53, 308.
  Weekly Register, 307, 397.
Noah, Mordecai Manasseh, 283, 287.
Nord Deutsche Algemeine Zeitung, 230.
North American, Philadelphia, 79, 175, 182.
North American Review, 381, 548.
Norton, Benjamin Hammett, 308.
Novels, Plays, Romances as News, 587.
Nullification, 249, 403, 407.

Observatore Romano, Official, 230.
Observer, New York, 289, 293, 296, 363.
  Salem, 170.
Ocean Cable, 616.
O'Conor, Charles, 34.
Offering, Lowell, 498.
Office Seekers, 553, 554, 681.
Official Patronage, 468, 553, 681.
Oil Regions, The first Paper in, 585.
Old Boy in Specs, 216.
Old Grimes, 112.
Old Newspapers, Files of, 55, 108, 388.
Oldstyle, Jonathan, 263.
Oliver, Andrew, 128.
"On to Richmond," 255, 678.
Oracle of Dauphin, 177.
Oregon Question, 530.
Organs, Official, 230.
Otis, James, 105, 107, 138.
Overland Express from Halifax, 531.
Owen, Robert Dale, 368, 417.

Packet, New York, 138, 144, 146.
  Pennsylvania, 136, 146.
Paine, Thomas, 136.
Palladium, New England, 155, 190.
Parker, James, 93, 105, 111, 121, 122.
Parks, William, 79, 135.
Party Papers, 144, 276, 410, 411.
Patriot, Albany, 400.
  Baltimore, 120, 226.
  Boston, 164.
  New Hampshire, 272, 274, 277.
  New York, 312.
  Washington, 260.
Paulding, James Kirke, 346.
Payne, John Howard, 338, 464.
Pekin Gazette, Official, 230.
Penmanship of Editors, 565, 576, 619.
Pennsylvanian, Philadelphia, 226, 410, 411.
Penny Press, 37, 410, 416, 417, 440, 505, 609, 679.
Percival, James G., 193.
Persecutions of the Press, 141.
Personal Advertisements, 472, 474.
Personal Description of an Editor, 94.
Personalities of the Press, 448, 459, 460.

Phillips, Wendell, 301, 500, 584.
Picayune, New Orleans, 256, 337, 493, 777.
Pierce, Franklin, 485.
  Richard, the first Newspaper Publisher in America, 44.
Pilot, Boston, 297.
Pilots, New York, and the Herald, 534, 609.
Pintard, John, 176.
Plaindealer, Leggett's, 221.
Pleasants, John H., 240, 271.
Plebeian, New York, 223, 489, 576.
  Ulster, 276.
Plough-Boy, 266.
Pneumatic Dispatch Lines, 776.
Poindexter, George, 252.
Political Parties, their Names, 143.
  Rewards, 549.
Polk, James K., 241, 399.
Porcupine, Cobbett's, 154, 310, 620.
Porter, Wm. T., "the Tall Son of York," 341.
Port-Folio, 229.
Post, Baltimore Evening, 307.
  Boston, 277, 309, 389, 390.
  Boston Evening, 80.
  Cincinnati Evening, 199.
  Morning, of New York, 417.
  New York Evening, 100, 146, 216, 225, 430.
  Pennsylvania Evening, 136.
Post-Boy, Albany, 132.
  Boston Weekly, 96.
  New York Weekly, 93.
Postmasters as Editors, 59, 195.
Poulson, Zachariah, 175.
Pranitelstoennii Vyestaik, Official, of Russia, 230.
Premiums for Subscribers, 73, 502, 526, 528.
Prentice, George D., 323, 325.
Prentiss, John, 163.
Presidential Aspirations, 555, 569.
Press in Austria, 659.
  in Congress, 697.
  in France, 21.
  in Russia, 231.
  in the World, 774.
  Philadelphia, 260.
Prime, William C., 373.
Printers' Cemetery at Woodlands, 515.
Printing: first Proof-slip, 28.
  History of, 22.
  its Discovery, 27.
Printing-House Square, 560, 573, 635.
Printing-presses, 46, 100, 110, 126, 197, 349, 381, 418.
Proclamation, The bogus, 373, 671.
Prospectus: first in America, 44.
  first in Europe, 38.
Publick Occurrences, of Boston, 39, 44.
Public Ledger, Philadelphia, 22, 100, 505, 507.
Public Printing, 49, 223, 240, 255, 268, 278, 284, 579.
Puffs, Editorial, 469, 539.
Punch, 690.

Quincy, Josiah, 105, 107.

Rags: Advertisements for them, 114.
  Appeals to Women, 115.
  Italy as a Rag-bag, 117.
Railroads, 381, 391, 431.
Randolph, John, 232, 234, 245, 308.
Raymond, Henry J., 22, 200, 346, 360, 525, 550, 552, 587, 622, 624, 631, 638, 662, 729.
Rebel News, 484.
Rebellion: its Effect on Newspapers, 483.
Recorder, American, 170.
  Boston, 289, 363.
  Catskill, 277.
  Chillicothe, 295.
Reformation, Washington, 238.
Register, Albany, 265.

Register, Albany State, 577.
    American, in Paris, 314.
    Christian, 297.
    Cincinnati Commercial, 197.
    Cobbett's Weekly Political, 309.
    Illinois State, 203.
    Mobile, 496.
    National Republican and Ohio Political, 196.
    Niles's Weekly, 307.
    Raleigh (N. C.), 227, 232.
    Salem, 170.
    Stage, 382.
Rehearsal, Boston Weekly, 79.
Reid, Whitelaw, 559.
Relf's Gazette, 78.
Religious Newspapers, 64, 289, 420, 667.
Reporter, Lexington (Ky.), 272.
Reporters, 227, 228, 232, 247, 258, 619, 720.
Reporting: Congressional, 228, 255.
    first in America, 57.
    Gales and Seaton, 232.
    James Madison as a Reporter, 233.
    Joseph Gales's début, 228.
    Major Russell as a Reporter, 149.
    New York Herald, 256, 446, 453.
    Religious, 304, 453, 721.
    Telegraphic, 605, 606.
Repository, Ohio, 201.
Republic, American, 577.
    New York, 238, 377, 577.
    Washington, 256.
Republican, Albany, 275.
    Chicago, 206, 678.
    Federal, 274.
    Petersburg, 232.
    Springfield (Mass.), 141, 301, 394, 582, 747.
    St. Louis, 202, 745, 778.
Revere, Paul, 106, 129.
Revolution, Woman's Organ, 498.
Revolutionary Journalists, 105.
Rhett, R. Barnwell, Jr., 407.
Richmond Junta, 265.
Richmond, William E., 316.
Rights of the Press, 751.
Riker, Richard, 145, 220, 264.
Rind, William, 120.
Riots: Abolition, in New York, 354, 367, 370.
    Draft, in New York, 557, 634.
    Free Trade and Sailor's Rights, 274.
    Political, in Philadelphia, 211, 214.
    Sons of Liberty, in New York, 122.
    The Woods, in New York, 355.
Ripley, George, 677.
Ritchie, Thomas, 241, 242, 268, 270.
    Thomas, Jr., 240, 271.
    William F., 271.
Rives, John C., 238, 242, 246, 251.
Rivington, James, 122, 132, 134.
Roberts, George, 352, 587.
Rogers, Charles O., 395.
Romer, Pilot-boat William J., 530.
Russell, Major Benjamin, 147, 161.

Sailor's Rights, 274.
Sanford, Edwards S., 182, 521, 615.
Sargent, Epes, 386, 577.
    John O., 256, 346, 577.
Schell, Richard, 359.
School Question in New York, 464.
Schools of Journalism, 712.
Schouler, William, 198, 392.
Scientific American, 709.
Scott, General Winfield, 480.
Seaton, William Winston, 22, 232, 247, 258.
Sedition Laws, 159, 213.
Sentinel, Boston, 308.
    Indianapolis State, 202.

Sentinel, New Hampshire, 163.
    New York, 323, 425.
    Vicksburg, 762.
Sermons, their publication, 102, 453.
Sewall, Jonathan, 54, 107, 128, 129.
Seward, Weed & Co., 549.
Seward, William H., 277, 287, 398.
Shay's Rebellion, 149.
Shed, Samuel, the Revolutionary Grocer, 105.
Shepard, Dr. Horatio David, 417, 524.
Shipping Journals, 335.
Shipping News, 180, 189, 262, 346, 445, 608.
Siècle, Paris, 537.
Simms, William Gilmore, 328.
Simonton, J. W., 560, 612, 616.
Size of Newspapers, 349, 352, 409.
Slamm, Bang & Co., 576.
Slavery, Abolition of, 192, 240, 363, 373, 400.
Sleeper, John S., 394.
Smith, Samuel Harrison, 228, 232.
    Seba, Jr., 176.
    Sol, 196, 688.
Snelling, William J., 384.
Snowden, Thomas, 284, 458.
Socialism, 525.
Soft Shells, 279.
Sons of Liberty, 105, 111, 122, 130.
Southwick, Solomon, Sr., 110.
    Solomon, Jr., 265.
Spectator of the East, 231.
    Washington, 241, 253.
Spirit of the Times, Philadelphia, 507.
    Porter & Wilkes's, 341.
Spooner, Alden, 225.
Sporting Press, 341.
Spy in Washington, 216, 349.
Spy, Massachusetts, 119, 127, 167.
    Western, and Hamilton (Ohio), Gazette, 196.
    Worcester, 131, 169.
Staats Anzarger, Berlin, Official, 230.
Stamp Act of 1765, 96, 105, 118, 121.
Standard, Anti-Slavery, 301, 386, 584.
    Charleston, 406.
    New York, 323, 411, 413.
Stanley, Henry M., 486, 717.
Stanton, Edwin M., 484, 521, 670, 673.
    Elizabeth Cady, 500.
Star, New York, 488.
    New York Evening, 287, 430.
    New York Morning, 287.
    Syracuse, 747.
    Washington, 257, 260.
Statesman, New York, 225, 266.
    Ohio, 201, 277.
Statistics of the Press, 770, 771, 772, 775.
Statue to Liberty of the Press, 32.
Steam-boats, 196, 431.
Steam Navigation, 440, 450.
Steam Printing-presses, 197, 349, 381, 418.
Stevenson's Expedition, 591.
Stewart, A. T., 505.
Stock or their Sales, 435.
Stockwell, Stephen N., 395.
Stone, David M., 372, 616.
    William L., 192, 194, 207, 280.
Stop my Paper, 315.
Story, Chief-Justice Joseph, 170, 173.
Style in Newspaper Writing, 76, 146, 467.
Summary, New London, 111.
Sun, Baltimore, 510.
    New York, 259, 287, 366, 417, 488, 500, 677, 681.
Sunday Newspapers, 337, 339.
Suppression of the first Newspaper in America, 48.
Swain, William M., 424, 505, 510, 513.
Swartwout, Colonel John, 264.
Swishelm, Jane G., 499.
Symmes's Hole, 197.

Tammany Ring, War on, 641, 642, 644.

Index. 789

Tappan, Arthur, 363.
    Lewis, 363, 367, 370.
Tariff Question, 318, 407, 526, 535.
Tasistro, Lewis Fitzgerald, 588.
Taxes on Newspapers, 141, 149, 164, 167, 724.
Taylor, Zachary, 256, 308.
Tea, Destruction of, in Boston Harbor, 106.
Telegram, New York, 520, 734.
Telegraph, American, 306.
    Boston, 363.
    New York, 323.
    United States, 235, 369.
Telegraphic Era, 595, 600.
    Dictation, 613.
    Monopoly, 614.
Telegraphs, Automatic, 616.
    Atlantic, 616.
    Electro-Magnetic, 480, 505, 509, 595, 599, 602, 607, 615.
    Newfoundland, 614.
    Semaphore, 365, 596, 597.
Texas Question, 240, 271.
Theatrical Advertisements in 1793 and 1872, 147.
Thomas, Frederick W., 200.
    Isaiah, 22, 115, 119, 129, 135, 145, 152, 167, 228.
    Reminiscences of E. S., 161, 199.
Tilton, Theodore, 298.
Time-Piece, New York, 187.
Times, Boston, 576.
    Chicago, 205.
    Cincinnati, 200, 759.
    Hartford, 277, 308.
    London, 350, 643, 698.
    New York, 222, 361, 618, 629, 634, 639, 640, 644, 747, 759.
    New York Sunday, 287.
    Washington, 254.
Toasts, Newspaper, 385.
Topliff, Samuel, 189.
Torpedoes and the New York Herald, 465.
Trade with England, Opposition to, 148.
Transcript, Boston, 386.
    New York, 424, 430.
    Philadelphia, 507.
Traveller, American, 382.
    Boston Daily, 393, 582.
    Boston Evening, 171, 201, 383.
Tribune, Chicago, 204.
    Lawrence (Kan.), 209.
    Mobile, 496.
    New York, 23, 183, 205, 207, 480, 483, 522, 526, 531, 557, 566, 777.
Triumvirate, Democratic, 268, 269.
True Woman, 503.
Truth Teller, New York, 302.
Turkie, Organ of the Sultan, 230.
Turner, Nat., 363.
Tyler, John, 214, 240, 241, 287, 575.

Uncle Tom's Cabin, 259.
Union, Nashville, 241, 277, 402, 736.
    Washington, 241, 254.
Union of Newspapers, 670.
United States Bank, 249, 273, 345, 447.
Universal Instructor in all the Arts and Sciences and Pennsylvania Gazette, 77.

Value, Financial, of Newspapers, 183, 200, 202, 204, 205, 304, 388, 395, 441, 506, 513, 537, 538, 728, 758, 760.

Van Buren, John, 238, 579.
    Martin, 240, 251, 271, 273, 276, 581.
Van Dam, Rip, 81.
Vanderbilt, Commodore Cornelius, 505, 532.
Van Dyck, Henry H., 579.
Vanity Fair, 690.
Verplanck, Gulian C., 182, 283.
    Johnston, 312.
Vienna Gazette, Official, 230.
Villager, Amesburg, 328.
Violation of Rules of Congress, 569.
Virginia, Resolutions of, 1798, 160.

Walsh, Robert, 322.
War Maps, 61, 446.
    of Editors, 58, 61, 152, 175.
    of 1812-15, 148.
    on the New York Herald, 456, 459.
    with the Blondes, 205.
Ward, Artemus, 692, 694.
Warren, General Joseph, 105, 137.
Washington, George, 152, 173, 175, 185, 210.
    Papers, 230, 261.
Watchman, American, 145.
    Montpelier (Vt.), 431.
Watchman and Reflector, 296.
Watch-Tower, Cooperstown (N. Y.), 266.
Waterloo, Battle of, 23.
Watterson, Henry, 326.
Webb, James Watson, 273, 281, 285, 313, 344, 348, 353, 413, 462, 533, 552, 623, 669.
Webster, Daniel, 233, 234, 240, 257, 328, 390, 392, 619, 711.
    Noah, 188, 191, 193.
Weed, Thurlow, 194, 207, 226, 278, 397, 402, 522, 549, 675, 746.
Welles, Gideon, 308.
Westcott, Senator, of Florida, 254.
Western Newspapers, 195.
Westminster Review on American Press, 463.
Wheaton, Henry, 282, 312.
Whig, Knoxville (Tenn.), 574.
    New York, 522.
    Richmond, 271, 768.
Whittier, John Greenleaf, 326.
Wikoff, Henry, the Chevalier. 238, 362, 577.
Williams, Eleazer, the Dauphin, 207.
Willis, Nathaniel, 125, 195, 289.
    Nathaniel P., 125, 314, 360.
Wilmot Proviso, 580.
Winthrop, Robert C., 390.
Wirt, William, 269.
Wisconsin Newspapers, 207.
Wise, Henry A., 120, 238, 249.
Witness, New York Daily, 303.
Wits, 323, 494, 688.
Woman's Rights, 388, 525.
Women as News-venders, 33.
Woodworth, Samuel, 314.
World, New York, 141, 183, 375, 611, 667, 669.
Worthington R., 383.
Wright, Fanny, 323, 368, 417, 499.

Yeadon, Richard, 262.
Yellow Fever, 211.
Young, Alexander, 188, 191.
    John Russell, 548, 555, 560, 682.
Youth's Companion, 293, 305.

Zenger, John Peter, 81, 741.